SOCIAL AND EMOTIONAL DEVELOPME
ATTACHMENT RELATIONSHIPS AND THE EMEI

Social and Emotional Development: Attachment Relationships and the Emerging Self

Karen S. Rosen, PhD

 macmillan education   palgrave

First published 2016 by
PALGRAVE

Palgrave in the UK is an imprint of Macmillan Publishers Limited, registered in England, company number 785998, of 4 Crinan Street, London, N1 9XW.

Palgrave Macmillan in the US is a division of St Martin's Press LLC, 175 Fifth Avenue, New York, NY 10010.

Palgrave is a global imprint of the above companies and is represented throughout the world.

Palgrave® and Macmillan® are registered trademarks in the United States, the United Kingdom, Europe and other countries.

ISBN 978-0-230-30346-1   ISBN 978-1-137-57901-0 (eBook)

DOI 10.1007/978-1-137-57901-0

This book is printed on paper suitable for recycling and made from fully managed and sustained forest sources. Logging, pulping and manufacturing processes are expected to conform to the environmental regulations of the country of origin.

A catalogue record for this book is available from the British Library.

A catalog record for this book is available from the Library of Congress.

Contents

Preface   x

Acknowledgments   xiii

1   Attachment Relationships During Infancy   1
The Early Roots of Attachment Theory   3
The Attachment Behavioral System   6
How Are Infants Prepared to Develop Attachment Relationships?   8
How Are Parents Prepared to Develop Attachments to Their Children?   10
The Neurobiological Basis of Parent–Child Interactions   11
Stages in the Development of Attachment   13
How Are Attachment Relationships Evaluated and Described?   16
What Contributes to the Development of Attachment Relationships?   19
    Caregiving   19
    Temperament   23
    Genetic and Environmental Influences on Attachment Security   26
What Are the Developmental Consequences of Early Attachment
Relationships?   28
Attachment Relationships Beyond Infancy   32
    Why Was Attachment Security Initially Studied Only In Infancy?   32
    Developments in the Measurement of Attachment Security   35
Is There Stability or Instability in Attachment Patterns?   39
The Effects of Child Care on Attachment Relationships   41
The Development of Multiple Attachments   44
The Neuroscience of Attachment Relationships   47
Clinical Implications of Attachment Theory and Research   52

2   Infant Individuality and the Origins of the Self   56
Temperament   57
How is Temperament Defined and Measured?   59
What Are the Biological Underpinnings of Temperament?   64
Is There Stability in Temperament Over Time?   66
How Does Temperament Influence Development and Does it Predict
Later Behavior?   70
Temperament: In Summary   72
Emotions   73
Emotional Development   73
Perspectives on Emotions and Emotional Development   75
Emotional Expressiveness   78
Emotion Display Rules   81
Emotion Understanding   83

Emotion Regulation 86

Early Emotion Regulation and Later Development 93

Relationships and Emotional Development 97

The Development of the Autonomous Self 99

Developmental Changes in Aspects of the Self 100

Attachment Relationships and the Developing Self 113

3   Sibling Relationships 116

Why Study Siblings? 117

Theoretical Perspectives For Studying Sibling Relationships 118

Sibling Relationships Across Different Developmental Periods 126

The Transition to Becoming a Sibling 126

Childhood 128

Adolescence 128

Emerging Adulthood 129

What Happens to Sibling Relationships Over Time? 130

How Are Sibling Relationships Described and Measured? Conflict,
Rivalry, and So Much More 131

Measurement Approaches For the Study of Sibling Relationships 136

Behavioral Observations 136

*Self-Report Measures and Multiple Perspectives on Sibling
Relationships* 138

Why Are Siblings So Different? 139

Differential Parental Treatment and Its Effects on Siblings 142

Other Influences on Sibling Relationship Quality 147

Sibling Relationships and Their Effects on Social and Emotional
Development 148

Sibling Relationships and Friendships 151

Now, What About Only Children? 156

4   Peer Relations and Friendship During Childhood 161

What Makes Peer Relationships a Unique Context For Studying Social,
Emotional, and Cognitive Development? 163

Developmental Changes in Peer Interactions 163

Developing Friendships in Childhood 167

Friendship Stability 170

What Influences Children's Friendship Choices? 173

Children's Understanding of Friendships 174

Individual Differences in Peer Status and Friendship Quality 175

Peer Status: What Happens When Children Are Accepted or Rejected? 175

Friendship Quality 178

The Effects of Friendships on Children's Socio-Emotional Functioning 180

The Links Between Children's Relationships With Parents and Peers 184

Some Final Considerations 191

5   The Development of Empathy, Prosocial Behavior, and Morality 194

Empathy 196

What is Empathy? 196

Empathy and Perspective Taking 200

Perspective Taking and Relationships 201

Prosocial Behavior 202
The Development of Prosocial Behavior 203
Individual Differences in Prosocial Behavior 205
What Are the Origins of Individual Differences in Prosocial Behavior? 206
What Happens When Children Do Not Develop a Concern For Others? 212
Morality 213
Emotions and Morality 214
How Are Moral Emotions Socialized? 218
Moral Judgments 221
Moral Behavior 229

6 **Adolescent Social Relations** **236**
The Context of Adolescence 237
The Adolescent in the Family 239
Parenting and Its Impact on Adolescent Adjustment 242
Peer Relationships in Adolescence 245
The Nature of Adolescent Friendships 248
The Broadened Social World of Adolescents 252
Attachment Relationships in Adolescence 257
How Do Emerging Cognitive, Social, and Emotional Competencies
Impact Adolescent Attachments? 258
The Hierarchy of Attachment Relationships in Adolescence 260
The Measurement of Attachment Relationships in Adolescence 262
Early and Later Attachment Security 267
Adolescent Attachment and Social and Emotional Functioning 270
Attachment Relationships and Friendships During Adolescence 273

7 **Adolescent Identity and the Consolidation of the Self** **278**
The Development of Autonomy and the Self 279
The Development of Self-Concept 284
Self-Descriptions of Adolescents 286
Internal Representations of the Self 288
Self-Esteem 291
Factors Influencing Self-Esteem 293
What Are the Consequences of Self-Esteem? 295
Identity Development 296
Identity Formation and Adjustment in Adolescence 297
Attachment and Identity Development 302
Contextual Influences on Identity Development 303
Recent Developments in the Study of the Self and Identity 305
Ethnic Identity 307
Gender Identity 309
Biological Influences on Gender and Sexuality 310
Gender, Sexuality, and Identity in Adolescence 311
Intimacy 314
Self-Disclosure and Authenticity in Adolescent Relationships 317
Emotional Development and the Self During Adolescence 318
Emotion Regulation in Adolescence 319
The Role of Mentalization in Emotion Regulation 322

Emotion Regulation and Empathy in Adolescence   324
The Self, Empathy, Moral Emotions, and Moral Behavior   326
What Comes Next in Emerging Adulthood?   329

References   331
Index   434

About the Author

Dr. Karen Rosen is Associate Professor in the Department of Psychology at Boston College, where she teaches courses in developmental and clinical psychology. She also serves as the Director of the Psychology Honors Program and of the Undergraduate Clinical Concentration. In addition, as a Senior Staff Psychologist at Brookline Psychological Services, her clinical practice focuses on a range of psychological issues, including attachment and self-related disorders.

Dr. Rosen received her PhD from Harvard University. Her research on parent–child attachment relationships and sibling relationships has been published in many scholarly journals and in several edited books. She has presented her work at both national and international conferences.

Preface

From the moment we are born we live in relation to other people. We depend upon our caregivers for comfort and welcome their calming presence, gentle touch, and warm embrace. We interact with our caregivers, first with emotional signals and gestures and later with language and emerging social skills. We rely on our caregivers for the safety and support they provide as we gradually move away from them to explore and discover our ever-expanding world. When hesitant, we may be encouraged by their loving assurance. When distressed, we seek contact with them and this may eventually calm and soothe us. Over time, and with repeated interactional experiences, we develop attachment relationships, first to our primary caregivers and then to other significant people in our social world. Ideally, we derive comfort from the security of our attachment relationships. They are essential to our social and emotional development. As our social world grows, we play and learn with our siblings and peers, helping and companioning each other, sharing new discoveries with curiosity and interest. We feel pleasure and joy, frustration and sadness, hurt and anger. Together, we build the foundation for new relational experiences that are woven into the deeper friendships that we ultimately come to form. We reciprocate confidences, cooperate, compete, and struggle, as we learn to negotiate and compromise. Through all of these interactions, our connections to others are transformed.

In this process of learning about our earliest attachment relationships, we also come to understand that we are individuals – autonomous, unique, and distinct from others. The self emerges in the first few months and years of life, influenced by, and developing parallel to, our emotionally significant attachment relationships. In infancy, we form a nascent sense of our separateness from our caregivers and come to physically recognize ourselves. We then begin, in childhood, to distinguish who we are, what we like, what we are good at, and how we compare to our siblings and peers. As we continue to build on our evolving understanding of our self over time, we learn to regulate our emotions and behaviors and to feel increasingly competent. It is this emerging sense of self that we then bring to our relationships and that allows us to negotiate new ways of interacting in our social world. Balancing our sense of self with a continued feeling of connection to others is our developmental challenge throughout the lifespan. Just as our attachments provide the starting point from which the self is born, so too does the self allow for evolving connections to others that are deeper and more meaningful. From the beginning, the interrelated themes of attachment and self form the foundation of our social and emotional worlds.

The themes of attachment and the self provide the organizing framework for this textbook. Issues relevant to these themes are examined in alternating chapters that consider developing attachments and aspects of the self from birth through adolescence and into emerging adulthood. We begin by exploring attachment relationships in infancy and then infant individuality and the origins of the self. Here, we consider the role of temperament, emotional development, and the initial emergence of the autonomous self. Then, relationships with siblings, peers, and friends are examined, as children's social worlds extend outside of the family and new connections are nurtured. The evolving sense of self is considered once again as it influences, and is influenced by, advances in children's cognitive, social, and emotional competencies. Thus, characteristics that contribute to, and reflect, children's unique sense of self are explored, including the development of empathy and perspective taking, the inclination to engage in prosocial behavior, the ability to regulate emotions, and the capacity for moral thought and decision making. Finally, adolescent social relations and the consolidation of the self in adolescence are examined. Theory and research findings are clearly presented. Controversial issues are addressed and questions that remain unanswered are highlighted. The reader is provided with a comprehensive understanding of the antecedents to, and developmental consequences of, attachment relationships and the emerging self from infancy through adolescence.

There are several additional aspects of the integrative approach adopted in this text that are noteworthy:

1. The focus is on understanding normative trends as well as individual differences. Questions about "what" develops "when" are examined. More important, however, is the exploration of "how" and "why" development occurs as the current research that is reviewed in the book examines underlying mechanisms and the multiple factors that influence developmental outcomes.

2. While developing attachment relationships and an evolving understanding of the self are considered as major developmental tasks in the social and emotional domains, emerging cognitive competencies underlie, and are in turn influenced by, social and emotional advances. Moreover, biological factors, such as temperament and evolving brain structures, influence developmental pathways. Thus, important advances from contemporary research in social-cognitive development and developmental social neuroscience are incorporated.

3. Children's experiences are deeply impacted by their families and the larger social and cultural context in which they live. Where it is relevant, and research findings are available, attention is drawn to cultural issues and the distinct values and beliefs that contribute in important ways to our understanding of developing social and emotional competencies in children around the world.

4. Understanding the pathways to both normal and atypical patterns of development raises questions about the risk and protective factors that contribute to vulnerability and resilience in children and adolescents. There are many difficulties that may arise in the course of development. Disruptions or disturbances in early attachment relationships, and threats to the emergence of the self, may contribute to individual fragility, lead to maladaptive patterns of behavior, and make the resolution of subsequent developmental challenges more problematic. Theoretical background and empirical findings will be presented that contribute to our understanding of individual and relational factors leading to adaptation or the development of psychopathology. Therefore, this book is relevant to the work of advanced students and developmental researchers, as well as to clinicians and those who are dedicated to improving the lives of children and families.

Acknowledgments

The intricate connection between attachment relationships and the emerging self has served as an organizing theme in my professional work, providing a coherence to my thinking as a professor, researcher, and clinical psychologist. Throughout my career, I have been fascinated by the study of early attachment relationships, their precursors and developmental consequences, and the role that they play in self-related thinking, feelings, and behaviors. The self, in turn, influences developing attachment relationships, not only during infancy but throughout the lifespan. Thus, these related themes are central to the questions I continue to ask in my ongoing research, to the framework I have adopted in my teaching, and to the way that I have come to understand many of the struggles and challenges of my patients in the clinical consulting room. It, therefore, seemed very appropriate to be structuring this book around the related themes of attachment and the self.

There are many people who have generously supported me while writing this book. I want to thank my colleagues in the Department of Psychology at Boston College for encouraging the kind of careful analysis and critical thinking that is essential to our role as teachers and scholars. I am especially fortunate to work with a group of wise and dedicated clinicians at Brookline Psychological Services: Cheryl Abel, Dr. Virginia Byron, Dr. Diane Kwasnick, and Mikele Rauch. We have offered each other, in our weekly consultation meetings, a safe haven for professional exploration and growth. Together, we have come to appreciate the relational, personal, and experiential challenges that may undermine secure attachments but, when understood, may ultimately lead to individual growth and new ways of maintaining connections. Many of our discoveries are reflected in this book.

In my work as a clinical psychologist, my patients have trusted me to listen, to make sense of their feelings, to respect the silences, and to help them sort through the repetitive relational patterns, betrayals, and emotional injuries that reflect their earlier attachments. I am humbled and impressed by their courage, respectful of their honesty and resilience, and grateful for all that I continue to learn from them. In our work together, we integrate and come to understand their personal and relational histories. Over time, they use this more cohesive narrative, and the insights that emerge from our clinical work, to promote healing. The security of our relationship serves as a transformative context for creating new opportunities for growth and change.

The many students I have taught over 30 years at Boston College have inspired and challenged me. This book was born out of successive semesters teaching both an undergraduate course and a graduate seminar on social and emotional development. The organization and structure of this book reflects a consolidation of the way I have conceptualized and taught these courses. My hope is that this book will serve as the foundation for others to learn about the related themes of attachment and the self. Supplementing this text with the many new research findings that continue to emerge on both of these topics will help readers appreciate the advances and controversies that stimulate new empirical studies and the development of appropriate clinical interventions.

I would like to acknowledge the editors at Palgrave, especially Paul Stevens and Isabel Berwick, whose support and patience, and confidence in the importance of this work, were instrumental in providing the context for me to write. You have skillfully guided this project and brought my thinking to a larger audience. It has been a pleasure working with you.

Finally, I would like to warmly thank my most special attachments. To my friends: Dr. Diane Kwasnick, your compassion, clarity, and insights, and our friendship, have been essential to me both personally and professionally. I am comforted knowing you are by my side. Robert Abel and Madelaine Abel, I have always appreciated your steady encouragement, unwavering support, and enduring friendship. To my children: Emily, Gabriel, and Rebecca Rosen, I cherish the connection that I have with each of you. I am always here to support and hold you securely, whether in close proximity or across a distance. I lovingly celebrate your unique and wonderful emerging selves. And to my husband: Dr. Ron Rosen, I am deeply grateful for your love and sustaining presence, your confidence in me, and your dedication to our relationship. You have helped me to stay emotionally grounded over the many years we have been together. You will always be my secure base.

Attachment Relationships During Infancy

How do infants develop emotionally significant attachments to their caregivers? And why are these relationships so important? The attachment process gradually unfolds in a manner that is biologically based but depends on parental, familial, and cultural influences. While all babies develop attachment relationships with their primary caregivers, the quality of these attachments will reflect contributions of each interactional partner and the history of their interactions over time. Ultimately, variations in the security of early attachment relationships have profound implications for later social and emotional development.

In this chapter, attachment theory and research will be explored. Beginning with the work of John Bowlby, the theoretical foundation will be provided for current thinking about attachment relationships. Research will be presented that has looked at the ways in which infants and caregivers are prepared to develop attachment relationships and the neurobiological basis of parent–child interactions. Methods for evaluating qualitative differences in attachment relationships will be critically discussed. Studies exploring the precursors to, and developmental consequences of, variations in attachment security will be reviewed. Integrated throughout will be empirical findings and provocative issues that have resulted in the reworking of earlier theory and/or the identification of some new lines of research. Questions about attachment relationships beyond the infancy period, and the development of multiple attachment relationships, will be examined. There will be a particular focus on studies that illuminate the processes involved in promoting continuity or discontinuity in attachment patterns over time. Contemporary trends in empirical work will be highlighted as well, including the effects of early child care and the neuroscience of attachment relationships. Finally, the clinical implications of attachment theory and research will be discussed.

A good place to begin our exploration is to consider two young girls, Katie and Anna, who have been friends for years. They both attended the same child care center from the age of about 2 months. At first, Katie was more calm and relaxed, whether alone in her bouncy seat or carried in the arms of a child care provider. Anna spent her awake time actively looking around the room, watching what others were doing, and preferring contact with adult caregivers. When Katie began to crawl, and then to walk, she was happy to explore the room, to involve herself in an independent activity, to spend time engaged in play with puzzles or toys, or to gradually approach other children to see what they were doing. When distressed or in need of help, Katie was effective in seeking out the child care providers for comfort or direction. By contrast, as Anna approached her first birthday, she had difficulty engaging in independent play. She was much happier when sitting near an adult and rarely moved off on her own to explore the toys or engage in activities, either alone or with other children. But she "liked" Katie and Katie "liked" her – they were interested in each other, moved towards one another as they became mobile, babbled, imitated sounds, and then eventually talked, enjoying their "conversations," laughing, and fully engaged. As they got older, they actively greeted each other every morning, seemed happiest when playing together, and had more difficulty at child care when one of them was not in attendance because of illness or changes in parental schedules. They had come to rely on one another for comfort and security, companionship and play.

Katie's mother came to get her from the child care center at the end of each day. When she was younger, her mother's entrance into the infant room brought a huge smile to Katie's face. She would wiggle and squeal and bounce in her infant seat. And as her mother approached her and picked her up out of her seat, Katie beamed while she snuggled into her mother's embrace. As she got older, if she was involved in an activity with Anna or some of the other children, Katie would wait for her mother to come to her side so she could show her, with great excitement, what she had been doing. She would chatter endlessly about the picture she was drawing, the structure she was building, or the game she had been playing with Anna and her other playmates. Sometimes Katie would run to her mother's side and drag her over to where she had been playing, insisting that her mom see what she had been doing in her absence. Then, when satisfied, Katie would collect her belongings and happily leave with her mom, but not before saying "goodbye" to Anna.

Anna's mom usually picked her up from child care after Katie had left to go home. Sometimes her father would pick her up if he was done with work before her mother. As an infant, Anna would generally be in one of the caregiver's arms, passive and seemingly content to be held. As she got older, she would often sit quietly with a child care provider after Katie left, not needing to be involved in activity so much as to avoid being by herself. Sometimes she would color alone or look at a book. When either of her parents appeared at the child care center, Anna was aware they had come in but barely acknowledged their entrance, quickly put her things away, and left without much emotion or conversation. Though happily engaged with Katie when playing together, Anna had difficulty involving herself in play with the other children in her classroom. Her affect was more muted and her play more restricted.

She watched, with great interest, what the other children were doing but had difficulty joining with them or getting involved in their play activities.

How can we come to understand the developmental precursors to Katie and Anna's ways of relating to each other, to their child care providers, and to the other children in their child care classrooms? How can we account for the observed differences in their personalities and behaviors? It is no longer relevant to ask whether infants are "blank slates" who are impacted by the entirety of their social experience or genetically programmed to develop with no influence from their parents. Rather, we now know that children develop in an interactive context and that "context" needs to be conceptualized broadly, on multiple levels, and over time. Some have argued that babies grow within the minds and behaviors of those around them (e.g., Winnicott, 1965/1996) so that the context is the psychological state of the mother. Others focus on relationship systems (Sroufe & Fleeson, 1986) or networks of relationships at successive levels of complexity (Hinde, 1987), or adopt a systems perspective for understanding dynamic processes that change over time (Minuchin, 1988; Sameroff & Chandler, 1975). Still others (Bronfenbrenner, 2004) consider individuals from a bio-ecological framework, taking into account the child's biological inheritance nested within the larger microsystems of family, school, and neighborhood, as well as the societal macrosystems. Thus, although Katie and Anna were each born with their own unique genetic endowments and temperamental predispositions, their experiences with their primary caregivers, in their own unique family and social contexts, undoubtedly impacted the emergence of particular patterns of interaction.

Given this complexity of contexts, and the nonlinear trajectories along which children develop, it is impossible to offer a single, clear pathway that accounts for the multitude of influences on young children's social and emotional development. Still, we can consider some of the key elements in children's lives that set them on their developmental course. We will begin by exploring, in this chapter, the experiences that children, like Katie and Anna, have in their first year of life that contribute to the development of their early attachments. The construct of attachment provides a way of characterizing the quality of the emotional relationship that infants form with their primary caregivers. In subsequent chapters, the attachment construct will also be used as the basis for considering the development of concepts about the self during infancy, childhood, adolescence, and emerging adulthood.

The Early Roots of Attachment Theory

Attachment theory originated from the very painful and poignant clinical observations, conducted in the 1940s and 1950s, of young children for whom relationships with their mothers were disrupted (e.g., Bowlby, 1944; Robertson & Bowlby, 1952). Through understanding what happened when things went "wrong," the mechanisms underlying the normal process of developing attachment relationships were uncovered. John Bowlby was a psychoanalyst who, early in his career, made the first observations that raised questions about the disruption of the maternal bond. Bowlby was especially intrigued by what he observed in young children with whom he worked at the London Child Guidance Clinic. He eventually came to report retrospectively on these children who had so profoundly impacted him and his thinking in a seminal paper, "Forty-Four Juvenile Thieves: Their Characters and Home Life" (Bowlby, 1944). Based on the attention that was increasingly being given to children's relationships with their mothers, Bowlby's clinical assessments of these children focused, in particular, on "the elucidation of the mother–child relationship in each and every case" (Bowlby, 1944, p. 20). Clinical interviews, and careful consideration of the delicate emotional material provided, led Bowlby to some important conclusions.

> [I]n several cases sympathetic discussions with the mothers of the children revealed that their apparent love for their child was only one aspect of their feelings about him. Often an intense, though perhaps unadmitted, dislike and rejection of him also came to light. Furthermore, very careful enquiries showed a remarkable proportion of children who, for one reason or another, had not lived securely in one home all their lives but had spent long periods away from home (Bowlby, 1944, p. 20).

Bowlby came to believe that when the child's relationship with the mother was interrupted by prolonged separation in the early years, this could provide an important clue to explaining the development of psychopathology later on.

A decade later, Bowlby, together with his colleague, John Robertson, observed that separation from the mother for extended periods, even if children are nurtured and nourished by others, can lead to a predictable response of angry protest followed by deep despair (Robertson & Bowlby, 1952). Mothers seemed to be extremely significant to young children and Bowlby continued to ask why this was the case. Others were documenting similar observations (e.g., Bender & Yarnell, 1941) that, taken together, led Bowlby to argue that the mother–child relationship is critical, both to children's current functioning and to their later development (Bowlby, 1969/1982). The idea that social relationships influence, and are impacted by, development and psychopathology was not new, as ego psychologists (Freud, 1965) and object relations theorists (Mahler, Pine, & Bergman, 1975; Winnicott, 1965/1996) emphasized the importance of early relationships for social and emotional functioning. However, Bowlby highlighted both the emotional significance of the early maternal attachment relationship and the implications of disruptions to this relationship resulting from prolonged maternal separation and loss.

Bowlby's ideas about *why* the early emotional comfort and security provided by the mother were essential to the child were novel, especially since secondary drive theories offered the prevailing explanation for why the child formed a close tie to the mother. Psychoanalytic and social learning theorists suggested that the infant's relationship with the mother develops because she feeds the infant; the mother's presence comes to be associated with the pleasure of satisfying hunger drives and so being near to the mother must be comforting as well (Freud, 1910/1957; Sears, Maccoby, & Levin, 1957). Bowlby became increasingly uncomfortable with these associative learning secondary drive theories, though at the time there were no alternatives (Bowlby, 1980). Moreover, ethological studies offered contradictory evidence. For example, Konrad Lorenz (1935/1957) observed that infant geese became attached to the first moving object in their view, whether or not it was the parent and even when it did not feed them. And in his classic studies, Harry Harlow (1958) demonstrated that infant rhesus monkeys that were stressed preferred the cloth-covered surrogate "mother" who provided security and comfort to the wire-mesh "mother" who provided food.

Over subsequent years, Bowlby went on to formulate attachment theory, drawing heavily on ideas from conversations with colleagues in the fields of ethology, evolutionary biology, cognitive science, developmental psychology, and control systems theory (Bowlby, 1969/1982). He argued that through the process of natural selection, a biologically based desire for close proximity to the mother emerged. Bowlby articulated his ideas more fully in his now seminal trilogy, *Attachment and Loss* (Vol. 1: Attachment (1969/1982), Vol. 2: Separation (1973), Vol. 3: Loss (1980)), though the "basic blueprint of attachment theory" (Bretherton, 1992, p. 762) was provided in his earlier paper, "The Nature of the Child's Tie to His Mother" (Bowlby, 1958). In his writings, Bowlby offered an evolutionary perspective on attachment behaviors (Bowlby, 1969/1982). He proposed that the infants of humans, as a species, have survived within an "environment of evolutionary adaptedness," where the behavioral propensities of babies and parents allow them to maintain proximity to one another. This physical closeness is essential because it allows the infant to be protected, thereby maximizing the possibility for survival. Thus, Bowlby referred to the "biological function" of attachment behaviors as protection from predators. This concept was then expanded when Bowlby incorporated the idea that infants are predisposed to seek out parents when distressed. While in proximity, infants are nourished, comforted and calmed, engage in social interaction, and learn about their environment. Consequently, maintaining proximity to attachment figures is essential for survival, support, and comfort and is a normal sign of emotional health. Indeed, Bowlby so wisely suggests: "All of us, from cradle to grave, are happiest when life is organized as a series of excursions, long or short, from the secure base provided by our attachment figures" (Bowlby, 1988, p. 62).

Bowlby's attachment theory focuses on the biological bases of attachment behaviors. These behaviors have the "set goal" of increasing the child's proximity to the attachment figure (who is usually the mother). Because human infants, unlike babies of other species, cannot move closer to or follow after adults for many months after birth, they rely on attachment behaviors or signals that encourage adults to come close to them. When babies smile or vocalize, these signals often bring the mother closer to the child, informing her that her baby is interested in interaction. When infants cry, this prepotent signal is also very effective in bringing the mother towards the baby, to pick up, comfort, and ultimately soothe the distressed infant. With time, increased physical and motor development lead to infant searching, approaching, and following, as well as physical attempts to initiate or maintain contact (e.g., reaching, holding on), which are more active behaviors that move the infant to the mother or keep him in proximity to her.

The effectiveness of these signals, of course, depends on the adult's predisposition to respond when the infant cries, smiles, vocalizes, or approaches. Crying, in particular, is an important attachment signal that alerts parents to their infant's distress (Soltis, 2004). Crying usually elicits empathic feelings in parents and motivates proximity and care with the goal of reducing distress. Crying also serves an evolutionary function in enhancing infant survival by stimulating parental responsiveness (Bowlby, 1969/1982). There are, however, important differences in sensitivity to infant crying. Indeed, maternal sensitivity to infant crying, as compared to sensitivity to other signals in nondistress situations, has been found to have greater explanatory power in predicting qualitative differences in infant attachment security (McElwain & Booth-LaForce, 2006). This suggests that crying plays a crucial role in the development of the mother–child attachment relationship. When parents have an aversive reaction to infant crying, they are more likely to respond insensitively (Dix, Gershoff, Meunier, & Miller, 2004; Riem, Bakermans-Kranenburg, van IJzendoorn, Out, & Rombouts, 2012), thereby undermining the development of a secure attachment.

Thus, Bowlby's conception of attachment is essentially a relational one; attachments develop out of interactions with significant caregivers. Over time, children and parents exert an influence on one another and establish a coordinated patterning of attachment-related behaviors. Their relationships are dynamic. Ultimately, the organization of the relational system is as important as is the contribution of each of the individuals within the relationship.

The Attachment Behavioral System

The concept of a behavioral system, which Bowlby borrowed from ethology (Bowlby, 1969/1982), refers to a species-specific set of behaviors that lead to certain expected and predictable consequences. The "attachment behavioral system" consists of behaviors that serve the goal of maintaining proximity, which in turn ensures survival. Bowlby argued that there is an inherent motivation to engage in these behaviors since they contribute to reproductive fitness. Whether or not parents are meeting the child's physiological needs, children engage in attachment behaviors and develop an attachment relationship. This relationship is not a consequence of basic processes or drives; rather the attachment behavioral system is activated on its own because it involves its own inherent motivation. Over time, in response to a history of interaction with the caregiver, attachment behaviors achieve an organization that is particular and unique to the dyad.

In their seminal paper, Sroufe and Waters (1977) elaborate on this idea and describe attachment as an *organizational construct*, arguing that

> attachment is not viewed as a static trait; rather, it has the status of an intervening variable or an organizational construct, to be evaluated in terms of its integrative power. It is not a set of behaviors that are constantly and uniformly operative (in the manner of a temperamental characteristic) or even operative with a fixed probability of occurrence. Neither is it reducible to the interaction between infant and caregiver, though it is a product of that interaction (as it is shaped by species general characteristics, cognitive development, and characteristics of the individual baby and caregiver). Rather, attachment refers to an affective tie between infant and caregiver and to a behavioral system, flexibly operating in terms of set goals, mediated by feeling, and in interaction with other behavioral systems. In this view, behavior is predictably influenced by context rather than constant across situations. (Sroufe & Waters, 1977, p. 1185)

When conceptualized in this way, different attachment behaviors may serve the same function. A child who is unable to move may reach out to and cry for the mother in order to achieve contact, while a crawling infant may achieve the same goal by moving to her side. Additionally, while discrete behaviors that serve the attachment system may vary, there will be stability across context and over time in the organization of attachment relationships, based on the history of the dyad's interactions. Both developmental and contextual changes will influence the precise behaviors used to achieve the set goal of proximity to mother (Cassidy, 2008).

Bowlby (1969/1982) argued that the attachment system is activated when the child is stressed or in danger. When, for example, the child is hungry or tired, or when the mother has left the room and the infant notices she is "missing," or when there is a loud and unexpected noise, attachment behaviors may be activated. The goal for the child is to reduce environmental or personal stress; that, in turn, reduces the activation of attachment behavior. So when the mother talks to, picks up, feeds, or rocks her baby, this "return" of the mother and associated contact with her is usually an effective intervention to reduce the infant's distress. Sometimes, the solution may simply be hearing her soothing voice; at other times, physical contact and touch may be essential. The extent to which the attachment system is activated will determine how much is required from the attachment figure to reduce the infant's distress. Thus, the goal is to return to a state where the infant is calmed and a feeling of security is achieved.

Sroufe and Waters (1977) also broadened Bowlby's account of the function of attachment behavior. They argued that, in many species, protection from danger was of primary importance. For human infants, however, the attachment figure serves as a secure base for exploration (Ainsworth, 1963, 1972). Moreover, Sroufe and Waters (1977) suggest that exploration is of paramount importance for human infants who rely on their caregivers to expose them to the social and object worlds, as they learn to flexibly approach new situations and problems and develop problem-solving skills. Attachment and exploration are, thus, two behavioral systems that operate in dynamic relation to one another (Ainsworth, 1972). When the infant is secure in her understanding of the caregiver's availability, the possibility for exploration is maximized (Sorce & Emde, 1981). When the attachment system is activated (e.g., upon separation from the attachment figure), or if the environment is threatening (e.g., too many novel stimuli, noises, or people), then exploration and playful exchanges are reduced in frequency. Thus, the two systems balance one another: attachment fosters exploration and exploration is enhanced in the presence of attachment figures.

Finally, Sroufe and Waters (1977) highlight the affective connection inherent in attachment relationships. They view attachments as the "psychological tether which binds infant and caregiver together" (Sroufe & Waters, 1977, p. 1186). Though dependent on cognitive abilities, such as object permanence and discrimination learning, the affective bond is evident in "the expressions of positive affect embodied in the bouncing, smiling greeting reactions to caregivers and the apparent security and comfort derived from the mere presence and later the internal representation of the caregiver" (Sroufe & Waters, 1977, p. 1186). When described in this way, attachment relationships are organized to reflect this affective bond (see also Sroufe, 1996). And while it cannot be observed directly, the affective bond is what allows the infant to use the attachment figure as a secure base, to explore in her presence, to be distressed by separation, to express pleasure on reunion, and to seek proximity when uncomfortable. It is also what accounts for the sequence of behaviors – protest, despair, detachment – observed to follow prolonged separation from attachment figures (Bowlby, 1969/1982; Robertson & Robertson, 1971). Attachment is thus a special emotional *relationship* between infant and caregiver, one that evolves over time, reflects the dyad's interactional history, and represents a mutual affective tie.

How Are Infants Prepared to Develop Attachment Relationships?

Many of their earliest perceptual abilities prepare infants to relate to faces and people and to be social beings. Infants generally seem to prefer to look at faces than to look at inanimate objects. In one early demonstration of this preference (Tronick & Brazelton, 1980), infants were filmed as a toy monkey, suspended on a wire, was brought almost within the infant's reach and then taken away from the baby. The infants responded with great excitement, attempting to grasp and explore the toy with irregular, uneven movements. When filmed while responding to their mothers, babies looked at, smiled, and responded to the mother in a more fluid and integrated manner, sometimes looking away before looking back at her. Infants also show a preference for high contrast colors and facial features. Black and white drawings of faces capture their attention even in the first few minutes of life. Newborns and their mothers often seek out each other's eyes following birth. And babies distinguish lines resembling the eyes, nose, and mouth; that is, they are attuned to face-like shapes (Music, 2011). Babies also show a preference for looking at pictures where the faces have eyes that are open rather than closed (Field, Cohen, Garcia, & Greenberg, 1984). Taken together, these research findings suggest that newborns are biologically prepared to recognize faces that, in turn, can elicit positive responses and promote interactive exchanges.

Studies of babies' responses to the mother's voice also demonstrate that there are clear preferences present from birth. Measures of the differences in fetal heart rate changes that occur when hearing tapes of a stranger's voice, as compared to the mother's voice, demonstrate that babies learn the sound of the mother's voice very early (Kisilevsky et al., 2009). When babies listen to their mother's voice, their brain waves are different from when they listen to the voice of another female. Babies are also much more interested in their mother's voices, can change their sucking rates to restore a recording of their mother's voices reading to them, and reveal, through sucking rate patterns, an ability to discriminate between stories, showing a preference for the one that was read to them *in utero* by the mother (DeCasper & Spence, 1986). However, newborns' capacity to discriminate faces and speech are compromised in babies of depressed mothers (Field et al., 1984). There is a disruption to the normal rhythm in face-to-face exchanges when children are interacting with a nonresponsive mother simulating the experience of depression (Tronick, 1989), suggesting that certain experiences may result in a "switching off" of these innate abilities. Thus, the infant's repertoire of potential social skills can only develop within a context of interaction with others who are responsive to their gestures, signals, and cues.

One skill that facilitates interaction is imitation. Infants have been found to be able to imitate their parents when parents stick out their tongues. As soon as 20 minutes after birth, babies watch carefully and, with some effort, proceed to stick out their own tongue (Meltzoff, 2007). They also can imitate, as soon as two days after birth, expressions such as smiling and frowning (Field, 2007), a remarkable demonstration of early attempts to communicate. They show increases in heart rates when they imitate gestures; when adults imitate their gestures, infants' heart rates slow (Trevarthen & Aitken, 2001). Babies also come to imitate sounds and gestures in a synchronized pattern as they listen to adults "baby talk". In sum, infants experience an emotional and physiological regulation that comes from interactions with parents who are attuned to them.

How Are Parents Prepared to Develop Attachments to Their Children?

While the hormones involved in pregnancy prepare mothers to become parents, there are also hormonal changes that occur in fathers anticipating their child's birth (Storey, Walsh, Quinton, & Wynne-Edwards, 2000). Even before a baby's entrance into the world, hormonal shifts prepare parents to engage in the type of behavior that is essential for developing attachments. Mothers become more sensitive to infant cries (Corter & Fleming, 2002). Mothers and fathers experience a range of neuroendocrine changes that provide the foundation for developing attachments (Feldman, Gordon, Schneiderman, Weisman, & Zagoory-Sharon, 2010; Samuel et al., 2015). In the postpartum period, prolactin levels rise when parents are involved in child care. During pleasurable interactions with their young babies, both mothers and fathers release oxytocin (Feldman, Gordon, & Zagoory-Sharon, 2010). Indeed, higher levels of prenatal oxytocin have been associated with more optimal maternal interactive behaviors in the postpartum period (Feldman, Gordon, & Zagoory-Sharon, 2011).

The core processes involved in effective parenting are dependent upon the functioning of particular brain regions or circuits (Hughes & Baylin, 2012). For example, when oxytocin is released from the medial preoptic area in the parent's brain, it activates dopamine neurons that then extend into the brain's reward system (the nucleus accumbens), resulting in the activation of parenting behavior (Numan & Stolzenberg, 2008). Recent research also suggests that, for fathers, vasopressin and prolactin combine with oxytocin, leading to similar brain changes that prepare them to parent. While mothers and fathers engage in distinct styles of interaction with their babies, the same brain reward system is involved, motivating mothers and fathers to engage in caregiving and to find it rewarding (Gordon, Zagoory-Sharon, Leckman, & Feldman, 2010). For some fathers, testosterone levels decrease when they begin to interact with their infant after birth. Men who have lower testosterone levels spend more time holding a baby doll and respond more to infant cries and other cues as compared to men who do not experience a decrease in testosterone (Fleming, Corter, Stallings, & Steiner, 2002). In fact, even before their babies are born, men who are more intimately involved with their wives during the pregnancy exhibit greater hormonal shifts. And more experienced fathers who already have a child have testosterone levels that are even lower than childless men (Gray, Yang, & Pope, 2006) and first-time fathers (Corter & Fleming, 2002).

Infant survival and development are dependent upon the provision of certain parental behaviors that organize the infant's physiological reactions and promote well-being and adaptation (Bowlby, 1969/1982; Leckman & Herman, 2002; Tronick, 1989). Mothers and fathers form internal cognitive representations of their baby even during pregnancy, suggesting that parents' relationships with their infant evolve before the child's birth, thereby facilitating the transition to parenthood and influencing caregiving behaviors and the developing attachment relationship (Benoit, Parker, & Zeanah, 1997; Theran, Levendosky, Bogat, & Huth-Bocks, 2005; Vreeswijk, Maas, Rijk, Braeken, & van Bakel, 2014). Thus, adults bring to their role as parents certain biological, behavioral, and psychological processes that promote their infant's growth (Carter et al., 2005).

Indeed, certain parental behaviors are evident immediately after birth and have been found to organize, in important ways, the infant's physiological and behavioral responses. Behaviors such as maternal gaze at the infant face, expression of positive affect, high-pitched vocalizations, and affectionate touching are critical to the developing relationship (Bowlby, 1969/1982). These parental behaviors help infants to organize and regulate their own emotions and behaviors within the developing attachment relationship. Initially, infants rely on the caregiver to help modulate their cries or their angry protests. They learn to initiate interactions with smiling or eye contact and to terminate interactions with gaze aversion or by falling asleep. Responding sensitively and appropriately to their infant's cries is a way that caregivers communicate their availability to their babies and help their infants decrease their arousal. Thus, caregivers' responsiveness contributes to the quality of the attachment relationship while helping the infant to regulate affect (Cassidy, 1994; Thompson & Meyer, 2007).

The Neurobiological Basis of Parent–Child Interactions

Parents need to adapt their behaviors to moments of infant responsiveness in order to maintain synchronous coordination between themselves and their babies (Feldman, 2007; Isabella & Belsky, 1991). In rodents, research has demonstrated that naturally occurring variations in maternal behavior lead to distinct processes that uniquely influence gene expression, organize the oxytocinergic system underlying formation of bonds in mammals, and impact lifetime ability to manage stress (Champagne, 2008; Weaver et al., 2004). Similarly, in humans, studies have demonstrated that the degree of interactional synchrony between parental behavior and infant responsiveness is associated with peripheral measures of oxytocin in the infant and the parent (Atzil, Hendler, Zagoory-Sharon, Weintraub, & Feldman, 2012; Feldman, Gordon, & Zagoory-Sharon, 2010). When mothers are anxious and disregard their infant's signals and cues, they may overstimulate their babies and engage in intrusive behavior. Interestingly, these synchronous or intrusive maternal styles appear to be relatively stable from birth through adolescence. They are also associated with particular patterns of parasympathetic and hypothalamic-pituitary-adrenal (HPA) axis responses in both children and mothers that are distinctively predictive of social and emotional outcomes in children and adolescence (Feldman, 2010; Feldman, Singer, & Zagoory, 2010; Sroufe, 2005).

Moreover, both sub-cortical motivational limbic regions and high-level emotion modulation networks support the neural basis of maternal behavior

(Hughes & Baylin, 2012). The relationship that develops between the mother and infant is based on the activation and balance of motivational mechanisms that signal stress, such as increased vigilance and threat detection, and reward (Leckman et al., 2004). Distinct motivational and threat-related networks support the formation of affiliative bonds and the stress and reward components of maternal attachment. In particular, the nucleus accumbens and amygdala are structures in the limbic system that have been found to play a role in maternal behavior and bond formation in mammals (Aron et al., 2005; Cardinal, Parkinson, Hall, & Everitt, 2002). The amygdala, in particular, has been identified as playing a critical role in affiliative tendencies and maternal attachment (Oxley & Fleming, 2000; Toscano, Bauman, Mason, & Amaral, 2009). Together with the nucleus accumbens, the amygdala works in conjunction with several cortical areas in mammals, including the medial preoptic area, which promotes parenting and integrates infant sensory cues (Insel & Young, 2000; Lee, Clancy, & Fleming, 2000), and the anterior cingulate and dorsomedial prefrontal cortex (Murphy, MacLean, & Hamilton, 1981; Slotnick, 1967). Because some of these cortical areas have been suggested to play a role in empathic abilities and theory of mind skills (Gallagher & Frith, 2003; Völlm et al., 2006), they may also be involved when human parents read and respond to their infant's signals.

Additionally, functional imaging studies (using fMRI) have highlighted the importance of the nucleus accumbens, the amygdala, and other discrete brain areas for parenting in humans (Barrett & Fleming, 2011; Strathearn, Fonagy, Amico, & Montague, 2009). For example, reward dopaminergic circuits, areas involving oxytocin projections (Strathearn et al., 2009), the hippocampus (Swain, Lorberbaum, Kose, & Strathearn, 2007), and the anterior cingulate and insula (Bartels & Zeki, 2004; Noriuchi, Kikuchi, & Senoo, 2008; Swain et al., 2007) have been identified as distinct regions critical to parental behavior. The coordinated functioning of neural networks, affiliation hormones, maternal behavior, and infant social signals has also been explored in human mothers (Atzil, Hendler, & Feldman, 2011). The limbic motivational network appears to be activated in response to infant stimuli; additionally, brain networks associated with attention and emotion modulation are activated and function in a coordinated manner. Unique integrative profiles of these three functional neural networks have been identified for mothers with synchronous, as compared to intrusive, parenting styles (Atzil et al., 2011). And there also appears to be synchrony in brain regions associated with empathy and social understanding that are activated in response to infant cues across mothers and fathers (Feldman, Bamberger, & Kanat-Maymon, 2013).

Interestingly, fathers who are homosexual and serve as primary caregivers, raising their infants without maternal involvement, show high amygdala activation associated with higher levels of oxytocin and greater synchrony in response to their infants. These primary caregiving fathers also show greater activation in the cortical circuits associated with social understanding and empathy, similar to what is seen in fathers involved as secondary caregivers (where their heterosexual partner is the primary caregiver). Moreover, for both primary and secondary male caregivers, the amount of time spent involved in caregiving is correlated with greater amygdala activation (Abraham et al., 2014). Thus, months of pregnancy may sensitize the amygdala, but fathers' active parenting may activate and sensitize this brain region as well. Similar results may be found in those circumstances where fathers in heterosexual relationships play an active parenting role, either as a stay-at-home dad or as a single father. Future work will contribute to our understanding of the social and emotional brain systems that are crucial to parenting and to the formation of parent–infant attachments.

Stages in the Development of Attachment

According to Bowlby (1969/1982), there are four stages in the development of attachment relationships: Indiscriminate Social Responsiveness (from birth through 1 or 2 months of age); Discriminating Sociability (from 1 or 2 months through 6 or 7 months); Attachment (from 7 to 24 months); and Goal-Corrected Partnership (from 24 to 30 months onward). While the stages have no clear boundaries, Bowlby detailed the internal processes that facilitate movement through the stages, such as the infant's developing capacity to orient, to signal the caregiver by smiling and crying, to communicate by babbling, and to promote proximity by reaching, grasping, and clinging. He also identified the maternal caretaking behaviors and emotional qualities that he considered central to the development of attachment relationships (Bowlby, 1969/1982).

Phase 1: *Indiscriminate Social Responsiveness.* During the first phase of developing attachment relationships, infants use a repertoire of signals that impact the adults around them. For example, when adults hear an infant's cry, physiological mechanisms are activated that motivate them to relieve the baby's distress (Frodi et al., 1978; Murray, 1979). The most common response is for the adult to pick up a crying infant; holding the baby is also the most effective way of quieting the cries (Bell & Ainsworth, 1972). This is a clear example of Bowlby's assumption that infants and adults possess behavioral predispositions that are biologically determined and that maximize the infant's chances of survival.

Crying is an attachment behavior that brings the baby into close proximity with the caregiver. When a baby cries, adults approach the baby because they want to terminate an aversive signal. Smiling, another attachment behavior that becomes part of the infant's behavioral repertoire during the second month of life, also impacts the caregiver. When an infant smiles, the caregiver wants to stay in close proximity and to continue the interaction because both partners find the interaction pleasurable. Thus, we see that crying and smiling are two attachment behaviors that affect the people in infants' early social environments. What is particularly noteworthy is that during this first phase in the development of attachment relationships, infants do not show preferences for the people who respond to them; they are satisfied with anyone who responds to their cries or smiles. They do not possess the perceptual or cognitive skills that allow them to discriminate among individuals or to recognize their mothers or fathers. It is when they begin to show a preference for those caregivers with whom they have the most consistent interaction that they make the transition into the second phase of *discriminating sociability.*

Phase 2: *Discriminating Sociability.* From the first weeks of life, infants are capable of using visual, auditory, olfactory, and kinesthetic cues to discriminate among people (Lamb, Bornstein, & Teti, 2002). They recognize their mother's face and can identify their mother by smell or voice (Bushnell, Sai, & Mullin, 1989). We do not know when infants develop multimodal ideas of people that allow them to realize these different features belong to the same person. But infants do begin to show a preference for familiar people; that is, for those with whom they share pleasurable encounters, such as cuddling, rocking, playing, and feeding, and who help to reduce their distress.

As babies' arousal levels becomes more regular, they spend less time sleeping and more time awake (Emde & Robinson, 1979). Their behavior becomes more coordinated and they are more likely to spend their awake time engaged in face-to-face interactions with their parents and other caregivers. While at first the adult assumes responsibility for maintaining the interaction, the baby increasingly plays a role in initiating, sustaining, and terminating these exchanges. What began as an adult-led activity eventually becomes a well-attuned dance where it is difficult for the observer to know who is leading and who is following; the coordinated exchange reflects the dyads' unique history of give and take. So the baby might smile, coo, then avert gaze, return to look at her mother's face, smile again, kick her feet in delight, gaze avert, then look again at her mom, move her tongue in and out, smile. And all of these movements and gestures are likely to be responded to with a similar action from the adult. From these repeated exchanges, several important lessons are learned: (1) *effectance:* the infant's behavior affects the other's behavior in a predictable and consistent way; (2) *reciprocity:* taking turns is part of all social interactions where each partner acts and reacts to the other; and (3) *trust:* the infant can rely on the caregiver to respond to her signals and cues (Lamb & Lewis, 2011). Additionally, these ideas are discovered in the context of adults' responses to infants' expressions of distress and pleasure. When caregivers approach their crying infants and attempt to soothe them, or move toward their smiling infants and try to engage them in playful exchanges, babies learn their effect on others and come to see their social world as predictable and coherent. Because certain specific people are more reliably involved in the baby's care, the history of their interaction leads infants and their caregivers to develop reliable sequences of exchanges that have profound consequences. The infant's level of confidence in the caregiver's responsiveness ultimately contributes to the overall quality of their attachment relationship. Similarly, qualitative differences in the way each caregiver responds to the baby will impact the baby's perceived effectance and level of trust in that particular caregiver.

Phase 3: *Attachment.* The hallmark of the transition into the next phase of a clear and specific affective bond between the infant and caregiver is the emergence of *separation protest.* Now, infants will cry when the caregiver leaves the room. They have achieved an awareness of the person to whom they are attached and respond with distress when that person goes away. Crying is usually the clear sign that the infant does not want or like separation from the attachment figure (Ainsworth, Blehar, Waters, & Wall, 1978). Babies react to the caregiver's departure and continue to be concerned about where the caregiver might be, as evidenced by attempts at looking for the attachment figure made possible by increased locomotor skills. Once babies are able to crawl, they can explore on their own and play a more active role in searching for the caregiver. When reunited, infants are then able to use the caregiver as a secure base for exploration.

Phase 4: *Goal-Corrected Partnership.* Children assume more and more responsibility for initiating and maintaining interactions with their attachment figures as they grow older. Their more sophisticated language skills, behaviors, and social responses help them to tolerate increasing distance when interacting with their attachment figures. Therefore, exchanges may occur through vocal dialogues, shared gaze, emotional expressions, and behavioral displays, either in close proximity or across some physical distance. Parents may comfort children with their words rather than with a physical approach; they may communicate their loving care with a smile across a room instead of a hug. As children become more familiar with daily routines, learn to tolerate separations from their attachment figures, and become immersed in their larger social world of siblings, peers, and unfamiliar adults, they begin to understand that their caregivers may have needs that are different from their own. Separations may be a part of their regular routine just as reunions provide lots of opportunities for reconnecting and sharing stories about their time apart. Thus, rudimentary role-taking skills and the capacity to take another's perspective help young children navigate the goal-corrected partnership of the attachment relationship.

All children progress through these stages of developing attachment relationships and, except for rare instances of extremely inconsistent contact or supreme neglect, develop an attachment relationship to their primary caregiver. However, not all attachment relationships are equal. Variations in child and caregiver characteristics and behaviors lead to differences in their patterns of interactions. Some children will come to learn that their caregivers are sensitive, reliable, and emotionally available, while others will have caregivers who are inconsistently responsive or insensitive to their infants and unable to meet their emotional needs. Some caregivers will ignore or reject their infant's signals and cues, while others will anticipate their baby's every need, thereby making it unnecessary for the infant to initiate interactions.

Some babies will, by their very nature, be extremely difficult to calm when distressed, while others may be so passive that they seemingly require very little attention from their caregivers. Over time, the history of interactive exchanges between infants and their caregivers will determine the overall quality of their attachment relationship.

How Are Attachment Relationships Evaluated and Described?

During the initial stages of Bowlby's development of attachment theory, Mary Salter Ainsworth, a Canadian developmental psychologist, responded to a newspaper advertisement for a position in a research lab. She was hired and began working with John Bowlby's research team. In the course of her work, Ainsworth conducted two groundbreaking naturalistic studies of infants and mothers in their home environments. These observational studies – one in Uganda in the early 1950s and the other in Baltimore, Maryland in the early 1960s – focused on the analyses of discrete parental and child behaviors that contribute to the attachment relationship. Thus, by applying ethological principles of attachment theory to her work, Ainsworth laid the foundation for continued formulations of Bowlby's attachment theory and offered her own significant contribution to the study of attachment relationships.

With time, Ainsworth, together with her colleagues, developed an assessment procedure, the "Strange Situation", for evaluating the quality of attachment relationships (Ainsworth, Blehar, Waters, & Wall, 1978). This procedure is perhaps one of the most widely used assessments of attachment relationships throughout the world. In the Strange Situation, the child is observed in a series of seven three-minute episodes that involve increasingly stressful experiences. A laboratory playroom is arranged with two chairs positioned to the side of the room (one for the mother and one for the "stranger") and a box of toys placed in the center. The parent and child are introduced to the room, the mother is asked to sit in one of the chairs, and the child is placed on the floor next to the toy box. The mother is instructed to sit quietly, only responding to her child's requests if s/he approaches her, gestures, talks, or offers a toy, but otherwise not to initiate contact with her child. In the first episode, the child is free to explore the toys. After three minutes, the stranger comes in to the room and sits in her chair quietly for the first minute, then talks to the mother for a minute, and then gets down on the floor and plays with the child. At the beginning of the next episode, the mother is signaled to leave the room, the stranger returns to her chair, and the child is now separated from the mother for the first time (though in the company of the stranger). The first reunion occurs in the next episode, when the mother enters to the room, pauses at the door (so that the child's reaction to her return may be observed), and then sits in her chair. After three minutes, the mother hears a signal indicating that she should leave the room again. Now, the child remains in the room alone until the stranger returns in the next three-minute episode. Finally, the mother returns to the playroom for the last episode and the stranger quietly leaves. As she enters the room, the mother is instructed to pause again, then to talk to and finally pick up her child, and then to place her child down near the toy box, returning to her chair for the remainder of this final episode. The entire sequence of episodes is videotaped. Several interactive behaviors are observed and coded from the videotapes of the 21-minute assessment, including proximity and contact seeking, contact maintenance, avoidance, resistance, search, and distance interaction (for a complete description of the Strange Situation procedure and coding guidelines, see Ainsworth, Blehar, Waters, & Wall, 1978).

The assumption behind the use of the Strange Situation is that the attachment behavioral system will be activated as a result of the stress of being in a new room, meeting an unfamiliar adult (the "stranger"), separating from the caregiver (in the company of the "stranger"), and then separating from the caregiver while alone in the room. The two separations, in particular, are thought to create the most stress and to elicit behaviors (e.g., proximity seeking, contact maintenance, search) reflecting the infant's need to reconnect with the caregiver which, in turn, reduces the stress of separation and facilitates a return to exploration. The organization of the infant's behaviors across the seven episodes, and especially during the two separation/reunion sequences, provides the coder with the information needed to classify the quality of the attachment relationship.

The Strange Situation originally allowed for the classification of infant–caregiver dyads into one of three patterns of attachment – secure, insecure anxious-avoidant, and insecure anxious-resistant (Ainsworth et al., 1978). A fourth pattern, insecure disorganized, was added many years later to describe infants who did not fit into one of the existing three categories. Each of these patterns is described below, with associated caregiving behaviors relevant to the patterns of attachment delineated.

Secure attachment (Group B): Infants in this category appear to be confident in their exploration of the room and toys and in their expectation that the caregiver is a stable secure base for exploration. These infants will, in response to their parent's departure from the room, temporarily inhibit exploration and make active attempts to bring the parent back to the room by vocalizing, crying, or searching for her. When the parent re-enters the room, they return to play and re-engage in interaction with the parent. If distressed by separation, they may seek to be held or cuddled but are then comforted by the parent's presence and are able to return to play. A similar set of responses, though perhaps of greater intensity, will occur during the second separation and reunion sequence. About 60–65% of all infants in the United States who are studied in the Strange Situation demonstrate this behavior. This pattern of *secure attachment* is rooted in consistent and reliable care, where the parent is responsive, in a predictable and sensitive manner, to the infant's expression of need. The message communicated to the infant is that s/he is worthy and valued; care is provided because the infant deserves to be loved.

Insecure anxious-avoidant attachment (Group A): Infants in this group are happy to explore without prompting from or interaction with the caregiver. These infants do not seek contact with the parent during exploration nor are they distressed by separation. They do not greet or seek proximity to the parent upon reunion, ignoring the parent's bids for contact and actively avoiding interaction. They are more inclined to approach and interact with an unfamiliar adult (the "stranger"), though increased stress (with increased activation of the attachment system) leads to more avoidance of both the stranger and the parent. These *insecure-avoidant* infants constitute about 15–20% of infants in US samples. A history of chronic and sustained emotional unavailability from, and/or rejection by, the parent underlies this pattern of attachment. The infant comes to view the self as unworthy of attention and care.

Insecure anxious-resistant attachment (Group C): When entering the new room with the parent, infants in this category show little or no exploration. They are not interested in the toys or the "stranger." Separation from the parent leads to distress which is usually more extreme during and after the second separation. These infants are extremely difficult to comfort and, even when calmed, cannot return to exploration or play. They may seek proximity or contact upon reunion, but this is mixed with angry rejection of the caregiver's overtures to calm them down. About 10–15% of babies in American samples show this ambivalent pattern of *insecure-resistant* attachment that results from inconsistent, chaotic care not tailored to the infant's needs. Continued vigilance by the infant is required to ensure that the parent is available, and even when seemingly available, the care provided is unpredictable, insensitive, and unreliable. The infant learns that s/he is ineffective in eliciting care.

Insecure disorganized attachment (Group D): Mary Main and her colleagues introduced a fourth category of attachment to describe infants whose behavior was difficult to classify using the original three attachment patterns and developed classification guidelines for this group of infants described as "disorganized" or "disoriented" (Main & Solomon, 1990). These infants appear to lack a coherent strategy with respect to using the attachment figure; their behavior reflects confusion about approaching their caregivers, manifested by undirected or incomplete movements, stereotypies, or contradictory behavioral patterns (e.g., moving towards the caregiver and then freezing or exhibiting disorientation). The antecedents to this pattern of attachment include parental depression, marital discord, dissociation, and frightening or disturbing parental behaviors (Main & Hesse, 1990; Schuengel, Bakermans-Kranenburg, van IJzendoorn & Blom, 1999). Disorganized attachments are more often seen in children who have been abused or neglected. Across several studies, about 48% of maltreated children are classified as disorganized, though about 15% of infants in middle-class and about 24% in lower socioeconomic status nonclinical samples have been classified as disorganized as well (van IJzendoorn, Schuengel, & Bakermans-Kranenburg, 1999).

The organization of attachment behaviors, considered in relation to the caregiver and across the episodes of the Strange Situation, is critical to observe.

The patterning of attachment behaviors, not the frequency of any discrete behavior, is assessed to determine the quality of the attachment relationship. The underlying assumption is that the increasingly stressful experiences that the infant needs to manage in the Strange Situation activate the attachment behavioral system. The infant's behavior reflects the ability to balance exploration of the new environment with the need for reassurance and comfort from the attachment figure. The infant and caregiver's interactional history is presumed to lead to certain beliefs and expectations regarding the availability of the caregiver, which are also reflected in the organization of the infant's attachment behaviors. Ultimately, the attachment classification assigned to the *relationship* is based on the careful observation and coding of the *infant's behavior* in relation to the caregiver.

What Contributes to the Development of Attachment Relationships?

Caregiving

Ainsworth and her colleagues initially tested, and found strong support for, the hypothesis that maternal behaviors during the first year predict attachment security at 12 months of age (Ainsworth, Bell, & Stayton, 1971; Ainsworth et al., 1978). Their idea was that when a mother is attuned and responds appropriately to her baby's particular expression of needs, and is capable of adapting her responses as she accepts and meets her baby's biological and emotional states, then her baby learns that her needs will be met and this leads to a secure pattern of attachment. On the other hand, a mother who repeatedly misreads or has difficulty understanding or accepting her infant's signals and cues may be inconsistent in her responsiveness and insensitive to her baby and an insecure attachment relationship is more likely to develop. The initial studies of maternal behaviors focused, in particular, on maternal sensitivity, though the maternal characteristics of acceptance, cooperation, and accessibility were also examined. Sensitivity was defined based on the mother's ability to notice, interpret, and respond to her baby's signals promptly and appropriately. Mothers who displayed higher levels of sensitivity were more likely to have infants who were classified as securely attached at 12 months of age. In addition, high maternal sensitivity was also associated with more acceptance, cooperation, and accessibility (Ainsworth et al., 1971). Maternal sensitivity has since been studied extensively.

There is considerable evidence supporting the notion that infants with more sensitive mothers are more likely to develop a secure attachment to them (for meta-analyses, see Atkinson et al., 2000; de Wolff & van IJzendoorn, 1997; Goldsmith & Alansky, 1987). While many researchers developed new observational measures that extend beyond the original definition of sensitivity, they continue to find meaningful associations with attachment security (Mesman &

Emmen, 2013). However, questions about the strength of this association have been raised (see, for example, Rosen & Rothbaum, 1993). Indeed, the results of the meta-analyses reveal only a modest effect size, thereby raising questions about whether the association between maternal sensitivity and attachment security is as strong as was originally believed.

Some investigators have suggested that the original definition of sensitivity, with a focus on the mother's contingent, prompt, and *appropriate* responsiveness to her infant (Ainsworth et al., 1971), has not been considered carefully enough by attachment researchers. Thus, the meta-analytic results may be influenced by variations in the definitions of sensitivity, thereby leading to the conclusion that "sensitivity plays an important but not exclusive role in the emergence of attachment security" (de Wolff & van IJzendoorn, 1997, p. 586). In fact, detailed coding and analyses of maternal sensitivity, consistent with Ainsworth's relational approach to the assessment of maternal behavior, have been found to yield more robust associations with attachment security (Pederson, Bailey, Tarabulsy, Bento, & Moran, 2014). However, alternative conceptions of parental behavior presumed to be related to attachment security have also been explored. There has been research, for example, focusing on aspects of "affect mirroring" (Fonagy, Gergely, Jurist, & Target, 2002), "mutual responsivity" (Kochanska, Aksan, Prisco, & Adams, 2008), and "affect attunement" (Jonsson & Clinton, 2006; Stern, Hofer, Haft, & Dore, 1985). These differences in the way that the construct of maternal sensitivity has been operationalized may be what accounts for variability in the association between sensitivity and attachment.

Some researchers have argued that other factors need to be considered that may promote or interfere with the development of a secure attachment (de Wolff & van IJzendoorn, 1997; Rosen & Rothbaum, 1993; Seifer & Schiller, 1995). The parent, as the more mature interactive partner, is usually assumed to be influencing her child. However, each member of the dyad influences the other and, thus, the developing attachment relationship. Support for this idea comes, for example, from recent research indicating that secure attachment at 19 months of age was predicted by positive affect in the infant at 4 months, together with highly positive maternal affect. However, insecure attachment was predicted by positive maternal affect together with negative or neutral infant affect at 4 months (Pauli-Pott & Meresacker, 2009). Thus, affective reactions in both mother and child influence the quality of their attachment relationship.

More recently, the construct of maternal sensitivity has been re-examined and elaborated, with an emphasis on the parent's understanding of, and capacity to reflect on, the infant's internal emotional world. This capacity for "mentalization" is seen to be critical to the developing attachment relationship. Moreover, mentalization appears to underlie the intricate connections between attachment processes and the child's growing ability to understand and interpret interpersonal behavior in terms of mental states (Fonagy et al., 2002; Fonagy, Steele, Steele, Higgitt, & Target, 1994).

Some researchers have also made an important distinction between sensitivity to children's emotional and physical needs and sensitivity to mental processes (Meins, 1997). The concept of "mind-mindedness" was introduced to describe the mother's tendency to "treat her infant as an individual with a mind rather than merely as a creature with needs that must be satisfied" (Meins, Fernyhough, Fradley, & Tuckey, 2001, p. 638). Reflective function, or the mother's ability to understand and "hold in mind" (Slade, Grienenberger, Bernbach, Levy, & Locker, 2005, p. 284) her own and her infant's mental states, is essential to creating a secure and comforting psychological environment for her baby. Terms such as mentalization, mind-mindedness, and reflective function, therefore, refer to the mother's ability to adopt and maintain a psychological perspective regarding her child; this capacity appears to be associated with responsive caregiving behavior (Grienenberger, Kelly, & Slade 2005) and with secure attachment (Sharp, Fonagy, & Goodyer, 2006). In turn, the self-reflective and interpersonal components of mentalization contribute, in important ways, to the infant's growing understanding of the self and others and to the developing capacity for emotional understanding, affect regulation, and empathy. In fact, deficits in mentalization, as are often observed in children who have been maltreated, have been found to result from, and to further impact, a disorganized attachment system (Cicchetti & Valentino, 2006; Fonagy, Gergely, & Target, 2008). When conceptualized in this way, mental functions that are part of the developing self-system, such as affect regulation and empathic abilities, may be seen to emerge within a relational context.

The concepts of mind-mindedness and maternal reflective function are consistent with Ainsworth et al.'s (1971) original notion that the sensitive mother is "capable of perceiving things from [the child's] point of view" (p. 43), thus making inferences from observing her child's behavior about her child's internal mental states. The "mind-minded mother" is sensitive to her child's behavior and is willing to adapt her responses in accordance with her interpretation of her child's cues. A mother of a child who forms a secure attachment to her is thus able to respond appropriately because she can accurately evaluate the reasons for her child's behavior and respond in accordance with that expression of need. Conversely, mothers of children who develop an insecure attachment either have more difficulty discerning why their child is behaving in a certain way or may be unwilling to understand the behavior; these mothers do not necessarily fail to respond to their baby but are more likely to respond in ways that do not match the need indicated by the child's behavior. Thus, for example, they might try to play with a sleepy infant, stimulate a baby when she needs to be calmed, or feed a baby who really just wants to engage in social interaction.

Five distinct measures of "mind-mindedness" were originally identified, each directed towards evaluating mothers' awareness and interpretation of their infants' behavior and mental processes (Meins, 2013; Meins et al., 2001). Four of these measures assess the mother's responses to her infant's behaviors (maternal responsiveness to a change in the infant's direction of gaze; maternal responsiveness to the infant's object-directed action; imitation; encouragement of autonomy); these responses suggest the infant's behaviors are viewed by the mother as goal-directed and intentional. The final measure evaluates the mother's tendency to comment on her infant's thoughts and feelings (i.e., mental processes) by making appropriate mind-related comments. In a study of 71 infants and their mothers, ratings from play interactions when the infants were 6 months were examined in relation to attachment classifications at 12 months. Clear associations were found between higher scores for appropriate mind-related comments and secure attachment. Maternal sensitivity ratings (as measured by Ainsworth et al.'s (1971) sensitivity scale) were also found to be related to attachment security, though the frequency of appropriate mind-related comments was found to be an independent and stronger predictor (Meins et al., 2001). A reanalysis of the original behavioral mind-mindedness scales elaborates on these findings, explores the comparative strength of composite behavioral and verbal responses, and documents the independent role of appropriate and nonattuned mind-related comments in predicting attachment security at 12 months (Meins, 2013). These results confirm that mind-mindedness is best conceptualized as a multidimensional construct that may also relate to other developmental abilities in young children.

In another line of research, mind-mindedness, sensitivity, and attachment security were explored together (Lundy, 2003). In this work, sensitivity was conceptualized as interactional synchrony, where parents are seen to respond appropriately to their infants when their responses are reciprocal, mutually rewarding, and connected to the infant's preceding behavior (cf. Isabella, Belsky, & von Eye, 1989; Lundy, 2002). Both mothers and fathers were included and the frequency of interactional synchrony was found to mediate the relation between mind-related comments and attachment security at 13 months (Lundy, 2003). Thus, it appears that parents who frequently consider their infants' perspective are likely to engage in more synchronized interactions that, in turn, are associated with attachment security. Consistent with these findings, mind-mindedness, sensitivity, and attachment were also found to be associated when more rigorous, independent measures were used, thereby supporting the idea that sensitivity mediates between mind-mindedness and attachment security (Laranjo, Bernier, & Meins, 2008). Thus, just as Ainsworth and her colleagues postulated in their original conception of sensitivity, parents need to first understand their children's signals and cues before they can respond sensitively to them.

Whether paternal behavior is associated with attachment security is a question that has been explored more in recent years. Many researchers have assumed that similar findings regarding this link in mothers and their infants would be obtained in studies with fathers and their infants. However, the results are quite mixed. Early studies of fathers' interactions with their infants, either at 6 and 9 months of age or concurrent with Strange Situation assessments at 12 months, found no association between paternal responsiveness and attachment security (Notaro & Volling, 1999; Volling & Belsky, 1992a). Modest, though significant, associations between paternal behavior and attachment security were found when assessed concurrently (Rosen & Rothbaum, 1993). A small, but significant, association was found between paternal sensitivity and infant–father attachment security in a meta-analysis of eight extant studies (van IJzendoorn & de Wolff, 1997). This association was weaker than what has been obtained in studies of maternal sensitivity and attachment, though the reasons for these differences are not readily apparent.

It may be that though levels of sensitivity and reciprocity are comparable, there are differences in the meaning of sensitivity and responsiveness across mothers and fathers. There may be distinct behavioral characteristics associated with coordinated, synchronous exchanges that are unique for mothers and for fathers with their children. And maternal and paternal sensitivity and responsiveness in infancy may differentially predict to developing attachments and other indices of adjustment and socio-emotional adaptation in childhood or adolescence (Feldman et al., 2013; Feldman & Eidelman, 2004; Kochanska et al., 2008). Moreover, controlling for maternal effects is necessary when assessing father effects, though very few studies have adopted this strategy (cf. Aldous & Mulligan, 2002; Stolz, Barber, & Olsen, 2005; Volling, Blandon, & Gorvine, 2006). Unique father effects may be especially evident when evaluating children's ability to negotiate conflict and manage aggression, whereas unique maternal effects have been observed in the ability to engage in reciprocal dialogues within positive social interactions (Feldman et al., 2013). Studies that continue to examine the unique and shared influences that maternal and paternal behaviors have on their children's developing attachments and other social competencies are critical to deepening our understanding of the importance of caregiving.

Mediational analyses reveal that mothers and fathers have different patterns of influence on their children's development (e.g., Kochanska et al., 2008; Lindsey, Cremeens, Colwell, & Caldera, 2009). These unique influences may have to do with how affectionate mothers and fathers are, how much time they spend with their children, their ability to connect and respond appropriately to their children, or their own attachment representations (Caldera, Huston, & O'Brien, 1995; Cox, Owen, Henderson, & Margand, 1992; van IJzendoorn, 1995). Whether these differences in the ways that mothers and fathers influence their children impact later social and emotional development is an important question we will return to later on.

Temperament

Questions about the associations between attachment and temperament in infancy, childhood, and adolescence have been posed for several decades (see, for example, Goldsmith & Alansky, 1987; Goldsmith & Harman,

1994; Seifer & Schiller, 1995). Overlapping behavioral characteristics that are relevant to theories of attachment and temperament, and interpretive claims made by attachment and temperament theorists, contribute to the controversy (see Vaughn, Bost, & van IJzendoorn, 2008, for a comprehensive review). Adding to this complex terrain is the issue that while there is a fairly coherent theoretical context within which attachment relationships are understood, and a well-validated and widely used procedure for assessing qualitative differences in attachment security (i.e., the Strange Situation), the conceptualization and measurement of temperament is more complicated. There are multiple theoretical approaches to the study of temperament, each with its own definition of, and measurement strategy for capturing, possible dimensions (Goldsmith et al., 1987). Despite these conceptual differences, most theorists now agree that temperamental variations appear early in life, are strongly influenced by biological factors, and show a fair degree of individual consistency over time.

A substantial body of research has continued to explore and elaborate many of the theoretical ideas central to temperament research (for a review, see Shiner et al., 2012). Current conceptions of temperament have more carefully elaborated the complex ways in which biological, genetic, and environmental factors interact across development and influence temperament. Experience and context are now viewed as playing a critical role in impacting the expression of a broader range of temperament dimensions that include activity, reactivity, emotionality, and sociability as well as attention and self-regulation (Rothbart, 2011; Zentner & Shiner, 2012). When considered in relation to the development of early attachments, questions about individual differences in temperament often focus on the "goodness of fit" between the infant and the mother (Chess & Thomas, 1984). When the infant's temperament and the caregiver's expectations, attitudes, or behaviors do not match, the infant is at risk for poor outcomes. Certain temperamental qualities, such as irritability, may lead to positive developmental outcomes (e.g., secure attachment) when there is a good caregiving environment that can sensitively respond to the particular challenges this temperamental quality presents; alternatively, when the caregiving environment is less optimal, infant irritability may be a risk factor for insensitive or harsh caregiving and negative developmental outcomes may arise (e.g., insecure attachment). Thus, temperamental characteristics may make some infants differentially susceptible to environmental influences (van IJzendoorn & Bakermans-Kranenburg, 2012). Infant temperament may also influence the caregiving context, parental behavior, and the attachment relationship (Bates, Schermerhorn, & Petersen, 2012). Considered together, both infant and parent continually influence one other as part of a dynamic, transactional process.

There are several ways of interpreting the data that has emerged from systematic exploration of the attachment–temperament link (see Vaughn et al., 2008, for a comprehensive review). First, the view that temperamental predispositions directly determine individual differences in attachment security has not been supported by existing empirical work (see, for example, Seifer, Schiller, Sameroff, Resnick, & Riordan, 1996). Behavioral indices of temperamental variations are not directly linked, when measured either concurrently or predictively, to differences in patterns of attachment. Proneness to distress, for example, a temperamental quality, is not associated with only one pattern of attachment. Securely attached babies may be distressed easily by separations in the Strange Situation, but the parent's return to the room is sufficient for the child to derive comfort in her presence and to return to exploration. By contrast, insecure anxious-resistant babies may be distressed easily by the separation as well, but their exploration both before and after the separations may be limited by their lack of confidence in being able to use the caregiver as a secure base. Thus, babies who are prone to distress, who are highly inhibited, or who have "difficult" temperaments, given the "right" kind of care may develop a particular pattern of attachment because there are multiple pathways to both security and insecurity (Sroufe, 2005). Therefore, temperament alone does not determine attachment security. Additionally, though often treated as a static trait, temperamental qualities have been found to change and may even be impacted by quality of care provided by parents (Belsky, Fish, & Isabella, 1991).

Second, the view that individual differences in temperament create a potentially more challenging context for parents to provide sensitive care for their children has only been weakly supported. It may that an infant's "difficult" temperament makes it more difficult for parents to provide optimal care. Or perhaps, when parents are already strained by psychological, social, or economic stressors, an infant's difficult temperament introduces another stress for the parent to manage (Vaughn et al., 2008). But not all observers would agree on what makes an infant "difficult". Moreover, temperament reports from different raters are only moderately associated (e.g., Seifer, Sameroff, Barrett, & Krafchuk, 1994), suggesting that observers' judgments may vary depending on their relationship to the infant being rated. And when adequate help and support is received from family members and friends, difficult infants are easier to manage and infants who are rated as "irritable" are no more likely to be rated as insecurely attached than are infants rated as "easy" (Crockenberg, 1981). By contrast, mothers with difficult infants who are socially isolated or have little support from other adults have more difficulty developing a secure attachment with their babies (Levitt, Weber, & Clark, 1986).

Thus, when examined alone, distinct indices of temperamental qualities have not been found to influence parenting and to be associated with attachment security (Vaughn et al., 2008). It is more likely that temperament indirectly influences parental behavior and, when considered together with other situational and contextual stressors, impacts the developing attachment relationship. This position emphasizes the contributions of both caregiving behaviors and temperamental factors in determining attachment security.

Genetic and Environmental Influences on Attachment Security

There is now considerable support for the view that the quality of early attach-ment relationships results from the dyad's history of interaction, influenced by temperamental characteristics of the child and parental caregiving behaviors. If temperament alone predicted attachment patterns, then we would expect infants to engender comparable caregiving behaviors and develop a similar pattern of attachment to both parents. Similarly, if parental caregiving behav-iors were all that was relevant, we would expect older and younger siblings to have the same quality of attachment to the same parent. However, extant research indicates that infants' attachments to their two caregivers are only modestly congruent (Fox, Kimmerly, & Schafer, 1991; Rosen & Burke, 1999; Sagi et al., 1995; Steele, Steele, & Fonagy, 1996). And two siblings do not necessarily have the same quality of attachment to the same caregiver, either when assessed when the two children are the same age (e.g., at 12 months (Ward, Vaughn, & Robb, 1988)) or when attachment is assessed at the same time using age-appropriate measures for younger and older siblings (Rosen & Burke, 1999). Thus, it appears that patterns of attachment reflect the interac-tional history of the dyad over time.

But are there genetic factors that influence attachment security as well? Sisters and brothers raised in the same family have parents who are likely to be similarly sensitive or insensitive to their children, to maintain a stable capacity for mentalization, mind-mindedness, or reflective function and, therefore, to relate in similar ways to their children. However, despite these shared aspects of the siblings' environment, there are also differences in how parents relate to each of their children, creating unique, different, or nonshared environmental influences (Hetherington, Reiss, & Plomin, 1994; Plomin & Daniels, 1987). Moreover, genetically determined child characteristics, such as temperament, influence mothers and fathers' capacity to respond sensitively to their child or may make children differentially susceptible to parental influences. Study-ing pairs of twins provides a unique opportunity to explore, within similar childrearing contexts, the influence of genetic factors on attachment security. The degree of concordance in attachment classifications would be expected to be significantly greater among identical (monozygotic (MZ)) than fraternal (dizygotic (DZ)) twins (or nontwin siblings) if genetically based child factors influence parental sensitivity (Goldsmith, Buss, & Lemery, 1997; Scarr & McCartney, 1983).

There are several studies that have assessed infant–mother attachment security using samples of MZ and DZ twins. For example, 60% of MZ twins and 57% of DZ twins, in a total sample of 157 twelve-month-old twin pairs and their mothers who were seen in the Strange Situation, were found to be concordant in attachment classifications (Bokhorst et al., 2003). Using behavior genetic modeling, 52% of the variance in attachment security within the organized secure and insecure categories was found to be attributable to shared environmental effects (for example, parental behaviors are similar across siblings), while the remainder of the variance was explained by nonshared environmental factors (for example, parental behaviors that are unique to a particular dyad) and measurement error. Substantial associations between twins' secure and insecure classifications were also obtained in a subsequent analysis of the data, excluding twin pairs with disorganized attachments, with similarities in shared environmental influences (Fearon et al., 2006). Moreover, nonshared environmental effects were found to create an inverse relation between sensitivity and attachment such that greater sensitivity to one, but not the other, twin was associated with a lower likelihood of secure attachment in the first twin. Thus, the relationship that the parent has with one twin appears to influence attachment security with the other twin. Comparable findings emerged from a study of older preschoolers, where high concordance was found in both MZ (70%) and DZ (64%) twin pairs (O'Connor & Croft, 2001). Again, these high rates of concordance indicate environmental, rather than genetic, influences on parent–child attachment relationships. By contrast, substantial genetic effects, and no shared environmental effects, were found in a sample of 18–24-month-old twin pairs, where 68% of the MZ twins, and only 39% of the DZ twins, were concordant in attachment security using an adapted attachment measure (Finkel, Wille, & Matheny, 1998). Taken together, these results suggest that there is a significant effect of shared (and nonshared) environmental factors on attachment security, while genetic effects appear to have relatively less influence (Belsky & Fearon, 2008). The similarity in twins' attachment classifications may be partially explained by consistencies in parental sensitivity; there is still a gap in our ability to account for nonshared influences on attachment relationships within the family.

In particular, this work highlights the significance of parental behaviors and helps to clarify their importance for attachment security in sibling and twin pairs. While parental sensitivity plays a critical role in influencing concordance in sibling attachment, this does not imply that the way sensitive parental behavior is expressed needs to be identical across all children in the same family. Parental behavior may objectively appear to be different when evaluated independently of interactive context, though it may still be "functionally similar" (O'Connor & Croft, 2001) in its degree of sensitivity to siblings' differing needs for affection, warmth, or control, or to siblings who are differentially responsive to parental behaviors. Thus, a secure attachment relationship may be the consequence of nonshared experiences, whereby different parenting behaviors may serve the same goal of sensitive and responsive care offered by the parent in response to each child's unique needs and temperamental characteristics. Moreover, developmental differences between siblings of different ages, and in the siblings over time, require frequent accommodations in discrete parental behaviors, though there may be consistency in overall parental sensitivity and responsiveness. However, even among identical (MZ) twins, there is only moderate similarity in parental behavior (Plomin, 1994). And, importantly, developmental changes in genetic influences, as well as in shared and nonshared environmental influences, also need to be considered given that shared environmental factors tend to be the largest in early childhood (McCartney, Harris, & Bernieri, 1990). Differential parental behavior, therefore, may be expected and necessary as parents accommodate their behavior to the particular needs of each of their children; these nonshared experiences may reflect changing contributions of genetics and environment to parental sensitivity and to the development of attachment relationships (Fearon et al., 2006).

Studies of siblings' and twins' attachment relationships with the same parent challenge attachment researchers to continue to explore the ways in which infant characteristics, parental behaviors, and familial factors may, alone or in combination, influence attachment security. Children's temperamental predispositions may be modified with time and maturation and these changes will undoubtedly impact parental behavior and the quality of dyadic interaction (e.g., Belsky et al., 1991). Similarly, parental behavior may alter the expression of individual differences in the child's particular temperamental profile and influence the developing attachment relationship. The family context, including marital relationship quality, psychosocial stressors, and availability of social supports, needs to be considered as well. Considered together, it appears that patterns of attachment reflect the dynamic interplay of genetic and environmental factors as the child and parent negotiate their relationship over time.

What Are the Developmental Consequences of Early Attachment Relationships?

John Bowlby (1969/1982) originally introduced the theoretical notion that qualitative differences in attachment security have significant implications for children's concurrent and later development. Ainsworth's development and validation of the Strange Situation procedure (Ainsworth et al., 1978) allowed Bowlby's idea to be empirically tested. Researchers have followed infants who were originally seen in the Strange Situation when they were 12 months of age. In general, the extant studies, spanning time periods ranging from several months to several decades, support the idea that secure attachment is related to better functioning in a variety of social, emotional, and cognitive domains. Thus, individual differences in attachment security appear to be associated with both concurrent and later development of exploration and play, curiosity, behavior with peers and friends, frustration tolerance, language development, self-recognition, quality of peer relationships, ego resilience and ego control, behavior problems, and many other developmental outcomes. There are important questions that need to be asked about *why* these associations might be expected and *under what circumstances* we would anticipate them to be found. It is also essential to understand what *mechanisms* or *processes* underlie these associations. These are the issues to which we will now turn our attention.

The concept of "internal working models" was introduced by Bowlby (1969/1982, 1980, 1988) to account for the internalized cognitive representations of relationships and the self that result from early attachment experiences. Bowlby argued that the infant who has early experiences with a sensitive caregiver expects similarly sensitive encounters in new relationships and behaves in ways that elicit this support. These early attachment experiences also lead the infant to view the self as worthy of sensitive and responsive care and to seek out experiences that confirm this perspective. Thus, working models are "interpretive filters through which children reconstruct their understanding of new relationships and experiences...(and) internalize conceptions of themselves from early relational experiences that form the basis for developing self-concept and other self-referential beliefs" (Thompson, 2008, p. 350). These models guide the ways in which children relate to others and think about the self, thereby confirming or disconfirming expectations about the self and relationships.

Working models are thus constructed during infancy. Secure infants, for example, use their parents as a base from which to explore, seek interaction and proximity when uncertain or frightened, derive comfort when distressed, and resume exploration when calmed. Their internal working models incorporate a view of their attachment figure as sensitive, available, and responsive in meeting their attachment and exploratory needs. Insecure-avoidant infants develop a working model of parents as unable to provide a safe haven when the infant needs one. This failure on the part of the parent leads the infant to turn away from the attachment figure, avoiding proximity and interaction when stressed. Insecure-resistant infants view their parents as unpredictable. They try to stay close to them in case they need them, but cannot derive comfort from them in ways that promote successful exploration. These organized strategies for managing attachment relationships, whether secure or insecure, are contrasted to the internal models of insecure-disorganized infants who view their parents as a source of danger or fear, leading them to behave in ways that are disoriented and/or frightened. Thus, internal working models are organized around the history of infant–caregiver interactions.

Internal working models may serve as the primary mechanism by which continuity is maintained between early attachment and later functioning. These models are developing over time as well, incorporating attributes of multiple caregivers, representations of significant attachment-related experiences, and developing understanding of the self and of others (Bretherton, 1991, 1993; Thompson, 1998). Additionally, distinct components of these models (e.g., autobiographical memories, relational expectations) may develop at varying times and have different influences on outcome measures during particular developmental periods. For example, because self-representations are expanding and increasingly refined at about the age of 5 or 6 years, a secure attachment at this age may be more influential on self-image than a secure attachment during infancy (Thompson, 2008). Finally, internal working models are formed, in part, as a result of shared conversations with others about the self, relationships, and experiences (Fivush, 1994; Oppenheim & Waters, 1995). Thus, caregivers influence working models, both in the care they provide to their children and in their interpretations offered in discourse about their children's relational experiences (Thompson, 2008).

There are, of course, circumstances under which we might not expect there to be continuity between early attachment and later social, emotional, and cognitive development. Family crises, marital disruption, life transitions, and other normative and unexpected events may influence the quality of the parent–child relationship. If there is continuity in the care provided by parents during these challenging periods, then this may provide the bridge between early attachment security, developing internal working models of the self and relationships, and later outcomes (Thompson, 2008). If, however, parents find it to be more difficult to maintain their responsiveness to their children when challenged by marital or financial stress, or to respond sensitively and appropriately to their child who is experiencing a normal developmental transition (such as problems when entering kindergarten), then these relational changes may disrupt the associations between early attachment security, internal models of self and relationships, and later developmental outcomes. Thus, when the same conditions that foster a secure attachment relationship are maintained over time, it is more likely that children will benefit from the continued support provided by sensitive parenting and will be open to the caregiver's socialization influences. Under these circumstances, attachment security will more likely be associated with a more positive view of the self, greater competence in social interactions, increased curiosity, and openness to experiences that promote cognitive growth. The initial internal models that guide the child's view of relationships and of the self continue to be modified and refined in the context of later interactions. If there is continuity in the quality of parent–child interactions, then we would expect there to be links between early attachments and later adjustment (Thompson, 2006). However, when the parent–child relationship is disrupted, or the quality of care is diminished, early attachments may not be associated with subsequent developmental outcomes.

Several significant longitudinal studies have explored these predictive links between early attachment and later competence (see Cassidy & Shaver, 2008; Grossman, Grossman, & Waters, 2005; Sroufe, Egeland, Carlson, & Collins, 2005a). Generally, there are three distinct outcomes on which these studies have focused: (1) functioning in interpersonal relationships, particularly peer interactions (e.g., Erickson, Sroufe, & Egeland, 1985; Schneider, Atkinson, & Tardif, 2001) and later romantic relationships (Roisman, Collins, Sroufe, & Egeland, 2005); (2) internalizing problems (e.g., Bosquet & Egeland, 2006; Groh, Roisman, van IJzendoorn, Bakermans-Kranenburg, & Fearon, 2012); and (3) externalizing problems (Fearon, Bakermans-Kranenburg, van IJzendoorn, Lapsley, & Roisman, 2010). The results tend to support the notion that individuals who are securely attached are more competent in their interpersonal relationships and exhibit lower levels of internalizing and externalizing behaviors. However, it is important to note that there is a dearth of longitudinal studies exploring attachment and later competence across socioeconomic and cultural groups, thereby limiting the conclusions that may be drawn from the extant body of research.

Moreover, there are an astounding number of short- and long-term follow-up studies that have explored many other developmental outcomes of early attachment relationships. There are some investigations that focus on relational outcomes with parents, siblings, peers, friends, and romantic partners. There are others that examine personality outcomes, self-concept, social cognition, and conscience development. And still other research has explored emotion regulation and emotion understanding (see Thompson, 2008, for a review). Generally, these studies support the notion that secure attachment relationships during infancy and early childhood provide children with many advantages and more optimal outcomes, regardless of the particular areas of development evaluated. Importantly, a few studies have examined attachment to both mothers and fathers and considered their association to later outcomes. When children are insecure in their attachment relationships with both parents at 15 months of age, they exhibit more behavior problems as reported by their teachers at 6½ years and by their parents at 8 years of age. A secure attachment with at least one parent appears to offset this risk, though a secure attachment to both parents does not provide any more protection than a secure attachment to only one parent (Kochanska & Kim, 2013). Insecure attachments to both parents at 25 months of age are also associated with more behavior problems 6 years later, though fewer behavior problems and greater competence are observed when children with insecure attachments to mothers have secure attachments with their fathers (Boldt, Kochanska, Yoon, & Nordling, 2014). Exploring the mechanisms that account for these associations, and continuing to examine the predictive power of attachment to both mothers and fathers, are important areas for future research.

There are several limitations to extant studies as well (see, for example, Roisman & Groh, 2011). Most importantly, the research does not disentangle the many possible reasons as to *why* early attachment security is related to later developmental outcomes. However, some significant clues have emerged. Early attachment may be more predictive of later development when there is continuity in the quality of parental caregiving (Sroufe et al., 2005a). High-quality mother–child conversations that elaborate and support developing social interactions and emotional competencies may be relevant as well (Fivush, 1994; Raikes & Thompson, 2006). Internal working models may direct memory and attention to experiences and relationships that are consistent with prior internal cognitive representations, thereby supporting the construction and maintenance of stable models over time (Bretherton & Munholland, 2008). These models may grow with conceptual development across childhood and adolescence. Thus, advances in event representation, theory of mind, and autobiographical memory may lead to consistencies in the ways in which social experiences are understood, encoded, and represented, thereby contributing to the understanding of the self in relation to others and to the continued use of attachment-related working models (Thompson, 2008). Children who are securely attached may have certain social-cognitive advantages that influence their social competence (Cassidy, Kirsh, Scolton, & Parke, 1996). And attachment security serves as a moderator in influencing the impact of parenting strategies on the child's moral development (Kochanska, Aksan, Knaack, & Rhines, 2004).

Given the predictive power of early attachment security, we need to ask what happens when there are problems in negotiating an early secure attachment relationship. Are there compensatory processes that may influence attachment relationships? For example, is it possible for an individual who has a history of an early, insecure attachment in infancy to achieve "earned security" (see, for example, Roisman, Padrón, Sroufe, & Egeland, 2002) or to develop secure representations of attachment in adulthood? Indeed, it has been demonstrated that adults who report early negative relationships with attachment figures have the capacity to turn to an alternative figure for comfort and emotional support when vulnerable or stressed and demonstrate the ability to ultimately form secure attachments with their own infants (Saunders, Jacobvitz, Zaccagnino, Beverung, & Hazen, 2011). Additionally, there may be certain developmental periods when the associations between early attachment security and later developmental outcomes are strongest. For example, links between attachment and peer functioning have been found to be of larger magnitude for peer relationships in the middle childhood and adolescent periods than for the early childhood period (Schneider et al., 2001). Mother–child and father–child attachment relationships may also differentially influence aspects of social and emotional functioning, depending upon the developmental periods assessed. Thus, future research needs to incorporate a developmentally sensitive lens when exploring the outcomes of early attachment relationships. Alternative pathways to achieving attachment security need to be better understood. Finally, examining the individual, relational, and contextual factors that may underlie the associations between attachment and later development, and adopting more sophisticated mediational models, represent important directions for future research.

Attachment Relationships Beyond Infancy

Why Was Attachment Security Initially Studied Only In Infancy?

There are several theoretical and methodological reasons as to why attachment theory and research began with an emphasis on the infancy period (Schneider-Rosen, 1990). Psychoanalytic thinking underscored the importance of significant early relationships and evolved to include the notion that anxiety is a signal to the threat of a meaningful interpersonal loss (Freud, 1940/1964). Early relationships were seen as the prototype for later relationships and for the emergence of the self (Breger, 1974; Erikson, 1950/1963; Klein, 1976; Loevinger, 1976; Mahler et al., 1975; Sandler, 1975; Sullivan, 1953). Attachment theory, with its roots in psychoanalytic thinking, therefore emphasized the importance of the infancy period. The first meaningful relationships, initially viewed as with only mothers, developed during the first year and were seen to have an enduring impact on the child's development (Ainsworth, 1969; Bowlby, 1958, 1969/1982).

Early attachment researchers adopted an organizational approach to development, with its emphasis on a set of developmental tasks or issues around which behavioral reorganizations occur (Sroufe, 1979; Sroufe & Rutter, 1984). According to this organizational perspective, development is a coherent process involving an integration of emerging capacities in the social, emotional, and cognitive domains. Early adaptation is thought to promote concurrent and later adaptation within and across domains, given consistency in the caregiving environment. Alternatively, difficulties in the resolution of stage-salient tasks may result in the development of compensatory mechanisms, which in turn create alternative pathways to achieving competence or leave the child vulnerable to developing psychopathology (see Cicchetti & Schneider-Rosen, 1984, for a review). Within this organizational perspective, establishing an attachment relationship is the first stage-salient task of infancy. Researchers, in their early efforts to demonstrate both the construct and predictive validity of the attachment construct, focused on individual differences in attachment and the role these early relationships play in influencing subsequent development. By then examining new competencies or tasks, such as exploration or mastery in the toddler period, negotiation of peer relationships in preschool, or curiosity and persistence in the early school years, researchers inadvertently perpetuated the idea that attachment relationships decrease in importance relative to these emerging abilities. But, in fact, we now know that attachment relationships remain critical to the individual in childhood and adolescence and remain so through the entire lifespan.

Attachment researchers highlighted the idea that achieving organized, predictable patterns of behavior for managing attachment-related needs was an essential task in infancy. While a secure pattern of attachment was seen to be the optimal outcome for most infants, in certain dyads and in particular caregiving environments an insecure pattern may be more adaptive (cf. Fonagy & Target, 2007; Schneider-Rosen, Braunwald, Carlson, & Cicchetti, 1985). Thus, the consideration of diverse populations, such as children raised in homes where there is trauma or abuse, encouraged attachment researchers to evaluate their theoretical assumptions, thereby extending and refining their work in significant ways. Additionally, researchers began to study children's attachments to both their mothers and fathers (e.g., Diener, Mangelsdorf, McHale, & Frosch, 2002; Verissimo et al., 2011; Rosen & Burke, 1999), recognizing that children develop unique relationships with each of their attachment figures. Attachment has been studied in infant–parent dyads from different socioeconomic backgrounds, as well as from families where there are marital challenges, emotional and psychological problems, and developmental disabilities. Together, this work has been critical to understanding the precursors to and consequences of early attachment patterns and to the exploration of attachment as a relational construct.

Attachment researchers have also examined attachment relationships in various cultural groups. Despite the fact that Ainsworth's (1967) original study of infant–mother attachment was conducted in Uganda, researchers began to raise some critical issues relevant to studying attachment in other cultures: (1) are attachment relationships important in all cultures? (2) does the classification scheme used in the United States have relevance for other cultural groups? (3) are there similar precursors to attachment security (e.g., maternal sensitivity) in other cultures? (4) what are the developmental sequelae of attachment patterns in other cultural groups? (5) what is the impact of experiences with multiple caregivers on attachment to the primary caregiver? (van IJzendoorn & Sagi-Schwartz, 2008). These important questions generated a substantial body of new research, highlighting the ways in which infants with varying caregiving experiences may behave differently in the Strange Situation.

Infants differ, for example, in their experiences with separation from the caregiver. Consequently, the Strange Situation, developed for use with parent–infant dyads in the United States, may have another meaning to infants from other cultural communities, thereby impacting infant behavior and raising questions about the validity of this method. Infants in Japan are in close contact with their mothers and are rarely left alone as their mothers carry them, hold them, and usually sleep in the same bed with them (Rothbaum, Weisz, Pott, Miyake, & Morelli, 2000). In Kenya, Gusii infants are held by their mothers for much of the day during the first year. Infants are kept in close contact with their mothers in Puerto Rico (Harwood, Miller, & Irizarry, 1995). In Uganda, infants do not experience brief separations but are separated from their mothers for long periods of time while their mothers work (Colin, 1996). And in Israel, communal sleeping arrangements with parents and caregivers are part of the upbringing for infants raised on kibbutzim (Sagi, Koren-Karie, Gini, Ziv, & Joels, 2002). Because of their experiences, infants from these cultures are more stressed by separations and have more difficulty being comforted upon reunion in the Strange Situation. They are more likely to be classified as ambivalent in their attachment relationship as compared to infants from the United States. By contrast, infants in Great Britain, Sweden, and Germany are encouraged by their parents to be independent, even more than what has been observed by parents in the United States. Infants from these countries are more likely to display behaviors that lead to an avoidant attachment classification in the Strange Situation (Colin, 1996). Researchers have found similarities across cultures in what attachment experts and parents conceptualize as the hallmarks of a securely attached child (Posada et al., 1995). However, the actual behaviors that are used to signify secure or insecure attachment patterns may be different across cultures. Thus, the assumptions underlying the use of the Strange Situation, and the criteria used for capturing security in parent–infant dyads in the United States, may not be appropriate when studying attachment relationships in children around the world.

Along with these theoretical considerations that have challenged attachment researchers, there are also methodological concerns that have emerged. The Strange Situation was the most commonly used measure to assess qualitative differences in attachment in 12- and 18-month-old infants. It was soon observed that older children, who have increased experiences with separation and improved coping skills, were less likely to respond to separations with heightened attachment behaviors and the Strange Situation could not be used to assess attachment security. Capturing individual differences in attachment security beyond infancy was not possible because measurement strategies were not available. As researchers began to acknowledge the significance of attachment relationships beyond the infancy period, they also wanted to examine questions about the stability of attachment over time. New developmentally appropriate coding schemes were required to capture the more advanced and relevant attachment behaviors activated in older children and to evaluate qualitative differences in patterns of attachment.

Developments in the Measurement of Attachment Security

Modifications to the original Strange Situation coding scheme were introduced, based on the understanding that developmental advances lead to new behavioral strategies for exploration, relating to the parent, and managing the stress of separation. These newer schemes assumed that age-related changes in overt behaviors may still be seen to reflect the same underlying organized patterns of attachment (see, for example, Cassidy, Marvin, & the MacArthur Attachment Working Group, 1992; Crittenden, 1994; Schneider-Rosen, 1990). An alternative to the Strange Situation, the California Attachment Procedure (CAP), was found to provide a valid attachment measure for children who are accustomed to routine separations from their parents (such as those involved in child care) (Clarke-Stewart, Goossens, & Allhusen, 2001). Rather than focusing on separation-reunion sequences, the CAP assesses the way a child who is stressed (by a scary robot or a loud noise) uses the mother as a secure base. The measure yields a score that is similar to Ainsworth's attachment types (secure, insecure-avoidant, or insecure-resistant). While there has not been an extensive body of research based on this attachment measure, it is a theoretically based assessment procedure that has been found to be strongly related to Strange Situation classifications and to ratings of maternal sensitivity.

Some attachment researchers have coded children's reunion behavior in the Strange Situation along specific scales, rather than considering children's behavior across all episodes and classifying overall security (Fraley & Spieker, 2003). Attachment behaviors activated in the separation-reunion sequences are coded on four of Ainsworth's original scales: proximity and contact seeking, contact maintenance, avoidance, and resistance. Through factor analysis, these scales are reduced to two dimensions: (1) the dimension of proximity seeking versus avoidance, which captures the extent to which the infant uses the caregiver as a secure base as opposed to minimizing contact with the caregiver; and (2) the dimension of anger versus resistance, which reflects the amount of overt anger and conflict expressed toward the caregiver. These continuous measures of attachment security offer ratings that are distinct from the traditional attachment categories. While the continuous nature of attachment classifications may ultimately prove to be useful and some researchers support these efforts (e.g., Cummings, 2003), others have questioned its usefulness (e.g., Cassidy, 2003; Sroufe, 2003). Whether or not they are appropriate alternatives to the Strange Situation for use with infants is still an empirical question. However, researchers who question the assumptions of the categorical or continuous approaches to studying attachment are promoting important discussions about the way in which attachment is conceptualized and measured.

Several alternatives to the Strange Situation procedure have also been developed for use with older children. While observations of the infant's behavior are used to draw inferences about the processes going on inside the infant and about the quality of the infant's relationship with attachment figures, the capacity for symbolic thought and language that emerges during the preschool years introduces new possibilities for what could, until this point, only be accomplished by physical proximity and contact. Now, the development of language serves the attachment system. Children may call out across a distance or communicate with a caregiver with words, thereby achieving comfort and reassurance. They may also tolerate longer separations. For example, a 4-year-old knows that a working parent will return at the end of the day and may be soothed by a picture, a phone call, a substitute object, or the anticipation of her return. Moreover, developmental advances result in the "move to the level of representation" (Main, Kaplan, & Cassidy, 1985, p. 66) and the construction of internal working models. These models contain perceptions and memories, including the affective content, of repeated relational exchanges with caregivers, encoded as scripts (Bowlby, 1969/1982; Bretherton, Grossman, Grossman, & Waters, 2005; Waters & Waters, 2006). Developed from their interactional experiences, these internal representational models are expected to parallel actual behaviors with the attachment figure. Therefore, concordance is anticipated between behavioral measures assessing secure-base behavior or behavior on reunion and representational measures (see Bretherton & Munholland, 2008).

Even though we may not have access to them until language develops, internal working models have been inferred from the infant's organization of attachment-related behaviors directed toward the caregiver in the Strange Situation. In older children, these models are reflected at the behavioral level in children's play and at the representational level in their verbalizations. Thus, new representational measures of attachment have been designed to parallel Ainsworth's original categorical system and/or to capture specific aspects of attachment security. Observations of children's doll play, with a focus on attachment-related themes, are an alternative approach to understanding attachment in childhood. Several protocols have been developed, each with their own method for evaluating and classifying attachment (see Solomon & George, 2008). For example, the Attachment Story Completion Task (Bretherton, Ridgeway, & Cassidy, 1990) relies on a doll-play procedure, originally developed for 4-year-olds, with a story stem introducing something that happened (e.g., a child's parents leave). The child is asked to enact with the dolls what happens next and the child's verbal responses and doll play are classified based on the predominant response to the stories. The coding criteria were designed based on anticipated consistencies between what the child describes and what is to be expected based on the well-documented reunion behaviors of children in each of the Ainsworth attachment groups. "Secure" (group B) children will enact coping in relation to a parent leaving by playing with the grandmother doll, "avoidant" (group A) children will ask for another story as a way of avoiding a response, "ambivalent" (group C) children do not have a consistent pattern of responding, and "disorganized" (group D) children provide unusual, incoherent responses such as throwing the doll on the floor. There is limited reliability and validity data available on this measure; however, the use of this measure does highlight the ways in which representational processes operate in young children in forms that parallel what have been identified in adolescents and adults. Secure children, for example, express their attachment behaviors in active and persistent ways and communicate affect (whether it is joy, sadness, or anger) openly and directly. They express confidence in the resolution of attachment-related concerns and anxieties. Alternative doll play and "projective" techniques for assessing attachment have also been used, including Cassidy's Incomplete Stories with Doll Family (Cassidy, 1988) and the Attachment Doll Play Assessment (e.g., George & Solomon, 1990/1996/2000). To the extent that these representational procedures actually activate the attachment behavioral system in young children, they may prove useful for further differentiating children with varying attachment patterns.

Another procedure, the Separation Anxiety Test, uses a series of six photographs, following a protocol originally developed for adolescents (Hansburg, 1972) and then modified for 4- to 7-year-old children (Klagsbrun & Bowlby, 1976). The pictures portray scenes, ranging from mildly stressful (a child in bed with a parent saying goodnight) to most stressful (a child watching as a parent leaves), that are expected to elicit attachment-related responses. An adult introduces each picture and asks the child to describe how the child in the picture is feeling and what the child will do. Representational models of attachment security are inferred based on the child's verbal responses. A classification scheme was developed (Kaplan, 1985) that focuses on 6-year-old children's emotional openness and their ability to come up with constructive solutions to the feelings stimulated by these pictures portraying separation scenarios. Children who are open and clear in their descriptions and cope with separation in constructive ways are classified as "resourceful" (group B).

When children express feelings of distress or vulnerability in response to separation but cannot elicit coping strategies, they are classified as "inactive" (group A). A mixture of emotional responses to the parent, especially when they are contradictory (e.g., wanting to please despite feeling angry toward the parent), results in an "ambivalent" (group C) classification. And the "fearful" (group D) classification is used for children who express fear, are disorganized in their thinking, and cannot offer constructive strategies for dealing with separation. While there is relatively little information regarding the reliability and validity of this coding scheme as it has been used with the Separation Anxiety Test, it has stimulated the development of other representational measures of attachment (see Solomon & George, 2008).

Many researchers believed that attachment could be assessed more easily when children could talk about their attachment experiences. However, attachment researchers have learned that language may not be more reliable than behavior in inferring attachment security. Increased regulation and control over thought and feelings, and the use of defensive processes in older children, adolescence, and adults, may make it more difficult to ascertain the "truth" about attachment relationships from language alone (Ainsworth, 1990). With the emergence of developmentally appropriate measures and coding schemes to capture attachment security in older children, the focus has been on internal working models of attachment that include an appreciation of the affective and cognitive dimensions of attachment relationships.

For middle childhood, self-report measures of strategies reflecting secure attachment (Kerns Security Scale (Kerns, Klepac, & Cole, 1996)) or avoidant and preoccupied attachment (Finnegan, Hodges, & Perry, 1996) have been used. The Separation Anxiety Test (Kaplan, 1985; Klagsbrun & Bowlby, 1976) was modified to assess attachment-related feelings and thoughts in late childhood and early adolescence (Resnick, 1993). Other projective techniques used for early adolescents have been developed to evaluate attachment-related representations of family members (Fury, Carlson, & Sroufe, 1997) and of attachment figures (Sroufe, Carlson, & Shulman, 1993). The Child Attachment Interview has been developed to assess representational processes (similar to those assessed in the Adult Attachment Interview (George, Kaplan, & Main, 1984, 1985, 1996)) in late childhood and early adolescence (Shmueli-Goetz, Target, Fonagy, & Datta, 2008; Target, Fonagy, Shmueli-Goetz, Datta, & Schneider, 1999). And the Experiences in Close Relationships scale (Brennan, Clark, & Shaver, 1998) has also been revised for children between the ages of 8 and 14 years, with demonstrated usefulness as an instrument for measuring attachment in children and young adolescents (Brenning, Soenens, Braet, & Bosmans, 2011).

Parents or trained observers may also complete attachment assessments by observing and rating children's secure-base behavior in the home. This method is quite different from those systems that classify attachment based on the child's behavior or using representational processes. The Attachment Q-Set (AQS: Waters, 1995) consists of a set of 90 cards containing descriptive phrases of children's attachment-related behaviors and is appropriate for use with children between the ages of 1 and 5. After observing the child at home for an extended period of time, an observer may complete the AQS; alternatively a parent or other caregiver who knows the child well may complete it. The set of cards is sorted, following a carefully prescribed method, into nine piles, ranging from those phrases that are most descriptive of the child to those that are least descriptive. The mother, other caregiver, or observer's sorting of the cards is then correlated with the standard criterion sort for a hypothetically "most secure" child; the final correlation reflects how similar to the secure child the child rated appears. Thus, children are seen as secure or insecure (based on the correlation to the hypothetical standard) but subtypes of attachment insecurity are not assigned. Scores from the AQS have been found to be moderately related to Strange Situation classifications in a meta-analysis of studies that have explored this association. Additionally, the AQS has been found to distinguish between children who have clinical problems and a nonclinical sample. Finally, observers' AQS ratings are more highly related to Strange Situation classifications (and thus more valid) than are mothers' ratings (van IJzendoorn, Vereijken, Bakermans-Kranenburg, & Riksen-Walraven, 2004). Thus, the AQS provides a useful method for exploring normative patterns of secure-base behavior and for identifying individual differences in attachment security beyond infancy.

When different techniques are used to assess attachment relationships, an important question to address is how consistent the findings are across measures. In general, associations between questionnaire and interview measures of attachment are typically quite low in middle childhood (Granot & Mayseless, 2001; Kerns, Tomich, Aspelmeier, & Contreras, 2000; Kerns, Abraham, Schlegelmilch, & Morgan, 2007) as well as in adolescence and adulthood (Crowell, Fraley, & Shaver, 2008). However, interpreting these low correlations is difficult. Do they reflect a lack of consistency across measures or are self-report and interview measures capturing different aspects of attachment and therefore not expected to be related? For example, while it has been incredibly useful to consider children and adolescents' organized internal representations of attachment, evaluated by interview techniques, there are also characteristics of particular attachment relationships that are critical to assess and that are the focus of self-report questionnaires. Still, it can be advantageous to use multiple measures in that they offer a broader assessment of the attachment construct and reduce the reliance on a single measurement strategy.

Is There Stability or Instability in Attachment Patterns?

Attachment researchers argue that despite developmental changes over time, continuity in attachment patterns is expected. Even though changes in particular attachment behaviors are expected, there should be stability in the overall organization of attachment relationships. Each partner continues to adapt to the other's interaction patterns, thereby contributing to the relationship's underlying stability (Sroufe & Waters, 1977). However, this continuity occurs only when there is stability in the quality of age-appropriate care provided to the child. It also depends on the child organizing attachment-related behaviors into internal models that tend to be resistant to change (Ainsworth, 1990). Under certain conditions, however, changes in attachment quality may be expected (see Cassidy & Shaver, 2008, for a comprehensive review of these issues).

In order to assess questions about the continuity of attachment patterns, longitudinal, prospective studies have been conducted that explore attachment security in participants first seen in infancy and followed into adulthood (see Grossman et al., 2006, for an overview). Several investigators have, for example, examined the long-term stability of attachment patterns within the toddler period (from 12 to 18 or 24 months), across early childhood (from 12 to 60 months), or across periods of developmental transitions (from infancy to childhood, adolescence, and early adulthood) (e.g., Weinfield, Sroufe, Egeland, & Carlson, 2008). During the preschool period, 68% of children who were first seen at 3–4 years of age in a modified separation-reunion procedure (Cassidy & Marvin, 1992) were found to have similar attachment classifications when tested again two years later (Moss, Cyr, Bureau, Tarabulsy, & Dubois-Comtois, 2005). Similarly, findings of high stability (over 70%) have been reported across shorter time periods (e.g., Hamilton, 2000; Main & Cassidy, 1988; Waters, 1978) though some researchers have also reported much lower levels of stability (Belsky, Campbell, Cohn, & Moore, 1996; Cassidy, Berlin, & Belsky, 1990). Across longer periods of time, 72% of infants who were classified as securely attached were found to be secure 20 years later (Waters, Merrick, Treboux, Crowell, & Albersheim, 2000). Fraley (2002) conducted a meta-analysis in which evidence was provided for significant, but modest, stability from infancy to young adulthood in attachment security.

There is some research that offers mixed evidence for stability and documents "lawful change," or change in attachment security over time that is theoretically consistent and meaningful (Hamilton, 2000; Waters et al., 2000; Weinfield, Sroufe, & Egeland, 2000). Other empirical findings are consistent with this idea that change may be lawful and expected. For example, a significant percentage of infants with insecure attachments were found to develop secure relationships by 4 (Fish, 2004) or 5 (Lounds, Borkowski, Whitman, Maxwell, & Weed, 2005) years of age. As mothers become more experienced, or better at understanding their children's emotional signals and needs, or as family circumstances change, so too might the quality of attachment relationship change from insecure to secure (Waters et al., 2000). And even secure attachments may become insecure over time when there are traumatic family situations or increases in parental hostility or conflict (Moss et al., 2005). Exploring questions about stability or instability in attachment patterns in populations who encounter relatively low levels of stress (e.g., intact,

White, middle-class American families) may yield a very different pattern of results than when looking at a lower socioeconomic status population or at children who are more likely to experience alterations in attachment relationships due to family, parental, or environmental stressors (see, for example, Booth-LaForce et al., 2014). Conducting longitudinal studies with more socioeconomically and culturally diverse populations continues to be an important direction for future work.

Finally, only relatively small numbers of individuals have been studied longitudinally from infancy to young adulthood (Roisman & Haydon, 2011) though recent studies are exploring attachment stability in larger samples (see, for example, Groh et al., 2014). And questions have been raised as to whether it is a mistake, or a misrepresentation of Bowlby's original ideas, to emphasize the need for stability from infancy to young adulthood (Roisman & Groh, 2011). Moreover, findings of stability in attachment do not mean that the child is protected against later insecurity; rather, parents who are sensitive and responsive, and who understand their role in providing a secure base for their infant, are more likely to continue to provide this essential support through childhood and adolescence. The general consensus is that early attachment patterns are not immutable. Rather, attachment patterns may be altered when environmental events, such as loss, illness, marriage, or divorce, *lead to* modifications of internal models because of changes in the caregiver's behavior toward the child and/or because of the child's changing views of the caregiver's responsiveness or sensitivity. Additionally, early clinical interventions that are targeted at affect regulation and affect communication in both the infant and the caregiver have the potential to alter the attachment relationship (Schore & Schore, 2008). Similarly, adults who have worked to develop secure representations or states of mind regarding attachments, by developing relationships with alternative support figures and/or by experience in therapy, have been successful in forming a secure attachment relationship with their infants (Phelps, Belsky, & Crnic, 1998; Roisman et al., 2002; Saunders et al., 2011).

The Effects of Child Care on Attachment Relationships

What happens when children routinely spend time away from their primary caregivers, starting at several weeks or months of life? How do these separations impact the developing attachment relationship? Questions about the experiences of children in child care, and the effects of separation from their mothers on attachment security, have been the focus of much research. It has been found that children in child care do form close relationships with their parents (Clarke-Stewart & Allhusen, 2005; Lamb & Ahnert, 2006). Still, there has been significant debate regarding the potential adverse effects of regular nonmaternal care, particularly with regard to attachment quality (Belsky & Steinberg, 1978; Fox & Fein, 1990; NICHD Early Child Care Research Network, 1997; Rutter, 1981).

Perhaps motivated by evidence provided by Bowlby (1973) linking early institutional rearing with deficits in affective and cognitive development, researchers began to raise questions about the prolonged separations experienced by children in child care. Indeed, several multi-study analyses of research findings supported the idea that the experience of child care during infancy was associated with attachment classifications. For example, some researchers found that 12-month-old infants who were involved in routine child care for 20 or more hours per week during the first year of life were less likely to be classified as securely attached than were infants with less than 20 hours of weekly child care (Belsky & Rovine, 1988). Other multi-study analyses (e.g., Clarke-Stewart, 1989; Lamb & Sternberg, 1990) obtained similar results; that is, more than 20 hours per week of child care during the first year was associated with an increased risk of insecure attachment.

But several, more contemporary questions have been raised regarding these data. For example, it is more common now than it was in the 1980s (when these data were collected) for mothers of infants to work full time outside of the home and to have some choices regarding the type and quality of substitute care. Today's mothers could represent a different population than those who were studied 30 years ago as today's mothers tend to be older and more educated. Moreover, today's moms may be more aware of the controversies and problems surrounding child care (educated, in part, by popular media reports and parenting books). As a result, they may be more selective in the kinds of child care environments they choose or more attentive to the need for providing sensitive, responsive care during the time they spend with their infants. In addition, mothers who choose to stay at home may differ from those who enter the work force in a number of significant ways. For example, they may have different values and parenting goals, different levels of education, skills, or abilities, and access to different resources. There may also be preexisting differences among children that influence a mother's decision to work as well as the developing attachment relationship. Thus, instead of considering maternal employment alone, it may be these other factors that account for observed differences in children (Caldwell, 1993). Some researchers (e.g., Clarke-Stewart, 1989) have even questioned the measure of attachment security that was used in these early studies since the Strange Situation relies on separation-reunion sequences for activating attachment behaviors; the separations may not be as stressful and therefore not valid for measuring attachment in children with experience in child care.

These more refined questions about the attachment relationships of children in child care have continued to be the focus of recent research. For example, in an extensive, prospective longitudinal study of infants from varying economic, ethnic, and educational backgrounds who were identified at birth at multiple hospitals across the United States, the NICHD Early Child Care Research Network (1997) explored the effects of early child care experiences on attachment security. While there were many advantages of this study, including the diversity of its participants, the variety of childcare options chosen (e.g., in-home caregivers, fathers, relatives, child care homes and centers), and the comprehensiveness of observational measures used, there were also some important limitations. For example, mothers under the age of 18 years were not included nor were infants requiring hospitalization after birth. Some 42% of the mothers invited to be part of the study declined, raising questions about the factors that might differentiate those who did or did not choose to participate in this research. Still, the behavior of infants in the Strange Situation (e.g., in terms of level of distress or exploratory tendencies) did not seem to vary based on child care experience, thus establishing the measure to be valid even for children for whom separations are more common. Consistent with prior studies showing that economic stress impacts quality of parental care (see McLoyd, 1990, for a review) and that children from poorer homes are more likely to be classified as insecurely attached (Spieker & Booth, 1988), a higher proportion of insecure attachments were found in children from economically disadvantaged homes (NICHD Early Child Care Research Network, 1997).

Maternal sensitivity and psychological adjustment were related to security of attachment, but no effects of child characteristics (gender, maternal-rated temperament) were found for attachment security. Also, after effects of children (e.g., gender, temperament) and of mothers (e.g., maternal sensitivity, psychological adjustment) were considered, the main effect of child care was examined. No significant differences in attachment security were found based on participation in early child care. Early stable, high-quality child care did not increase the likelihood that the infant would be securely attached to the mother, just as extensive, unstable, poor-quality care did not increase the tendency towards insecure attachment. These findings differ from those of prior reports such as Belsky and Rovine's (1988) and Clarke-Stewart's (1989) findings. Is it that today's parents are more sensitized to the possible negative effects of child care based on the increased availability of media reports on the topic? Perhaps parents who use child care make a special effort to provide sensitive care to their infants when they are with them?

Alternatively, the more complex interaction effects found in the NICHD study between maternal characteristics and child care may help to illuminate the results. Specifically, it appears that when considered alone, child care does not put the child at increased risk for insecure attachment. However, when maternal care is insensitive or nonresponsive, then extensive involvement in unstable, poor-quality child care increases the risk of insecure attachment. Stated another way, children whose child care providers were least responsive and sensitive to their needs, and whose mothers were also less sensitive and responsive, were found to be the most insecure. But high-quality care may play a compensatory role for children with poor-quality maternal care such that they may be more likely to develop a secure attachment because of the high-quality care they receive outside of the home. Thus, the results from this important, ongoing longitudinal study demonstrate there is a moderating effect of child care on the association between maternal sensitivity and attachment security.

The Development of Multiple Attachments

Infants develop attachments to more than one person during the first year of life. The concept of a hierarchy of attachments was originally put forth by Bowlby (1969/1982, 1988) when he wrote:

> There is abundant evidence that almost every child habitually prefers one person, usually his mother-figure, to whom to go when distressed but that, in her absence, he will make do with someone else, preferably someone whom he knows well. On these occasions, most children show a clear hierarchy of preference so that in extremity and with no one else available, even a kindly stranger may be approached. Thus, whilst attachment behavior may in differing circumstances be shown to a variety of individuals, an enduring attachment, or attachment bond, is confined to very few. Should a child fail to show such clear discrimination, it is likely he is very disturbed. (Bowlby, 1988, p. 28)

In this brief passage, several important concepts are introduced: (1) the mother is usually the primary attachment figure; (2) children form a hierarchy of attachments; (3) an enduring attachment relationship is developed with a few significant figures; and (4) it is unusual for the child not to seek out an attachment figure when distressed; in these cases, there are likely to be problems in the child's capacity to develop or maintain attachment relationships.

Bowlby's seminal ideas have been supported by several important research studies. During the first year of life, the primary caregiver for most infants is usually the mother. She is also the first person to whom most infants develop an attachment (Roopnarine, Fouts, Lamb, & Lewis-Elligan, 2005). Then, once this foundation is established, infants form attachments to other familiar people, developing a hierarchy of attachments (Bretherton & Munholland, 2008; Steele et al., 1996). From an evolutionary perspective, this makes a lot of sense as the capacity to form multiple attachments with a variety of caregivers ensures the infant's survival if at some point the caregiver becomes unavailable. This concept is especially important as it allows for a consideration of cultural variations in caregiving arrangements that sometimes include multiple caregivers from the very early months of life (Sagi et al., 1985; van IJzendoorn, Sagi, & Lambermon, 1992). It also acknowledges the fact that children develop preferences for certain caregivers since they may play different roles in meeting children's needs.

Infants develop attachments to both their mothers and fathers, even though they typically spend more time with their mothers than with their fathers (Lamb, 2002; Lamb & Lewis, 2010). In order for an attachment to develop, it is not the amount of time spent together that matters but rather the quality of the interaction. Fathers assume a special and unique role as a playmate in their infant's life, spending much more time playing with them than actually caring for them (Pleck & Masciadrelli, 2004). Still, fathers, as well as older siblings and alternative caregivers, become attachment figures so long as they have consistent and meaningful interactions with the infant (Ahnert, Pinquart, & Lamb, 2006; Goosens & van IJzendoorn, 1990; Grossman, Grossman, Kindler, & Zimmerman, 2008; Howes & Spieker, 2008; Stewart & Marvin, 1984; Teti & Ablard, 1989; van IJzendoorn & de Wolff, 1997). These multiple attachments become organized in a hierarchy such that there is a preference for the principal attachment figure, especially when comfort is needed (a concept Bowlby termed "monotropy" (1969/1982)). When babies are with more than one attachment figure and the situation is stress-free, they may show no consistent preference for one person over another. If infants become distressed by the possibility of separation, or if they are fatigued, uncertain, or frightened, mothers are the more frequent attachment figure infants seek for consolation; it is only when she is absent that infants seek out other attachment figures for reassurance (Cassidy, 2008). When both parents are present, 10- to 18-month-old distressed infants still tend to prefer their mothers (Lamb & Lewis, 2011). In fact, Ainsworth (1982) provided early support for these ideas when she compared the less substantial distress she observed in response to infants' separations from secondary attachment figures to their greater distress in response to separation from the primary attachment figure.

Why has monotropy evolved in human infants? The infant's preference for the primary attachment figure ensures that care will be provided and increases the infant's likelihood of survival when faced with danger. Moreover, "reciprocal hierarchical bonding" (Cassidy, 2008) implies that infants will develop an attachment to the person who is most invested in, and has the most to gain from, their healthy development. This process of reciprocal hierarchical bonding could also account for why mothers tend to be the principle attachment figure, since only she devotes her bodily resources during the pregnancy, knows the baby's true biological origin, and has fewer chances to bear offspring than do fathers (Cassidy, 2008).

What happens to multiple attachments relationships over time? We know that infants may develop two or three attachments during the first year, usually with the mother and other family members or significant people involved in their care. New opportunities for developing attachment relationships emerge during childhood and adolescence as social worlds expand and children spend more time with peers and adults outside of the immediate family. Finally, sexual partners may also become attachment figures during late adolescence and early adulthood (Bowlby, 1988; Cassidy, 2008). How these new attachment relationships become organized in relation to already existing attachments (e.g., to parents and siblings) is a question that has not been fully addressed to date.

Which attachment relationship is most significant in predicting subsequent functioning is also a question that has been difficult to resolve. Most studies have only examined maternal attachment as it predicts later social and emotional functioning. But it may be that paternal attachment predicts to some areas of competence, while maternal attachment predicts to others.

Alternatively, one secure relationship may be all that is needed to promote competence in later development. Extant research indicates that a secure attachment to mother (and an insecure attachment to father or another attachment figure) leads to more competent behavior than a secure attachment to father or another attachment figure (and an insecure attachment to mother). Thus, attachment relationships with the primary attachment figure, who is usually the mother, could be the most influential for the child's later development (Boldt et al., 2014; Cassidy, 2008). But having two secure relationships leads to the best functioning later on, while two insecure relationships leads to the least competent behavior (Howes, Rodning, Galluzzo, & Myers, 1988; Main & Weston, 1981; Sagi-Schwartz & Aviezer, 2005). Still, attachment relationships are best viewed within the family system so that any assessment of the child's emotional security, and of the links between early attachment relationships and later development, should include both parents (Mikulincer, Florian, Cowan, & Cowan, 2002; Parke & Buriel, 2006) as well as any other adults (e.g., child care providers, nannies, grandparents) who are significant in the child's world (Howes & Spieker, 2008).

Similarly, the extent to which these multiple attachment relationships, and the internal working models associated with them, become integrated and impact the individual's view of relationships and of the self is unknown (Cassidy, 2008). If children develop an internal model of relationships based on the history of interaction with the primary attachment figure, and we expect that model to serve as the template for all other relationships, will the model be transformed based on ongoing attachment experiences with other caregivers? If the child's attachment-related experiences with a sensitive caregiver contribute to a model of the self as worthy of responsive care, but the child's experiences with the other parent are more negative and rejecting, will an integrated model of relationships be constructed? Or will one relationship be more salient in determining the child's emerging internal model of relationships and of the self? And what happens when the internal models are formed simultaneously as compared to sequentially? Children use their affective experiences developed in their early attachment relationships, together with their growing cognitive and social competencies, to construct models of relationships that develop during the same developmental periods (e.g., with mother and father during the early years) or over subsequent periods (e.g., with child care providers, adoptive or step-parents in early or later childhood).

Finally, there are several possible ways in which these internal working models of relationships may be organized. These include: (1) the *hierarchical organization* model, where the child's primary attachment figure is the most important in developing internalized models of self and others but secondary attachments are sought out when the primary figure is unavailable (Bretherton, 1985); (2) the *integrative organization* model, where the child develops a single model, integrating experiences and knowledge from multiple attachments, and uses this model to understand the self and others (van IJzendoorn et al., 1992); and (3) the *independent organization* model of multiple attachment relationships, where qualitatively different attachment relationships develop (for example, with mothers and fathers) and impact different areas of the child's development (Bretherton, 1985; Steele & Steele, 2005). Empirical evidence in support of these different models has been offered, either by focusing on the concordance of attachment security across caregivers (e.g., Ahnert et al., 2006; Boldt et al., 2014; Fox et al., 1991; Rosen & Burke, 1999) or on the prediction of later outcomes based on attachment security with different caregivers (e.g., Howes, Hamilton, & Phillipsen, 1998; Howes, Matheson, & Hamilton, 1994; Howes & Tonyan, 2000; Sagi-Schwartz & Avierzer, 2005, van IJzendoorn et al., 1992). Ultimately, determining which model is most relevant when accounting for the development of multiple attachment relationships may depend on the developmental period examined and the outcomes for which predictions are being made. These are important questions that continue to warrant further investigation.

The Neuroscience of Attachment Relationships

There has been a great deal of interest in integrating the study of attachment relationships with the field of neuroscience. Our earliest relationships influence, and are impacted by, the neural systems involved in the way we react to stress, regulate emotions, and develop attachments (Coan, 2008). Attachment researchers have used two approaches to evaluate the links between psychological and physiological processes. One approach is to examine individual differences in physiological responses that are associated with particular kinds of behaviors and the other is to observe behavioral responses and then assess the physiological systems related to those behaviors (Fox & Hane, 2008). Thus, for example, researchers have used tasks that are intended to provoke a stress response and then measured activity of the hypothalamic-pituitary-adrenal (HPA) axis. When an individual responds to stress, such as a threat to the attachment system, the assumption is that there will be changes in the level of activation of the HPA axis (Gunnar & Donzella, 2002). Measures of cortisol changes are used to index HPA activity and provide an indirect measure of stress reactivity (Fox & Hane, 2008). Alternatively, researchers have measured autonomic system activation in response to stressful situations. In these studies, physiological arousal, as indexed by measures of heart rate, skin conductance, and respiration, is seen to reflect sympathetic or parasympathetic activity in response to a relational challenge (Phillips, Carroll, Hunt, & Der, 2006). Varying states of attention have also been indexed by measures of autonomic activity, where, for example, sustained attention in response to particular sights or sounds is indexed by sustained heart rate deceleration in even preverbal infants (Courage, Reynolds, & Richars, 2006).

There has been a long history of viewing attachment relationships as reflecting the organization of multiple behavioral and physiological systems that are intended to provide a sense of security (Bowlby, 1969/1982).

Measures of physiological systems provide indirect information regarding the ways in which the mind and the body respond to situational demands, particularly those that reflect relational challenges. However, unlike neuroscientific approaches, they are not measuring actual brain activity. Brain imaging techniques, such as measures of evoked response potentials (ERPs), provide greater accuracy in charting the neural circuitry of certain behaviors and in understanding the temporal course of neural events. And techniques such as fMRI provide better clues as to the underlying structural features of areas of brain activity. While psychophysiological approaches have been used more easily with infants and young children (assessing, for example, heart rate, respiration, or cortisol activity associated with individual differences in the security of attachment relationships), neuroimaging techniques have been especially helpful in better understanding the activation of brain regions involved in adult attachment. Both approaches have been critical to advancing the study of attachment relationships (see Fox & Hane, 2008, for an extensive review).

The findings that have emerged from this burgeoning area of research have informed attachment researchers and challenged them to consider the reciprocal influences of biological predispositions and relationship experiences. Thus, for example, physiological markers of temperament (such as measures of cortisol levels or EEG asymmetry) have been identified that appear to underlie individual differences in reactivity to stress and affect expression and that potentially influence behavior in laboratory-based measures of attachment security, such as the Strange Situation (Calkins, Fox, & Marshall, 1996; Fox & Davidson, 1988; Henriques & Davidson, 1990; Pizzagalli, Sherwood, Henriques, & Davidson, 2005). In one interesting line of research, infant behavior and autonomic and brain electrical activity were explored in a modified Strange Situation (Dawson et al., 2001). Infants identified as insecurely attached in this modified Strange Situation (i.e., mother plays with the infant, a stranger enters, a familiar experimenter plays with the infant, and then the mother leaves) showed more activity on the right side of the prefrontal cortex, and less activity on the left side, as compared to infants who were securely attached. The right prefrontal cortex has been found to be specialized for the expression of fear, distress, and disgust (Coan, Allen, & McKnight, 2006). Indeed, infants who were found to be insecurely attached showed more anger towards their mothers or withdrew from them, a finding consistent with greater activity on the right side. The left prefrontal cortex, which is specialized for joy, interest, and other positive emotions, was found to be more active in securely attached infants; these secure infants were also happier and more likely to be interested in interaction with their mothers. Thus, a clear correspondence between brain activity and attachment was confirmed.

As we continue to learn more about the neural mechanisms by which the attachment system functions, the temperamental, situational, and contextual factors that activate the underlying neural components of attachment will be better understood (Coan, 2008; Schore, 1994). Research in interpersonal neurobiology has emphasized the ways in which brain development is impacted by early experience and relational trauma (Fonagy & Target, 2005; Leckman & March, 2011; Schore, 2003). Moreover, attachment experiences may actually interact with, and moderate or buffer, initial temperamental predispositions, thereby influencing physiological processes. Indeed, research with human infants, building on findings from animal studies (e.g., Caldji et al., 1998; Francis, Diorio, Liu, & Meaney, 1999), supports these claims. Maternal caregiving behavior has been found to influence the neurological systems involved in stress reactivity; moreover, the expression of negative affect during interactions with mothers influences the quality of care received, thereby impacting the infant's subsequent behavior (Hane & Fox, 2006). Taken together, this research supports the notion that biology and experience interact in complex ways. Caregiver behavior alters the expression of the infant's innate physiological tendencies by impacting neurological systems involved in stress reactivity and affect regulation, while these changes may lead to subsequent alterations in the caregiving environment.

In adults, certain physiological responses and neurological systems may be associated with caregiving behavior and attachment patterns as well (Fox & Hane, 2008). There are some studies documenting changes in adults' physiological responses to their own and unfamiliar infants; these changes are associated with distinct behavioral responses (Donovan & Leavitt, 1985; Donovan, Leavitt, & Ballling, 1978, Frodi et al., 1978; Wiesenfeld & Klorman, 1978). Moreover, when mothers view images of their own 7-month-old infants' happy or sad faces, there is greater activation of brain reward regions in mothers with more secure attachment relationships (assessed using the Adult Attachment Interview during pregnancy). Thus, the development of reward and affiliation brain circuits that promote sensitive and contingent responsiveness to her own infant's cues may be influenced by the mother's own childhood attachment experiences. These early experiences shape the neural circuits that impact her perception and responsiveness to her infant's signals years later. Mothers with anxious attachments were found, by fMRI measures of activation, to experience their infants as less rewarding compared to mothers with secure attachment (Strathearn et al., 2009). These differences in neural activation, in turn, resulted in variations in interactive behaviors between mothers and their infants, which may then contribute to developing attachment relationships.

Additionally, individual differences in adult attachment organization have been linked to variations in autonomic reactivity and to patterns of emotion regulation (Diamond, 2001). And neuroimaging techniques have been used to explore the brain regions involved in emotion expression and other attachment-related behaviors (e.g., Leibenluft, Gobbini, Harrison, & Haxby, 2004), as well as to differentiate the neural underpinnings of emotion regulation strategies in adults with secure, anxious, or avoidant attachment styles (e.g., Gillath, Bunge, Shaver, Wendelken, & Mikulincer, 2005). Individuals with insecure attachment representations have been found to show increased activation of the amygdala when they hear infant cries. This heightened amygdala activity may lead adults with insecure, as compared to secure, attachment representations to exhibit more negative emotions in response to infant crying and result in inconsistent or rejecting parental behavior (Riem et al., 2012). Further research in this area will help to highlight the neural circuitry involved in cognitive processing and emotion regulation associated with differences in adult attachment organization. Moreover, this research could extend our understanding of the physiological and neural underpinnings of caregiving behaviors.

The study of memory also provides indirect clues to the neuroscience of attachment relationships. The implicit and explicit memory systems contain various subtypes of memory that are organized by distinct neural systems. Implicit memory includes emotional, sensory, and procedural memories of early caregiving, which are influenced by, and continue to shape experiences in, relationships (Cozolino, 2014). These early memories are organized by specific neural systems, including the amygdala, thalamus, cerebellum, and orbital medial prefrontal structures. It is not until the brain matures that systems of explicit memory begin to develop. As the hippocampus, temporal lobes, and lateral prefrontal lobes mature, systems of explicit memory begin to organize; these neural structures are essential for encoding, storage, and consolidation of memories (Fuster, 1996; Selden, Everitt, Jarrard, & Robbins, 1991). Especially important to developing attachments are the aspects of explicit memory that allow us to recognize and remember familiar faces, learn language and social rules, regulate emotions, and narrate autobiographical memories, thus combining semantic, episodic, and emotional memories with an awareness of the self (Cozolino, 2014). Eventually, implicit and explicit memory systems are interwoven, forming the core of our attachment schema, or internal cognitive models or representations of significant attachment relationships, and the foundation for our experience of the self in relationships.

Attachment schemas develop based on our experiences with our primary caregivers. These schemas are a form of implicit social memory; they develop out of experience-dependent networks that are formed over time, linking the orbital frontal cortex and the amygdala and resulting in the many connections responsible for regulating emotion, arousal, and affect (Coan, 2008; Cozolino, 2014). Interactions with specific caregivers are associated, within these neural networks, with feelings of warmth and safety, or alternatively, with fear and anxiety. The child's experiences with supportive, loving, and responsive caregivers promote the development of positive and secure attachment schemas. These, in turn, foster the establishment of a biochemical environment in the brain that encourages affect regulation, psychological growth, and ideal immunological functioning (Coan, 2008).

A great deal has been learned about the coordination of these coherent memory systems, together with the systems regulating affect and behaviors, by studying what happens when there is a lack of integration, as is the case in trauma. The amygdala, which plays a central role in emotional and somatic processing of experiences, is functionally connected to the hippocampus and higher cortical structures that are necessary for the development of conscious memory and for cooperative social functioning (Tsoory et al., 2008). The quality of their connection is influenced by temperament, stress, and epigenetic factors (Canli et al., 2006). The amygdala and hippocampus are involved in affect regulation, learning, anxiety and arousal states, and the successful management of relationships (Irle et al., 2010). When there is trauma, memory systems may be disrupted and disturbances in memory, emotion, behavior, and cognition may result (Cozolino, 2014; Dozier, Stovall-McClough, & Albus, 2008).

Indeed, decreases in hippocampal volume, which have been documented in adult women with histories of childhood abuse, are associated with deficits in encoding short-term into long-term memories; thus, the hippocampus appears to play an important role in the integration of memories into a personal narrative about the past (Bremner et al., 1997; Stein, Koverola, Hanna, Torchia, & McClarty, 1997). The consequence may be a lack of coherent recall or a dissociation of memory and experiences (Cozolino, 2014). Still, the memories may be "held" in the body and remain there until some later time, when therapeutic intervention may release these implicit social memories in a context where they can be safely explored and understood. The emotional nature of the therapeutic relationship, and the possibility of the "working through" of unconscious memories, allow for the recall and examination of implicit social memories and resulting psychological change (Cozolino, 2002). Therefore, experiences in the early years, which provide the foundation for attachment relationships, may be difficult to remember because of the immaturity of the hippocampal-cortical networks that are necessary for the conscious recall of early experiences. These experiences, in turn, exert a profound impact on developing attachment schema.

While attachment schemas appear to be relatively consistent over time, they are subject to change with alterations in the caregiving environment or changes in specific relationship experiences. Thus, while negative or insecure attachment schemas may be linked to emotional difficulties and physical illness throughout life (Fox & Hane, 2008), there is the possibility that they may be modified. Attachment schemas are therefore a prime example of implicit social memories at work (Cozolino, 2014). They are formed in the context of early experiences with caregivers and they are activated in subsequent relationships where we, without even knowing it, re-enact our early experiences by either seeking or avoiding proximity, intimacy, and connection. These schemas influence our reactions to stress, playing a central role in determining whether we turn to and use our attachment relationships to modulate arousal and regulate affect. And they may be modified with repeated exposure to new relational experiences and conscious processing that alter attachment schemas (Suomi, 2008). Thus, attachment schemas reflect the integration of the underlying experiential, physiological, and neurological bases of attachment relationships.

Clinical Implications of Attachment Theory and Research

Attachment theory was developed based on John Bowlby's assertions about the impact of maternal deprivation and the effects of early relational trauma on young children. His clinical observations and theoretical writings highlight the importance of early attachment relationships for normative development (Bowlby, 1969/1982, 1973, 1980). Developmental psychologists have been deeply inspired by Bowlby's ideas, and attachment theory and research has been at the forefront of their work for more than 50 years. An extensive body of research supports Bowlby's idea that early attachment relationships play a critical role in the development of concurrent and later social, emotional, and cognitive competencies. The emotional significance of early attachment relationships is profound and extends throughout the lifespan.

Researchers have extended beyond the focus on normative development and studied the developmental outcomes of children who experience threats to the availability of caregivers or disruptions in attachment bonds (for example, when there is parental hostility or inconsistency, maltreatment, or maternal depression). Additionally, attachment theory has been used to guide empirical questions about *how* early relationships influence the development of particular processes central to adaptation or maladaptation. Thus, for example, developmental researchers have explored the influence of early attachment experiences on developing emotion regulation, behavioral organization, coping strategies, and the construction of cognitive models for representing the self and relationships (for reviews, see DeKlyen & Greenberg, 2008; Egeland & Carlson, 2004; Kobak, Cassidy, Lyons-Ruth, & Ziv, 2006). The quality of the early attachment relationship has been found either to buffer against other risks and serve as a protective factor (for example, secure attachment may protect against the traumatizing effects of abuse) or to increase the risk of maladaptive solutions to developmental tasks (Cicchetti, Toth, & Lynch, 1995). Profound disturbances in attachment relationships have been associated with impairments in children's social and emotional functioning and may serve as a risk factor for developing psychopathology.

These empirical findings have not only deepened our understanding of the processes involved in the development of pathology, but they have also opened new directions for clinical intervention programs. Mental health professionals have become increasingly aware of the importance of supporting parents and children by promoting the development of secure attachment relationships (Berlin, Zeanah, & Lieberman, 2008; Oppenheim & Goldsmith, 2007). Interventions geared toward assessing parental working models, building reflective functioning capacities, and improving parent–child interactions in the early years have been designed with the hope that positive changes may improve the overall quality of the attachment relationship (Steele, Murphy, & Steele, 2010). Clinicians have also recognized that, with particular populations, there may be increased challenges to developing a secure attachment relationship. What happens, for example, when parents' experiences with unresolved trauma or loss threaten their reflective capacities and their parenting behaviors? When parents experience social isolation and multiple stresses, or when their personal histories include physical abuse, neglect, foster care placements, sexual abuse, substance abuse, domestic and community violence, incarceration, or psychopathology, the quality of their parenting, and their developing attachment relationships with their children, may be at risk. Even with high-risk samples of parents and children, clinical interventions may be targeted at fostering secure attachment relationships. Programs that involve parents in enhancing nurturance and support of their children, while promoting parental reflective functioning, emotional attunement, and affect regulation, have been found to be extremely effective, especially when clinicians themselves model emotional availability and reflective capacities in their work with their patients (see, for example, Murphy, Steele, & Steele, 2013).

Interestingly, even though Bowlby was a psychoanalyst and practicing clinician, the psychoanalytic community did not welcome his ideas, in part because he challenged some of the central tenets underlying psychoanalytic thinking (Slade, 2008). Despite the fact that Bowlby was interested in the study of psychopathology and in the application of his ideas to clinical work (Bowlby, 1988), it is only in the last few decades that clinicians have begun to understand and treat disorders through the lens of attachment theory. Bowlby's ideas about the importance of early attachment relationships, and the implications of attachment theory for clinical interventions, are being explored in clinical settings and theoretical writings (Friedman, Ertegun, Lupi, Beebe, & Deutsch, 2013; Murphy et al., 2013; Slade, 2000, 2004, 2008). There are many ways in which attachment and psychoanalytic theories are now seen to overlap. Despite points of divergence, there are enormous possibilities for mutual enhancement and exchange of ideas (Blom & Bargman, 2013; Fonagy et al., 2008; Fonagy & Target, 2007; Steele & Steele, 1998). Thus, an appreciation of the strengths and limitations of attachment and psychoanalytic theories has been mutually beneficial. Perhaps more importantly, it has led to the delineation of empirical questions for future research and strategic interventions for clinicians working with children, adolescents, and adults.

A central focus of attachment research has been on the roles of parental sensitivity and responsiveness and the importance of mutual regulation in the infant–parent relationship. Attachment-based thinking, integrated with more traditional psychoanalytic perspectives, pioneered the development of microanalytic investigative techniques for analyzing infant–parent interactions. Contingent responsiveness, optimal cueing, and the correspondence of affective states have been explored with a clinical lens (Beebe, 2003; Jaffe, Beebe, Feldstein, Crown, & Jasnow, 2001; Stern, 1971, 1995). Achieving mutual regulation is considered to be optimal for the infant's security, where infant and mother are flexibly attuned to one another and mothers, in particular, make fine adjustments to the tempo and affective states of their infants (Beebe, 2005; Tronick, 2007). By "holding" (p. 44) the infant in the nurturing environment of a "good enough" (p. 145) mother (Winnicott, 1965/1996), the infant is offered contingent responsiveness by a sensitive and responsive parent. This "good enough" mother at once offers nurturing and regulation of affect while encouraging autonomy and self-regulation; she is attentive without being intrusive and can tolerate the infant's need for gradual separation and exploration while staying present and affectively attuned. Together, through their mutual exchanges, mothers and infants build states of mind and co-create mental representations of their dyadic relationship that reflect their successes and failures in managing their interactions. A moderate degree of coordination and disruption (neither too much nor too little of either state) allows the infant to build a stable internal representation of attachment to the mother, as well as to maintain an optimal level of contact with the attachment figure while developing the capacity for self-regulation and exercising emerging autonomy.

Attachment-based clinical work incorporates a dynamic, dyadic-systems approach to exploring the contributions of infants and parents to the process of developing an attachment relationship. Inherent to this approach is the assumption that patterns of relational behavior are activated and terminated by both infants and mothers within a social context (Bowlby, 1958, 1969/1982). Thus, mutual regulation is critical to attachment-based clinical work. Parents need to be offered tools for understanding their children's needs, based in part on the activation of their own attachment-related affects, cognitions, and behaviors, and then trained to mobilize their responses with the goal of improving the attachment relationship with their infants (Beebe et al., 2000). Videotapes of infant–parent interactions are often used in the clinical setting to improve face-to-face interactions (Beebe & Stern, 1977), to assess secure-base behavior and educate parents (as in the "Circle of Security" project (Marvin, Cooper, Hoffman, & Powell, 2002)), and to increase maternal reflective functioning in interventions with high-risk dyads (Lyons-Ruth, Yellin, Melnick, & Atwood, 2005; Slade, 2008). Videotaped parent–infant interaction and feedback have also been used quite successfully to promote maternal sensitivity and positive parenting in home-based interventions (Juffer, Bakermans-Kranenburg, & van IJzendoorn, 2007; Klein Velderman, Bakermans-Kranenburg, Juffer, & van IJzendoorn, 2006).

Effective intervention programs also need to incorporate an awareness that developmental changes in the parent–child relationship, during infancy, childhood, and adolescence, necessitate new goals for clinical intervention. Children's developmental advances require that parents learn to flexibly adapt, continuing to be available and responsive in new ways. Increased autonomy on the part of the child, for example, needs to be understood and promoted within the context of the child's developing cognitive, social, and emotional competencies and needs. Cooperation and negotiation around achieving particular goals, while concurrently establishing clear limits and discipline, are critical to the child's exploration and mastery. Therefore, enhancing patterns of emotional communication and establishing expectancies regarding parental behavior are all important to the child's developing internal models of attachment relationships and of the self. Continued support among clinicians for integrating new, well-validated attachment measures for older children into dynamic, family-systems-based clinical models of intervention, will direct attention to developing child–caregiver interactions during each stage of development. The benefits of this developmentally sensitive integration of attachment concepts into clinical work highlights the therapeutic value of the rich exchange of ideas between researchers and clinicians.

Attachment theory and research also have implications for therapy with adolescents and adults. Clinical thinking and interventions may be informed by a rich understanding of the nature of early attachments, the dynamics of attachment relationships, and the importance of early relational experiences for internal representations of relationships. Attachment theory, therefore, offers important ideas to therapists as they make meaning of their patients' relational experiences, their capacity for affect regulation, and their defensive strategies. In their ongoing clinical work, therapists may use this understanding, together with other theoretical ideas, to guide their clinical work, their thinking about their patients, and the therapeutic relationship they develop. Moreover, therapists' own attachment representations may impact the treatment, thereby requiring the therapist to be aware and able to make use of attachment-related feelings and cognitions (Slade, 2008; Wallin, 2007). Thus, both the patient's and therapist's attachment histories have the potential to influence the process and outcome of therapy. To the extent that the clinician listens for and attends to attachment narratives, and understands the ways in which attachment patterns and processes need to be incorporated into the treatment, the course of therapy may be enriched and transformed.

In summary, advances in attachment theory, and the impressive body of research that it has motivated, continue to offer critical ideas to clinical researchers and practicing therapists. Understanding adults' working models of relationships, or sensitizing parents to their behavioral interactions with their children, may ultimately serve to modify parent–infant interactions in ways that promote and enhance the quality of early attachment relationships. The developing competencies that are impacted by early insecure attachment patterns may be targeted as areas appropriate for clinical interventions in young children. Thus, improving emotion regulation skills, social-cognitive understanding, and empathic responsiveness may benefit young children as they approach new challenges in their expanding social network. And in clinical work with children, adolescents, and adults, the principles of attachment theory may help to guide clinicians' understanding of themselves in the therapeutic relationship, and to use their interpretation and understanding of their patients' attachment-related thoughts, feelings, behaviors, and narratives, to promote therapeutic change.

Infant Individuality and the Origins of the Self

2

The quality of infants' early attachment relationships affects their feelings about themselves. These are the feelings and impressions that children then bring to their relationships with others. If their attachment relationships are secure, then infants are likely to have had caregivers who are sensitive and responsive to their needs; this kind of care, in turn, communicates to infants that they are valued and worthy of responsive care. Therefore, attachment experiences are critical early in life because they influence the sense of self that emerges in infancy. Still, the development of a sense of self is an ongoing, complex process that involves more than early attachment experiences.

What constitutes the self-system? Does it comprise feelings about internal characteristics and psychological functioning? Or does it consist of social and personality characteristics? Is it a conceptual system involving attitudes and thoughts about oneself or about one's physical features? Does it incorporate notions of change and continuity? How does the young child define the self? Or is the self defined in the reflections of others? And does the self remain the same or does it change over time? These are the questions that will be explored in this chapter. Clearly, understanding the self is important because it is the way individuals view and feel about themselves that influences and, in turn, is influenced by, feelings of competence and well-being. These feelings will impact subsequent ways of relating to others. What we will come to see is that it is out of relationships, especially early attachment relationships, that children come to know the self as distinct from others; concomitantly, how children think about themselves (their identity) and how they feel about themselves (their esteem) impacts their understanding of others and their ways of relating to them. Thus, the inextricable link between attachment and self is evidenced from a very early age.

Indeed, children's sense of self emerges in their interactions with people who are important to them. Though initially dependent on others to care for them, babies come into the world with their own temperamental predispositions and emotional competencies, as well as an evolving awareness of the self as distinct from others. These qualities establish a unique profile to which others respond; others also recognize these qualities as part of what makes the individual distinct. As such, they represent the early foundation of personality (Thompson, Winer, & Goodvin, 2011). One child in a family may be inhibited and withdrawn, keenly sensitive to noises and sounds, and very difficult to soothe when distressed. Caregivers may learn to respond quickly to this baby's cries, picking her up to quiet her, knowing that without immediate contact and holding, she will quickly escalate into a state of distress that will be much more difficult to calm. Her parents may describe her, mostly lovingly but sometimes with clear frustration, as "the sensitive one." Another child in the same family may be more rhythmic and relaxed. She may not cry often and may have the amazing ability to fall asleep in her infant seat even when there is a lot of noise and commotion. She awakens quietly, kicking and squirming with delight when she sees her older brother, and if she becomes distressed she is soothed by her mother's voice even from across the room. She is described as "the calm one." Each baby requires a different kind of response from her parents and, in turn, is characterized and defined by her parents in a distinct way. And so, the early roots of personality are planted.

Temperamental variations are important to consider because they exert an influence on others from the moment a baby is born. As infants begin to express emotions, to understand emotional expressions, and to regulate their emotional responses, their affective world expands, allowing for new ways of understanding themselves and others. Cognitive advances contribute to changes in self-understanding; in turn, advances in self-understanding allow the child to organize inborn temperamental qualities and emotional responses into a coherent and meaningful definition of the self. Thus, the emerging self reflects the dynamic, evolving process by which inborn tendencies and the child's social world interact to influence the child's evolving personality (Thompson et al., 2011).

Over a relatively short period of time, there are dramatic shifts in social and emotional functioning as the self emerges from infancy (birth to 1 year of age), through toddlerhood (1–3 years of age), and into the preschool (3–5 years of age), early childhood (ages 5–7 years), middle childhood (ages 7–9 years), and late childhood (ages 9–11 years) periods. In this chapter, we will consider temperament, emotions, and the development of the autonomous self. Research on temperamental characteristics will be presented and we will explore the contribution of these unique individual difference variables, together with the development of emotion and emotion regulation, to individuality and the origins of the self in infancy and childhood.

Temperament

An infant's individuality is expressed, almost immediately after birth, in qualities that reflect temperament. These individual differences are assumed to have a biological or genetic basis and to distinguish an active baby from a more passive one, an easy-going infant from a more demanding baby, a happy baby who is adaptable and calm from a more fussy one who is difficult to settle. While parents cannot "know" their babies' temperament just by looking at them, they can observe the behavioral manifestations of temperament by watching and learning how their babies engage with them and their world. Sometimes, parents will accommodate their behavior to adapt to their infant's needs; at other times, they may try to modify their baby's behavior with the hope that they can change the expression of temperament. Particular temperamental characteristics may evoke certain responses from others. Thus, an easy baby with a cheerful disposition is likely to elicit smiles from siblings, peers, and adults; these reactions, in turn, may influence the child's sociability in a way that is different from the responses social partners might offer to a child who is more negative or difficult temperamentally. Parents also use their understanding of their baby's temperament to predict what they think their child's personality might be (for example, "He'll be the social one" or "She'll be the focused, serious one"). In this way, the construct of temperament captures the significant and early contribution that children make to their own development.

Early developmental scholars (e.g., Gesell, 1928; Shirley, 1933) identified temperamental differences among children even as they were attempting to establish normative patterns of behavior. Their work highlighted several important ideas, most notably that temperamental dimensions are relatively stable and provide the core of personality. They also documented the way in which developmental outcomes may be similar for children with different temperaments or different for children with similar temperaments (Rothbart & Bates, 2008). The roots of current research on temperament lie in the work of Thomas and Chess (Thomas, Chess, Birch, Hertzig, & Korn, 1963). Their longitudinal examination of children's behavioral styles, which they later called temperament, documented the role of temperament in emotional functioning and social adaptation. Following Thomas and Chess, early temperament researchers continued to explore questions about how to best classify and measure temperamental characteristics as well as about the stability of temperament over time. More recent longitudinal work has examined the role that temperament plays in social interaction and functioning in general and in the development of psychopathology in particular (Pulkkinen, Kokko, & Rantanen, 2012; Rothbart, 2011).

Today, most temperament researchers agree that temperament is constitutionally based, relatively stable, and reflected in an individual's emotional, motoric, and attentional responses across different situations. They also agree that temperamental dimensions do not translate into discrete behaviors; rather, a child's temperament reflects behavioral tendencies that may be modified over time by maturation and experience. Thus, researchers who incorporate the study of temperament into their empirical investigations are promulgating the idea that development depends on both biology and experience in the world. There has been considerable disagreement, however, regarding several issues, including: (1) identifying the key behavioral dimensions that constitute temperament; (2) determining how to best measure temperament in ways that are developmentally appropriate and sensitive to context and informant; (3) understanding how temperament is related to motivation and emotion; and (4) establishing how temperament develops over time (see, for example, Goldsmith et al., 1987; Shiner et al., 2012).

How is Temperament Defined and Measured?

Early studies of infant temperament were conducted by clinical researchers and resulted in the publication of the New York Longitudinal Study (Thomas et al., 1963). The researchers asked parents of young infants to consider their children's responses to common situations that they could easily observe. Parents were interviewed extensively about their children's behavioral style, documenting patterns of their children's behaviors across a variety of stimuli and situations. What evolved from a content analysis of the parents' detailed descriptions were nine discrete behavioral dimensions, including: activity level, approach/withdrawal, adaptability, mood, threshold, intensity, distractibility, rhythmicity, and attention span/persistence. These dimensions clustered into three types, thus characterizing children as "easy," "difficult," or "slow-to-warm-up" (Chess & Thomas, 1986; Thomas & Chess, 1977). Easy babies (about 40% of the babies studied) were happy, friendly, and adapted easily. Difficult babies (about 10%) had irregular sleeping and eating patterns, were fussy and cried a lot, and became upset easily in new situations. And babies who were slow-to-warm-up adapted slowly to new stimuli and experiences after an initial negative reaction; they tended to show a negative response to something new but gradually showed interest (Chess & Thomas, 1986).

Concurrent with these reports, developmental researchers were beginning to emphasize the role that individual children play in their own social and cognitive development (Bell, 1968; Kohlberg, 1969; Sears et al., 1957). The result was a surge of interest in identifying the key temperament constructs that could account for individual differences in how children make sense of themselves, their emotions, and their social worlds, and how these individual differences influence their development. Thus, other researchers, stimulated by Thomas and Chess's seminal work, began to explore the idea that certain inborn qualities contributed to children's later behavior. In turn, they developed measurement strategies to characterize these qualities. Today, a variety of methods have been used to assess observable behavioral indices of temperament. There are differences in the number of dimensions proposed, the relative emphasis on behaviors as opposed to emotions, and the position taken with regard to environmental influences (Fox, Henderson, & Marshall, 2001; Goldsmith et al., 1987). These measurement approaches have included both laboratory-based assessments as well as questionnaires completed by the caregiver or someone who is extremely familiar with the child.

The various assessment strategies developed and used reflect the underlying definition of temperament adopted by the researchers. For example, some researchers have used measurement strategies that rely on parents (usually mothers) completing questionnaires that rate the frequency of specific behaviors observed during a one-week time period. In general, the dimensions reflect the child's activity level, emotionality, and attention (Buss & Plomin, 1984; Rothbart, 1981). Other researchers have concentrated on the propensity to experience and express specific emotions (e.g., fear, anger) in particular contexts (Goldsmith & Campos, 1990), with little regard for interactional factors that might influence the emotions being expressed. Some researchers elaborated on Thomas and Chess's notion of "goodness of fit," arguing that any measurement of temperament needs to consider context together with infant and parental behavior as well as parental expectations (Seifer et al., 1996). Others challenged Chess and Thomas's (1986) list of temperament traits, arguing they are not empirically distinct (De Pauw & Mervielde, 2010). Instead, they used more sophisticated statistical models to identify alternative typologies to the easy, difficult, and slow-to-warm-up categories (e.g., "resilient," "undercontrolled," and "overcontrolled" (Caspi & Shiner, 2006)). And challenges to the "difficult" type, in particular, have raised questions about differences in parents' perceptions of, and responses to, more "difficult" children (Bates & McFadyen-Ketchum, 2000; Paulussen-Hoogeboom, Stams, Hermanns, Peetsma, & van den Wittenboer, 2008). Finally, some researchers restricted their study of temperament to discrete, defined dimensions, such as identifying two extreme groups of children who are either inhibited or uninhibited (Kagan, 1994). Inhibited children are sensitive to new people, stimuli, and situations and tend to withdraw from stimulation, whereas uninhibited children are eager to approach novelty and more outgoing. These two characteristic patterns of approach and withdrawal have been found to reflect distinct biobehavioral profiles which are unique to these extremes and remain stable across childhood (Kagan & Snidman, 1991).

Mary Rothbart and her colleagues focused on two broad dimensions of temperament – reactivity and self-regulation – and the subscales subsumed by these dimensions (Derryberry & Rothbart, 1997; Rothbart & Bates, 2006). Reactivity and self-regulation are used to organize a range of temperamental qualities. The reactive component of temperament reflects the infant's behavioral and physiological responses to different sensory stimuli; it is measured by latency and intensity of affect, motor activity, and related responses, as well as threshold of response, time to peak intensity, and recovery time. Present and observable at birth, reactivity is considered to be a relatively stable quality in the child (Rothbart, Derryberry, & Hershey, 2000) influenced by control systems that regulate the expression and stability of reactive traits (Rothbart, 2011). Though initially quite general and undifferentiated (e.g., generalized distress characterized by facial and vocal signs of negativity), early reactions become more differentiated and sophisticated over time (e.g., sadness, anger, and fear), reflecting cognitive development and the emergence of self-awareness (Bronson, 2000; Rothbart, 2011). When conceptualized in this way, reactivity is influenced by the integration of affective and cognitive systems (Derryberry & Tucker, 2006).

Self-regulation emerges during the first few years of life and reflects attentional and behavioral control mechanisms (e.g., approach-withdrawal, behavioral inhibition, attention, self-soothing). These processes, influenced by developing biological systems, emerge in infancy and serve the purpose of modulating reactivity. With maturation, variations in specific behavioral indices of reactivity and self-regulation may appear yet reveal an underlying process that is stable. Thus, for example, approach-withdrawal or inhibition in infancy may be evident in different developmentally appropriate forms in childhood or adolescence yet still reflect stability in underlying attentional and self-regulatory processes (Laucht, Becker, & Schmidt, 2006; Rothbart, 2011; Schwartz et al., 2012).

What has emerged from the use of reactivity and self-regulation as an organizing framework for studying temperament is an extensive body of research that supports the idea that there are three broad dimensions reflecting attention/regulation and emotions (with corresponding specific temperamental traits). These dimensions are: (1) orienting/regulation (in infants) or effortful control (e.g., attentional focus, perceptual sensitivity, low-intensity pleasure, inhibitory control) (in older children); (2) extraversion/surgency (e.g., activity level, smiling and laughter, sociability, high-intensity pleasure); and (3) negative emotionality (e.g., sadness, anger, fear, physical discomfort, soothability) (Rothbart, Ahadi, Hershey, & Fisher, 2001; Rothbart & Bates, 2008). Interestingly, these three dimensions are similar to what has been identified in studies of nonhuman animals, thereby providing clues to the psychobiology of temperamental differences (Gosling & John, 1999). There are now questionnaire, observational, and laboratory measures that capture these temperament dimensions (Goldsmith & Rothbart, 1993; Putnam, Ellis, & Rothbart, 2001). Moreover, the broad factors of reactivity and self-regulation have been identified not only in studies in the United States but in Japan and China as well (Ahadi, Rothbart, & Ye, 1993; Kochanska, DeVet, Goldman, Murray, & Putnam, 1993; Rothbart et al., 2001). And strong conceptual parallels have been found between childhood temperament dimensions and personality factors in adults (Ahadi & Rothbart, 1994; Evans & Rothbart, 2007), thus illustrating the links between early temperament and later personality.

The capacity to sustain attention or shift focus serves to amplify, at a neural level, the stimuli attended to, thereby modifying the individual's affective experience (Rothbart, Posner, & Rosicky, 1994). Early gaze, affect synchrony, and joint attention skills are examples of the kinds of interactive behaviors that facilitate effective self-regulation (Henderson & Mundy, 2013). There are qualitative changes in emotional regulation during the first year that parallel shifts in attentional skills during this same time period; there are also clear differences in how well infants can use attention to regulate emotions. These observations highlight the role of attention and other control mechanisms that bridge temperamental reactivity and adjustment, even in the early years.

Ultimately, it may be these regulatory abilities that determine how well young children master developmental challenges and negotiate social skills or alternatively develop disruptive behavior problems (Calkins, 2009).

Together, these dimensions of reactivity and self-regulation are seen by Rothbart and her colleagues to constitute the core of personality. But personality involves a whole lot more, reflecting an elaboration of temperament and experience into the social and cognitive models we construct of the world (Rothbart, 2007; Rutter, 1987). While children's reactivity and self-regulation are biologically based, the behavioral expression of temperament is modified over time by maturation, heredity, and experiences (Rothbart, 1989; Rothbart & Derryberry, 1981). In particular, self-regulation involves the gradual transfer of external control of behavior, thought, and emotion to internal sources (Henderson & Mundy, 2013; Kopp, 2002; Rothbart & Derryberry, 1981). Precisely how this transfer occurs is not clear, though the internalization of control is likely to be influenced by attachment experiences (Cassidy, 1994), parents' success in managing their child's level of arousal (Schore, 1994), sibling experiences (Volling, 2001), and peer influences (Cassidy, 1994). Therefore, both the quality and quantity of dyadic and triadic social interactions predict to developing self-regulatory skills (e.g., Feldman, Greenbaum, & Yirmiya, 1999; Lecuyer & Houck, 2006; Schore, 1996).

Some researchers have relied on direct observations of temperament, either in the home or the laboratory, as a way of validating maternal ratings by questionnaires. For example, the Laboratory Temperament Assessment Battery, or LAB-TAB (Goldsmith & Rothbart, 1993) is one such measure that uses a standard set of tasks to assess temperament in a laboratory setting. The observations are scored along several dimensions yielding ratings of fear, frustration, and positive affection. Laboratory-based measures allow for direct observation of specific behaviors in a more controlled and objective context. All children are observed in similar conditions, with unbiased observers rating their behavior. However, these approaches are more time consuming and expensive to implement and are limited in the range of situations and contexts in which children may be studied. Moreover, laboratory-based observational assessments may be biased because of relatively brief periods of time in which the child's behavior is rated or limitations in the range of behaviors that are observed. Still, these ratings may then be used to provide convergent validity with behavioral observations in the home; they may also be used to evaluate temperament and its association with social adjustment (see, for example, Buss & Goldsmith, 1998; Calkins & Dedmon, 2000).

Parents may provide useful information about their child's temperamental characteristics because they have a long history of observing their child in multiple situations. Parental report is a quick, easy, and inexpensive way to collect important data about temperament. However, parents may be biased in their assessments, highlighting certain qualities they deem acceptable and minimizing the presence of those that are not as positive or consistent with the view of their child that they want to maintain. Their judgments may be influenced by the relationship they have with their child and their ability to adapt to the challenges presented by their child's temperamental profile. Thus, questions persist regarding the validity of parental reports and whether or not it is appropriate to rely on them (Rothbart & Bates, 2006).

Naturalistic observations of children and assessments of temperamental characteristics in real-life situations (e.g., home, child care, playground) are similarly constrained and time consuming. For example, there is limited control over the range of situations in which children might be observed, the people present, or the behaviors elicited. One child might look extremely inhibited because several older children appear on the playground during the time the observer's temperament ratings are being made, though in the safety and familiarity of the classroom the same child may appear completely relaxed and free to explore.

Evaluating the behavioral component of temperament requires the use of reliable and valid measurement strategies. But if the traits or qualities assessed represent the observable behavioral manifestations of an underlying biological process, then psychobiological assessments of temperament could provide convergent validation as well. Various measures have been used to document physiological responses that accompany emotional reactions (Calkins & Mackler, 2011). For example, cortisol, which is a hormone that can be measured in blood, saliva, or urine and regulates the body's response to stressors, has been used as a measure of emotional reactivity. Basal cortisol levels vary during the course of the day and there are developmental changes in patterns of cortisol activity as well. Still, so long as changes from baseline to stressor conditions are considered relative to the daily cycle of the adrenocortical system, cortisol may be used as a measure of emotional reactivity (e.g., Gunnar & Davis, 2003).

In some studies, extremely inhibited children, as compared to uninhibited children, display faster and less variable heart rates, which is thought to reflect differences in sympathetic activation between the two groups (e.g., Kagan, Reznick, & Snidman, 1987). In other studies, researchers have focused on the relation between emotional reactivity and vagal tone, or heart rate variability that reflects parasympathetic activity and cycles with breathing (respiratory sinus arrhythmia). For example, infants with high vagal tone have been found to be more emotionally reactive and more competent at emotion regulation (Porges, 1991; Porter, Porges, & Marshall, 1988). Developmental shifts in emotion expression may be the result of normative changes in vagal tone (Porges, 1991). Moreover, suppression of respiratory sinus arrhythmia, and the associated vagal regulation of the heart, may be a physiological response that enables active coping, sustained attention, and emotional regulation that we begin to see in preschool-aged children (Porges, 1996; Wilson & Gottman, 1996).

Patterns of electrical activity in the right and left brain hemispheres have been recorded and ratio or difference scores used to determine the degree to which one hemisphere shows greater activation than the homologous region. The link between these differences and individual variation in temperamental qualities, such as emotionality, has been explored in infants. For example, in a baseline condition prior to maternal separation, infants with less left-side activation in the frontal region were more likely to cry when the mother left the room (Fox & Davidson, 1987). Right-sided frontal activation may be characteristic of a lower threshold for negative emotion (Fox & Davidson, 1991). And longitudinal studies reveal greater relative right frontal activation seen in infants with temperamental characteristics predictive of inhibition (Calkins et al., 1996) as well as in those who continue to show inhibition in childhood (Fox, Schmidt, Calkins, Rubin, & Coplan, 1996).

In sum, we see that there are many different ways of measuring temperament, each with its own advantages and disadvantages (Rothbart & Bates, 2008; Rothbart & Goldsmith, 1985). Thus, a multi-method approach to measuring temperament is recommended. Observational assessments and physiological responses in a structured environment (e.g., a research lab) may be used in combination with parental measures or questionnaires to validate parental reports and offer temperament ratings that consider behaviors over several days or weeks (Calkins, Dedmon, Gill, Lomax, & Johnson, 2002). A multi-method approach also allows for the unique and shared variance of each measure to be explored (see, for example, Kochanska, 1995) and for more sophisticated, developmentally appropriate questions to be examined.

What Are the Biological Underpinnings of Temperament?

The biological basis of temperament is complex. While certain genetic predispositions influence activity level, emotionality, inhibitory control, fearfulness, sociability, and other temperamental characteristics (Caspi & Shaver, 2006; Goldsmith, 2002; Kagan & Fox, 2006), they interact with development and experience as well in determining an individual's temperament profile. Advances in molecular genetics have allowed researchers to identify some genetic polymorphisms that are related to particular personality and temperamental characteristics and may result in differential sensitivity to environmental influences (Thompson et al., 2011). For example, these involve polymorphisms in the dopamine D4 receptors (DRD4), associated with impulsivity and novelty seeking, and in the serotonin transporter promoter region (5-HTTLPR), linked to avoidance of harm and negative emotionality (Bakermans-Kranenburg, van IJzendoorn, Pijlman, Mesman, & Juffer, 2008; Ebstein, Benjamin, & Belmaker, 2000). Moreover, genetic individuality may be communicated in many physiological systems. Thus, for example, we see individual differences in neuroendocrine functioning (Gunnar & Vasquez, 2006), cerebral asymmetry (Fox, Schmidt, & Henderson, 2000), reactivity of subcortical structures and the sympathetic nervous system (Kagan & Fox, 2006), regulation of the parasympathetic system (Porges, 2007), attentional processes (Rothbart, 2007; Rothbart, Posner, & Kieras, 2006), and other psychobiological processes (see reviews in Martin & Fox, 2006; Rothbart & Bates, 2006). Individual differences in biological systems, which emerge in the early weeks and months of life, influence social and emotional competencies. But these biological systems are not static. As they develop, the growth of neuroendocrine, neocortical, neurological, and other systems will impact temperamental qualities as well. Additionally, social experiences may play a moderating role in determining how these biological systems impact temperament. For example, sensitive caregivers may influence physiological responsiveness in children who are temperamentally reactive to danger (Nachmias, Gunnar, Mangelsdorf, Parritz, & Buss, 1996). Likewise, cortisol levels and other biological markers of stress responses can be altered by early experiences, such as abuse or neglect, resulting in increased wariness and irritability (Wiik & Gunnar, 2009). Therefore, biology and experience interact to influence temperament. But temperament may impact the development and maturation of biological systems as well and, ultimately, the child's social and emotional behavior.

There are also neurochemical and neurological underpinnings to individual differences in temperament. Neurochemicals such as dopamine, epinephrine, oxytocin, and vasopressin all seem to play a role in temperamental variations (Irizarry & Galbraith, 2004). And activity in the anterior and lateral prefrontal areas of the brain has been associated with variations in impulsivity, proneness to frustration, and effortful control (Posner & Rothbart, 2007). Infants and children who are timid and highly reactive to novel events show more activation in the amygdala region than do bold children who are low in reactivity. Neuroimaging studies have identified two complementary and interconnected neural systems involved in emotion regulation (Dennis, O'Toole, & DeCicco, 2013). The ventral system (including the amygdala, the insula, the striatum, and the medial orbitofrontal cortex) is activated under conditions of emotional arousal; evaluative and motivational processes are involved in modulating arousal. The dorsal system (including the lateral prefrontal cortex, the medial prefrontal cortex, the lateral orbitofrontal cortex, and the anterior cingulate cortex) is involved in attention regulation and executive control functions. These brain regions are activated when implementing cognitive control strategies, such as effortful control, directed attention, and planning actions, and serve to modulate emotional experiences (Critchley, 2005; Dennis et al., 2013; Luu, Tucker, & Derryberry, 1998). Recent studies have charted brain maturation during infancy, childhood, and adolescence. These investigations provide evidence for structural and functional brain changes related to developing emotion regulatory abilities as well as for individual differences in developing psychopathology (Adrian, Zeman, & Veits, 2011; Cole, Mischel, & Teti, 1994; Paus, Keshavan, & Giedd, 2008).

The identification of critical periods in the development of emotion regulation, and the specification of neural models of "mature" emotion regulation, are some of the research areas that need to be explored further from a developmental neuroscience perspective (Dennis, Buss, & Hastings, 2012; Dennis et al., 2013). This growing area of inquiry is critical to identifying possible vulnerability factors for disorders in childhood and adolescence and expanding our understanding of the neurobiological factors underlying both adaptive and maladaptive regulatory processes. For example, the neural systems underlying attentional mechanisms continue to mature into adulthood. These changes may modify the developmental trajectories of more reactive traits and contribute to competence and resilience (Shiner & Masten, 2012). Moreover, recent research has documented the neural activation differences in children with serious behavioral problems, such as aggression and anxiety, as well as the distinct neural activation patterns that predict individual treatment responses to cognitive behavior therapy techniques (Pizzagalli et al., 2001). Changes in brain activations have been found to be associated with cognitive behavior therapy, leading to modified neural circuits involved in regulating negative emotional states (Linden, 2006; Porto et al., 2009). Considered together, this research has great potential for illuminating the neural mechanisms that maintain behavior problems in children as well as for better understanding the changes in emotion regulation abilities that may result from successful therapeutic interventions. Ultimately, this work may help to identify and target treatment strategies for children at risk for difficulties in emotion regulation which, if left untreated, may lead to more serious disturbances in adolescence (Hum & Lewis, 2013).

Is There Stability in Temperament Over Time?

Certain temperamental characteristics may be detected even before a child is born. Pregnant women often note how active, rhythmic, or responsive their babies are *in utero*; they may even comment on differences from a previous pregnancy and wonder what these differences might mean for their newborn's temperament. In one study, fetuses that were more active *in utero* were found to be more unpredictable and difficult at 3 and 6 months of age (DiPietro, Hodgson, Costigan, & Johnson, 1996). Immediately after birth, there are apparent differences in distress and soothability. By around 2–3 months, variations may be seen in how much babies smile and approach social stimuli or cry and express negative emotions (e.g., anger, frustration). By 3 months, most infants develop the capacity to engage in self-soothing behavior (e.g., thumb sucking) that helps them to modulate their levels of arousal. Between 3 and 9 months, infants attend and respond to their environment by reaching and grasping for toys and objects that are near to them (Kopp, 2002). Over the first 2 years, children begin to control and regulate the expression of positive and negative emotions, reflecting effortful control, another temperamental dimension that continues to develop and becomes more stable by early childhood (Kochanska & Knaack, 2003; Rothbart, Sheese, & Posner, 2007). How quickly, intensely, and persistently children respond, and how much they approach or avoid new stimuli or become distracted by external sights and sounds, are all relevant to the measurement of temperamental traits during the first 2 years. And not all temperamental traits are expected to be stable. As control systems mature, they may alter the expression and stability of more reactive temperamental dimensions (Rothbart, 2011).

Because temperamental qualities are often inferred from observations of behavior, there is an essential problem inherent in trying to measure stability or change in temperament. We expect that behavior will change with development. Thus, an infant who is highly inhibited will manifest this inhibition differently than a highly inhibited preschooler or adolescent. Change in overt behaviors will therefore be expected. But there may still be an underlying stability in the organizing temperamental dimension. This idea leads to several questions: Can we use developmentally appropriate measures to assess the same temperamental quality at different ages? Is there a significant association between comparable measures of a particular temperament characteristic over time that would allow us to conclude that the temperamental dimension is stable? And if no association exists, does this mean there is lack of stability in the temperamental quality? Or might it be that the two indices, though developmentally appropriate measures of a particular underlying dimension, do not adequately capture the same temperamental quality of interest, thereby leading to errors in evaluating stability or change? Whether an individual maintains the same relative position on a measure of the dimension of interest may be a better way of evaluating stability (e.g., Roberts & DelVecchio, 2000). That is, when compared to her peers, does the child rank similarly on the same temperamental dimension at varying ages? And are there new developmentally appropriate indices of temperamental traits that need to be incorporated when studying children and adolescents, rather than simply looking at qualities that have been identified in infants (see, for example, Ganiban, Suadino, Ulbricht, Neiderhiser, & Reiss, 2008)?

The answers to these questions differ depending on the specific temperamental quality measured and the ages at which they are examined. For example, there are weak or inconsistent relations between measures of distress, attention, and activity level when assessed during the first few months of life and compared to assessments later on (Thompson et al., 2011). As the biological systems that express these temperamental qualities mature, individual variation in these dimensions are likely to be observed, thereby leading to instability in these temperamental characteristics. The newborn initially manifests a generalized distress reaction which becomes more differentiated over the first year; neurophysiological systems mature and the infant become more competent in appraisal processes that contribute to distinctions between cries of fear, frustration, and anger (Buss & Goldsmith, 1998). Early signs of wariness and behavioral inhibition arise by about 8–9 months of age that may affect activity level and negative emotional reactivity (Thompson & Limber, 1990). Concurrent with these advances, there are changes in attention span and control over visual attention that result from neocortical maturation. Consequently, maturation both within and between the neurobiological, cognitive, and perceptual systems leads to apparent instability in certain discrete temperamental qualities.

However, evidence for stability has also been found during the first year of life. When the Infant Behavior Questionnaire (Rothbart, 1981, 2011), the most widely used parent-report temperament measure, was used in two coordinated studies of infant temperament and maternal ratings, two consistent factors emerged: positive affectivity (smiling and laughter, soothability, and duration of orienting) and negative affectivity (activity level, fear, and distress to limitation). Considerable and significant stability was observed across relatively brief periods (from 2 to 5 months and between 5 and 13 months), though the magnitude of stability was slightly lower when examined across the larger time period (from 2 to 13 months). The rank order of infants was evaluated across assessments as well; despite rapid social, emotional, motoric, linguistic, and cognitive changes across distinct developmental periods, the infants preserved their relative standing. Several potential moderators of stability were explored; stability was quite robust across gender, term status, socioeconomic status, and birth order (Bornstein et al., 2015). During the first year, these developmentally sensitive analyses confirm consistent stability for the positive and negative affectivity temperament factors. Moreover, temperament is relatively stable across multiple contrasting samples, though discrete qualities may manifest differently and be impacted by environmental and parenting factors over time.

After the first year of life, there does appear to be greater stability, at least over the short term, in certain temperamental qualities. Using developmentally appropriate measures to assess characteristics, such as positive emotionality, effortful control, behavioral inhibition, and activity level, moderate stability has been found over several months or even years (Thompson et al., 2011). And certain temperamental characteristics measured in infancy have been found to predict later personality characteristics. For example, differences in reactivity and regulation during infancy predict problems with emotion regulation in preschool and anxiety problems in childhood (Bosquet & Egeland, 2006). Also, infants who are highly reactive to novelty appear to be more anxious about the future as adolescents (Kagan, Snidman, Kahn, & Townsley, 2007). However, many other studies reveal weak or inconsistent relations between early temperament measures and later assessments of developmental outcomes, thereby suggesting that individual differences in temperament during the first few years of life continue to be quite variable and links to later behavior are limited.

There is some research that indicates that temperament traits show substantial stability by the preschool years and, with age, become more consistent (Roberts & DelVecchio, 2000). Long-term continuities have been found between temperament measured after the second year of life and developmental outcome assessed in young adulthood (see, for example, Caspi et al., 2003). However, not all studies have yielded such strong associations for all children (see, for example, Pfeifer, Goldsmith, Davidson, & Rickman, 2002). Still, there are many reasons why temperamental dimensions are expected to be more stable after infancy (Thompson et al., 2011). Some of the core neurobiological systems that underlie temperament mature and become increasingly organized during the first few years. As a result, an individual's temperament profile is likely to be more consolidated and to be expressed more consistently. Additionally, the child may begin to perceive and understand individual characteristics that comprise their sense of self (e.g., "I am shy," "I like to run and play all the time") and differentiate themselves from others. As such, they may choose interactional partners who are similar to them and engage in activities consistent with their preferences. These choices serve to reinforce certain temperamental dispositions as well as the perceptions that others may have of them.

The stability of early temperamental qualities may also be influenced by interactions with caregivers. Positive affection is likely to be enhanced, and fear and anger to be minimized, when parents are warm and sensitive. Parents may teach their children how to regulate their emotions and this, in turn, may change the expression of negative emotions or distress reactions (Putnam & Stifter, 2008). Recent research has demonstrated that preschoolers who were socially wary were more poorly adjusted at 9 years of age (as assessed by internalizing and anxiety-related problems, measures of social skills, and school performance) when they have highly overprotective mothers or low respiratory sinus arrhythmia (a measure of parasympathetic regulation). When preschoolers are low on social wariness and have low respiratory sinus arrhythmia, maternal overprotectiveness appears to be related to better adjustment. Thus, both internal self-regulatory abilities and parental support for autonomy and competence appear to be beneficial for socially wary children (Hastings, Kahle, & Nuselovici, 2014). This work demonstrates the complex relation between temperamental measures and qualities of the caregiving environment in predicting developmental outcome.

In conclusion, studies that examine the stability of temperament from infancy into adolescence need to consider the transactional nature of influences. Parents may play a role in modifying the expression of certain traits in their children as they age (e.g., reactivity (Kagan et al., 2007)) just as the adolescent–parent relationship and parenting practices may be influenced by temperament (e.g., anger reactivity (Katainen, Raikkonen, & Keltikangas-Jarvinen, 1998)). Thus, stability in temperament may result from the consolidation of these individual difference variables and result in greater prediction to later behavioral characteristics. Some researchers believe that this stability will be greater within, rather than between, developmental periods because of the reorganization of competencies that occurs in the transitions from infancy to childhood or from childhood to adolescence (Goldsmith et al., 1987). Certainly more research on these topics, using developmentally appropriate indices and considering contextual factors that elicit certain temperamental qualities, will extend our understanding of when and why continuities in temperament, and between temperament and later personality characteristics, might be expected.

How Does Temperament Influence Development and Does it Predict Later Behavior?

While temperament is often thought of as directly influencing development, temperamental qualities may also be influenced by other developmental processes and interactions with caregivers. Several studies have revealed that the influence of temperament is mediated by environmental factors (Crockenberg, Leerkes, & Lekka, 2007; Porter, Wouden-Miller, Silva, & Porter, 2003; Sheese, Voelker, Rothbart, & Posner, 2007). Parental sensitivity and responsiveness, social stresses and demands, and the availability of other social influences all play a role in mediating the impact of temperamental variations. Thus, for children with both "easy" or "difficult" temperaments, how others interpret and respond to them, and the environmental supports available, will impact developmental outcomes. Temperament also interacts with cultural values and beliefs that influence parents' interpretations of and responses to children's particular temperamental characteristics (Chen, Yang, & Fu, 2012; Cole & Packer, 2011). For example, while US mothers find certain levels of fussiness and proximity seeking to be indicative of developmental problems, Japanese mothers actually value these same behaviors (Rothbaum et al., 2000). It may be more appropriate, therefore, to suggest that early discrete temperamental dispositions do not always foreshadow the child's personality later on. The dynamic transaction between temperamental characteristics and the environment in which the child is developing is more likely to lead to discontinuity and change than to predict a smooth, continuous process of personality development.

Questions about the consequences of temperamental variations for children's later social development have been explored in several longitudinal studies. Many interesting findings have emerged from this work. It appears that more psychological problems develop in children who are emotional, impulsive, irritable, or difficult (Goldsmith, Aksan, Essex, Smider, & Vandell, 2001; Rothbart & Bates, 2006). Internalizing problems, such as sadness, fear, anxiety, withdrawal, and guilt, are more likely to arise in shy or fearful children (Lindhout, Markus, Hoogendijk, & Boer, 2009; Muris et al., 2009; Rothbart, 2007). Externalizing behavior problems, such as hyperactive, aggressive, and disruptive behavior, are often seen in children with low effortful control (Ormel et al., 2005; Valiente et al., 2003). Both types of problems may appear in children with high negative emotionality.

Why are temperamental variations linked to these later problems? There are several possible explanations. Researchers have examined the ways in which the child's temperamental profile may influence their social interactions (Scarr & McCartney, 1983). Cheerful, easy babies elicit positive reactions from others (e.g., parents, siblings, caregivers, peers), thereby leading to more engaged, enduring interactive exchanges. Babies who are fearful or negative are more difficult for others to involve in interaction and social exchanges are therefore more challenging. The child's temperament may also lead to the choice of certain activities or social partners that are consistent with their natural dispositions, thereby restricting opportunities for different kinds of experiences. A highly inhibited child may choose not to join an activity at child care, preferring quiet puzzles and drawing alone and thus limiting social play, exploration, and experimenting with new interests. And temperamental characteristics may impact children's reactions to environmental stressors, thereby leaving some children either more resilient or more vulnerable (Rothbart & Bates, 2006). Thus, children with more difficult temperaments may be more difficult to care for and elicit unfavorable reactions from others; parents may be less sensitive and more critical and other children and adults may be more rejecting. There may also be an indirect effect of difficult temperament such that children who are more stressed and irritable become targets for angry comments or punitive behavior from their parents. Additionally, it may be that children with difficult temperaments react more negatively to stress and find it to be more challenging to adapt to situational demands (Reiss, Neiderhiser, Hetherington, & Plomin, 2000).

There may also be an interaction between temperament and environmental conditions. For example, children who are more fearful, and whose parents use harsh discipline, are more likely, as compared to children who are not temperamentally fearful or whose parents are not harsh, to evidence depression (Colder, Lochman, & Wells, 1997) and low levels of conscience (Kochanska, 1997). When mothers of children with timid temperaments are negative, depressed, or unsupportive, their children are more likely to have negative moods and to be less adept at regulating their negative emotions (Feng et al., 2008). They are also more likely to continue to be socially withdrawn (Hane, Cheah, Rubin, & Fox, 2008) and fearful (Gilissen, Bakermans-Kranenburg, van IJzendoorn, & van der Veen, 2008). If, however, their parents use gentle rather than harsh discipline, fearful children may develop more self-control (Kagan & Snidman, 2004).

Children are more likely to develop externalizing problems when they have a difficult temperament and their parents have marital conflict, are under stress, or lack social supports, as compared to when their parents are under less conflict and the home environment is less stressful (Morris et al., 2002; Tschann, Kaiser, Chesney, Alkon, & Boyce, 1996). The combination of a child with a difficult temperament being raised by an insensitive or harsh mother is more likely, as compared to a child with only one of these disadvantages, to evidence academic and social difficulties (Stright, Gallagher, & Kelley, 2008), depression (Paulussen-Hoogeboom et al., 2008) and to be aggressive or engage in acting-out behaviors (Miner & Clarke-Stewart, 2008). Even children who have "easy" temperaments, who are raised by parents who are cold or insensitive and in an environment where behavioral demands are inappropriate or excessive, may develop behavior problems later on.

Taken together, these research findings illustrate the combined effects of temperament and parental behavior. If parents are able to accept their child's unique temperamental qualities and adapt their behavior to their understanding of what their child needs, then development is likely to be more smooth in part because of the "goodness of fit" between them (Thomas & Chess, 1986). But the match (or mismatch) between the child's temperament and parental behavior may be altered with changes in the environment. Parents and teachers expect more of children as they mature. Entrance into school and participation in other organized activities (e.g., sports, music, or art lessons) require greater self-control, cooperation, initiative, compliance, and flexibility. Cultural demands and gender-role expectations also play a role in establishing norms for appropriate behaviors in different contexts. Therefore, certain temperamental dimensions may be well matched to particular environmental circumstances at one age (high activity level and low attention span when playing in an infant child care setting) but not at another (when entering kindergarten). Different expectations may be placed on the child by parents or teachers, potentially contributing to a more strained interactional dynamic; this may, in turn, lead to modifications in the child's temperamental profile and/or the appearance of developmental problems.

Finally, a relatively recent line of research has explored genetic and environmental factors involved in determining risk and resiliency (Shiner et al., 2012). Some temperamental traits, such as infant irritability, may make certain children more susceptible to environmental influences. This *differential susceptibility* may lead a highly irritable infant toward a positive developmental outcome if raised in a "good" environment but toward a negative outcome if raised in a "bad" environment (Belsky & Pluess, 2009; van IJzendoorn & Bakermans-Kranenburg, 2012). The ongoing transaction between children and their contexts needs to be better understood in order to more clearly illuminate the ways in which children's temperamental variations influence, and are influenced by, the contexts in which they develop.

Temperament: In Summary

The current view of temperament, maintained by contemporary theorists and researchers, is very different from the more traditional notion that biologically based dispositions result in relatively constant profiles of temperament across situations and over time. Now, temperamental dimensions are considered to be evolving, becoming more consistent with development. Stability is more likely to be reflected in developmentally appropriate expressions of the same underlying temperamental dimension (see, for example, Bornstein et al., 2015; Schwartz et al., 2012). Basic temperamental dispositions include the domains of activity, attention, emotionality, sociability, reactivity, and self-regulation (Shiner et al., 2012). Moreover, the qualities that define what is unique about each individual become organized into behavioral tendencies; these are ways of interacting with social partners, of approaching and evaluating new experiences, and of organizing and regulating emotional reactions that both reflect and define the self. Temperamental differences reflect the interaction of biology and experience, influencing development in intricate ways. Thus, biology and experience impact temperament before a child's birth (Huizink, 2012) and continue to have an effect after birth (Champagne & Mashood, 2009), with new genetic influences even appearing later in development (Saudino & Wang, 2012). These unique, individual difference variables may, in turn, make some children more vulnerable, while others become more resilient, when facing challenges and stressors, depending on the environmental and caregiving supports they receive.

Emotions

Emotions are complex, reflect many interrelated developmental processes, and serve a variety of purposes for young children. Emotions may be transient or persistent. They may be experienced or expressed only in certain situations or across many contexts. Children communicate their feelings to others through emotional expressions, language, and actions, and their understanding of emotions changes over time. Emotional expressions may influence, or be influenced by, others' behavior. And emotional development is associated with psychobiological maturation, cognitive advances, and social interactions, reflecting the developing capacity to appraise experiences, to understand the self and others, to be aware of social rules, and to exert self-control.

Emotional Development

Infants begin to detect emotions in others and to engage in affective exchanges with their caregivers as early as 2 months of age (Abe & Izard, 1999). In their reciprocal exchanges, infants have been found to modify their affective displays and behaviors in response to their perceptions of their caregiver's affect (Tronick, 1989). When the caregiver does not express any emotion, for example, during the Still-Face Paradigm, infants have been observed to become quite distressed, reflecting their anticipation of discernable emotional expressions from their interactive partners (Mesman, van IJzendoorn, & Bakermans-Kranenburg, 2009). This expectation, that they will participate in affective exchanges with others, is an important foundation for later emotional communication and regulation through social interactions.

In infancy, we tend to see extremes of emotions that are generally either pleasant or unpleasant. There is little regulation of emotional states other than when a sensitive caregiver intervenes. Infants have not learned how to conceal their emotions and so their displeasure, disgust, distress, or delight are readily apparent. In fact, during the infancy period, emotion regulation is quite dependent on the context and the caregiver (Cassidy, 1994). Basic emotions of joy, anger, interest, and sadness are present from the early months of life; by 7 or 8 months, infants can express fear, disgust, and surprise (Izard,

Huebner, Risser, McGinnes, & Dougherty, 1980). These emotions are directly related to the causal events that preceded them and serve an adaptive function (Izard et al., 2011). Distress in response to a shot in the doctor's office, fear following separation from a parent, or joy when interacting with a sibling are all evident on infants' faces. Moreover, emotions are identifiable by researchers who use elaborate coding schemes, such as the Maximally Discriminative Facial Movement (Max) Coding System (Izard & Dougherty, 1982), to distinguish these basic emotions by focusing on different parts of the face (eyelids, forehead, lips) and specific patterns of movement.

Infants are able to react to others' facial expressions of emotions as well. Neural processing studies demonstrate that, in response to human faces, there is activation in the amygdala which indicates that infants can detect emotions (Leppänen & Nelson, 2009). Neural activation during the processing of fearful and angry faces, as indicated by differential arousal patterns in event-related potentials (ERPs), suggests infants can detect and distinguish different emotion expressions as well (Hoehl & Striano, 2008). And infants do not only react to the emotions of others but they use others' emotion expressions to manage their interactions. For example, social referencing, or using others' emotional expressions as a source of information in ambiguous situations (Campos, 1983; Walden & Ogan, 1988), begins at around 9 months of age. By 1 year, infants can use an experimenter's affect and visual gaze to predict which object they will reach for and take (Phillips, Wellman, & Spelke, 2002). Thus, infants are using their emotional knowledge, from a very early age, in adaptive ways.

By the end of the second year, new emotions appear, such as guilt, shame, pride, jealousy, empathy, and embarrassment. These self-conscious or social emotions depend on children's developing ability to be aware of and talk about themselves in relation to other people (Lewis, 2007; Tracy, Robins, & Tangney, 2007). These emotions also depend on children valuing appropriate standards of conduct and then being able to apply those standards to their own behavior. Initially, feelings of guilt or pride come from parental evaluations in a relational context ("I am so proud of how you shared your toys"). Gradually, preschoolers rely on a combination of "checking out" their parent's reactions as they work on a difficult task (e.g., "You're doing a good job with that") and looking for their parent's emotional responses when the task is completed (e.g., when a mother says, with a big smile on her face, "Good for you! You figured it out"). In this way, children are learning about standards and expectations for appropriate behavior. They begin to experience and express the feelings of pride or self-worth that result from meeting these standards. Growing self-understanding is occurring within the parent–child relationship, again a reminder of the way emotional development occurs in context and of the potential negative consequences that may result when there is a difficult or challenging parent–child relationship.

Preschoolers begin to comprehend the causes of emotional experiences (e.g., "She is sad because he wouldn't let her take a turn") and the way that emotions can impact social interactions (e.g., "We don't want to play with him today because he is angry"). The self-conscious emotions also play a significant role in social development. Children's feelings about themselves and others are defined by their own feelings of pride and shame. When they perceive others as having something more or better than they do, they experience jealousy. When they finish a task that they thought might be too hard for them to complete, they feel pride. They are motivated to apologize when they have transgressed and feel guilty. And prosocial acts are performed when children understand and share another person's feelings and feel empathic toward them. Thus, the experience and expression of emotions during the preschool period become more complex, reflecting the ability to evaluate the self as well as to manage emotional expressiveness, regulate arousal, and understand the expressions of others (Lewis, 1998; Saarni, Campos, Camras, & Witherington, 2006).

When children reach the age of 5 or 6 years, they are much more competent at regulating their emotional experiences, though this is a process that begins earlier in infancy as well. Now, children may use a behavioral tactic (such as walking away from a difficult situation) or a cognitive strategy (such as distraction) to modify their emotional responses or to reduce the intensity or duration of their reactions (Denham et al., 2010). Moreover, children are better able to understand others' feeling states and to genuinely empathize with another person, even when the "other" is not there (e.g., they can respond to stories of other people who are in trouble, distressed, or suffering). The social emotions are further refined and elaborated. By middle childhood, children are able to use emotional display rules to help them understand what emotions can be expressed under particular circumstances. They learn when and with whom they can talk about and share their feelings. Emotional development continues well into adolescence, as cognitive advances and more complex emotional understanding and social interactions contribute to a deeper psychological understanding of both personal emotional experiences and of others' emotional states.

Perspectives on Emotions and Emotional Development

Several different theoretical positions have been advanced to account for the many factors that influence children's emotional development. There are some theorists who believe that the expression of basic emotions is innate, rooted in human evolution, and that there are discrete, universally recognized emotional expressions (Darwin, 1872; Ekman, 1972, 1984, 1993; Izard, 1991, 2007). Indeed, Darwin (1872) first suggested that there are certain anatomical features that correspond to basic emotions and that are universal. Some research has confirmed that the facial expressions for happiness, sadness, anger, fear, surprise, and disgust are the same in different cultures (Ekman, 1972), although this view has been increasingly challenged and cross-cultural studies have provided contradictory evidence (Kayyal & Russell, 2013; Nelson &

Russell, 2013; Russell, 1994). Moreover, a substantial body of research supports the claim that distinct facial muscles are associated with discrete emotional expressions (Ekman, 2003). However, questions still persist as to whether emotions are universally expressed and recognized.

Cognitive neuroscientists have provided evidence that different brain regions are involved with emotions. The expression of fear is controlled by the right cerebral hemisphere while joy is controlled by the left hemisphere (Davidson, 1994; Fox, 1991). Emotion is rooted in primitive regions of the brain, such as the limbic system and especially the amygdala (Armony, 2013), but more sophisticated regions of the cerebral cortex, such as the prefrontal cortex, guide emotions (Davidson, Fox, & Kalin, 2007). Hormones and neurotransmitters (regulated by different brain areas) also impact emotional responses (Gunnar & Vasquez, 2006). And neurophysiological and neuroendocrine processes change rapidly (LeDoux, 2000), impacting emotional behavior as well. For example, maturational changes in parasympathetic regulation and adrenocortical activation contribute to the ability to modulate and control arousal states (Gunnar & Davis, 2003). And emotion regulation during childhood is facilitated by the development of functional connections between subcortical and frontal systems (Ochsner & Gross, 2007). Thus, biological factors clearly play a role in the expression and regulation of emotions. Finally, research with infant twins shows that the age at which they smile, the frequency of smiling, the general degree of emotional inhibition, and the onset of fear reactions are more similar in identical (monozygotic) twins than in fraternal (dizygotic) twins (Plomin, DeFries, McClearn, & McGuffin, 2001; Robinson, Kagan, Reznick, & Corley, 1992; Rutter, 2006). Considered together, a variety of research studies provide convergent evidence that biological processes, including genes, anatomy, and brain organization, both constrain and contribute to emotion expression.

But parents, siblings, peers, and caregivers also influence the development of emotions. It is in the context of relationships that children learn to express their emotional states. Parents serve as models for emotional expressiveness and regulation. Indeed, researchers have found that children are similar to their parents in the types of emotions they express and in their levels of expressiveness. Children will display more positive emotions, be more negative or hostile, or express more empathy when their parents demonstrate these same reactions (Ayoub et al., 2006; Denham, Bassett, & Wyatt, 2007; Halberstadt, Denham, & Dunsmore, 2001). And children learn to regulate their emotions in their interactions with their parents. Some parents encourage emotional expressiveness or reward particular emotional displays, while others may be punitive, dismissing, or rejecting when their children express certain emotions. The consequence is that children learn what emotions are acceptable to express, whether or not their emotional expressions will be responded to, and how to modulate or dampen their emotional reactions based on the responses of their significant social partners. Moreover, specific events or situations may contribute to the learning of particular emotional reactions such as fear. A painful shot during a doctor's visit, for example, may classically condition an infant to fear the doctor. Fear in reaction to seeing a dog may be learned by observing a sibling scream and run away from the animal. And an adverse consequence, such as a bad fall off of a bicycle, may lead a child to acquire fear through operant conditioning. Regardless of the type of learning processes involved, these examples illustrate the ways in which children's negative or positive emotions may be modified by the learning environment.

There are those theorists who believe that emotions serve a very important purpose or function for children. Emotions motivate children to achieve survival or social goals. When in a dangerous or threatening situation, fear arises and leads the child to flee. When anticipating a special event or meeting a new person, hope and excitement help the child to prepare for the interaction. This functionalist perspective emphasizes the ways in which emotions help children to reach their goals, establish and maintain relationships, and adapt to the environment (Saarni et al., 2006). Emotions are conceptualized more broadly and serve a biologically adaptive role (Malatesta, 1990). While there are important distinctions between the different versions of these functionalist theories, many focus on the innate communicative and motivational roles of emotion (Saarni, Mumme, & Campos, 1998). Thus, emotional reactions from others provide feedback that should be helpful in guiding subsequent behavior. The way a parent responds when a child approaches to hug him will determine how the child feels and behaves. If the parent smiles and receives the child with open arms, the child will be happy and accept the embrace. On the other hand, if the parent withdraws, freezes, or turns away, the child is likely to feel confused, hurt, or sad and to withdraw. And memories of past interactions will also determine a child's response in a new situation. When meeting new friends, if a child has been successful in engaging others in positive interactions, she will be more confident and approach someone she does not know with more assurance; if the child has had difficulty being welcomed and accepted by her peers, she will be more emotionally withdrawn and others might turn away.

Emotions are thus seen to serve a very important function, providing vital information about others' underlying mental states and expected behaviors. At the same time, emotions function to facilitate goal-directed behavior that is adaptive. Cognitive advances, socialization experiences, and biological maturation all serve to motivate and organize adaptive emotional functioning (Denham, 1998; Saarni et al., 1998). Moreover, while emotions generally serve an adaptive purpose, emotional functioning may be disrupted by biological and social stresses, leading to the development of psychopathology (Malatesta & Wilson, 1988; Plutchik, 1993). Even maladaptive outcomes may be understood by considering disruptions in the effective use of emotions for goal-directed behavior and interpersonal communication.

Finally, other theorists consider emotions to be psychological constructs (Barrett, 2009; Barrett & Russell, 2014; Kuppens, Tuerlinckx, Russell, & Barrett, 2013; Russell, 2009, 2014). Rather than viewing emotions as a singular event, emotions are seen to have varying causes, to be influenced by core affect, and to be constructed by differing processes (Russell, 2014). The underlying dimensions of pleasure-displeasure and activation-deactivation are integrated to form a unified, subjective feeling (Russell, 2003). This view stands in contrast to biological constructionist views, inherent in basic emotion theory (e.g., Ekman, 1972; Izard, 1971), and to social constructionist perspectives that emphasize the cultural determinants of emotion (e.g., Dashiell, 1928; Landis, 1924). Instead, the psychological constructionist view posits that emotional experiences are unique and subjective. Cognitive neuroscience research, highlighting brain regions involved in cognitive and affective processing, supports the position that attention, perception, and emotional language all come together in the construction of a diverse range of emotions (Barrett, 2009). Emotions are context- and person-specific, influenced by physiology, core affect, action tendencies, and appraisals. Emotions derive meaning from the individual's own appraisals and experiences which are dynamic, change over time, and lead to nuanced emotional experiences and responses that transcend simple combinations of basic emotions (Ellsworth & Scherer, 2003; Kuppens, Stouten, & Mesquita, 2009). Individual differences in the duration and intensity of emotions are expected. Understanding these differences in normality and pathology are critical to the constructionist view (e.g., Tomarken & Keener, 1998; Verduyn, Delvaux, Van Coillie, Tuerlinckx, & Van Mechelen, 2009; Whittle et al., 2008). Therefore, in accordance with this view, the natural course of emotions, and the determinants of the ways in which specific emotion components vary over time, depend on a consideration of the individual and the situation.

Together, these different perspectives – biological, learning, functionalist, and constructionist – offer valuable starting points for understanding critical aspects of emotional development. We will now consider developmental advances in emotional expressiveness, the use of display rules, emotion understanding, and emotion regulation and conclude with a discussion of relationships and emotional development.

Emotional Expressiveness

From the start, children are able to let others know how they feel, as well as what they like and dislike, through their emotions. Learning how to express, interpret, and regulate emotions is critical to children's emotional development and social success (Goleman, 2005). These three essential abilities – emotional expressiveness, understanding, and regulation – are interrelated. While these developing aspects of emotional competence may be studied separately, it will quickly become clear that there are significant ways in which they are inherently connected.

Important individual differences in emotional expressiveness are evident early in life. Some babies are not disturbed by loud noises or novel events while others react with fear; some babies smile more easily and laugh energetically while others are more subdued and reserved. These variations in emotional expressiveness are related to temperament, suggesting that the intensity of children's reactions to arousing stimuli and situations may be biologically based.

During infancy, emotion expressiveness serves the purpose of communication and usually leads caregivers to attend to their infant's needs. For example, sad expressions and crying are ways that infants signal their distress to caregivers; they will likely respond in an effort to ease their babies' discomfort. Similarly, joyful expressions attract the caregiver to share positive affective exchanges and sustain the interaction. Shared communication occurs as infants and caregivers rely on vocalizations and facial expressions of emotion. Significantly, these emotional exchanges contribute to the infant's capacity for emotion regulation and facilitate the development of an attachment relationship (Cassidy, 1994). Thus, caregivers respond to their infant's emotional expressions and infants develop positive expectations that their caregivers will help them to regulate their emotions. When caregivers are unavailable, infants are less likely to be successful in regulating their emotions (Bridges, Grolnick, & Connell, 1997). The predominant method for regulating emotional expressions in infancy, therefore, is through the infant–caregiver relationship. While there are some self-soothing and autonomous regulatory behaviors that infants may use as well (cf. Woltering & Lewis, 2009), infants depend on their caregivers to comfort and soothe them, reduce distress, sustain positive exchanges, and provide the relational support for emotion regulation.

During the preschool years, emotional expressions become more significant in social communication. Emerging language skills facilitate communication. Now, the labeling of emotions helps children make sense of their emotional states (cf. Barrett, Lindquist, & Gendron, 2007; Cole, Dennis, Smith-Simon, & Cohen, 2009). Children begin to use words to describe their feelings. They develop emotion schemas as they connect their feelings and associate them with appropriate cognitions. For example, they now understand that angry expressions on another's face may be linked to aggressive intentions or behaviors. Children acquire this knowledge in the context of their home and social environment (Izard et al., 2011). Parents and teachers serve as models for emotional expressions, emotion-related language, and behavior (Cunningham, Kliewer, & Garner, 2009; Garner, Dunsmore, & Southam-Gerrow, 2007; Warren & Stifter, 2008). The development of the ability to understand others' emotion expressions allows children to move beyond basic emotion experiences. With increases in emotion regulation and emotional knowledge, preschoolers are now more successful in managing their positive and negative emotional reactions and begin to learn that they can experience multiple feelings at the same time.

Additionally, significant neurobiological changes, especially in the orbitofrontal cortex and the anterior cingulate cortex, are believed to be involved in children's acquisition of emotion knowledge. These areas are not fully developed in preschoolers (Lewis & Todd, 2007). Researchers have found high variability among preschool children in their capacity to maintain attentional focus and engage in inhibitory control. These individual differences may impact how children focus and modulate their behaviors and their emotional reactions. Thus, because emotion knowledge influences children's ability to regulate their emotional expressions and experiences, we see that the social and neurobiological processes that influence emotion knowledge also influence emotion expression and regulation in preschoolers (Izard et al., 2011).

Parents continue to play a critical role in helping children learn to regulate their emotional expressions through the preschool and early childhood periods. If parents offer constructive responses when their children are angry, or provide comfort when they are sad or upset, children learn how to display their emotions and regulate them better (McDowell & Parke, 2005). Alternatively, if parents frequently berate their children (e.g., "You're such a baby!") or punish them ("You can't cry now. Go to your room!") when they express emotions, children have trouble regulating their own emotions (Parke, McDowell, Cladis, & Leidy, 2006; Valiente & Eisenberg, 2006). Moreover, when parents are good at regulating their own emotional expressions, they provide for their children lessons that help them to manage their positive and negative feelings too (Perlman, Camras, & Pelphrey, 2008). Children are less likely to experience problems regulating their emotions if their parents settle arguments between them in constructive ways (Cummings & Davies, 2010). But when parents' marital conflicts are pervasive, children become highly sensitive to anger and distress and are often overinvolved in their parents' difficulties; this leads to insecurity and difficulty managing the emotions aroused in them (Sturge-Apple, Davies, Winter, Cummings, & Schermerhorn, 2008).

Children who are exposed to domestic violence (Katz, Hessler, & Annest, 2007) or who are maltreated (Edwards, Shipman, & Brown, 2005; Shipman et al., 2007) are particularly poor at regulating their emotions. And when parents suffer from depression or other affective disorders, their children are vulnerable to problems with emotion regulation (Goodman & Gotlib, 1999). Therefore, when parent–child relationships are disturbed, there are consequences for children's emotional expressiveness (Thompson & Goodman, 2010). Considered together, it is the quality of parental caregiving that interacts with the child's temperament and genetic vulnerability that may buffer them against developing problems with expressing and regulating their emotions or make them more vulnerable to developing difficulties later on. Again we see the importance of early attachment relationships, and the emotional support derived from them, for the child's emotional development.

Siblings and peers also exert an influence on emotional expressiveness. Siblings offer models of positive and negative responses to emotion (Denham et al., 2007; Dunn, 1988), often "tattling" when a brother or sister has an angry outburst or joining in the fun when "silliness" sets in. Intervention programs have focused on improving sibling relationships by teaching children skills (e.g., identifying, evaluating, and monitoring their feelings) that help them to modify their emotional reactions to their brothers and sisters (Kennedy & Kramer, 2008), thus highlighting the communicative value of emotional expressiveness. Children also learn about other people's feelings by engaging in pretend play with their siblings and peers (Dunn & Hughes, 2001). When children have good relationships with their peers, they learn about the subtle nuances of emotions (Dunsmore & Karn, 2004). And, it is in interactions with their peers that children learn they will experience disapproval or be rejected when they are angry or be accepted and receive approval when they are happy (Denham et al., 2007). Consequently, children serve as powerful models for emotional reactions.

Research has demonstrated that individual differences in positive and negative emotionality are associated with children's overall adjustment. For example, children who are emotionally more positive tend to be more socially competent, have higher self-esteem, and better overall adjustment, whereas children have a higher rate of developmental problems when they express more negative emotions (Goldsmith et al., 2001; Lengua, 2002; Rothbart & Bates, 2006). And emotional expressiveness is associated with children's physical and emotional health. When a child is despondent, expressing mostly sadness and little joy, this may indicate problems associated with social withdrawal, difficulty concentrating, and more general signs of depression. Physical health may also be affected by conditions that lead to problems managing stress and anxiety. For example, heightened cortisol levels may lead to physical problems (Gunnar, 2000; Rutter, 2002) and parental hostility and conflict may also impair health (Gottman, Katz, & Hooven, 1996). Taken together, there are many reasons as to why it is important to better understand developmental changes in emotional expressiveness. Though influenced by biological factors, there are significant relational experiences that help children to learn how to regulate the expression of their emotional states. We will now consider, in particular, the use of emotion display rules before considering more fully the importance of emotion regulation.

Emotion Display Rules

Emotions are expressed in social contexts and communicate a lot about a person to others. But do people always display in their emotional expressions what they are really feeling inside? While hiding one's real feelings may not be healthy or adaptive, for the individual or the relationship, there are still many ways in which emotion display rules are used to hide or mask the expression of true feelings. Why might we hide our true feelings? It is more likely that feelings will be hidden or masked when expressing those feelings might hurt someone else (e.g., anger at someone who forgot to bring you the toy they borrowed), reveal insecurity or self-doubt (e.g., embarrassment over missing the ball when up at bat), or impact an important relationship (e.g., distress when a friend does not stick up for you). Young children do not understand the rules around socially acceptable emotional displays. This is why a 3-year-old might burst into tears and declare to a friend, "It is time for you to leave now" when he is tired and cranky and wants a play date to end, or why a 3½-year-old might get angry and tell her older sister, who shared her most precious doll with her younger sibling, "You gave me an ugly doll to play with." It is also why a child might, out of discomfort or distress, laugh when another child cries or gets angry. However, with development, children gradually learn the rules for regulating the expression of their true emotions.

Children as young as 4 years of age are capable of modulating or controlling their expressions to protect another person's feelings (Banerjee, 1997). But it is not until about 6 or 7 years of age that children have the cognitive skills necessary to appreciate the significance of, and reasons for using, emotional display rules (Saarni, 1999). With this increased understanding, children learn that they can disguise their own feelings and their emotions may remain private. They also learn that others may not reveal what they are truly feeling. Display rules may vary by gender and culture, as current research has demonstrated (see, for example, Cole & Tan, 2007). They may also vary for different types of emotions expressed. Thus, there may be different rules regarding the expression of discrete negative emotions, such as anger, fear, and sadness, depending upon context as well as age and gender of the child (Roberts & Strayer, 1996). For example, girls are taught that it is more acceptable for them to reveal their fear or sadness, whereas these feelings are less acceptable for boys to share (Fivush, 1994).

There are several different types of display rules that may be used to alter the emotions expressed when in the presence of others (Ekman & Friesen, 1975). A child might "maximize" the distress he feels, crying more loudly when a sibling takes away a toy when a caregiver is present. Alternatively, a child might "minimize" the emotion she actually feels, thereby reducing the impact of her real feelings. For example, she might seem not to care when everyone else gets a gift from a relative but she does not get one, or he may show little distress when he is being reprimanded by a parent in front of his friends. When a child wants to hide how she really feels, she might "neutralize" her expression of emotion, maintaining no expression on her face at all while her teacher reprimands her. Or he might "mask" his emotional expression, replacing what he is really feeling with the opposite expression. Thus, he might smile and congratulate his friend who made the team for which he was not chosen (Ekman, 2003; Thompson et al., 2011). Each of these rules serves an important communicative function and has an impact on social partners.

Because emotions are inherently social and part of the language of social exchanges, children need to understand emotion display rules in order to successfully negotiate their social interactions. As they develop, children learn to apply display rules. They come to discover and understand that what the other reveals in their emotional expressions may not be what that person is truly feeling inside. In the process, children also learn that they can reveal or disguise their own emotions. Eventually, more sophisticated rules are elaborated for when, where, and with whom one is comfortable expressing his or her true feelings. Therefore, internal emotional states may be disguised to social partners by the display of more "appropriate" emotional expressions, even though the honest expression and sharing of emotional states is critical for being known in more intimate connections. While there are many individual, relational, familial, and cultural factors that impact the use of display rules, children as young as 6 years of age begin to recognize the conventions for the display of positive and negative emotions (Cole & Tan, 2007) and may modify their emotional expressions based on contextual variables (Thompson et al., 2011).

Emotion Understanding

Expressing emotions, and using emotion display rules to regulate their expression, are only part of developing social competence. Children also need to understand emotions and be able to recognize feeling states in themselves and in others. They also need to learn about the different precursors to and consequences of emotions. With development, they discover ways to manage their own and others' emotions and learn about the contexts where it is appropriate to express or display emotions. The early roots of emotion recognition occur in face-to-face interactions with caregivers. During the first few months of life, emotions are communicated through facial expressions and tone of voice. Though babies do not use language, they are able to recognize some emotions, discerning positive emotions earlier and more often than negative ones (Denham et al., 2007), in a sequence that matches the pattern of infants' own displays, where smiling and laughter appear before frowning (LaFreniere, 2000). Babies recognize their mother's expressions earlier than they do their father's. Moreover, those babies who spend more time with their mothers are more adept (compared to those spending less time with their mothers) at recognizing her expressions (Montague & Walker-Andrews, 2002). Thus, early experience appears to influence emotion recognition.

The development of self-understanding during the late second and early third years of life also contributes to emotion understanding. As children become more physically and psychologically aware of the self as distinct from others, and develop a new sense of autonomy, they evidence an emergence of the self-conscious emotions such as pride, shame, embarrassment, and guilt (Lagattuta & Thompson, 2007; Lewis, 1992a; Lewis, Alessandri, & Sullivan, 1992). Now, children can feel pride when positively evaluating the self after doing something well or when praised by a trusted adult. Children can also experience the "bad self" (Erikson, 1950/1963) or shame when exposed and vulnerable, feeling defeat and lacking in dignity or worth (Sroufe, 1996; Tomkins, 1963). These emotions are only possible when children have increased self-awareness, an understanding that the self can make things happen (the self as agent), and an appreciation of the standards for appropriate behavior. It may be that pride and guilt necessitate an internalized set of behavioral standards, rather than responding to externally guided parental standards, though shame may be an earlier precursor to guilt. Moreover, shame and pride may be experienced even without another person present whereas guilt and embarrassment depend on an understanding that one's behavior has been observed by someone else (Sroufe, 1996). These self-conscious emotions result from the increased understanding of the connection between one's own behavior, associated feelings, and consequent outcomes, which are all central to the sense of self (Sroufe, 1996). And it is within a relational context that children come to rely on their own emotional reactions, and the responses from others ("Wow, you really did a great job building that block tower!" said by a parent with a big smile on her face), as the basis for the self-conscious emotions. In turn, these emotions offer children important cues regarding their own self-worth and impact their subsequent social interactions with others.

By 3 or 4 years of age, children can recognize and correctly identify the emotions of happiness, sadness, fear, and anger. These abilities continue to improve with age, as children learn about the causes of emotions, the kinds of situations that elicit different emotions, and the subtle ways to discriminate the expression of emotions (Denham et al., 2010). Children's emotion understanding is influenced by their interactions with their parents. When the quality of their relationship is compromised, then there are consequences for their understanding of emotion. For example, children who were abused and experienced high levels of hostility in their relationship with their parents are better than nonabused children at discerning expressions of anger and less competent at identifying expressions of sadness (Pollak & Sinha, 2002). Deficits in emotion understanding are also seen in children who were neglected rather than abused (Sullivan, Bennett, Carpenter, & Lewis, 2008). Thus, social experiences impact children's ability to recognize emotions. Similarly, developmental advances in emotion understanding contribute to social interactions, success in the peer group, and interpersonal competence (Saarni et al., 2006).

Emotion understanding also involves children's thinking about emotions in themselves and others. As their naïve "theory of mind" expands, 4- and 5-year-olds begin to appreciate the complex connections between emotions and beliefs, thoughts and expectations (Thompson & Lagattuta, 2006). Now, children can see that emotions may be linked to the satisfaction or frustration of beliefs ("I can't wait to go home and see my grandma," though the child does not know that her grandmother's flight was cancelled and she could not come to visit) or of wishes and desires ("I hope I can have a chocolate ice cream cone!"). Children think more deeply about the range of emotions they might feel and about whether they can experience more than one emotion at the same time ("If I get to stay home from school today, I will be happy because I can play in the snow and have hot chocolate with my Dad, but I will be sad because I won't be able to see my friends or play basketball at recess"). However, while by 6 years of age children can experience two emotions of the same valence (e.g., "happy" and "proud" or "mad" and "upset" (Harter, 2006)), it is not until 10 or 12 years of age that children can experience two different, even conflicting, emotions (e.g., "happy" and "disappointed" (Harter, 2006)). These advances in emotion understanding are related to children's developing awareness of the self; moreover, they inform children's self and other awareness and influence their social relationships.

Children also go through different periods in their thinking about emotions and their understanding of how emotions might be experienced and expressed (Pons, Harris, & de Rosnay, 2004). For example, while 3-year-olds can use external features to recognize basic emotions (happiness, sadness, fear, and anger), it is not until 5 years of age that children can understand and identify external causes of these basic emotions. Thus, they can understand that a child might be sad if they break a favorite toy. But they also can appreciate that two different children in the same situation might have different desires and therefore feel different feelings. For example, one child might be happy to get a birthday gift because it is exactly what she wanted, whereas another child might be disappointed because she did not get the toy she had asked for. Understanding that emotions have a psychological component begins at about age 7, when children can begin to appreciate that emotional expressions reflect not just the external situation but also inner states. Thoughts and beliefs might influence the person's emotional reactions and external expressions may not match the person's inner feelings. The child who is disappointed not to receive the gift she had asked for may still smile and say "Thank you!" to the gift giver because she knows it would be rude and ungrateful to express her disappointment. By 9 years of age and on, children see that it is possible to reflect on a situation and to consider it from multiple perspectives. Different emotions may be associated with a particular situation, and these emotions may be ambivalent, contradictory, or mixed. The hierarchical organization of this developmental progression requires that earlier understanding is attained before more sophisticated understanding may be achieved (Pons et al., 2004).

Emotional scripts, or internal cognitive representations that facilitate children's understanding that certain events lead to particular emotional reactions, help reduce uncertainty for children as they learn which emotions are linked to which situations. By 3 or 4 years of age, children are capable of describing the types of situations that lead to fear, surprise, or excitement (Cole & Tan, 2007). By 5 years, more complex emotional scripts allow them to know that particular situations lead to emotions that are associated with certain behaviors (e.g., crying implies the person is sad) or have discernable facial displays (e.g., frowning indicates anger). Seven-year-old children can appreciate the kinds of situations that might elicit emotions (worry, jealousy or pride) that have more ambiguous expressions or behaviors associated with them, and by 10 years of age, they can recognize situations evoking disappointment or relief (Harris, Olthof, Meerum Terwogt, & Hardman, 1987). While the content of these emotional scripts vary in different countries, this developmental sequence has been observed not only in the United States but in Great Britain, the Netherlands, and Nepal as well (Harris, 1989).

How do children expand their emotion understanding? Cognitive advances and developing social experiences provide rich opportunities for children to learn about their emotions. Conversations with parents, siblings, and peers enhance their learning as well (Lagattuta & Wellman, 2002; Thompson,

2006). Children spontaneously share their experiences in stories and running accounts of events that happened, social exchanges they participated in or witnessed, or feelings they experienced. Parents may question, elaborate, interpret, and offer information that extends understanding, illuminates the antecedents and consequences of emotions, and communicates expectations about appropriate emotional reactions and behavior (Thompson & Meyer, 2007). In this way, parents are conveying significant messages that are relevant to the child's understanding and that reflect their own emotional understanding embedded within a cultural and psychological context. For example, US mothers include discussion of their child's and others' feelings and thoughts twice as often as Korean mothers do when talking about past events with their children (Mullen & Yi, 1995). Additionally, the child's personal characteristics will impact the messages offered and the way they are received. Research has demonstrated that parents offer different lessons about emotion based on their child's gender. For boys, parents attribute emotions to external causes (e.g., anger is the result of rain interfering with swimming), discuss anger more often than sadness, and offer few options for resolving negative emotions. By contrast, for girls, parents are more likely to explain emotions based on relational factors (e.g., sadness is the result of a friend being mean), discuss sadness more than anger, and suggest reconciliation and reassurance when negative emotions are expressed (Fivush, 1994).

We see that children's growing social competence depends on their capacity to express emotions, to use emotion display rules, and to understand their own and others' emotions. But the capacity to regulate emotions is also important to socially competent behavior. Unlike the use of display rules, which serve to regulate the *expression* of emotions, emotion regulation strategies influence the *emotion* itself (Eisenberg & Spinrad, 2004). Moreover, as we will come to see, the capacity for emotion regulation emerges out of early social interactions and, in turn, impacts social interactions.

Emotion Regulation

Why do children need to learn to regulate themselves? Children generally feel better when they are able to modulate their emotional reactions and reduce the intensity and duration of their arousal or negative affect. When they are successful at regulating their emotions, others respond more positively to them and want to be with them. It makes sense, then, that competence in emotion regulation is related to more general social competence. The study of emotion regulation is concerned with the ways in which emotional experiences are modulated, constrained, or enriched by emotion regulation processes. These processes include strategies, behaviors, and skills that operate either automatically or deliberately (Calkins & Mackler, 2011; Eisenberg, Hofer, & Vaughan, 2007; Gross & Thompson, 2007) and that serve the function of helping the individual to achieve particular goals (Thompson, 2014; Thompson, Virmani, Waters, Raikes, & Meyer, 2013).

While infants have a limited capacity to regulate themselves and their emotions, they learn, through interactions with caregivers, to engage in mutual dyadic regulation. Eventually, they develop additional emotion regulation strategies that help them modulate their emotions over the toddler and preschool years. Over time, children learn to regulate their own emotions as well as to regulate how others respond to them (see, for example, Campos, Frankel, & Camras, 2004; Cole, Martin, & Dennis, 2004). Ultimately, adaptive emotion regulation does not simply imply that children are able to reduce their negative emotions or turn negative emotions into positive ones. Rather, most theoretical approaches to emotion regulation suggest that adaptive regulation involves the capacity to experience genuine emotions, to initiate, maintain, and move flexibly between positive and negative emotional states, and to diminish heightened states of positive or negative emotional arousal when necessary (Bridges, Denham, & Ganiban, 2004; Thompson, 2014). Thus, emotion regulation involves altering the dynamics of emotions, rather than the valence, in a manner that is consistent with the individual's goals (Thompson, 1990). When viewed in this way, emotion regulation facilitates confidence in the self and competence in social interactions.

Researchers have considered a variety of issues, including the influence of temperamental qualities, such as reactivity (Rothbart & Bates, 1998), and of attentional processes, such as effortful control (Valiente et al., 2003), on emotion regulation. There is a substantial body of literature, for example, that supports the direct impact of temperament on emotion regulation (Cole et al., 2004). Emotion regulation includes both the dimensions of emotional reactivity and emotional control; these dimensions, which operate in dynamic relation to one another, may be difficult to untangle. While emotional reactivity, a temperament dimension, is influenced by genetic and biological factors and present in the early few months, emotional control develops over time and reflects efforts to manage emotions (Fox & Calkins, 2003). Multiple models of the causal relations between temperament and developmental outcomes, such as emotion regulation, have been offered, including consideration of the moderating role of the caregiving environment (Bates & McFadyen-Ketchum, 2000). There has been less of an emphasis, however, on exploring the *processes* involved in accounting for the association between temperament characteristics, environmental factors, and emotion regulation. It may be, for example, that variations in temperament impact emerging emotion regulation skills that, in turn, have an effect on the parent–child relationship. Temperamental qualities may directly constrain the regulatory behaviors that are critical to behavioral control, they may be moderated by caregiving behaviors that then impact emotion regulation, or they might be mediated by attention or other regulatory processes that influence emotion regulation in context (see Calkins & Mackler (2011) for a discussion of these alternatives).

As the infant's nervous system matures during the first year of life, inhibitory and excitatory processes are stabilized (Thompson, Easterbrooks, & Padilla-Walker, 2003). Thus, while subcortical structures are active from birth, there is rapid maturation of certain cortical structures associated with the sympathetic nervous system over the first year (Sroufe, 1996). During this time, there is also a much more gradual maturation of the finely tuned inhibitory processes that are associated with the parasympathetic nervous system (Thompson, 1990). By the second year, there is further maturation of the frontal lobe, which plays an essential role in the development of self-regulatory behavior (Dawson, Panagiotides, Klinger, & Hill, 1992). In particular, maturation of the lateral tegmental (inhibitory) limbic circuit in the orbitofrontal cortex allows this system to be integrated with the ventral tegmental (excitatory) circuit, which has already achieved maturation earlier in development (Sroufe, 1996). There is evidence that the orbital prefrontal areas are directly involved in attachment relationships (Steklis & Kling, 1985), especially as these cortical areas are important to the processing of social signals. Now, the hierarchical organization of the excitatory and inhibitory systems allows for the homeostatic regulation of emotional and motivational states as well. The result is that delayed response capacities, as well as rapid shifts between varying emotion states, are possible. These advances, therefore, have implications for the toddler's emotional development (see Schore, 2003, for further explication of the neurobiology and psychobiology of attachment relationships and self-development).

Developmental changes in the central nervous system, together with ongoing relationships with attachment figures, have implications for emotion regulation. As the child moves from dyadic regulation (in the context of the attachment relationship) to self-regulation, development of the central nervous system both supports, and is influenced by, these advances (Schore, 1994). Thus, while emotion regulation is a process that appears to be impacted by temperamental qualities, attentional processes, and developing neurobiology, especially in the prefrontal cortex (Davidson et al., 2007), it is also influenced by the parent–child relationship. Socialization processes interact with developing neural systems and temperament over time and impact the capacity for emotion regulation.

During infancy, babies are almost completely dependent on caregivers to help regulate their emotional states. Parents attempt to modulate their infant's states of arousal, provide appropriate levels of stimulation, and reciprocate and support emotional reactions. In turn, infants respond to their caregivers' initiatives and stimulation and contingently react to emotional expressions, thus regulating their caregivers' emotions. This reciprocal "dance" leads to a finely tuned exchange of emotional behaviors that are contingent upon emotional communication and contribute to the infant's ability to regulate. When a baby is distressed, for example, it is the caregiver who can calm the baby by picking her up or offering her a pacifier. By about 6 months of age, babies participate more purposefully in eliciting responses from the caregiver by, for example, raising their arms in an effort to initiate being picked up. They may even approach the parent by crawling or call out to the parent, thereby adjusting their behavior until they achieve the desired response. Therefore, infants engage more actively in dyadic regulation (Sroufe, 2000), using the growth of intentional abilities that emerge during the first year. Parents may modify the demands of the child's familiar settings in accordance with what the child needs or coach their child on strategies for managing emotions (e.g., "It's okay to hold your blankie when you're scared"). Guided self-regulation, where the caregiver supports the toddler as she gradually acquires the beginning capacities for self-control, gives way to the toddler being able to manage a wider range of emotions, tolerate frustration and disappointments, and regulate her emotional states independently of the caregiver. Genuine self-regulation requires that parents monitor their child's efforts at regulation, offer clear guidelines for expected emotional and behavioral reactions, and provide opportunities for practice and mastery (Sroufe, 2000). Now, the toddler may turn away from a stranger, cover her face, or put her thumb in her mouth. She may hold a favorite teddy bear when afraid, seek an alternate activity when the one she wants is not available, or play with a sibling when the parent is occupied. These alternative activities serve the purpose of diminishing fear or anger, thereby allowing the child to self-regulate and ultimately engage in an alternative solitary or social activity.

While infants develop a broader range of emotional reactions, they also become more capable at minimizing the intensity and duration of these emotional reactions. As they approach toddlerhood, children are better able to regulate their emotional arousal; therefore, they may delay their emotional reactions or adopt alternative coping strategies other than fleeing or reacting intensively to stressors. Consequently, regulating emotions and behavioral reactions may moderate between social demands and anticipated social outcomes (Saarni, Campos, Camras, & Witherington, 2008). For example, sustaining the duration of an expression of fear, or intensifying one's fear reactions, may increase the likelihood that one's interactive partner will remain in close proximity, thereby serving the toddler's need to avoid separation from the caregiver.

Advances in cognitive and motor skills and conceptual advances in emotion understanding during the toddler and preschool periods allow for a broader range of emotion regulation abilities than were possible in infancy (Kopp & Neufeld, 2003; Thompson, 1994). During the toddler period, aggressive outbursts appear to be most frequent and caregivers often need to calm their distressed toddlers (Kochanska, Murray, & Harlan, 2000). However, growing competence with effortful control during the preschool period leads to increased use of adaptive self-regulatory strategies. Young preschoolers are often able to use distraction as a way of focusing on the more positive, rather than the distressing, aspects of a situation, which in turn leads to fewer behavioral problems. Self-distraction and reorienting attention, or movement toward or away from a situation, are common regulatory tactics used in the preschool years. Children also begin to use objects and interactions with others in more complex ways (Diener & Mangelsdorf, 1999).

Over time, emotion regulation strategies that children use incorporate the behaviors and techniques learned from their caregivers. When parents respond in an accepting and supportive manner to children's displays of negative emotions, children learn to cope in more adaptive ways and develop more constructive emotion regulation strategies (Denham, 1998). These strategies, in turn, impact children's biological responses and behavioral adaptations (Calkins, Graziano, Berdan, Keane, & Degnan, 2008; Calkins & Hill, 2007). So, for example, a child will learn to be positive and enthusiastic when approaching an emotionally arousing situation, such as a visit to the doctor, because she can anticipate the treat she will get when the visit is over. Young children also begin to see that there is a connection between the effort they make to regulate themselves and the feelings they have. They might still be afraid, upset, angry, or frustrated, but they can cry or complain or pout without the temper tantrums and screaming, angry outbursts characteristic of the toddler period. Developmental advances, in the context of supportive parent–child relationships, thus facilitate, and are facilitated by, emotion regulation.

At times, the toddler may be able to regulate her behavior successfully while periodically falling back on the caregiver for assistance or guidance. The caregiver may also anticipate the need for support, thereby enabling the toddler's emerging self-regulatory activities. A sensitive caregiver will encourage the child's control and management of her behavior and affect, anticipating when help is needed (e.g., when the child experiences frustration or is beginning to lose control) and taking control in highly charged affective states (e.g., when the child becomes increasingly angry). This dynamic "dance" allows the child to learn how to manage arousal while still protected by the caregiver's presence (Sroufe, 1996). At the same time, the child gradually learns to inhibit impulses (e.g., grabbing, pushing) and strong expressions of affect (e.g., temper tantrums). With the caregiver as her guide, the toddler is learning to regulate her emotional states by expressing affect directly while also modulating and controlling her expression. In the safety of the infant–caregiver relationship, the infant has already learned, from face-to-face interactions, that feelings can be expressed and responded to in a "dance" that builds confidence and trust in the caregiver as an interactive partner. Similarly, the attachment–exploration balance provides the infant with confidence in moving away from the caregiver while knowing she can return for comfort, support, or assistance. The toddler can now build on this foundation and learn that strong feelings can be expressed but that they also need to be modulated and contained with assistance from the caregiver. Thus, it is out of the foundation that was established during infancy that emotion regulation is achieved (Sroufe, 1996, 2000).

The development of language represents another significant milestone in emerging regulatory abilities. Children may be encouraged to talk about their feelings and parents may help them understand the antecedents to and consequences of their feeling states (Campos et al., 2004). Over time, children become more flexible in using their language, behavior, and social skills and, while impacted by earlier levels of physiological regulation, the result is an increase in regulation and a decrease in emotional reactivity (Blandon, Calkins, Keane, & O'Brien, 2008). Now, in interaction with parents and siblings, children are able to better understand their emotions as they observe first hand the emotional climate of the family (Morris, Silk, Steinberg, Myers, & Robinson, 2007). However, there are variations in the extent to which parents express, discuss, and regulate their own emotions; these differences may, in turn, contribute to their children's developing capacities for regulating emotions. Conversations with parents about emotions lead children to better understand the normative expectations for managing emotions and provide the conceptual base for creating their own understanding of emotion regulation. Additionally, familial messages regarding ways to assess, process, activate, or modulate emotional responses are embedded within a cultural context. Thus, for example, children in Western cultures are encouraged to use problem-focused strategies while children in Asian societies are expected to endure negative feeling states to maintain social harmony (Lee & Yang, 1998). Children incorporate familial and cultural values and gender expectations into their developing conceptions of emotion and emotion regulation.

Emotion knowledge expands as children move beyond the preschool years and begin to understand the consequences of emotions as well as the ways they can use emotions in constructive ways (Denham, 1998; Izard, 2009). Developing neurobiological, emotional, social, and cognitive systems provide the foundation for using emotions more effectively. Now, for example, emotions (especially negative ones) may be increasingly differentiated and their positive regulatory functions understood (Barrett, Gross, Christensen, & Benvenuto, 2001). Thus, the regulation of children's anger-related behavior may be influenced by the arousal of feelings of guilt that serve to inhibit negative responses and promote adaptive alternatives (Kochanska, Barry, Jimenez, Hollatz, & Woodard, 2009). Consistent with the constructivist view of emotion, children's growing understanding of emotion includes an awareness of the associations between emotions and desires, beliefs, expectations, and goals. Children's deepening emotion knowledge, therefore, helps them to make meaning of their emotions; this then facilitates the use of self-regulatory strategies with greater confidence and competence.

By the time children are ready to enter kindergarten, they generally are capable of more active emotion regulation. Children can now integrate their own knowledge of emotions, or emotion schemas, together with an understanding of the links between emotion, cognition, and behavior, to facilitate social information processing and regulation of their emotional reactions (Lemerise & Arsenio, 2000). They have a wider range of regulatory skills that allow them to adapt to the academic and social pressures of the more demanding school setting. Now, children can use cognitive and behavioral coping strategies. They might reevaluate a frustrating situation, interpret disappointment in more positive ways, and actively use distraction as a way of managing their feelings (Kalpidou, Power, Cherry, & Gottfried, 2004). Some of these methods, such as reappraisal, may promote learning, whereas other methods, such as rumination, do not (Davis & Levine, 2013). Additionally, errors in attribution patterns may interfere with adaptive social behavior. For example, more aggressive behavior in 5- to 7-year-old children is associated with the use of a hostile attribution bias (that is, the tendency to attribute hostile intent to others in situations where there is ambiguous information) (Halligan, Cooper, Healy, & Murray, 2007). Therefore, if no help is provided to develop strategies for controlling reactivity to challenging circumstances, early problem behaviors and difficulties with emotion regulation can lead to later academic and social difficulties (Burr, Obradovic, Long, & Masten, 2008).

At the onset of puberty, increases in risk-taking and sensation-seeking behaviors may be the result of increases in arousal levels prior to maturation of regulatory abilities and of the systems necessary for the detection of risk and reward (Calkins & Mackler, 2011; Steinberg, 2005b). Throughout adolescence, heightened emotional lability and negative emotional experiences may be the result of fluctuations in hormone levels (Rosenblum & Lewis, 2003), even as adolescents learn to better distinguish and anticipate long-term consequences of their behaviors (Moilanen, 2007). Caregivers continue to play a role in influencing their adolescent's emotion regulation skills, although their influence continues to interact with biological processes. For example, when mothers diminish or invalidate their adolescent's positive affect, adolescents, in turn, engage in dysregulating strategies associated with symptoms of depression and display negative behaviors with their mothers as well (Yap, Allen, & Ladouceur, 2008).

During adolescence, as children spend more time with their peer group, there is continued maturation of the brain regions associated with emotion regulation processes, including the prefrontal cortex, amygdala, and anterior cingulate cortex (Beauregard, Levesque, & Paquette, 2004). These changes within the brain, together with physical growth and hormonal shifts, interact with changes in the adolescent's social world. As their social world shifts from the home to the peer group, adolescents are both impacted and constrained by the biological changes they are experiencing. They may use regulatory techniques they have already learned to be personally helpful, such as talking to a friend, exercising, or listening to music, to regulate their emotions. Emotion schemas during this period are more sophisticated and involve more complex cognitive processes. Emotion regulation now depends on cognitive appraisals, thoughts, and ideas (Izard, 2009). There is a continued interaction between the cognitive, emotional, and behavioral components of emotions, with consequences for their motivational, regulatory, and functional capacities (Izard et al., 2011). As we will come to learn, how adolescents organize themselves, regulate their emotions, and adapt to the many changes of the teenage years will affect their long-term adjustment.

Clearly, the developmental shifts in emotion regulation require that researchers adapt their conceptualization and measurement of emotion regulation processes to the developmental period of interest (Bridges et al., 2004). Attentional processes, for example, may be most relevant in infancy, whereas emotion awareness, appraisal, and monitoring may be more relevant in childhood and adolescence. Because there is no single widely accepted definition of emotion regulation, measurement strategies vary as well (Cole et al., 2004). For example, studies of infants rely on assessments of the reflexive and dyadic regulation of distress. During the toddler and preschool period, researchers have used developmentally appropriate structured observations of attempts that children make to modulate negative emotion. And research with older children has focused on the analysis of emotion dynamics in interpersonal interactions (Trentacosta & Shaw, 2009). Research in naturalistic and laboratory settings has been conducted, and comparisons of emotion regulation have been made in contrasting conditions where, for example, social circumstances are manipulated (e.g., child alone or with mother or stranger present) or different emotional reactions are induced (e.g., anger or fear), allowing researchers to more carefully document the regulation of particular emotions activated in differing conditions (Cole et al., 2004). Ultimately, the convergence of multiple measures of emotion regulation, including self-report, behavioral observations, and manipulations of experimental conditions, and the evaluation of emotion expression, observed behaviors, and physiological responses associated with regulation, will provide a richer approach to understanding developmental shifts in emotion regulation.

Early Emotion Regulation and Later Development

While eventually all children learn to regulate their emotions, some are more competent regulators than others. Researchers have documented that early emotion regulation abilities are important predictors of later adjustment (Fox & Calkins, 2003). For example, 4- to 6-year-old children who display high emotional intensity demonstrate lower levels of constructive coping and more distractibility (lower levels of attentional control), are seen by their peers as less desirable playmates, and are viewed by their teachers as less socially mature (Eisenberg et al., 1993). Children who are better able to regulate their emotions get more attention and approval and are responded to more positively by adults (Howes, 2000). They are also liked better by their peers and more socially competent when they are aware of social display rules regarding emotions (Parke et al., 2006). And children are less disruptive and aggressive at kindergarten entry when they have learned in preschool to modulate their anger by shifting attention away from frustrating situations (Gilliom, Shaw, Beck, Schonber, & Lukon, 2002). Thus, individual differences in emotion regulation exist early on, appear to be relatively stable, and are remarkably predictive of later self-regulatory competence and social functioning (Eigsti et al., 2006).

Some children are born with a "temperamental advantage" that makes it easier for them to modify the duration and intensity of their emotional reactions. They seem to be biologically less reactive and better at controlling their attention through activities such as gaze aversion (Rothbart & Bates, 2006). Other children are temperamentally more reactive and less competent at controlling their attention and are therefore poor regulators from the start. They (and their caregivers) have to work harder to focus or to recover from an intense emotional experience. In fact, their difficulties are reflected in and confirmed by biological indices. When faced with a frustrating task (e.g., waiting for a prize), children who are less competent at regulating themselves have lower cardiac vagal tone and higher levels of negative affectivity (Santucci et al., 2008). They need to work harder to develop the ability to regulate their emotions. Children who are born with higher negative emotionality (higher frequency and intensity of negative emotions in response to emotionally arousing situations) may also overtax their emotion regulation abilities (Kochanska & Coy, 2002).

While there is likely to be a reciprocal influence between negative emotionality and emotion regulation, more effective emotion regulation may eventually diminish the tendency to respond with negative emotions. Alternatively, children with more positive emotionality (who experience more positive emotions and can induce positive responses) can recover more quickly from the arousal of negative emotions and may be more effective at emotion regulation (Izard, 2009). These early appearing temperamental variations may impact emotion regulation abilities and influence later development. Moreover, research findings suggest that these temperamental influences may be quite potent since, without intervention, individual differences in emotion regulation tend to be stable over time (Raffaelli, Crockett, & Shen, 2005).

Variations in emerging emotion regulatory processes, which are dependent on biologically determined constraints and aspects of the social environment, impact children's development (Bridges et al., 2004). Adaptive self-regulatory strategies at early periods in development have been related to later adaptation (e.g., Silk, Shaw, Skuban, Oland, & Kovacs, 2006). The ability to use self-regulatory strategies and delay gratification in a waiting task during the preschool period, for example, is associated with academic and social competence later in adolescence (Mischel, Shoda, & Peake, 1988). However, problematic outcomes may arise when children are not able to master adaptive emotional self-regulation strategies during the preschool period. Maladaptive and dysregulated styles, or the use of inflexible responses to changes in the environment, may lead to impaired social competence and externalizing problems (Denham et al., 2003; Dishion & Patterson, 2006). Research has found, for example, that at 3½ years of age, the use of focused attention on a delay object (e.g., a cookie) in a frustration task is associated with more teacher-rated externalizing behavior problems reported three years later, while the ability to use distraction strategies during a frustration task is associated with fewer externalizing behavior problems reported three years later by teachers (Gilliom et al., 2002). Moreover, the use of adaptive emotional self-regulation strategies (such as active distraction) during a waiting task in early childhood is directly related to lower peer rejection in middle childhood. Peer rejection, in turn, predicts to antisocial behavior in early adolescence. Thus, while self-regulation in early childhood is not directly linked to later antisocial behavior, it is indirectly associated through its link to peer rejection (Trentacosta & Shaw, 2009). In sum, it appears that the effective use of regulatory strategies and the capacity to apply alternative strategies, depending upon contextual and desired emotional goals, are critical to later developmental outcomes. Fostering adaptive self-regulation strategies in young children may reduce the risk of later social and emotional problems.

It is important to recognize, however, that in certain circumstances, individuals with clinical problems or who are at risk for developing pathology may develop a pattern of emotion regulation that is adaptive in helping them deal with a current difficult situation (such as where they experience abuse or neglect). Even though the regulatory solution may create risk in other competencies, such as developing social relationships, assessed concurrently or at later points in development, the manner in which "at risk" individuals regulate their emotional responses may serve an adaptive function in the current context. A child who, as a result of her early experience of trauma and abuse, shows heightened sensitivity to internal cues of anxiety, interprets others' behavior as potentially aggressive, and is hypervigilant to threatening events may develop a self-regulatory strategy for avoiding anxiety-provoking encounters based on prior experience and learning. This constellation of emotional behaviors serves the purpose of self-protection and security when with an abusive parent and therefore reflects adaptive emotion regulation in the parent–child context, though it may interfere with competent functioning in the peer group. When considering particular family processes or temperamental vulnerabilities that may increase the risk for developing pathology, it is important to understand the emotional goals that children are seeking to achieve. These goals serve a critical function as they may lead to the development of emotion regulation strategies that are the most adaptive for a child in a particular circumstance, though they may potentially lead to or perpetuate a maladaptive solution over the long term.

Is it possible to intervene and help children become better at emotion regulation? We know that children who use their emotion knowledge to regulate their feelings are more competent at achieving desired goals (Izard, 2002, 2007). And research has demonstrated that the classroom environment, and the learning process itself, is improved when children are able to regulate their emotions in adaptive ways (Trentacosta & Izard, 2007). The capacity to distinguish between one's own and others' thoughts and feelings, or to understand theory of mind, may be facilitated by adaptive emotion regulation (Wellman, Cross, & Watson, 2001). By contrast, the inability to link feelings, thoughts and behaviors, to identify emotion expressions, or to modulate emotion reactions may interfere with adaptive emotion regulation (Izard et al., 2011).

Interventions that focus on the recognition and identification of emotions may ultimately help children to modulate and control neurobiological responses. Children need to be taught the labels for emotions and the functions of different emotions, including the positive and negative consequences associated with expressing different emotions (Izard et al., 2001, 2008). When children learn the adaptive functions of emotions, they may also learn adaptive emotion schemas. Thus, for example, if they learn that a fearful expression lets others know you are afraid, then they may also come to associate fear with the incentive to get help, find support, or move to a different environment where fear can be reduced (Izard et al., 2011).

Learning to slow down or inhibit typical rapid responses in emotion-eliciting situations is another intervention that may be productive. Children may benefit especially from interventions that incorporate the use of distraction as an adaptive means of dealing with distressing situations (Trentacosta & Shaw, 2009). Indeed, successful prevention programs may help children to develop the emotion self-regulation skills that reduce later social difficulties. There are some existing early childhood prevention programs that focus on helping children understand and manage their emotions and have obtained positive results for emotional self-regulation (Domitrovich, Cortes, & Greenberg, 2007; Izard et al., 2008). Additionally, research that has focused on neurobiological development and the emergence of executive control in young children demonstrates that there are individual differences in preschoolers' ability to use effortful control to regulate emotion processes (Blair & Diamond, 2008; Rhoades, Greenberg, & Domitrovich, 2009). Teaching children to attend to the emotion as it is first felt may help to moderate high arousal levels, thereby reducing the challenge to inhibitory systems by helping children to diminish prepotent responses. Using these behavioral strategies may be especially helpful to children as they continue to develop their regulatory abilities. If children can learn to understand their emotional reactions in different situations, they will be better able to control their responses and behaviors (Izard et al., 2011). Ultimately, these skills will help them to access adaptive emotion schemes that enable children to distinguish their own emotional reactions from others', be empathic, take another's perspective, and have better relationships with their peers (Vaish, Carpenter, & Tomasello, 2009); these are all competencies that facilitate the transition to the school environment.

Finally, whether emotion regulation is congruent with coping is another controversial issue (Saarni et al., 2008). Coping may be an important feature of emotion regulation; when presented with challenging circumstances, purposeful or effortful reactions may be necessary (see, for example, Compas, 1987). Emotion regulation and coping may both be required in stressful situations and thus both terms have been used interchangeably (Brenner & Salovey, 1997). However, when facing a stressful situation, emotion regulation may occur first as the child attempts to modulate emotional arousal before trying to resolve the situation and coping with the inherent challenges of the stressful circumstance. The question remains as to whether indeed this temporal path exists or whether there is a more reciprocal dynamic between emotion regulation and coping (Campos et al., 2004). Examining the developmental precursors to individual differences in emotion regulation and coping, as well as in their dynamic connection over time and in their predictive association to later outcomes, remain important areas for further exploration.

Relationships and Emotional Development

As we have come to see, it is in the context of our most significant early relationships that we begin to learn about emotions – how and when to express them, how to understand them, and how to modulate and control them. The quality of attachments to mothers and fathers influence how children come to understand, experience, and interpret emotions. When these relationships are secure, children rely on their attachment figures to support their emotional development through shared conversations, emotional guidance, assistance in regulating emotions, and sensitive instruction (Laible & Thompson, 2007). When these supports are missing, such as when the early attachment relationship is insecure, or when parental psychopathology or marital conflicts are present, emotional development is impacted (Thompson & Goodman, 2010). Thus, children's understanding of emotions, and developing emotion regulation skills, emerge in a relational context.

Early attachment experiences have been linked to emotional development both theoretically (Cassidy, 1994) and empirically (see Cassidy & Shaver, 2008). Interestingly, over the first three years of life, children with different attachment histories develop a tendency to experience different emotions (Kochanska, 2001). Securely attached children, when placed in situations intended to elicit anger and fear, display these emotions less than children with insecure attachments. Infants who are classified as insecure-avoidant become more fearful, infants who are insecure-resistant have difficulty reacting with pleasure or joy, and infants with disorganized attachments become more angry over time. Mothers of securely attached infants comment about positive and negative emotions more when they are interacting with their 1-year-olds, whereas mothers of insecurely attached infants talk primarily about negative emotions or do not comment on feelings at all (Goldberg, MacKay-Soroka, & Rochester, 1994). There is also evidence that securely attached preschoolers are more advanced in their emotion understanding as they talk more about emotions in their everyday interactions with their mothers and have mothers who tend to elaborate and extend conversations about emotions with their children (Thompson, 2006). Moreover, boys who are securely attached at 18 months use more constructive strategies to manage their anger at 3½ years of age (Gilliom et al., 2002).

During the infancy period, caregivers in secure attachment relationships are more sensitive to and accepting of their infant's expressions of positive and negative emotions. Their babies, in turn, learn that the caregiver is available to help regulate emotional reactions. As changes in physiological and emotional states are understood and responded to by the caregiver (e.g., soothing the baby's cry, smiling while holding the baby closely, calming the infant's distress), the infant learns that the caregiver is there to comfort, calm, and help establish equilibrium. When the caregiver is present, the baby discovers that arousal will not lead to disorganization but rather will be met by the caregiver's attempts to soothe and regulate. As the baby develops expectations regarding the caregiver, internal working models (Bowlby, 1973) are formed from these regulatory experiences with an available and responsive caregiver. When a caregiver "mirrors" an infant's experience of physiological, affective, and behavioral arousal, the infant can organize his/her experience by perceiving, and internally representing, the caregiver's state. In turn, this internal representation comes to be interpreted by the infant as his/her "self-state," thereby providing a "higher order representation of the child's experience" (Fonagy et al., 2002, p. 30). If the caregiver mirrors the infant's reactions (e.g., distress) too precisely, then this might produce a fear reaction in the infant; if the caregiver does not mirror the infant's reactions, or does so in a way that is biased by the caregiver's own preoccupations, then the development of the self may be challenged (Fonagy et al., 2002).

What is evident in the early representational mapping between the affect of the self (the infant) and of others (the caregiver) is the beginning development of the understanding of internal states; it is this understanding that ultimately contributes to the labeling of emotions and the regulation of affect. Children in secure relationships have mothers who are more open to talking with them about their emotional states. This, in turn, leads to greater emotional awareness, deeper emotion understanding, and a greater capacity to modulate emotions (Thompson, 2014). Therefore, children who are securely attached learn to attribute mental states to others and this learning helps them to account for others' behavior. By contrast, children in insecure relationships have mothers who are less comfortable talking with them about difficult emotions. They are less likely to respond to their children's expressions of emotions in sensitive and responsive ways. Their children are more limited in their understanding of emotions and more easily dysregulated, especially when dealing with stressful situations (Thompson, 2014). Children who are insecure and avoidant may ignore the mental states of self and others, while those who are insecure and resistant may focus only on their own internal states and ward off or exclude interactions that could overwhelm them with affect. And children who are disorganized in their attachment relationships tend to maintain a heightened state of vigilance and may therefore be acutely sensitized to the caregiver's state, creating a mental representation of the caregiver's behavior but not learning to effectively organize his/her own internal states (Fonagy & Target, 1997). Thus, secure attachment appears to enhance, whereas insecure attachment appears to interfere with, the development of emotion regulation which in turn impacts autonomy and self-worth, enhances self-organization, and prepares the child for reflective functioning that promotes agency and self-control.

In conclusion, we see that the expression and understanding of emotions and emotion regulation evolve within a social context and influence social relationships. While genetic predispositions, or particular caregiving experiences, may protect children against problems in emotional development, they may also make them more vulnerable to developmental difficulties. Exploring the transaction between temperament, neurobiology, parenting, and social context is critical to our understanding of emotional development and its impact on the emerging self.

The Development of the Autonomous Self

Advances in social, emotional, and cognitive functioning during the first few years of life, and the process of differentiation between self and others, gradually lead to the emergence of autonomous functioning. This developing awareness of self progresses through a series of stages (Bertenthal & Fischer, 1978; Damon & Hart, 1982) and reflects the organization of underlying developmental advances (Case, 1991). Different theoretical approaches to studying the self in young children have been offered. For example, Spitz (1957) proposed that increased awareness of intentions leads to the toddler's experience of the "I." Erikson (1950/1963) wrote extensively about self-control and autonomy that begins to emerge at about 2 years of age and leads the child, through a sequence of stages, to initiate actions while mastering the environment, to be industrious, and to achieve a sense of identity. Mahler and her colleagues (Mahler et al., 1975) described the process of separation and individuation that occurs as the infant moves away from the mother through a series of stages that reflect an increased awareness of the self.

Developmental researchers have identified some of the apparent advances that move the child toward autonomous functioning, including the acquisition of motor skills (crawling, walking, climbing) and the emergence of representation (language). Toddlers assert their autonomy by insisting, "I okay!" or "Me do it!" as they increasingly move away and explore on their own, sometimes out of sight of their caregivers. They are more comfortable relying on shared gaze, affective signals, distance interaction, or vocalization as opposed to physical contact. Toddlers are increasingly able to spend time apart from the caregiver, exploring their social and nonsocial worlds. When faced with uncertainty, toddlers will still seek reassurance from their caregivers by returning to their side or by social referencing; that is, they may, across a distance, look to their caregiver and rely on the caregiver's positive or negative affective signals to "decide" how to proceed (Boccia & Campos, 1989).

At the same time that toddlers are evidencing increased autonomy in their behavior, there is a developing awareness of the self as a social being. James (1892) wrote about the subjective self, or the self who experiences, feels, thinks, and acts upon the world around her. This subjective or "I-self" has self-awareness as one of its most basic functions. Knowledge of the self as subject is followed by knowledge of the self as object. As the observer, the "I-self" becomes aware of the "Me-self," or the self as observed as an object by the other. The "Me-self" reflects all the characteristics that others come to know.

Thus, young children begin to describe themselves using the concrete terms that others might use to describe them. At first, these reflect physical characteristics, family roles, and possessions but will later include more abstract psychological qualities, such as feelings, values, and beliefs (Damon & Hart, 1982; Harter, 1998b).

Developmental Changes in Aspects of the Self

Learning about the self is a process that starts very early (Legerstee, 2006; Rochat, 2009). *Self-awareness* begins to develop in the early months of life as young infants organize everyday routines and experiences into a subjective awareness of the self (Meltzoff, 2007). The result of visceral sensations, such as being held, touched, and moved around, is that infants become physically aware of their bodies. As they interact with their early social partners, infants acquire a sense of agency. They also learn about the consequences of their actions, especially when their caregivers respond contingently to them. For example, infants learn that if they reach both their arms up toward a caregiver, the caregiver will likely pick them up. And, together with the awareness of new emotions while in social interactions, these experiences contribute to the emergence of a subjective self within the first 6 to 8 months of life (Thompson et al., 2011). During the second year, infants come to learn that other people have subjective states, just as they do. They are increasingly able to match their mental state with their caregiver's in relation to a third person or object when they engage in joint attention. They may also use social referencing, attending to the caregiver or another person when in situations involving cognitive uncertainty and relying on their affective reactions to determine what to do or how to feel. Through activities such as joint attention, social referencing, and re-engaging with a partner after gaze aversion or inattention, infants come to see that they can affect, and be affected by, the subjective states of other people.

Visual self-recognition, or the capacity to recognize what they look like, is achieved towards the end of the toddler's second year and is another early precursor in the ontogenetic sequences of self-awareness in both infants and primates (Amsterdam, 1972; Bertenthal & Fischer, 1978; Dixon, 1957; Gallup, 1977; Lewis & Brooks-Gunn, 1979). Toddlers who have the capacity for visual self-recognition now identify themselves in a photograph, mirror, or video recording, understanding that a visual representation of the self is reflected in the image. When babies younger than 1 year of age are held in front of a mirror, they happily look at their reflections but they do not understand that they are looking at an image of themselves. Infants may smile or vocalize toward their mirror image or even touch the mirror as if they are looking at a playmate. Between 5 and 18 months of age, this mirror-directed behavior is quite common. Empirical work demonstrates that it is through correspondences between proprioceptive feedback of their own movement and visual cues provided by movements of the mirror image that infants begin to discriminate their own image from those of opposite sex babies, older children, and adults (Lewis & Brooks-Gunn, 1979).

During the second year, children no longer need to rely solely on contingency cues as they develop the ability to recognize their own image on the basis of features of the image alone (Amsterdam & Greenberg, 1977). For example, now toddlers can demonstrate self-recognition in noncontingent situations such as the observation of photographs of themselves (Harter, 2006). They are able to use internal schema to maintain visual images of themselves and others that they can then compare to external observations of their own mirror image or of other people in their immediate environment. Thus, toddlers become capable of differentiating between themselves and others in both contingent and noncontingent situations (Lewis & Brooks-Gunn, 1979). This process is facilitated by the active construction and use of internal representations of self and others. By the middle of the second year, mirror directed behavior decreases with a concomitant increase in self-conscious reactions. Thus, by about 15 months, we begin to see behaviors such as blushing, glancing, and, toward the end of the second year, averting gaze and strutting. These self-conscious reactions suggest a nascent self-awareness that is revealed in both an admiring of the self and an embarrassment in seeing the self.

Visual self-recognition tasks have been used to document developmental shifts in self-awareness. By the middle of the second year (between 15 and 18 months of age), some children begin to recognize themselves and by 22 months of age, most are capable of recognizing their mirror image (Amsterdam, 1972). How is visual self-recognition assessed? Following a procedure originally used with young chimpanzees (Gallup, 1970), researchers position a young child in front of a mirror and then turn the child away to surreptitiously put a spot of red rouge on her nose. When placed back in front of a mirror, the critical behavior that indicates self-recognition is when the child touches her rouge-marked nose while simultaneously looking at her mirror image (Brooks-Gunn & Lewis, 1984; Bullock & Lutkenhaus, 1990). Children who recognize themselves seem to know that the rouge is on them; the mark-directed behavior results from this awareness. They have a representation of what they are supposed to look like, see that the image now violates that representation, and "comment" on the discrepancy by touching their nose.

Prior to 15 months of age, no children demonstrate this understanding. While they tend to be quiet, curious, and attentive when they see their rouge-marked noses, it is not until they engage in mark-directed behavior that we also see them acting coy or embarrassed (Lewis & Brooks-Gunn, 1979). Some children even laugh or act silly at the sight of their rouge-marked nose. Thus, there are affective parallels to visual self-recognition. An increase in positive emotional expressions, as well as in the display of coy and self-admiring reactions (e.g., strutting, preening), may be seen when children recognize themselves in the mirror or in pictures (Schneider-Rosen & Cicchetti, 1991). And the capacity for self-recognition is tied to advances in cognitive development as well (Mans, Cicchetti, & Sroufe, 1978). For example, beginning at about 15–18 months of age, there is an increase in the use of personal pronouns such as "I" and "me" (Lewis & Ramsay, 2004) and some children even name themselves as they gaze at their image (Bates, 1990) suggesting a rudimentary concept of the self. Thus, self-descriptive statements and personal pronouns are used as children describe their actions and behaviors. By about 18 to 20 months, children begin to use terms to denote emotional states and to describe the affective experiences of self and others (Bretherton, McNew, & Beeghly-Smith, 1981).

Studies examining individual differences within age groups suggest that early experiences with caregivers impact visual self-recognition. For example, self-recognition at 19 months has been found to reflect the quality of the mother–child attachment relationship (Schneider-Rosen & Cicchetti, 1984), with more children who are able to recognize themselves at this age found to be secure in their attachment to their mothers. Secure attachment has also been found to be associated with greater self-knowledge at 2 to 3 years of age (Pipp, Easterbrooks, & Harmon, 1992). The early emergence of self-awareness develops within the child's social world and reflects qualitative differences in early experiences (Keller et al., 2004). Mirror self-recognition has been studied in children from across four different sociocultural environments. Interestingly, while the capacity for visual self-recognition increases with age in all contexts, the earlier emergence of this ability occurs in cultural contexts where mothers value and support their children's development of autonomy. Familiarity with mirrors and cultural norms regarding expressive behavior do not impact mirror self-recognition. And children who recognize themselves also use personal pronouns more (Kärtner, Keller, Chaudhary, & Yovsi, 2012). Thus, visual self-recognition appears to be a valid index of an early representation of the self and to reflect the development of the self as it emerges in a culturally specific manner (Greenfield, Keller, Fuligni, & Maynard, 2003).

In the context of the early parent–child relationship, children also begin to learn *self-regulation* or *self-control*. There are several phases in the development of self-regulation (Kopp, 2002). Initially, in the *control* phase, children rely on the adults around them for directives and reminders about acceptable behavior. In the *self-control* phase, children comply with what they know is expected of them even when they are not being watched. It is in the *self-regulation* phase when children can use their own plans and strategies to guide their behavior and resist temptations and impulsive actions. This capacity to delay gratification increases during the second and third years as children continue to develop self-regulation (Kochanska, Coy, & Murray, 2001). When toddlers are told that they need to wait for something that they really want (e.g., a special treat that they want to eat or an activity they really enjoy) they are increasingly able to delay gratification and tolerate the frustration inherent in waiting. Concomitant with this shift is a decrease in the frequency of temper tantrums associated with the "terrible twos." These tantrums are best seen as the expression of frustration at needing to wait, not getting their way, not getting what they want, or not being able to control others. The decrease in their frequency marks a significant shift in toddlers' developing self-regulation.

While children may still have a long way to go before they can more fully control their behavior, their ability to differentiate the self from others, and to understand that others may have needs that are different from their own, helps in the process of learning to regulate their behavior and reactions. Moreover, advances in the development of the frontal cortex also accompany these shifts to more mature self-regulation (Shonkoff & Phillips, 2000). And temperamental qualities appear to be related to individual differences in self-regulatory abilities as well. In particular, effortful control leads to deliberate and conscious attempts to actively inhibit behavior, reflected in children's increased capacity to pay attention, slow motor actions, or respond to directives to suppress ongoing activity or initiate behaviors. Children who are capable of inhibiting their behaviors and actions early on become better at self-regulation in early childhood (Kochanska et al., 2000, 2001). They comply more with rules, even in the absence of adults, and demonstrate a greater internalization of the rules for appropriate behavior. For children who are more fearful and inhibited in temperament, gentle discipline techniques that focus on positive motivation foster self-regulation (Kochanska, 1995, 1997).

As children continue to develop the capacity to regulate their behavior in the early elementary school years, they are better able to manage themselves in various social contexts. So, for example, they now understand they need to sit quietly and pay attention in the classroom whereas they can engage in more active behavior outside during recess or in organized gym classes. Children become more competent at how they present themselves to others, especially with regard to the expression of emotions. Now, their developing emotion regulation skills allow them to determine what feelings they want others to see (Saarni, 1999). At the same time, there is an increase in children's perceptions of their social competence (Cole et al., 2001). Thus, the increasingly mature social self is much more self-conscious and acutely aware of how it appears to others, while also mindful of the need to respond appropriately in different social situations and to diverse social demands.

Another parallel understanding that emerges is the awareness that the self and others are agents of action. Young children begin to appreciate they can be in charge of their actions and make things happen; they can find a hidden object, complete a puzzle, pretend to "read" a book, or build a block tower. This *sense of agency* is a manifestation of the "I-self," reflecting a belief that one's thoughts and actions can be controlled by the self. During the second year, toddlers experiment with their developing autonomy by attempting to control their own behaviors and the behaviors of others. They begin to recognize themselves as active agents who are independent from others and can effect change in the environment. They are able to use internal representations of themselves and others to conceptualize plans for action that they may then demonstrate by their deliberate movements and verbalizations and by their active attempts to control others' behaviors.

The emotional reactions that accompany toddlers' activities suggest a developing awareness of the self as an agent during the second year as well. We may now see joy over the completion of a task that has been conceptualized and planned, interest in the process of detecting and understanding means–ends relations or causal sequences in the execution of a task, or distress in the face of uncertainty over the ability to solve a problem. An increase in positive expressions, usually reflecting pleasure and pride, indicate the young child's feelings about her self as an agent of action because she now knows that she made an outcome happen. For example, the toddler demonstrates less pleasure when an experimenter completes a task and much more pleasure when she does it on their own (Stipek, Recchia, & McClintic, 1992). She now recognizes her responsibility for her behavior, feeling good when something is done correctly and experiencing shame when told she has done something wrong.

Toddlers also begin to understand that others people's actions may be goal-directed and purposeful (Thompson, 2006). They seem to know, for example, that someone is interested in an object when they look at, reach for, or point at the object (Woodward, 2003). They can also create joint attentional states with an adult by using their own actions, such as pointing or reaching, to encourage the adult to look at an object with them (Tomasello & Rakoczy, 2003). As toddlers become increasingly aware of rules and standards guiding appropriate behavior, they are also more aware of the violations of those standards. They recognize that a red spot on the nose is not how they are supposed to look (as in the visual self-recognition paradigm) or that when an object breaks it is not how the object is supposed to appear.

Even by the middle of the second year, toddlers very much want to please their caregivers by showing they understand rules and can control their behavior (Maccoby, 1980). They know that certain behaviors are forbidden and so they may, while looking directly at their caregiver, "test" the limits of the rules by starting and stopping the forbidden behavior (Kochanska, 1993; Kopp, 1989). When things are not the way they should be, or they cannot do something they are asked to do, they may become distressed (Emde, Biringen, Clyman, & Oppenheim, 1991; Stipek et al., 1992). They are also aware of others' transgressions (Dunn & Munn, 1985) and show a sensitivity to others' distress (Zahn-Waxler, Radke-Yarrow, Wagner, & Chapman, 1992). However, during the second year, their distress reactions are not differentiated (did they violate a parental rule or a behavioral standard?) but may be best seen as generalized arousal reflecting uncertainty and discomfort in response to doing something they know they should not have done (Kochanska, 1993). Perhaps most importantly, these reactions indicate that children are beginning to understand that their behavior may be the basis for the emotional responses of pride, guilt, or shame (Sroufe, 1996). They are distressed if they transgress a rule (e.g., breaking a toy or spilling milk on the floor) and generally respond to directives to stop doing something they know is not allowed (e.g., climbing onto a table). However, their adherence to standards still seems to be dependent on an adult's presence.

By the end of the second year of life, toddlers have developed a rudimentary sense of themselves as active agents, independent of others. They have acquired an understanding of their invariant physical features that enable them to recognize their own image. They have internalized schema for themselves and others that may help them to plan actions, conceptualize alternatives, and regulate their behaviors. They have begun to employ verbal labels to identify themselves and to account for internal emotional states and ongoing activities. And they demonstrate emotional reactions that represent the affective concomitants to a developing understanding of the self, social rules, and appropriate behavioral responses.

Toddlers become increasingly aware, during the third year of life, of social norms and scripts for their own and others' routines: "I brush my teeth and then you read me a book," "Mommy goes to work and then Mommy comes back home," "Daddy always sits next to me at the table." Toddlers' knowledge of these scripts contributes to their understanding of the world around them and makes things more predictable. It also gives them a sense of control over their environment and helps them to understand what is going on or what will happen next. Scripts for social routines, such as family rituals, bedtime routines, or what to do when they arrive at child care, become familiar to children by the end of their second year and they can use these scripts to describe their routines to others (Bauer, 2002; Nelson, 1993). These early scripts provide the foundation for later social understanding as they detail, for example, how to follow rules of games, introduce oneself to a new friend, or follow routines in child care and later in school.

Continuing into the third year, toddlers evidence multiple advances that reflect emerging awareness of the self through *self-representation*. They reference the self ("That's me!") and their belongings ("my doll"), use their name ("Jason") when they see their mirror image, and describe internal states ("I am happy") using emotion labels (Bretherton, Fritz, Zahn-Waxler, & Ridgeway, 1986). Self-conscious emotions begin to emerge, such as shame, pride, and guilt (Lagattuta & Thompson, 2007). Toddlers assert their competence and independence ("I can do it myself") (Bullock & Lutkenhaus, 1988; Stipek, Gralinski, & Kopp, 1990) and identify the self by gender ("I am a big girl!") (Ruble, Martin, & Berenbaum, 2006). With time, 3-year-olds begin to understand standards and rules (Kochanska et al., 2008) and show signs of a developing conscience (Thompson, Flood, & Goodvin, 2006). Children's increased understanding of internal states during the preschool years helps them to make sense of their own psychological states as well as those of others. As they develop a rudimentary "theory of mind" (Miller, 2012; Wellman, 2002), they incorporate their own, and gradually others', desires, intentions, feelings, thoughts, and beliefs into their understanding of mental states. They become capable of thinking about themselves and incorporate these thoughts into their representation of the self.

Now, young children are sensitive to how their parents evaluate them and their behavior. They are motivated to avoid negative reactions and they seek out parental approval. Children also incorporate parental standards into their view of themselves. In fact, one of the distinctive features of young preschoolers' self-representations is a deep concern with how significant people in their lives view them (Lagattuta & Thompson, 2007). If Jenny's mommy hugs her and praises her for "doing a really nice job putting away her toys," Jenny knows that her mother expects her to put her toys away, that her efforts were appreciated, and that she feels the outcome was good. She may also internalize a good feeling, knowing her mother was proud of her. These small everyday exchanges provide the young child with clear messages about the self. They implicitly convey the caregiver's view of the child. In recounting these experiences in everyday conversations, parents communicate to children lessons about the self: "Remember, Kayla, how hard it was for you to put your clothes on this morning and get ready for preschool? We had quite a struggle, didn't we? And it was sad we had to leave the house with you crying. But we had to get you to preschool, didn't we?" Here, Kayla's mother is saying that Kayla was crying because there was some difficulty getting ready for preschool, that Kayla was uncooperative, and that they had to leave the house on time. Kayla's representation of this event might include a message that what she did was "wrong" or "bad," or that she was tired and did not want to get dressed and leave her house (and her mommy), depending on the way her mother structures and elaborates the shared recollection of the earlier event.

The recounting of an event or personal experience together with the child is one way in which parents can begin to provide the foundation for autobiographical memories and personal narratives (Nelson & Fivush, 2004; Welch-Ross, 1995; Welch-Ross, Fasig, & Farrar, 1999). Research has supported this idea. When parents talk to their young children about the personal importance of experiences and events, using rich emotional language to evaluate positive events and highlighting the causes and consequences of negative emotions, children begin to understand the personal meaning of their experiences, incorporate them into their self-representations, and continuity of their self-concept is enhanced (Bird & Reese, 2006; Reese, Bird, & Tripp, 2007). Parents, therefore, promote self-awareness through the narratives they use that help their children understand themselves. They provide their children with stories that are then integrated, together with their own thoughts and feelings, in constructing autobiographical memories. Parents will undoubtedly talk about encounters they think are important, thereby reinforcing the memory of certain aspects of the child's present and past experiences (Haden, 2003; Nelson, 2003). Therefore, parents play a critical role as they contribute to their children's construction of a narrative about themselves, allowing them to reflect on experiences or behaviors and to collaborate with their caregivers in forming a portrait of the self.

Interestingly, mothers and fathers have been found to adopt different narrative styles when talking to their sons and daughters about shared experiences. For example, mothers discuss social relationships and emotions more in their conversations with daughters than with their sons (Fivush & Buckner, 2003; Hayne & MacDonald, 2003). These parental differences, together with other cultural factors (evident in children's toys, clothing, books, television, advertising), contribute to gender differences in the structure and content of children's self-representations (Fivush & Buckner, 2003; Harter, 2012). As children's language skills develop, they begin to take on a more active role in co-constructing, together with their parents, personal narratives about the self (Nelson & Fivush, 2004; Reese, 2002; Rogoff, 1990). Thus, autobiographical accounts of the self are created and there is a critical sense of continuity and permanence that becomes part of the child's self-representation (Nelson, 2003). The retelling of personal experiences reinstantiates memories and underscores their meaning for the child. In turn, these experiences are integrated into a network of representations that are meaningful because of their significance to the child's developing sense of self (Thompson et al., 2011).

Children are limited in their self-awareness prior to the age of 3. They also have not begun to develop the ability to view the self as enduring over time (Povinelli & Simon, 1998). They have little capacity to represent experiences autobiographically (Nelson & Fivush, 2004). The result is that most people have difficulty recalling events that occurred before the age of three, a phenomenon that has been called infantile or childhood amnesia (Harley & Reese, 1999). Early in the fourth year, as an awareness of the continuity of the self and the capacity to have meaningful conversations with parents develop, children's autobiographical narratives, or working models of the self, begin to emerge (Reese, 2002; Thompson, 2006). Memories may now be stored as experiences referring to the self or happening to "me" (Howe, 1998).

Consequently, we see that parents play an important role in reflecting on past events, sometimes using an elaborative style that contributes to autobiographical memory (Harley & Reese, 1999). The reminiscing may incorporate the caregivers' perceptions of the child (reflected in their shared recollections), as well as the emotional language, moral values, and attributions that parents use when describing the child to the child (in personal conversations) or to others. For younger children, these conversations exert a profound impact on the child's self-representations. Not surprisingly, young children's views of themselves are similar to the way their mothers view them (Brown, Mangelsdorf, Agathen, & Ho, 2008). If the mother views the child as difficult, moody, controlling, or shy, she will likely include in her recollection of daily events or past experiences examples that concur with these impressions (e.g., "Remember how you wouldn't eat your breakfast?" or "That wasn't nice when you didn't let your sister play with your trucks. It made her cry when you told her to go away"). These are the same qualities that will then be included in the child's view of the self ("I can be difficult" or "I can be bossy"). As children get older, they are less dependent on conversations with parents to recall and consolidate memories into their self-representations. However, early judgments and evaluations by parents tend to persist, influencing the organization and structure of the child's self-representations. Thus, again we see that early relationships impact emerging notions of the self.

Children's self-descriptions are also influenced by what they learn about themselves in the context of their earliest relationships. Depending on their age and developmental level, *self-descriptions* will be based on different criteria. For example, in the earliest years, self-descriptions are based on observable physical characteristics. A typical preschooler will say, for example, "I am a boy," or "I am 3 years old," or "I have blue eyes and blond hair." Later on, behaviors and psychological qualities are incorporated into self-descriptions that children provide when they have increased verbal abilities. Now, children will refer to particular behaviors ("I can hop" or "I like puzzles") and attributes ("I am friendly" or "I am shy") using language that reflects the "I-self's" awareness of the "Me-self" (Harter, 2012). Three- to four-year-old boys are more likely to include in their descriptions the activities and skills they have mastered (e.g., "I know all of my ABC's...I can run real fast..." (Harter, 2012, p. 29)) while girls are more likely to incorporate emotional, social, and relational descriptions (Fivush & Buckner, 2003). For example, a 4-year-old girl might say: "I live with my mommy and daddy and they really love me" or "I have a nice teacher at preschool..."(Harter, 2012, p. 29), or "I'm really happy playing baby dolls with my friends.... I'm sad when my grandma has to leave" (p. 30). Interestingly, when researchers employ methods that do not rely on descriptions in response to general questions but rather incorporate a forced-choice format (i.e., asking children to select which of two possible statements most describe themselves), even the responses of 3½-year-old children reflect an emerging understanding of psychological qualities (e.g., social closeness, aggression) that is consistent across dimensions and stable over time (Eder, 1990).

Theoretical accounts and research findings support the idea that these early self-descriptions reflect the very concrete cognitive representations of what young children are able to observe about themselves (Damon & Hart, 1988; Griffin, 1992; Harter, 2006; Watson, 1990). They often incorporate descriptions of things they possess (e.g., "I have a kitty that is orange...and a television in my own room, it's all mine!" (Harter, 2012, p. 29)). Children are also eager to demonstrate their abilities and skills, as when a young boy says, "I'm really strong. I can lift this chair, watch me!" (p. 30). From a cognitive-developmental perspective, it is evident that the self-descriptions of young children are very much tied to their behavior, possessions, emotional reactions, and those qualities that may be observed by others. They may appear to be disjointed and incoherent, disparate fragments of descriptive accounts, yet quite typical of young children's thinking at this age.

There are also certain cognitive limitations that impact children's self-descriptions, making them unrealistically positive (Harter, 2012; Trzesniewski, Kinal, & Donnellan, 2010). For example, young children are not able to differentiate between their actual competence and their ideal or desired competence. Their self-descriptions may include abilities or talents that are overstated and transcend their real competencies (e.g., "I can kick a soccer ball *real* far, all the way from one end of the field to the other" (Harter 2012, p. 29)). This overly optimistic view of the self may also reflect a difficulty in making social comparisons (Ruble & Frey, 1991). Rather than spontaneously evaluating their abilities against the competencies of others, they are more likely to compare their behavior to their more limited skills at an earlier age (e.g., "Remember when I wasn't able to do these puzzles? I am really smart now!"). Limited perspective-taking abilities in young children mean they do not take into account the opinions of significant others who may be critical of them, thereby contributing to overly positive views of the self as well (Harter, 2006). Additionally, many parents today tend to indulge their children with overly positive appraisals ("You are the smartest girl in your class!" or "Everyone loves being your friend") or resort to providing constant assistance to their children so they have little experience with failure. As a result, there is a tendency toward children staying "stuck" in this place of limited perspective taking so that their self-descriptions remain overly positive, one sided, and unrealistically grand. And this inclination to think about the self and one's competencies in extremes, as one way or another ("smart" or "stupid"), without considering a range of talents ("smart in math but not so good in reading"), also contributes to an unrealistically more positive view of the self (e.g., "I always do good work at school") or, alternatively, to an inflexible negative view (e.g., "I am just so bad at school that I may as well not try") (e.g., Fischer & Bidell, 2006; Harter, 2012).

By middle childhood, children begin to incorporate specific examples of a trait or characteristic into generalizations about themselves (Harter, 2003). For example, if a boy sees himself as friendly, this may be because he talked to his friends at school, said hello to the bus driver on the way home, and waved to his neighbor as he walked into his home. Social comparison processes are more developed and spontaneously incorporated into self-evaluations in middle childhood (Harter, 2012). Children compare their abilities with others, looking to see where they stand in relation to their peers (Frey & Ruble, 1990). Self-descriptions now often include a more relational orientation, identifying themselves as "well liked by my friends" or "helpful to my brother and sister." Therefore, self-descriptions in middle childhood are influenced by how children feel others view them and incorporate more psychological and interpersonal attributes.

Cognitive advances lead children to begin to coordinate concepts of the self during middle childhood, allowing them to move beyond compartmentalizing (Case, 1991). They can now view themselves as good at a number of activities or across contexts (e.g., "I am good at math, singing, and playing basketball," "I am helpful at home, school, and when I play with my friends"). Children develop more realistic and differentiated views of themselves and can begin to understand that they may be competent in some areas but not in others (Cole et al., 2001). They are capable of offering a more refined, distinctive view of the self ("I am a really good friend, I like art and music, but really don't do well in sports. My favorite subject is English and I struggle a lot in math"). Social pressures, school policies, and organized activities (both in and out of school) contribute to the use of social comparison as a basis for describing the self (Wigfield, Eccles, Schiefele, Roeser, & Davis-Kean, 2006). It is no longer expected that praise will be offered for simply trying one's best. Now, distinctions are made within and across age groups and between those who are more or less competent in varying domains. As a result, children have clear information that they may use to gauge their performance in relation to their peers.

At this point, children's self-descriptions are more likely to contain both strengths and limitations and to consider multiple domains, such as physical appearance, behavioral conduct, academic achievement, athletic prowess, peer popularity (Cole et al., 2001; Harter, 2006). Additionally, children begin to appreciate the fact that individual differences are not easily modified and might even constrain possible choices or levels of achievement (e.g., a relatively uncoordinated, short girl will not likely be a top player on her school's basketball team). They are more accurate when predicting how they will fare, especially if they are able to use personal self-awareness and past performance to guide their predictions (Thompson et al., 2011). And we continue to see qualitative changes in adolescents' self-descriptions. Because they can now understand the multiple roles they assume (daughter, sister, student, friend, club member), they are more likely to distinguish themselves in these different roles, recognizing some they may fulfill better than others (e.g., "I am a really kind friend but I am not so patient or understanding with my sister"). Self-descriptions become even more differentiated, complex, and insightful in adolescence. Adolescents use a greater number of dimensions than younger children to describe themselves, though they may continue to include some of the earlier descriptions (e.g., physical characteristics) that still remain important to them (Damon & Hart, 1988).

We have come to see that once children are able to recognize themselves, they begin to show the early characteristics of the "Me-self," the categorical self or the self as an object observed by others. Children's descriptions of the self progress from physical recognition (as in the mirror-and-rouge paradigm) to assigning labels to describe the self based on physical characteristics (e.g., age, gender, ethnic or racial group) to identifying character traits (e.g., friendly, strong, shy) and finally to integrating motivations, attitudes, thoughts, feelings. These components of self-definition ultimately allow for social comparisons and more differentiated self-descriptions (Cole et al., 2001; Harter, 2006). Internalizing the evaluations of others, combined with a growing understanding of the self, contribute to self-evaluations (Stipek, 1995). There are developmental changes in children's feelings about the self, or the perception of the self as good or bad, based on these early evaluations.

The evaluative component of the self is alternatively referred to as *self-esteem* (Rosenberg, 1979) or *self-worth* (Harter, 1982). Indeed, the terms are often used interchangeably. However, there is some value in making a clear distinction between global self-esteem or self-worth, referring to "one's perceived worth as a person" (Harter, 2012, p. 24), and domain-specific self-esteem or self-worth, referring to the specific domains of behavioral conduct, physical appearance, cognitive competence, physical competence, and peer acceptance. Young children are capable of evaluating themselves in terms of how they look and behave, their physical and cognitive competencies, and their friendships, yet they are not able to clearly distinguish these domains from one another (Harter, 1990, 2012; Harter & Pike, 1984). A prerequisite to forming a concept of one's overall value as a person is to first be able to provide differentiated descriptions of attributes in various domains (Harter, 2012). However, the same cognitive limitations that limit young children's self-descriptions also limit their ability to integrate the distinct domain-specific qualities and verbally represent their global self-esteem or overall self-worth (Harter, 2012). It is not until about the age of 8 that children can verbalize a global evaluation of the self (Harter, 2012).

Measuring self-esteem in young children requires that teachers, or other adults who know the child well, rate specific behaviors reflective of global worth. This approach incorporates the notion that young children manifest their self-esteem through observable behaviors. Displays of curiosity, confidence, initiative, and independence, and the capacity to react adaptively to changes or stress, are hallmarks of high self-esteem in young children (Harter, 2012). Developmentally sensitive measurement approaches have been used to tap age-appropriate, domain-specific, manifestations of specific areas of competence (cognitive and physical competence, peer acceptance, physical appearance, and behavioral conduct) and global self-worth as well (see, for example, Harter, 2012). Additionally, studies of the predictors and consequences of self-esteem highlight the many factors that contribute to global self-worth; these factors may vary, depending upon the age and developmental level considered.

Early socialization experiences with parents, caregivers, teachers, and the broader sociocultural context have been found to influence young children's self-descriptions and self-esteem (Harter, 2008). While children play an active role in the construction of the self, their self-worth is impacted by their interactions with, and by the reactions of, significant others. Parents who support their children with tangible expressions of affection, praise, and admiration are providing them with important early precursors to high self-esteem. When other significant adults treat young children as lovable, valued, and competent, this also lays the foundation for global positive self-esteem (Harter, 2012). Even before this can be seen in children's verbal self-descriptions, however, high or low self-esteem may be revealed first in young children's behavior.

Indeed, young children with high self-esteem are defined by teachers as being independent learners, taking initiative, exploring with curiosity, and displaying confidence, while demonstrating more adaptive behaviors in response to stress, such as being able to manage transitions and tolerate frustration. Children with low self-esteem, by contrast, are less likely to actively approach new situations or challenges with confidence and more likely to avoid exploration. When dealing with stress or change, these children react by giving up easily, expressing frustration, or behaving inappropriately (Harter, 2012). Confidence does not seem to derive in younger children from competence in the display of certain skills. Rather, certain parental behaviors, such as support, responsiveness, encouragement of curiosity, exploration and mastery, promote confidence that, in turn, contributes to higher self-esteem (Harter, 2012). Older children may then bring this confidence to new developmental tasks, thereby developing competencies and skills that will ultimately become part of how they define their esteem. Parental socialization practices, therefore, play an important role in the young child's esteem.

As children approach the middle childhood years, we know that socialization practices that support exploration, mastery, and a sense of competence continue to promote high self-esteem. However, during this developmental period, children's cognitive advances, increased social understanding, and improved social comparison processes result in self-descriptions that are more accurate reflections of their evaluation of their self-worth. The more realistic assessments that are made during middle childhood are also associated with a drop in self-esteem. Children are now more self-critical. There is a decline in their views of their intellectual and physical competencies (Wigfield et al., 2006). It is not surprising, then, that we begin to see the motivational implications of differences in self-esteem in middle childhood (Dweck, 2002). By late childhood and early adolescence, parental processes and peer approval and support are linked, once again, to high self-esteem (Allen, 2008; Harter, 2006; Thompson, 2006).

Questions continue to persist as to whether self-esteem is a useful construct and whether it causes, or is a consequence of, positive or negative outcomes. Some researchers (e.g., Baumeister, Campbell, Kreuger, & Vohs, 2003) argue that high self-esteem is simply the result of positive life experiences. Others contend that variations in self-esteem influence choices that people make and are therefore useful to consider (e.g., Swann, Chang-Schneider, & McClarty, 2007). To the extent that the self is constructed within the context of interpersonal relationships in general, and is dependent upon socialization experiences within the family in particular, there are ways in which self-development may be disrupted. Distortions in the narrative that parents co-construct with their children, or misrepresentations of reality that are defensively used to protect the self, may lead to an inauthentic or false view of the self (Harter, 2002) which could, in turn, lead to negative affect and low self-esteem (Impett, Sorsoli, Schooler, Henson, & Tolman, 2008). Distinctions between the real and ideal self, the construction of multiple selves, and a preoccupation with what others are thinking about the self, especially during adolescence, may contribute to inauthenticity, low self-esteem, anxiety, and depression (Harter, 2012). Thus, the value of studying self-esteem may lie in its relation to developing psychopathology.

In sum, we see that while there are early signs of the emerging self-system in young infants, developmental changes in self-awareness, self-regulation, sense of agency, representations of the self, evaluation processes, and self-esteem occur over a protracted period of time. The sense of self provides a subjective lens for understanding not only oneself and one's own experiences, but also for understanding other people and their experiences as well (Harter, 2006; Sroufe, 1996; Stern, 1985). The self grows out of relational roots and, in turn, influences subsequent relationships.

Attachment Relationships and the Developing Self

Early attachment relationships offer children the foundation for developing representations of the self. Through regular and predictable routines, infants learn to anticipate certain actions and events. Infants are prepared to rely on attachment behaviors, such as crying and smiling, to communicate to their caregivers (Bowlby, 1973, 1988). Moreover, they expect caring and appropriate responses to these signals (Bretherton & Munholland, 2008). Within a consistent and emotionally responsive emotional environment, parents respond to their babies' signals and cues and teach them that their initiatives and signals are meaningful. A sense of self becomes organized based on the positive, loving reactions of sensitive parents and children incorporate a view of the self as worthy, valued, important and good. Thus, developmental precursors to the emerging sense of self include parental sensitivity, support, and contingent responsiveness, the very behaviors that are critical to developing a secure attachment relationship (Thompson, 2006).

But when the attachment relationship is insecure, parents may be rejecting, inconsistently responsive, insensitive, or irritated with their babies. Children come to integrate into their working models of relationships the notion that others are not to be counted on and to develop a view of the self as someone who is not worthy of care. Additionally, comments that are disparaging (e.g., "You're such a *bad* boy!"), harsh (e.g., "You *always* get into trouble!"), and nonsupportive ("Why do you have to be *so* difficult?") undermine the development of positive self-representations during the early years. Therefore, even before the toddler can verbally express feelings about the self, we may see avoidance of new experiences, insecurity and shame, lack of initiative, and little enthusiasm or positive affect. The consequence of the same parental behaviors that contribute to insecure attachment relationships during infancy may also be in their impact on the young toddler's developing self-representations during the second and third years of life (Goodvin, Meyer, Thompson, & Hayes, 2008). When there are failures in affective mirroring, and dysregulated, nonreflective caregiving, self-development in infancy and childhood may be disrupted in profound ways (Fonagy et al., 2002; Slade, 2005).

It is in the context of their earliest interactions, both with parents and other social partners, that children are also exposed to different subjective viewpoints that are incorporated into their developing sense of self. Through verbal and nonverbal communication, social referencing, observation, and early play, infants and toddlers practice the skills necessary to learn about others' ideas and perspectives. Parents may provide their toddlers with opportunities to practice their burgeoning independence, offering contexts in which emerging skills can be executed so their children may feel pride or shame. Parents may also reinforce their children's developing self-representations by expressing pride or disappointment in their children's behavior. In turn, these experiences offer their children a mirror (the "looking glass self" (Mead, 1934)) of how others see them and through which they begin to view themselves (Thompson et al., 2011). Parents' evaluative comments ("You're such a smart girl!" "Your behavior is *so* bad today!") or descriptive statements ("You're such a tall boy!"), whether positive or negative, are incorporated over time into their children's evaluations of and feelings about themselves.

It is clearly evident that the same behaviors that contribute to a secure attachment relationship also should be associated with more positive views of the self. Those infants who are securely attached to their caregivers will have a greater potential for exploring their social and nonsocial environment with confidence and trust in the accessibility of the caregiver. Their affective growth will promote the skills that underlie early self-development, such as the capacity for visual self-recognition. Indeed, toddlers who are securely attached to their caregivers evidence this ability relatively earlier than those who are insecurely attached (Schneider-Rosen & Cicchetti, 1984). Moreover, children who demonstrate visual self-recognition also reveal more positive spontaneous affective reactions to their mirror self-images, an early reflection of children's feelings about themselves (Schneider-Rosen & Cicchetti, 1991). The direction of effects needs to be considered further, though the exploration of individual differences provides important insights into those factors that contribute to the development of the self-system. It may be that positive feelings about the self lead to self–other differentiation or recognizing the self as distinct from others leads to more positive feelings about the self. Alternatively, the ability to distinguish self from others, and the experience of more positive feelings about the self, may both be influenced by the quality of the parent–child relationship (cf. Schneider-Rosen & Cicchetti, 1984).

As another illustrative example, attachment theory and research also have relevance to our understanding of the personal narratives that are incorporated into autobiographical memories. The elaborative style of attachment figures impacts the quality of children's narrative reports (Haden, 2003). It is within secure attachment relationships that mothers use more internal state language with an emotional focus (Newcombe & Reese, 2004). Mothers of securely attached children also reflect more on their children's experiences using elaborative descriptions, leading to more coherent and connected themes in their children's later autobiographical memories (Reese, 2002). Thus, while the causal direction of the association needs to be explored further, we see that there is a clear connection between the quality of early relationships and developing self-representations.

What happens when early childhood experiences lead to problems in self-development? It may not be only insecure attachment patterns that lead to difficulties in the child's sense of self, but parenting stress, trauma, lack of social support, and ineffective parenting practices may all play a role. Moreover, child abuse and/or neglect may interfere with a developing awareness of the self and consequently impact "I-self" and "Me-self" functions (see Harter, 1998b, for a thorough elaboration). Because the maltreated child remains hypervigilant to external dangers and others' reactions, there is little opportunity to focus on one's own thoughts, needs, or feelings that are important to developing self-awareness (Briere, 1992). Indeed, there is a substantial body of research that supports the idea that early experiences of abuse and neglect may impact early self-development. For example, maltreated toddlers use less descriptive speech to account for their own feelings and actions (Coster, Gersten, Beeghly, & Cicchetti, 1989) and less internal state language (describing negative feelings and physiological reactions) than nonmaltreated children (Cicchetti, 1989). Older maltreated children also describe feelings and inner states less than nonmaltreated children (Gralinsky, Fesbach, Powell & Derrington, 1993). It therefore appears that the attention and alertness to others' reactions that is defensively employed by maltreated children may interfere with their awareness of internal feelings and thoughts. Moreover, maltreated children are more likely to develop insecure attachment relationships with their caregivers (Cicchetti, Rogosch, & Toth, 2006), thus affecting internal models of relationships and of the self.

The quality of the early attachment relationship may interact with young children's genetic vulnerabilities, temperamental characteristics, parenting behaviors, and situational stresses and either promote resilience or enhance risk of emerging problems in the developing self-system. Close relationships provide the support children need to differentiate themselves from others, as well as to be aware of the self, regulate the self and control behavior, develop a sense of agency, represent and describe the self in increasingly more differentiated ways, and evaluate the self. These self-related competencies, which develop from infancy through childhood and into adolescence, are best facilitated when children are provided with sensitivity and emotional support in their earliest relationships. Unfortunately, problems in these emerging aspects of the self may contribute to difficulties in current or future social and emotional development. Therefore, it is within an interpersonal context that children develop meaningful connections to others and critical self-related competencies; in turn, the emerging sense of self evolves over time and contributes to ongoing connections and future relationships.

Sibling Relationships

3

The experience of sharing childhood with a sibling has a profound effect on development. In ways that are subtle or obvious, siblings influence personality, emotional functioning, academic performance, and relationships both inside and outside of the family. Most children spend more time in direct interaction with their siblings than with their parents or other significant people in their lives. And yet there has been relatively less research focused on relationships with sisters and brothers as compared to studies of children's relationships with their mothers and fathers. Sibling relationships have the potential to be one of the most enduring relationships throughout the lifespan. They influence, and are influenced by, relationships with parents as well as with peers and other adults. Because 80–85% of children worldwide grow up with at least one sibling (Dunn, 2007), it is critical to consider sibling relationships and their impact on social and emotional functioning.

Initially, researchers examining the influence of siblings focused on sibling status variables, such as birth order, gender, or age spacing, and explored their possible association to developmental outcomes, such as self-esteem, IQ, or achievement as an adult. There is now an extensive literature on these status or family constellation variables. A lot of conclusions have been drawn from this work about the behavior of firstborn as compared to later-born children, about whether it is best for children if they are the same gender or different genders, or about whether a larger age spread is better or worse than a smaller age difference. However, the conclusions vary from one study to the next, due in part to sampling and methodological differences across studies. Moreover, a significant challenge to this type of correlational research is in the interpretation of the results. Any observed link between birth order, gender, or age spacing and some developmental outcome cannot be attributed solely to the status variable per se. There may be other variables influencing the association, such as differences in child temperament, parent–child interaction, or parental attention. Perhaps most importantly, this kind of research does not take us very far toward understanding the quality of the relationship that develops between young siblings.

116

The model for siblings' relationships, and for their ways of connecting to others in their social world, is their first attachment to their parents. Thus, once again the theme of attachment is relevant as we explore in this chapter children's expanding social worlds. Sisters and brothers are part of that world. From childhood to old age, children negotiate relationships with their siblings as they influence each other's development within the larger family system. Researchers have attempted to understand different patterns of sibling relationships and to explore the factors that lead to variations in the quality of sibling relationships. For example, differential parental treatment and the quality of the parents' relationship have been associated with variations in sibling relationship quality. The consequences of these variations, in terms of each individual's social and emotional development, have also been studied. Poor-quality sibling relationships have, for example, been found to be linked to higher levels of depression. Sibling conflict, and difficulties resolving that conflict, have been linked to problems in peer relationships. In discussing this work, questions about reciprocity, complementarity, and the balance of discrete qualities of sibling relationships will be addressed, as will issues of continuity and discontinuity in sibling relationship quality over time. Finally, the status of only children will also be explored, with a focus on the inconsistencies in the research literature and an appreciation of the significance of only child status for theory development.

Why Study Siblings?

While the parent–child relationship has a clear influence on development, the relationship that children have with their sisters and brothers is also significant but often overlooked. Young children interact with their siblings frequently, sibling bonds have the potential to last longer than connections to parents, and the emotional intensity of the sibling relationship is profound. The vast majority of children in the United States grow up with at least one sibling; indeed, children are more likely to be in a household with a brother or sister than with a father (McHale, Kim, & Whiteman, 2006). By middle childhood, more time is spent together with siblings than with parents (McHale & Crouter, 1996). The *reciprocal* nature of their relationships, as relatively equal interactional partners, means that siblings develop an emotionally significant relationship where there are lots of opportunities for active engagement, social understanding, and social support as well as for conflict, competition, and rivalry. Moreover, there are ways in which siblings complement one another, offering models for social competence, school engagement, and peer relationships. The *hierarchical* nature of their relationship, defined by birth order and age differences, means that older siblings are more likely to serve caregiving, teaching, and socializing roles, whereas younger siblings are more likely to imitate their older brothers and sisters and to want to be just like them. While children have no choice when it comes to selecting their sisters and brothers, their connections are powerful; whether the quality of those connections is positive and adaptive, or problematic and conflictual, sibling relationships impact experiences both within and outside of the family and have a considerable influence on identity and development.

Theoretical Perspectives For Studying Sibling Relationships

Attachment theorists originally described the attachment relationship as an enduring emotional connection that develops between infants and their primary caregivers. This relatively narrow definition has been broadened to include other attachment figures during later developmental periods. Sibling relationships have been viewed by attachment theorists as providing children with a sense of security (Ainsworth, 1989) or an affectional bond (Berlin, Cassidy, & Appleyard, 2008). When infants develop secure attachments with their primary caregivers, they internalize a model of the self as worthy and of others in their social world as responsive and trustworthy (Bowlby, 1973; Bretherton, 1985). These internal models influence the child's understanding, expectations, and feelings regarding other relationships. Accordingly, secure attachments to parents, with consequent expectations of warmth, positive affect, and trust in dyadic relationships, are likely to lead to positive sibling experiences. Insecure attachments, with resulting expectations of fear, negativity, and mistrust, are likely to lead to negative sibling experiences.

Sibling relationship quality, therefore, should be associated with each sibling's attachment to his or her primary caregiver (Berlin et al., 2008). From the perspective of attachment theory, early attachments lay the groundwork for the development of sibling relationships. Siblings each bring their own internal working model to their relationship; these models influence their developing relationship and, in turn, are likely to be modified by their ongoing attachment experiences. Developmental shifts in significant elements of their relationships, and changes that occur as new relationships are incorporated into their social worlds, are likely to influence the quality of the sibling relationship as well. However, there is limited research that has examined the quality of sibling relationships from the perspective of attachment theory.

There are, however, several related lines of research that are relevant to understanding the implications of attachment theory for sibling relationships. Some investigators have examined security of parent–child attachment when there are multiple children in the same family. Most studies find moderate concordance – between 40% and 70% – in parents' attachment to each member of the sibling pair (O'Connor & Croft, 2001; Rosen & Burke, 1999; van IJzendoorn et al., 2000). Consistent with the tenets of attachment theory, concordance is expected given that parental behavior plays a key role in the development of secure or insecure attachments. Indeed, available data support the idea that parental sensitivity and responsiveness are related to attachment security, though meta-analyses reveal the magnitude of the effect is only moderate (Atkinson et al., 2000; de Wolff & van IJzendoorn, 1997; Goldsmith & Alansky, 1987). Moreover, parental sensitivity and responsiveness are presumed to be regulated and guided by an internal model of relationships; there is empirical support for the association between parental internal working models and the quality of the infant–parent attachment relationship (van IJzendoorn, 1995). Thus, when studying attachment relationships between a parent and two children in the same family, the assumption is that there should be concordance in attachment classifications because parental behavior toward their children is similar.

However, the finding of only a moderate degree of concordance suggests that parents may develop distinct patterns of attachment with each of their children. This raises the question of whether differential sensitivity might be expected. Additionally, there may be other factors that account for differences in attachment quality within the same family, such as gender and age differences between siblings, marital relationship quality, and life stresses that might lead to instability of parental behavior (Rosen & Burke, 1999). Whether internal working models are specific to relationships with particular children in the family also needs to be explored (Slade, Belsky, Aber, & Phelps, 1999). Still, evidence from studies examining the similarity of siblings' attachments to their parents represents one way of beginning to understand sibling relationships within the framework of attachment theory.

Another line of research that is relevant to understanding sibling relationships is the exploration of early attachment to parents and subsequent behavior toward siblings. Indeed, security of infant–mother attachment is related to children's more positive treatment of, and from, an older sibling (Teti & Ablard, 1989). Thus, when younger siblings have a secure attachment to their mothers, they are, in turn, less likely to become distressed when their mothers focus their attention on their older sibling. Moreover, older siblings who are securely attached to their mothers are also more likely to be sensitively responsive to their younger siblings' distress, providing comfort in the mother's absence. And younger siblings are more likely to seek care from an older sibling only when the older sibling is securely attached to the mother (Teti & Ablard, 1989). Security of the older sibling's attachment to mother, but not to father (assessed when the older sibling was 12 and 13 months old, respectively), is also associated five years later with less sibling conflict and aggression in the home (Volling & Belsky, 1992b). Similarly, children classified as anxious-resistant in their attachment to mothers at 12 months, who were then seen at 4 years of age in a laboratory assessment of sibling interaction, showed more conflict and hostility with a younger sibling; the quality of attachment to father at 12 months was not significantly related to 4-year-olds' emotional responses to their younger sibling (Volling, 2001). Though not grounded in an attachment framework, some research even indicates that the presence of an older sibling facilitates infant exploration, providing the security that allows for greater locomotion away from the mother (Samuels, 1980). Thus, early attachment relationships with mothers, in particular, influence subsequent interactions with siblings.

In studies of older sibling dyads, attachment representations have also been found to play a role in sibling relationships in young adults (Fortuna, Roisman, Haydon, Groh, & Holland, 2011). Working models of 18- to 25-year-old siblings' early attachment experiences with their parents have been found to predict emotion regulation in the context of negotiating conflict with the sibling as well as sibling relationship quality. Dismissing states of mind regarding attachment relationships (measured with the Adult Attachment Interview (George et al., 1984, 1985, 1996)) are associated with less affective expression during contentious negotiations with the sibling. If one sibling is dismissive in his/her representations of attachment experiences and needs, then the current sibling relationship is perceived as less affectionate and supportive. Strong expressions of negative affect in conflict negotiations are found in sibling dyads with preoccupied states of mind regarding early attachment experiences and the sibling relationship is perceived as more conflictual (Fortuna et al., 2011; Haydon, Roisman, & Burt, 2012). Thus, early attachment experiences appear to influence current sibling interactions and perceptions of the sibling relationship in young adulthood. Future work is essential to better understand the reciprocal influences of internal models of multiple relationships and the underlying developmental processes involved in the organization and operation of these models.

Whether older siblings take on the role of the attachment figure or provide a secure base for their younger siblings is also a question that has been addressed by researchers. Of course, the likelihood that siblings serve in this capacity is dependent upon the individual, familial, and contextual factors that impact the overall quality of their relationship. Still, an increase in the quality of sibling relationships occurs in the early adolescent period, particularly as adolescents share similar social experiences (Buist, Deković, Meeus, & van Aken, 2002). Moreover, when there are stressful circumstances, siblings may offer one another a secure base and a source of emotional comfort and support at varying points throughout the lifespan (Cicirelli, 1995; Kim, McHale, Osgood, & Crouter, 2006; Voorpostel & Blieszner, 2008). And even studies of adult twins indicate that shared experiences, empathic responsiveness, support, and other features of attachment relationships are important to explore (Cicirelli, 1995; Neyer, 2002; Tancredy & Fraley, 2006). Thus, siblings may act as attachment figures for one another, providing comfort, security, and closeness during childhood, adolescence, and adulthood. Younger siblings may use the older sibling as a source of support and older siblings may engage in caring and helping behavior. These attachment behaviors, involving seeking and maintaining closeness, are consistent with the notion that siblings develop strong attachments to one another and these attachments are likely to be sustained across the lifespan.

Just as researchers have explored the consequences of secure attachment relationships with mothers and fathers for developing social and emotional competencies, there is a growing body of research that has also supported the association between different qualities of sibling relationships (e.g., warmth, support, conflict) and later competence. For example, sibling warmth has been associated with the development of fewer internalizing problems in childhood and adolescence (East & Rook, 1992; Kim, McHale, Crouter, & Osgood, 2007; Noller, 2005; Pike, Coldwell, & Dunn, 2005). And when dealing with stressful life events, supportive sibling relationships buffer against the development of internalizing problems (Gass, Jenkins, & Dunn, 2007). Moreover, higher levels of sibling warmth are associated with better emotion regulation (Kennedy & Kramer, 2008) and more prosocial behavior (Pike et al., 2005), thereby potentially protecting against the development of externalizing problems (see, for example, DeKlyen & Greenberg, 2008). Thus, more adaptive strategies for managing and regulating emotions may be promoted within positive sibling attachment experiences; these strategies, in turn, may reduce the likelihood of developing depression, anxiety, or aggressive behavior problems (Guttmann-Steinmetz & Crowell, 2006). Warmth and support in the sibling relationship, therefore, are particular characteristics that promote emotional competence and adaptive social functioning.

Attachment theory provides a solid foundation for exploring sibling relationships from infancy through adolescence. There may be similarities between sibling and parent–child attachments, and certain characteristics of adaptive and maladaptive sibling interactions may have their roots in early attachment experiences. The precursors to and consequences of differences in sibling relationship quality continue to be important to examine as siblings have the capacity to maintain their relationships across the lifespan. Therefore, studying sibling relationships contributes to the understanding of continuity and change in relationship quality over time. Attachment theory provides a critical framework for future work in this area. Moreover, the study of siblings may help to refine and clarify some of the important principles of attachment theory.

Social learning theorists offer an alternative theoretical framework for studying sibling relationships. Social learning theorists argue that children acquire new behaviors, as well as beliefs and attitudes, through the processes of observation and reinforcement (Bandura, 1977). Parents, for example, educate their children about how to resolve conflicts in the way they manage their own disputes. They also teach their children when they praise them for getting along or for resolving their own conflicts, or when they intervene and control their children's disagreements and struggles. Children may be impacted by parents' poor conflict resolution strategies or by observing and imitating positive or negative behaviors or interactions between a sibling and a parent (Whiteman, McHale, & Soli, 2011). Just as cooperation, closeness, and sharing may be fostered in well-functioning families, aggressive and antisocial behavior may be learned and practiced in poorly functioning families where sibling competition and aggression, without intervention from adults, may lead to later interpersonal problems. Thus, the family is an essential training ground for social learning. It is in the context of their sibling relationships where specific patterns of interaction and skills for social understanding may be acquired that are then generalized to other relationships. Moreover, siblings provide one another with opportunities for practicing social skills and styles of interaction, as well as ways of managing conflicts and disputes, that shape their own relationship and that can then be used in their social interactions outside of the family (Stauffacher & DeHart, 2006).

Younger children often imitate and learn from their older siblings, who in turn serve as teachers, supervisors, and models for their younger sibling's behavior. It is more likely that children will imitate models who are nurturing and warm, viewed as competent, powerful, and higher in status, and perceived to be similar to them (Bandura, 1977; Furman & Buhrmester, 1985a). Siblings who are older and of the same gender may be especially powerful models. Social modeling processes are more likely when brothers and sisters share a warm and close relationship. Indeed, these relationship quality variables have been found to influence adolescent outcomes (East & Khoo, 2005; Gamble, Yu, & Card, 2010).

However, sibling characteristics that potentially impact social learning processes need to be examined further instead of inferring, based on observed similarities in behavior, the potency of sibling socialization processes (Whiteman, Becerra, & Killoren, 2009; Whiteman, McHale, & Soli, 2011). Older brothers and sisters may function as "gatekeepers" by limiting or extending experiences with other children outside of the family (Zukow-Goldring, 2002). Children may also learn indirectly from observing parents interacting with their siblings (Dunn, 1993). They may, for example, identify similarities or differences in how parents manage an older or younger sibling. Their perceptions of these parental behaviors, and of the interactions their siblings have with their parents, may also lead to certain attributions and emotional reactions. Through all of these experiences, much can be learned about complex social emotions such as jealousy and rivalry, as well as about differential parental treatment, and their effect on sibling behaviors.

The sibling relationship may be the context within which aggression and hostile behavior is learned. Some research, for example, has explored the way in which, in normative samples of children, one sibling's aggressive behavior may be linked to more aggression by the other sibling (Brody, Stoneman, & Burke, 1987; Dunn & Munn, 1986a). Younger children are more likely to imitate an older sibling's aggressive behavior and older siblings are more likely to be the initiator of aggression in the dyad (Abramovitch, Corter, & Lanso, 1979: Dunn & Kendrick, 1982). Siblings may learn to get what they want by escalating their level of hostility in a conflictual exchange with a brother or sister. When the other sibling relents, the aggressive sibling is positively reinforced for increasing negativity while the sibling who gave in is negatively reinforced. This cycle leads to increased negativity in subsequent interactions and both siblings learn that they can get their way by being more negative. Indeed, when young school-aged aggressive children have been studied, more intense and frequent conflict and aggression, and longer cycles of negative interactions, have been observed in sibling interactions (Aguilar, O'Brien, August, Aoun, & Hektner, 2001; Loeber & Tengs, 1986; Patterson, 1984, 1986). Thus, sibling relationships provide a context for learning aggressive behaviors that may, in turn, lead to later adjustment problems during adolescence; that is, as early conflicts persist, sibling behavior may escalate toward more verbally aggressive, and, as they get older, intense physically aggressive, behavior in a negative coercive cycle (Patterson, 1986; Slomkowski, Rende, Conger, Simons, & Conger, 2001). In fact, concurrent and longitudinal studies of brothers involved in coercive conflictual relationships have found that they are more likely to become involved in delinquent behaviors (Bank, Patterson, & Reid, 1996). Studies of sisters in early and middle adolescence have revealed the same findings (Slomkowski et al., 2001).

Sibling conflict in early childhood is also associated with concurrent and later internalizing behavior problems (Dunn, Slomkowski, Beardsall, & Rende, 1994). For example, sibling conflict in early childhood is linked with a decrease in the likelihood that children will discuss their own feelings or the feelings of others (Howe, Petrakos, & Rinaldi, 1998) and with poor self-esteem, loneliness, and depressed mood in elementary school (Stocker, 1994). Sibling conflict in middle childhood has also been found to predict later depressed mood, anxiety, and delinquent behavior in early adolescence, even after controlling for earlier marital conflict and parent–child hostility (Stocker, Burwell, & Briggs, 2002). When sibling relationships become less conflictual in the transition from middle childhood to adolescence, and there is an increase in warmth between the siblings over time, children's depressed mood declines. Conversely, increases in conflict and decreases in warmth lead to an increase in depressive symptoms (Richmond, Stocker, & Rienks, 2005).

Taken together, these studies suggest that conflict in early sibling relationships may lead, as social learning theorists suggest, to developing a pattern of interaction that is then brought to other relational contexts. However, it may also be that what is learned when there is conflict in the early sibling relationship influences children's developing emotion regulation skills or social understanding, thereby undermining the development of empathy and perspective taking (see Chapter 5 for further elaboration of these abilities). Indeed, in early adolescent sibling dyads, high levels of conflict and low levels of empathy are associated with sibling bullying and victimization, which are in turn related to bullying and victimization with peers (Menesini, Camodeca, & Nocentini, 2010). Moreover, sibling conflict may lead to internalizing a global, stable, negative attributional style regarding the self in relationships. This cognitive style may put children at risk for depression or other internalizing difficulties (Nolen-Hoeksema, Girgus, & Seligman, 1992). Thus, a high degree of sibling conflict may be a risk factor for developing internalizing problems (Kim et al., 2007; Stocker et al., 2002; Vogt Yuan, 2009), with some studies suggesting more sibling conflict leads to increases over time in symptoms of depression (Brody, 1998; Richmond et al., 2005). And sibling conflict is also a risk factor for externalizing difficulties in childhood and adolescence as well (Kim, Hetherington, & Reiss, 1999;

Natsuaki, Ge, Reiss, & Neiderhiser, 2009). These findings indicate that direct efforts to improve sibling relationship quality may help to buffer against some of the challenges brought on by the transition to adolescence.

Parents may play a role in shaping sibling relationships by regulating and influencing their interactions. When parents intervene in their children's disputes and model appropriate reasoning techniques or scaffold children's strategies for conflict resolution, there is a positive effect on the children's relationship. Children are then more likely to use ignoring, compliance, and perspective taking as effective skills for de-escalating and resolving their disagreements (Perlman & Ross, 1997). The benefits of parental intervention may vary, however, depending upon the ages of the siblings, with relatively younger dyads benefiting more than older dyads. Intervention programs have been effective in promoting social understanding, discussion of emotions, and positive interactions, thereby leading to a reduction in sibling conflict, when parents are trained to use mediation strategies with their younger children (Siddiqui & Ross, 2004). Yet, older children and adolescents do not seem to benefit in the same way. By contrast to younger children, older children respond more negatively when parents intervene in their conflicts (Kramer, Perozynski, & Chung, 1999). Mothers' use of control (punishment, threats, distraction) or child-centered (encouraging communication, negotiation, and compromise) strategies may be perceived by older siblings as pressure to resolve their difficulties and to get along, even when they do not want parental intervention or may choose not to resolve their conflicts (Dunn, 1988). This may, in turn, lead to or exacerbate an already distant relationship between siblings.

The value of parental interventions may also depend on maternal and paternal responsiveness to conflict and parental enactment of conflict resolution strategies (Kramer et al., 1999). Moreover, parental influence may extend beyond observational learning. Parents may indirectly model appropriate behaviors for effective social interactions, or maladaptive exchanges that undermine social relations, in the context of their marital relationship or in their dealings with their children (Whiteman, McHale, & Soli, 2011). A number of studies have documented associations between marital and sibling conflict. For example, when there are high levels of conflict between parents, there is more negativity and greater frequency of conflict between siblings (Brody, Stoneman, McCoy, & Forehand, 1992; Erel, Margolin, & John, 1998). Hostility in the mother–partner relationship has also been found to be associated with negativity in the sibling relationship four years later (Dunn, Deater-Deckard, Pickering, & Golding, 1999). However, it appears that siblings do not simply model their behavior on what they observed between their parents. Rather, conflict resolution in the parent–child/adolescent relationship appears to mediate between interparental and sibling conflict resolution (Dunn et al., 1999; Reese-Weber, 2000; Reese-Weber & Kahn, 2005; Stocker & Youngblade, 1999). Therefore, children seem to learn conflict patterns from their interactions with their parents, and then, through "interaction-based transmission," use these patterns with their siblings (Noller, Feeney, Sheehan, & Peterson, 2000).

When there are difficulties in the marital relationship, there tend to be more hostile parent–child relationships and more conflict in sibling relationships (Cox, 2010; Minuchin, 1985). Some siblings may turn to each other for support when there is intense marital conflict. Many siblings experience conflict even when the marital relationship provides appropriate models for negotiation and management of conflict. However, the observed links between conflict in sibling, parent–child, and marital relationships highlight the importance of exploring further the processes underlying the development of sibling relationships. It may also be that the reciprocal influences between sibling, parent–child, and marital relationships vary depending upon other stresses and conflicts on the family system, including the transition to adolescence (e.g., Kim et al., 2006), parental separation and divorce (e.g., Sheehan, Darlington, Noller, & Feeney, 2004), and the oldest sibling's leaving home (Whiteman, McHale, & Crouter, 2011).

Social comparison theory (Festinger, 1954) has also been used to understand sibling behavior. Children and adults use social comparison, especially with those who are similar and physically close, as a way of evaluating themselves. Sibling relationships provide a context for the kinds of comparisons that may contribute to developing self-esteem. Moreover, as children compare the way their parents treat them and their siblings, perceptions of differential treatment may lead to relational difficulties between brothers and sisters. Thus, if a parent is more affectionate and loving toward one child, or more critical of one child in the family over the other, this may lead to confusion, insecurity, feelings of unfairness, and anxiety in the less favored child (Boyle et al., 2004; Feinberg, Neiderhiser, Simmens, Reiss, & Hetherington, 2000). This perceived discrepancy influences the esteem of the sibling who is treated worse (contributing to lower self-worth) as well as of the sibling who feels favored (confusion over why s/he is favored, guilt over and downplaying of the qualities that may have led to being favored, or fear of losing their favored status) (Buist, Deković, & Prinzie, 2013). Additionally, it impacts the quality of the sibling relationship, as the siblings are "set up" by the parents' differential treatment for confusion, animosity, and tension. This may lead to increased competition and conflict between siblings and ambivalent or negative feelings between them. The less favored child may attempt to garner parental attention by acting out in ways that lead to more negative responsiveness from parents, thereby participating in perpetuating the differential treatment.

Sibling rivalry has been a central focus of much of the early research on sibling relationships. Rooted in Adler's notion of the "inferiority complex," and his modification of traditional psychoanalytic theory, the power dynamics and social comparison inherent in families are seen as central to the individual's developing sense of self (Adler, 1927). According to his account of sibling experiences, Adler argued that sibling rivalry occurs in an effort to gain recognition in the family and to secure limited parental resources. By differentiating themselves from one another, siblings develop unique personal qualities and distinct niches for themselves, thereby ensuring a share of parental love and attention. This sibling deidentification process (Ansbacher & Ansbacher, 1956; Whiteman, Becerra, & Killoren, 2009) is presumed to lead to more harmonious interactions between siblings, with less conflict and decreased feelings of inferiority. However, when parents show clear preferences for one child over another, this ultimately leads to and reinforces poor sibling relationships.

Sulloway (1996) also placed sibling rivalry, and competition for parental time and attention, at the center of his argument when he maintained that sibling rivalry, and the subsequent differentiation between siblings that occurs, serves to minimize competition within families. By occupying unique niches that will, in turn, increase access to limited resources, differences between siblings are adaptive (in an evolutionary sense) and promote more positive sibling relationships. However, there is still very little research that explores the processes involved in sibling differentiation and their association with sibling competition and rivalry. Some research does suggest that differentiation leads to improved sibling relationships (Feinberg, McHale, Crouter, & Cumsille, 2003; Whiteman & Christiansen, 2008). However, the results of these studies are not conclusive (e.g., Whiteman, Bernard, & McHale, 2010; Whiteman, McHale, & Couter, 2007) and there is a need for more research that explores the emergence of distinct characteristics, abilities, and behaviors in siblings and the role these play in determining overall sibling relationship quality.

Sibling relationships vary across developmental periods and there may be no single theoretical perspective that best accounts for all of the observed family, developmental, and group differences (Whiteman, McHale, & Soli, 2011). Indeed, some dynamics (such as attachment relationships or social learning experiences) may be more relevant during certain developmental periods than others. Sibling rivalry may be important to consider, but it may not be the only way to characterize interactions between brothers and sisters. Moreover, particular processes, such as differential treatment, and contexts, for example familial, school, and peer groups, need to be considered in future studies exploring the quality of sibling relationships. There are many variables that may mediate between family experiences and sibling relationship quality (Brody, 1998). Thus, complex questions still remain surrounding the shared (and nonshared) parental and environmental experiences of sisters and brothers and the impact of these experiences on the quality of the sibling relationship.

Sibling Relationships Across Different Developmental Periods

The Transition to Becoming a Sibling

There is very little research that has explored the impact of a newborn sibling's arrival on the older child in the family. While some studies have indicated the transition following the birth of a new child is stressful for both the parents and the older sibling (e.g., Field & Reite, 1984; Nadelman & Begun, 1982), there are great variations in the older sibling's reaction to the birth of a new sibling. Indeed, many children experience both excitement and distress; they may also display behaviors such as a desire to be involved in the baby's care or aggression toward the baby. These ambivalent reactions are quite common (Dunn & Kendrick, 1982). Some older siblings express a combination of deep concern about their baby sister or brother while also manifesting regression in language, toilet training, and cooperative behaviors. There are multiple individual, familial, and contextual adjustments that occur concurrently with the birth of a new sibling that may also impact the older sibling's behavior (Volling, 2005). Studies that follow the developmental trajectories of older siblings (e.g., Stewart, Mobley, Van Tuyl, & Salvador, 1987), though rare, provide an important opportunity to explore the factors that account for individual differences in the older sibling's adjustment to the arrival of a younger sister or brother.

The firstborn child's initial reactions to the birth of a new sibling, and the shift in family roles and responsibilities that may accompany the new child's birth, may influence the emotional tone of the family system during the firstborn's transition and the new baby's first year. Older siblings who manifest behavior problems following the birth of a younger sibling, and continue to display difficulties beyond the first few weeks and months of the new sibling's entrance into the family, may increase parental stress. This stress, in turn, could result in harsh parenting techniques, contribute to postpartum depression, and/or create or exacerbate relational challenges that compromise marital quality. A developmental ecological systems model that considers changes in child and family functioning during the transition to siblinghood is a fruitful direction for future research (Volling, 2005). By simultaneously considering multiple dynamic systems across time, including psychological characteristics of the children and parents, as well as the family setting and the larger social context in which the family is functioning, researchers may more accurately capture the complexity of the siblings' current adjustment and of developmental outcomes.

The transition to becoming an older sibling may be different for children who were the only child in the family, as compared to for second or third children expecting a new sibling, since these later-born children only know the experience of being in a family that includes other children. The age of the older child(ren) when the new sibling is born is also likely to impact adjustment, as is the availability of supports, both to the older children and to the family as a whole. Cultural and ethnic group differences in the role of the older sibling in the care of younger siblings, and socioeconomic differences and the work status of parents as they are caring for one or more children in the family, are all likely to impact the older sibling's adjustment as well. Finally, while the focus of much of the research on the transition to being a sibling is on the older child's jealousy and negative reactions, there are also benefits to being an older sibling (Dunn & Kendrick, 1982). Important learning lessons may result from early experiences with siblings; these may translate into increased competence in perspective taking, empathic responsiveness, and emotional understanding not only between brothers and sisters but in other relationships outside of the family as well. Thus, future research on the transition to siblinghood needs to consider the multiple patterns of change that are possible.

Childhood

Younger children do not become active reciprocal participants in sibling interactions (with their older brothers and sisters) until about the age of 4 years (Dunn, Creps, & Brown, 1996). At this point, older siblings begin to take more interest in being with their younger siblings and to see them as potential playmates. Now, younger brothers and sisters can be interactive partners and companions. During middle childhood, sibling interactions become more egalitarian (e.g., Buhrmester & Furman, 1990). It is not clear whether this is the result of younger siblings increasingly trying to exert their power, or older siblings needing to exercise their dominance, or both. Older siblings are still involved in their relationships with their younger siblings before the outside pressures of adolescence potentially impact the intensity and warmth of the sibling relationship (Dunn, 2002).

There is a substantial body of research demonstrating associations between sibling relationship quality, and conflict in particular, and individual children's adjustment (see, for example, reviews by Brody, 1998 and Volling, 2003). Longitudinal associations have also been reported, with differences in each child's adjustment in middle childhood related to preschool sibling relationship quality (Dunn, Slomkowski, Beardsall, et al., 1994). Positive aspects of sibling relationships during childhood are also linked with higher levels of interpersonal skills, such as empathy, cooperation, and sharing (Downey & Condron, 2004; Pike et al., 2005). It may be that both positive and negative peer interactions contribute to sibling relationship quality and therefore the direction of effects needs to be explored further in future research.

Adolescence

While there appears to be continuity in the quality of sibling relationships from childhood into adolescence (Dunn, 1996a), a good relationship with siblings during childhood does not necessarily translate into a good sibling relationship in adolescence. There is more symmetry and equality in the sibling relationship when siblings enter adolescence due to the similarity in developmental status and competence (Buhrmester, 1992). At the same time, there may be less time spent in interaction with siblings, as well as decreased intimacy and affection, though the sibling relationship may still be important and marked by closeness. The quality of sibling relationships may also be modified due to important biological changes and developing social and cognitive competencies (Yeh & Lempers, 2004). And siblings may continue to serve important roles, such as providing emotional support, even as other social resources become available to adolescents.

During early adolescence, relationships with brothers and sisters are often described as no different from parents in terms of their differential power and status. Siblings are seen as providing assistance and satisfaction in a manner that is similar to relationships with parents. However, sibling relationships are also now seen as more similar to friendships in terms of their importance and their offering of companionship to young adolescents (Furman & Buhrmester, 1985a). Still, conflicts tend to increase in the transition from childhood to early adolescence (Brody, Stoneman, & McCoy, 1994) and there is more reported negativity with siblings than there is with friends (Buhrmester & Furman, 1990). During middle and later adolescence, relationships between siblings become more supportive and egalitarian and high levels of conflict decrease (just as has been found with parent–adolescent conflicts), even as relationships continue to expand more outside of the family (Hetherington, Henderson, & Reiss, 1999). The sharing of more equal status and relative power in later adolescence leads to a greater sense of feeling understood and respected by siblings. There is, consequently, a preference for seeking help from brothers and sisters rather than from parents in later adolescence, especially around issues such as dating, sexual exploration, and problems with friends, as increased separation from parents and attempts to gain autonomy lead adolescents to rely less on their parents (Moser, Paternite, & Dixon, 1996). Thus, connections to the family may be maintained by close sibling relationships, even as the adolescent is navigating increased autonomy and independence.

Emerging Adulthood

Sibling relationships continue to evolve during the period between 18 and 25 years of age, or "emerging" adulthood (Arnett, 2000), when increased independence and new responsibilities bring important changes (Conger & Little, 2010). By contrast to the period of adolescence, most siblings spend far less time together in emerging adulthood. When older siblings leave home, they are not only separating from their parents but also from their younger brothers and sisters. They may be living in different cities, states, or countries. Now, contact is more effortful and needs to be more deliberate. Despite the physical distance, siblings may stay connected through social media, video chatting, phone calls, texting, and e-mail. They may also continue to share free time, recreational activities, and visits. While ambivalent feelings toward siblings may persist, the relationships are less intense with less frequent interaction (Hetherington & Kelly, 2002). This may lead either to a dissolution or a working through and resolution of old conflicts, or conflict may lead to continued distance and alienation. The choices that siblings make about continued involvement in one another's lives both reflect, and contribute to, sibling relationship quality.

In emerging adulthood, as their social interaction patterns and attachment networks are modified even further, sibling contact tends to decrease because of increasing work and family responsibilities, especially for those who have children of their own (Noller, 2005). Siblings may provide role models for leaving home, pursuing and completing a college education, and participation in the working world. Moreover, marriage and childbearing are two additional role transitions that can bring siblings closer or exacerbate old conflicts (Conger & Little, 2010). These role changes usually occur at different points in time, thereby complicating further the readjustments required and the consequences for the siblings' relationship. Then, in later adulthood, as childrearing responsibilities gradually decline, siblings may again have more contact, particularly if they are caring for aging parents. Of course, the number and gender of the siblings, the family's expectations regarding sibling care, the emotional closeness of the sibling relationship, and the siblings' experiences with managing and resolving conflict will all impact the amount and quality of contact between siblings in adulthood. Siblings may be increasingly important for older childless individuals and those without a partner, as adults' attachment networks expand to include friends, partners, and siblings. For some adults, siblings serve the critical attachment functions of providing a secure base and safe haven, with proximity seeking and protest around separation reportedly high (Doherty & Feeney, 2004).

What Happens to Sibling Relationships Over Time?

While there is a significant body of research on parent–child attachment relationships over time, and the predictive significance of attachments to mothers and fathers for children's developmental outcomes, there is a relative dearth of longitudinal research on the continuity of sibling relationship quality. From the few extant studies, it appears that the quality of sibling relationships is generally quite consistent from the time a new sibling is born through late adolescence, so long as there are few stressors or significant life changes (Slomkowski & Manke, 2004). Evidence for continuity in the quality of sibling relationships also comes from Judy Dunn's classic longitudinal study of 40 families in Cambridge, England. In the early 1980s, these families were expecting their second child. They were studied and then followed when the older siblings were 9-, 11-, and 13-years-old (Dunn, Slomkowski, & Beardsall, 1994). Based on maternal reports of the older children's positive and negative behaviors toward their younger siblings, there was moderate stability over seven years, especially during the middle childhood period. This stability may result from continuities in family circumstances, in family dynamics, and in children's personality characteristics. However, with the onset of adolescence, there was a decrease in sibling closeness and intimacy (Dunn et al., 1994), perhaps resulting from developmental changes in social competencies and in views of themselves and of relationships outside of the family.

Consistent with these findings, other investigators have found decreased intimacy in sibling relationships as children enter adolescence, in part because of the increased involvement with peers in more diverse social opportunities outside of the family (Buhrmester, 1992; Conger, Bryant, & Brennom, 2004; Dunn et al., 1994; Dunn, Slomkowski, Beardsall et al., 1994). Additionally, some investigators have reported an improvement in the quality of sibling relationships as brothers and sisters become more differentiated from their parents (Feinberg et al., 2003). Moreover, family stressors, such as marital separations and divorce, may lead to either a decrease in sibling relationship quality (Dunn, Slomkowski, Beardsall et al., 1994; Hetherington, 1988) or increased closeness, where the sibling relationship serves a protective function in compensating for difficult family circumstances (Jenkins, 1992). Family hardships, including economic stresses, may indirectly affect sibling relationships. The disruptions in parenting that are caused by familial stressors may in turn lead to more negative interactions between siblings (Conger & Conger, 1996). Thus, interpersonal and familial variables need to be examined more fully when addressing questions regarding stability or change in the quality of sibling relationships. In the future, longitudinal studies will help to illuminate the supportive role that siblings might play in promoting adaptation and resilience during adulthood. Exploring the impact of individual role transitions, together with family dynamics and cultural values, will continue to contribute to our understanding of the importance of sibling relationships across the life course.

How Are Sibling Relationships Described and Measured? Conflict, Rivalry, and So Much More

Conflict is common between siblings, though it is only one of many different dimensions of sibling relationships (Conger & Kramer, 2010; Howe, Ross, & Recchia, 2011). Siblings spend time together playing, sharing, helping, competing, guiding, fighting, and resolving conflict. And, at different points in development, they may assume some roles more than others. For example, younger siblings spend more time together in shared activities (e.g., playing games and sports), in creative activities (such as music, art, and hobbies), watching television and movies, playing computer games, eating meals, and hanging out. Adolescent sibling relationships may include all of these activities, but they may also serve as emotional supports, sharing ideas and providing advice and comfort, communicating about difficult issues, and engaging in contentious exchanges. Adolescent sibling relationships tend to be more egalitarian than they were in childhood, though not as intense or close (East, 2009).

The initial research on sibling relationships focused primarily on conflict and rivalry. Conflict between siblings is normative, parents are especially concerned about how to manage conflict between their children, and many parenting books are directed at reducing sibling rivalry and conflict (e.g., Faber & Mazlish, 1998). Some researchers make important distinctions between rivalry and negative emotions, such as jealousy, in the sibling relationship. Jealousy occurs when one person believes that there is another individual who stands in the way of a significant person's attention and affection. With siblings, this social triangle usually involves one child (e.g., the jealous older sibling) who experiences another person (e.g., the newborn younger sibling) as a threat to love and attention from the desired adult (e.g., the mother or father). Jealousy is therefore a complex social emotion that involves cognitive appraisal, affective reactions, and behavioral consequences (Volling, Kennedy, & Jackey, 2013). The jealous child may interpret the parent's attention to another sibling as a betrayal, leading to feelings of loss and anger, and resulting in aggressive acts toward the "favored" sibling. Sibling jealousy has not been studied extensively, though it appears to be evident even in preschool-aged sibling dyads. Older siblings' jealous reactions strongly predict the overall quality of the sibling relationship, and sibling conflict in particular, when assessed over a two-year time period, especially when the children were observed with their fathers (Kolak & Volling, 2011).

By contrast, sibling conflict has been studied much more extensively. On the surface, conflict between siblings may appear to be similar to jealous reactions but conflict and jealousy can reflect differing underlying motivations. Conflict involves negative dynamics between siblings that may be motivated by jealousy or result from competitive rivalry for parental attention; however, there may be other factors that motivate conflict between siblings so that conflict may simply be the result of differing needs or goals. Identifying the reasons for sibling conflict, as well as exploring the distinctions between conflict and competitive rivalry, is important to the understanding of the developmental course of conflict and rivalry (Whiteman, McHale, & Soli, 2011). Moreover, strategies used to resolve conflicts have been examined and differing outcomes for the sibling relationship have been associated with age, relative birth order, sibling relationship quality, and caregivers' interventions (Recchia & Howe, 2009; Smith & Ross, 2007). Sibling relationship quality has been positively associated with constructive conflict strategies, such as more problem solving, fewer accusations, and less contention; the negotiations of siblings with higher quality relationships are more likely to end in compromise resolutions rather than stand-offs (Howe, Rinaldi, Jennings, & Petrakos, 2002; Ram & Ross, 2001; Ross, Ross, Stein, & Trabasso, 2006).

To date, the primary focus has been on describing and measuring conflict in sibling relationships. When studied developmentally, conflict seems to peak during early adolescence (Laursen, Coy, & Collins, 1998), though studies have explored conflict in early and middle childhood as well. For example, comparisons of sibling conflict among third-, sixth-, ninth-, and twelfth-grade younger siblings led to the conclusion that sibling conflict was reported the most by the sixth graders (Buhrmester & Furman, 1990). The strategies that siblings use in early and middle childhood to resolve their conflicts vary (Howe et al., 2002) and the issues that they disagree about appear to most often involve the sharing of personal possessions (McGuire, Manke, Eftekhari, & Dunn, 2000). By adolescence, the most common causes of conflict include invasion of the personal domain (as opposed to fights over fairness and equality between siblings). These conflicts, involving threats to the self and to relationships (e.g., with friends), are reported to be the most intense and frequent by early adolescent (about 13 years of age) older siblings (Campione-Barr & Smetana, 2010), causing more anxiety and impacting self-esteem (Campione-Barr, Greer, & Kruse, 2013), perhaps because these adolescents are beginning to negotiate issues of autonomy and agency. Thus, evaluating the issues that cause conflict, considering both the siblings' and the parents' perspective, is important to understanding their differential links to developmental outcomes.

What are the long-term effects of sibling conflict? In a study of 5-year-old low-income boys, sibling conflict was found to be associated with conduct problems, even after controlling for maternal hostility and children's earlier adjustment (Garcia, Shaw, Winslow, & Yaggi, 2000). Additionally, the adjustment of middle-class young adolescents is predicted by the target child's reports of sibling conflict evaluated two years earlier, again after controlling for maternal and paternal hostility (Stocker et al., 2002). Moreover, there can be detrimental consequences to sibling conflict, especially when it occurs together with ineffective parenting (East, 2009; Kramer, 2010; Milevsky, 2011). When sibling conflict (fighting, hitting, cheating, stealing) was considered in combination with ineffective parenting (weak supervision, parent–adolescent conflict, poor problem-solving skills) in a sample of 10- to 12-year-olds, associations are found with poor peer relations and antisocial behavior at 12–16 years of age (Bank, Burraston, & Snyder, 2004). And in another longitudinal study, increases in sibling conflict (from the time the older sibling was about 12–17 years of age, and the younger sibling was, on average, 9–15 years of age) are found to be related to youth reports of increased symptoms of depression, while increases in intimacy between siblings are linked to higher perceived peer competence and, for girls, lower reported symptoms of depression (Kim et al., 2007).

What are the mechanisms by which these negative aspects of sibling relationships lead to negative outcomes for adolescents? There may be direct modeling of an older sibling's behavior, so that a young sibling may learn to engage in delinquent behavior, use drugs or alcohol, or adopt poor study habits because that is what they learn from their older sibling. Or there may be carryover from the parent–child relationship to the sibling relationship and the family environment may support such learning. The associations among positive and negative sibling relationship qualities and individual adjustment have been explored in several recent studies, controlling for the influence of the parent–child relationship, parenting behavior, and the general family environment. The results indicate that the association between sibling relationship quality and adjustment persists, even with the impact of parenting and parent–child relationship quality controlled (Kim et al., 2007; Pike et al., 2005; Stocker et al., 2002).

Importantly, longitudinal studies have explored reciprocal associations between the quality of the sibling relationship and individual adjustment. For example, adolescents with higher self-esteem appear to have less conflict in their sibling relationships, just as less conflict in the sibling relationship is linked to higher self-esteem (Yeh & Lempers, 2004). Sibling conflict influences changes in internalizing symptoms over time, and internalizing symptoms in one sibling contributes to problems in the sibling relationship. When there are stressful circumstances in an adolescent's life, siblings may help to buffer against the negative effects and promote adaptive functioning (East, 2009). Moreover, moderators of these associations, including ordinal position and gender composition of the dyad, have been identified (Campione-Barr et al., 2013). Investigators are now better able to explore these moderating influences, over time, using more sophisticated data analytical techniques that examine relationship processes as well as differences at the family or dyadic level of analysis (e.g., multilevel modeling which controls for interdependence of siblings nested within dyads (Kim et al., 2007) or the actor–partner interdependence model (Kenny, Kashy, & Cook, 2006)).

While the primary focus in studies of siblings has been on conflict, we now know that siblings do not just manage competition, antagonism, and conflict in their relationships. Sisters and brothers also share affectionate, cooperative, helpful, and supportive exchanges as well. And the absence of conflict does not guarantee a more positive sibling relationship, just as being more engaged and affectionate with one's siblings does not mean there is no conflict. How can we best characterize sibling relationships? Sibling relationships may be described in different ways, using variations in emotional quality, familiarity, and intimacy (Dunn, 2007). These dimensions may, in fact, be quite overlapping and related. Because siblings know each other so well, they may use this understanding to support and help one another or to tease and expose one another's vulnerabilities. Depending upon the situation and the quality of their relationship, siblings may use their deep knowledge of one another in positive or negative ways. They may, for example, display unwavering loyalty in the face of a threat to one sibling or know just which "buttons" to push, thereby provoking one another in times of distress. And during certain periods of development, siblings might describe their relationship more positively than during other periods, influenced, in part, by the other stresses and strains they experience individually as well as in their relationship. Thus, there may be considerable variation in the way that siblings feel about one another. At times, they may describe their relationship as warm and supportive and feel quite affectionate toward one another, expressing intense positive feelings, whereas other times they may focus on how irritating and annoying a sibling is, focusing only on negative feelings toward their siblings. Most siblings, however, would characterize the emotional quality of their relationship as variable and mixed.

There is evidence of varying combinations of positive and negative affects and behaviors in sibling relationships, yet we do not know what the ideal balance might be and whether this varies during different developmental periods. If siblings do not experience conflict in their relationship, then they may be deprived of the opportunity to learn the skills necessary for managing conflict in other relationships such as with peers (Shantz & Hobart,

1989). They may learn to deny negative affects in relationships or maintain distance from their brother or sister when conflict arises and appear distant and detached. If there is too much conflict, this might disrupt family coherence (Kramer & Baron, 1995) or reflect more general disturbances in family functioning that the siblings are re-enacting. By contrast, constructive and moderate forms of conflict between brothers and sisters may help children to tolerate negative affects (Katz, Kramer, & Gottman, 1992), develop conflict management skills (Vandell & Bailey, 1992), and promote social understanding (Dunn & Slomkowski, 1992). Research efforts should be directed toward understanding the ideal levels of positive and negative sibling behaviors, which may be differentiated by gender composition of the sibling dyad and vary at different points in development (Kramer, 2010).

There are several qualities that characterize a more balanced sibling relationship, one that integrates both positive and negative experiences and feelings (Rosen, 2015). An emerging list of these competencies include: shared experiences, positive engagement, emotion regulation, cohesiveness, and perspective taking, as well as conflict negotiation and problem-solving skills and open discussions about differential parental treatment (Kramer, 2010). Based on prior research findings that identify and support the development of these skills in sibling dyads, the delineation of these competencies may help to guide prevention and intervention efforts directed toward creating more successful relationships (see, for example, Kennedy & Kramer, 2008). Still, this work needs to be refined in accordance with the evolving competencies of brothers and sisters during different developmental periods. For example, conversations about differential parental treatment will not likely happen between siblings until early adolescence (e.g., Kowal, Krull, & Kramer, 2006), whereas the early roots of emotion regulation in the context of sibling relationships may be seen in the preschool and early childhood periods (Volling, McElwain, & Miller, 2002). Thus, adaptive and maladaptive manifestations of these varying competencies need to be considered with a sensitivity to developmentally appropriate measures of each, and continuities and discontinuities over time need to be explored in terms of the relative salience of these competencies to the sibling dyad. Tracking the developmental course of positive sibling behaviors, such as cooperation, sharing, support, openness, and nurturance, should be a research priority so as to round out the portrait of relevant sibling behaviors that emerge and develop over the lifespan of the relationship.

As sibling relationships develop over time, brothers and sisters are more likely to describe feelings of closeness and support as each sibling negotiates new developmental tasks. In particular, the development of relationships outside of the family, as well as each sibling's self- and identity development, may deepen attachments between siblings and reduce conflict and rivalry. Moreover, it may be that the positive qualities of sibling relationships, such as support, affection, and cooperation, and negative qualities, such as competition, conflict, and control, are consolidated into more stable patterns of interaction that then characterize the sibling relationship over time

(Kramer, 2010). Ultimately, describing sibling relationships in terms of these qualitative patterns of interaction may be more fruitful. For example, varying combinations of positive and negative sibling behaviors lead to patterns of sibling relationships that may be described as harmonious, conflicted, hostile, balanced, or detached (see, for example, Brody et al., 1994; Hetherington, 1989; Rosen, 2015). Thus, rather than characterizing sibling dyads as high or low in conflict, there are other alternatives that need to be considered. It is this more comprehensive view of sibling relationships that should be incorporated into future research and that will likely lead to a deeper understanding of sibling relationships.

Measurement Approaches For the Study of Sibling Relationships

Behavioral Observations

Early studies of young siblings relied on the observation of sibling interactions in the home or the research lab. Positive (or prosocial) and negative (or agonistic) behaviors were coded from naturalistic observations and/or videotapes. Some commonly occurring prosocial behaviors that were identified and coded included laughing, affectionate touching, smiling, offering help, providing comfort, and sharing toys. Behaviors in the agonistic category included yelling, hitting, screaming, pushing, insulting, rejecting, and taking and throwing toys. Usually, the behaviors were then aggregated in some way to determine the relative frequency or proportion of positive (e.g., cooperative, prosocial, and play sequences (Dunn & Munn, 1986b)) and/or negative (e.g., conflictual (Dunn & Munn, 1986a)) behavior in the dyad. This method proved to be quite useful in providing positive and negative characterizations of the sibling relationship (as either good (positive behaviors) or bad (negative behaviors)). However, the reliance on this dichotomy implicated a value judgment inherent in the positive and negative distinction and suggested that the quality of the relationship was static. Moreover, other variables began to be considered as they were seen to influence the context in which the dyad was interacting, including the antecedent conditions and the other interactional partners present. Seemingly negative behaviors (such as taking away a toy) could have prosocial intent if, for example, the behavior was executed so as to protect a younger child from danger. Alternatively, it could have the intent of getting an emotionally unavailable parent involved, by generating conflict and requiring parental intervention. Likewise, a string of prosocial behaviors (such as teaching, helping, sharing toys) could be carried out with resentment or in a controlling manner without much positive affect or shared enthusiasm.

Thus, an alternative method for documenting sibling behavior was developed by creating categories of behaviors and rating them on global scales. Some researchers created these scales from observations, while others used statistical techniques, such as factor analysis, to categorize sibling behaviors (e.g., Stocker, Dunn, & Plomin, 1989). For example, the four factors or dimensions of warmth/closeness, relative status/power, conflict, and rivalry were identified from open-ended interviews of siblings in late childhood (Furman, Jones, Buhrmester, & Adler, 1989). Similar dimensions were derived through factor analyses of laboratory observations of siblings, aged 4–11 years, yielding categories of power/status, teaching, helping, conflict, positive tone, companionship, and self-praise (Vandell, Minnett, & Santrock, 1987). Judy Dunn and her colleagues reworked these dimensions to better reflect observable behaviors in young sisters and brothers (Stocker & Dunn, 1990; Stocker et al., 1989). They created four scales to measure children's behaviors toward their siblings – cooperation, control, conflict, and competition – and used these scales to reliably differentiate sibling interactions. These scales set the standard for other sibling researchers and were introduced in an attempt to move the research beyond the study of conflict and rivalry alone. Yet, these behaviors still reflected a preoccupation with the more negative aspects of sibling relationships.

Later, researchers began to attend to the more emotionally laden, positive aspects of sibling relationships, including affection, nurturance, and sensitivity. Additionally, they acknowledged the lack of independence between the positive and negative sibling dimensions. Thus, for example, some studies of sibling relationship quality identified and measured elements of sibling affection and protection together with rivalry (Brody, 1998; Stocker, 1994). When there are high levels of conflict between siblings, without much affection and warmth, children are more likely to be aggressive with their siblings as well as with their peers (Brody, 2004). Alternatively, sibling dyads characterized by a balance of affection and conflict provide children with a natural context to learn about others' emotions and perspectives and to develop social skills.

Researchers also began to code behaviors for each sibling separately and to then organize sibling behaviors into patterns or styles that reflect contributions of each sibling. For example, two studies of siblings in middle childhood through adolescence identified "sibling styles" in nondivorced families, including harmonious, typical, and conflicted (Brody et al., 1994). These styles were similar to those identified in a study of families with varying marital status, i.e., nondivorced, divorced, and remarried, where the styles included compassionate-caring, ambivalent, and hostile-alienated, respectively (Hetherington, 1989). A fourth style, enmeshed, was also identified in this sample. Still other research has examined dyadic behaviors and the affective quality of the sibling relationship, documenting four patterns of sibling relationships, including harmonious, balanced, hostile, and detached, in young sibling dyads (18- to 24-month-old younger siblings and 4- to 5-year-old older siblings) that similarly reflect varying combinations of observed sibling behaviors (Rosen, 2015). Taken together, this work indicates that the relative balance of positive and negative behaviors in sibling dyads is much more important to consider, rather than simply observing and coding the two distinct positive and negative dimensions or considering a continuum of relational quality. Patterns of interaction are organized within the sibling relationship that are more meaningful than simple descriptions of discrete positive or negative behaviors. Studying these patterns over time, and in sibling pairs from diverse cultural and socioeconomic backgrounds, will help to illuminate the developmental and contextual factors that may influence the way these sibling patterns evolve.

Self-Report Measures and Multiple Perspectives on Sibling Relationships

While behavioral observations of young siblings may offer valuable information about the quality of their relationship, they are constrained by the context, task demands, people present, and coding methods used. Consequently, many investigators also rely on children's and/or the parents' perceptions of sibling relationships. Brothers and sisters have their own views about the quality of their relationships that need to be considered (Kowal & Kramer, 1997). The Sibling Relationship Questionnaire (Furman & Buhmester, 1985b) has been used extensively to assess several dimensions of sibling relationship quality including: warmth/closeness (companionship, affection, admiration, intimacy, and prosocial behavior), relative status/power (dominance over, and nurturance of, sibling), conflict (antagonism and quarreling), and rivalry (parental partiality and competition). This questionnaire is the most widely used when children's perceptions of their sibling relationship are being evaluated (Volling, 2003). It has also been used when studying early adolescents' reports of their sibling relationships (Hetherington & Clingempeel, 1992; Stocker & McHale, 1992).

Ratings made on the Sibling Relationship Questionnaire reflect perceptions of the siblings' interactions in a variety of contexts, but they are likely to be influenced by the siblings' memories and subjective evaluations of their experiences together. The questionnaire has often been used to assess the subjective experience of only one member of the sibling dyad. In order to capture the interpersonal relationship, researchers need to obtain *both* siblings' perspectives. Additionally, researchers will frequently ask parents to describe their children's relationship using similar measures, such as the Maternal Interview of Sibling Relationships (Stocker et al., 1989). The assumption is that parents have high exposure to, and some understanding of, the relationship they are describing. Again, it is essential to have *both* parents' perspectives on the quality of the sibling relationship rather than relying on only maternal reports as representative of the parents' view. For these reasons, some researchers argue that *both* parents' and *both* children's perceptions of the sibling relationship should be assessed and similarities or discrepancies in their ratings should be considered.

Do parents and children agree on their overall assessments of the sibling relationship? Extant research has demonstrated that children's perceptions are generally consistent with their siblings' and parents' ratings (Pike et al., 2005). Mothers and fathers are most consistent on their ratings of sibling warmth, conflict, and relative power/status, though their ratings of rivalry tend to differ (Kramer & Baron, 1995). Interestingly, when all family members share their perceptions of sibling relationships, then they are more likely to be stable and cohesive as a family unit (Minuchin, 1974); this cohesiveness influences the nature of relationships within the family and is associated with more positive adjustment (Howe, Karos, & Aquan-Assee, 2011; Kowal et al., 2006). If their perceptions are not shared, then this may indicate low cohesiveness and more problematic relationships within the family (Rinaldi & Howe, 2003).

When there are differences in parental perceptions of the sibling relationship, this may be due to relative differences in the knowledge that parents have about their children's interactions, how much parents know about levels of intimacy or conflict between their children, how much the children are willing to honestly share about their relationship, and the depth of children's (or parents') understanding of the meaning of the siblings' interactive behaviors (Dunn, 1988). Moreover, parental expectations regarding the way their children "should" get along, how much warmth and closeness or antagonism and rivalry there "should" be in the sibling dyad, may bias their perceptions and influence their ratings of sibling relationship quality. Parents have their own investment in viewing their children, or in presenting them, in a particular way. They also may be influenced by their own sibling experiences. Therefore, parental descriptions may be biased and ultimately may not correspond with one another or with outside observers' ratings (e.g., Furman et al., 1989). Indeed, research indicates that parents overestimate the consistency of their relationships with different children in the family (Pike, Reiss, Hetherington, & Plomin, 1996), perhaps due to expectations that parents have that their relationships "should" be consistent. Similarly, parents may maintain standards for how their children "should" behave. These standards may, in turn, influence parents' socialization practices as well as their own and their children's perceptions of sibling relationships (Howe et al., 2011). Future work should continue to incorporate multiple perspectives and use multiple methods to assess perceptions of, and observed interactive behaviors within, the sibling dyad in order to obtain a more comprehensive and meaningful view of sibling relationships.

Why Are Siblings So Different?

Most parents are remarkably aware of the differences that exist in their children's temperament and behavior. Parents often muse, "It's hard to believe that they came from the same family!" when they attempt to account for perceived differences between their children. Even when children are raised in the same family, there are certain experiences that they have that are not similar. These varying experiences are presumed to create nonshared environments. Differences that emerge between siblings, in personality, adjustment, and developmental outcomes, are then usually explained in terms of these nonshared influences (Daniels & Plomin, 1985; Rowe & Plomin, 1981; Turkheimer & Waldron, 2000). Nonshared environmental factors include age, birth order, relationships with parents, disabilities or illnesses, differential parental treatment, school experiences, and relationships with friends (Dunn & Plomin, 1990; Harris, 2006). These factors contribute to making siblings different from one another (Hetherington et al., 1994; Pike, Manke, Reiss, & Plomin, 2000; Plomin & Daniels, 1987; Vandell, 2000). However, there is still substantial controversy over the issue of how much these nonshared environmental variables account for the variance in developmental or behavioral outcomes (see, for example, Plomin, Asbury, & Dunn, 2001).

Initially, constellation variables such as age spacing, gender composition of sibling pairs, and birth order were examined in an attempt to understand the factors that could lead to differences between brothers and sisters. Some studies, for example, explored the effect of age spacing on sibling relationship quality. This research has yielded mixed results, with some studies finding no significant effect of age on relationship quality (e.g., Lee, Mancini, & Maxwell, 1990) and others finding lower quality relationships between sibling pairs with a smaller age difference between them (e.g., Milevsky, Smoot, Leh, & Ruppe, 2005). It appears that when the firstborn is relatively older (4–5 years of age) when s/he becomes a sibling, there is less competition and rivalry in the relationship when the siblings reach adolescence than when the siblings are three years apart or less. When the quality of the firstborn's relationship with the mother before the new sibling is born is explored in relation to the quality of the sibling relationship in adolescence, significant positive associations are found; moreover, analyses indicate a stronger link when the firstborn is older (4–5 years of age) as compared to younger (Kramer & Kowal, 2005). Thus, age spacing may make a difference in overall sibling relationship quality, though other factors, such as early relational competence with mothers or friends, may be important to consider as well.

Gender composition of the sibling dyad may also have an impact on sibling relationship quality (Brody, 1996). Sisters appear to be more supportive and affectionate and to experience less antagonism and conflict as compared to brothers (Dunn, 2002; Hetherington et al., 1999). By contrast, brothers tend to demonstrate more threatening and hostile behaviors, including bullying and physical violence, and to engage in more frequent conflict with their siblings (Brody, 2004). Studies have also shown that same-sex sibling pairs (especially sisters) have higher quality relationships than mixed-sex sibling pairs. Boys with older brothers tend to differ from boys with older sisters and the lowest quality relationships are seen in older brother/younger sister pairs (Aguilar et al., 2001; Buist, 2010). And sibling gender appears to impact psychosocial adaptation (e.g., delinquency), with greater similarity in delinquent behavior found for same-sex sibling pairs (Fagan & Najman, 2003; Rowe & Gulley, 1992; Slomkowski et al., 2001).

Researchers have studied birth order as well and have found that there are certain personality characteristics that are linked to sibling birth order. For example, firstborns tend to be more conscientious, intelligent, self-controlled, and achievement-oriented. They tend to identify with parents and maintain the status quo. By contrast, later-borns are more agreeable and liberal, creative and rebellious, and likely to reject the status quo (Paulhus, Trapnell, & Chen, 1999; Sulloway, 1996). Because firstborns receive exclusive care and attention from parents before the birth of their siblings, they may identify more easily with authority figures and demonstrate more authoritarian behavior toward their younger siblings (Sulloway, 1996). Firstborns may therefore appear more detached and differentiated from their younger siblings, whereas later-borns may seek affinity with and connection to older siblings (Dunn, 2002). However, studies that explore the impact of birth order tend to rely on correlational findings and to report only modest differences; thus, many sibling researchers have extended beyond the focus on birth order to consider other variables that might impact developmental outcomes.

Older and younger children in the same family assume different roles, both in relation to their parents and to their siblings. Attempts have been made to understand the different roles that older and younger siblings play and the consequence of these varying roles for siblings' relationships. Older siblings tend to be more dominant and controlling (Vandell et al., 1987) and to feel more resentful when they perceive differential treatment by parents toward their younger siblings. This, in turn, may have an impact on the sibling relationship. There is, however, a decrease in firstborns' efforts to control their younger siblings during the early and middle adolescent period (Tucker, Updegraff, & Baril, 2010), consistent with the notion that sibling relationships become more egalitarian during adolescence (Buhrmester, 1992). Additionally, second-borns are more likely to initiate conflict with their older siblings, especially in those dyads where there is more balanced control (similar to what is seen in peer relationships) or where the younger sibling is more dominant (Tucker et al., 2010).

Now, many researchers argue that birth order is only one of many important family constellation variables to consider. Indeed, age spacing and gender patterns also need to be examined as they may influence observed differences between the behavior of firstborns and later-borns. Moreover, the observed effects of these constellation variables may vary depending upon the developmental period in which the siblings are observed. They may, for example, be much more important during early and middle childhood than they are during adolescence and emerging adulthood. The impact of these constellation variables may also vary depending upon the family's social and cultural context. The experiences of adopted, foster, half-, or step-siblings may differ from siblings in more traditional families. Additionally, circumstances such as developmental disorders or chronic illness in a sibling, parental illness, or abuse in the family may lead to different sibling outcomes as well.

Researchers have also begun to emphasize the importance of considering multiple sibling dyads within the same family (e.g., Jenkins, Rasbash, Leckie, Gass, & Dunn, 2012). Therefore, later-borns need to be differentiated into whether they are the last of two siblings or the middle child in a family of three or more siblings. Later-borns tend to be more social with their peers, perhaps because they were born into a family where other children were always there and they have more experience interacting with others. Middle-borns tend to be mediators in the family, often negotiating conflicts and disputes between siblings. Last-borns are usually considered the "baby" of the family even when they are adolescents or adults. They are regarded as uninformed, immature, and unsophisticated in terms of competence, experiences, preferences, and opinions even when external criteria (e.g., academic success, social achievements) prove otherwise (Sutton-Smith, 1982).

In sum, the effects of sibling birth order, age spacing, and gender have been examined as they influence individual adaptation. But, children who are raised in the same family may also have differing temperaments, or other genetic predispositions, suggesting yet another group of factors that may not be shared by brothers and sisters. Thus, the current view, emerging from socialization theories and behavioral-genetic research, is that both constellation variables and genetic factors create differing environments for brothers and sisters, thereby potentially influencing and contributing to differing developmental outcomes.

Parents may also respond to their children differently, based on some of the very same constellation variables that impacted their own sibling relationships. Mothers may, for example, identify more with their daughter(s) and/or with the child of their same birth order and attempt to replicate old patterns from their own sibling or family relationships in their current family. A responsible oldest brother in a family of three children may, as a father, expect his oldest son to assume the same role in relation to his siblings. However, current individual, familial, cultural, or economic factors may dictate a different pattern of behavior for this oldest son, thereby creating tension in the parent–child relationship and/or conflict between siblings in this next generation. Thus, parental expectations, early experiences with their own brothers and sisters, and current circumstances may all influence parental behavior toward their own children, subsequently impacting the relationships they develop as brothers and sisters.

Differential Parental Treatment and Its Effects on Siblings

Most parents recognize that their children have unique personalities, behaviors, and needs. Accommodating to these distinctive qualities and responding to differences in age and gender are necessary so that parents can be sensitive and responsive to their children's individual differences (Kowal & Kramer, 1997). Parents may even exaggerate the differences between their children in some temperamental dimensions (e.g., "He needs to be moving all the time but she is so content to be playing quietly" or "She loves talking to everyone but he is so shy") or areas of interests (e.g., "She's the athlete" or "He's the musician"). This tendency, in turn, may impact their expectations for their children's behavior and result in parents treating their children differently.

Parents justify differential treatment in accordance with their perceptions of their children's individual personalities, interests, and needs (Atzaba-Poria & Pike, 2008; McHale & Crouter, 2003; Plomin & Daniels, 1987; Saudino, Wertz, Gagne, & Chawla, 2004). Yet, siblings may have difficulty understanding why these differences in parental treatment are important and, in fact, come to resent the differences. Variations in parental warmth or hostility, or in parents' responses to sibling conflicts, may impact children's relationships with one another. Moreover, interactions between child and parent variables may also influence how siblings get along. For example, siblings tend to get along better when they both have "easy" temperaments and they are treated relatively equally by their parents. When one or both siblings have "difficult" temperaments, or when parents offer preferential treatment to one sibling, the siblings have more problems in their relationship (Brody, 1998; Brody et al., 1987). Thus, differential treatment has been examined as an important part of the nonshared environment that may impact siblings' personal characteristics and relationships.

Studies exploring the nonshared environments of siblings typically focus on differential parental treatment (e.g., affection and control), though there are also differences in nonmutuality of sibling interactions (e.g., sibling antagonism, caretaking, jealousy, and closeness), differences in experiences with their peers (e.g., delinquency, popularity, school/college orientation), and events specific to each sibling (e.g., romantic relationships, relationships with teachers, accidents) (Daniels & Plomin, 1985; Harris, 1998). Behavior geneticists contend that differences between siblings become more apparent across development, suggesting that it may be more common to find differential treatment of adolescents than of children (McCartney et al., 1990; Scarr & McCartney, 1983). Parents of children and adolescents have been found to treat their children differently, depending on parent gender and the age and gender constellation of the siblings. The particular aspect of parental treatment assessed (e.g., warmth or control) also influences the differences observed. Thus, sibling dyads with two boys report lower levels of maternal warmth and involvement, relative to other sibling gender combinations, and parents are more involved with the sibling of his or her gender in mixed-gender sibling dyads (McHale, Updegraff, Jackson-Newson, Tucker, & Crouter, 2000). There are many factors, therefore, that contribute to differences in parental treatment.

Early research on the effects of parental differential treatment supported the idea that differential treatment leads to poorer individual siblings' adjustment and more negative sibling relationship quality (Brody et al., 1987; Dunn, Stocker, & Plomin, 1990; Volling & Belsky, 1992b). When parents treat their children differently, there may be detrimental consequences for psychosocial functioning in children and adolescents as well (Boyle et al., 2004; Coldwell, Pike, & Dunn, 2008). In general, differential treatment has been found to have a stronger effect on externalizing problems than on internalizing problems (Richmond et al., 2005). Differential parental warmth and negativity (Feinberg & Hetherington, 2001) and differential parental conflict (Mekos, Hetherington, & Reiss, 1996) have been associated with more externalizing behavior problems. Mixed results have been found for internalizing problems, with some studies concluding there are limited or no effects of differential affection (Kowal, Kramer, Krull, & Crick, 2002; Richmond et al., 2005) and others indicating differential conflict and warmth are associated with depressive symptoms (Shanahan, McHale, Crouter, & Osgood, 2008). Interestingly, differential treatment of siblings appears to be more strongly associated with internalizing behavior problems in children than in adolescents (Buist et al., 2013), consistent with the notion that family and sibling influences appear to be stronger in childhood and decrease with increased peer influences on behavior during adolescence. It appears that the developmental period in which siblings are studied is an important moderator of the effects of differential treatment on developmental outcome.

Children are quite sensitive to the differences in how parents treat them, as compared to their brothers and sisters, and these perceived differences are associated with developing behavioral problems. A comprehensive meta-analysis of extant research found that less differential treatment of siblings by parents and more warmth and less conflict between siblings were related to fewer internalizing and externalizing problems in the children (Buist et al., 2013). Children appear to benefit from interactions with their parents where parents are attentive and sensitively responsive to each child's individual needs. In this context, the well-being of each child and the quality of the sibling relationship are subsequently enhanced. However, when children perceive differential treatment, this may lead to behavior problems as children act out, or become anxious or depressed, in an attempt to compensate for the perceived lack of attention. Alternatively, perceptions of personality or behavioral differences in their children may lead parents to treat their children differently. When internalizing and externalizing behavior problems emerge, therefore, they may be either the cause or the outcome of differential parental treatment.

It is the perceptions that siblings have of these differences, whether seen as fair and legitimate or leading to feelings of jealousy and rivalry, that are associated with measures of sibling relationship quality and of individual well-being. For example, when siblings perceive differential treatment to be reasonable and fair, and they describe their own treatment to be equal or favored relative to their sibling, they report higher self-esteem and more positive regard for their brothers or sisters. However, those siblings who perceive their own disfavored treatment as fair report lower self-esteem. Thus, siblings' perceptions of parental fairness (McHale et al., 2000), and their attributions regarding whether parents' differential treatment is justified (Kowal & Kramer, 1997), are critical to consider. It is not the magnitude of differential treatment, but rather the meaning that children make of these differences, that matters.

In certain domains (e.g., discipline, parental warmth and support, assignment of chores), and with certain children (depending upon age, cognitive and physical abilities), equal treatment may not be practical or beneficial. Oldest children in the family may be more attuned to differential treatment (Reid, Ramey, & Burchinal, 1990). They may also be more sophisticated in their perspective taking and empathic abilities, thereby more likely to understand the reasons for these differences. Moreover, this capacity to justify differential treatment based on varying sibling needs suggests that siblings are not solely motivated by feelings of resentment, jealousy, and rivalry (Kowal & Kramer, 1997). There may also be cultural factors that impact the meaning attributed to differential treatment. In collectivistic cultures, where expectations and roles are more differentiated by age and gender, there may be clear reasons for, and fewer negative attributions regarding, differential treatment (Nuckolls, 1993; Weisner, 1993). By contrast, in individualistic cultures, differential treatment may have more negative repercussions (McHale, Updegraff, Shanahan, Crouter, & Killoren, 2005).

The direction of effects here is not clear, since those with lower self-esteem may justify their disfavored treatment as fair or, alternatively, siblings may accept the parent's differential treatment as fair and this may lead to low self-esteem (McHale et al., 2000). Differential parenting may be elicited by both children and parents (Reiss et al., 1995). Parenting may be reactive to more difficult children (Jenkins, Rasbash, & O'Connor, 2003; Zadeh, Jenkins, & Pepler, 2010) and difficult children may elicit more negative parenting (Lytton & Romney, 1991). Whichever the direction of effects, these results suggest that siblings' subjective evaluations of their experiences of differential treatment need to be considered in future research exploring the processes through which parental differential treatment has implications for sibling outcomes.

There also may be other factors that interact with differential treatment and lead to differences in sibling adjustment. Older siblings appear to be more sensitive to differential treatment (Feinberg et al., 2000; Shebloski, Conger, & Widaman, 2005) so age needs to be considered when exploring links between differential treatment and outcome. Moreover, sibling relationship quality and adjustment, for both siblings, may depend on differential parental treatment and therefore need to be considered using statistical models that consider their dependence, such as hierarchical linear modeling (Richmond et al., 2005). Children's and adolescents' appraisals of differential treatment affect the sibling relationship as well as the parent–child relationship (Kowal & Kramer, 1997; Kowal, Krull, & Kramer, 2004). Communication about the differences in parents' behavior may facilitate children's understanding and experience of differential treatment. Finally, more complex models exploring the mechanisms of influence need to be considered. For example, in one study, adolescent twins (15–18 years old) who reported being disfavored as compared to their co-twin also reported greater attachment insecurity and lower psychological adjustment; moreover, attachment insecurity was found to mediate the link between the twins' reports of differential maternal affection and of higher anxiety as well as between the twins' reports of differential paternal affection and of lower self-esteem (Sheehan & Noller, 2002). Future research using longitudinal designs with more diverse and larger samples will help to validate these pathways of influence.

Additionally, measurement of differential treatment varies, with some studies relying on parental or sibling report, others using observational measures, and some using both. Using multiple methods and informants is advantageous, with reports of differential parental treatment found to be associated with objectively rated negative relationship dynamics, characterized by poor communication, which could perpetuate a vicious cycle of aggressive sibling behavior (Bedford & Volling, 2004; Sheehan, 1997). In one longitudinal study of 384 adolescent sibling pairs, observers rated parents' hostility (angry, critical, rejecting behavior), angry coerciveness (blaming, threatening, or demanding behavior), and antisocial behavior (insensitive or inconsiderate demeanor) toward each child. Only 26% of mothers and 30% of fathers were found to treat their children equally across three annual assessments. Moreover, older siblings perceived that their younger sibling was given preferential treatment in terms of parents taking sides, treating the younger sibling better, and giving the younger sibling more attention at all three assessments but only in terms of taking sides at the third assessment (Shebloski et al., 2005).

Clearly, the child's perspective on the magnitude of differential treatment by mothers and fathers is important to consider. Moderate differences in parental treatment may not trigger comparison with brothers and sisters, may be seen as justified, and therefore may not impact sibling relationship quality (Coldwell et al., 2008; Kowal et al., 2006). Additionally, research on differential treatment needs to extend beyond the almost exclusive focus on only two children in the family, since this may not accurately represent the dynamics inherent in larger families and may confound the effects of differential treatment (Meunier, Bisceglia, & Jenkins, 2012). Studying multiple sibling dyads within families using multilevel modeling techniques allows for the examination of family processes that may account for the way siblings relate to one another over time (Jenkins et al., 2012).

In sum, as research has continued to evolve, differential treatment is no longer viewed as unusual or consistently associated with negative outcomes for siblings. In fact, differential parental treatment may be necessary. And the consequences of such differential treatment have been found to account for only a small part of nonshared environmental influences on siblings' personal characteristics after controlling for genetic factors (Plomin et al., 2001). Researchers now believe that the subjective meaning children attribute to differences in treatment, especially the legitimacy and fairness of these differences, accounts for individual differences in outcomes (Kowal & Kramer, 1997; McHale & Pawletko, 1992). The less favored sibling appears to be affected the most, manifesting low self-esteem, poor relational communication, and the most behavior problems (Brody et al., 1987; McHale et al., 2000). Conversely, the favored sibling who receives preferred treatment may also be at risk for developing problems (Meunier et al., 2012). The results of research on differential treatment indicate that parents should be more sensitive to children's emotional responses to differential treatment, offer explanations about the reasons for and legitimacy of differential treatment, and minimize unfair differences in their treatment of their children.

Other Influences on Sibling Relationship Quality

Sibling relationship quality may be influenced by many other factors that have not been adequately examined to date. There is an increased need to consider siblings in ethnically and structurally diverse families in order to better understand the impact of these unique family experiences on relationship quality (McGuire & Shanahan, 2010). For example, siblings in nonimmigrant, ethnically diverse families (e.g., across the many Asian American subgroups in the United States), many of whom live in extended, multigenerational households, have not been extensively studied (Taylor, 2001). Children in step-families, half siblings, and foster and adopted children may also have unique experiences that impact their evolving sibling relationships and lead to differences in adjustment. Internationally adopted children may be of particular interest to investigate; their sibling relationships may influence their adjustment as well as their racial and ethnic identity (Lee, Grotevant, Hellerstedt, Gunnar, and the Minnesota International Adoption Project Team, 2006). And siblings who are placed together in foster care may serve a protective function in managing stress and promoting resilience, even in the face of family disruptions (Linares, Li, Shrout, Brody, & Pettit, 2007). Exploring sibling experiences in families headed by same-sex partners would also contribute to our understanding of family context and the role of gender in parental differential treatment. Moreover, studies of sexual-minority adolescents and their sibling relationships would highlight the role of sibling experiences in identity development (Gottlieb, 2005).

Finally, exploring factors outside the larger family context may also serve an important role in deepening our understanding of sibling relationships. Qualities of the siblings' shared environment, such as socioeconomic status and the neighborhood in which the family lives, are important to examine so as to understand their role in determining sibling relationship quality. Those studies that have examined the impact of socioeconomic status or neighborhoods have yielded inconsistent results. Some report more positive sibling relationships in families of lower socioeconomic status (McHale, Whiteman, Kim, & Crouter, 2007) while others find more negative sibling relationship quality (Updegraff, McHale, Whiteman, Thayer, & Delgado, 2005). Additionally, neighborhood characteristics and resources, such as parks and playgrounds, are related to sibling experiences as well (Updegraff & Obeidallah, 1999). When neighborhoods offer more opportunities for interactions with peers, adolescents' interpersonal experiences are more likely to be influenced by these contextual factors, leading to variations in sibling relationship patterns. Older adolescents' sibling experiences are also more likely to be impacted by new technologies that allow for communication and contact even as brothers and sisters leave younger siblings to attend college (Whiteman, McHale, & Soli, 2011). Now, the availability of text messaging, social media platforms, video chatting, and email exchanges make contact possible between siblings who are geographically separated. The impact of these communication resources for sustaining feelings of connection and support, as well as for repairing conflicts and difficulties, need to be studied in future research.

Cultural forces also influence sibling relationships. In fact, some theorists believe that culture is the single most important factor to consider when exploring sibling relationships, as sibling relationships are embedded in larger ethnic, racial, and cultural niches (Weisner, 1993). Cultural values impact parenting practices and shape experiences that are unique to distinct cultural groups (e.g., discrimination, family loyalty, gender roles). For example, research on African American siblings identifies ethnic identity, extended family involvement, and experiences with discrimination as central cultural factors associated with sibling relationship quality (McHale et al., 2007). Interdependence among family members, solidarity, and family obligations in Mexican American families are associated with sibling closeness (Updegraff et al., 2005). In some non-Western cultures, where older siblings are expected to assume caregiving responses and the structure of sibling roles is hierarchically organized, qualities of sibling relationships, such as competition, rivalry, and cooperation, are likely to vary (Maynard, 2004; Nuckolls, 1993; Zukow, 1989). While future research needs to explore the reciprocal influences between sociocultural factors, sibling relationship quality, and psychosocial development, extant research highlights the importance of testing more complex models of family conditions that are related to individual differences in the quality of sibling relationships.

Sibling Relationships and Their Effects on Social and Emotional Development

The emotional intensity of the sibling relationship, and the amount of time that sisters and brothers spend with one another, make interactions between siblings a primary context for influencing social competencies and emotion socialization. The contribution of siblings may be direct, reflecting the quality of the sibling relationship. Alternatively, sibling influences may be indirect, reflecting one child's impact on its parents which subsequently influences the other sibling(s). Siblings growing up in the same family may have experiences that, in turn, make them very different from one another. Siblings also create different environments for one another, simply as a function of being there (Dunn & Plomin, 1990). Older siblings, for example, who attend to and respond positively to their younger preschool-aged siblings' emotions play a role in the younger siblings' developing emotion knowledge (e.g., understanding the causes of emotions and appropriate display rules) and prosocial responsiveness. This influence is moderated by the age of the younger sibling, the interval between siblings, and the gender of the older sibling (Sawyer et al., 2002). During middle childhood, the quality of the older sibling's caretaking (e.g., encouragement of autonomy, nurturance, and discipline) is related to the younger sibling's perspective taking and empathy (Bryant, 1989). Social understanding is promoted when siblings manage conflict between them (Dunn, Slomkowski, Donelan, & Herrera, 1995; Kramer & Conger, 2009). Thus, because younger siblings display more positive and negative affect during their interactions (as compared to during child–parent interaction (Dunn et al., 1996)), sibling relationships provide a context where children learn a great deal about emotions and appropriate social competencies.

Some research has suggested that siblings may have a stronger socializing influence than do parents or peers. Sibling relationship quality in middle childhood has been linked to positive peer relationships as well as overall adjustment in early adolescence (Stocker et al., 2002). Adolescents' positive sibling relationships are associated with positive self-worth, increased autonomy, and greater sociability and academic competence (Hetherington et al., 1999). Because they are closer in age, a sibling may help an adolescent to deal with or understand social problems (for example, with peers or first sexual relationships) in a way that a parent cannot. When experiencing stressful life events (such as separations, deaths, accidents, illnesses, marital or family problems), sibling affection moderates the association between the stressful event and internalizing symptoms, though it does not affect the link between stressful events and externalizing symptoms. The protective effect of sibling affection is independent of the quality of the parent–child relationship (Gass et al., 2007). Additionally, siblings may play an important distracting role, enabling children to shift their focus away from stress by engaging one another in alternative activities. Close relationships with sisters and brothers may reduce the negative effects of marital conflict and hostility on children's adjustment (Conger, Stocker, & McGuire, 2009; Deković & Buist, 2005). Thus, siblings may serve as attachment figures who are sought out for comfort and security when children are stressed.

Siblings view one another as sources of guidance and support for scholastic and social activities as well (Tucker, McHale, & Crouter, 2001). Sibling warmth promotes positive behavioral and emotional adaptation for children who are bullied by their peers. And a close relationship with a brother or sister can compensate for the negative consequences of not having a close friend (East & Rook, 1992). However, siblings may also influence one another in negative ways. Some research has indicated that positive sibling relationships, particularly within brother pairs where there is a delinquent or aggressive sibling, may be a risk factor for externalizing problems (Fagan & Najma, 2003; Rende, Slomkowski, Lloyd-Richardson, & Niaura, 2005). Moreover, siblings adopt similar problem behaviors (Slomkowski et al., 2001), such as early sexual behavior and pregnancy risk (East & Jacobson, 2001) as well as aggressive and delinquent behavior and drug use (Rowe, Rodgers, Meseck-Bushey, & St. John, 1989). In fact, even when controlling for other factors in adolescent siblings' shared environment, such as parent substance use and neighborhood risk, the older and younger adolescent siblings' attitudes about, and actual use of, substances are related (Pomery et al., 2005).

There are differences in the impact of sibling relationships on psychological adjustment, depending on whether the focus is on sibling warmth and support or on sibling conflict. Effects for sibling conflict on problem behavior appear to be stronger than for sibling warmth or differential treatment (Buist et al., 2013). Studies of sibling conflict indicate that when children fight with their siblings, or observe hostile behavior between their siblings, they learn negative behaviors that they may generalize to other contexts (Stauffacher & DeHart, 2006). Additionally, some studies have extended beyond the focus on normative samples. Research on aggressive children's sibling relationships has primarily focused on negative behaviors in the dyad. However, when positive behaviors, such as support and warmth, are examined as well, greater emotional control and social competence have been found in dyads where there are moderate levels of warmth and conflict. By contrast, more behavior problems and difficulties with peers are found when aggressive children's sibling relationships are characterized by conflict in the absence of support and warmth (Stormshak, Bellanti, & Bierman, 1996).

Thus, sibling relationship quality may have both positive and negative developmental outcomes (e.g., Deater-Deckard, Dunn, & Lussier, 2002; Gass et al., 2007; Modry-Mandell, Gamble, & Taylor, 2007). Positive sibling relationships may promote adjustment in general or they may moderate the impact of negative peer, parent, and family experiences on social and emotional adaptation. There may also be bidirectional influences of adjustment on sibling relationship quality such that positive adjustment facilitates higher quality interactions between siblings. Moreover, questions remain regarding the pathways through which sibling relationship dynamics affect developmental outcomes. It may be, for example, that skills learned in early sibling relationships, such as social perspective taking, emotion regulation, or internalizing positive working models of relationships, are directly transferred to later peer relationships or, alternatively, they may mediate the influence of sibling relationships on later adaptation.

There are also several potential processes that may be operating when there is negativity in early sibling relationships. Children may re-enact the negative interactions they have with their siblings outside of the family, thereby developing a coercive interaction style with their peers and in school settings (Patterson, 1986). Siblings who experience conflict in their relationship may also be more susceptible to peer pressure; they may, in turn, collude in deviant behaviors with peers as a result of talking about, engaging in, or imitating aggressive or antisocial activities associated with sibling deviancy training (Slomkowski et al., 2001; Snyder, Bank, & Burraston, 2005). Finally, sibling conflict may have evocative effects on parenting, exerting stress and disrupting the parents' ability to competently monitor and manage their children's relationships (Brody, 2003; Dishion, Nelson, & Bullock, 2004). Recent studies suggest the underlying mechanisms of bidirectional influences between parents and children may reflect environmental, genetic, and genotype-environmental interaction processes (Marceau et al., 2013). Consistent with this view, sibling conflict may both increase, and result from, parental negativity. Genetic effects of both parents and children may be implicated in determining and perpetuating negative sibling and parent–child interactions. Thus, there are multiple pathways through which sibling relationships may impact individual adaptation and family dynamics. This perspective highlights the need to explore reciprocal developmental influences both within and outside the family.

This broader theoretical framework has the potential to target intervention programs aimed at reducing sibling conflict and promoting positive sibling and family dynamics. Several intervention programs have been developed and used with young siblings (Stormshak, Bullock, & Falkenstein, 2009). For example, parent management training has been advocated for siblings who are at heightened risk for developing conduct disorders (Bank et al., 2004). The *More Fun with Sisters and Brothers* program has been used with 4- to 8-year-old sibling pairs and focuses on developing emotion regulation skills that are intended to reduce conflict and enhance prosocial relationships (Kennedy & Kramer, 2008). Parents have been taught to mediate conflicts between their children; helping siblings in middle childhood to recognize and resolve their problems leads to more compromise and less conflict in their relationship (Smith & Ross, 2007). And the *Siblings are Special* program has been used to teach fifth graders and their younger siblings emotion regulation and problem-solving skills. Building on the idea that negative sibling relationship experiences may be a risk factor for adjustment problems in adolescence, the interventions are focused on enhancing the sibling relationship (Feinberg, Sakuma, Hostetler, & McHale, 2013). By encouraging sibling pairs to engage in constructive activities together, as well as with their parents, enhanced closeness and decreased conflict is expected to lead to more positive relationships with peers and fewer problems with substance use and in school (Feinberg, Solmeyer, & McHale, 2012). Including parents in monitoring sibling interactions, and educating them regarding the ways in which sibling relationships may be a training ground for deviant behavior, are also anticipated to encourage techniques for reducing sibling conflict and parental stress and for promoting family warmth. Thus, deepening our understanding of the causal processes whereby siblings influence, and are influenced by, one another and their family dynamics will continue to contribute to future prevention and intervention efforts.

Sibling Relationships and Friendships

Do children's early social experiences with siblings generalize directly to relationships with their close friends? Attachment theorists predict causal links between early attachment security and children's relationships with siblings and close friendships (Berlin et al., 2008). The expectation is that early experiences in parent–child relationships become organized in internal models of attachment relationships. These models then guide children's behavior in, and expectations for, their relationships with siblings and friends with whom they maintain close affectional bonds (as compared to peers and nonfriends). Additionally, the emotional significance, intensity, and closeness of sibling relationships provides an arena for children to develop and practice relationship skills that may be the same competencies needed to form close friendships. Friends are similar to siblings in that relationships with close friends are intense and significant; there is also affection, sharing, and reciprocity between siblings and close friends. Therefore, positive associations are expected across these relational systems and the quality of sibling relationships and friendships should be similar.

However, there are also many reasons as to why significant differences between friendships and sibling relationships might be expected as well. Friends and siblings differ in their commitment to and trust in one another, friends are chosen whereas siblings are not, and siblings are inherently more competitive as they are required to share parental love and attention. Whether sibling relationships and friendships are evaluated using measures of specific and discrete interactive behaviors, or more general assessments of overall relationship quality, may impact the associations as well. Siblings are usually studied in the home (a context where they may be more likely to display a range of positive and negative emotions and behaviors) whereas friends are studied outside of the home, often in school settings with different expectations and demands (Cutting & Dunn, 2006). Thus, when questions about the similarities and/or differences across sibling relationships and friendships are explored, these inherent distinctions in the relationships themselves, as well as in the methods used to evaluate them, need to be considered.

There is some evidence supporting the idea that there is a direct "carryover" effect across relationships. For example, young children do learn, from engaging in cooperative and pretend play with their siblings, the skills necessary for prosocial understanding (Dunn, 1999). And social competencies developed in early sibling relationships may lay the foundation for subsequent relationships with friends (McCoy, Brody, & Stoneman, 2002). However, there is a substantial body of research demonstrating a lack of association between particular aspects of sibling relationships and friendships in childhood (Abramovitch, Corter, Pepler, & Stanhope, 1986; Mendelson, Aboud, & Lanthier, 1994). Differences between siblings and friends have been found in conflict, cooperation, shared pretend play, and features of communication (Cutting & Dunn, 2006; Stocker & Dunn, 1990). Interestingly, even within the same study, both positive and negative associations have been found (e.g., Updegraff & Obeidallah, 1999; Volling, Youngblade, & Belsky, 1997).

When differences are identified in the quality of children's relationships with siblings and friends, they appear to be influenced by other factors, such as age, birth order, and sibling gender (Dunn, 1993, 2004). Familial variables, such as inconsistent parental discipline and low parental monitoring, together with negative sibling behaviors during childhood, have been found to contribute to poor relationships and antisocial behavior as well as to academic difficulties, depression, anxiety, and phobias in adolescence (Bank et al., 1996). Additionally, particular qualities of sibling relationships (warmth and conflict) mediate between aspects of the family environment (such as marital conflict and the quality of each siblings' relationships with parents) assessed in childhood and the quality of best friendships evaluated in early adolescence (McCoy, Brody, & Stoneman, 1994). The role of self-esteem in influencing sibling relationships and friendships has also been considered. Adolescents who report more warmth and low conflict both in sibling relationships and in friendships also report the highest levels of self-esteem and lowest levels of loneliness. That is, high-quality relationships with both siblings and friends that are warm and supportive are associated with more positive feelings about the self. Higher self-esteem, in turn, may enhance social competence across relational domains (Sherman, Lansford, & Volling, 2006). The influence of sibling relationship quality on later adaptation may also be mediated by friendship quality and self-esteem considered together (Feinberg et al., 2012). In sum, it appears that more complex linkages across sibling relationships and close friendships have been found. Consideration of the processes and mechanisms that influence these associations, using more sophisticated analytic models, is an important direction for future research.

There are also studies that have explored bidirectional influences, assuming that not only do sibling relationships influence friendships but relationships with friends also have an impact on the quality of sibling relationships (Kramer & Gottman, 1992; Kramer & Kowal, 2005). It has been found, for example, that adaptation to the birth of a new sibling is facilitated by positive relationships with friends. Four-year-old children behave more positively toward a new sibling (assessed when the new sibling was 6 and 14 months) when the older sibling has a more positive interaction style with a best friend and is better able to manage negative affect and conflict in the relationship with the best friend (Kramer & Gottman, 1992). It is likely that interpersonal competence is enhanced by firstborn children's interactions with a best friend; this competence then impacts the emerging sibling relationship. In early and middle childhood, friends continue to provide social support and help children learn important social competencies (Berndt & Perry, 1986; Parker & Asher, 1993). Thus, friendships may remain important in shaping the developing sibling relationship throughout childhood. These results have practical implications for parents, as it may be that fostering early social and emotional competencies encourages the kinds of prosocial interactions with friends that, in turn, lead to more positive sibling relationships.

When facing the challenges inherent in negotiating sibling relationships, children who have developed friendships are likely to respond more effectively. Friends have closer connections than do peers, thus accounting for the even stronger linkages that have been reported between relationships with friends (as opposed to with peers) and siblings (Stocker & Dunn, 1990). The associations between sibling relationships and friendship may vary across development and depend, to some extent, upon sibling gender composition (Conger et al., 2004). Continuity has also been found in the link between early and later friendships and between early friendship quality and less negative sibling relationships in adolescence as well (Kramer & Kowal, 2005). Thus, early friendships may establish positive representations, or "working models" (Howes, 1996), on which children draw, which may contribute to the link between early and later friendships as well (Dunn, Cutting, & Fisher, 2002).

A relationship perspective to developmental outcomes may be especially meaningful, particularly when considering interactional processes and competencies across relational partners. Relationships with brothers and sisters are unique in that they incorporate complementary (hierarchical, such as caretaking and teaching) and reciprocal (equal, such as sharing and playing) qualities (Dunn, 1983). Reciprocal interactions between siblings are comparable to their interactions with friends. When children interact with friends, they develop and practice some of the interpersonal skills that are necessary for their interactions with brothers and sisters. For example, they may learn more about managing conflict in their interactions with friends than when in direct interaction with their parents; they can then bring this learning to their sibling interactions. Additionally, unlike hierarchical parent–child interactions, where sensitive parents attempt to modify their behavior to accommodate to their children's needs and emotional states, friends may be limited in their capacity to make these adjustments. When interacting with friends, therefore, children need to work harder to justify their needs or express their feelings within these relationships (Kramer & Gottman, 1992). Once they learn these skills, children can then bring these competencies to their interactions with their younger or older siblings. Again we see the importance of dynamic influences across relational partners.

Additionally, some research has even documented that when other social relationships are problematic, sibling relationships may play a compensatory role in providing gratifying alternatives. For example, having at least one positive relationship (with a sibling, mother, or friend) plays a role in protecting children from developing conduct problems (McElwain & Volling, 2005; Stocker, 1994). And positive relationships with a favorite sibling protect socially isolated children from developing adjustment difficulties (East & Rook, 1992). These findings justify and support the implementation of intervention programs geared toward improving sibling relationship quality. Social skills training programs with 4- to 6-year-olds have been found to be effective in enhancing positive, and decreasing negative, relationships that older children have with their younger siblings (Kramer, 2004). Four- to eight-year-old children who are involved in learning more adaptive emotion regulation skills also show improved sibling relationship quality (Kennedy & Kramer, 2008). These interventions may have a positive impact in promoting skills, such as perspective taking, conflict management, and self-control, that may ultimately improve children's relationships not only with siblings but also with close friends.

Interestingly, by adolescence, sibling support does not compensate for low support from friends (Sherman et al., 2006; van Aken & Asendorpf, 1997). Rather, the linkages among parent–child and sibling relationships and friendships now appear to be more complex. Perceptions of the quality of their relationships with their parents have been found to influence adolescents' ratings of the quality of their relationships with their siblings that, in turn, influence their peer relationships (MacKinnon-Lewis, Starnes, Volling, & Johnson, 1997). Some research has attempted to identify the mechanisms underlying these causal connections between sibling relationships and friendships in adolescence. For example, high-quality sibling relationships in early adolescence have been found to impact the quality of friendships and self-esteem one year later (though early friendship quality does not predict as strongly to sibling relationship quality one year later). There is also a bidirectional relationship between positive sibling relationships and higher self-esteem. Adolescents with better sibling relationships are also less depressed, less lonely, and engage in less delinquent behavior two years after the initial assessment (Yeh & Lempers, 2004). Therefore, early sibling relationships may affect later adjustment indirectly by promoting more positive friendships and higher self-esteem. The testing of these more sophisticated longitudinal predictive models will continue to enhance our understanding of the linkages between relational systems.

In summary, research to date has explored the ways in which sibling experiences are useful in providing children with the skills that they may bring to other relationships. Most of this research examines associations between specific positive or negative aspects of sibling relationships and friendships. Thus, for example, conflict in relationships with siblings and friends is not associated (Cutting & Dunn, 2006; East & Rook, 1992; Mendelson et al., 1994; Stocker & Dunn, 1990) whereas prosocial interactions with friends and siblings are related (Kramer & Kowel, 2005). Rather than expecting consistency in discrete behaviors, it may be more meaningful to assess the overall quality of these relationships. Future work should explore the organization of sibling behaviors within the dyad (e.g., Kramer, 2010; Rosen, 2015; Sherman et al., 2006) and their significance for developing better quality friendships.

Extant research on sibling relationship quality and association to friendships has resulted in two divergent views: either harmonious sibling relationships serve a protective role in buffering against later relational problems and deviant behaviors or, alternatively, poor sibling relationships are a potential training ground for interactional difficulties and interfere with establishing healthy relationships. The quality of each of these relationships may be related to some developmental outcomes more than others and the predictive associations may vary across developmental periods. Exploring the processes underlying these associations is critical. Understanding the compensatory role that siblings and friends may play in promoting social and emotional adaptation, at different points in development, is another important direction for future research. Ultimately, appreciating the significance of sibling relationships may have practical implications for parents and clinicians interested in improving children's emotional competencies and relational skills.

Now, What About Only Children?

There are generations of happy, productive, socially competent only children who challenge the notion, originally perpetuated by psychoanalytic writers and thinkers, that having siblings is an essential key to a successful life (Kluger, 2011). Historically, however, there has been a long-standing prejudice against only children (Brill, 1922; Fenton, 1928) and a general impression that only children tend to be self-centered, dependent, and demanding, to lack self-control, and to be generally anxious, unhappy, and spoiled (Falbo & Polit, 1986; Thompson, 1974). Based on his study with a very small sample of only children, the pioneering psychologist G. Stanley Hall concluded, in 1898 (as reported by Fenton, 1928), that "being an only child is a disease in itself" (p. 547). His negative view perpetuated a more general perspective that still prevails today, suggesting that only children are spoiled and lonely (Roberts & Blanton, 2001), and a belief that parents of only children overprotect and overindulge them, thereby contributing to their general unhappiness, selfishness, and isolation (Veenhoven & Verkuyten, 1989).

Spending one's childhood being doted on by adoring parents is thought to result in poor social skills, narcissism, and inflexibility. Indeed, relative to children with siblings, only children tend to be more aggressive and victimized in their peer group, and less well liked by classmates, which may result from the lack of experience managing conflict with siblings at home (Kitzmann, Cohen, & Lockwood, 2002). The negative stereotypes about only children are quite persistent and appear to be prevalent across cultural groups, as demonstrated by research in Korea (Doh & Falbo, 1999), the Netherlands (Veenhoven & Verkuyten, 1989), China (Falbo & Poston, 1993), and Great Britain (Laybourn, 1990). Moreover, information about birth order has been found to influence perceptions of one's own and others' personalities (Herrera, Zajonc, Wieczorkowska, & Cichomski, 2003; Nyman, 1995) and even to impact clinicians' initial impressions of hypothetical clients (Stewart, 2004). Thus, the potency of negative stereotypes of only children prevail despite empirical attempts to explore the validity of these claims (see, for example, Mancillas, 2006).

From the 1920s to the 1980s, there were more than 200 empirical papers that attempted to document the challenges and consequences of growing up without brothers and sisters (Falbo & Polit, 1986). Some of these papers yielded findings indicating there were no differences between only children and children with siblings, while others revealed clear developmental consequences for children with no brothers or sisters. Many researchers have argued that exploring birth order is an unnecessary waste of effort and time (Ernst & Angst, 1983), that variations in methodologies and a lack of a guiding theoretical framework make it challenging to interpret the results (Polit & Falbo, 1987; Sulloway, 1996), and that variations in demographics of research participants make it impossible to draw meaningful conclusions (Falbo & Poston, 1993). Recent research, incorporating better methodology, has resulted in more reliable and valid findings. There appear to be many positive consequences for only children who, for example, seem to benefit from having the undivided attention of their parents and, in turn, to perform as well, if not better than, children with siblings on measures of cognitive and social functioning. Only children, for example, score higher on intelligence tests and on measures of achievement motivation than do later-born children. As adults, they also finish more years of education and achieve positions of higher status (Falbo & Poston, 1993; Herrera et al., 2003; Mellor, 1990; Polit & Falbo, 1987; Travis & Kohli, 1995).

However, the exclusive attention from their parents may also be experienced by only children as pressure to achieve, with parental expectations and family responsibility focused only on their one child. These pressures are even more intense in China, where the one-child policy was introduced nearly 35 years ago although it has been inconsistently applied. For example, enforcement of this policy has been less strict in rural areas and wealthier families have found ways of "buying" the privilege of having more than one child, leading to a class divide in family size. Additionally, the financial and employment incentives that were intended to restrict family size to one child led to a huge number of Chinese babies who were abandoned and subsequently adopted overseas, or the selective abortion of girls, as boys were considered essential to carrying on the family name and more likely to guarantee family status and wealth (Kluger, 2011). The consequence is a huge disparity in gender balance and the emergence of a generation of (especially male) Chinese children who are at risk of extreme entitlement and concurrently bear the huge burden of achieving success. And still, there are mixed results about the outcomes for only children in China, with many studies finding higher academic achievement in only children but fewer consistent differences in personality between only children and children with siblings (Falbo & Poston, 1993).

Unfortunately, much of the extant research on only children has not been guided by a coherent theoretical framework. Many studies have compared outcomes for only children and children with siblings and then attempted to offer an explanation for observed similarities or differences. Varying interpretive lenses have been used to account for the findings. For example, disadvantages for only children are explained in terms of sibling deprivation (e.g., Belmont, Wittes, & Stein, 1977). Thus, lower levels of intelligence or problems in interpersonal communication, identity formation, or autonomy development in only children have been explained based on the notion that only children are deprived of siblings who could provide critical learning experiences for one another. Alternatively, advantages are often accounted for by the distinct, unique aspects of being the only child (e.g., Adler, 1964). Therefore, studies that find only children to be more autonomous, to assume leadership positions, or to be more mature and cooperative cite the uniqueness of the only child and the critical ways in which only children are different from first- and last-borns (Falbo & Polit, 1986).

The parent–child relationship is also viewed as an important explanatory mechanism in accounting for developmental outcomes in only children. Questions have been raised, such as whether only children are more mature and cooperative since they spend more time with adults (Falbo & Cooper, 1980) or whether they are at greater risk of maladjustment due to excessive involvement by parents who indulge them or expect too much from their only child (Polit & Falbo, 1987). Parents are presumed to influence developmental outcomes for only children, just as they do for firstborns, in that first-time parents are more anxious, have less experience parenting, and pay more attention to their children (Falbo & Cooper, 1980). But exclusive attention from parents may cause firstborn and only children to be more selfish and dependent as well as to be more achievement-oriented and mature (though the status of firstborns shifts when they are "dethroned" with the arrival of a sibling).

Parents with only one child tend to be more anxious; this may, in turn, influence their childrearing practices. They often expect their only child to maintain their same core values and beliefs and to be just like them. Unlike in a larger family, where there is room to accommodate varying roles, attitudes, and developmental trajectories, in families with only one child, widely divergent opinions, ideas, and traits are considered less tolerable and, in extreme cases, unacceptable. The intense scrutiny, and the sense that they need to fulfill the parents' hope to "do it right," makes many only children internalize an enormous pressure either to conform or to diverge only to the outer limits of what parents can tolerate (Sandler, 2013). Indeed, without other siblings to help mitigate the impact of parental expectations, or to serve as confidants in managing the strains of adolescence and/or changes in familial circumstances (e.g., parental unemployment), only children feel especially vulnerable and experience their relationships with their parents as particularly intense (Roberts & Blanton, 2001; Veenhoven & Verkuyten, 1989).

One consistent challenge that only children appear to face is the concern about their aging parents and the role they will play as their sole caregiver (Roberts & Blanton, 2001). Additionally, worries prevail about providing their parents with grandchildren, about parenting their own child(ren), and about how to divide time and attention between several children (if they choose to have more than one child) (Mancillas, 2006). Finally, parents of only children lack the experience that may influence their expectations, for example, regarding developmental milestones. Placing high standards on their children may heighten achievement motivation which, in turn, could lead to greater achievement in only children (and firstborns). However, parents of only children may also realize that because their child is the only one they will have, they need to develop and maintain a more positive relationship.

This positive relationship may, in turn, help to diminish the potential negative consequences of high parental expectations, thereby promoting their child to develop a more positive self-image and high achievement motivation.

A meta-analysis of 115 studies comparing children with siblings to only children found that developmental outcomes do not differ, only children are not at a disadvantage relative to children with siblings, and a more positive relationship with their parents appears to contribute to more positive developmental outcomes in only children. While many worry that only children will be more lonely children, the meta-analysis revealed that on self-report measures and in the perceptions of others, only children were no different on measures of loneliness (Falbo & Polit, 1986). Indeed, only children learn to companion themselves, to value their time alone, and to be more independent and self-sufficient (Pickhardt, 2008). Moreover, several studies have explored the outcomes of only children as adults and found that their social skills and overall social competence are no different from that of adults from larger families (Glenn & Hoppe, 1984; Polit, Nuttall, & Nuttall, 1980). Additionally, in interviews documenting the subjective experiences of young adults who are only children, many reported being appreciative of the parental resources and attention they received and of the close relationships they had with their parents. They valued their time alone and the creativity it fostered. They felt they were more mature than their peers and therefore better able to connect with adults (Roberts & Blanton, 2001). While these reports may be biased by current adaptation and/or a need to validate their only child status, extant empirical evidence indicates that only children are similar in many important ways to their peers with siblings and appears to contradict the negative stereotypes about only children.

There are, however, several intervening variables that need to be considered because of the role they may play in determining developmental outcomes for both only children and children with siblings. Economic and maturational differences among parents of only born, firstborn, and later-born children may influence outcomes. The quality of the marital relationship, and parental encouragement of separation and autonomy for only children and for children with siblings, also need to be considered. Moreover, outcomes may vary depending on the age and developmental period explored. For example, the experience of being an only child may be wonderful for newborns and infants (who know nothing other than their only child status) but change when social comparison processes lead to an awareness of relative sibling status with all its concomitant effects. It may also change when external academic and social demands invoke parental pressures and necessitate adaptations, when normal developmental transitions (e.g., beginning school or leaving for college) are negotiated, and when unexpected challenges (e.g., dealing with parental separation or divorce or caring for a sick or aging parent) present themselves. Comparing the outcomes of only children and children with siblings may also vary, depending on whether the comparison group is firstborns, later-borns and/or last-borns. Firstborns and only children may be more similar when it comes to the expectations that new parents have for their infants and toddlers, whereas only children may be more similar to last-borns in adolescence since they share the position of being the last (or only) child to separate and leave home.

A further examination of the personality characteristics of only children indicates that only children do not differ from children with siblings in their personality or social skills. Their experiences in intense interaction with their parents may compensate for the lack of sibling experiences thought to contribute, in particular, to the development of those skills that lead to successful interpersonal interactions (Polit & Falbo, 1987). And just as interactions with parents may "compensate" for the lack of siblings in only children, the availability of sisters and brothers may "compensate" for the lack of an exclusive relationship with their parents in children with siblings. In turn, only children and children with siblings are similar in terms of a range of personality characteristics. Thus, rather than viewing only child status as something negative for which the child needs to "compensate," it may be more fruitful to consider the special advantages of being an only child *or* a child with siblings.

Finally, there is a burgeoning literature on the many political and economic issues related to the family and parenting, including important books by Crittenden (2010), Folbre (2010), Last (2014), and McKibben (1999). These authors highlight the changing demographics of families and the economic, social, ethical, and personal issues that are deeply entwined in the choice to parent and in decisions regarding family size. Certainly, the more that researchers examine questions about parenting and families using reliable and valid methods, and continue to challenge the negative views and stereotypes about only children, the more that parents, educators, health professionals, and policy makers can make informed decisions about children and their families.

Peer Relations and Friendship During Childhood

4

As children's social worlds expand, so too do the network of connections that they make. While attachments to parents and sibling relationships continue to be important during childhood, they also lay the groundwork for interactions with peers. In this chapter, we will consider the special nature of peer relationships and their implications for children's social development. Developmental patterns in peer interactions and emerging friendships during childhood will be explored. Changes in children's conceptions of friendships, and the factors that influence friendship choices, will be examined. Current research will be reviewed that investigates the role that friendships play in young children's lives, the factors that influence their quality, and the social and emotional consequences of peer relationships and close friendships. Particular topics, such as the possible costs of friendship, especially for children with behavioral problems, and the painful experience of peer rejection and loneliness, will be considered. The integrated social worlds of children will be examined, with a particular focus on the connection between relationships with parents, peers, and friends. Some of the factors that may impact these associations between relational systems will be explored. Gender differences, and the clinical implications of this research, will also be discussed. Taken together, these issues illustrate the interrelated themes of attachment and separation, as connections, or lack of connections, to others during childhood both reflect and impact feelings about the self.

But first, let's consider some illustrative examples of the kinds of relationships we might see developing between young children.

Lauren and Rebecca met soon after they were born. Their mothers were very close friends so, as babies, they spent hours together even before they could speak. The evolving friendship between the young girls was born of a profound connection similar to, yet distinct from, what is seen between siblings. Sharing time and activities, companionship, affection, and understanding, these friends were forever linked by their invisible bond lovingly forged in early infancy. They found strength and comfort

161

in their friendship. When in new settings, they maintained an openness to developing relationships with other children. Still, their preference was to be together, supporting each other's interests, sharing confidences and worries, and feeling secure in their deep and enduring connection.

Michael and Zachary met on the first day of kindergarten. Similar in temperament and intellectual abilities, they were both quite athletic and musical. They chose to sit together, ate lunch together, partnered with one another in class and on the playing field, and though they shared free time and play with other peers, they ultimately turned to each other whenever they could. They both had an endearing sense of humor and a capacity to intensely involve themselves, with focus, curiosity, and enthusiasm, in their school work and play. Outside of school, they happily spent hours together, and whether they were cooperating and sharing or resolving minor disagreements between them, their commitment to their friendship prevailed.

Sara and Marissa were 10-years-old when they first met each other at a summer camp program. They each had a close circle of friends in their respective schools; their special contact was during the precious eight weeks they spent together at their overnight camp. Their families lived far apart, so phone calls, text messages, and e-mail exchanges allowed them to continue to stay connected over long periods of separation. Occasional visits during school breaks were long anticipated and time together was spent in nonstop conversations and sharing of confidences. They were each the oldest children in their families, relatively mature in their social-cognitive understanding, and responsive and sensitive to their younger siblings. They knew each other so well they could finish each other's sentences and respect the other's personal preferences and moods. They learned to resolve their differences fairly and defended one another in the face of any conflict with their peers.

As we think about these early friendships, we are provided with a window into the thoughts and feelings, the minds and hearts, that connect close friends, regardless of the age at which they met or the other connections they share. We see loyalty and commitment, shared understanding, security, and deep care. When conflicts arise, they are talked about; when disagreements inevitably occur, they are worked through. There are many factors that might account for how these relationships evolve. We have already considered early attachment relationships and the roots of the developing self in infancy and childhood. The quality of early relationships, the child's temperamental characteristics, aspects of the child's developing emotional competence, and conceptions of and feelings about the self may all influence children's emerging relationships with friends. Moreover, the presence of siblings, and the quality of sibling relationships, may impact peer interactions and friendships as well. We will consider, in this chapter, the influence of early attachment relationships on peer relationships and friendships. Then, in the next chapter, we will explore developing aspects of the self that also have their roots in early relationships and continue to enrich relationships and elaborate evolving conceptions of the self.

What Makes Peer Relationships a Unique Context For Studying Social, Emotional, and Cognitive Development?

There are several reasons as to why studying the peer group is essential to our understanding of individual development (cf. Bukowski, Buhrmester, & Underwood, 2011). First, because they spend so much time together, peers provide innumerable opportunities for play and social learning. Through playful exchanges and ongoing interactions over time, peers offer rewards (or punishments) for the specific behaviors and emotional reactions deemed acceptable (or prohibited) by the larger peer group. Second, the social world of peers is quite distinct from the world of adults. Peers become role models for one another, offering opportunities for the imitation of desirable (e.g., altruism) or undesirable (e.g., aggression) behaviors. Piaget (1932) believed that by sharing experiences and equal status, peers offer one another a critical context for discussing disparate views, negotiating ideas, and engaging in conflict resolution, all essential to understanding the thoughts, affective states, and intentions of others. For Piaget, this "co-construction" of ideas that emerge from these shared experiences with peers is critical since peer interactions, relative to interactions with adults, are more egalitarian and less hierarchically structured. Vygotsky (1978) also argued that when children resolve problems together through cooperation, they capitalize on each other's areas of strength and stimulate cognitive development. And Sullivan (1953) suggested that opportunities for learning about the self and others are enhanced when children interact, as peers offer a context for self-validation and a perspective on how children are perceived. Third, the experience of not having any friends places children at risk for various adjustment problems throughout childhood, adolescence, and adulthood (Bagwell, Newcomb, & Bukowski, 1998). And fourth, numerous studies have provided evidence supporting the idea that problems with peers (e.g., peer rejection) in childhood and adolescence are associated with behavioral difficulties, ranging from internalizing problems such as low self-esteem, loneliness, and depression (Ladd & Troop-Gordon, 2003; Sandstrom, Villessen, & Eisenhower, 2003) to externalizing problems including attentional difficulties, conduct disorder, substance abuse, and antisocial behavior (Boivin, Vitaro, & Poulin, 2005; Kupersmidt & Coie, 1990).

Developmental Changes in Peer Interactions

When we consider children's interactions with peers, there are profound developmental differences that we can observe across a relatively short time period from infancy through late childhood. Infants, for example, are quite limited in their abilities to initiate and sustain interactions. Still, they are able to engage in socially directed behaviors toward their peers. Even 2-month-old infants can be aroused by the presence of their peers and engage in mutual gaze (Eckerman, 1979). During the first 6 months of life, infants have also been observed as they smile, reach out, and vocalize toward their peers (Fogel, 1979). And during the second half of the first year, directed looks, smiles, and vocalizations are more common, as are similar gestures in response to the looks and vocalizations of peers (Hay, Pederson, & Nash, 1982). Infants reach out and touch each other, usually in "friendly" ways, though sometimes they may also hit or push one another (Hay, Castle, & Davies, 2000). These socially oriented behaviors increase dramatically over the first year of life. Infants not only initiate these behaviors but they also increasingly respond to social overtures, particularly as they approach their first birthdays (Jacobson, 1981). While often conceptualized as imitative acts, focused on the use of objects (Mueller & Silverman, 1989), these behaviors represent the first examples of infants' shared meaning, an important precursor to later cooperative play. Still, these exchanges tend to be brief, infrequent, and unpredictable.

It is not until the second year of life that we begin to see significant changes in the toddlers' repertoire of social skills (Brownell & Kopp, 2007). Advances in motor, cognitive, and linguistic skills lead to social exchanges that become increasingly complex and lengthy (Adolph & Berger, 2010; Dunn, 1993, 2005; MacWhinney, 2010; Ross & Conant, 1992; Rubin, Bukowski, & Parker, 2006). Now, toddlers engage in more coordinated interactive sequences that may take the form of playful games. With the emergence of turn-taking sequences (Howes, 1988; Ross, Lollis, & Elliot, 1982; Warneken, Chen, & Tomasello, 2006), these games often involve reciprocal imitation, give-and-take, and reversal of roles in play. Positive social interactions are accompanied by smiles and laughter (Mueller & Brenner, 1977), with increases in shared positive affect (Denham, McKinley, Couchoud, & Holt, 1990). And toddlers increasingly show a preference for interaction with peers rather than with adults (Eckerman, Whatley, & Kutz, 1975).

During the late toddler and early preschool period, the most important social advance is the ability for children to share meaning in playful exchanges (Howes & Matheson, 1992; Mueller, 1989). Children now take on complementary roles as they play with each other. And their developing language skills contribute significantly to their social competence as well. For example, now one child may declare that she wants to be the "mommy" to the baby doll until the other says "It's my turn now!" and takes the doll into her arms. These children communicate the shared understanding of their imaginary roles as the first child who has relinquished the "baby" now gets the doll-sized stroller for the second "mommy" to use. The ability to share meaning during pretense, or what has been called intersubjectivity (Trevarthen, 1979), allows children to play a broader range of pretend games. Advances in the intersubjectivity of social exchanges occur between 3 and 4½ years of age (Goncu, 1993), leading to greater coordination of roles and rules in longer periods of pretend play.

Pretend play allows children to take on the roles of others and to experience their feelings in a playful context. When engaged in pretend play, children need to coordinate their activities with other children and to collaborate as part of a social group. Therefore, pretend play is critical to the development of social competence in early childhood. It usually begins when the child is in interaction with a parent or older sibling, but peers become more common partners as children have more opportunities to meet and interact with other children (Dunn, 1988; Haight & Miller, 1993). More importantly, the quality of pretend play shifts with age. At 3 years, though pretense may be complex and dramatic, all children may want to take on a particular self-defined role (e.g., Daddy, Mommy, Doctor, Batman) and have difficulty waiting their turn if someone else claims that same role. By 4 years, children can accept taking on another role assigned to them, knowing that they will have their turn later to take on the more "desired" role. Five-year-olds engage in more elaborate, prolonged pretend games where they dress up and act out complex scenes, staging weddings, doctors' offices, classrooms, dangerous rescues, or slow-motion gang fights.

These pretend activities take on new meaning with development but children continue to engage in a variety of play activities. Six social participation categories have been identified to describe children's pretend play; these categories follow a particular developmental course over time (Parten, 1932). Specifically, prior to age 3 years, children spend much of their time in unoccupied behavior, solitary play, onlooker behavior (observing but not participating in another's activity), or parallel play (playing in similar activities without engaging one another). Between the ages of 3 and 5 years, children engage in fewer bouts of these types of play and instead engage in more frequent associative play (playing and sharing with others) and cooperative play (where children share a common goal). Subsequent research suggests that children do not replace one type of play activity for another; rather, they still spend time in all types of play activities. The major developmental change that occurs in the play of preschoolers seems to be not in the type of activity but rather in the cognitive maturity of these activities (Rubin, Watson, & Jambor, 1978). Even at 5 years of age, children spend a considerable amount of time alone or near others, playing in solitary or parallel activities, when at school or on the playground. But the quality of these solitary and parallel interactions, as well as of group activities, differs depending on the child's social and cognitive maturation. For example, associative games with rules are played more frequently as children grow in their understanding of the meaning of these rules.

In addition to the shifts in observed forms of interaction, there are also qualitative differences in the meaning of their interactions. Preschoolers engage in both prosocial (helping and sharing) and aggressive social exchanges. From toddlerhood through the preschool and middle childhood years, there are significant advances in social-cognitive and affective perspective-taking abilities (Paulus, 2014). It is this more advanced social understanding that likely leads to increases in helping and sharing behaviors (Benenson, Markovits,

Roy, & Denko, 2003; Eisenberg, Fabes, & Spinrad, 2006; Warneken, 2015) and to more frequent cooperative play with children working together toward a common goal (Brownell, Ramani, & Zerwas, 2006). Indeed, preschool children who are more cooperative and helpful with their peers are rated as more likable and popular (Howes et al., 1998; Slaughter, Dennis, & Pritchard, 2002).

However, early peer play is not only positive and cooperative. There are often highly arousing and emotional interchanges between preschoolers. Disputes over toys may lead to physical and verbal aggression. In fact, aggression is at its peak during this period of development (Campbell, 2002). The emerging ability to regulate behavior and emotions (both positive and negative) appears to be critical for competent interaction with peers. It is during the preschool period that we begin to see the roots of emotional and behavioral regulation in social interactions, as well as the emotional and social problems associated with dysregulation. For example, preschool aged children begin to understand and appreciate the fact that other people have thoughts, feelings, and intentions that may be different from their own (Izard, 2009). This may require that children delay the gratification of their own needs or talk about and coordinate their own and their peers' varying needs and goals, which ultimately helps them to negotiate differences, achieve social goals, and resolve interpersonal conflicts (Rubin & Rose-Krasnor, 1992). Children continue to become more skilled in establishing shared meaning with their peers (Goldstein, Kaczmarek, & English, 2002); a more sophisticated understanding of how others think and feel promotes the early development of empathy during the preschool years. Some researchers have suggested it may be the continued development of empathic responsiveness that, in turn, leads to more prosocial and altruistic behavior in peer interactions (Vaish et al., 2009). The increased understanding of others' motives and intentions also impacts children's negative social interactions. While instrumental aggression, or fights over objects and toys, decreases from toddlerhood into the preschool years (NICHD Early Child Care Research Network, 2001), social and relational aggression increases. Now, preschoolers begin to understand that their words can hurt others and can communicate hostile intent.

A major shift that occurs when children enter school is that they decrease the frequency of their social interactions with adults while they increase further their social exchanges with other children. By contrast to the vertical or hierarchical nature of parent–child relationships, peer relationships are more *horizontal* in that they are more even and balanced. Accordingly, peers are central for developing notions of fairness and equality. Interactions with peers shift in quality as generosity and helpfulness increase and physical aggression decreases (Eisenberg, Fabes, et al., 2006). In middle childhood, there is a greater concern about fitting in and being accepted by peers and particular friends begin to assume special status. Children are more likely to enjoy being with their friends and to ascribe positive characteristics to their playful exchanges with their friends. Relative to interactions with nonfriends, children show more emotional intensity, affective reciprocity, and increased levels of emotional understanding when interacting with their friends (Newcomb & Bagwell, 1995). Now, friends are more likely to resolve conflicts in ways that preserve their friendship and promote its continuity (Laursen, Finkelstein, & Townsend Betts, 2001).

The peer group serves several important functions during childhood. Peers continue to provide information, offering valuable perspectives on acceptable social norms and popular culture. During middle and later childhood, comparisons with peers offer direct and indirect feedback that informs children's behaviors and attitudes. The peer group provides a critical context for learning social skills, such as compromise, cooperation, and conflict resolution, as well as social-cognitive skills, such as perspective taking. Finally, identification with the peer group helps children to feel accepted and to establish aspects of their own identity as well.

Developing Friendships in Childhood

Establishing close friendships with specific peers during childhood is a major developmental task. The mutual, close, and affectionate ties between friends evolve out of, and have important implications for, each individual's emotional security and comfort. Making and keeping friends is a significant endeavor that has consequences extending far beyond childhood into adolescence and emerging adulthood. The factors that contribute to the formation and maintenance of friendships vary with development. The psychological meaning of friendships also changes over time. We will come to see that friendships are essential, at each developmental stage, not only to children's sense of connection to others but also to their growing sense of self. Early friendships lay an important foundation for friendships across differing developmental periods (Ladd, 2005) and the capacity to form friendships in early childhood relates to later positive adjustment (Hay, Payne, & Chadwick, 2004).

Friendships provide children with reassurance, opportunities for intimacy and self-disclosure, validation of the self, support and guidance, and self-esteem enhancement. Friendships influence children's goals, attitudes, and behaviors through processes such as providing direct examples, modeling, and peer pressure (Berndt & Murphy, 2002). They also serve as models for later intimate and parental relationships (Newcomb & Bagwell, 1995; Sullivan, 1953). Friends offer children a safe place from which they may explore the effects of their behaviors on their peers and on the larger social world (Rubin, Coplan, Chen, Bowker, & McDonald, 2011). And as children continue to define their personal identities, friends provide essential feedback and support. Thus, friendships are not unlike attachment figures, serving several important functions (though the specific functions they serve are quite distinct from those of primary attachment figures); moreover, these functions change at different points in development. And when friendships are missing, as is the case with children who are rejected or lonely, there are profound consequences for the child's sense of self and capacity to connect to others in the future.

What is it that is so unique about friendships and distinguishes them from peer relationships? Friendships extend beyond how well a child is accepted by his or her peers. That is, a child may be largely accepted by classmates but not have a close friend; alternatively, a child may have one close friend but be rejected by her classmates. So how do we define friendship? A friendship is a close, intimate relationship where there is mutual affection, reciprocity, and sharing. Friends are companions who find pleasure in being together and are comfortable doing things with and for one another.

From a developmental perspective, friendships differ in the infancy, pre-school, and childhood periods (Howes, 1996; Parker & Gottman, 1989). In infancy, children show *preferences* for particular playmates (Ross & Lollis, 1989). These preferences are not transient in that 50–70% of these "friend-ships" continue for more than one year (Howes, 1996) and sometimes even for several years (Dunn, 2005). Friendships are evidenced by a mutual prefer-ence for interaction, shared affect, and complementary and reciprocal play (Howes, 1983). When defining friendships using these behavioral terms, 75% of preschoolers have a friend, and even younger children show clear prefer-ences (Dunn, 1993). Considered together, we see that the foundation for estab-lishing friendships is laid down early, as infants and toddlers demonstrate a preference for specific peers, express positive affect, and learn to help, share, and engage in sustained and reciprocal play. However, not all infants and toddlers have opportunities to form relationships with children outside of the family. Moreover, these relationships may not be developmentally significant in the same way that they are for older children (Bagwell & Schmidt, 2011). Thus, we do not know whether friends in toddlerhood offer significant contri-butions to social and emotional development beyond that of parents, siblings, and other peers.

During the preschool years, children generally begin to spend more time with their peers. Now, friends share common activities and interests and are fun to be with, and friendships typically revolve around play (Lindsey, 2002; Sebanc, 2003). Three- to five-year-old children have been observed to share feelings, elaborate each other's play, ask and answer questions, communicate with and understand one another, engage in shared activities, and resolve conflicts (Gottman, 1983). The social, emotional, and cognitive skills that are essential for establishing friendships are also developed further within friendships. Thus, preschool children learn that friends take care of each other and support, help, and rely on one another. They understand that a friend is someone who you like and who likes you. While preschool friendships are generally not as stable as they are for older children, they may last for at least a year or even longer (Howes, 1988). Still, there is variability in the way preschoolers use the notion of friendship to indicate who they do or do not like ("You can't be my friend today") or to control others ("You can be my friend if you let me have that doll"). Parents and teachers refer to friends when trying to teach children appropriate social skills and how to get along with others ("We don't treat our friends that way" or "You need to share with your friends") (Bagwell & Schmidt, 2011).

Those children who are more successful in forming friendships in the pre-school years have more mature social-cognitive skills. They are more adept at understanding others' social intentions, reading others' emotions, sending emotional signals, and regulating their own emotional states (Dunsmore, Noguchi, Garner, Casey, & Bhullar, 2008). Additionally, those preschool-ers who have stable friendships over the school year evidence the greatest increases in the sophistication of their play (Howes, 1983) and those with more complex play are also more prosocial and less aggressive (Howes & Phillipsen, 1992). While the direction of effects is not specified, we can see from these associations that stable friendships have emotional and social-cognitive benefits for preschoolers.

Emerging from the early relationships of toddlerhood and the preschool years, children in early, middle, and later childhood expand their social connections beyond their immediate families and interact with peer groups in school, on the playground, in neighborhoods, organized activities, and unstructured groups. Thus, the period between the end of preschool and the onset of adolescence, once thought to be a relatively quiescent time, is actually a significant watershed. Friendships during this period help children acquire knowledge about behavioral norms. They also help children to learn the skills that are necessary for presenting the self to others (Rubin et al., 2011). Friendships have new meaning now as children take their place in a wider social network.

Though often an overlooked period of development, there are many crucial changes that occur during middle childhood in particular (Lancy & Grove, 2011). Most notably, we now know that the brain is at its peak for learning since it has achieved an organization that allows for mastery of certain basic cognitive tasks, yet it remains elastic and open to new learning and new ideas. This is the time when children divide along gender lines and become focused on girls playing with girls and boys playing with boys. More importantly, it is when children have a well-developed "theory of mind" and learn that other people have wishes, plans, desires, and minds of their own; these changes in children's understanding of other's thoughts and feelings lead to more complex and effective social exchanges (Slaughter, Imuta, Peterson, & Henry, 2015). Acutely aware of issues of fairness and justice, they also notice when others are selfish, mean, or nasty. Rules of social interaction are paramount now, and children pay attention and then hold on to the local social rules guiding dress, behavior, speech, and how to get along with others.

These social-cognitive changes influence, and are influenced by, children's entry into school and the entire childhood period is, therefore, a time when friendships become increasingly sophisticated. Children between 5 and 11 years of age describe spending time and playing together as important for best friends. Expectations for friendships now include companionship, sharing, helpfulness, acceptance, and commitment; it is not until early adolescence that the deeper qualities of intimacy, understanding, loyalty, and trust are expected (Berndt, 1986, 2004). Indeed, a meta-analysis of 80 studies comparing the actual behavioral and affective manifestations of friendships of children and early adolescents revealed the clearest distinctions between friends and nonfriends in the areas of loyalty, liking one another, and closeness. Friends, as compared to nonfriends, do appear to be better at resolving conflicts, are more positively involved with one another (e.g., positive affect, sharing, and cooperation), and are better at task-related activities, though some of these differences, while significant, are quite small (Newcomb & Bagwell, 1995; Simpkins & Parke, 2002). Thus, the characteristics of positive engagement, sharing, cooperating, positive affect, and companionship seem to be relevant for friendships from preschool through childhood and into early adolescence. However, the deeper properties of relationships, including loyalty, intimacy, and closeness, appear to be most relevant as adolescence approaches (Bagwell & Schmidt, 2011). We see that the qualities of children's friendships change over time, reflecting shifts in beliefs and expectations as well as in social behaviors and emotional competencies. It is with friends that children learn about commitment and loyalty, companionship and intimacy, and together they develop the ability to manage conflict. Children's friendships, therefore, provide a critical context for developing interpersonal skills.

Friendship Stability

Unlike family members, friends are free to choose one another and may terminate their relationship as well. With friends, time spent together and displays of care, affection, loyalty, and commitment are all balanced with negotiation and compromise. Learning to express differences and resolve disagreements is also critical. Moreover, developmental changes in the capacity for commitment and intimacy that each individual brings to a friendship are important to the stability of the relationship. Empirical studies support the idea that friendship stability increases over time. For example, across a school year, first graders maintain about 50% of their friendships while fourth graders keep about 75% of theirs. By contrast, cliques tend to be less stable, with only about 30% of them remaining the same over the school year (Poulin & Chan, 2010). By early adolescence, approximately one-third to one-half of friendships are unstable (Bowker, 2004; Cantin & Bouvin, 2004) reflecting not only the consequence of the transition to a new school (for example, from elementary to middle school), with its concomitant reconfiguring of social opportunities and networks, but also the impact of the many biological, social, and cognitive changes that occur during this time. During late adolescence, friendship stability increases, with between 50% and 75% of friendships being maintained over the school year (Degirmencioglu, Urberg, Tolson, & Richard, 1998) and more old friends lost than new ones developed (Berndt & Hoyle, 1985). More intimate relationships with fewer close friendships seem to characterize the adolescent period. Additionally, larger social networks seem to be more stable, with 50% to 80% of cliques remaining intact over the year (Degirmencioglu et al., 1998). While different methodologies have been used to compare friendship stability across age groups, developmental changes in stability appear to be present from childhood into adolescence (Poulin & Chan, 2010).

What are the factors that influence the stability of friendships in childhood? There are several relational and contextual characteristics that researchers interested in this question have explored, ranging from the composition of friendships (e.g., age, gender, and race) to the quality of friendships and the social and environmental contexts in which friendships occur (e.g., Nangle, Erdley, Newman, Mason, & Capenter, 2003; Poulin & Chan, 2010; Rubin, Wojslawowicz, Rose-Krasnor, Booth-LaForce, & Burgess, 2006; Vitaro, Tremblay, & Bukowski, 2001). Researchers have found that friendships are more likely to be developed and maintained over time when they are formed between children who are similar in age, gender, and race. The structure of most school settings leads to same-age groupings through much of elementary, middle, and even high school. Very little is known about mixed-age friendships during these time periods. While mixed-age friendships are more common as adolescents enter high school, the developmental differences may still be quite pronounced, potentially leading to greater conflict and instability in friendships (Poulin & Chan, 2010).

Same-sex friendships are most common across all age groups. Girls tend to interact in dyads or small groups, to disclose and share more about themselves, and to be more affected by possible threats to their friendships (Poulin & Chan, 2010). Girls are also inclined to be more exclusive in their friendships, a finding that may lead to greater stability. Boys, on the other hand, are oriented toward activity-based interactions with multiple participants, some of whom may be acquaintances but not friends. There are mixed findings on whether there are gender differences in friendship stability; when differences are found (e.g., Benenson & Christakos, 2003), boys' friendships tend to be more stable. Cross-sex friendships begin to be formed during adolescence (Feiring, 1999; Maccoby, 1998) with a greater increase in cross-sex friendships for girls than for boys (Poulin & Pedersen, 2007). However, girls report that there is greater instability in their cross-sex friendships (Chan & Poulin, 2007), a finding that might be explained by the fact that the boys tend to be older and from outside of school (Poulin & Pedersen, 2007). Finally, same-race friendships have been found to be more stable than cross-race friendships (Aboud, Mendelson, & Purdy, 2003; Lee, Howes, & Chamberlain, 2007). And cross-race friendships, which typically decrease in frequency by high school, tend to be rated as lower in intimacy, a finding that may explain the greater instability in these friendships (Aboud & Janani, 2007; Poulin & Chan, 2010). Importantly, methodological concerns, such as the definition of friendship, the procedures used to collect friendship data, and the time interval assessed, may limit the conclusions that may be drawn from extant research (Poulin & Chan, 2010).

Qualitative features of children's friendships have also been explored in an attempt to see how they may affect friendship stability. When friendship quality is defined by positive features such as self-disclosure, intimacy, and prosocial behavior, high levels of these features have been linked to greater friendship stability (Berndt, Hawkins, & Hoyle, 1986; Branje, Frijns, Finkenauer, Engels, & Meeus, 2007; Schneider, Fonzi, Tani, & Tomada, 1997). Whether less intimacy with, loyalty to, and affection for friends is the cause or consequence of less stable friendships, the fact is that those children who have trouble developing and maintaining high-quality friendships are likely to experience more instability. Similarly, lower friendship stability is associated with higher levels of conflict (Bukowski, Hoza, & Boivin, 1994). However, it appears that the strategy adopted to resolve conflicts seems to be more critical than the experience of conflict itself. Girls are more likely to maintain friendships when they use assertive or confrontational strategies, while boys' friendships are more stable when they adopt a strategy of minimizing problems (Bowker, 2004).

The environment and social context in which the friendship occurs have also been found to influence friendship stability (Poulin & Chan, 2010). For example, when school classroom groupings are maintained from one year to the next, social networks remain significantly more stable (Neckerman, 1996). When school transitions occur (between elementary and middle school or between middle and high schools), friendship stability decreases. Expanding social networks that include neighborhood and extracurricular activities expose children to different learning experiences and to opportunities for friendships across multiple contexts. In fact, research demonstrates that friendships that involve both school and nonschool contexts tend to be more stable than those that occur in only one context (Chan & Poulin, 2007). Some have speculated that friendship quality is enhanced when it is extended beyond one setting because it allows for more intimacy and sharing. Alternatively, it may be that stable friendships in one context are more likely to extend to others over time (Poulin & Chan, 2010). So, the girls who are already friends in their fourth-grade classroom may ask their parents if they can join the same extramural soccer team or take an art class together at a local community center.

In addition to these contextual influences, there are variations in friendship stability that reflect individual differences in behavioral characteristics and personal adjustment (Poulin & Chan, 2010). For example, friendship instability has been found in children who are depressed (Chan & Poulin, 2009) and children who maintain stable friendships are less likely to be victimized by their peers (Wojslawowicz, Rubin, Burgess, Booth-LaForce, & Rose-Krasnor, 2006). Friendship stability is lower in children who display externalizing behavior. Thus, for example, maintaining friendships is affected by relational and overt aggression (Ellis & Zarbatany, 2007a) and making friends is more difficult for girls with attention deficit/hyperactivity disorder (Blachman & Hinshaw, 2002). While the direction of influence again remains unclear, these findings suggest strong links between certain behavioral difficulties or personal characteristics and friendship instability.

What Influences Children's Friendship Choices?

In preschool, children often choose interactional partners based on similarities in age and gender. They also express their preferences by choosing friends who help to organize their behavior in the face of arousal, maximizing positive experiences and minimizing negative states (Rubin et al., 2011). Therefore, children who are active and extroverted are more likely to seek each other out, while those who are more reserved and introverted are drawn together. Even in preschool, friends behave differently with each other than they do with those who are not their friends. They cooperate more, show more positive behaviors, and seek interaction with their friends (Dunn, 2005). These friendships may be exclusive (Sebanc, 2003) and have been found to provide comfort and support (Howes & Farver, 1987). And although conflicts may arise between preschool friends, they are more likely to be resolved and then followed by continued interaction than are conflicts between nonfriends (Hartup, Laursen, Stewart, & Eastenson, 1988).

By middle childhood, friends are more similar than nonfriends in prosocial and antisocial/delinquent behaviors (Popp, Laursen, Kerr, Burk, & Stattin, 2008), internalized distress and shyness (Rubin, Wojslawowicz, et al., 2006) and popularity and acceptance (Kupersmidt, DeRosier, & Patterson, 1995). When interacting with their friends, we see greater sophistication in their play (e.g., more positive fantasy play, more negotiation and compromise) (Simpkins & Parke, 2002). Cooperation, generosity, helpfulness, and other altruistic behaviors increase with age (Berndt, 1985) and similarities in these characteristics are found across friends.

What role do these similarities play in influencing children's selection of friends in middle and later childhood? Children may seek out others whose personal characteristics and behaviors are similar to their own and friendships may develop as a result; the similarity in these qualities offers reinforcement and support. On the other hand, it may be that as friendships persist, children influence one another and become more similar over time. One way to disentangle the effects of selection and socialization on similarity between friends is to study children's friendships over time. Longitudinal research has demonstrated that both processes appear to play a role in determining similarity between friends. When children's characteristics and social competence were assessed in fifth grade, prior to their transition to a larger middle school, interpersonal similarity was an antecedent to developing friendships (Newcomb, Bukowski, & Bagwell, 1999). Additionally, dissimilar friendship pairs who continued their relationship over the course of their first school year together (that is, they were found to be reciprocal friends in both the fall and spring terms) were more similar in social competence and aggression. Thus, children appear to select certain friends who then offer them particular socialization experiences. Certainly, more process-oriented studies that extend beyond simple associations between friends, and that adopt multiple methods for identifying who children's friends are and the similarity between them, are necessary to further understand children's choices of friends and the ways in which children are influenced by their friendship choices (Bagwell & Schmidt, 2011).

Children's Understanding of Friendships

How do children think about and come to understand the meaning of friendship? And how do they define friendship? When asked the question "What is a best friend?" children of all ages consider reciprocity and the capacity to give and take as key characteristics (Hartup & Stevens, 1999). But there are striking developmental differences in children's descriptions of friendships that reflect an increased understanding of friendship and a greater sophistication in the need for intimacy over time. For example, up to the age of 5 or 6 years, friends are "kids who live near to me" or "kids that have toys that are nice that I like to play with." During the early school years, friends are expected to share rules and values, to like the same activities, and to be loyal to and stick up for one another. By middle childhood, friendship is seen to have an enduring quality, to be characterized by intimate knowledge of one another (Berndt, 2002), and thoughts about friends are more differentiated and integrated (Peevers & Secord, 1975). It is likely that the increased tendency, by middle childhood, to resolve conflicts so as to preserve the continuity of the relationship is the result of this conception of friendship as cohesive, unified, and enduring.

What accounts for these changes in children's conceptions of friendships? Some researchers have suggested that perspective-taking abilities are at the core of children's understanding of friendships (e.g., Selman & Schultz, 1990). In the preschool years, when children have difficulty understanding that others may think and feel about things differently from the way they do, they are more likely to see their friends as those who have things they like to play with or who are physically close to them. When children enter school, the shift from egocentrism to mutual perspective taking helps them to take on the viewpoints of others and to understand friendships in terms of shared loyalties, activities, overt characteristics, and values. Now, the need for companionship dominates children's friendships. When children are asked about the meaning of friendship, they talk about helping one another or sharing common activities (McDougall & Hymel, 2007).

It is not until later childhood and early adolescence, when children can begin to view themselves and their relationships from the perspective of someone outside of the relationship, that shifts occur again in friendship understanding. Cognitive advances and social changes bring about emerging concepts of loyalty and reciprocity and increasingly sophisticated problem-solving skills. With a more mature conception of friendship, notions of intimacy and self-disclosure deepen and adolescents now look for and engage in more emotional support in their friendships. Intimacy in adolescence is defined as more than simply sharing activities and self-disclosure; it now includes feelings of connection, commitment, and mutual affect between friends (Bauminger, Finzi-Dottan, Chason, & Har-Even, 2008; Radmacher & Azmitia, 2006). Gender differences are also seen, with self-disclosure considered to be primary for girls as a way of achieving feelings of closeness and intimacy, whereas shared activities are important to establishing intimacy for boys (McNelles & Connolly, 1999). Adolescents are more autonomous in their selection of friends, thereby exerting more control over whom they choose to have as friends, the level of intimacy they want in their friendships, and the ways in which their friendships are maintained.

Individual Differences in Peer Status and Friendship Quality

The developmental shifts that we see in children's peer interactions and friendships reflect and influence changes in their capacity to connect to others and in their understanding of themselves. There are differences in the ways in which children manage their interactions in the peer group, leading them to be accepted or rejected by their peers; there are also changes in the quality of their close friendships. Individual differences in both peer status and friendship quality have been identified and studied in an effort to explore the variety of ways in which children navigate the developmental task of adapting to their expanding social worlds.

Peer Status: What Happens When Children Are Accepted or Rejected?

Children's sense of belonging and feelings about themselves are deeply impacted by the way that they are viewed by their peers. Peer status is a measure of how well liked and accepted, or disliked and rejected, children are in their peer group. If they are accepted, then children tend to feel good about themselves, are willing to give back to their peers, and want to do all that they can to sustain the feeling that they belong to their larger peer group. But if they are rejected, children may struggle with trying to understand the reason(s) for not being included. They may feel badly about themselves and either try harder to be included or back away in order to protect themselves. Unlike friendship, which defines a specific relationship between individuals, peer status represents how other children feel about a child and has meaning only in the context of the peer group (Rubin, Bukowski, et al., 2006). However, because some of the same social competencies and skills that contribute to children being able to make friends also enhance social acceptance, peer acceptance has been found to predict the number of reciprocal friends a child has (Ladd, Kochenderfer, & Coleman, 1996; Parker & Asher, 1993). Whatever the reasons for being accepted or rejected, children make a contribution to their own peer status and, in turn, are impacted by their status. So how can we study peer acceptance or rejection and what contributes to a child's status within the peer group?

Sociometric ratings, where children are asked how much they like or dislike each other, are the most common methods for studying children's peer status (Hymel, Closson, Caravita, & Vaillancourt, 2010). In one method, called the "roster and rating" sociometric technique (Parker & Asher, 1993), children are given a list of all of their classmates. They are then asked to use a 5-point scale to rate, for example, how much they like to play with or to work with each of them. Children's average ratings are then used to determine each child's level of acceptance. Thus, this method helps researchers to determine how each child feels about every other child in the classroom.

An alternative method, called the "nomination" sociometric technique, is relatively quick and easy to use (Coie, Dodge, & Coppotelli, 1982). Children are asked to name a specific number of peers (e.g., three) in their class whom they like the most and then the same number they like the least. Scores are added for the most- and least-liked nominations for each child and summary ratings are created. Those who receive the highest number of most-liked nominations, together with the fewest number of least-liked nominations, are described as *popular*. Children who are *rejected* receive the most least-liked nominations and the fewest most-liked scores. *Average* children are those who receive some of both types of scores, though not as many most-liked ratings as those who are popular. Children who are *neglected* receive very few most-liked and very few least-liked ratings; they are isolated children who are not disliked but simply ignored. Finally, children who are *controversial* receive a large number of most- and least-liked nominations, indicating there is something that leads others to have strong positive or negative feelings toward them. These nomination techniques have been criticized as having the potential to increase social problems for kids who are already not well liked by their peers. However, when administered carefully, they can effectively, and without risk, address questions regarding peer status in a classroom setting (Mayeux, Underwood, & Risser, 2007).

What factors influence children's peer status? Whether or not a child is accepted, rejected, or neglected depends on many factors, including behaviors (such as friendliness, prosocial behavior, aggression), biological predispositions (such as temperament, cortisol levels), and socio-cognitive skills (understanding others' mental states, awareness of and understanding of emotions). Additionally, physical appearance and the capacity to "blend in" have been linked to popularity in numerous studies (e.g., Langlois et al., 2000). During both the preschool and childhood periods, peer status is related to children's sensitivity to and understanding of others' mental states (see Slaughter et al., 2015, for a meta-analysis of extant studies). Children who are accepted by their peers tend to be more socially competent and cooperative. They communicate well and are effective at regulating their emotions. By contrast, children who are rejected show more immature, impulsive behaviors and tend to be more aggressive and disruptive.

Peer status and friendship are empirically and conceptually related, though they have been associated with different measures of adjustment (Bukowski,

Hoza, & Boivin, 1993). Peer rejection, for example, appears to be a risk factor for a range of academic, behavioral, and psychological problems, including loneliness, antisocial behavior, delinquency, and victimization, whether assessed concurrently or over time (Bierman, 2004; Deater-Deckard, 2001; Newcomb, Bukowski, & Pattee, 1993). The friendships of accepted and rejected children differ in significant ways. Rejected children tend to have lower quality friendships (Parker & Asher, 1993) and, when observed in interaction with their friends, show less maturity and poorer conflict resolution skills as compared to children who are accepted by their peers (Lansford et al., 2006). Thus, children who are rejected may miss out on the many benefits that could be provided by interactions in higher quality friendships. It may not be rejection, per se, that leads to poor outcomes but rather the experiences that rejected children have in low-quality friendships that limit opportunities for growth.

There has been a great deal of interest in understanding whether the exact timing of peer rejection has an impact on subsequent functioning (Pedersen, Vitaro, Barker, & Borge, 2007). Interestingly, while peer rejection is negatively related to the development of reciprocal friendships more generally, many children who are rejected still maintain at least one close friend (and many popular children are not able to manage dyadic friendships) (Asher & Paquette, 2003). Explorations of the impact of these interrelated peer experiences in childhood on subsequent internalizing and externalizing behavior problems in early adolescence have led to some important conclusions. In particular, of the many pathways of influence explored, it appears that behavior problems in the early school years predict peer rejection and problems with developing close friendships in middle childhood; the lack of reciprocal, close friendships in middle childhood then lays the foundation for internalizing problems in early adolescence (Pedersen et al., 2007). Thus, early behavior problems, such as disruptive behavior, put young children at risk for later negative peer experiences and adjustment difficulties.

Children who behave aggressively are generally not very well liked by their peers. In fact, there is considerable research evidence supporting an association between aggressive behavior and peer rejection. During the elementary school years, one of the best predictors of peer rejection is aggressive behavior (Coie, Dodge, & Kupersmidt, 1990; Parker & Asher, 1987). Additionally, peer rejection also leads to aggression in the future (e.g., Coie, Lochman, Terry, & Hyman, 1992). It makes sense that because children learn, within the peer group, adaptive social behavior, rejection by their peers will deprive them of these learning opportunities and may even perpetuate negative social interactions (Dodge et al., 2003). Moreover, cognitive mechanisms may influence the way children interpret events, such as experiences with peer rejection, which in turn may impact their response to that rejection. Social information processing theory (Crick & Dodge, 1994) proposes that children's interpretations of social events will determine whether they respond aggressively. Similarly, peer rejection may lead to deficits in processing information in social situations, including, for example, making incorrect inferences about others' hostile intentions (Dodge et al., 2003).

Recent research on peer rejection, within the framework of developmental psychopathology, has extended beyond the study of early risk factors as they impact later developmental outcome. The value of a more nuanced "developmental cascade model" (Masten, Burt, & Coatsworth, 2006) is that it considers the reciprocal and transactional links between pairs of variables that influence and potentially exacerbate one another. For example, by considering environmental (peer rejection), cognitive (social information processing), and behavioral (peer aggression) factors together, it is possible to go beyond considering links between pairs of variables (e.g., between peer rejection and social information processing, between social information processing and aggression, and between peer rejection and aggression) and to explore the ways in which they all impact each other over time. In a large-scale study of children between kindergarten and third grade, peer rejection, social information processing, and aggression were all found to be related to each other as both predictors and outcomes in a series of demonstrated cascade effects over time (Lansford, Malone, Dodge, Pettit, & Bates, 2010). While the model of precise predictors and outcomes may change depending upon the developmental period studied, this research powerfully demonstrates the importance of early intervention efforts that may disrupt the cascading effects of aggression, deficits in social information processing, and peer rejection, thereby providing children with compensatory mechanisms for developing more adaptive outcomes.

Friendship Quality

While exploring peer status is critical for understanding children in the context of their larger peer group, the experience of friendships throughout childhood is also meaningful. The significance of particular friendships and the impact of these relationships on children's development are important to consider as well. As we have already seen, children begin to show preferences for particular peers during the early years, even before they can talk about their friendships. Preschoolers, especially those who are more socially competent and aware, have been found to have "best friends." The experience of having a best friend, which is even more likely among children in kindergarten and first grade, and more common among girls than boys, offers children positive social experiences in the peer group. Those young children who do have a best friend exhibit a higher level of prosocial behavior and are more accepted by their peers (Sebanc, Kearns, Hernandez, & Galvin, 2007). The ability to form reciprocal friendships, also more common among girls, is related to young children's capacity to communicate and regulate emotions (Dunsmore et al., 2008) and promotes social skills and positive adjustment (Hay et al., 2004), Thus, while the direction of effects remains unclear, we see that developing friendships in early childhood prepares young children for more mature, stable, and enduring friendships during childhood and adolescence.

Because friendships are reciprocal, dyadic relationships, assessing the presence and quality of friendships requires techniques, such as reciprocal nominations, that capture mutuality in a relationship (Newcomb & Bagwell, 1995). While parents or teachers are sometimes asked to report on children's friendships, there are problems with these assessments. For example, there is a reliance on limited observations of children's interactions in only one setting (e.g., in the classroom or outside of school) (Bagwell & Schmidt, 2011; Gest, 2006). Asking children about their friendships appears to provide a more reliable and valid assessment. Methods involving mutual friendship nominations may be used where children are asked, for example, to nominate three friends and then select the one friend they consider to be their "very best friend" (Parker & Asher, 1993). If the target child names a "very best friend" who also considers that child to be one of his or her three nominated friends, then the relationship is considered a "best friendship." Using this method, children can have up to three "best friendships" but only one "very best friend." It is not enough for a child to like another friend or to indicate that they wish to be someone's friend. Rather, it is reciprocity in nominated friends that matters (Newcomb & Bagwell, 1995).

Problems with this method may still arise if studies are limited to school friends, who must all be participants in the assessment, thereby precluding the naming of friends outside of school (Kiesner, Kerr, & Stattin, 2004). Moreover, there are variations to this technique that allow children to make unlimited nominations of friends or to restrict the definition of friendship to one exclusive relationship where both friends identify each other as their best friend (Bagwell et al., 1998). This more restrictive method is especially helpful when researchers are interested in evaluating friendship quality with a focus on one particular, mutually agreed upon friendship.

Understanding individual differences in the quality of children's friendships requires an exploration of the essential characteristics of children's friendships, such as companionship, intimacy, self-disclosure, jealousy, rivalry, and conflict (Bagwell & Schmidt, 2011; Berndt, 2002). Despite the specific features measured, when there are primarily positive characteristics in a friendship it is considered to be a high-quality relationship that provides both children with comfort and satisfaction. By contrast, low-quality friendships consists of many negative and few, if any, positive features and are not very satisfying.

Variations in friendship quality have been explored as they may influence children's current adaptation and future adjustment. Empirical studies have relied on interviews and self-report questionnaires that ask about children's perceptions of particular aspects of a specific friendship. There are many controversies in the use of these measures, including questions about how many dimensions or characteristics should be measured, whether the characteristics measured should be specific (e.g., companionship, help, closeness, conflict) or global (positive vs. negative), and whether there are consistencies between children's perceptions of the same relationship or across children and outside observers' ratings. Evaluations of friendship quality should ideally rely on the use of multiple measures and consider the views of both friends in the friendship as well as other informants (Bagwell & Schmidt, 2011). Then, a more reliable understanding is possible of the differences between friendships and peer relationships as well as of the distinct features of particular friendships and their association with various outcome measures. We see, therefore, that the ways in which individual differences in children's friendships are assessed ultimately affect what we learn about the relationship.

The Effects of Friendships on Children's Socio-Emotional Functioning

The experiences that children have in their friendships reflect and affect how they think and feel about themselves and their subsequent relationships. We generally assume that good quality friendships lead to all kinds of positive outcomes, just as problems in friendships result from, and contribute to, difficulties for children. Conceptions of friendship provided by Harry Stack Sullivan's (1953) interpersonal theory offer theoretical justification for these assumptions and influence many of the contemporary empirical questions raised by developmental researchers. Consistent with Sullivan's views, investigators have been interested in exploring whether high-quality friendships lead to positive outcomes, such as high self-esteem and good adjustment, which in turn provide the foundation for continued close relationships and protect against feelings of loneliness, anxiety, and depression. Sullivan's theoretical notions about friendship have been expanded to include an understanding of the critical social competencies, such as empathy and perspective-taking skills, that arise out of social interactions during each developmental period (Buhrmester & Furman, 1986). Other theorists have focused on the importance of reciprocity, cooperation, and responsibility in friendships and highlighted developmental changes in interpersonal understanding that are consistent with Piaget's theory of cognitive development (Youniss, 1980). And still others have described friendship as a significant context for development across the lifespan, emphasizing the importance of having friends, distinct characteristics of friendships, and differences in the quality of these relationships (Hartup, 1996; Hartup & Stevens, 1999). Thus, Sullivan's ideas, inspired by his clinical work as a psychiatrist treating patients with interpersonal difficulties, stimulated many important empirical questions that have been explored by developmental researchers.

There is some evidence in support of Sullivan's (1953) proposition that friendships provide validation for self-worth. For example, high-quality friendships are correlated with higher levels of self-esteem (Bukowski, Motzoi, & Meyer, 2009). However, there is little support for the idea that friendship quality leads to changes in self-esteem, either positive or negative, over time (Keefe & Berndt, 1996). Positive associations have also been found between high-quality friendships and peer-rated sociability and leadership (Berndt,

Hawkins, & Jiao, 1999). Good, supportive friendships are linked to lower levels of loneliness (Parker & Asher, 1993) and, among shy children, to lower levels of trait anxiety (Fordham & Stevenson-Hinde, 1999). In late childhood and early adolescence, friendship quality is associated with good social competence and high self-worth (Erdley, Nangle, Newman, & Carpenter, 2001; Rubin et al., 2004). Having high-quality, stable friendships helps children during especially stressful times of transition. For example, the challenges and demands of a new school may be negotiated better when children have high-quality, stable friendships, whether they are entering elementary school (Ladd et al., 1996) or junior high school (Aikins, Bierman, & Parker, 2005). And having friends may compensate for early stressful socialization experiences in the home, thereby reducing the likelihood of peer victimization (Schwartz, Dodge, Petit, Bates, & Conduct Problems Prevention Research Group, 2000). Thus, friendships appear to play a buffering or protective role, particularly during times of stress.

There is also a substantial body of literature focused on children with poor-quality or no friendships, perhaps because these are the children who are brought to the attention of clinicians and are of interest to researchers exploring the developmental roots of psychopathology. Children with no or poor-quality friends have lower self-esteem (Berndt, 2002) and are more lonely than those with good quality friends (Parker & Asher, 1993; Renshaw & Brown, 1993), especially when their friendships are unstable or they have unreasonable expectations for their friends (Asher & Paquette, 2003). Fifth-grade children who are shy/withdrawn have friends who are also shy/withdrawn, their friendships are of lower quality, and they are more likely to be victimized by their peers than those who are nonaggressive and nonwithdrawn (Rubin, Wojslawowicz, et al., 2006). When there is lack of mutuality and more conflict in friendships, children (especially girls) exhibit more symptoms of depression (Prinstein, Borelli, Cheah, Simon, & Aikins, 2005). And, in some cases, more aggressive and disruptive behavior problems in school are seen in children who have friends but whose friendships are marked by more disagreements and greater hostility, as reinforcement is provided for increasingly disruptive behaviors (Hoza, Molina, Bukowski, & Sippola, 1995; Poulin, Dishion, & Haas, 1999). However, there is less delinquency evidenced if these children, especially boys, do not participate in deviancy training (discussing, imitating, or engaging in aggressive or antisocial activities) with other at-risk youth or do not have friends (Dishion, McCord, & Poulin, 1999; Vitaro, Brendgen, & Wanner, 2005). In sum, a substantial body of evidence supports the conclusion that poor-quality or no friendships in childhood are associated with a range of negative developmental outcomes, including internalizing behavior problems (such as loneliness, low self-esteem, and depression), externalizing behavior problems (such as aggression, delinquency, and conduct disorder), as well as poor academic achievement and school dropout.

Whether friendship quality is the cause or consequence of various positive or negative developmental outcomes, or whether some other variable(s) impact friendship experiences and outcomes, is not clear. It may be, for example, that when children with poor-quality friendships exhibit more delinquent behavior, both friendship quality and delinquency are caused by low group status or rejection within the peer group. Thus, group status, rather than friendship quality per se, may be linked to delinquency (Vitaro, Boivin, & Bukowski, 2009). Moreover, friendship quality may serve as a buffer against problems and help children avoid negative developmental outcomes. For example, children from at-risk families develop fewer problems when they have high-quality friendships as compared to low-quality or no friends (Bukowski et al., 2009).

Additionally, having a best friend decreases the effects of peer victimization in fourth and fifth graders and buffers against negative adjustment (Hodges, Boivin, Vitaro, & Bukowski, 1999). Peer victimization is most likely to occur when children are at risk because they have internalizing or externalizing behavior problems; however, having a best friend is related to decreases in victimization for fourth and fifth graders, regardless of whether the children have behavior problems. Particularly noteworthy is the finding that friendship quality plays a role such that when children with internalizing problems perceive a high level of protection from a friend, there is no association between internalizing problems and victimization. The results of this work suggest that children with behavior problems are at risk for victimization, particularly if they do not have a best friend. Having a good quality friendship can help mitigate the likelihood of peer victimization and also prevent behavior problems from getting worse as a result of victimization (Hodges et al., 1999).

While friendships become increasingly important in middle and late childhood and early adolescence, relationships with parents are still essential. In fact, the quality of parent–child relationships may interact with friendships to predict social and emotional functioning (Booth-LaForce, Rubin, Rose-Krasnor, & Burgess, 2005). Attachment security and friendship quality may each make unique contributions to children's functioning. Alternatively, it may be that attachment security is a predictor of later social and emotional competencies, though it is mediated by friendship characteristics. That is, attachment security may be related to particular friendship characteristics which, in turn, predict later outcomes. Or friendships may moderate between attachment security and adjustment such that friends play a compensatory role, potentially reducing the negative effects of lack of maternal support or of insecurity.

In fact, several studies have supported the idea that friendship quality moderates between early family characteristics and developmental outcome. For example, quality of friendship in children in grades 4, 5, and 6 predicts general self-worth and perceived social competence more strongly when children come from families with less than optimal family experiences. Specifically, high-quality friendships buffer children whose families are low in cohesion and adaptability. The link between these family measures and children's adjustment is stronger for children whose friendship quality is poor, as compared to those with higher quality friendships, and for children who do not have friends relative to those who do have friends. (Gauze, Bukowski, Aquan-Assee, & Sippola, 1996). In other work, preschoolers who experience harsh home environments, including marital conflict, abuse, or maternal hostility, are more likely to be victimized by peers (Schwartz et al., 2000), especially when the children have a lower number of friendships. And when the association between family adversity and children's externalizing behavior problems is explored, no link is found for children who have a large network of friendships (Criss, Pettit, Bates, Dodge, & Lapp, 2002). Still, because of the variability in how friendship quality and adjustment have been assessed, and because few longitudinal investigations have been conducted exploring the effects of friendship quality on adjustment over time, there is a need for more work that can untangle the role that friendships play in children's adjustment.

Despite the very important findings that have emerged from empirical studies to date, there are several problems with extant research in this area. There are many reasons to expect that friendships provide a developmental context for enhancing esteem, promoting social and emotional competence, offering support, giving help when navigating transitions, and protecting against loneliness, depression, and anxiety. However, there is a great deal of variability in the definition of, and indices used to measure, the quality of friendships. Friendship quality may be determined by a number of different factors, including the quality of parent–child relationships, sibling relationships, prior peer experiences, temperamental factors, gender, or socio-cultural variables. There is very little research that has clarified the role that these factors, either alone or in combination, may play in determining friendship quality (Bagwell & Schmidt, 2011). Moreover, any of these variables may also influence developmental outcomes in unique ways. Thus, it is unclear, for example, whether it is friendship quality per se or some combination of family and friendship experiences that lead to low self-esteem. Exploring friendship quality as it may mediate or moderate developmental outcome is especially important for future research. Additionally, we do know that low-quality and high-quality friendships provide different contexts within which children function, offering distinct experiences for children in their relationships and thereby influencing developmental outcomes in potentially disparate ways (Bagwell & Schmidt, 2011). Exploring the possible causal mechanisms through which good quality friendships lead to positive outcomes in children or young adolescents is essential to deepening our understanding of the developmental implications of friendships in young children's lives. Finally, clarifying the contexts in which friendships play a protective role, or may increase vulnerability to problems, has enormous implications for clinicians interested in promoting adaptation and reducing peer victimization and bullying.

The Links Between Children's Relationships With Parents and Peers

Children are socialized by their parents and their peers. While some investigators maintain that parents' socialization of their children has little influence on children's peer relationships (e.g., Harris, 1995), others see strong connections between children's experiences in their family and the quality of their relationships with peers (e.g., Booth-LaForce & Kerns, 2009; Sroufe, Egeland, & Carlson, 1999). Questions regarding the relative influence of each of these forces on children's social development are complex and many conceptual and theoretical issues remain unanswered (cf. Knoester, Haynie, & Stephens, 2006). Still, there are compelling theoretical reasons for exploring the associations between these relational systems and their relative influence on subsequent development.

Attachment theorists argue that parents provide the earliest models for establishing relationships. If children experience sensitive and responsive parenting, then they learn about reciprocity in social interactions (Elicker, Englund, & Sroufe, 1992) and begin to develop an empathic and prosocial orientation (Clark & Ladd, 2000) that affords them a set of social skills to be used in relationships outside of the family. The secure base provided by a caregiver to whom a child is securely attached allows the child to explore the social world, to develop the competencies and skills necessary to interact and play with peers, and to form positive expectations regarding relationships (Sroufe, 1988). Alternatively, when care is inconsistent or unpredictable, children develop poor social skills, negative expectations about relationships, emotion regulation difficulties, and negative attributions about peer behavior (Cassidy, 1994; Cassidy et al., 1996). It is through these experiences that children come to internalize models or cognitive representations of relationships and of the self (Bowlby, 1980; Sroufe & Fleeson, 1986). Thus, early experiences in attachment relationships are represented, cognitively, affectively, and dynamically, in ways that influence self-understanding and guide the development of new relationships.

According to attachment theorists, therefore, peer relationships will be heavily influenced by the quality of the early parent–child attachment relationship. Several empirical studies have indeed confirmed this theoretical assumption. Children who are securely attached to their mothers are more competent with peers (Waters, Wippman, & Sroufe, 1979), liked better by peers (LaFreniere & Sroufe, 1985), are more empathic and less hostile toward others (Sroufe, 1983), and display more positive affect in peer interactions (Sroufe, Schork, Motti, Lawroski, & LaFreniere, 1984). Securely attached children are found to be in more positive, synchronous friendships with peers at 5 years of age (Youngblade & Belsky, 1992) and attachment security is associated with peer acceptance in 6-year-olds (Cohn, 1990). Attachment security has been associated with behavioral tendencies to be sociable with peers (Belsky & Cassidy, 1994) and to be socially competent and popular

(Kerns et al., 1996; Sroufe et al., 1993) in early and middle childhood. Other studies support the association between attachment and friendship quality in preschoolers (Park & Waters, 1989) and find that securely attached preschoolers are less likely to be a victim or a bully (Troy & Sroufe, 1987). Children who, at 15 months, have insecure-avoidant attachment relationships display more instrumental aggression at 3 years than do those with secure or insecure-resistant attachments, and children with insecure-resistant, as compared to insecure-avoidant, attachments are less assertive in their interactions with friends (McElwain, Cox, Burchinal, & Macfie, 2003). In the early elementary school years, securely attached children are less aggressive with their peers (Renken, Egeland, Marvinney, Mangelsdorf, & Sroufe, 1989), while children with insecure-disorganized attachments demonstrate more aggressive behavior problems in the peer group (Lyons-Ruth, 1996).

Attachment security is also related, both concurrently and over time, to peer acceptance and rejection in independent samples of preschoolers and elementary school children (Cassidy et al., 1996; Shulman, Elicker, & Sroufe, 1994). In a follow-up study of children from low-income families, secure infants, as compared to those who were insecure, developed higher quality friendships and were rated by teachers and camp counselors as more competent with their peers (Shulman et al., 1994; Sroufe, Egeland, & Kreutzer, 1990). And other studies have continued to provide support for predictive associations between secure attachment in infancy and greater social competence in early childhood (e.g., Belsky & Fearson, 2002; Stams, Juffer, & van IJzendoorn, 2002), between attachment in infancy and social functioning in early childhood (e.g., Bohlin, Hagekull, & Rydell, 2000), and between attachment and peer competence assessed concurrently in middle childhood (e.g., Contreras, Kerns, Weimer, Gentzler, & Tomich, 2000).

Finally, there are also studies examining links between attachment and peer acceptance that have focused on middle childhood, including samples of children between the ages of 8 and 11 years. Mixed results have been obtained. For example, no associations were found for child–mother or child–father attachment security and peer popularity (Lieberman, Doyle, & Markiewicz, 1999). However, other studies report associations between secure child–father attachment (but not child–mother attachment) and peer popularity (Verschueren & Marcoes, 2002, 2005) and between attachment security and peer acceptance (Bohlin et al., 2000; Granot & Mayseless, 2001). It may be that some of the characteristics that have been found to lead to peer acceptance, such as adaptive emotion regulation strategies, are more likely to be found in securely attached children but that other qualities, such as physical attractiveness, are not (Booth-LaForce & Kerns, 2009). It may also be that during middle childhood, most children have at least one friend so examining associations between attachment security and general aspects of peer relationships is less relevant to explore.

By contrast, consistent findings have been reported in studies linking attachment security to the quality of children's friendships (e.g., Howes &

Tonyan, 1999; McElwain & Volling, 2004; Rubin et al., 2004). Early secure attachment relationships are associated with more positive friendship quality (e.g., greater intimacy, cooperation, ability to get along, positive affect, cooperation) in fourth grade (Lucas-Thompson & Clarke-Stewart, 2007), higher friendship competence in middle childhood (Freitag, Belsky, Grossman, Grossman, & Scheuerer-Englisch, 1996), and the capacity to choose friends with similar attachment histories and greater competence in making friends in childhood (Elicker et al., 1992). In a meta-analysis of 63 studies exploring the link between attachment security and peer group functioning (Schneider et al., 2001), a small-to-moderate effect size was obtained. While these findings are compelling, the more relevant link is between secure attachments and friendships since friendships are more similar to the intimacy, intensity, and closeness expected in secure parent–child relationships. Indeed, a larger effect size was obtained when attachment security was linked with friendship rather than peer relationships more generally (Hodges, Finnegan, & Perry, 1999; Schneider et al., 2001).

In an expanded meta-analysis, drawing on data from 80 samples and including over 4,000 children, early attachment was moderately associated with children's peer competence (Groh et al., 2014). Specifically, early secure attachment was found to promote, and insecure attachment to undermine, social competence with peers. While subtypes of insecurity were distinguished (avoidant, resistant, and disorganized), they all appeared to confer similar risk for diminishing children's peer competence. These results did not vary with age at which social competence was measured, though the magnitude of the association did vary depending on the attachment measure used (and age and type of attachment assessment were confounded). And unlike the earlier meta-analysis (Schneider et al., 2001), attachment security contributed significantly to children's competence with both friends and nonfriends. In fact, the findings were strongest when social competence with nonfriends, as compared to friends, was assessed. This unexpected result was explained by sampling and methodological differences as well as by the inclusion criteria used across meta-analytic reviews and the current availability of more studies. Considered together, early attachment security appears to have broad significance for children's peer competence, regardless of friendship status (Groh et al., 2014).

Children in the transition from middle childhood to early adolescence who feel that their mothers are available if needed, and who develop a sense of autonomy, report more supportive and close friendships. Moreover, children who are secure in their relationships with their mothers and fathers, and who turn to them during stressful times, have higher quality friendships with low levels of conflict (Lieberman et al., 1999) and more reciprocated friendships (Kerns et al., 1996) as compared to those with less secure attachments. Thus, unlike what has been found with more general measures of acceptance or popularity, parent–child attachment security appears to be associated with the deeper aspects of children's friendships in later childhood, such as trust, intimacy, and security, that are relevant to close relationships.

What we can see from this review of extant literature is that early attachment history appears to play a role in peer relationships and friendships. But just how do these experiences in early attachment relationships contribute to expectations and behaviors with peers? Attachment theorists argue that children develop internal representations of parents, the self, and relationships (Bowlby, 1969/1982: Sroufe & Fleeson, 1986). Over time, these representations generalize to representations of others, including peers, incorporate a view of the self in relation to others, and then influence actual behavior with peers (Cassidy et al., 1996). Thus, positive representations lead to positive behaviors with peers (Dodge, Murphy, & Buchsbaum, 1984). These positive behaviors, in turn, help the child to be well liked by his or her peers (Dodge, 1983), which increases opportunities for peers to direct positive behavior toward the child (Dodge & Frame, 1982), thereby contributing to positive representations of peers.

This self-perpetuating cycle originates with parental caregiving behavior. Initial representations of primary attachment relationships, which are usually with the mother, may then contribute to the development of new representations. Because these representations emerge out of a history of sensitivity, availability, and responsiveness of specific caregivers, they may differ for different attachment figures. Attachment security to mothers and fathers may not be related (e.g., Belsky & Rovine, 1987; Rosen & Burke, 1999); therefore, children's representations of these relationships may differ. There may also be other significant influences on children's representational models, such as experiences with siblings and substitute caregivers. How these representations of multiple attachment relationships are then organized and used to influence behavior with peers may depend on the generalization of attachment representations (see, for example, Bretherton, 1990; Main et al., 1985) and on the attachment hierarchy (Cassidy, 2008; Kobak, Rosenthal, & Serwik, 2005). While early representations are thought to show consistency over time, clinical and research evidence substantiate the idea that attachment-related behaviors, and their representations, may change (e.g., Mason & Mendoza, 1998; Suomi, 2008). Thus, controversy persists as to whether there are relationship-specific internal models or more general working models of relationships. There is also debate over how these models impact other intimate relationships, such as friendships.

Some investigators have argued that attachment security has been found to explain only a small portion of the variance in children's functioning in close relationships (Thompson, 2008). Rather than relying on the compelling notion of internal models to explain all developmental outcomes, questions have been raised as to whether there is theoretical or empirical justification for the link between internal representational models of attachment and specific aspects of the child's social and emotional development (see, for example, Hinde, 1988; Thompson & Raikes, 2003). Accordingly, it might be best to view Bowlby's notion of the internal working model as a conceptual metaphor (Thompson, 2005) and not as a descriptive frame that can account for all empirical findings. If, for example, an association is found between attachment security and peer competence, it may be because of a direct link between attachment and peer relationships (influenced by working models of relationships), because of a mediational influence (where, for example, emotion regulation plays a role), or because they both derive from an association with other influences (for example, parental support) (Thompson, 2005). When viewed in this way, internal models of attachment security may serve a critical role in guiding the empirical questions that are asked but do not provide definitive explanatory templates.

There is also the issue that Bowlby originally articulated which has to do with the fact that not all relationships are attachment relationships (Bowlby, 1982). Children may have many other close relationships with, for example, siblings, substitute caregivers, aunts and uncles, or grandparents. When there is a divorce, remarriage, or single parenthood, new caregivers may become attachment figures and existing attachment figures may have more limited contact or influence in children's lives. Thus, questions about the reorganization of attachment relationships, and the permeability of boundaries between attachment and other close relationships as children age (cf. Thompson, 2005), become increasingly important. Additionally, mothers and fathers serve roles that extend beyond solely that of an attachment figure. Mothers and fathers serve as playmates, teachers, socializers, and models for appropriate behavior. The developing mother–child and father–child relationships more generally, rather than attachment security alone, may influence children's behavior in other relationships.

And a related question that persists in the attachment literature is whether associations between early attachment security and later developmental outcomes are the result of some "prototype" or internal model that guides the selection of later experiences (Sroufe et al., 1990) or of some ongoing stability in the quality of the mother–child or father–child relationship. The prototype model does not imply high stability of individual differences but rather argues that early experiences exert an enduring influence (Roisman et al., 2005). As such, early secure attachment relationships make certain developmental pathways (e.g., better quality friendships) more likely. Alternatively, the "revisionist" view (Fraley, 2002) maintains that continuity in ongoing social experiences leads to stability in attachment security and that when changes are observed they result from some change in the quality of interaction. Thus, increased marital stress, child maltreatment, or other adverse experiences may diminish the quality of mother–child interaction, lead to a shift in the quality of attachment over time, and result in interactional difficulties in other close relationships. Research examining transactional influences on developmental outcomes needs to carefully examine the caregiving environment, as well as individual, familial, and social stresses, that may impact the child. Integrating these possible alternatives into studies examining the links between early attachments and later relationships has implications for our understanding of the role of working models.

It is for these reasons that a more nuanced, conceptually rich and appealing framework for explaining associations between early attachment and peer relationships may be more appropriate. One such perspective suggests that attachment security may support the development of peer relationships because of the expectations derived from early attachments (Sroufe, Egeland, Carlson, & Collins, 2005b). Specifically, there is:

(1) a motivational base, involving expectations of connectedness; (2) an attitudinal base, involving expectations of responsiveness; (3) an instrumental base centered on exploratory and play capacities; (4) an emotional base, including entrained capacities for arousal and emotional regulation; and (5) a relational base, involving empathy and expectations of mutuality (Sroufe et al., 2005b, p. 57).

These expectations, as well as particular interactive skills and abilities, are carried over to relationships with others. Thus, the more specific, dynamic, and transactional processes involved in the presumed links between attachment and peer relationships need to be identified and explored empirically as well.

Indeed, alternatives to the notion of internal working models have been suggested and studied. It may be, for example, that children who are securely attached to their parents are liked by others because they are well able to tolerate frustration, competent at regulating their affect and behavior, and feel good about themselves in general (Elicker et al., 1992; Sroufe, 1983). If they perceive themselves as competent and evaluate themselves positively, this may help them to be liked by others, and if they are well liked by their peers, this in turn might lead to positive peer representations. Therefore, the representations of peers may not be generalized only from the representation of attachment figures (cf. Cassidy et al., 1996) but positive views of the self and of emotion regulation may be critical to developing representations of peer relationships.

In fact, there is research supporting this view that emotion regulation abilities are related to both attachment security and peer relationships. Attachment theorists argue that one of the functions of the attachment system is emotion regulation. Securely attached children can rely on the parent to help them regulate their positive and negative emotions (Bowlby, 1982; Cassidy, 1994; Sroufe & Waters, 1977). The same parental characteristics that contribute to a secure attachment relationship (e.g., sensitivity, responsiveness, open communication) also provide children with examples of effective emotion regulation (Contreras & Kerns, 2000). Additionally, children come to internalize the patterns of emotion regulation that are learned within the parent–child dyad and then use those patterns in other social interactions (Cassidy, 1994). Securely attached preschoolers, for example, use positive affect to initiate and maintain peer interactions and to respond to their peers (Sroufe et al., 1984). They also express sadness after failing a competitive task more openly than do children who are avoidant in their attachment relationship (Lutkenhaus,

Grossman, & Grossman, 1985). As compared to insecurely attached children, preschoolers who are securely attached also display less negative affect when playing with their familiar peers (Sroufe et al., 1984). And, preschool friend pairs who are both securely attached to their mothers show more positive affect during play when compared to secure-insecure pairs (Park & Waters, 1989). Therefore, there appears to be a significant association between attachment and emotion regulation.

The association between emotion regulation and children's peer relationships has also been established. Managing the demands of interpersonal interactions, such as resolving conflicts, requires certain emotion regulation skills. Associations have been observed between emotion regulation measures and children's socially appropriate behaviors (Eisenberg et al., 1995; Eisenberg, Fabes, et al., 1997). For example, those children who use less effective coping skills (e.g., venting, aggression) in social situations demonstrate less competent social behavior. And children who tend to experience negative emotional states use less appropriate social behavior both at school and at home. Moreover, when children exhibit high negative emotionality, emotion regulation is more strongly related to socially appropriate behavior. Thus, negative emotionality moderates the association between particular aspects of regulation, such as behavioral regulation and attentional control, and competent behaviors directed toward peers (Eisenberg, Guthrie, et al., 1997).

Perhaps most significantly, an exploration of emotion regulation as a potential mediator between attachment and competence in the peer group allows for an examination of another mechanism by which early parent–child attachment may be associated with peer relationships. Indeed, emotion regulation skills have been found to play a mediating role between parent–child attachment and competence in peer relationships. In one study, 9- to 11-year-old children who used constructive coping strategies (as rated by their parents) were those who were well able to seek support and engage in cognitive decision making or problem solving, and less likely to rely on aggressive or avoidant coping strategies, when facing a problem or emotionally upset. Constructive coping was associated with measures of attachment (as reported by the children) and competence in the peer group (as rated by the teachers). Moreover, constructive coping was found to mediate the association between attachment and peer competence (Contreras et al., 2000). While there are sampling and methodological limitations that preclude definitive conclusions, this research represents an example of a growing body of literature that explores the underlying processes or mechanisms accounting for the link between early parent–child attachment security and children's social relationships.

Attachment theorists also predict that the early attachment relationship is associated with the child's view of the self, which in turn is carried into other relationships (e.g., Bretherton, 1985; Cassidy, 1990). A limited number of studies have explored the link between attachment and the self in middle childhood. Still, attachment security to mother and father has been found to predict perceptions of self-worth and social competence (Rubin et al., 2004).

Some research has documented the association between security of attachment to mother and self-esteem among kindergarten children (Verschueren & Marcoen, 1999) and in early adolescence (Engels, Finkenauer, Meeus, & Deković, 2001). Additionally, perceptions of self-worth have been associated with social and emotional outcomes in middle childhood, such as school adjustment (e.g., Verschueren, Buyck, & Marcoen, 2001), peer competence and behavior problems (negatively) (e.g., Easterbrooks & Abeles, 2000), perceptions of social acceptance among shy children and loneliness and anxiety (negatively) (Fordham & Stevenson-Hinde, 1999), and friendship quality (Franco & Levitt, 1998). Given these findings, the question of whether the child's perception of self-worth plays a mediating role between attachment and children's close relationships is important to explore in future investigations.

Similarly, according to attachment theory, perceptions of emotional support may mediate between early attachment security and socio-emotional functioning in social relationships outside of the family. Indeed, some research supports this idea as well. For example, attachment security of 4-year-olds predicted social support networks, which mediated between attachment and social competence (Bost, Vaughn, Washington, Cielinski, & Bradbard, 1998). Similarly, early attachment security was related to social support in 6-year-old children and social support was, in turn, found to mediate between early attachment security and later adjustment (Anan & Barnett, 1999).

So how might these constructs be conceptually linked? Several extant studies have now explored a conceptual model linking attachment security, friendship, and psychosocial functioning in middle childhood; they concurrently evaluated the mediating roles of perceptions of emotional support and of self-worth (for a review, see Booth-LaForce et al., 2005). Perhaps most significantly, a consistent finding that has emerged from this impressive body of work supports the idea that perceptions of self-worth play a mediating role in the association between attachment security and both friendship quality and psychosocial functioning (Booth-LaForce et al., 2006). Future studies are needed that examine the mediating role of self-worth across various points in time and consider other processes (e.g., internal working models, emotion regulation) that might also mediate associations between early attachment relationships and later friendships.

Some Final Considerations

There are several remaining issues that the extant literature on links between attachment and peer relationships has raised (cf. Booth-LaForce & Kerns, 2009). There may be, for example, some additional, unmeasured "third variable" (e.g., parents' valuing of relationships (e.g., Kerns, Cole, & Andrews, 1998) or the mother's competence at teaching appropriate social behaviors (e.g., Contreras & Kerns, 2000)) that influences both attachment security and peer relationships. Mothers' conversations with their 2-year-old children about cognitive mental states (similar to maternal mind-mindedness (Meins, 1997) and reflective function (Fonagy & Target, 1997)) appear to be more frequent in the context of a secure attachment; they also appear to be related to more positive friendships, both observed and mother-reported, and to more rapid decreases in mother-reported negative friendships between 54 months and first grade. Thus, mothers' cognitive mental state talk appears to be an intervening mechanism between attachment and friendship (McElwain, Booth-LaForce, & Wu, 2011). The differential role of mother–child and father–child attachment security in predicting aspects of children's friendships, at different developmental periods, needs to be considered. For example, father–child security appears to be associated, in middle childhood, with the quality of children's best friend relationships (Rubin et al., 2004) and with lower conflict in these best friend dyads (Lieberman et al., 1999). Early elementary school-aged children who, two years earlier, were found to have a secure relationship with their fathers have more reciprocal friends (Verissimo et al., 2011). Mothers and fathers may have different interaction styles and play patterns that promote different developmental consequences in friendships.

It might be that friendship quality moderates the association between attachment and social competence with peers (cf. Booth-LaForce et al., 2005). The role that close friends play in compensating for insecure attachment relationships, or in weakening the association between attachment history and later outcomes, is not clear. Moreover, attachment security may impact particular components of friendship, such as initiating or developing friendships, differently than other aspects, such as maintaining or repairing friendships. Finally, to the extent that children form friendships with others with similar attachment histories, intervention strategies might be helpful in promoting social competence in children with insecure attachment histories.

Friendships are embedded within a constellation of relationships. Each friend brings a network of relationships to their developing friendships and characteristics of this larger network are likely to impact the development and continuity of particular friendships (Bukowski, Newcomb, & Hartup, 1996). In the future, research needs to explore the social contexts that promote or inhibit friendships. For example, we know very little about the association between sibling relationships and friendship (cf. Kramer & Gottman, 1992). Family influences on friendships usually emphasize the role of the parent–child relationship, yet sibling relationships are in many ways more comparable to children's relationships with their friends. Do children transfer patterns of interaction with siblings to their friendships? Do children with multiple siblings have less (or more) of a need for friends than do only children? The multiple motivations for developing friendships, and for sustaining particular friendships, need to be explored further. What role do personal characteristics and relational properties play in facilitating and influencing friendships? And how do these factors change over time? Studies of cultural differences in friendships are especially important, particularly as they demonstrate that the values and goals of a culture are reflected in areas of competence promoted by larger social support networks (Bagwell & Schmidt, 2011).

Perhaps most importantly, researchers are now focusing on the role of mediating variables, such as children's self-esteem (Booth-LaForce et al., 2006; Verschueren & Marcoen, 2002) and emotion regulation strategies (Contreras & Kerns, 2000; Kerns et al., 2007). This reflects an acknowledgment that it is essential to understand the processes involved in the link between early relational experiences and social competence with peers. While attachment theorists purport that internal working models are critical for understanding this link, more refined questions focusing on specific areas where links to early attachment experiences might be expected, during different developmental periods and in particular developmental contexts, need to be explored in future work (Booth-LaForce & Kerns, 2009).

In conclusion, it is essential for researchers to adopt a developmental framework that allows for the examination of specific questions about the early social experiences that impact peer relationships and friendships. There is a general consensus that by the preschool years, peers are important interactive partners. Indeed, the focus shifts during early childhood from communicating shared meaning to developing social knowledge about the peer group (Howes, 1988). Children move from coordinated interaction and positive engagement with peers to inclusion and greater investment in the larger peer world in middle and later childhood. Learning to select partners and to coordinate and sustain interactions gives way to developing close friendships and functioning in stable peer groups. These developmental shifts have implications for exploring links among attachments, peer relationships, and friendships. Moreover, age-appropriate methods for assessing attachment security in childhood need to be used (see, for example, Kerns & Richardson, 2005; Solomon & George, 2008) when examining associations with developmentally salient aspects of peer relationships (Sroufe et al., 1999). Thus, for example, exploring links between attachment and coordinated peer interaction is most relevant during early childhood, whereas examining connections between attachment and friendship quality remains a question for middle and later childhood and adolescence. Finally, it appears that current research is no longer focused on the question of *whether* peer relationships and friendships are influenced by parent–child relationships. Rather, the underlying processes and mechanisms that may help to explain the links among these relational systems are important to understand. This knowledge may ultimately have implications for elucidating patterns of adaptation and maladaptation and may facilitate the identification of developmentally appropriate interventions that can enhance children's experiences in their larger social world of peers and friends.

The Development of Empathy, Prosocial Behavior, and Morality

5

Children need to feel empathy, or to share another person's emotions or feelings, in order to act in prosocial ways. Prosocial behaviors, such as helping, sharing, and comforting others, are voluntary actions intended to benefit other people. We know that children who are especially empathic are also more prosocial (Eisenberg, Fabes, et al., 2006). The differentiation between self and other seems to be a precursor to empathic responsiveness; this differentiation allows the individual to understand the other's feeling states and to avoid self-focused responses while fostering other-oriented concern (Bischof-Köhler, 2012). Yet, the experiential core of empathy – namely, the shared affect between self and other – also requires the capacity to connect to others. Empathy is often defined by prosocial responses, such as expressing concern or helping others, which require certain interpersonal competencies. Thus, we see that early relationships and self–other differentiation appear to be critical to our understanding of empathy and prosocial behavior.

With development, children's ability to empathize with others grows as they become better at interpreting and responding appropriately to others' emotional states. Children first become aware of their own emotions and then learn to distinguish and understand others' emotions. There has been much theorizing and research on children's capacity to perceive others' emotional expressions and to realize that others may have beliefs, intentions, or feelings that may be different from their own (Denham, 1998; Harris, 2000; Thompson et al., 2003). Of course, this development occurs concurrently with children's increasing awareness of their own emotional experiences, with the ability to understand the causes and behavioral consequences of varying emotional states, and with the capacity to empathize (Saarni et al., 2008).

Though young babies have been found to fuss upon hearing the cries of another infant (Hay, Nash, & Pedersen, 1981; Sagi & Hoffman, 1976), these responses reflect more of an "emotional contagion" than an understanding of the feelings of others. Infants continue to be distressed and to exhibit contagious crying throughout the first year (Geangu, Benga, Stahl, & Striano, 2010), especially when the other's distress is intense, expressed for long periods of time, or in an unfamiliar environment. While some investigators have argued that there is evidence of concern for others in the first year of life, others maintain that it is not until the second year that children begin to develop a sense of themselves as distinct individuals, their responses to other's change, and we see some of the earliest forms of empathic responses (Davidov, Zahn-Waxler, Roth-Hanania, & Knafo, 2013; Roth-Hanania, Davidov, & Zahn-Waxler, 2011). Upon observing their mother's distress, toddlers will now react with concerned attention (Zahn-Waxler, 2000) as empathic concern for the mother increases from the middle to the end of the second year (van der Mark, van IJzendoorn, & Bakermans-Kranenburg, 2002). Toddlers shift from a concern for their own comfort to a wish to comfort others. However, cognitive limitations and overall immaturity make it difficult for them to adopt another's point of view. This may lead, for example, to an 18-month-old offering his or her own special teddy bear to an adult who is upset. Between 18 and 36 months, children demonstrate behaviors in response to another's sadness that reflect increases in understanding their own emotional and personal distress, and older children express more concern for others in pain relative to sadness (Bandstra, Chambra, McGrath, & Moore, 2011).

During the preschool and early childhood periods, as children learn to distinguish their own emotional needs from those of others, they can respond in ways that are less egocentric and more sensitive. They will sometimes make an effort to comfort the person who is distressed or to offer other forms of prosocial behavior. Indeed, prosocial helping, sharing, and caring become more frequent with age, as 4-year-olds direct more prosocial behavior toward their peers than do 3-year-olds (Benenson et al., 2003). Still, the motivation to help is complicated and does not always reflect empathy alone (Eisenberg, Spinrad, & Sadovsky, 2006). Indeed, the question of whether empathy leads to prosocial behavior is a controversial issue (see Eisenberg, 2003, for a review). What we will come to see is that children's developing affective and cognitive understanding of their own and others' emotional experiences impacts the development of empathy. Moreover, self-development and relationships with parents, siblings, and peers are likely to influence, and be influenced by, children's developing empathic abilities and prosocial behaviors. Thus, again we are reminded of the interconnections between attachments to others and the development of the self.

The social, emotional, and cognitive competencies associated with the developing awareness of the self also influence children's ideas of right and wrong. While specific values and behaviors regarded as desirable vary among cultures, and even within families, adults help children to learn moral rules. Initially, parents control their young children's actions as they teach them rules for appropriate behavior. With time and maturity, children begin to regulate their own behavior so that, in the absence of external constraints, they exert self-control. There are various components of morality – emotional, cognitive, and behavioral – that have been studied by developmental researchers. These components will be discussed with a focus on the self in relationships as a way of understanding developmental changes in moral reasoning and behavior.

Empathy

What is Empathy?

Empathy is an immediate emotional response that connects us to others. Empathy occurs when we witness someone else's emotional state, take their perspective, and experience the emotion that we believe they are feeling. It is distinct from sympathy, which is when we feel concern or sorrow for a person in distress (even when, for example, we read about the unfortunate experiences of someone we do not know). With sympathy, we do not necessarily experience the negative emotional response ourselves (Eisenberg, 2003). Empathy requires that the individual be able to understand another person's feeling state (a cognitive component) as well as to share that feeling state (an affective component) (Feshbach, 1975; Hoffman, 1983; Strayer, 1987). It also necessitates an ability to regulate the negative emotional arousal that results from feeling the emotion, such as distress or anxiety, similar to the one experienced by the other. Research has demonstrated that empathic concern is greater when children have the ability to regulate negative emotions; when self-regulatory capacities are poor, children are more likely to maintain their distressed state and not respond to the other with concern (Davidov & Grusec, 2006; Eisenberg, Fabes, et al., 2006).

The capacity to be empathic has important implications for children's prosocial behavior, social competence, and the development of psychopathology (Strayer & Roberts, 2004). In fact, several studies have been conducted where children view others in distress or in need of help. Physiological, facial, or behavioral markers of empathy have been found to be associated with young children's prosocial behavior (Holmgren, Eisenberg, & Fabes, 1998; Zahn-Waxler, Cole, Welch, & Fox, 1995; Zahn-Waxler, Radke-Yarrow, et al., 1992). Empathy has been studied, therefore, both as the capacity to know what another person is thinking and feeling and as a motivator to relieve the suffering of the other person for whom empathic feelings are felt (Batson, 2009).

Several different types of empathic responsiveness in young children have been delineated (Hoffman, 2000). The earliest signs of empathic responding may be seen in *rudimentary empathic responding*, that is, when a newborn cries in response to hearing another baby cry. By the end of the first year, infants become distressed or agitated when they hear another child cry. As a result, they seek comfort for themselves. This *egocentric empathic distress* does not lead them to help the other child but to feel agitated, aroused, and distressed as a result of what the other appears to be feeling. It is not until the beginning of the second year that they are more likely to approach and try to comfort a distressed child. Now, because they begin to differentiate the self from the other, they can experience true concern for someone else's distress. These empathic feelings may lead to early prosocial behavior. Thus, by about 18 months of age, we begin to see children offer help that is more specific and focused. For example, instead of offering a cookie to a child whose toy was taken away by another peer (thinking the cookie will make her feel better), the toddler will find a new toy that might make her happy. This *quasi-egocentric empathic distress* still reflects children's own feelings as they are unable to clearly distinguish their own and others' feeling states. As toddlers further develop a sense of themselves as distinct from others, later in the second year, they are capable of *true empathic distress* as they respond to another's distress with more appropriate behaviors (for example, by bringing a tissue to a crying toddler who fell down or choosing to sit quietly with a peer who is too tired to run around but does not want to sit alone).

Initially, children can only experience empathy when the other person is present, with a clear developmental progression when responding to both peers' (Lamb & Zakhireh, 1997) and mothers' (van der Mark et al., 2002) distress. It is not until they are older that children can listen to stories of other people's distress and respond empathically. Understanding another person's general condition (such as being poor, disabled, or seriously ill) is something that occurs in middle childhood, whereas it is not until adolescence when cognitive advances allow for a deeper understanding of the psychological state of those who are less fortunate (e.g., populations who are undernourished or politically oppressed) and a consideration of alternative courses of action that might lead to real change.

Individual differences in empathy are likely to be determined by a number of variables, such as experiences with parents and caregivers (Bischof-Köhler, 2012; Davidov & Grusec, 2006; Hoffman, 1975; Kiang, Moreno, & Robinson, 2004) and the infant's temperamental predispositions (e.g., fearfulness, irritability, sociability, regulation) (Eisenberg, 2000; van der Mark et al., 2002; Young, Fox, & Zahn-Waxler, 1999). For example, variations in self-regulation at 4 months have been linked to infants' responses to others' distress at 1 year (Ungerer et al., 1990). Moreover, individual differences in affective and cognitive empathic responses at 8 and 10 months have been found to be associated with more prosocial behavior during the second year (Roth-Hanania et al., 2011). Fearfulness in infancy has been linked with empathic concern at school age as reported by parents (Rothbart, Ahadi, & Hershey, 1994). And infants who are highly reactive in the first year and less inhibited in their reactions to unfamiliar adults at 2 years also show more empathy to an unfamiliar adult's distress as compared to more inhibited children (van der Mark et al., 2002; Young et al., 1999).

Empathy communicated by caregivers in their attempts to understand their baby's emotional needs may be one of the earliest foundations for the development of empathy. There is some evidence that maternal sensitivity to infants' emotional needs and signals predicts empathy in young children (e.g., Kiang et al., 2004; Robinson, Zahn-Waxler, & Emde, 1994; Zahn-Waxler & Radke-Yarrow, 1990). This sensitivity leads the caregiver to meet the child's needs while responding to emotional cues, thereby providing a foundation of security and safety. It also communicates an orientation of compassionate care for others (Hastings, Utendale, & Sullivan, 2007). Parental socialization practices are likely to continue to play a role in the development of empathy (see Grusec & Sherman, 2011, for an extensive review). Additionally, there may not be a direct correspondence between parents' and their children's empathic abilities. Rather, associations may be influenced by affective reactions such as anger. For example, parents who are more empathic have children who are less angry and more empathic. By contrast, parents who are less empathic are also more controlling and have children who are less empathic and more angry (Strayer & Roberts, 2004). In an observational study of 240 six-year-old children, more frequent displays of parental anger were found to be associated with more frequent anger, and less sadness and fear, in the children (Snyder, Stoolmiller, Wilson, & Yamamoto, 2003). These children learn that anger is the way to express all negative feeling states, making them less likely to display their vulnerability when sad or afraid and more likely to have difficulties understanding and responding to more differentiated emotions in themselves or others.

Genetic factors may account for early differences in children's empathy, as documented in studies of identical (monozygotic) and fraternal (dizygotic) twins, although parental behavior may continue to play a role (Zahn-Waxler, Robinson, & Emde, 1992). For example, more empathy in the second year has been found to be associated with maternal warmth (Robinson et al., 1994). Supportive, sensitive parental behavior provides a model for empathic interactions, especially if it is part of a secure attachment relationship (van IJzendoorn, 1997). In fact, several studies have demonstrated that attachment security is associated with the development of empathy. Securely attached children have been found to be more empathic toward their peers in preschool (Kestenbaum, Farber, & Sroufe, 1989; Waters, Wippman, & Sroufe, 1979) and more likely to respond, in their mother's absence, to their younger sibling's distress with empathic caregiving (Teti & Ablard, 1989).

When interactions between maternal affective state, children's affect regulation, and attachment security have been explored, an interesting pattern of results has been observed. Specifically, 2- to 4-year-old children of non-depressed or moderately depressed mothers who are securely attached and have no problems in affect regulation demonstrate moderate frequencies of empathic responses, whereas children of severely depressed mothers, to whom they are securely attached but who have problems with affect regulation themselves, show the highest frequencies of empathic responses. Perhaps these children are overly involved in "inappropriate" maternal caregiving, abandoning their own emotional needs, failing to learn necessary affect regulation skills, and manifesting the caregiving behaviors more typically displayed by children with disorganized attachments (van IJzendoorn et al., 1999). Thus, securely attached children are more likely to experience caregiving characterized by sensitivity and empathic responsiveness. In turn, these children tend to be more emotionally expressive and to communicate their emotions more accurately, and these are the very skills that are necessary for true empathy. Additionally, parental affective state, as well as insensitive, unresponsive, or rejecting caregiving behaviors, may impact, among other things, children's development of emotion understanding and contribute to problems in empathic responsiveness.

Interestingly, while gender differences in empathy have been postulated, research findings provide inconsistent evidence. Some studies report differences between boys and girls in their empathic concern or prosocial responding (e.g., Knafo, Zahn-Waxler, Van Hulle, Robinson, & Rhee, 2008; Volbrecht, Lemery-Chalfant, Aksan, Zahn-Waxler, & Goldsmith, 2007) while others do not (Roth-Hanania et al., 2011; Vaish, Carpenter, & Tomasello, 2009). In studies of older children, girls have consistently been found to be more empathic than boys (Eisenberg, Fabes, et al., 2006), though this may reflect an internalization of socially acceptable gender roles and behavior that is congruent with these expectations rather than any inherent gender difference in empathic abilities.

Contemporary cognitive neuroscientists have studied empathy in the context of higher brain structures, including the cortex (Lamm, Batson, & Decety, 2007). Researchers exploring the neural mechanisms required for the expression of empathy have determined that at least some of the underlying physiological substrates are shared with more general qualities of emotionality, including sociability (Carter, Harris, & Porges, 2009). Empathy and emotionality are dependent on lower brain structures and on the autonomic nervous system as well. An examination of the neural and endocrine systems required for detecting and responding to bodily states is helpful for understanding feelings and emotional states. Empathy may consequently be viewed in terms of the regulation of emotions and of arousal levels and requires adaptive autonomic and neuroendocrine processes (Porges, 2007). Furthermore, the ability to feel what another person is feeling, to perceive another's emotion and experience the same emotion, is thought to result from an overlap in brain circuits (Decety & Meyer, 2008; Preston & de Waal, 2002), though what might be experienced is a combination of self-distress and empathic concern (Davidov et al., 2013).

Empathy has also been distinguished from more general theory of mind abilities. Whereas theory of mind involves a cognitive process that allows for reasoning about other people's mental states, empathy is considered an affective reaction that involves sensitivity to, and understanding of, others' emotions (Wellman, 1991). Developing theory of mind abilities is a process that extends throughout childhood (Wellman & Lui, 2004). By contrast, the automatic affective aspects of empathy, such as affective sharing and emotional contagion, are present in infants and toddlers, while the more advanced cognitive perspective-taking abilities that influence empathic responsiveness are developed throughout childhood (Hoffman, 2000). These affective and cognitive components of empathy have been supported by evidence from neuroscience research. Specifically, the brain regions involved in perspective taking, self–other differentiation, and mentalizing tasks suggest that distinct neural correlates provide explicit cognitive support for empathy in ways that are quite different from those involved in other kinds of social and nonsocial cognitive tasks (such as some theory of mind tasks) (Pfeifer & Dapretto, 2009).

Moreover, the mirror neuron system appears to be involved with the affective processes supporting empathic responsiveness and interpersonal competence in children (Pfeifer, Iacoboni, Mazziotta, & Dapretto, 2008). Indeed, there is extremely consistent evidence for dysfunction in the mirror neuron system in individuals with autism spectrum disorder (Oberman & Ramachandran, 2007). While the mirror neuron system appears to be associated with individual differences in the affective components of empathy, the role this system plays in the cognitive aspects of empathy (e.g., perspective taking) is less apparent (Pfeifer & Dapretto, 2009). The developmental social neuroscience perspective has clearly offered many important insights into the affective and cognitive components of empathy. Ultimately, future research will continue to inform our understanding of the neural systems involved across development and provide direction for intervention strategies that might promote the development of social-cognitive skills.

Finally, some of what we have learned about empathy comes from the study of the absence of empathy and its associated social dysfunction. For example, infants and young children with autism spectrum disorders or conduct disorders, and children and adolescents with externalizing and other antisocial behaviors, experience deficiencies in empathic responsiveness as well as in their social relationships (although the underlying reasons for these deficiencies vary) (Blair, 2005; Miller & Eisenberg, 1988; Oberman & Ramachandran, 2007; Preston & de Waal, 2002). Children who have been maltreated, or who have problems discriminating emotions and comprehending others' emotional expressions and affective states, have difficulty empathizing with others or engaging in prosocial behavior (see, for example, Pollak, Cicchetti, Hornung, & Reed, 2000). Early detection of empathic deficits may be helpful in screening for certain developmental disorders, thereby allowing for intervention to be provided earlier in the child's life. If children's empathy and prosocial behaviors are closely linked to their ability to accurately recognize and respond to others' emotional states, then we see once more the importance of early emotional relationships with caregivers as the training ground for later social and emotional competence.

Empathy and Perspective Taking

Perspective taking is the ability to understand the point of view of another person. The capacity for perspective taking has been found to be associated with prosocial behavior (Strayer & Roberts, 2004; Zahn-Waxler et al., 1995). However, it may be that perspective taking itself is not enough to lead a child to act in prosocial ways. That is, the motivation to help may also require the capacity for empathy (Denham, 1998). In fact, several studies have demonstrated that children who demonstrated good perspective-taking abilities and who were more competent at understanding another's feelings acted in more prosocial ways as compared to those who were good at perspective taking alone (Denham, 1998; Knight, Johnson, Carlo, & Eisenberg, 1994; Stams, Deković, Brugman, Rutten, Van den Wittenboer, Tavecchio, Hendriks, & Van Schijndel, 2008). When an explicit model was tested predicting that perspective taking contributes to empathy and empathy in turn contributes to prosocial behavior (Roberts & Strayer, 1996), the model was supported for groups of 5-, 9-, and 13-year-old children. Additionally, for girls, empathy was a more significant predictor of prosocial behavior toward friends, perhaps because they are closer to and more intimate with friends than are boys.

Studies of affective perspective taking have focused on the ability to put oneself in someone else's place, make inferences about their affective state, and then respond based on those assumptions (Hoffman, 1984; Thompson, 1987). Recent research, using developmentally sensitive measures of sympathy reactions, has documented the appearance of this ability in children as young as 2 years of age (Vaish et al., 2011). It is relevant to note that similar results were obtained by researchers who documented theory of mind abilities in children as young as 2 years of age when using age-appropriate measures (Onishi & Baillargeon, 2005; Southgate, Senju, & Csibra, 2007). Thus, affective and cognitive perspective-taking abilities are likely to be interrelated, such that an affective reaction to another's state may lead to a cognitive understanding, or alternatively, a cognitive construction may generate an affective response. Moreover, this understanding may motivate prosocial behavior, even in very young children, and measurement approaches need to incorporate developmentally appropriate assessments of these competencies.

Perspective Taking and Relationships

There has been an increased interest in exploring children's understanding of others' minds. How do children come to understand the inner states and feelings of others? And how do they learn to associate others' thoughts, desires, or beliefs with their behaviors? Indeed, much cognitive-developmental research in the past two decades has focused on theory of mind, broadening findings on the age range at which an understanding of theory of mind is achieved and exploring theory of mind abilities in different cultural groups. Moreover, the association between children's affective and cognitive understanding of others' emotional states and the impact of this understanding on the quality of their social relationships are areas of increasing concern to developmental researchers (Dunn, 2000). For example, it has been argued that an early understanding of others' emotional states gives rise to an understanding of their cognitive states (for example, *why* they do what they do) (Bartsch & Wellman, 1995). And the developmental sequelae of individual differences in these two related competencies are important to consider given the impact of cognitive and affective perspective taking on social relationships more generally (Dunn, 2000). Thus, for example, more sophisticated peer relationships, characterized by much connected communication and frequent role play, have been associated with early mind-reading skills (Dunn, 1996b). And later popularity with peers, advanced understanding of emotions, and moral awareness are related to early emotion understanding abilities (Dunn, 1995; Dunn, Cutting, & Demetriou, 2000). Security of attachment is also associated with mind-reading skills later on (Meins, 1997). While the direction of effects is unclear, and other processes may mediate these associations, increased interest in these areas of research reflect a growing acknowledgment of the intricate connection between cognitive and affective development.

Perhaps most importantly, children's affective or cognitive understanding of others' emotional states is likely to be associated with the quality of the relationship they have with their primary attachment figure and to have consequences for their social development (see, for example, Dunn & Cutting, 1999; Fonagy, Redfern, & Charman, 1997). Additionally, the nature of the relationship (e.g., with mothers, friends, siblings) seems to influence how children use their understanding of others' internal states (Dunn, 1996b). Children's behavior, when engaging in imaginative play, conversing about mental states, and managing conflict, has been found to vary with different interactive partners. Indeed, general developmental trends in theory of mind abilities have been shown to be affected by experiences with siblings (Perner, Ruffman, & Leekam, 1994; Ruffman, Perner, Naito, Parkin, & Clements, 1998). Again, this research highlights the important connections among mind, emotions, and social understanding. It also emphasizes the need to clarify normative patterns of development as well as alternative pathways that may be seen in children with behavioral and emotional problems such as autism spectrum disorders, conduct disorders, and attentional problems. Ultimately, this work will contribute to our growing understanding of the essential affective and cognitive abilities that impact children's social relationships.

Prosocial Behavior

When children engage in behavior that is intended to help someone else, such as helping, sharing, comforting, cooperating, or acting kindly, and they do so without the other requesting their help, we say that they are displaying prosocial behavior. When prosocial behavior is displayed without any apparent concern for how it will benefit the person engaging in prosocial acts and without any need for acknowledgment, approval, or reciprocity, then the behavior is altruistic. While prosocial behavior may be seen in young infants, it is only in childhood that we begin to see truly altruistic behavior (Eisenberg, Fabes, et al., 2006).

Interestingly, the study of prosocial behavior is much more complicated than is the study of antisocial behavior. Researchers tend to be more concerned with the disruptive, maladaptive behaviors that can be clearly identified and may potentially cause harm, whereas the detection of helpful behaviors that express concern and care for others is more challenging. The actions that constitute prosocial behavior are not universally agreed upon, thus necessitating careful attention to how prosocial behaviors are operationalized and studied and restricting conclusions to only those behaviors that have been carefully defined and examined (Grusec & Sherman, 2011). Moreover, assumptions about the motivations for engaging in prosocial behavior, or the meaning of prosocial behaviors for the doer and the recipient, are not believed to be universal. Again, these considerations raise important questions for researchers to explore.

The Development of Prosocial Behavior

Most babies are biologically prepared to pay attention to social partners and to engage in social interactions. Newborns show a preference for prosocial stimuli, such as happy facial expressions, as compared to neutral or fear expressions (Farroni, Menon, Rigato, & Johnson, 2007). As early as 3 months of age, infants demonstrate an ability to evaluate others' behavior in preferential looking tasks and appear to have an aversion for antisocial actors (Hamlin, Wynn, & Bloom, 2010). Additionally, 6- and 10-month-old infants selectively attend to and approach actors who have helped another reach a goal (Hamlin & Wynn, 2011; Hamlin, Wynn, & Bloom, 2007). Thus, social evaluations seem to result from the observation of others' social behaviors, even without direct experience with the consequences of others' good or bad actions.

A certain moral sensitivity appears to be present even in very young infants (Decety & Howard, 2013). Infants' reactions to social stimuli may be the result of emotional arousal and have little to do with cognitive abilities (Vaish & Warneken, 2012). These internal, arousal-based reactions to both positive and negative stimuli may be influenced by early developing neural systems (Decety, 2010). Later increases in activity in affective-processing brain regions, such as the insula and orbitofrontal cortex (Blasi et al., 2011), together with developing inferential social-cognitive abilities and social learning experiences, may provide the basis for more active prosocial responsiveness, including sharing, helping, and altruistic responses (Decety & Howard, 2013). Indeed, even young children can infer, based on minimal cues, when help is needed and respond flexibly in prosocial ways, whether driven by empathic concern in response to emotional distress (Eisenberg, Fabes, et al., 2006; Hoffman, 2000) or by a desire to help others achieve more pragmatic goals (Warneken, 2015).

There is a developmental progression in children's tendency to engage in prosocial behavior. Early signs of sharing include participating in joint attention or infants pointing to objects and interesting things that they have seen and want others to look at (Hay, 1994). By 12–18 months of age, children are eager to give toys and objects to others without direction or the need to be reinforced (Warneken & Tomasello, 2007). There are cognitive achievements that appear to play a role in prosocial behavior. Beginning at 2 years of age, children will help by inferring the other person's needs using observations of their prior behavior, though some children may help even in the absence of behavioral signals or cues (Pettygrove, Hammond, Karahuta, Waugh, & Brownell, 2013; Warneken, 2013, 2015). During the second year, children will touch or verbally comfort a distressed child. They now have a rudimentary sense of the self as distinct from others and will sometimes offer their own teddy bear or blanket, assuming it will comfort the other just as it soothes them. By 2 years of age, we see an increase in a variety of prosocial behaviors such as helping, protecting, offering advice, and sharing (Garner, Jones, & Palmer, 1994). Now capable of recognizing themselves in the mirror, and of taking another's perspective, more advanced prosocial behaviors are possible. Thus, as compared to empathy, prosocial behavior may appear later because it requires both a cognitive understanding of, and feeling concern for, another's distress (Decety & Meyer, 2008). Prosocial behavior also requires an integration of affect, cognition, and behavior in order to engage in a goal-directed response. During the second and third years of life, important advances in false-belief attributions (Baillargeon, Scott, & He, 2010), in emotion regulation (McGuigan & Nunez, 2006), in the capacity to maintain effortful control (Kochanska et al., 2000), and in theory of mind (Carlson, 2009) all contribute to and promote prosocial behavior. We tend to see fairly rapid growth of prosocial behavior in the toddler and preschool period, with relatively slower but continued growth into childhood, adolescence, and early adulthood (Hastings et al., 2007).

Neuroimaging studies that have examined the underlying neural processes involved in prosocial responsiveness and morality in young children are limited. However, some studies exploring the perception of morally salient situations reveal developmental changes in structures involved in processing emotionally laden experiences (for example, the insula and amygdala). A decrease in activation with age and a concomitant increase in medial and ventral prefrontal cortex activity are reflected in more advanced moral evaluations (Decety & Howard, 2013). Thus, the capacity to assess intent to harm and the consequences of immoral behaviors reflects an understanding of others' mental states, supported by distinct neural networks linking cognitive processes with affective and motivational states involved in moral judgments (Young & Dungan, 2012). Future research exploring developmental changes in neural connections and activation of brain regions will provide important insights into the brain systems involved in moral reasoning, as well as those individual and connected networks that may result in immoral behavior (Decety & Howard, 2013).

As children become increasingly mature in their cognitive abilities and emotional understanding, they are able to detect more subtle emotional cues, discern when others need help, and engage in more targeted and appropriate prosocial behavior (Eisenberg, Fabes, et al., 2006). Despite advances in moral sensitivity that are made possible with development, it is also conceivable that young children will display insensitive or inappropriate responses, such as ignoring, laughing, or acting aggressively, when others are distressed (Radke-Yarrow, Zahn-Waxler, & Chapman, 1982). Longitudinal studies will contribute to our understanding of the individual and environmental factors that lead to prosocial behavior. For example, there is some research that has documented low-to-moderate stability of individual differences in prosocial characteristics during early childhood (Hay, Castle, Davies, Demetriou, & Stimson, 1999; Zahn-Waxler, Radke-Yarrow, et al., 1992), with increased stability in empathy during childhood (Zhou et al., 2002) and in prosocial behavior toward peers during adolescence (Wentzel, Barry, & Caldwell, 2004). What accounts for these individual differences in prosocial behavior? And what are the origins of these individual differences in children's developing abilities to behave in a prosocial manner? These are the issues to which we will now turn.

Individual Differences in Prosocial Behavior

Children vary in their tendency to engage in prosocial behavior. These individual differences appear early on and are relatively stable over time. For example, 2-year-old children's responses to their mother's distress are similar to the way they respond when observed again at 7 years of age (Radke-Yarrow & Zahn-Waxler, 1984). From preschool through the elementary school years, there is moderate stability in children's nurturant and sympathetic behaviors toward peers (Baumrind, 1971). Across the elementary school years, children are consistent in their willingness to donate to needy children, help an adult, and offer assistance to their peers (Eisenberg, Fabes, et al., 2006). There is relative stability in prosocial behavior in adolescence (Wentzel et al., 2004) and in reasoning about and valuing concern for others in young adulthood (Pratt, Skoe, & Arnold, 2004).

There are also gender differences in prosocial behavior, though these also depend on the particular behavior studied (Eisenberg, Fabes, et al., 2006). For example, girls are consistently more likely than boys to display consideration and kindness, to experience emotions felt by others, and to be empathic (Zahn-Waxler, Schiro, Robinson, Emde, & Schmitz, 2001). Girls, as compared to boys, have been found to show more concern for others from the age of 2 years through adolescence (Eisenberg & Fabes, 1998). And small but significant differences have been found in sharing, comforting, donating, and instrumental helping, with girls more likely to engage in these behaviors than boys. Moreover, 2-year-old children who engage in more sharing behavior with their peers are also more likely to be sensitive, and react negatively, to peers' distress (Hay et al., 1999).

Interestingly, when prosocial acts are anonymous, there appear to be no gender differences (Carlo, Hausmann, Christiansen, & Randall, 2003). And gender differences are more striking when self-report data or responses from family members are examined (Hastings, Rubin, & DeRose, 2005). When data are obtained from objective observers, gender differences are minimal. Parents are more likely to stress the value of prosocial behavior for their daughters and to assume they result from inborn tendencies whereas boys' prosocial behavior is often seen to be the result of socialization. Also, gender differences appear to increase with age (Eisenberg, Fabes, et al., 2006). Thus, the obtained gender differences may reflect gendered ideas about how girls and boys are supposed to behave rather than what they actually do (Hastings et al., 2007). Moreover, as children become more aware of gender stereotypes and incorporate them into their self-image, they are more likely to incorporate these views into their self-representations and to report behaviors consistent with these stereotypes (Eisenberg, Fabes, et al., 2006).

Individual differences in empathy should also be considered in combination with other variables, such as moral values, to predict prosocial behavior (Saarni et al., 2008). Empathy is believed to be a precursor to moral development. Empathic children have been found to show more concern, offer more helpful and other prosocial behaviors, be less aggressive, and display more advanced moral judgment (Mehrabian, Young, & Sato, 1988; van IJzendoorn, 1997). In order for moral reasoning or behavior to occur, children need to know the difference between themselves and others, take the perspective of another, and be motivated to offer supportive moral behavior. The cognitive and emotional prerequisites for empathy and moral development are established in the second year of life (Kagan, 1981; Lamb, 1993) and impact subsequent prosocial behavior through childhood and into adolescence. For example, youth with conduct disorders have been found to exhibit failures in empathy (Cohen & Strayer, 1996). Additionally, lack of empathy has been identified as one of the potential mediators between moral values and bullying (Arsenio & Lemerise, 2004). And children are more likely to engage in prosocial behavior when helping others is something for which they feel personally responsible (Chapman, Zahn-Waxler, Cooperman, & Iannotti, 1987). Thus, future research exploring multiple variables and adopting more sophisticated statistical models may help to illuminate the many factors that account for individual differences in children's tendency to engage in prosocial behavior.

What Are the Origins of Individual Differences in Prosocial Behavior?

Evolutionary theorists have contributed to and informed the approach that developmental psychologists have taken to understanding the causes of prosocial behavior (McAndrew, 2002). The evolutionary perspective focuses on the distal causes, or the origins and functions, of prosocial behavior, thereby serving as a reminder to developmentalists that all humans have a tendency to act in prosocial ways. This prosocial inclination is quite adaptive for humans. It allows us to be helpful and cooperative and it contributes to the forging of social bonds within reciprocal relationships while concurrently establishing trust within larger social groups (Sober & Wilson, 1998). Developmental psychologists tend to focus on the more immediate, or proximal, causes of prosocial behavior and are concerned with better understanding individual differences that may be explained by genes, experiences, or some combination of these two influences (Grusec & Sherman, 2011). Both evolutionary and developmental theorists inform one another, emphasizing the evolved predispositions, normative patterns, and social influences that influence prosocial behavior. Moreover, behavior genetics researchers have also focused on the development of prosocial behavior and found both genetic and shared environmental effects.

Interestingly, the contribution of heritability to prosocial behaviors is low for toddlers and young children compared to the influence of shared environment (Knafo & Plomin, 2006; Zahn-Waxler et al., 2001). However, there are cultural factors that influence shared environmental effects (Knafo & Israel, 2009). The significance of either the influence of genes or shared environment has been found to differ depending on the specific prosocial behavior examined (Grusec & Sherman, 2011). With age, shared environment effects appear to decrease while genetic effects increase. This shift is due, in part, to the fact that cognitive capacities appearing between the ages of 2 and 7 years, such as perspective-taking abilities, influence prosocial behavior, thereby adding to the importance of genetic influences. Shared environmental influences become insignificant by 7 years of age (Knafo & Plomin, 2006) as the diversity of social experiences increases, parental behaviors interact with children's temperamental proclivities, and children choose environments and social partners who are well suited to their temperaments (Grusec & Sherman, 2011). By adolescence and young adulthood, genetic influence continues to be significant (as high as 70% or more), while there is little influence of shared environment (Knafo & Plomin, 2006). This may be the result of methodological factors since self-report measures are used in studies of adolescents and adults (as opposed to the observer ratings used for measuring younger children's prosocial behaviors) and these are subject to response biases (Grusec & Sherman, 2011). Still, we see the developmental impact of biology and environment working in tandem as children's behavior influences, and is influenced by, their environment (Bell, 1968; Sameroff, 1975). Both genetic and shared environmental influences, therefore, appear to play a role in the development of children's prosocial behavior (Scourfield, John, Martin, & McGuffin, 2004; Zahn-Waxler, Robinson, et al., 1992).

Furthermore, molecular genetics researchers have identified specific genes associated with prosocial behavior. For example, polymorphisms of the dopamine D4 receptor gene have been associated with preschool-aged twins sharing with one another (DiLalla, Elam, & Smolen, 2009). Polymorphisms in the oxytocin receptor gene and in the gene responsible for arginine vasopressin activity have been linked to behaviors such as social bonding and affiliation (Israel et al., 2008). Many more genes may be discovered to be involved in prosocial behavior (see, for example, Chakrabarti et al., 2009). Researchers are continuing to explore the differential timing of gene activation related to prosocial behaviors, as well as gene-by-gene and gene-by-environment interactions (Grusec & Sherman, 2011), thereby providing more support for the role of genes in the development of specific prosocial behaviors.

However, while genes play a role in empathy and prosocial behavior (Zahn-Waxler et al., 2001), they may not tell the whole story. In fact, early socialization experiences, and attachment relationships in particular, appear to be critical for prosocial development. It is in the dynamic affective exchanges that occur in early attachment relationships that we see some of the earliest roots of prosocial and altruistic behavior. Indeed, as a result of joint attention, interactive exchanges, and turn-taking, the infant and caregiver "create a world of shared meaning, empathic understanding, and appropriate linking of one's own emotions with those of others that then generalize beyond the parent–child dyad" (Zahn-Waxler, 1991, p. 156). Thus, while maternal sensitivity facilitates the development of a secure attachment relationship, it is also through the history of their interactions that parents communicate to their children their willingness to respond to their signals and cues. When parents are available to offer their infants relief from distress, comfort and support when needed, and developmentally appropriate responses to their signals, infants in turn develop expectations regarding current and future interactions. They also learn about how to respond to others in sensitive and helpful ways.

Research exploring the associations between infants' early attachment security and children's later prosocial behavior has found strong links. Specifically, attachment security at 12 and 18 months is associated with more sympathetic reactions and helpful behavior directed toward a peer in distress at 3½ years (Waters et al., 1979) and at 4 years of age (Kestenbaum et al., 1989). More securely attached toddlers are also more prosocial with their peers when studied three years later; independent measures of maternal behavior do not predict prosocial behavior with peers as strongly as does attachment security (Iannotti, Cummings, Pierrehumbert, Milano, & Zahn-Waxler, 1992). Secure attachment relationships may lead to prosocial competence because of the associated internal working models that contain components of care and concern, engaging with others in empathic ways, and being prepared to respond to another's signals and cues (see, for example, Mikulciner & Shaver, 2005). Additionally, secure attachment, born of experiences of effective calming and soothing from parents, supports the development of early emotion regulation (especially when seeing someone else in distress), which in turn may lead to a greater sensitivity to the other and a willingness to offer support and help (Cassidy, 1994).

Parents play a primary role in the socialization of prosocial behavior during infancy. When mothers sensitively respond to their infant's distress, they promote the development of neurobiological systems associated with stress (Gunnar, 2000) and foster children's capacity to cope with their own and others' distress and negative emotions (Cassidy, 1994). By the second and third years, children are also more competent at displaying empathy toward others and responding to them in helpful ways, in part because of their ability to regulate their own emotional arousal in the face of stress (Grusec & Sherman, 2011). Thus, by distinguishing their own reactions from those of others, made possible by their more general understanding of the self as separate from others, children can ward off feelings of being overwhelmed by the other's personal distress, remain focused on the other's problem or difficulty, and try to do something to improve the situation (Davidov & Grusec, 2006; Eisenberg, Fabes, et al., 2006; Eisenberg, Wentzel, & Harris, 1998).

When children's social worlds expand in the preschool and early childhood years, peers, teachers, and other adults assume an increasingly important role in the socialization of prosocial behavior. Parents continue to be concerned with how their children deal with negative emotions in particular. Research has found that mothers play a significant role in influencing the frequency and quality of comforting behaviors offered to others in their 8- to 11-year-olds, both sons and daughters (Eisenberg, Fabes, & Murphy, 1996). And when mothers know what helped to comfort their 10- to 12-year-old children when distressed, their children are, in turn, found to cope better and to be rated by their teachers as more prosocial (Vinik, Almas, & Grusec, 2011). Parents, teachers, and other adults impact children by modeling and offering information about prosocial behavior. They also encourage appropriate, and discourage inappropriate, prosocial responses, and cultivate an emotional climate that supports prosocial development (Eisenberg & Murphy, 1995). Moreover, siblings play an important role in fostering perspective taking and social understanding, thereby promoting empathy and prosocial responsiveness (Tucker, Updegraff, McHale, & Crouter, 1999).

Only recently has prosocial behavior been explored in adolescents (see, for example, Smetana, Campione-Barr, & Metzger, 2006). With increased autonomy, and more time spent away from family and together with peers (Larson, Richards, Moneta, Holmbeck, & Duckett, 1996), prosocial behavior is initiated and perpetuated in peer groups (Bukowski & Sippola, 1996). This is especially true among the more influential adolescent groups who are physically attractive (especially for girls) and members of sports teams (Ellis & Zarbatany, 2007b). There are also negative consequences of peer influences, especially when it comes to prosocial behaviors. Pairs of delinquent male friends are less likely to engage in prosocial conversations and more likely to react positively to topics having to do with breaking of rules (Dishion, Spracklen, Andrews, & Patterson, 1996). Still, despite the enormous influence of peers in adolescence, mothers and fathers continue to impact moral reasoning and prosocial behavior (Carlo, Fabes, Laible, & Kupanoff, 1999). For example, adolescents who share more with their mother and turn to her for emotional support are more likely to report internalization of moral values such as kindness, fairness, and honesty (Barry, Padilla-Walker, Madsen, & Nelson, 2008). And secure attachments with parents in adolescence are associated with various prosocial behaviors as well (Laible, Carlo, & Roesch, 2004).

Finally, the socialization of emotion, which involves promoting children's developing understanding of their own and others' emotional experiences, has been explored as it encompasses parents' efforts to foster their children's regulation of emotions and may therefore influence prosocial behavior. Parents, through supporting emotional competence, may in turn have children who are more kind, helpful, and empathic (Hastings et al., 2007). While there are no longitudinal studies exploring these ideas, several maternal behaviors have been found to be associated with distinct measures of prosocial behavior. For example, mothers who offer explanations, talk about emotions, and encourage the expression of emotions, while also controlling the expression of emotions that might hurt others, have children who are more prosocial (Eisenberg et al., 1996; Eisenberg, Fabes, Schaller, Carlo, & Miller, 1991; Garner et al., 2007). Some research supports the idea that the link between parental behaviors and children's prosocial behavior is mediated by empathy, but few studies have explored the processes by which empathy is affected by parental socialization practices (Hastings et al., 2007). In one study, children's basic affective processes (such as emotional expressiveness, emotional insight, anger) were found to mediate the association between parental socialization practices (such as warmth, maturity demands, encouragement of emotional expressiveness) and empathy (Strayer & Roberts, 2004). Those children who were more insightful and expressive and less angry were found to display more empathy. But more research is needed before we can conclude that parents who support the development of children's empathy, the affective state central to engaging in prosocial behavior, are in turn promoting prosocial development in their children.

Studies on the father's role in children's prosocial development have been more limited. Specifically, correlational studies reveal that fathers who display more warmth, and who use more inductive reasoning and discipline, have children who are more prosocial (Janssens & Gerris, 1992; Sturgess, Dunn, & Davies, 2001), though fathers tend to be less attuned than mothers to prosocial behavior in their children (Grusec, Goodnow, & Cohen, 1996). And there is some longitudinal work indicating that children display more prosocial behavior toward their fathers (Eberly & Montemayor, 1999) and siblings (Volling & Belsky, 1992b) when fathers offer supportive parenting, though there is also some evidence that this is not always the case (Hastings et al., 2005). Consequently, it is unclear whether fathers' influence is distinct from mothers' when it comes to socializing prosocial behavior in their children.

Questions have been asked about the role that siblings play in prosocial development. The idea that has been explored is that prosocial behavior is facilitated when children interact with their siblings, since sharing and playing with brothers and sisters requires a certain kind of sensitivity and accommodation to another's needs. Whether siblings are older or younger, or of the same or a different gender, may influence how much prosocial behavior is displayed (Hay et al., 1999). There are limited studies exploring the influence of siblings, especially by contrast to those that have examined the impact of peers and friends.

Children who are more prosocial, as compared to those who are less prosocial, have been found to be more well liked, to be more popular, and to have close friends (Clark & Ladd, 2000; Deković & Gerris, 1994; Gest, Graham-Bermann, & Hartup, 2001). But the direction of effects is unclear. Are children who are well liked and who have close friends more likely to be prosocial? Or are more prosocial children likely to be more well liked and popular? There are several longitudinal studies that have explored these questions (e.g., Haselager, Cillessen, Van-Lieshout, Riksen-Walraven, & Hartup, 2002; Persson, 2005; Wentzel, 2003; Wentzel et al., 2004). The general conclusion is that more prosocial behavior seems to lead to more positive reactions from others. Having friends who are cooperative and kind continues to support the development of prosocial behavior. And mothers' and fathers' childrearing styles appear to influence children's prosocial behavior as well as their social competence, popularity, and acceptance from their peer group. Moreover, prosocial behavior partially mediates the relation between childrearing and children's sociometric status (Deković & Janssens, 1992).

Teachers impact children's prosocial behavior in significant ways as well. When teachers are warm and their relationship with their students is close and not conflicted, children tend to act in more prosocial ways (Birch & Ladd, 1998; Howes, 2000). When children are secure in their attachment to their teachers, they also tend to be more competent in their prosocial behaviors (Copeland-Mitchell, Denham, & DeMulder, 1997). Similarly, when teachers work to praise positive behaviors and diminish children's anger using school-based intervention strategies, children report that they engage in more sharing and helpful behaviors and are more likely to apologize for mistakes (Flannery et al., 2003).

Some researchers have explored other factors that may influence prosocial behavior. For example, early child care experiences have been examined. Children with more experience in out-of-home infant and toddler care have been found to be more prosocial, though the quality of the child care seems to matter more than the amount of time children spend there (NICHD Early Child Care Research Network, 2002). Finally, children who are engaged in volunteer community work learn about the value of helping, caring, and giving back, which ultimately may foster prosocial activities in the future (Pancer & Pratt, 1999). And several studies have explored socioeconomic status (e.g., Lichter, Shanahan, & Gardner, 2002) as well as the role of collectivistic, as opposed to individualistic, cultural values (e.g., Carlo, Koller, Eisenberg, DaSilva, & Frohlich, 1996; Zaff, Moore, Papillo, & Williams, 2003) as they relate to children's developing prosocial orientations.

In conclusion, we see that there is likely a very complex interaction between social and evolutionary adaptation, genetically determined predispositions, and social experiences both within and outside of the family that all make a significant contribution to prosocial behavior. The intricacies of these influences, when considered together with the different ways in which prosocial behavior has been defined and measured, have led to difficulties in drawing general conclusions from extant research in this area. Much remains to be learned about the ways in which children develop an orientation toward care and concern for others, the early roots of empathy and prosocial behavior, and the consequences of individual differences in these competencies for later adaptation.

What Happens When Children Do Not Develop a Concern For Others?

While perspective-taking abilities and a sensitivity to others promote social responsibility and reduce the likelihood of engaging in behavior that is harmful to others' well-being (Feshbach, 1975; Hoffman, 1982), what happens when children do not develop this interpersonal concern? Children diagnosed with conduct disorders commonly evidence limited empathy or guilt. When these aggressive, oppositional children act impulsively, or in ways that are harmful to others, they appear to have little concern for the impact of their behavior in social contexts and to have no feelings of remorse. They may threaten or intimidate others, initiate or engage in physical fights, harm, damage, or steal property, or engage in behavior that violates parental rules or prohibitions (American Psychiatric Association, 2013). It is unclear whether the lack of prosocial concern is the cause or consequence of conduct disorders or of other externalizing behavior problems such as aggression or poor impulse control. What is clear, however, is that children with conduct disorders show little concern for how others might feel or for the impact of their own behavior on others.

Some studies have found no differences in concern for others between preschoolers with disruptive behavior problems and those without these problems (e.g., MacQuiddy, Maise, & Hamilton, 1987). Other studies, however, have found toddlers who were poor self-regulators (as measured by disobedience) to be less likely to offer prosocial responses to stories involving wrongdoings against others when seen again six to eight years later (Kochanska, 1991). Disruptive or aggressive behavior in early elementary school has been associated with low concern for others (Tremblay, Vitaro, Gagnon, Piche, & Royer, 1992). And antisocial adolescents have been found to show a lack of concern for others as well (Cohen & Strayer, 1996). Thus, aggressive or antisocial behavior that emerges early seems to be a risk factor for later problems in prosocial behavior. By contrast, more prosocial toddlers and preschoolers have fewer externalizing problems and are less aggressive when they enter elementary school (Hay & Pawlby, 2003). Interestingly, concern for others has been found to moderate the stability of disruptive behaviors and externalizing problems over time. Children who are identified as high in externalizing behaviors in preschool but who also demonstrate a high concern for others evidence a decrease in externalizing behavior in middle childhood (Hastings, Zahn-Waxler, Robinson, Usher, & Bridges, 2000).

These results have implications for intervention strategies, especially given that maternal socialization practices have been found to be associated with prosocial development in children with or without behavior problems. For example, mothers who are inconsistent in establishing rules, who are punitive and harsh, and who freely express disappointment and anger have children who are less prosocial. Considered together with other studies demonstrating a complex relation between angry parental behavior and externalizing problems in high-risk children (e.g., Denham et al., 2000), it may be that these maternal behaviors are especially impactful on prosocial behaviors when children already display aggressive or disruptive behavior. That is, these children may be less likely to develop any concern for others and more likely to maintain or increase their problematic behavior (Hastings et al., 2000). Certainly, developmentally appropriate interventions that encourage or maintain concern for others, particularly in children who evidence early aggression and poor impulse control, may result in more desirable outcomes. Research in this area, therefore, has important implications for clinicians working with young children.

Morality

Why do some children obey rules and others not? Why do some children transgress, without concern for how their behavior may impact another child, while others are more interested in sharing, helping, and complying? What contributes to these variations in children's moral behavior? There is a substantial philosophical literature on morality. Psychologists, too, have written about and studied questions about the nature of morality and how moral behavior develops. There has been much research and theorizing on the issues of moral emotions, moral judgments or how children think about rules, and moral behavior or how children act in moral ways. We will now consider this work as it reflects considerations of these important aspects of the developing self and their impact on others in relationships.

The early roots of psychological theory and work on morality may be found in Freud's (1923/1961) psychoanalytic writings on the development of the superego. Freud proposed that it is through the process of identification with the same-sex parent, in the resolution of the Oedipal or Electra conflict, that children internalize standards for appropriate behavior; the superego thus develops, contains our conscience (as well as the ego ideal), and guides and constrains behavior. Children also internalize the emotional mechanisms for regulating their moral behavior. Freud's ideas were countered by B. F. Skinner's (1938) position that moral behaviors are shaped by environmental contingencies. Skinner believed that children learn to behave in particular ways based on what they have learned about the consequences of their behaviors. The likelihood that a behavior will be repeated again in the future depends upon whether it was followed, in the past, by reinforcement or punishment. Moral behaviors, in particular, are learned not because they are intrinsically good or bad; rather, they are also seen as conditioned responses consistent with the values of the social group to which one belongs. Skinner eventually went on to argue that affective and cognitive processes were considered to be irrelevant (Skinner, 1971).

Jean Piaget (1932/1977) offered a cognitive-developmental approach to moral judgment. Through reciprocal interactions in the context of games and other social exchanges with peers and adults, children construct an understanding of their experiences and gradually form judgments about rules, relationships, authority, and transgressions. Piaget offered a stage theory of moral development, suggesting that children's cognitive abilities, which are built on concepts acquired in earlier stages, influence their level of moral reasoning. Kohlberg (1969) extended Piaget's work, focusing on children's judgments and reasoning about morally relevant issues and seeking uniform processes characterizing developmental changes, while others (Gilligan, 1982; Gilligan & Attanucci, 1988) uncovered distinct variations in moral reasoning based on a morality of care rather than a morality of justice.

Social-cognitive theorists continued in this historical tradition, with a focus on the cognitive representation of moral rules (Smetana, 1997; Turiel, 1998; Turiel, Killen, & Helwig, 1997). However, they offered an expanded view that incorporates children's interactions with parents and peers. And developmental researchers, following in the tradition of socialization theorists (e.g., Maccoby, 1984; Sears, Rau, & Alpert, 1965), explored questions about how children come to experience and express moral emotions and when they learn to behave in ways that are consistent with rules and values even without external monitoring (Grusec, 1997; Kagan, 2005). Developmental researchers have also studied morally relevant emotions, cognitions, and behaviors, across contexts and time, and the processes and factors associated with individual differences in children's developmental pathways (e.g., Eisenberg, 1998; Hoffman, 1983; Kochanska, 1995). For example, recent research highlights the distinct contributions that siblings and friends make to children's understanding of themselves and others as agents of moral behavior (Recchia, Wainryb, & Pasupathi, 2013). Thus, contemporary work has continued to inform our understanding of both normal developmental pathways and of individual differences, thereby contributing to the research of developmental psychopathologists (e.g., Blair, 1995; Frick & Ellis, 1999). Considered together, these theorists offer ideas about moral development, highlighting the three essential components of moral emotions, moral thoughts, and moral behaviors. These aspects change with age, are influenced by the family and the peer group, and are embedded within a social and cultural context. Children have feelings about their "right" and "wrong" behaviors, they learn about ethical rules, judge moral actions, and think about moral dilemmas, and when in situations requiring moral decisions, they may behave in "good" or "bad" ways.

Emotions and Morality

Children appear to have a moral sense from a very young age. Kagan (1981) proposed that young children have an awareness of standards – of how things should look or be – and that their interest in, and distress over, a violation of standards reflects an emerging sense of what is right and wrong. In fact, researchers have found consistency between the emotional reactions of 2- and

3-year-olds to flawed objects and then to their own wrongdoings in a contrived laboratory-based assessment (Kochanska, Casey, & Fukumoto, 1995). Children are distressed when they are led to believe that they caused damage to the examiner's presumed valuable objects, displaying negative affect, apologizing, and making attempts to repair them. In related research, a comparison of responses when a rigged toy falls apart reveals age-related changes from 22 to 45 months of age. As children get older, there is an increase in bodily tension, with a decrease in negative affect and overall distress reactions, along with a decrease in avoiding gaze (Kochanska, Gross, Lin, & Nichols, 2002). It appears that with increased skills in emotion regulation, children are able to maintain a socially appropriate reaction to mishaps and to modulate, or mask, their expression of negative affect, despite the fact that their distress may be revealed in bodily tension and changes in posture (e.g., squirming, hanging their head, hunching their shoulders). These studies suggest that even 2-year-olds have an ability to appreciate standards and a general concern about what is right and wrong (Kagan, 1984), perhaps reflecting an early sign of conscience (Kochanska & Thompson, 1997; Stipek et al., 1990) or "moral instinct" (Pinker, 2008).

Guilt, shame, and embarrassment are considered to be the self-conscious moral emotions. These emotions or feeling states involve the individual's understanding and appraisal of the self (Eisenberg, 2000). During the second year, as self-awareness develops, children recognize themselves in the mirror (Lewis & Brooks-Gunn, 1979), use the personal pronouns of "me" and "I" (Pipp, Fischer, & Jennings, 1987), assert their agency (Mascolo & Fischer, 1998), and begin to experience and express these early moral, self-conscious emotions (Mascolo & Fischer, 2007; Zahn-Waxler & Kochanska, 1990). Embarrassment is the least negative and serious emotion, involving surprise at events that occur by accident with minimal anger at the self (Keltner & Buswell, 1997). As such, embarrassment does not play a major role in morality. Guilt reflects the emergence of the child's conscience (Groenendyk & Volling, 2007) and is effective in motivating individuals to engage in moral behavior (Tangney, Stuewig, & Mashek, 2007). This is especially the case when the person feels responsibility for a behavior that goes against internalized standards or wants to make amends for a wrongdoing that causes someone else to be distressed (Tangney, 1991). Guilt is therefore an example of a self-conscious moral emotion that, like shame, influences and is influenced by the child's developing awareness of the self within a social context (Mascolo & Fischer, 2007).

There is a great deal of controversy regarding the distinction between shame and guilt (see Tangney et al., 2007, for a review). For example, some have argued that shame and guilt lead to different actions or behaviors (Sheikh & Janoff-Bulman, 2010). Shame is self-focused, where the flaws of the self, the sense of failing to inhibit immoral behavior, often motivate the individual to hide, deny, or escape the situation that induced the shame. With shame, the individual feels that his/her self is diminished in the eyes of another person.

The wish to hide comes from a sense of being exposed. Unlike guilt, where the focus is on the act, with shame, the focus is on the self as viewed by others. The experience of shame requires not only self-awareness but also the child's ability to use social and moral guidelines to evaluate the self as others view him or her. We see important age-related changes in the child's experience of shame over the second and third years of life, reflecting cognitive advances that allow for increased evaluation of the self and one's own behavior as well as an awareness of standards, rules, and desirable goals (see Mascolo & Fischer, 2007). In childhood, continued evaluations of the self, and perceived experiences of the self as inadequate, defective, or inferior in someone else's eyes, result in negative evaluations and threats to the self, thereby influenced by and impacting self-related affects and cognitions.

Research has even found associated physiological markers that reflect psychobiological responses to threats to the social self. For example, children react during laboratory tasks to nonverbal expressions of shame, more than to other nonverbal expressions, with greater changes in cortisol levels (Lewis & Ramsay, 2002). Shame may also elicit characteristic postural changes reflecting deference and self-concealment. Thus, shame is an affective state that serves to organize motivational, biological, and behavioral changes (Dickerson, Gruenaewald, & Kemeny, 2004) with the goal of hiding from others. By contrast, the experience of guilt does not require social exposure. We might feel guilt in not living up to perceived expectations for appropriate behavior or when we experience failure in a particular situation, even without another person knowing. However, rather than concealing ourselves from others, guilt often motivates interpersonal repair and behavioral change (Barrett, Zahn-Waxler, & Cole, 1993).

Guilt and shame are also differentially linked to empathy. When someone is guilty, s/he is more likely to take another's perspective and demonstrate empathic concern. However, when an individual feels shame, this emotion leads to a greater focus on one's own distress and disrupts the person's ability to feel empathic toward the other (Tangney & Dearing, 2002). Empathy and guilt both involve a concern for someone else's distress and a sense of responsibility toward doing something to ease it (Hoffman, 1982). Just as empathy underlies the experience of guilt, anxiety appears to be the cause of shame (Sheikh & Janoff-Bulman, 2010). This anxiety is associated with the self-oriented focus on the "bad self," or one's personal flaws, defects, and failures, that then interferes with the ability to connect empathically to others (Tangney et al., 2007). Feelings of shame (in contrast to guilt) are also often associated with anger at others and the tendency to blame them for one's problems (Bennett, Sullivan, & Lewis, 2005), thereby supporting the painful and relationally destructive shame–rage spiral (Lewis, 1971; see Scheff, 1987, for a clear clinical illustration) and interfering with the capacity for empathy.

Finally, proneness to either shame or guilt has particular significance for the development of psychopathology as well as for implementing effective interventions with children (Tangney, Burggraf, & Wagner, 1995). Clinical research indicates that guilt and shame are linked to different psychological symptoms. Shame leads to a range of problems, from low self-esteem and depression to anxiety, eating disorders, and posttraumatic stress disorder (see a review in Tangney & Dearing, 2002). Guilt may lead to rumination and chronic self-blame (Freud, 1924/1961; Hartmann & Loewenstein, 1962). However, unless it becomes fused with shame, guilt may also serve an adaptive role, especially for interpersonal behavior, as guilt leads to an acknowledgment of responsibility and proactive attempts to make amends (Baumeister, Stillwell, & Heatherton, 1994; Tangney, 1995; Tangney et al., 2007). Thus, guilt may motivate reparative actions and apologies, whereas shame leads to withdrawal and self-punishment and is therefore a more painful experience than guilt (Lewis, 1971; Morrison, 1996; Tangney, Wagner, Fletcher, & Gramzow, 1992). It is, of course, possible for both emotions to occur together. And certain transgressions may elicit either emotion. For example, a child may deliberately "trick" a friend in order to win a game or get a better prize. The experience of guilt or shame will depend on whether the child focuses on his cheating behavior, which is immoral and may result in shame, or whether the child focuses on his failure to help his friend win or get the better prize, which may result in guilt.

Researchers now generally agree that the period between 2 and 3 years is when we first see the appearance of guilt in young children. However, guilt does not have a distinct "signature," a clear expression like some of the basic emotions such as happiness or anger (Darwin, 1872), and there appear to be developmental changes in the expression of guilt. In addition, there are individual differences in children's guilt reactions. Girls tend to display more guilt than boys. We see these gender differences in early childhood (Kochanska et al., 2002) as well as in middle childhood (Zahn-Waxler, 2000). And infants who are rated by parents as more fearful tend to be more prone to guilt in childhood (Rothbart, Ahadi, et al., 1994). Additionally, 18-month-old children who show early signs of self-development (reported by mothers) exhibit more intense guilt reactions after laboratory-based "planned" transgressions at 33 months. Moreover, children who, at 22 and 45 months of age, displayed more guilt subsequently provide descriptions of the self at 56 months that are more "moral," including a stronger commitment to rule-congruent behavior and a greater concern for rules (Kochanska et al., 2002).

During the preschool years, children begin to see objects, actions, or events as either consistent with, or violating of, standards. This sensitivity is learned in the context of family conversations and interactions (Dunn, 1987, 1988), sets the stage for the development of conscience, and reflects an early morality (Emde et al., 1991; Lamb, 1993). Indeed, moral behavior may be motivated by trying to avoid negative emotions associated with violations of standards, such as guilt, shame, and embarrassment. Moral behavior may also be motivated by positive emotions, such as empathy and pride, related to doing what is "right" or "correcting" a wrongdoing. All these feelings require an awareness of the self. Furthermore, the moral emotions play an important role in helping us to think through situations requiring moral actions and in regulating moral behaviors.

How Are Moral Emotions Socialized?

There are many socialization factors that interact with the child's developing self and influence moral emotions. Distinct qualities of the parent–child relationship contribute to the development of guilt (Kochanska et al., 2005). For example, mothers who share positive affect with their 14-month-old infants in turn have children who display more guilt at 22 months. Maternal responsiveness and shared affect during the first two years of life are associated with greater guilt at preschool (Kochanska, Forman, & Coy, 1999; Kochanska, Aksan, & Carlson, 2005). Parental behavior also plays an important role in determining children's moral emotions. Children are more likely to internalize their parents' emotional reactions, such as shame and guilt, and to listen to and respond to their parent's communications if the parents offer supportive and responsive care (Kochanska et al., 2008). Parents who are warm and affectionate promote the notion that being a moral person implies caring for others and an inclination toward maintaining warm and loving relationships (Zahn-Waxler & Kochanska, 1990).

Interestingly, parents who themselves are prone to shame tend to be more restrictive with their children; the strategies they use to regulate their own shame reactions may, in turn, heighten their children's anxiety about the acceptability of the self (Mills et al., 2007). When parents provide their children with explanations for rules and reasons for not violating them, their children are more likely to feel guilt and remorse if they misbehave. If, however, parents assert their power and authority by punishing their children for transgressions without explanation, children are less likely to feel guilty (Forman, Aksan, & Kochanska, 2004). Parents also play a role in teaching their children the moral emotions associated with misbehavior or rule violations. If a parent, for example, tells her child, "Stop throwing your food on the floor. You are a bad boy!", he uses her global appraisal to evaluate himself in emotional terms as a bad person who does bad things (which, if repeated enough, will be internalized into his self-evaluations and descriptions, i.e., "I am a bad boy," rather than "I am a good boy who sometimes does bad things."). If a parent says, "You should be ashamed of yourself for breaking Tommy's truck," the wrongdoing is associated with the moral emotion of shame (Stipek et al., 1992). These parental messages, though intended to ward off future misbehavior, teach children the moral emotions of shame and guilt that are associated with the breaking of rules.

Parents who openly express their emotional reactions may also influence their children's moral emotions. Children are more likely to focus on the harm or problem they caused when parents are clear in expressing their anger and offer understandable messages as to why they are distressed (Arsenio & Lemerise, 2004). When mothers respond in a way that is affectively neutral, as opposed to expressing negative affect, their children are less likely to try to repair their moral transgressions (Grusec, Dix, & Mills, 1982). It is helpful, therefore, for parents to honestly express their emotional reactions in response to their children's misbehavior or wrongdoings. However, parents generally should not express their anger in dramatic, intense, or frightening ways because this can be too difficult for children to process. If, in response to their parent's emotional expressions, children are scared or overly aroused, they may react with fear or sadness, inhibit their own feelings, or withdraw and worry about how to protect themselves emotionally. By contrast, we know that when children express guilt, remorse, or shame, parents who take the time to respond to these emotional expressions in positive and constructive ways help their children learn that even when parents reprimand them it is still possible to repair and restore the relationship (Thompson, Meyer, & McGinley, 2006).

Questions about the impact of extreme childrearing experiences on moral development warrant further investigation. What happens, for example, when children are abused or neglected and parental expressions of disappointment, anger, criticism, or rejection are frequent? There is some research that has demonstrated that maltreated, as compared to nonmaltreated, preschool-aged children show more rigid, fearful, and "compulsive" compliance, with less committed compliance, in response to maternal requests to clean up a laboratory playroom. There are also clear differences in emotions and behaviors based on the type of maltreatment experienced (Koenig, Cicchetti, & Rogosch, 2000). These observed distinctions may reflect a maladaptive pathway in the development of the self (Crittenden & DiLalla, 1988), in the internalization of moral standards, and in the moral emotions of guilt and shame in children who have been abused or neglected. This work has critical implications for clinicians. The secrecy and lack of disclosure that is typically associated with physical, emotional, and sexual abuse, for example, often lead to profound shame. Sensitivity to, and understanding of, the legacy of shame and its resulting impact on the developing self in maltreated children and adolescents is essential for clinical interventions geared towards uncovering the emotional and psychological consequences of early abuse histories.

Socialization experiences also interact with children's temperamental predispositions and impact moral emotions. Parental responses are especially important for children who are temperamentally uninhibited. A rule-oriented approach and consistent discipline (though not one that includes physical punishment) help uninhibited children develop feelings of guilt. By contrast, parenting is not related to levels of guilt in inhibited preschool-aged children (Cornell & Frick, 2007). Thus, temperament influences the nature and quality of specific parental behaviors that ultimately are associated with particular child outcomes, reminding us that there is no single causal process that leads to an adaptive or maladaptive developmental outcome (see, for example,

Cicchetti & Rogosch, 1996). Additionally, clinical interventions need to consider the interaction between temperament and parental behaviors. For example, promoting moral development in an attempt to prevent conduct disorders in temperamentally at-risk children (such as those who are uninhibited) requires specific parental interventions and practices consistent with the child's temperamental style (Hawes & Dadds, 2005).

Finally, it is important to note that most of the research conducted on children's guilt, as well as on other aspects of moral development, has used low-risk, relatively homogeneous populations. Guilt may serve maladaptive functions in high-risk environments and its developmental course may be different than in low-risk families (Zahn-Waxler, 2000; Zahn-Waxler, Kochanska, Krupnick, & McNew, 1990). Moreover, cross-cultural work has revealed variations in relevant variables associated with the development of guilt, including children's temperament (Kagan et al., 1994), self-development and self-conscious emotions (Kitayama, Markus, & Matsumoto, 1995), socialization of guilt and shame and the cultural meanings associated with these emotions (Miyake & Yamazaki, 1995), and early family relationships (Rothbaum, Pott, Azuma, Miyake, & Weisz, 2000). Future work needs to explore these cultural differences so as to provide a more comprehensive understanding of the deeply embedded practices and cultural values that contribute to the development of moral emotions.

How do moral emotions influence children's behaviors? The moral emotions, such as the experience, or anticipated experience, of shame and guilt, play an important role in regulating moral behavior (Sheikh & Janoff-Bulman, 2010). As such, they seem to serve a positive function in children's moral development. In one study that explored the association between children's guilt reactions and their moral behaviors, children's responses to rules set out by their mothers (e.g., to not touch an appealing set of objects when she left the room or to finish cleaning up toys in her absence) or an experimenter (e.g., to not cheat on a difficult guessing game) were not influenced by moral emotions until the children were 4 years of age (Aksan & Kochanska, 2005). In another study, 4½-year-old children were less likely to play with toys that were forbidden if they had expressed more guilty reactions when assessed at an earlier age. They anticipated feeling guilty and this in turn influenced their subsequent behavior, making them less likely to disobey the rules (Kochanska et al., 2002). And children (especially boys) who were found to show early signs of guilt evidenced higher "moral self" scores on dimensions such as empathy, guilt or affective discomfort after transgressions, sensitivity to violations of standards, internalized conduct, confession, apology, and concern about good feelings with their parent (Kochanska, 2002). Thus, it appears that young children have a rich variety of moral emotions that impact moral behavior in important ways.

Moral emotions and behavior are also associated in older children and adolescents. For example, after controlling for family income and maternal education levels, fifth graders who were more prone to guilt were less likely to be arrested, convicted, or incarcerated during adolescence (Tangney & Dearing, 2002). And even when imagining that they were involved in committing immoral acts, adolescents who said they felt more intense moral emotions were less involved in delinquent behavior (Krettenauer & Eichler, 2006). Interestingly, guilt is more effective than shame in inspiring moral behavior. Moreover, vulnerability to guilt is associated with measures of perspective taking and empathy (Tangney & Dearing, 2002). Guilt proneness appears to play a more powerful inhibitory function than shame (Stuewig & McCloskey, 2005), whereas shame may actually be detrimental, leading to more externalizing behavior in children (Ferguson, Stegge, Miller, & Olsen, 1999) and inclinations toward illegal behavior in adolescence (Tibbetts, 1997). Therefore, guilt may be the moral emotion that is most relevant in fostering moral behavior (Tangney et al., 2007).

Moral Judgments

Jean Piaget (1932) studied children's moral reasoning using two methods: (1) he observed children playing games and examined their attitudes about the rules of their games; and (2) he examined children's judgments about the seriousness of transgressions. Consistent with his notion that children actively construct their understanding of the world by interacting directly with their environment, Piaget explored children's awareness and practice of rules in the everyday games that they play. He also talked to children about moral situations that require them to reason about immoral acts or transgressions (such as lying or stealing). Ultimately, Piaget developed his stage theory based on these observations. He maintained the perspective that judgments about laws, rules, and authority result from children's experiences in the social world with other children and adults. Moral judgment is influenced by these experiences, as well as by emotional reactions such as empathy and sympathy, and develops through a series of stages that occur in sequence.

During the premoral stage, children are not aware of or concerned about the rules of the games they play. Rather, they play for the purpose of exploring and having fun. At about the age of 5 years, children's *heteronomous* view leads them to strictly adhere to rules which come from authority figures (such as parents) and cannot be questioned or changed. This strict adherence to rules and obedience to authority results from young children's limitations in cognitive abilities; specifically, because young children cannot take into account someone else's perspective concurrently with their own, they are absolutely sure that "the rule is the rule" everywhere in the world because moral absolutism prevails ("that is just the way it is"). And rules are right because "my mommy (or daddy) says so." When rules are broken, "immanent justice" prevails; that is, a punishment will automatically result when there is any deviation from the rules. A child might think, for example, that he got what he deserved when his favorite toy broke after he did not listen to his father.

Through continued peer interactions and experiences in the social world, children begin to evaluate the rules that guide them. By about the age of 11 years, when playing games, solving problems, or making decisions, children begin to consider rules more critically. This *autonomous* orientation suggests that rules and norms are established through cooperation, reciprocity, and mutual respect. Children may now consider the other person's perspective, along with their own, as they come to understand that rules may sometimes be broken and transgressions do not always lead to punishment. When punishments are invoked, they need to be appropriate to the misbehavior and to the transgressor's intentions and they should compensate for whatever harm was done. The punishment should also offer a lesson to the wrongdoer so as to avoid this misbehavior in the future. Thus, it is in the context of interpersonal interactions that Piaget believed children learn about equality, reciprocity, and equal justice. The shift in thinking that allows children to take the other's perspective allows them to work out rules that are fair, considering all involved.

There are many who have been critical of Piaget's theory, arguing that his ideas regarding the shift from moral realism to moral reciprocity is not universal across cultural groups (Havighurst & Neugarten, 1955). Some have also questioned Piaget's ideas regarding the age at which certain cognitive abilities appear, thereby underestimating children's capacity to consider moral situations (Chandler, Greenspan, & Barenboim, 1973; Helwig, Zelazo, & Wilson, 2001; Zelazo, Helwig, & Lau, 1996). Over time, researchers have refined Piaget's ideas. They have learned, for example, that children's moral judgments depend in part on distinctions children come to make between whether wrongdoings are accidental or intentional and whether these wrongdoings lead to positive or negative consequences.

Lawrence Kohlberg (1969) modified and expanded Piaget's stages and had a major influence on research on moral development. He maintained the same assumption that provided the foundation for Piaget's work, namely, that children's level of moral reasoning builds on cognitive competencies achieved at an earlier stage. But he studied moral development by focusing on the ways in which children and adolescents reason about hypothetical situations involving conflicts around relational obligations, life, law, authority, and trust. He identified six stages of moral reasoning (grouped into three levels) that extended beyond the childhood period, arguing that achieving mature moral thinking is a long, gradual process. Kohlberg believed that the stages are passed through in sequence, though this progression may occur at different ages for different individuals. Once an individual has reached a certain level of reasoning, s/he will not return to an earlier level, and not all people achieve the highest level (Colby & Kohlberg, 1987). Moreover, the sequence of stages is universal, though the highest level of moral reasoning may vary both within and across cultures (Kohlberg, 1985).

Kohlberg (1969) distinguished three levels of moral reasoning and identified two stages within each level as follows: Level I – *Preconventional* morality: Stage 1 – Obedience and punishment orientation; Stage 2 – Naïve hedonistic and instrumental orientation; Level II – *Conventional* morality: Stage 3 – Good boy/good girl morality; Stage 4 – Authority and morality that maintain social order; Level III – *Postconventional* morality: Stage 5 – Morality of contract, individual rights, and democratically accepted law; Stage 6 – Morality of individual principles and conscience. At the first *preconventional* level, moral reasoning is based on an individualistic, concrete perspective. Within this level, Stage 1 judgments focus on not breaking rules, thereby avoiding punishment. This heteronomous orientation is similar to Piaget's notion that reasoning reflects an inability to consider others' perspectives. Moral reciprocity begins to emerge in Stage 2, where there is a focus on the practical value of a behavior. There is a sense in which what is right or fair reflects an agreement or exchange and that the individual will follow the rules when immediate self-interests can be met. When there is conflict, the individual determines and justifies what is right in a relative sense (e.g., "You hurt me so I can hurt you."). The rules and norms guiding social exchanges do not serve to guide reasoning at this level. It is not until the second *conventional* level where these norms and conventions are understood as necessary and used to guide moral reasoning. There is greater conformity with the laws and rules that are now used more consistently. A person in Stage 3 will conform with the rules learned from people close to him or her (e.g., family or community members). Getting approval from others and being loyal to the group are all-important. By Stage 4, there is a shift to defining what is right based on the norms and rules of the larger social system. Now, being moral requires that one follow society's laws (except in those cases where there is a conflict between the law and other prescribed social responsibilities) because the laws are intended to protect everyone. Finally, it is at the third *postconventional* level where moral reasoning is based on an ethical code that may be applied independently, without uniform adherence to rules and norms. At Stage 5, reasoning is based on the fundamental principles supporting societal norms and rules, and conflicts are resolved through prescribed measures. It is only at Stage 6 where morality is based on a consideration of human rights, fairness, and a regard for life that extends beyond societal and cultural dictates. Laws are not automatically followed; rather, they are evaluated in terms of how consistent they are with the more abstract principles of what is fair and just.

Kohlberg's sequence reflects a shift from the ages at which Piaget proposed children move from heteronomous to autonomous thought. Kohlberg argued that children do not maintain a respect for authority or rules until the conventional level of reasoning in adolescence, whereas Piaget believed this respect was possible in young children at the heteronomous level of moral judgment. Moreover, Kohlberg believed that the concepts of justice and mutual respect do not emerge until late adolescence, and maybe not even until adulthood (in the postconventional level), and not, as Piaget suggested, in late childhood's or early adolescence's autonomous reasoning. But Kohlberg's influence extended beyond the stage theory that he proposed. He argued for the need to ground the study of moral development in philosophical considerations about morality (Kohlberg, 1971). He also emphasized the importance of social interactions in children's constructions of moral judgments. Now, broader questions stemming from Kohlberg's theorizing are the focus of contemporary research, including the role of gender-related experiences and of emotions on the study of moral judgment, the impact of peers and schooling on moral reasoning, as well as the consideration of individualistic and collectivistic orientations and of locally based and universal moral perspectives (see, for example, Turiel, 2008). For example, it has been found that children may be taught to shift their moral reasoning to a higher stage using peer modeling or role-playing (Turiel, 2006). Unique domains of morality have been identified in studies exploring cultural similarities and differences (Shweder, Much, Mahapatra, & Park, 1997). And historical, political, and economic factors have been found to influence moral judgments as well (Rest, Narvaez, Thoma, & Bebeau, 2000; Turiel, 2002).

Additionally, two independent lines of research have been pursued in the past two decades that have been increasingly regarded as related: (1) young children's moral judgments; and (2) theory of mind or the understanding of others' mental states. In order to make more advanced moral judgments, it is assumed that it is necessary to have a more sophisticated understanding of others' mental states. Indeed, many studies have supported the idea that the development of theory of mind underlies children's moral judgments during the preschool years (Flavell, Mumme, Green & Flavell, 1992; Killen, Mulvey, Richardson, Jampol, & Woodward, 2011; Lane, Wellman, Olson, LaBounty, & Kerr, 2010). Other research has supported the alternative position; that is, that moral judgments impact theory of mind understanding, in both children (Leslie, Knobe, & Cohen, 2006) and adults (Knobe, 2005, 2010). Finally, the idea that theory of mind and early moral judgments develop as transactional, bidirectional processes during the preschool years has been supported by recent work (Smetana, Jambon, Conry-Murray, & Sturge-Apple, 2012).

Children not only think about and come to understand other's mental states. They also reflect on their social world as they try to make sense of their social relationships, make decisions about what is right and wrong, and fully involve themselves in interactions with others. Piaget and Kohlberg focused on rules, laws, and the consequences of misbehavior; they did not emphasize positive moral emotions or the complexity of moral judgments as they are rooted in parental, sibling, and peer relationships (cf. Turiel, 2008). A broadened view of the moral domain now includes not only a morality of justice but also a morality of care and concern for others. This expanded perspective emerged first in research with young girls and women, who showed patterns of moral reasoning in response to hypothetical moral dilemmas that were distinct from boys and men (Gilligan, 1982, 1993). The females' responses reflected an interpersonal focus, where the individual came to be understood as connected to social networks, and moral reasoning was oriented toward the fulfillment of responsibilities to others within this context of care. Current explorations of the morality of care have included many studies of boys and men; they have been found to reason about hypothetical dilemmas in ways that are not significantly different from girls and women. Thus, a perspective of care and justice is now seen to be relevant for males and females as they reason about both hypothetical and real-life moral dilemmas.

Interestingly, neuroimaging studies provide evidence supporting the idea that different parts of the brain are activated when making decisions regarding issues of caring and issues of justice (Robertson et al., 2007). Moreover, research has expanded our understanding of the specific network of brain regions involved in mediating moral judgments more generally. For example, the regions that play a critical role in emotional processing also influence personal moral decision making – the medial prefrontal cortex, the posterior cingulate and angular gyrus on the left and right sides (Greene & Haidt, 2002; Raine & Yang, 2006). The right temporoparietal junction is an area that appears to be involved in moral state reasoning (Young, Camprodon, Hauser, Pascual-Leone & Saxe, 2010), facilitating the discrimination of intentions and consequences when making moral judgments. While much of this research has focused on adults, methodological advances have allowed for the examination of brain regions involved in theory of mind reasoning in young children. Results suggest that the same brain regions are recruited by both children and adults when reasoning about someone else's thoughts (Saxe, Whitfield-Gabrieli, Scholz, & Pelphrey, 2009). Further research using neuroimaging techniques will contribute to our understanding of important developmental questions that continue to arise regarding the systems used for reasoning about other people's minds (see, for example, Saxe, Carey, & Kanwisher, 2004).

When the development of moral reasoning is considered in the context of social interactions, emotional experiences are also seen to play a more central role. There is an acknowledgment that social and emotional experiences influence, and are influenced by, moral thinking and reasoning. It is within this perspective that both hypothetical and real-life situations have been used to study moral decision making. The assumption is that in real life, we usually know and have a history with the person experiencing moral conflict. The conflict may also elicit strong emotions for us and we may be especially concerned about the outcome (Frank, 2001; Greene, Sommerville, Nystrom, Darley, & Cohen, 2001; Haidt, 2001). Hypothetical and real situations have been used to study children's concepts of sharing and distribution of goods (Damon, 1977, 1988), as well as prosocial moral reasoning or judgments about helping, giving, and other positive social actions (Eisenberg, Miller, Shell, McNalley, & Shea, 1991).

Another direction in which the study of moral development has expanded has been through the elaboration of social domain theory (Helwig & Turiel, 2010; Smetana, 2006). Morality is considered to be one of several domains of children's social knowledge and is structured by considerations of fairness, welfare, and the effects our actions have on others. But there are other aspects of the social world as well, such as concerns about personal choices, emotions, and privacy (personal domain), as well as knowledge about social norms, systems, and relationships (social-conventional domain). These matters of social convention result from rules that are predictable, socially agreed upon, and essential to the functioning of a social group. The initial focus of researchers interested in social domain theory was on the similarities and differences between children's understanding of the rules pertaining to the moral, social-conventional, and personal domains. For example, how do individuals form "personal" judgments concerning behaviors outside the specific domains of moral rules or social judgments? What has emerged within this exploration of domains of social judgment is the finding that young children do indeed differentiate between conventional, moral, and personal domains.

The distinctions between moral and conventional wrongdoings appear in children as young as 3 years of age (Smetana & Braeges, 1990) and are fairly consistent by 4 to 5 years of age (Turiel, 2008). Children view moral violations (such as lying, stealing, or hitting someone) as worse than breaches of social-conventional rules (such as eating a meal with fingers instead of utensils or addressing a teacher by his or her first name) (Turiel, 2006; Turiel & Wainryb, 2000). It seems that children make this distinction in part because they view moral transgressions as going against concepts of welfare, fairness, and justice and these violations result in harm to other persons (Turiel, 1983). However, the ability to make this distinction happens only when considering familiar situations based in early social experiences. The capacity to differentiate between familiar and unfamiliar situations does not happen until the age of 9 or 10 years (Turiel, 2006). Moreover, there is a developmental progression in children's understanding of what constitutes harm (Smetana, 2006). While moral rules are seen as universal and absolute, children's views about harm shift from early childhood to adolescence, thereby contributing to the more complex distinctions that older children make between moral violations and transgressions of social conventions. Finally, social conventions are increasingly understood as dependent upon social expectations and norms and the expectations of parents or teachers (Helwig, 2006; Wainryb, 2006).

More recent research has focused on exploring children's social reasoning in multiple domains, leading to an appreciation of the complexity in both the criteria used when thinking about a domain and in the justifications offered for particular actions (Turiel, 2008). This work has identified the psychological domain as yet another important domain of social knowledge, distinct from the moral and social-conventional domains, that has been explored by social domain theorists. Issues relevant to the psychological domain reflect an understanding of the self and others. Also considered are distinctions between *psychological* concerns, involving knowledge about the self and others and choices about personal disclosure, *personal* concerns, such as choices about appearance, friends, and hobbies that impact only the self, and *prudential* concerns, or issues of safety, health, and welfare that are immediately relevant to the self.

Research has shown, for example, that young children view moral transgressions, which impact another person, as more serious than prudential transgressions, which only harm the self (Smetana, 1988; Tisak & Turiel, 1984). With increasing age, children are able to distinguish between personal concerns and moral rules (Nucci, 2002; Yau & Smetana, 2003), often resorting to personal choice when justifying moral rules or behavior. And when faced with issues that invoke complex judgments, such as whether or not it is okay to exclude others from a social group, children consider social-conventional, moral, and personal reasons to justify particular behaviors (Killen & Stangor, 2001; Killen, Lee-Kim, McGlothlin, & Stangor, 2002; Killen, Margie, & Sinno, 2006). For example, they might be opposed to excluding others, based on moral principles of what is fair and just, if they themselves have friends from other races or gender groups but less likely to oppose exclusion if their friendship choices are homogenous (based on a conventional justification). If their friendship choices are made based on decisions about expertise ("we are the smarter students") or the nature of the relationship ("I must include my sister"), then personal or social-conventional arguments may be used to justify exclusion.

Older children and young adolescents are more likely to offer multiple perspectives regarding exclusion, providing a convincing rationale for each choice. They may believe, for example, that it is up to the child to decide who they want to include (a personal choice), or that it is reasonable to separate groups by gender when the distinctions help them to get along better (a conventional choice), or that it is unacceptable to exclude others because it creates different experiences and opportunities for racial or gender groups (a moral choice) (Clarke-Stewart & Parke, 2014). Thus, age, experience, and reasoning abilities all contribute to children's judgments about more complex issues involving multiple social domains. These domains are important for children all over the world, though the content of social conventions will vary across cultural groups in accordance with cultural traditions and norms. Still, despite these differences in content, transgressions in the social-conventional and psychological domains are universally viewed by children across cultures as less serious than they are in the moral domain (Clarke-Stewart & Parke, 2014).

How do children learn about and distinguish between the different social domains? While we have been considering morality as an essential aspect of the developing self-system, it is here where we can see, once again, the importance of relationships as they influence, and are influenced by, the self. Social domain theorists argue that through their experiences with significant others, children construct social knowledge that is then used to guide their moral reasoning. During the second year of life, children begin to make distinctions between what is right and wrong. Observations of young children interacting with their mothers reveal that mothers teach their children about social and moral rules and that, by the age of 3, children are able to understand both moral and social-conventional reasoning (Dunn, 2006; Dunn, Bretherton, & Munn, 1987). Parents are effective in helping promote their children's reasoning when they offer explanations for decisions, support democratic discussions among family members, and provide a rationale for discipline (Walker, Hennig, & Krettenauer, 2000). By encouraging children to think about the consequences of their behavior and its effects on others' feelings, especially when it violates a moral rule, parents are supporting their children's moral development.

In the context of family interactions, children learn the difference between the consequences of hitting their sister or taking a toy (behaviors that violate a moral standard) and the consequences of spilling food on the floor, putting their shoes on the wrong feet, or forgetting to flush the toilet (behaviors that violate social-conventional standards). It is more likely, for example, that a parent will respond to a moral wrongdoing by inviting the child to think about the other person's rights and feelings ("How would you feel if Jane hurt you in the way that you just hurt her?"). When responding to social-conventional transgressions, the focus is more likely to be on the mess that was made or on what needed to be done to rectify the violation (Nucci, 1984; Smetana, 2006). These differences in parental responses help children to understand the varying qualities and consequences of moral and social-conventional violations, where moral rules are more clearly defined and absolute while social conventions are more flexible and personal. Moreover, responses from different adults, such as teachers and parents, help children to understand the domains in which the authority of these adults prevail (school vs. home) and the similarities and differences in their responses to children's wrongdoings (Killen, Breton, Ferguson, & Handler, 1994; Smetana, 1997, 2006).

The domain appropriateness of adults' messages influences their effectiveness; children are more likely to accept messages when they are domain appropriate. The age appropriateness of adults' explanations also influences the extent to which children learn from them and expand their moral understanding (Turiel, 2006). Moreover, as children get older, parental regulation of moral behavior may be acceptable in certain domains (e.g., moral, prudential) but not in others (e.g., personal) (Hasebe, Nucci, & Nucci, 2004; Padilla-Walker & Carlo, 2006). Indeed, as adolescents mature, conflicts between their parents and them occur more often and with increased frequency around personal issues (Smetana, 2006). Parents who allow their adolescents to increasingly gain control over issues in the personal domain (e.g., choice of clothes or music), while continuing to regulate social-conventional and prudential issues, encourage their adolescents' sense of autonomy.

Siblings and peers also play a role in helping children understand the rules across social domains. It is in the context of playful exchanges with other young children that rules may be learned about sharing, turn-taking, possession of games and toys, teasing, exclusion, and caring for or hurting others. Thus, children's experiences with their interactive partners influence their moral development. For example, 4-year-olds who have close friends, as compared to those without close friends, provide more mature reasoning when considering hypothetical moral transgressions (Dunn et al., 2000). Children who have close relationships with their siblings at 2 and 3 years of age, as compared to those who experience high levels of sibling rivalry, are more mature in their moral reasoning at 5 or 6 years of age (Dunn, Brown, & Maguire, 1995). They understand how the other person might feel, especially when they are excluded, and use their experiences of loyalty and betrayal to learn about moral situations (Singer & Doornenbal, 2006). And even when interacting with other children, moral violations are considered by 2- and 3-year-olds to be more problematic and, subsequently, to evoke more intense reactions than social-conventional wrongdoings (Smetana, 2006). Children's experiences with parents, peers, and siblings are varied, just as the contexts in which these experiences occur also differ. These variations contribute to children's learning about and differentiating conventional, moral, and personal issues. In conversation and play, young children learn moral and social rules, and then use these rules to justify their behavior, verbalize the dictates that guide what is right or wrong, and manage their social interactions.

Moral Behavior

Moral development does not only involve learning about what is right or ethical or fair. It also involves learning to follow the rules. And the capacity to follow rules and resist temptation to act willfully, impulsively, or without regard for others is dependent upon the development of self-control. Once again, therefore, we see that the development of the self, and in particular, self-regulation, is essential to the ways in which children function in, and maintain connections to, their broader social worlds. As we have already seen, self-regulation is considered to be an important dimension of temperament that is biologically based, emerges across development, helps in managing more reactive emotional systems, and is susceptible to social and environmental influences (Rothbart, 2011; Rothbart, Ahadi, & Evans, 2000; Rothbart & Bates, 2006). Self-regulation includes the processes that facilitate the ability to modulate arousal, reactivity, and impulsivity, influence inhibition of behavior, and engage in effortful control (Rothbart, Ellis, & Posner, 2011). The capacity for self-regulation develops across childhood. Indeed, recent studies indicate that there are profound changes in self-regulation, at the behavioral and neurobiological levels, well into adolescence (Dahl, 2004; King, Lengua, & Monahan, 2013; Monahan, Steinberg, Cauffman, & Mulvey, 2009).

Initially, children require external support for inhibiting their impulses, managing limits, and behaving in socially acceptable ways. Over time, they progress through three stages in developing self-regulation that are relevant to moral behavior (Kopp, 1982; 1991). Children rely on parents and other adults to remind them about appropriate moral behavior in the first *control* phase. Gradually, they are able to act in accordance with adults' expectations, even without adults monitoring their behavior, in the *self-control* phase. They direct their own behavior, using strategies they have learned, to avoid temptations or the violation of moral standards when they are in the *self-regulation* phase. The development of self-regulation is critical to successful adaptation. Indeed, poor self-regulation is associated with an increased risk of social and behavioral problems in childhood and adolescence, including internalizing and externalizing problems, low empathy, substance use, and social and academic problems (Eisenberg, Valiente, et al., 2003; Kochanska, Murray, Jacques, Koenig, & Vandegeest, 1996; Krueger et al., 2002; Rudolph, Troop-Gordon, & Liewellyn, 2013). And youth who are relatively slow in developing self-regulation across adolescence are at greater risk for antisocial behavior (Monahan et al., 2009; Monahan, Steinberg, Cauffman, & Mulvey, 2013).

Children show an increased ability for self-control, especially between the ages of 18 months and 3 years of age, as they learn to tolerate frustration and delay gratification (Vaughn, Kopp, & Krakow, 1984). Their capacity for self-regulation continues to improve during the preschool years (Kochanska et al., 2001), a process facilitated in part by maturation of the frontal cortex (Shonkoff & Phillips, 2000). Moreover, during this time period, there is evidence of increasing "committed compliance," particularly in contexts where children are asked not to do something, such as not to touch attractive toys on a shelf (Kochanska, 2002). Committed compliance reflects an internal motivation to comply with and accept parental values and ideals without necessitating external control (as compared to situational compliance, which is dependent on sustained parental control) and is associated with positive emotion and pride. These affective reactions, the internalization of parental values and beliefs, and developing self-regulatory competencies together constitute an important part of the child's emerging sense of self (Stipek et al., 1992). Ultimately, the child comes to view the self as a "good" and moral person. This notion of the moral self in turn serves to regulate moral behavior, especially for boys and in contexts where their mothers are asking them not to do something (e.g., "don't touch the toys") (Kochanska, 2002). Thus, this dynamic and transactional position affirms the importance of the "self" as the guide to regulating behavior; parental values are incorporated into internalized standards that direct moral conduct (cf. Harter, 1998a; Stipek et al., 1990), which in turn contribute to developing notions about the self.

But there are individual differences in the way children progress from control by others to self-control to self-regulation. Some children move through these phases and are capable of self-regulation by the age of 4 or 5 years while others can only comply with rules when relying on the adults around them. Those children who are early self-regulators are able to control their behavior despite needing to delay gratification. They also advocate and internalize values and rules learned from their parents and appear to have a stronger "moral self" (Kochanska et al., 2001). And there are also differences in the relative consistency in moral behavior over time. Children who follow moral rules at 22 months tend to follow rules at 45 months of age as well (Aksan & Kochanska, 2005). Moreover, children who are capable of delaying gratification in preschool are found to be better self-regulators in adolescence (Shoda, Mischel, & Peake, 1990). And limitations in children's internalization of rules and impaired moral emotions in childhood appear to lead to immoral behavior in adolescence and adulthood (Frick, Cornell, Barry, Bodin, & Dane, 2003; Shaw & Winslow, 1997).

So what factors are associated with individual differences in self-regulation? There are two related lines of research that are relevant to this question. First, there are studies that have focused on parenting dimensions, such as parental restrictiveness and nurturance, considered separately as well as in varying combinations of parenting styles (Baumrind, 1966, 1967, 1991; Maccoby & Martin, 1983). These parenting dimensions are central to socialization research and have been found to play a role in regulating children's behavior. Parental restrictiveness, where inflexible and demanding control practices are used that are unresponsive to children's needs, involves monitoring and setting of rigid limits for children and socializes a primary focus on immorality and (self-oriented) anxiety. It is parenting with an emphasis on obedience and inhibition of behavior ("should nots" and "don'ts") that, because of the use or threat of punishment, as well as physical and/or psychological control, is likely to induce anxiety in the child (Sheikh & Janoff-Bulman, 2010). While some restrictiveness is necessary to keep children from getting involved in situations or behaviors that may be harmful or even dangerous, it is best used when enforcing limits and communicating expectations for mature behavior in a respectful, warm, and supportive manner. By contrast, a prevalence of restrictive, punitive parenting, with little warmth and nurturance, may signal to the child that s/he is likely to be immoral or engage in immoral behavior and therefore needs to be restrained. This produces anxiety in the child, who will continue to yearn for strict, proscriptive messages so as not to behave immorally and will therefore find it difficult to be self-reliant. In fact, research has documented a positive association between parental restrictiveness and anxiety in adolescence. Additionally, restrictiveness has been linked to adolescent loneliness, high self-derogation, low self-reliance, low self-esteem, and low academic achievement (see Barber & Harmon, 2002, for a review). Thus, the anxiety that is a consequence of highly restrictive parenting leads to self-focused attempts to diminish this distressing affective state, thereby interfering with the child's capacity to feel concern for others. In fact, past research has demonstrated that lower levels of empathy and prosocial behavior are found in children with punitive parents (see Eisenberg, Spinrad, et al., 2006, for a review).

Parental nurturance, involving praise, encouragement, affection, and warmth expressed in the context of parent–child interactions, inculcates an emphasis on morality and (other-oriented) empathy (Sheikh & Janoff-Bulman, 2010). When parents are nurturing, children are interested in offering reciprocal care and concern so as to sustain warm, loving relationships. Therefore, children are more likely to offer help to others when parents establish clear expectations for them (the "shoulds"). The message to children is that they are respected and cherished; thus, these warm and nurturing interactions lead to increases in empathic concern and prosocial helping (Grusec et al., 1996) as well as to a sense of being valued and able to care for others (Sheikh & Janoff-Bulman, 2010). This view is consistent with the work of attachment researchers who have argued that the development of empathic concern is rooted in the early attachment relationship (Bowlby, 1969). Indeed, maternal responsiveness and secure attachment relationships have been linked to children's current and future empathic responses (Eisenberg, Spinrad, et al., 2006; Kochanska et al., 1999). It would be helpful if research could explore further the role that attachment relationships play in the development of morality. If, for example, sensitive and responsive parenting contributes to a secure attachment and the child's emerging autonomy, then the secure attachment should also promote committed compliance and enhance the child's ability to incorporate parental ideals and values into a core sense of self. How these attachment experiences and internalized beliefs are then associated with children's autobiographical memories and integrated into cognitive representations of the self, others, and interactions between them, and, in turn, influence moral conduct, are empirical questions worth exploring.

Second, there is a substantial body of literature that has centered on parental discipline in response to children's transgressions (e.g., Dienstbier, 1984; Hoffman, 1983; Maccoby, 1999; Maccoby & Martin, 1983). Evidence from this research supports the finding that gentle parental discipline strategies that deemphasize power assertion and rely on inductive methods promote children's desire and willingness to cooperate with parental rules. Another related area of research has focused on the parent–child relationship, exploring links to parental sensitivity and availability, concepts that are central to the developing attachment relationship (Londerville & Main, 1981; Matas, Arend, & Sroufe, 1978; Parpal & Maccoby, 1985; van IJzendoorn, 1997; Volling, McElwain, Notaro, & Herrera, 2002). Children who have a loving, responsive relationship with their parents, and whose parents are more sensitive and available, are more likely to internalize their standards and moral values at a younger age. They are also more eager to comply with parental directives and internalized rules because they want to maintain a positive, cooperative relationship with their parents. These internalized values help guide children's behavior even when they are not with their parents (Kochanska & Murray, 2000).

Thus, although proposed mechanisms of influence vary from one conceptual framework to another, the theme common to these ideas is that early reciprocal, secure relationships represent a critical context for the development of conscience and autonomous self-regulation (Kochanska & Aksan, 2006). Additionally, the reciprocal, supportive parent–child relationship that is mutually responsive and permeated by positive feelings leads to the construction of a *mutually responsive orientation* (Aksan, Kochanska, & Ortmann, 2006; Kochanska, 2002). Parental responsiveness, mutual cooperation, and shared positive affect between a parent and child, essential components of this mutually responsive orientation, all contribute to the development of conscience (Kochanska & Murray, 2000) and have implications for subsequent moral behavior.

But children's regulation of moral behavior does not arise only from their interactions with their parents. There are also two aspects of child temperament that may play a role in influencing self-regulation and that have been found to be critical to children's normal and atypical functioning in a variety of domains: (1) passive inhibition, which is linked to fear and anxiety and operates unconsciously; and (2) active inhibition, which is linked to effortful control and is both deliberate and mindful (see, for example, Caspi, Henry, McGee, Moffitt, & Silva, 1995; Derryberry & Rothbart, 1997; Kagan & Snidman, 1999; Kochanska et al., 2001; Posner & Rothbart, 2000). Active inhibition may be accomplished by children slowing their motor movements, initiating a purposeful movement or suppressing a behavior in response to specific directives (e.g., in a game such as Simon Says), or clearly focusing attention. Children who can actively inhibit their behavior are better at self-regulation. They internalize rules for appropriate conduct and adhere to guidelines and directives even when adults are not watching (Kochanska, Murray, & Koy, 1997). These associations have been found, both concurrently and longitudinally, from the toddler period to early school age (Kochanska et al., 1996). For children who are passive inhibitors and more fearful (particularly in the face of novel situations and persons), their anxious arousal during transgressions promotes internalized moral conduct (Kochanska et al., 2001).

And an interesting interaction between temperament and parental behavior has been found to impact the development of self-regulation. Parental discipline techniques need to be modified for children who display passive inhibition. Because these children are more fearful or anxious, they need gentle discipline that promotes the development of conscience and instills positive motivation that, in turn, encourages self-regulation, both concurrently and over time (Kochanska, 1997). By contrast, for children higher in effortful control (who tend to be more fearless), maternal responsiveness and attachment security are associated, both concurrently and longitudinally, with internalized conduct (Kochanska, 1995). Said another way, for those children who are more fearless, the same parental behaviors that contribute to a secure attachment relationship, and that reflect a mutually responsive, positive interpersonal orientation, provide the motivational basis for children to take on and adhere to parental values (Kochanska & Aksan, 2006).

It appears that one of the main structures responsible for the association between early conscience and later self-regulation of moral behavior is the developing self-system (Kochanska & Aksan, 2006). Just how self and morality are integrated and a moral self is formed in the adolescent years remains an important area for future research. We do know, for example, that there are developmental shifts in self-understanding during adolescence that make it possible for moral ideals to be integrated into the adolescent's self-concept (Damon & Hart, 1988). Additionally, there are changes in the metacognitive understanding of moral knowledge that support the integration of moral beliefs into personal belief systems. The notion that the self and morality are more integrated in adolescence is supported by the finding that there is an association between confidence in moral judgment and self-attributed moral emotions in adolescents. Thus, the process of coordinating moral emotion attributions and moral judgment that begins in childhood continues well into adolescence (Krettenauer & Eichler, 2006).

Finally, the development of conscience encompasses the three related mechanisms of emotion, cognition, and behavior and may best be viewed as an inner system of self-regulation (Kochanska & Aksan, 2006). Children follow different pathways to the development of conscience, and the ultimate organization of this self-regulatory system is influenced by child temperament and socialization within the family. The assumption made by theorists exploring the development of conscience (Hoffman, 1983), as well as others examining the role of emotions in moral socialization (Dienstbier, 1984) and in the development of behavior disorders (Gray, 1991; Quay, 1988), is that anxious arousal is the affective state most children experience following a wrongdoing. It is this uncomfortable feeling state that ultimately fosters the internalization of rules of conduct and suppresses subsequent transgressions (Damasio, 1994).

Importantly, while we have been discussing moral emotions, thoughts, and behaviors as distinct elements of moral development, it is also clear that these components develop in parallel and gradually become quite coherent over time. Before the second birthday and into the third year of life, children show individual differences in their ability to follow rules and in their distress following transgressions. When children are 3 or 4 years old, there is growing cohesiveness between moral emotions and behavior (Kochanska et al., 2005). Now, children are able to engage in moral behavior and abide by rules without supervision. They are more likely to feel moral emotions, such as guilt, when they disobey a rule or even anticipate a transgression. The two components of moral emotions and rule-compatible conduct have been found to be consistent across situation and stable over time (Kochanska & Akson, 2006). Increasingly, children develop an understanding of social contracts, moral rules, and the consequences of violating standards for themselves and others, as cognitive advances allow them to incorporate the cognitive components of morality into their behavior and emotional reactions.

Most children have a nascent but growing moral self, or conscience, by the time they enter kindergarten. They appreciate the importance of rules, try to refrain from actions that are prohibited, understand the consequences of transgressions, and feel guilty if they violate rules. The integration of the cognitive and emotional components of morality ultimately guides moral choices and activities and is reflected in children's moral behavior. But what happens when children fail to integrate the emotional, cognitive, and behavioral components of moral development? They may not be able to anticipate the consequences of their behavior or have limited understanding of social interactions. They may also feel little guilt or remorse if they transgress a rule. Increasingly, connections have been drawn between research on the development of morality and conscience and the development of psychopathology (Blair, 1995; Frick & Ellis, 1999; Quay, 1988). Thus, in the extreme, we may see children who fail to develop the essential affective and cognitive aspects of a moral system engage in behaviors that interfere with adaptive social functioning. Once again, these interrelated components of morality reflect, and influence, the self-system that continues to develop through childhood and into adolescence and to impact, and be impacted by, emotionally significant relationships.

Adolescent Social Relations

6

As adolescents' social worlds expand, their relationships with friends take on deeper meaning as well. Developmental changes in understanding the self and others lead to changes in the nature of friendships, their meaning and significance, and their influence on social and emotional functioning. Adolescents' growing understanding of their own and others' feelings often results in an increased desire for self-disclosure and for emotional intimacy. Differences in how much adolescents trust others and choose to share their private confidences in authentic ways may be related to early and current attachment relationships. Additionally, social and cognitive advances contribute to adolescents' choices of friends and conflict resolution strategies. The quality of their friendships may, in turn, impact adolescents' academic, social, and emotional development. These issues, as well as emerging sexual exploration and the development of romantic relationships during adolescence, will be discussed.

Attachment relationships continue to be important in adolescence. While the form and function of adolescent attachments change in developmentally appropriate ways, their organization and significance evolve out of earlier attachment experiences in infancy and childhood. An internal working model of secure attachment relationships allows adolescents to independently explore their identity, interests, ideas, and values. At the same time, secure models allow adolescents to challenge assumptions and ideas about themselves, as well as about their connections to others and their social worlds, without threatening their attachment relationships. When these relationships are secure, the inevitable disagreements that arise with parents during identity exploration, for example, may ultimately strengthen their connection if the conflicts are resolved in a manner that is respectful of both partners' feelings and needs. Therefore, the comfort and support of a secure attachment is still critical, both to sustaining connections and to burgeoning adolescent identity. Alternatively, when relationships are insecure, adolescents may struggle with understanding and asserting their own thoughts and feelings and, in turn, feel less confident in establishing their autonomy. When conflicts arise, they may adopt methods for resolving disagreements that diminish or deny their own needs while prioritizing those of others or they may go along with their parents' needs and beliefs while undermining their own. Early insecure relationships heighten insecurities and uncertainties about the self, thereby contributing to both ongoing and future difficulties as adolescents navigate more complex relational experiences. Exploring attachment relationships during the adolescent period is therefore critical to understanding their precursors, as well as the developmentally appropriate consequences and the cascading impact of attachments on other relationships outside of the family. We will come to see that attachment relationships continue to be crucial to the adolescent's evolving sense of self as the themes of autonomy and connection remain intricately linked.

Issues of measuring attachment security in adolescence will be discussed and critically reviewed in this chapter. Empirical findings from longitudinal studies examining the stability of attachment patterns from infancy through childhood into adolescence will be considered. Research exploring the links between attachment to parents, social competence, and emotional adjustment in adolescence will be reviewed and potential mechanisms accounting for these associations will be identified. Finally, questions about the developmental pathways of adolescents who have early insecure attachments will be examined and issues of resiliency and the capacity for change will be highlighted.

The Context of Adolescence

What is this period that we call adolescence? While the term "adolescence" is usually used to refer to the period between childhood and adulthood, it is actually a rather protracted period of development that begins at puberty and is associated with major transformations in social and emotional functioning. Biological changes lead to significant alterations in the adolescent's physical appearance and functioning. Emerging cognitive abilities allow the adolescent to now engage in more abstract thought processes. Developing interpersonal skills, as well as advances in the capacity for moral reasoning and decision making, reflect these more sophisticated cognitive competencies. Connections within already established relationships (with parents, siblings, peer groups, and friendships) and in emerging relationships (with romantic partners, best friends, and other adults) are transformed. And more sophisticated emotional competencies and skills lead to increased independence and autonomy.

Still, there are striking differences between the thoughts, feelings, behaviors, and capacities of a young, as compared to an older, adolescent. Psychologists and developmental researchers, therefore, often differentiate between early (between the ages of 11 and 13 years), middle (between the ages of 14 and 16 years), and late (17 years and older) adolescence. This conceptualization reminds us that there is not a sudden and dramatic shift from childhood to adolescence. Rather, over an extended period of time, the personal and interpersonal worlds of adolescents evolve. And the term "emerging adulthood" has been used to refer to the developmental period during which those in their late teens and early twenties are navigating the beginning of adulthood, with distinct identity, family, romantic relationship, and friendship issues (Arnett, 2000, 2007). There are many associated challenges of this period, both for the emerging adults and for their family members (Arnett & Fishel, 2013). Several research studies have begun to document the expected developmental changes in self-esteem, independence, and relationships that occur during emerging adulthood as well (Arnett, 2004; Galambos, Barker, & Krahn, 2006; Schulenberg & Zarrell, 2006).

There is a need to look both within and across the three stages of adolescence to understand the ways in which developing cognitive, social, and emotional competencies become consolidated and influence adolescents' functioning. There are new and varying relational challenges involving the capacity to seek support effectively, negotiate conflict, cooperate and collaborate with peers and adults, and create and maintain connections. At the same time, adolescents are influenced by both their families and their peer groups, as well as by the network of relationships they develop with other significant adults and teachers, all within a broader social and cultural context. The challenge for adolescents is to negotiate transformations in their interpersonal relationships by managing changes within and outside of the family, maintaining their own personal integrity and independence, and sustaining important attachments.

As children approach adolescence, biological, social, and cognitive changes occur that disrupt the equilibrium that was previously established in the parent–child relationship during childhood. In particular, biological maturation of the brain and related changes in cognition, decision making, and self-regulation occur during this time of significant growth and development (Paus, 2005; Steinberg & Sheffield Morris, 2001). Longitudinal studies using neuroimaging techniques have examined structural changes in the brain and established that the brain continues to develop throughout the adolescent period and into emerging adulthood. After puberty, the area of the brain where the most significant change occurs is in the prefrontal cortex, which is involved in "executive" functions such as attending, planning, organizing, monitoring, problem solving, and other mental processes involved in managing mental activity. The prefrontal cortex is also associated with increases in impulse control (Nelson, Thomas, & deHaan, 2008). Of all of the brain regions, the prefrontal cortex has one of the longest periods of development (Luciana, 2003). Indeed, cognitive developmentalists and neuroscientists have documented that the high-level cognitive functions involving executive processes mature over a relatively prolonged period of time and typically do not reach adult levels of performance until late in adolescence (Anderson, Anderson, Northam, Jacobs, & Catroppa, 2001) or even into emerging adulthood (Blakemore & Choudhury, 2006). Studies of patients with lesions in the prefrontal cortex have also found that injury to this area results in disturbances in behavioral regulation, manifested by socially inappropriate behavior and impulsivity, as well as difficulties in focused attention, working memory, and planning (Fuster, 1997).

Taken together, the developmental cognitive neuroscience literature has established a very clear association between the development of the prefrontal cortex and of executive functioning skills (Nelson et al., 2008). While these skills appear to improve with practice and age, they also influence, and are influenced by, individual differences in motivation, intelligence, and experience. In particular, neuroimaging research has documented two kinds of changes in neuronal connections that are at least in part driven by experience – one that involves a pruning or reduction of those neuronal connections that are not used and the other that involves enhanced myelination of established connections that thereby become more efficient. Thus, the adolescent's involvement in certain activities will influence which neuronal connections are strengthened and which are "pruned" or weakened. These neurological changes continue to support a specialization of activities that reflect a true reciprocal interaction between biology and experience and contribute to variations in the adolescent's cognitive and social functioning (Kuhn & Franklin, 2008).

The Adolescent in the Family

The biological, social, and cognitive changes of adolescence impact the family as a whole and, consequently, family relationships are altered (Collins & Steinberg, 2008). Researchers have identified three dimensions along which parent–child relationships change, including autonomy, conflict, and harmony (Collins & Laursen, 2004). Adolescents want to exert more control over decision making and to be able to make some decisions for themselves. They also want parental support for the choices they make. However, parents may have difficulty relinquishing control or supporting their children when the decisions they make are in contrast to parental values or standards for appropriate behavior. Similarly, adolescents may react to parental resistance to their autonomy with anger and conflict. Indeed, as they spend less time with their parents and struggle to develop autonomy, a moderate degree of conflict is expectable and normal. Conflict with parents tends to be highest in early to middle adolescence. By middle to late adolescence, the frequency of conflict generally decreases with a concomitant increase in its intensity (DeGoede, Branje, & Meeus, 2009; Laursen, Coy, & Collins, 1998). Thus, while frequent, high-intensity fighting is not the norm throughout the entire adolescent period, disagreements are common and there tends to be a lot of bickering. And still, research suggests that the overall emotional closeness that adolescents have achieved with their parents remains stable across age, despite the conflict that occurs (Mayseless, Wiseman, & Hai, 1998; Smetana, Metzger, & Campione-Barr, 2004).

Much of this conflict, and the manner in which it is resolved, is a consequence of shifts in adolescents' reasoning abilities. Now, the young adolescent questions parental authority. Adolescents, to varying degrees, begin to examine their parents' values and beliefs. Frequently, in an effort to assert themselves and to demonstrate their capacity to regulate their own behavior, they argue about moral issues, practical decisions, or personal matters. Sometimes these arguments take on a life of their own, and the argument itself becomes more salient than the issues underlying the disagreement. However, with increased sophistication in reasoning abilities, adolescents begin to discern when challenging adult authority makes the most sense (e.g., when moral issues are at stake) and adults learn which "battles" are worth fighting with their adolescent children (e.g., when safety or long-term goals are at issue). The manner in which conflicts are typically resolved during adolescence may also create frustration for both parents and their children. During the early and middle adolescent periods, conflicts tend to be settled through submission (e.g., "Okay, you win!") or disengagement (e.g., walking away). Discussion and compromise are distinctly less common (Laursen & Collins, 1994) and angry or neutral affect tends to predominate (Adams & Laursen, 2001). By contrast, there tends to be more discussion, clarification of issues, and a willingness to compromise when older adolescents and their parents are able to talk through their differences and recognize that the process of resolving the conflict is as important as is the outcome.

There are also shifts in the expression of affect and feelings of closeness toward parents during adolescence. Indeed, less frequent expressions of positive affect, and more frequent displays of negative emotions, have been reported by parents and their children in middle adolescence, whereas reports by parents and younger adolescents include more frequent expressions of positive affect. Yet, following a decrease in positive affect during the early teen years, more positive feelings during family interactions have been reported by older adolescents (Larson et al., 1996). Additionally, there is evidence indicating a decrease in subjective feelings of closeness, as well as in objective measures of interdependence, across the period of adolescence (Collins & Repinski, 2001). Still, children who had connected, close relationships with their parents during middle and late childhood are likely to remain close to them during adolescence despite the fact that the overall frequency of their positive interactions decreases (Collins & Laursen, 2004).

Finally, consistent findings have emerged from studies examining variations in autonomy, harmony, and conflict in adolescent–parent relationships. It appears that adolescents do best in family environments characterized by warmth, where they are encouraged to express their own individuality while staying connected to their parents (McElhaney & Allen, 2001). A reported feeling of being close to their parents is associated with higher scores on measures of self-reliance, academic performance, and self-esteem, as well as with fewer social problems including drug and alcohol abuse and depression (Steinberg & Silk, 2002). Similarly, adolescents who are involved in joint decision making with their parents, and who are encouraged to offer their opinions even though parents have the final word, fare better than when parents (or adolescents) unilaterally make decisions (Lamborn, Dornbusch, & Steinberg, 1996). Thus, there are clear benefits when a balance is achieved between autonomy and connectedness. By contrast, problems arise when parents are overinvolved or intrusive, which may lead to difficulties in establishing autonomy and consequent problems with anxiety or depression (McElhaney & Allen, 2001). And when adolescents are granted too much autonomy and feel distant or detached from their parents, there are negative consequences for their adjustment as well (Ryan & Lynch, 1989). In these instances, there may be more "testing" of the limits, as adolescents alternatively seek to prove they can be autonomous while, at the same time, act out and engage in potentially risky behavior. Here, the "acting out" may be seen as "crying out" for limit setting and parental involvement.

Mothers' and fathers' attachment styles have been considered as they influence parents' thoughts, feelings, and behaviors in their relationships with their adolescents. In particular, attachment styles are believed to impact the extent to which parents grant autonomy and communicate warmth and closeness which, in turn, may guide adolescents' behavior toward their parents or, alternatively, contribute to difficulties in the relationship. It is important to note that the term "attachment style" refers to an assessment derived from self-report measures developed by social psychologists to describe experiences in close relationships (see, for example, Brennan, Clark, & Shaver, 1998; Mikulincer & Shaver, 2007). This stands in contrast to the assessment of internal working models of attachment that are captured in measures used by researchers to assess quality of attachment in adolescence and adulthood. Recent work has explored the extent to which parents' attachment styles relate to secure-base behaviors in their interactions with their adolescents, considering the family context as well. Thus, for example, parental hostile behavior toward their adolescent, marital quality, and parental psychological distress have been examined. Complex patterns of results have been obtained regarding the associations among parental attachment style, adolescents' perceptions of their parents, and secure-base use when adolescents are involved in a conflict discussion task with their parents (Jones & Cassidy, 2014; Jones, Cassidy, & Shaver, 2015). Still, this work represents an exciting new direction for future research exploring models of association between parents' attachment styles and adolescents' behavior toward their parents. Moreover, it is consistent with the idea that adolescents and their parents are involved in a dynamic, transactional process where each contributes in significant ways to the quality of their relationship over time.

Many parents have found ways of staying involved in their adolescents' lives, striking a balance between granting autonomy and maintaining connection while not being too constrictive or controlling. Adolescents typically disclose less to their parents over the teenage years, yet it is still critically important for parents to learn about their children's activities and friends (Cheung, Pomerantz, & Dong, 2012; Keijers, Frijns, Branje, & Meeus, 2009). Parental monitoring allows parents to communicate their expectations, to keep track of their teens' activities, friends, and responsibilities, and to convey (and hopefully follow through with) the consequences when rules are broken (Guilamo-Ramos, Jaccard, & Dittus, 2010). Parents may begin monitoring their children even before adolescence begins, but it is especially important throughout the teen years. They may monitor through active conversation and spending time with their teens and their teens' friends as well as through the use of cell phones, e-mail, and/or social networking sites. In fact, research has demonstrated that when monitoring is effective, teens show more positive adjustment and higher levels of academic achievement; they are less likely to smoke, drink alcohol, engage in early sexual activity, be physically aggressive, make poor decisions, or skip school (Brendgen, Vitaro, Tramblay, & Lavoie, 2001; Li, Feigelman, & Stanton, 2000; Markham et al., 2010).

Whether the beneficial outcomes of monitoring result from monitoring per se, or whether they are the result of the parent and adolescent having developed a relationship where there is openness and the teen is willing to disclose information to the parent, is important to consider (Stättin & Kerr, 2000). Additionally, disclosure in the context of a good parent–child relationship, where autonomy support is high and parental control is low, promotes academic adjustment and autonomous motivation more than when it occurs in a poor parent–child relationship or where the parent is controlling, thereby undermining the child's autonomy and motivation to succeed (Cheung et al., 2012). Therefore, how parents obtain knowledge about their teen's activities and behaviors is as critical to understand as is what they learn about their teen (Collins & Steinberg, 2008) and the socialization context in which disclosure occurs. Considered together, these ideas extend the concept of monitoring in important ways.

Parenting and Its Impact on Adolescent Adjustment

What do we mean when we talk about parenting? Is it something we can measure by observing behaviors? Or are we talking about attitudes, beliefs, and feelings about raising children? There are multiple ways to study parenting, in part because of its complexity and the difficulties inherent in definition and measurement. Some researchers have advocated a social learning orientation, viewing the main role of parents as delivering rewards and punishments to their children. Others have focused instead on the effects that a child's characteristics or particular behaviors may have in eliciting certain parental responses. Parental attitudes, beliefs, and knowledge about their children have been explored, with an emphasis on the ways in which parents' thinking influences their behavior. More recent longitudinal studies have examined associations between parental behaviors and child outcomes, incorporating newer statistical methods (such as structural equation modeling) to examine those variables that might mediate or moderate these associations. Finally, the most well-established and popular approach is to identify categories of parenting traits or styles and to examine their impact on adolescent development (Holden, Vittrup, & Rosen, 2011).

While there are many different parenting schemes that have been studied (Holden & Miller, 1999), the best-known typological approach is the result of Baumrind's (1971) research. In her work, three childrearing styles emerged based on varying combinations of parental warmth and structure. Warmth is defined as the degree to which the parent is sensitive and responsive to, and supportive of, the child's feelings and needs. Structure is defined as demandingness or the extent to which the parent attempts to control the child's behavior. *Authoritative* parents are high in both warmth and structure. They are responsive to their child, maintaining clear expectations for appropriate behavior and using consistent discipline when necessary. Authoritative parents encourage discussion with their child, share their reasoning, and support their child's autonomy in ways that are age appropriate. *Authoritarian* parents are rigid, demanding, and unresponsive to their child. They do not consider the child's needs or viewpoint and hesitate to grant the child autonomy. *Permissive* parents are responsive and supportive but not demanding. They do not set limits but rather prematurely grant autonomy and decision making to their child (Baumrind, 1971). A fourth category of parenting was later introduced (Baumrind, 2005; Maccoby & Martin, 1983). *Uninvolved (or rejecting/neglecting)* parents are neither responsive nor demanding. They offer little warmth or sensitivity and provide minimal structure or demands. They may also neglect their caregiving responsibilities and reject their child, maintaining more of a focus on their own needs rather than being child-centered.

A substantial body of research has explored the connections between these varying parenting styles and developmental outcomes. In general, authoritative parenting is linked to more positive outcomes in adolescence, including greater responsibility, self-assuredness, social competence, and academic success. By contrast, adolescents whose parents are authoritarian are typically more passive and dependent and less self-assured, socially adept, and intellectually curious. Adolescents whose parents are permissive tend to be more irresponsible, less mature, and more conforming to peer pressures. And those whose parents are uninvolved are more likely to exhibit impulsive or delinquent behavior, to experience disruptions in peer relationships, cognitive development, and school performance, and to prematurely experiment with alcohol or drugs or engage in sexual behavior (Steinberg & Silk, 2002). Thus, evidence supports the association between authoritative parenting and healthy adolescent development. In fact, studies have confirmed these results not only in the United States but also internationally and across a variety of social classes, ethnic groups, and family structures (Steinberg, 2001). Some researchers have found, however, that under certain circumstances, such as when children are raised in high-risk environments where there may be increased threat and danger, the use of authoritarian (as opposed to authoritative) strategies is more common and leads to more positive outcomes (Dodge, McLoyd, & Lansford, 2005; Furstenberg, Cook, Eccles, Elder, & Sameroff, 1999).

It is important to note that these results are correlational and limited attention has been directed toward the processes involved that account for the observed associations. Questions have been raised about bidirectional influences and the role of other significant variables that might influence parenting styles and outcomes (see, for example, Sameroff, 1994). It might be that certain parenting styles reflect parental responses to their adolescent's temperament or behavioral characteristics or differences in the goals that parents have for their children. Identifying the processes through which parenting influences adolescent development, and the factors that might mediate observed associations, is also critical. Different developmental periods necessitate varying parenting styles; therefore, flexibility in parenting style is expected when increases in autonomy granting become important during adolescence, though this may also depend on parental values, cultural practices, and the adolescent's emotional preparedness (Darling & Steinberg, 1993). More attention needs to be directed toward understanding the contextual factors that impact parenting styles and the dynamic, transactional nature of child characteristics and parenting behavior.

An interesting line of research has explored the distinct influences of mothers and fathers on their relationships with their adolescents, as well as the role of co-parenting on adolescent development (e.g., Holmes, Dunn, Harper, Dyer, & Day, 2013). This research has been influenced by the work of family systems theorists (e.g., Minuchin, 1974, 1985), who stress the impact of interdependent subsystems, such as the parent–adolescent and the co-parenting relationship, on one another. Positive mother–adolescent relationships, for example, have been found to be associated with higher levels of prosocial behavior (Day & Padilla-Walker, 2009), lower rates of internalizing and externalizing behaviors (Kim & Cicchetti, 2004), and less risky sexual behavior (Jaccard, Dittus, & Gordon, 1996). Researchers have explored associations between maternal gatekeeping and both the father–child relationship (Allen & Hawkins, 1999; Cannon, Schoppe-Sullivan, Mangelsdorf, Brown, & Sokolowski, 2008; DeLuccie, 1995; Fagan & Barnett, 2003; Gaunt, 2008) and the mother–adolescent relationship (Holmes et al., 2013). Co-parenting has been studied in relation to its effects on adolescent outcomes, indicating that conflict in co-parenting increases adolescent antisocial behavior (Feinberg, Kan, & Hetherington, 2007) and adolescent risky behavior (Baril, Crouter, & McHale, 2007). And co-parenting interactions, rather than marital relationships per se, have been found to have a greater impact on child outcomes (McHale, 2009; Teubert & Pinquart, 2010). Certainly, there may be other variables, such as parental psychological control, that mediate between co-parenting or parental gatekeeping and developmental outcome in adolescence (cf. Holmes et al., 2013). Future longitudinal studies examining these and other important parenting variables are needed to better understand the direct and indirect effects of parenting on adolescent adjustment.

Of course, it might be the case that adolescents who are more difficult to begin with may elicit more punitive or harsh discipline or lead to parenting practices that are more distant or passive (Rueter & Conger, 1998). It may be easier to respond to children with warmth, flexibility, and careful guidance when parents see their adolescents as curious, responsible, self-assured, and competent. Moreover, difficult adolescents may cause more problems in the co-parenting relationship that could lead to conflict between the parents; this, in turn, may influence adolescent adjustment in negative ways. Alternatively, there may be a reciprocal cycle whereby the adolescent's competence leads to more authoritative parenting or more collaborative and shared parenting experiences that, in turn, support and nurture further psychosocial competence (Collins & Steinberg, 2008).

Finally, while the study of parenting styles and behavioral outcomes has provided much useful information, there are some who have objected to the idea that there are distinct parenting styles. Even Baumrind (1971) acknowledged that not all parents can be neatly fitted into one of the categories. Additionally, fathers were not included when the original longitudinal study was conducted that established the parenting categories. There is limited research on parenting in non-Western countries (cf. Ng, Pomerantz, & Deng, 2014). Even within the United States, there are families of diverse ethnic backgrounds who are not adequately represented in studies of parenting behaviors and their effects on children (Garcia Coll & Pachter, 2002). And, perhaps most significantly, parental behavior is not static over time. Parents may respond differently to each of their children and, even with the same child, parental behavior may vary across developmental periods and contexts. Interactions between parental factors and child factors may lead to varying parental practices as well. And, particularly during adolescence, there may be other powerful influences on development, such as the peer group (Harris, 1995). While parents may affect peer involvement, supporting or constraining access to, time spent with, and attitudes about their adolescent's peer group, peers also need to be considered as playing a critical role in socialization.

Peer Relationships in Adolescence

There are important transformations in peer relationships during adolescence. Teenagers acquire the ability to reason, explore, and consider multiple alternatives. These cognitive skills result in a more mature and deeper understanding of others. Adolescents also learn about their own inner feeling states and emotional reactions to others, become more aware of their impact on their peers, and progress in their self-understanding. Personal identity develops; being part of a peer group helps adolescents define themselves and offers them opportunities to experiment with new roles and responsibilities. Deeper connections to their peers, together with a more evolved sense of self, lead to increased sharing and disclosure in same-sex and opposite-sex friendships and lay the groundwork for more intimate, romantic relationships.

There are many important distinctions between relationships with peers and with family members. The power differential that is inherent in parent–child or even sibling relationships is generally not salient in peer relationships as peer relationships are more likely to be symmetrical and equal in status. Peer relationships are not considered to be as permanent as familial connections tend to be; rather, they are voluntary and potentially more transient, where members initiate and maintain their connections or choose to dissolve them when mutually gratifying terms cannot be achieved. Moreover, there are different levels of social complexity in peer relations. *Friendships* are specific dyadic peer relations that are distinct from peer interactions (where acceptance and rejection are salient constructs) and peer groups (where larger peer networks are examined) (Bagwell & Schmidt, 2011). The socialization experiences that adolescents have with their peers are unique, especially as they develop into deeper friendships and the potential for romantic relationships arises during this important period of development.

Some adolescents are well liked by their peers while others are not. There are many ways of characterizing the kinds of relationships that adolescents have with their peers. Acceptance or rejection, as measured by peer or sociometric status ratings, is the dimension of peer relations that has been most studied (Bagwell & Schmidt, 2011). These ratings reflect others' feelings toward the adolescent in the context of the peer group; they do not capture individual characteristics that make the adolescent more likely to be accepted or rejected (see Rubin, Bukowski, et al., 2006). We know that children who are accepted are more cooperative and effective at regulating their emotions, more socially competent, sensitive to and aware of others. By contrast, rejected children are more aggressive, impulsive, and disruptive, less likely to engage in prosocial behavior, and at greater risk for concurrent and future adjustment problems (Bierman, 2004).

Adolescents' experiences in peer groups may also be linked to an individual's status in the larger social hierarchy of their school (Eder, 1985). These peer networks are usually formed through shared activities and common interests. There may be dyadic friendships embedded within these larger peer groups, though not every adolescent has a reciprocal friendship with every other person. Peer networks provide a structure for adolescents, offering powerful socialization influences and critical cultural knowledge (Adler & Adler, 1998). Adolescents are exposed to the attitudes, values, and behaviors that are deemed important by the larger group (Harris, 1995). Moreover, within these peer networks, members tend to be similar to one another in important qualities considered salient to that group, such as popularity, academic motivation, participation in sports, achievement, and/or aggression and bullying (e.g., Bagwell, Coie, Terry, & Lochman, 2000; Cairns, Cairns, Neckerman, Gest, & Gariepy, 1988; Duffy & Nesdale, 2009; Sijsema et al., 2010). It is in the context of these larger networks that peer relationships exert a powerful impact on adolescents, independent from their more intimate, reciprocal friendships.

These larger networks are now established and maintained, in part, through the dominant, pervasive influence of social media. Social networks, such as Facebook, Twitter, and Instagram, offer adolescents a multitude of options for creating and sustaining their larger network of "friends." Within these networks, adolescents may create long lists of "friends," individuals who have been "friended" or mutually chosen. This term reflects a relatively new use of the word "friend" as a verb, "to friend," characterized by individuals accepting a request to be friends with someone on the Facebook social media site. As adolescents' friend groups expand, and the number of "friends" who have been "friended" enlarges, it might appear to the individual (and anyone else who examines his/her social media site) that s/he has many friends. In reality, however, the rapidly expanding social circle reflects, like a pebble that casts concentric circles in a still pond, a network of connections that increases without limit. So long as a friendship request is accepted, someone becomes your "friend." However, no distinction is made as to whether this "friend" is someone with whom the adolescent has a deep or peripheral connection, nor is there any indication of the significance of this "friend" in the adolescent's social experiences.

Despite all that psychologists know about the normative development of friendships, the characteristics and qualities of friendships, and the developmental consequences of friendships, social media sites have transformed the use of the term "friend," as well as children's and adolescents' concepts about the power and importance of friendships. Now, friends are people you know, whether intimately or more distantly, and to whom you are connected in a relatively indiscriminate manner through your social media network. There are no apparent distinctions made between qualitatively different friendships, other than perhaps by the frequency of contact, inclusion of photographs, or who "writes on your wall." "Talking" to friends happens on cell phones by "texting," and online through iMessage, Facebook Messenger, gchat, and Skype. Conversations happen less often by telephone or in person. In fact, recent reports indicate that 73% of adolescents in the United States who have internet access use social networking sites (Purcell, 2011); 75% of adolescents in the United States own a cell phone and use text messaging as the dominant form of communication with their peers (Lenhart, Ling, Campbell, & Purcell, 2010). More research is needed that is focused on understanding the meaning and development of online friendships, as well as the use of social network sites and text messaging for sustaining and terminating friendships. Whether adolescents view themselves as having multiple "levels" of Facebook friends and whether their reported friendship quality mimics patterns in real life are questions that need to be explored. Researchers are beginning to examine the role that digital media plays in friendship and identity during adolescence (Davis, 2012). Advances in technology have led to a deep concern about adolescents' preoccupation with staying connected virtually. Parents and professionals worry about the potential psychological costs to the individual and to relationships when the compelling pull to be continuously "connected" actually leaves many feeling isolated and alone (Turkle, 2012). More studies need to examine the developmental implications of online and text communications that are now such an integral part of adolescents' lives.

We do know that the internet (e.g., social media sites, instant messaging) and mobile technologies (e.g., text messaging) have unfortunately been used in aggressive or destructive ways that deliberately cause harm to others. Nasty rumors may be spread, humiliating or sexually inappropriate pictures posted, and aggressive attacks issued against children and adolescents. Cyberstalking and cyberbullying others, while increasingly the focus of schools and the legal system, are particularly serious activities because they can be carried out anonymously and without supervision. Victims are often not aware that they are being bullied or stalked for some time, yet the victimization may be widespread and intense. Parents and teachers may play a critical role in educating children about the healthy use of social media sites and in monitoring for potential problems related to cyberbullying, sexting, exposure to inappropriate content, and addictive behavior. There have been many instances where the aggression and psychological abuse that occur on social media sites have been so intense that they have led to devastating consequences, including suicide, for the victim (Hinduja & Patchin, 2007, 2009). Clearly, much remains to be learned about the power of digital communication as parents and schools grapple with setting limits and maintaining policies that protect children and adolescents.

The Nature of Adolescent Friendships

Outside of their connections to family members, friends are the next most important relationships in adolescents' lives. Friendships differ from peer relationships in that they are dyadic, reciprocal, and based on mutual affection and liking. Friends of all ages describe their relationships as supportive and mutually gratifying, where give-and-take is expected and there is a balance of sharing and need fulfillment. The essence of friendship, or the "deep structure," is reciprocity, which remains relatively consistent across age (Hartup & Stevens, 1997). The more specific interactions and exchanges (or "surface structure") may change across the lifespan, depending upon the developmental period and specific needs expressed. Thus, intimacy is characteristic of adolescent friendships, whereas sharing and playful exchanges define friendships among younger children (Hartup & Stevens, 1997).

Friendships are quite distinct from status within the peer group because friendships define a relationship between two people. Indeed, not all popular children have friends while some rejected children still do (Bagwell & Schmidt, 2011; Gest et al., 2001). However, it has been found that the social competencies that lead to social acceptance and popularity also help children make friends. More popular children have more chances to form friendships (Erdley et al., 2001) and popularity also appears to mediate the link between children's social competence and the development of a mutual friendship (Newcomb et al., 1999). Interestingly, however, in early adolescence, research exploring these complex associations has found that popularity is linked to feelings of belongingness while friendship, but not popularity, is linked to feelings of loneliness (Bukowski et al., 1993). Thus, popularity is linked to loneliness through its association with friendship; that is, less popular adolescents are less likely to have a friend and more likely to feel lonely (Bagwell & Schmidt, 2011). And longitudinal studies support the finding that adolescent participation in mutual friendships and experiences with acceptance or rejection are unique predictors of later adjustment (Berndt, 1996). Specifically, having a mutual friend (but not peer rejection) has been found to be linked to higher self-worth and lower levels of depressive symptoms in early adulthood, whereas rejection (but not friendship) is associated with lower school adjustment and aspiration level and less participation in social activities (Bagwell, Newcomb, et al., 1998).

Differences in the quality of friendships have also been found in self-reports of popular and rejected children (Parker & Asher, 1993). There is some conflicting data, however, indicating that rejected girls do not differ from average or popular girls in reported friendship quality. What does differ is that rejected girls and their friends' reports of the quality of their friendship do not correspond as strongly as they do for average and popular girls, suggesting that rejected girls may have trouble reporting that their friendships are of low quality because they might then feel the need to terminate them (Lansford et al., 2006). Observational studies have demonstrated that boys and girls in dyads of two friends with high sociometric ratings, or high-accepted friendship dyads, are more sensitive and coordinated in their behavior than those in dyads of two low-accepted friends. Low-accepted friends disagree more and their interactions are less positive than those of high-accepted friend dyads (Phillipsen, 1999). When compared to interactions between higher status girls and their friends, more immaturity and poorer conflict resolution skills are found in the interactions of rejected girls with their friends. Rejected girls also display less prosocial behavior and lower levels of social competence, more negative affect, and more bossiness as compared to average and popular girls (Lansford et al., 2006). Consequently, friendship quality appears to be different for popular and unpopular children, highlighting the need for continued exploration of the importance of peer status (acceptance and rejection) and friendship (its meaning and significance) for adolescents (Bagwell & Schmidt, 2011).

How adolescents feel about themselves in friendship is a significant part of their overall sense of competence (Masten et al., 1995). Friendships provide adolescents with a model for close relationships (Sullivan, 1953) and offer them an opportunity to consider themselves and their choices in these relationships (Brown, 2004). Indeed, preferences for different friends tend to be somewhat fluid as adolescents navigate their own identity issues. Moreover, there tends to be instability in friendships resulting from school transitions, academic tracking, and involvement in a range of school and extracurricular activities (Hardy, Bukowski, & Sippola, 2002). If new friends offer more positive role models or goals, then changing friends can be quite beneficial and promote adjustment (Berndt et al., 1999). Additionally, adolescents are more likely to develop mixed-gender friendships, as compared to in middle childhood where segregation by gender is more common (Maccoby, 1990). Therefore, exposure to varying gender roles, values, and ideas, managing transitions in friendships, and integrating what is learned in friendship into the adolescent's developing sense of self are all central to the adolescent period.

There are multiple layers or levels of friendships, so that "best friends" are distinct from "close" friends, more "casual" friends, "soccer friends," "chorus friends," "camp friends," and the larger group of "other" friends in the broader peer group (e.g., Adler & Adler, 1998). Adolescents appear to be quite adept at distinguishing between these different types of friends (Berndt, 1996). Although the term "friend" may be used to refer to *all* of these peer relationships, it is important to distinguish between types of friends (Berndt, 1996; Hartup & Stevens, 1997) because they impact the adolescent in distinct ways. Friendships in adolescence transcend the boundaries of the classroom or school environment, thereby requiring initiative and effort in maintaining relationships (Hardy et al., 2002). Friends may satisfy different needs as well. A best friend may satisfy the need for intimacy, while friends on the soccer team provide support and summer camp friends satisfy the need for companionship. Accordingly, these friends may be rated by adolescents as "more" or "less" close or important. Ratings of different types of friends, therefore, need to consider their inherent complexity and the specific social and emotional needs they satisfy, especially for older adolescents.

Adolescents' beliefs about and concepts of friendships become increasingly sophisticated and more complex from the early to the later adolescent periods (Selman, 1980). Expectations of their friendships change as well, so that now sharing and companionship are essential for closeness but so too are intimacy and commitment (Youniss & Smoller, 1985). Young adolescents report that friends are expected to confide in each other, to feel emotionally close, and to trust one another (Gummerum & Keller, 2008; Selman, 1980). Providing support and security, and offering opportunities to share thoughts and feelings, are increasingly important in adolescent friendships (Shulman, Laursen, Kalman, & Karpovsky, 1997). While mutual support and self-disclosure increase in frequency in adolescence (Furman & Buhrmester, 1992; McNelles & Connolly, 1999), leading to greater satisfaction in friendships, this also makes the possibility of conflict more likely. Same-sex friendships serve as a primary source of intimacy and support in adolescence and are therefore especially important (Chow, Roelse, Buhrmester, & Underwood, 2011).

Friendships that are high in conflict may threaten psychological well-being (Sherman et al., 2006) just as supportive friendships in adolescence have been found to be linked to better psychological adjustment (Bagwell et al., 2005). Disagreements and disappointments may arise and, when they lead to conflict, the "threat" may be greater for adolescents who have achieved more intimacy in their friendships. While there are likely to be individual differences in the capacity for intimacy, there are also consequences that result from self-disclosure and sharing that may be hurtful (e.g., if a confidence is "used" against the person who shared) or damaging (e.g., if a trust is broken). Cognitive advances and improved negotiation skills may make for more effective resolution of conflicts that are then less likely to disrupt relationships (Laursen et al., 2001). However, it is especially critical to understand the role of negotiation and compromise, and the capacity for conflict resolution, in the context of adolescents' relationships that differ in levels of intimacy.

Additionally, there may be differences in the perceived significance of achieving particular social or personal goals in adolescent friendships. For example, some adolescents may pursue a friendship to meet more self-focused goals (e.g., to gain status), while others may approach a friendship with the goal of increased intimacy and sharing with another. Indeed, these friendship goals may lead to different patterns of interaction. Adolescents who have a strong desire for intimacy will choose a friend with whom they can disclose their own feelings, be sensitive to their friend's open expression of feelings, offer and receive social support, and carefully negotiate conflict (cf. Sanderson, Rahm, & Beigbeder, 2005). Pursuing the goal of intimacy, as opposed to status, thus leads the adolescent to choose and develop a specific friendship that provides a distinct context for greater intimacy to be achieved. At this point, more research is needed that illuminates the nature of intimacy in friendships, its developmental course and significance at different ages, and the short- and long-term correlates and consequences of intimacy in friendships (Bagwell & Schmidt, 2011).

We can see that while a substantial literature exists that has established the normative experience of friendships and documented developmental changes from childhood through adolescence (see, for example, Bukowski et al., 1996; Hartup, 1996; Hartup & Stevens, 1997; Ladd, 1999; Newcomb & Bagwell, 1996; Rubin, Bukowski, et al., 2006), some of the more interesting questions that have been the focus of recent research are related to friendship quality and the characteristics of friendships. We know, for example, that the "deeper" components of friendship, including intimacy, support, and loyalty, develop gradually over time rather than emerging suddenly (Berndt, 2004). Additionally, there are similarities and differences in characteristics of friendships across childhood and adolescence. For example, there is a belief that liking, helping, and spending time together, while talking and laughing, are important components of friendship at all ages. Children and adolescents recognize that companionship is essential to friendship; they understand that intimacy as well as support or similarity constitute important elements of friendship (Bagwell & Schmidt, 2011). But by late adolescence, there are more sophisticated displays of intimacy that reflect enhanced cognitive abilities and social experiences. Empathy, for example, has been found to affect friendship quality, particularly in the context of same-sex adolescent friendships, though it appears to be mediated by the capacity for intimacy and competence at managing conflict (Chow, Ruhl, & Buhrmester, 2013). In turn, the improved capacity for intimacy influences adolescents in significant ways, making their friendships unique contexts for sharing deeper connections and promoting identity development.

It is important to consider developmental shifts in the nature of friendships across the periods of adolescence rather than viewing adolescence as a unitary stage. In early adolescence, friendships help in the process of exploring the self and in identity formation. Friends try to understand each other, share similar ideas and interests, and engage in more intimate self-disclosure (Schneider & Tessier, 2007). These behavioral similarities continue into later adolescence, where friends tend to be similar to one another in their attitudes about academic aspirations, school involvement, and the use of drugs and alcohol (e.g., Vitaro, Brendgen, & Wanner, 2005). There is an increase in empathy and sharing, an increase in expectations of friendships, a decrease in the number of conflicts, and relative stability or an increase in intimacy from early to late adolescence (Claes, 1998). Self-disclosure and sustained intimate affect have been found to be increasingly important to intimacy between the ages of 14 and 17 years, especially for girls, while boys continue to rely on shared activities to establish and sustain intimacy from early to middle adolescence (McNelles & Connolly, 1999). Adolescents' perceptions of their friendships also shift between the ages of 12 and 20 years. Friendships are viewed as more supportive by both boys and girls, though an increase is reported in negative interactions for boys that then decrease by the end of adolescence (DeGoede, Branje, & Meeus, 2009). Certainly, future longitudinal studies that follow the development of friendships, using both self-reports and naturalistic observations, and that document normative trends as well as individual differences related to the resolution of other stage-salient tasks (e.g., the development of the self), will contribute to our understanding of the nature of friendships across adolescence.

The Broadened Social World of Adolescents

The development of friendships, expanded peer groups, and growing connections to other adults (e.g., family friends, relatives, teachers) result in a significantly wider social world in adolescence that extends beyond the established relationships that children have with their parents and siblings. Peers now occupy more of their time, as adolescents not only engage in more activities with them but the nature of their friendships changes and close ties deepen. Still, adolescents continue to rely on significant adults who provide them with security, guidance, and support. More complex attachment relationships develop, and adolescents continue to include additional attachment figures into their internal models of relationships. Thus, the challenges of adolescent social relationships include balancing connections with peers, friends, and parents.

The onset of adolescence is usually associated with changes in parent–child relationships, as increased conflict and less support are often reported

(Ammaniti, van IJzendoorn, Speranza, & Tambelli, 2000; Arnett, 1999). Friendships become increasingly important. The quality of and satisfaction in close friendships have been found to be associated with lower levels of psychological distress (Kenny, Dooley, & Fitzgerald, 2013; LaGreca & Harrison, 2005). Adolescents' friendship choices become a way for them to both exercise their autonomy and assert their preferences in a domain they feel they, not their parents, control (Mounts, 2001). Moreover, interactions with friends become more exclusive, loyal, and supportive (Berndt & Perry, 1990; Damon, 1983) and take on some of the meaning they will have in later adolescence and adulthood. Friends provide important feedback about relevant social behaviors, offer information about acceptable social behavior, influence attitudes, provide intimacy and closeness, serve as attachment figures and, ultimately, as sexual and relational partners (Ainsworth, 1989; Allen, 2008; Collins & Laursen, 2000; Hartup, 1989, 1992). Negative associations have been found between supportive friendships and loneliness, identity problems, depression, and school difficulties. Positive associations have been obtained for self-esteem, psychosocial adjustment, success in other relationships, and school achievement, especially for girls (Bukowski et al., 1993). Thus, negotiating successful relationships with close friends is a critical developmental task in adolescence.

The intimacy of adolescent friendships, particularly in same-sex friendships (Berndt, 1989; Collins & Repinski, 1994) and especially for girls (Berndt & Perry, 1990), leads to feelings of being accepted, loved, and understood (Buhrmester, 1990; Reis & Shaver, 1988). The similarity between intimacy, closeness, trust, and communication in adolescent friendships, and these qualities in adolescent attachments, has led many to consider attachment theory as a model of friendship and to explore friendships within the attachment framework (Ainsworth, 1989; Nickerson & Nagle, 2005). Indeed, several researchers have argued that parent–child attachment relationships serve as a prototype for close relationships and explored attachment in adolescence and adulthood (Ainsworth, 1989; Bartholomew, 1993; Collins & Feeney, 2000; Fraley & Shaver, 2000; Hazan & Shaver, 1994; Rice, 1990).

There are, however, several critical characteristics that are the hallmark of attachment relationships alone. Attachment figures continue to serve the primary function of being those to whom the infant, child, or adolescent seeks proximity, offering comfort when distressed, feeling joy upon reunion or grief at loss, and providing a secure base for exploration (Ainsworth, 1989; Nickerson & Nagle, 2005). The form of these behaviors (i.e., seeking proximity, offering comfort, expressing joy or grief, and exploration away from the secure base) changes with age, thereby leading to differences in children's and adolescents' behavior in attachment relationships. For example, unlike infant–parent attachments, attachments in adolescents are reciprocal. Each member of the dyad receives care and provides care. In later adolescence, attachment figures may be close friends or romantic partners, and "felt security" is represented internally in expectations and beliefs (unlike the behavioral measures of infancy).

Moreover, anxiety and distress motivate proximity-seeking behavior in infants, while adolescents seek attachment figures to provide comfort and support, reduce anxiety and distress, and maintain intimacy (Allen & Land, 1999). These characteristics, and the varying developmental forms they take, remind us of the different functions served by attachment figures and friendships at varying points in the lifespan. While in childhood friends appear to be quite distinct from attachment figures in the functions they serve, these differences may become less obvious when adolescent friendships are examined. Indeed, adolescent friendships may take on the special functions of attachment relationships, though the intensity and coordination of these functions may be different from the way they were in earlier parent–child relationships (Allen, 2008).

Before discussing attachment relationships in adolescence, we will first consider the social world of adolescents. While family relationships remain salient, adolescents spend relatively more time now with people outside of the family and these extrafamilial relationships become especially important. Thus, the social world of adolescents includes an extended peer group, more intimate friendships, and new romantic partners. Adolescents' relationships with their friends are likely to be close, just as their relationships with parents may be as well. However, there are multiple ways of conceptualizing closeness within these relationships and parents and friends may provide unique contributions (Bagwell & Schmidt, 2011). For example, in a study of 13- to 17-year-olds, mothers (as compared to fathers or friends) reported having more frequent interactions with, and a stronger influence on, their adolescent children, while adolescents reported feeling closer to, and experiencing more positive and negative emotions with, their friends (as compared to their parents) (Repinski & Zook, 2005). While adolescents feel increasingly close and emotionally connected to their friends, as expected during the adolescent period, they maintain frequent interactions with their mothers. Additionally, adolescents studied longitudinally between the ages of 9 and 18 years continue to perceive friends and parents as equally supportive. However, emotional support from friends exceeded that from parents between the ages of 16 and 18 years (Bokhorst, Sumter, & Westenberg, 2010).

Of course, parents can directly influence friend choices by selectively choosing particular neighborhoods and schools for their children (Parke & Bhavnagri, 1989), and characteristics of children's schools influence their educational outcomes beyond the impact of significant people in their lives (Buchmann & Dalton, 2002). Additionally, through supervision and monitoring, parents influence who is in their children's network of friendships (Warr, 2005). For example, there is some research that indicates that adolescents are more likely to have an academically oriented friendship group when parental monitoring is high; when parents fail to monitor their children, adolescents are more likely to associate with delinquent friendship groups (Brown, Mounts, Lamborn, & Steinberg, 1993). Therefore, parents can shape the developing network of friends that their children choose, especially if they have a good-quality relationship with their children (Knoester et al., 2006).

It may be that parental and peer influences depend upon the domain examined, the context, or the way in which the influence is measured (Bagwell & Schmidt, 2011). For example, it has been found that parents continue to have influence over their adolescent's decisions, though this influence differs depending upon the issues at stake. Adolescents may still be influenced more by their parents for decisions that have long-lasting consequences, such as alcohol or substance use or academic achievement, whereas their friends may be more influential for decisions with short-term consequences, such as clothing or music preferences (Bengtson, Biblarz, & Roberts, 2002). Thus, it may be that both peers and parents continue to be important and that perceptions of closeness and support may be reciprocal. Indeed, adolescents' perceptions of their relationships with their parents have been found to generalize to their relationships with friends, and the relational skills they learn in their friendships are used in their relationships with their parents (DeGoede, Branje, Delsing, & Meeus, 2009). Still, parental influence decreases, while the influence of friends increases, by middle to late adolescence, again validating the notion that friends and parents continue to be important but that they influence adolescents in different ways, depending upon the domain studied (Bagwell & Schmidt, 2011).

Friends also impact the development of romantic relationships in adolescence. Adolescents include opposite-gender friends in their expanding social networks. In the context of these friendships, they learn to negotiate, compromise, cooperate, and resolve conflict. They begin to share more about themselves, thereby establishing a foundation for the kind of intimacy that is inherent in romantic relationships. Biological and physical maturation, as well as cultural and social expectations, independently influence the onset of dating and the development of romantic relationships (Feldman, Turner, & Aroujo, 1999). Certainly, the peer group is also a primary context for communicating these expectations since being in a romantic relationship seems to be central to achieving status and fitting in to the peer group (Connolly, Craig, Goldberg, & Pepler, 1999; Giordano, 2003). Spending time in mixed-gender groups facilitates social interactions and provides opportunities for adolescents to identify and pursue their attraction to one another (Connolly & Goldberg, 1999). Thus, peer networks seem to support romantic pairings while being in a romantic relationship promotes peer connections (Brown, 2004; Collins & Steinberg, 2008).

The timing of involvement in dating and sexual activity has been linked to adolescent development, with earlier involvement found to place adolescents at risk for both current and later difficulties (Zimmer-Gembeck, Siebenbruner, & Collins, 2001). Those younger adolescents who engage in "pseudomature" behavior and early romantic relationships, for example, may have failed to develop the positive social skills and meaningful friendships that lead to more intimate connections (Allen, Schad, Oudekerk, & Chango, 2014). In later adolescence, being involved in a romantic relationship is associated with romantic self-concept and positive feelings about the self (Kuttler, LaGreca, & Prinstein, 1999), and longitudinal studies have confirmed that perceived competence in romantic relationships is associated with general competence by late adolescence (Masten et al., 1995). While causal relations cannot be confirmed, it appears that further research needs to clarify these associations. Moreover, it is not just the experience of being in a romantic relationship but rather the particular social and emotional processes that are involved in negotiating the relationship that are important to explore. Experiences with sharing intimacies, being vulnerable, and managing compromise and conflict resolution, as well as with navigating the balance between spending time with friends and with romantic partners (alone and together with larger groups), are all significant aspects of adolescent relationships.

The "hooking up" culture has also impacted adolescents' views regarding sexuality and its place in their lives. "Hookups," defined as sexual encounters that may occur once or several times but where no commitment is expected (Bogle, 2008; Stepp, 2007), are now considered culturally normative for adolescents of both sexes (Garcia, Reiber, Massey, & Merriweather, 2012). While much of the research on hooking up has been conducted with college students, studies of younger adolescents (from as early as 12 years of age) indicate that among those who are sexually active, between 60% and 70% of them report having had uncommitted sex (Grello, Welsh, Harper, & Dickson, 2003; Manning, Giordano, & Longmore, 2006). During emerging adulthood, the period of developmental transition where adolescents are typically in college, intimacy and sexuality are usually explored (Arnett, 2000). Now, between 60% and 80% of US college students engage in a hookup experience as part of this exploration (Garcia et al., 2012).

The hookup culture may be the result of the women's movement, popular media, and shifting cultural norms, as well as the convergence of social and evolutionary forces. Popular media portrayals of sexuality in books, literature, and film contribute to the representation of uncommitted sex as pleasurable and without consequence. There are a variety of motives associated with hooking up, including physical or emotional gratification, attraction to the partner, intoxication and/or a wish to feel desirable (Fielder & Carey, 2010). Some have suggested that pluralistic ignorance leads to hooking up, with individuals overestimating others' comfort with hookups and feeling pressure to participate despite feelings of confusion or conflict (Peterson & Muehlenhard, 2007; Reiber & Garcia, 2010). Whatever the motives, there may be profound emotional and psychological consequences which are not fully understood to date. While some have argued that hooking up is empowering for women, allowing them to delay commitment and marriage while exploring their sexuality, others are concerned that hookup experiences may reflect or result in low self-esteem, loneliness, and depression. There is certainly a need to further explore both the positive and negative aspects of hooking up for both males and females and during different stages of the adolescent's experience.

There are individual differences in relationship experiences which impact behavior, influence expectations, and alter interpretations of current relationships. For example, the quality of relationships with both parents and peers, and young adults' recollections of earlier attachment relationships with their parents, have been found to be associated with the development of romantic relationships (Collins & Van Dulmen, 2006a). The link between attachment relationships and hooking up has yet to be more fully understood, with extant studies offering contradictory findings (Owen, Rhoades, Stanley, & Fincham, 2010; Paul, McManus, & Hayes, 2000; Snapp, Lento, Ryu, & Rosen, 2014). Clearly, providing a more nuanced and sophisticated view of close relationships in adolescence and young adulthood continues to be an important objective for future research.

Thus, while longitudinal studies have established that friendships in early adolescence promote adjustment and well-being in later adolescence and young adulthood (e.g., Bagwell, Schmidt, Newcomb, & Bukowski, 2001; Coie, Terry, Lenox, Lochman, & Hyman, 1995; Woodward & Fergusson, 1999), the direction of effects remains unclear. There may be certain vulnerabilities that make establishing and maintaining friendships more difficult or that present cumulative risk factors for later maladjustment. Alternatively, friendships may mediate the relation between early vulnerabilities and later problems (Bagwell, Newcomb, et al., 1998). However, simply having friends does not guarantee later adjustment (Pettit, 1997); that is, having poor-quality friendships may be a risk factor, just as having no friends or being rejected by peers may lead to adjustment difficulties. Similarly, having friendships does not necessarily serve as a protective factor. While supportive friendships do protect at-risk children from peer victimization, provide validation and encouragement, and help children cope with life stressors, there are particular types of friends, or characteristics of friendships, that may place some children at risk for negative outcomes. For example, when friendships are filled with conflict, children may be more disruptive in school (Berndt, 1996). Children develop greater acceptance for aggression when their friends are more aggressive (Newcomb et al., 1999). And the communication patterns of antisocial children and adolescents who are friends serve to escalate deviant behavior (Dishion, Andrews, & Crosby, 1995). Thus, future work that explores the developmental significance of close friendships in adolescence needs to consider the mechanisms through which friendships influence later adjustment, recognizing there may be different processes that moderate the outcome for adolescents with multiple risk factors.

Attachment Relationships in Adolescence

Even as adolescents mature and their social worlds expand beyond the immediate family, their attachment relationships with their parents remain important. Adolescents are continuing to develop autonomy, master increasingly complex cognitive skills, and manage peer relationships. Their developing emotional competencies and increased self-understanding allow for more mature, deeply connected friendships. Still, their attachments to their parents are essential as adolescents face new developmental challenges.

Adolescents continue to need their parents as a secure base, a safe haven, and a source of reassurance, just as parents continue to play a critical role in supporting and guiding their adolescent's exploration. The underlying set goal for the attachment system is now availability of the attachment figure, as opposed to the earlier goal of proximity, and there are qualitative differences in the ways in which availability is communicated and security and support are achieved (Bowlby, 1969/1982). The need for availability will vary depending upon the adolescent's circumstances and the extent to which the attachment figure is responsive to the adolescent's needs, physically and emotionally accessible, and able to communicate openly with the adolescent. While fatigue, distress, the experience of anything frightening, parental unresponsiveness, and lack of availability are some of the conditions that activate attachment behaviors in infants and young children, adolescents are more likely to prefer proximity and contact with attachment figures when in emergency situations where protection from danger is needed (Goldberg, Grusec, & Jenkins, 1999) or when the availability of the attachment figure is threatened (Kobak & Madsen, 2008). And the specific attachment behaviors used by adolescents reflect age-appropriate expressions of proximity seeking, distress upon separation, and secure-base and safe-haven needs (Campa, Hazan, & Wolfe, 2009). Thus, the nature of the circumstances that elicit attachment behaviors, and the ways in which attachment relationships are organized, are unique in later developmental periods. Adolescents and their parents modify and transform their attachment relationships, sharing responsibility for maintaining contact in what becomes a truly negotiated partnership.

How Do Emerging Cognitive, Social, and Emotional Competencies Impact Adolescent Attachments?

As adolescents come to understand themselves better, they grow to understand others better as well. They become more aware of their own inner thoughts, feelings, and motives and they assume that others also develop an awareness of their own internal worlds. Thus, a more coherent sense of self emerges along with a more complete understanding of others. The understanding of self and others develops in parallel, thereby influencing how adolescents conceptualize themselves as well as other people and relationships. Adolescents, as compared to younger children, have a greater capacity for mutual understanding (Hartup & Stevens, 1999). While younger children understand the importance of reciprocity and give-and-take, they do not fully understand others as complete individuals. By adolescence, they recognize that others have feeling states and emotional reactions, just as they do. This capacity for mutual understanding results in an increase in self-disclosure and a desire to share. Relationships develop, becoming deeper and more intimate, when friends disclose inner feelings and experiences in real and authentic ways. There is a greater capacity and desire for intimacy in friendships from middle childhood through to middle adolescence (Hartup & Stevens, 1999; Rubin, Bukowski, et al., 2006). There is also a greater commitment to keeping confidences and to maintaining loyalty and trust. By later adolescence, the capacity to coordinate multiple relationships, and to balance the competing demands of a broader range of friendships, results from improved cognitive abilities. Emerging cognitive competencies, therefore, have a direct influence on adolescents' social functioning.

The adolescent shift to more abstract, logical thought also makes possible the construction of an integrated, overarching framework for thinking about and approaching attachment relationships (Main et al., 1985). Drawing from their interactional histories with multiple attachment figures during infancy and childhood, adolescents develop a generalized perspective toward attachment that guides their interactions in, and thinking about, attachment relationships. Attachment security in adolescence and adulthood is now assessed as a generalized internal state of mind (Main & Goldwyn, 1998) rather than as a feature of, or reflecting specific behavior unique to, a particular attachment relationship. This view of attachment as an organizational construct, incorporating aspects of thought and behavior, has implications for interactions with mothers, fathers, and friends in adolescence (Allen et al., 2003; Allen, Porter, McFarland, McElhaney, & Marsh, 2007).

The capacity to think about and make meaning of their relationships, which results from the emergence of more sophisticated cognitive abilities, allows adolescents to evaluate their attachment figures, comparing them to each other and to an imagined ideal. Their ability to maintain a more consistent view of the self and of their own needs, independently of those of their caregivers, results from increased differentiation of self and other (Selman, 1980). Adolescents are more inclined to recognize that their needs may be met more by one attachment figure than another. And they can now view their parents in both positive and negative ways, leading them to diminish their idealization of them (Steinberg, 2005a). Thus, the ability to engage in abstract thought and to entertain alternative possibilities, reflecting cognitive advances in formal operational thinking, allows adolescents to thoughtfully consider their different attachment relationships. This process may lead to an angry preoccupation with the disappointment in a parent who "fails" them or to a dismissive attitude toward the parent who is absent or deficient in some essential way. Alternatively, it may result in a more objective, coherent, and balanced view of attachment relationships that is reflective of a secure attachment organization in adolescents (Allen & Land, 1999; Kobak & Duemmler, 1994). For example, an adolescent boy may be more inclined to acknowledge flaws in his relationship with his father, while understanding that his mother may be completely responsive and supportive when he is stressed. Still, the adolescent now has the capacity to think more generally about attachment relationships, rather than focusing on one specific relationship, and to construct his own organized state of mind regarding attachment.

With increases in autonomy and differentiation between themselves and others, adolescents also construct more internally based views of the self that are less dependent on a particular relationship or behavioral interaction (Allen & Land, 1999). They can detect inconsistencies in themselves and others and reflect on the way things are and how they might be (Sroufe et al., 2005a). All of this contributes to the development of a more stable view of the self as well, a view that is anchored in early attachment experiences but that gradually consists of the adolescent's conception of self apart from their interactions with others (e.g., caregivers, siblings, friends, other adults). The capacity to reflect on the self, to think about one's own feelings and thoughts as well as those of others and to engage in *reflective function* (Fonagy et al., 2002; Fonagy, Steele, Steele, Moran, & Higgit, 1991; Fonagy & Target, 1997), constitutes a critical developing skill that encompasses both an interpersonal and intrapersonal dimension (Benbassat & Priel, 2012). Adolescents learn to think about others' thoughts, feelings, and needs, just as they develop the capacity for self-awareness and understanding. Conceptualized within the attachment framework, reflective function relies on internal mental representations of self and other. Indeed, longitudinal studies have demonstrated an association between parents' capacity for reflective function and the security of their attachment relationships with their children (Fonagy Steele, Steele, Moran, et al., 1991). Moreover, parental reflective function is linked to more positive adolescent outcomes, including adolescent reflective function and social competence (Benbassat & Priel, 2012). Thus, given that adolescence extends over a protracted period of years, during which abstract thinking and logical reasoning abilities continue to grow, the adolescent increasingly reflects upon, modifies, and organizes his or her states of mind regarding attachment relationships and the self.

The Hierarchy of Attachment Relationships in Adolescence

What happens to attachment relationships as children move from childhood into adolescence? Not only do developmental advances and expanding social experiences provide new opportunities for continuities and discontinuities in attachment relationships, but now children have typically formed significant relationships with several adults. Many children have also experienced familial disruptions and reconfigurations resulting from separation, divorce, and remarriage, as well as other disturbances in relationships with their biological parents (Kobak, Little, Race, & Acosta, 2011). Moreover, some theorists maintain that as adolescents begin to spend more time with their close friends during the teen years they develop attachment relationships with them (Hazan & Shaver, 1994). Increased engagement with close friends enhances the likelihood that emotional support and security will be felt and that significant emotional connections will be forged. Now, the easy accessibility of friends and time spent together in close proximity increases the possibility that friends may be attachment figures who are sought out when needed. In older adolescents and emerging adults, close friendships and romantic partnerships may also be viewed as attachment relationships (Fraley & Shaver, 2000; Hazan & Shaver, 1994; Weiss, 1986). Thus, by adolescence, attachment functions may gradually transfer from mothers and fathers to close friends and eventually to romantic partners (Hazan & Zeifman, 1994), though attachment relationships with parents still remain critical.

A question of particular importance is how friends become incorporated into the hierarchy of attachments. The daily stressors and challenges of school and social situations may result in close friends meeting attachment needs in nonemergency situations where parents are not easily accessible (Kobak et al., 2007). Attachment behaviors directed toward parents may still be activated in emergency situations where there is a threat to the self or to the attachment figure's availability (Waters & Cummings, 2000). Importantly, the need for close physical proximity decreases as young adolescents incorporate into their working models the availability and responsiveness of their parents and close friends; these internalized representations of attachment-related experiences, expectations, and beliefs provide adolescents with a feeling of security, even when not physically proximate (Crowell & Waters, 1994).

Friendships resemble attachment relationships as the attachment hierarchy expands, though there are critical differences between close friends and parents in terms of the functions they serve. Close friends are sought out for proximity and offer a safe haven, as adolescents come to rely on their emotional support, comfort, and meaningful companionship. But parents remain critical in providing a secure base during times of high stress and as adolescents explore their autonomy (Allen, 2008; Nickerson & Nagle, 2005; Sroufe & Waters, 1977). Both parents and close friendships are therefore important in adolescence, fulfilling different but complementary roles (Paterson, Field, & Pryor, 1994). These multiple attachments are organized into a hierarchy; the primary attachment figure may be preferred but others may be sought out to satisfy particular attachment-related functions or when the attachment system is activated and the primary attachment figure is not emotionally accessible (Ainsworth, 1989; Bowlby, 1969/1982; Cassidy, 2008). Thus, in situations involving danger or distress, such as when there are threats of abandonment (Bowlby, 1973), when bearing witness to parental conflict (Davies & Cummings, 1994), or when there are disruptions in attachment relationships (Kobak et al., 2001), adolescents may not be able to count on the availability of the primary attachment figure (Ainsworth, 1991). They may, as a result, look to their closest friends to fulfill their attachment-related needs. Additionally, some theorists suggest that romantic partners may take the place of parents as the primary attachment figure in later adolescence. Major changes occur in the attachment hierarchy (Furman & Wehner, 1994; Hazan & Zeifman, 1994) as relationships with romantic partners incorporate the broader functions of the affiliative, caregiving, and sexual behavioral systems (Furman & Wehner, 1997). Thus, we see that during adolescence, attachment relationships are highly selective, distinct from other supportive social relationships, and serve unique and important functions (Rosenthal & Kobak, 2010; van IJzendoorn & Bakermans-Kranenburg, 2010).

Identifying the critical relationships in an adolescent's attachment hierarchy and then assessing the quality of these different attachment relationships will contribute to our understanding of the impact of multiple attachments and the differential role that attachment figures may play in influencing adaptation (Kobak et al., 2005). Parents continue to serve as significant attachment figures, especially in satisfying secure-base needs during adolescence and even into emerging adulthood (Fraley & Davis, 1997; Fraley & Shaver, 2000; Freeman & Brown, 2001). The fact that they may be sought out less frequently for reassurance or physical proximity suggests that, in adolescence, different attachment-related needs may be served by different attachment figures. Future research should illuminate the particular roles that close friends and significant adults other than parents may play in the attachment hierarchy, the ways in which attachment functions may be "delegated" to friends and romantic partners, and the compensatory role that attachment figures may play when there are disturbances in attachment relationships with parents.

Interestingly, comparisons of older adolescents' attachment hierarchies indicate that mothers remain as important attachment figures while fathers are more likely to be "relinquished" (Rosenthal & Kobak, 2010). Moreover, romantic partners increase in importance in the attachment hierarchy through later adolescence and into early adulthood (Markiewicz, Lawford, Doyle, & Haggart, 2006). Whether romantic partners increase in importance when fathers are not involved in adolescents' lives is an important question for future research. Similarly, the relative placement of friends in adolescents' attachment hierarchies is a critical issue to explore further; higher placement of friends over parents has been associated with an increased risk for internalizing and externalizing problems (Rosenthal & Kobak, 2010). The reliance on friends as attachment figures may serve to compensate for problems in the parent–child attachment relationship but make the adolescent more vulnerable to emotional difficulties. Alternatively, adolescents with behavior problems may have difficulty forming or maintaining attachment relationships with parents and friends more generally. These are important issues that warrant longitudinal investigation to better understand developmental differences and the potential for reorganization of attachment hierarchies.

The Measurement of Attachment Relationships in Adolescence

The quality of attachment relationships in adolescence and emerging adulthood is most often measured by self-report (Armsden & Greenberg, 1987, 2009; Greenberg, Siegel, & Leitch, 1983; Hazan & Shaver, 1987) or interview (Bartholomew & Horowitz, 1991; Kobak & Sceery, 1988; Main et al., 1985) measures. For example, the Attachment History Questionnaire (Pottharst, 1990) was developed to assess memories of attachment-related experiences in childhood. The Inventory of Parent and Peer Attachment (Armsden & Greenberg, 1987, 2009) was created to evaluate adolescents' perceptions of current relationships with parents and peers, including degree of trust and respect for feelings, quality of communication, and degree of anger and alienation. Both of these measures were designed to assess attachment history, behaviors, and feelings of security in relationships with parents and peers; they were not developed to identify and differentiate between secure and insecure attachment patterns. By contrast, the Experiences in Close Relationships inventory (Brennan et al., 1998) and the Experiences in Close Relationships – Revised (Fraley, Waller, & Brennan, 2000) are self-report measures of attachment-related emotions, expectations, and behaviors, or attachment styles, as they are reflected in adult romantic relationships (Crowell et al., 2008; Mikulincer & Shaver, 2007). And the Adult Attachment Interview (George et al., 1984, 1985, 1996) poses questions about childhood attachment-related experiences and the influence of those experiences on current functioning. These measures were designed to evaluate the underlying organization of the attachment system, yielding descriptions of secure and insecure attachment patterns similar to those originally identified by Ainsworth and her colleagues (Ainsworth et al., 1978).

The focus of the Experiences in Close Relationships inventory is on providing information about the person's experiences regarding the two attachment-related dimensions of attachment avoidance and attachment anxiety. Individuals who are high on attachment avoidance are not willing to approach others for support and comfort, whereas those who are high on attachment anxiety fear abandonment by or loss of others. When there is relatively little attachment avoidance or anxiety, then the individual displays a secure attachment style. The attachment styles captured by the Experiences in Close Relationships inventory are presumed to reflect childhood attachment experiences. Indeed, research supports this view, indicating that those adults with insecure attachment styles retrospectively report more negative attachment-related experiences as compared to those with secure attachment styles (for a review, see Mikulincer & Shaver, 2007). More recently, the Relationships Structures questionnaire of the Experiences in Close Relationships – Revised (Fraley et al., 2000) has been used to assess attachment in multiple relational contexts (with mother, father, romantic partners, and friends), relying on a common set of items that allows for the assessment of individual differences across attachment relationships (Fraley, Heffernan, Vicary, & Brumbaugh, 2011). Some researchers have developed attachment style questionnaires that yield attachment categories of secure, avoidant, and ambivalent-anxious/resistant (Hazan & Shaver, 1987, 1990) and an additional fearful (Bartholomew & Horowitz, 1991) attachment group. While these attachment style classifications may be viewed as similar to those that emerge from interview measures, these self-report and interview measures are actually quite distinct, statistically unrelated, and measure different aspects of working models (Roisman, 2009; Roisman et al., 2007).

The Adult Attachment Interview (George et al., 1984, 1985, 1996) was developed as a semi-structured interview for adults to report on their childhood attachment experiences, especially their early relationships with their parents and the meaning attached to those experiences. Individuals are asked questions intended to elicit memories of being hurt, ill, or upset, as well as memories of separation, rejection, and loss (Main, Hesse, & Goldwyn, 2008). The Adult Attachment Interview is the interview measure most often used to assess attachment during adolescence as well (Allen, 2008; Crowell et al., 2008; Hesse, 2008). Some researchers have even used the Adult Attachment Interview when evaluating attachment security in late childhood and early adolescence (Ammaniti et al., 2000) though the Child Attachment Interview, a modification of the Adult Attachment Interview, has been developed to assess attachment representations in 7- to 12-year-old children (Target, Fonagy, & Shmueli-Goetz, 2003).

The assumption underlying the use of the Adult Attachment Interview is that the questions elicit an individual's *state of mind* regarding attachment relationships, independent of the particular early attachments that the individual may have had with the mother or father. The individual's responses to questions about early attachment experiences, current relationships with parents and children, and recent losses are evaluated. Moreover, internalized strategies that have been used to regulate attention and affect related to early attachment experiences are identified. Using a well-delineated classification system, coders rate verbatim transcripts of these interviews with a focus on the language used to describe attachment-related experiences and the impact of these experiences on development and current functioning. Directly expressed material, as well as salient characteristics of the text, are considered. The coder uses a series of 9-point scales, reflecting the inferred quality of childhood experiences reported by the individual (e.g., parental behavior that was loving and attentive) as well as the individual's current state of mind (e.g., coherent or incoherent) with regard to attachment. The overall coherence of the narratives is considered. Passages that are brief, unusually long, contradictory, or irrelevant are highlighted and consistencies or inconsistencies in the text are evaluated. It is the attachment-relevant *language* used, rather than *inferences drawn* about the individual's attachment history (using behavioral observations or affective cues as is done with younger children), that provides the basis for classifying attachment (Hesse, 2008). Scoring is therefore dependent on the evaluation of the respondents' narratives regarding early attachment figures, as well as on the overall coherence and consistency of the words used to describe these experiences and the individual's ability to provide an integrated and meaningful account of these early experiences. The scores are then integrated and used by the coder to classify the resulting transcribed text from the interview into one of five categories.

There are several "organized" state-of-mind categories into which responses from these interviews may be placed. Individuals who are *secure-autonomous* value attachment relationships, are objective with respect to individual relationship experiences, and describe childhood experiences coherently. Individuals classified as *insecure-dismissing* devalue, dismiss, or cut themselves off from attachment experiences and relationships. They often present a positive global picture of their past relationships without offering specific supporting details or examples. Individuals who are *insecure-preoccupied* demonstrate a preoccupation with, and continued concern about, early attachments and attachment-related experiences. They may be passive or confused, unobjective or angry (Main, Goldwyn, & Hesse, 2008). These categories parallel the three infant attachment classifications (secure, insecure-avoidant, and insecure-resistant) identified by Ainsworth et al. (1978). The two adult "insecure" categories reflect incoherent or inconsistent explanations where the respondent's appraisals of his or her early experiences are not well matched by the accounts provided of actual parental behaviors. Classification into one of these two categories reflects the strategies that have been used to manage the anxiety resulting from having a parent who was rejecting (dismissing strategy) or over-involving (preoccupied strategy). The discourse typical of a dismissing classification includes discomfort talking about attachment-related issues, a denial of the importance of early attachments, and an idealization of early experiences along with difficulty remembering specific events. Individuals who are classified as preoccupied often experienced a role reversal in their early parental relationships, where their responsibility was to attend and respond to parental needs rather than the other way around. The individual's descriptions are often confused or ambivalent; they may alternate between anger and indifference and reflect a continued focus on or preoccupation with the relationship.

There are two additional "disorganized" categories that were developed after the original classification scheme was proposed for the Adult Attachment Interview. These additional categories, which are now well delineated, are *unresolved/disorganized* or *cannot classify* (Hesse, 1996; Hesse & Main, 2000). Individuals who are classified as *unresolved/disorganized* demonstrate disorganization and confusion when talking about early attachment-related traumas associated with abuse and/or loss. And *cannot classify* is reserved for those instances where the transcript cannot be classified into one of the major categories. In those rare circumstances, for example, where one parent is described with a great deal of anger while the other is idealized, the result may be a great deal of incoherence in the interview transcript, thereby resulting in a "cannot classify" designation (Hesse, 1996, 2008).

In most research examining middle-class samples, the predominant classification is the secure-autonomous category (e.g., Benoit & Parker, 1994; Das Eiden, Teti, & Corns, 1995; Fonagy, Steele, & Steele, 1991). However, in high-risk samples, for example, with adolescent mothers (Ward & Carlson, 1995) or where there is child maltreatment or maternal depression (Cicchetti & Valentino, 2006; Weinfield et al., 2000), a high proportion of insecure-dismissing classifications have been obtained. Several alternative methods are available for scoring the Adult Attachment Interview, such as the Adult Attachment Q-Set (Kobak, 1993) and the Reflective Functioning Scoring System (Fonagy et al., 2008; Fonagy, Steele, Steele, Moran, et al., 1991). Moreover, there has been a substantial body of research exploring the meaning of adult attachment classifications and the defensive processes at play that might influence adults' recall and discourse regarding attachment-related experiences and affects (Mikulincer & Shaver, 2007).

Interestingly, researchers have found that both the Adult Attachment Interview and the attachment styles measures are similarly associated, in theoretically meaningful and expected ways, to a variety of attachment-related constructs such as emotion regulation (see Mikulincer & Shaver, 2008 for a review), social information processing (Dykas & Cassidy, 2011), and functioning in romantic relationships (Roisman, Madsen, Hennighausen, Sroufe, & Collings, 2001). Researchers have also documented associations between adult attachment classifications (using the Adult Attachment Interview) and the speakers' responsiveness and attachment to their own children and links between adult attachment and clinical status (see Hesse, 2008, and Crowell et al., 2008, for reviews). For example, meta-analytic data reveal a substantial association (effect size = 0.72) between the Adult Attachment Interview and parental caregiving behavior (van IJzendoorn, 1995). Additionally, there is strong concordance between parental Adult Attachment Interview classifications and infants' attachment classifications in the Strange Situation (van IJzendoorn, 1995). Studies that have attempted to explore the transmission of attachment, as well as limitations or gaps in extant research and some possible alternative ways to explore parenting antecedents to attachment security (such as autonomy support), represent exciting new directions for research in this area (Bernier, Matte-Gagné, Bélanger, & Whipple, 2014). A higher proportion of insecure attachments are found in clinical populations than in the general population, although particular associations with the insecure-dismissing or insecure-preoccupied have not been found (Riggs & Jacobvitz, 2002; van IJzendoorn & Bakermans-Kranenburg, 1996; Wallis & Steele, 2001). Together, this research has expanded our understanding of the intergenerational transmission of patterns of attachment and the links between development and psychopathology (Lyons-Ruth & Jacobvitz, 2008). It has generated ideas for the timing and potential role of intervention approaches directed toward improving parent–child interactions, as well as for modifying maternal attachment representations (Cicchetti et al., 2006). Finally, it has raised questions regarding the potential for reorganizations in attachment patterns over time and the possible adaptive functions of particular attachment strategies (see, for example, Belsky, 2005, and Hrdy, 2005).

In conclusion, we see that the techniques used for assessing attachment security in adolescence have focused primarily on internal states of mind regarding attachments rather than on attachment as a feature of a particular relationship (Main & Goldwyn, 1998). Adopting an organizational perspective (Sroufe & Waters, 1977) to an understanding of attachment in adolescence leads to the view that attachment security will be reflected in both ongoing relationships and in internal representations of relationships (Allen et al., 2007). Indeed, "generalized states of mind" (Allen, 2008) regarding attachments appear to emerge during adolescence that are synthesized and constructed from the multiple models that have been formed of earlier attachment relationships. This integrated view of attachment relationships is predictive of how adolescents will develop new attachments and how they will eventually assume caregiving roles themselves (Grossman, Grossman, & Waters, 2005; Steele et al., 1996).

Early and Later Attachment Security

Is there continuity between attachment behaviors at 1 year of age and representations in adolescence? Because there are now developmentally appropriate measures that can be used to assess qualitative differences in attachment, researchers have been able to explore questions about the continuity of attachment security or insecurity from infancy through childhood and into adolescence. Some research has found consistency (Main et al., 1985) even though there are clear distinctions in the way attachment is assessed at different ages. In infancy and early childhood, attachment is typically evaluated in terms of the security of a particular relationship and there tends to be continuity across assessments of attachment security (Weinfield et al., 2008). In adolescence and emerging adulthood, most research focuses on the assessment of internal representations of attachment, transcending any specific relationship. When continuity is examined from infancy to adolescence, moderate stability (63–64%) has been found in attachment in low-risk samples (Hamilton, 2000; Waters, Merrick, et al., 2000). In particular, stability in the caregiving environment and in attachment experiences seems to be essential to continuity of attachment classifications. Even in families where the children were adopted before 6 months of age, high levels of maternal sensitivity in early childhood and in adolescence predict continuity in attachment security from infancy to adolescence, and a change from insecurity in infancy to security in adolescence is associated with a relative increase in maternal sensitivity over this time (Beijersbergen, Juffer, Bakermans-Kranenburg, & van IJzendoorn, 2012).

By contrast, there is also research that has documented a lack of continuity between attachment in infancy and particular behaviors in childhood (Belsky, Spritz, & Crnic, 1996; Thompson & Lamb, 1983) or attachment representations in adolescence (Lewis, Feiring, & Rosenthal, 2000; Zimmermann, Fremmer-Bombik, Spangler, & Grossman, 1997). Lower attachment stability from infancy to adolescence and adulthood (38–39%) has been found in studies of high-risk samples (Lewis et al., 2000; Weinfield et al., 2000). Discontinuity is more likely to be found when there are more challenging environmental circumstances and major negative life events (Hamilton, 2000; Sroufe, 1997;

Waters, Hamilton, & Weinfield, 2000; Weinfield et al., 2000; Weinfield, Whaley, & Egeland, 2004). Parental divorce, for example, is associated with insecure attachment representations in adolescence (Lewis et al., 2000; Zimmermann et al., 1997). Poverty, emotional enmeshment with mothers, and adolescent depression have all been found to predict change in security over the period of adolescence (Allen, McElhaney, Kuperminc, & Jodl, 2004). In addition, stressful events such as child maltreatment, parental drug or alcohol use, life-threatening illnesses, or parental death predict changes in attachment representations over time. Thus, stability between infancy and young adulthood is primarily attributed to continuity in secure attachment representations, whereas instability, or the move from security in infancy to insecurity in young adulthood, is associated with experiences of maltreatment, more life stressors (for boys), and lower levels of parental support in early adolescence (Sroufe et al., 2005a).

While we do know that challenging or stressful circumstances lead to expected changes in the security of attachment representations, what is less clear is *how* these experiences bring about these shifts in an adolescent's state of mind regarding attachment. Even in low-risk samples, stressful life events are associated with changes in attachment representations (e.g., Waters, Merrick, et al., 2000). In these low-risk groups, it may be that follow-up assessments are needed to determine if these changes reflect temporary perturbations rather than long-term changes in attachment representations (Aikins, Howes, & Hamilton, 2009). It may also be that limited self-regulatory and cognitive abilities make it more challenging for adolescents to manage life stressors and that low caregiver accessibility and support, along with parental expectations that adolescents should be better at managing life stress, lead to changes in attachment representations. Understanding the mechanisms that lead to discontinuity in attachment, in both low- and high-risk samples, is certainly an important direction for future research.

Interestingly, some longitudinal studies have demonstrated that infant attachment status is associated with particular qualities of adolescents' close relationships. In fact, these associations may be even stronger than when infant attachment is linked to measures of adolescent or adult attachment (Allen, 2008; Grossman, Grossman, & Kindler, 2005; Sroufe et al., 2005a). Moreover, attachment representations in adolescence are only moderately correlated with maternal attachment security (Allen et al., 2004). Thus, taken together, there appears to be modest continuity from infant to adolescent measures of attachment and between parental attachment status and adolescents' attachment representations (Allen, 2008). There also appears to be stability across the adolescent period in attachment representations (e.g., Allen et al., 2004; Ammaniti et al., 2000; Zimmermann & Becker-Stoll, 2002), although these studies use relatively small sample sizes and varying methodologies for measuring and coding attachment patterns. Still, we do know that under particular conditions and in specific contexts, adolescents' attachment representations may remain stable.

By contrast, when attachment relationship quality is assessed using the Inventory of Parent and Peer Attachment, qualitative changes in attachment have been found across the period of 11–17 years of age (using a cohort-sequential design), with gender of the adolescent and of the attachment figure influencing the patterns of change (Buist et al., 2002). For example, quality of attachment to mother shows a linear decline for girls across the period from 11 to 17 years, whereas change in mean level of attachment quality is nonlinear for boys. For attachment to father, there is a linear decline in attachment quality for boys and a nonlinear change for girls. Moreover, gender composition of sibling dyads is associated with differential development of quality of attachment. While these results come from the use of only one self-report instrument, and the children were from a Dutch sample of adolescents from two-parent middle-class families, they still provide interesting data on the developmental patterns of adolescent attachment and raise important questions about the individual, familial, and relational characteristics that may influence these patterns.

It is also important to consider the possibility that enduring patterns of attachment may not be reflected in adolescent states of mind (as evaluated by the Adult Attachment Interview) or predictive of future attachment representations. In fact, some variability in representations of attachment may be expected (Weinfield et al., 2004). Moreover, some adolescents may have had negative life experiences that they deny, thereby leading to a dismissing classification, especially if they have not gained autonomy from their family of origin and find it too difficult to acknowledge the poor treatment they received from a parent on whom they still depend. However, if some rethinking and analysis of these childhood experiences and increased autonomy occur, these adolescents may actually achieve a secure classification in spite of these negative experiences (Waters, Weinfield, & Hamilton, 2000). Thus, therapeutic interventions may lead to shifts from insecurity to security in attachment representations. Relationships with teachers in middle childhood and quality of friendships in early adolescence may also play an important role in predicting trajectories of internal representations of attachment (Aikins et al., 2009). Still, extant research offers interesting directions for future studies that will illuminate further the construct of attachment and the usefulness of current assessment techniques for evaluating attachment security across multiple developmental periods.

The research on attachment from infancy to adolescence has profound implications for understanding adolescent attachment and emotional adjustment. The organizational approach to development offers a framework for considering the early origins of later maladaptive patterns of development (Sroufe, 2005; Sroufe et al., 2005b). Accordingly, while early events, such as attachment relationship experiences, establish a course for later adaptation, the pathways are not firmly determined. Later experiences may solidify these developmental trajectories or alternatively lead to changes and reorganizations. The subsequent resolution of stage-salient developmental tasks, the experiences children have, and the competencies they acquire are all likely to have an impact as well. Children are also influenced by other relationships, with siblings, friends, teachers, or other significant adults, as they continue to consolidate their early attachment experiences. Therefore, children who begin life with insecure attachment relationships may be at a relative disadvantage when it comes to managing other interpersonal relationships, as well as concurrent or subsequent stage-salient tasks. But all hope is not lost. There is the potential for change. When considering pathways from early infancy to later adolescence, early attachment experiences may establish a likely course for later representations of attachment. However, intervening circumstances may also contribute to outcomes in adolescence and, together with current stressors and experiences, predict outcomes better than early experiences or attachment representations alone (Aikins et al., 2009; Sroufe et al., 2005a). Relationships outside of the family, particularly with peers and teachers, may, for example, offer alternative possibilities for interpersonal experiences that may be incorporated into current attachment representations. Future research exploring attachment continuity with high- and low-risk samples will contribute to our understanding of the degree to which attachment representations are modified or reorganized during adolescence.

Adolescent Attachment and Social and Emotional Functioning

During adolescence, the attachment system achieves an organization that has developed over time, is relatively stable, and is predictive of functioning both within the family and in relationships outside of the family (Allen, 2008; Hesse, 2008). Indeed, attachment patterns have been found to be positively associated with social competence and interpersonal functioning in adolescence (Allen & Land, 1999; Bagwell, Newcomb, et al., 1998; Black & McCartney, 1997) and negatively associated with antisocial behavior (Marcus & Betzer, 1996). While attachment security appears to be more relevant to functioning in close relationships than in broader peer interactions (Hazan & Shaver, 1987; Lieberman et al., 1999), associations have also been found between attachment security, general peer competence, and working models of peer relationships (e.g., Allen, Moore, Kuperminc, & Bell, 1998; Allen et al., 2007; Furman, Simon, Shaffer, & Bouchey, 2002). Thus, attachment security is relevant to functioning in close relationships with friends as well as to overall popularity, acceptance, and friendship quality.

Securely attached adolescents are more comfortable with emotional intimacy in close friendships (Weimer, Kerns, & Oldenburg, 2004; Zimmerman, 2004). They are more competent at seeking emotional support while resisting peer pressure. Moreover, adolescents' working models of relationships with parents are similar to those with romantic partners and friends, thereby supporting the role that attachment-related thoughts, feelings, and experiences play in influencing emerging romantic relationships (Allen, 2008; Furman et al., 2002, Hazan & Shaver, 1994). Secure attachment representations (assessed with the Adult Attachment Interview) are also associated with better quality interactions with romantic partners (Roisman et al., 2001). Thus, just as we have seen in infancy, attachment security appears to play an important role in impacting social relationships in adolescence. As relationships with friends become increasingly important, these friendships may influence adjustment directly or they may mediate the associations between parent-child attachment and later adjustment.

For college students, attachment relationships with mothers and fathers have been found to be associated with concurrent measures of emotional adjustment (Kenny, 1987; Love & Murdock, 2004: McCarthy, Moller, & Fouladi, 2001). The transition to living away from home requires that adolescents negotiate the developmental tasks of separating from their families while developing new relationships and support systems (Hinderlie & Kenny, 2002). Interestingly, there has been some research that has examined social skills as they mediate between attachment and emotional adjustment. Differential effects have been found. Specifically, stronger attachment to mothers predicts greater competence in conflict resolution, which in turn is associated with greater relational competence and better emotional adjustment. Stronger attachment to fathers has been found to predict better social skills, leading to greater relational competence and higher emotional adjustment (Ross & Fuertes, 2010). Whether mothers serve as a secure base, particularly in high-conflict situations, which then helps adolescents to learn the kinds of skills necessary to manage conflict in interpersonal situations and sustain their secure attachment relationships, is an interesting question that warrants further exploration. Moreover, this research confirms the idea that relationships with mothers, fathers, and peers are essential and play complementary roles in adolescents' emotional adjustment (Noom, Deković, & Meeus, 1999).

Attachment security has also been explored in relation to the development of psychopathology, with insecure attachment, in particular, believed to be a risk factor for maladjustment (Bowlby, 1973; Burgess, Marshall, Rubin, & Fox, 2003; Greenberg, Speltz, & DeKlyen, 1993; Sroufe, 1997). Some research has indeed found a concurrent association between attachment and psychopathology in adolescence (Cole-Detke & Kobak, 1996; Kobak & Sceery, 1988; Kobak, Sudler, & Gamble, 1991; Lewis et al., 2000; Rosenstein & Horowitz, 1996). Across adolescence, attachment security has been found to be linked to higher levels of depressive symptoms and to a pattern of increasing levels of externalizing symptoms in both at-risk samples (Allen et al., 2002; Marsh, McFarland, Allen, McElhaney, & Land, 2003) and community samples (Allen et al., 2007; Dawson, Allen, Marston, Hafen, & Schad, 2014). More interpersonal difficulties have been found in insecurely attached individuals (Crowell et al., 2008). And in a comprehensive review and meta-analysis of studies exploring concurrent and longitudinal associations between attachment security or insecurity and anxiety, depression, and global internal-izing symptoms, associations have been found to be stronger in preadolescence and adolescence than in childhood (Brumariu & Kerns, 2010).

Whether different types of internalizing problems are related to specific patterns of insecure attachment, and whether attachments to fathers play a role in the development of internalizing symptoms, are questions that warrant further attention (Brumariu & Kerns, 2010). Because the approaches to meas-uring attachment differ across studies, with questionnaires appearing to be the most frequently used assessment procedure, future research that reduces the influence of response biases and shared method variance is needed. Research-ers need to control for initial levels of internalizing symptoms, since mood may influence attachment ratings (Roisman, Fortuna, & Holland, 2006); this may help to clarify and illuminate the possibility of bidirectional effects between internalizing symptoms and attachment (Brumariu & Kerns, 2010). Moreover, additional longitudinal studies are needed to explore social and contextual factors, such as characteristics of the child and the caregiving envi-ronment (e.g., family functioning, socioeconomic background), that may help to account for the obtained associations between early attachment and later psychopathology (Raudino, Fergusson, & Horwood, 2013).

A number of potential mechanisms have been proposed to account for the link between insecure attachment and maladaptive behaviors. For example, insecure attachment could lead to difficulties with emotion regulation (Cassidy, 1994; Thompson, 1994). Aggressive behavior may result from models of attachment that are characterized by mistrust, anger, and fear (Bretherton, 1985) as well as by negative attribution biases (Dodge & Newman, 1981). Feelings of social isolation and loneliness (Kerns et al., 1996) and internal-izing problems (Granot & Mayseless, 2001) may result from views of the self as unworthy. Recent empirical work has explored these propositions. For example, maladaptive coping strategies have been found to play a role in mediating the association between adolescent insecure attachment organi-zation and later reports of externalizing behavior in emerging adulthood (Dawson et al., 2014). Thus, specific child characteristics, including difficul-ties identifying, understanding, and regulating emotions, cognitive biases, and perceived self-worth, should be examined further (Brumariu & Kerns, 2010). Additionally, parental psychopathology, gender, and the effect of insecure attachment on biochemical and neurophysiological processes should all be studied in relation to the development of psychopathology.

Moreover, factors that have been found to moderate the relation between attachment and internalizing symptoms, such as child temperament, stress, poor parenting, or economic risk, should be explored further so as to clarify their role in potentiating, either alone or in combination, the likelihood of internalizing symptoms, depression, or anxiety (cf. Brumariu & Kerns, 2013; DeKlyen & Greenberg, 2008). The interactive and combined effects of multi-ple risk factors in determining internalizing (or externalizing) problems may be more relevant than the exploration of any single variable alone. And finally, consistent with cascade models of psychopathology (Masten & Cicchetti, 2010), insecure attachment may be associated with more internalizing problems in part because of particular experiences, such as difficulties getting along with their peers and regulating emotions, that heighten a child's risk for anxiety (Kerns & Brumariu, 2014). Ultimately, future research has enormous potential for developing models for understanding psychopathology and for promoting targeted clinical interventions.

Attachment Relationships and Friendships During Adolescence

Maintaining a secure attachment relationship throughout adolescence requires that parents are able to provide a sense of "felt security" and protection while supporting the older child's need for exploration and autonomy. Children must still be able to clearly communicate their expectations and needs. And parents and children together must negotiate new ways of communicating across greater distances (a process that is indeed facilitated by new technologies). When children reach middle and later childhood, they also develop close friendships and, in adolescence, they may have their first experiences with dating and intimacy (Furman et al., 2002). Now, multiple attachment relationships coexist (Allen, 2008) as adolescents work to balance close connections to family members with expanded social networks that include attachments to peers and romantic partners. It is a paradox, then, when we acknowledge the predictable struggle of most adolescents: they both want, and resist, their connection to their earlier attachments. It is within the security of parental attachment relationships that adolescent autonomy is most easily established (Allen, Hauser, Bell, & O'Connor, 1994; Fraley & Davis, 1997, Nickerson & Nagle, 2005) and new attachment relationships are formed. Yet, adolescents seem determined to purposefully "escape" the perceived restraint of their attachments with parents as they continue to manage more autonomously and negotiate new connections. And their inevitable conflicts with their attachment figures play an integral role in the development of autonomy. Earlier attachments, therefore, provide the anchoring and the security that facilitate the development of autonomy while also serving as a template for connecting to others.

Indeed, as attachment theorists suggest, the attachment relationship provides a secure base for exploring other relationships and leads to the development of internal working models of self, others, and relationships. In turn, these early experiences and internal models together shape subsequent relationships. Researchers have provided evidence supporting these claims, as secure attachment has been found to predict greater competence in interpersonal functioning in children and adolescents (Black & McCartney, 1997; Elicker et al., 1992; Rice, 1990). Children with histories of secure attachments are more capable at making friends, tend to choose friends who similarly have histories of secure attachments (Elicker et al., 1992), and have more positive interactions with a close friend in fourth grade (Lucas-Thompson & Clarke-Stewart, 2007). And when adolescents describe their parents as warm and accepting, they are also more likely to describe their experiences with their best friends as intimate and close (Madden-Derdich, Estrada, Sales, Leonard, & Updegraff, 2002). Adolescents have been found to have higher quality friendships with less conflict when they rate their parents as available, report feeling secure with their parents, and know they can count on them during times of stress as compared to those with less secure attachments (Lieberman et al., 1999). Moreover, adolescents have more difficulty discussing problems and concerns with a best friend when they have more dismissing, rather than secure, models of relationships (Shomaker & Furman, 2009).

While associations between adolescent and young adult attachments to friends and parents have been found, the correlations are relatively low (*rs* range from 0.15 to 0.31 across measures), indicating unique attachments for different relationships (Crowell, et al., 2008; Fraley et al., 2011). There is also evidence to suggest that some adolescents who have insecure attachments with their parents may seek friends to fulfill their attachment needs. In these cases, friends may compensate for what is missing in their relationships with their parents (Freeman & Brown, 2001; Schneider & Younger, 1996). Thus, adolescents who view attachments to parents as less secure are more likely to view their relationships with friends as secure (Furman et al., 2002) and to turn to their friends for proximity-seeking and secure-base functions (Nickerson & Nagle, 2005). Additionally, some research suggests that insecure attachments in adolescents may lead to their prematurely seeking romantic relationships to meet attachment needs (Hazan & Zeifman, 1994).

If friends become the central source of emotional support and companionship in adolescence, especially for those who have less secure attachments to their parents, then the development of peer relationships and friendships during this important developmental period should be encouraged. There is a substantial body of research suggesting that close peer relationships are associated with positive outcomes for youth (Bukowski et al., 1993; Reis & Shaver, 1988). Indeed, several studies indicate that friendship quality may mediate between early attachment and later psychological adjustment (Booth-LaForce et al., 2005; Rubin et al., 2004). Moreover, adolescents with secure attachments to both parents and friends are found to have low internalizing and externalizing problems, while those who are insecurely attached to parents but secure with friends have fewer problem behaviors than those who are secure with parents but insecure with friends (Laible, Carlo, & Raffaelli, 2000). The clinical implications of these findings are profound. Promoting competency and resilience in children and adolescents is critical (Masten, 2014). Fostering close peer relationships in schools and community settings, through peer tutoring, for example, may lead to positive academic outcomes and promote cooperative social relationships across racial and ethnic groups (see, for example,

Nickerson & Nagle, 2005). Educators and mental health providers working with adolescents should recognize and support the role of friends in managing leisure activities, emotional conflicts, and interpersonal relationships. While close friendships may not protect against all possible outcomes associated with insecure attachment relationships, they may still buffer the adolescent and serve some compensatory role.

Certainly future research may help to flesh out the aspects of friendship that are influenced most by attachment history and to examine the attachment patterns of both interactional partners. It may be, for example, that children with secure attachment experiences are more likely to seek out and befriend others with secure histories, where beginning and maintaining friendships is easier for them and/or they expect and offer more intimacy and support in the friendship. Exploring the consequences of an insecure attachment history for adolescents' initiation of friendships, for sustaining a trusting and open connection, or for negotiating conflict may help to identify the particular challenges that require intervention strategies. Finally, while internal working models have been described as playing a central role in the relation between early attachment experiences and later friendships, there may be some other factors that account for the association. Early attachment security may contribute to the developing sense of self, resulting in a view of the self as competent and confident, which then impacts the child's orientation to friendships. Greater feelings of self-worth, and an expectation of reciprocity and social support, may result from the kinds of early social experiences that contribute to secure attachment and high-quality friendships (Booth-LaForce et al., 2005). Research designs that incorporate measures of other features of the parent–adolescent relationship, cognitive representations of friendships and attachments, and measures of self-understanding and perceived competence may provide important clues to better understanding the association between attachment and friendship (Bagwell & Schmidt, 2011).

Emotion regulation may also play a role in mediating the association between attachment relationships to parents and the development of friendships in adolescence. Indeed, attachment theorists propose that both working models and emotion regulation skills (or the behaviors and strategies used to modulate emotional arousal) are important to explore (Bowlby, 1973; Bretherton, 1987). Researchers have documented the role that constructive coping, an emotion regulation strategy, plays in mediating between attachment and peer competence in late childhood, especially for those with high negative emotionality (Contreras et al., 2000; Kerns et al., 2007). Children who are securely attached to their mothers are more likely to use constructive coping strategies and are rated as higher in peer competence. Teachers also rate children who use more constructive coping as more competent with their peers (Contreras et al., 2000). Thus, the capacity to regulate emotions in adaptive ways and across contexts may help to explain the finding that more adaptive social functioning, including the ability to develop high-quality peer relationships, is found in children who are securely attached (Contreras & Kerns,

2000). Examining the mediating role of emotion regulation in adolescence would represent an important extension of this work.

Similarly, clarifying the role that internal working models play in processing social information is another important direction taken in recent research (Dykas & Cassidy, 2011). This work is based on the assumption that an individual's experiences in close interpersonal relationships will lead to differences in how they process information in their social environments (Bowlby, 1969/1982, 1973, 1980; Dykas & Cassidy, 2011). In one study, for example, the link was explored between attachment (using the security composite score from the Experiences in Close Relationships inventory) and the social information to which adolescents attend. More secure adolescents were found to seek out more positive feedback about the self and to engage in schematic processing that is more positively biased (Cassidy, Ziv, Mehta, & Feeney, 2003). In another study, adolescents and their mothers' reconstructed perceptions of adolescent–parent conflict were found to be affected by attachment security (measured by the Adult Attachment Interview). Insecure adolescents report less favorable conflict-related discussions as compared to secure adolescents; both secure and insecure adolescents also perceive their conflict-related discussions to be less negative than observer ratings though, over time, only the secure adolescents' bias toward negativity decreased (Dykas, Woodhouse, Ehrlich, & Cassidy, 2010). In related work (also using the Adult Attachment Interview and including mothers and fathers), adolescents in the insecure-dismissing group were found to engage in a deactivating strategy leading to difficulty remembering new attachment-related information and negative (as compared to positive) information about their own parents, whereas those in the preoccupied group had more memories of emotional childhood events, reflecting hyperactivation and difficulty regulating emotional distress (Dykas, Woodhouse, Jones, & Cassidy, 2014). Secure adolescents have also been found to have expectations and make attributions about others that are more positively biased while insecure adolescents process information in a negatively biased manner. For example, those with lower Adult Attachment Interview coherence of mind scores are more likely to expect rejection by others (Dykas, Cassidy, & Woodhouse, 2009). Moreover, insecurely attached adolescents (using the Adult Attachment Interview) also have insecure models of friends (and of romantic partners) if their Adult Attachment Interview classification is insecure-preoccupied (Furman et al., 2002). By contrast, more secure adolescents have more positive attributions regarding closeness and emotional support in friendships (Zimmermann, 2004); they also have greater access to feelings and more flexible expectations and attributions when evaluating rejection by peers (Zimmermann, 1999). Considered together, this research suggests that attachment-related defensive strategies appear to influence social information processing and memory processes, thus highlighting the complex connections between attachment, emotion regulation, and memory for attachment-relevant information.

In summary, it appears that adolescent attachments influence relationships with peers and close friends, the capacity for emotional regulation, and patterns of adaptation and maladaptation in adolescence and young adulthood. Intimacy in adolescent relationships develops from the cumulative history of earlier experiences in the family and depends upon the capacity for trust and the ability to regulate affect. In the context of early relationships, children learn to engage in reciprocal give-and-take, tolerate a range of affects, be attentive and responsive to others, take another person's perspective, develop empathy, and negotiate and resolve conflicts; these are all essential components to developing intimacy. Adolescents' experiences of early care, ongoing support, and responsiveness from parents, and subsequent successes and challenges in peer interactions and friendships, allow for feelings of vulnerability and the self-disclosure and authentic emotional sharing inherent in intimate connections. Clearly, competencies that arise in the context of early attachment relationships support later attachments as well, but they are integrated, practiced, and refined within close friendships throughout childhood and adolescence. When there is continuity in the caregiving environment across developmental periods, we can predict coherence of adaptation over time. However, when there are stressors that impact the child, parents, family, or caregiving environment, developmental outcomes may vary in less predictable ways (Sroufe et al., 2005a). Understanding these different developmental trajectories, and the various pathways to adaptation and maladaptation, will continue to inform the work of developmental researchers and clinicians.

Adolescent Identity and the Consolidation of the Self

7

One of the major tasks of adolescence is to establish a sense of the self as integrated and coherent. The process of identity development is complex, involving an understanding of the self as well as an understanding of the self in relation to others. Social, emotional, and cognitive advances contribute to changes in adolescent self-concept, as internal representations of the self are modified and self-esteem is altered. Adolescents are now more equipped to use regulatory strategies to guide their behavior, inhibit their impulsive reactions, and modify their emotional responses; consequently, their relationships with peers and family members are transformed. Most adolescents achieve a new level of closeness with peers and their connections with parents are modified in developmentally appropriate ways. Adolescence is a time of continuing the process of becoming a separate individual while remaining connected to others. Thus, adolescents are navigating the balance between connection and autonomy once again.

Families continue to provide the emotional setting for promoting identity development by offering adolescents comfort and security while encouraging them to develop a unique sense of self. In fact, it is in the context of secure attachments to parents that adolescents develop the capacity to establish autonomy while maintaining connections to significant attachment figures. Questions about gender, ethnic, and sexual identity, though influenced by familial and cultural values, need to be resolved in a manner that is meaningful to adolescents. And issues around intimacy and self-disclosure become more salient as adolescents manage multiple relationships with significant adults, teachers, and friends. All of these topics will be considered in this chapter. The role of emotion regulation and empathy, as well as of moral emotions and moral behavior, in the capacity to connect to others will also be discussed.

For some adolescents, it is in working through the challenge of identity formation that social and emotional difficulties may arise. Research on the development of internalizing problems (disturbances in mood or emotion such as anxiety and depression) and externalizing problems (such as delinquency, alcohol and substance abuse) during adolescence will be woven throughout, with a focus on controversial issues such as why some adolescents are more vulnerable than others to developing psychological problems. What we will come to see is that adolescent identity and the consolidation of the self are meaningful not only to the individual; a clear sense of self also impacts the nature and quality of connections that adolescents are able to negotiate within their larger social worlds. Therefore, it is during adolescence that we can most clearly see the tension between these two critical developmental tasks of managing connections to significant others and continuing to develop an autonomous self. The way this tension is resolved provides a useful framework for understanding developmental risk factors for later patterns of adaptation and maladaptation.

The Development of Autonomy and the Self

It is during adolescence that individuals begin to ask questions such as "Who am I?" "How do I want others to view me?" and "How do I fit into the larger social world?" Now, psychological characteristics of the self are explored and examined. Erikson provided the seminal theory that accounts for adolescent identity development, highlighting the critical identity crisis that occurs during adolescence (Erikson, 1968). More recent theory and research suggests that identity work extends into late adolescence (Levy-Warren, 1999) or even beyond, into the period of emerging adulthood (Arnett, 2000). In Western societies, the transition to adulthood is generally more protracted. Thus, the period of emerging adulthood, between 18 and 25 years, is now viewed as a separate phase in life marked by intensive exploration (Arnett, 2004). There are frequent changes in various domains of functioning (e.g., work, relationships, living situations) with few stable commitments made during this time (Arnett, 2000). Adolescents are in the process of making the critical transition from being dependent children to independent young adults.

It is important to note, however, that this process of "becoming independent" implies that the adolescent is separating from and developing autonomy *in relation to* a significant other, usually the parent(s). There is much more research on the outcome of this process of establishing independence than there is on the individual and relational transformations that promote and support the outcome (Collins & Steinberg, 2008). Moreover, while many developmental theories conceptualize achieving autonomy as a critical developmental outcome for adolescents (McElhaney, Allen, Stephenson, & Hare, 2009), independence is valued differently across cultural and socioeconomic groups (Feldman & Quatman, 1988; Manzi, Regalia, Pelucchi, & Fincham, 2012). Middle-class European Americans, for example, value individual autonomy, encouraging independence in functioning and decision making and confidence in asserting one's own opinions (even if they run counter to one's elders or the attitudes and pressures of one's peers). When adolescents are not capable of behavioral and emotional autonomy, they are often seen as dependent and immature, though these impressions are grounded in specific cultural values that provide the lens through which individuals are viewed. By contrast, groups that value collective responsibility (e.g., working-class Mexican Americans, middle-class Japanese) believe that attending to the good of the larger group is much more important than expressing personal desires and that symbiotic harmony and accommodating others is valued over individuation (Rothbaum, Pott, et al., 2000).

There are, therefore, significant variations across cultural groups in the value placed on autonomy and relatedness as developmental goals as well as on the correlates and consequences of adolescent independence (see Tamis-LeMonda et al., 2008, for a review of individualism and collectivism as cultural value systems). For non-Western cultures that do not promote or value individual autonomy, where developing an autonomous identity is not a developmental goal for adolescents, parenting styles, such as autonomy support and control, need to be understood differently in relation to adolescent adjustment (Mason, Walker-Barnes, Tu, Simons, & Martinez-Arrue, 2004; Roland, 1987; Soenens & Beyers, 2012). Within particular cultural groups (e.g., those that value collectivistic ideals), parenting that does not promote autonomy is not viewed as placing the adolescent at risk for problems such as anxiety and depression (Rothbaum & Trommsdorff, 2007; Trommsdorff, 2005). Additionally, adolescents' perceptions of their parents' support of, and respect for, their autonomy may influence their inclination toward independence (Sher-Censor, Oppenheim, & Sagi-Schwartz, 2012). Therefore, the contextual and socialization experiences that potentially lead to problems in the process of developing autonomy need to be acknowledged and explored further. Even within Western cultural groups, for example, we need to ask why is it that some adolescents continue to be dependent on their parents, incapable of autonomous functioning or making independent decisions that are thoughtful and principled. Why do some adolescents rely on parents excessively for, or alternatively dismiss and reject, emotional support? Indeed, there is limited empirical research that explores parental behaviors related to maladaptive outcomes (such as dysfunctional dependence or independence) in the separation process (Kins, Soenens, & Beyers, 2012).

The process of developing autonomy from parents begins in infancy and early childhood and continues to evolve through adolescence and emerging adulthood. There are many different ways of thinking about autonomy, including autonomous thought, autonomous decision making, and physical separation (Soenens et al., 2007). There are also varying ways in which parents promote and encourage each of these dimensions of autonomy which are, in turn, interpreted and valued differently by diverse cultural groups (Manzi et al., 2012). Adolescents from varying cultural backgrounds will ascribe different interpretations and affective meanings to parental behaviors in a manner that is consistent with the underlying goals of their cultural background. So, for example, the domain of physical autonomy (concerning free time and physical space) remains relatively unimportant for Italian first year university students, whereas it is of great importance in the United States (Manzi et al., 2012). For many first year university students in the United States, encouragement of physical autonomy is also accompanied by a move out of the parental home. This move may, in turn, be marked by a pronounced shift in the power balance, transforming the parental relationship into one that is more mutual as opposed to hierarchical. But even when living together, the process of separation and individuation unfolds within the family context; thus it influences, and is influenced by, parental factors such as psychological control (Kins et al., 2012) and by important cultural factors as well (Chao & Aque, 2009; Rothbaum & Trommsdorff, 2007). Therefore, there may be important *within family* differences, such as the family's tolerance for and encouragement of independence, which interact with cultural values and play an important role in the resolution of this developmental task.

Psychodynamic theorists emphasize the importance of emotional independence from parents and view conflict in the parent–child relationship as the normal consequence of a process of detachment (Freud, 1958). When there is too much harmony in the adolescent parent–child relationship, it is seen as symptomatic of an intrapsychic immaturity that is potentially stunting of the adolescent's growth and development (Freud, 1958). However, it is not necessary for there to be active rebellion or complete repudiation of parents either; rather, such extreme rejection of parents by the adolescent is more likely to foreshadow developmental problems related to autonomy and psychosocial functioning (Steinberg, 1990). Thus, a moderate degree of conflict and disagreement between adolescents and their parents is to be expected. Ultimately, this leads to both internal and relational transformations. Moreover, there is a growing interest in the adjustments that parents need to make in their parenting of their older children. Parents, too, are managing their own relational and work transitions, physical health, psychological growth, and potential responsibilities for elderly parents (Kins, Soenens, & Beyers, 2011; Pardini, 2008; Wiley & Berman, 2012). These developmental changes for parents may, in turn, exert an influence on their adolescent's developing autonomy.

For families rooted in Western cultural traditions, navigating the tension between independence and relatedness is one of the many struggles of adolescence, where the transition from earlier dependency and parent-regulation leads to greater independence and increased self-regulation (Tanner, 2006). But during the period between early and middle adolescence (from about 11 to 17 years of age), mature self-regulation is not yet part of adolescents' behavioral repertoire, despite the fact that many of them are already looking for more autonomy from their parents. Adolescents want to assume greater responsibility for themselves and, at the same time, they want their parents to relinquish control over them (Collins & Steinberg, 2008). Managing this transition, while respecting and honoring the emotional needs of both children and their parents, is a considerable challenge throughout the entire adolescent period.

Interestingly, important advances from developmental neuroscience research help to inform our understanding of significant gaps between aspects of adolescent development, parental control, and brain maturation (Steinberg et al., 2006). In particular, for some adolescents, the inclination toward risk-taking and sensation-seeking behaviors, which requires more independence from and less control by parents, is associated with changes in the limbic system. The growth of the limbic system occurs before maturation of the pre-frontal cortex, the brain area responsible for executive functioning skills such as planning, regulating affect, and controlling impulses. The consequence of this asynchrony in development is that some adolescents may seek autonomy before they are capable of executing sound judgment in decision making, leaving them vulnerable to problems in managing situations that require more mature self-regulation, especially when with their peers (Collins & Steinberg, 2008; Nelson et al., 2002; Steinberg & Scott, 2003).

Moreover, while adolescents seem to function best when there is con-gruence between their own and their parents' desires and expectations for autonomy (Juang, Lerner, McKinney, & von Eye, 1999), it is not uncommon to find that adolescents believe they are ready to be granted autonomy much earlier than do their parents (Ruck, Peterson-Badali, & Day, 2002). Cultural and ethnic differences in expectations for and timing of behavioral autonomy have also been found (Collins & Steinberg, 2008). In America, Australia, and Hong Kong, Anglo adolescents and their parents endorse expectations for behavioral autonomy (e.g., going out on dates, freedom in spending money) earlier than Asian adolescents and their parents living in the same countries (Feldman & Quatman, 1988; Rosenthal & Feldman, 1990). It is not clear whether the comparative differences in these expectations lead to, or result from, Asian adolescents being less likely to seek autonomy from their parents as compared to their Anglo peers.

Additionally, gender and birth order differences in expectations for auto-nomy have been explored, though there are few consistent findings (Collins & Steinberg, 2008). Parental attitudes toward gender roles, and the particu-lar constellation of daughters and sons in the family, seem to be related to parental tendencies toward granting autonomy. For example, when parents hold more traditional views of gender roles, they are more likely to be con-trolling of their daughters than of their sons (Bumpus, Crouter, & McHale, 2001). Also, counter to popular belief, parents extend more autonomy to their firstborn than to their second-born children, particularly when the firstborn child is a girl and the second-born is a boy (Bumpus et al., 2001). And gender differences in autonomy granting by parents seem to be especially striking in African American households, where boys are given more freedom and girls less freedom, as compared to adolescents in other ethnic groups (Bulcroft, Carmody, & Bulcroft, 1996).

The developmental stages of adolescence may require qualitatively differ-ent forms of autonomy support from parents, depending on the social and emotional demands on the adolescent, particular family circumstances, and parental objectives. For example, if a parent wants his child to be a bit more assertive, he might allow a young adolescent to make a decision regarding an after-school activity that empowers her to pursue a burgeoning interest. If a parent wants her older adolescent to learn to be in social situations while also being able to stand up for herself and not succumb to peer pressure, she might encourage her child to make a decision about going to a party where there is adequate parental supervision and offer a concrete plan for what to do if she is feeling unsafe or wants to leave. Or the parent might make the decision not to allow an adolescent to attend a party that is not adequately supervised, even if she is trying to support more autonomy in the adolescent, so as to foster good judgment in assessing those situations that are appropriate to be in and those that might be risky or problematic.

Across all the periods of adolescence, parents are usually quite concerned about their adolescent's ability to respond appropriately when exposed to strong peer influences, to be responsible and self-reliant, and to be personally accountable for their decisions and behaviors. In their relationships with parents and peers, adolescents become increasingly competent at discerning when they need emotional support and how to ask for it. Managing peer pressure is, at the same time, one of the strongest challenges to emerging autonomy while in social relationships. Indeed, balancing connections to peers with maintaining autonomy in relation to peer pressures has consequences both for adaptive behavior and friendships (Allen, Chango, & Szwedo, 2014).

Establishing secure models of attachment relationships with parents helps adolescents to form peer relationships where they can maintain their autonomy and resist peer pressures. When these attachments are secure, adolescents are more likely to function autonomously while sustaining connections to their parents. They are also more likely to rely on both parents and best friends for emotional support (Allen et al., 2007). When attachments to parents are insecure, however, adolescents may be at risk for relational problems and have little practice at identifying and asserting their own independent ways of thinking and making decisions, especially when exposed to peer influences. Moreover, with little autonomy support from parents, adolescents have much more difficulty managing relational challenges, maintaining autonomy with friends, and resisting peer pressures (Allen, Chango, Szwedo, Schad, & Marston, 2012; Allen & Loeb, 2015; Oudekerk, Allen, Hessel, & Molloy, 2014).

Thus, when there are problems in the resolution of the balance between autonomy and relatedness, there may be a tendency to seek constant connection to others at the expense of achieving autonomy or, alternatively, there may be a strong preoccupation with independence and an avoidance of connection. Associations between these maladaptive developmental outcomes and particular attachment styles have been identified, with attachment avoidance linked to a tendency to keep others at a distance and avoid intimacy and attachment anxiety related to a fear of loss and anxiety around separation from others (Kins, Beyers, & Soenens, 2013). The security of adolescents' attachment relationships, therefore, continues to impact their developing ability to be autonomous while maintaining social relatedness.

Ultimately, the adolescent comes to see the self as more independent, mature, and in control while also developing a new view of the parent, and the parent alters his/her view of the child and of him- or herself, as the relationship eventually becomes more egalitarian (Collins, 1995; Steinberg, 1990). The process of beginning to discover that one has a separate identity, or a "second individuation" from parents (Blos, 1967), seems to be most salient at the beginning of adolescence, while the process of identity development, or discovering just what that identity is, becomes much more salient during middle and late adolescence (Collins & Steinberg, 2008; Nurmi, 2004). Indeed, many contemporary psychologists now see the development of a coherent identity continuing through emerging adulthood. Thus, researchers have shifted their lens away from the identity crisis (Erikson, 1968) and toward exploring self-understanding and the developing self-concept as important aspects of identity development throughout the period of adolescence (Steinberg & Morris, 2001).

The Development of Self-Concept

Extant studies have offered normative descriptions of developmental shifts in self-concept, both in US samples (e.g., Harter, 1999; Jacobs, Lanza, Osgood, Eccles, & Wigfield, 2002) and in samples of adolescents in Australia (e.g., Watt, 2004) and Canada (Shapka & Keating, 2005). The cognitive advances of the early adolescent period result in more abstract characterizations of the self (Damon & Hart, 1982; Selman, 1980). Now, self-concepts become more differentiated as adolescents begin to be aware of opposing self-attributes and may even behave differently in different contexts (Harter, 2006). Their self-concept reflects specific self-evaluations in particular domains.

Harter's Self-Perception Profile is an example of a widely used measure that evaluates self-concept in various domains of functioning, including academic, social, physical, and general self-worth (Harter, 1989). For some adolescents, the awareness of diverse role-dependent selves may lead to confusion over who is the "true self" (Harter & Monsour, 1992). They may describe themselves in ways that are inconsistent (e.g., "shy at school" but "outgoing with siblings"). They have the ability to compare different attributes about the self but they still have difficulty integrating varying abstract concepts into a coherent and organized description. Adolescents may even be troubled by the differences in their behavior depending upon the social context (e.g., school versus home or the classroom versus the playing field).

Theoretical accounts suggest that because adolescents integrate into their self-views other peoples' evaluations of them, variability across time and context in self-concept is to be expected (Cairns & Cairns, 1988). This variability may be more salient during early adolescence, when there is heightened concern about how they are perceived and a great deal of inconsistency in the external feedback young adolescents receive about their social and academic competence (Bukowski, Sippola, & Newcomb, 2000; Dweck, 2002).

It is not until late adolescence when the content and substance of the adolescent's self-concept changes in significant ways. At this point, adolescents' self-understanding, reflected in their self-concepts, continues to incorporate advances in their thinking about abstract ideas. They can now consider contradictions within themselves and make distinctions between what is true and real and what is false or more of an ideal self to which they aspire. Adolescents integrate into their self-concepts an increasing awareness of their multiple "selves" or variations in behaviors and feelings across different relationships, contexts, and roles.

Adolescents' self-concept eventually becomes more organized and continuous over time (Harter & Monsour, 1992), reflecting both parental ideals and their own sense of who they are (Hart & Fegley, 1995). By late adolescence and emerging adulthood, individuals establish a more coherent and integrated understanding of themselves and are less likely to be distressed by potentially incongruous attributes. They come to rely much less on direct social comparisons with their peers, or feedback from others, as they adhere to, and view themselves more in terms of, personal standards and moral beliefs (Harter, 1998a). Thus, self-concept continues to develop, in important ways, across the period of adolescence and into emerging adulthood.

Recent empirical studies have extended beyond advancing our understanding of normative trends in the development of self-concept to documenting fluctuations within specific domains of self-concept. Investigators have also begun to explore the factors that may make some adolescents more vulnerable to stable or unstable self-concepts and the consequences of these variations for the development of later academic and social competence (Molloy, Ram, & Gest, 2011). For example, intra-individual factors, such as the timing of puberty and its effects on self-concept, have been examined (e.g., Wiesner & Ittel, 2002). Environmental influences, such as school climate, academic pressures, and the quality of relationships with parents and peers, may also influence domains of self-concept. Peer victimization has been associated with negative self-concept in adolescents, with victimization experiences developmentally preceding negative self-perceptions and offering a direct focus for intervention efforts (Bellmore & Cillessen, 2006).

Additionally, parents have been viewed as playing an important role in contributing to adolescents' self-evaluations (Litovsky & Dusek, 1985; Ohannessian, Lerner, Lerner, & Von Eye, 1998). During the adolescent period, changes in family dynamics, with concomitant increases in parenting stress, may result from less frequent parent–adolescent interactions, shifting power dynamics, lower perceived acceptance from parents, and the potential for increased conflict (Collins & Russell, 1991). The link between adolescent self-concept and parenting stress has been studied by considering the stresses arising from difficulties in the adolescent's behavior, in the parent's ability to fulfill parenting responsibilities, or in dysfunctional parent–child interactions. Direct and indirect relations among parenting stress, adolescents' perceptions of their parents, and their developing self-concept have been explored. Indirect links have been observed, such that parenting stress is associated with adolescents' perceptions of specific parenting behaviors in mothers and fathers, which are, in turn, related to particular domains of adolescent self-concept (Putnick et al., 2005). Future work exploring these more complex causal models will contribute to our growing understanding of the multiple factors that influence adolescents' self-concept, as well as to improving and targeting more effective interventions for adolescents at risk for problems resulting from negative self-concepts.

Self-Descriptions of Adolescents

When adolescents are asked to describe themselves, there are distinct differences from their descriptions in earlier developmental periods, reflecting the changes in self-concept that begin in the early adolescent period (Damon & Hart, 1988; DeHart, Sroufe, & Cooper, 2004; Harter, 1998, 1999). Self-descriptions become more differentiated during adolescence and shift from a focus on concrete, external features (e.g., demographic, physical, and behavioral attributes that may be observed) to characteristics that are more abstract, reflecting emotions, attitudes, and the interior world. Adolescents tend to describe themselves along more dimensions, relative to when they were younger, and to see themselves in more complex ways. They understand, for example, that the way they are will vary from one situation to the next. Thus, their self-descriptions gradually become more differentiated across settings, relationships, and areas of competence. Now, an adolescent might say he is well behaved at school but more likely to act up at home, or that she is moody with her parents but happy with her friends, or plays the piano beautifully but does not do so well at school. This capacity to offer varying self-descriptions results in part from a developing ability to be more introspective and to think about the self in more complex ways. The ability to engage in self-reflection means that adolescents are more capable of making their own choices about what they think and how they will behave as they search for a deeper understanding of themselves (Montemayor, Adams, & Gullotta, 1990).

When younger children are asked to describe themselves, they are likely to look for similarities between themselves and their peers and to describe themselves in terms of what they share in common. By early adolescence, however, their self-concepts become more individuated. Now, adolescents incorporate into their descriptions those aspects that make them unique and different from others. An adolescent may focus now on what s/he does that is especially important or noteworthy (e.g., "I am a loyal and caring friend," or "I am very honest and would never do anything to hurt other people"). Their descriptions reflect a deeper understanding of themselves, highlighting the value of their own special qualities. Adolescents now see their unique place in their social networks and recognize the role they play in relation to their friends ("I like to plan the things that my friends and I then do" or "My friends rely on me to take the lead on our school projects"). Personal beliefs and maintaining standards for appropriate behavior are more important to adolescents and their self-concept reflects less concern with social comparison (Steinberg & Morris, 2001). Still, adolescents are aware of their interactions with others, often defining themselves in terms of their social characteristics within their network of relationships (Damon & Hart, 1988). Thus, self-descriptions may include, for example, an awareness of their friendliness toward others, their popularity at school, or their ability to lead their team.

By late adolescence, self-descriptions become increasingly coherent as the older adolescent attempts to integrate disparate characteristics of the self over time. Adolescents are now more introspective and can therefore make their own choices about behaviors and values. Cognitive changes allow them to consider a range of alternatives, examining the present sense of self, relating it to past behaviors, and projecting the self into the future. Now, the view of the self becomes more unified as the adolescent coordinates multiple perspectives and ideas in an attempt to reconcile discrepancies between behavior in different situations and across time. Consequently, rather than just describing differences in behavior across relationships or situations, the older adolescent can now account for some of the reasons for these differences. For example, an 18-year-old might say, "I work really hard at school because getting good grades is important to me and will help me get in to a good college. But I don't work really hard at my job because my boss is disrespectful and the work is not very difficult to perform."

Many of the changes in adolescents' self-descriptions reflect an overall decline in the fragility of the sense of self as tentative beliefs about the self are increasingly confirmed ("I *am* smart in math!") and self-consciousness decreases. In early adolescence, there is a great deal of vulnerability related to adolescents' uncertainty about how they feel about themselves and about how others view them as well. With time, increased experiences and opportunities to appraise their competence, along with support from family members, friends, and trusted adults, lead to a consolidation in adolescents' beliefs about themselves. As a result, adolescents, in turn, become less self-conscious (Harter, 1998). A developing understanding of the self, and more accurate appraisals of the self in terms of both strengths and weaknesses, successes and failures, ultimately lead to a more stable and coherent sense of self. There is a general decline in vulnerability about the self by late adolescence (DeHart et al., 2004).

There are many instances, however, where adolescents' self-concepts are not coherent or stable, there is still a great deal of vulnerability in their self-concepts, and threats to the sense of self prevail. For example, when problems with self-definition persist in adolescence, it is more likely that externalizing problems such as aggression and delinquency will develop, especially in adolescent males. By contrast, an excessive preoccupation with views of the self in relation to others has been linked to the development of internalizing problems, such as depression, in adolescent females (Leadbeater, Kuperminc, Blatt, & Hertzog, 1999). While the direction of effects need to be disentangled, we see that individual vulnerability is associated with social functioning. Thus, self-definition and interpersonal relatedness are closely linked in adolescent self-concepts, a view that is consistent with current perspectives on adaptive psychological functioning and the development of psychopathology (Luyten & Blatt, 2013).

Internal Representations of the Self

We know from the work of attachment researchers that the construct of internal models, or mental representations of attachment relationships, has been used to account for the ways in which attachment experiences influence subsequent social and emotional development. Central to the thinking of attachment researchers is the idea that concurrent models of the self are developing as well. Children transform their early interactions with significant caregivers into mental representations of the self that then guide, regulate, and direct future behavior. These cognitive-affective schemes, relevant to theoretical work in psychoanalysis, cognitive science, and developmental psychology, reflect the interpersonal framework within which adolescents come to understand how they think and feel about themselves and others in their social world (Besser & Blatt, 2007). Thus, this relational model is critical to understanding the importance of developing representations of the self during adolescence. However, there has only been a limited focus in the empirical literature on internal mental representations of the self.

Bowlby (1973) theorized that attachment experiences influence an individual's developing sense of self. Experiences in attachment relationships are used as a source of information about the self. Consequently, it is through learning about the self within the relationship, and observing and experiencing interactions with the attachment figure, that components of the attachment figure and the relationship are incorporated into the self (Sroufe & Fleeson, 1986). When adolescents have had experiences in earlier secure relationships where they felt valued and loved they, in turn, will come to feel special and valuable. But experiences of rejection, neglect, or abuse, inconsistency in care, or lack of emotional availability will leave the adolescent, to varying degrees, with the sense that the self is bad, not valued, worthless, or easy to dismiss. Moreover, when adolescents maintain representations of sensitive and caring relationships with their caregivers, they are able to preserve a certain degree of integration and to regulate their emotions and behaviors even when interpersonal support is not immediately available (Behrends & Blatt, 1985; Mikulincer & Shaver, 2008). Additionally, these positive internal models of early relationships contribute to more secure models of the self and predict to more adaptive functioning (Fonagy & Target, 1997). By contrast, adolescents who are insecure in their early attachment relationships are less able to regulate affect, adopt less constructive coping strategies, and are less likely to rely on others in times of need (Mikulincer & Shaver, 2008).

When models of attachment relationships are secure, adolescents are able to engage in the exploration of their own identity, to establish their autonomy, and to develop representations of the self without concern about sacrificing relatedness (Allen et al., 1994). Alternatively, when adolescents are insecure in their attachment relationships and either avoidant or dismissive of their attachment needs, they are unable to use others to modulate arousal, cope constructively, or regulate behavior. In turn, these adolescents may experience increased relational conflict as they attempt to explore their autonomy and manifest more fragile, insecure internal models of the self.

Interestingly, while there is theoretical justification for exploring internal models of the self, the operationalization of these internal models is more complicated. There is some research that has explored associations between attachment history and the self in adults (e.g., Bartholomew & Horowitz, 1991; Griffin & Bartholomew, 1994). However, much of this work focuses on self-esteem rather than on the more complex notion of the self from a cognitive perspective; this perspective incorporates multiple aspects of the self and considers the self as perceived not only by the individual but also by others. In an in-depth exploration of associations between attachment style and self-representations in high school students, differences were observed across attachment styles. These differences were found not only in the affective tone of their self-evaluations but also in the capacity to integrate both positive and negative self-attributes as well as in the coherence and organization of aspects of the self (Mikulincer, 1995). In another study of 18- to 25-year-old college students, associations between attachment to family and friends, models of self and others, and perceptions of social support were explored. The combination of secure attachments to others and a positive model of the self was linked to perceptions of higher social support from family and friends as well as to stronger attachments to friends. By contrast, either a negative view of the self or insecure attachments to others was associated with weaker attachments to friends and perceptions of less social support from family and friends (Blain, Thompson, & Whiffen, 1993).

The results of these studies confirm the notion that internal models of the self generally parallel internal models of attachment experiences in adolescents and are important to examine in relation to adolescent development and adjustment. However, the direction of effects is unclear and the cross-sectional design of extant research does not allow for an exploration of influences over time. Moreover, attachment history has been assessed in these studies using a measure of attachment style, rather than of internal models (e.g., by using the Adult Attachment Interview (George et al., 1984, 1985, 1996)), and patterns of interaction with attachment figures are not observed. These self-report measures tap affective/cognitive and behavioral dimensions of attachment styles rather than behaviorally-based representations of the self and others. Still, in spite of these concerns, this work is critical in providing initial support for Bowlby's (1973) idea that attachment experiences are incorporated into mental representations of the self and influence the way the individual perceives, organizes, and responds to new experiences.

In yet another interesting line of research, security of attachment in adolescence has been examined together with the capacity to negotiate autonomy needs while maintaining a sense of relatedness (Allen et al., 2003). When there is a secure state of mind regarding attachment to mothers, fathers, and peers in adolescence, the process of negotiating autonomy, while maintaining a sense of relatedness (i.e., by valuing attachment), is enhanced. Additionally, measures of internalizing (e.g., depressive symptoms) and externalizing (e.g., aggressive, hyperactive, hostile, or delinquent) behaviors, reflecting affective and cognitive states and emotion regulation capacities, have been found to be linked to attachment security (Allen et al., 2007). Together, these findings suggest that working models of attachment relationships are associated with models of the self and that attachment security is related to patterns of psychological adaptation and maladaptation.

Thus, it appears that internal mental representations of the self are connected to models of others and developed in a relational context. Studying the capacity for reflective functioning is another way of extending our understanding of internal representations of self. Reflective functioning is the ability to reflect on the self and on one's own thoughts and feelings, as well as those of others, and to attribute mental states, such as needs, desires, emotions, and beliefs, to oneself and others (Fonagy, Steele, Steele, Moran, et al., 1991). This concept, developed within the framework of attachment theory (Fonagy & Target, 1997), involves both an affective process (i.e., experiencing, holding, and regulating emotions) and a cognitive process (i.e., thinking about and understanding one's own and another's perspective). Moreover, it forms the basis for self-representations as well as for engaging oneself fully in significant relationships (Fonagy et al., 2002; Slade, 2005). Parental reflective functioning has been found to be associated with adolescent reflective functioning and social competence; it also moderates the association between particular parenting behaviors and psychological adjustment in adolescence (see, for example, Benbassat & Priel, 2012). Further examination of reflective functioning in adolescence will deepen our understanding of its importance for constructing meaning from attachment relationships, for thinking about the self in relation to others, and for establishing an internalized view of the self.

There may also be other ways of approaching the study of internal representations of the self. There is a significant cognitive component to these internal models that has traditionally been studied by developmental, cognitive, and personality psychologists and is reflected in measures of self-concept and self-understanding. And there is also an affective component that has been explored by developmental, personality, and clinical psychologists and is reflected in measures of self-esteem. We have already explored the cognitive aspects. It is the affective part of the self to which we will now turn. It is important to keep in mind that although we are distinguishing here between the affective and cognitive components of the self, in fact they are probably best viewed in terms of their interconnections and reflected in integrated working models of the self and of the self in relationships. Future empirical work directed toward more carefully exploring internal models of the self will enhance our understanding of these cognitive-affective schemes that organize representations of the self.

Self-Esteem

The evaluative aspect of the self, or self-esteem, has been a topic of great interest for developmental psychologists. Self-esteem refers to the more global evaluation of the self and is also called self-image or self-worth. Many traditional theories focused on the development of self-esteem proposed that social experiences lead to the formation of perceptions of self-worth. Early symbolic interactionists, for example, maintained that children observe others' reactions to their behavior and then interpret and internalize these reactions (Cooley, 1902; Mead, 1934). Self-perception theorists asserted that when adults interpret and label children's behavior, children then acquire knowledge about themselves (Bem, 1972). Young adolescents' self-esteem has been found to be influenced by support from parents and other significant adults (Harris et al., 2015; Harter, 1999, 2008; Markus & Cross, 1990; Rosenberg, 1986).

Research has explored age-related changes in self-esteem, as well as the factors that influence self-esteem and the consequences of self-esteem for concurrent and future development. General trends have been identified indicating that self-esteem is typically high in childhood, becomes lower over the course of the adolescent period, then tends to rise over early and middle adulthood but drops again in old age (Marsh, 1989). However, individuals' self-esteem also remains quite consistent over time, such that *relative* self-esteem in childhood is likely to be maintained in adolescence and adulthood as well (Robins, Trzesniewski, Tracy, Gosling, & Potter, 2002). The measure of self-esteem used and the domains of competence evaluated undoubtedly impact the observed developmental trends. The number of dimensions of self-esteem that can be measured also increases with development. For example, the domains of scholastic competence, peer acceptance, behavioral conduct, physical appearance, and athletic competence, as well as global self-worth, are typically assessed in middle childhood, while close friendships, romantic relationships, and job competence are added in adolescence (Harter, 1999). Thus, adolescents' self-esteem often depends on their perceptions of competence in valued domains.

While self-esteem has been conceptualized as a multidimensional construct, global self-esteem is considered and retained in most current self-esteem measures (Bracken, 1996; Harter, 1985, 1989; March, 1986; Rosenberg, 1979). Some theorists and researchers view global self-esteem as the overarching construct within which particular domains or dimensions of esteem are hierarchically nested (L'Ecuyer, 1992; March, 1987). Global self-esteem is indexed by a single score reflecting the individual's general satisfaction with him- or herself as a person. There are also domain-specific measures of self-esteem that may or may not be related to the global self-esteem measure (Harter, 2012). Thus, adolescents evaluate themselves on the Self-Perception Profile for Adolescents (Harter, 1989) along a global dimension of self-esteem as well as along several more specific dimensions (e.g., academics, appearance, social relations, athletics, and moral conduct). Indeed, varying associations among the specific dimensions of self-concept and global self-esteem have been found, as have differences in self-concept across time and contexts (Steinberg & Morris, 2001).

There are many interesting results that have emerged from this burgeoning body of research. Global self-esteem has been found to increase slightly during the early adolescent period and then remains fairly stable. Younger adolescents report more daily fluctuations in self-esteem than older adolescents (Alsaker & Olweus, 1992; Harter, 1998). Indeed, it is believed that there is a baseline sense of self around which variations may occur across time and situation, especially during adolescence (Blos, 1962; Demo & Savin-Williams, 1992; Harter, Stocker, & Robinson, 1996). Moreover, views of the self have been found to vary across roles. So, for example, adolescents may view themselves differently when they are with their classmates, close friends, parents, teachers, and romantic partners (Hart, 1988; Harter, Bresnick, Bouchey, & Whitesell, 1998). Their self-descriptions also vary depending upon interpersonal contexts (Gergen, 1991; Harter, 1998; Ogilvie & Clark, 1992). Consequently, the approval and support an adolescent perceives that they receive in a relationship is related to their self-esteem in the context of that relationship (Harter, Waters, & Whitesell, 1998).

It appears that judgments of overall self-worth may vary as a function of the specific relationships and interpersonal situations considered. Adolescents' views of themselves may be influenced by others' views of them and they may, in turn, like themselves more in some relationships (e.g., parents) than in others (e.g., peers). The "looking-glass self" is the term used to account for the social mirrors that others hold up, offering reflections that the individual then evaluates and which become incorporated into the individual's self-worth (Cooley, 1902). These reflected appraisals lead to individuals seeing themselves as others perceive and evaluate them (Mead, 1934). Substantial research has supported the conclusion that there is a stronger association between reflected appraisals and self-appraisals than between actual appraisals by others and self-appraisals (Berndt & Burgy, 1996).

Adolescents seem to rely on others' views of them to determine their global self-esteem (i.e., reflected appraisals). They evaluate themselves based on their perceptions of support from their relationship partners, especially their parents, and of their competence in valued domains (Ojanen & Perry, 2007). This may be part of the reason why self-esteem is so unstable during the adolescent period (Harter, 2006; Harter & Whitesell, 2003). Adolescents have also been found to present a "false self" and to act in ways that are not honest or authentic, especially when they are with classmates and in romantic relationships. The reasons for engaging in false-self behavior have been found to have consequences for adolescents' mental health. For example, adolescents who engage in false-self behavior in order to please others do not suffer from depression, whereas those who present with false-self behavior because they devalue their real self do suffer from depression (Harter, Marold, Whitesell, & Cobbs, 1996). While some false-self behavior may be expected in adolescence, the antecedents to and motivations for high levels of false-self behavior need to be better understood.

Factors Influencing Self-Esteem

There are many other factors that may influence self-esteem. Behavioral geneticists have argued, for example, that genetics and nonshared environments exert a greater impact on overall self-esteem and specific areas of competence (e.g., academic or athletic) than familial or shared environments (McGuire et al., 1999; Neiss, Sedikides, & Stevenson, 2002). Therefore, the influence of genes on physical attractiveness, which is strongly related to self-esteem, may account for the fact that identical (or monozygotic) twins' self-concepts are correlated more strongly than those of fraternal (or dizygotic) twins or nontwin siblings (Harter, 2006; McGuire et al., 1999). Developmental and social changes (e.g., school transitions) may challenge adolescent self-esteem (Wigfield & Eccles, 1994), whereas protective factors such as social support and academic achievement have been found to decrease the impact of school transitions (Wigfield, Eccles, MacIver, Reuman, & Midgley, 1991). More generally, protective factors such as positive peer and family relationships and a more positive emotional status lead some adolescents to show higher and more stable levels of self-esteem in high school (Deihl, Vicary, & Deike, 1997).

Meta-analyses indicate that self-esteem may vary depending upon race, with higher self-esteem among Black as compared to White adolescents (Gray-Little & Hafdahl, 2000). Additionally, some researchers report no gender differences in self-esteem (Mullis, Mullis, & Normandin, 1992; Wigfield & Eccles, 1994), while others find that female adolescents have lower self-esteem than their male counterparts, especially during the transition to high school (Alsaker & Olweus, 1992; Kling, Hyde, Showers, & Buswell, 1999; Lord, Eccles, & McCarthy, 1994; Wigfield & Eccles, 1994). However, other studies indicate that over the course of adolescence and into early adulthood, many girls show a steady increase in self-esteem (Baldwin & Hoffmann, 2002; Kling et al., 1999). This is especially true for adolescent girls who in the eighth grade score high on measures of relationship authenticity (i.e., in their capacity to represent themselves, and how they think and feel, accurately in relationships). These girls were found to show greater increases in self-esteem between eighth and twelfth grade as compared to those who scored low in authenticity (Impett et al., 2008). Gender differences that are consistent with gender stereotypes have also been found in specific areas of functioning. Male adolescents have higher self-esteem in mathematics, sports, and physical appearance whereas female adolescents have higher self-esteem in interpersonal relationships and reading abilities (Harter, 1999). Several explanations have been offered to account for these gender differences in self-evaluations, including socialization by parents and other adults, underlying motivational differences, and gender stereotyping (Pomerantz, Saxon, & Kenney, 2001).

Parenting behaviors and attachment styles have also been found to be associated with self-esteem. Consistent with attachment theory, secure attachment relationships should lead to the individual developing a view of others as available, consistent, and reliable and of the self as worthy of acceptance and love. Associations have been found between these positive internal models of the self and high self-esteem in children (Cassidy, 1988; Mikulincer, 1995; Verschueren, Marcoen, & Schoefs, 1996). By contrast, children who are insecurely attached are expected to develop internal models of the self as incompetent, unlovable, and devalued and of attachment figures as unavailable and rejecting (Bretherton & Munholland, 2008). These children, in turn, are expected to develop either more negative or idealized views of the self, whereas securely attached children develop more realistic and positive views of the self. The impact of these different attachment histories, and their consequences for the adolescent's developing working models of the self and of others, is important to consider in future research.

Parenting styles and parental behaviors also impact self-esteem, especially in adolescence but during earlier periods of development as well. For example, in middle childhood, an authoritative parenting style, where parents set clear limits for acceptable behaviors while also being warm and affectionate, is associated with high self-esteem (Lamborn, Mounts, Steinberg, & Dornbusch, 1991). And numerous studies have demonstrated that there is a positive association between adolescent self-esteem and supportive family characteristics (Allen et al., 1994; Barber, Chadwick, & Oerter, 1992; Harris et al., 2015). By contrast, children whose parents are abusive hold views of themselves that are universally negative and undifferentiated, a pattern that we typically see in younger children especially when there is abuse or neglect (Harter, 1999; Toth, Cicchetti, Macfie, & Emde, 1997). Moreover, disruptions in parenting that are associated with problems, such as maternal depression, can also adversely influence adolescents' self-esteem (Jaenicke et al., 1987; Killen & Forehand, 1998). In adolescence, lower self-esteem has been related to views of the mother as unaffectionate and psychologically controlling and to views of the self as untrusting, debilitated (high in fearfulness and self-blame), and defiant (high in disobedience, aggression, and opposition) (Ojanen & Perry, 2007). Alternatively, when adolescents perceive their parents as approving and supportive of them, they are more likely to report high self-esteem within the context of the parent–adolescent relationship (Ojanen & Perry, 2007).

Children and adolescents often report that they believe their parents know them better than they know themselves (Rosenberg, 1979). Thus, they are particularly sensitive to parents' emotional responses to them, their attitudes, and their behavior; these parental responses may, in turn, have a profound effect on child and adolescent self-esteem. However, it is important to consider that adolescents may also use their own self-appraisals, project these onto their parents, and then interpret parental behavior as consistent with these views (Felson, 1989). For example, they may see their parents as critical and nonsupportive if their esteem is low. Thus, there may be reciprocal relations between parental support and adolescents' self-esteem (Felson & Zielinski, 1989). Importantly, the relational context in which the assessment of self-esteem is made is critical to consider, as perceived approval from others is incorporated into judgments of self-worth through a gradual internalization process (Harter, Waters, & Whitesell, 1998). Self-esteem may be best viewed within a transactional model of parent–adolescent relations (Killeen & Forehand, 1998; Sameroff & Chandler, 1975). In accordance with this model, there are indirect effects of adolescent and parental characteristics on self-esteem. These effects are mediated by the actual behavior of both parents and adolescents, as well as by the affective and cognitive interpretations of one another's behaviors.

What Are the Consequences of Self-Esteem?

Questions about how to best define self-esteem, and what measurement strategies are most appropriate to evaluate self-esteem, are linked to important concerns about the consequences of self-esteem for concurrent and future adaptation. Is self-esteem a useful construct and, if so, is self-esteem the cause of later outcomes or might it be the consequence of critical experiences? Some contend that self-esteem does impact a person's choices and developmental outcomes, thereby validating the usefulness of the construct (e.g., Swann et al., 2007). This appears to be especially true when the measure of self-esteem is linked to the outcome of interest (e.g., grades are better predicted by academic self-concept than by overall self-esteem). Other researchers argue instead that high self-esteem is a consequence, rather than a cause, of positive life experiences (e.g., Baumeister et al., 2003). Regardless of the direction of causality, research indicates that high self-esteem is related to adjustment, peer support, parental approval, and school success (DuBois, Bull, Sherman, & Roberts, 1998; Luster & McAdoo, 1995; Steinberg & Morris, 2001). Additionally, negative outcomes have been associated with low self-esteem in childhood and adolescence. Studies have found, for example, that low self-esteem is associated with school dropout, substance abuse, depression, risky sexual behavior, teen pregnancy, and criminal behavior (Barry, Grafeman, Adler, & Pickard, 2007; Crockenberg & Soby, 1989; Ethier et al., 2006; Lan & Lanthier, 2003; Reinherz et al., 1993; Rumberger, 1995; Trzesniewski et al., 2006).

In young children, it is difficult to evaluate global self-esteem because of lack of verbal abilities and limitations in the capacity to understand or assess aspects of the self. Researchers have therefore relied more heavily on the assessment of behavioral correlates of self-esteem, such as taking the initiative in goal-directed behavior, displaying assurance in exploration, persistence, and flexibility. Children with high self-esteem have been found, as reported by teachers or other adults, to be more independent and confident and to react in more adaptive ways to stress (Harter, 2012). With age, self-evaluations become more accurate as a result of both cognitive development and changes in the criteria used to evaluate competence in particular domains. For example, those children with higher levels of cognitive development have more accurate self-perceptions as compared to their peers with lower levels of cognitive development (Bouffard, Markovits, Vezeau, Boisvert, & Dumas, 1998). Older children's perceptions of their academic ability are more closely tied to their school grades (Chapman & Tunmer, 1995; Stipek & Mac Iver, 1989). Moreover, it is common to find that adolescents and adults who do not expect to be successful in a particular domain devalue the importance of that domain so that their success or failure does not impact their overall self-esteem (Major, Spencer, Schmader, Wolfe, & Crocker, 1998).

There are many concerns among researchers and clinicians that the emphasis among parents and teachers to promote self-esteem in young children may lead to inflated self-esteem, entitlement, and an inconsistency between actual competence and positive self views (Twenge, 2006), though the empirical findings are controversial (Trzesniewski, Donnellan, & Robins, 2008). Still, several different interventions have been proposed and implemented with the goal of increasing self-esteem. Ultimately, these programs are likely to be most effective when they target increases in behavior and performance in a particular domain and then assess self-esteem in that same domain and when they are theoretically based and specifically focused (Haney & Durlak, 1998).

The important role that self-esteem plays in social development has been established by studies demonstrating that self-esteem may predict children's and adolescents' emotional functioning (Lei, Swartz, Dodge, & McBride-Chang, 2003), social skills and adjustment (Barber, Olsen, & Shagle, 1994; Pettit, Laird, Dodge, Bates, & Criss, 2001), and the likelihood of peer victimization (Egan & Perry, 1998). Thus, it continues to be important to better understand the early roots of self-esteem. Cognitive views of social development support the idea that children and adolescents internalize models of relationships and social interactions that then influence their sense of self (Andersen & Chen, 2002; Crittenden, 1990). And developmental models continue to explore the balance between social support and self-esteem over time and their implications for later emotional and behavioral adjustment across adolescence (DuBois et al., 2002).

Identity Development

Identity development, or the process of coming to know who one is in the context of past history and future possibilities, is a complex task that takes center stage in adolescence (Erikson, 1980; Finkenauer, Engels, Meeus, &

Oosterwegel, 2002). There are components of one's identity that are assigned, such as gender and physical attributes, and others that are selected, involving decisions around interpersonal relationships, sexuality, work and career directions, religious, political, and moral beliefs (Bennion & Adams, 1986; Grotevant, 1992). Self-conceptions and evaluations provide the framework for the identity development process; adolescents use their growing understanding of who they are, of their competencies and skills in a variety of domains, and of their attitudes and beliefs to form a personal identity. While some aspects of identity, such as race and ethnicity, are predetermined and provide important elements of personal identity (Ruble et al., 2004), there are many other aspects of identity about which the individual may have some choice. Indeed, membership in social groups may play an important role in establishing personal identity (Brewer & Gardner, 1996), although there are individual and contextual factors that determine the relative importance of social identity to the individual (Turner & Brown, 2007). The factors that influence identity formation, and the correlates and consequences of identity for other aspects of psychological adjustment, have been a focus of much research, especially in recent years.

Identity Formation and Adjustment in Adolescence

Erikson proposed a stage model of development that spans eight periods, from infancy to old age (Erikson, 1950/1963, 1980). According to Erikson, the formation and expression of an identity and the capacity for intimacy are the major developmental tasks for the periods of adolescence and early adulthood. Psychosocial development occurs in parallel with biological maturation (using the concept of *epigenesis* to refer to "processes inherent to the organism" (Erikson, 1950/1963, p. 34)) and cognitive development, influenced by historical and cultural factors. Like all stage theorists (cf. Freud's theory of psychosexual development), Erikson believed that the developmental timing and order of a series of crises is predetermined but that the way these crises are resolved is not. The psychosocial tasks reflect opposite ends of a continuum characterizing an essential aspect of development that he considered most dominant during a particular stage. So, for example, the crisis of the infancy period is one of trust versus mistrust. It is interesting to note that this crisis parallels Bowlby's emphasis on the evolutionary adaptiveness of establishing and maintaining an attachment relationship (Bowlby, 1969/1982).

While Erikson did not focus on the exact processes by which the crisis of each stage was resolved, he did offer the idea that positive and negative experiences within a stage were uniquely organized, leading to a resolution that then allowed for subsequent development. Resolutions that were more positive (e.g., despite both positive and negative experiences in early relationships, resolving the first crisis in infancy toward trust) then led to healthier, more positive resolutions of subsequent crises. Thus, Erikson identified the crises of trust versus mistrust in infancy; autonomy versus shame and doubt in toddler-hood; initiative versus guilt in early childhood; industry versus inferiority in middle and late childhood; identity versus role confusion in adolescence; intimacy versus isolation in young adulthood; generativity versus self-absorption and stagnation in adulthood; and integrity versus despair in old age (Erikson, 1950/1963). Erikson did not believe that early problematic resolutions of these crises (e.g., mistrust, shame and doubt, guilt, etc.) were immutable. Rather, he argued that resolutions of later crises could alter earlier resolutions, thereby offering a dynamic and positive view of development and of the capacity for change.

During adolescence, the critical task that needs to be resolved is the development of identity. Erikson postulated that the first four stages provided the foundation for identity development. In the context of the child's early social relationships, the development of trust or mistrust depends on the primary caregiver's sensitivity and responsiveness to the baby's needs. Subsequent developmental tasks reflect the child's expanding social network, as siblings, peers, and teachers become part of the child's world. Children gain skills in interacting with others, cooperating, collaborating, and navigating an ever-increasing circle of significant others. In adolescence, peers and ultimately romantic partners become more salient as the former dominance of the family diminishes (Larson et al., 1996). It is in the context of day-to-day experiences in these social exchanges that children receive feedback and learn about their role in relationships, their capacity to take initiative, and their ability to impact others. Erikson (1980) called the self-descriptions that derive from what others say about the individual *identifications*. When a child hears, for example, "Ben, you did such a nice job helping me clean up this afternoon," this supports his developing notion that he takes initiative and can be very helpful. When another child hears, "Claire, you tried to help me but you just made things so much worse," this undermines her initiative and ridicules her efforts, contributing to an emerging view of herself as unhelpful and unable to get things done.

By adolescence, these identifications, and increasingly more sophisticated self-descriptions made possible by advancing cognitive abilities, are then consolidated into the individual's psychosocial identity. The stage of identity versus role confusion requires the physical, cognitive, and social maturity characteristic of adolescence. Erikson believed that it was at this point when individuals could make decisions and answer questions regarding personal, ethical, and moral values, including career choices, what it means to be male or female, and relationship preferences. Personal identity provides the individual with coherent and meaningful ways of defining the self and of viewing others over time. The resolution of prior stage-salient tasks prepares the individual for the task of defining identity; this understanding of identity is then brought to subsequent developmental tasks (intimacy versus isolation, generativity versus self-absorption and stagnation, and integrity versus despair) that need to be negotiated.

In particular, the consolidation of one's identity is necessary for healthy intimacy. Erikson believed that openness and vulnerability are part of intimate relationships and can only occur when there is a well-developed sense of identity (Erikson, 1950/1963). Establishing an identity, or determining who one really is, allows the individual to choose with whom to share this understanding while also remaining open to the other's understanding of his or her identity. Identity and intimacy are actually quite interconnected, as recent theory and research suggest (Bosma & Gerlsma, 2003; Dyk & Adams, 1987, 1990; Pittman, Keiley, Kerpelman, & Vaughn, 2011; Zimmer-Gembeck & Petherick, 2006). Adolescents and young adults who have a clearer sense of their identity are more willing to share intimacy (Montgomery, 2005). Indeed, Erikson (1950/1963) acknowledged the implications of establishing identity for subsequent intimacy when he proposed that "adolescent love is an attempt to arrive at a definition of one's identity by projecting one's diffused ego image on another and by seeing it thus reflected and gradually clarified" (p. 262). The capacity for establishing intimate relationships is therefore influenced by the progress that has been made in identity formation, and the two processes continue to evolve and remain interconnected through adolescence and into young adulthood (Adams & Archer, 1994; Markstrom & Kalmanir, 2001). Identity formation, though often conceptualized as an individual process of exploration and commitment, is deeply grounded in an interpersonal context (Erikson, 1950/1963; Grotevant, 1987; Kerpelman, Pittman, & Lamke, 1997; Lichtwarck-Aschoff, van Geert, Bosma, & Kunnen, 2008). Consequently, significant others, including intimate partners and attachment figures, may provide feedback that leads to a reconsideration of particular identity content or that supports and validates identity commitments when identity threats occur (Pittman et al., 2011).

Some researchers have attempted to translate Erikson's ideas into a paradigm of identity outcomes. Most notably, Marcia (1966, 1980) focused on the processes of exploration and commitment, rather than on the content of one's emerging identity, as they lead to identity consolidation. Exploration of identity includes considering different options and actively questioning possible alternatives, whereas commitment implies making firm choices about values and goals and behaving in a manner that is consistent with these decisions (Crocetti, Rubini, & Meeus, 2008). Marcia (1966) believed that though it is difficult to directly observe the processes of identity formation, the processes of exploration and commitment may be recognized in the outcome and may be directly assessed. He proposed different combinations of high and low exploration and commitment to offer a way of characterizing an individual's current identity outcome: (1) if exploration and commitment have occurred, then an adolescent's identity is "achieved"; (2) if commitment has occurred without exploration, then the adolescent's identity is "foreclosed"; (3) if exploration has occurred without commitment, the adolescent is in "moratorium"; and (4) if neither exploration nor commitment have occurred, then identity is "diffused" (Marcia, 1966).

The course of identity development may vary for different individuals. Some may progress from a less mature status (i.e., identity foreclosure or diffusion) to a more mature status (i.e., identity moratorium or achievement). Others may stay stuck in the same status and never progress. While Marcia's theory is not a developmental theory (cf. Bosma & Kunnen, 2001), but rather a typology of outcomes of the normative identity crisis, he does suggest that the most typical developmental course begins with identity foreclosure, then moves to moratorium, and finally transitions to achievement (Marcia, 2002). Cross-sectional studies of males (Meilman, 1979) and females (Archer, 1982) have found an increasing number of individuals classified as "identity achieved" across the period of adolescence into young adulthood. However, not all individuals follow this course, some continue to develop their identity into adulthood, and significant life changes may challenge identity status and lead to transitions from identity achievement back to less mature identity status (Arnett, 2000; Sneed, Whitourne, & Culang, 2006; Stephen, Fraser, & Marcia, 1992).

Narrative approaches have also been used to study the complexity of identity development (McAdams, 1993, 2006). Some researchers have relied on a combination of the identity status approach (Marcia, 1966) and the narrative life story model (Dumas, Lawford, Tieu, & Pratt, 2009), thereby offering a deeper conceptualization of the processes and characteristics of identity development. The capacity to provide narrative accounts of life events (including significant turning points as well as high and low points in one's personal history), and to interpret and incorporate personal life stories in a coherent manner, reflects individuals' attempts to make meaning of their lives and of the role they play in them (McAdams, 1993). Identifying and describing personal changes over time, and differentiating between representations of the self in the past and the present, are important components of self-processing and contribute to the formation and consolidation of a stable identity during late adolescence and early adulthood (McAdams, 2001). Coherence in the narratives of these life stories reflects not only an understanding of the disparate events in one's life but also of the self across situations and time. Thus, coherence in personal narratives has been related to more advanced identity development. Additionally, the ability to derive meaning from significant life turning points, where an experience causes meaningful change in a person, has also been associated with identity status (McLean & Pratt, 2006). For example, lower levels of meaning making in personal narratives were found among adolescents with higher levels of identity diffusion or foreclosure. And researchers have also found a connection between positive affect in individuals' life story narratives and emotional adjustment (McAdams, Reynolds, Lewis, Patten, & Bowman, 2001). Extant research supports the view that narrative meaning making, or the ability to reflect on past events and to learn something about the self, is one of the major processes by which one's identity is constructed during adolescence and adulthood (McLean & Breen, 2009).

Other researchers have offered more complex models of identity development. For example, a recent meta-analysis of extant research postulates a longer course of identity development such that the process of identity formation continues well into late adolescence and early adulthood; moreover, there is significant variation in the way in which mature identity states are achieved (Kroger, Martinussen, & Marcia, 2010). Linkages have been identified between personality measures, the family context, and identity development in emerging adulthood (Syed & Seiffge-Krenke, 2013). And still other researchers have proposed descriptive developmental models of identity status where developmental maturity is used as the basis for rank ordering status, from diffusion to foreclosure, moratorium, and achievement. Patterns of growth from less advanced (diffusion and foreclosure) to more advanced (moratorium and achievement) identity status are seen to reflect corresponding changes in cognitive and social-cognitive development (Waterman, 1984). Additionally, different sequential patterns of identity status have been documented through development. Thus, for example, the pattern may be: *stable*, where the individual stays at the same status over time; it may be *progressive*, where there is movement from lower to higher status; it may be *regressive*, with movement from higher to lower status; or it may be *fluctuating* between higher and lower and back again to higher status (Waterman, 1982, 1999). There is some support for the idea that early adolescents are more likely to be diffused or foreclosed, whereas later adolescents more often move into moratorium or achieved. However, longitudinal evidence regarding the status sequence patterns is mixed (Bosma & Kunnen, 2008), leading some to question the usefulness of the status model in explaining shifts in identity status across development (van Hoof, 1999).

Many have criticized Marcia's scheme, arguing that it oversimplifies Erikson's ideas and places too much emphasis on identity outcomes and not enough focus on the actual process of identity formation (Côté & Levine, 1988). In spite of these criticisms, some researchers have investigated in more detail the role of exploration as it impacts the commitments that become part of one's identity (Berzonsky, 1990). Additionally, there is some work that has proposed a two-cycle process of exploring and committing to identity choices. In the first phase, tentative commitments are made only after a process of broad exploration. Then, using the tentative choices made in the first phase, a more in-depth exploration follows that may lead to an investment in the identity selected or a return to broad exploration (Luyckx, Goossens, Soenens, & Beyers, 2006; Luyckx, Goossens, Soenens, Beyers, & Vansteenkiste, 2005). This model has been elaborated even further into the late adolescent period (Luyckx et al., 2008). Clearly, longitudinal studies that extend over longer periods of time, from early adolescence through emerging adulthood, would contribute significantly to our understanding of the process of identity development in general and to our understanding of individual differences.

Attachment and Identity Development

Adolescents rely less on their parents as their secure base and begin to reevaluate their internalized representations of attachment figures. Increased autonomy from family and greater involvement with peers offers an expanded social context within which friendships and close relationships are explored. A history of secure attachment should promote more exploration as part of the process of identity formation. The secure attachment relationship should also lead the adolescent to more actively and intentionally explore options, be responsive to feedback, and remain open to experiences gained through exploration. In turn, the security of the early attachment relationship should promote confidence in the ability to make decisions about identity options and, in turn, lead to identity commitments (Marcia, 1988; Pittman et al., 2011). There is a limited body of research that has explored the links between attachment and identity formation in adolescence, and within this work there are variations in the ways these constructs are operationalized. Rather than evaluating working models of self and others, some studies have relied on self-reports of specific relationships, such as with parents and peers (Meeus, Oosterwegel, & Vollebergh, 2002) or parents and romantic partners (Ávila, Cabral, & Matos, 2012). Secure attachments to parents and experiences in romantic relationships have been found to encourage identity development. However, few direct links between parent–adolescent relationships and identity development have been revealed in an important review of extant research (Meeus & de Wied, 2007), suggesting that there may be other factors that influence this association that are important to consider. Adolescents' relationships with peers or romantic partners, for example, may be impacted by qualities of the earlier or current relationships with parents and these may in turn mediate the influence of parental relationships on identity development.

Interestingly, several studies have found attachment patterns in parent–adolescent relationships to be linked to identity commitment but not to identity exploration (Benson, Harris, & Rogers, 1992; Samuolis, Layburn, & Schiaffino, 2001). Indeed, this pattern has been confirmed in a recent meta-analysis, indicating an association between attachment security and identity commitment (Arseth, Kroger, Martinussen, & Marcia, 2009). These findings appear to be consistent with the view of identity exploration and commitment as a two-cycle process (Luyckx et al., 2005). Adolescents with secure attachments may be more likely to carefully consider their options prior to identity commitment; in turn, they may then re-examine, following a preliminary commitment, their choices. While the potential threat to and disconfirmation of an initial identity commitment may be distressing, adolescents with secure representations of attachment figures are more likely to engage in this in-depth process; the confidence they have derived from the security of their relationships helps them to be more active and intentional in exploration. By contrast, adolescents with negative models of others (including attachment representations that are fearful or dismissing) may be more likely to avoid exploration or commitment, leading to identity diffusion. And adolescents with negative models of the self (including self-representations that are fearful or anxious) may be more likely to commit to an identity without exploration, leading to identity foreclosure (Pittman et al., 2011).

Future research that examines these insecure working models of self and relationships would help to illuminate and clarify the interconnections between attachment relationships and identity development during adolescence. Moreover, because each partner in an intimate relationship brings his/her own working models of relationships, and his/her own identity challenges, the negotiation of intimacy becomes that much more complex. Each partner is not only constructing his/her own identity but is also providing the context for the other's identity exploration. Similarly, each partner's attachment history will impact proximity seeking in the face of identity threats and identity exploration in the context of new experiences (Bartholomew, 1990; Crowell et al., 2002). The consideration of attachment and developing identity in adolescence provides a rich foundation from which important questions about self and relationships may be raised and testable hypotheses proposed. Indeed, some of this work has already begun (see, for example, Kerpelman et al., 2012; Pittman, Kerpelman, Soto, Adler-Baeder, 2012). We can see that attachment representations are important not only to the process of identity formation, but also to the development of subsequent relationships. In the context of intimate relationships, those with insecure attachment representations may be challenged to resolve identity issues and their partners may validate, exacerbate, or provide new opportunities to work through these identity challenges.

Contextual Influences on Identity Development

Not all adolescents are equally successful in managing the task of identity formation. Some are well able to establish an integrated and clear identity while others are confused about their identity. Erikson (1968) emphasized the interpersonal context and the role of society in supporting and shaping the adolescent's identity. Researchers have continued to examine the interpersonal context (parents, peers, school) as it shapes, defines, and influences the process of identity development (Galliher & Kerpelman, 2012). There are also ways in which relationships and contextual factors can undermine the development of a stable and coherent identity by limiting the opportunities and kinds of experiences that contribute to a strong sense of self. Poor educational options, low socioeconomic status, parental psychopathology, and child maltreatment are all examples of contextual factors that may negatively impact identity development. Identity formation is therefore best conceptualized as a transactional process between the individual and his or her social and interpersonal context.

There is some research that has explored interactional patterns in families and their association with identity status. The assumption underlying this work is that parents play a critical role in their adolescents' identity development. Parents who offer their children affection, who are open and communicative, and who allow their children the opportunity to explore while providing them with a secure base will in turn have adolescents who are in a state of either identity achievement or identity moratorium. Adolescents who are emotionally close to and rely heavily on their parents for security and who engage in little independent exploration are likely to be foreclosed in their identity. And adolescents who are distant from their families, who see their parents as indifferent, detached or rejecting, are in the state of identity diffusion (Campbell, Adams, & Dobson, 1984; Grotevant & Cooper, 1985). These correlational findings are interesting, though they need to be considered with caution since they may be true for some, but not all, of the adolescents in each family situation and/or identity status classification. Additionally, the direction of effects is not clear, since some interaction patterns may either cause, or be the consequence of, particular identity status groups.

The role of peer relationships in the process of identity exploration has also been studied. Peers provide adolescents with many opportunities to learn about themselves, about social rules and mores, as well as about attitudes, values, and beliefs. Close friendships are especially important as they provide adolescents with the emotional security that allows them to talk about and explore their identity in a supportive context that is neither critical nor judgmental (Azmitia, 2002). In one empirical study exploring the beneficial effects of friendship on the development of identity, undergraduate students who had strong attachments to friends were found to be more likely to explore occupational choices and career options (Felsman & Blustein, 1999). And there is also empirical evidence supporting the notion that even though there is an increase in peer influence during adolescence, parents continue to influence identity development as well (Hill, Bromell, Tyson, & Flint, 2007; McLean & Jennings, 2012). For example, parental psychological control has been found to be associated with experiences of anxiety and avoidance in romantic attachments during adolescence. Moreover, attachment avoidance is negatively related to exploration of dating identity during adolescence (Pittman et al., 2012). Therefore, we see that adolescent exploration of romantic relationships, and the development of identity linked with these relationships, may be supported or inhibited by the quality of the parent–adolescent relationship. The relative importance of parents and peers for identity development thus continues to be debated (Meeus et al., 2002) and many theorize that each contributes in important and unique ways (Schacter & Ventura, 2008; Weeks & Pasupathi, 2010).

Identity development has also been studied in relation to vulnerability to peer pressures and involvement in delinquent behaviors (Ellis & Zarbatany, 2007b; Steinberg & Monahan, 2007). Specifically, though identity development has been linked to engagement in risky behavior (Jones & Hartmann, 1988), recent research has demonstrated that identity development (in particular, exploration and commitment) moderates between the experience of peer pressure and the reported frequency of substance use and generally deviant behaviors in high school students (Dumas, Ellis, & Wolfe, 2012). Thus, fostering identity development within the family context (Perosa, Perosa, & Tam, 2002) or the school environment (Oyserman & Destin, 2010) may help diminish teens' involvement in risky behaviors, particularly in those contexts where there is strong peer pressure to conform. This research serves as a reminder that peers and parents both play an important role in identity development. Moreover, the compensatory or complementary roles that peers may play, in addition to parental influences on identity formation, warrant further investigation (see, for example, Galliher & Kerpelman, 2012).

Schools can exert a very powerful role in supporting the process of identity formation as well. Adolescents' relationships with their teachers may offer students the support they need to explore their identity. Teachers may encourage their students to discover new interests through, for example, offering courses that incorporate service learning (Pascarella & Terenzini, 2005; Yates & Youniss, 1996). Adolescents learn, through community service activities, to reflect on social and political issues and to consider their role in effecting progress and change (Waterman, 1989). Open classroom discussions about identity-related issues, career and college fairs, and self-reflective writing assignments all offer students important opportunities to engage in identity-promoting experiences.

Finally, the larger socio-historical context within which the adolescent lives may promote or inhibit identity development (Bosma & Kunnen, 2001). Factors such as socioeconomic status, educational opportunities, familial obligations and commitments, geographic isolation, and parental values and traditions may all impose limitations and/or barriers to exploring identity. Moreover, the social, political, and economic influences on identity development depend on historical conditions as well (Baumeister & Muraven, 1996). For example, the increased access for both men and women to college education and career possibilities, fueled in part by the women's movement, has challenged long-established notions about relationships, family functioning, work-life balance, and parental responsibilities and opened up a range of identity-related questions for all adolescents and young adults.

Recent Developments in the Study of the Self and Identity

Newer methodologies, such as advanced neuroimaging techniques, are being used in research on the self and identity (LeDoux & Debiec, 2003). Some researchers have explored the ways in which the self comes to be understood as a distinct entity that has control and agency over one's own actions (Farrer et al., 2003). Other investigators have examined self–other differentiation (Heatherton et al., 2006), self-reflection across time (Conway, 2005; D'Argembeau et al., 2008; McAdams, 2001), and self-face and self-voice recognition (Kaplan, Aziz-Zadeh, Uddin, & Iacoboni, 2008). For example, during tasks involving self-other discriminations or visual self-recognition, neuroimaging studies have indicated that there is selective activation of the right frontoparietal network (Devue et al., 2007; Uddin, Kaplan, Molnar-Szakacs, Zaidel, & Iacoboni, 2005). Additionally, researchers have examined the cognitive organization of autobiographical memory (Conway, 2005), the development of the capacity to differentiate one's own feelings and thoughts from others' (Astington, Harris, & Olson, 1988), and the social psychological causes and consequences of decisions individuals make about their past and future selves (Liberman & Trope, 1998). The neural and cognitive systems that contribute to a sense of the continuity of the self, from the past to the present and into the future, have been identified (Wheeler, Stuss, & Tulving, 1997). The evidence from this growing body of research supports the idea that the neural processes involved in distinguishing the self from others are also involved in constructing a sense of the self across time (Libby, Eibach, & Gilovich, 2005; Pronin & Ross, 2006).

The brain regions involved in representing the self across different life periods have also been examined. Specifically, there is greater activation in cortical midline structures when thinking about the current self. These are the same regions involved in representing distinctions between self and other in the past and the present (D'Argembeau et al., 2008). These findings are consistent with a meta-analysis suggesting these brain structures are more engaged when thinking about the self in the present (Northoff et al., 2006), since activity in the cortical medial structures appears to be sensitive to temporal (present and past) perspectives on the self. Whether the cortical midline structures are activated when thinking about the current self across contexts, when in social roles that are consistent (or vary) across relational contexts, or when constructing a view of the self into the future are important questions to explore (Libby, 2008).

Investigators have also found activations in cortical midline structures when people reflect on their own psychological characteristics (Craik et al., 1999; Ochsner et al., 2005; Saxe, Moran, Scholz, & Gabrieli, 2006) as well as on those of others (Amodio & Frith, 2006). While most of these studies have been conducted with adult participants, there are some preliminary studies that have used fMRI imaging with young infants and children. In one study, 15- to 30-month-old children referred for evaluations of possible neurological problems were included in this research after no neurological problems were found (Lewis & Carmody, 2008). Behavioral measures of pretend play and visual self-recognition in the mirror, and mothers' reports of personal pronoun use, were combined to yield a self-representation score. These scores were then compared to the neuroimaging results. An association was found between higher self-representation scores and greater maturation of the temporoparietal junction, independent of the child's age. Taken together with the work on older subjects, this research suggests that brain development and environmental factors may together influence self-representations and highlights important directions for using neuroimaging techniques in future research.

Ethnic Identity

Ethnic identity involves a sense of oneself as belonging to or being part of an ethnic group. The development of ethnic identity involves the interconnected processes of exploration and commitment (Phinney, 1996), though it is based on a gradual understanding of, and sense of connection to, cultural and ethnic traditions and the larger ethnic community. When youth are encouraged to explore what their ethnicity means to them within the larger cultural context, optimal developmental outcomes may be fostered and ultimately lead to a commitment and stable sense of belonging to the larger ethnic group (Galliher, Jones, & Dahl, 2011; Ghavami, Fingerhut, Peplau, Grant, & Wittig, 2011). Questions regarding the development of ethnic identity have been raised since the early 1990s, with more recent studies extending beyond a focus on Black adolescents (e.g., Marshall, 1995) to include studies of ethnic identity among Asian, Latino, and Native American adolescents (Lysne & Levy, 1997; Spencer & Markstrom-Adams, 1990; Ying & Lee, 1999).

Identifying oneself as a member of a racial or ethnic group with whom one affiliates is especially salient for minority or non-dominant ethnic groups. Identifying and defining oneself as a group member, feeling a sense of belonging to the group, and participating in cultural practices and traditions are all components of ethnic identity (Hill & Witherspoon, 2011; Phinney, 1990; Weisner, 2011). The course of identity development is complicated for adolescents in any ethnic minority group because there are decisions that need to be made about the importance and place of their own group and the more dominant group. The processes of exploring and committing to one's ethnic identity are embedded within important relationships and broader social interactions. Parents may attempt to instill ethnic awareness in their children and to foster a sense of belonging and pride in their ethnic or racial heritage and traditions. They may also attempt to protect their children against racism and guide them in ways of dealing with discrimination. In fact, several studies have demonstrated that adolescents report a more coherent and positive ethnic identity, and are better able to manage experiences with discrimination, when their parents engage in higher levels of racial or ethnic socialization (for a review, see Hughes et al., 2006).

One way to study ethnic identity has been to explore the extent to which individuals integrate their ethnic minority status and their identification with the dominant culture. Some adolescents abandon their ethnic identity and completely integrate into the majority cultural group, others may try to hold on to their cultural identity and separate themselves from the dominant culture, some try to hold on to their cultural identity while also participating in the majority group culture, and still others fail to identify with any group and stay on the "margins" (Berry, 1997; Phinney & Alipuria, 1990). While extant research provides a useful way of conceptualizing an individual's relative status regarding their acceptance of, and integration into, the mainstream culture, many important questions remain. For example, do adolescents work their way through various stages in their development of ethnic identity? What factors influence this process? And how does establishing one's racial and ethnic identity impact psychosocial functioning, academic adjustment, and behaviors and attitudes about health risks in adolescents? These are some of the many relevant questions that are now being examined more carefully by developmental researchers and scholars (see, for example, Umaña-Taylor et al., and the Ethnic and Racial Identity in the 21st Century Study Group, 2014).

Ethnic identity development may involve a gradual transition from identifying with the dominant culture, to encountering discrimination, which may lead to a greater awareness and upholding of the values of their own group, to a rejecting of the dominant group values, and finally to an integration of personal and cultural identities (Cross, 1987). Alternatively, a three-stage model of ethnic identity development, based on Marcia's (1966) ego identity status framework, has also been useful for conceptualizing adolescents' status regarding their evolving interest in and commitment to their racial or ethnic group (Phinney, 1989, 1996). In the first stage, when individuals are not interested in their ethnic identity or it is unexamined, they are said to be in a state of diffusion. Alternatively, their parents may expose them to, and prescribe their involvement with, their ethnic identity and heritage, leading to a state of foreclosure. When exploration of culture and history occurs in the second stage, individuals begin to consider the meaning of their ethnic group's values and practices in relation to themselves. This is a period of moratorium. Finally, when individuals identify with and commit to their ethnic group, achievement of an ethnic identity is accomplished. Perceptions of discrimination have been found to increase with ethnic identity development (Brown & Bigler, 2005). However, it may be that ethnic identity is impacted by these perceptions of ethnic and racial discrimination (Hughes et al., 2006); therefore, directions of influence still need to be better understood.

A stronger ethnic identity in minority adolescents has been found to be related to higher self-esteem, more positive social relationships, stronger academic motivation, and better psychological adjustment (Carlson, Uppal, & Prosser, 2000; Kiang, Witkow, & Champagne, 2013; Phinney, Cantu, & Kurtz, 1997; Umaña-Taylor, 2004). Factors that may impact the process of identity development for ethnic minorities include the ethnic composition of the school environment, the amount of time since the family's immigration, and the contrast between the parents' ethnic identities and the adolescent's social experiences (Quintana, Castaneda-English, & Ybarra, 1999). In general, the limited available research has found that experiences with discrimination may serve as a catalyst for the exploration of ethnic identity (Greene, Way, & Pahl, 2006; Pahl & Way, 2006). Moreover, a strong and positive identification with one's ethnic group may buffer adolescents against the negative effects of discrimination over time. Some recent research has even suggested that in adolescence, peers may assume the socialization functions previously assumed by family members; therefore, interactions among friends may lead to mutual conversations about ethnicity and race and contribute to ethnic identity

(Syed & Juan, 2012). And identity status relative to the dominant culture may shift, depending upon developmental changes, stresses (such as school transitions), and other pressures (French, Seidman, Allen, & Aber, 2006; Kiang et al., 2013). At different points in development, minority adolescents may be challenged by their association with "mainstream" culture and either reject it, live within it but feel like an "outsider," reject their own culture, or maintain ties to both the minority and majority cultures (Phinney & Alipuria, 1990). More longitudinal studies are needed that distinguish between and within ethnic groups and explore the multiple influences on developmental outcomes during adolescence. Finally, some studies have reported gender differences in the process of ethnic identity, thus highlighting the need to explore variability between males and females in terms of the influence of both familial and peer socialization (Umaña-Taylor & Guimond, 2010). Ethnic identity may not be a static variable but may change, depending upon other developmental challenges. At this point, we do know that growing up as a member of a minority group within a larger cultural community challenges the process of identity formation in complex ways.

Gender Identity

Developing a sense of oneself as either male or female constitutes gender identity. Children usually begin to be aware of themselves as male or female at the age of 2½ years, when they are likely to describe themselves as a "boy" or a "girl" (Ruble et al., 2007). With development, gender identity includes an awareness of oneself as possessing gender-typed traits, characteristics, and competencies, having interests in and preferences for activities that are gender-typed, and maintaining a sense of oneself as a typical (or an atypical) member of a gender group (Ruble et al., 2006). Several theoretical perspectives and explanatory models have been offered to account for the development of gender-typed behavior and of gender identity. Many focus on the role that gender-related cognitions play in influencing behavior (e.g., Bussey & Bandura, 1999). However, an alternative framework has been proposed suggesting that either gender-related beliefs influence behavior (the *attitudinal-pathway* model) or individual preferences and characteristics influence gender-related beliefs (the *personal-pathway* model). Incorporated into this framework is a consideration of the extent to which the individual believes that gender is an important construct, or the idea of *gender schematicity,* which is determined by both individual and situational influences. While there are aspects of both the attitudinal- and personal-pathway models in all individuals, personal, developmental, and situational factors influence which model tends to prevail at a particular point in time (Liben & Bigler, 2002).

By adolescence, a key developmental task is to come to terms with the biological changes brought on by puberty and the associated development of gender and sexual identity (Erikson, 1968). Now, increased sexual awareness and interest needs to be integrated into the adolescent's developing sense of self. How do the biological changes of adolescence impact developing identity and how do gender differences impact sexuality in adolescence? These are the topics to which we will now turn.

Biological Influences on Gender and Sexuality

The biological changes of puberty begin long before adolescence and any visible signs of physical changes become apparent. For boys, this process begins at about the age of 9½ years, whereas for girls it begins as early as 7 years of age (Kroger, 2007). About a year before any noticeable signs of puberty, there are changes in the endocrine system, that part of the body that regulates levels of hormones circulating throughout the body. Like a thermostat, the endocrine system receives messages from the central nervous system, primarily the brain, and controls secretions of hormones. While functionally connected to and controlled by the hypothalamus, the pituitary gland, which is part of this finely tuned endocrine system, secretes hormones and regulates homeostasis. Between infancy and puberty, the pituitary gland inhibits levels of sex hormones circulating within the body. However, there is a change in the regulating system, with rising levels of sex hormones, about one year before the appearance of physical signs of puberty (Archibald, Graber, & Brooks-Gunn, 2003); as a consequence, the many biological changes of puberty become apparent. There is evidence that nutrition, illness, stress, extreme thinness, and excessive exercise may all impact the timing of puberty (Kroger, 2007). Early family experiences that have been found to relate to the earlier onset of puberty include situations that may involve conflict and stress in social contexts, including low socioeconomic status, father absence, maternal harshness, family conflict, child maltreatment, and early substance use (Arim, Tramonte, Shapka, Dahinten, & Willms, 2011). The timing of puberty onset is important to consider, given that numerous studies have identified early pubertal maturation as a potential risk factor for behavioral and mental health problems in adolescence (Arim & Shapka, 2008; Ge, Brody, Conger, & Simons, 2006; Graber, Lewinsohn, Seeley, & Brooks-Gunn, 1997).

The biological changes associated with puberty are the result of two primary classes of sex hormones called androgens and estrogens. Testosterone is an androgen that plays a primary role in pubertal development for males. Increasing levels of testosterone lead to an enlargement of the testicles and penis, the appearance of pubic hair, minor voice changes, the first ejaculation, a growth spurt in height, more voice changes, and the appearance of facial and body hair. In females, pubertal development is influenced by the estrogen called estradiol, as well as by some androgens. The initial physical changes include breast development, the growth of pubic hair, widening of hips, increase in height, and the beginning of menstruation (Kroger, 2007; Rabin & Chrousos, 1991). The increase in height usually occurs about two years earlier for girls than for boys. Interestingly, the growth spurt occurs before girls are capable of reproduction, while for boys the capacity to reproduce occurs before their skeletal growth spurt (Archibald et al., 2003). Some have speculated that there are important adaptive, evolutionary reasons for the ordering of puberty in males and females which may, in turn, have important implications for identity (Bogin, 1994). Moreover, recent research indicates that the timing and pacing of pubertal changes, which vary between individuals, is strongly inherited (Dick, Rose, Pilkkinen, & Kapiro, 2001). Clear ethnic differences have also been observed, independent of weight, geographic location, or socioeconomic status. For example, African American females seem to mature relatively earlier than Mexican American girls and White American girls mature relatively later than both groups (Chumlea et al., 2003).

There are important identity-related issues associated with the physical changes of puberty and the timing of pubertal development relative to one's peers. Adolescents tend to be very preoccupied with their appearance as the physical changes of puberty unfold. For girls, there is a general dissatisfaction with their increase in body fat and weight that violate cultural ideals and the media's focus on slimness (McCabe & Riccardelli, 2003; Petersen & Leffert, 1995). Boys, on the other hand, seem to find an advantage in their increased muscle mass, size, and physical strength, viewing these biological changes more positively than girls (Dorn, Crockett, & Petersen, 1988). Interestingly, however, ethnic group differences in valued body types are increasingly emerging that may shift the cultural ideals for some minority groups (Parker et al., 1995; Snapp, 2009). Moreover, pubertal changes have implications for body image and self-esteem, as female adolescents are generally dissatisfied with their bodies and would like to be thinner (Gardner, Friedman, & Jackson, 1999), are more self-conscious and have lower self-esteem than adolescent boys (Simmons & Blyth, 1987), and feel best when they are slightly underweight (whereas boys prefer to be of average weight) (Brooks-Gunn, 1991). When female adolescents mature early, they tend to feel less positive about their bodies and less attractive than their peers, whereas when males mature early, they seem to have a more positive body image (Brooks-Gunn, 1991). Additionally, early maturing girls tend to have a higher incidence of eating-related problems and may be vulnerable to other adjustment difficulties as well. For example, some research has found that early maturing females are more vulnerable to depression (though this was found only in Caucasian Americans and not among Hispanic or African American females) (Archibald et al., 2003) and more likely to engage in early sexual behaviors and to become pregnant (Stattin & Magnusson, 1990).

Gender, Sexuality, and Identity in Adolescence

Researchers who study gender differences distinguish between three components of an individual's sexual self: sexual or gender identity, sex or gender roles, and sexual orientation (Kroger, 2007). During the transition to puberty, there are important changes that occur in one's sexual identity. Biological maturation, and the meaning of the associated physical changes that occur, need to be incorporated into the adolescent's identity. Now, adolescents have a greater awareness of their physical strengths and limitations. They begin to distinguish those physical features they can modify or change (e.g., hair style and color, weight, muscle tone) and those that are more permanent (e.g., height, bone structure), which eventually leads to a greater acceptance of the observable signs of puberty. As growth rates decline and sexual maturation is completed, increased musculature makes a significant contribution to weight gain in late adolescence. After puberty, there are gender differences in body fat, bone mass, and muscle mass. Females now have about twice the body fat as compared to males, and males have about one and a half times the bone mass and lean muscle mass as females (Grumbach & Styne, 1998). These physical differences have implications for identity development as well, since males and females need to integrate into their sense of self an appreciation of their changed stature, size, strength, and overall physical capabilities, relative to what they once were when they were younger and relative to their peers.

Adolescents incorporate into their personal identity an internal sense of being a man or a woman, which is then expressed in their behavior and personality. By mid-adolescence, the biological changes of puberty lead to an increased recognition of feelings of sexual arousal and a need to find appropriate outlets for sexual expression (Graber, Brooks-Gunn, & Galen, 1998). The process of developing a sexual self-concept evolves over time and may be structured differently for adolescent men and women. For example, females do not distinguish the emotional from the relationship dimensions of sexuality, whereas males do appear to differentiate between these dimensions (Breakwell & Millward, 1997). For women, but not for men, maintaining some control over where and when sexual intercourse occurs is important to the adolescent's sexual self-concept. Males who are more concerned with the relationship dimension of sexuality are less likely to have sex or to engage in risky sexual behaviors. Females are more likely to incorporate into their sexual identity a combination of assertiveness and initiative as they approach their sexual encounters, together with a receptivity to and acceptance of their sexuality. It may be that the loosening of stereotyped sexual behaviors, together with the use of safer sex practices and a greater sense of sexual freedom and options for women more generally, are contributing to changes in sexual identity for both males and females in adolescence. Still, there are enormous cultural and societal pressures to conform to particular gender, ethnic, religious, or racial group values or more rigidly defined roles that are difficult for many adolescents to transcend. This may result in continued confusion, exploration, and struggle, and/or a need to more firmly establish comfortable expressions of sexuality and gender roles.

Adolescents are increasingly aware of the gendered roles of males and females. Several studies have examined the question of whether gender roles become more differentiated early in adolescence. Some researchers, for example, have found an intensification of attitudes about gender roles, while others find factors such as family socialization practices, the maintenance of traditional sex roles, and cultural/societal differentiation of gender roles to be associated with increased differences in masculinity, femininity, and sex role attitudes (Kroger, 2007). Ultimately, the consolidation of physical changes, together with developing notions of gender roles and sexual identity, occur toward the end of the teenage years (Blos, 1967). This is a time when adolescents now begin to assume more responsibility for the decisions and choices in their own lives. While this continues to be a process encouraged more in Western than in non-Western cultures, it is part of what leads adolescents to establish social relationships that include various forms of intimacy and sexual expression as they begin to explore and/or assume their sexual orientation.

Research on the development and experience of sexual orientation in adolescents has been relatively limited. There has been some research, however, exploring sexual identity from the perspective of adolescents who are in the sexual minority (e.g., lesbian and gay youth) (Savin-Williams, 2001); this work may, in turn, result in an expanding body of research on sexuality and sexual identity more generally among adolescents of all sexual orientations. Within this area of research, inconsistencies in developmental trajectories have been reported for men and women. Moreover, samples of ethnically and socioeconomically diverse participants have rarely been included and retrospective self-reports of feelings, perceptions, and events are most commonly used (Diamond, 1998). Longitudinal studies, though potentially quite difficult to execute, would help to clarify the developmental progression of sexual orientation from childhood into adolescence. This research might serve to highlight some of the early indicators of sexual orientation, as well as the alternative pathways leading to the emergence of same-sex attraction in adolescent men and women.

It is critical that more empirically based conceptual models of sexual orientation be proposed and tested that can represent the range of experiences and developmental challenges for sexual minority (e.g., homosexual and bisexual) men and women. Issues of definition and measurement of sexual orientation need to be considered. Moreover, work that disentangles the concepts of affectional feelings and sexual desire will contribute to the growing body of research on the development of sexual orientation and the processes of "coming out." Theoretical models that integrate biobehavioral associations between love and desire, within the context of social, cultural, and interpersonal influences, have implications for our understanding of gender differences in sexuality and sexual orientation (Diamond, 2001, 2003; Peplau & Garnets, 2000). Finally, more research is needed exploring the direction of influences and factors (such as attachment styles or self-esteem) that place some sexual minority adolescents at increased risk for mental health problems and suicide. The range of experiences and different patterns of adaptive and maladaptive developmental outcomes need to be explored within diverse groups of sexual minority adolescents so as to better understand the factors that promote resilience as well; ultimately, this work will deepen our understanding of sexuality and its place in developing identity.

Intimacy

Intimacy in relationships is dependent upon a certain degree of responsiveness and mutual openness between social partners. It may therefore be seen to have its roots in earlier relationships. In fact, research confirms associations between early family relationships and the degree of openness and support in adolescents' close relationships (Collins & Van Dulmen, 2006b). Thus, for example, a positive association has been found between cohesion, respect for privacy, and flexible control in the family and intimacy in romantic relationships in late adolescence, especially for women (Feldman, Gowen, & Fisher, 1998). Additionally, negative emotionality in adolescent–parent dyads has been linked to poor-quality interactions and negative emotionality with romantic partners in late adolescence (Kim, Conger, Lorenz, & Elder, 2001). It appears that ineffective parental monitoring, inconsistent discipline, and negative affect (parental hostility and coercion) mediate this association (Conger, Cui, Bryant, & Elder, 2000), thereby supporting the notion that intimacy has strong interpersonal roots (Collins & Steinberg, 2008).

Increased sophistication in understanding social relationships and in the ability to infer the feelings and thoughts of others results from cognitive advances that contribute to the adolescent's improved capacity for intimacy (Selman, 1980). Adolescents who spend longer periods of time with their peers may become more comfortable with them, thereby encouraging an openness to sharing one's own thoughts and to listening to others' private thoughts. The support and comfort that peers may offer to one another, especially regarding the salient issues they believe are unique and "not something that adults can understand," leads to an increased need to communicate, whether by phone, text, social networking sites, or in person. The biological changes of adolescence, in particular, may foster the sharing of worries and concerns regarding physical changes, appropriate dress and appearance, dating, and sex. Adolescents are more likely to turn to their friends when attempting to master new social challenges, or to find ways of surviving in the face of disappointments, frustrations, and rejections. They prefer spending more time with peers, and less with parents, as they seek opportunities for self-disclosure, sharing, and intimacy. Now, rather than engaging in physical or structured activities, they yearn for support and closeness, with the potential for trust, loyalty, mutual concern, responsiveness, and the sharing of confidences (Newcomb & Bagwell, 1995).

Indeed, many studies have documented the increased frequency of mutual self-disclosure, frankness, trust, loyalty, and sensitivity toward friends over the period of early adolescence through the early college years (e.g., Furman & Buhrmester, 1985a, 1992; Sharabany, Gershoni, & Hofmann, 1981). Additionally, gender differences in intimacy have been examined and researchers have found that males and females increasingly engage in discussion and self-disclosure with close friends, though the manner in which intimacy is achieved differs. Females are more likely to achieve intimacy through talking and sharing, while males are more likely to establish intimacy in the context of shared activities (McNelles & Connolly, 1999). There is some concern that adolescent girls who extensively discuss their feelings and talk about their problems may co-ruminate (Rose, 2002), thereby focusing on negative feelings, discussing problems, concerns, and unanswerable questions, and increasing the likelihood of internalizing symptoms (Tompkins, Hockett, Abraibesh, & Witt, 2011). However, co-rumination with friends has also been associated with positive relationship qualities, such as relationship satisfaction (Calmes & Roberts, 2008; Rose, Carlson, & Waller, 2007), and may be more likely to occur when adolescents also engage in co-rumination with their mothers (Waller & Rose, 2013).

Adolescent friendships provide essential experiences that impact later close relationships and help to overcome loneliness (Furman & Wehner, 1994; Sullivan, 1953). But we also know that earlier relationships with parents and friends impact relationships in adolescence (Carlson, Sroufe, & Egeland, 2004; Collins & Van Dulmen, 2006b; Owens, Crowell, Treboux, O'Connor, & Pan, 1995; Waters, Merrick, et al., 2000). Research has documented links across relationships. Research has documented links across relationships. For example, associations have been found between representations of friendships in middle and late adolescence and romantic relationships assessed concurrently, as well as between displays of safe-haven and secure-base behaviors with best friends and dating partners (Collins & Van Dulmen, 2006b; Furman, Simon, Shaffer, & Bouchey, 2002; Treboux, Crowell, Owens, & Pan, 1994). Critical questions remain regarding the commonalities across all of these relationships and whether the competencies developed in early attachment relationships, for example, necessarily translate to successful negotiation of subsequent relationships over time and across relationships. It may be that there is some additional variable that accounts for this association across relationships. More specifically, it may be that the individual's sense of self, which is rooted in early attachment relationships, is what is carried forward in to all subsequent relationships and influences their quality and organization. Therefore, the capacity to develop intimate friendships and romantic relationships, where the adolescent feels cared for, supported, and loved, and experiences mutual self-disclosure, may reflect important aspects of adolescent identity. In other words, the capacity to negotiate intimacy emerges from a well-formed identity, a concept that Erikson (1968) originally put forth. Some have even suggested that Erikson's model needs to be modified, since identity formation and intimacy may emerge concurrently (Dyk & Adams, 1987; Montgomery, 2005; Pittman et al., 2012).

There are some empirical studies that have explored Erikson's prediction that individuals who are more advanced in identity development are more likely to have developed intimate relationships (Arseth et al., 2009; Beyers & Seiffge-Krenke, 2010; Dyk & Adams, 1990; Hartup, 1996; Tesch & Whitbourne, 1982). However, the direction of influence cannot be firmly established in these correlational studies, nor are other developmental influences, such as qualitative differences in early attachment relationships, considered as they may impact both identity and intimacy in adolescence. For example, internal representations of sensitive and responsive attachment figures may be another mechanism that plays an important role in the development of identity and of relationships outside of the family. These internal representations incorporate attachment-relevant scripts (Waters, Rodrigues, & Ridgeway, 1998), which in turn have effects on mental representations of self and others and on affect regulation (Mikulincer & Shaver, 2008). When attachment figures are responsive, representations develop incorporating positive expectations and beliefs about the continued availability of a caring and trustworthy partner.

These positive representations contribute to a view that others are available to help manage distress and negative emotions, without criticizing, shaming, rejecting, or disapproving. In turn, these positive representations of attachment figures also encourage the individual to seek out others, ask for help when needed, and express feelings, hopes, and vulnerabilities in close relationships. Therefore, with this profound confidence in the availability of the other comes a greater willingness to explore, to consider and try new experiences, to act in prosocial ways, and to effectively seek support from others when needed. As a result, there is a decrease in dependency and an increase in autonomy over time, a concept that is consistent with the view that secure attachments to parents during adolescence promote adolescent autonomy (Allen, 2008). In adult romantic relationships, it has also been found that individuals who are sensitive to distress cues and accepting of proximity seeking and dependency needs, in turn, have partners who function more autonomously and are less dependent (Feeney, 2007).

Early experiences with sensitive and responsive attachment figures empower individuals to feel good about themselves even when faced with difficulties or challenges. Secure adolescents view themselves as competent and valuable (Cooper, Shaver, & Collins, 1998), have higher self-esteem relative to those with an anxious attachment style (Bartholomew & Horowitz, 1991; Mickelson, Kessler, & Shaver, 1997), and hold views of themselves that are more positive, balanced, and coherent than those of insecure adolescents (Mikulincer, 1995). Additionally, in the face of stress, self-worth is maintained by self-representations that are grounded in positive evaluations by attachment figures and in identification with traits and characteristics of attachment figures who are caring and supportive (Mikulincer & Shaver, 2004). Secure individuals can draw on representations of themselves as being valued and loved even in times of stress, thereby providing comfort, enhancing affect regulation, and minimizing the use of defensive strategies to manage distress. Consequently, a stable sense of self and the capacity to maintain emotional balance derive from early attachment experiences and contribute, in turn, to greater confidence in the self and authentic self-esteem in adolescence and young adulthood.

Intimacy is an emerging aspect of relationships that is rooted in earlier attachment experiences as well as in the adolescent's developing sense of self. The physical, cognitive, and social changes of adolescence contribute to the developing capacity for intimacy. However, intimacy in relationships also reflects a balance between an understanding of the self and an openness to others and therefore provides a rich example of the close interconnection between attachment and the self system.

Self-Disclosure and Authenticity in Adolescent Relationships

Developmental researchers have found that adolescents who are more competent at disclosing their personal feelings are more likely to offer support to others and to have more intimate friendships (Buhrmester, 1990; Buhrmester, Furman, Wittenberg, & Reis, 1988; Chow & Buhrmester, 2011; Reis & Shaver, 1988). Self-disclosure requires both an understanding of the self as well as the capacity to tolerate the potential risk that making oneself vulnerable to another might introduce (e.g., the possibility of rejection, humiliation, invalidation). Self-disclosure has also been associated with relationship quality (Buhrmester, 1990). Furthermore, the capacity for empathy appears to make some adolescents more likely to self-disclose, which in turn leads to closer friendships. Thus, self-disclosure appears to mediate between empathic responsiveness and friendship closeness (Chow et al., 2013).

Related to the research on self-disclosure is the capacity to be authentic and to express oneself openly and honestly in relationships. Because adolescence is a period when concerns about acceptance and approval by peers are especially salient, authenticity is particularly relevant to consider. Authenticity has been studied as a relational variable that may be both a risk and a protective factor for social and emotional outcomes. In order to be authentic in relationships, the adolescent needs to know and represent his/her own self (Harter, 1997), voice (Gilligan, Lyons, & Hammer, 1990), and emotional reactions; moreover, the authentic adolescent needs to experience consistency between feelings and thoughts as well as between how he or she behaves and what he or she communicates in relational contexts (Impett et al., 2008). Some adolescents may silence themselves (Jack, 1991) and present false-self behavior (Harter, 2002) as a way of protecting themselves from exposure or possible rejection if their thoughts, feelings, and behaviors are contradictory, do not comply with parental expectations, and/or do not conform to societal norms.

Authenticity was studied initially in terms of its effects on individual development, with research documenting an association between higher levels of authenticity in relationships and more positive and stable self-esteem (Impett et al., 2008) and between lower levels of authenticity and depression, eating disorders, and low self-esteem in adolescence (Harter, Marold, et al., 1996; Smolak & Munstertieger, 2002; Tolman, Impett, Tracy, & Michael, 2006). More recently, however, authenticity has been explored in terms of its association with adolescents' developing relationships with friends and family members (e.g., Harter, Waters, Whitesell, & Kastelic, 1998; Miller, Jordan, Kaplan, Stiver, & Surrey, 1997; Theran, 2010). This research focus reflects an acknowledgment that expressions of one's own authenticity, and encouragement of authenticity in the other, are important within and across relational contexts in adolescence and in emerging adulthood as well.

The precursors to, and relational consequences of, authenticity have been examined. Security of attachment has been found to be associated with adolescent girls' authenticity with authority figures (Theran, 2009). Particular maternal behaviors, such as perceived parental support, are positively associated with authenticity, while high levels of perceived parental criticism are associated with low levels of authenticity, in female adolescents and young adults (Abel, 2014). Authenticity in relationships with authority figures (e.g., mothers, fathers, and teachers) and with peers (e.g., classmates and best friends) has also been found to be associated with greater intimacy in adolescents' closest friendships (Theran, 2010). Thus, particular parental behaviors may contribute to the development of authenticity in adolescents' relationships with their parents, though alternatively it may be that levels of authenticity influence parental behavior. Moreover, while establishing authenticity is an important predictor of closeness in adolescent friendships, it may also be that in the context of close friendships, adolescents experience increased self-awareness and thus greater authenticity.

Longitudinal investigations with larger and more diverse samples will extend these findings, clarify the developmental precursors to and consequences of authenticity in relationships, and continue to explore more complex causal models. For example, maternal support has been examined as it moderates the relation between particular emotion regulation strategies and authenticity in relationships with mothers and fathers (Abel, 2014). High levels of approval and emotional support from the family appear to protect against low levels of authenticity in relationships with authority figures and moderate psychological well-being and symptoms of depression (Theran, 2010). And level of authenticity has been found to mediate between early adverse circumstances and later mental health outcomes (Theran & Han, 2013). Further examination of risk and protective factors (including, for example, particular emotion regulation strategies or parental variables) will illuminate the possibilities for clinical interventions geared toward reducing symptoms of anxiety, depression, and low self-esteem in adolescents with lower levels of authenticity.

Emotional Development and the Self During Adolescence

Adolescents can be incredibly engaging and passionate, spirited and joyful, as well as combative, self-involved, moody, and difficult. They can test the limits, challenge authority, and leave parents feeling worn out and distressed. And yet they also can be articulate and funny, thoughtful and endearing. The variable emotional states of young adolescents, characterized by extreme fluctuations and the tendency to "blow up" at their parents, siblings, or close friends with little provocation, may be the consequence of significant hormonal changes.

The typical increase in negative emotions in adolescents may also be related to stress, school transitions, social relationships, changes in eating patterns, and sexual pressures. In fact, these environmental stresses may be more important in accounting for mood fluctuations than hormonal changes (Susman & Dorn, 2009). While it may be very difficult to be around adolescents because of their intense emotional reactions and moodiness, most adolescents emerge from this period and become quite competent adults who can more successfully regulate their emotional states. For some, however, the intensely negative emotions may reflect serious problems that, depending upon the timing of their onset, the familial and social circumstances in which they arise, and the adolescent's general functioning, may warrant clinical intervention.

Managing emotions is an especially important challenge of adolescent development. Greater self-awareness may influence the context in which adolescents allow themselves to really "let down" and communicate to others what they are feeling. For example, it is likely easier for them to share their honest reactions when with a close friend as opposed to when with someone to whom they feel attracted. An increased ability to understand their own emotional reactions may also lead some adolescents to have feelings about their feelings or about their emotional displays. Now, the adolescent might feel angry at herself for feeling jealous of someone else's success or she might feel guilty for expressing her anger at her younger sibling. Adolescents also become more adept at communicating their feelings in constructive ways, thereby contributing to the overall quality of their relationships.

There are developmental changes in adolescents' awareness that the expression of emotions plays a significant role in relationships (Saarni, 1999). Adolescents now begin to understand that their emotional expressions may in fact have an effect on others and that they may have inner affective states that do not directly correspond to overt expressions. They are increasingly competent at reading and responding to others' affective states and continue to develop emotion regulation strategies to help cope with their own emotions. With increases in inhibitory control over emotional arousal, adolescents learn to use affective appraisals and expectancies to regulate their emotions (Kober et al., 2008). While their emotions become more intense and labile during adolescence (Dahl, 2001; Rosenblum & Lewis, 2003), these regulation strategies serve to reduce the duration and intensity of their emotional states while helping adolescents to not become overwhelmed by them.

Emotion Regulation in Adolescence

Emotion regulation involves evaluating, monitoring, and modulating emotional reactions so as to meet individual goals and promote adaptive social functioning (Thompson, 1994). The use of emotion regulation strategies impacts the emotional responses manifested, depending upon where the strategies are implemented in the process of managing emotions. Specifically, antecedent-focused strategies are used early in the process, when emotions are first elicited and efforts are made to regulate them before the activation of a complete emotional response. Response-focused strategies, which are generally regarded as less effective regulation strategies, are used after the activation of an emotional response and are directed toward modifying an emotion that has already been activated (Gross & John, 2003; Gross & Thompson, 2007).

Adolescents have already begun to develop the capacity to regulate their emotions. During early childhood, they tend to rely on the assistance and guidance of their parents to help them in this process (Kopp, 1989; Morris et al., 2007) though they also develop behavioral and cognitive skills that gradually help them to manage their emotional reactions more autonomously (Kalpidou et al., 2004). By adolescence, the ability to regulate emotions becomes more independent of parental support, emotion regulation strategies are increasingly more differentiated and varied (Eschenbeck, Kohlmann, & Lohaus, 2007; Gullone, Hughes, King, & Tonge, 2010), and boys and girls differ in the preferred strategies used (Gullone et al., 2010; Perry-Parrish & Zeman, 2011). Recent research has focused on the biological processes involved in regulating emotional reactions. Specifically, maturation of the prefrontal cortex occurs as adolescents move into young adulthood; this may be responsible, in part, for the developmental shift in the capacity for emotion regulation (Casey, Jones, & Somerville, 2011; Gogtay & Thompson, 2010; Thompson et al., 2013). Individual differences in the types of strategies used, the circumstances under which they are employed, and the consequences of these strategies for adolescents' sense of self and for their relationships are areas of continued interest for researchers and clinicians.

Emotion regulation in adolescence is important to understand, as challenges to emotion regulation occur across many different contexts (e.g., family, school, peer group) and much of this regulation influences, and is influenced by, the quality of social relationships (Allen & Manning, 2007). Attachment researchers have explored the ways in which individual differences in attachment during adolescence lead to varying strategies for regulating emotional distress which could, in turn, influence emotional and social adjustment (e.g., Brenning, Soenens, Braet, & Bosmans, 2012). Indeed, many factors, ranging from temperament to early attachment relationships and experiences managing stress and negotiating peer relationships, impact the continuing development of emotion regulation strategies (Allen & Miga, 2010).

Interestingly, emotion regulation has typically been studied by examining single strategies and the associations of these single strategies, such as emotion suppression, to particular psychosocial outcomes, such as heightened emotional responses, disturbances in interpersonal communication, decreased well-being, and difficulties regulating anger (Butler et al., 2003; Gross, 2001; Gross & John, 2003; Szasz, Szentagotai, & Hoffman, 2011). However, most individuals typically adopt a range of emotion regulation strategies (Bonanno, Papa, Lalande, Westphal, & Coifman, 2004). It may be more adaptive to use multiple strategies rather than relying on the exclusive use of only one

(Westphal, Seivert, & Bonanno, 2010). It is important for adolescents to learn that the circumstances may determine which strategies are more effective than others (Campos, Walle, Dahl, & Main, 2011; Halberstadt & Parker, 2007). Therefore, emotion regulation in adolescence may be best viewed as the *adaptive* and *flexible* use of a range of emotion regulation strategies, depending upon the specific situational demands and the desired outcome (Campos et al., 2011; Lougheed & Hollenstein, 2012).

The strategies that are most likely to be used to regulate emotions in adolescence include: *reappraisal*, or the ability to modify the emotional effect of a situation by thinking about it differently; *suppression*, or decreasing both the experience and the expression of emotions (Gullone et al., 2010); *adjusting*, or using emotional information to respond to the demands of a situation or to solve problems (Eschenbeck et al., 2007); *emotional engagement*, or the understanding and acceptance of emotions and the awareness that emotions are manageable (Weinberg & Klonsky, 2009); and *concealing*, or the ability to hide emotions (Perry-Parrish & Zeman, 2011). Research exploring adolescents' simultaneous use of these strategies indicates that distinct profiles of emotion regulation emerge that reflect an organized pattern of dealing with emotionally arousing situations. Additionally, there is an association between these profiles and particular interpersonal outcomes and psychosocial difficulties. In general, adolescents who use a broader range of emotion regulation strategies tend to experience greater psychosocial well-being (Lougheed & Hollenstein, 2012). However, adolescents differ in the range of emotion regulation strategies used, in their flexibility in transitioning between emotional states (which may also be influenced by regulation strategies used), and in their capacity to regulate emotions across different situational contexts (Campos et al., 2011; Halberstadt & Parker, 2007; Hollenstein, 2007; Lougheed & Hollenstein, 2012).

The emotion regulation strategies used by adolescents have also been explored in relation to their role in predicting individual developmental outcomes, with difficulties in emotion regulation identified as a potential risk factor for psychopathology (e.g., Allen & Sheeber, 2008; Barrett, 2013; McLaughlin, Hatzenbuehler, Mennin, & Nolen-Hoeksema, 2011; Zeman, Cassano, & Adrian, 2013). Indeed, most adolescents are increasingly competent at dealing effectively with their fluctuating emotional states and managing challenging personal and interpersonal experiences, thereby developing a certain kind of emotional resourcefulness and resilience. Adolescents need to learn not only what regulatory strategies are adaptive in one context or at one point in time but also how to flexibly adapt in anticipation of future events and demands since what is adaptive in one context or time period may not be in another (Barrett, 2013).

Some adolescents, either because of individual, familial, social, or contextual experiences, may have ongoing emotion regulation difficulties or continue to struggle as they attempt to modulate their emotional responses to psychosocial stressors and developmental challenges. For example, when adolescents are supported and protected to an extreme, where opportunities to be challenged or to struggle are met by parental interventions in the service of reducing frustration and disappointment, adolescents miss out on the chance to manage their own vulnerability with regulatory responses. The "downside of privilege," whether defined by affluence or "helicopter parents" or the availability of a disproportionately high level of access to support, is that these adolescents do not develop adaptive emotion regulation strategies and coping skills (Luthar, 2003; Luthar & Becker, 2002; Luthar & Latendresse, 2002). Without this experience, individuals may be more vulnerable to maladaptive coping efforts and problem solving that may, in turn, interfere with managing their emotions and establishing a positive sense of self (Spencer, 2008).

Consequently, adolescents who do not have the opportunity to be exposed to and learn both adaptive and maladaptive coping responses may be more vulnerable to poor emotional regulation, anxiety, depression, anger, and other psychological problems. Adolescence is a time when we begin to see manifestations of more serious emotional difficulties that warrant intervention. And if these problems are not addressed, they may have a deleterious effect on the adolescent's behavior, leading to academic problems, truancy, delinquency, eating disorders, drug and alcohol abuse, or other serious disorders (Saarni et al., 2006). Future research that explores emotion regulation profiles in larger and more diverse samples, and investigates the emergence and stability of patterns of regulatory strategies used across the entire period of adolescence, will help to further illuminate the role of emotion regulation in managing the self in interpersonal relationships.

The Role of Mentalization in Emotion Regulation

As developmental researchers have explored more deeply the concept of mentalization, they have come to articulate the importance of children's ability to make sense of their own and others' behavior in terms of mental states (Fonagy & Target, 1997) or the ability to think about states of mind and "read people's minds" (Baron-Cohen, Tager-Flusberg, & Cohen, 1993). The behavior of others becomes more meaningful when children and adolescents attribute them to mental states, that is, to their conception of the feelings, thoughts, beliefs, or plans that lead to certain behaviors. With development, adolescents continue to use their understanding of others' mental states to help them determine their own adaptive response in interpersonal interactions. They do this by drawing on representations of the self and others that have been formed from prior experiences (Fonagy & Target, 1997). Developing the ability to derive meaning in others' behaviors and psychological experiences (usually beginning in the parent–child relationship) precedes the child's learning to meaningfully interpret and label their own (Fonagy, Steele, Steele, Moran, et al., 1991). Thus, the capacity to mentalize, a key determinant of self-organization, is acquired in the context of early attachment relationships (Fonagy, 2006). Emotionally attuned parents mirror their child's internal states, reflecting on and expressing emotions that the child then gradually comes to see as mental states that can be recognized, accepted, and shared. Ultimately, understanding one's own and others' mental states provides a foundation for "affect regulation, impulse control, self-monitoring, and the experience of self-agency, the building blocks of the organization of the self" (Fonagy & Target, 1997, p. 680). The cognitive capacity for mentalization, therefore, provides the foundation and structure for defining features of the developing self (Fonagy et al., 2002).

Mentalization allows children and adolescents to monitor and regulate their emotional and behavioral responses and to enhance self-understanding. Indeed, while many factors may influence parental mentalization (including, for example, child temperament, parental psychopathology, stressful life events), parental mentalization may also influence children's and adolescents' developing emotional regulation abilities. Longitudinal studies of children and adolescents will illuminate the more complex mechanisms involved when reduced mentalization capacities lead to deficient emotion regulation processes, perhaps putting the adolescent at risk for developing psychopathology (Fonagy, 1991; Fonagy et al., 2002; Sharp & Fonagy, 2008; Sharp et al., 2011).

Additionally, the capacity to understand others' emotional states and to use affective mentalizing skills enhances the ability to empathize with others and promotes successful interpersonal exchanges (Shamay-Tsoory, Tomer, Goldsher, Berger, & Aharon-Peretz, 2004). That is, in order to empathize with another person, it is necessary to infer or imagine the emotional experience of that person. This affective representation of the other's emotional experience can then be used to observe, understand, and share their own emotional response as well as to motivate prosocial behavior. Indeed, recent research indicates that neural activity in those brain regions related to mentalizing and emotion (specifically, the medial prefrontal cortex, temporal poles, somatosensory-related cortices, inferior frontal gyrus, and thalamus) are also involved when making predictions about future emotional responses. There is greater neural activity in the primary emotion-related regions of the brain as well, including the bilateral thalamus and the right somatosensory-related cortices, when predicting others' emotional responses and completing self-reported empathy measures (Hooker, Verosky, Germine, Knight, & D'Esposito, 2008). Enhanced neural responsivity in those structures involved in emotion processing appears to be linked to both internal representations of affect, which promote the understanding of the self and others' thoughts and feelings, and to empathic responsiveness. Thus, self-awareness and the awareness of others' mental states are closely associated in terms of the brain areas involved (Fonagy, 2006). Attempts to understand the emotional experiences of others may be facilitated by particular neural systems responsible for generating and using affective information that, in turn, lead to greater empathy and improved interpersonal relationships. In sum, we see that the capacity for mentalization organizes the self, is associated with emotion regulation, and is critical to adaptive social relationships.

Emotion Regulation and Empathy in Adolescence

Empathy is the ability to understand and experience the feelings of others as they are experiencing those feelings themselves. Researchers have provided compelling evidence for the evolutionary roots of empathic behaviors, as empathic responses are observable across species where cooperative kin relationships are present and where empathy is seen to have important benefits for survival (de Waal, 2008). The neuroanatomy of empathic skills has been studied as well. Investigators exploring the activation of mirror neurons provided cellular evidence for the experience and understanding of others' feelings (di Pellegrino, Fadiga, Fogassi, Gallese, & Rizzolatti, 1992), though more recent fMRI studies on empathy have not found consistent evidence of mirror neuron regions activated during the performance of an empathy task (Fan, Duncan, DeGreck, & Northoff, 2011). Still, many question the precision of studies examining the neuroscience of empathy as more complex cognitive and affective processes are involved in the psychological experience of empathy. Psychologists are therefore more interested in processes involved in empathic responsiveness, such as theory of mind, affective sharing, and self-and-other differentiation, whereas neuroimaging studies, until recently, focused more on associations between stimuli and brain activity and less on behavioral responses. Advances in recent neuroscience research, such as some studies using naturalistic social-cognitive paradigms and others exploring brain–behavior links, will contribute to greater understanding of the neural processes involved in empathic understanding (Zaki & Ochsner, 2012).

The capacity to be empathic is related to perspective-taking abilities (Findlay, Girardi, & Coplan, 2006) and prosocial behavior (Eisenberg, 2000). Moreover, empathy is negatively associated with aggressive behavior (Hastings et al., 2000) and bullying (Caravita, DiBlasio, & Salmivalli, 2009). Thus, empathy has been described as a necessary condition for socially competent behavior (Wölfer, Cortina, & Baumert, 2012). Despite the fact that there is a strong theoretical justification for a link between the quality of social relationships and the capacity to express empathy, there is little research that has specifically investigated this association in adolescence. The mother–infant relationship has been explored as an important context for children's developing social understanding (Carpendale & Lewis, 2004; Saarni, 1990). Attachment processes and emotion regulation have been linked to one another and to empathy. In particular, because attachment figures serve the role of helping infants to manage their frustration, distress, and other negative emotions, they consequently promote the development of the regulatory processes that may lead to empathy.

Interestingly, researchers have demonstrated that the regulation of pain plays an important role in the development of empathy (Tucker, Luu, & Derryberry, 2005). As significant progress has been made in understanding the neural mechanisms that may help to shape psychological capacities, evidence has supported the patterns of activation of brain structures, such as the amygdala and cingulate cortex, that are involved in the regulation of pain. The pain pathway has been found to extend into the cortex, including the anterior cingulate cortex and the orbitofrontal cortex, and the mechanisms used in more complex self-regulation appear to be extensions of the same mechanisms that evolved for evaluating and reacting to pain (Tucker et al., 2005). Thus, a model for understanding empathy may involve the neural structures related to pain evaluation, recognition of another's affect, and the capacity to tolerate negative states. The neural processes that evolved from the pain system may, in turn, be linked to the brain structures involved in self-regulation. Additionally, sensitive parenting may help children develop the self-regulatory abilities that modulate the pain system involved in attachment and the development of empathy (Tucker et al., 2005). Indeed, sensitive and supportive parenting and secure attachment relationships have been linked to higher levels of self-regulation in children (Eisenberg, Smith, Sadovsky, Spinrad, 2004), as well as to empathy (Eisenberg, Fabes, et al., 2006) and understanding of others' internal states and emotions (Thompson, 2006). Neurologically based self-regulatory processes, therefore, appear to be critical for empathic responding.

Only recently has research on the social experiences that promote empathic responsiveness been extended into adolescence, even though the required social knowledge that underlies empathy is likely to continue to be constructed from both early and current social interactions. There is a substantial body of research that supports the value of social connections, especially during adolescence, when peer status and social relationships are vitally important (LaFontana & Cillessen, 2009). Social isolation and physical danger appear to activate the same pain-inducing, neurocognitive threat system (Eisenberger, Lieberman, & Williams, 2003). Moreover, the adolescent's expanding social network introduces increased demands for cooperation and support, managing conflicts, and regulating relationships, thereby enhancing social skills as well as providing opportunities for their further development. Less socially involved adolescents miss opportunities to develop social understanding (Parker & Asher, 1987), whereas involvement with peers helps to shape empathic responses. In particular, perception of another person's behavior appears to activate the individual's own internal representation of this behavior. "State-matching" responses in the motor areas of the brain, over many interactions across diverse situations, enhance an individual's capacity to experience and understand the other (Preston & de Waal, 2002). With increased social experiences, the quantity and quality of shared representations of the other are enhanced and empathic processes are improved (Wölfer et al., 2012).

Indeed, small-to-moderate associations have been found between adolescents' peer relationships and some aspects of empathy, such as empathic accuracy (Gleason, Jenson-Campbell, & Ickes, 2009) and emotional intelligence (Ciarrochi, Chan, & Bajgar, 2001). Additionally, empathy has been explored in relation to the social demands and friendship patterns of adolescents. These experiences have been found to shape social understanding and empathic skills (Oberle, Schonert-Reichl, & Thomson, 2009; Wölfer et al., 2012) and, in turn, empathy likely influences the quality of social relationships. Social exclusion has been found to cause a lack of empathy (DeWall & Baumeister, 2006) and to interfere with the capacity for empathic understanding (Twenge, Baumeister, DeWall, Ciarocco, & Bartels, 2007). And adolescent girls, in particular, appear to be more integrated into their social networks; the need to manage increased social demands may impact their developing empathic skills and ultimately lead to improved social understanding (Wölfer et al., 2012). Alternatively, there are contextual factors (e.g., the peer group, the school context) that may lead some strongly integrated adolescents to direct their higher social understanding into aggressive, as opposed to prosocial, behavior. Exploring these adaptive and maladaptive developmental pathways in future empirical investigations has important implications for clinical intervention (Rodkin, Farmer, Pearly, & Van Acker, 2006; Wölfer et al., 2012).

In sum, the capacity to be empathic is contingent on both affective and cognitive competencies. Empathic behavior is highly influenced by age and dependent on individual and contextual factors (Feshbach, 1975, 1978). The related capacities to discriminate the other's emotional state, to experience the other's emotions in an appropriate manner, and to take on the perspective of the other are all directly linked to the emerging self and critical to the development of empathy in adolescence.

The Self, Empathy, Moral Emotions, and Moral Behavior

Understanding the self has been highlighted as a prerequisite for empathic responsiveness and moral behavior, both by psychologists (e.g., Blasi, 1983, 1984; Damon & Hart, 1992, 1995; Lewis, 2002; Wegner, 1980) and philosophers (Flanagan, 1991). While empathy is not a discrete emotion, it is an emotional process that has consequences for moral behavior (Tangney, Stuewig, & Mashek, 2007). Self-awareness has been viewed as a necessary condition before inferences may be made about the mental and emotional states of others (Gallup, 1982). Indeed, research with children has revealed that visual self-recognition is related to the understanding of others' feelings and the emergence of prosocial and altruistic behavior (Carruthers & Smith, 1996; Johnson, 1982). Studies of individuals who are deficient or delayed in mirror self-recognition reveal their difficulties in understanding what others are thinking (Frith, 1997; Gallup & Platek, 2002; Platek & Gallup, 2002; Spiker & Ricks, 1984). Additionally, individuals with "empathy disorders," such as autism, sociopathy, and even anorexia nervosa, have impairments in the ability to express emotions, verbalize feelings, and conceptualize mental states. Brain area dysfunctions in the prefrontal system have been found in individuals with these disorders; these are the same brain areas found to be involved in empathy (Gillberg, 1992, 1999; Preston & de Waal, 2002). Thus, there appear to be links between self-understanding and the higher order perspective-taking abilities involved in empathy and moral behavior and these may have similar neural correlates (Keenan & Wheeler, 2002).

There is evidence supporting the idea that empathic behavior develops in a sequential manner through adolescence and may be hierarchically organized to incorporate cognitive changes that occur in understanding the self and others (see, for example, Commons & Wolfsont, 2002). Moral emotions, such as shame and guilt, appear to be well established by middle childhood and to have consequences for moral behavior as well (Tangney & Dearing, 2002). Though much of the extant work on moral emotions has been based on North American and Western European cultures, a growing body of research indicates that guilt and shame may take multiple forms, both across and within cultural groups (see, for example, Li, Wang, & Fischer, 2004; Mascolo, Fischer, & Li, 2002; Scheff, 2000). These self-conscious emotions influence, and are influenced by, early socialization experiences as well as the adolescent's developing capacity to evaluate and regulate the self within his/her social context. Accordingly, the organization of the self-conscious emotions has profound implications for the adolescent's adjustment.

Shame- and guilt-proneness reflect dispositional tendencies to experience these self-conscious emotions across a range of situations (Tangney et al., 2007). What is it that makes an adolescent prone to shame or guilt? It appears that certain experiences make some individuals more likely to anticipate shame or guilt in response to particular triggers, behaviors, or situations; when a failure or transgression actually does occur, these individuals are more likely, relative to their less shame- or guilt-prone peers, to experience intense feelings of shame or guilt. While there are multiple pathways to developing these self-conscious emotions, insensitive parenting and problems with emotion regulation may set the stage for later difficulties (Mascolo & Fischer, 2007). For example, proneness to shame-free guilt (guilt-proneness) has been linked to high levels of externalizing behaviors in girls but to low levels of externalizing behaviors in boys (Ferguson et al., 1999). Among adolescents, negative associations between proneness to shame-free guilt and delinquency have also been found (Stuewig & McCloskey, 2005). And fifth graders who were prone to shame-free guilt were less likely to be arrested, convicted, and incarcerated in adolescence. Moreover, they were less likely to abuse drugs and more likely to practice safe sex (Tangney & Dearing, 2002). Guilt-proneness in college students is negatively related to risky behavior (Tangney, 1994) and self-reported criminal activity (Tibbetts, 2003), and college students who are prone to guilt are less likely to abuse alcohol and drugs (Dearing, Stuewig, & Tangney, 2005).

Interestingly, in contrast to guilt, shame does not serve the same inhibitory function in children, adolescents, or college students (Stuewig & McCloskey, 2005; Tangney, Wagner, Hill-Barlow, Marschall, & Gramzow, 1996). Rather, shame-prone individuals are actually more vulnerable to a variety of difficulties, including low self-esteem (Woien, Ernst, Patock-Peckham, & Nagoshi, 2003), problems managing anger (Hoglund & Nicholas, 1995), and psychological difficulties (Tangney et al., 1995). Shame-proneness in fifth graders predicts early alcohol and drug use, a decreased likelihood of practicing safe sex, and risky driving in adolescence (Tangney & Dearing, 2002). And shame-proneness is associated with drug and alcohol abuse in adulthood (Dearing et al., 2005).

Feelings of shame involve a global negative feeling about the self, usually in response to some shortcoming or misdeed. Shame can be debilitating to one's core sense of self (Lewis, 1971) and may involve a self-defeating cycle of negative affect, blaming the other, and/or engaging in self-defeating activities such as drug or alcohol abuse. All of these reactions are intended to dampen the painful affects associated with shame. Shame, with its focus on the self as defective, has also been found to impair empathic abilities which can, in turn, lead to a range of interpersonal problems (Leith & Baumeister, 1998). By contrast, feelings of guilt involve negative emotions about an event, rather than about the self (Lewis, 1971). While painful, guilt appears to be less disabling than shame, often encouraging the individual to engage in more positive behavior intended to repair or remediate a situation (Baumeister, Stillwell, & Heatherton, 1995). Consequently, just as we observed in younger children, guilt may be effective in motivating moral behavior, leading adolescents and adults to accept personal responsibility and to act in constructive ways. Indeed, research indicates that proneness to shame-free guilt is not related to psychological symptoms (Tangney et al., 1995). Rather, shame-free guilt is positively associated with appropriate responses to anger (Tangney, 1995) and enhanced empathic responsiveness (Leith & Baumeister, 1998). Therefore, shame and guilt are examples of two moral emotions that impact personal and moral behavior in varying ways. The capacity for guilt is more likely to foster moral behavior, making it the "moral emotion of choice" when considering its impact on the self and relationships (Tangney et al., 2007).

There are distinct physiological correlates that have been identified that correspond to experiences of shame in adolescents and adults. For example, increased proinflammatory cytokine activity has been found to occur following laboratory manipulations designed to increase self-reported shame (Dickerson, Kemeny, Aziz, Kim, & Fahey, 2004). Cortisol levels have been found to increase significantly in individuals tested in shame-eliciting situations (Gruenewald, Kemeny, Aziz, & Fahey, 2004). And cardiovascular changes have been observed in participants' reactions to laboratory conditions designed to elicit shame (Herrald & Tomaka, 2002). Although these results were obtained in laboratory settings, the findings have important implications for understanding clinicians' reports of the heightened experience of shame in adolescent and adult patients who experienced early trauma. The secretive and hidden nature of maltreatment elicits profound feelings of shame (Deblinger & Runyon, 2005). Indeed, recent empirical studies support these clinical observations. Adolescents of punitive and authoritarian parents, who use insults and are emotionally abusive to their children, are vulnerable to feeling high levels of shame (Tangney & Dearing, 2002). Patients with early histories of emotional, physical, and/or sexual abuse continue, as adolescents and adults, to struggle with profound shame (see Tangney et al., 2007, for a review) and are much more vulnerable to autoimmune and stress-related illnesses and poor psychological outcomes.

Finally, pride is the more positive moral emotion that is often experienced when the individual feels s/he is socially valued as a person or responsible for some outcome for which s/he is responsible (Mascolo & Fischer, 1995). Pride is often felt in contexts where there has been some achievement (e.g., academic, athletic, professional). However, pride may also be a very powerful motivator in morally relevant situations where control over emotions, inhibition of immoral impulses, or meeting appropriate and valued behavioral or emotional standards are accomplished. Thus, the achievement of some desired emotional outcome might lead to feelings of pride. Distinctions have been made by some researchers between pride in one's behavior and pride in the self. The extent to which individual differences in pride are associated with the capacity to regulate the self or to engage in moral behavior has not been studied extensively. Some researchers speculate that using feelings of pride for self-serving purposes, to express dominance or power, to enhance the self, or to boost esteem (i.e., "hubris" (Lewis, 1992b; Tracy & Robins, 2004)) may lead to interpersonal difficulties (Tangney et al., 2007). However, feelings of pride may also motivate prosocial behavior, such as cooperation, caregiving, and achievement. Thus, pride may be an important moral emotion to explore further. Pride, similar to the moral emotions of shame and guilt, has implications for adolescent moral behavior and decision making. In sum, the experience and expression of these moral emotions are influenced by important cognitive, social, and emotional factors and, in turn, impact adolescents' social and emotional functioning.

What Comes Next in Emerging Adulthood?

The development of attachment relationships and the consolidation of the self in adolescence together lay the groundwork for what lies ahead in emerging adulthood. Certainly, the issues that we have considered throughout this book remain critical as adolescents in their late teens and early twenties navigate new relational and individual challenges. In fact, concerns about attachment relationships and the evolving self persist throughout the lifespan, alternating between the foreground and the background of our everyday lives. The different stages of adulthood bring many new questions about relational commitments, educational goals, job uncertainties, babies and parenting, work and family, housing and health, aging parents, professional growth, and ongoing connections to siblings and friends. Old conflicts reemerge, new problems arise, individuals struggle, and relationships are transformed. There are a multitude of ways in which we all come to manage the many issues that need to be resolved within the two interrelated developmental tasks of balancing attachments to others and the developing self. It is now clear that while conceptualized as two separate strands of development, they are actually inextricably linked: good quality relationships generally support the development of the self, just as a clear sense of self contributes to emotionally significant attachment relationships. Alternatively, difficulties in attachment relationships compromise the developing self, leaving the individual vulnerable to emotional difficulties and relational challenges.

Attention to the precursors and consequences of both attachment relationships and the consolidation of the self in emerging adulthood continues to be important to researchers and clinicians who want to understand the trajectories of adaptive and maladaptive solutions to these developmental tasks. Ultimately, the journey we all travel from infancy through adolescence and eventually into adulthood serves as a reminder that the very issues we navigate when we come into the world continue to foreshadow what lies ahead. And as we find our way in the balance between relational connections and our ever-evolving understanding of the self, we often draw on what has come before. We may re-enact old experiences or chart a new course. There are myriad possibilities for continuity or change, even in the face of unanticipated challenges and stresses, as we transform attachments and rediscover the self on the developmental path we all travel across the lifespan.

References

Abe, J. A., & Izard, C. E. (1999). The developmental functions of emotions: An analysis in terms of differential emotions theory. *Cognition and Emotion, 13,* 523–549.

Abel, M. R. (2014). *Authenticity in adolescents and young adults' relationships: The roles of emotion regulation and perceived parental feedback.* Unpublished manuscript, Wellesley College, Wellesley, MA.

Aboud, F. E., & Janani, S. (2007). Friendship and identity in a language-integrated school. *International Journal of Behavioral Development, 31,* 445–453.

Aboud, F. E., Mendelson, M. J., & Purdy, K. T. (2003). Cross-race peer relations and friendship quality. *International Journal of Behavioral Development, 27,* 165–173.

Abraham, E., Hendler, T., Shapira-Lichter, I., Kanat-Maymon, Y., Zagoory-Sharon, O., & Feldman, R. (2014). Father's brain is sensitive to childcare experiences. *Proceedings of the National Academy of Sciences, 111,* 9792–9797

Abramovitch, R., Corter, C., & Lando, B. (1979). Sibling interaction in the home. *Child Development, 50,* 997–1003.

Abramovitch, R., Corter, C., Pepler, D. J., & Stanhope, L. (1986). Sibling and peer interaction: A final follow-up and a comparison. *Child Development, 57,* 217–229.

Adams, G. R., & Archer, S. L. (1994). Identity: A precursor to intimacy. In S. L. Archer (Ed.), *Interventions for adolescent identity development* (pp. 193–213). Thousand Oaks, CA: Sage Publications.

Adams, R., & Laursen, B. (2001). The organization and dynamics of adolescent conflict with parents and friends. *Journal of Marriage and Family, 63,* 97–110.

Adler, A. (1927). *Understanding human nature: The psychology of personality.* New York, NY: Greenberg.

Adler, A. (1964). *Problems of neurosis.* New York, NY: Harper and Row.

Adler, P. A., & Adler, P. (1998). *Peer power: Preadolescent culture and identity.* New Brunswick, NJ: Rutgers University Press.

Adolph, K. E., & Berger, S. E. (2010). Physical and motor development. In M. H. Bornstein & M. E. Lamb (Eds.), *Developmental science: An advanced textbook* (6th ed., pp. 241–302). Hove: Psychology Press.

Adrian, M., Zeman, J., & Veits, G. (2011). Methodological implications of the affect revolution: A 35-year review of emotion regulation assessment in children. *Journal of Experimental Child Psychology, 110,* 171–197.

Aguilar, B., O'Brien, K. M., August, G. J., Aoun, S. L., & Hektner, J. M. (2001). Relationship quality of aggressive children and their siblings: A multiinformant, multimeasure investigation. *Journal of Abnormal Child Psychology, 29,* 479–489.

Ahadi, S. A., & Rothbart, M. K. (1994). Temperament, development, and the big five. In C. F. Halverson, G. A. Kohnstamm, & R. P. Martin (Eds.), *The developing structure of temperament and personality from infancy to adulthood* (pp. 189–207). Hillsdale, NJ: Erlbaum.

Ahadi, S. A., Rothbart, M. K., & Ye, R. (1993). Children's temperament in the United States and China: Similarities and differences. *European Journal of Personality, 7,* 359–378.

Ahnert, L., Pinquart, M., & Lamb, M. E. (2006). Security of children's relationships with nonparental care providers: A meta-analysis. *Child Development, 74,* 664–679.

Aikins, J. W., Bierman, K. L., & Parker, J. G. (2005). Navigating the transition to junior high school: The influence of pre-transition friendship and self-system characteristics. *Social Development, 14,* 42–60.

Aikins, J. W., Howes, C., & Hamilton, C. (2009). Attachment stability and the emergence of unresolved representations during adolescence. *Attachment & Human Development, 11,* 491–512.

Ainsworth, M. D. S. (1963). The development of infant–mother interaction among the Ganda. In B. M. Foss (Ed.), *Determinants of infant behavior* (Vol. 2, pp. 67–112). New York, NY: Wiley.

Ainsworth, M. D. S. (1967). *Infancy in Uganda: Infant care and the growth of love.* Baltimore, MD: Johns Hopkins University Press.

Ainsworth, M. D. S. (1969). Object relations, dependency, and attachment: A theoretical review of the infant–mother relationship. *Child Development, 40,* 969–1025.

Ainsworth, M. D. S. (1972). Attachment and dependency: A comparison. In J. L. Gewirtz (Ed.), *Attachment and dependency* (pp. 97–137). Washington, DC: V.H. Winston.

Ainsworth, M. D. S. (1982). Attachment: Retrospect and prospect. In C. M. Parkes & J. Stevenson-Hinde (Eds.), *The place of attachment in human behavior* (pp. 3–30). New York, NY: Basic Books.

Ainsworth, M. D. S. (1989). Attachments beyond infancy. *American Psychologist, 44,* 709–716.

Ainsworth, M. D. S. (1990). Epilogue: Some considerations regarding theory and assessment relevant to attachments beyond infancy. In M. T. Greenberg, D. Cicchetti, & E. M. Cummings (Eds.), *Attachment in the preschool years: Theory, research, and intervention* (pp. 463–488). Chicago, IL: University of Chicago Press.

Ainsworth, M. D. S. (1991). Attachments and other affectional bonds across the life cycle. In C. M. Parkes, J. Stevenson-Hinde, & P. Marris (Eds.), *Attachment across the life cycle* (pp. 33–51). London: Routledge.

Ainsworth, M. D. S., Bell, S. M., & Stayton, D. J. (1971). Individual differences in Strange Situation behavior of one-year-olds. In H. R. Schaffer (Ed.), *The origins of human social relations* (pp. 17–52). New York, NY: Academic Press.

Ainsworth, M. D. S., Blehar, M., Waters, E., & Wall, S. (1978). *Patterns of attachment: A psychological study of the Strange Situation.* Hillsdale, NJ: Erlbaum.

Aksan, N., & Kochanska, G. (2005). Conscience in childhood: Old questions, new answers. *Developmental Psychology, 41,* 506–516.

Aksan, N., Kochanska, G., & Ortmann, M. R. (2006). Mutually responsive orientation between parents and their young children: Toward methodological advances in the science of relationships. *Developmental Psychology, 42,* 833–848.

Aldous, J., & Mulligan, G. M. (2002). Fathers' child care and children's behavior problems. *Journal of Family Issues, 23,* 624–647.

Allen, J. P. (2008). The attachment system in adolescence. In J. Cassidy & P. R. Shaver (Eds.), *Handbook of attachment: Theory, research, and clinical applications* (2nd ed., pp. 419–435). New York, NY: Guilford Press.

Allen, J. P., Chango, J., & Szwedo, D. (2014). The adolescent relational dialectic and the peer roots of adult social functioning. *Child Development, 85,* 192–204.

Allen, J. P., Chango, J., Szwedo, D., Schad, M., & Marston, E. (2012). Predictors of susceptibility to peer influence regarding substance use in adolescence. *Child Development, 83,* 337–350.

Allen, J. P., Hauser, S. T., Bell, K. L., & O'Connor, T. G. (1994). Longitudinal assessment of autonomy and relatedness in adolescent–family interactions as predictors of adolescent ego development and self-esteem. *Child Development, 65,* 179–194.

Allen, J. P., & Land, D. (1999). Attachment in adolescence. In J. Cassidy & P. R. Shaver (Eds.), *Handbook of attachment: Theory, research, and clinical applications* (pp. 319–335). New York, NY: Guilford Press.

Allen, J. P., & Loeb, E. L. (2015). The autonomy-connection challenge in adolescent peer relationships. *Child Development Perspectives, 9,* 101–105.

Allen, J. P., & Manning, N. (2007). From safety to affect regulation: Attachment from the vantage point of adolescence. *New Directions for Child and Adolescent Development, 117,* 23–39.

Allen, J. P., Marsh, P., McFarland, C., McElhaney, K. B., Land, D. J., Jodl, K. M., & Peck, S. (2002). Attachment and autonomy as predictors of the development of social skills and delinquency during midadolescence. *Journal of Consulting and Clinical Psychology, 70,* 56–66.

Allen, J. P., McElhaney, K. B., Kuperminc, G. P., & Jodl, K. M. (2004). Stability and change in attachment security across adolescence. *Child Development, 75,* 1792–1805.

Allen, J. P., McElhaney, K. B., Land, D. J., Kuperminc, G. P., Moore, C. M., O'Beirne-Kelley, H., & Kilmer, S. L. (2003). A secure base in adolescence: Markers of attachment security in the mother–adolescent relationship. *Child Development, 74,* 292–307.

Allen, J. P., & Miga, E. M. (2010). Attachment in adolescence: A move to the level of emotion regulation. *Journal of Social and Personal Relationships, 27,* 181–190.

Allen, J. P., Moore, C., Kuperminc, G., & Bell, K. (1998). Attachment and adolescent psychosocial functioning. *Child Development, 69,* 1406–1419.

Allen, J. P., Porter, M., McFarland, C., McElhaney, K. B., & Marsh, P. (2007). The relation of attachment security to adolescents' paternal and peer relationships, depression, and externalizing behavior. *Child Development, 78,* 1222–1239.

Allen, J. P., Schad, M. M., Oudekerk, B., & Chango, J. (2014). What ever happened to the "cool" kids? Long-term sequelae of early adolescent pseudomature behavior. *Child Development, 85,* 1866–1880.

Allen, N. B., & Sheeber, L. B. (2008). The importance of affective development for the emergence of depressive disorder during adolescence. In N. B. Allen & L. B. Sheeber (Eds.), *Adolescent emotional development and the emergence of depressive disorders* (pp. 1–10). Cambridge: Cambridge University Press.

Allen, S. M., & Hawkins, A. J. (1999). Maternal gatekeeping: Mothers' beliefs and behaviors that inhibit greater father involvement in family work. *Journal of Marriage and Family, 61,* 199–212.

Alsaker, F., & Olweus, D. (1992). Stability of global self-evaluations in early adolescence: A cohort longitudinal study. *Journal of Research on Adolescence, 1,* 123–145.

American Psychiatric Association. (2013). *Diagnostic and statistical manual of mental disorders* (5th ed.). Washington, DC: Author.

Ammaniti, M., van IJzendoorn, M. H., Speranza, A. M., & Tambelli, R. (2000). Internal working models of attachment during late childhood and early adolescence: An exploration of stability and change. *Attachment & Human Development, 2,* 328–346.

Amodio, D. M., & Frith, C. D. (2006). Meeting of minds: The medial frontal cortex and social cognition. *Nature Reviews Neuroscience, 7,* 268–277.

Amsterdam, B. (1972). Mirror self-image reactions before age two. *Developmental Psychology, 5,* 297–305.

Amsterdam, B., & Greenberg, L. M. (1977). Self-conscious behavior of infants: A videotape study. *Developmental Psychobiology, 10,* 1–6.

Anan, R. N., & Barnett, D. (1999). Perceived social support mediates between prior attachment and subsequent adjustment: A study of urban African American children. *Developmental Psychology, 35,* 1210–1222.

Andersen, S. M., & Chen, S. (2002). The relational self: An interpersonal social-cognitive theory. *Psychological Review, 109,* 619–645.

Anderson, V., Anderson, P., Northam, E., Jacobs, R., & Catroppa, C. (2001). Development of executive functions through late childhood and adolescence in an Australian sample. *Developmental Neuropsychology, 20,* 385–406.

Ansbacher, H. L., & Ansbacher, R. R. (Eds.). (1956). *The individual psychology of Alfred Adler: A systematic presentation in selections from his writings.* Oxford: Basic Books, Inc.

Archer, S. L. (1982). The lower age boundaries of identity development. *Child Development, 53,* 1551–1556.

Archibald, A. B., Graber, J. A., & Brooks-Gunn, J. (2003). Pubertal processes and physiological growth in adolescence. In G. R. Adams & M. D. Berzonsky (Eds.), *Blackwell handbook of adolescence* (pp. 24–47). Oxford: Blackwell.

Arim, R. G., & Shapka, J. D. (2008). The impact of pubertal timing and parental control on adolescent problem behaviors. *Journal of Youth and Adolescence, 37,* 445–455.

Arim, R. G., Tramonte, L., Shapka, J. D., Dahinten, V. S., & Willms, J. D. (2011). The family antecedents and the subsequent outcomes of early puberty. *Journal of Youth and Adolescence, 40,* 1423–1435.

Armony, J. L. (2013). Current emotion research in behavioral neuroscience: The role(s) of the amygdala. *Emotion Review, 5,* 104–115.

Armsden, G. C., & Greenberg, M. T. (1987). The Inventory of Parent and Peer Attachment: Individual differences and their relationship to psychological well-being in adolescence. *Journal of Youth and Adolescence, 16*, 427–454.

Armsden, G. C., & Greenberg, M. T. (2009). *Inventory of Parent and Peer Attachment.* Unpublished manuscript, Pennsylvania State University, State College, PA.

Arnett, J. J. (1999). Adolescent storm and stress, reconsidered. *American Psychologist, 54*, 317–326.

Arnett, J. J. (2000). Emerging adulthood: A theory of development from the late teens through the twenties. *American Psychologist, 55*, 469–480.

Arnett, J. J. (2004). *Emerging adulthood: The winding road from the late teens through the twenties.* New York, NY: Oxford University Press.

Arnett, J. J. (2007). Emerging adulthood: What is it, and what is it good for? *Child Development Perspectives, 1*, 68–73.

Arnett, J. J., & Fishel, E. (2013). *When will my grown-up kid grow up? Loving and understanding your emerging adult.* New York, NY: Workman Publishing.

Aron, A., Fisher, H., Mashek, D. J., Strong, G., Li, H., & Brown, L. L. (2005). Reward, motivation, and emotion systems associated with early-stage intense romantic love. *Journal of Neurophysiology, 94*, 327–337.

Arsenio, W. F., & Lemerise, E. A. (2004). Aggression and moral development: Integrating social information processing and moral domain models. *Child Development, 75*, 987–1002.

Årseth, A. K., Kroger, J., Martinussen, M., & Marcia, J. E. (2009). Meta-analytic studies of identity status and the relational issues of attachment and intimacy. *Identity, 9*, 1–32.

Asher, S. R., & Paquette, J. A. (2003). Loneliness and peer relations in childhood. *Current Directions in Psychological Science, 12*, 75–78.

Astington, J. W., Harris, P. L., & Olson, D. R. (1988). *Developing theories of mind.* New York, NY: Cambridge University Press.

Atkinson, L., Niccols, A., Paglia, A., Coolbear, J., Parker, K. C. H., Poulton, L., ... Sitarenios, G. (2000). A meta-analysis of time between maternal sensitivity and attachment assessments: Implications for internal working models in infancy/toddlerhood. *Journal of Social and Personal Relationships, 17*, 791–810.

Atzaba-Poria, N., & Pike, A. (2008). Correlates of parental differential treatment: Parental and contextual factors during middle childhood. *Child Development, 79*, 217–232.

Atzil, S., Hendler, T., & Feldman, R. (2011). Specifying the neurobiological basis of human attachment: Brains, hormones, and behavior in synchronous and intrusive mothers. *Neuropsychopharmacology, 36*, 22603–22615.

Atzil, S., Hendler, T., Zagoory-Sharon, O., Weintraub, Y., & Feldman, R. (2012). Synchrony and specificity in the maternal and paternal brain: Relations to oxytocin and vasopressin. *Journal of the American Academy of Child and Adolescent Psychiatry, 51*, 798–811.

Ávila, M., Cabral, J., & Matos, P. M. (2012). Identity in university students: The role of parental and romantic attachment. *Journal of Adolescence, 35*, 133–142.

Ayoub, C. C., O'Connor, E., Rappolt-Schlichtmann, G., Fischer, K. W., Rogosch, F. A., Toth, S. L., & Cicchetti, D. (2006). Cognitive and emotional differences in young maltreated children: A translational application of dynamic skill theory. *Development and Psychopathology, 18*, 679–706.

Azmitia, M. (2002). Self, self esteem, conflicts, and best friendships in early adolescence. In T. M. Brinthaupt & R. P. Lipka (Eds.), *Understanding early adolescent self and identity: Applications and interventions* (pp. 167–192). Albany, NY: University of New York Press.

Bagwell, C. L., Bender, S. E., Andreassi, C. L., Kinoshita, T. L., Montarello, S. A., & Muller, J. G. (2005). Friendship quality and perceived relationship changes predict psychosocial adjustment in early adulthood. *Journal of Social and Personal Relationships, 22*, 235–354.

Bagwell, C. L., Coie, J. D., Terry, R. A., & Lochman, J. E. (2000). Peer clique participation and social status in preadolescence. *Merrill-Palmer Quarterly, 46*, 280–305.

Bagwell, C. L., Newcomb, A., & Bukowski, W. M. (1998). Preadolescent friendship and rejection as predictors of adult adjustment. *Child Development, 69*, 140–153.

Bagwell, C. L., & Schmidt, M. E. (2011). *Friendships in childhood and adolescence.* New York, NY: Guilford Press.

Bagwell, C. L., Schmidt, M. E., & Bukowski, W. M. (1998). Preadolescent friendship and peer rejection as predictors of adult adjustment. *Child Development, 69,* 140–153.

Bagwell, C. L., Schmidt, M. E., Newcomb, A. F., & Bukowski, W. M. (2001). Friendship and peer rejection as predictors of adult adjustment. *New Directions for Child and Adolescent Development, 91,* 25–49.

Baillargeon, R., Scott, R. M., & He, Z. (2010). False-belief understanding in infants. *Trends in Cognitive Sciences, 14,* 110–118.

Bakermans-Kranenburg, M. J., van IJzendoorn, M. H., Pijlman, F. T. A., Mesman, J., & Juffer, F. (2008). Experimental evidence for differential susceptibility: Dopamine D4 receptor polymorphism (DRD4 VNTR) moderates intervention effects on toddlers' externalizing behavior in a randomized controlled trial. *Developmental Psychology, 44,* 293–300.

Baldwin, S. A., & Hoffmann, J. P. (2002). The dynamics of self-esteem: A growth-curve analysis. *Journal of Youth and Adolescence, 31,* 101–113.

Bandstra, N. F., Chambers, C. T., McGrath, P., & Moore, C. (2011). The behavioral expression of empathy to others' pain versus others' sadness in young children. *Pain, 152,* 1074–1082.

Bandura, A. (1977). *Social learning theory.* Englewood Cliffs, NJ: Prentice Hall.

Banerjee, M. (1997). Hidden emotions: Preschoolers' knowledge of appearance-reality and emotion display rules. *Social Cognition, 15,* 107–132.

Bank, L., Burraston, B., & Snyder, J. (2004). Sibling conflict and ineffective parenting as predictors of boys' antisocial behavior and peer difficulties: Additive and international effects. *Journal of Research on Adolescence, 14,* 99–125.

Bank, L., Patterson, G. R., & Reid, J. B. (1996). Negative sibling interaction patterns as predictors of later adjustment problems in adolescent and young adult males. In G. H. Brody (Ed.), *Sibling relationships: Their causes and consequences* (pp. 197–229). Norwood, NJ: Ablex.

Barber, B. K., Chadwick, B. A., & Oerter, R. (1992). Parental behaviors and adolescent self-esteem in the United States and Germany. *Journal of Marriage and the Family, 54,* 128–141.

Barber, B. K., & Harmon, E. L. (2002). Violating the self: Parental psychological control of children and adolescents. In B. K. Barber (Ed.), *Intrusive parenting: How psychological control affects children and adolescents* (pp. 15–52). Washington, DC: American Psychological Association.

Barber, B. K., Olsen, J., A., & Shagle, S. (1994). Associations between parental psychological and behavioral control and youth internalized and externalized behaviors. *Child Development, 65,* 1120–1136.

Baril, M. E., Crouter, A. C., & McHale, S. M. (2007). Processes linking adolescent well-being, marital love, and coparenting. *Journal of Family Psychology, 21,* 645–654.

Baron-Cohen, S., Tager-Flusberg, H., & Cohen, D. J. (1993). *Understanding other minds: Perspectives from autism.* Oxford: Oxford University Press.

Barrett, J., & Fleming, A. S. (2011). Annual Research Review: All mothers are not created equal: Neural and psychobiological perspectives on mothering and the importance of individual differences. *The Journal of Child Psychology and Psychiatry, 52,* 368–397.

Barrett, K. C. (2013). Adaptive and maladaptive regulation of and by emotion: Process, context, and relation to self-regulation. In K. C. Barrett, N. A. Fox, G. A. Morgan, D. J., Fidler, & L. A. Daunhauer (Eds.), *Handbook of self-regulatory processes in development: New directions and international perspectives* (pp. 61–78). New York, NY: Psychology Press.

Barrett, K. C., Zahn-Waxler, C., & Cole, P. M. (1993). Avoiders versus amenders: Implications for the investigation of guilt and shame during toddlerhood? *Cognition and Emotion, 7,* 481–505.

Barrett, L. F. (2009). Variety is the spice of life: A psychological constructionist approach to understanding variability in emotion. *Cognition and Emotion, 23,* 1284–1306.

Barrett, L. F., Gross, J., Christensen, T. C., & Benvenuto, M. (2001). Knowing what you're feeling and knowing what to do about it: Mapping the relation between emotion differentiation and emotion regulation. *Cognition and Emotion, 15,* 713–724.

Barrett, L. F., Lindquist, K. A., & Gendron, M. (2007). Language as context for the perception of emotion. *Trends in Cognitive Sciences, 11,* 327–332.

Barrett, L. F., & Russell, J. A. (Eds.). (2014). *The psychological construction of emotion.* New York, NY: Guilford Press.

Barry, C. M., Padilla-Walker, L. M., Madsen, S. D., & Nelson, L. J. (2008). The impact of maternal relationship quality on emerging adults' prosocial tendencies: Indirect effects via regulation of prosocial values. *Journal of Youth and Adolescence, 37,* 581–591.

Barry, C. T., Grafeman, S. J., Adler, K. K., & Pickard, J. D. (2007). The relations among narcissism, self-esteem, and delinquency in a sample of at-risk adolescents. *Journal of Adolescence, 30,* 933–942.

Bartels, A., & Zeki, S. (2004). The neural correlates of maternal and romantic love. *NeuroImage, 21,* 1155–1166.

Bartholomew, K. (1990). Avoidance of intimacy: An attachment perspective. *Journal of Social and Personal Relationships, 7,* 147–178.

Bartholomew, K. (1993). From childhood to adult relationships: Attachment theory and research. In S. Duck (Ed.), *Learning about relationships* (pp. 30–62). Newbury Park, CA: Sage Publications.

Bartholomew, K., & Horowitz, L. M. (1991). Attachment styles among young adults: A test of a four-category model. *Journal of Personality and Social Psychology, 61,* 226–244.

Bartsch, K., & Wellman, H. M. (1995). *Children talk about the mind.* Oxford: Oxford University Press.

Bates, E. (1990). Language about me and you: Pronominal reference and the emerging concept of self. In D. Cicchetti & M. Beeghly (Eds.), *The self in transition: Infancy to childhood* (pp. 165–182). Chicago, IL: University of Chicago Press.

Bates, J. E., & McFadyen-Ketchum, S. (2000). Temperament and parent–child relations as interacting factors in children's behavioral adjustment. In V. J. Molfese & D. L. Molfese (Eds.), *Temperament and personality development across the lifespan* (pp. 141–176). Mahwah, NJ: Erlbaum.

Bates, J. E., Schermerhorn, A. C., & Petersen, I. T. (2012). Temperament and parenting in developmental perspective. In M. Zentner & R. L. Shiner (Eds.), *Handbook of temperament* (pp. 425–441). New York, NY: Guilford Press.

Batson, C. S. (2009). These things called empathy: Eight related but distinct phenomena. In J. Decety & W. Ickes (Eds.), *The social neuroscience of empathy* (pp. 1–15). Cambridge, MA: The MIT Press.

Bauer, P. J. (2002). Long-term recall memory: Behavioral and neuro-developmental changes in the first 2 years of life. *Current Directions in Psychological Science, 11,* 137–141.

Baumeister, R. F., Campbell, J. D., Kreuger, J. I., & Vohs, K. D. (2003). Does high self-esteem cause better performance, interpersonal success, happiness, or healthier lifestyles? *Psychological Science in the Public Interest, 4,* 1–44.

Baumeister, R. F., & Muraven, M. (1996). Identity as adaptation to social, cultural, and historical context. *Journal of Adolescence, 19,* 405–416.

Baumeister, R. F., Stillwell, A. M., & Heatherton, T. F. (1994). Guilt: An interpersonal approach. *Psychological Bulletin, 115,* 243–267.

Baumeister, R. F., Stillwell, A. M., & Heatherton, T. F. (1995). Personal narratives about guilt: Role in action control and interpersonal relationships. *Basic and Applied Social Psychology, 17,* 173–198.

Bauminger, N., Finzi-Dottan, R., Chason, S., & Har-Even, D. (2008). Intimacy in adolescent friendship: The roles of attachment, coherence, and self-disclosure. *Journal of Social and Personal Relationships, 25,* 409–428.

Baumrind, D. (1966). Effects of authoritative control on child behavior. *Child Development, 37,* 887–890.

Baumrind, D. (1967). Child care practices anteceding three patterns of preschool behavior. *Genetic Psychology Monographs, 75,* 43–87.

Baumrind, D. (1971). Current patterns of parental authority. *Developmental Psychology Monographs, 4*(1, Pt. 2), 1–103.

Baumrind, D. (1991). The influence of parenting style on adolescent competence and substance use. *The Journal of Early Adolescence, 11,* 56–95.

Baumrind, D. (2005). Patterns of parental authority and adolescent autonomy. *New*

Directions for Child and Adolescent Development, 108, 61–69.

Beauregard, M., Levesque, J., & Paquette, V. (2004). Neural basis of conscious and voluntary self-regulation of emotion. In M. Beauregard (Ed.), *Consciousness, emotional self-regulation, and the brain* (pp. 163–194). Amsterdam: Benjamins.

Bedford, V., & Volling, B. (2004). A dynamic ecological systems perspective on emotion regulation development within the sibling relationship. In F. Lang & K. Fingerman (Eds.), *Growing together: Personal relationships across the lifespan* (pp. 76–101). New York, NY: Cambridge University Press.

Beebe, B. (2003). Brief mother–infant treatment: Psychoanalytically informed video feedback. *Infant Mental Health Journal, 24,* 24–52.

Beebe, B. (2005). Mother–infant research informs mother–infant treatment. *Psychoanalytic Study of the Child, 60,* 7–46.

Beebe, B., Jaffe, J., Lachmann, F. M., Feldstein, S., Crown, C., & Jasnow, J. (2000). Systems models in development and psychoanalysis: The case of vocal rhythm coordination and attachment. *Infant Mental Health Journal, 21,* 99–122.

Beebe, B., & Stern, D. (1977). Engagement-disengagement and early object experience. In M. Freedman & S. Grenel (Eds.), *Communicative structures and psychic experiences* (pp. 33–55). New York, NY: Plenum.

Behrends, R., & Blatt, S. J. (1985). Internalization and psychological development throughout the life cycle. *Psychoanalytic Study of the Child, 40,* 11–39.

Beijersbergen, M. D., Juffer, F., Bakermans-Kranenburg, M. J., & van IJzendoorn, M. H. (2012). Remaining or becoming secure: Parental sensitive support predicts attachment continuity from infancy to adolescence in a longitudinal adoption study. *Developmental Psychology, 48,* 1277–1282.

Bell, R. Q. (1968). A reinterpretation of the direction of effects in studies of socialization. *Psychological Review, 75,* 81–95.

Bell, S. M., & Ainsworth, M. D. S. (1972). Infant crying and maternal responsiveness. *Child Development, 43,* 1171–1190.

Bellmore, A. D., & Cillessen, A. H. N. (2006). Reciprocal influences of victimization, perceived social preference, and self-concept in adolescence. *Self and Identity, 5,* 209–229.

Belmont, L., Wittes, J., & Stein, Z. (1977). Relation of birth order, family size, and social class to psychological functions. *Perceptual and Motor Skills, 45,* 1107–1116.

Belsky, J. (2005). The development and evolutionary psychology of intergenerational transmission of attachment. In C. S. Carter, L. Ahnert, K. E. Grossman, S. B. Hrdy, M. E. Lamb, S. W. Porges, & N. Sachser (Eds.), *Attachment and bonding: A new synthesis* (pp. 169–198). Cambridge, MA: The MIT Press.

Belsky, J., Campbell, S. B., Cohn, J. F., & Moore, G. (1996). Instability of infant–parent attachment security. *Developmental Psychology, 32,* 921–924.

Belsky, J., & Cassidy, J. (1994). Attachment: Theory and evidence. In M. L. Rutter, D. F. Hay, & S. Baron-Cohen (Eds.), *Development through life: A handbook for clinicians* (pp. 373–402). Oxford: Blackwell.

Belsky, J., & Fearon, R. M. P. (2002). Early attachment security, subsequent maternal sensitivity, and later child development: Does continuity in development depend upon continuity of caregiving? *Attachment & Human Development, 4,* 361–387.

Belsky, J., & Fearon, R. M. P. (2008). Precursors of attachment security. In J. Cassidy & P. R. Shaver (Eds.), *Handbook of attachment: Theory, research, and clinical applications* (2nd ed., pp. 295–316). New York, NY: Guilford Press.

Belsky, J., Fish, M., & Isabella, R. (1991). Continuity and discontinuity in infant negative and positive emotionality: Family antecedents and attachment consequences. *Developmental Psychology, 27,* 421–431.

Belsky, J., & Pluess, M. (2009). The nature (and nurture?) of plasticity in early human development. *Perspectives in Psychological Science, 4,* 345–351.

Belsky, J., & Rovine, M. (1987). Temperament and attachment security in the Strange Situation: An empirical rapprochement. *Child Development, 58,* 787–795.

Belsky, J., & Rovine, M. (1988). Nonmaternal care in the first year of life and the security of infant–parent attachment. *Child Development, 59,* 157–167.

Belsky, J., Spritz, B., & Crnic, K. (1996). Infant attachment security and affective-cognitive information processing at age 3. *Psychological Science, 7*, 111–114.

Belsky, J., & Steinberg, L. (1978). The effects of day care: A critical review. *Child Development, 49*, 929–949.

Bem, D. J. (1972). Self-perception theory. In L. Berkowitz (Ed.), *Advances in experimental social psychology* (Vol. 6, pp. 1–62). New York, NY: Academic Press.

Benbassat, N., & Priel, B. (2012). Parenting and adolescent adjustment: The role of parental reflective function. *Journal of Adolescence, 35*, 163–174.

Bender, L., & Yarnell, H. (1941). An observation nursery. *American Journal of Psychiatry, 97*, 1158–1174.

Benenson, J. F., & Christakos, A. (2003). The greater fragility of females' versus males' closest same-sex friendships. *Child Development, 74*, 1123–1129.

Benenson, J. F., Markovits, H., Roy, R., & Denko, P. (2003). Behavioural rules underlying learning to share: Effects of development and context. *International Journal of Behavioural Development, 27*, 116–121.

Bengtson, V. L., Biblarz, T. J., & Roberts, R. E. L. (2002). *How families still matter: A longitudinal study of youth in two generations*. New York, NY: Cambridge Universities Press.

Bennett, D. S., Sullivan, M. W., & Lewis, M. (2005). Young children's adjustment as a function of maltreatment, shame, and anger. *Child Maltreatment, 10*, 311–323.

Bennion, L. D., & Adams, G. R. (1986). A revision of the extended version of the Objective Measure of Ego Identity Status: An identity instrument for use with late adolescents. *Journal of Adolescent Research, 1*, 183–197.

Benoit, D., & Parker, K. (1994). Stability and transmission of attachment across three generations. *Child Development, 65*, 1444–1456.

Benoit, D., Parker, K. C. H., & Zeanah, C. H. (1997). Mothers' representations of their infants assessed prenatally: Stability and association with infants' attachment classifications. *Journal of Child Psychology and Psychiatry, 38*, 307–313.

Benson, M. J., Harris, P. B., & Rogers, C. S. (1992). Identity consequences of attachment to mothers and fathers among late adolescents. *Journal of Research on Adolescence, 2*, 187–204.

Berlin, L. J., Cassidy, J., & Appleyard, K. (2008). The influence of early attachments on other relationships. In J. Cassidy & P. R. Shaver (Eds.), *Handbook of attachment: Theory, research, and clinical applications* (2nd ed., pp. 333–347). New York, NY: Guilford Press.

Berlin, L. J., Zeanah, C. H., & Lieberman, A. F. (2008). Prevention and intervention programs for supporting early attachment security. In J. Cassidy & P. R. Shaver (Eds.), *Handbook of attachment: Theory, research, and clinical applications* (pp. 745–761). New York, NY: Guilford Press.

Berndt, T. J. (1985). Prosocial behavior between friends in middle childhood and adolescence. *Journal of Adolescence, 5*, 307–313.

Berndt, T. J. (1986). Children's comments about their friendships. In M. Perlmutter (Ed.), *Cognitive perspectives on children's social and behavioral development. The Minnesota Symposium on Child Psychology* (Vol. 18, pp. 189–211). Hillsdale, NJ: Erlbaum.

Berndt, T. J. (1989). Obtaining support from friends during childhood and adolescence. In D. Belle (Ed.), *Children's social networks and social supports* (pp. 308–331). New York, NY: John Wiley & Sons.

Berndt, T. J. (1996). Exploring the effects of friendship quality on social development. In W. M. Bukowski, A. F. Newcomb, & W. W. Hartup (Eds.), *The company they keep: Friendship in childhood and adolescence* (pp. 346–365). New York, NY: Cambridge University Press.

Berndt, T. J. (2002). Friendship quality and social development. *Current Directions in Psychological Science, 11*, 7–10.

Berndt, T. J. (2004). Children's friendships: Shifts over a half-century in perspectives on their development and their effects. *Merrill-Palmer Quarterly, 50*, 206–223.

Berndt, T. J., & Burgy, L. (1996). The social self-concept. In B. A. Bracken (Ed.), *Handbook of self-concept: Developmental, social, and clinical considerations* (pp. 171–209). Oxford: Wiley.

Berndt, T. J., Hawkins, J. A., & Hoyle, S. G. (1986). Changes in friendship during a school year: Effects of children's and adolescent's impressions of friendships and sharing with friends. *Child Development, 57,* 1284–1297.

Berndt, T. J., Hawkins, J. A., & Jiao, Z. (1999). Influences of friends and friendships on adjustment to junior high school. *Merrill-Palmer Quarterly, 45,* 13–41.

Berndt, T. J., & Hoyle, S. G. (1985). Stability and change in childhood and adolescent friendships. *Developmental Psychology, 21,* 1007–1015.

Berndt, T. J., & Murphy, L. M. (2002). Influences of friends and friendships: Myths, truths, and research recommendations. In R. V. Kail (Ed.), *Advances in child development and behavior* (Vol. 30, pp. 275–310). San Diego, CA: Academic Press.

Berndt, T. J., & Perry, T. B. (1986). Children's perceptions of friendships as supportive relationships. *Developmental Psychology, 22,* 640–648.

Berndt, T. J., & Perry, T. B. (1990). Distinctive features and effects of early adolescent friendships. In R. Montemayor, G. R. Adams, & T. P. Gullotta (Eds.), *From childhood to adolescence: A transitional period?* (pp. 269–287). Newbury Park, CA: Sage Publications.

Bernier, A., Matte-Gagné, C., Bélanger, M.-E., & Whipple, N. (2014). Taking stock of two decades of attachment transmission gap: Broadening the assessment of maternal behavior. *Child Development, 85,* 1852–1865.

Berry, J. W. (1997). Immigration, acculturation, and adaptation. *Applied Psychology: An International Review, 46,* 5–68.

Bertenthal, B. L., & Fischer, K. W. (1978). Development of self-recognition in the infant. *Developmental Psychology, 14,* 44–50.

Berzonsky, M. D. (1990). Self-construction over the life span: A process perspective on identity formation. In G. J. Neimeyer & R. A. Neimeyer (Eds.), *Advances in personal construct theory* (Vol. 1, pp. 155–186). Greenwich, CT: JAI Press.

Besser, A., & Blatt, S. J. (2007). Identity consolidation and internalizing and externalizing problem behaviors in early adolescence. *Psychoanalytic Psychology, 24,* 126–149.

Beyers, W., & Seiffge-Krenke, I. (2010). Does identity precede intimacy? Testing Erikson's theory on romantic development in emerging adults of the 21st century. *Journal of Adolescent Research, 25,* 387–415.

Bierman, K. L. (2004). *Peer rejection: Developmental processes and intervention strategies.* New York, NY: Guilford Press.

Birch, S. H., & Ladd, G. W. (1998). Children's interpersonal behaviors and the teacher–child relationship. *Developmental Psychology, 34,* 934–946.

Bird, A., & Reese, E. (2006). Emotional reminiscing and the development of an autobiographical self. *Developmental Psychology, 42,* 613–626.

Bischof-Köhler, D. (2012). Empathy and self-recognition in phylogenetic and ontogenetic perspective. *Emotion Review, 4,* 40–48.

Blachman, D. R., & Hinshaw, S. P. (2002). Patterns of friendship among girls with and without attention-deficit/hyperactivity disorder. *Journal of Abnormal Child Psychology, 30,* 626–640.

Black, K. A., & McCartney, K. (1997). Adolescent females' security with parents predicts the quality of peer interactions. *Social Development, 6,* 91–110.

Blain, M. D., Thompson, J. M., & Whiffen, V. E. (1993). Attachment and perceived social support in later adolescence: The interaction between working models of self and others. *Journal of Adolescent Research, 8,* 226–241.

Blair, C., & Diamond, A. (2008). Biological processes in prevention and intervention: The promotion of self-regulation as a means of preventing school failure. *Development and Psychopathology, 20,* 899–911.

Blair, R. J. R. (1995). A cognitive developmental approach to morality: Investigating the psychopath. *Cognition, 57,* 1–29.

Blair, R. J. R. (2005). Responding to the emotions of others: Dissociating forms of empathy through the study of typical and psychiatric populations. *Consciousness and Cognition, 14,* 698–718.

Blakemore, S.-J., & Choudhury, S. (2006). Development of the adolescent brain: Implications for executive function and social cognition. *Journal of Child Psychology and Psychiatry, 47,* 296–312.

Blandon, A. Y., Calkins, S. D., Keane, S. P., & O'Brien, M. (2008). Individual differences in trajectories of emotion regulation processes: The effects of maternal depressive symptomatology and children's physiological regulation. *Developmental Psychology, 44,* 1110–1123.

Blasi, A. (1983). Moral cognition and moral action: A theoretical perspective. *Developmental Review, 3,* 178–210.

Blasi, A. (1984). Moral identity: Its role in moral functioning. In W. Kurtines & J. Gewirtz (Eds.), *Morality, moral behavior, and moral development* (pp. 128–139). New York, NY: Wiley.

Blasi, A., Mercure, E., Lloyd-Fox, S., Thomson, A., Brammer, M., Sauter, D., … Murphy, D. G. M. (2011). Early specialization for voice and emotion processing in the infant brain. *Current Biology, 21,* 1220–1224.

Blom, I., & Bergman, A. (2013). Observing development: A comparative view of attachment theory and separation-individuation theory. In J. E. Bettmann & D. D. Friedman (Eds.), *Attachment-based clinical work with children and adolescents* (pp. 9–43). New York, NY: Springer.

Blos, P. (1962). *On adolescence.* New York, NY: Free Press.

Blos, P. (1967). The second individuation process of adolescence. *Psychoanalytic Study of the Child, 22,* 162–186.

Boccia, M., & Campos, J. (1989). Maternal emotional signals, social referencing, and infants' reactions to strangers. In N. Eisenberg (Ed.), *Empathy and related emotional responses: New directions for child development* (pp. 25–49). San Francisco, CA: Jossey Bass.

Bogin, B. (1994). Adolescence in evolutionary perspective. *Acta Paediatrica Supplement, 406,* 29–35.

Bogle, K. A. (2008). *Hooking up: Sex, dating, and relationships on campus.* New York, NY: New York University Press.

Bohlin, G., Hagekull, B., & Rydell, A. M. (2000). Attachment and social functioning: A longitudinal study from infancy to middle childhood. *Social Development, 9,* 24–39.

Boivin, M., Vitaro, F., & Poulin, F. (2005). Peer relationships and the development of aggressive behavior in early childhood. In R. E. Tremblay, W. W. Hartup, & J. J. Archer (Eds.), *Developmental origins of aggression* (pp. 376–397). New York, NY: Guilford Press.

Bokhorst, C. L., Bakermans-Kranenburg, M. J., Fearon, R. M. P., van IJzendoorn, M. H., Fonagy, P., & Schuengel, C. (2003). The importance of shared environment in mother–infant attachment security: A behavioral genetic study. *Child Development, 74,* 1769–1782.

Bokhorst, C. L., Sumter, S. R., & Westenberg, P. M. (2010). Social support from parents, friends, classmates, and teachers in children and adolescents aged 9 to 18 years: Who is perceived as most supportive? *Social Development, 19,* 417–426.

Boldt, L. J., Kochanska, G., Yoon, J. E., & Nordling, J. K. (2014). Children's attachment to both parents from toddler age to middle childhood: Links to adaptive and maladaptive outcomes. *Attachment & Human Development, 16,* 211–229.

Bonanno, G. A., Papa, A., Lalande, K., Westphal, M., & Coifman, K. (2004). The importance of being flexible. *Psychological Science, 15,* 482–487.

Booth-LaForce, C., Groh, A. M., Burchinal, M. R., Roisman, G. I., Owen, M. T., & Cox, M. J. (2014). Caregiving and contextual sources of continuity and change in attachment security from infancy to late adolescence. *Monographs of the Society for Research in Child Development, 79*(3), 67–84.

Booth-LaForce, C., & Kerns, K. A. (2009). Child–parent attachment relationships, peer relationships, and peer group functioning. In K. H. Rubin, W. M. Bukowski, & B. Laursen (Eds.), *Handbook of peer interactions, relationships, and groups.* (pp. 490–507). New York, NY: Guilford Press.

Booth-LaForce, C., Oh, W., Kim, A. H., Rubin, K. H., Rose-Krasnor, L., & Burgess, K. (2006). Attachment, self-worth, and peer-group functioning in middle childhood. *Attachment & Human Development, 8,* 309–325.

Booth-LaForce, C., Rubin, K. H., Rose-Krasnor, L., & Burgess, K. B. (2005). Attachment and friendship predictors of psychosocial functioning in middle childhood and the mediating roles of social support and self-worth. In K. Kerns & R. A. Richardson (Eds.), *Attachment in middle childhood* (pp. 161–188). New York, NY: Guilford Press.

Bornstein, M. H., Putnick, D. L., Gartstein, M. A., Hahn, C.-S., Auestad, N., & O'Connor, D. L. (2015). Infant temperament: Stability by age, gender, birth order, term status, and socioeconomic status. *Child Development, 86*, 844–863.

Bosma, H. A., & Gerlsma, C. (2003). From early attachment to relations to the adolescent and adult organization of self. In J. Valsiner & K. J. Connolly (Eds.), *Handbook of developmental psychology* (pp. 450–488). London: Sage Publications.

Bosma, H. A., & Kunnen, E. S. (2001). Determinants and mechanisms in ego identity development: A review and synthesis. *Developmental Review, 21*, 39–66.

Bosma, H. A., & Kunnen, E. S. (2008). Identity-in-context is not yet identity development-in-context. *Journal of Adolescence, 31*, 281–289.

Bosquet, M., & Egeland, B. (2006). The development and maintenance of anxiety symptoms from infancy through adolescence in a longitudinal sample. *Development and Psychopathology, 18*, 517–550.

Bost, K. K., Vaughn, B. E., Washington, W. N., Cielinski, K., & Bradbard, M. R. (1998). Social competence, social support, and attachment: Demarcation of construct domains, measurement, and paths of influence for preschool children attending Head Start. *Child Development, 69*, 192–218.

Bouffard, T., Markovits, H., Vezeau, C., Boisvert, M., & Dumas, C. (1998). The relation between accuracy of self-perception and cognitive development. *British Journal of Educational Psychology, 68*, 321–330.

Bowker, A. (2004). Predicting friendship stability during early adolescence. *Journal of Early Adolescence, 24*, 85–112.

Bowlby, J. (1944). Forty-four juvenile thieves: Their characters and home life. *International Journal of Psycho-Analysis, 25*, 19–52, 107–127.

Bowlby, J. (1958). The nature of the child's tie to his mother. *International Journal of Psycho-Analysis, 39*, 350–373.

Bowlby, J. (1969/1982). *Attachment and loss: Vol. 1. Attachment.* New York, NY: Basic Books.

Bowlby, J. (1973). *Attachment and loss: Vol. 2. Separation: Anxiety and anger.* New York, NY: Basic Books.

Bowlby, J. (1980). *Attachment and loss: Vol. 3. Loss: Sadness and depression.* New York, NY: Basic Books.

Bowlby, J. (1982). Attachment and loss: Retrospect and prospect. *American Journal of Orthopsychiatry, 52*, 664–678.

Bowlby, J. (1988). *A secure base: Clinical applications of attachment theory.* New York, NY: Basic Books.

Boyle, M. H., Jenkins, J. M., Georgiades, K., Cairney, J., Duku, E., & Racine, Y. (2004). Differential-maternal parenting behavior: Estimating within- and between-family effects on children. *Child Development, 75*, 1457–1476.

Bracken, B. (1996). Clinical applications of a context-dependent multi-dimensional model of self-concept. In B. Bracken (Ed.), *Handbook of self-concept* (pp. 463–505). New York, NY: Wiley.

Branje, S. J. T., Frijns, T., Finkenauer, C., Engels, R., & Meeus, W. (2007). You are my best friends: Commitment and stability in adolescents' same-sex friendships. *Personal Relationships, 14*, 587–603.

Breakwell, G. M., & Millward, L. J. (1997). Sexual self-concept and risk-taking. *Journal of Adolescence, 20*, 29–41.

Breger, L. (1974). *From instinct to identity.* Englewood Cliffs, NJ: Prentice Hall.

Bremner, J. D., Randall, P., Vermetten, E., Staib, L., Bronen, R. A., Mazure, C., ... Charney, D. S. (1997). Magnetic resonance imaging-based measurement of hippocampal volume in posttraumatic stress disorder related to childhood physical and sexual abuse – A preliminary report. *Biological Psychiatry, 41*, 23–32.

Brendgen, M., Vitaro, R., Tremblay, R. E., & Lavoie, F. (2001). Reactive and proactive aggression: Predictions to physical violence in different contexts and moderating effects of parental monitoring and caregiving behavior. *Journal of Abnormal Child Psychology, 29*, 293–304.

Brennan, K. A., Clark, C. L., & Shaver, P. R. (1998). Self-report measurement of adult romantic attachment: An integrative approach. In J. A. Simpson & W. S. Rhodes (Eds.), *Attachment theory and close relationships* (pp. 46–76). New York, NY: Guilford Press.

Brenner, E., & Salovey, P. (1997). Emotion regulation during childhood: Developmental, interpersonal, and individual considerations. In P. Salovey & D. Sluyter (Eds.), *Emotional literacy and emotional development* (pp. 168–192). New York, NY: Basic Books.

Brenning, K. M., Soenens, B., Braet, C., & Bosmans, G. (2011). An adaptation of the

Experiences in Close Relationships Scale-Revised for use with children and adolescents. *Journal of Social and Personal Relationships, 28,* 1048–1072.

Brenning, K. M., Soenens, B., Braet, C., & Bosmans, G. (2012). Attachment and depressive symptoms in middle childhood and early adolescence: Testing the validity of the emotion regulation model of attachment. *Personal Relationships, 19,* 445–464.

Bretherton, I. (1985). Attachment theory: Retrospect and prospect. In I. Bretherton & E. Waters (Eds.), Growing points of attachment theory and research. *Monographs of the Society for Research in Child Development, 50*(1–2, Serial No. 209), 3–35.

Bretherton, I. (1987). New perspectives on attachment relations: Security, communication, and internal working models. In J. D. Osofsky (Ed.), *Handbook of infant development* (2nd ed., pp. 1061–1100). New York, NY: Wiley.

Bretherton, I. (1990). Open communication and internal working models: Their role in the development of attachment relationships. In R. A. Thompson (Eds.), *Nebraska Symposium on Motivation: Social-emotional development.* Lincoln: University of Nebraska Press.

Bretherton, I. (1991). Pouring new wine into old bottles: The social self as internal working model. In M. R. Gunnar & L. A. Sroufe (Eds.), *Minnesota Symposia on Child Psychology: Vol. 23. Self processes in development* (pp. 1–41). Hillsdale, NJ: Erbaum.

Bretherton, I. (1992). The origins of attachment theory: John Bowlby and Mary Ainsworth. *Developmental Psychology, 28,* 759–775.

Bretherton, I. (1993). From dialogue to internal working models: The co-construction of self in relationship. In C. A. Nelson (Ed.), *Minnesota Symposia on Child Psychology: Vol. 26. Memory and affect in development* (pp. 237–263). Hillsdale, NJ: Erlbaum.

Bretherton, I., Fritz, J., Zahn-Waxler, C., & Ridgeway, D. (1986). Learning to talk about emotions: A functionalist perspective. *Child Development, 57,* 529–548.

Bretherton, I., Grossman, K. E., Grossman, K., & Waters, E. (2005). In pursuit of the internal working model construct and its relevance to attachment relationships. In K. E. Grossman, K. Grossman, & E. Waters

(Eds.), *Attachment from infancy to adulthood: The major longitudinal studies* (pp. 13–47). New York, NY: Guilford Press.

Bretherton, I., McNew, S., & Beeghly-Smith, M. (1981). Early person knowledge as expressed in gestural and verbal communication: When do infants acquire a "theory of mind"? In M. Lamb & L. Sherrod (Eds.), *Infant social cognition: Theoretical and empirical considerations* (pp. 333–373). Hillsdale, NJ: Erlbaum.

Bretherton, I., & Munholland, K. A. (2008). Internal working models in attachment relationships: Elaborating a central construct in attachment theory. In J. Cassidy & P. R. Shaver (Eds.), *Handbook of attachment: Theory, research, and clinical applications* (2nd ed., pp. 102–127). New York, NY: Guilford Press.

Bretherton, I., Ridgeway, D., & Cassidy, J. (1990). Assessing internal working models of the attachment relationship: An attachment story completion task for 3-year-olds. In M. T. Greenberg, D. Cicchetti, & E. M. Cummings (Eds.), *Attachment in the preschool years* (pp. 273–308). Chicago, IL: University of Chicago Press.

Brewer, M. B., & Gardner, W. (1996). Who is this "We"? Levels of collective identity and self representations. *Journal of Personality and Social Psychology, 71,* 83–93.

Bridges, L. J., Denham, S. A., & Ganiban, J. M. (2004). Definitional issues in emotion regulation research. *Child Development, 75,* 340–345.

Bridges, L. J., Grolnick, W. S., & Connell, J. P. (1997). Infant emotion regulation with mothers and fathers. *Infant Behavior & Development, 20,* 47–57.

Briere, J. (1992). Methodological issues in the study of sexual abuse effects. *Journal of Consulting and Clinical Psychology, 60,* 196–203.

Brill, A. A. (1922). *Psychoanalysis: Its theories and practical applications.* Philadelphia, PA: Saunders.

Brody, G. H. (1996). *Sibling relationships: Their causes and consequences.* Norwood, NJ: Ablex.

Brody, G. H. (1998). Sibling relationship quality: Its causes and consequences. *Annual Review of Psychology, 49,* 1–24.

Brody, G. H. (2003). Parental monitoring: Action and reaction. In A. C. Crouter & A.

Booth (Eds.), *Children's influence on family dynamics: The neglected side of family relationships* (pp. 163–169). Mahwah, NJ: Lawrence Erlbaum Publishers.

Brody, G. H. (2004). Siblings' direct and indirect contributions to child development. *Current Directions in Psychological Science, 13,* 124–126.

Brody, G. H., Stoneman, Z., & Burke, M. (1987). Child temperaments, maternal differential behavior and sibling relationships. *Developmental Psychology, 23,* 354–362.

Brody, G. H., Stoneman, Z., & McCoy, J. (1994). Forecasting sibling relationships in early adolescence from child temperaments and family processes in middle childhood. *Child Development, 65,* 771–784.

Brody, G. H., Stoneman, Z., McCoy, J., & Forehand, R. (1992). Contemporaneous and longitudinal association of sibling conflict with family relationship assessments and family discussions about sibling problems. *Child Development, 63,* 391–400.

Bronfenbrenner, U. (2004). *Making human beings human: Bioecological perspectives on human development.* Newbury Park, CA: Sage Publications.

Bronson, M. B. (2000). *Self-regulation in early childhood: Nature and nurture.* New York, NY: Guilford Press.

Brooks-Gunn, J. (1991). Maturational timing variations in adolescent girls, antecedents of. In R. M. Lerner, A. C. Petersen, & J. Brooks-Gunn (Eds.), *Encyclopedia of adolescence* (Vol. 2, pp. 609–612). New York, NY: Garland.

Brooks-Gunn, J., & Lewis, M. (1984). The development of early visual self-recognition. *Developmental Review, 4,* 215–239.

Brown, B. (2004). Adolescents' relationships with peers. In R. Lerner & L. Steinberg (Eds.), *Handbook of adolescent psychology* (2nd ed., pp. 363–394). Hoboken, NJ: Wiley.

Brown, B. B., Mounts, N., Lamborn, S. D., & Steinberg, L. (1993). Parenting practices and group affiliation in adolescence. *Child Development, 64,* 467–482.

Brown, C. S., & Bigler, R. S. (2005). Children's perceptions of discrimination: A developmental model. *Child Development, 76,* 533–553.

Brown, G. L., Mangelsdorf, S. C., Agathen, J. M., & Ho, M. (2008). Young children's psychological selves: Convergence with maternal reports of child personality. *Social Development, 17,* 161–182.

Brown, J. D. (1998). *The self.* New York, NY: McGraw-Hill.

Brownell, C. A., & Kopp, C. B. (2007). *Socioemotional development in the toddler years: Transitions and transformations.* New York, NY: Guilford Press.

Brownell, C. A., Ramani, G. B., & Zerwas, S. (2006). Becoming a social partner with peers: Cooperation and social understanding in one- and two-year-olds. *Child Development, 77,* 803–821.

Brumariu, L. E., & Kerns, K. A. (2010). Parent–child attachment and internalizing symptoms in childhood and adolescence: A review of empirical findings and future directions. *Development and Psychopathology, 22,* 177–203.

Brumariu, L. E., & Kerns, K. A. (2013). Pathways to anxiety: Contributions of attachment history, temperament, peer competence, and ability to manage intense emotions. *Child Psychiatry and Human Development, 44,* 504–515.

Bryant, B. (1989). The child's perspective of sibling caretaking and its relevance to understanding social-emotional functioning and development. In P. S. Zukow (Ed.), *Sibling interaction across cultures* (pp. 143–164). New York, NY: Springer-Verlag.

Buchmann, C., & Dalton, B. (2002). Interpersonal influences and educational aspirations in 12 countries: The importance of institutional context. *Sociology of Education, 75,* 99–122.

Buhrmester, D. (1990). Intimacy of friendship, interpersonal competence, and adjustment during middle childhood and adolescence. *Child Development, 61,* 1101–1111.

Buhrmester, D. (1992). The developmental courses of sibling and peer relationships. In F. Boer & J. Dunn (Eds.), *Children's sibling relationships: Developmental and clinical issues* (pp. 19–40). Hillsdale, NJ: Erlbaum.

Buhrmester, D., & Furman, W. (1986). The changing functions of friends in childhood: A neo-Sullivanian perspective. In V. G. Derlega & B. A. Winstead (Eds.), *Friendship and social interaction* (pp. 41–62). New York, NY: Springer-Verlag.

Buhrmester, D., & Furman, W. (1990). Perceptions of sibling relationships during middle childhood and adolescence. *Child Development, 61,* 1387–1396.

Buhrmester, D., Furman, W., Wittenberg, M. T., & Reis, H. T. (1988). Five domains of interpersonal competence in peer relationships. *Journal of Personality and Social Psychology, 55,* 991–1008.

Buist, K. L. (2010). Sibling relationship quality and adolescent delinquency: A latent growth curve approach. *Journal of Family Psychology, 24,* 400–410.

Buist, K. L., Deković, M., Meeus, W., & van Aken, M. A. G. (2002). Developmental patterns in adolescent attachment to mother, father and sibling. *Journal of Youth and Adolescence, 31,* 167–176.

Buist, K. L., Deković, M., & Prinzie, P. (2013). Sibling relationship quality and psychopathology of children and adolescents: A meta-analysis. *Clinical Psychology Review, 33,* 97–106.

Bukowski, W. M., Buhrmester, D., & Underwood, M. K. (2011). Peer relations as a developmental context. In M. K. Underwood & L. H. Rosen (Eds.), *Social development: Relationships in infancy, childhood, and adolescence.* New York, NY: Guilford Press.

Bukowski, W. M., Hoza, B., & Boivin, M. (1993). Popularity, friendship, and emotional adjustment during early adolescence. In W. Damon (Series Ed.) & B. Laursen (Vol. Ed.), *New directions for child development* (Vol. 60, pp. 23–37). San Francisco, CA: Jossey-Bass.

Bukowski, W. M., Hoza, B., & Boivin, M. (1994). Measuring friendship quality during pre- and early adolescence: The development and psychometric properties of the friendship qualities scales. *Journal of Social and Personal Relationships, 11,* 471–484.

Bukowski, W. M., Motzoi, C., & Meyer, F. (2009). Friendship as process, function, and outcome. In K. H. Rubin, W. M. Bukowski, & B. Laursen (Eds.), *Handbook of peer interactions, relationships, and groups* (pp. 217–231). New York, NY: Guilford Press.

Bukowski, W. M., Newcomb, A. F., & Hartup, W. W. (1996). Friendship and its significance in childhood and adolescence: Introduction and comment. In W. M. Bukowski, A. F. Newcomb, & W. W. Hartup (Eds.), *The company they keep: Friendship in childhood and adolescence* (pp. 3–18). New York, NY: Cambridge University Press.

Bukowski, W. M., & Sippola, L. K. (1996). Friendship and morality. In W. M. Bukowski & A. F. Newcomb (Eds.), *The company they keep: Friendship in childhood and adolescence* (pp. 238–261). Cambridge: Cambridge University Press.

Bukowski, W. M., Sippola, L. K., & Newcomb, A. F. (2000). Variations in patterns of attraction of same- and other-sex peers during early adolescence. *Developmental Psychology, 36,* 147–154.

Bulcroft, R., Carmody, D., & Bulcroft, K. (1996). Patterns of parental independence giving to adolescents: Variations by race, age, and gender of child. *Journal of Marriage and the Family, 58,* 866–883.

Bullock, M., & Lutkenhaus, P. (1988). The development of volitional behavior in the toddler years. *Child Development, 59,* 664–674.

Bullock, M., & Lutkenhaus, P. (1990). Who am I? Self-understanding in toddlers. *Merrill-Palmer Quarterly, 36,* 217–238.

Bumpus, M. F., Crouter, A. C., & McHale, S. M. (2001). Parental autonomy granting during adolescence: Exploring gender differences in context. *Developmental Psychology, 37,* 163–173.

Burgess, K. B., Marshall, P., Rubin, K. H., & Fox, N. A. (2003). Infant attachment and temperament as predictors of subsequent behavior problems and psychophysiological functioning. *Journal of Child Psychology and Psychiatry and Allied Discipline, 44,* 1–13.

Burr, K. B., Obradovic, J., Long, J. D., & Masten, A. S. (2008). The interplay of social competence and psychopathology over 20 years: Testing transactional and cascade models. *Child Development, 79,* 359–374.

Bushnell, I. W. R., Sai, F., & Mullin, J. T. (1989). Neonatal recognition of the mother's face. *British Journal of Developmental Psychology, 7,* 3–15.

Buss, A. H., & Goldsmith, H. H. (1998). Fear and anger regulation in infancy: Effects on the temporal dynamics of affective expression. *Child Development, 69,* 359–374.

Buss, A. H., & Plomin, R. (1984). *Temperament: Early developing personality traits.* Hillsdale, NJ: Erlbaum.

Bussey, K., & Bandura, A. (1999). Social cognitive theory of gender development and differentiation. *Psychological Review, 106,* 676–713.

Butler, E. A., Egloff, B., Wilhelm, F. H., Smith, N. C., Erickson, E. A., & Gross, J. J. (2003). The social consequences of expressive suppression. *Emotion, 3,* 48–67.

Cairns, R. B., & Cairns, B. D. (1988). The sociogenesis of self-concepts. In N. Bolger, A. Caspi, G. Downey, & M. Moorehouse (Eds.), *Persons in context: Developmental processes* (pp. 181–202). New York, NY: Cambridge University Press.

Cairns, R. B., Cairns, B. D., Neckerman, H. J., Gest, S. D., & Gariepy, J. (1988). Social networks and aggressive behavior: Peer support or peer rejection? *Developmental Psychology, 24,* 815–823.

Caldera, Y. M., Huston, A. C., & O'Brien, M. (1995). *Antecedents of father–infant attachment: A longitudinal study.* Paper presented at the Society for Research in Child Development, Indianapolis, IN.

Caldji, C., Tannenbaum, B., Sharma, S., Francis, D., Plotsky, P. M., & Meaney, M. J. (1998). Maternal care during infancy regulates the development of neural systems mediating the expression of fearfulness in the rat. *Proceedings of the National Academy of Sciences USA, 95,* 5335–5340.

Caldwell, B. (1993). Impact of day care on the child. *Pediatrics, 91,* 225–228.

Calkins, S. D. (2009). Regulatory competence and early disruptive behavior problems: The role of physiological regulation. In S. Olson & A. Sameroff (Eds.), *Regulatory processes in the development of behavior problems: Biological, behavioral, and social-ecological interactions* (pp. 86–115). New York, NY: Cambridge University Press.

Calkins, S. D., & Dedmon, S. (2000). Physiological and behavioral regulation in two-year-old children with aggressive/destructive behavior problems. *Journal of Abnormal Child Psychology, 28,* 103–118.

Calkins, S. D., Dedmon, S., Gill, K., Lomax, L., & Johnson, L. (2002). Frustration in infancy: Implications for emotion regulation, physiological processes, and temperament. *Infancy, 3,* 175–198.

Calkins, S. D., Fox, N. A., & Marshall, T. R. (1996). Behavioral and physiological antecedents of inhibited and uninhibited behavior. *Child Development, 67,* 523–540.

Calkins, S. D., Graziano, P. A., Berdan, L. E., Keane, S. P., & Degnan, K. A. (2008). Predicting cardiac vagal regulation in early childhood from maternal–child relationship quality during toddlerhood. *Developmental Psychobiology, 50,* 751–766.

Calkins, S. D., & Hill, A. (2007). Caregiver influences on emerging emotion regulation. In J. J. Gross (Ed.), *Handbook of emotion regulation* (pp. 229–248). New York, NY: Guilford Press.

Calkins, S. D., & Mackler, J. S. (2011). Temperament, emotion regulation, and social competence. In M. K. Underwood & L. H. Rosen (Eds.), *Social development: Relationships in infancy, childhood, and adolescence* (pp. 44–70). New York, NY: Guilford Press.

Calmes, C. A., & Roberts, J. E. (2008). Rumination in interpersonal relationships: Does co-rumination explain gender differences in emotional distress and relationship satisfaction among college students? *Cognitive Therapy and Research, 32,* 577–590.

Campa, M. I., Hazan, C., & Wolfe, J. E. (2009). The form and function of attachment behavior in the daily lives of young adults. *Social Development, 18,* 288–304.

Campbell, E., Adams, G. R., & Dodson, W. R. (1984). Familial correlates of identity formation in late adolescence: A study of the predictive utility of connectedness and individuality in family relations. *Journal of Youth and Adolescence, 13,* 509–525.

Campbell, S. B. (2002). *Behavior problems in preschool children: Clinical and developmental issues* (2nd ed.). New York, NY: Guilford Press.

Campione-Barr, N., Greer, K. B., & Kruse, A. (2013). Differential associations between domains of sibling conflict and adolescent emotional adjustment. *Child Development, 84,* 938–954.

Campione-Barr, N., & Smetana, J. G. (2010). "Who said you could wear my sweater?" Adolescent siblings' conflicts and associations with relationship quality. *Child Development, 81,* 464–471.

Campos, J. J. (1983). The importance of affective communication in social referencing: A commentary on Feinman. *Merrill Palmer Quarterly, 29,* 83–87.

Campos, J. J., Frankel, C. B., & Camras, L. (2004). On the nature of emotion regulation. *Child Development, 75,* 377–394.

Campos, J. J., Walle, E., Dahl, A., & Main, A. (2011). Reconceptualizing emotion regulation. *Emotion Review, 3,* 26–35.

Canli, T., Qiu, M., Omura, K., Congdon, E., Haas, B. W., Amin, Z., ... Lesch, K. P. (2006). Neural correlates of epigenesis. *Proceedings of the National Academy of Sciences, 103,* 16033–16038.

Cannon, E. A., Schoppe-Sullivan, S. J., Mangelsdorf, S. C., Brown, G. L., & Sokolowski, M. S. (2008). Parent characteristics as antecedents of maternal gatekeeping and fathering behavior. *Family Process, 47,* 501–519.

Cantin, S., & Bouvin, M. (2004). Change and stability in children's social network and self-perceptions during transition from elementary to junior high school. *International Journal of Behavioral Development, 28,* 561–570.

Caravita, S. C. S., Di Blasio, P., & Salmivalli, C. (2009). Unique and interactive effects of empathy and social status on involvement in bullying. *Social Development, 18,* 140–163.

Cardinal, R. N., Parkinson, J. A., Hall, J., & Everitt, B. J. (2002). Emotion and motivation: The role of the amygdala, ventral striatum, and prefrontal cortex. *Neuroscience and Biobehavioral Reviews, 26,* 321–352.

Carlo, G., Fabes, R. A., Laible, D., & Kupanoff, K. (1999). Early adolescence and prosocial moral behavior: II. The role of social and contextual influences. *Journal of Early Adolescence, 19,* 133–147.

Carlo, G., Hausmann, A., Christiansen, S., & Randall, B. A. (2003). Sociocognitive and behavioral correlates of a measure of prosocial tendencies for adolescents. *Journal of Early Adolescence, 23,* 107–134.

Carlo, G., Koller, S. H., Eisenberg, N., DaSilva, M. S., & Frohlich, C. B. (1996). A cross-national study on the relations among prosocial moral reasoning, gender role orientations, and prosocial behaviors. *Developmental Psychology, 32,* 231–240.

Carlson, C., Uppal, S., & Prosser, E. C. (2000). Ethnic differences in processes contributing to the self-esteem of early adolescent girls. *Journal of Early Adolescence, 20,* 44–67.

Carlson, E. A., Sroufe, L. A., & Egeland, B. (2004). The construction of experience: A longitudinal study of representation and behavior. *Child Development, 75,* 66–83.

Carlson, S. M. (2009). Social origins of executive function development. In C. Lewis & J. I. M. Carpendale (Eds.) & R. Larson & L. Jensen (Series Eds.), *Social interaction and the development of executive function. New Directions for Child and Adolescent Development* (pp. 87–98). San Francisco, CA: Jossey Bass.

Carpendale, J. I. M., & Lewis, C. (2004). Constructing an understanding of mind: The development of children's social understanding within social interaction. *Behavioral and Brain Sciences, 27,* 79–151.

Carruthers, P., & Smith, P. K. (1996). *Theories of theories of mind.* Cambridge: Cambridge University Press.

Carter, C. S., Ahnert, L., Grossman, K. E., Hrdy, S. B., Lamb, M. E., Porges, S. W., & Sachser, N. (2005). *Attachment and bonding: A new synthesis.* Cambridge, MA: The MIT Press.

Carter, C. S., Harris, J., & Porges, S. W. (2009). Neural and evolutionary perspectives on empathy. In J. Decety & W. Ickes (Eds.), *The social neuroscience of empathy* (pp. 169–182). Cambridge, MA: The MIT Press.

Case, R. (1991). Stages in the development of the young child's first sense of self. *Developmental Review, 11,* 210–230.

Casey, B. J., Jones, R. M., & Somerville, L. H. (2011). Braking and accelerating of the adolescent brain. *Journal of Research on Adolescence, 21,* 21–33.

Caspi, A., Harrington, H., Milne, B., Amell, J. W., Theodore, R. F., & Moffitt, T. E. (2003). Children's behavioral styles at age 3 are linked to their adult personality traits at age 26. *Journal of Personality, 71,* 495–513.

Caspi, A., Henry, B., McGee, R. O., Moffitt, T. E., & Silva, P. A. (1995). Temperamental origins of child and adolescent behavior problems: From age three to age fifteen. *Child Development, 66,* 55–68.

Caspi, A., & Shiner, R. L. (2006). Personality development. In W. Damon & R. M. Lerner (Eds.) & N. Eisenberg (Vol. Ed.), *Handbook of child psychology, Vol. 3: Social, emotional and personality development* (6th ed., pp. 300–365). New York, NY: Wiley.

Cassidy, J. (1988). Child–mother attachment and the self in six-year-olds. *Child Development, 59*, 121–134.

Cassidy, J. (1990). Theoretical and methodological considerations in the study of attachment and the self in young children. In M. T. Greenberg, D. Cicchetti, & E. M. Cummings (Eds.), *Attachment in the preschool years: Theory, research, and intervention* (pp. 87–119). Chicago, IL: University of Chicago Press.

Cassidy, J. (1994). Emotion regulation: Influences of attachment relationships. In N. A. Fox (Ed.), The development of emotion regulation: Biological and behavioral considerations. *Monographs of the Society for Research in Child Development, 59*(2–3, Serial No. 240), 228–249.

Cassidy, J. (2003). Continuity and change in the measurement of infant attachment: Comment on Fraley and Spiker (2003). *Developmental Psychology, 39*, 409–412.

Cassidy, J. (2008). The nature of the child's ties. In J. Cassidy & P. Shaver (Eds.), *Handbook of attachment: Theory, research, and clinical implications* (2nd ed., pp. 3–22). New York, NY: Guilford Press.

Cassidy, J., Berlin, L., & Belsky, J. (1990, April). *Attachment organization at age 3: Antecedent and concurrent correlates.* Paper presented at the biennial meetings of the International Conference on Infant Studies, Montreal.

Cassidy, J., Kirsh, S. J., Scolton, K. L., & Parke, R. D. (1996). Attachment and representations of peer relationships. *Developmental Psychology, 32*, 892–904.

Cassidy, J., & Marvin, R. S. with the MacArthur Attachment Working Group. (1992). *Attachment organization in preschool children: Coding guidelines* (4th ed.). Unpublished manuscript, University of Virginia, Charlottesville, VA.

Cassidy, J., & Shaver, P. R. (Eds.). (2008). *Handbook of attachment: Theory, research, and clinical applications* (2nd ed.). New York, NY: Guilford Press.

Cassidy, J., Ziv, Y., Mehta, T. G., & Feeney, B. C. (2003). Feedback seeking in children and adolescents: Associations with self-perceptions, attachment representations, and depression. *Child Development, 74*, 612–628.

Chakrabarti, B., Dudbridge, E., Kent, L., Wheelwright, S., Hill-Cawthorne, G., Allison, C., ... Baron-Cohen, S. (2009). Genes related to sex steroids, neural growth, and social-emotional behavior are associated with autistic traits, empathy, and Asperger syndrome. *Autism Research, 2*, 157–177.

Champagne, F. A. (2008). Epigenetic mechanisms and the transgenerational effects of maternal care. *Frontiers in Neuroendocrinology, 29*, 386–397.

Champagne, F. A., & Mashoodh, R. (2009). Genes in context. *Current directions in Psychological Science, 18*, 127–131.

Chan, A., & Poulin, F. (2007). Monthly changes in the composition of friendship networks in early adolescence. *Merrill-Palmer Quarterly, 53*, 578–602.

Chan, A., & Poulin, F. (2009). Monthly instability in early adolescent friendship networks and depressive symptoms. *Social Development, 18*, 1–23.

Chandler, M. J., Greenspan, S., & Barenboim, C. (1973). Judgments of intentionality in response to videotaped and verbally presented moral dilemmas: The medium is the message. *Child Development, 44*, 315–320.

Chao, R. K., & Aque, C. (2009). Interpretations of parental control by Asian immigrant and European American youth. *Journal of Family Psychology, 23*, 342–354.

Chapman, J. W., & Tunmer, W. E. (1995). Development of young children's reading self-concepts: An examination of emerging subcomponents and their relationship with reading achievement. *Journal of Educational Psychology, 87*, 154–167.

Chapman, M., Zahn-Waxler, C., Cooperman, G., & Iannotti, R. (1987). Empathy and responsibility in the motivation of children's helping. *Developmental Psychology, 23*, 140–145.

Chen, X., Yang, F., & Fu, R. (2012). Culture and temperament. In M. Zentner & R. L. Shiner (Eds.), *Handbook of temperament* (pp. 462–478). New York, NY: Guilford Press.

Chess, S., & Thomas, A. (1984). *Origins and evolution of behavior disorders.* New York, NY: Bruner/Mazel.

Chess, S., & Thomas, A. (1986). *Temperament in clinical practice.* New York, NY: Guilford Press.

Cheung, C. S.-S., Pomerantz, E. M., & Dong, W. (2012). Does adolescents' disclosure to their parents matter for their academic adjustment? *Child Development, 84,* 693–710.

Chow, C. M., & Buhrmester, D. (2011). Interdependent patterns of coping and support among close friends. *Journal of Social and Personal Relationships, 28,* 684–705.

Chow, C. M., Roelse, H., Buhrmester, D., & Underwood, M. K. (2011). Transformations in friend relationships across the transition into adulthood. In B. Laursen & W. A. Collins (Eds.), *Relationship pathways: From adolescence to young adulthood* (pp. 91–111). Thousand Oaks, CA: Sage Publications.

Chow, C. M., Ruhl, H., & Buhrmester, D. (2013). The mediating role of interpersonal competence between adolescents' empathy and friendship quality: A dyadic approach. *Journal of Adolescence, 36,* 191–200.

Chumlea, W. C., Schubert, C. M., Roche, A. F., Kulin, H. E., Lee, P. A., Himes, J. H., & Sun, S. S. (2003). Age at menarche and racial comparisons in US girls. *Pediatrics, 111,* 110–113.

Ciarrochi, J., Chan, A. Y. C., & Bajgar, J. (2001). Measuring emotional intelligence in adolescents. *Personality and Individual Differences, 31,* 1105–1119.

Cicchetti, D. (1989). How research on child maltreatment has informed the study of child development: Perspectives from developmental psychology. In D. Cicchetti & V. Carlson (Eds.), *Child maltreatment: Theory and research on the causes and consequences of child abuse and neglect* (pp. 309–350). New York, NY: Cambridge University Press.

Cicchetti, D., & Rogosch, F. A. (1996). Equifinality and multifinality in developmental psychopathology. *Development and Psychopathology, 4,* 597–600.

Cicchetti, D., Rogosch, F. A., & Toth, S. L. (2006). Fostering secure attachment in infants in maltreating families through preventive interventions. *Development and Psychopathology, 18,* 623–649.

Cicchetti, D., & Schneider-Rosen, K. (1984). Theoretical and empirical considerations in the investigation of the relationship between affect and cognition in atypical populations of infants. In C. Izard, J. Kagan, & R. Zajonc (Eds.), *Emotions, cognition, and behavior* (pp. 366–406). New York, NY: Cambridge University Press.

Cicchetti, D., Toth, S. L., & Lynch, M. (1995). Bowlby's dream comes full circle: The application of attachment theory to risk and psychopathology. In T. H. Ollendick & R. J. Prinz (Eds.), *Advances in clinical child psychology* (Vol. 17, pp. 1–75). New York, NY: Plenum Press.

Cicchetti, D., & Valentino, K. (2006). An ecological-transactional perspective on child maltreatment: Failure of the average expectable environment and its influence on child development. In D. Cicchetti & D. J. Cohen (Eds.), *Developmental psychopathology: Vol. 3. Risk, disorder, and adaptation* (2nd ed., pp. 129–201). Hoboken, NJ: Wiley.

Cicirelli, V. G. (1995). *Sibling relationships across the life span.* New York, NY: Plenum Press.

Claes, M. (1998). Adolescents' closeness with parents, siblings, and friends in three countries: Canada, Belgium, and Italy. *Journal of Youth and Adolescence, 27,* 165–184.

Clark, K. E., & Ladd, G. W. (2000). Connectedness and autonomy support in parent–child relationships: Links to children's socioemotional orientation and peer relationships. *Developmental Psychology, 36,* 485–498.

Clarke-Stewart, A., & Allhusen, V. D. (2005). *What do we know about childcare?* Cambridge, MA: Harvard University Press.

Clarke-Stewart, A., & Parke, R. D. (2014). *Social development* (2nd ed.). New York, NY: John Wiley & Sons, Inc.

Clarke-Stewart, K. A. (1989). Infant day care: Maligned or malignant? *American Psychologist, 44,* 266–273.

Clarke-Stewart, K. A., Goossens, F. A., & Allhusen, V. D. (2001). Measuring infant–mother attachment: Is the Strange Situation enough? *Social Development, 10,* 143–169.

Coan, J. A. (2008). Toward a neuroscience of attachment. In J. Cassidy & P. R. Shaver (Eds.), *Handbook of attachment: Theory, research, and clinical applications* (2nd ed., pp. 241–268). New York, NY: Guilford Press.

Coan, J. A., Allen, J. J. B., & McKnight, P. E. (2006). A capability model of individual differences in frontal EEG asymmetry. *Biological Psychiatry, 72,* 198–207.

Cohen, D., & Strayer, J. (1996). Empathy in conduct-disordered and comparison youth. *Developmental Psychology, 32,* 988–998.

Cohn, D. A. (1990). Child–mother attachment of six-year-olds and social competence at school. *Child Development, 61,* 152–162.

Coie, J. D., Dodge, K. A., & Coppotelli, H. (1982). Dimensions and types of social status: A cross-age perspective. *Developmental Psychology, 18,* 557–570.

Coie, J. D., Dodge, K. A., & Kupersmidt, J. (1990). Peer group behavior and social status. In S. R. Asher & J. D. Coie (Eds.), *Peer rejection in childhood* (pp. 17–59). New York, NY: Cambridge University Press.

Coie, J. D., Lochman, J. E., Terry, R., & Hyman, C. (1992). Predicting early adolescent disorder from childhood aggression and peer rejection. *Journal of Consulting and Clinical Psychology, 60,* 783–792.

Coie, J. D., Terry, R., Lenox, K., Lochman, J. E., & Hyman, C. (1995). Childhood peer rejection and aggression as predictors of stable patterns of adolescent disorder. *Development and Psychopathology, 7,* 697–714.

Colby, A., & Kohlberg, L. (1987). *The measurement of moral judgement* (Vols. 1–2). New York, NY: Cambridge University Press.

Colder, C. R., Lochman, J. E., & Wells, K. C. (1997). The moderating effects of children's fear and activity level on relations between parenting practices and childhood symptomatology. *Journal of Abnormal Child Psychology, 25,* 251–263.

Coldwell, J., Pike, A., & Dunn, J. (2008). Maternal differential treatment and child adjustment: A multi-informant approach. *Social Development, 17,* 596–612.

Cole, A. K., & Kerns, K. A. (2001). Perceptions of sibling qualities and activities of early adolescents. *Journal of Early Adolescence, 21,* 204–227.

Cole, D. A., Maxwell, S. E., Martin, J. M., Peeke, L. G., Seroczynski, A. D., Tram, J. M., ... Maschman, T. (2001). The development of multiple domains of child and adolescent self-concept: A cohort sequential longitudinal design. *Child Development, 72,* 1723–1746.

Cole, M., & Packer, M. (2011). Culture in development. In M. E. Lamb & M. H. Bornstein (Eds.), *Social and personality development: An advanced textbook* (pp. 67–123). Hove, East Sussex: Psychology Press.

Cole, P. M., Dennis, T. A., Smith-Simon, K. E., & Cohen, L. H. (2009). Preschoolers' emotion regulation strategy understanding: Relations with emotion socialization and child self-regulation. *Social Development, 18,* 324–352.

Cole, P. M., Martin, S. E., & Dennis, T. A. (2004). Emotion regulation as a scientific construct: Methodological challenges and directions for child development research. *Child Development, 75,* 317–333.

Cole, P. M., Mischel, M. K., & Teti, L. O. (1994). The development of emotion regulation and dysregulation: A clinical perspective. In N. Fox (Ed.), The development of emotion regulation: Biological and behavioral considerations. *Monographs of the Society for Research in Child Development, 59*(2–3, Serial No. 240), 73–100.

Cole, P. M., & Tan, P. Z. (2007). Emotion socialization from a cultural perspective. In J. E. Grusec & P. Hastings (Eds.), *Handbook of socialization* (pp. 516–542). New York, NY: Guilford Press.

Cole-Detke, H., & Kobak, R. (1996). Attachment processes in eating disorder and depression. *Journal of Consulting and Clinical Psychology, 64,* 282–290.

Colin, V. L. (1996). *Human attachment.* New York, NY: McGraw Hill.

Collins, N. L., & Feeney, B. C. (2000). A safe haven: An attachment theory perspective on support seeking and caregiving in intimate relationships. *Journal of Personality and Social Psychology, 78,* 1053–1073.

Collins, W. A. (1995). Relationships and development: Family adaptation to individual change. In S. Shulman (Ed.), *Close relationships and socioemotional development* (pp. 128–154). New York, NY: Ablex.

Collins, W. A., & Laursen, B. (2000). Adolescent relationships: The art of fugue. In C. Hendrick & S. S. Hendrick (Eds.), *Close relationships: A sourcebook* (pp. 59–69). Thousand Oaks, CA: Sage Publications.

Collins, W. A., & Laursen, B. (2004). Parent-adolescent relationships and influences. In R. Lerner & L. Steinberg (Eds.), *Handbook of adolescent psychology* (2nd ed., pp. 331–361). Hoboken, NJ: Wiley.

Collins, W. A., & Repinski, D. J. (1994). Relationships during adolescence: Continuity and change in interpersonal perspective. In R. Montemayor, G. R. Adams, & T. P. Gullotta (Eds.), *Personal relationships during adolescence* (pp. 7–36). Thousand Oaks, CA: Sage Publications.

Collins, W. A., & Repinski, D. J. (2001). Parents and adolescents as transformers of relationships: Dyadic adaptations to developmental change. In J. R. M. Gerris (Ed.), *Dynamics of parenting: International perspectives on nature and sources of parenting* (pp. 429–443). Leuven: Garant.

Collins, W. A., & Russell, G. (1991). Mother-child and father–child relationships in middle childhood and adolescence: A developmental analysis. *Developmental Review, 11,* 99–136.

Collins, W. A., & Steinberg, L. (2008). Adolescent development in interpersonal context. In W. Damon & R. M. Lerner (Eds.), *Child and adolescent development: An advanced course* (pp. 551–590). Hoboken, NJ: John Wiley & Sons.

Collins, W. A., & Van Dulmen, M. (2006a). "The course of true love(s)...": Origins and pathways in the development of romantic relationships. In A. Booth & A. Crouter (Eds.), *Romance and sex in adolescence and emerging adulthood: Risks and opportunities* (pp. 63–86). Mahwah, NJ: Erlbaum.

Collins, W. A., & Van Dulmen, M. (2006b). Friendships and romantic relationships in emerging adulthood: Continuities and discontinuities. In J. J. Arnett & J. Tanner (Eds.), *Emerging adults in America: Coming of age in the 21st century* (pp. 219–234). Washington, DC: American Psychological Association.

Commons, M. L., & Wolfsont, C. A. (2002). A complete theory of empathy must consider stage changes. *Behavioral and Brain Sciences, 25,* 30–31.

Compas, B. E. (1987). Coping with stress during childhood and adolescence. *Psychological Bulletin, 101,* 393–403.

Conger, K. J., Bryant, C. M., & Brennom, J. M. (2004). The changing nature of adolescent sibling relationships: A theoretical framework for evaluating the role of relationship quality. In R. D. Conger, F. O. Lorenz,

& K. A. S. Wickrama (Eds.), *Continuity and change in family relations: Theory, methods, and empirical findings* (pp. 319–344). Mahwah, NJ: Erlbaum.

Conger, K. J., & Conger, R. D. (1996). Sibling relationships. In R. Simons (Ed.), *Understanding differences between divorced and intact families* (pp. 104–121). Thousand Oaks, CA: Sage Publications.

Conger, K. J., & Kramer, L. (2010). Introduction to the special section: Perspectives on sibling relationships: Advancing child development research. *Child Development Perspectives, 4,* 69–71.

Conger, K. J., & Little, M. L. (2010). Sibling relationships during the transition to adulthood. *Child Development Perspective, 4,* 87–94.

Conger, K. J., Stocker, C., & McGuire, S. (2009). Sibling socialization: The effects of stressful life events and experiences. In L. Kramer & K. J. Conger (Eds.), *Siblings as agents of socialization. New Directions for Child and Adolescent Development* (Vol. 126, pp. 45–60). San Francisco, CA: Jossey-Bass.

Conger, R. D., Cui, M., Bryant, C. M., & Elder, G. H., Jr. (2000). Competence in early adult romantic relationships: A developmental perspective on family influences. *Journal of Personality and Social Psychology, 79,* 224–237.

Connolly, J. A., Craig, W., Goldberg, A., & Pepler, D. (1999). Conceptions of cross-sex friendships and romantic relationships in early adolescence. *Journal of Youth and Adolescence, 28,* 481–494.

Connolly, J. A., & Goldberg, A. (1999). Romantic relationships in adolescence: The role of friends and peers in their emergence and development. In W. Furman, B. B. Brown, & C. Feiring (Eds.), *The development of romantic relationships in adolescence* (pp. 266–290). New York, NY: Cambridge University Press..

Contreras, J. M., & Kerns, K. A. (2000). Emotion regulation processes: Explaining links between parent–child attachment and peer relationships. In K. A. Kerns, J. M. Contreras, & A. M. Neal-Barnett (Eds.), *Family and peers: Linking two social worlds* (pp. 1–26). Westport, CT: Praeger Publisher.

Contreras, J. M., Kerns, K. A., Weimer, B. L., Gentzler, A. L., & Tomich, P. L. (2000). Emotion regulation as a mediator of associations between mother–child attachment and peer relationships in middle childhood. *Journal of Family Psychology, 14,* 111–124.

Conway, M. (2005). Memory and the self. *Journal of Memory and Language, 53,* 594–628.

Cooley, C. H. (1902). *Human nature and the social order.* New York, NY: Charles Scribner's Sons.

Cooper, M., Shaver, P. R., & Collins, N. L. (1998). Attachment styles, emotion regulation, and adjustment in adolescence. *Journal of Personality and Social Psychology, 74,* 1380–1397.

Copeland-Mitchell, J. M., Denham, S. A., & DeMulder, E. K. (1997). Q-sort assessment of child–teacher attachment relationships and social competence in the preschool. *Early Education and Development, 8,* 27–39.

Cornell, A. H., & Frick, P. J. (2007). The moderating effects of parenting styles in the association between behavior inhibition and parent-reported guilt and empathy in preschool children. *Journal of Clinical Child & Adolescent Psychology, 36,* 305–318.

Corter, C., & Fleming, A. S. (2002). Psychobiology of maternal behavior in human beings. In M. H. Bornstein (Ed.), *Handbook of parenting: Vol. 2. Biology and ecology of parenting* (2nd ed., pp. 141–182). Mahwah, NJ: Erlbaum.

Coster, W. J., Gersten, M. S., Beeghly, M., & Cicchetti, D. (1989). Communicative functioning in maltreated toddlers. *Developmental Psychology, 25,* 1020–1029.

Côté, J. E., & Levine, C. (1988). A critical examination of the ego identity status paradigm. *Developmental Review, 8,* 147–184.

Courage, M. L., Reynolds, G. D., & Richars, J. E. (2006). Infants' attention to patterned stimuli: Developmental change from 3 to 12 months of age. *Child Development, 77,* 680–695.

Cox, M. (2010). Family systems and sibling relationships. *Child Development Perspectives, 4,* 95–96.

Cox, M. J., Owen, M. T., Henderson, V. K., & Margand, N. A. (1992). Prediction of infant–father and infant–mother attachment. *Developmental Psychology, 28,* 474–483.

Cozolino, L. (2002). *The neuroscience of psychotherapy: Building and rebuilding the human brain.* New York, NY: Norton.

Cozolino, L. (2014). *The neuroscience of human relationships: Attachment and the developing social brain* (2nd ed.). New York, NY: Norton.

Craik, F. I. M., Moroz, T. M., Moscovitch, M., Stuss, D. T., Winocur, G., Tulving, E., & Kapur, S. (1999). In search of the self: A positron emission tomography study. *Psychological Science, 10,* 26–34.

Crick, N. R., & Dodge, K. A. (1994). A review and reformulation of social-information processing mechanisms in children's social adjustment. *Psychological Bulletin, 115,* 74–101.

Criss, M. M., Pettit, G. S., Bates, J. E., Dodge, K. A., & Lapp, A. L. (2002). Family adversity, positive peer relationships, and children's externalizing behavior: A longitudinal perspective on risk and resilience. *Child Development, 74,* 1220–1237.

Critchley, H. D. (2005). Neural mechanisms of autonomic, affective, and cognitive integration. *Journal of Comparative Neurology, 493,* 154–166.

Crittenden, A. (2010). *The price of motherhood: Why the most important job in the world is still the least valued.* New York, NY: Picador.

Crittenden, P. M. (1990). Internal representational models of attachment relationships. *Infant Mental Health Journal, 11,* 259–277.

Crittenden, P. M. (1994). *Preschool Assessment of Attachment* (2nd ed.). Unpublished manuscript, Family Relations Institute, Miami, FL.

Crittenden, P. M., & DiLalla, D. L. (1988). Compulsive compliance: The development of an inhibitory coping strategy in infancy. *Journal of Abnormal Psychology, 16,* 585–599.

Crocetti, E., Rubini, M., & Meeus, W. (2008). Capturing the dynamics of identity formation in various ethnic groups: Development and validation of a three-dimensional model. *Journal of Adolescence, 31,* 207–222.

Crockenberg, S. B. (1981). Infant irritability, mother responsiveness, and social support influences on the security of infant–mother attachment. *Child Development, 52,* 857–865.

Crockenberg, S. B., & Soby, B. A. (1989). Self-esteem and teenage pregnancy. In A. M. Mecca, N. J. Smelser, & J. Vasconcellos (Eds.), *The social importance of self-esteem* (pp. 125–164). Berkeley: University of California Press.

Crockenberg, S. C., Leerkes, E. M., & Lekka, S. K. (2007). Pathways from marital aggression to infant emotion regulation: The development of withdrawal in infancy. *Infant Behavior and Development, 30,* 97–113.

Cross, W. E. (1987). A two-factor theory of Black identity: Implications for the study of identity development in minority children. In J. S. Phinney & M. J. Rotheram (Eds.), *Children's ethnic socialization: Pluralism and development* (pp. 117–133). Newbury Park, CA: Sage Publications.

Crowell, J. A., Fraley, R. C., & Shaver, P. R. (2008). Measurement of individual differences in adolescent and adult attachment. In J. Cassidy & P. R. Shaver (Eds.), *Handbook of attachment: Theory, research, and clinical applications* (2nd ed., pp. 599–634). New York, NY: Guilford Press.

Crowell, J. A., Treboux, D., Gao, Y., Fyffe, C., Pan, H., & Waters, E. (2002). Assessing secure base behavior in adulthood: Development of a measure, links to adult attachment representations, and relations to couples' communication and reports of relationships. *Developmental Psychology, 38,* 679–693.

Crowell, J. A., & Waters, E. (1994). Bowlby's theory grown up: The role of attachment in adult love relationships. *Psychological Inquiry, 5,* 31–34.

Cummings, E. M. (2003). Toward assessing attachment on an emotional security continuum: Comment on Fraley and Spieker (2003). *Developmental Psychology, 39,* 405–408.

Cummings, E. M., & Davies, P. (2010). Emotional regulation and marital conflict. In P. K. Smith & C. H. Hart (Eds.), *Wiley-Blackwell handbook of childhood social development* (2nd ed.). Oxford: Wiley-Blackwell.

Cunningham, J. N., Kliewer, W., & Garner, P. W. (2009). Emotion socialization, child emotion understanding and regulation, and adjustment in urban African American families: Differential associations across child gender. *Development and Psychopathology, 21,* 261–283.

Cutting, A. L., & Dunn, J. (2006). Conversations with siblings and with friends: Links between relationship quality and social understanding. *British Journal of Developmental Psychology, 24,* 73–87.

Dahl, R. E. (2001). Affect regulation, brain development, and behavioral/emotional health in adolescence. *CNS Spectrums, 6,* 60–72.

Dahl, R. E. (2004). Adolescent brain development: A period of vulnerabilities and opportunities. *Annals of the New York Academy of Sciences, 1021,* 1–22.

Damasio, A. R. (1994). *Descartes' error: Emotion, reason, and the human brain.* New York, NY: Avon Books.

Damon, W. (1977). *The social world of the child.* San Francisco, CA: Jossey-Bass.

Damon, W. (1983). *Social and personality development: Infancy through adolescence.* New York, NY: Norton.

Damon, W. (1988). *The moral child: Nurturing children's natural moral growth.* New York, NY: Free Press.

Damon, W., & Hart, D. (1982). The development of self-understanding from infancy through adolescence. *Child Development, 53,* 841–864.

Damon, W., & Hart, D. (1988). *Self-understanding in childhood and adolescence.* New York, NY: Cambridge University Press.

Damon, W., & Hart, D. (1992). Social understanding, self-understanding, and morality. In M. Bornstein & M. E. Lamb (Eds.), *Developmental psychology: An advanced textbook* (3rd ed., pp. 421–464). Hillsdale, NJ: Erlbaum.

Damon, W., & Hart, D. (1995). Prosocial behavior and caring in adolescence: Relations to self-understanding and social judgment. *Child Development, 66,* 1346–1359.

Daniels, D., & Plomin, R. (1985). Differential experiences of siblings in the same family. *Developmental Psychology, 21,* 747–760.

D'Argembeau, A., Feyers, D., Majerus, S., Collette, F., Van Der Linden, M., Maquet,

P., & Salmon, E. (2008). Self-reflection over time: Cortical midline structures differentiate between present and past selves. *Social Cognitive and Affective Neuroscience, 3,* 244–252.

Darling, N., & Steinberg, L. (1993). Parenting style as context: An integrative model. *Psychological Bulletin, 113,* 487–496.

Darwin, C. (1872). *The expression of emotions in man and animals.* London: John Murray.

Das Eiden, R., Teti, D., & Corns, K. (1995). Maternal working models of attachment, marital adjustment, and the parent–child relationship. *Child Development, 66,* 1504–1518.

Dashiell, J. F. (1928). Are there any native emotions? *Psychological Review, 35,* 319–327.

Davidov, M., & Grusec, J. E. (2006). Untangling the links of parental responsiveness to distress and warmth to child outcomes. *Child Development, 77,* 44–58.

Davidov, M., Zahn-Waxler, C., Roth-Hanania, R., & Knafo, A. (2013). Concern for others in the first year of life: Theory, evidence, and avenues for research. *Child Development Perspectives, 7,* 126–131.

Davidson, R. J. (1994). Temperament, affective style, and frontal lobe symmetry. In G. Dawson & K. W. Fischer (Eds.), *Human behavior and the developing brain* (pp. 518–536). New York, NY: Guilford Press.

Davidson, R. J., Fox, N. A., & Kalin, N. H. (2007). Neural bases of emotion regulation in non-human primates and humans. In J. J. Gross (Ed.), *Handbook of emotion regulation* (pp. 47–68). New York, NY: Guilford Press.

Davies, P., & Cummings, E. M. (1994). Marital conflict and child adjustment: An emotional security hypothesis. *Psychological Bulletin, 116,* 387–411.

Davis, E. L., & Levine, L. J. (2013). Emotion regulation strategies that promote learning: Reappraisal enhances children's memory for educational information. *Child Development, 84,* 361–374.

Davis, K. (2012). Friendship 2.0: Adolescents' experiences of belonging and self-disclosure online. *Journal of Adolescence, 35,* 1527–1536.

Dawson, A. E., Allen, J. P., Marston, E. G., Hafen, C. A., & Schad, M. M. (2014). Adolescent insecure attachment as a predictor of maladaptive coping and externalizing behaviors in emerging adulthood. *Attachment & Human Development, 16,* 462–478.

Dawson, G., Ashman, S. B., Hessl, D., Spieker, S., Frey, K., Panagiotides, H., & Embry, L. (2001). Autonomic and brain electrical activity in securely- and insecurely-attached infants of depressed mothers. *Infant Behavior and Development, 24,* 135–149.

Dawson, G., Panagiotides, H., Klinger, L. G., & Hill, D. (1992). The role of frontal lobe functioning in the development of infant self-regulatory behavior. *Brain and Cognition, 20,* 152–175.

Day, R. D., & Padilla-Walker, L. (2009). Mother and father connectedness and involvement during early adolescence. *Journal of Family Psychology, 23,* 900–904.

Dearing, R. L., Stuewig, J., & Tangney, J. P. (2005). On the importance of distinguishing shame from guilt: Relations to problematic alcohol and drug use. *Addictive Behaviors, 30,* 1392–1404.

Deater-Deckard, K. (2001). Annotation: Recent research examining the roles of peer relationships in the development of psychopathology. *Journal of Child Psychology and Psychiatry, 42,* 565–579.

Deater-Deckard, K., Dunn, J., & Lussier, G. (2002). Sibling relationships and social-emotional development in different family contexts. *Social Development, 11,* 571–590.

Deblinger, E., & Runyon, M. (2005). Understanding and treating feelings of shame in children who have experienced maltreatment. *Child Maltreatment, 10,* 364–376.

DeCasper, A. J., & Spence, M. J. (1986). Prenatal maternal speech influences newborns' perception of speech sounds. *Infant Behavior and Development, 9,* 133–150.

Decety, J. (2010). The neurodevelopment of empathy in humans. *Developmental Neuroscience, 32,* 257–267.

Decety, J., & Howard, L. H. (2013). The role of affect in the neurodevelopment of morality. *Child Development Perspectives, 7,* 49–54.

Decety, J., & Meyer, M. (2008). From emotion resonance to empathic understanding: A social developmental neuroscience account. *Development and Psychopathology, 20,* 1053–1080.

Degirmencioglu, S. M., Urberg, K. A., Tolson, J. M., & Richard, P. (1998). Adolescent friendship networks: Continuity and change over the school year. *Merrill-Palmer Quarterly, 44,* 313–337.

DeGoede, I. H. A., Branje, S. J. T., Delsing, M. J. M. H., & Meeus, W. H. J. (2009). Linkages over time between adolescents' relationships with parents and friends. *Journal of Youth and Adolescence, 38,* 1304–1315.

DeGoede, I. H. A., Branje, S. J. T., & Meeus, W. H. J. (2009). Developmental changes and gender differences in adolescents' perceptions of friendships. *Journal of Adolescence, 32,* 1105–1123.

DeHart, G. B., Sroufe, L. A., & Cooper, R. G. (2004). *Child development: Its nature and course* (5th ed.). New York, NY: McGraw Hill.

Deihl, L. M., Vicary, J. R., & Deike, R. C. (1997). Longitudinal trajectories of self-esteem from early to middle adolescence and related psychosocial variables among rural adolescents. *Journal of Research in Adolescence, 7,* 393–411.

DeKlyen, M., & Greenberg, M. T. (2008). Attachment and psychopathology in childhood. In J. Cassidy & P. R. Shaver (Eds.), *Handbook of attachment: Theory, research, and clinical applications* (2nd ed., pp. 637–665). New York, NY: Guilford Press.

Deković, M., & Buist, K. L. (2005). Multiple perspectives within the family: Family relationship patterns. *Journal of Family Issues, 26,* 467–490.

Deković, M., & Gerris, J. R. M. (1994). Developmental analyses of social cognitive and behavioral differences between popular and rejected children. *Journal of Applied Developmental Psychology, 15,* 367–386.

Deković, M., & Janssens, J. M. (1992). Parents' child-rearing style and child's sociometric status. *Developmental Psychology, 28,* 925–932.

DeLuccie, M. F. (1995). Mothers as gatekeepers: A model of maternal mediators of father involvement. *The Journal of Genetic Psychology, 156,* 115–131.

Demo, D. H., & Savin-Williams, R. C. (1992). Self-concept stability and change during adolescence. In R. P. Lipka & T. M. Brinthaupt (Eds.), *Self-perspectives across the life span* (Vol. 4, pp. 116–150). Albany, NY: State University of New York Press.

Denham, S. A. (1998). *Emotional development in young children.* New York, NY: Guilford Press.

Denham, S. A., Bassett, H. H., & Wyatt, T. (2007). The socialization of emotional competence. In J. E. Grusec & P. Hastings (Eds.), *Handbook of socialization* (pp. 516–542). New York, NY: Guilford Press.

Denham, S. A., Blair, K. A., DeMulder, E., Levitas, J., Sawyer, K., Auerbach-Major, S., & Queenan, P. (2003). Preschool emotional competence: Pathway to social competence? *Child Development, 74,* 238–256.

Denham, S. A., McKinley, M., Couchoud, E., & Holt, R. (1990). Emotional and behavioral predictors of preschool peer ratings. *Child Development, 61,* 1145–1152.

Denham, S. A., Warren, H., von Salisch, M., Benga, O., Chin, J.-C., & Geangu, E. (2010). Emotions and social development in childhood. In P. K. Smith & C. H. Hart (Eds.), *Wiley-Blackwell handbook of childhood social development* (2nd ed.). Oxford: Wiley-Blackwell.

Denham, S. A., Workman, E., Cole, P. M., Weissbrod, C., Kendziora, K. T., & Zahn-Waxler, C. (2000). Prediction of behavior problems from early to middle childhood: The role of parental socialization and emotion expression. *Development and Psychopathology, 12,* 23–45.

Dennis, T. A., Buss, K. A., & Hastings, P. D. (Eds.). (2012). Physiological measures of emotion from a developmental perspective: State of the science. *Monographs of the Society for Research in Child Development, 77*(2).

Dennis, T. A., O'Toole, L. J., & DeCicco, J. M. (2013). Emotion regulation from the perspective of developmental neuroscience: What, where, when, and why. In K. C. Barrett, N. A. Fox, G. A. Morgan, D. J. Fidler, & L. A. Daunhauer (Eds.), *Handbook of self-regulatory processes in development: New directions and international perspectives* (pp. 135–172). New York, NY: Psychology Press.

De Pauw, S. S. W., & Mervielde, I. (2010). Temperament, personality and developmental psychopathology: A review based on the conceptual dimensions underlying childhood traits. *Child Psychiatry and Human Development, 41,* 313–329.

Derryberry, D., & Rothbart, M. K. (1997). Reactive and effortful processes in the organization of temperament. *Development and Psychopathology, 9*, 633–652.

Derryberry, D., & Tucker, D. E. (2006). Motivation, self-regulations, and self-organization. In D. Cicchetti & D. J. Cohen (Eds.), *Developmental psychopathology: Vol. 2. Developmental neuroscience* (2nd ed., pp. 502–532). New York, NY: Wiley.

Devue, C., Collette, F., Balteau, E., Degueldre, C., Luxen, A., Maquet, P., & Brédart, S. (2007). Here I am: The cortical correlates of visual self-recognition. *Brain Research, 1143*, 169–182.

de Waal, F. B. M. (2008). Putting the altruism back into altruism: The evolution of empathy. *Annual Review of Psychology, 59*, 279–300.

deWall, C. N., & Baumeister, R. F. (2006). Alone but feeling no pain: Effects of social exclusion on physical pain tolerance and pain threshold, affective forecasting, and interpersonal empathy. *Journal of Personality and Social Psychology, 91*, 1–15.

de Wolff, M. S., & van IJzendoorn, M. H. (1997). Sensitivity and attachment: A meta-analysis on parental antecedents of infant attachment. *Child Development, 68*, 571–591.

Diamond, L. M. (1998). Development of sexual orientation among adolescent and young adult women. *Developmental Psychology, 34*, 1085–1095.

Diamond, L. M. (2001). Contributions of psychophysiology to research on adult attachment: Review and recommendations. *Personality and Social Psychology Review, 5*, 276–295.

Diamond, L. M. (2003). What does sexual orientation orient? A biobehavioral model distinguishing romantic love and sexual desire. *Psychological Review, 110*, 173–192.

Dick, D., Rose, R., Pulkkinen, L., & Kapiro, J. (2001). Measuring puberty and understanding its impact: A longitudinal study of adolescent twins. *Journal of Youth and Adolescence, 30*, 385–400.

Dickerson, S. S., Gruenewald, T. L., & Kemeny, M. E. (2004). When the social self is threatened: Shame, physiology, and health. *Journal of Personality, 72*, 1191–1216.

Dickerson, S. S., Kemeny, M. E., Aziz, N., Kim, K. H., & Fahey, J. L. (2004). Immunological effects of induced shame and guilt. *Psychosomatic Medicine, 66*, 124–131.

Diener, M. L., & Mangelsdorf, S. C. (1999). Behavioral strategies for emotion regulation in toddlers: Associations with maternal involvement and emotional expressions. *Infant Behavior and Development, 22*, 569–583.

Diener, M. L., Mangelsdorf, S. C., McHale, J. L., & Frosch, C. A. (2002). Infants' behavioral strategies for emotion regulation with fathers and mothers: Associations with emotional expressions and attachment quality. *Infancy, 5*, 151–172.

Dienstbier, R. A. (1984). The role of emotion in moral socialization. In C. Izard, J. Kagan, & R. B. Zajonc (Eds.), *Emotions, cognitions and behavior* (pp. 484–513). New York, NY: Cambridge University Press.

DiLalla, L. F., Elam, K. K., & Smolen, A. (2009). Genetic and gene-environment interaction effects on preschoolers' social behaviors. *Developmental Psychobiology, 51*, 451–464.

di Pellegrino, G., Fadiga, L., Fogassi, L., Gallese, V., & Rizzolatti, G. (1992). Understanding motor events: A neurophysiological study. *Experimental Brain Research, 91*, 176–180.

DiPietro, J. A., Hodgson, D. M., Costigan, K. A., & Johnson, T. R. B. (1996). Fetal antecedents of infant temperament. *Child Development, 67*, 2568–2583.

Dishion, T. J., Andrews, D. W., & Crosby, L. (1995). Antisocial boys and their friends in early adolescence: Relationship characteristics, quality, and interactional process. *Child Development, 65*, 139–151.

Dishion, T. J., McCord, J., & Poulin, F. (1999). When interventions harm: Peer groups and problem behavior. *American Psychologist, 54*, 755–764.

Dishion, T. J., Nelson, S. E., & Bullock, B. M. (2004). Premature adolescent autonomy: Parent disengagement and deviant peer process in the amplification of problem behavior. *Journal of Adolescence, 27*, 515–530.

Dishion, T. J., & Patterson, G. R. (2006). The development and ecology of antisocial behavior in children and adolescents. In D. Cicchetti & D. J. Cohen (Eds.),

Developmental psychopathology: Vol. 3. Risk, disorder, and adaptation (pp. 503–541). New York, NY: Wiley.

Dishion, T. J., Spracklen, K. M., Andrews, D. M., & Patterson, G. R. (1996). Deviancy training in male adolescent friendships. *Behavior Therapy, 27,* 373–390.

Dix, T., Gershoff, E. T., Meunier, L. N., & Miller, P. C. (2004). The affective structure of supportive parenting: Depressive symptoms, immediate emotions, and child-oriented motivation. *Developmental Psychology, 40,* 1212–1227.

Dixon, J. C. (1957). Development of self-recognition. *Journal of Genetic Psychology, 91,* 251–256.

Dodge, K. A. (1983). Behavioral antecedents of peer social status. *Child Development, 54,* 1386–1399.

Dodge, K. A., & Frame, C. L. (1982). Social cognitive biases and deficits in aggressive boys. *Child Development, 53,* 620–635.

Dodge, K. A., Lansford, J. E., Burks, V. S., Bates, J. E., Pettit, G. S., Fontaine, R., & Price, J. M. (2003). Peer rejection and social information-processing factors in the development of aggressive behavior problems in children. *Child Development, 74,* 374–393.

Dodge, K. A., McLoyd, V. C., & Lansford, J. E. (2005). The cultural context of physically disciplining children. In V. C. McLoyd, N. E. Hill, & K. A. Dodge (Eds.), *African American family life* (pp. 245–263). New York, NY: Guilford Press.

Dodge, K. A., Murphy, R. R., & Buchsbaum, L. (1984). The assessment of attention-cue detection skills in children: Implications for developmental psychopathology. *Child Development, 55,* 163–173.

Dodge, K. A., & Newman, J. P. (1981). Biased decision-making processes in aggressive boys. *Journal of Abnormal Psychology, 90,* 375–379.

Doh, H., & Falbo, T. (1999). Social competence, maternal attentiveness, and overprotectiveness: Only children in Korea. *International Journal of Behavioral Development, 23,* 149–162.

Doherty, N. A., & Feeney, J. A. (2004). The composition of attachment networks throughout the adult years. *Personal Relationships, 11,* 469–488.

Domitrovich, C. E., Cortes, R. C., & Greenberg, M. T. (2007). Improving young children's social and emotional competence: A randomized trial of the preschool PATHS curriculum. *Journal of Primary Prevention, 28,* 67–91.

Donovan, W. L., & Leavitt, L. A. (1985). Physiologic assessment of mother–infant attachment. *Journal of the American Academy of Child Psychiatry, 24,* 65–70.

Donovan, W. L., Leavitt, L. A., & Balling, J. D. (1978). Maternal physiological response to infant signals. *Psychophysiology, 15,* 68–74.

Dorn, L. D., Crockett, L. J., & Petersen, A. C. (1988). The relation of pubertal status to intrapersonal changes in young adolescents. *Journal of Early Adolescence, 8,* 405–419.

Downey, D. B., & Condron, D. J. (2004). Playing well with others in kindergarten: The benefit of siblings at home. *Journal of Marriage and Family, 66,* 333–350.

Dozier, M., Stovall-McClough, K. C., & Albus, K. E. (2008). Attachment and psychopathology in adulthood. In J. Cassidy & P. R. Shaver (Eds.), *Handbook of attachment: Theory, research, and clinical applications* (2nd ed., pp. 718–744). New York, NY: Guilford Press.

DuBois, D. L., Bull, C. A., Sherman, M. D., & Roberts, M. (1998). Self-esteem and adjustment in early adolescence: A social-contextual perspective. *Journal of Youth and Adolescence, 27,* 557–583.

DuBois, D. L., Burk-Braxton, C., Swenson, L. P., Tevendale, H. D., Lockerd, E. M., & Moran, B. L. (2002). Getting by with a little help from self and others: Self-esteem and social support as resources during early adolescence. *Developmental Psychology, 38,* 822–839.

Duffy, A. L., & Nesdale, D. (2009). Peer groups, social identity, and children's bullying behavior. *Social Development, 18,* 121–139.

Dumas, T. M., Ellis, W. E., & Wolfe, D. A. 2012). Identity development as a buffer of adolescent risk behaviors in the context of peer group pressure and control. *Journal of Adolescence, 35,* 917–927.

Dumas, T. M., Lawford, H., Tieu, T.-T., & Pratt, M. W. (2009). Positive parenting in adolescence and its relation to low point narration and identity status in emerging adulthood: A longitudinal analysis. *Developmental Psychology, 45,* 1531–1544.

Dunn, J. (1983). Sibling relationships in early childhood. *Child Development, 54,* 787–811.

Dunn, J. (1987). The beginnings of moral understanding: Development in the second year. In J. Kagan & S. Lamb (Eds.), *The emergence of morality in young children* (pp. 91–112). Chicago, IL: University of Chicago Press.

Dunn, J. (1988). *The beginnings of social understanding.* Cambridge, MA: Harvard University Press.

Dunn, J. (1993). *Young children's close relationships: Beyond attachment.* Newbury Park, CA: Sage Publications.

Dunn, J. (1995). Children as psychologists: The later correlates of individual differences in understanding of emotions and other minds. *Cognition and Emotion, 9,* 187–201.

Dunn, J. (1996a). Brothers and sisters in middle childhood and early adolescence: Continuity and change in individual differences. In G. H. Brody (Ed.), *Sibling relationships: Their causes and consequences* (pp. 31–46). Norwood, NJ: Ablex.

Dunn, J. (1996b). The Emanuel Miller Memorial Lecture 1995: Children's relationships: Bridging the divide between cognitive and social development. *Journal of Child Psychology and Psychiatry and Allied Disciplines, 37,* 507–548.

Dunn, J. (1999). Making sense of the social world: Mindreading, emotion, and relationships. In P. D. Zelazo, J. W. Astington, & D. R. Olson (Eds.), *Developing theories of intention: Social understanding and self-control* (pp. 229–242). Mahwah, NJ: Erlbaum.

Dunn, J. (2000). Mind-reading, emotion understanding, and relationships. *International Journal of Behavioral Development, 24,* 142–144.

Dunn, J. (2002). Sibling relationships. In P. K. Smith & C. H. Hart (Eds.), *Wiley-Blackwell handbook of childhood social development* (pp. 223–237). Oxford: Blackwell.

Dunn, J. (2004). *Children's friendships: The beginnings of intimacy.* London: Blackwell.

Dunn, J. (2005). Commentary: Siblings in their families. *Journal of Family Psychology, 19,* 654–657.

Dunn, J. (2006). Moral development in early childhood and social interaction in the family. In M. Killen & J. G. Smetana (Eds.), *Handbook of moral development* (pp. 331–350). Mahwah, NJ: Erlbaum.

Dunn, J. (2007). Siblings and socialization. In J. E. Grusec & P. D. Hastings (Eds.), *Handbook of socialization* (pp. 309–327). New York, NY: Guilford Press.

Dunn, J., Bretherton, I., & Munn, P. (1987). Conversations about feeling states between mothers and their young children. *Developmental Psychology, 23,* 132–139.

Dunn, J., Brown, J. R., & Maguire, M. (1995). The development of children's moral sensibility: Individual differences and emotional understanding. *Developmental Psychology, 31,* 649–659.

Dunn, J., Creps, C., & Brown, J. (1996). Children's family relationships between two and five: Developmental changes and individual differences. *Social Development, 5,* 230–250.

Dunn, J., & Cutting, A. (1999). Understanding others, and individual differences in friendship interactions in young children. *Social Development, 8,* 201–219.

Dunn, J., Cutting, A., & Demetriou, H. (2000). Moral sensibility, understanding other, and children's friendship interactions in the preschool period. *British Journal of Developmental Psychology, 18,* 159–177.

Dunn, J., Cutting, A. L., & Fisher, N. (2002). Old friends, new friends: Prediction of children's perspectives on their friends at school. *Child Development, 73,* 621–635.

Dunn, J., Deater-Deckard, K., Pickering, K., & Golding, J. (1999). Siblings, parents, and partners: Family relationships within a longitudinal community study. *Journal of Child Psychology and Psychiatry, 40,* 1025–1037.

Dunn, J., & Hughes, C. (2001). "I got some swords and you're dead!" Violent fantasy, antisocial behavior, friendship, and moral sensibility in young children. *Child Development, 72,* 491–505.

Dunn, J., & Kendrick, C. (1982). *Siblings: Love, envy, and understanding.* Cambridge, MA: Harvard University Press.

Dunn, J., & Munn, P. (1985). Becoming a family member: Family conflict and the development of social understanding in the second year. *Child Development, 56,* 480–492.

Dunn, J., & Munn, P. (1986a). Sibling quarrels and maternal intervention: Individual understanding and aggression. *Journal of Child Psychology and Psychiatry, 27,* 583–595.

Dunn, J., & Munn, P. (1986b). Siblings and prosocial development. *International Journal of Behavioral Development, 9,* 265–284.

Dunn, J., & Plomin, R. (1990). *Separate lives: Why siblings are so different.* New York, NY: Basic Books.

Dunn, J., & Slomkowski, C. (1992). Conflict and the development of social understanding. In C. U. Shantz & W. W. Hartup (Eds.), *Conflict in child and adolescent development* (pp. 70–92). Cambridge: Cambridge University Press.

Dunn, J., Slomkowski, C., & Beardsall, L. (1994). Sibling relationships from the preschool period through middle childhood and adolescence. *Developmental Psychology, 30,* 315–324.

Dunn, J., Slomkowski, C., Beardsall, L., & Rende, R. (1994). Adjustment in middle childhood and early adolescence: Links with earlier and contemporary sibling relationships. *Journal of Child Psychology and Psychiatry, 35,* 491–504.

Dunn, J., Slomkowski, C., Donelan, N., & Herrera, C. (1995). Conflict, understanding, and relationships: Developments and differences in the preschool years. *Early Education and Development, 6,* 303–316.

Dunn, J., Stocker, C. M., & Plomin, R. (1990). Nonshared experiences within the family: Correlates of behavioral problems in middle childhood. *Development and Psychopathology, 2,* 113–126.

Dunsmore, J. C., & Karn, M. A. (2004). The influence of peer relationships and maternal socialization on kindergartners' developing emotion knowledge. *Early Education and Development, 15,* 39–56.

Dunsmore, J. C., Noguchi, R. J. P., Garner, P. W., Casey, E. C., & Bhullar, N. (2008). Gender specific linkages of affective social competence with peer relations in preschool children. *Early Education and Development, 19,* 211–237.

Dweck, C. S. (2002). The development of ability conceptions. In A. Wigfield & J. S. Eccles (Eds.), *Development of achievement motivation* (pp. 57–88). San Diego, CA: Academic.

Dyk, P. H., & Adams, G. R. (1987). The association between identity development and intimacy during adolescence: A theoretical treatise. *Journal of Adolescent Research, 2,* 223–235.

Dyk, P. H., & Adams, G. R. (1990). Identity and intimacy: An initial investigation of three theoretical models using cross-lag panel correlations. *Journal of Youth and Adolescence, 19,* 91–110.

Dykas, M. J., & Cassidy, J. (2011). Attachment and the processing of social information across the life span: Theory and evidence. *Psychological Bulletin, 137,* 19–46.

Dykas, M. J., Cassidy, J., & Woodhouse, S. S. (2009, April). Rejection sensitivity in adolescence: The role of attachment behavior and representations. In K. B. Ehrlich & J. Cassidy (Co-Chairs), *Fear of social rejection in adolescence: Physiological, behavioral, and relationship processes.* Symposium conducted at the biennial meeting of the Society for Research in Child Development, Denver, CO.

Dykas, M. J., Woodhouse, S. S., Ehrlich, K. B., & Cassidy, J. (2010). Adolescents and parents reconstruct memories about their conflict as a function of adolescent attachment? *Child Development, 81,* 1445–1459.

Dykas, M. J., Woodhouse, S. S., Jones, J. D., & Cassidy, J. (2014). Attachment-related biases in adolescents' memory. *Child Development, 85,* 2185–2201.

East, P. L. (2009). Adolescents' relationships with siblings. In R. M. Lerner & L. Steinberg (Eds.), *Handbook of adolescent psychology: Vol. 2: Contextual influences on adolescent development* (3rd ed., pp. 43–73). New York, NY: Wiley.

East, P. L., & Jacobson, L. J. (2001). The younger siblings of teenage mothers: A follow-up of their pregnancy risk. *Developmental Psychology, 37,* 254–264.

East, P. L., & Khoo, S. T. (2005). Longitudinal pathways linking family factors and sibling relationship qualities to adolescent substance use and sexual risk behaviors. *Journal of Family Psychology, 19,* 571–580.

East, P. L., & Rook, K. S. (1992). Compensatory patterns of support among children's peer relationships: A test using school friends, nonschool friends, and siblings. *Developmental Psychology, 28,* 163–172.

Easterbrooks, M. A., & Abeles, R. (2000). Windows to the self in 8-year-olds: Bridges to attachment representation and behavioral adjustment. *Attachment & Human Development, 2,* 85–106.

Eberly, M. B., & Montemayor, R. (1999). Adolescent affection and helpfulness towards parents: A 2-year follow-up. *Journal of Early Adolescence, 19,* 226–248.

Ebstein, R. P., Benjamin, J., & Belmaker, R. H. (2000). Personality and polymorphism of genes involved in aminergic neurotransmission. *European Journal of Pharmacology, 410,* 205–214.

Eckerman, C. O. (1979). The human infant in social intersection. In R. Cairns (Ed.), *The analysis of social interactions: Methods, issues, and illustrations* (pp. 163–178). Hillsdale, NJ: Lawrence Erlbaum Associates.

Eckerman, C. O., Whatley, J. L., & Kutz, S. L. (1975). Growth of social play with peers during the second year of life. *Developmental Psychology, 11,* 42–49.

Eder, D. (1985). The cycle of popularity: Interpersonal relations among female adolescents. *Sociology of Education, 58,* 154–165.

Eder, R. A. (1990). Uncovering young children's psychological selves: Individual and developmental differences. *Child Development, 61,* 849–863.

Edwards, C. P., Shipman, K., & Brown, A. (2005). The socialization of emotional understanding: A comparison of neglectful and nonneglectful mothers and their children. *Child Maltreatment, 10,* 293–304.

Egeland, B., & Carlson, B. (2004). Attachment and psychopathology. In L. Atkinson & S. Goldberg (Eds.), *Attachment issues in psychopathology and intervention* (pp. 27–48). Mahwah, NJ: Erlbaum.

Eigsti, I.-M., Zayas, V., Mischel, W., Shoda, Y., Ayduk, O., Dadlani, M. B., ... Casey, B. J. (2006). Predicting cognitive control from preschool to late adolescence and young adulthood. *Psychological Science, 17,* 478–484.

Eisenberg, N. (1998). Introduction. In W. Damon (Series Ed.) & N. Eisenberg (Vol Ed.), *Handbook of child psychology: Vol. 3. Social, emotional, and personality development* (5th ed., pp. 1–24). New York, NY: Wiley.

Eisenberg, N. (2000). Emotion, regulation, and moral development. *Annual Review of Psychology, 51,* 665–697.

Eisenberg, N. (2003). Prosocial behavior, empathy, and sympathy. In M. Bornstein & L. Davidson (Eds.), *Well-being: Positive development across the life course* (pp. 253–265). Mahwah, NJ: Erlbaum.

Eisenberg, N., & Fabes, R. A. (1998). Prosocial development. In W. Damon (Series Ed.) & N. Eisenberg (Vol. Ed.), *Handbook of child psychology: Vol. 3. Social, emotional, and personality development* (5th ed., pp. 701–778). New York, NY: Wiley.

Eisenberg, N., Fabes, R. A., Bernzweig, J., Karbon, M., Poulin, R., & Hanish, L. (1993). The relations of emotionality and regulation to preschoolers' social skills and sociometric status. *Child Development, 64,* 1418–1438.

Eisenberg, N., Fabes, R. A., & Murphy, B. C. (1996). Parents' reactions to children's negative emotions: Relations to children's social competence and comforting. *Child Development, 67,* 2227–2247.

Eisenberg, N., Fabes, R. A., Murphy, B., Maszk, P., Smith, M., & Karbon, M. (1995). The role of emotionality and regulation in children's social functioning: A longitudinal study. *Child Development, 66,* 1360–1384.

Eisenberg, N., Fabes, R. A., Schaller, M., Carlo, G., & Miller, P. A. (1991). The relations of parental characteristics and practices to children's vicarious emotional responding. *Child Development, 62,* 1393–1408.

Eisenberg, N., Fabes, R. A., Shepard, S. A., Murphy, B. C., Guthrie, I. K., Jones, S., ... Maszk, P. (1997). Contemporaneous and longitudinal prediction of children's social functioning from regulation and emotionality. *Child Development, 68,* 642–664.

Eisenberg, N., Fabes, R. A., & Spinrad, T. L. (2006). Prosocial development. In W. Damon & R. M. Lerner (Series Eds.) & N. Eisenberg (Vol. Ed.), *Handbook of child psychology: Vol. 3. Social, emotional, and personality development* (6th ed., pp. 646–718). Hoboken, NJ: Wiley.

Eisenberg, N., Guthrie, I., Fabes, R. A., Reiser, M., Murphy, B., Holgren, R., ... Losoya, S. (1997). The relations of regulation and emotionality to resiliency and competent social functioning in elementary school children. *Child Development, 68,* 295–311.

Eisenberg, N., Hofer, C., & Vaughan, J. (2007). Effortful control and its socioemotional consequences. In J. J. Gross (Ed.), *Handbook of emotion regulation* (pp. 287–306). New York, NY: Guilford Press.

Eisenberg, N., Miller, P. A., Shell, R., McNalley, S., & Shea, C. (1991). Prosocial development in adolescence: A longitudinal study. *Developmental Psychology, 27,* 849–857.

Eisenberg, N., & Murphy, B. (1995). Parenting and children's moral development. In M. H. Bornstein (Ed.), *Handbook of parenting. Vol. 4: Applied and practical parenting* (pp. 227–257). Mahwah, NJ: Erlbaum.

Eisenberg, N., Smith, C. L., Sadovsky, A., & Spinrad, T. L. (2004). Effortful control: Relations with emotion regulation, adjustment, and socialization in childhood. In R. F. Baumeister & K. D. Vohs (Eds.), *Handbook of self-regulation: Research, theory, and applications* (pp. 259–282). New York, NY: Guilford Press.

Eisenberg, N., & Spinrad, T. L. (2004). Emotion-related regulation: Sharpening the definition. *Child Development, 75,* 334–339.

Eisenberg, N., Spinrad, T. L., & Sadovsky, A. (2006). Empathy-related responding in children. In M. Killen & J. G. Smetana (Eds.), *Handbook of moral development* (pp. 517–549). Mahwah, NJ: Lawrence Erlbaum Associates.

Eisenberg, N., Valiente, C., Fabes, R. A., Smith, C. L., Reiser, M., Shepard, S. A., ... Cumberland, A. J. (2003). The relations of effortful control and ego control to children's resiliency and social functioning. *Developmental Psychology, 39,* 761–776.

Eisenberg, N., Wentzel, M., & Harris, J. D. (1998). The role of emotionality and regulation in empathy-related responding. *School Psychology Review, 27,* 506–521.

Eisenberger, N. I., Lieberman, M. D., & Williams, K. D. (2003). Does rejection hurt? An fMRI study of social exclusion. *Science, 302,* 290–292.

Egan, S. K., & Perry, D. G. (1998). Does low self-regard invite victimization? *Developmental Psychology, 34,* 299–309.

Ekman, P. (1972). Universals and cultural differences in facial expressions of emotion. In J. Cole (Ed.), *Nebraska Symposium on Motivation, 1971* (pp. 207–283). Lincoln: University of Nebraska Press.

Ekman, P. (1984). Expression and the nature of emotion. In K. Sherer & P. Ekman (Eds.), *Approaches to emotion* (pp. 329–343). New York, NY: Prentice Hall.

Ekman, P. (1993). Facial expressions and emotion. *American Psychologist, 48,* 384–392.

Ekman, P. (2003). *Emotions revealed.* New York, NY: Times Books.

Ekman, P., & Friesen, W. (1975). *Unmasking the face.* Englewood Cliffs, NJ: Prentice Hall.

Elicker, J., Englund, M., & Sroufe, L. A. (1992). Predicting peer competence and peer relationships in childhood from early parent–child relationships. In R. D. Parke & G. W. Ladd (Eds.), *Family–peer relationships: Modes of linkage* (pp. 77–106). Hillsdale, NJ: Erlbaum.

Ellis, W. E., & Zarbatany, L. (2007a). Explaining friendship formation and friendship stability: The role of children's and friends' aggression and victimization. *Merrill-Palmer Quarterly, 53,* 79–104.

Ellis, W. E., & Zarbatany, L. (2007b). Peer group status as a moderator of group influence on children's deviant, aggressive, and prosocial behavior. *Child Development, 78,* 1240–1254.

Ellsworth, P. C., & Scherer, K. R. (2003). Appraisal processes in emotion. In R. J. Davidson, K. R. Scherer & H. H. Goldsmith (Eds.), *Handbook of affective sciences* (pp. 572–595). New York, NY: Oxford University Press.

Emde, R. N., Biringen, Z., Clyman, R., & Oppenheim, D. (1991). The moral self of infancy: Affective core and procedural knowledge. *Developmental Review, 11,* 251–270.

Emde, R. N., & Robinson, J. (1979). The first two months: Recent research in developmental psychology and the changing view of the newborn. In J. Noshpitz & J. Call (Eds.), *Basic handbook of child psychiatry* (pp. 72–105). New York, NY: Basic Books.

Engels, R. C. M. E., Finkenauer, C., Meeus, W., & Deković, M. (2001). Parental attachment and adolescents' emotional adjustment: The associations with social skills and relational competence. *Journal of Counseling Psychology, 48,* 428–439.

Erdley, C. A., Nangle, D. W., Newman, J. E., & Carpenter, E. M. (2001). Children's friendship experiences and psychological adjustment: Theory and research. In D. W. Nangle & C. A. Erdley (Eds.), *The role of friendship in psychological adjustment. New Directions for Child and Adolescent Development, 91,* 5–24.

Erel, O., Margolin, G., & John, R. S. (1998). Observed sibling interaction: Links with the marital and the mother–child relationship. *Developmental Psychology, 34,* 288–298.

Erickson, M. F., Sroufe, L. A., & Egeland, B. (1985). The relationship between quality of attachment and behavior problems in preschool in a high-risk sample. In I. Bretherton & E. Waters (Eds.), Growing points of attachment theory and research. *Monographs of the Society for Research in Child Development, 50*(1–2, Serial No. 209), 147–166.

Erikson, E. H. (1950/1963). *Childhood and society* (2nd ed.). New York, NY: Norton.

Erikson, E. H. (1968). *Identity: Youth and crisis.* Oxford: Norton.

Erikson, E. H. (1980). *Identity and the life cycle.* Oxford: International Universities Press.

Ernst, C., & Angst, J. (1983). *Birth order: Its influence on personality.* New York, NY: Springer.

Eschenbeck, H., Kohlmann, C. W., & Lohaus, A. (2007). Gender difference in coping strategies in children and adolescents. *Journal of Individual Differences, 28,* 18–26.

Ethier, K. A., Kershaw, T. S., Lewis, J. B., Milan, S., Niccolai, L. M., & Ickovics, J. R. (2006). Self-esteem, emotional distress and sexual behavior among adolescent females: Inter-relationships and temporal effects. *Journal of Adolescent Health, 38,* 268–274.

Evans, D., & Rothbart, M. K. (2007). Developing a model for adult temperament. *Journal of Research in Personality, 41,* 868–888.

Faber, A., & Mazlish, E. (1998). *Siblings without rivalry.* New York, NY: HarperCollins.

Fagan, A. A., & Najman, J. M. (2003). Sibling influences on adolescent delinquent behavior: An Australian longitudinal study. *Journal of Adolescence, 26,* 546–558.

Fagan, J., & Barnett, M. (2003). The relationship between maternal gatekeeping, paternal competence, mothers' attitudes about the father role, and father involvement. *Journal of Family Issues, 24,* 1020–1043.

Falbo, T., & Cooper, C. R. (1980). Young children's time and intellectual ability. *Journal of Genetic Psychology, 173,* 299–300.

Falbo, T., & Polit, D. (1986). Quantitative review of the only child literature: Research evidence and theory development. *Psychological Bulletin, 100,* 176–189.

Falbo, T., & Poston, D. L. (1993). The academic, personality, and physical outcomes of only children in China. *Child Development, 64,* 18–35.

Fan, Y., Duncan, N. W., DeGreck, M., & Northoff, G. (2011). Is there a core neural network in empathy? An fMRI based quantitative meta-analysis. *Neuroscience Biobehavioral Reviews, 35,* 903–911.

Farrer, C., Franck, N., Georgieff, N., Frith, C. D., Decety, J., & Jeannerod, M. (2003). Modulating the experience of agency: A positron emission tomography study. *Neuroimage, 18,* 324–333.

Farroni, T., Menon, E., Rigato, S., & Johnson, M. H. (2007). The perception of facial expressions in newborns. *European Journal of Developmental Psychology, 4,* 2–13.

Fearon, R. M. P., Bakermans-Kranenburg, M. J., van IJzendoorn, M. H., Lapsley, A., & Roisman, G. I. (2010). The significance of insecure attachment and disorganization in the development of children's externalizing behavior: A meta-analytic study. *Child Development, 81,* 435–456.

Fearon, R. M. P., van IJzendoorn, M. H., Fonagy, P., Bakermans-Kranenburg, M. J., Schuengel, C., & Bokhorst, C. L. (2006). In search of shared and nonshared environmental factors in security of attachment: A behavior-genetic study of the association between sensitivity and attachment security. *Developmental Psychology, 42,* 1026–1040.

Feeney, B. C. (2007). The dependency paradox in close relationships: Accepting dependence promotes independence. *Journal of Personality and Social Psychology, 92,* 268–285.

Feinberg, M. E., & Hetherington, E. M. (2001). Differential parenting as a within-family variable. *Journal of Family Psychology, 15,* 22–37.

Feinberg, M. E., Kan, M. L., & Hetherington, E. M. (2007). The longitudinal influence of coparenting conflict on parental negativity and adolescent maladjustment. *Journal of Marriage and Family, 69*, 687–702.

Feinberg, M. E., McHale, S. M., Crouter, A. C., & Cumsille, P. (2003). Sibling differentiation: Sibling and parent relationship trajectories in adolescence. *Child Development, 74*, 1261–1274.

Feinberg, M. E., Neiderhiser, J. M., Simmens, S., Reiss, D., & Hetherington, E. M. (2000). Sibling comparison of differential parental treatment in adolescence: Gender, self-esteem, and emotionality as predictors of the parenting-adjustment association. *Child Development, 71*, 1611–1628.

Feinberg, M. E., Sakuma, K.-L., Hostetler, M., & McHale, S. M. (2013). Enhancing sibling relationships to prevent adolescent problem behaviors: Theory, design and feasibility of Siblings Are Special. *Evaluation and Program Planning, 36*, 97–106.

Feinberg, M. E., Solmeyer, A. R., & McHale, S. M. (2012). The third rail of family systems: Sibling relationships, mental and behavioral health, and preventive intervention in childhood and adolescence. *Clinical Child and Family Review, 15*, 43–57.

Feiring, C. (1999). Other-sex friendship networks and the development of romantic relationships in adolescence. *Journal of Youth and Adolescence, 28*, 495–512.

Feldman, R. (2007). Parent–infant synchrony and the construction of shared timing: Physiological precursors, developmental outcomes, and risk conditions. *Journal of Child Psychology and Psychiatry, 48*, 329–354.

Feldman, R. (2010). The relational basis of adolescent adjustment: Trajectories of mother–child interactive behaviors from infancy to adolescence shape adolescents' adaptation. *Attachment & Human Development, 12*, 173–192.

Feldman, R., Bamberger, E., & Kanat-Maymon, Y. (2013). Parent-specific reciprocity from infancy to adolescence shapes children's social competence and dialogical skills. *Attachment & Human Development, 15*, 407–423.

Feldman, R., & Eidelman, A. I. (2004). Parent–infant synchrony and the social-emotional development of triplets. *Developmental Psychology, 40*, 1133–1147.

Feldman, R., Gordon, I., Schneiderman, I., Weisman, O., & Zagoory-Sharon, O. (2010). Natural variations in maternal and paternal care are associated with systematic changes in oxytocin following parent–infant contact. *Psychoneuroendocrinology, 35*, 1133–1141.

Feldman, R., Gordon, I., & Zagoory-Sharon, O. (2010). The cross-generation transmission of oxytocin in humans. *Hormones and Behavior, 58*, 669–676.

Feldman, R., Gordon, I., & Zagoory-Sharon, O. (2011). Maternal and paternal plasma, salivary, and urinary oxytocin and parent–infant synchrony: Considering stress and affiliation components of human bonding. *Developmental Science, 14*, 752–761.

Feldman, R., Greenbaum, C. W., & Yirmiya, N. (1999). Mother–infant affect synchrony as an antecedent of the emergence of self-control. *Developmental Psychology, 40*, 1133–1147.

Feldman, R., Singer, M., & Zagoory-Sharon, O. (2010). Touch attenuates infants' physiological reactivity to stress. *Developmental Science, 13*, 271–278.

Feldman, S. S., Gowen, L. K., & Fisher, L. (1998). Family relationships and gender as predictors of romantic intimacy in young adults: A longitudinal study. *Journal of Research on Adolescence, 8*, 263–286.

Feldman, S. S., & Quatman, T. (1988). Factors influencing age expectations for adolescent autonomy: A study of early adolescents and parents. *Journal of Early Adolescence, 8*, 325–343.

Feldman, S. S., Turner, R., & Araujo, K. (1999). Interpersonal context as an influence on sexual timetables of youths: Gender and ethnic effects. *Journal of Research on Adolescence, 9*, 25–52.

Felsman, D. E., & Blustein, D. L. (1999). The role of peer relatedness in late adolescent career development. *Journal of Vocational Behavior, 54*, 279–295.

Felson, R. B. (1989). Parents and the reflected appraisal process: A longitudinal analysis. *Journal of Personality and Social Psychology, 56*, 965–971.

Felson, R. B., & Zielinski, M. A. (1989). Children's self-esteem and parental support. *Journal of Marriage and the Family, 51*, 727–735.

Feng, X., Shaw, D. S., Kovacs, M., Lane, T., O'Rourke, F. E., & Alarcon, J. H. (2008). Emotion regulation in preschoolers: The roles of behavioral inhibition, maternal affective behavior, and maternal depression. *Journal of Child Psychology and Psychiatry, 49*, 132–141.

Fenton, N. (1928). The only child. *Journal of Genetic Psychology, 35*, 546–556.

Ferguson, T. J., Stegge, H., Miller, E. R., & Olsen, M. E. (1999). Guilt, shame, and symptoms in children. *Developmental Psychology, 35*, 347–357.

Feshbach, N. (1975). Empathy in children: Some theoretical and empirical considerations. *Counseling Psychologist, 5*, 25–30.

Feshbach, N. (1978). Studies of empathic behavior in children. *Progress in Experimental Personality Research, 8*, 1–47.

Festinger, L. (1954). A theory of social comparison processes. *Human Relations, 7*, 117–140.

Field, T., & Reite, M. (1984). Children's responses to separation from mother during the birth of another child. *Child Development, 55*, 1308–1316.

Field, T. M. (2007). *The amazing infant.* London: Wiley.

Field, T. M., Cohen, C., Garcia, R., & Greenberg, R. (1984). Mother–stranger face discrimination by the newborn. *Infant Behavior and Development, 7*, 19–25.

Fielder, R. L., & Carey, M. P. (2010). Prevalence and characteristics of sexual hookups among first-semester female college students. *Journal of Sex and Marital Therapy, 36*, 346–359.

Findlay, L. C., Girardi, S., & Coplan, R. J. (2006). Links between empathy, social behavior, and social understanding in early childhood. *Early Childhood Research Quarterly, 21*, 347–359.

Finkel, D., Wille, D. E., & Matheny, A. P., Jr. (1998). Preliminary results from a twin study of infant–caregiver attachment. *Behavior Genetics, 28*, 1–8.

Finkenauer, C., Engels, R. C. M. E., Meeus, W., & Oosterwegel, A. (2002). Self and identity in early adolescence: The pains and gains of knowing who and what you are. In T. M. Brinthaupt & R. P. Lipka (Eds.), *Understanding early adolescent self and identity: Applications and interventions* (pp. 22–56). Albany, NY: University of New York Press.

Finnegan, R. A., Hodges, E. V. E., & Perry, D. G. (1996). Preoccupied and avoidant coping during middle childhood. *Child Development, 67*, 1318–1328.

Fischer, K. W., & Bidell, T. R. (2006). Dynamic development of action, thought, and emotion. In W. Damon & R. M. Lerner (Eds.) & R. M. Lerner (Vol. Ed.), *Handbook of child psychology: Vol. 1. Theoretical models of human development* (6th ed., pp. 313–399). New York, NY: Wiley.

Fish, M. (2004). Attachment in infancy and preschool in low socioeconomic status rural Appalachian children: Stability and change and relations to preschool and kindergarten competence. *Development and Psychopathology, 16*, 293–312.

Fivush, R. (1994). Constructing narrative, emotion, and self in parent–child conversations about the past. In U. Neisser & R. Fivush (Eds.), *The remembering self: Construction and accuracy in the self-narrative* (pp. 136–157). Cambridge: Cambridge University Press.

Fivush, R., & Buckner, J. P. (2003). Creating gender and identity through autobiographical narratives. In R. Fivush & C. A. Haden (Eds.), *Autobiographical memory and the construction of a narrative self* (pp. 149–168). Mahwah, NJ: Erlbaum.

Flanagan, O. (1991). *Varieties of moral personality: Ethics and psychological realism.* Cambridge, MA: Harvard University Press.

Flannery, D. J., Vazsonyi, A. T., Liau, A. K., Guo, S., Powell, K. E., Atha, H., ... Embry, D. (2003). Initial behavior outcomes for the PeaceBuilders universal school-based violence prevention program. *Developmental Psychology, 39*, 292–308.

Flavell, J. H., Mumme, D. L., Green, F. L., & Flavell, E. R. (1992). Young children's understanding of different types of beliefs. *Child Development, 63*, 960–977.

Fleming, A. S., Corter, C., Stallings, J., & Steiner, M. (2002). Testosterone and prolactin are associated with emotional responses to infant cries in new fathers. *Hormones and Behavior, 42*, 399–413.

Fogel, A. (1979). Peer- vs. mother-directed behavior in 1- to 3-month-old infants. *Infant Behavior and Development, 2*, 215–226.

Folbre, N. (2010). *Valuing children: Rethinking the economics of the family.* Cambridge, MA: Harvard University Press.

Fonagy, P. (1991). Thinking about thinking: Some clinical and theoretical considerations in the treatment of a borderline patient. *International Journal of Psychoanalysis, 72,* 639–656.

Fonagy, P. (2006). The mentalization-focused approach to social development. In J. G. Allen & P. Fonagy (Eds.), *Handbook of mentalization-based treatment* (pp. 53–100). West Sussex: John Wiley & Sons, Ltd.

Fonagy, P., Gergely, G., Jurist, E. L., & Target, M. (2002). *Affect regulation, mentalization, and the development of the self.* New York, NY: Other Press.

Fonagy, P., Gergely, G., & Target, M. (2008). Psychoanalytic constructs and attachment theory and research. In J. Cassidy & P. R. Shaver (Eds.), *Handbook of attachment: Theory, research, and clinical applications* (2nd ed., pp. 783–810). New York, NY: Guilford Press.

Fonagy, P., Redfern, S., & Charman, A. (1997). The relationship between belief–desire reasoning and a projective measure of attachment security. *British Journal of Developmental Psychology, 15,* 51–61.

Fonagy, P., Steele, H., & Steele, M. (1991). Maternal representations of attachment during pregnancy predict the organization of infant–mother attachment at one year of age. *Child Development, 62,* 891–905.

Fonagy, P., Steele, H., Steele, M., Moran, G. S., & Higgitt, A. C. (1991). The capacity for understanding mental states: The reflective self in parent and child and its significance for security of attachment. *Infant Mental Health Journal, 12,* 201–218.

Fonagy, P., Steele, M., Steele, H., Higgitt, A. C., & Target, M. (1994). The Emmanuel Miller Memorial Lecture 1992: The theory and practice of resilience. *Journal of Child Psychology and Psychiatry, 25,* 231–257.

Fonagy, P., & Target, M. (1997). Attachment and reflective function: Their role in self-organization. *Development and Psychopathology, 9,* 679–700.

Fonagy, P., & Target, M. (2005). Bridging the transmission gap: An end to an important mystery of attachment research? *Attachment & Human Development, 7,* 333–343.

Fonagy, P., & Target, M. (2007). The rooting of the mind in the body. *Journal of the American Psychoanalytic Association, 55,* 411–456.

Fordham, K., & Stevenson-Hinde, J. (1999). Shyness, friendship quality, and adjustment during middle childhood. *Child Development, 67,* 1318–1328.

Forman, D. R., Aksan, N., & Kochanska, G. (2004). Toddlers' responsive imitation predicts preschool-age conscience. *Psychological Science, 15,* 699–704.

Fortuna, K., Roisman, G. I., Haydon, K. C., Groh, A. M., & Holland, A. S. (2011). Attachment states of mind and the quality of young adults' sibling relationships. *Developmental Psychology, 47,* 1366–1373.

Fox, N. A. (1991). If it's not left, it's right: Electroencephalograph asymmetry and the development of emotion. *American Psychologist, 46,* 863–872.

Fox, N. A., & Calkins, S. D. (2003). The development of self-control of emotion: Intrinsic and extrinsic influences. *Motivation and Emotion, 27,* 7–26.

Fox, N. A., & Davidson, R. J. (1987). Electroencephalogram asymmetry in response to the approach of a stranger and maternal separation in 10-month-old infants. *Developmental Psychology, 23,* 233–240.

Fox, N. A., & Davidson, R. J. (1988). Patterns of brain electrical activity during the expression of discrete emotions in ten-month-old infants. *Developmental Psychology, 24,* 230–236.

Fox, N. A., & Davidson, R. J. (1991). Hemispheric asymmetry and attachment behaviors: Developmental processes and individual differences in separation protest. In J. L. Gewirtz & W. M. Kurtines (Eds.), *Intersections with attachment* (pp. 147–164). Hillsdale, NJ: Erlbaum.

Fox, N. A., & Fein, G. (1990). *Infant day care: The current debate.* Norwood, NJ: Ablex.

Fox, N. A., & Hane, A. A. (2008). Studying the biology of human attachment. In J. Cassidy & P. R. Shaver (Eds.), *Handbook of attachment: Theory, research, and clinical applications* (2nd ed., pp. 217–240). New York, NY: Guilford Press.

Fox, N. A., Henderson, H. A., & Marshall, P. J. (2001). The biology of temperament: An integrative approach. In C. A. Nelson & M. Luciana (Eds.), *The handbook of developmental cognitive neuroscience* (pp. 631–646). Cambridge, MA: The MIT Press.

Fox, N. A., Kimmerly, N. L., & Schafer, W. D. (1991). Attachment to mother/attachment to father: A meta-analysis. *Child Development, 62,* 210–225.

Fox, N. A., Schmidt, L. A., Calkins, S. D., Rubin, K. H., & Coplan, R. J. (1996). The role of frontal activation in the regulation and dysregulation of social behavior during the preschool years. *Development and Psychopathology, 8,* 89–102.

Fox, N. A., Schmidt, L. A., & Henderson, H. A. (2000). Developmental psychophysiology: Conceptual and methodological perspectives. In J. T. Cacioppo, L. G. Tassinary, & G. G. Berntson (Eds.), *Handbook of psychophysiology* (2nd ed., pp. 665–686). New York, NY: Cambridge University Press.

Fraley, R. C. (2002). Attachment stability from infancy to adulthood: Meta-analysis and dynamic modeling of developmental mechanisms. *Personality and Social Psychology Review, 6,* 123–151.

Fraley, R. C., & Davis, K. E. (1997). Attachment formation and transfer in young adults' close friendships and romantic relationships. *Personal Relationships, 4,* 131–144.

Fraley, R. C., Heffernan, M. E., Vicary, A. M., & Brumbaugh, C. C. (2011). The Experiences in Close Relationships-Relationship Structure Questionnaire: A method for assessing attachment orientations across relationships. *Psychological Assessment, 23,* 615–625.

Fraley, R. C., & Shaver, P. R. (2000). Adult romantic attachment: Theoretical developments, emerging controversies, and unanswered questions. *Review of General Psychology, 4,* 132–154.

Fraley, R. C., & Spieker, S. J. (2003). Are infant attachment patterns continuously or categorically distributed? A taxometric analysis of Strange Situation behavior. *Developmental Psychology, 39,* 387–404.

Fraley, R. C., Waller, N. G., & Brennan, K. A. (2000). An item response theory analysis of self-report measures of adult attachment. *Journal of Personality and Social Psychology, 78,* 350–365.

Francis, D. D., Diorio, J., Liu, D., & Meaney, M. J. (1999). Nongenomic transmission across generations of maternal behavior and stress responses in the rat. *Science, 286,* 1155–1158.

Frank, R. H. (2001). Cooperation through emotional commitment. In R. M. Nesse (Ed.), *Evolution and the capacity for commitment* (pp. 57–76). New York, NY: Russell Sage Foundation.

Freeman, H., & Brown, B. B. (2001). Primary attachment to parents and peers during adolescence: Differences by attachment style. *Journal of Youth and Adolescence, 30,* 653–674.

Freitag, M. K., Belsky, J., Grossman, K., Grossman, K. E., & Scheuerer-Englisch, H. (1996). Continuity in parent–child relationships from infancy to middle childhood and relations with friendship competence. *Child Development, 67,* 1437–1454.

French, S. E., Seidman, E., Allen, L., & Aber, J. L. (2006). The development of ethnic identity during adolescence. *Developmental Psychology, 42,* 1–10.

Freud, A. (1958). Adolescence. In R. Eissler, A. Freud, H. Hartman, & M. Kris (Eds.), *Psychoanalytic study of the child* (Vol. 13, pp. 255–278). New York, NY: International Universities Press.

Freud, A. (1965). *Normality and pathology in childhood.* New York, NY: International Universities Press.

Freud, S. (1910/1957). Five lectures on psychoanalysis. In J. Strachey (Ed. & Trans.). *The standard edition of the complete psychological works of Sigmund Freud* (Vol. XI, pp. 3–56). London: Hogarth.

Freud, S. (1923/1961). The ego and the id. In J. Strachey (Ed. & Trans.), *The standard edition of the complete psychological works of Sigmund Freud* (Vol. XIX, pp. 3–66). London: Hogarth.

Freud, S. (1924/1961). The dissolution of the Oedipus complex. In J. Strachey (Ed. & Trans.), *The standard edition of the complete psychological works of Sigmund Freud* (Vol. XIX, pp. 173–179). London: Hogarth.

Freud, S. (1940/1964). An outline of psychoanalysis. In J. Strachey (Ed. & Trans.), *The standard edition of the complete psychological works of Sigmund Freud* (Vol. XXIII, pp. 139–207). London: Hogarth.

Frey, K. S., & Ruble, D. N. (1990). Strategies for comparative evaluation: Maintaining a sense of competence across the life span. In R. J. Sternberg & J. Kolligian, Jr. (Eds.), *Competence considered* (pp. 167–189). New Haven, CT: Yale University Press.

Frick, P. J., Cornell, A. H., Barry, C. T., Bodin, S. D., & Dane, H. E. (2003). Callous-unemotional traits and conduct problems in the prediction of conduct problem severity, aggression, and self-report of delinquency. *Journal of Abnormal Child Psychology, 31*, 457–470.

Frick, P. J., & Ellis, M. L. (1999). Callous-unemotional traits and subtypes of conduct disorder. *Clinical Child and Family Psychology Review, 2*, 149–168.

Friedman, D. D., Ertegun, L., Lupi, T., Beebe, B., & Deutsch, S. (2013). Securing attachment: Mother–infant research informs attachment-based clinical practice. In J. E. Bettmann & D. D. Friedman (Eds.), *Attachment-based clinical work with children and adolescents* (pp. 45–60). New York, NY: Springer.

Frith, C. D. (1997). Functional brain imaging and the neuropathology of schizophrenia. *Schizophrenia Bulletin, 23*, 525–527.

Frodi, A. M., Lamb, M. E., Leavitt, L. A., Donovan, W. L., Neff, C., & Sherry, D. (1978). Fathers' and mothers' responses to the faces and cries of normal and premature infants. *Developmental Psychology, 14*, 490–498.

Furman, W., & Buhrmester, D. (1985a). Children's perceptions of the personal relationships in their social networks. *Developmental Psychology, 21*, 1016–1024.

Furman, W., & Buhrmester, D. (1985b). Children's perceptions of the qualities of sibling relationships. *Child Development, 56*, 448–461.

Furman, W., & Buhrmester, D. (1992). Age and sex differences in perceptions of networks of personal relationships. *Child Development, 63*, 103–115.

Furman, W., Jones, L., Buhrmester, D., & Adler, T. (1989). Children's, parents', and observers' perspectives on sibling relationships. In P. G. Zukow (Ed.), *Sibling interactions across cultures* (pp. 165–183). New York, NY: Springer-Verlag.

Furman, W., Simon, V. A., Shaffer, L., & Bouchey, H. A. (2002). Adolescents' working models and styles for relationships with parents, friends, and romantic partners. *Child Development, 73*, 241–255.

Furman, W., & Wehner, E. A. (1994). Romantic views: Toward a theory of adolescent romantic relationships. In R. Montemayor, G. R. Adams, & T. P. Gullotta (Eds.), *Advances in adolescent development: An annual book series* (Vol. 6, pp. 168–195). Thousand Oaks, CA: Sage Publications.

Furman, W., & Wehner, E. A. (1997). Adolescent romantic relationships: A developmental perspective. *New Directions for Child and Adolescent Development, 1997*, 21–36.

Furstenberg, F. F., Jr., Cook, T. D., Eccles, J., Elder, G. H., Jr., & Sameroff, A. (1999). *Managing to make it: Urban families and adolescent success.* Chicago, IL: University of Chicago Press.

Fury, G., Carlson, E. A., & Sroufe, L. A. (1997). Children's representations of attachment relationships in family drawings. *Child Development, 68*, 1154–1164.

Fuster, J. M. (1996). Frontal lobe and the cognitive foundation of behavioral action. In A. R. Damasio, H. Damasio, & Y. Christen (Eds.), *Neurobiology of decision-making* (pp. 47–61). New York, NY: Springer-Verlag.

Fuster, J. M. (1997). *The prefrontal cortex: Anatomy, physiology, and neuropsychology of the frontal lobe* (3rd ed.). Philadelphia, PA: Lippincott-Raven Press.

Galambos, N. L., Barker, E. T., & Krahn, H. J. (2006). Depression, self-esteem, and anger in emerging adulthood: Seven-year trajectories. *Developmental Psychology, 42*, 350–365.

Gallagher, H. L., & Frith, C. D. (2003). Functional imaging of 'theory of mind.' *Trends in Cognitive Science, 7*, 77–83.

Galliher, R. V., Jones, M. D., & Dahl, A. (2011). Concurrent and longitudinal effects of ethnic identity and experiences of discrimination on psychosocial adjustment of Navajo adolescents. *Developmental Psychology, 47*, 509–526.

Galliher, R. V., & Kerpelman, J. L. (2012). The intersection of identity development and peer relationship processes in adolescence and young adulthood: Contributions of the special issue. *Journal of Adolescence, 35*, 1409–1415.

Gallup, G. G., Jr. (1970). Chimpanzees: Self-recognition. *Science, 167,* 86–87.

Gallup, G. G., Jr. (1977). Self-recognition in primates: A comparative approach to the bidirectional properties of consciousness. *American Psychologist, 32,* 329–338.

Gallup, G. G., Jr. (1982). Self-awareness and the emergence of mind in primates. *American Journal of Primatology, 2,* 237–248.

Gallup, G. G., Jr., & Platek, S. M. (2002). Cognitive empathy presupposes self-awareness: Evidence from phylogeny, ontogeny, neuropsychology, and mental illness. *Behavioral and Brain Sciences, 25,* 36–37.

Gamble, W. C., Yu, J. J., & Card, N. A. (2010). Self-representations in early adolescence: Variations in sibling similarity by sex composition and sibling relationship qualities. *Social Development, 19,* 148–169.

Ganiban, J. M., Saudino, K. J., Ulbricht, H., Neiderhiser, J. M., & Reiss, D. (2008). Stability and change in temperament during adolescence. *Journal of Personality and Social Psychology, 95,* 222–236.

Garcia, J. R., Reiber, C., Massey, S. G., & Merriwether, A. M. (2012). Sexual hookup culture: A review. *Review of General Psychology, 16,* 161–176.

Garcia, M. M., Shaw, D. S., Winslow, E. B., & Yaggi, K. E. (2000). Destructive sibling conflict and the development of conduct problems in young boys. *Developmental Psychology, 36,* 44–53.

Garcia Coll, C. G., & Pachter, L. M. (2002). Ethnic and minority parenting. In M. H. Bornstein (Ed.), *Handbook of parenting: Vol. 4. Social conditions and applied parenting* 2nd ed., pp. 1–20). Mahwah, NJ: Erlbaum.

Gardner, R. M., Friedman, B. N., & Jackson, N. A. (1999). Hispanic and white children's judgments of perceived and ideal body size in self and others. *Psychological Record, 49,* 555–564.

Garner, P. W., Dunsmore, J. C., & Southam-Gerow, M. (2007). Mother–child conversations about emotions: Linkages to child aggression and prosocial behavior. *Social Development, 17,* 259–277.

Garner, P. W., Jones, D. C., & Palmer, D. J. (1994). Social cognitive correlates of preschool children's sibling caregiving behavior. *Developmental Psychology, 30,* 905–911.

Gass, K., Jenkins, J., & Dunn, J. (2007). Are sibling relationships protective? A longitudinal study. *Journal of Child Psychology and Psychiatry, 48,* 167–175.

Gaunt, R. (2008). Maternal gatekeeping antecedents and consequences. *Journal of Family Issues, 29,* 373–395.

Gauze, C., Bukowski, W. M., Aquan-Assee, J., & Sippola, L. K. (1996). Interactions between family environment and friendship and associations with self-perceived well-being during adolescence. *Child Development, 67,* 2201–2216.

Ge, X., Brody, G. H., Conger, R. D., & Simons, R. L. (2006). Pubertal maturation and African American children's internalizing and externalizing symptoms. *Journal of Youth and Adolescence, 35,* 531–540.

Geangu, E., Benga, O., Stahl, D., & Striano, T. (2010). Contagious crying beyond the first days of life. *Infant Behavior and Development, 33,* 279–288.

George, C., Kaplan, N., & Main, M. (1984). *Adult Attachment Interview protocol.* Unpublished manuscript, University of California, Berkeley, CA.

George, C., Kaplan, N., & Main, M. (1985). *Adult Attachment Interview protocol* (2nd ed.). Unpublished manuscript, University of California, Berkeley, CA.

George, C., Kaplan, N., & Main, M. (1996). *Adult Attachment Interview protocol* (3rd ed.). Unpublished manuscript, University of California, Berkeley, CA.

George, C., & Solomon, J. (1990/1996/2000). *Six-year attachment doll play classification system.* Unpublished manuscript, Mills College, Oakland, CA.

Gergen, K. J. (1991). *The saturated self.* New York, NY: Basic Books.

Gesell, A. L. (1928). *Infancy and human growth.* New York, NY: Macmillan.

Gest, S. D. (2006). Teacher reports of children's friendships and social groups: Agreement with peer reports and implications for studying peer similarity. *Social Development, 15,* 248–259.

Gest, S. D., Graham-Bermann, S. A., & Hartup, W. W. (2001). Peer experience: Common and unique features of number of friendships, social network centrality, and sociometric status. *Social Development, 10,* 23–240.

Ghavami, N., Fingerhut, A., Peplau, L. A., Grant, S. K., & Wittig, M. A. (2011). Testing a model of minority identity achievement, identity affirmation, and psychological well-being among ethnic minority and sexual minority individuals. *Cultural Diversity & Ethnic Minority Psychology, 17,* 79–88.

Gilissen, R., Bakermans-Kranenburg, M. J., van IJzendoorn, M. H., & van der Veen, R. (2008). Parent–child relationship, temperament, and physiological reactions to fear-inducing film clips: Further evidence for differential susceptibility. *Journal of Experimental Child Psychology, 99,* 182–195.

Gillath, O., Bunge, S. A., Shaver, P. R., Wendelken, C., & Mikulincer, M. (2005). Attachment-style differences in the ability to suppress negative thoughts: Exploring the neural correlates. *NeuroImage, 28,* 835–847.

Gillberg, C. L. (1992). The Emanuel Miller Memorial Lecture 1991: Autism and autistic-like conditions: Subclasses among disorders of empathy. *Journal of Child Psychology and Psychiatry and Allied Disciplines, 33,* 813–842.

Gillberg, C. L. (1999). Neurodevelopmental processes and psychological functioning in autism. *Development and Psychopathology, 11,* 567–587.

Gilligan, C. (1982). *In a different voice: Psychological theory and women's development.* Cambridge, MA: Harvard University Press.

Gilligan, C. (1993). Women's place in man's life cycle. In A. Dobrin (Ed.), *Being good and doing right: Readings in moral development* (pp. 37–54). Lanham, MD: University Press of America.

Gilligan, C., & Attanucci, J. (1988). Two moral orientations: Gender differences and similarities. *Merrill-Palmer Quarterly, 34,* 223–237.

Gilligan, C., Lyons, N. P., & Hammer, T. J. (1990). *Making connections: The relational worlds of adolescent girls at Emma Willard School.* Cambridge, MA: Harvard University Press.

Gilliom, M., Shaw, D. S., Beck, J. E., Schonberg, M. A., & Lukon, J. L. (2002). Anger regulation in disadvantaged preschool boys: Strategies, antecedents, and the development of self-control. *Developmental Psychology, 38,* 222–235.

Giordano, P. C. (2003). Relationships in adolescence. *Annual Review of Sociology, 29,* 257–281.

Gleason, K. A., Jenson-Campbell, L. A., & Ickes, W. (2009). The role of empathic accuracy in adolescents' peer relations and adjustment. *Personality and Social Psychology Bulletin, 35,* 997–1011.

Glenn, N., & Hoppe, S. (1984). Only children as adults: Psychological well-being. *Journal of Family Issues, 5,* 363–382.

Gogtay, N., & Thompson, P. M. (2010). Mapping gray matter development: Implications for typical development and vulnerability to psychopathology. *Brain and Cognition, 72,* 6–15.

Goldberg, S., Grusec, J. E., & Jenkins, J. M. (1999). Confidence in protection: Arguments for a narrow definition of attachment. *Journal of Family Psychology, 13,* 475–483.

Goldberg, S., MacKay-Soroka, S., & Rochester, M. (1994). Affect, attachment, and maternal responsiveness. *Infant Behavior and Development, 17,* 335–339.

Goldsmith, H. H. (2003). Genetics of emotional development. In R. J. Davidson, K. R. Scherer, & H. H. Goldsmith (Eds.), *Handbook of affective sciences.* New York, NY: Oxford University Press.

Goldsmith, H. H., Aksan, N., Essex, M., Smider, N. A., & Vandell, D. L. (2001). Temperament and socioemotional adjustment to kindergarten: A multi-informant perspective. In T. D. Wachs & G. A. Kohnstamm (Eds.), *Temperament in context* (pp. 103–138). Mahwah, NJ: Erlbaum.

Goldsmith, H. H., & Alansky, J. (1987). Maternal and infant temperamental predictors of attachment: A meta-analytic review. *Journal of Consulting and Clinical Psychology, 55,* 805–816.

Goldsmith, H. H., Buss, K. A., & Lemery, K. S. (1997). Toddler and childhood temperament: Expanded content, stronger genetic evidence, new evidence for the importance of environment. *Developmental Psychology, 33,* 891–905.

Goldsmith, H. H., Buss, A. H., Plomin, R., Rothbart, M. K., Thomas, A., Chess, S., … McCall, R. R. (1987). Roundtable: What is temperament? Four approaches. *Child Development, 58*, 505–529.

Goldsmith, H. H., & Campos, J. (1990). The structure of temperamental fear and pleasure in infants: A psychometric perspective. *Child Development, 61*, 1944–1964.

Goldsmith, H. H., & Harman, C. (1994). Temperament and attachment: Individuals and relationships. *Current Directions in Psychological Science, 3*, 53–57.

Goldsmith, H. H., & Rothbart, M. K. (1993). *The Laboratory Temperament Assessment Battery (LAB-TAB).* Madison, WI: University of Wisconsin.

Goldstein, H., Kaczmarek, L. A., & English, K. M. (2002). *Promoting social communication: Children with developmental disabilities from birth to adolescence.* Baltimore, MD: Brookes.

Goleman, D. (2005). *Emotional intelligence.* New York, NY: Bantam Books.

Goncu, A. (1993). Development of intersubjectivity in the dyadic play of preschoolers. *Early Childhood Research Quarterly, 8*, 99–116.

Goodman, S. H., & Gotlib, I. H. (1999). Risk for psychopathology in the children of depressed mothers: A developmental model for understanding mechanisms of transmission. *Psychological Review, 106*, 458–490.

Goodvin, R., Meyer, S., Thompson, R. A., & Hayes, R. (2008). Self-understanding in early childhood: Associations with attachment security, maternal perceptions of the child, and maternal emotional risk. *Attachment & Human Development, 10*, 433–450.

Goossens, F. A., & van IJzendoorn, M. (1990). Quality of infants' attachments to professional caregivers: Relation to infant–parent attachment and daycare characteristics. *Child Development, 61*, 832–837.

Gordon, I., Zagoory-Sharon, O., Leckman, J. F., & Feldman, R. (2010). Oxytocin and the development of parenting in humans. *Biological Psychiatry, 68*, 377–382.

Gosling, S. D., & John, O. P. (1999). Personality dimensions in nonhuman animals: A cross-species review. *Current Directions in Psychological Science, 8*, 69–75.

Gottlieb, A. R. (2005). *Side by side: On having a gay or lesbian sibling.* New York, NY: Harrington Park Press.

Gottman, J. M. (1983). How children become friends. *Monographs of the Society for Research in Child Development, 48*(3, Serial No. 201).

Gottman, J. M., Katz, L., & Hooven, C. (1996). *Meta-emotion.* Mahwah, NJ: Erlbaum.

Graber, J. A., Brooks-Gunn, J., & Galen, B. R. (1998). Betwixt and between: Sexuality in the context of adolescent transitions. In N. R. Jessor (Ed.), *New perspectives on adolescent risk behavior* (pp. 270–316). Cambridge: Cambridge University Press.

Graber, J. A., Lewinsohn, P. M., Seeley, J., & Brooks-Gunn, J. (1997). Is psychopathology associated with the timing of pubertal development? *Journal of the American Academy of Child and Adolescent Psychiatry, 36*, 1768–1776.

Gralinsky, J., Fesbach, N. D., Powell, C., & Derrington, T. (1993). *Self-understanding: Meaning and measurement of maltreated children's sense of self.* Paper presented at the meeting of the Society for Research in Child Development, New Orleans, LA.

Granot, D., & Mayseless, O. (2001). Attachment security and adjustment to school in middle childhood. *International Journal of Behavioral Development, 25*, 530–541.

Gray, J. (1991). Neural systems, emotion and personality. In J. Madden IV (Ed.), *Neurobiology of learning, emotion and affect* (pp. 273–306). New York, NY: Raven Press.

Gray, P., Yang, C. J., & Pope, H. G. Jr. (2006). Fathers have lower salivary testosterone levels than unmarried men and married non-fathers in Beijing, China. *Proceedings of the Royal Society: B, 273*, 333–339.

Gray-Little, B., & Hafdahl, A. R. (2000). Factors influencing racial comparisons of self-esteem: A quantitative review. *Psychological Bulletin, 126*, 26–54.

Greenberg, M. T., Siegel, J. M., & Leitch, C. J. (1983). The nature and importance of attachment relationships to parents and peers during adolescence. *Journal of Youth and Adolescence, 12*, 373–386.

Greenberg, M. T., Speltz, M. L., & DeKlyen, M. (1993). The role of attachment in the early development of disruptive problems. *Development and Psychopathology, 5*, 191–213.

Greene, J., & Haidt, J. (2002). How (and where) does moral judgment work? *Trends in Cognitive Sciences, 6,* 517–523.

Greene, J. D., Sommerville, R. B., Nystrom, L. E., Darley, J. M., & Cohen, J. D. (2001). An fMRI investigation of emotional engagement in moral judgment. *Science, 293,* 2105–2108.

Greene, M. L., Way, N., & Pahl, K. (2006). Trajectories of perceived adult and peer discrimination among Black, Latino, and Asian American adolescents: Patterns and psychological correlates. *Developmental Psychology, 39,* 606–617.

Greenfield, P. M., Keller, H., Fuligni, A., & Maynard, A. (2003). Cultural pathways through universal development. *Annual Review of Psychology, 54,* 461–490.

Grello, C. M., Welsh, D. P., Harper, M. S., & Dickson, J. W. (2003). Dating and sexual relationship trajectories and adolescent functioning. *Adolescent and Family Health, 3,* 103–112.

Grienenberger, J. F., Kelly, K., & Slade, A. (2005). Maternal reflective functioning, mother–infant affective communication, and infant attachment: Exploring the link between mental states and observed caregiving behavior in the intergenerational transmission of attachment. *Attachment & Human Development, 7,* 299–311.

Griffin, D., & Bartholomew, K. (1994). Models of the self and other: Fundamental dimensions underlying measures of adult attachment. *Journal of Personality and Social Psychology, 67,* 430–445.

Griffin, S. (1992). Structural analysis of the development of their inner world: A neo-structural analysis of the development of intrapersonal intelligence. In R. Case (Ed.), *The mind's staircase* (pp. 189–206). Hillsdale, NJ: Erlbaum.

Groenendyk, A. E., & Volling, B. L. (2007). Co-parenting and early conscience development in the family. *Journal of Genetic Psychology, 168,* 201–224.

Groh, A. M., Fearon, R. P., Bakermans-Kranenburg, M. J., van IJzendoorn, M. H., Steele, R. D., & Roisman, G. I. (2014). The significance of attachment security for children's social competence with peers: A meta-analytic study. *Attachment & Human Development, 16,* 103–136.

Groh, A. M., Roisman, G. I., Booth-LaForce, C., Fraley, R. C., Owen, M. T., Cox, M. J., & Burchinal, M. R. (2014). Stability of attachment security from infancy to late adolescence. *Monographs of the Society for Research in Child Development, 79*(3), 51–66.

Groh, A. M., Roisman, G. I., van IJzendoorn, M. H., Bakermans-Kranenburg, M. J., & Fearon, R. P. (2012). The significance of insecure and disorganized attachment for children's internalizing symptoms: A meta-analytic study. *Child Development, 83,* 591–610.

Gross, J. J. (2001). Emotion regulation in adulthood: Timing is everything. *Current Directions in Psychological Science, 10,* 214–219.

Gross, J. J., & John, O. P. (2003). Individual differences in two emotion regulation processes: Implications for affect, relationships, and well-being. *Journal of Personality and Social Psychology, 85,* 348–362.

Gross, J. J., & Thompson, R. A. (2007). Emotion regulation: Conceptual foundations. In J. J. Gross (Ed.), *Handbook of emotion regulation* (pp. 3–24). New York, NY: Guilford Press.

Grossman, K., Grossman, K. E., Kindler, H., & Zimmerman, P. (2008). A wider view of attachment and exploration: The influence of mothers and fathers on the development of psychological security from infancy to young adulthood. In J. Cassidy & P. R. Shaver (Eds.), *Handbook of attachment: Theory, research, and clinical applications* (2nd ed., pp. 857–879). New York, NY: Guilford Press.

Grossman, K. E., Grossman, K., & Kindler, H. (2005). Early care and the roots of attachment and partnership representations: The Bielefeld and Regensburg longitudinal studies. In K. E. Grossman, K. Grossman, & E. Waters (Eds.), *Attachment from infancy to adulthood: The major longitudinal studies* (pp. 98–136). New York, NY: Guilford Press.

Grossman, K. E., Grossman, K., & Waters, E. (Eds.). (2005). *Attachment from infancy to adulthood: The major longitudinal studies.* New York, NY: Guilford Press.

Grotevant, H. D. (1987). Toward a process model of identity formation. *Journal of Adolescent Research, 2,* 203–222.

Grotevant, H. D. (1992). Assigned and chosen identity components: A process perspective on their integration. In G. R. Adams,

T. P. Gullota, & R. Montemayor (Eds.), *Adolescent identity formation* (pp. 73–90). Thousand Oaks, CA: Sage Publications.

Grotevant, H. D., & Cooper, C. R. (1985). Patterns of interaction in family relationships and the development of identity exploration in adolescence. *Child Development, 56,* 415–428.

Gruenewald, T. L., Kemeny, M. E., Aziz, N., & Fahey, J. L. (2004). Acute threat to the social self: Shame, social self-esteem, and cortisol activity. *Psychosomatic Medicine, 66,* 915–924.

Grumbach, M. M., & Styne, D. M. (1998). Puberty: Ontogeny, neuroendocrinology, physiology, and disorders. In J. D. Wilson, D. W. Foster, H. M. Kronenberg, & P. R. Larsen (Eds.), *Williams textbook of endocrinology* (pp. 1509–1625). Philadelphia, PA: W. B. Sanders.

Grusec, J. E. (1997). A history of research on parenting strategies and children's internalization of values. In J. E. Grusec & L. Kuczynski (Eds.), *Parenting and children's internalization of values: A handbook of contemporary theory* (pp. 3–22). New York, NY: Wiley.

Grusec, J. E., Dix, T., & Mills, R. (1982). The effects of type, severity, and victim of children's transgressions on maternal discipline. *Canadian Journal of Behavioral Science, 14,* 276–289.

Grusec, J. E., Goodnow, J. J., & Cohen, L. (1996). Household work and the development of concern for others. *Developmental Psychology, 32,* 999–1007.

Grusec, J. E., & Sherman, A. (2011). Prosocial behavior. In M. K. Underwood & L. H. Rosen (Eds.), *Social development: Relationships in infancy, childhood, and adolescence* (pp. 263–286). New York, NY: Guilford Press.

Guilamo-Ramos, V., Jaccard, J., & Dittus, P. (Eds.). (2010). *Parental monitoring of adolescents: Current perspectives for researchers and practitioners.* New York, NY: Columbia University Press.

Gullone, E., Hughes, E. K., King, N. J., & Tonge, B. (2010). The normative development of emotion regulation strategy use in children and adolescents: A 2-year follow-up study. *Journal of Child Psychology and Psychiatry, 51,* 567–574.

Gummerum, M., & Keller, M. (2008). Affection, virtue, pleasure, and profit: Developing an understanding of friendship closeness and intimacy in western and Asian societies. *International Journal of Behavioral Development, 32,* 218–231.

Gunnar, M. R. (2000). Early adversity and the development of stress reactivity and regulation. In C. A. Nelson (Ed.), *Minnesota Symposia on Child Psychology: Vol. 31. The effects of early adversity on neurobehavioral development* (pp. 163–200). Mahwah, NJ: Erlbaum.

Gunnar, M. R., & Davis, E. P. (2003). Stress and emotion in early childhood. In R. M. Lerner, M. A. Easterbrooks, & J. Mistry (Eds.), *Handbook of psychology: Developmental psychology* (pp. 113–134). Hoboken, NJ: Wiley.

Gunnar, M. R., & Donzella, B. (2002). Social regulation of the cortisol levels in early human development. *Psychoneuroendocrinology, 27,* 199–220.

Gunnar, M. R., & Vasquez, D. (2006). Stress neurobiology and developmental psychopathology. In D. Cicchetti & D. Cohen (Eds.), *Developmental psychopathology, Vol. 1: Developmental neuroscience* (2nd ed., pp. 533–577). New York, NY: Wiley.

Guttmann-Steinmetz, S., & Crowell, J. A. (2006). Attachment and externalizing disorders: A developmental psychopathology perspective. *Journal of American Academy of Child & Adolescent Psychiatry, 45,* 440–451.

Haden, C. A. (2003). Joint encoding and joint reminiscing: Implications for young children's understanding and remembering of personal experiences. In R. Fivush & C. A. Haden (Eds.), *Autobiographical memory and the construction of a narrative self* (pp. 49–70). Mahwah, NJ: Erlbaum.

Haidt, J. (2001). The emotional dog and its rational tail: A social intuitionist approach to moral judgment. *Psychological Review, 108,* 814–834.

Haight, W. L., & Miller, P. J. (1993). *Pretending at home: Early development in sociocultural context.* Albany, NY: State University of New York Press.

Halberstadt, A. G., Denham, S. A., & Dunsmore, J. C. (2001). Affective social competence. *Social Development, 10,* 79–119.

Halberstadt, A. G., & Parker, A. E. (2007). Function, structure, and process as independent dimensions in research on emotion.

Clinical Psychology: Science and Practice, 14, 402–406.

Halligan, S. L., Cooper, P. J., Healy, S. J., & Murray, L. (2007). The attribution of hostile intent in mothers, fathers, and their children. *Journal of Abnormal Child Psychology, 35,* 594–604.

Hamilton, C. E. (2000). Continuity and discontinuity of attachment from infancy through adolescence. *Child Development, 71,* 690–694.

Hamlin, J. K., & Wynn, K. (2011). Five- and 9-month-old infants prefer prosocial to antisocial others. *Cognitive Development, 26,* 30–39.

Hamlin, J. K., Wynn, K., & Bloom, P. (2007). Social evaluation by preverbal infants. *Nature, 450,* 557–559.

Hamlin, J. K., Wynn, K., & Bloom, P. (2010). Three-month-olds show a negativity bias in their social evaluations. *Developmental Science, 13,* 923–929.

Hane, A. A., Cheah, C., Rubin, K. H., & Fox, N. A. (2008). The role of maternal behavior in the relation between shyness and social reticence in early childhood and social withdrawal in middle childhood. *Social Development, 17,* 795–811.

Hane, A. A., & Fox, N. A. (2006). Ordinary variations in maternal caregiving of human infants influence stress reactivity. *Psychological Science, 17,* 550–556.

Haney, P., & Durlak, J. A. (1998). Changing self-esteem in children and adolescents: A meta-analytic review. *Journal of Clinical Child Psychology, 27,* 423–433.

Hansburg, H. G. (1972). *Adolescent separation anxiety: A method for the study of adolescent separation problems.* Springfield, IL: Charles C. Thomas.

Hardy, C. L., Bukowski, W. M., & Sippola, L. K. (2002). Stability and change in peer relationships during the transition to middle-level school. *Journal of Early Adolescence, 22,* 117–142.

Harley, K., & Reese, E. (1999). Origins of autobiographical memory. *Developmental Psychology, 35,* 1338–1348.

Harlow, H. F. (1958). The nature of love. *American Psychologist, 13,* 673.

Harris, J. R. (1995). Where is the child's environment? A group socialization theory of development. *Psychological Review, 102,* 458–489.

Harris, J. R. (1998). *The nurture assumption.* New York, NY: Free Press.

Harris, J. R. (2006). *No two alike: Human nature and human individuality.* New York, NY: Norton.

Harris, M. A., Gruenenfelder-Steiger, A. E., Ferrer, E., Donnellan, M. B., Allemand, M., Fend, H., …Trzesniewski, K. H. (2015). Do parents foster self-esteem? Testing the prospective impact of parent closeness on adolescent self-esteem. *Child Development, 86,* 995–1013.

Harris, P. L. (1989). *Children and emotion: The development of psychological understanding.* New York, NY: Wiley-Blackwell.

Harris, P. L. (2000). Understanding emotion. In M. Lewis & J. Haviland (Eds.), *Handbook of emotion* (2nd ed., pp. 281–292). New York, NY: Guilford Press.

Harris, P. L, Olthof, T., Meerum Terwogt, M., & Hardman, C. E. (1987). Children's knowledge of the situations that provide emotion. *International Journal of Behavioral Development, 10,* 319–343.

Hart, D. (1988). The adolescent self-concept in social context. In D. K. Lapsley & F. C. Power (Eds.), *Self, ego, and identity* (pp. 71–90). New York, NY: Springer-Verlag.

Hart, D., & Fegley, S. (1995). Prosocial behavior and caring in adolescence: Relations to self-understanding and social judgment. *Child Development, 66,* 1346–1359.

Harter, S. (1982). The perceived competence scale for children. *Child Development, 53,* 87–97.

Harter, S. (1985). *The Self-Perception Profile for Children.* Unpublished manual, University of Denver, Denver, CO.

Harter, S. (1989). *The Self-Perception Profile for Adolescents.* Unpublished manual, University of Denver, Denver, CO.

Harter, S. (1990). Adolescent self and identity development. In S. S. Feldman & G. R. Elliott (Eds.), *At the threshold: The developing adolescent* (pp. 352–387). Cambridge, MA: Harvard University Press.

Harter, S. (1997). The personal self in social context: Barriers to authenticity. In R. D. Ashmore & L. J. Jussim (Eds.), *Self and identity: Fundamental issues* (Vol. 1, pp. 81–105). New York, NY: Oxford University Press.

Harter, S. (1998a). The development of self-representations. In W. Damon (Series Ed.)

& N. Eisenberg (Vol. Ed.), *Handbook of child psychology: Vol. 3. Social, emotional, and personality development* (5th ed., pp. 553–617). New York, NY: Wiley.

Harter, S. (1998b). The effects of child abuse on the self-system. In B. B. Rosman & M. S. Rosenberg (Eds.), *Multiple victimization of children: Conceptual, developmental, research, and treatment issues.* New York, NY: Guilford Press.

Harter, S. (1999). *The construction of the self: Developmental and sociocultural foundations.* New York, NY: Guilford Press.

Harter, S. (2002). Authenticity. In C. R. Snyder & S. J. Lopez (Eds.), *Handbook of positive psychology* (pp. 382–394). New York, NY: Oxford University Press.

Harter, S. (2003). The development of self-representations during childhood and adolescence. In M. R. Leary & J. P. Tangney (Eds.), *Handbook of self and identity* (pp. 610–642). New York, NY: Guilford Press.

Harter, S. (2006). The self. In W. Damon & R. Lerner (Eds.) & N. Eisenberg (Vol. Ed.), *Handbook of child psychology: Vol. 3, Social, emotional, and personality development* (6th ed., pp. 505–570). New York, NY: Wiley.

Harter, S. (2008). The developing self. In W. Damon & R. M. Lerner (Eds.), *Child and adolescent development: An advanced course* (pp. 216–260). Hoboken, NJ: John Wiley & Sons.

Harter, S. (2012). *The construction of the self: Developmental and sociocultural foundations* (2nd ed.). New York, NY: Guilford Press.

Harter, S., Bresnick, S., Bouchey, H. A., & Whitesell, N. R. (1998). The development of multiple role-related selves during adolescence. *Development and Psychopathology, 9,* 835–854.

Harter, S., Marold, D. B., Whitesell, N. R., & Cobbs, G. (1996). A model of the effects of perceived parent and peer support on adolescent false self behavior. *Child Development, 67,* 360–374.

Harter, S., & Monsour, A. (1992). Developmental analysis of conflict caused by opposing attributes in the adolescent self-portrait. *Developmental Psychology, 28,* 251–260.

Harter, S., & Pike, R. (1984). The pictorial scale of perceived competence and social acceptance for young children. *Child Development, 55,* 1969–1982.

Harter, S., Stocker, C., & Robinson, N. S. (1996). The perceived directionality of the link between approval and self-worth: The liabilities of a looking glass self orientation among young adolescents. *Journal of Adolescence, 6,* 285–308.

Harter, S., Waters, P., & Whitesell, N. R. (1998). Relational self-worth: Differences in perceived worth as a person across interpersonal contexts among adolescents. *Child Development, 69,* 756–766.

Harter, S., Waters, P. L., Whitesell, N. R., & Kastelic, D. (1998). Level of voice among female and male high school students: Relational context, support, and gender orientation. *Developmental Psychology, 34,* 892–901.

Harter, S., & Whitesell, N. R. (2003). Beyond the debate: Why some adolescents report stable self-worth over time and situation, whereas others report changes in self-worth. *Journal of Personality, 71,* 1027–1058.

Hartmann, E., & Loewenstein, R. (1962). Notes on the superego. *Psychoanalytic Study of the Child, 17,* 42–81.

Hartup, W. W. (1989). Social relationships and their developmental significance. *American Psychologist, 44,* 120–126.

Hartup, W. W. (1992). Friendships and their developmental significance. In H. McGurk (Ed.), *Childhood social development: Contemporary perspectives* (pp. 175–205). Hillsdale, NJ: Erlbaum.

Hartup, W. W. (1996). The company they keep: Friendships and their developmental significance. *Child Development, 67,* 1–13.

Hartup, W. W., Laursen, B., Stewart, M. I., & Eastenson, A. (1988). Conflict and the friendship relations of young children. *Child Development, 59,* 1590–1600.

Hartup, W. W., & Stevens, N. (1997). Friendships and adaptation in the life course. *Psychological Bulletin, 121,* 355–370.

Hartup, W. W., & Stevens, N. (1999). Friendships and adaptation across the life span. *Current Directions in Psychological Science, 8,* 76–79.

Harwood, R. L., Miller, J. G., & Irizarry, N. L. (1995). *Culture and attachment: Perceptions of the child in context.* New York, NY: Guilford Press.

Hasebe, Y., Nucci, L. P., & Nucci, M. S. (2004). Parental control of the personal domain and adolescent symptoms of psychopathology: A cross-national study in the United States and Japan. *Child Development, 75,* 815–828.

Haselager, G. J. T., Cillessen, A. H. N., Van-Lieshout, C. F. M., Riksen-Walraven, J. M. A., & Hartup, W. W. (2002). Heterogeneity among peer-rejected boys across middle childhood: Developmental pathways of social behavior. *Developmental Psychology, 38,* 446–456.

Hastings, P. D., Kahle, S., & Nuselovici, J. M. (2014). How well socially wary preschoolers fare over time depends on their parasympathetic regulation and socialization. *Child Development, 85,* 1586–1600.

Hastings, P. D., Rubin, K., & DeRose, L. (2005). Links among gender, inhibition, and parental socialization in the development of prosocial behavior. *Merrill-Palmer Quarterly, 51,* 501–527.

Hastings, P. D., Utendale, W. T., & Sullivan, C. (2007). The socialization of prosocial behavior. In J. E. Grusec & P. D. Hastings (Eds.), *The handbook of socialization* (pp. 638–664). New York, NY: Guilford Press.

Hastings, P. D., Zahn-Waxler, C., Robinson, J., Usher, B., & Bridges, D. (2000). The development of concern for others in children with behavior problems. *Developmental Psychology, 36,* 531–546.

Havighurst, R. F., & Neugarten, B. L. (1955). *American Indian and White children.* Chicago, IL: University of Chicago Press.

Hawes, D. J., & Dadds, M. R. (2005). The treatment of conduct problems in children with callous-unemotional traits. *Journal of Consulting and Clinical Psychology, 73,* 737–741.

Hay, D. F. (1994). Prosocial development. *Journal of Child Psychology and Psychiatry, 35,* 29–71.

Hay, D. F., Castle, J., & Davies, L. (2000). Toddlers' use of force against familiar peers: A precursor of serious aggression? *Child Development, 71,* 457–467.

Hay, D. F., Castle, J., Davies, L., Demetriou, H., & Stimson, C. A. (1999). Prosocial action in very early childhood. *Journal of Child Psychology and Psychiatry, 40,* 905–916.

Hay, D. F., Nash, A., & Pedersen, J. (1981). Responses of six-month-olds to the distress of their peers. *Child Development, 52,* 1071–1075.

Hay, D. F., & Pawlby, S. (2003). Prosocial development in relation to children's and mothers' psychological problems. *Child Development, 74,* 1314–1327.

Hay, D. F., Payne, A., & Chadwick, A. (2004). Peer relations in childhood. *Journal of Child Psychology and Psychiatry, 45,* 84–108.

Hay, D. F., Pederson, J., & Nash, A. (1982). Dyadic interaction in the first year of life. In K. H. Rubin & H. S. Ross (Eds.), *Peer relationships and social skills in childhood.* New York, NY: Springer-Verlag.

Haydon, K. C., Roisman, G. I., & Burt, K. B. (2012). In search of security: The latent structure of the Adult Attachment Interview revisited. *Development and Psychopathology, 24,* 589–606.

Hayne, H., & MacDonald, S. (2003). The socialization of autobiographical memory in children and adults: The roles of culture and gender. In R. Fivush & C. A. Haden (Eds.), *Autobiographical memory and the construction of a narrative self* (pp. 99–120). Mahwah, NJ: Erlbaum.

Hazan, C., & Shaver, P. (1987). Romantic love conceptualized as an attachment process. *Journal of Personality and Social Psychology, 52,* 511–524.

Hazan, C., & Shaver, P. (1990). Love and work: An attachment-theoretical perspective. *Journal of Personality and Social Psychology, 59,* 270–280.

Hazan, C., & Shaver, P. (1994). Attachment as an organizational framework for research on close relationships. *Psychological Inquiry, 5,* 1–22.

Hazan, C., & Zeifman, D. (1994). Sex and the psychological tether. In K. Bartholomew & D. Perlman (Eds.), *Advances in personal relationships* (Vol. 5, pp. 151–177). London: Jessica Kingsley.

Heatherton, T. F., Wyland, C. L., Macrae, C. N., Demos, K. E., Denny, B. T., & Kelley, W. M. (2006). Medial prefrontal activity differentiates self from close others. *Social Cognitive and Affective Neuroscience, 1,* 18–25.

Helwig, C. C. (2006). Rights, civil liberties, and democracy across cultures. In M. Killen & J. G. Smetana (Eds.), *Handbook of moral development* (pp. 185–210). Mahwah, NJ: Erlbaum.

Helwig, C. C., & Turiel, E. (2010). Children's social and moral reasoning. In P. K. Smith & C. H. Hart (Eds.), *Wiley-Blackwell handbook of childhood social development* (2nd ed.), Oxford: Wiley-Blackwell.

Helwig, C. C., Zelazo, P. D., & Wilson, M. (2001). Children's judgments of psychological harm in normal and noncanonical situations. *Child Development, 72,* 66–81.

Henderson, H. A., & Mundy, P. C. (2013). The integration of self and other in the development of self-regulation: Typical and atypical processes. In K. C. Barrett, N. A. Fox, G. A. Morgan, D. J. Fidler, & L. A. Daunhauer (Eds.), *Handbook of self-regulatory processes in development: New directions and international perspectives* (pp. 113–134). New York, NY: Psychology Press.

Henriques, J. B., & Davidson, R. J. (1990). Regional brain electrical asymmetries discriminate between previously depressed and healthy control subjects. *Journal of Abnormal Psychology, 99,* 22–31.

Herrald, M. M., & Tomaka, J. (2002). Patterns of emotion-specific appraisal, coping, and cardiovascular reactivity during an ongoing emotional episode. *Journal of Personality and Social Psychology, 83,* 434–450.

Herrera, N., Zajonc, R., Wieczorkowska, G., & Cichomski, B. (2003). Beliefs about birth rank and their reflection in reality. *Journal of Personality and Social Psychology, 85,* 142–150.

Hesse, E. (1996). Discourse, memory, and the Adult Attachment Interview: A note with emphasis on the emerging cannot classify category. *Infant Mental Health Journal, 17,* 4–11.

Hesse, E. (2008). The Adult Attachment Interview: Protocol, method of analysis, and empirical studies. In J. Cassidy & P. R. Shaver (Eds.), *Handbook of attachment: Theory, research, and clinical applications* (2nd ed., pp. 552–598). New York, NY: Guilford Press.

Hesse, E., & Main, M. (2000). Disorganized infant, child, and adult attachment: Collapse in behavioral and attentional strategies. *Journal of the American Psychoanalytic Association, 48,* 1097–1127.

Hetherington, E. M. (1988). Parents, children and siblings six years after divorce. In R. Hinde & J. Stevenson-Hinde (Eds.), *Relationships within families* (pp. 311–331). Cambridge: Cambridge University Press.

Hetherington, E. M. (1989). Coping with family transitions: Winners, losers, and survivors. *Child Development, 60,* 1–14.

Hetherington, E. M., & Clingempeel, W. G. (1992). Coping with marital transitions: A family systems perspective. *Monographs of the Society for Research in Child Development, 57*(2–3, Serial No. 227).

Hetherington, E. M., Henderson, S., & Reiss, D. (1999). Adolescent siblings in stepfamilies: Family functioning and adolescent adjustment. *Monographs of the Society for Research in Child Development, 64*(4, Serial No. 259).

Hetherington, E. M., & Kelly, J. (2002). *For better or for worse: Divorce reconsidered.* New York, NY: Norton.

Hetherington, E. M., Reiss, D., & Plomin, R. (Eds.). (1994). *Separate social worlds of siblings: The impact of nonshared environment on development.* Hillsdale, NJ: Erlbaum.

Hill, N. E., Bromell, L., Tyson, D. F., & Flint, R. (2007). Developmental commentary: Ecological perspectives on parental influences during adolescence. *Journal of Clinical Child and Adolescent Psychology, 36,* 367–377.

Hill, N. E., & Witherspoon, D. P. (2011). Race, ethnicity, and social class. In M. K. Underwood & L. H. Rosen (Eds.), *Handbook of social development* (pp. 316–346). New York, NY: Guilford Press.

Hinde, R. A. (1987). *Individuals, relationships and culture: Links between ethology and the social sciences.* Cambridge: Cambridge University Press.

Hinde, R. A. (1988). Continuities and discontinuities: Conceptual issues and methodological considerations. In M. Rutter (Ed.), *Studies of psychosocial risk: The power of longitudinal data* (pp. 367–383). Cambridge: Cambridge University Press.

Hinderlie, H. H., & Kenny, M. (2002). Attachment, social support, and college adjustment among Black students at predominantly White universities. *Journal of College Student Development, 43,* 327–340.

Hinduja, S., & Patchin, J. W. (2007). Offline consequences of online victimization: School violence and delinquency. *Journal of School Violence, 6,* 89–112.

Hinduja, S., & Patchin, J. W. (2009). *Bullying beyond the schoolyard: Preventing and responding to cyberbullying*. Thousand Oaks, CA: Corwin Press.

Hodges, E. V. E., Boivin, M., Vitaro, F., & Bukowski, W. M. (1999). The power of friendship: Protection against an escalating cycle of peer victimization. *Developmental Psychology, 35*, 94–101.

Hodges, E. V. E., Finnegan, R. A., & Perry, D. G. (1999). Skewed autonomy-relatedness in preadolescents' conceptions of their relationships with mother, father, and best friend. *Developmental Psychology, 35*, 737–748.

Hoehl, S., & Striano, T. (2008). Neural processing of eye gaze and threat-related emotional facial expressions in infancy. *Child Development, 79*, 1752–1760.

Hoffman, M. L. (1975). Altruistic behavior and the parent–child relationship. *Journal of Personality and Social Psychology, 31*, 937–943.

Hoffman, M. L. (1982). Development of prosocial motivation: Empathy and guilt. In N. Eisenberg (Ed.), *The development of prosocial behavior* (pp. 281–313). New York, NY: Academic Press.

Hoffman, M. L. (1983). Affective and cognitive processes in moral internalization. In E. T. Higgins, D. N. Ruble, & W. W. Hartup (Eds.), *Social cognition and social development: A sociocultural perspective* (pp. 236–274). Cambridge: Cambridge University Press.

Hoffman, M. L. (1984). Interaction of affect and cognition in empathy. In C. E. Izard, J. Kagan, & R. B. Zajonc (Eds.), *Emotions, cognition, and behavior* (pp. 103–131). Cambridge: Cambridge University Press.

Hoffman, M. L. (2000). *Empathy and moral development: Implications for caring and justice*. Cambridge: Cambridge University Press.

Hoglund, C. L., & Nicholas, K. B. (1995). Shame, guilt, and anger in college students exposed to abusive family environments. *Journal of Family Violence, 10*, 141–157.

Holden, G. W., & Miller, P. C. (1999). Enduring and different: A meta-analysis of the similarity in parents' child rearing. *Psychological Bulletin, 125*, 223–254.

Holden, G. W., Vittrup, B., & Rosen, L. H. (2011). Families, parenting, and discipline. In M. K. Underwood & L. H. Rosen (Eds.), *Social development: Relationships in infancy, childhood, and adolescence*. New York, NY: Guilford Press.

Hollenstein, T. (2007). State space grids: Analyzing dynamics across development. *International Journal of Behavioral Development, 31*, 384–396.

Holmes, E. K., Dunn, K. C., Harper, J., Dyer, W. J., & Day, R. D. (2013). Mother knows best? Inhibitory maternal gatekeeping, psychological control, and the mother–adolescent relationship. *Journal of Adolescence, 36*, 91–101.

Holmgren, R. A., Eisenberg, N., & Fabes, R. A. (1998). The relations of children's situational empathy-related emotions to dispositional prosocial behavior. *International Journal of Behavioral Development, 22*, 169–193.

Hooker, C. I., Verosky, S. C., Germine, L. T., Knight, R. T., & D'Esposito, M. (2008). Mentalizing about emotion and its relationship to empathy. *Social Cognitive and Affective Neuroscience, 3*, 204–217.

Howe, M. L. (1998). Language is never enough: Memories are more than words reveal. *Applied Cognitive Psychology, 12*, 475–481.

Howe, N., Karos, L. K., & Aquan-Assee, J. (2011). Sibling relationship quality in early adolescence: Child and maternal perceptions and daily interactions. *Infant and Child Development, 20*, 227–245.

Howe, N., Petrakos, H., & Rinaldi, C. M. (1998). "All the sheeps are dead. He murdered them": Sibling pretense, negotiation, internal state language, and relationship quality. *Child Development, 69*, 182–191.

Howe, N., Rinaldi, C., Jennings, M., & Petrakos, H. (2002). "No! The lambs can stay out because they got cozies": Constructive and destructive sibling conflict, pretend play, and social understanding. *Child Development, 73*, 1360–1473.

Howe, N., Ross, H. S., & Recchia, H. (2011). Sibling relationships in early and middle childhood. In P. K. Smith & C. H. Hart (Eds.), *Wiley-Blackwell handbook of childhood social development* (2nd ed., pp. 356–372). New York, NY: Wiley.

Howes, C. (1983). Patterns of friendship. *Child Development, 54,* 1041–1053.

Howes, C. (1988). Peer interaction of young children. *Monographs of the Society for Research in Child Development, 53*(1, Serial No. 217).

Howes, C. (1996). The earliest friendships. In W. M. Bukowski, A. F. Newcomb, & W. W. Hartup (Eds.), *The company they keep: Friendships in childhood and adolescence* (pp. 66–86). New York, NY: Cambridge University Press.

Howes, C. (2000). Social-emotional classroom climate in child care, child–teacher relationships and children's second grade peer relations. *Social Development, 9,* 191–204.

Howes, C., & Farver, J. (1987). Toddlers' responses to the distress of their peers. *Journal of Applied Developmental Psychology, 8,* 441–452.

Howes, C., Hamilton, C., & Phillipsen, L. C. (1998). Stability and continuity of child–caregiver and child–peer relationships. *Child Development, 69,* 418–426.

Howes, C., & Matheson, C. C. (1992). Sequences in the development of competent play with peers: Social and social pretend play. *Developmental Psychology, 28,* 961–974.

Howes, C., Matheson, C. C., & Hamilton, C. E. (1994). Maternal, teacher, and child care history correlates of children's relationships with peers. *Child Development, 55,* 257–273.

Howes, C., & Phillipsen, L. (1992). Gender and friendship: Relationships with peer groups of young children. *Social Development, 1,* 230–242.

Howes, C., Rodning, C., Galluzzo, D. C., & Myers, L. (1988). Attachment and child care: Relationships with mother and caregiver. *Early Childhood Research Quarterly, 3,* 703–715.

Howes, C., & Spieker, S. (2008). Attachment relationships in the context of multiple caregivers. In J. Cassidy & P. Shaver (Eds.), *Handbook of attachment: Theory, research, and clinical applications* (2nd ed., pp. 317–332). New York, NY: Guilford Press.

Howes, C., & Tonyan, H. (1999). Peer relations. In L. Balter & C. S. Tamis-LeMonda (Eds.), *Child psychology: A handbook of contemporary issues* (pp. 143–157). New York, NY: Psychology Press.

Howes, C., & Tonyan, H. A. (2000). Links between adult and peer relations across four developmental periods. In K. A. Kerns, J. Contreras, & A. Neal-Barnett (Eds.), *Examining associations between parent–child and peer relationships* (pp. 84–114). New York, NY: Greenwood.

Hoza, B., Molina, B. S. G., Bukowski, W. M., & Sippola, L. (1995). Peer variables as predictors of later childhood adjustment. *Development and Psychopathology, 7,* 787–802.

Hrdy, S. (2005). Evolutionary context of human development: The cooperative breeding model. In C. S. Carter, L. Ahnert, K. E. Grossman, S. B. Hrdy, M. E. Lamb, S. W. Porges, & N. Sachser (Eds.), *Attachment and bonding: A new synthesis* (pp. 9–32). Cambridge, MA: The MIT Press.

Hughes, D. A., & Baylin, J. (2012). *Brain-based parenting: The neuroscience of caregiving for healthy attachment.* New York, NY: Norton.

Hughes, D., Rodriguez, J., Smith, E., Johnson, D., Stevenson, H., & Spicer, P. (2006). Parents' ethnic-racial socialization practices: A review of research and directions for future study. *Developmental Psychology, 42,* 747–770.

Huizink, A. (2012). Prenatal influences on temperament. In M. Zentner & R. L. Shiner (Eds.), *Handbook of temperament* (pp. 297–314). New York, NY: Guilford Press.

Hum, K. M., & Lewis, M. D. (2013). Neural mechanisms of emotion regulation in children: Implications for normative development and emotion-related disorders. In K. C. Barrett, N. A. Fox, G. A. Morgan, D. J. Fidler, & L. A. Daunhauer (Eds.), *Handbook of self-regulatory processes in development: New directions and international perspectives* (pp. 173–198). New York, NY: Psychology Press.

Hymel, S., Closson, L. M., Caravita, S. C. S., & Vaillancourt, T. (2010). Social status among peers: From sociometric attraction to peer acceptance to perceived popularity. In P. K. Smith & C. H. Hart (Eds.), *Wiley-Blackwell handbook of childhood social development* (2nd ed., pp. 375–392). Oxford: Wiley-Blackwell.

Iannotti, R. J., Cummings, E. M., Pierrehumbert, B., Milano, M. J., & Zahn-Waxler, C. (1992). Parental influences on prosocial behavior and empathy in early childhood. In J. M. A. M. Janssens & J. R. M. Gerris (Eds.), *Child rearing: Influence on prosocial and moral development* (pp. 77–100). Amsterdam: Swets & Zeitlinger.

Impett, E. A., Sorsoli, L., Schooler, D., Henson, J. M., & Tolman, D. L. (2008). Girls' relationship authenticity and self-esteem across adolescence. *Developmental Psychology, 44*, 722–733.

Insel, T. R., & Young, L. J. (2001). The neurobiology of attachment. *Nature Reviews Neuroscience, 2*, 129–136.

Irizarry, K. J., & Galbraith, S. J. (2004). Complex disorders reloaded: Causality, action, reaction, cause, and effect. *Molecular Psychiatry, 9*, 431–432.

Irle, E., Ruhleder, M., Lange, C., Seidler-Brandler, U., Salzer, S., Dechent, P., … Leichsenring, F. (2010). Reduced amygdalar and hippocampal size in adults with generalized social phobia. *Journal of Psychiatry and Neuroscience, 35*, 126–131.

Isabella, R. A., & Belsky, J. (1991). Interactional synchrony and the origins of infant–mother attachment: A replication study. *Child Development, 62*, 373–384.

Isabella, R. A., Belsky, J., & von Eye, A. (1989). Origins of infant–mother attachment: An examination of interactional synchrony during the infant's first year. *Developmental Psychology, 25*, 12–21.

Israel, S., Lerer, E., Shalev, I., Uzefovsky, F., Reibold, M., Bachner-Melman, R., … Ebstein, R. P. (2008). Molecular genetic studies of the arginine vasopressin 1a receptor (AVPR1a) and the oxytocin receptor (OXTR) in human behavior: From autism to altruism with some notes in between. *Progress in Brain Research, 170*, 435–449.

Izard, C. E. (1971). *The face of emotion.* New York, NY: Appleton-Century-Crofts.

Izard, C. E. (1991). *The psychology of emotions.* New York, NY: Plenum.

Izard, C. E. (2002). Emotion knowledge and emotion utilization facilitate school readiness. *Social Policy Report, 16*, 7.

Izard, C. E. (2007). Basic emotions, natural kinds, emotion schemas, and a new paradigm. *Perspectives on Psychological Science, 2*, 260–280.

Izard, C. E. (2009). Emotion theory and research: Highlights, unanswered questions, and emerging issues. *Annual Review of Psychology, 60*, 1–25.

Izard, C. E., & Dougherty, L. M. (1982). Two complementary systems for measuring facial expressions in infants and children. In C. E. Izard (Ed.), *Measuring emotions in infants and children* (pp. 97–126). New York, NY: Cambridge University Press.

Izard, C. E., Fine, S., Schultz, D., Mostow, A., Ackerman, B., & Youngstrom, E. (2001). Emotion knowledge as a predictor of social behavior and academic competence in children at risk. *Psychological Science, 12*, 18–23.

Izard, C. E., Huebner, R. R., Risser, D., McGinnes, G. C., & Dougherty, L. M. (1980). The young infant's ability to produce discrete emotion expressions. *Developmental Psychology, 16*, 132–140.

Izard, C. E., King, K. A., Trentacosta, C. J., Laurenceau, J. P., Morgan, J. K., Krauthamer-Ewing, E. S., & Finlon, K. J. (2008). Accelerating the development of emotion competence in Head Start children. *Development and Psychopathology, 20*, 369–397.

Izard, C. E., Woodburn, E. M., Finlon, K. J., Krauthamer-Ewing, E. S., Grossman, S. R., & Seidenfeld, A. (2011). Emotion knowledge, emotion utilization, and emotion regulation. *Emotion Review, 3*, 44–52.

Jaccard, J., Dittus, P. J., & Gordon, V. V. (1996). Maternal correlates of adolescent sexual and contraceptive behavior. *Family Planning Perspectives, 28*, 159–165.

Jack, D. C. (1991). *Silencing the self: Women and depression.* Cambridge, MA: Harvard University Press.

Jacobs, J. E., Lanza, S., Osgood, D. W., Eccles, J. S., & Wigfield, A. (2002). Changes in children's self-competence and values: Gender and domain differences across grades one through twelve. *Child Development, 73*, 509–527.

Jacobson, J. L. (1981). The role of inanimate objects in early peer interaction. *Child Development, 52*, 618–626.

Jaenicke, C., Hammen, C., Zupan, B., Hiroto, D., Gordon, D., Adrian, C., & Burge, D. (1987). Cognitive vulnerability in children at risk for depression. *Journal of Abnormal Child Psychology, 15*, 559–572.

Jaffe, J., Beebe, B., Feldstein, S., Crown, C. L., & Jasnow, M. D. (2001). Rhythms of dialogue in infancy: Coordinated timing in development. *Monographs of the Society for Research in Child Development, 66*(2, Serial No. 231).

James, W. (1892). *Text-book of psychology.* London: Macmillan and Co.

Janssens, J. M. A. M., & Gerris, J. R. M. (1992). Child rearing, empathy, and prosocial development. In J. M. A. M. Janssens & J. R. M. Gerris (Eds.), *Child rearing: Influence on prosocial and moral development* (pp. 57–75). Amsterdam: Swets & Zeitlinger.

Jenkins, J. (1992). Sibling relationships in disharmonious homes: Potential difficulties and protective effects. In F. Boer & J. Dunn (Eds.), *Children's sibling relationships: Developmental and clinical issues* (pp. 125–138). Hillsdale, NJ: Erlbaum.

Jenkins, J., Rasbash, J., Leckie, G., Gass, K., & Dunn, J. (2012). The role of maternal factors in sibling relationship quality: A multilevel study of multiple dyads per family. *Journal of Child Psychology and Psychiatry, 53,* 622–629.

Jenkins, J. M., Rasbash, J., & O'Connor, T. G. (2003). The role of the shared family context in differential parenting. *Developmental Psychology, 39,* 99–113.

Johnson, D. B. (1982). Altruistic behavior and the development of the self in infants. *Merrill-Palmer Quarterly, 28,* 379–388.

Jones, J. D., & Cassidy, J. (2014). Parental attachment style: Examination of links with parent secure base provision and adolescent secure base use. *Attachment & Human Development, 16,* 437–461.

Jones, J. D., Cassidy, J., & Shaver, P. R. (2015). Parents' self-reported attachment styles: A review of links with parenting behaviors, emotions, and cognition. *Personality and Social Psychology Review, 19,* 44–76.

Jones, R. M., & Hartmann, B. R. (1988). Ego identity: Developmental differences and experimental substance use among adolescents. *Journal of Adolescence, 11,* 347–360.

Jonsson, C.-O., & Clinton, D. (2006). What do mothers attune to during interactions with their infants? *Infant and Child Development, 15,* 387–402.

Juang, L. P., Lerner, J. V., McKinney, J. P., & von Eye, A. (1999). The goodness of fit in autonomy timetable expectations between Asian-American late adolescents and their parents. *International Journal of Behavioral Development, 23,* 1023–1048.

Juffer, F., Bakermans-Kranenburg, M. J., & van IJzendoorn, M. H. (Eds.). (2007). *Promoting positive parenting: An attachment-based intervention.* Mahwah, NJ: Erlbaum.

Kagan, J. (1981). *The second year: The emergence of self-awareness.* Cambridge, MA: Harvard University Press.

Kagan, J. (1984). *The nature of the child.* New York, NY: Basic Books.

Kagan, J. (1994). On the nature of emotion. In N. A. Fox (Ed.), The development of emotion regulation: Behavioral and biological considerations. *Monographs of the Society for Research in Child Development, 59*(2–3, Serial No. 240), 7–24.

Kagan, J. (2005). Human morality and its variants. In A. Dientsbier (Series Ed.) & G. Carlo & C. P. Edwards (Vol. Eds.), *Nebraska Symposium on Motivation: Vol. 51. Moral motivation through the lifespan.* Lincoln: University of Nebraska Press.

Kagan, J., Arcus, D., Snidman, N., Feng, W. Y., Hendler, J., & Greene, S. (1994). Reactivity in infants: A cross-national comparison. *Developmental Psychology, 30,* 342–345.

Kagan, J., & Fox, N. A. (2006). Biology, culture, and temperamental biases. In W. Damon & R. M. Lerner (Eds.), *Handbook of child psychology. Vol 3: Social, emotional and personality development* (6th ed., pp. 167–225). New York, NY: Wiley.

Kagan, J., Reznick, J. S., & Snidman, N. (1987). The physiology and psychology of behavioral inhibition in children. *Child Development, 58,* 1459–1473.

Kagan, J., & Snidman, N. (1991). Temperamental factors in human development. *American Psychologist, 46,* 856–862.

Kagan, J., & Snidman, N. (1999). Early childhood predictors of adult anxiety disorders. *Biological Psychiatry, 46,* 1536–1541.

Kagan, J., & Snidman, N. (2004). *The long shadow of temperament.* Cambridge, MA: Harvard University Press.

Kagan, J., Snidman, N., Kahn, V., & Towsley, S. (2007). The preservation of two infant temperaments into adolescence. *Monographs of the Society for Research in Child Development, 72*(2, Serial No. 287).

Kalpidou, M. D., Power, T. G., Cherry, K. E., & Gottfried, N. W. (2004). Regulation of emotion and behavior among 3- and 5-year-olds. *Journal of General Psychology, 131,* 159–178.

Kaplan, J. T., Aziz-Zadeh, L., Uddin, L. Q., & Iacoboni, M. (2008). The self across the senses: An fMRI study of self-face and self-voice recognition. *Social Cognitive and Affective Neuroscience, 3,* 218–223.

Kaplan, N. (1985). *Procedures for the administration of the Hansburg Separation Anxiety Test for younger children adapted from Klagsbrun and Bowlby.* Unpublished manuscript, University of California, Berkeley, CA.

Kärtner, J., Keller, H., Chaudhary, N., & Yovsi, R. D. (2012). The development of mirror self-recognition in different sociocultural contexts. *Monographs of the Society for Research in Child Development, 77*(4, Serial No. 305).

Katainen, S., Raikkonen, K., & Keltikangas-Jarvinen, L. (1998). Development of temperament: Childhood temperament and the mother's childrearing attitudes as predictors of adolescent temperament in a 9-year follow-up study. *Journal of Research on Adolescence, 8,* 485–509.

Katz, L. F., Hessler, D. M., & Annest, A. (2007). Domestic violence, emotional competence, and child adjustment. *Social Development, 16,* 513–538.

Katz, L. F., Kramer, L., & Gottman, J. M. (1992). Conflict and emotions in marital, sibling, and peer relationships. In C. U. Shantz & W. W. Hartup (Eds.), *Conflict in child and adolescent development* (pp. 122–149). Cambridge: Cambridge University Press.

Kayyal, M. H., & Russell, J. A. (2013). Palestinians and Americans judge spontaneous facial expressions of emotion. *Emotion, 13,* 891–904.

Keefe, K., & Berndt, T. J. (1996). Relations of friendship quality to self-esteem in early adolescence. *The Journal of Early Adolescence, 16,* 110–129.

Keenan, J. P., & Wheeler, M. A. (2002). Elucidation of the brain correlates of cognitive empathy and self-awareness. *Behavioral and Brain Sciences, 25,* 40–41.

Keijers, L., Frijns, T., Branje, S. J. T., & Meeus, W. (2009). Developmental links of adolescent disclosure, parental solicitation, and control with delinquency: Moderation by parental support. *Developmental Psychology, 45,* 1314–1327.

Keller, H., Yovsi, R., Borke, J., Kartner, J., Jensen, H., & Papaligoura, Z. (2004). Developmental consequences of early parenting experiences: Self-recognition and self-regulation in three cultural communities. *Child Development, 75,* 1745–1760.

Keltner, D., & Buswell, B. (1997). Embarrassment: Its distinct form and appeasement functions. *Psychological Bulletin, 122,* 250–270.

Kennedy, D. E., & Kramer, L. (2008). Improving emotional regulation and sibling relationship quality: The More Fun with Sisters and Brothers Program. *Family Relations, 57,* 567–578.

Kenny, D. A., Kashy, D. A., & Cook, W. L. (2006). *Dyadic data analysis.* New York, NY: Guilford Press.

Kenny, M. (1987). The extent and function of parental attachment among first-year college students. *Journal of Youth and Adolescence, 16,* 17–29.

Kenny, R., Dooley, B., & Fitzgerald, A. (2013). Interpersonal relationships and emotional distress in adolescence. *Journal of Adolescence, 36,* 351–360.

Kerns, K. A., Abraham, M. M., Schlegelmilch, A., & Morgan, T. A. (2007). Mother–child attachment in later middle childhood: Assessment approaches and associations with mood and emotion regulation. *Attachment & Human Development, 9,* 33–53.

Kerns, K. A., & Brumariu, L. E. (2014). Is insecure parent–child attachment a risk factor for the development of anxiety in childhood and adolescence? *Child Development Perspectives, 8,* 12–17.

Kerns, K. A., Cole, A., & Andrews, P. B. (1998). Attachment security, parent peer management practices, and peer relationships in preschoolers. *Merrill-Palmer Quarterly, 44,* 504–522.

Kerns, K. A., Klepac, L., & Cole, A. (1996). Peer relationships and preadolescents' perceptions of security in the child–mother relationship. *Developmental Psychology, 32,* 457–466.

Kerns, K. A., & Richardson, R. A. (Eds.). (2005). *Attachment in middle childhood.* New York, NY: Guilford Press.

Kerns, K. A., Tomich, P. L., Aspelmeier, J. E., & Contreras, J. M. (2000). Attachment based assessments of parent–child relationships in middle childhood. *Developmental Psychology, 36,* 614–626.

Kerpelman, J. L., Pittman, J. F., Cadely, H. S.-E., Tuggle, F. J., Harrell-Levy, M. K., & Adler-Baeder, F. M. (2012). Identity and intimacy during adolescence: Connections among identity styles, romantic attachment and identity commitment. *Journal of Adolescence, 35,* 1427–1439.

Kerpelman, J. L., Pittman, J. F., & Lamke, L. K. (1997). Toward a microprocess perspective on adolescent identity development: An identity control theory approach. *Journal of Adolescent Research, 12,* 325–346.

Kestenbaum, R., Farber, E. A., & Sroufe, L. A. (1989). Individual differences in empathy among preschoolers: Relation to attachment history. *New Directions for Child Development, 44,* 51–64.

Kiang, L., Moreno, A., & Robinson, J. L. (2004). Maternal preconceptions about parenting predict child temperament, maternal sensitivity, and children's empathy. *Developmental Psychology, 40,* 1081–1092.

Kiang, L., Witkow, M. R., & Champagne, M. C. (2013). Normative changes in ethnic and American identities and links with adjustment among Asian American adolescents. *Developmental Psychology, 49,* 1713–1722.

Kiesner, J., Kerr, M., & Stattin, H. (2004). "Very important persons" in adolescence: Going beyond in-school, single friendships in the study of peer homophily. *Journal of Adolescence, 27,* 545–560.

Killeen, M. R., & Forehand, R. (1998). A transactional model of adolescent self-esteem. *Journal of Family Psychology, 12,* 132–138.

Killen, M., Breton, S., Ferguson, H., & Handler, K. (1994). Preschoolers' evaluations of teacher methods of intervention in social transgressions. *Merrill-Palmer Quarterly, 40,* 399–415.

Killen, M., Lee-Kim, J., McGlothlin, H., & Stangor, C. (2002). How children and adolescents evaluate gender and racial exclusion. *Monographs of the Society for Research in Child Development, 67*(4, Serial No. 271).

Killen, M., Margie, N. G., & Sinno, S. (2006). Morality in the context of intergroup relationships. In M. Killen & J. G. Smetana (Eds.), *Handbook of moral development* (pp. 155–184). Mahwah, NJ: Erlbaum.

Killen, M., Mulvey, L., Richardson, C., Jampol, N., & Woodward, A. (2011). The accidental transgressor: Morally relevant theory of mind. *Cognition, 119,* 197–215.

Killen, M., & Stangor, C. (2001). Children's social reasoning about inclusion and exclusion in gender and race peer group contexts. *Child Development, 72,* 174–186.

Kim, J., & Cicchetti, D. (2004). A longitudinal study of child maltreatment, mother–child relationship quality and maladjustment: The role of self-esteem and social competence. *Journal of Abnormal Child Psychology, 32,* 341–354.

Kim, J. E., Hetherington, E. M., & Reiss, D. (1999). Associations among family relationships, antisocial peers, and adolescents' externalizing behaviors: Gender and family type differences. *Child Development, 70,* 1209–1230.

Kim, J. Y., McHale, S. M., Crouter, A. C., & Osgood, D. W. (2007). Longitudinal linkages between sibling relationships and adjustment from middle childhood through adolescence. *Developmental Psychology, 43,* 960–973.

Kim, J. Y., McHale, S. M., Osgood, D. W., & Crouter, A. C. (2006). Longitudinal course and family correlates of sibling relationships from childhood through adolescence. *Child Development, 77,* 1746–1761.

Kim, K., Conger, R. D., Lorenz, F. O., & Elder, G. H., Jr. (2001). Parent–adolescent reciprocity in negative affect and its relation to early adult social development. *Developmental Psychology, 37,* 775–790.

King, K. M., Lengua, L. J., & Monahan, K. C. (2013). Individual differences in the development of self-regulation during preadolescence: Connections to context and adjustment. *Journal of Abnormal Child Psychology, 41,* 57–69.

Kins, E., Beyers, W., & Soenens, B. (2013). When the separation-individuation process goes awry: Distinguishing between dysfunctional dependence and dysfunctional independence. *International Journal of Behavioral Development, 37,* 1–12.

Kins, E., Soenens, B., & Beyers, W. (2011). "Why do they have to grow up so fast?" Parental separation anxiety and emerging adults' pathology of separation-individuation. *Journal of Clinical Psychology, 67,* 647–664.

Kins, E., Soenens, B., & Beyers, W. (2012). Parental psychological control and dysfunctional separation-individuation: A tale of two different dynamics. *Journal of Adolescence, 35,* 1099–1109.

Kisilevsky, B., Hains, S. M., Brown, C. A., Lee, C. T., Cowperthwaite, B., Stutzman, S. S., ... Wang, Z. (2009). Fetal sensitivity to properties of maternal speech and language. *Infant Behavior and Development, 32,* 59–71.

Kitayama, S., Markus, H. R., & Matsumoto, H. (1995). Culture, self, and emotion: A cultural perspective on "self conscious" emotions. In J. P. Tangney & K. W. Fischer (Eds.), *Self-conscious emotions: The psychology of shame, guilt, embarrassment, and pride* (pp. 439–464). New York, NY: Guilford Press.

Kitzmann, K., Cohen, R., & Lockwood, R. (2002). Are only children missing out? Comparison of the peer-related social competence of only children and siblings. *Journal of Social and Personal Relationships, 19,* 299–316.

Klagsbrun, M., & Bowlby, J. (1976). Responses to separation from parents: A clinical test for young children. *British Journal of Projective Psychology and Personality Study, 21,* 7–27.

Klein, G. S. (1976). *Psychoanalytic theory: An exploration of essentials.* New York, NY: International Universities Press.

Klein Velderman, M., Bakermans-Kranenburg, M. J., Juffer, F., & van IJzendoorn, M. H. (2006). Effects of attachment-based interventions on maternal sensitivity and infant attachment: Differential susceptibility of highly reactive infants. *Journal of Family Psychology, 20,* 266–274.

Kling, K. C., Hyde, J. S., Showers, C. J., & Buswell, B. N. (1999). Gender differences in self-esteem: A meta-analysis. *Psychological Bulletin, 125,* 470–500.

Kluger, J. (2011). *The sibling effect: What the bonds among brothers and sisters reveal about us.* New York, NY: Riverhead Books.

Knafo, A., & Israel, S. (2009). Genetic and environmental influences on prosocial behavior. In M. Mikulincer & P. R. Shaver (Eds.), *Prosocial motives, emotions, and behavior* (pp. 149–167). Washington, DC: American Psychological Association.

Knafo, A., & Plomin, R.(2006). Prosocial behavior from early to middle childhood: Genetic and environmental influences on stability and change. *Developmental Psychology, 42,* 771–786.

Knafo, A., Zahn-Waxler, C., Van Hulle, C., Robinson, J. L., & Rhee, S. H. (2008). The developmental origins of a disposition toward empathy: Genetic and environmental contributions. *Emotion, 8,* 737–752.

Knight, G. P., Johnson, L. G., Carlo, G., & Eisenberg, N. (1994). A multiplicative model of the dispositional antecedents of a prosocial behavior: Predicting more of the people more of the time. *Journal of Personality and Social Psychology, 66,* 178–183.

Knobe, J. (2005). Theory of mind and moral cognition: Exploring the connections. *Trends in Cognitive Sciences, 9,* 357–359.

Knobe, J. (2010). The person as moralist account and its alternatives. *Behavioral and Brain Sciences, 33,* 353–365.

Knoester, C., Haynie, D. L., & Stephens, C. M. (2006). Parenting practices and adolescents' friendship networks. *Journal of Marriage and Family, 68,* 1247–1260.

Kobak, R. (1993). *The Attachment Interview Q-Set.* Unpublished manuscript, University of Delaware, Newark, DE.

Kobak, R., Cassidy, J., Lyons-Ruth, K., & Ziv, Y. (2006). Attachment, stress, and psychopathology: A developmental pathways model. In D. Cicchetti & D. J. Cohen (Eds.), *Developmental psychopathology: Vol. 1. Theory and method* (2nd ed., pp. 333–369). Hoboken, NJ: Wiley.

Kobak, R., & Duemmler, S. (1994). Attachment and conversation: Toward a discourse analysis of adolescent and adult security. In K. Bartholomew & D. Perlman (Eds.), *Advances in personal relationships: Volume 5. Attachment processes in adulthood* (pp. 121–149). London: Jessica Kingsley.

Kobak, R., Little, M., Race, E., & Acosta, M. (2001). Attachment disruptions in seriously emotionally disturbed children: Implications for treatment. *Attachment & Human Development, 3,* 243–258.

Kobak, R., & Madsen, S. (2008). Disruptions in attachment bonds: Implications for theory, research, and clinical intervention. In J. Cassidy & P. R. Shaver (Eds.), *Handbook of attachment: Theory, research, and clinical applications* (2nd ed., pp. 23–47). New York, NY: Guilford Press.

Kobak, R., Rosenthal, N., & Serwik, A. (2005). The attachment hierarchy in middle childhood: Conceptual and methodological issues. In K. Kerns & R. A. Richardson (Eds.), *Attachment in middle childhood* (pp. 71–88). New York, NY: Guilford Press.

Kobak, R., Rosenthal, N. L., Zajac, K., & Madsen, S. (2007). Adolescent attachment hierarchies and the search for an adult pair bond. In M. Scharf & O. Mayseless (Eds.), *New directions in child development: Adolescent attachment.* New York, NY: Jossey-Bass.

Kobak, R., & Sceery, A. (1988). Attachment in late adolescence: Working models, affect regulation, and representations of self and others. *Child Development, 59,* 135–146.

Kobak, R., Sudler, N., & Gamble, W. (1991). Attachment and depressive symptoms during adolescence: A developmental pathways analysis. *Development and Psychopathology, 3,* 461–474.

Kober, H., Barrett, L. F., Joseph, J., Bliss-Moreau, E., Lindquist, K., & Wager, T. D. (2008). Functional grouping and cortical–subcortical interactions in emotion: A meta-analysis of neuroimaging studies. *NeuroImage, 42,* 998–1031.

Kochanska, G. (1991). Socialization and temperament in the development of guilt and conscience. *Child Development, 62,* 1379–1392.

Kochanska, G. (1993). Toward a synthesis of parental socialization and child temperament in early development of conscience. *Child Development, 64,* 325–347.

Kochanska, G. (1995). Children's temperament, mothers' discipline, and security of attachment: Multiple pathways to emerging internalization. *Child Development, 66,* 597–615.

Kochanska, G. (1997). Multiple pathways to conscience for children with difficult temperaments: From toddlerhood to age 5. *Developmental Psychology, 33,* 228–240.

Kochanska, G. (2001). Emotional development in children with different attachment histories: The first three years. *Child Development, 72,* 474–490.

Kochanska, G. (2002). Committed compliance, moral self, and internalization: A mediational model. *Developmental Psychology, 38,* 339–351.

Kochanska, G., & Aksan, N. (2006). Children's conscience and self-regulation. *Journal of Personality, 74,* 1587–1617.

Kochanska, G., Aksan, N., & Carlson, J. J. (2005). Temperament, relationships, and young children's receptive cooperation with their parents. *Developmental Psychology, 41,* 648–660.

Kochanska, G., Aksan, N., Knaack, A., & Rhines, H. (2004). Maternal parenting and children's conscience: Early security as a moderator. *Child Development, 75,* 1229–1242.

Kochanska, G., Aksan, N., Prisco, T. R., & Adams, E. E. (2008). Mother–child and father–child mutually responsive orientation in the first 2 years and children's outcomes at preschool age: Mechanisms of influence. *Child Development, 79,* 30–44.

Kochanska, G., Barry, R. A., Jimenez, N. B., Hollatz, A. L., & Woodard, J. (2009). Guilt and effortful control: Two mechanisms that prevent disruptive developmental trajectories. *Journal of personality and Social Psychology, 97,* 322–333.

Kochanska, G., Casey, R. J., & Fukumoto, A. (1995). Toddlers' sensitivity to standard violations. *Child Development, 66,* 643–656.

Kochanska, G., & Coy, K. C. (2002). Child emotionality and maternal responsiveness as predictors of reunion behaviors in the Strange Situation: Links mediated and unmediated by separation distress. *Child Development, 73,* 228–240.

Kochanska, G., Coy, K. C., & Murray, K. T. (2001). The development of self-regulation in the first four years of life. *Child Development, 72,* 1091–1111.

Kochanska, G., DeVet, K., Goldman, M., Murray, K. T., & Putnam, S. P. (1993). Maternal reports of conscience development and temperament in young children. *Child Development, 65,* 852–868.

Kochanska, G., Forman, D., Aksan, N., & Dunbar, S. (2005). Pathways to conscience: Early mother–child mutually responsive orientation and children's moral emotion, conduct and cognition. *Journal of Child Psychology and Psychiatry, 46,* 19–34.

Kochanska, G., Forman, D., & Coy, K. C. (1999). Implications of the mother–child relationship in infancy for socialization in the second year of life. *Infant Behavior and Development, 22,* 249–265.

Kochanska, G., Gross, J. N., Lin, M.-H., & Nichols, K. E. (2002). Guilt in young children: Development, determinants, and relations with a broader system of standards. *Developmental Psychology, 73,* 461–482.

Kochanska, G., & Kim, S. (2013). Early attachment organization with both parents and future behavior problems: From infancy to middle childhood. *Child Development, 84,* 283–296.

Kochanska, G., & Knaack, A. (2003). Effortful control as a personality characteristic of young children: Antecedents, correlates, and consequences. *Journal of Personality, 71,* 1087–1112.

Kochanska, G., & Murray, K. T. (2000). Mother–child mutually responsive orientation and conscience development: From toddler to early school age. *Child Development, 71,* 417–431.

Kochanska, G., Murray, K. T., & Coy, K. C. (1997). Inhibitory control as a contributor to conscience in childhood: From toddler to early school age. *Developmental Psychology, 68,* 263–277.

Kochanska, G., Murray, K. T., & Harlan, E. (2000). Effortful control in early childhood: Continuity and change, antecedents, and implications for social development. *Developmental Psychology, 36,* 220–232.

Kochanska, G., Murray, K. T., Jacques, T. Y., Koenig, A. L., & Vandegeest, K. A. (1996). Inhibitory control in young children and its role in emerging internalization. *Child Development, 67,* 420–507.

Kochanska, G., & Thompson, R. A. (1997). The emergence and development of conscience in toddlerhood and early childhood. In J. E. Grusec & L. Kuczynski (Eds.), *Parenting and children's internalization of values: A handbook of contemporary theory* (pp. 53–77). New York, NY: Wiley.

Koenig, A. L., Cicchetti, D., & Rogosch, F. A. (2000). Child compliance/noncompliance and maternal contributors to internalization in maltreating and nonmaltreating dyads. *Child Development, 71,* 1018–1032.

Kohlberg, L. (1969). Stage and sequence: The cognitive developmental approach to socialization. In D. A. Goslin (Ed.), *Handbook of socialization theory and research* (pp. 347–480). Chicago, IL: Rand McNally.

Kohlberg, L. (1971). From is to ought: How to commit the naturalistic fallacy and get away with it in the study of moral development. In T. Mischel (Ed.), *Psychology and genetic epistemology* (pp. 151–235). New York, NY: Academic Press.

Kohlberg, L. (1985). *The psychology of moral development.* San Francisco, CA: Harper & Row.

Kolak, A. M., & Volling, B. L. (2011). Sibling jealousy in early childhood: Longitudinal links to sibling relationship quality. *Infant and Child Development, 20,* 213–226.

Kopp, C. (1982). The antecedents of self-regulation. *Developmental Psychology, 18,* 199–214.

Kopp, C. (1989). Regulation of distress and negative emotions: A developmental view. *Developmental Psychology, 25,* 343–354.

Kopp, C. (1991). Young children's progression to self-regulation. In M. Bullock (Ed.), *The development of intentional action: Cognitive, motivational, and interactive processes* (pp. 38–54). Basel: Karger.

Kopp, C. (2002). Commentary: The codevelopments of attention and emotion regulation. *Infancy, 3,* 199–208.

Kopp, C., & Neufeld, S. J. (2003). Emotional development during infancy. In R. J. Davidson, K. R. Scherer, & H. H. Goldsmith (Eds.), *Handbook of affective sciences* (pp. 347–374). New York, NY: Oxford University Press.

Kowal, A., & Kramer, L. (1997). Children's understanding of parental differential treatment. *Child Development, 68,* 113–126.

Kowal, A., Kramer, L., Krull, J. L., & Crick, N. R. (2002). Children's perceptions of the fairness of parental preferential treatment and their socioemotional well-being. *Journal of Family Psychology, 16,* 297–306.

Kowal, A. K., Krull, J. L., & Kramer, L. (2004). How the differential treatment of siblings is linked with parent–child relationship quality. *Journal of Family Psychology, 18,* 658–665.

Kowal, A. K., Krull, J. L., & Kramer, L. (2006). Shared understanding of parental differential treatment in families. *Social Development, 15,* 276–295.

Kramer, L. (2004). Experimental interventions in sibling relationships. In R. D. Conger, F. O. Lorenz, & K. A. S. Wickrama (Eds.), *Continuity and change in family relations: Theory, methods, and empirical findings* (pp. 345–380). Mahwah, NJ: Erlbaum.

Kramer, L. (2010). The essential ingredients of successful sibling relationships: An emerging framework for advancing theory and practice. *Child Development Perspectives, 4,* 80–86.

Kramer, L., & Baron, L. A. (1995). Parental perceptions of children's sibling relationships. *Family Relations, 44,* 95–103.

Kramer, L., & Conger, K. J. (2009). What we learn from our sisters and brothers: For better or for worse. In L. Kramer & K. J. Conger (Eds.), *Siblings as agents of socialization. New Directions for Child and Adolescent Development* (Vol. 126, pp. 1–12). San Francisco, CA: Jossey-Bass.

Kramer, L., & Gottman, J. M. (1992). Becoming a sibling: "With a little help from my friends." *Developmental Psychology, 28,* 685–699.

Kramer, L., & Kowal, A. K. (2005). Sibling relationship quality from birth to adolescence: The enduring contributions of friends. *Journal of Family Psychology, 19,* 503–511.

Kramer, L., Perozynski, L. A., & Chung, T. (1999). Parental responses to sibling conflict: The effects of development and parent gender. *Child Development, 70,* 1401–1414.

Krettenauer, T., & Eichler, D. (2006). Adolescents' self-attributed moral emotions following a moral transgression: Relations with delinquency, confidence in moral judgment and age. *British Journal of Developmental Psychology, 24,* 489–506.

Kroger, J. (2007). *Identity development: Adolescence through adulthood.* Thousand Oaks, CA: Sage Publications.

Kroger, J., Marinussen, M., & Marcia, J. E. (2010). Identity status change during adolescence and young adulthood: A meta-analysis. *Journal of Adolescence, 33,* 683–698.

Krueger, R. F., Hicks, B. M., Patrick, C. J., Carlson, S. R., Iacono, W., & McGue, M. (2002). Etiologic connections among substance dependence, antisocial behavior, and personality: Modeling the externalizing spectrum. *Journal of Abnormal Psychology, 111,* 411–424.

Kuhn, D., & Franklin, S. (2008). The second decade: What develops (and how)? In W. Damon & R. M. Lerner (Eds.), *Child and adolescent development: An advanced course* (pp. 517–550). New York, NY: John Wiley & Sons.

Kupersmidt, J. B., & Coie, J. D. (1990). Preadolescent peer status, aggression, and school adjustment as predictors of externalizing problems in adolescence. *Child Development, 61,* 1350–1362.

Kupersmidt, J. B., DeRosier, M., & Patterson, C. (1995). Similarity as the basis for children's friendships: The roles of sociometric status, aggressive and withdrawn behavior, academic achievement and demographic characteristics. *Journal of Social and Personal Relationships, 12,* 439–452.

Kuppens, P., Stouten, J., & Mesquita, B. (2009). Individual differences in emotion components and dynamics: Introduction to the special issue. *Cognition and Emotion, 23,* 1249–1258.

Kuppens, P., Tuerlinckx, F., Russell, J. A., & Barrett, L. F. (2013). The relation between valence and arousal in subjective experience. *Psychological Bulletin, 139,* 917–940.

Kuttler, A., LaGreca, A. M., & Prinstein, M. J. (1999). Friendship qualities and social-emotional functioning of adolescents with close, cross-sex friendships. *Journal of Research on Adolescence, 9,* 339–366.

Ladd, G. W. (1999). Peer relationships and social competence during early and middle childhood. *Annual Review of Psychology, 50,* 333–359.

Ladd, G. W. (2005). *Children's peer relationships and social competence: A century of progress.* New Haven, CT: Yale University Press.

Ladd, G. W., Kochenderfer, B. J., & Coleman, C. C. (1996). Friendship quality as a predictor of young children's early school adjustment. *Child Development, 67,* 1103–1118.

Ladd, G. W., & Troop-Gordon, W. (2003). The role of chronic peer difficulties in the development of children's psychological adjustment problems. *Child Development, 74,* 1344–1367.

LaFontana, K., & Cillessen, A. (2009). Developmental changes in the priority of perceived status in childhood and adolescence. *Social Development, 19,* 130–147.

LaFreniere, P. J. (2000). *Emotional development: A biosocial perspective.* Belmont, CA: Wadsworth.

LaFreniere, P. J., & Sroufe, L. A. (1985). Profiles of peer competence in the preschool: Interrelations between measures, influence of social ecology, and relation to attachment history. *Developmental Psychology, 21,* 56–69.

Lagattuta, K. H., & Thompson, R. A. (2007). The development of self-conscious emotions: Cognitive processes and social influence. In R. W. Robins & J. Tracy (Eds.), *Self-conscious emotions* (2nd ed., pp. 91–113). New York, NY: Guilford Press.

Lagattuta, K. H., & Wellman, H. M. (2002). Differences in early parent–child conversations about negative versus positive emotions: Implications for the development of emotion understanding. *Developmental Psychology, 38,* 564–580.

LaGreca, A. M., & Harrison, H. M. (2005). Adolescent peer relations, friendships, and romantic relationships: Do they predict social anxiety and depression? *Journal of Clinical Child and Adolescent Psychology, 34,* 49–61.

Laible, D. J., Carlo, G., & Raffaelli, M. (2000). The differential relations of parent and peer attachment to adolescent adjustment. *Journal of Youth and Adolescence, 29,* 45–59.

Laible, D. J., Carlo, G., & Roesch, S. C. (2004). Pathways to self-esteem in late adolescence: The role of parent and peer attachment, empathy, and social behaviors. *Journal of Adolescence, 27,* 703–716.

Laible, D. J., & Thompson, R. A. (2007). Early socialization: A relational perspective. In J. Grusec & P. Hastings (Eds.), *Handbook of socialization* (pp. 181–207). New York, NY: Guilford Press.

Lamb, M. E. (2002). Infant–father attachments and their impact on child development. In C. S. Tamis-LeMonda & N. Cabrera (Eds.), *Handbook of father involvement* (pp. 93–118). Mahwah, NJ: Lawrence Erlbaum Associates.

Lamb, M. E., & Ahnert, L. (2006). Childcare and youth programs. In W. Damon & R. M. Lerner (Series Eds.) & K. A. Renninger & I. E. Sigel (Vol. Eds.), *Handbook of child psychology: Vol. 4. Child psychology in practice* (6th ed., pp. 950–1016). Hoboken, NJ: Wiley.

Lamb, M. E., Bornstein, M. H., & Teti, D. M. (2002). *Development in infancy* (4th ed.). Mahwah, NJ: Lawrence Erlbaum Associates.

Lamb, M. E., & Lewis, C. (2010). The development and significance of father–child relationships in two-parent families. In M. E. Lamb (Ed.), *The role of the father in child development* (5th ed., pp. 94–153). Hoboken, NJ: Wiley.

Lamb, M. E., & Lewis, C. (2011). The role of parent–child relationships in child development. In M. E. Lamb & M. H. Bornstein (Eds.), *Social and personality development: An advanced textbook* (pp. 250–308). New York, NY: Psychology Press.

Lamb, M. E., & Sternberg, K. (1990). Do we really know how day-care affects children? *Journal of Applied Developmental Psychology, 11,* 351–379.

Lamb, S. (1993). First moral sense: An examination of the appearance of morally related behaviours in the second year of life. *Journal of Moral Education, 22,* 97–109.

Lamb, S., & Zakhireh, B. (1997). Toddlers' attention to the distress of peers in a day care setting. *Early Education and Development, 8,* 105–118.

Lamborn, S. D., Dornbusch, S. M., & Steinberg, L. (1996). Ethnicity and community context as moderators of the relation between family decision-making and adolescent adjustment. *Child Development, 66,* 283–301.

Lamborn, S. D., Mounts, N. S., Steinberg, L., & Dornbusch, S. M. (1991). Patterns of competence and adjustment among adolescents from authoritative, authoritarian, indulgent, and neglectful families. *Child Development, 62,* 1049–1065.

Lamm, C., Batson, C. D., & Decety, J. (2007). The neural substrate of human empathy: Effects of perspective-taking and cognitive appraisal. *Journal of Cognitive Neuroscience, 19,* 42–58.

Lan, W., & Lanthier, R. (2003). Changes in students' academic performance and perceptions of school and self before dropping out of schools. *Journal of Education for Students Placed at Risk, 8,* 309–332.

Lancy, D. F., & Grove, M. A. (2011). Getting noticed: Middle childhood in cross-cultural perspective. *Human Nature, 22,* 281–302.

Landis, C. (1924). Studies of emotional reactions: II. General behavior and facial expressions. *Comparative Psychology, 4,* 447–501.

Lane, J. D., Wellman, H. N., Olson, S. L., LaBounty, J., & Kerr, D. C. R. (2010). Theory of mind and emotion understanding predict moral development in early childhood. *British Journal of Developmental Psychology, 28,* 871–889.

Langlois, J. E., Kalakanis, L., Rubenstein, A. J., Larson, A., Hallam, N., & Smoot, M. (2000). Maxims or myths of beauty: A meta-analytic and theoretical review. *Psychological Bulletin, 126,* 390–423.

Lansford, J. E., Malone, P. S., Dodge, K. A., Pettit, G. S., & Bates, J. E. (2010). Developmental cascades of peer rejection, social information processing biases, and aggression during middle childhood. *Development and Psychopathology, 22,* 593–602.

Lansford, J. E., Putallaz, M., Grimes, C. L., Schiro-Osman, K. A., Kupersmidt, J. B., & Coie, J. D. (2006). Perceptions of friendship quality and observed behaviors with friends: How do sociometrically rejected, average, and popular girls differ? *Merrill-Palmer Quarterly, 52,* 694–720.

Laranjo, J., Bernier, A., & Meins, E. (2008). Associations between maternal mind-mindedness and infant attachment security: Investigating the mediating role of maternal sensitivity. *Infant Behavior and Development, 31,* 688–695.

Larson, R. W., Richards, M. H., Moneta, G., Holmbeck, G., & Duckett, E. (1996). Changes in adolescents' daily interactions with their families from ages 10 to 18: Disengagement and transformation. *Developmental Psychology, 32,* 744–754.

Last, J. V. (2014). *What to expect when no one's expecting: America's coming demographic disaster.* New York, NY: Encounter Books.

Laucht, M., Becker, K., & Schmidt, M. H. (2006). Visual exploratory behavior in infancy and novelty seeking in adolescence: Two developmentally specific phenotypes of DRD4? *Journal of Child Psychology and Psychiatry, 47,* 1143–1151.

Laursen, B., & Collins, W. (1994). Interpersonal conflict during adolescence. *Psychological Bulletin, 115,* 197–209.

Laursen, B., Coy, K., & Collins, W. (1998). Reconsidering changes in parent–child conflict across adolescence: A meta-analysis. *Child Development, 69,* 817–832.

Laursen, B., Finkelstein, B., & Betts, N. T. (2001). A developmental meta-analysis of peer conflict resolution. *Developmental Review, 21,* 423–449.

Laybourn, A. (1990). Only children in Britain: Popular stereotype and research evidence. *Children & Society, 4,* 386–400.

Leadbeater, B. J., Kuperminc, G. P., Blatt, S. J., & Hertzog, C. (1999). A multivariate model of gender differences in adolescents' internalizing and externalizing problems. *Developmental Psychology, 35,* 1268–1282.

Leckman, J. F., Feldman, R., Swain, J. E., Eicher, V., Thompson, N., & Mayes, L. C. (2004). Primary parental preoccupation: Circuits, genes, and the crucial role of the environment. *Journal of Neural Transmission, 111,* 753–771.

Leckman, J. F., & Herman, A. E. (2002). Maternal behavior and developmental psychopathology. *Biological Psychiatry, 51,* 27–43.

Leckman, J. F., & March, J. S. (2011). Editorial: Developmental neuroscience comes of age. *Journal of Child Psychology and Psychiatry, 52,* 333–338.

Lecuyer, E., & Houck, G. M. (2006). Maternal limit-setting in toddlerhood: Socialization strategies for the development of self-regulation. *Infant Mental Health Journal, 27,* 344–370.

L'Ecuyer, R. (1992). An experiential-developmental framework and methodology to study the transformations of the self-concept from infancy to old age. In T. M. Brinthaupt & R. P. Lipka (Eds.), *The self: Definitional and methodological issues* (pp. 96–136). Albany, NY: State University of New York Press.

LeDoux, J. E. (2000). Emotion circuits in the brain. *Annual Review of Neuroscience, 23,* 155–184.

LeDoux, J. E., & Debiec, J. (2003). Preface: The self: From soul to brain. *Annals of the New York Academy of Sciences, 1001,* vii–viii.

Lee, A., Clancy, S., & Fleming, A. S. (2000). Mother rats bar-press for pups: Effects of lesions of the mpoa and limbic sites on maternal behavior and operant responding for pup-reinforcement. *Behavioral Brain Research, 108,* 215–231.

Lee, L., Howes, C., & Chamberlain, B. (2007). Ethnic heterogeneity of social networks and cross-ethnic friendships of elementary school boys and girls. *Merrill-Palmer Quarterly, 53,* 325–346.

Lee, M. L., & Yang, G. S. (1998). Endurance in Chinese people: Conceptual analysis and empirical study. *Indigenous Psychological Studies, 10,* 3–68.

Lee, R. M., Grotevant, H. D., Hellerstedt, W. L., Gunnar, M. R., and the Minnesota International Adoption Project Team (2006). Cultural socialization in families with internationally adopted children. *Journal of Family Psychology, 20,* 571–580.

Lee, T. R., Mancini, J. A., & Maxwell, J. W. (1990). Sibling relationships in adulthood: Contact patterns and motivations. *Journal of Marriage and the Family, 52,* 431–440.

Legerstee, M. (2006). *Infants' sense of people: Precursors to a theory of mind.* New York, NY: Cambridge University Press.

Lei, C., Swartz, D., Dodge, K. A., & McBride-Chang, C. (2003). Harsh parenting in relation to child emotion regulation and aggression. *Journal of Family Psychology, 17,* 598–606.

Leibenluft, E., Gobbini, M. I., Harrison, T., & Haxby, J. V. (2004). Mothers' neural activation in response to pictures of their children and other children. *Biological Psychiatry, 56,* 225–232.

Leith, K. P., & Baumeister, R. F. (1998). Empathy, shame, guilt, and narratives of interpersonal conflicts: Guilt-prone people are better at perspective taking. *Journal of Personality, 66,* 1–37.

Lemerise, E. A., & Arsenio, W. F. (2000). An integrated model of emotion processes and cognition in social information processing. *Child Development, 71,* 107–118.

Lengua, L. J. (2002). The contribution of emotionality and self-regulation to the understanding of children's response to multiple risk. *Child Development, 73,* 144–161.

Lenhart, A., Ling, R., Campbell, S., & Purcell, K. (2010). *Teens and mobile phones (Pew Internet & American Life Project).* Retrieved from: http://www.pewinternet.org/~/media//Files/Reports/2010/PIP-Teens-and-Mobile-2010-with-topline.pdf.

Leppänen, J. M., & Nelson, C. A. (2009). Tuning the developing brain to social signals of emotion. *Nature Reviews Neuroscience, 10,* 37–47.

Leslie, A., Knobe, J., & Cohen, A. (2006). Acting intentionally and the side-effect effect: "Theory of mind" and moral judgment. *Psychological Science, 17,* 421–427.

Levitt, M. J., Weber, R. A., & Clark, M. C. (1986). Social network relationships as sources of maternal support and well-being. *Developmental Psychology, 22,* 310–316.

Levy-Warren, M. H. (1999). I am, you are, and so are we: A current perspective on adolescent separation-individuation theory. In A. H. Esman, L. T. Flaherty, & H. A. Horowitz (Eds.), *Adolescent psychiatry: Developmental and clinical studies, Vol. 24* (pp. 3–24). Hillsdale, NJ: Analytic Press.

Lewis, H. B. (1971). *Shame and guilt in neurosis.* New York, NY: International Universities Press.

Lewis, M. (1992a). The self in self-conscious emotions: Commentary. In D. Stipek, S. Recchia, S. McClintic, & M. Lewis (Eds.), Self–evaluation in young children. *Monographs of the Society for Research in Child Development, 57*(1, Serial No. 226), 85–95.

Lewis, M. (1992b). *Shame: The exposed self.* New York, NY: The Free Press.

Lewis, M. (1998). Emotional competence and development. In D. Pushkar, W. M. Bukowski, A. E. Schwartzman, D. M. Stack, & D. R. White (Eds.), *Improving competence across the lifespan* (pp. 27–36). New York, NY: Plenum Press.

Lewis, M. (2002). Empathy requires the development of the self. *Behavioral and Brain Sciences, 25,* 42.

Lewis, M. (2007). *The rise of consciousness and the development of emotional life.* New York, NY: Guilford Press.

Lewis, M., Alessandri, S., & Sullivan, M. (1992). Differences in shame and pride as a function of children's gender and task difficulty. *Child Development, 63,* 630–638.

Lewis, M., & Brooks-Gunn, J. (1979). *Social cognition and the acquisition of self.* New York, NY: Plenum.

Lewis, M., & Carmody, D. P. (2008). Self-representation and brain development. *Developmental Psychology, 44,* 1329–1334.

Lewis, M., Feiring, C., & Rosenthal, S. (2000). Attachment over time. *Child Development, 71,* 707–720.

Lewis, M., & Ramsay, D. (2002). Cortisol response to embarrassment and shame. *Child Development, 73,* 1034–1045.

Lewis, M., & Ramsay, D. (2004). Development of self-recognition, personal pronoun use, and pretend play during the second year. *Child Development, 75,* 1821–1831.

Lewis, M. D., & Todd, R. M. (2007). The self-regulating brain: Cortical–subcortical feedback and the development of intelligent action. *Cognitive Development, 22,* 406–430.

Li, J., Wang, L., & Fischer, K. W. (2004). The organization of shame words in Chinese. *Cognition and Emotion, 18,* 767–797.

Li, X., Feigelman, S., & Stanton, B. (2000). Perceived parental monitoring and health risk behaviors among urban low-income African-American children and adolescents. *Journal of Adolescent Health, 27,* 43–48.

Libby, L. K. (2008). A neural signature of the current self. *Social Cognitive and Affective Neuroscience, 3,* 192–194.

Libby, L. K., Eibach, R. P., & Gilovich, T. (2005). Here's looking at me: The effect of memory perspective on assessments of personal change. *Journal of Personality and Social Psychology, 88,* 50–62.

Liben, L. S., & Bigler, R. S. (2002). The developmental course of gender differentiation: Conceptualizing, measuring, and evaluating constructs and pathways. *Monographs of the Society for Research in Child Development, 67*(2, Serial No. 269).

Liberman, N., & Trope, Y. (1998). The role of feasibility and desirability considerations in near and distant future decisions: A test of temporal construal theory. *Journal of Personality and Social Psychology, 75,* 5–18.

Lichter, D. T., Shanahan, M. J., & Gardner, E. L. (2002). Helping others? The effects of childhood poverty and family instability on prosocial behavior. *Youth and Society, 34,* 89–119.

Lichtwarck-Aschoff, A., van Geert, P., Bosma, H., & Kunnen, S. (2008). Time and identity: A framework for research and theory formation. *Developmental Psychology, 28,* 370–400.

Lieberman, M., Doyle, A.-B., & Markiewicz, D. (1999). Developmental patterns in security of attachment to mother and father in late childhood and early adolescence: Associations with peer relations. *Child Development, 70,* 202–213.

Linares, L. O., Li, M., Shrout, P. E., Brody, G. H., & Pettit, G. S. (2007). Placement shift, sibling relationship quality, and child outcomes in foster care: A controlled study. *Journal of Family Psychology, 21,* 736–743.

Linden, D. E. (2006). How psychotherapy changes the brain – the contribution of functional neuroimaging. *Molecular Psychiatry, 11,* 528–538.

Lindhout, I. E., Markus, M. T., Hoogendijk, T. H. G., & Boer, F. (2009). Temperament and parental child-rearing style: Unique contributions to clinical anxiety disorders in childhood. *European Child & Adolescent Psychiatry, 18,* 439–446.

Lindsey, E. W. (2002). Preschool children's friendships and peer acceptance: Links to social competence. *Child Study Journal, 32,* 145–156.

Lindsey, E. W., Cremeens, P. R., Colwell, M. J., & Caldera, Y. M. (2009). The structure of parent–child dyadic synchrony in toddlerhood and children's communication competence and self-control. *Social Development, 18,* 375–396.

Litovsky, V. G., & Dusek, J. B. (1985). Perceptions of child rearing and self-concept development during the early adolescent years. *Journal of Youth and Adolescence, 14,* 373–387.

Loeber, R., & Tengs, T. (1986). The analysis of coercive chains between children, mothers, and siblings. *Journal of Family Violence, 1,* 51–70.

Loevinger, J. (1976). *Ego development.* San Francisco, CA: Jossey-Bass.

Londerville, S., & Main, M. (1981). Security of attachment, compliance and maternal training methods in the second year of life. *Developmental Psychology, 17,* 289–299.

Lord, S. E., Eccles, J. S., & McCarthy, K. A. (1994). Surviving the junior high school transition: Family processes and self-perceptions as protective and risk factors. *Journal of Early Adolescence, 14,* 162–199.

Lorenz, K. Z. (1935/1957). Companionship in bird life: Fellow members of the species as releasers of social behavior. In C. H. Schiller (Ed. & Trans.), *Instinctive behavior: The development of a modern concept* (pp. 83–128). New York, NY: International Universities Press.

Lougheed, J. P., & Hollenstein, T. (2012). A limited repertoire of emotion regulation strategies is associated with internalizing problems in adolescence. *Social Development, 21,* 704–721.

Lounds, J. J., Borkowski, J. G., Whitman, T. L., Maxwell, S. E., & Weed, K. (2005). Adolescent parenting and attachment during infancy and early childhood. *Parenting: Science and Practice, 5,* 91–117.

Love, K. M., & Murdock, T. B. (2004). Attachment to parents and psychological well-being: An examination of young adult college students in intact families and stepfamilies. *Journal of Family Psychology, 18,* 600–608.

Lucas-Thompson, R., & Clarke-Stewart, K. A. (2007). Forecasting friendship: How marital quality, maternal mood, and attachment security are linked to children's peer relationships. *Journal of Applied Developmental Psychology, 28,* 499–514.

Luciana, M. (2003). The neural and functional development of human prefrontal cortex. In M. de Haan & M. H. Johnson (Eds.), *The cognitive neuroscience of development* (pp. 157–179). London: Psychology Press.

Lundy, B. L. (2002). Paternal socio-psychological factors and infant attachment: The mediating role of synchrony in father–infant interaction. *Infant Behavior and Development, 25,* 220–235.

Lundy, B. L. (2003). Father- and mother-infant face-to-face interactions: Differences in mind-related comments and infant attachment? *Infant Behavior and Development, 26,* 200–212.

Luster, T., & McAdoo, H. P. (1995). Factors related to self-esteem among African American youths: A secondary analysis of the High/Scope Perry Preschool data. *Journal of Research on Adolescence, 5,* 451–467.

Luthar, S. S. (2003). *Resilience and vulnerability: Adaptation in the context of childhood adversities.* Cambridge: Cambridge University Press.

Luthar, S. S., & Becker, B. E. (2002). Privileged but pressured? A study of affluent youth. *Child Development, 73,* 1593–1610.

Luthar, S. S., & Latendresse, S. J. (2002). Adolescent risk: The cost of affluence. *New Directions in Youth Development, 95,* 101–121.

Lutkenhaus, P., Grossman, K. E., & Grossman, K. (1985). Infant–mother attachment at 12 months and style of interaction with a stranger at the age of three years. *Child Development, 56,* 1538–1542.

Luu, P., Tucker, D. M., & Derryberry, D. (1998). Anxiety and the motivational basis of working memory. *Cognitive Therapy and Research, 22,* 577–594.

Luyckx, K., Goossens, L., Soenens, B., & Beyers, W. (2006). Unpacking commitment and exploration: Preliminary validation of an integrative model of late adolescent identity formation. *Journal of Adolescence, 29,* 361–378.

Luyckx, K., Goossens, L., Soenens, B., Beyers, W., & Vansteenkiste, M. (2005). Identity statuses based upon four rather than two identity dimensions: Extending and refining Marcia's paradigm. *Journal of Youth and Adolescence, 34,* 605–618.

Luyckx, K., Schwartz, S. J., Berzonsky, M. D., Soenens, B., Vansteenkiste, M., Smits, I., & Goossens, L. (2008). Capturing ruminative exploration: Extending the four-dimensional model of identity formation in late adolescence. *Journal of Research in Personality, 42,* 58–82.

Luyten, P., & Blatt, S. J. (2013). Interpersonal relatedness and self-definition in normal and disrupted personality development. *American Psychologist, 68,* 172–183.

Lyons-Ruth, K. (1996). Attachment relationships among children with aggressive behavior problems: The role of disorganized early attachment patterns. *Journal of Consulting and Clinical Psychology, 64,* 64–73.

Lyons-Ruth, K., & Jacobvitz, D. (2008). Attachment disorganization: Genetic factors, parenting contexts, and developmental transformation from infancy to adulthood. In J. Cassidy & P. R. Shaver (Eds.), *Handbook of attachment: Theory, research, and clinical applications* (2nd ed., pp. 666–697). New York, NY: Guilford Press.

Lyons-Ruth, K., Yellin, C., Melnick, S., & Atwood, A. (2005). Expanding the concept of unresolved mental states: Hostile/helpless states of mind on the Adult Attachment Interview are associated with disrupted mother–infant communication and infant disorganization. *Development and Psychopathology, 17,* 1–23.

Lysne, M., & Levy, G. D. (1997). Differences in ethnic identity in Native American adolescents as a function of school context. *Journal of Adolescent Research, 12,* 372–388.

Lytton, H., & Romney, D. M. (1991). Parents' differential socialization of boys and girls: A meta-analysis. *Psychological Bulletin, 109,* 267–296.

Maccoby, E. E. (1980). *Social development.* New York, NY: Harcourt, Brace, Jovanovich.

Maccoby, E. E. (1984). Socialization and developmental change. *Child Development, 55,* 317–328.

Maccoby, E. E. (1990). Gender and relationships. *American Psychologist, 45,* 513–520.

Maccoby, E. E. (1998). *The two sexes: Growing up apart, coming together.* Cambridge, MA: Harvard University Press.

Maccoby, E. E. (1999). The uniqueness of the parent–child relationship. In W. A. Collins & B. Laursen (Eds.), *Minnesota symposium on child psychology: Vol. 30. Relationships as developmental contexts* (pp. 157–175). Mahwah, NJ: Erlbaum.

Maccoby, E. E., & Martin, J. (1983). Socialization in the context of the family: Parent-child interaction. In P. H. Mussen (Series Ed.) & E. M. Hetherington (Vol. Ed.), *Handbook of child psychology: Vol. 4. Socialization, personality, and social development* (pp. 1–101). New York, NY: Wiley.

MacKinnon-Lewis, C., Starnes, R., Volling, B., & Johnson, S. (1997). Perceptions of parenting as predictors of boys' sibling and peer relations. *Developmental Psychology, 33,* 1024–1031.

MacQuiddy, S. L., Maise, S. J., & Hamilton, S. B. (1987). Empathy and affective perspective-taking skills in parent-identified conduct-disordered boys. *Journal of Child Clinical Psychology, 16,* 260–268.

MacWhinney, B. (2010). Language development. In M. H. Bornstein & M. E. Lamb (Eds.), *Developmental sciences: An advanced textbook* (6th ed., pp. 389–424). Hove: Psychology Press.

Madden-Derdich, D. A., Estrada, A. U., Sales, L. J., Leonard, S. A., & Updegraff, K. A. (2002). Young adolescents' experiences with parents and friends: Exploring the connections. *Family Relations, 51,* 72–80.

Mahler, M. S., Pine, F., & Bergman, A. (1975). *The psychological birth of the human infant.* New York, NY: Basic Books.

Main, M., & Cassidy, J. (1988). Categories of response to reunion with the parent at age 6: Predictable from infant attachment classifications and stable over a 1-month period. *Developmental Psychology, 24,* 415–426.

Main, M., & Goldwyn, R. (1998). *Adult attachment scoring and classification system.* Unpublished manuscript, University of California, Berkeley, CA.

Main, M., Goldwyn, R., & Hesse, E. (2008). *The Adult Attachment Interview: Scoring and classification system, version 8.* Unpublished manuscript, University of California, Berkeley, CA.

Main, M., & Hesse, E. (1990). Parents' unresolved traumatic experiences are related to infant disorganized attachment status: Is frightened and/or frightening parental behavior the linking mechanism? In M. T. Greenberg, D. Cicchetti, & E. M. Cummings (Eds.), *Attachment in the preschool years: Theory, research, and intervention* (pp. 161–182). Chicago, IL: University of Chicago Press.

Main, M., Hesse, E., & Goldwyn, R. (2008). Studying differences in language usage in recounting attachment history: An introduction to the AAI. In H. Steele & M. Steele (Eds.), *Clinical applications of the Adult Attachment Interview* (pp. 31–68). New York, NY: Guilford Press.

Main, M., Kaplan, N., & Cassidy, J. (1985). Security in infancy, childhood, and adulthood: A move to the level of representation. In I. Bretherton & E. Waters (Eds.), Growing points of attachment theory and research. *Monographs of the Society for Research in Child Development, 50*(1–2, Serial No. 209), 66–104.

Main, M., & Solomon, J. (1990). Procedures for identifying infants as disorganized/disoriented during the Ainsworth Strange Situation. In M. T. Greenberg, D. Cicchetti, &

E. M. Cummings (Eds.), *Attachment in the preschool years: Theory, research, and intervention* (pp. 121–160). Chicago, IL: University of Chicago Press.

Main, M., & Weston, D. (1981). The quality of the toddler's relationship to mother and to father: Related to conflict behavior and the readiness to establish new relationships. *Child Development, 52,* 932–940.

Major, B., Spencer, S., Schmader, T., Wolfe, C., & Crocker, J. (1998). Coping with negative stereotypes about intellectual performance. *Personality and Social Psychology Bulletin, 24,* 34–50.

Malatesta, C. (1990). The role of emotions in the development and organization of personality. In R. Thompson (Ed.), *Nebraska Symposium on Motivation, Vol. 36: Socioemotional development* (pp. 1–56). Lincoln, NE: University of Nebraska Press.

Malatesta, C., & Wilson, A. (1988). Emotion/cognition interaction in personality development: A discrete emotions, functionalist analysis. *British Journal of Social Psychology, 27,* 91–112.

Mancillas, A. (2006). Challenging the stereotypes about only children: A review of the literature and implications for practice. *Journal of Counseling & Development, 84,* 268–275.

Manning, W. S., Giordano, P. C., & Longmore, M. A. (2006). Hooking up: The relationship contexts of "nonrelationship" sex. *Journal of Adolescent Research, 21,* 459–483.

Mans, L., Cicchetti, D., & Sroufe, L. A. (1978). Mirror reactions of Down's syndrome infants and toddlers: Cognitive underpinning of self-recognition. *Child Development, 49,* 1247–1250.

Manzi, C., Regalia, C., Pelucchi, S., & Fincham, F. D. (2012). Documenting different domains of promotion of autonomy in families. *Journal of Adolescence, 35,* 289–298.

Marceau, K., Horwitz, B. N., Narusyte, J., Ganiban, J. M., Spotts, E. L., Reiss, D., & Neiderhiser, J. M. (2013). Gene-environment correlation underlying the association between parental negativity and adolescent externalizing problems. *Child Development, 84,* 2031–2046.

March, H. W. (1986). Global self-esteem: Its relation to specific facets of self-concept and their importance. *Journal of Personality and Social Psychology, 52,* 1224–1236.

March, H. W. (1987). The hierarchical structure of self-concept: An application of hierarchical confirmatory factor analysis. *Journal of Educational Measurement, 24,* 17–19.

Marcia, J. E. (1966). Development and validation of ego identity status. *Journal of Personality and Social Psychology, 5,* 551–558.

Marcia, J. E. (1980). Identity in adolescence. In J. Adelson (Ed.), *Handbook of adolescent psychology* (pp. 159–1887). New York, NY: Wiley.

Marcia, J. E. (2002). Adolescence, identity, and the Bernardone family. *Identity, 2,* 199–209.

Marcus, R. F., & Betzer, P. D. S. (1996). Attachment and antisocial behavior in early adolescence. *Journal of Early Adolescence, 16,* 229–249.

Markham, C. M., Lormand, D., Gloppen, K. M., Peskin, M. F., Flores, B., Low, B., & House, L. D. (2010). Connectedness as a predictor of sexual and reproductive health outcomes for youth. *Journal of Adolescent Health, 46*(3, Supplement), S23–S41.

Markiewicz, D., Lawford, H., Doyle, A. B., & Haggert, N. (2006). Developmental differences in adolescents' and young adults' use of mothers, fathers, best friends, and romantic partners to fulfill attachment needs. *Journal of Youth and Adolescence, 35,* 127–140.

Markstrom, C. A., & Kalmanir, H. M. (2001). Linkages between the psychosocial stages of identity and intimacy and the ego strengths of fidelity and love. *Identity, 1,* 179–196.

Markus, H., & Cross, S. (1990). The interpersonal self. In L. A. Pervin (Ed.), *Handbook of personality: Theory and research* (pp. 576–608). New York, NY: Guilford Press.

Marsh, H. W. (1989). Age and sex effects in multiple dimensions of self-concept: Preadolescence to early adulthood. *Journal of Educational Psychology, 81,* 417–430.

Marsh, P., McFarland, F. C., Allen, J. P. McElhaney, K. B., & Land, D. J. (2003). Attachment, autonomy, and multifinality in adolescent internalizing and risky behavioral symptoms. *Development and Psychopathology, 15,* 451–467.

Marshall, S. (1995). Ethnic socialization of African American children: Implications for parenting, identity development, and academic achievement. *Journal of Youth and Adolescence, 24,* 377–396.

Martin, J. N., & Fox, N. A. (2006). Temperament. In K. McCartney & D. Phillips (Eds.), *The Blackwell handbook of early childhood development* (pp. 126–146). London: Blackwell.

Marvin, R., Cooper, G., Hoffman, K., & Powell, B. (2002). The Circle of Security project: Attachment-based intervention with caregiver–pre-school child dyads. *Attachment & Human Development, 4,* 107–124.

Mascolo, M. F., & Fischer, K. W. (1995). Developmental transformations in appraisals for pride, shame, and guilt. In J. P. Tangney & K. W. Fischer (Eds.), *Self-conscious emotions: The psychology of shame, guilt, embarrassment, and pride* (pp. 64–113). New York, NY: Guilford Press.

Mascolo, M. F., & Fischer, K. W. (1998). The development of self through the coordination of component systems. In M. Ferrari & R. Sternberg (Eds.), *Self-awareness: Its nature and development* (pp. 332–384). New York, NY: Guilford Press.

Mascolo, M. F., & Fischer, K. W. (2007). The co-development of self and socio-moral emotions during the toddler years. In C. A. Brownell & C. B. Kopp (Eds.), *Socioemotional development in the toddler years: Transitions and transformations* (pp. 66–99). New York, NY: Guilford Press.

Mascolo, M. F., Fischer, K. W., & Li, J. (2003). Dynamic development of component systems of emotions: Pride, shame, and guilt in China and the United States. In R. J. Davidson, K. R. Scherer, & H. H. Goldsmith (Eds.), *Handbook of affective sciences* (pp. 375–408). Oxford: Oxford University Press.

Mason, C. A., Walker-Barnes, C. J., Tu, S., Simons, J., & Martinez-Arrue, R. (2004). Ethnic differences in the affective meaning of parental control behaviors. *The Journal of Primary Prevention, 25,* 59–79.

Mason, W. A., & Mendoza, S. P. (1998). Generic aspects of primate attachments: Parents, offspring, and mates. *Psychoneuroendocrinology, 23,* 765–778.

Masten, A. S. (2014). *Ordinary magic: Resilience in development.* New York, NY: Guilford Press.

Masten, A. S., Burt, K. B., & Coatsworth, J. D. (2006). Competence and psychopathology in development. In D. Cicchetti & D. J. Cohen (Eds.), *Developmental Psychopathology* (Vol. 3, 2nd ed., pp. 696–738). Hoboken, NJ: Wiley.

Masten, A. S., & Cicchetti, D. (Eds.). (2010). Developmental cascades. *Development and Psychopathology, 22,* 491–495.

Masten, A. S., Coatsworth, J. D., Neeman, J., Gest, S. D., Tellegen, A., & Garmezy, N. (1995). The structure and coherence of competence from childhood through adolescence. *Child Development, 66,* 1635–1659.

Matas, L., Arend, R. A., & Sroufe, L. A. (1978). Continuity of adaptation in the second year: The relationship between quality of attachment and later competence. *Child Development, 49,* 547–556.

Mayeux, L., Underwood, M. K., & Risser, S. D. (2007). Perspectives on the ethics of sociometric research with children: How children, peers, and teachers help to inform the debate. *Merrill-Palmer Quarterly, 53,* 53–78.

Maynard, A. E. (2004). Sibling interactions. In U. P. Gielen & J. Roopnarine (Eds.), *Childhood and adolescence: Cross-cultural perspectives and applications. Advances in applied developmental psychology* (pp. 229–252). Westport, CT: Praeger.

Mayseless, O., Wiseman, H., & Hai, I. (1998). Adolescents' relationships with father, mother, and same-gender friend. *Journal of Adolescent Research, 13,* 101–123.

McAdams, D. P. (1993). *The stories we live by: Personal myths and the making of the self.* New York, NY: Morrow.

McAdams, D. P. (2001). The psychology of life stories. *Review of General Psychology, 5,* 100–122.

McAdams, D. P. (2006). The problem of narrative coherence. *Journal of Constructivist Psychology, 19,* 109–125.

McAdams, D. P., Reynolds, J., Lewis, M., Patten, A. H., & Bowman, P. J. (2001). When bad things turn good and good things turn bad: Sequences of redemption and contamination in life narrative and their relation to psychosocial adaptation in midlife adults and in students. *Personality and Social Psychology Bulletin, 27,* 474–485.

McAndrew, F. T. (2002). New evolutionary perspectives on altruism: Multi-level selection and costly-signaling theories. *Current Directions in Psychological Science, 11,* 79–82.

McCabe, M. P., & Ricciardelli, L. A. (2003). Sociocultural influences on body image and body changes among adolescent boys and girls. *Journal of Social Psychology, 143,* 5–26.

McCarthy, C. J., Moller, N. P., & Fouladi, R. T. (2001). Continued attachment to parents: Its relationship to affect regulation and perceived stress among college students. *Measurement and Evaluation in Counseling and Development, 33,* 198–211.

McCartney, K., Harris, M. J., & Bernieri, F. (1990). Growing up and growing apart: A developmental meta-analysis of twin studies. *Psychological Bulletin, 107,* 226–237.

McCoy, J., Brody, G., & Stoneman, Z. (1994). A longitudinal analysis of sibling relationships as mediators of the link between family processes and youths' best friendships. *Family Relations, 43,* 400–408.

McCoy, J., Brody, G., & Stoneman, Z. (2002). Temperament and the quality of best friendships: Effect of same-sex sibling relationships. *Family Relations, 51,* 248–255.

McDougall, P., & Hymel, S. (2007). Same-gender versus cross-gender friendship conceptions: Similar or different? *Merrill-Palmer Quarterly, 53,* 347–380.

McDowell, D. J., & Parke, R. D. (2005). Parental control and affect as predictors of children's display rule use and social competence with peers. *Social Development, 14,* 440–457.

McElhaney, K. B., & Allen, J. P. (2001). Autonomy and adolescent social functioning: The moderating effect of risk. *Child Development, 72,* 220–231.

McElhaney, K. B., Allen, J. P., Stephenson, J. C., & Hare, A. L. (2009). Attachment and autonomy during adolescence. In R. Lerner & L. Steinberg (Eds.), *Handbook of adolescent psychology* (Vol. 1, 3rd ed., pp. 358–403). Hoboken, NJ: John Wiley & Sons, Inc.

McElwain, N. L., & Booth-LaForce, C. (2006). Maternal sensitivity to infant distress and nondistress as predictors of infant–mother attachment security. *Journal of Family Psychology, 20,* 247–255.

McElwain, N. L., Booth-LaForce, C., & Wu, X. (2011). Infant–mother attachment and children's friendship quality: Maternal mental-state talk as an intervening mechanism. *Developmental Psychology, 47,* 1295–1311.

McElwain, N. L., Cox, M. J., Burchinal, M. R., & Macfie, J. (2003). Differentiating among insecure mother–infant attachment classifications: A focus on child–friend interaction and exploration during solitary play at 36 months. *Attachment & Human Development, 5,* 136–164.

McElwain, N. L., & Volling, B. L. (2004). Attachment security and parental sensitivity during infancy: Associations with friendship quality and false-belief understanding at age 4. *Journal of Social and Personal Relationships, 21,* 639–667.

McElwain, N. L., & Volling, B. L. (2005). Preschool children's interactions with friends and older siblings: Relationship specificity and joint contributions to problem behavior. *Journal of Family Psychology, 19,* 486–496.

McGuigan, N., & Nunez, M. (2006). Executive functioning by 18–24-month-old children: Effects of inhibition, working memory demands, and narrative in a novel detour-reaching task. *Infant and Child Development, 15,* 519–542.

McGuire, S., Manke, B., Eftekhari, A., & Dunn, J. (2000). Children's perceptions of sibling conflict during middle childhood: Issues and sibling (dis)similarity. *Social Development, 9,* 173–190.

McGuire, S., Manke, B., Saudino, K. J., Reiss, D., Hetherington, E. M., & Plomin, R. (1999). Perceived competence and self-worth during adolescence. *Child Development, 70,* 1283–1296.

McGuire, S., & Shanahan, L. (2010). Sibling experiences in diverse family contexts. *Child Development Perspectives, 4,* 72–79.

McHale, J. (2009). Shared child rearing in nuclear, fragile, and kinship family systems: Evolution, dilemmas, and promise of a coparenting framework. In M. Schulz, M. Pruett, P. Kerig, & R. Parke (Eds.), *Strengthening couple relationships for optimal child development: Lessons from research and intervention* (pp. 77–94). Washington, DC: American Psychological Association.

McHale, S. M., & Crouter, A. C. (1996). The family contexts of children's sibling relationships. In G. H. Brody (Ed.), *Sibling relationships: Their causes and consequences. Advances in applied developmental psychology* (Vol. 10, pp. 173–195). Norwood, NJ: Ablex Publishing Corporation.

McHale, S. M., & Crouter, A. C. (2003). How do children exert an impact on family life? In A. C. Crouter & A. Booth (Eds.), *Children's influence on family dynamics: The neglected side of family relationships* (pp. 207–220). Mahwah, NJ: Erlbaum.

McHale, S. M., Kim, J. -Y., & Whiteman, S. D. (2006). Sibling relationships in childhood and adolescence. In P. Noller & J. Feeney (Eds.), *Close relationships: Functions, forms and processes* (pp. 127–150). New York, NY: Psychology Press.

McHale, S. M., & Pawletko, T. (1992). Differential treatment of siblings in two family contexts. *Child Development, 63*, 68–81.

McHale, S. M., Updegraff, K. A., Jackson-Newsom, J., Tucker, C. J., & Crouter, A. C. (2000). When does parents' differential treatment have negative implications for siblings? *Social Development, 9*, 149–172.

McHale, S. M., Updegraff, K. A., Shanahan, L., Crouter, A. C., & Killoren, S. E. (2005). Siblings' differential treatment in Mexican American families. *Journal of Marriage and Family, 67*, 1259–1274.

McHale, S. M., Whiteman, S. D., Kim, J., & Crouter, A. C. (2007). Characteristics and correlates of sibling relationships in two-parent African American families. *Journal of Family Psychology, 21*, 227–235.

McKibben, B. (1999). *Maybe one: A case for smaller families.* New York, NY: Simon & Schuster.

McLaughlin, K. A., Hatzenbuehler, M. L., Mennin, D. S., & Nolen-Hoeksema, S. (2011). Emotion dysregulation and adolescent psychopathology: A prospective study. *Behavior Research and Therapy, 49*, 544–554.

McLean, K. C., & Breen, A. V. (2009). Processes and content of narrative identity development in adolescence: Gender and well-being. *Developmental Psychology, 45*, 702–710.

McLean, K. C., & Jennings, L. E. (2012). Teens telling tales: How maternal and peer audiences support narrative identity development. *Journal of Adolescence, 35*, 1455–1469.

McLean, K. C., & Pratt, M. W. (2006). Life's little (and big) lessons: Identity statuses and meaning-making in the turning point narratives of emerging adults. *Developmental Psychology, 42*, 714–722.

McLoyd, V. C. (1990). The impact of economic hardship on black families and children: Psychological distress, parenting, and socioemotional development. *Child Development, 61*, 311–346.

McNelles, L. R., & Connolly, J. A. (1999). Intimacy between adolescent friends: Age and gender differences in shared affect and behavioral form. *Journal of Research on Adolescence, 9*, 143–159.

Mead, G. H. (1934). *Mind, self, and society from the standpoint of a social behaviorist.* Chicago, IL: University of Chicago Press.

Meeus, W., & de Wied, M. (2007). Relationship with parents and identity in adolescence: A review of 25 years of research. In M. Watzlawik & A. Born (Eds.), *Capturing identity: Quantitative and qualitative methods* (pp. 131–145). Lanham, MD: University Press of America.

Meeus, W., Oosterwegel, A., & Vollebergh, W. (2002). Parental and peer attachment and identity development in adolescence. *Journal of Adolescence, 25*, 93–106.

Mehrabian, A., Young, A. L., & Sato, S. (1988). Emotional empathy and associated individual differences. *Current Psychology: Research and Reviews, 7*, 221–240.

Meilman, P. (1979). Cross-sectional age changes in ego identity status during adolescence. *Developmental Psychology, 15*, 230–231.

Meins, E. (1997). *Security of attachment and the social development of cognition.* Hove: Psychology Press.

Meins, E. (2013). Sensitive attunement to infants' internal states: Operationalizing the construct of mind-mindedness. *Attachment & Human Development, 15*, 524–544.

Meins, E., Fernyhough, C., Fradley, E., & Tuckey, M. (2001). Rethinking maternal sensitivity: Mothers' comments on infants' mental processes predict security of attachment at 12 months. *Journal of Child Psychiatry and Psychology, 42,* 637–648.

Mekos, D., Hetherington, E. M., & Reiss, D. (1996). Sibling differences in problem behavior and parental treatment in nondivorced and remarried families. *Child Development, 67,* 2148–2165.

Mellor, S. (1990). How do only children differ from other children? *Journal of Genetic Psychology, 151,* 221–230.

Meltzoff, A. N. (2007). 'Like me': A foundation for social cognition. *Developmental Science, 10,* 126–134.

Mendelson, M., Aboud, F., & Lanthier, R. (1994). Kindergartners' relationships with siblings, peers, and friends. *Merrill Palmer Quarterly, 40,* 416–427.

Menesini, E., Camodeca, M., & Nocentini, A. (2010). Bullying among siblings: The role of personality and relational variables. *British Journal of Developmental Psychology, 28,* 921–939.

Mesman, J., & Emmen, R. A. G. (2013). Mary Ainsworth's legacy: A systematic review of observational instruments measuring parental sensitivity. *Attachment & Human Development, 15,* 485–506.

Mesman, J., van IJzendoorn, M. H., & Bakermans-Kranenburg, M. J. (2009). The many faces of the Still-Face Paradigm: A review and meta-analysis. *Developmental Review, 29,* 120–162.

Meunier, J. C., Bisceglia, R., & Jenkins, J. M. (2012). Differential parenting and children's behavioral problems: Curvilinear associations and mother–father combined effects. *Developmental Psychology, 48,* 987–1002.

Mickelson, K. D., Kessler, R. C., & Shaver, P. R. (1997). Adult attachment in a nationally representative sample. *Journal of Personality and Social Psychology, 73,* 1092–1106.

Mikulincer, M. (1995). Attachment style and the mental representation of the self. *Journal of Personality and Social Psychology, 69,* 1203–1215.

Mikulincer, M., Florian, V., Cowan, P. A., & Cowan, C. P. (2002). Attachment security in couple relationships: A systematic model and its implications for family dynamics. *Family Process, 41,* 405–434.

Mikulincer, M., & Shaver, P. R. (2004). Security-based self-representations in adulthood: Contents and processes. In W. S. Rholes & J. A. Simpson (Eds.), *Adult attachment: Theory, research, and clinical implications* (pp. 159–195). New York, NY: Guilford Press.

Mikulincer, M., & Shaver, P. R. (2005). Mental representations of attachment security: Theoretical foundation for a positive social psychology. In M. W. Baldwin (Ed.), *Interpersonal cognition* (pp. 233–266). New York, NY: Guilford Press.

Mikulincer, M., & Shaver, P. R. (2007). *Attachment in adulthood: Structure, dynamics, and change.* New York, NY: Guilford Press.

Mikulincer, M., & Shaver, P. R. (2008). Adult attachment and affect regulation. In J. Cassidy & P. R. Shaver (Eds.), *Handbook of attachment: Theory, research, and clinical applications* (pp. 503–531). New York, NY: Guilford Press.

Milevsky, A. (2011). *Sibling relationships in childhood and adolescence: Predictors and outcomes.* New York, NY: Columbia University Press.

Milevsky, A., Smoot, K., Leh, M., & Ruppe, A. (2005). Familial and contextual variables and the nature of sibling relationships in emerging adulthood. *Marriage and Family Review, 37,* 123–141.

Miller, J. B., Jordan, J. V., Kaplan, A. G., Stiver, I. P., & Surrey, J. L. (1997). Some misconceptions and reconceptions of a relational approach. In J. V. Jordan (Ed.), *Women's growth in diversity: More writings from the Stone Center* (pp. 25–49). New York, NY: Guilford Press.

Miller, P. A., & Eisenberg, N. (1988). The relation of empathy to aggressive and externalizing/antisocial behavior. *Psychological Bulletin, 103,* 324–344.

Miller, S. A. (2012). *Theory of mind: Beyond the preschool years.* New York, NY: Psychology Press.

Mills, R. S. L., Freeman, W. S., Clara, I. P., Elgar, F. J., Walling, B. R., & Mak, L. (2007). Parents' proneness to shame and the use of psychological control. *Journal of Child and Family Studies, 16,* 359–374.

Miner, J. L., & Clarke-Stewart, K. A. (2008). Trajectories of externalizing behavior from age 2 to age 9: Relations with gender, temperament, ethnicity, parenting, and rater. *Developmental Psychology, 44,* 771–786.

Minuchin, P. (1985). Families and individual development: Provocations from the field of family therapy. *Child Development, 56,* 289–302.

Minuchin, P. (1988). Relationships within the family: A systems perspective on development. In R. A. Hinde & J. Stevenson-Hinde (Eds.), *Relationships within families: Mutual influences* (pp. 7–26). Oxford: Oxford University Press.

Minuchin, S. (1974). *Families and family therapy.* Cambridge, MA: Harvard University Press.

Mischel, W., Shoda, Y., & Peake, P. K. (1988). The nature of adolescent competencies predicted by preschool delay of gratification. *Journal of Personality and Social Psychology, 54,* 687–696.

Miyake, K., & Yamazaki, K. (1995). Self-conscious emotions, child rearing, and child psychopathology in Japanese culture. In J. P. Tangney & K. W. Fischer (Eds.), *Self-conscious emotions: The psychology of shame, guilt, embarrassment, and pride* (pp. 488–504). New York, NY: Guilford Press.

Modry-Mandell, K. L., Gamble, W. C., & Taylor, A. R. (2007). Family emotional climate and sibling relationship quality: Influences on behavioral problems and adaptation in preschool-aged children. *Journal of Child and Family Studies, 16,* 59–71.

Moilanen, K. L. (2007). The Adolescent Self-Regulatory Inventory: The development and validation of a questionnaire of short-term and long-term self-regulation. *Journal of Youth and Adolescence, 36,* 835–848.

Molloy, L. E., Ram, N., & Gest, S. D. (2011). The storm and stress (or calm) of early adolescent self-concepts: Within- and between-subjects variability. *Developmental Psychology, 47,* 1589–1607.

Monahan, K. C., Steinberg, L., Cauffman, E., & Mulvey, E. P. (2009). Trajectories of antisocial behavior and psychosocial maturity from adolescence to young adulthood. *Developmental Psychology, 45,* 1654–1668.

Monahan, K. C., Steinberg, L., Cauffman, E., & Mulvey, E. P. (2013). Psychosocial (im)maturity from adolescence to early adulthood: Distinguishing between adolescence-limited and persisting antisocial behavior. *Development and Psychopathology, 25,* 1093–1105.

Montague, D. P. F., & Walker-Andrews, A. S. (2002). Mothers, fathers, and infants: The role of person familiarity and parental involvement in infants' perception of emotion expressions. *Child Development, 75,* 1339–1352.

Montemayor, R., Adams, G. R., & Gullotta, T. P. (1990). *From childhood to adolescence: A transitional period?* (Vol. 2). Newbury Park, CA: Sage Publications.

Montgomery, M. J. (2005). Psychosocial intimacy and identity: From early adolescence to emerging adulthood. *Journal of Adolescent Research, 20,* 346–374.

Morris, A. S., Silk, J. S., Steinberg, L., Myers, S. S., & Robinson, L. R. (2007). The role of the family context in the development of emotion regulation. *Social Development, 16,* 361–388.

Morris, A. S., Silk, J. S., Steinberg, L., Sessa, F. M., Avenevoli, S., & Essex, M. J. (2002). Temperamental vulnerability and negative parenting as interacting predictors of child adjustment. *Journal of Marriage and Family, 64,* 461–471.

Morrison, A. (1996). *The culture of shame.* New York, NY: Ballantine Books.

Moser, M. R., Paternite, C. E., & Dixon, W. E., Jr. (1996). Late adolescents' feelings toward parents and siblings. *Merrill-Palmer Quarterly, 42,* 537–553.

Moss, E., Cyr, C., Bureau, J.-F., Tarabulsy, G. M., & Dubois-Comtois, K. (2005). Stability of attachment during the preschool period. *Developmental Psychology, 41,* 773–783.

Mounts, N. S. (2001). Young adolescents' perceptions of parental management of peer relationships. *Journal of Early Adolescence, 16,* 229–249.

Mueller, E. (1989). Toddlers' peer relations: Shared meaning and semantics. In W. Damon (Ed.), *Child development today and tomorrow* (pp. 312–331). San Francisco, CA: Jossey-Bass.

Mueller, E., & Brenner, J. (1977). The origins of social skills and interaction among playgroup toddlers. *Child Development, 48,* 854–861.

Mueller, E., & Silverman, N. (1989). Peer relations in maltreated children. In D. Cicchetti & V. Carlson (Eds.), *Child mistreatment: Theory and research on the causes and consequences of child abuse and neglect* (pp. 529–578). New York, NY: Cambridge University Press.

Mullen, M. K., & Yi, S. (1995). The cultural context of talk about the past: Implications for the development of autobiographical memory. *Cognitive Development, 10,* 407–419.

Mullis, A. K., Mullis, R. L., & Normandin, D. (1992). Analysis of age effect in longitudinal studies of adolescent self-esteem. *Developmental Psychology, 18,* 372–379.

Muris, P., Bos, A. E. R., Mayer, B., Verkade, R., Thewissen, V., & Dell'Avvento, V. (2009). Relations among behavioral inhibition, big five personality factors, and anxiety disorder symptoms in non-clinical children. *Personality and Individual Differences, 46,* 525–529.

Murphy, A., Steele, M., & Steele, H. (2013). From out of sight, out of mind to in sight and in mind: Enhancing reflective capacities in a group attachment-based intervention. In J. E. Bettmann & D. D. Friedman (Eds.), *Attachment-based clinical work with children and adolescents* (pp. 237–257). New York, NY: Springer.

Murphy, M. R., MacLean, P. D., & Hamilton, S. C. (1981). Species-typical behavior of hamsters deprived from birth of the neocortex. *Science, 213,* 459–461.

Murray, A. D. (1979). Infant crying as an elicitor of parental behavior: An examination of two models. *Psychological Bulletin, 86,* 191–215.

Music, G. (2011). *Nurturing natures: Attachment and children's emotional, sociocultural, and brain development.* New York, NY: Psychology Press.

Nachmias, M., Gunnar, M., Mangelsdorf, S., Parritz, R. H., & Buss, K. (1996). Behavioral inhibition and stress reactivity: The moderating role of attachment security. *Child Development, 67,* 508–522.

Nadelman, L., & Begun, A. (1982). The effect of the newborn on the older sibling: Mothers' questionnaires. In M. E. Lamb & B. Sutton-Smith (Eds.), *Sibling relationships: Their nature and significance across the lifespan* (pp. 13–38). Hillsdale, NJ: Erlbaum.

Nangle, D. W., Erdley, C. A., Newman, J. E., Mason, C. A., & Carpenter, E. M. (2003). Popularity, friendship quantity, and friendship quality: Interactive influences on children's loneliness and depression. *Journal of Clinical Child and Adolescent Psychology, 32,* 546–555.

Natsuaki, M. N., Ge, X., Reiss, D., & Neiderhiser, J. M. (2009). Aggressive behavior between siblings and the development of externalizing problems: Evidence from a genetically sensitive study. *Developmental Psychology, 45,* 1009–1018.

Neckerman, H. J. (1996). The stability of social groups in childhood and adolescence: The role of the classroom social environment. *Social Development, 5,* 131–145.

Neiss, M. B., Sedikides, C., & Stevenson, J. (2002). Self-esteem: A behavioral genetic perspective. *European Journal of Personality, 16,* 351–368.

Nelson, C. A., Bloom, F., Cameron, J., Amaral, D., Dahl, R., & Pine, D. (2002). An integrative, multidisciplinary approach to the study of brain-behavior relations in the context of typical and atypical development. *Development and Psychopathology, 14,* 499–520.

Nelson, C. A., Thomas, K. M., & de Haan, M. (2008). Neural bases of cognitive development. In W. Damon & R. M. Lerner (Eds.), *Child and adolescent development: An advanced course* (pp. 19–53). New York, NY: John Wiley & Sons.

Nelson, K. (1993). The psychological and social origins of autobiographical memory. *Psychological Science, 4,* 7–14.

Nelson, K. (2003). Narrative and self, myth and memory: Emergence of the cultural self. In R. Fivush & C. A. Haden (Eds.), *Autobiographical memory and the construction of a narrative self* (pp. 3–28). Mahwah, NJ: Erlbaum.

Nelson, K., & Fivush, R. (2004). The emergence of autobiographical memory: A socio-cultural developmental theory. *Psychological Review, 111,* 486–511.

Nelson, N., & Russell, J. A. (2013). Universality revisited. *Emotion Review, 5,* 8–15.

Newcomb, A. F., & Bagwell, C. L. (1995). Children's friendship relations: A meta-analytic review. *Psychological Bulletin, 117,* 306–347.

Newcomb A. F., & Bagwell, C. L. (1996). The developmental significance of children's friendship relations. In W. M. Bukowski, A. F. Newcomb, & W. W. Hartup (Eds.), *The company they keep: Friendship in childhood and adolescence* (pp. 289–321). New York, NY: Cambridge University Press.

Newcomb, A. F., Bukowski, W. M., & Bagwell, C. L. (1999). Knowing the sounds: Friendship as a developmental context. In W. A. Collins & B. Laursen (Eds.), *Relationships as developmental contexts* (pp. 63–84). Mahwah, NJ: Erlbaum.

Newcomb, A. F., Bukowski, W. M., & Pattee, L. (1993). Children's peer relations: A meta-analytic review of popular, rejected, neglected, controversial, and average sociometric status. *Psychological Bulletin, 113,* 99–128.

Newcombe, R., & Reese, E. (2004). Evaluations and orientations in mother–child narratives as a function of attachment security: A longitudinal investigation. *International Journal of Behavioral Development, 28,* 230–245.

Neyer, F. J. (2002). Twin relationships in old age: A developmental perspective. *Journal of Social and Personal Relationships, 19,* 155–177.

Ng, F. F.-Y., Pomerantz, E. M., & Deng, C. (2014). Why are Chinese mothers more controlling than American mothers? "My child is my report card." *Child Development, 85,* 355–369.

NICHD Early Child Care Research Network. (1997). The effects of infant child care on infant–mother attachment security: Results of the NICHD Study of Early Child Care. *Child Development, 68,* 860–879.

NICHD Early Child Care Research Network. (2001). Child care and children's peer interaction at 24 and 36 months: The NICHD study of early child care. *Child Development, 72,* 1478–1500.

NICHD Early Child Care Research Network. (2002). The interaction of child care and family risks in relation to child development at 24 and 36 months. *Applied Developmental Science, 6,* 144–156.

Nickerson, A. B., & Nagle, R. J. (2005). Parent and peer attachment in late childhood and early adolescence. *Journal of Early Adolescence, 25,* 223–249.

Nolen-Hoeksema, S., Girgus, J. S., & Seligman, M. E. P. (1992). Predictors and consequences of childhood depressive symptoms: A 5-year longitudinal study. *Journal of Abnormal Psychology, 101,* 405–422.

Noller, P. (2005). Sibling relationships in adolescence: Learning and growing together. *Personal Relationships, 12,* 1–22.

Noller, P., Feeney, J. A., Sheehan, G., & Peterson, C. (2000). Marital conflict patterns: Links with family conflict and family members' perceptions of one another. *Personal Relationships, 7,* 79–94.

Noom, M. J., Deković, M., & Meeus, W. H. (1999). Autonomy, attachment and psychosocial adjustment during adolescence: A double-edged sword? *Journal of Adolescence, 22,* 771–783.

Noriuchi, M., Kikuchi, Y., & Senoo, A. (2008). The functional neuroanatomy of maternal love: Mother's response to infant's attachment behaviors. *Biological Psychiatry, 63,* 415–423.

Northoff, G., Heinzel, A., de Greck, M., Bermpohl, F., Dobrowolny, H., & Panksepp, J. (2006). Self-referential processing in our brain – A meta-analysis of imaging studies on the self. *NeuroImage, 31,* 440–457.

Notaro, P. C., & Volling, B. L. (1999). Parental responsiveness and infant–parent attachment: A replication study with fathers and mothers. *Infant Behavior and Development, 22,* 345–352.

Nucci, L. P. (1984). Evaluating teachers as social agents: Students' ratings of domain appropriate and domain inappropriate teacher responses to transgressions. *American Educational Research Journal, 21,* 367–378.

Nucci, L. P. (2002). The development of moral reasoning. In U. Goswami (Ed.), *Blackwell handbook of childhood cognitive development* (pp. 303–325). Malden, MA: Blackwell.

Nuckolls, C. W. (1993). An introduction to the study of cross-cultural sibling relations. In C. W. Nuckolls (Ed.), *Siblings in South Asia* (pp. 19–44). New York, NY: Guilford Press.

Numan, M. T., & Stolzenberg, D. S. (2008). Hypothalamic interaction with the mesolimbic dopamine system and the regulation of maternal responsiveness. In R. Bridges (Ed.), *Neurobiology of the parental brain* (pp. 3–22). London: Academic Press.

Nurmi, J.-E. (2004). Socialization and self-development: Channeling, selection, adjustment, and reflection. In R. Lerner & L. Steinberg (Eds.), *Handbook of adolescent psychology* (2nd ed., pp. 85–124). Hoboken, NJ: Wiley.

Nyman, L. (1995). The identification of birth order personality attributes. *Journal of Psychology, 129,* 51–59.

Oberle, E., Schonert-Reichl, K. A., & Thomson, K. C. (2009). Understanding the link between social and emotional well-being and peer relations in early adolescence: Gender-specific predictors of peer acceptance. *Journal of Youth and Adolescence, 39,* 1330–1342.

Oberman, L. M., & Ramachandran, V. S. (2007). The simulating social mind: The role of the mirror neuron system and simulation in the social and communicative deficits of autism spectrum disorders. *Psychological Bulletin, 133,* 310–327.

Ochsner, K. N., Beer, J. S., Robertson, E. R., Cooper, J. C., Gabrieli, J. D. E., Kihlstrom, J. F., & D'Esposito, M. (2005). The neural correlates of direct and reflected self-knowledge. *NeuroImage, 28,* 797–814.

Ochsner, K. N., & Gross, J. J. (2007). The neural architecture of emotion regulation. In J. J. Gross (Ed.), *Handbook of emotion regulation* (pp. 87–109). New York, NY: Guilford Press.

O'Connor, T. G., & Croft, C. M. (2001). A twin study of attachment in preschool children. *Child Development, 72,* 1501–1511.

Ogilvie, D. M., & Clark, M. D. (1992). The best and worst of it: Age and sex differences in self discrepancy research. In R. P. Lipka & T. M. Brinthaupt (Eds.), *Self-perspectives across the life span.* Albany, NY: State University of New York Press.

Ohannessian, C. M., Lerner, R. M., Lerner, J. V., & von Eye, A. (1998). Perceived parental acceptance and early adolescent self-competence. *American Journal of Orthopsychiatry, 68,* 621–629.

Ojanen, T., & Perry, D. G. (2007). Relational schemas and the developing self: Perceptions of mother and of self as joint predictors of early adolescents' self-esteem. *Developmental Psychology, 43,* 1474–1483.

Onishi, K. H., & Baillargeon, R. (2005). Do 15-month-old infants understand false beliefs? *Science, 308,* 255–258.

Oppenheim, D., & Goldsmith, D. F. (Eds.). (2007). *Attachment theory in clinical work with children: Bridging the gap between research and practice.* New York, NY: Guilford Press.

Oppenheim, D., & Waters, H. A. (1995). Narrative processes and attachment representations: Issues of development and assessment. In E. Waters, B. E. Vaughn, G. Posada, & K. Kondo-Ikemura (Eds.), Caregiving, cultural, and cognitive perspectives on secure-base behavior and working models: New growing points of attachment theory and research. *Monographs of the Society for Research in Child Development, 60*(2–3, Serial No. 244), 197–215.

Ormel, J., Oldehinkel, A. J., Ferdinand, R. F., Hartman, C. A., De Winter, A. F., Veenstra, R., ... Verhulst, F. C. (2005). Internalizing and externalizing problems in adolescence: General and dimension-specific effects of familial loadings and preadolescent temperament traits. *Psychological Medicine, 35,* 1825–1835.

Oudekerk, B. A., Allen, J. P., Hessel, E. T., & Molloy, L. E. (2014). The cascading development of autonomy and relatedness from adolescence to adulthood. *Child Development, 86,* 472–485.

Owen, J. J., Rhoades, G. K., Stanley, S. M., & Fincham, F. D. (2010). "Hooking up" among college students: Demographic and psychosocial correlates. *Archives of Sexual Behavior, 39,* 653–663.

Owens, G., Crowell, J., Pan, H., Treboux, D., O'Connor, E., & Waters, E. (1995). The prototype hypothesis and the origins of attachment working models: Adult relationships with parents and romantic partners. In E. Waters, B. E. Vaughn, G. Posada, & K. Kondo-Ikemura (Eds.), Caregiving, cultural, and cognitive perspectives on secure-base behavior and working models: New growing points of attachment theory and research. *Monographs of the Society for Research in Child Development, 60*(2–3, Serial No. 244), 216–233.

Oxley, G., & Fleming, A. S. (2000). The effects of medial preoptic area and amygdala lesions on maternal behavior in the juvenile rat. *Developmental Psychobiology, 37,* 253–265.

Oyserman, D., & Destin, M. (2010). Identity-based motivation: Implications for intervention. *The Counseling Psychologist, 38,* 1001–1043.

Padilla-Walker, L. M., & Carlo, G. (2006). Adolescent perceptions of appropriate parental reactions in moral and conventional social domains. *Social Development, 15,* 480–500.

Pahl, K., & Way, N. (2006). Longitudinal trajectories of ethnic identity among urban Black and Latino adolescents. *Child Development, 7,* 1403–1415.

Pancer, S. M., & Pratt, M. W. (1999). Social and family determinants of community service involvement in Canadian youth. In M. Yates & J. Youniss (Eds.), *Roots of civic identity: International perspectives on community service and activism in youth* (pp. 32–55). New York, NY: Cambridge University Press.

Pardini, D. A. (2008). Novel insights into long-standing theories of bidirectional parent–child influences: Introduction to the special section. *Journal of Abnormal Child Psychology, 36,* 627–631.

Park, K. A., & Waters, E. (1989). Security of attachment and preschool friendships. *Child Development, 60,* 1076–1081.

Parke, R. D., & Bhavnagri, N. P. (1989). Parents as managers of children's peer relationships. In D. Belle (Ed.), *Children's social networks and social supports* (pp. 241–259). New York, NY: Wiley.

Parke, R. D., & Buriel, R. (2006). Socialization in the family: Ethnic and ecological perspectives. In W. Damon & R. M. Lerner (Series Eds.) & N. Eisenberg (Vol. Ed.), *Handbook of child psychology: Vol. 3. Social, emotional, and personality development* (6th ed., pp. 429–504). Hoboken, NJ: Wiley.

Parke, R. D., McDowell, D. J., Cladis, M., & Leidy, M. S. (2006). Family and peer relationships: The role of emotion regulatory processes. In D. K. Snyder, J. A. Simpson, & J. N. Hughes (Eds.), *Emotion regulation in couples and families: Pathways to dysfunction and health* (pp. 143–162). Washington, DC: American Psychological Association.

Parker, J. G., & Asher, S. R. (1987). Peer relations and later personal adjustment: Are low-accepted children at risk? *Psychological Bulletin, 102,* 357–389.

Parker, J. G., & Asher, S. R. (1993). Friendship and friendship quality in middle childhood: Links with peer group acceptance and feelings of loneliness and social dissatisfaction. *Developmental Psychology, 29,* 611–621.

Parker, J. G., & Gottman, J. M. (1989). Social and emotional development in a relational context: Friendship interaction from early childhood to adolescence. In T. J. Berndt & G. W. Ladd (Eds.), *Peer relations in child development* (pp. 15–45). New York, NY: Wiley-Interscience.

Parker, S., Nichter, M., Nichter, N., Vuckovic, N., Sims, C., & Ritenbaugh, C. (1995). Body image and weight concerns among African American and White adolescent females: Differences that make a difference. *Human Organization, 54,* 103–115.

Parpal, M., & Maccoby, E. E. (1985). Maternal responsiveness and subsequent child compliance. *Child Development, 56,* 1326–1334.

Parten, M. (1932). Social participation among preschool children. *Journal of Abnormal and Social Psychology, 28,* 231–241.

Pascarella, E., & Terenzini, P. (2005). *How college affects students: A third decade of research.* San Francisco, CA: Jossey Bass.

Paterson, J. E., Field, J., & Pryor, J. (1994). Adolescents' perceptions of their attachment relationships with their mothers, fathers, and friends. *Journal of Youth and Adolescence, 23,* 579–600.

Patterson, G. R. (1984). Siblings' fellow travelers in coercive family processes. In R. J. Blanchard (Eds.), *Advances in the study of aggression* (pp. 174–213). New York, NY: Academic Press.

Patterson, G. R. (1986). The contribution of siblings to training for fighting: A microsocial analysis. In D. Olweus, J. Block, & M. Radke-Yarrow (Eds.), *Development of antisocial and prosocial behavior: Research theories, and issues* (pp. 235–261). New York, NY: Academic Press.

Paul, E. L., McManus, B., & Hayes, A. (2000). "Hookups": Characteristics and correlates of college students' spontaneous and anonymous sexual experiences. *Journal of Sex Research, 37,* 76–88.

Paulhus, D. L., Trapnell, P. D., & Chen, D. (1999). Birth order effects on personality and achievement within families. *Psychological Science, 10,* 482–488.

Pauli-Pott, U., & Mertesacker, B. (2009). Affect expression in mother–infant interaction and subsequent attachment development. *Infant Behavior and Development, 32,* 208–215.

Paulus, M. (2014). The emergence of prosocial behavior: Why do infants and toddlers help, comfort, and share? *Child Development Perspectives, 8,* 77–81.

Paulussen-Hoogeboom, M. C., Stams, G. J. J. M., Hermanns, J. M. A., Peetsma, T. T. D., & van den Wittenboer, G. L. H. (2008). Parenting style as a mediator between children's negative emotionality and problematic behavior in early childhood. *Journal of Genetic Psychology, 169,* 209–226.

Paus, T. (2005). Mapping brain maturation and cognitive development during adolescence. *Trends in Cognitive Science, 9,* 60–68.

Paus, T., Keshavan, M., & Giedd, J. N. (2008). Why do many psychiatric disorders emerge during adolescence? *Nature Reviews: Neuroscience, 9,* 947–957.

Pedersen, S., Vitaro, F., Barker, E. D., & Borge, A. I. H. (2007). The timing of middle-childhood peer rejection and friendship: Linking early behavior to early-adolescent adjustment. *Child Development, 78,* 1037–1051.

Pederson, D. R., Bailey, H. N., Tarabulsy, G. M., Bento, S., & Moran, G. (2014). Understanding sensitivity: Lessons learned from the legacy of Mary Ainsworth. *Attachment & Human Development, 16,* 261–270.

Peevers, B. H., & Secord, P. F. (1973). Developmental changes in attribution of descriptive concepts to persons. *Journal of Personality and Social Psychology, 27,* 120–128.

Peplau, L. A., & Garnets, L. D. (2000). A new paradigm for understanding women's sexuality and sexual orientation. *Journal of Social Issues, 56,* 329–350.

Perlman, M., & Ross, H. S. (1997). The benefits of parental intervention in children's disputes: An examination of concurrent changes in children's fighting styles. *Child Development, 68,* 690–700.

Perlman, S. B., Camras, L. A., & Pelphrey, K. (2008). Physiology and functioning: Parents' vagal tone, emotion socialization, and children's emotion knowledge. *Journal of Experimental Child Psychology, 100,* 308–315.

Perner, J., Ruffman, T., & Leekam, S. R. (1994). Theory of mind is contagious: You catch it from your sibs. *Child Development, 65,* 1228–1238.

Perosa, L. M., Perosa, S. L., & Tam, H. P. (2002). Intergenerational systems theory and identity development in young adult women. *Journal of Adolescent Research, 17,* 235–259.

Perry-Parrish, C., & Zeman, J. (2011). Relations among sadness regulation, peer acceptance, and social functioning in early adolescence: The role of gender. *Social Development, 20,* 135–153.

Persson, G. E. B. (2005). Young children's prosocial and aggressive behaviors and their experiences of being targeted for similar behaviors by peers. *Social Development, 14,* 206–228.

Petersen, A. C., & Leffert, N. (1995). What is special about adolescence? In M. Rutter (Ed.), *Psychosocial disturbances in young people: Challenges for prevention* (pp. 3–36). Cambridge: Cambridge University Press.

Peterson, Z. D., & Muehlenhard, C. L. (2007). Conceptualizing the "wantedness" of women's consensual and nonconsensual sexual experiences: Implications for how women label their experiences with rape. *Journal of Sex Research, 44,* 72–88.

Pettit, G. (1997). The untold story of childhood friendships. *PsycCRITIQUES, 42,* 807–808.

Pettit, G. S., Laird, R. D., Dodge, K. A., Bates, J. E., & Criss, M. M. (2001). Antecedents and behavior-problem outcomes of parental monitoring and psychological control in early adolescence. *Child Development, 72,* 583–598.

Pettygrove, D. M., Hammond, S. I., Karahuta, E. L., Waugh, W. E., & Brownell, C. (2013). From cleaning up to helping out: Parental socialization and children's early prosocial behavior. *Infant Behavior and Development, 36,* 843–846.

Pfeifer J. H., & Dapretto, M. (2009). "Mirror, mirror, in my mind": Empathy, interpersonal competence, and the mirror neuron system. In J. Decety & W. Ickes (Eds.), *The social neuroscience of empathy* (pp. 183–197). Cambridge, MA: The MIT Press.

Pfeifer, J. H., Iacoboni, M., Mazziotta, J. C., & Dapretto, M. (2008). Mirroring others' emotions relates to empathy and interpersonal competence in children. *NeuroImage, 39*, 2076–2085.

Pfeifer, M., Goldsmith, H. H., Davidson, R. J., & Rickman, M. (2002). Continuity and change in inhibited and uninhibited children. *Child Development, 73*, 1474–1485.

Phelps, J. L., Belsky, J., & Crnic, K. (1998). Earned security, daily stress, and parenting: A comparison of five alternative models. *Development and Psychopathology, 10*, 21–38.

Phillips, A. C., Carroll, D., Hunt, K., & Der, G. (2006). The effects of the spontaneous presence of a spouse/partner and others in cardiovascular reactions to an acute psychological challenge. *Psychophysiology, 43*, 633–640.

Phillips, A. T., Wellman, H. M., & Spelke, E. S. (2002). Infants' ability to connect gaze and emotional expression to intentional action. *Cognition, 85*, 53–78.

Phillipsen, L. C. (1999). Associations between age, gender, and group acceptance and three components of friendship quality. *Journal of Early Adolescence, 19*, 438–464.

Phinney, J. S. (1989). Stages of ethnic identity development in minority group adolescents. *Journal of Early Adolescence, 9*, 34–49.

Phinney, J. S. (1990). Ethnic identity in adolescents and adults: Review of research. *Psychological Bulletin, 108*, 499–514.

Phinney, J. S. (1996). When we talk about American ethnic groups, what do we mean? *American Psychologist, 51*, 918–927.

Phinney, J. S., & Alipuria, L. L. (1990). Ethnic identity in college students from four ethnic groups. *Journal of Adolescence, 13*, 171–183.

Phinney, J. S., Cantu, C. L., & Kurtz, D. A. (1997). Ethnic and American identity as predictors of self-esteem among African American, Latino, and White adolescents. *Journal of Youth and Adolescence, 26*, 165–185.

Piaget, J. (1932). *The moral judgment of the child.* New York, NY: Harcourt, Brace.

Pickhardt, C. E. (2008). *The future of your only child: How to guide your child to a happy and successful life.* New York, NY: Palgrave Macmillan.

Pike, A., Coldwell, J., & Dunn, J. (2005). Sibling relationships in early/middle childhood: Links with individual adjustment. *Journal of Family Psychology, 19*, 523–532.

Pike, A., Manke, B., Reiss, D., & Plomin, R. (2000). A genetic analysis of differential experiences of adolescent siblings across three years. *Social Development, 9*, 96–114.

Pike, A., Reiss, D., Hetherington, E. M., & Plomin, R. (1996). Using MZ differences in the search for nonshared environmental effects. *The Journal of Child Psychology and Psychiatry, 37*, 695–704.

Pinker, S. (2008, January 13). The moral instinct. *New York Times Magazine*, pp. 32–37, 52–58.

Pipp, S., Easterbrooks, M. A., & Harmon, R. J. (1992). The relation between attachment and knowledge of self and mother in one-to three-year-old infants. *Child Development, 63*, 738–750.

Pipp, S. L., Fischer, K. W., & Jennings, S. L. (1987). The acquisition of self and mother knowledge in infancy. *Developmental Psychology, 23*, 86–96.

Pittman, J. F., Keiley, M. K., Kerpelman, J. L., & Vaughn, B. E. (2011). Attachment, identity, and intimacy: Parallels between Bowlby's and Erikson's paradigms. *Journal of Family Theory & Review, 3*, 32–46.

Pittman, J. F., Kerpelman, J. L., Soto, J. B., & Adler-Baeder, F. M. (2012). Identity exploration in the dating domain: The role of attachment dimensions and parenting practices. *Journal of Adolescence, 35*, 1485–1499.

Pizzagalli, D., Pascual-Marqui, R. D., Nitschke, J. B., Oakes, T. R., Larson, C. L., Abercrombie, H. C., ... Davidson, R. J. (2001). Anterior cingulate activity as a predictor of degree of treatment response in major depression: Evidence from brain electrical tomography analysis. *American Journal of Psychiatry, 158*, 405–415.

Pizzagalli, D. A., Sherwood, R., Henriques, J. B., & Davidson, R. J. (2005). Frontal brain asymmetry and reward responsiveness. *Psychological Science, 16*, 805–813.

Platek, S. M., & Gallup, G. G. Jr. (2002). Self-face recognition is affected by schizotypal personality traits. *Schizophrenia Research, 57*, 311–315.

Pleck, J. H., & Masciadrelli, B. P. (2004). Paternal involvement by U.S. residential fathers: Levels, sources, and consequences. In M. E. Lamb (Ed.), *The role of the father in child development* (4th ed., pp. 222–271). Hoboken, NJ: Wiley.

Plomin, R. (1994). *Genetics and experience.* Newbury Park, CA: Sage Publications.

Plomin, R., Asbury, K., & Dunn, J. (2001). Why are children in the same family so different? Nonshared environment a decade later. *Canadian Journal of Psychiatry, 46,* 225–233.

Plomin, R., & Daniels, D. (1987). Why are children in the same family so different from one another? *Behavioral and Brain Sciences, 10,* 1–16.

Plomin, R., DeFries, J. C., McClearn, G. E., & McGuffin, P. (2001). *Behavioral genetics* (4th ed.). New York, NY: Worth.

Plutchik, R. (1993). Emotions and their vicissitudes: Emotions and psychopathology. In M. Lewis & J. Haviland (Eds.), *Handbook of emotions* (pp. 53–66). New York, NY: Guilford Press.

Polit, D. F., & Falbo, T. (1987). Only children and personality development: A quantitative review. *Journal of Marriage and the Family, 49,* 309–325.

Polit, D. F., Nuttall, R., & Nuttall, E. (1980). The only child grows up: A look at some characteristics of adult only children. *Family Relations, 29,* 99–106.

Pollak, S. D., Cicchetti, D., Hornung, K., & Reed, A. (2000). Recognizing emotion in faces: Developmental effects of child abuse and neglect. *Developmental Psychology, 36,* 679–688.

Pollak, S. D., & Sinha, P. (2002). Effects of early experience on children's recognition of facial displays of emotion. *Developmental Psychology, 38,* 784–791.

Pomerantz, E. M., Saxon, J. L., & Kenney, G. A. (2001). Self-evaluation: The development of sex differences. In G. B. Moskowitz (Ed.), *Cognitive social psychology: The Princeton symposium on the legacy and future of social cognition* (pp. 59–73). Mahwah, NJ: Erlbaum.

Pomery, E. A., Gibbons, F. X., Gerrard, M., Cleveland, M. J., Brody, G. H., & Wills, T. A. (2005). Families and risk: Prospective analyses of familial and social influences on adolescent substance use. *Journal of Family Psychology, 19,* 560–570.

Pons, F., Harris, P. L., & de Rosnay, M. (2004). Emotion comprehension between 3 and 11 years: Developmental periods and hierarchical organization. *European Journal of Developmental Psychology, 1,* 127–152.

Popp, D., Laursen, B., Kerr, M., Burk, W., & Stattin, H. (2008). Modeling homophily over time with an actor–partner interdependence model. *Developmental Psychology, 44,* 1028–1039.

Porges, S. W. (1991). Vagal tone: An autonomic mediator of affect. In J. A. Garber & K. A. Dodge (Eds.), *The development of affect regulation and dysregulation* (pp. 111–128). New York, NY: Cambridge University Press.

Porges, S. W. (1996). Physiological regulation in high-risk infants: A model for assessment and potential intervention. *Development and Psychopathology, 8,* 43–58.

Porges, S. W. (2007). The polyvagal perspective. *Biological Psychology, 74,* 116–143.

Porter, C. L., Wouden-Miller, M., Silva, S. S., & Porter, A. E. (2003). Marital harmony and conflict: Linked to infants' emotional regulation and cardiac vagal tone. *Infancy, 4,* 297–307.

Porter, F. L., Porges, S. W., & Marshall, R. E. (1988). Newborn pain cries and vagal tone: Parallel changes in response to circumcision. *Child Development, 59,* 495–505.

Porto, P. R., Oliveira, L., Mari, J., Volchan, E., Figueira, I., & Ventura, P. (2009). Does cognitive behavioral therapy change the brain? A systematic review of neuroimaging in anxiety disorders. *Journal of Neuropsychiatry and Clinical Neurosciences, 21,* 114–125.

Posada, G., Gao, Y., Wu, F., Posada, R., Tascon, M., Schöelmerich, A., ... Synnevaag, B. (1995). The secure-base phenomenon across cultures: Children's behavior, mothers' preferences, and experts' concepts. In E. Waters, B. E. Vaughn, G. Posada, & K. Kondo-Ikemura (Eds.), Caregiving, cultural, and cognitive perspectives on secure-base behavior and working models: New growing points of attachment theory and research. *Monographs of the Society for Research in Child Development, 60*(2–3, Serial No. 244), 27–48.

Posner, M. I., & Rothbart, M. K. (2000). Developing mechanisms of self-regulation. *Development and Psychopathology, 12,* 427–441.

Posner, M. I., & Rothbart, M. K. (2007). *Educating the human brain.* Washington, DC: American Psychological Association.

Pottharst, K. (Ed.). (1990). *Explorations in adult attachment.* New York, NY: Peter Lang.

Poulin, F., & Chan, A. (2010). Friendship stability and change in childhood and adolescence. *Developmental Review, 30,* 257–272.

Poulin, F., Dishion, T., & Haas, E. (1999). The peer influence paradox: Friendship quality and deviancy training within male adolescent friendships. *Merrill-Palmer Quarterly, 45,* 42–61.

Poulin, F., & Pedersen, S. (2007). Developmental changes in gender composition of friendship networks in adolescent girls and boys. *Developmental Psychology, 43,* 1484–1495.

Povinelli, D. J., & Simon, B. B. (1998). Young children's understanding of briefly versus extremely delayed images of self: Emergence of the autobiographical stance. *Developmental Psychology, 34,* 188–194.

Pratt, M. W., Skoe, E. E., & Arnold, M. L. (2004). Care reasoning development and family socialization patterns in later adolescence: A longitudinal analysis. *International Journal of Behavioral Development, 28,* 139–147.

Preston, S. D., & de Waal, F. B. M. (2002). Empathy, its ultimate and proximate bases. *Behavioral and Brain Sciences, 25,* 1–20, Discussion 20–71.

Prinstein, M. J., Borelli, J. L., Cheah, C. S. L., Simon, V. A., & Aikins, J. W. (2005). Adolescent girls' interpersonal vulnerability to depressive symptoms: A longitudinal examination of reassurance-seeking and peer relationships. *Journal of Abnormal Psychology, 114,* 676–688.

Pronin, E., & Ross, L. (2006). Temporal differences in trait self-ascription: When the self is seen as an other. *Journal of Personality and Social Psychology, 90,* 197–209.

Pulkkinen, L., Kokko, K., & Rantanen, J. (2012). Paths from socioemotional behavior in middle childhood to personality in middle adulthood. *Developmental Psychology, 48,* 1283–1291.

Purcell, K. (2011). *Trends in teen communication and social media use (Pew Internet & American Life Project).* Presentation given at Joint Girl Scout Research Institute/Pew Internet Webinar. Retrieved from http://www.pewinternet.org/Presentations/2011/Feb/PIP-Girl-Scout-Webinar.aspx

Putnam, S. P., Ellis, L. K., & Rothbart, M. K. (2001). The structure of temperament from infancy through adolescence. In A. Eliasz & A. Angleitner (Eds.), *Advances in research on temperament* (pp. 165–182). Lengerich, Germany: Pabst Scientist Publisher.

Putnam, S. P., & Stifter, C. A. (2008). Reactivity and regulation: The impact of Mary Rothbart on the study of temperament. *Infant and Child Development, 17,* 311–320.

Putnick, D. L., Bornstein, M. H., Hendricks, C., Painter, K. M., Suwalsky, J. T. D., & Collins, W. A. (2008). Parenting stress, perceived parenting behaviors, and adolescent self-concept in European American families. *Journal of Family Psychology, 22,* 752–762.

Quay, H. C. (1988). The behavioral reward and inhibition systems in childhood behavior disorder. In L. M. Bloomingdale (Ed.), *Attention deficit disorder* (Vol. 3, pp. 176–186). New York, NY: Spectrum.

Quintana, S. M., Castaneda-English, P., & Ybarra, V. C. (1999). Role of perspective-taking abilities and ethnic socialization in development of adolescent ethnic identity. *Journal of Research in Adolescence, 9,* 161–184.

Rabin, D. S., & Chrousos, G. P. (1991). Androgens, gonadal. In R. M. Lerner, A. C. Petersen, & J. Brooks-Gunn (Eds.), *Encyclopedia of adolescence* (Vol. 1, pp. 56–59). New York, NY: Garland.

Radke-Yarrow, M., & Zahn-Waxler, C. (1984). Roots, motives, and patterns in children's prosocial behavior. In J. Reykowski, T. Karylowski, D. Bar-Tal, & E. Staub (Eds.), *Origins and maintenance of prosocial behaviors* (pp. 81–99). New York, NY: Plenum Press.

Radke-Yarrow, M., Zahn-Waxler, C., & Chapman, M. (1982). Children's prosocial dispositions and behavior. In E. M. Hetherington (Ed.), *Handbook of child psychology: Vol. 4. Socialization, personality and social development* (pp. 469–546). New York, NY: Harper Row.

Radmacher, K., & Azmitia, M. (2006). Are there gendered pathways to intimacy in early adolescents' and emerging adults' friendships? *Journal of Adolescent Research, 21,* 415–448.

Raffaelli, M., Crockett, L. J., & Shen, Y. (2005). Developmental stability and change in self-regulation from childhood to adolescence. *Journal of Genetic Psychology, 166,* 54–75.

Raikes, H. A., & Thompson, R. A. (2006). Family emotional climate, attachment security, and young children's emotion understanding in a high-risk sample. *British Journal of Developmental Psychology, 24,* 89–104.

Raine, A., & Yang, Y. (2006). Neural foundations to moral reasoning and antisocial behavior. *Social Cognitive and Affective Neuroscience, 1,* 203–213.

Ram, A., & Ross, H. S. (2001). Problem-solving, contention, and struggle: How siblings resolve a conflict of interests. *Child Development, 72,* 1710–1722.

Raudino, A., Fergusson, D. M., & Horwood, L. J. (2013). The quality of parent/child relationships in adolescence is associated with poor adult psychosocial adjustment. *Journal of Adolescence, 36,* 331–340.

Recchia, H., Wainryb, C., & Pasupathi, M. (2013). "Two for flinching": Children's and adolescents' narrative accounts of harming their friends and siblings. *Child Development, 84,* 1459–1474.

Recchia, H. E., & Howe, N. (2009). Sibling relationship quality moderates the associations between parental interventions and siblings' independent conflict strategies and outcomes. *Journal of Family Psychology, 23,* 551–561.

Reese, E. (2002). Social factors in the development of autobiographical memory: The state of the art. *Social Development, 11,* 124–142.

Reese, E., Bird, A., & Tripp, G. (2007). Children's self-esteem and moral self: Links to parent–child conversations regarding emotion. *Social Development, 16,* 460–478.

Reese-Weber, M. (2000). Middle and later adolescents' conflict resolution skills with siblings: Associations with interparental and parent–adolescent conflict resolution. *Journal of Youth and Adolescence, 29,* 97–711.

Reese-Weber, M., & Kahn, J. H. (2005). Familial predictors of sibling and romantic-partner conflict resolution: Comparing late adolescents from intact and divorced families. *Journal of Adolescence, 28,* 479–493.

Reiber, C., & Garcia, J. R. (2010). Hooking up: Gender differences, evolution, and pluralistic ignorance. *Evolutionary Psychology, 8,* 390–404.

Reid, M., Ramey, S. L., & Burchinal, M. (1990). Dialogues with children about their families. *New Directions for Child Development, 48,* 5–27.

Reinherz, H. Z., Giaconia, R. M., Pakiz, B., Silverman, A. B., Frost, A. K., & Lefkowitz, E. S. (1993). Psychosocial risks for major depression in late adolescence: A longitudinal community study. *Journal of the American Academy of Child and Adolescent Psychiatry, 32,* 1155–1163.

Reis, H. T., & Shaver, P. (1988). Intimacy as an interpersonal process. In S. W. Duck, D. F. Hay, S. E. Hobfoll, W. Ickes, & B. M. Montgomery (Eds.), *Handbook of personal relationships: Theory, research, and interventions* (pp. 367–389). Oxford: John Wiley and Sons.

Reiss, D., Hetherington, E. M., Plomin, R., Howe, G. W., Simmens, S. J., Henderson, S. H., ... & Law, T. (1995). Genetic questions for environmental studies: Differential parenting and psychopathology in adolescence. *Archives of General Psychiatry, 52,* 925–936.

Reiss, D., Neiderhiser, J. M., Hetherington, E. M., & Plomin, R. (2000). *The relationship code: Deciphering genetic and social influences on adolescent development.* Cambridge, MA: Harvard University Press.

Rende, R., Slomkowski, C., Lloyd-Richardson, E., & Niaura, R. (2005). Sibling effects on substance use in adolescence: Social contagion and genetic relatedness. *Journal of Family Psychology, 19,* 611–618.

Renken, B., Egeland, B., Marvinney, D., Mangelsdorf, S., & Sroufe, L. A. (1989). Early childhood antecedents of aggression and passive-withdrawal in early elementary school. *Journal of Personality, 57,* 257–282.

Renshaw, P., & Brown, P. (1993). Loneliness in middle childhood: Concurrent and longitudinal predictors. *Child Development, 64,* 1271–1284.

Repinski, D. J., & Zook, J. M. (2005). Three measures of closeness in adolescents' relationships with parents and friends:

Variations and developmental significance. *Personal Relationships, 12,* 79–102.

Resnick, G. (1993). *Manual for the administration, coding, and interpretation of the Separation Anxiety Test for 11- to 14-year-olds.* Rockville, MD: Westat.

Rest, J. R., Narvaez, D., Thoma, S. J., & Bebeau, M. J. (2000). A neo-Kohlbergian approach to morality research. *Journal of Moral Education, 29,* 381–395.

Rhoades, B. L., Greenberg, M. T., & Domitrovich, C. E. (2009). The contribution of inhibitory control to preschoolers' social-emotional competence. *Journal of Applied Developmental Psychology, 30,* 310–320.

Rice, K. G. (1990). Attachment in adolescence: A narrative and meta-analytic review. *Journal of Youth and Adolescence, 19,* 511–538.

Richmond, M. K., Stocker, C. M., & Rienks, S. L. (2005). Longitudinal associations between sibling relationship quality, parental differential treatment, and children's adjustment. *Journal of Family Psychology, 19,* 550–559.

Riem, M. M. E., Bakermans-Kranenburg, M. J., van IJzendoorn, M. H., Out, D., & Rombouts, S. A. R. B. (2012). Attachment in the brain: Adult attachment representations predict amygdala and behavioral responses to infant crying. *Attachment & Human Development, 14,* 533–551.

Riggs, S. A., & Jacobvitz, D. (2002). Expectant parents' representations of early attachment relationships: Associations with mental health and family history. *Journal of Consulting and Clinical Psychology, 70,* 195–204.

Rinaldi, C., & Howe, N. (2003). Perceptions of constructive and destructive conflict within and across family subsystems. *Infant and Child Development, 12,* 441–459.

Roberts, B. W., & DelVecchio, W. F. (2000). The rank-order consistency of personality traits from childhood to old age: A quantitative review of longitudinal studies. *Psychological Bulletin, 126,* 25–30.

Roberts, L., & Blanton, P. (2001). "I always knew mom and dad loved me best": Experiences of only children. *Journal of Individual Psychology, 57,* 125–140.

Roberts, W., & Strayer, J. (1996). Empathy, emotional expressiveness, and prosocial behavior. *Child Development, 67,* 449–470.

Robertson, D., Snarey, J., Ousley, O., Bowman, D., Harenski, K., & Kilts, C. (2007). The neural processing of moral sensitivity to issues of justice and care: An fMRI study. *Neuropsychologia, 45,* 755–766.

Robertson, J., & Bowlby, J. (1952). Responses of young children to separation from their mothers. *Courrier du Centre International de l'enfance, 2,* 131–142.

Robertson, J., & Robertson, J. (1971). Young children in brief separation: A fresh look. *The Psychoanalytic Study of the Child, 36,* 264–315.

Robins, R. W., Trzesniewski, K. H., Tracy, J. L., Gosling, S. D., & Potter, J. (2002). Global self-esteem across the life span. *Psychology and Aging, 17,* 423–434.

Robinson, J. L., Kagan, J., Reznick, J. S., & Corley, R. (1992). The heritability of inhibited and uninhibited behavior: A twin study. *Developmental Psychology, 28,* 1030–1037.

Robinson, J. L., Zahn-Waxler, C., & Emde, R. N. (1994). Patterns of development in early empathic behavior: Environmental and child constitutional influences. *Social Development, 3,* 125–145.

Rochat, P. (2009). *Others in mind: Social origins of self-consciousness.* New York, NY: Cambridge University Press.

Rodkin, P., Farmer, T., Pearl, R., & Van Acker, R. (2006). They're cool: Social status and peer group supports for aggressive boys and girls. *Social Development, 15,* 175–204.

Rogoff, B. (1990). *Apprenticeship in thinking.* New York, NY: Oxford University Press.

Roisman, G. I. (2009). Adult attachment: Toward a rapprochement of methodological cultures. *Current Directions in Psychological Science, 18,* 122–126.

Roisman, G. I., Collins, W. A., Sroufe, L. A., & Egeland, B. (2005). Predictors of young adults' representations of and behavior in their current romantic relationship: Prospective tests of the prototype hypothesis. *Attachment & Human Development, 7,* 105–121.

Roisman, G. I., Fortuna, K., & Holland, A. (2006). An experimental manipulation of retrospectively defined earned and continuous attachment security. *Child Development, 77,* 59–71.

Roisman, G. I., & Groh, A. M. (2011). Attachment theory and research in developmental psychology: An overview and appreciative critique. In M. K. Underwood & L. H. Rosen (Eds.), *Social development: Relationships in infancy, childhood, and adolescence* (pp. 101–126). New York, NY: Guilford Press.

Roisman, G. I., & Haydon, K. C. (2011). Earned security in retrospect: Emerging insights from longitudinal, experimental, and taxometric investigations. In D. Cicchetti & G. I. Roisman (Eds.), *Minnesota symposia on child psychology: The origins and organization of adaptation and maladaptation* (pp. 109–154). Hoboken, NJ: Wiley.

Roisman, G. I., Holland, A., Fortuna, K., Fraley, R., Clausell, E., & Clarke, A. (2007). The Adult Attachment Interview and self-reports of attachment style: An empirical rapprochement. *Journal of Personality and Social Psychology, 92,* 678–697.

Roisman, G. I., Madsen, S. D., Hennighausen, K. H., Sroufe, L. A., & Collins, W. A. (2001). The coherence of dyadic behavior across parent–child and romantic relationships as mediated by the internalized representation of experience. *Attachment & Human Development, 3,* 156–172.

Roisman, G. I., Padrón, E., Sroufe, L. A., & Egeland, B. (2002). Earned-secure attachment status in retrospect and prospect. *Child Development, 73,* 1204–1219.

Roland, A. (1987). The familial self, the individualized self, and the transcendent self. *Psychoanalytic Review, 74,* 237–250.

Roopnarine, J. L., Fouts, H. N., Lamb, M. E., & Lewis-Elligan, T. Y. (2005). Mothers' and fathers' behaviors towards their 3- to 4-month-old infants in lower, middle, and upper socioeconomic African American families. *Developmental Psychology, 41,* 723–732.

Rose, A. J. (2002). Co-rumination in the friendships of girls and boys. *Child Development, 73,* 1830–1843.

Rose, A. J., Carlson, W., & Waller, E. M. (2007). Prospective associations of co-rumination with friendship and emotional adjustment: Considering the socioemotional trade-offs of co-rumination. *Developmental Psychology, 43,* 1019–1031.

Rosen, K. S. (2015). *Invisible threads: The enduring connections between sisters and brothers.* Unpublished manuscript, Boston College, Chestnut Hill, MA.

Rosen, K. S., & Burke, P. (1999). Multiple attachment relationships within families: Mothers and fathers with two young children. *Developmental Psychology, 35,* 436–444.

Rosen, K. S., & Rothbaum, F. (1993). Quality of parental caregiving and security of attachment. *Developmental Psychology, 29,* 358–367.

Rosenberg, M. (1979). *Conceiving the self.* New York, NY: Basic Books.

Rosenberg, M. (1986). Self-concept from middle childhood through adolescence. In J. Suls & A. Greenwald (Eds.), *Psychological perspectives on the self* (Vol. 3, pp. 107–136). Hillsdale, NJ: Erlbaum.

Rosenblum, G. D., & Lewis, M. (2003). Emotional development in adolescence. In G. R. Adams & M. D. Berzonsky (Eds.), *Blackwell handbook of adolescence* (pp. 269–289). Malden, MA: Blackwell.

Rosenstein, D. S., & Horowitz, H. A. (1996). Adolescent attachment and psychopathology. *Journal of Consulting and Clinical Psychology, 64,* 244–253.

Rosenthal, D. A., & Feldman, S. S. (1990). The acculturation of Chinese immigrants: Perceived effects on family functioning of length of residence in two cultural contexts. *The Journal of Genetic Psychology, 151,* 495–514.

Rosenthal, N. L., & Kobak, R. (2010). Assessing adolescents' attachment hierarchies: Differences across developmental periods and associations with individual adaptation. *Journal of Research on Adolescence, 20,* 678–706.

Ross, H. S., & Conant, C. L. (1992). The social structure of early conflict: Interactions, relationships, and alliances. In C. U. Shantz & W. W. Hartup (Eds.), *Conflict in child and adolescent development* (pp. 153–185). Cambridge: Cambridge University Press.

Ross, H. S., & Lollis, S. P. (1989). A social relations analysis of toddler peer relationships. *Child Development, 60,* 1082–1091.

Ross, H. S., Lollis, S. P., & Elliot, C. (1982). Toddler-peer communication. In K. H. Rubin & H. S. Ross (Eds.), *Peer relationships and social skills in childhood.* New York, NY: Springer-Verlag.

Ross, H. S., Ross, M., Stein, N., & Trabasso, T. (2006). How siblings resolve their conflicts: The importance of first offers, planning and limited opposition. *Child Development, 77,* 1730–1745.

Ross, J., & Fuertes, J. (2010). Parental attachment, interparental conflict, and young adults' emotional adjustment. *The Counseling Psychologist, 38,* 1050–1077.

Roth-Hanania, R., Davidov, M., & Zahn-Waxler, C. (2011). Empathy development from 8 to 16 months: Early signs of concern for others. *Infant Behavior and Development, 34,* 447–458.

Rothbart, M. K. (1981). Measurement of temperament in infancy. *Child Development, 52,* 569–578.

Rothbart, M. K. (1989). Temperament and development. In G. Kohnstamm, J. Bates, & M. K. Rothbart (Eds.), *Temperament in childhood* (pp. 187–248). Chichester: Wiley.

Rothbart, M. K. (2007). Temperament, development, and personality. *Current Directions in Psychological Science, 16,* 207–212.

Rothbart, M. K. (2011). *Becoming who we are: Temperament and personality in development.* New York, NY: Guilford Press.

Rothbart, M. K., Ahadi, S. A., & Evans, D. E. (2000). Temperament and personality: Origins and outcomes. *Journal of Personality and Social Psychology, 78,* 122–135.

Rothbart, M. K., Ahadi, S. A., & Hershey, K. L. (1994). Temperament and social behavior in childhood. *Merrill-Palmer Quarterly, 40,* 21–39.

Rothbart, M. K., Ahadi, S. A., Hershey, K. L., & Fisher, P. (2001). Investigations of temperament at 3 to 7 years: The Children's Behavior Questionnaire. *Child Development, 72,* 1394–1408.

Rothbart, M. K., & Bates, J. E. (1998). Temperament. In W. Damon (Series Ed.) & N. Eisenberg (Vol. Ed.), *Handbook of child psychology. Vol 3: Social, emotional and personality development* (5th ed., pp. 105–176). New York, NY: Wiley.

Rothbart, M. K., & Bates, J. E. (2006). Temperament. In W. Damon & R. M. Lerner (Eds.), *Handbook of child psychology. Vol 3: Social, emotional and personality development* (6th ed., pp. 99–166). New York, NY: Wiley.

Rothbart, M. K., & Bates, J. E. (2008). Temperament. In W. Damon & R. M. Lerner (Eds.), *Child and adolescent development: An advanced course* (pp. 54–92). Hoboken, NJ: John Wiley & Sons, Inc.

Rothbart, M. K., & Derryberry, D. (1981). Development of individual differences in temperament. In M. E. Lamb & A. L. Brown (Eds.), *Advances in developmental psychology* (Vol. 1, pp. 37–86). Hillsdale, NJ: Erlbaum.

Rothbart, M. K., Derryberry, D., & Hershey, K. (2000). Stability of temperament in childhood: Laboratory infant assessment to parent report at seven years. In V. Molfese & D. Molfese (Eds.), *Temperament and personality development across the lifespan* (pp. 85–119). Mahwah, NJ: Erlbaum.

Rothbart, M. K., Ellis, L. K., & Posner, M. I. (2011). Temperament and self-regulation. In R. F. Baumeister & K. D. Vohs (Eds.), *Handbook of self-regulation: Research, theory and applications* (2nd ed., pp. 441–460). New York, NY: Guilford Press.

Rothbart, M. K., & Goldsmith, H. H. (1985). Three approaches to the study of infant temperament. *Developmental Review, 5,* 237–260.

Rothbart, M. K., Posner, M. I., & Kieras, J. (2006). Temperament, attention, and the development of self-regulation. In K. McCartney & D. Phillips (Eds.), *The Blackwell handbook of early childhood development* (pp. 328–357). London: Blackwell.

Rothbart, M. K., Posner, M. I., & Rosicky, J. (1994). Orienting in normal and pathological development. *Development and Psychopathology, 6,* 635–652.

Rothbart, M. K., Sheese, B. E., & Posner, M. I. (2007). Executive attention and effortful control: Linking temperament, brain networks, and genes. *Child Development Perspectives, 1,* 2–7.

Rothbaum, F., Pott, M., Azuma, H., Miyake, K., & Weisz, J. (2000). The development of close relationships in Japan and the United States: Paths of symbiotic harmony and generative tension. *Child Development, 71,* 1121–1142.

Rothbaum, F., & Trommsdorff, G. (2007). Do roots and wings complement or oppose one another? The socialization of relatedness and autonomy in cultural context. In J. Grusec & P. Hastings (Eds.), *Handbook of socialization: Theory and research* (pp. 461–489). New York, NY: Guilford Press.

Rothbaum, F., Weisz, J., Pott, M., Miyake, K., & Morelli, G. (2000). Attachment and culture: Security in the United States and Japan. *American Psychologist, 55,* 1093–1104.

Rowe, D. C., & Gulley, B. L. (1992). Sibling effects on substance use and delinquency. *Criminology, 30,* 217–233.

Rowe, D. C., & Plomin, R. (1981). The importance of nonshared (E-sub-1) environmental influences in behavioral development. *Developmental Psychology, 17,* 517–531.

Rowe, D. C., Rodgers, J. L., Meseck-Bushey, S., & St. John, C. (1989). Sexual behavior and nonsexual deviance: A sibling study of their relationship. *Developmental Psychology, 25,* 61–69.

Rubin, K. H., Bukowski, W. M., & Parker, J. G. (2006). Peer interactions, relationships, and groups. In W. Damon & R. M. Lerner (Series Eds.) & N. Eisenberg (Vol. Ed.), *Handbook of child psychology: Vol. 3. Social, emotional, and personality development* (6th ed., pp. 571–645). Hoboken, NJ: Wiley.

Rubin, K. H., Coplan, R., Chen, X., Bowker, J., & McDonald, K. L. (2011). Peer relationships in childhood. In M. E. Lamb & M. H. Bornstein (Eds.), *Social and personality development: An advanced textbook* (pp. 308–360). New York, NY: Psychology Press.

Rubin, K. H., Dwyer, K. M., Booth-LaForce, C. L., Kim, A. H., Burgess, K. B., & Rose-Krasnor, L. (2004). Attachment, friendship, and psychosocial functioning in early adolescence. *Journal of Early Adolescence, 24,* 326–356.

Rubin, K. H., & Rose-Krasnor, K. (1992). Interpersonal problem solving. In V. B. Van Hassett & M. Hersen (Eds.), *Handbook of social development* (pp. 283–323). New York, NY: Plenum.

Rubin, K. H., Watson, K., & Jambor, T. (1978). Free play behaviors in preschool and kindergarten children. *Child Development, 49,* 534–536.

Rubin, K. H., Wojslawowicz, J. C., Rose-Krasnor, L., Booth-LaForce, C., & Burgess, K. B. (2006). The best friendships of shy/withdrawn children: Prevalence, stability, and relationship quality. *Journal of Abnormal Child Psychology, 34,* 139–153.

Ruble, D. N., Alvarez, J., Bachman, M., Cameron, J., Fuligni, A., Garcia Coll, C., & Rhee, E. (2004). The development of a sense of "we": The emergence and implications of children's collective identity. In M. Bennett & F. Sani (Eds.), *The development of the social self* (pp. 29–76). New York, NY: Psychology Press.

Ruble, D. N., & Frey, K. S. (1991). Changing patterns of comparative behavior as skills are acquired: A functional model of self-evaluation. In J. Suls & T. A. Wills (Eds.), *Social comparison: Contemporary theory and research* (pp. 70–112). Hillsdale, NJ: Erlbaum.

Ruble, D. N., Martin, C. L., & Berenbaum, S. A. (2006). Gender development. In W. Damon & R. M. Lerner (Series Ed.) & N. Eisenberg (Vol. Ed.), *Handbook of child psychology, Vol. 3: Social, emotional, and personality development* (6th ed., pp. 858–932). New York, NY: Wiley.

Ruble, D. N., Taylor, L. J., Cyphers, L., Greulich, F. K., Lurye, L. E., & Shrout, P. E. (2007). The role of gender constancy in early gender development. *Child Development, 78,* 1121–1136.

Ruck, M. D., Peterson-Badali, M., & Day, D. M. (2002). Adolescents' and mothers' understanding of children's rights in the home. *Journal of Research on Adolescence, 12,* 373–398.

Rudolph, K. D., Troop-Gordon, W., & Llewellyn, N. (2013). Interactive contributions of self-regulation deficits and social motivation to psychopathology: Unraveling divergent pathways to aggressive behavior and depressive symptoms. *Development and Psychopathology, 25,* 407–418.

Rueter, M., & Conger, R. D. (1998). Reciprocal influences between parenting and adolescent problem-solving behavior. *Developmental Psychology, 34,* 1470–1482.

Ruffman, T., Perner, J., Naito, M., Parkin, L., & Clements, W. A. (1998). Older (but not younger) siblings facilitate false belief understanding. *Developmental Psychology, 34,* 161–174.

Rumberger, R. W. (1995). Dropping out of middle school: A multilevel analysis of students and schools. *American Educational Research Journal, 32,* 583–625.

Russell, J. A. (1994). Is there universal recognition of emotion from facial expression? A review of the cross-cultural studies. *Psychological Bulletin, 115,* 102–141.

Russell, J. A. (2003). Core affect and the psychological construction of emotion. *Psychological Review, 110,* 145–172.

Russell, J. A. (2009). Emotion, core affect, and psychological construction. *Cognition and Emotion, 23,* 1259–1283.

Russell, J. A. (2014). My psychological constructionist perspective. In L. F. Barrett & J. A. Russell (Eds.), *The psychological construction of emotion* (pp. 183–208). New York, NY: Guilford Press.

Rutter, M. (1981). Socioemotional consequences of daycare for preschool children. *American Journal of Orthopsychiatry, 51,* 4–28.

Rutter, M. (1987). Continuities and discontinuities from infancy. In J. D. Osofsky (Ed.), *Handbook of infant development* (pp. 1150–1198). New York, NY: Wiley.

Rutter, M. (2002). Family influences on behavior and development: Challenges for the future. In J. McHale & W. S. Grolnick (Eds.), *Retrospect and prospect in the psychological study of families* (pp. 321–351). Mahwah, NJ: Erlbaum.

Rutter, M. (2006). *Genes and behavior.* New York, NY: Blackwell.

Ryan, R., & Lynch, J. (1989). Emotional autonomy versus detachment: Revisiting the vicissitudes of adolescence and young adulthood. *Child Development, 60,* 340–356.

Saarni, C. (1990). Emotional competence: How emotions and relationships become integrated. In R. A. Thompson (Ed.), *Socioemotional development. Nebraska Symposium on Motivation* (pp. 115–182). Lincoln, NE: University of Nebraska Press.

Saarni, C. (1991). *The development of emotional competence.* New York, NY: Guilford Press.

Saarni, C. (1999). *The development of social competence.* New York, NY: Guilford Press.

Saarni, C., Campos, J. J., Camras, L. A., & Witherington, D. (2006). Emotional development: Action, communication, and understanding. In W. Damon & R. M. Lerner (Series Eds.) & N. Eisenberg (Vol. Ed.), *Handbook of child psychology: Vol. 3. Social, emotional, and personality*

development (6th ed., pp. 226–299). Hoboken, NJ: Wiley.

Saarni, C., Campos, J. J., Camras, L. A., & Witherington, D. (2008). Principles of emotion and emotional competence. In W. Damon & R. M. Lerner (Eds.), *Child and adolescent development: An advanced course* (pp. 361–405). New York, NY: Wiley.

Saarni, C., Mumme, D. L., & Campos, J. (1998). Emotional development: Action, communication, and understanding. In N. Eisenberg (Ed.) & W. Damon (Series Ed.), *Handbook of child psychology: Vol. 3. Social, emotional, and personality development* (5th ed., pp. 237–309). New York, NY: Wiley.

Sagi, A., & Hoffman, M. L. (1976). Empathic distress in the newborn. *Developmental Psychology, 12,* 175–176.

Sagi, A., Koren-Karie, N., Gini, M., Ziv, Y., & Joels, T. (2002). Shedding further light on the effects of various types and quality of early child care on infant–mother attachment relationship: The Haifa study of early child care. *Child Development, 73,* 1166–1186.

Sagi, A., Lamb, M., Lewkowicz, K. S., Shoham, R., Dvir, R., & Estes, D. (1985). Security of infant–mother, –father and –metapelet attachments among kibbutz-reared Israeli children. In I. Bretherton & E. Waters (Eds.), Growing points of attachment theory and research. *Monographs of the Society for Research in Child Development, 50*(1–2, Serial No. 209), 257–275.

Sagi, A., van IJzendoorn, M. H., Aviezer, O., Donnell, F., Koren-Karie, N., Joels, T., & Harel, Y. (1995). Attachments in multiple-caregiver and multiple-infant environment: The case of the Israeli kibbutzim. In E. Waters, B. E. Vaughn, G. Posada, & K. Kondo-Ikemura (Eds.), Caregiving, cultural, and cognitive perspectives on secure-base behavior and working models: New growing points of attachment theory and research. *Monographs of the Society for Research in Child Development, 60*(2–3, Serial No. 244), 71–91.

Sagi-Schwartz, A., & Aviezer, O. (2005). Correlates of attachment to multiple caregivers in kibbutz children from birth to emerging adulthood: The Haifa longitudinal study. In K. E. Grossman, K. Grossman, & E. Waters

(Eds.), *Attachment from infancy to adulthood: The major longitudinal studies* (pp. 165–197). New York, NY: Guilford Press.

Sameroff, A. (1994). Developmental systems and family functioning. In R. D. Parke & S. G. Kellam (Eds.), *Exploring family relationships with other social contexts* (pp. 199–214). Hillsdale, NJ: Erlbaum.

Sameroff, A. J. (1975). Early influences on development: Fact or fancy? *Merrill-Palmer Quarterly, 21,* 267–294.

Sameroff, A. J., & Chandler, M. (1975). Reproductive risk and the continuum of caretaking casualty. In F. Horowitz (Ed.), *Review of child development research* (Vol. 4, pp. 187–244). Chicago, IL: University of Chicago Press.

Samuel, S., Hayton, B., Gold, I., Feeley, N., Carter, C. S., & Zelkowitz, P. (2015). Attachment security and recent stressful life events predict oxytocin levels: A pilot study of pregnant women with high levels of cumulative psychosocial adversity. *Attachment & Human Development, 17,* 272–287.

Samuels, H. R. (1980). The effect of an older sibling on infant locomotor exploration of a new environment. *Child Development, 51,* 607–609.

Samuolis, J., Layburn, K., & Schiaffino, K. M. (2001). Identity development and attachment to parents in college students. *Journal of Youth and Adolescence, 30,* 373–384.

Sanderson, C. A., Rahm, K. B., & Beigbeder, S. A. (2005). The link between the pursuit of intimacy goals and satisfaction in close same-sex friendships: An examination of the underlying processes. *Journal of Social and Personal Relationships, 22,* 75–98.

Sandler, L. (1975). Infant and caretaking environment. In E. J. Anthony (Ed.), *Explorations in child psychiatry* (pp. 129–166). New York, NY: Plenum.

Sandler, L. (2013). One and only: The freedom of having an only child, and the joy of being one. New York, NY: Simon and Schuster.

Sandstrom, M. J., Cillessen, A. H. N., & Eisenhower, A. (2003). Children's appraisal of peer rejection experiences: Impact on social and emotional adjustment. *Social Development, 12,* 530–550.

Santucci, A. K., Silk, J. S., Shaw, D. S., Gentzler, A., Fox, N. A., & Kovacs, M. (2008). Vagal tone and temperament as predictors of emotion regulation strategies in young children. *Developmental Psychology, 50,* 205–216.

Saudino, K. J., & Wang, M. (2012). Quantitative and molecular genetic studies of temperament. In M. Zentner & R. L. Shiner (Eds.), *Handbook of temperament* (pp. 315–346). New York, NY: Guilford Press.

Saudino, K. J., Wertz, A. E., Gagne, J. R., & Chawla, S. (2004). Night and day: Are siblings as different in temperament as parents say they are? *Journal of Personality and Social Psychology, 87,* 698–706.

Saunders, R., Jacobvitz, D., Zaccagnino, M., Beverung, L. M., & Hazen, N. (2011). Pathways to earned-security: The role of alternative support figures. *Attachment & Human Development, 13,* 403–420.

Savin-Williams, R. C. (2001). A critique of research on sexual-minority youths. *Journal of Adolescence, 24,* 5–13.

Sawyer, K. S., Denham, S., DeMulder, E., Blair, K., Auerbach-Major, S., & Levitas, J. (2002). The contribution of older siblings' reactions to emotions to preschoolers' emotional and social competence. *Marriage & Family Review, 34,* 182–212.

Saxe, R., Carey, S., & Kanwisher, N. (2004). Understanding other minds: Linking developmental psychology and functional neuroimaging. *Annual Review of Psychology, 55,* 87–124.

Saxe, R., Moran, J. M., Scholz, J., & Gabrieli, J. (2006). Overlapping and nonoverlapping brain regions for theory of mind and self reflection in individual subjects. *Social Cognitive and Affective Neuroscience, 1,* 229–234.

Saxe, R., Whitfield-Gabrieli, S., Scholz, J., & Pelphrey, K. A. (2009). Brain regions for perceiving and reasoning about other people in school-aged children. *Child Development, 80,* 1197–1209.

Scarr, S., & McCartney, K. (1983). How people make their own environments: A theory of genotype-environment effects. *Child Development, 54,* 424–435.

Schacter, E. P., & Ventura, J. J. (2008). Identity agents: Parents as active and reflective participants in their children's identity formation. *Journal of Research on Adolescence, 18,* 449–476.

Scheff, T. J. (1987). The shame–rage spiral: A case study of an interminable quarrel.

In H. B. Lewis (Ed.), *The role of shame in symptom formation* (pp. 109–149). Hillsdale, NJ: Erlbaum.

Scheff, T. J. (2000). Shame and the social bond: A sociological theory. *Sociological Theory, 18,* 84–99.

Schneider, B. H., Atkinson, L., & Tardif, C. (2001). Child–parent attachment and children's peer relations: A quantitative review. *Developmental Psychology, 37,* 86–100.

Schneider, B. H., Fonzi, A., Tani, F., & Tomada, G. (1997). A cross-cultural exploration of the stability of children's friendships and the predictors of their continuation. *Social Development, 6,* 322–339.

Schneider, B. H., & Tessier, N. (2007). Close friendship as understood by socially withdrawn, anxious early adolescents. *Child Psychiatry & Human Development, 38,* 339–351.

Schneider, B. H., & Younger, A. J. (1996). Adolescent–parent attachment and adolescents' relations with their peers: A closer look. *Youth and Society, 28,* 95–108.

Schneider-Rosen, K. (1990). The developmental reorganization of attachment relationships: Guidelines for classification beyond infancy. In M. T. Greenberg, D. Cicchetti, & E. M. Cummings (Eds.), *Attachment in the preschool years: Theory, research, and intervention* (pp. 185–220). Chicago, IL: University of Chicago Press.

Schneider-Rosen, K., Braunwald, K., Carlson, V., & Cicchetti, D. (1985). Current perspectives in attachment theory: Illustration from the study of maltreated infants. In I. Bretherton & E. Waters (Eds.), Growing points of attachment theory and research. *Monographs of the Society for Research in Child Development, 50*(1–2, Serial No. 209), 194–210.

Schneider-Rosen, K., & Cicchetti, D. (1984). The relationship between affect and cognition in maltreated infants: Quality of attachment and the development of visual self-recognition. *Child Development, 55,* 648–658.

Schneider-Rosen, K., & Cicchetti, D. (1991). Early self-knowledge and emotional development. *Developmental Psychology, 27,* 471–478.

Schore, A. N. (1994). *Affect regulation and the origin of the self: The neurobiology of emotional development.* Hillsdale, NJ: Erlbaum.

Schore, A. N. (1996). The experience-dependent maturation of a regulatory system in the orbital prefrontal cortex and the origin of developmental psychopathology. *Development and Psychopathology, 8,* 59–87.

Schore, A. N. (2003). *Affect regulation and the repair of the self.* New York, NY: Norton.

Schore, J. R., & Schore, A. N. (2008). Modern attachment theory: The central role of affect regulation in development and treatment. *Clinical Social Work Journal, 36,* 9–20.

Schuengel, C., Bakermans-Kranenburg, M., van IJzendoorn, M. H., & Blom, M. (1999). Unresolved loss and infant disorganization: Links to frightening maternal behavior. In J. Solomon & C. George (Eds.), *Attachment disorganization* (pp. 71–94). New York, NY: Guilford Press.

Schulenberg, J. E., & Zarrett, N. R. (2006). Mental health during emerging adulthood: Continuity and discontinuity in courses, causes, and functions. In J. J. Arnett & J. L. Tanner (Eds.), *Emerging adults in America: Coming of age in the 21st century* (pp. 135–172). Washington, DC: APA Books.

Schwartz, C., Kunwar, P. S., Greve, D. N., Kagan, J., Snidman, N. C., & Bloch, R. B. (2012). A phenotype of early infancy predicts reactivity of the amygdala in male adults. *Molecular Psychiatry, 17,* 1042–1050.

Schwartz, D., Dodge, K. A., Pettit, G. S., & Bates, J. E., and Conduct Problems Prevention Research Group (2000). Friendship as a moderating factor in the pathway between early harsh home environment and later victimization in the peer group. *Developmental Psychology, 36,* 646–662.

Scourfield, J., John, B., Martin, N., & McGuffin, P. (2004). The development of prosocial behavior in children and adolescents: A twin study. *Journal of Child Psychology and Psychiatry, 45,* 927–935.

Sears, R. R., Maccoby, E. E., & Levin, H. (1957). *Patterns of child rearing.* Evanston, IL: Row, Peterson.

Sears, R. R., Rau, L., & Alpert, R. (1965). *Identification and child rearing.* Stanford, CA: Stanford University Press.

Sebanc, A. M. (2003). The friendship features of preschool children: Links with prosocial behavior and aggression. *Social Development, 12,* 249–268.

Sebanc, A. M., Kearns, K. T., Hernandez, M. D., & Galvin, K. B. (2007). Predicting having a best friend in young children: Individual characteristics and friendship features. *Journal of Genetic Psychology, 168,* 81–95.

Seifer, R., Sameroff, A. J., Barrett, L. C., & Krafchuk, E. (1994). Infant temperament measured by multiple observations and mother report. *Child Development, 65,* 1478–1490.

Seifer, R., & Schiller, M. (1995). The role of parenting sensitivity, infant temperament, and dyadic interaction in attachment theory and assessment. In E. Waters, B. E. Vaughn, G. Posada, & K. Kondo-Ikemura (Eds.), Caregiving, cultural, and cognitive perspectives on secure-base behavior and working models: New growing points of attachment theory and research. *Monographs of the Society for Research in Child Development, 60*(2–3, Serial No. 244), 146–174.

Seifer, R., Schiller, M., Sameroff, A. J., Resnick, S., & Riordan, K. (1996). Attachment, maternal sensitivity, and infant temperament during the first year of life. *Developmental Psychology, 32,* 12–55.

Selden, N. R. W., Everitt, B. J., Jarrard, L. E., & Robbins, T. W. (1991). Complementary roles for the amygdala and hippocampus in aversive conditioning to explicit and contextual cues. *Neuroscience, 42,* 335–350.

Selman, R. L. (1980). *The growth of interpersonal understanding: Developmental and clinical analyses.* New York, NY: Academic Press.

Selman, R. L., & Schultz, L. (1990). *Making a friend in youth: Developmental theory and pair therapy.* Chicago, IL: University of Chicago Press.

Shamay-Tsoory, S. G., Tomer, R., Goldsher, D., Berger, B. D., & Aharon-Peretz, J. (2004). Impairment in cognitive and affective empathy in patients with brain lesions: Anatomical and cognitive correlates. *Journal of Clinical and Experimental Neuropsychology, 26,* 1113–1127.

Shanahan, L., McHale, S. M., Crouter, A. C., & Osgood, D. W. (2008). Linkages between parents' differential treatment, youth depressive symptoms, and sibling relationships. *Journal of Marriage and Family, 70,* 480–494.

Shantz, C. U., & Hobart, C. J. (1989). Social conflict and development. In T. J. Berndt & G. W. Ladd (Eds.), *Peer relationships in child development* (pp. 71–94). New York, NY: Wiley.

Shapka, J. D., & Keating, D. P. (2005). Structure and change in self-concept during adolescence. *Canadian Journal of Behavioral Science, 37,* 83–96.

Sharabany, R., Gershoni, R., & Hofmann, J. (1981). Girlfriend, boyfriend: Age and sex differences in intimate friendship. *Developmental Psychology, 17,* 800–808.

Sharp, C., & Fonagy, P. (2008). The parent's capacity to treat the child as a psychological agent: Constructs, measures, and implications for developmental psychopathology. *Social Development, 17,* 737–754.

Sharp, C., Fonagy, P., & Goodyer, I. (2006). Imagining your child's mind: Psychosocial adjustment and mothers' ability to predict their children's attributional response styles. *British Journal of Developmental Psychology, 24,* 197–214.

Sharp, C., Pane, H., Ha, C., Venta, A., Patel, A., Sturek, J., & Fonagy, P. (2011). Theory of mind and emotion regulation difficulties in adolescents with borderline traits. *Journal of the American Academy of Child & Adolescent Psychiatry, 50,* 563–573.

Shaw, D. S., & Winslow, E. B. (1997). Precursors and correlates of antisocial behavior from infancy to preschool. In D. M. Stoff, J. Breiling, & J. D. Maser (Eds.), *Handbook of antisocial behavior* (pp. 148–158). Hoboken, NJ: Wiley.

Shebloski, B., Conger, K. J., & Widaman, K. F. (2005). Reciprocal links among differential parenting, perceived partiality, and self-worth: A three-wave longitudinal study. *Journal of Family Psychology, 19,* 633–642.

Sheehan, G. (1997). Adolescent sibling conflict. *Family Matters, 46,* 37–39.

Sheehan, G., Darlington, Y., Noller, P., & Feeney, J. (2004). Children's perceptions of their sibling relationships during parental separation and divorce. *Journal of Divorce and Remarriage, 41,* 69–94.

Sheehan, G., & Noller, P. (2002). Adolescents' perceptions of differential parenting: Links with attachment style and adolescent adjustment. *Personal Relationships, 9,* 173–190.

Sheese, B. E., Voelker, P. M., Rothbart, M. K., & Posner, M. I. (2007). Parenting quality interacts with genetic variation in dopamine receptor D4 to influence temperament in early childhood. *Development and Psychopathology, 19,* 1039–1046.

Sheikh, S., & Janoff-Bulman, R. (2010). Tracing the self-regulatory bases of moral emotions. *Emotion Review, 2,* 386–396.

Sher-Censor, E., Oppenheim, D., & Sagi-Schwartz, A. (2012). Individuation of female adolescents: Relations with adolescents' perceptions of maternal behavior and with adolescent–mother discrepancies in perceptions. *Journal of Adolescence, 35,* 397–405.

Sherman, A. M., Lansford, J. E., & Volling, B. L. (2006). Sibling relationships and best friendships in young adulthood: Warmth, conflict, and well-being. *Personal Relationships, 13,* 151–165.

Shiner, R. L., Buss, K. A., McClowry, S. G., Putnam, S. P., Saudino, K. J., & Zentner, M. (2012). What is temperament *now?* Assessing progress in temperament research on the twenty-fifth anniversary of Goldsmith et al. (1987). *Child Development Perspectives, 6,* 436–444.

Shiner, R. L., & Masten, A. S. (2012). Childhood personality as a harbinger of competence and resilience in adulthood. *Development and Psychopathology, 24,* 507–528.

Shipman, K. L., Schneider, R., Fitzgerald, M. M., Sims, C., Swisher, L., & Edwards, A. (2007). Maternal emotion socialization in maltreating and non-maltreating families: Implications for children's emotion regulation. *Social Development, 16,* 268–285.

Shirley, M. M. (1933). *The first two years: A study of 25 babies.* Minneapolis, MN: University of Minnesota Press.

Shmueli-Goetz, Y., Target, M., Fonagy, P., & Datta, A. (2008). The child attachment interview: A psychometric study of reliability and discriminant validity. *Developmental Psychology, 44,* 939–956.

Shoda, Y., Mischel, W., & Peake, P. K. (1990). Predicting adolescent cognitive and self-regulatory competencies from preschool delay of gratification: Identifying diagnostic conditions. *Developmental Psychology, 26,* 978–986.

Shomaker, L. B., & Furman, W. (2009). Parent–adolescent relationship qualities, internal working models, and attachment styles as predictors of adolescents' interactions with friends. *Journal of Social and Personal Relationships, 26,* 579–603.

Shonkoff, J. P., & Phillips, D. (Eds.). (2000). *From neurons to neighborhoods.* Washington, DC: National Academy Press.

Shulman, S., Elicker, J., & Sroufe, L. A. (1994). Stages of friendship growth in preadolescence as related to attachment history. *Journal of Social and Personal Relationships, 11,* 341–361.

Shulman, S., Laursen, B., Kalman, Z., & Karpovsky, S. (1997). Adolescent intimacy revisited. *Journal of Youth and Adolescence, 26,* 597–617.

Shweder, R. A., Much, N. C. Mahapatra, M., & Park, L. (1997). The "big three" of morality (autonomy, community, divinity) and the "big three" explanations of suffering. In A. M. Brandt & P. Rozin (Eds.), *Morality and health* (pp. 119–169). Florence, KY: Taylor & Frances/Routledge.

Siddiqui, A., & Ross, H. S. (2004). Mediation as a method of parent intervention in children's disputes. *Journal of Family Psychology, 18,* 147–159.

Sijsema, J. J., Ojanen, T., Veenstra, R., Lindenberg, S., Hawley, P. H., & Little, T. D. (2010). Forms and functions of aggression in adolescent friendship selection and influence: A longitudinal social network analysis. *Social Development, 19,* 515–534.

Silk, J. S., Shaw, D. S., Skuban, E. M., Oland, A. A., & Kovacs, M. (2006). Emotion regulation strategies in offspring of childhood-onset depressed mothers. *Journal of Child Psychology and Psychiatry, 47,* 69–78.

Simmons, R. G., & Blyth, D. A. (1987). *Moving into adolescence: The impact of pubertal change and school context.* New York, NY: Aldine.

Simpkins, S., & Parke, R. (2002). Do friends and nonfriends behave differently? A social relations analysis of children's behavior. *Merrill-Palmer Quarterly, 48,* 263–283.

Singer, E., & Doornenbal, J. (2006). Learning morality in peer conflict: A study of school children's narratives about being betrayed by a friend. *Childhood: A Global Journal of Child Research, 13,* 225–245.

Skinner, B. F. (1938). *The behavior of organisms.* New York, NY: Appleton-Century-Crofts.

Skinner, B. F. (1971). *Beyond freedom and dignity.* New York, NY: Knopf.

Slade, A. (2000). The development and organization of attachment: Implications for psychoanalysis. *Journal of the American Psychoanalytic Association, 48,* 1147–1174.

Slade, A. (2004). Two therapies: Attachment organization and the clinical process. In L. Atkinson & S. Goldberg (Eds.), *Attachment issues in psychopathology and intervention* (pp. 181–206). Mahwah, NJ: Erlbaum.

Slade, A. (2005). Parental reflective functioning: An introduction. *Attachment & Human Development, 7,* 269–281.

Slade, A. (2008). The implications of attachment theory and research for adult psychotherapy: Research and clinical perspectives. In J. Cassidy & P. R. Shaver (Eds.), *Handbook of attachment: Theory, research, and clinical applications* (2nd ed., pp. 762–782). New York, NY: Guilford Press.

Slade, A., Belsky, J., Aber, J. L., & Phelps, J. L. (1999). Mothers' representations of their relationships with their toddlers: Links to adult attachment and observed mothering. *Developmental Psychology, 35,* 611–619.

Slade, A., Grienenberger, J., Bernbach, E., Levy, D., & Locker, A. (2005). Maternal reflective functioning, attachment, and the transmission gap: A preliminary study. *Attachment & Human Development, 7,* 283–298.

Slaughter, V., Dennis, M. J., & Pritchard, M. (2002). Theory of mind and peer acceptance in preschool children. *British Journal of Developmental Psychology, 20,* 545–564.

Slaughter, V., Imuta, K., Peterson, C. C., & Henry, J. D. (2015). Meta-analysis of theory of mind and peer popularity in the preschool and early school years. *Child Development, 86,* 1159–1174.

Slomkowski, C., & Manke, B. (2004). Sibling relationships during childhood: Multiple perceptions from multiple observers. In R. D. Conger, F. O. Lorenz, & K. A. S. Wickrama (Eds.), *Continuity and change in family relations: Theory, methods, and empirical findings* (pp. 293–318). Mahwah, NJ: Erlbaum.

Slomkowski, C., Rende, R., Conger, K. J., Simons, R. L., & Conger, R. D. (2001). Sisters, brothers, and delinquency: Evaluating social influence during early and middle adolescence. *Child Development, 72,* 271–283.

Slotnick, B. M. (1967). Disturbances of maternal behavior in the rat following lesions of the cingulate cortex. *Behaviour, 29,* 204–236.

Smetana, J. G. (1988). Concepts of self and social convention: Adolescents' and parents' reasoning about hypothetical and actual family conflicts. In M. R. Gunnar & W. A. Collins (Eds.), *Minnesota Symposia on Child Psychology: Vol. 21. Development during the transition to adolescence* (pp. 79–122). Hillsdale, NJ: Erlbaum.

Smetana, J. G. (1997). Parenting and the development of social knowledge reconceptualized: A social domain analysis. In J. E. Grusec & L. Kuczynski (Eds.), *Parenting and children's internalization of values: A handbook of contemporary theory* (pp. 162–192). New York, NY: Wiley.

Smetana, J. G. (2006). Social domain theory: Consistencies and variations in children's moral and social judgments. In M. Killen & J. G. Smetana (Eds.), *Handbook of moral development* (pp. 119–154). Mahwah, NJ: Erlbaum.

Smetana, J. G., & Braeges, J. L. (1990). The development of toddlers' moral and conventional judgments. *Merrill-Palmer Quarterly, 36,* 329–346.

Smetana, J. G., Campione-Barr, N., & Metzger, A. (2006). Adolescent development in interpersonal and societal contexts. *Annual Review of Psychology, 57,* 255–284.

Smetana, J. G., Jambon, M., Conry-Murray, C., & Sturge-Apple, M. L. (2012). Reciprocal associations between young children's developing moral judgments and theory of mind. *Developmental Psychology, 48,* 1144–1155.

Smetana, J. G., Metzger, A., & Campione-Barr, N. (2004). African American late adolescents' relationships with parents: Developmental transitions and longitudinal patterns. *Child Development, 75,* 932–947.

Smith, J., & Ross, H. (2007). Training parents to mediate sibling disputes affects children's negotiation and conflict understanding. *Child Development, 78,* 790–805.

Smolak, L., & Munstertieger, B. F. (2002). The relationship of gender and voice to depression and eating disorders. *Psychology of Women Quarterly, 26,* 234–241.

Snapp, S. (2009). Internalization of the thin ideal among low-income ethnic minority adolescent girls. *Body Image, 6,* 311–314.

Snapp, S., Lento, R., Ryu, E., & Rosen, K. S. (2014). Why do they hook up? Attachment style and sexual motives in college students. *Personal Relationships, 21,* 468–481.

Sneed, J. R., Whitbourne, S. K., & Culang, M. E. (2006). Trust, identity, and ego integrity: Modeling Erikson's core stages over 34 years. *Journal of Adult Development, 13,* 148–157.

Snyder, J., Bank, L., & Burraston, B. (2005). The consequences of antisocial behavior in older male siblings for younger brothers and sisters. *Journal of Family Psychology, 19,* 643–653.

Snyder, J., Stoolmiller, M., Wilson, M., & Yamamoto, M. (2003). Child anger regulation, parental responses to children's anger displays, and early child antisocial behavior. *Social Development, 12,* 335–360.

Sober, E., & Wilson, D. S. (1998). *Unto others: The evolution and psychology of unselfish behavior.* Cambridge, MA: Harvard University Press.

Soenens, B., & Byers, W. (2012). The cross-cultural significance of control and autonomy in parent–adolescent relationships. *Journal of Adolescence, 35,* 243–248.

Soenens, B., Vansteenkiste, M., Lens, W., Luyckx, K., Goossens, L., Beyers, W., & Ryan, R. M. (2007). Conceptualizing parental autonomy support: Adolescent perceptions of promotion of independence versus promotion of volitional functioning. *Developmental Psychology, 43,* 633–646.

Solomon, J., & George, C. (2008). The measurement of attachment security and related constructs in infancy and early childhood. In J. Cassidy & P. R. Shaver (Eds.), *Handbook of attachment: Theory, research, and clinical applications* (2nd ed., pp. 383–416). New York, NY: Guilford Press.

Soltis, J. (2004). The signal functions of early infant crying. *Behavioral and Brain Sciences, 27,* 443–490.

Sorce, J., & Emde, R. (1981). Mother's presence is not enough: Effect of emotional availability on infant exploration. *Developmental Psychology, 17,* 737–745.

Southgate, C., Senju, A., & Csibra, G. (2007). Action anticipation through attribution of false belief in two-year-olds. *Psychological Science, 18,* 587–592.

Spencer, M. B. (2008). Phenomenological and ecological systems theory: Development of diverse groups. In W. Damon & R. M. Lerner (Eds.), *Child and adolescent development: An advanced course* (pp.

696–740). Hoboken, NJ: John Wiley & Sons.

Spencer, M. B., & Markstrom-Adams, C. (1990). Identity processes among racial and ethnic minority children in America. *Child Development, 61,* 290–310.

Spieker, S. J., & Booth, C. L. (1988). Maternal antecedents of attachment quality. In J. Belsky & T. Nezworski (Eds.), *Clinical implications of attachment* (pp. 95–135). Hillsdale, NJ: Erlbaum.

Spiker, D., & Ricks, M. (1984). Visual self-recognition in autistic children: Developmental relationships. *Child Development, 55,* 214–225.

Spitz, R. (1957). *No and yes.* New York, NY: International Universities Press.

Sroufe, L. A. (1979). Socioemotional development. In J. Osofsky (Ed.), *Handbook of infant development* (pp. 462–516). New York, NY: Wiley.

Sroufe, L. A. (1983). Infant–caregiver attachment and patterns of adaptation in preschool: The roots of maladaptation and competence. In M. Perlmutter (Eds.), *Minnesota Symposium on Child Psychology* (Vol. 16, pp. 41–81). Hillsdale, NJ: Erlbaum.

Sroufe, L. A. (1988). The role of infant–caregiver attachment in development. In J. Belsky & T. Nezworski (Eds.), *Clinical implications of attachment* (pp. 18–38). Hillsdale, NJ: Erlbaum.

Sroufe, L. A. (1996). *Emotional development: The organization of emotional life in the early years.* Cambridge: Cambridge University Press.

Sroufe, L. A. (1997). Psychopathology as an outcome of development. *Development and Psychopathology, 9,* 251–268.

Sroufe, L. A. (2000). Early relationships and the development of children. *Infant Mental Health Journal, 21,* 67–74.

Sroufe, L. A. (2003). Attachment categories as reflections of multiple dimensions: Comment on Fraley and Spieker (2003). *Developmental Psychology, 39,* 413–416.

Sroufe, L. A. (2005). Attachment and development: A prospective longitudinal study from birth to adulthood. *Attachment & Human Development, 7,* 349–367.

Sroufe, L. A., Carlson, E. A., & Shulman, S. (1993). Individuals in relationships: Development from infancy through adolescence. In D. C. Funder, R. D. Parke, C.

Tomlinson-Keasey, & K. Widaman (Eds.), *Studying lives through time* (pp. 315–342). Washington, DC: American Psychological Association.

Sroufe, L. A., Egeland, B., & Carlson, E. A. (1999). One social world: The integrated development of parent–child and peer relationships. In W. A. Collins & B. Laursen (Eds.), *Minnesota Symposia on Child Psychology: Vol. 30. Relationships in developmental contexts: Festschrift in honor of William W. Hartup* (pp. 241–261). Mahwah, NJ: Erlbaum.

Sroufe, L. A., Egeland, B., Carlson, E. A., & Collins, W. A. (2005a). *The development of the person: The Minnesota study of risk and adaptation from birth to adulthood.* New York, NY: Guilford Press.

Sroufe, L. A., Egeland, B., Carlson, E. A., & Collins, W. A. (2005b). Placing early attachment experiences in developmental context. In K. E. Grossman, K. Grossman, & E. Waters (Eds.), *Attachment from infancy to adulthood: The major longitudinal studies* (pp. 48–70). New York, NY: Guilford Press.

Sroufe, L. A., Egeland, B., & Kreutzer, T. (1990). The fate of early experience following developmental change: Longitudinal approaches to individual adaptation in childhood. *Child Development, 61,* 1363–1373.

Sroufe, L. A., & Fleeson, J. (1986). Attachment and the construction of relationships. In W. W. Hartup & Z. Rubin (Eds.), *Relationships and development* (pp. 51–71). Hillsdale, NJ: Erlbaum.

Sroufe, L. A., & Rutter, M. (1984). The domain of developmental psychopathology. *Child Development, 55,* 17–29.

Sroufe, L. A., Schork, E., Motti, F., Lawroski, N., & LaFreniere, P. (1984). The role of affect in social competence. In C. Izard, J. Kagan, & R. Zajonc (Eds.), *Emotions, cognition, and behavior* (pp. 289–319). Cambridge: Cambridge University Press.

Sroufe, L. A., & Waters, E. (1977). Attachment as an organizational construct. *Child Development, 48,* 1184–1199.

Stams, G. J. M., Deković, M., Brugman, D., Rutten, E. A., Van den Wittenboer, G. L. H., Tavecchio, L. W. C., ... Van Schijndel, M. (2008). The relationship of punishment- and victim-based moral orientation to prosocial, externalizing, and norm trespassing behavior in delinquent and nondelinquent adolescents: A validation study of the Moral Orientation Measure. *Journal of Experimental Criminology, 4,* 41–60.

Stams, G.-J. J. M., Juffer, F., & van IJzendoorn, M. H. (2002). Maternal sensitivity, infant attachment, and temperament in early childhood predict adjustment in middle childhood: The case of adopted children and their biologically unrelated parents. *Developmental Psychology, 38,* 806–821.

Stättin, H., & Kerr, M. (2000). Parental monitoring: A reinterpretation. *Child Development, 71,* 1072–1085.

Stättin, H., & Magnusson, D. (1990). *Paths through life, Vol. 2. Pubertal maturation in female development.* Hillsdale, NJ: Lawrence Erlbaum.

Stauffacher, K., & DeHart, G. B. (2006). Crossing social contexts: Relational aggression between siblings and friends during early and middle childhood. *Journal of Applied Developmental Psychology, 27,* 228–240.

Steele, H., & Steele, M. (1998). Attachment and psychoanalysis: Time for a reunion. *Social Development, 7,* 92–119.

Steele, H., & Steele, M. (2005). The construct of coherence as an indicator of attachment security in middle childhood: The Friends and Family Interview. In K. Kerns & R. A. Richardson (Eds.), *Attachment in middle childhood* (pp. 137–160). New York, NY: Guilford Press.

Steele, H., Steele, M., & Fonagy, P. (1996). Associations among attachment classifications of mothers, fathers, and their infants. *Child Development, 67,* 541–555.

Steele, M., Murphy, A., & Steele, H. (2010). Identifying therapeutic action in an attachment-centered intervention with high risk families. *Clinical Social Work, 38,* 61–72.

Stein, M. B., Koverola, C., Hanna, C., Torchia, M. G., & McClarty, B. (1997). Hippocampal volume in women victimized by childhood sexual abuse. *Psychological Medicine, 27,* 951–959.

Steinberg, L. (1990). Autonomy, conflict and harmony in the family relationship. In S. S. Feldman & G. R. Elliott (Eds.), *At the threshold: The developing adolescent* (pp. 255–276). Cambridge, MA: Harvard University Press.

Steinberg, L. (2001). We know some things: Adolescent–parent relationships in retrospect and prospect. *Journal of Research on Adolescence, 11,* 1–19.

Steinberg, L. (2005a). *Adolescence.* New York, NY: McGraw Hill.

Steinberg, L. (2005b). Cognitive and affective development in adolescence. *Trends in Cognitive Sciences, 9,* 69–74.

Steinberg, L., & Monahan, K. C. (2007). Age differences in resistance to peer influence. *Developmental Psychology, 43,* 1531–1543.

Steinberg, L., & Morris, A. S. (2001). Adolescent development. *Annual Review of Psychology, 52,* 83–110.

Steinberg, L., & Scott, E. S. (2003). Less guilty by reason of adolescence: Developmental immaturity, diminished responsibility, and the juvenile death penalty. *American Psychologist, 58,* 1009–1018.

Steinberg, L., & Sheffield Morris, A. (2001). Adolescent development. *Annual Review of Psychology, 52,* 83–101.

Steinberg, L., & Silk, J. (2002). Parenting adolescents. In M. Bornstein (Ed.), *Handbook of parenting: Vol. 1. Children and parenting* (2nd ed., pp. 103–133). Mahwah, NJ: Erlbaum.

Steinberg, L. A., Dahl, R., Keating, D., Kupfer, D., Masten, A., & Pine, D. (2006). The study of developmental psychopathology in adolescence: Integrating affective neuroscience with the study of context. In D. Cicchetti & D. J. Cohen (Eds.), *Developmental psychopathology: Vol. 2. Developmental neuroscience* (2nd ed., pp. 710–741). Hoboken, NJ: Wiley.

Steklis, H. D., & Kling, A. (1985). Neurobiology of affiliative behavior in nonhuman primates. In M. Reite & T. Field (Eds.), *The psychobiology of attachment and separation* (pp. 93–134). Orlando, FL: Academic Press.

Stephen, J., Fraser, E., & Marcia, J. E. (1992). Moratorium-achievement (Mama) cycles in lifespan identity development: Value orientations and reasoning system correlates. *Journal of Adolescence, 15,* 283–300.

Stepp, L. S. (2007). *Unhooked: How young women pursue sex, delay love and lose at both.* New York, NY: Riverhead Books.

Stern, D. N. (1971). A microanalysis of the mother–infant interaction. *Journal of the American Academy of Child Psychiatry, 10,* 501–507.

Stern, D. N. (1985). *The interpersonal world of the infant.* New York, NY: Basic Books.

Stern, D. N. (1995). *The motherhood constellation.* New York, NY: Basic Books.

Stern, D. N., Hofer, L., Haft, W., & Dore, J. (1985). Affect attunement: The sharing of feeling states between mother and infant by means of inter-modal fluency. In T. Field & N. Fox (Ed.), *Social perception in infants* (pp. 249–268). Norwood, NJ: Ablex.

Stewart, A. (2004). Can knowledge of client birth order bias clinical judgment? *Journal of Counseling & Development, 82,* 167–176.

Stewart, R. B., & Marvin, R. S. (1984). Sibling relations: The role of conceptual perspective-taking in the ontogeny of sibling caregiving. *Child Development, 55,* 1322–1332.

Stewart, R. B., Mobley, L. A., Van Tuyl, S. S., & Salvador, M. A. (1987). The firstborn's adjustment to the birth of a sibling: A longitudinal assessment. *Child Development, 58,* 341–355.

Stipek, D. (1995). The development of pride and shame in toddlers. In J. P. Tangney & K. W. Fischer (Eds.), *Self-conscious emotions* (pp. 237–252). New York, NY: Guilford Press.

Stipek, D., Gralinski, J. H., & Kopp, C. B. (1990). Self-concept development in the toddler years. *Developmental Psychology, 26,* 972–977.

Stipek, D., & Mac Iver, D. (1989). Developmental change in children's assessment of intellectual competence. *Child Development, 60,* 521–538.

Stipek, D., Recchia, S., & McClintic, S. (1992). Self-evaluation in young children. *Monographs of the Society for Research in Child Development, 57*(Serial No. 226).

Stocker, C. M. (1994). Children's perceptions of relationships with siblings, friends, and mothers: Compensatory processes and links with adjustment. *Journal of Child Psychology and Psychiatry, 35,* 1447–1459.

Stocker, C. M., Burwell, R. A., & Briggs, M. L. (2002). Sibling conflict in middle childhood predicts children's adjustment in early adolescence. *Journal of Family Psychology, 16,* 50–57.

Stocker, C. M., & Dunn, J. (1990). Sibling relationships in childhood: Links with friendships and peer relationships. *British Journal of Developmental Psychology, 8,* 227–244.

Stocker, C. M., Dunn, J., & Plomin, R. (1989). Sibling relationships: Links with child temperament, maternal behavior, and family structure. *Child Development, 60,* 715–727.

Stocker, C. M., & McHale, S. M. (1992). The nature and family correlates of preadolescents' perceptions of their sibling relationships. *Journal of Social and Personal Relationships, 9,* 179–195.

Stocker, C. M., & Youngblade, L. (1999). Marital conflict and parent hostility: Links with children's sibling and peer relationships. *Journal of Family Psychology, 13,* 598–609.

Stolz, H. E., Barber, B. K., & Olsen, J. A. (2005). Toward disentangling fathering and mothering: An assessment of relative importance. *Journal of Marriage and Family, 67,* 1076–1092.

Storey, A. E., Walsh, C. J., Quinton, R. L., & Wynne-Edwards, K. E. (2000). Hormonal correlates of paternal responsiveness in new and expectant fathers. *Evolution and Human Behavior, 21,* 79–95.

Stormshak, E. A., Bellanti, C. J., & Bierman, K. L. (1996). The quality of sibling relationships and the development of social competence and behavioral control in aggressive children. *Developmental Psychology, 32,* 79–89.

Stormshak, E. A., Bullock, B. M., & Falkenstein, C. A. (2009). Harnessing the power of sibling relationships as a tool for optimizing social-emotional development. In L. Kramer & K. J. Conger (Eds.), *Siblings as agents of socialization. New Directions for Child and Adolescent Development* (Vol. 126, pp. 61–77). San Francisco, CA: Jossey-Bass.

Strathearn, L., Fonagy, P., Amico, J. A., & Montague, P. R. (2009). Adult attachment predicts mother's brain and oxytocin response to infant cues. *Neuropsychopharmacology, 34,* 2655–2666.

Strayer, J. (1987). Affective and cognitive perspectives on empathy. In N. Eisenberg & J. Strayer (Eds.), *Empathy and its development* (pp. 218–244). New York, NY: Cambridge University Press.

Strayer, J., & Roberts, W. (2004). Children's anger, emotional expressiveness, and empathy: Relations with parents' empathy, emotional expressiveness, and parenting practices. *Social Development, 13,* 229–254.

Stright, A. D., Gallagher, K. C., & Kelley, K. (2008). Infant temperament moderates relations between maternal parenting in early childhood and children's adjustment in first grade. *Child Development, 79,* 186–200.

Stuewig, J., & McCloskey, L. A. (2005). The relation of child maltreatment to shame and guilt among adolescents: Psychological routes to depression and delinquency. *Child Maltreatment, 10,* 324–336.

Sturge-Apple, M. L., Davies, P. T., Winter, M. A., Cummings, E. M., & Schermerhorn, A. (2008). Interparental conflict and children's school adjustment: The explanatory role of children's internal representations of interparental and parent–child relationships. *Developmental Psychology, 44,* 1678–1690.

Sturgess, W., Dunn, J., & Davies, L. (2001). Young children's perceptions of their relationships with family members: Links with family setting, friendships, and adjustment. *International Journal of Behavioral Development, 25,* 521–529.

Sullivan, H. S. (1953). *The interpersonal theory of psychiatry.* New York, NY: Norton.

Sullivan, M. W., Bennett, D. S., Carpenter, K., & Lewis, M. (2008). Emotion knowledge in young neglected children. *Child Maltreatment, 13,* 301–306.

Sulloway, F. J. (1996). *Born to rebel: Birth order, family dynamics, and creative lives.* New York, NY: Pantheon.

Suomi, S. J. (2008). Attachment in rhesus monkeys. In J. Cassidy & P. R. Shaver (Eds.), *Handbook of attachment: Theory, research, and clinical application* (2nd ed., pp. 173–191). New York, NY: Guilford Press.

Susman, E. J., & Dorn, L. D. (2009). Puberty: Its role in development. In R. M. Lerner & L. Steinberg (Eds.), *Handbook of adolescent psychology* (3rd ed., pp. 116–151). New York, NY: Wiley.

Sutton-Smith, B. (1982). Birth order and sibling status effects. In M. E. Lamb & B. Sutton-Smith, B. (Eds.), *Sibling relationships: Their* nature and significance across the life span (pp. 153–165). Hillsdale, NJ: Erlbaum.

Swain, J. E., Lorberbaum, J. P., Kose, S., & Strathearn, L. (2007). Brain basis of early parent–infant interactions: Psychology, physiology, and *in vivo* functional neuroimaging studies. *Journal of Child Psychology and Psychiatry, 48,* 262–287.

Swann, W. B., Jr., Chang-Schneider, C., & McClarty, K. (2007). Do our self-views matter?: Self-concept and self-esteem in everyday life. *American Psychologist, 62,* 84–94.

Syed, M., & Juan, M. J. D. (2012). Birds of an ethnic feather? Ethnic identity homophily among college-age friends. *Journal of Adolescence, 35,* 1505–1514.

Syed, M., & Seiffge-Krenke, I. (2013). Personality development from adolescence to emerging adulthood: Linking trajectories of ego development to the family context and identity formation. *Journal of Personality and Social Psychology, 104,* 371–384.

Szasz, P. L., Szentagotai, A., & Hoffman, S. G. (2011). The effect of emotion regulation strategies on anger. *Behavior Research and Therapy, 49,* 114–119.

Tamis-LeMonda, C. S., Way, N., Hughes, D., Yoshikawa, H., Kahana-Kalman, R., & Niwa, E. (2008). Parents' goals for children: The dynamic coexistence of individualism and collectivism in cultures and individuals. *Social Development, 17,* 183–209.

Tancredy, C. M., & Fraley, R. C. (2006). The nature of adult twin relationships: An attachment-theoretical perspective. *Journal of Personality and Social Psychology, 90,* 78–93.

Tangney, J. P. (1991). Moral affect: The good, the bad, and the ugly. *Journal of Personality and Social Psychology, 61,* 598–607.

Tangney, J. P. (1994). The mixed legacy of the superego: Adaptive and maladaptive aspects of shame and guilt. In J. M. Masling & R. F. Bornstein (Eds.), *Empirical perspectives on object relations theory* (pp. 1–28). Washington, DC: American Psychological Association.

Tangney, J. P. (1995). Shame and guilt in interpersonal relationships. In J. P. Tangney & K. W. Fischer (Eds.), *Self-conscious emotions: The psychology of shame, guilt, embarrassment, and pride* (pp. 114–139). New York, NY: Guilford Press.

Tangney, J. P., Burggraf, S. A., & Wagner, P. E. (1995). Shame-proneness, guilt-proneness, and psychological symptoms. In J. P. Tangney & K. Fischer (Eds.), *Self-conscious emotions: The psychology of shame, guilt, embarrassment, and pride* (pp. 343–367). New York, NY: Guilford Press.

Tangney, J. P., & Dearing, R. L. (2002). *Shame and guilt.* New York, NY: Guilford Press.

Tangney, J. P., Stuewig, J., & Mashek, D. J. (2007). Moral emotions and moral behavior. *Annual Review of Psychology, 58,* 345–372.

Tangney, J. P., Wagner, P., Fletcher, C., & Gramzow, R. (1992). Shamed into anger? The relation of shame and guilt to anger and self-reported aggression. *Journal of Personality and Social Psychology, 62,* 669–675.

Tangney, J. P., Wagner, P. E., Hill-Barlow, D., Marschall, D. E., & Gramzow, R. (1996). Relation of shame and guilt to constructive versus destructive responses to anger across the lifespan. *Journal of Personality and Social Psychology, 70,* 797–809.

Tanner, J. L. (2006). Recentering during emerging adulthood: A critical turning point in life span human development. In J. J. Arnett & J. L. Tanner (Eds.), *Emerging adults in America: Coming of age in the 21st century* (pp. 21–55). Washington, DC: American Psychological Association.

Target, M., Fonagy, P., & Shmueli-Goetz, Y. (2003). Attachment representations in school-age children: The development of the Child Attachment Interview (CAI). *Journal of Child Psychotherapy, 29,* 171–186.

Target, M., Fonagy, P., Shmueli-Goetz, Y., Datta, A., & Schneider, T. (1999). *The child attachment interview (CAI) protocol* (6th ed.). Unpublished manuscript, University College London, London, England.

Taylor, R. (2001). *Minority families in the United States: A multicultural perspective* (3rd ed.). Upper Saddle River, NJ: Prentice Hall.

Tesch, S. A., & Whitbourne, S. K. (1982). Intimacy and identity status in young adults. *Journal of Personality and Social Psychology, 43,* 1041–1051.

Teti, D., & Ablard, K. E. (1989). Security of attachment and infant–sibling relationships: A laboratory study. *Child Development, 60,* 1519–1528.

Teubert, D., & Pinquart, M. (2010). The association between coparenting and child adjustment: A meta-analysis. *Parenting: Science and Practice, 10*, 286–307.

Theran, S. A. (2009). Predictors of level of voice in adolescent girls: Ethnicity, attachment, and gender role socialization. *Journal of Youth and Adolescence, 38*, 1027–1037.

Theran, S. A. (2010). Authenticity with authority figures and peers: Girls' friendships, self-esteem, and depressive symptomatology. *Journal of Social and Personal Relationships, 27*, 519–534.

Theran, S. A., & Han, S. C. (2013). Authenticity as a mediator of the relation between child maltreatment and negative outcomes for college women. *Journal of Aggression, Maltreatment, & Trauma, 22*, 1096–1116.

Theran, S. A., Levendosky, A. A., Bogat, G., & Huth-Bocks, A. C. (2005). Stability and change in mothers' internal representations of their infants over time. *Attachment & Human Development, 7*, 253–268.

Thomas, A., & Chess, S. (1977). *Temperament and development*. New York, NY: Brunner/Mazel.

Thomas, A., & Chess, S. (1986). The New York Longitudinal Study: From infancy to early adult life. In R. Plomin & J. Dunn (Eds.), *The study of temperament: Changes, continuities, and challenges* (pp. 39–52). Hillsdale, NJ: Erlbaum.

Thomas, A., Chess, S., Birch, H. G., Hertzig, M. E., & Korn, S. (1963). *Behavioral individuality in early childhood*. New York: New York University Press.

Thompson, R. A. (1987). Empathy and emotional understanding: The early development of empathy. In N. Eisenberg & J. Strayer (Eds.), *Empathy and its development* (pp. 119–143). New York, NY: Cambridge University Press.

Thompson, R. A. (1990). Emotion and self-regulation. *Nebraska Symposium on Motivation, 1988: Socioemotional development. Current theory and research in motivation* (Vol. 36, pp. 383–483). Lincoln, NE: University of Nebraska Press.

Thompson, R. A. (1994). Emotion regulation: A theme in search of definition. In N. A. Fox (Ed.), The development of emotion regulation: Biological and behavioral considerations. *Monographs of the Society for Research in Child Development, 59*(2–3, Serial No. 240), 25–52.

Thompson, R. A. (1998). Early sociopersonality development. In W. Damon (Series Ed.) & N. Eisenberg (Vol. Ed.), *Handbook of child psychology: Vol. 3. Social, emotional, and personality development* (5th ed., pp. 25–104). New York, NY: Wiley.

Thompson, R. A. (2005). Multiple relationships multiply considerably. *Human Development, 48*, 102–107.

Thompson, R. A. (2006). The development of the person: Social understanding, relationships, self, conscience. In W. Damon & R. M. Lerner (Series Eds.) & N. Eisenberg (Vol. Ed.), *Handbook of child psychology: Vol. 3. Social, emotional, and personality development* (6th ed., pp. 24–98). Hoboken, NJ: Wiley.

Thompson, R. A. (2008). Early attachment and later development: Familiar questions, new answers. In J. Cassidy & P. R. Shaver (Eds.), *Handbook of attachment: Theory, research, and clinical applications* (2nd ed., pp. 348–365). New York, NY: Guilford Press.

Thompson, R. A. (2014). Socialization of emotion and emotion regulation in the family. In J. J. Gross (Ed.), *Handbook of emotion regulation* (2nd ed., pp. 173–186). New York, NY: Guilford Press.

Thompson, R. A., Easterbrooks, M. A., & Padilla-Walker, L. (2003). Social and emotional development in infancy. In R. Lerner, M. A. Easterbrooks, & J. Mistry (Eds.), *Handbook of psychology: Vol. 6. Developmental psychology* (pp. 91–112). Hoboken, NJ: Wiley.

Thompson, R. A., Flood, M. F., & Goodvin, R. (2006). Social support and developmental psychopathology. In D. Cicchetti & D. Cohen (Eds.), *Developmental psychopathology. Vol. III: Risk, disorder, and adaptation* (2nd ed., pp. 1–37). New York, NY: Wiley.

Thompson, R. A., & Goodman, M. (2010). Development of emotion regulation: More than meets the eye. In A. Kring & D. Sloan (Eds.), *Emotion regulation and psychopathology* (pp. 38–58). New York, NY: Guilford Press.

Thompson, R. A., & Lagattuta, K. (2006). Feeling and understanding: Early emotional development. In K. McCartney &

D. Phillips (Eds.), *The Blackwell handbook of early childhood development* (pp. 317–337). Oxford: Blackwell.

Thompson, R. A., & Lamb, M. E. (1983). Individual differences in dimensions of socioemotional development in infancy. In R. Plutchik & H. Kellerman (Eds.), *Emotion: Theory, research, and experience: Vol. 2. Emotions in early development* (pp. 87–114). New York, NY: Academic Press.

Thompson, R. A., & Limber, S. (1990). "Social anxiety" in infancy: Stranger wariness and separation distress. In H. Leitenberg (Ed.), *Handbook of social and evaluation anxiety* (pp. 85–137). New York, NY: Plenum.

Thompson, R. A., & Meyer, S. (2007). The socialization of emotion regulation in the family. In J. J. Gross (Ed.), *Handbook of emotion regulation* (pp. 249–268). New York, NY: Guilford Press.

Thompson, R. A., Meyer, S., & McGinley, M. (2006). Understanding values in relationship: The development of conscience. In M. Killen & J. G. Smetana (Eds.), *Handbook of moral development* (pp. 267–297). Mahwah, NJ: Erlbaum.

Thompson, R. A., & Raikes, H. A. (2003). Toward the next quarter-century: Conceptual and methodological challenges for attachment theory. *Development and Psychopathology, 15,* 691–718.

Thompson, R. A., Virmani, E. A., Waters, S. F., Raikes, H. A., & Meyer, S. (2013). The development of emotion self-regulation: The whole and the sum of the parts. In K. C. Barrett, N. A. Fox, G. A. Morgan, D. J., Fidler, & L. A. Daunhauer (Eds.), *Handbook of self-regulatory processes in development: New directions and international perspectives* (pp. 5–26). New York, NY: Psychology Press.

Thompson, R. A., Winer, A. C., & Goodvin, R. (2011). The individual child: Temperament, emotion, self, and personality. In M. E. Lamb & M. H. Bornstein (Eds.), *Social and personality development: An advanced textbook* (pp. 217–258). New York, NY: Psychology Press.

Thompson, V. D. (1974). Family size: Implicit policies and assumed psychological outcomes. *Journal of Social Issues, 30,* 93–124.

Tibbetts, S. G. (1997). Shame and rational choice in offending decisions. *Criminal Justice and Behavior, 24,* 234–255.

Tibbetts, S. G. (2003). Self-conscious emotions and criminal offending. *Psychological Reports, 93,* 101–126.

Tisak, M. S., & Turiel, E. (1984). Children's conceptions of moral and prudential rules. *Child Development, 55,* 1030–1039.

Tolman, D. L., Impett, E. A., Tracy, A. J., & Michael, A. (2006). Looking good, sounding good: Femininity ideology and adolescent girls' mental health. *Psychology of Women Quarterly, 30,* 85–95.

Tomarken, A. J., & Keener, A. D. (1998). Frontal brain asymmetry and depression: A self-regulatory perspective. *Cognition and Emotion, 12,* 387–420.

Tomasello, M., & Rakoczy, H. (2003). What makes human cognition unique? From individual to shared to collective intentionality. *Mind and Language, 18,* 121–147.

Tomkins, S. (1963). *Affect, imagery, consciousness: Vol. 2. The negative affects.* New York, NY: Springer.

Tompkins, T. L., Hockett, A. R., Abraibesh, N., & Witt, J. L. (2011). A closer look at co-rumination: Gender, coping, peer functioning and internalizing/externalizing problems. *Journal of Adolescence, 34,* 801–811.

Toscano, J. E., Bauman, M. D., Mason, W. A., & Amaral, D. G. (2009). Interest in infants by female rhesus monkeys with neonatal lesions of the amygdala or hippocampus. *Neuroscience, 162,* 881–891.

Toth, S. L., Cicchetti, D., Macfie, J., & Emde, R. N. (1997). Representations of self and others in the narratives of neglected, physically abused, and sexually abused preschoolers. *Development and Psychopathology, 9,* 781–796.

Tracy, J. L., & Robins, R. W. (2004). Show your pride: Evidence for a discrete emotion expression. *Psychological Science, 15,* 194–197.

Tracy, J. L., Robins, R. W., & Tangney, J. P. (Eds.). (2007). *The self-conscious emotions: Theory and research.* New York, NY: Guilford Press.

Travis, R., & Kohli, V. (1995). The birth order factor: Ordinal position, social strata, and educational achievement. *Journal of Social Psychology, 135,* 499–507.

Treboux, D., Crowell, J. A., Owens, G., & Pan, H. S. (1994, February). *Attachment behaviors and working models: Relations to best friendship and romantic relationships.* Paper presented at the Society for Research on Adolescence, San Diego, CA.

Tremblay, R. E., Vitaro, F., Gagnon, C., Piche, C., & Royer, N. (1992). A prosocial scale for the preschool behavior questionnaire: Concurrent and predictive correlates. *International Journal of Behavioral Development, 15,* 227–245.

Trentacosta, C. J., & Izard, C. E. (2007). Kindergarten children's emotion competence as a predictor of their academic competence in first grade. *Emotion, 7,* 77–88.

Trentacosta, C. J., & Shaw, D. S. (2009). Emotional self-regulation, peer rejection, and antisocial behavior: Developmental associations from early childhood to early adolescence. *Journal of Applied Developmental Psychology, 30,* 356–365.

Trevarthen, C. (1979). Communication and cooperation in early infancy: A description of primary intersubjectivity. In M. Bullowa (Ed.), *Before speech* (pp. 321–347). Cambridge: Cambridge University Press.

Trevarthen, C., & Aitken, K. J. (2001). Infant intersubjectivity: Research, theory, and clinical applications. *Journal of Child Psychology and Psychiatry and Allied Disciplines, 42,* 3–48.

Trommsdorff, G. (2005). Parent–child relations over the life-span: A cross-cultural perspective. In K. H. Rubin & O. B. Chung (Eds.), *Parenting beliefs, behaviors, and parent–child relations: A cross-cultural perspective* (pp. 143–183). New York, NY: Psychology Press.

Tronick, E. Z. (1989). Emotions and emotional communication in infants. *American Psychologist, 44,* 112–119.

Tronick, E. Z. (2007). *The neurobehavioral and social-emotional development of infants and children.* New York, NY: Norton.

Tronick, E. Z., & Brazelton, T. B. (1980). Preverbal communication between mothers and infants. In D. R. Olson (Ed.), *The social foundations of language and thought* (pp. 299–315). New York, NY: Norton.

Troy, M., & Sroufe, L. A. (1987). Victimization among preschoolers: The role of attachment relationship history. *Journal of the American Academy of Child Psychiatry, 26,* 166–172.

Trzesniewski, K. H., Donnellan, M. B., Moffitt, T. E., Robins, R. W., Poulton, R., & Caspi, A. (2006). Low self-esteem during adolescence predicts poor health, criminal behavior, and limited economic prospects during adulthood. *Developmental Psychology, 42,* 381–390.

Trzesniewski, K. H., Donnellan, M. B., & Robins, R. W. (2008). Do today's young people really think they are so extraordinary?: An examination of secular trends in narcissism and self-enhancement. *Psychological Science, 19,* 181–188.

Trzesniewski, K. H., Kinal, M. P., & Donnellan, M. B. (2010). Self-enhancement and self-protection in a developmental context. In M. D. Alicke & C. Sedikides (Eds.), *Handbook of self-enhancement and self-protection* (pp. 341–357). New York, NY: Guilford Press.

Tschann, J. M., Kaiser, P., Chesney, M. A., Alkon, A., & Boyce, W. T. (1996). Resilience and vulnerability among preschool children: Family functioning, temperament, and behavior problems. *Journal of the American Academy of Child and Adolescent Psychiatry, 35,* 184–192.

Tsoory, M. M., Vouimba, R. M., Akirav, I., Kavushansky, A., Avital, A., & Richter-Levin, G. (2008). Amygdala modulation of memory-related processes in the hippocampus: Potential relevance to PTSD. *Progress in Brain Research, 167,* 35–49.

Tucker, C. J., McHale, S. M., & Crouter, A. C. (2001). Conditions of sibling support in adolescence. *Journal of Family Psychology, 15,* 254–271.

Tucker, C. J., Updegraff, K., & Baril, M. E. (2010). Who's the boss? Patterns of control in adolescents' sibling relationships. *Family Relations, 59,* 520–532.

Tucker, C. J., Updegraff, K. A., McHale, S. M., & Crouter, A. C. (1999). Older siblings as socializers of younger siblings' empathy. *Journal of Early Adolescence, 19,* 176–198.

Tucker, D. M., Luu, P., & Derryberry, D. (2005). Love hurts: The evolution of empathic concern through the encephalization of nociceptive capacity. *Development and Psychopathology, 17,* 699–713.

Turiel, E. (1983). *The development of social knowledge: Morality and convention.* Cambridge: Cambridge University Press.

Turiel, E. (1998). The development of morality. In W. Damon (Series Ed.) & N. Eisenberg (Vol. Ed.), *Handbook of child psychology: Vol. 3. Social, emotional, and personality development* (5th ed., pp. 863–932). New York, NY: Wiley.

Turiel, E. (2002). *The culture of morality.* New York, NY: Cambridge University Press.

Turiel, E. (2006). The development of morality. In W. Damon & R. M. Lerner (Series Ed.) & N. Eisenberg (Vol. Ed.), *Handbook of child psychology: Vol. 3. Social, emotional, and personality development* (6th ed., pp. 789–857). Hoboken, NJ: Wiley.

Turiel, E. (2008). The development of morality. In W. Damon & R. M. Lerner (Eds.), *Child and adolescent development: An advanced course* (pp. 473–514). New York, NY: John Wiley & Sons, Inc.

Turiel, E., Killen, M., & Helwig, C. C. (1997). Morality: Its structure, functions, and vagaries. In J. Kagan & S. Lamb (Eds.), *The emergence of morality in young children* (pp. 155–244). Chicago, IL: University of Chicago Press.

Turiel, E., & Wainryb, C. (1998). Concepts of freedoms and rights in a traditional, hierarchically organized society. *British Journal of Developmental Psychology, 16,* 375–395.

Turiel, E., & Wainryb, C. (2000). Social life in cultures: Judgments, conflict, and subversion. *Child Development, 71,* 250–256.

Turkheimer, E., & Waldron, M. (2000). Nonshared environment: A theoretical, methodological, and quantitative review. *Psychological Bulletin, 126,* 78–108.

Turkle, S. (2012). *Alone together: Why we expect more from technology and less from each other.* New York, NY: Basic Books.

Turner, K. L., & Brown, C. S. (2007). The centrality of gender and ethnic identities across individuals and contexts. *Social Development, 16,* 700–719.

Twenge, J. M. (2006). *Generation me: Why today's young Americans are more confident, assertive, entitled – and more miserable than ever before.* New York, NY: Free Press.

Twenge, J. M., Baumeister, R. F., DeWall, C. N., Ciarocco, N. J., & Bartels, J. M. (2007). Social exclusion decreases prosocial behavior. *Journal of Personality and Social Psychology, 92,* 56–66.

Uddin, L. Q., Kaplan, J. T., Molnar-Szakacs, I., Zaidel, E., & Iacoboni, M. (2005). Self-face recognition activates a frontoparietal 'mirror' network in the right hemisphere: An event-related fMRI study. *NeuroImage, 25,* 926–935.

Umaña-Taylor, A. J. (2004). Ethnic identity and self-esteem: Examining the role of social context. *Journal of Adolescence, 27,* 139–146.

Umaña-Taylor, A. J., & Guimond, A. B. (2010). A longitudinal examination of parenting behaviors and perceived discrimination predicting Latino adolescents' ethnic identity. *Developmental Psychology, 46,* 636–650.

Umaña-Taylor, A. J., Quintana, S. M., Lee, R. M., Cross Jr., W. E., Rivas-Drake, D., Schwartz, S. J., ... Seaton, E., and the Ethnic and Racial Identity in the 21st Century Study Group. (2014). Ethnic and racial identity during adolescence and into young adulthood: An integrated conceptualization. *Child Development, 85,* 21–39.

Ungerer, J. A., Dolby, R., Brent, W., Barnett, B., Kelk, N., & Lewin, V. (1990). The early development of empathy: Self-regulation and individual differences in the first year. *Motivation and Emotion, 14,* 93–106.

Updegraff, K. A., McHale, S. M., Whiteman, S. D., Thayer, S. M., & Delgado, M. Y. (2005). Adolescent sibling relationships in Mexican American families: Exploring the role of familism. *Journal of Family Psychology, 19,* 512–522.

Updegraff, K. A., & Obeidallah, D. A. (1999). Young adolescents' patterns of involvement with siblings and friends. *Social Development, 8,* 52–69.

Vaish, A., Carpenter, M., & Tomasello, M. (2009). Sympathy through affective perspective-taking and its relation to prosocial behavior in toddlers. *Developmental Psychology, 45,* 534–543.

Vaish, A., & Warneken, F. (2012). Social-cognitive contributors to young children's empathic and prosocial behavior. In J. Decety (Ed.), *Empathy – From bench to bedside* (pp. 131–146). Cambridge, MA: The MIT Press.

Valiente, C., & Eisenberg, N. (2006). Parenting and children's adjustment: The role of children's emotion regulation. In D. K. Snyder, J. A. Simpson, & J. N. Hughes (Eds.), *Emotion regulation in couples and families:*

Pathways to dysfunction and health (pp. 123–142). Washington, DC: American Psychological Association.

Valiente, C., Eisenberg, N., Smith, C. L., Reiser, M., Fabes, R. A., Losoya, S., ... Murphy, B. C. (2003). The relations of effortful control and reactive control to children's externalizing problems: A longitudinal assessment. *Journal of Personality, 71,* 1171–1196.

van Aken, M. A. G., & Asendorpf, J. B. (1997). Support by parents, classmates, friends, and siblings in preadolescence: Covariation and compensation across relationships. *Journal of Social and Personal Relationships, 14,* 79–93.

Vandell, D. L. (2000). Parents, peer groups, and other socializing influences. *Developmental Psychology, 36,* 699–710.

Vandell, D. L., & Bailey, M. D. (1992). Conflicts between siblings. In C. U. Shantz & W. W. Hartup (Eds.), *Conflict in child and adolescent development* (pp. 242–269). Cambridge: Cambridge University Press.

Vandell, D. L., Minnett, A., & Santrock, J. W. (1987). Age differences in sibling relationships during middle childhood. *Journal of Applied Developmental Psychology, 8,* 247–257.

van der Mark, I. L., van IJzendoorn, M. H., & Bakermans-Kranenburg, M. J. (2002). Development of empathy in girls during the second year of life: Associations with parenting, attachment, and temperament. *Social Development, 11,* 451–468.

van Hoof, A. (1999). The identity status approach: In need of fundamental revision and qualitative change. *Developmental Review, 19,* 622–647.

van IJzendoorn, M. H. (1995). Adult attachment representations, parental responsiveness, and infant attachment: A meta-analysis of the predictive validity of the Adult Attachment Interview. *Psychological Bulletin, 117,* 387–403.

van IJzendoorn, M. H. (1997). Attachment, emergent morality, and aggression: Toward a developmental socioemotional model of antisocial behavior. *International Journal of Behavioral Development, 21,* 703–727.

van IJzendoorn, M. H., & Bakermans-Kranenburg, M. J. (1996). Attachment representations in mothers, fathers, adolescents and clinical groups: A meta-analytic search for normative data. *Journal of Clinical and Consulting Psychology, 64,* 8–21.

van IJzendoorn, M. H., & Bakermans-Kranenburg, M. J. (2010). Stretched until it snaps: Attachment and close relationships. *Child Development Perspectives, 4,* 109–111.

van IJzendoorn, M. H., & Bakermans-Kranenburg, M. J. (2012). Integrating temperament and attachment: The differential susceptibility paradigm. In M. Zentner & R. L. Shiner (Eds.), *Handbook of temperament* (pp. 403–424). New York, NY: Guilford Press.

van IJzendoorn, M. H., & de Wolff, M. S. (1997). In search of the absent father – Meta-analyses of infant–father attachment: A rejoinder to our discussion. *Child Development, 68,* 604–609.

van IJzendoorn, M. H., Moran, G., Belsky, J., Pederson, D., Bakermans-Kranenburg, M. J., & Kneppers, K. (2000). This similarity of siblings' attachments to their mothers. *Child Development, 71,* 1086–1098.

van IJzendoorn, M. H., Sagi, A., & Lambermon, M. W. E. (1992). The multiple caregiver paradox: Data from Holland and Israel. In R. C. Pianta (Ed.), *New directions for child development: Beyond the parent: The role of other adults in children's lives* (Vol. 57, pp. 5–24). San Francisco, CA: Jossey-Bass.

van IJzendoorn, M. H., & Sagi-Schwartz, A. (2008). Cross-cultural patterns of attachment: Universal and contextual dimensions. In J. Cassidy, & P. R. Shaver (Eds.), *Handbook of attachment: Theory, research, and clinical applications* (2nd ed., pp. 880–905). New York, NY: Guilford Press.

van IJzendoorn, M. H., Schuengel, C., & Bakermans-Kranenburg, M. J. (1999). Disorganized attachment in early childhood: Meta-analysis of precursors, concomitants, and sequelae. *Development and Psychopathology, 11,* 225–249.

van IJzendoorn, M. H., Vereijken, C. M. J. L., Bakermans-Kranenburg, M. J., & Riksen-Walraven, J. M. (2004). Assessing attachment security with the attachment Q sort: Meta-analytic evidence for the validity of the observer AQS. *Child Development, 75,* 1188–1213.

Vaughn, B. E., Bost, K. K., & van IJzendoorn, M. H. (2008). Attachment and temperament: Additive and interactive influences on behavior, affect, and cognition during infancy and childhood. In J. Cassidy & P. R. Shaver (Eds.), *Handbook of attachment: Theory, research, and clinical application* (2nd ed., pp. 192–216). New York, NY: Guilford Press.

Vaughn, B. E., Kopp, C. B., & Krakow, J. B. (1984). The emergence and consolidation of self-control from eighteen to thirty months of age: Normative trends and individual differences. *Child Development, 55,* 990–1004.

Veenhoven, R., & Verkuyten, M. (1989). The well-being of only children. *Adolescence, 24,* 155–166.

Verduyn, P., Delvaux, E., Van Coillie, H., Tuerlinckx, F., & Van Mechelen, I. (2009). Predicting the duration of emotional experience: Two experience sampling studies. *Emotion, 9,* 83–91.

Verissimo, F., Santos, A. J., Vaughn, B. E., Torres, N., Monteiro, L., & Santos, O. (2011). Quality of attachment to father and mother and number of reciprocal friends. *Early Child Development and Care, 181,* 27–38.

Verschueren, K., Buyck, P., & Marcoen, A. (2001). Self-representations and socioemotional competence in young children: A 3-year longitudinal study. *Developmental Psychology, 37,* 126–134.

Verschueren, K., & Marcoen, A. (1999). Representation of self and socio-emotional competence in kindergartners: Differential and combined effects of attachment to mother and to father. *Child Development, 70,* 183–201.

Verschueren, K., & Marcoen, A. (2002). Perceptions of self and relationship with parents in aggressive and nonaggressive rejected children. *Journal of School Psychology, 40,* 501–522.

Verschueren, K., & Marcoen, A. (2005). Perceived security of attachment to mother and father: Developmental differences and relations to self-worth and peer relationships at school. In K. A. Kerns & R. A. Richardson (Eds.), *Attachment in middle childhood* (pp. 212–230). New York, NY: Guilford Press.

Verschueren, K., Marcoen, A., & Schoefs, V. (1996). The internal working model of the self, attachment, and competence in five-year-olds. *Child Development, 67,* 2493–2511.

Vinik, J., Almas, A. N., & Grusec, J. E. (2011). Mothers' knowledge of what distresses and what comforts their children predicts children's coping, empathy, and prosocial behavior. *Parenting: Science and Practice, 11,* 56–71.

Vitaro, F., Boivin, M., & Bukowski, W. M. (2009). The role of friendship in child and adolescent psychosocial development. In K. Rubin, W. M. Bukowski, & B. Laursen (Eds.), *Handbook of peer interactions, relationships, and groups* (pp. 568–588). New York, NY: Guilford Press.

Vitaro, F., Brendgen, M., & Wanner, B. (2005). Patterns of affiliation with delinquent friends during late childhood and early adolescence: Correlates and consequences. *Social Development, 14,* 82–108.

Vitaro, F., Tremblay, R. E., & Bukowski, W. M. (2001). Friends, friendships, and conduct disorders. In J. Hill & B. Maughan (Eds.), *Conduct disorder in childhood* (pp. 346–378). Cambridge: Cambridge University Press.

Vogt Yuan, A. S. (2009). Sibling relationships and adolescents' mental health: The interrelationship of structure and quality. *Journal of Family Issues, 30,* 1221–1244.

Volbrecht, M. M., Lemery-Chalfant, K., Aksan, N., Zahn-Waxler, C., & Goldsmith, H. H. (2007). Examining the familial link between positive affect and empathy development in the second year. *The Journal of Genetic Psychology, 168,* 105–129.

Volling, B. L. (2001). Early attachment relationships as predictors of preschool children's emotion regulation with a distressed sibling. *Early Education and Development, 12,* 185–207.

Volling, B. L. (2003). Sibling relationships. In M. H. Bornstein, L. Davidson, C. L. M. Keyes, & K. A. Moore (Eds.), *Well-being: Positive development across the life course* (pp. 205–220). Mahwah, NJ: Erlbaum.

Volling, B. L. (2005). The transition to siblinghood: A developmental ecological systems perspective and directions for future research. *Journal of Family Psychology, 19,* 542–549.

Volling, B. L., & Belsky, J. (1992a). Infant, father, and marital antecedents of infant–father attachment security in dual-earner and single-earner families. *Journal of Behavioral Development, 15,* 83–100.

Volling, B. L., & Belsky, J. (1992b). The contribution of mother–child and father–child relationships to the quality of sibling interaction: A longitudinal study. *Child Development, 63,* 1209–1222.

Volling, B. L., Blandon, A. Y., & Gorvine, B. J. (2006). Maternal and paternal gentle guidance and young children's compliance from a within-family perspective. *Journal of Family Psychology, 20,* 514–524.

Volling, B. L., Kennedy, D. E., & Jackey, L. M. H. (2013). The development of sibling jealousy. In M. Legerstee & S. Hart (Eds.), *Handbook of jealousy: Theory, research, and multidisciplinary approaches* (pp. 387–417). Malden, MA: Blackwell Publishers.

Volling, B. L., McElwain, N. L., & Miller, A. L. (2002). Emotion regulation in context: The jealousy complex between young siblings and its relation with child and family characteristics. *Child Development, 73,* 581–600.

Volling, B. L., McElwain, N. L., Notaro, P., & Herrera, C. (2002). Parents' emotional availability and infant emotional competence: Predictors of parent–infant attachment and emerging self-regulation. *Journal of Family Psychology, 16,* 447–465.

Volling, B. L., Youngblade, L. M., & Belsky, J. (1997). Young children's social relationships with siblings and friends. *American Journal of Orthopsychiatry, 67,* 102–111.

Völlm, B. A., Taylor, A. N. W., Richardson, P., Corcoran, R., Stirling, J., McKie, S., ... Elliott, R. (2006). Neuronal correlates of theory of mind and empathy: A functional magnetic resonance imaging study in a nonverbal task. *NeuroImage, 29,* 90–98.

Voorpostel, M., & Blieszner, R. (2008). Intergenerational solidarity and support between adult siblings. *Journal of Marriage and Family, 70,* 157–167.

Vreeswijk, C. M., Mass, A. J., Rijk, C. H., Braeken, J., & van Bakel, H. J. (2014). Stability of fathers' representations of their infants during the transition to parenthood. *Attachment & Human Development, 16,* 292–306.

Vygotsky, L. (1978). *Mind in society: The development of higher mental processes.* Cambridge, MA: Harvard University Press.

Wainryb, C. (2006). Moral development in culture: Diversity, tolerance, and justice. In M. Killen & J. G. Smetana (Eds.), *Handbook of moral development* (pp. 211–240). Mahwah, NJ: Erlbaum.

Walden, T. A., & Ogan, T. A. (1988). The development of social referencing. *Child Development, 59,* 1230–1240.

Walker, L. J., Hennig, K. H., & Krettenauer, T. (2000). Parent and peer contexts for children's moral reasoning development. *Child Development, 71,* 1033–1048.

Waller, E. M., & Rose, A. J. (2013). Brief report: Adolescents' co-rumination with mothers, co-rumination with friends, and internalizing symptoms. *Journal of Adolescence, 36,* 429–433.

Wallin, D. (2007). *Attachment in psychotherapy.* New York, NY: Guilford Press.

Wallis, P., & Steele, H. (2001). Attachment representations in adolescence: Further evidence from psychiatric residential settings. *Attachment & Human Development, 3,* 259–268.

Ward, M. J., & Carlson, E. (1995). Associations among adult attachment representations, maternal sensitivity, and infant–mother attachment in a sample of adolescent mothers. *Child Development, 66,* 69–79.

Ward, M. J., Vaughn, B. E., & Robb, M. D. (1988). Socio-emotional adaptation and infant–mother attachment in siblings: Role of the mother in cross-sibling consistency. *Child Development, 59,* 643–651.

Warneken, F. (2013). Young children proactively remedy unnoticed accidents. *Cognition, 126,* 101–108.

Warneken, F. (2015). Precocious prosociality: Why do young children help? *Child Development Perspectives, 9,* 1–6.

Warneken, F., Chen, F., & Tomasello, M. (2006). Cooperative activities in young children and chimpanzees. *Child Development, 77,* 640–663.

Warneken, F., & Tomasello, M. (2007). Helping and cooperation at 14 months of age. *Infancy, 11,* 271–294.

Warr, M. (2005). Making delinquent friends: Adult supervision and children's affiliations. *Criminology, 43,* 77–106.

Warren, H. K., & Stifter, C. A. (2008). Maternal emotion-related socialization and preschoolers' developing emotion self-awareness. *Social Development, 17,* 239–258.

Waterman, A. S. (1982). Identity development from adolescence to adulthood: An extension of theory and a review of research. *Developmental Psychology, 18,* 341–358.

Waterman, A. S. (1984). *The psychology of individualism.* New York, NY: Praeger.

Waterman, A. S. (1989). Curricula interventions for identity change: Substantive and ethical considerations. *Journal of Adolescence, 28,* 397–409.

Waterman, A. S. (1999). Identity, the identity statuses, and identity status development: A contemporary statement. *Developmental Review, 19,* 591–621.

Waters, E. (1978). The reliability and stability of individual differences in infant–mother attachment. *Child Development, 49,* 483–494.

Waters, E. (1995). Appendix A: The Attachment Q-Set (Version 3.0). *Monographs of the Society for Research in Child Development, 60*(2–3), 234–246.

Waters, E., & Cummings, E. M. (2000). A secure base from which to explore close relationships. *Child Development, 71,* 164–172.

Waters, E., Hamilton, C. E., & Weinfield, N. S. (2000). The stability of attachment security from infancy to adolescence and early adulthood: General introduction. *Child Development, 71,* 678–683.

Waters, E., Merrick, S., Treboux, D., Crowell, J., & Albersheim, L. (2000). Attachment security in infancy and early adulthood: A twenty-year longitudinal study. *Child Development, 71,* 684–689.

Waters, E., Weinfield, N. S., & Hamilton, C. E. (2000). The stability of attachment security from infancy to adolescence and early adulthood: General discussion. *Child Development, 71,* 703–706.

Waters, E., Wippman, J., & Sroufe, L. A. (1979). Attachment, positive affect, and competence in the peer group: Two studies in construct validation. *Child Development, 50,* 821–829.

Waters, H. S., Rodrigues, L. M., & Ridgeway, D. (1998). Cognitive underpinnings of narrative attachment assessment. *Journal of Experimental Child Psychology, 71,* 211–234.

Waters, H. S., & Waters, E. (2006). The attachment working models concept: Among other things, we build script-like representations of secure base experiences. *Attachment & Human Development, 8,* 185–198.

Watson, M. (1990). Aspects of self-development reflected in children's role playing. In D. Cicchetti & M. Beeghly (Eds.), *The self in transition: Infancy to childhood* (pp. 123–144). Hillsdale, NJ: Erlbaum.

Watt, H. M. G. (2004). Development of adolescents' self-perceptions, values, and task perceptions according to gender and domain in 7th through 11th grade Australian students. *Child Development, 75,* 1556–1574.

Weaver, I. C. G., Cervoni, N., Champagne, F. A., D'Alessio, A. C., Sharma, S., Seckl, J. R., … Meaney, M. J. (2004). Epigenetic programming by maternal behavior. *Nature Neuroscience, 7,* 847–854.

Weeks, T. L., & Pasupathi, M. (2010). Autonomy, identity, and narrative construction with parents and friends. In K. C. McLean & M. Pasupathi (Eds.), *Narrative development in adolescence: Creating the storied self* (pp. 65–91). New York, NY: Springer Science & Business Media.

Wegner, D. (1980). The self in prosocial action. In D. Wagner & R. Vallacher (Eds.), *The self in social psychology* (pp. 131–157). New York, NY: Oxford University Press.

Weimer, B. L., Kerns, K. A., & Oldenburg, C. M. (2004). Adolescents' interactions with a best friend: Associations with attachment style. *Journal of Experimental Child Psychology, 88,* 102–120.

Weinberg, A., & Klonsky, E. D. (2009). Measurement of emotion dysregulation in adolescents. *Psychological Assessment, 21,* 616–621.

Weinfield, N. S., Sroufe, L. A., & Egeland, B. (2000). Attachment from infancy to early adulthood in a high-risk sample: Continuity, discontinuity, and their correlates. *Child Development, 71,* 695–702.

Weinfield, N. S., Sroufe, L. A., Egeland, B., & Carlson, E. (2008). Individual differences in infant–caregiver attachment. In J. Cassidy & P. R. Shaver (Eds.), *Handbook of attachment: Theory, research, and clinical applications* (2nd ed., pp. 78–101). New York, NY: Guilford Press.

Weinfield, N. S., Whaley, G. J. L., & Egeland, B. (2004). Continuity, discontinuity, and coherence in attachment from infancy to late adolescence: Sequelae of organization and disorganization. *Attachment & Human Development, 6*, 73–97.

Weisner, T. S. (1993). Overview: Sibling similarity and difference in different cultures. In C. W. Nuckolls (Ed.), *Siblings in South Asia* (pp. 1–18). New York, NY: Guilford Press.

Weisner, T. S. (2011). Culture. In M. K. Underwood & L. H. Rosen (Eds.), *Social development: Relationships in infancy, childhood, and adolescence* (pp. 372–399). New York, NY: Guilford Press.

Weiss, R. S. (1986). Continuities and transformation in social relationships from childhood to adolescence. In W. W. Hartup & Z. Rubin (Eds.), *Relationships and development* (pp. 95–110). Hillsdale, NJ: Erlbaum.

Welch-Ross, M. K. (1995). An integrative model of the development of autobiographical memory. *Developmental Review, 15*, 338–365.

Welch-Ross, M. K., Fasig, L. G., & Farrar, M. J. (1999). Predictors of preschoolers' self-knowledge: Reference to emotion and mental states in mother–child conversation about past events. *Cognitive Development, 14*, 401–422.

Wellman, H. M. (1991). From desires to beliefs: Acquisition of a theory of mind. In A. Whiten (Ed.), *Natural theories of mind: Evolution, development and simulation of everyday mindreading* (pp. 19–38). Cambridge, MA: Blackwell.

Wellman, H. M. (2002). Understanding the psychological world: Developing a theory of mind. In U. Goswami (Ed.), *Blackwell handbook of childhood cognitive development* (pp. 167–187). Oxford: Blackwell.

Wellman, H. M., Cross, D., & Watson, J. (2001). Meta-analysis of theory-of-mind development: The truth about false belief. *Child Development, 72*, 655–684.

Wellman, H. M., & Lui, D. (2004). Scaling of theory-of-mind tasks. *Child Development, 75*, 523–541.

Wentzel, K. R. (2003). Sociometric status and adjustment in middle school: A longitudinal study. *Journal of Early Adolescence, 23*, 5–28.

Wentzel, K. R., Barry, C. M., & Caldwell, K. A. (2004). Friendships in middle childhood: Influences on motivation and school adjustment. *Journal of Educational Psychology, 96*, 195–203.

Westphal, M., Seivert, N. H., & Bonanno, G. A. (2010). Expressive flexibility. *Emotion, 10*, 92–100.

Wheeler, M. A., Stuss, D. T., & Tulving, E. (1997). Toward a theory of episodic memory: The frontal lobes and autonoetic consciousness. *Psychological Bulletin, 121*, 331–354.

Whiteman, S. D., Becerra, J. M., & Killoren, S. (2009). Mechanisms of sibling socialization in normative family development. In L. Kramer & K. J. Conger (Eds.), *Siblings as agents of socialization* (Vol. 126, pp. 29–43). *New Directions for Child and Adolescent Development.* San Francisco, CA: Jossey-Bass.

Whiteman, S. D., Bernard, J. M., & McHale, S. M. (2010). The nature and correlates of sibling influence in two-parent African American families. *Journal of Marriage and Family, 72*, 267–281.

Whiteman, S. D., & Christiansen, A. (2008). Processes of sibling influence in adolescence: Individual and family correlates. *Family Relations, 57*, 24–34.

Whiteman, S. D., McHale, S. M., & Crouter, A. C. (2007). Competing processes of sibling influence: Observational learning and sibling deidentification. *Social Development, 16*, 642–661.

Whiteman, S. D., McHale, S. M., & Crouter, A. C. (2011). Family relationships from adolescence to early adulthood: Changes in the family system following firstborns' leaving home. *Journal of Research on Adolescence, 21*, 461–474.

Whiteman, S. D., McHale, S. M., & Soli, A. (2011). Theoretical perspectives on sibling relationships. *Journal of Family Theory & Review, 3*, 124–139.

Whittle, S., Yap, M. B. H., Yücel, M., Fornito, A., Simmons, J. G., Barrett, A., … Allen, N. B. (2008). Prefrontal and amygdala volumes are related to adolescents' affective behaviors during parent–adolescent interactions. *Proceedings of the National Academy of Sciences, 105*, 3652–3657.

Wiesenfeld, A. R., & Klorman, R. (1978). The mother's psychophysiological reactions to contrasting expressions by her own and unfamiliar infant. *Developmental Psychology, 14,* 294–304.

Wiesner, M., & Ittel, A. (2002). Relations of pubertal timing and depressive symptoms to substance use in early adolescence. *Journal of Early Adolescence, 22,* 5–23.

Wigfield, A., & Eccles, J. S. (1994). Children's competence beliefs, achievement values, and general self-esteem: Change across elementary and middle school. *Journal of Early Adolescence, 14,* 107–138.

Wigfield, A., Eccles, J. S., MacIver, D., Reuman, D. A., & Midgley, C. (1991). Transitions during early adolescence: Changes in children's domain-specific self-perceptions and general self-esteem across the transition to junior high school. *Developmental Psychology, 27,* 522–565.

Wigfield, A., Eccles, J. S., Schiefele, U., Roeser, R. W., & Davis-Kean, P. (2006). Development of achievement motivation. In W. Damon & R. M. Lerner (Eds.), *Handbook of child psychology. Vol. 3: Social, emotional, and personality development* (6th ed., pp. 933–1002). New York, NY: Wiley.

Wiik, K. L., & Gunnar, M. R. (2009). Development and social regulation of stress neurobiology in human development: Implications for the study of traumatic memories. In J. A. Quas & R. Fivush (Eds.), *Emotion and memory in development: Biological, cognitive, and social considerations* (pp. 256–277). New York, NY: Oxford University Press.

Wiley, R. E., & Berman, S. L. (2012). The relationships among caregiver and adolescent identity status, identity distress and psychological adjustment. *Journal of Adolescence, 35,* 1203–1213.

Wilson, B., & Gottman, J. (1996). Attention – The shuttle between emotion and cognition: Risk, resiliency, and physiological bases. In E. Hetherington & E. Blechman (Eds.), *Stress, coping and resiliency in children and families* (pp. 189–228). Mahwah, NJ: Erlbaum.

Winnicott, D. W. (1965/1996). *The maturational processes and the facilitating environment: Studies in the theory of emotional development.* New York, NY: International Universities Press.

Woien, S. L., Ernst, H. A. H., Patock-Peckham, J. A., & Nagoshi, C. T. (2003). Validation of the TOSCA to measure shame and guilt.

Personality and Individual Differences, 35, 313–326.

Wojslawowicz, J. C., Rubin, K. H., Burgess, K. B., Booth-LaForce, C., & Rose-Krasnor, L. (2006). Behavioral characteristics associated with stable and fluid best friendship patterns in middle childhood. *Merrill-Palmer Quarterly, 52,* 671–693.

Wölfer, R., Cortina, K. S., & Baumert, J. (2012). Embeddedness and empathy: How the social network shapes adolescents' social understanding. *Journal of Adolescence, 35,* 1295–1305.

Woltering, S., & Lewis, M. D. (2009). Developmental pathways of emotion regulation in childhood: A neuropsychological perspective. *Mind, Brian, and Education, 3,* 160–169.

Woodward, A. L. (2003). Infants' developing understanding of the link between looker and object. *Developmental Science, 6,* 297–311.

Woodward, L. J., & Fergusson, D. M. (1999). Childhood peer relationship problems and psychosocial adjustment in late adolescence. *Journal of Abnormal Child Psychology, 27,* 87–104.

Yap, M. B. H., Allen, N. B., & Ladouceur, C. D. (2008). Maternal socialization of positive affect: The impact of invalidation on adolescent emotion regulation and depressive symptomatology. *Child Development, 79,* 1415–1431.

Yates, M., & Youniss, J. (1996). Community service and political-moral identity in adolescents. *Journal of Research on Adolescence, 6,* 271–284.

Yau, J., & Smetana, J. (2003). Adolescent–parent conflict in Hong Kong and Shenzhen: A comparison of youth in two cultural contexts. *International Journal of Behavioral Development, 27,* 201–211.

Yeh, H. C., & Lempers, J. D. (2004). Perceived sibling relationships and adolescent development. *Journal of Youth and Adolescence, 33,* 133–147.

Ying, Y.-W., & Lee, P. A. (1999). The development of ethnic identity in Asian-American adolescents: Status and outcome. *American Journal of Orthopsychiatry, 69,* 194–208.

Young, L., Camprodon, J. A., Hauser, M., Pascual-Leone, A., & Saxe, R. (2010). Disruption of the right temporoparietal junction with transcranial magnetic stimulation reduces the role of beliefs in moral judgments. *Proceedings of the National Academy of Sciences, 107,* 6753–6758.

Young, L., & Dungan, J. (2012). Where in the brain is morality? Everywhere and maybe nowhere. *Social Neuroscience, 7,* 1–10.

Young, S. K., Fox, N. A., & Zahn-Waxler, C. (1999). The relations between temperament and empathy in 2-year-olds. *Developmental Psychology, 35,* 1185–1197.

Youngblade, L., & Belsky, J. (1992). Parent–child antecedents of five-year-olds' close friendships: A longitudinal analysis. *Developmental Psychology, 28,* 700–713.

Youniss, J. (1980). *Parents and peers in social development: A Sullivan-Piaget perspective.* Chicago, IL: University of Chicago Press.

Youniss, J., & Smoller, J. (1985). *Adolescent relations with mothers, fathers, and friends.* Chicago, IL: University of Chicago Press.

Zadeh, Z. Y., Jenkins, J., & Pepler, D. (2010). A transactional analysis of maternal negativity and child externalizing behavior. *International Journal of Behavioral Development, 34,* 218–228.

Zaff, J. F., Moore, K. A., Papillo, A. R., & Williams, S. (2003). Implications of extracurricular activity participation during adolescence on positive outcomes. *Journal of Adolescent Research, 18,* 599–630.

Zahn-Waxler, C. (1991). The case for empathy: A developmental review. *Psychological Inquiry, 2,* 155–158.

Zahn-Waxler, C. (2000). The development of empathy, guilt, and internalization of distress: Implications for gender differences in internalizing and externalizing problems. In R. J. Davidson (Ed.), *Anxiety, depression, and emotion* (pp. 222–265). New York, NY: Oxford University Press.

Zahn-Waxler, C., Cole, P. M., Welsh, J. D., & Fox, N. A. (1995). Psychophysiological correlates of empathy and prosocial behaviors in preschool children with behavior problems. *Development and Psychopathology, 7,* 27–48.

Zahn-Waxler, C., & Kochanska, G. (1990). The origins of guilt. In R. A. Thompson (Ed.), *Nebraska symposium on motivation: Vol. 36. Socioemotional development* (pp. 182–258). Lincoln: University of Nebraska Press.

Zahn-Waxler, C., Kochanska, G., Krupnick, J., & McKnew, D. (1990). Patterns of guilt in children of depressed and well mothers. *Developmental Psychology, 26,* 51–59.

Zahn-Waxler, C., & Radke-Yarrow, M. (1990). The origins of empathic concern. *Motivation and Emotion, 14,* 107–130.

Zahn-Waxler, C., Radke-Yarrow, M., Wagner, E., & Chapman, M. (1992). Development of concern for others. *Developmental Psychology, 28,* 126–136.

Zahn-Waxler, C., Robinson, J. L., & Emde, R. N. (1992). The development of empathy in twins. *Developmental Psychology, 28,* 1038–1047.

Zahn-Waxler, C., Schiro, K., Robinson, J. L., Emde, R. N., & Schmitz, S. (2001). Empathy and prosocial patterns in young MZ and DZ twins: Development and genetic and environmental influences. In R. N. Emde & J. K. Hewitt (Eds.), *Infancy to early childhood* (pp. 141–162). New York, NY: Oxford University Press.

Zaki, J., & Ochsner, K. N. (2012). The neuroscience of empathy: Progress, pitfalls and promise. *Nature Neuroscience, 15,* 675–680.

Zelazo, P. D., Helwig, C. C., & Lau, A. (1996). Intention, act, and outcome in behavioral prediction and moral judgment. *Child Development, 67,* 2478–2492.

Zeman, J., Cassano, M., & Adrian, M. C. (2013). Socialization influences on children's and adolescents' emotional self-regulation processes: A developmental psychopathology perspective. In K. C. Barrett, N. A. Fox, G. A. Morgan, D. J., Fidler, & L. A. Daunhauer (Eds.), *Handbook of self-regulatory processes in development: New directions and international perspectives* (pp. 79–106). New York, NY: Psychology Press.

Zentner, M., & Shiner, R. L. (Eds.). (2012). *Handbook of temperament.* New York, NY: Guilford Press.

Zhou, Q., Eisenberg, M., Losoya, S. H., Fabes, R. A., Reiser, M., Guthrie, I. K., … Shepard, S. A. (2002). The relations of parental warmth and positive expressiveness to children's empathy-related responding and social functioning: A longitudinal study. *Child Development, 73,* 893–915.

Zimmer-Gembeck, M. J., & Petherick, J. (2006). Intimacy dating goals and relationship satisfaction during adolescence and emerging adulthood: Identity formation, age and sex as moderators. *International Journal of Behavioral Development, 30,* 167–177.

Zimmer-Gembeck, M. J., Siebenbruner, J., & Collins, W. A. (2001). Diverse aspects of dating: Associations with psychosocial functioning from early to middle adolescence. *Journal of Adolescence, 24,* 1–24.

Zimmermann, P. (1999). Structure and functions of internal working models of attachment and their role for emotional regulation. *Attachment & Human Development, 1,* 291–206.

Zimmermann, P. (2004). Attachment representations and characteristics of friendship relations during adolescence. *Journal of Experimental Child Psychology, 88,* 83–101.

Zimmermann, P., & Becker-Stoll, F. (2002). Stability of attachment representations during adolescence: The influence of ego-identity status. *Journal of Adolescence, 25,* 107–124.

Zimmermann, P., Fremmer-Bombik, E., Spangler, G., & Grossman, K. E. (1997). Attachment in adolescence: A longitudinal perspective. In W. Koops, J. B. Hoeksma, & D. C. van den Boom (Eds.), *Development of interaction and attachment: Traditional and non-traditional approaches* (pp. 281–291). Amsterdam: North-Holland.

Zukow, P. G. (Ed.). (1989). *Sibling interaction across cultures: Theoretical and methodological issues.* New York, NY: Springer-Verlag.

Zukow-Goldring, P. (2002). Sibling caregiving. In M. H. Bornstein (Ed.), *Handbook of parenting: Vol. 3. Being and becoming a parent* (pp. 253–286). Mahwah, NJ: Erlbaum.

Index

A

abuse
  attachment security and, 268
  developing self, 114–115
  emotional understanding and, 84
  emotion regulation and, 95
  friendship quality, effect on, 183
  guilt, resulting from, 219
  insecure-disorganized attachment and, 18
  internal representations of self and, 288
  memory formation, effect on, 51
  moral development, effect on, 219
  self-esteem, effect on, 294
  shame, resulting from, 219, 328–329
acceptance, peer, 175–178, 246
  and friendships, 249
  prosocial behavior and, 178
active inhibition, 233
adjusting, as emotion regulation strategy, 321
adjustment, 43
  in adolescence, 241–245, 289–290
  emotional regulation and, 93
  friendships and, 163, 182–183, 249–250, 271
  and identity formation, 297–301
  parent-child relationships and, 69, 158
  social competence and, 81
adolescence
  and attachment
    classifying, 265–266
    security, 267–270, 283, 315–317
    styles of, 241
    transferring, 261
  attachment relationships in, 253–254, 257, 273–274
    hierarchy of, 260–262
    measuring, 262–267
    quality of, 269
  autonomy during, 240–242, 279–284
  competencies' impact on, 258–260
  defining, 237–239
  development during, 223, 233–234, 279–284

emotional support in, 254
emotion regulation in, 92, 319–322
emotions in, 318–319, 327–328
empathy in, 324–326
and ethnic identity, 307–309
exploration in, 258
friendships during, 253, 273–274
identity formation during, 278–279, 296–297, 298
neuroscience of, 238–239
parent-adolescent relationships, 240–244, 257–258
peer pressures in, 283
peer relationships in, 245–248
puberty and, 311
reflective function in, 260
romantic relationships during, 255–257
secure-base behaviors in, 241
self concept, stability of, 287
self-esteem and, 291
self-regulation in, 281
self-understanding and, 258–259
sense of self in, 278–279
sexuality during, 255–257, 312–313
sibling relationships in, 128–129, 132–133
social world in, 252–257
stages of, 237–238
  and autonomy support, 282–283
  early, 237
  and friendships, 252
  later, 237
  middle, 237
transition to adulthood, 279, 329–330
adolescents. see also parent-adolescent relationships
  attachment relationships, 236–237
    and emotion regulation, 275–276
    and exploration, 273–274
    framework for, 259
    hierarchies of, 261–262
    and internal working models, 275–276
    romantic, 261–262, 271
  attachments
    characteristics of, 253–254

compensating for insecure, 274
    and emotional functioning, 270–273
    self-reporting, 262–264
    social functioning and, 270–273
and authenticity, 317–318
challenging authority, 240
college, impact of, 271
confidence over time, 287
conflicts with parents, 239–240
decision-making, 255
developing empathy, 197
emotional development in, 75
emotional displays by, 240
family and, 239–242
friendships, 248–252
    compensating with, 274
    conflict in, 250–251
    and empathy, 251–252
    and gender, 250, 252
    goals for, 251
    and identity, 249–250
    online, 247–248
    vs. parent-adolescent relationships,
        252–253
    quality of, 251–252
    reciprocity in, 248
    vs. sibling relationships, 155
    stability of, 170–171
    types of, 250
    understanding of, 174–175
gender roles and, 312–313
intimacy and, 251, 253, 259
monitoring, 241–242
moral emotions in, 220–221
prosocial behavior in, 209
self-description by, 110, 286–288
self-disclosure and, 317–318
self-reflection in, 286–288
sibling relationships and, 120, 122–124,
    149
social media and, 247–248
social world, elements of, 254
temperament in, 67, 69, 244
therapy for, 55
adrenocortical activation, 76
Adult Attachment Interview, 120, 263,
    264–266, 276
Adult Attachment Q-Set, 266
adulthood, 329–330
    "emerging", 237–238
    and self-concept, 285
    sibling relationships in, 129–130
    therapy in, and attachment theory, 55

transition to, 279
affective reactions, 8, 20
agency, sense of, 103–105
age spacing in siblings, 140
aggression
    attachment security and, 185
    choosing friendships and, 173–174
    empathy and, 212, 324
    insecure attachment relationships and, 272
    peer relationships and, 177–178, 326
    in preschoolers, 168
    and self-concept problems, 287–288
    in siblings, 122–123
    social media and, 248
Ainsworth, Mary Salter, 16–18, 19–23, 35–37,
    263
altruistic behavior, 202
amygdala
    emotions and, 74, 76
    empathy and, 325
    insecure attachment representations and,
        49–51
    maternal attachment and, 12
    prosocial behavior and, 204
    temperament and, 65
androgens, 310–311
anger, 198
antisocial behavior
    empathy and, 200, 212
    friendships and, 173
    peer rejection and, 95, 177
    self-regulation and, 230
    sibling relationships and, 133, 153
anxiety
    in adolescence, 241, 253–254
    only children and, 158
    parental restrictiveness and, 231
    shame and, 217
attachment
    in adolescence, 253–254, 268–269,
        270–273
    anxiety, 263
    avoidance, 263
    brain regions linked to, 47–48, 50
    classifying, 264, 265–266
    clinical approaches to, 54–55
    competence and, 30–32
    continuity, 267–270
    delegating functions of, 262
    development, 19–23
    differential treatment and, 145–146
    discontinuity, 268–270
    evolutionary function of, 5–6

attachment (*continued*)
  exploration and, 8
  "goodness of fit", 24, 60
  hierarchy of, 44
  identity development and, 302–308
  internal working models and, 29, 41
  memory and, 50–51
  neurobiological basis for, 11–13
  preparation for, 8–9, 10–11
  psychophysiological approaches to, 47–49
  research, areas of focus, 53–54
  in siblings, 118–120, 130, 151–152
  stages of development, 13–16
    attachment, 15
    discriminating sociability, 14–15
    goal-corrected partnership, 15
    indiscriminate social responsiveness,
      13–14
  Strange Situation procedure for, 16–17
  stress, as response to, 7–8
  temperament, effect on, 49
attachment categories, 263–265
  cannot classify, 265
  insecure-dismissing, 265
  insecure-preoccupied, 265
  secure-autonomous, 265
  unresolved/disorganized, 265
Attachment Doll Play Assessment, 37
Attachment History Questionnaire, 263
Attachment Q-Set (AQS), 38–39
attachment relationships, 6–7. *see also* specific
    types of attachment relationships
  in adolescence, 236–237, 253–254, 257,
      273–274
  in adolescence, measuring, 262–267
  adolescent framework for, 259–262
  vs. adolescent friendships, 253
  adult, 329–330
  affective reactions in, 8, 20
  developing multiple, 44–47
  developmental outcomes of, 28–32, 52
  in diverse populations, 33–34
  emotional development and, 97–98
  evaluating and describing, 16–19
  friendships as, 167
  insecure anxious-avoidant, 18
  insecure anxious-resistant, 18
  insecure-disorganized, 18
  internal models of self and, 289–290
  mentalization and, 322–323
  neuroscience of, 47–51
  nonmaternal child care, effects of, 41–43
  in non-U.S. cultures, 34–35
  and origins of prosocial behavior, 208

  romantic relationships and, 257
  secure, 17
  sense of self and, 56, 113–115, 190–191
  state of mind regarding, 264–265
  and temperament, 23–25
  ways of organizing, 46–47
attachment schemas, 50–51
attachment security
  abuse and, 268
  in adolescents, 270–271
  conflict perceptions and, 276
  continuity through childhood, 267–270
  developmental outcomes and, 31–32
  friendship quality and, 182
  genetic and environmental influences on,
      26–28, 268
  interactional synchrony and, 22
  internal working models and, 36–37, 41,
      290
  "lawful change" in, 40–41
  measuring, 35–39
  paternal behavior and, 22–23
  peer relationships and, 184–185
  prosocial behavior and, 208
  psychopathology and, 271–273
  romantic relationships and, 271
  self-esteem and, 191, 294
  sense of self and, 275
  in siblings, 27–28
  stability of, 267–270
  trauma and, 40, 265
  in twins, 26–28
Attachment Story Completion Task, 37
attachment styles, 241, 266
attachment theory
  adolescent friendships and, 253
  biological basis for, 5
  clinical implications of, 52–55
  early roots of, 3–6
  emphasis on infancy, 32–35
  John Bowlby and, 4–8, 13–16
  and links between parents and peers,
      184–191
  Mary Salter Ainsworth and, 16–19
  personal narratives and, 114
  reflective functioning and, 290
  siblings and, 118–121
  trauma amd, 52
attention, 61, 89–90
attitudinal-pathway model for gender identity,
    309
authenticity, 317–318
authoritarian parents, 243
authoritative parents, 243

authority, adolescent challenges to, 240
autism spectrum disorders, 200, 202
autobiographical memories, 232, 306
autonomic system, 47
autonomous orientation, 222
autonomy
    adolescent, 244, 260
    attachment security and, 290
    brain maturation and, 281–282
    cultural background and, 279–281
    development of, 279–284
    emotional understanding and, 83
    expectations of, 282
    family differences in, 281
    intimacy and, 316
    parent-adolescent relationships and, 273,
        282
    parental support for, 282–283
    and parent development, 281
    peer relationships maintaining, 283
    self-regulation and, 281
    support, 282–283
    in toddlers, 103
    ways of conceptualizing, 280–281

B
babies. *see* infants
balance, in sibling relationships, 134–135
Baumrind, Diana, 243, 245
behavior
    influence of moral emotions, 220–221
    modeling, among siblings, 122–123, 133
    moral *vs.* social, 228
    temperament as predictor of, 70–72
behavioral coping strategies, 91–92
behavior problems
    adolescent monitoring and, 241–242
    friendships and, 172, 181
    identity development and, 304–305
    insecure attachment relationships and,
        272
    and lack of empathy, 212
    peer relationships and, 176–177
    self-regulation and, 230
    shame and, 218
    in siblings, 122–124, 127, 143–144,
        149–150
"best friends", 178–179, 182
biological basis
    for attachment theory, 5
    for emotional reactions, 320
    for emotion regulation, 93–94
    for emotions, 75–77, 78–79
    for gender and sexuality, 310–311
    for temperament, 64–66
biological inheritance
    and development, 3
birth order, 116, 140–141, 282
bossiness, 249
Bowlby, John, 4–6, 188
    attachment theory, 6–8, 28, 44, 288
    and Erikson's model of development, 297
    and internal working models, 29
    reception of his work, 52–53
    stages of attachment, 13–16
brain regions
    for attachment, 10, 47–48, 50
    and emotions, 76, 88–89, 320
    for empathy, 199, 326–327
    mentalization and, 323–324
    and moral reasoning, 204, 225
    in parent-child interactions, 11–13
    for prosocial behavior, 203
    representing self, 306
    and temperament, 63–65
bullying
    and lack of empathy, 206
    in siblings, 123
    social media and, 248

C
California Attachment Program (CAP), 35
cannot classify attachment category, 265
caregivers
    attachment to, 19–23, 97–98
    empathy and, 197–198
    responding to emotion expressiveness, 79
    siblings as, 149
    temperament and, 69
    toddlers wanting to please, 104
Cassidy's Incomplete Stories with Doll Family,
    37
Chess, Stella, 59–60
Child Attachment Interview, 38, 264
child care experiences, and prosocial behavior,
    211
childhood amnesia, 107
children. *see also* adolescents; infants;
        preschoolers; toddlers
    and "best friends", 178
    developing empathy, 197
    differential treatment and, 146
    emotional development of, 75
    emotional understanding in, 81–85
    and emotion regulation, 91–92
    friendless, 181
    friendships among, 167–170, 173–175
    links between parents and peers, 184–191

children (*continued*)
  moral emotions in, 220–221
  peer relationships among, 165–167
  prosocial behavior in, 209
  self-descriptions by, 109–110
  self-esteem and, 111–113
  self-regulation and, 103
  sibling relationships and, 128, 132–133,
    138–139
  temperament in, 67, 69
children, only, 156–160
China's one-child policy, 157
cliques, 170
cognitive coping strategies, 91–92
cognitive development
  identity formation and, 301
  internal models of self and, 290–291
  self-descriptions in, 108–109
  self-esteem and, 296
  and visual self-recognition, 101–102
coherence, 287, 300
cohesiveness, in sibling relationships, 135, 139
college, impact on adolescents, 271
commitment processes, 299, 301–303
"committed compliance", 230
competencies
  attachment and, 30–32
  father-adolescent relationships and, 271
  friendships and, 173–174
  impact on adolescence, 258–260
  in peer relationships, 186, 274–275
  prosocial behavior and, 209–210
  romantic relationships and, 255–256
  sibling relationships and, 121, 128–129,
    135–136, 148–151
concealing, as emotion regulation strategy,
  321
conduct disorders, 206, 212
confidence, in adolescents, 287
conflict
  in friendships, 170, 250–251
  insecure models of self and, 289
  and moral judgments, 225
  parent-adolescent, 239–240, 271
  perceptions of, and attachment security, 276
  sibling, 122–124, 131–133
conscience, 105, 215, 232–235
constructionism, 78
constructive coping, 275
constructs, psychological, 77–78, 112
contagious crying, 194–195
context, for child development, 3
control, and emotion regulation, 87
control phase of self-regulation, 102, 229

conventional morality, 223
conventional wrongdoing, 226
co-parenting, 244
coping, constructive, 275
coping strategies, 91–92, 190
cortical medial structures, 306
cortical midline structures, 306
co-rumination, 315
crying
  attachment development and, 13–14
  contagious, 194–195
  insecure attachment representations and,
    49–51
  role of, in attachment theory, 6
cultural background
  attachment relationships and, 34–35
  and autonomy, 279–282
  for emotional scripts, 85
  emotion display rules and, 82
  in emotion regulation, 91
  empathy and, 327
  friendships and, 192–193
  guilt and, 220
  identity development and, 307–309
  morality and, 224
  only children and, 156
  parenting styles and, 145, 245
  personal narratives and, 106–107
  prosocial behavior and, 207
  and puberty, 311
  sibling relationships and, 148
  temperament and, 70, 72

D
depression
  in adolescents, 92, 241
  attachment security and, 268
  authenticity and, 317
  friendships and, 180–181, 183
  parental, 18, 52
  peer relationships and, 163
  self-concept problems and, 112, 287–288
  self-esteem and, 295–296
  shame and, 217
  temperament and, 71
despair, 4, 8, 298
detachment, 8, 281
development
  adulthood and, 330
  attachment relationships' effect on, 28–32
  and "best friends", 178
  cognitive, and identity formation and, 301
  cognitive, and internal models of self,
    290–291

early attachment experiences and, 267–270
Erikson's stage model for, 297–298
as preparation for identity formation, 297–298
sibling relationships' effects on, 148–151
temperament changes during, 67
"developmental cascade model", 178
developmental contexts, 3
developmental outcomes
of attachment relationships, 52
co-parenting and, 244
differential treatment and, 143–144
emotion regulation and, 93–97, 321
in only children, 159–160
parenting styles and, 243–244
self-regulation and, 94–95
sibling relationships and, 143–144, 150–151, 154–155
temperamental influence on, 70–72
developmental psychology, and prosocial behavior, 206–207
developmental stages, 126–130, 168, 282–283
differential susceptibility, 72
differential treatment, 143–146
discriminating sociability, 14–15
discrimination, and ethnic identity, 308–309
disorganized attachment relationships, 18
display rules, of emotions, 81–83
distractions, 89, 91–92, 94, 96, 149
distress, and development of morality, 215
diverse populations
adolescent sexuality in, 313
attachment relationships in, 33–34
attachment security in, 40–41
guilt in, 220
identity development in, 307–309
nonmaternal child care, effects on, 42–43
only children from, 157
parenting styles in, 245
puberty, onset in, 311
sibling relationships in, 141, 147
dopamine, 10, 65
Dunn, Judy, 130, 137

E

early adolescence, 237
eating disorders, 217
effectance, 14
effortful control, 61, 66, 96, 103
egocentric empathic distress, 196–197
Electra conflict, 213
emerging adulthood. see adulthood
"emotional contagion", 194–195
emotional control, 87

emotional development, 73–75
in adolescence, 318–319
and attachment relationships, 97–98
environmental influences on, 76–77
identity development and, 318–319
managing emotions and, 83
mirroring and, 98
and parent-child relationships, 76–77, 97–99
perspectives on, 75–78
sense of self and, 74–75, 318–319
emotional engagement, as emotion regulation strategy, 321
emotional expressiveness, 78–81, 319
emotional functioning, 270–273
emotionality vs. empathy, 199
emotional reactivity, 87
emotional schemas, 91, 96
emotional scripts, 85
emotional understanding, 83–86
emotion modulation network, 11, 12
emotion regulation, 86–93
abuse and, 95
in adolescence, 92, 319–322
Adult Attachment Interview and, 266
in attachment relationships, 90, 320
adolescent, 275–276
insecure, 272
mediating between, 190
attachment styles and, 266
coping strategies and, 91–92, 96
developmental outcomes from, 93–97, 321
development of, 87
empathy and, 324
exploration and, 90
facilitating, 95–96
gender and, 320
in infants, 88–89
language and, 90–91
measurement strategies for, 93
mentalization and, 322–324
parent-child relationships and, 76–77, 80, 88–92
peer relationships and, 92, 189–190
in preschoolers, 89–90
prosocial behavior and, 204
self-regulation and, 89–90
strategies for, 320–321
adjusting, 321
concealing, 321
emotional engagement, 321
reappraisal, 321
suppression, 321
temperament and, 87, 93–94
in toddlers, 89–90

emotions, 73, 75–78
  adaptive functions of, 96
  in adolescence, 318–319
  biological basis for, 75–76, 320
  causes of, 85
  displaying, in adolescence, 240
  display rules for, 81–83, 93
  empathy and, 194
  health of, 81
  learning from siblings, 148–151
  moral, 214–218, 328–329
  neuroscience of, 76, 78, 320
  perspectives on, 75–78
  as psychological constructs, 77–78
  purpose of, 77
empathy, 74, 196–202
  in adolescence, 251–252, 324–326
  affective components of, 199
  aggression and, 198, 212, 324
  antisocial behaviors and, 200, 212
  and attachment, 198, 232, 324
  autism spectrum disorders and, 200, 202
  behavioral problems and, 212
  cognitive components of, 199
  cultural differences and, 327
  development of, 197–198, 327
  and emotion regulation, 324
  and emotions, 194
  evolutionary theory and, 324
  friendships and, 325–326
  gender and, 199, 327
  guilt and, 216
  identity development and, 324–326
  individual differences in, 197
  lack of, 206, 212–213
  mentalization and, 323–324
  mirror neuron systems and, 200, 324
  and morality, 217–218
  neuroscience of, 199, 324
  pain regulation and, 325
  parent-child relationships and, 197–198,
    210, 231–232, 324
  peer relationships and, 166, 325–326
  perspective taking and, 200–201, 324
  prosocial behavior and, 194–196, 206, 324
  and self-regulation, 196
  self-regulation and, 197, 325
  self-understanding and, 326–329
  shame and, 216, 328
  similarity of emotionality, 199
  "state-matching" responses and, 325
  vs. sympathy, 196
  theory of mind and, 199, 202
  in toddlers, 195

  types of responses, 196–197
    egocentric empathic distress, 196–197
    quasi-egocentric empathic distress, 197
    rudimentary empathic responding, 196
    true empathic distress, 197
empathy disorders, 326–327
environmental influences
  on attachment security, 26–28, 268
  on emotional development, 76–77
  on friendships, 172, 182–183
  prosocial behavior and, 207
  on self-concept, 285
  on self-esteem, 293
  and sibling relationships, 140, 143,
    147–148
  on temperament, 24, 64, 70–71
epigenesis, 297
epinephrine, 65
Erikson, Erik, 279, 303, 315–316
  stage model of development, 297–298
estrogen, 310–311
ethnic identity, 307–309
evolutionary theory
  attachment hierarchies and, 44
  emotions and, 75
  empathy and, 324
  function of attachment behaviors and, 5–6
  prosocial behavior, origins of, 206–207
Experiences in Close Relationships, 38, 263
explicit memory, 50
exploration
  in adolescence, 258
  attachment as base for, 8
  and classifying attachments, 16–19
  and emotion regulation, 90
  and identity development, 302–303
  and secure adolescent attachment, 273–274
  and siblings, 119–120
exploration processes, 299, 301
externalizing behaviors, 30, 70
  friendship quality and, 172, 181
  gender and, 327–328
  and insecure attachment, 271–272, 290
  peer rejection and, 177
  prosocial behavior and, 212
  self-regulation and, 94, 230
  sibling relationships and, 123–124, 143–144
extraversion/surgency, 61

F
Facebook, 247
faces, infant preference for, 8–9
fairness, 144–145, 166, 169, 222, 226
false-belief attributions, 204

"false" self, 292–293
father-child relationships, 11–13, 192
fathers
  attachment preparation, 10–11
  attachment security and, 22–23, 44, 46, 269
  authenticity and, 318
  emotional understanding and, 83
  empathy and, 210
  and greater competencies, 271
  homosexual, 12–13
  personal narratives and, 106–107
fearfulness, 197
feedback, in adolescence, 284–285
"felt security", 273
fluctuating identity, 301
Freud, Sigmund, 213
friendships, 161–163
  abuse, effects on, 183
  during adolescence, 155, 248–253, 273–274
  in adolescent attachment hierarchies, 261
  assessment of, 179–180
  attachment and, 151–152, 182, 185–186
  as attachment relationships, 167
  "best friends", 178, 182
  characteristics of, 179, 248–252
  children's, 167–170, 174–175
  choosing, 173–174, 227
  conflicts in, 170, 250–251
  cultural differences in, 192–193
  developmental outcomes and, 182–183
  developmental stages and, 168
  empathy and, 325–326
  environmental influence on, 182–183
  gender and, 169, 171, 249–250
  and identity development, 304
  individual differences in, 175–178
  infants and, 168
  intimacy and, 314–315
  lack of, 181
  loneliness and, 181, 249
  mediating attachment and adjustment, 274–275
  mediating variables in, 193
  motivations for, 192
  online, 247–248
  parent-child relationships and, 182, 186, 192
  peer relationships and, 168, 177, 246, 248–249
  play, and successful, 169
  popularity and, 248–249
  preschoolers, 168–169
  quality of, 178–183
    poor, effect of, 181

  and prosocial behavior, 172
  and reciprocal nominations, 179
  self-worth and, 180–181, 249
  sibling relationships and, 129, 151–156, 192
  stability in, 170–172
  theory of mind and, 169
  toddlers, 168
functionalist theories of emotions, 77

G

gchat, 247
gender
  adolescent attachments and, 269
  autonomy expectations and, 282
  "best friends" and, 178
  biological influences on, 310–311
  emotional understanding and, 82, 86
  emotion regulation and, 320
  empathy and, 199, 327
  and externalizing behaviors, 327–328
  friendships and, 169, 171, 175, 249, 250, 252
  and guilt, 217
  intimacy and, 314–315
  personal narratives by, 106–107
  perspective taking and, 201
  prosocial behavior and, 205–206
  roles, and adolescence, 312–313
  self-descriptions and, 105, 108
  self-esteem and, 293–294
  siblings and, 116, 140
  temperament and, 72
gender identity, 309–314
  attitudinal-pathway model, 309
  biological underpinnings of, 310–311
  frameworks for understanding, 309
  personal-pathway model, 309
  sexual orientation and, 311–313
gender schematicity, 309
genetics
  attachment security and, 26–28
  prosocial behavior and, 207–208
  self-esteem and, 293
global self-esteem, 291–292
"goodness of fit", 24, 60, 72
guilt, 74, 83, 215–217
  and abuse, 219
  adaptive role of, 217
  and adolescence, 327–328
  cultural background and, 220
  intervention strategies for, 216–217
  maternal responsiveness and, 218
  as moral emotion, 328

guilt (*continued*)
    and neglect, 219
    in parent-child relationships, 218
    psychopathology and, 216–217
    responding to, 219

H

harm, understanding, 226–227
Harter's Self-Perception Profile, 284
health, and emotional expressiveness, 81
heteronomous orientation, 221, 223
hierarchical organization model, 46
hierarchies
    of attachments, 44
    in peer relationships, 246
    in sibling relationships, 117–118
hippocampus, 12, 50–51
homosexuality, 12–13, 311–313
"hooking up", 256–257
hormones, 10, 310
hypothalamic-pituitary-adrenal (HPA) axis,
    11, 47

I

"identifications" and self-description, 298
identity commitment, 302–303
identity components, assigned *vs.* selected, 297
identity formation, 296–297
    adjustment and, 297–301
    in adolescence, 278–279
    attachment and, 299, 302–308
    authenticity and, 317–318
    behavioral problems and, 304–305
    as critical task, 298
    cultural background and, 307–309
    developmental preparation for, 297–298
    emotional development and, 318–319
    empathy and, 324–326
    ethnic identity and, 307–309
    exploration and, 302–303
    exploration and commitment processes of,
        299, 301
    and friendships, 304
    gender identity and, 309–314
    "identifications" as components of, 298
    influences on, 303–305
    intimacy and, 299, 303, 314–417
    mentalization and, 322–324
    parent-adolescent relationships and,
        302–304
    peer relationships and, 304–305
    romantic relationships and, 302, 304
    self-definition and, 298

    self-disclosure and, 317–318
    self-representations and, 300
    shame and, 327–329
    typical courses for, 300
identity, recent studies of, 305–306
iMessage, 247
imitation, in infants, 9
implicit memory, 50
impulse control, 212, 238, 323
independence. *see* autonomy
independent organization model, 46–47
indiscriminate social responsiveness, 13–14
Infant Behavior Questionnaire, 68
infantile amnesia, 107
infants. *see also* adolescents; children; pre-
    schoolers; toddlers
    and attachment
        multiple, 44–47
        responses to, 47
        stability, 40
    attachment security continuity and,
        267–270
    "emotional contagion" and, 194–195
    emotional development in, 73–74
    emotional expressiveness in, 78–79
    emotion regulation and, 88–89
    as focus of attachment theory, 32–35
    friendships among, 168
    guilt in, 217
    imitation and, 9
    influence of attachments on adolescents,
        268–269
    moral sensitivity in, 203
    peer interactions among, 163–164
    preference for faces and voices, 8–9
    preference for prosocial stimuli, 203
    preparation for attachment, 8–9
    reciprocal hierarchical bonding in, 45
    recognizing parents, 14–15
    self-awareness and, 100
    self-development and, 99, 113–114
    temperament in, 66–67, 69
inferior frontal gyrus, 323
inferiority complex, 125–126
insecure attachment relationships
    adolescent autonomy and, 283
    adolescent compensation for, 274
    aggression and, 272
    anxious-avoidant, 18
    anxious-resistant, 18
    behavior problems arising from, 31–32, 272
    emotional development and, 97–98
    emotion regulation and, 272

insecure-disorganized, 18
and internalizing problems, 272
internal working models in, 29
measurement procedures for, 35–39
nonmaternal child care and, 42
premature romantic relationships and, 274
psychopathology arising from, 271–273
recalling information and, 276
self-esteem, effects on, 294
self-reporting, 263
insecure-dismissing attachment category, 265
insecure-preoccupied attachment category, 265
insula, 12, 203
integrative organization model, 46
interactional synchrony, 11, 22
internalizing behaviors, 30, 70
attachment relationships and, 244, 272
friendships and, 181–182, 262
and intimacy, 314–315
peer rejection and, 163, 177
self-regulation and, 230
sibling relationships and, 121–124, 134, 143–144
internal models of self, 289–291, 303
internal representations, and intimacy, 315–316
internal working models, 29
adolescent attachment relationships and, 275–276
alternatives to, 189
attachment security and, 36–37
peer relationships and, 187–188
ways of organizing, 46–47
intervention strategies
for developing attachment relationships, 52–55
for emotion regulation, 95–96
for guilt and shame, 216–217
for lack of empathy, 212–213
for parent-adolescent relationships, 266
for sibling relationships, 80, 124, 151, 154–155
intimacy, 314–417
in adolescence, 253–254, 259
attachment security and, 315–317
and autonomy, 316
and friendship conflicts, 250–251
friendships and, 250–251, 314–315
gender and, 314–315
identity formation and, 299, 303
internalizing behaviors and, 314–315
internal representations and, 315–316
sense of self and, 315

Inventory of Parent and Peer Attachment, 263, 269

J
James, William, 99–100
jealousy, between siblings, 131–132
justice, morality of, 224–226

K
Kagan, Jerome, 214–215
Kohlberg, Lawrence, 214, 222–224

L
Laboratory Temperament Assessment Battery (LAB-TAB), 62
language
classifying attachments with, 264
emotion regulation and, 90–91
expressing emotion through, 79
measuring attachment security with, 38
self-representation and, 107
visual self-recognition and, 101–102
later adolescence, 237
"lawful change" in attachment security, 40–41
limbic system, 11, 12, 76, 282
London Child Guidance Clinic, 4
loneliness
in adolescence, 231, 249, 253, 315
and friendships, 181
friendships and, 180–181, 249, 253, 315
insecure attachment and, 272
in only children, 159
from peer rejection, 177
vs. popularity, 249
self-esteem and, 153
sibling conflict and, 123, 155
"looking-glass self", 292

M
Main, Mary, 18
maltreatment. see abuse; neglect
Marcia, James, 299–300, 301, 308
masking emotions, 82
Maternal Interview of Sibling Relationships, 138
maternal responsiveness, 218, 232
maternal sensitivity. see also paternal sensitivity
attachment security and, 6, 19–23, 26–28
definitions of, 20
empathy and, 197–198
nonmaternal child care and, 43
prosocial behavior and, 208

maternal warmth, 143, 198
Maximally Discriminative Facial Movement
    (Max) Coding System, 74
maximizing emotions, 82
medial prefrontal cortex, 225, 323
memories
    attachment relationships and, 50–51, 276
    autobiographical, recent research in, 306
    self-development and, 114
    self-representation and, 106–107
    trauma and, 50–51
mentalization, 20, 322–323, 322–324
middle adolescence, 237
mind-mindedness, 21–22
mind-reading. *see* perspective taking
minimizing emotions, 82
mirroring, 98, 114
mirror neuron system, 200, 324
mirrors, and visual self-recognition, 100–101
modeling among siblings, 122–123, 133
"monotropy", 45
moral absolutism, 221
moral behavior, 229–235
    anxiety and, 231
    cognitive representations and, 232
    development of moral self and, 230
    guilt and, 328
    individual differences in, 230–231
    mutually responsive orientations and,
        232–233
    parents and, 228, 231
    self-regulation and, 229–230
    self system and, 233–234
    and self-understanding, 326–329
moral development
    abuse, effect of, 219
    in adolescence, 223
    morality and, 234–235
    parental discipline and, 232
    and psychopathology, 235
    self-regulation and, 229
    stage theory of (Kohlberg), 222–223
    stage theory of (Piaget), 221–222
    temperament and, 220
moral emotions, 214–218, 328–329
    in adolescents, 220–221
    in children, 220–221
    honesty about, 218–219
    in preschoolers, 220
    socialization of, 218–221
morality, 213–214
    attachment and, 232
    autonomous orientation, 222

of care, *vs.* justice, 224–225, 226
components of, 195
components of, failure to integrate,
    234–235
conventional, 223
cultural background and, 224
emotions and, 214–219
empathy and, 217–218
exclusion, justifying, 227
fairness and, 226
friendship choices and, 227
gender and, 224–225
harm, understanding and, 226
heteronomous orientation, 221
moral development and, 234–235
peer relationships and, 224
postconventional, 223
preconventional, 222–223
in preschoolers, 217–218
sense of self and, 215
moral judgment, 221–229
    conflict and, 225
    neuroscience of, 225
    and parents, 227–228
    social domain theory and, 225–228
    theory of mind and, 224
    transgressions and, 221–222
moral reasoning, 225–228
moral reciprocity, 222, 223
moral self, 230, 233–234
moral transgressions, 227
moral wrongdoing, 226
More Fun with Sisters and Brothers, 151
mother-child relationships. *see also* father-
    child relationships; parent-adolescent
    relationships; parent-child relationships
    attachment and, 8–9, 19–23
    empathy and, 324
    importance of, 4–6
    infant temperament and, 24–25
    neurobiology of, 11–13
    nonmaternal child care, effects on, 42–43
    self-recognition and, 102
    stress and, 12
mothers
    and adolescents
        attachment hierarchies, 262
        attachment quality, 269
        conflict resolution among, 271
        influence on, 254
        transitions, 186
    in attachment hierarchies, 44, 46
    attachment preparation, 10–11

authenticity and, 318
crying and, 6
depression in
  and disruption of infant exchanges, 9
  and empathy, 198
  and insecure disorganized attachment, 18
emotional understanding and, 83
"good enough", 53–54
infants and, 4–6, 8–9
mediating attachment and friendships,
  191–192
moral judgments and, 227–228
personal narratives and, 106–107, 114
prosocial behavior and, 209–210
self-esteem and, 294
sibling attachments and, 119–120
mutually responsive orientations, 232–233

N

negative emotionality, 61
neglect
  and developing self, 115
  emotion regulation and, 95
  guilt, arising from, 219
  insecure-disorganized attachment and, 18
  internal representations of self and, 288
  moral development, effect on, 219
  self-esteem, effect on, 294
  shame arising from, 219, 328–329
neuroendocrine system, 10, 199
neuroimaging, 48–49, 65, 204, 225, 238–239,
  305–306
neuroscience
  of adolescence, 238–239
  of attachment relationships, 47–51
  emotion regulation and, 88–89
  of emotions, 76, 78
  of empathy, 199, 324
  moral judgment and, 225
  of parent-child interactions, 11–13
  of prosocial behavior, 204
  of temperament, 65–66
neutralizing emotions, 82
New York Longitudinal Study, 59
"nomination" sociometric technique, 176
nucleus accumbens, 12

O

Oedipal conflict, 213
only children, 156–160
  challenges of being, 158–159
  developmental outcomes in, 159–160
  vs. siblings, 156–157, 160

orbitofrontal cortex, 65, 79, 88, 203, 325
orienting/regulation, 61
oxytocin, 10, 12, 65

P

pain regulation, 325
parasympathetic nervous system, 11, 76, 88
parent-adolescent relationships, 236–237,
  239–242, 257–258, 271. see also father-
  child relationships; mother-child relationships; parent-child relationships; parents
  adolescent decisions and, 255
  vs. adolescent friendships, 252–253
  attachment and, 261–262
  autonomy and, 240–242, 273, 281–282
  conflict in, 239–240, 271
  cultural background and, 280
  and detachment, 281
  developmental outcomes in, 244
  friendship quality and, 274
  identity development and, 302–303
  intervention strategies for, 266
  intimacy and, 314
  self-esteem and, 294–295
parental expectations, 139, 157
parental monitoring, 241–242
parental restrictiveness, 231
parental warmth, 240–241, 243
parent-child relationships. see also father-child
  relationships; mother-child relationships;
  parent-adolescent relationships; parents
  emotional development and, 74, 97–98
  emotion regulation and, 88–89, 92
  friendship quality and, 182, 186
  guilt arising from, 218
  moral development and, 219–220, 232
  neuroscience of, 11–13, 39
  only children and, 158–159
  peer relationships and, 184–185, 188
  prosocial behavior and, 205–206, 208–210
  shame arising from, 218
  stability in, 188
parenting, 242–243
parenting styles, 231, 243
  and adolescence, 243–244
  cultural differences and, 245, 280
  developmental outcomes and, 243–244
  self-esteem and, 294
parent management training, 151
parents. see also father-child relationships;
  mother-child relationships; parent-
  adolescent relationships; parent-child
  relationships

parents (*continued*)
attachment formation by, 10–11, 52–53
authoratative, 243
authoritarian, 243
crying, response to, 6
ethnic identity development and, 307
"felt security" in adolescence, 273
and identity development, 303–304
infant recognition of, 14–15
influence on
adolescent adjustment, 242–245
emotional regulation, 76–77, 80
emotional understanding, 85–86
internal working models, 29
moral behavior, 227–228
self-concept, 285–286
self-esteem, 111–112
self-regulation, 231–233
siblings, 124–125, 133, 142–147
modeling empathy, 198
peers, links with, 184–191
permissive, 243
post-birth behaviors, 11
and self-representation, 105
sensitivity, comparative, 22–23
sibling relationships and, 117, 118–120,
138–139, 144–145
temperament and, 25, 57–60, 71–72
uninvolved, 243
passive inhibition, 233
paternal sensitivity, 22–23, 26–28
peer acceptance, 175–178, 246
and authenticity, 317
vs. friendships, 168, 249
peer competence, 185–186, 190, 275
peer pressures, 270, 283, 304–305
peer rejection, 94–95, 175–178, 246, 249
peer relationships, 161–163
in adolescence, 245–248, 255
aggression and, 177–178, 326
and attachment
hierarchies of, 187, 246
representations, 187
security, 185
"third variable" between, 191–193
authenticity and, 317
behavioral problems and, 176–177
"best friends", 178
children's, 165–167
developmental changes in, 163–167
and emotion regulation, 92, 189–190
empathy and, 166, 325–326
factors influencing, 176

friendships and, 168, 177, 246, 248–249
functions of, 167
horizontal quality of, 166–167
and identity development, 304
individual differences in, 175–178
infants, 163–164
influence of parent-child relationships,
184–185
and internal working models, 187–188
and intimacy, 314–315
and maintaining autonomy, 283
popularity and, 176, 185, 248–249
preschoolers, 164–166, 189–190
romantic relationships and, 255–257
social media and, 247–248
stability of, 188, 246
toddlers, 164–165
peers
acceptance and rejection by, 175–178
and emotional expressiveness, 80–81
links with parents, 184–191
and self-definition, 245
and self-description, 109–110
understanding social domains and, 228–229
permissive parents, 243
personality
foundations of, 56–57
predicting, from temperament, 58
temperament as core of, 62
personal narratives, 106–107, 114
personal-pathway model for gender identity,
309
perspective taking
affective *vs.* cognitive, 201–202
attachment relationships and, 201–202
empathy and, 324
prosocial behavior and, 200–201, 204
self-description and, 109
Piaget, Jean, 163, 180, 213, 221–224
play
emotional expressiveness through, 80–81
friendships and, 169, 173
peer relationships and, 164
pretend, categories of, 165
prosocial behavior and, 169
polymorphisms, 64
popularity, 248–249
attachment security and, 185
friendships and, 248–249
peer relationships and, 176
prosocial behavior and, 210–211, 249
postconventional morality, 223
posterior cingulate, 225

post-traumatic stress disorder, 217
preconventional morality, 222–223
prefrontal cortex, 238–239, 320
premoral stage, 221
preschoolers. *see also* adolescents; children;
    infants; toddlers
  aggression in, 168
  and attachment stability, 40
  "best friends" among, 178
  emotional development of, 74–75, 84
  emotional expressiveness in, 79–80
  emotion regulation in, 89–90
  friendships among, 168–169, 173–174
  importance of self-regulation in, 94–95
  morality in, 217–218, 220
  peer relationships among, 164–166,
    189–190
  prosocial behavior and adult influences, 209
  self-representations of, 105–106, 108
  temperament in, 67–69
pride, 74–75, 83, 329
privilege, and adolescent development, 322
progressive identity, 301
prosocial behavior, 202–203
  in adolescents, 209
  vs. altruistic behavior, 202
  attachment relationships and, 208
  brain regions for, 203–204
  development of, 203–208
  and emotional competence, 209
  emotion regulation and, 204
  empathy and, 194–195, 196, 206, 324
  false-belief attributions and, 204
  and friendship quality, 172
  individual differences in, 205–211
  lack of, 212–213
  mentalization and, 323–324
  neuroscience of, 204
  nonmaternal child care and, 211
  origins of, 206–211
  parent-child relationships and, 205–206,
    208–210, 231
  peer relationships and, 178, 209
  perspective taking and, 200–201, 204
  popularity and, 210–211, 249
  in preschoolers, 195
  pretend play and, 169
  sense of self and, 208–209
  in siblings, 121, 136, 209, 210
  in toddlers, 203–204
  visual self-recognition and, 204, 326
protest, as response to separation, 8, 15
prudential transgressions, 227
psychopathology

cascade models of, 272–273
conscience and, 235
emotional functioning and, 77
insecure attachment relationships and,
    271–273
moral development and, 235
self-esteem and, 112
shame and, 216–217
psychophysiological approaches, 47–49, 63
puberty, onset of, 310

Q

quasi-egocentric empathic distress, 197

R

race
  friendships and, 171
  and onset of puberty, 311
  self-esteem and, 293
reactivity, 60–62, 87
reappraisal, as emotion regulation strategy,
    321
reciprocal hierarchical bonding, 45
reciprocal nominations, 179
reciprocal relationships, between siblings,
    117–118
reciprocity, 14, 248
recounting, and personal narratives, 106
reflective functioning, 21, 260, 290
Reflective Functioning Scoring System, 266
regressive identity, 301
rejection, peer, 175–178, 246, 249, 288
romantic relationships
  and adolescence, 255–257, 261–262, 271
  attachment relationships and, 257
  attachment security and, 271
  and competence, 255–256
  identity development and, 302, 304
  individual differences in, 256–257
  and peer relationships, 255–257
  premature, and insecure attachment, 274
"roster and rating" sociometric technique,
    176
Rothbart, Mary, 60–62
rudimentary empathic responding, 196
rules
  emotional display, 75, 81–83
  moral development and, 213–214, 219–220,
    229–234
  moral judgments and, 221–226
  pretend play and, 165
  social, 169, 195
    vs. moral, 227–228
  toddlers' awareness of, 104

S

same-race friendships, 171
same-sex friendships, 171
"second individuation", 284
secure attachment relationships, 17
   in adolescence, 273–274, 283
   developing self and, 114
   developmental outcomes of, 31–32
   emotional development and, 97–98
   hierarchy outcomes and, 46
   identity development and, 302
   internal working models in, 29, 288–289
   and maternal sensitivity, 19–23
   measurement procedures for, 35–39
   self-esteem and, 294
   self-reporting, 263
   from therapeutic intervention, 269
secure-autonomous attachment category, 265
secure-base behaviors, 241
self
   autonomous, 99–100
   brain regions representing, 306
   continuity of, 306
   developing, 100–113, 279–284
      and attachment relationships, 113–115
      and personal narratives, 114
   false, 292–293
   feedback about, in adolescence, 284–285
   internal working models of, 29–30,
      288–291
   "looking-glass", 292
   moral, development of, 230
   recent studies about, 305–306
   subjective, 99–100
self-awareness, 100
self-concepts
   adulthood and, 285
   development of, 284–286
   influences on, 285–286
   instability of adolescent, 287–288
   stability in, 285, 287
   victimization and, 285
self-control, 102
self-control phase, 229–230
self-descriptions, 107–110
   by adolescents, 110, 286–288
   cognitive development and, 108–109
   coherence in, 287
   gender and, 108
   "identifications" and, 298
   perspective taking and, 109
   self-esteem and, 112
self-disclosure, 317–318
self-distraction, 89–90

self-esteem, 110–113, 291–293
   adolescence and, 291
   attachment security and, 191, 294
   authenticity and, 317
   children's, 111–113
   cognitive development and, 296
   consequences of, 295–296
   as a construct, 112
   depression and, 295–296
   differential treatment and, 145
   dimensions of, 291
   ethnic identity and, 308–309
   factors influencing, 293–295
   friendship quality and, 180–181
   global, 291–292
   internal models and, 290–291
   measuring, 111
   peer relationships and, 175
   procedures for evaluating, 292
   psychopathology and, 112
   puberty and, 311
   self-descriptions and, 112
   self-evaluation and, 291
   self-perception theory and, 291
   vs. self-worth, 110
   shame, effect on, 217, 328
   sibling relationships and, 125, 133–134,
      153, 155
   stress and, 296
   twins and, 293
Self-Perception Profile for Adolescents, 292
self-perception theory, 291
self-recognition, 102
self-reflection, 286–288
self-regulation, 24, 61, 88–90, 102–103
   in adolescence, 281
   behavioral problems and, 230
   in children, 103
   conscience and, 233
   and developmental outcomes, 94–95,
      230–231
   and empathy, 196, 197, 212, 325
   factors in development of, 231–233
   moral behavior and, 229–230
   parents' effect on, 231–233
   phases of
      control, 229
      self-control, 229–230
      self-regulation, 229–230
   temperament and, 60–62, 72, 103, 233
self-regulation phase, 229–230
self-report measures
   for adolescent attachments, 262–264, 289
   attachment security and, 38

for friendships, 179, 249
only children and, 159
prosocial behavior and, 205
for sibling relationships, 138–139
self-representations, 105–107
attachment and, 289–290
identity formation and, 300
self, sense of
in adolescence, 278–279
agency and, 83
attachment relationships and, 56, 329–330
attachment security and, 275
conflict arising from, 289
and early attachments, 190–191
elements of
emotions, 73, 75–78
temperament, 57–59, 69
emergence of, 56–57
emotional development and, 318–319
intimacy and, 315
mentalization and, 323
moral behavior and, 233–234
morality and, 215
personal narratives and, 106
prosocial behavior and, 208–209
relationship quality and, 315
shame and, 216
self-understanding
in adolescence, 258–259
emotional development and, 74–75
and emotional understanding, 83–84
empathy and, 326–329
moral behavior and, 326–329
self-disclosure amd, 317
shame and, 327–329
self, unique, 286–288
self-worth, 110–111
emotional understanding and, 84
friendships and, 180–181, 249
mediating role of, 191
vs. self-esteem, 110
siblings' comparisons and, 125
sense of agency, 103–105
separation
classifying attachments and, 16–19
influence on children, 4
nonmaternal child care and, 41–43
responses to, 8
Separation Anxiety Test, 37–38
separation protest, 8, 15
sexual activity, in adolescence, 255–257
sexuality, 310–313
sexual orientation, 311–313
shame, 74–75, 83, 215–217

abuse and, 219, 328–329
in adolescence, 327–328
behavior problems and, 218
vs. guilt, 215–216
identity development and, 327–329
intervention strategies for, 216–217
as moral emotion, 328
neglect and, 219, 328–329
parents instilling, 218
physiology of, 328–329
psychopathology and, 216–217
responding to, 219
self-esteem and, 217, 328
and self-understanding, 327–329
trauma and, 328
sibling deprivation, 157
Sibling Relationship Questionnaire, 138
sibling relationships, 116–117
in adolescence, 128–129, 155
in adulthood, 120, 129–130
attachment and, 151–152
balance in, 134–135
behavioral observations, 136–138
characteristics of, 134–136
in childhood, 128
and cohesiveness, 135, 139
compensating role of, 154–155
and competence, 121
conflict in, 131–133
and cultural background, 148
describing and measuring, 131–136
developmental outcomes and, 143–144,
154–155
developmental stages and, 126–130
in diverse populations, 141, 147
effects on development, 148–151
environment and, 143, 147–148
friendships and, 151–156, 192
comparison, 152–153
impact on, 153–154
hierarchical, 117–118
importance of multiple perspectives, 138–139
measuring, 136–139
other influences on, 147–148
and parental expectations, 139
reciprocal, 117–118
and self-esteem, 133–134, 153, 155
self-reporting and, 138–139
social media and, 147–148
stability of, 130–131
theoretical perspectives on, 118–126
siblings
age spacing between, 116, 127, 140
and aggression, 122–123

siblings (*continued*)
  as attachment figures, 120, 149
  attachment security among, 27–28
  and attachment theory, 118–121
  becoming, 126–128
  behavior problems among, 149–150
  birth order among, 116, 127–128, 140–141
  as caregivers, 149
  comparisons among, and self-esteem, 125
  conflict between, 122–124, 133, 150–151
  differences between, 139–142
  differential treatment of, 143–144, 146
  as distractions, 149
  and emotional expressiveness, 80–81
  friendships between, 129
  gender among, 116
  importance of, 116
  intervention strategies for, 80, 124
  learning from, 148–151, 228–229
  modeling behavior among, 122–123, 133
  observing, 136–138
  vs. only children, 156–157, 160
  parents
    attachments between, 117, 118–120
    influence of, 124–125, 142–147
    treatment by, 144–146
  prosocial behaviors among, 136, 209, 210
  reactions to new, 126–128
  reasons to study, 117–118
  rivalry between, 125–126, 131–132
  roles played by, 141
  social comparison theory and, 125–126
  social learning theory and, 121–125
Siblings are Special, 151
"sibling styles", 137–138
sibling warmth, 121, 149–150
Skinner, Burrhus Frederic, 213
Skype, 247
smiling, 13–14, 76
social comparison theory, 125–126
social competence, 103, 249
social constructionism, 78
social domains, 227–229, 255
social domain theory, 225–228
social functioning, in adolescence, 270–273
social information processing, 266
social learning theory, 5, 121–125
social media, 147–148, 247–248
social reasoning, 225–228
social world of adolescents, 252–257
sociometric techniques for evaluating peer
    relationships, 176
Sroufe, L. Alan, 7–8

stability
  in attachment patterns, 39–41
  in attachment relationships, 7
  of attachment security, 267–270
  effect on parent and peer relationships, 188
  in friendships, 170–172
  in prosocial behavior, 205
  of self-concept, 285, 287
  in sibling relationships, 130–131
  of temperament, 58, 66–69
stable identity, 301
stage model of development (Erikson),
    297–298
"state-matching" responses, 325
state of mind, 264–265, 269
Still-Face Paradigm, 73
Strange Situation procedure, 16–17
  and Adult Attachment Interview, 266
  vs. Attachment Q-Set (AQS), 39
  modifications to, 35–36
  nonmaternal child care and, 42, 43
  psychophysiological approaches and, 48
stress
  and adolescent attachments, 261
  attachment behavior and, 7–8, 16–19
  attachment security and, 268
  and developing self, 114–115
  friendships and, 181
  infant temperament as source, 25
  mother-child relationship and, 12
  self-esteem and, 296
  temperament and, 65, 71
subjective self, 99–100
Sullivan, Harry Stack, 163, 180–181
suppression, as emotion regulation strategy,
    321
sympathy, *vs.* empathy, 196

T
teachers
  adolescent identity and, 292, 305, 318
  as developmental models, 79, 111, 228
  expectations, 72, 93, 226, 296
  parents as, 188
  prosocial behavior and, 209, 211
  siblings as, 122
temperament, 24, 57–59, 72–73
  attachment relationships and, 23–25
  biological basis for, 64–66, 73
  brain regions and, 63–65
  caregiving and, 69
  cultural background and, 70
  defining and measuring, 59–64, 67

development, in infants, 66–67
dimensions of, 61, 72
emotion regulation and, 87, 93–94
environment and, 24, 64, 70–71
and "goodness of fit", 24, 60, 72
influence on development, 70–72, 220
parenting and, 71–72, 142–143, 244
personality and, 58, 62
polymorphisms and, 64
as predictor of behavior, 70–72
reactivity and, 60–62
self-regulation and, 60–62, 103, 233
stability of, 58, 66–69
stress and, 65
in utero, 66
"temperamental advantage", 93–94
testosterone, 10, 310
texting, 247
theory of mind, 169, 199, 202, 224
"third variable", between attachment and peer
relationships, 191–193
Thomas, Alexander, 59–60
toddlers. see also adolescents; children; infants; preschoolers
agency, sense of, 103–105
emotional development in, 74, 83–84
emotion regulation, 89–90
empathy and, 195–197
friendships among, 168
peer relationships among, 164–165
prosocial development in, 203–204
rules, awareness of, 104–105
self-development, 99, 113–114
self-regulation, 102–103
visual self-recognition, 100–102
transgressions, 214, 217
conscience and, 234
and moral judgments, 221–222, 226

moral vs. prudential, 227–228
toddlers' awareness of, 104
trauma
attachment security and, 40, 52, 265
memory, effect on, 50–51
self, problems developing and, 115
self-regulation, effect on, 95
and shame, 217, 328
true empathic distress, 197
"true" self, 284
trust, and attachment development, 14, 114,
118, 186, 253, 297
twins
attachment security among, 26–28
self-esteem among, 293
smiling in, 76

U

uninvolved parents, 243
unresolved/disorganized attachment, 265

V

vagal tone, 63
vasopressin, 10, 65
ventral system, 65, 88, 204
victimization
among siblings, 123
by peers, 177, 181–183, 257, 285
social media and, 248
videotaping, usefulness of, 54
visual self-recognition, 100–102, 204, 326
voices, infant preference for, 9
volunteer work, 211
Vygotsky, Lev, 163

W

Waters, Everett, 7–8
women's movement, 256

Printed by Printforce, the Netherlands

Slipping Through The Cracks

Curious and Cautionary Tales

by

Richard Henthorn

Can we ever know what lies beneath the cracks; the cracks in our everyday lives; the cracks in the universe, in time itself? Do we really want to know? Mostly they lie hidden, these fissures, until . . . . until some event, some incident occurs and one opens up. It opens and inexorably we are drawn through. Sometimes we feel ourselves slipping and desperately try to hold on to our reality. At other times we suddenly find ourselves there, in a new reality. And it isn't easy to return; to go back. We search and search but cannot find a way. The crack has closed.

Two roads diverged in a wood, and I----
I took the one less travelled by,
And that has made all the difference.

Robert Frost (1875 – 1963)

Tales

The Cottage In The Dunes . 6

The Rescue. . . . 53

Homecoming. . . . 65

A Child's Story. . . . 119

Remote Control . . . 127

My Exciting Adventure. . . 135

A Helping Hand.. . . 148

Not Cricket. . . . 158

The Old News Seller. . . 199

The Coastal Retreat. . . 229

The Missed Train. . . 248

Fever. 263

Michael.. . . . 269

The Cottage in the Dunes

It was a late evening in early September. Pippa and I were out on our habitual evening run up the Northumberland coast and back to the cottage. As usual we had run out along the beach (Pippa more in the sea than on the beach) and were now heading back along the top of the dunes. It was more tiring that way round but I liked to make the last leg harder, so that I was really ready for a hot shower and a nightcap.

It was Pippa who spotted her first. We were running along one of the highest points on the dunes when she stopped suddenly and looked out across the beach. I almost fell over her.

'Hey, steady on old girl,' I said somewhat crossly, 'you almost tripped me up there'.

Ignoring me she gave a sharp bark, as if to say 'hey look at this' and continued to stare out towards the sea. I followed her gaze. The tide was only just past full so the extent of beach was not very great and the setting sun was reflecting on the small clouds out over the North Sea, making them appear like so much pink candyfloss. The evening light was fading and I couldn't see anything at first until I spotted a head and raised arm about two hundred metres out from the shore. Stevie Smith's poem came immediately to mind. Waving? Drowning? There was a moderate offshore breeze and this, together with the sound of the surf, could be drowning out any cries for help.

'Well spotted Pips,' I said. 'Come on girl'.

We ran down the steep face of the dune and onto the beach. It was then I noticed the small pile of clothes at the bottom of the dune, together with a rucksack and a mountain bike. We ran on across the sand to the edge of the surf. I could now hear indistinct cries but could not make out any words.

'I think she's in trouble Pips,' I said, quickly taking off my trainers. 'You stay here.'

Pippa obediently sat down on her haunches, still staring intently out to sea. I only had on thin, tight leggings and a T-shirt and so, not wanting to waste any time, I waded into the surf without taking them off. I am a strong swimmer and made good progress. Even though it was the North Sea the water was not too cold after a long hot summer and I made good progress. However, now I was in the water I could no longer see the person I was aiming for. When I judged I was about far enough out I stopped swimming and, treading water, called out 'hello there'. An answering cry came from further out and a little to my right. Oh hell, I thought, the current is taking her out with the tide.

'Keep calling,' I shouted. 'I'm coming.'

I struck out as hard as I could towards the cries and after about half a minute I saw a young, pale, frightened face reflected in the setting sun. As I reached her I could see she was near the end of her tether; her head kept going under and she had stopped waving.

'Cramp,' she managed to splutter.

'You're safe now,' I said. 'Just try to relax. Turn around, lean back against me and kick your legs if you can. We'll have you back on the beach in no time at all.'

In saying this I was hoping I sounded more confident than I felt. At least she was being sensible, or maybe too exhausted to panic and was laying quietly, her back against my chest, as I held her under the armpits and kicked for the shore.

The next twenty minutes was a nightmare and I seriously began to doubt if we would make it as I struggled against the outgoing tide, whilst trying to keep her head above water. She said nothing further, just kicking out weakly. Fortunately the sea was reasonably calm and finally I heard the waves breaking and knew we must be nearing the shore. I heard a bark and suddenly there was Pippa swimming beside us.

'Good girl,' I spluttered. 'Show us the way home'. Hearing the word "home" Pippa answered with two more barks and almost immediately I felt the touch of sand under my flailing feet. Seconds later I was able to stand upright and began to wade backwards up the beach through the surf, pulling the woman with me.

'Can you walk,' I gasped, when I knew her feet must also be on the sand.

'I think so,' she answered weakly, with what sounded like a slight Scottish accent. 'Thank you.'

As soon as we cleared the shallows we both sank exhausted onto the sand and lay there breathing heavily without speaking, whilst Pippa ran around us giving an occasional bark of encouragement. After a couple of minutes I began to shiver and, raising my head, took my first good look at the woman I had risked my life for. She was wearing a one piece black or very dark bathing costume, lying on her back with her eyes closed, breathing heavily and also shivering. She looked young, about mid twenties at a guess, slim and quite pretty from what I could see in the gathering dusk, with medium length fair hair, currently plastered against her face and covered in sand.

'We need to move now and get you into dry clothes and warmed up before hypothermia sets in,' I said gently. 'Do you think you can walk?'

She opened two large eyes, possibly blue and set attractively wide apart, pushed a lock of matted hair back from a high forehead and gave me the benefit of a rueful smile which transformed an already pretty face into a quite beautiful one.

'I'm so sorry. I didn't think you were going to hear me. I don't know what I would have done if you hadn't.'

You would almost certainly have drowned, I thought to myself.

'It was Pippa who saw you, or heard you; I don't think I would have.'

'Thank you Pippa,' she said reaching out a hand, which Pippa promptly nuzzled her nose into. 'What a lovely colour; a sort of light chocolate. What breed is she?'

'She's a Cockapoo,' I replied. 'Come on, we should get moving.' Getting slowly to my feet I helped her up.

'I've never heard of a Cockapoo, but she's very cute.'

'She's a cross between a Cocker Spaniel and a Poodle. Listen, my cottage is only a quarter of a mile from here if you think you can make it. You can have a hot bath there if you wish and then I can take you home.'

'There was a few seconds pause. 'I — I'm on a cycling holiday. At least I think I am.'

'You think?'

She suddenly looked frightened. 'I'm not sure. I can't really remember.'

'If you're on holiday you must be staying the night somewhere; Bamburgh perhaps?'

'Bamburgh; yes perhaps Bamburgh,' she replied, uncertainly.

9

'Well don't worry about it. You've had quite a scare,' I said. 'I'm sure it will soon come back to you. Can you manage to put on your clothes whilst I go and try to find my trainers? I promise not to peek.'

'Your what?' she asked, looking puzzled.

'Running Shoes.'

'Oh! Yes of course.'

'Pippa! Find trainers' I said, and off she shot down the beach. Without Pips I might not have found them because it was now almost dark, but I followed her barks and there she was standing over them.

'Good girl. Let's go home now.'

'Woof, Woof.'

I was still shivering, but had nothing to change into. I took off my T-Shirt and wrung it out as best I could. By the time we got back she was wearing shorts which almost came down to her knees and a shirt, both of which appeared to be khaki coloured. She was also wearing sensible looking shoes and a short dark coat. She was just pushing her swimsuit into the front of her rucksack. Well she certainly wasn't on a night out I thought.

'Do you have any identification?' I asked. She looked at me blankly.

'In your rucksack; a purse or anything that will have your name and other personal details.'

'Oh, I see what you mean. Shall I go through it?'

'Well, don't worry about it yet; it's almost dark and we're both very cold. You can look back at the cottage. There's a stream which cuts through the dunes onto the beach just up there,' I said. 'We can get onto the farm track that passes by my cottage from there.'

'Yes, that's how I got my bicycle here.'

'Well, give me your rucksack,' I said. 'If you can manage to walk OK, I'll push your bike along.

We negotiated the path by the stream with a few stumbles and gained the farm track, which was much easier going.

'This way,' I said, indicating south along the track. We began to walk.

'The sea looked really lovely and I couldn't resist going in,' she said, after we had walked a little way. 'When I found it wasn't too cold I decided to have a swim. I didn't realise I had gone so far out and suddenly I started to get cramp in my legs. Then I saw you running along the dunes and waved and shouted.'

'You were very lucky. It's dangerous to swim hereabouts when the tide is going out. I ought to introduce myself. My name is Duncan; Duncan Bryant.'

'Mine is . . . . Oh no, I can't even remember my name.'

'Look, don't worry about it. You're remembering some things. That's a good sign.'

'Well at least I can say for certain that I'm *extremely* pleased to make your acquaintance,' she said solemnly, holding out her hand.

Although I could not distinguish her features clearly by this time I discerned a half laugh in her voice.

'My pleasure entirely.' I smiled in return and we briefly shook hands. Her hand was small and delicate.

'You must be Scottish with a name like Duncan,' she continued.

11

'Only on my father's side. My mother was Welsh.'

'A Celt then.'

'I suppose; although I've lived in the Home Counties all my life, until I moved up to Northumberland six months ago.'

'Why did you move all the way up here?'

'Well that's a long story.'

'I'm sorry, I didn't mean to pry.'

'Oh that's OK, it's no big secret.'

I was thinking, if I keep talking about myself that may distract her from her memory loss. In any case it might be cathartic and talking to a stranger who one will probably never meet again is sometimes easier than confiding in a friend.

'My wife died suddenly from a brain tumour two years ago,' I continued. 'She was only twenty seven.'

'Oh, I'm so sorry,' she interrupted. 'Please don't talk any more about it. It must upset you.'

'I don't mind. I'm beginning to become reconciled to it now. My mother and father have also now both passed away and so I had no family ties in London, being an only child. I carried on working in the south east for a year or so after Laura died and then decided a complete change of scenery and life-style might be just what I needed. I work from home as a web designer and so can do that from anywhere with a decent internet connection.'

'Are you in the fishing industry then? You design webbing and different kinds of nets?'

I tried not to laugh. My goodness, I though, it looks like her memory loss could be quite serious after all. She remembers some things, like Celts, but can't remember what the web or internet is.

'Well not exactly,' I continued, not wanting to upset her further by revealing how much she could not remember. 'Anyway, I saw this small cottage on the int . . . , I mean I phoned around the local estate agents and they sent me details of a number of places within my budget. We had always rented in London and so I didn't have an enormous amount of capital. I saw this little cottage nestling in the dunes which quite intrigued me and so I came up to look at it. It had been rented out for many years by the current owner and needed a lot of updating, but it was well within my budget and I thought it had a lot of potential, so I bought it. It's quite adequate to live in whilst I do the renovations. I'm doing as much of the work myself as I can and using local tradesmen where I don't have the necessary skills. It's just around this next bend behind those trees.'

I suddenly realised she was looking back along the track.

'Are you OK?' I asked.

'I thought I heard something,' she replied, 'and then when I turned around I thought I saw someone step off the track behind those gorse bushes.' She shuddered and took a step closer to me.

I looked for Pippa, but she had run on ahead. 'I'll go and take a look.'

'No. No please don't go. It was only a shadow; probably just my imagination. My nerves are rather on edge.'

'Well — if you're sure.'

'Yes, I'm quite sure.' She started walking again. 'So what about your friends? You've left them all behind in London.'

I took a last look back down the track and then followed her.

'Laura and I didn't have that many friends; we were quite a private couple. Anyway the east coast line is a good service and the cottage will have three decent bedrooms once I've finished. I've already had a couple of friends to visit and I'm getting to know the locals up here who are much friendlier than Londoners. Everyone says hello to me down in the village. You could walk around the streets all day in London without anyone saying a word to you. Well, here we are.'

She looked up at my recently whitewashed cottage reflecting the light of a full moon which had just risen above the pine trees and stopped suddenly.

'What's wrong?' I asked.

She didn't answer for a few seconds. 'I know this place,' she said finally. 'I've been here before.'

'That's a coincidence. Have you any idea when?'

'I don't know. I think it was a long time ago. There's something about it I should remember. I know I'm being silly but it frightens me.'

'Well, perhaps the white paint does make it look a little eerie in the moonlight, but I can assure you it's quite comfortable and cosy inside. If you're not happy though I can get the car out and run you down into Bamburgh. I'm sure you'll be able to find a room there at this time of the season, even if you haven't booked.'

She seemed to give a little shiver and then lifted her chin determinedly.

'No, I'm just being stupid. It's very kind of you to offer but it would be unforgiveable to refuse your hospitality when you have just saved my life.'

'I don't mind taking you, but if you're sure.'

'I'm sure. It looks like a lovely cottage. It's just this silly memory thing making my imagination run wild.'

I propped her bicycle against the side of the house and we entered by the back door, which faced the dunes. She hesitated on the threshold and then came slowly into the kitchen.

'Do you recognise anything?' I asked. 'I haven't done much to the downstairs yet. I started at the top and am working my way down. I'm afraid it's quite old fashioned.'

'Helen,' she said quietly.

'Excuse me?'

'My name; I think it must be Helen. The name just came into my head.'

'Well, that's good. Your memory is coming back.' She looked doubtful though. 'I can still get the car out and take you into Bamburgh,' I said, sensing her continued unease.'

'No, I'm fine. A hot bath would be very welcome.'

'Do you want to have a look in your rucksack before you're bath?'

'Oh yes. Yes of course'.

She rummaged through the different compartments of the rucksack. Eventually she looked up at me with an expression somewhere between dismay and fear. 'I don't understand. There's nothing here except my swimsuit, a hat, a book about

15

Northumberland and a map of the area. Why would I not have a purse with me?'

'Perhaps you just popped out of your hotel for a ride and didn't think you would need any money. Anyway, don't worry about it now. Have your bath, or a shower and you'll feel much better. The stairs are through the lounge. Just follow me. I'll light the wood burner in a moment,' I said, pointing to the stove in the inglenook, 'but there will be lots of hot water already.'

I led the way up the stairs from the lounge and along the corridor to the bathroom at the other end of the house.

'There you are. There are plenty of towels. Make yourself at home. I'll grab some dry clothes from my bedroom and see you downstairs when you're ready. I'll make a hot drink, or a meal too if you're feeling hungry.'

She looked around, her eyes widening. 'This is lovely; very unusual.'

'Well it isn't that special,' I said, feeling rather pleased none the less. 'I did most of it myself, except for the electrics.'

'What's that on the wall,' she asked, pointing towards the bath.

'That's the electric shower. You can use it instead of a bath if you wish.'

'An electric shower? I've never seen one of those before. Isn't electricity very dangerous with water?'

'Well it might be if I had installed it, but I can assure you it's quite safe.'

'I'll use the bath I think.'

I left, closing the door behind me and walked back down the corridor to my bedroom. She must have used an electric

16

shower before, I thought to myself. It's this loss of memory again. I may have to take her to hospital if she doesn't start remembering things soon. It was a relief to peel off my wet running gear and put on dry clothing. I then went downstairs, lit the stove and poured myself a generous tumbler of single malt.

'Well it's been an exciting evening Pips,' I said, settling into my old rocking chair by the inglenook. 'What do you think of Helen then; she's very pretty isn't she?'

'Woof,' replied Pippa, already settled into her favourite position on the rug in front of the already blazing stove.

What am I going to do with her though, I wondered? I can't just dump her at a hotel unless she remembers who she is. I may have to take her all the way to the nearest Accident and Emergency. I had better not have another one of these then, swirling the amber liquid in my glass, just in case I have to drive.

I began to go over in my mind the events of the past hour or so. It was strange how an ordinary evening could suddenly become extraordinary. If fortune had been against us back there we could both have died and no one would have known how it had happened. Certainly if I hadn't come along with Pippa, Helen would undoubtedly have drowned. I took another sip of whisky and put the glass down on the small table by my chair, ruminating on fate and feeling suddenly very tired, the adrenalin rush of the rescue having completely evaporated. The heat from the stove was radiating over me and I began to relax.

Suddenly I realised that Pippa was growling. She was no longer on the rug beside me. I looked around and she was stood at the bottom of the stairs, baring her teeth in a low insistent growl.

'What's up Pips? It's only Helen up there. I thought you liked her.'

Pippa turned briefly to look at me and then resumed her growling. Perhaps Helen had called for me, I thought and I hadn't heard her. Getting wearily to my feet I walked over and shouted up the stairs. 'Are you OK Helen? Do you need anything?'

Receiving no reply I began to climb the stairs. Perhaps she had fallen asleep in the bath, which could be dangerous if she was as exhausted as I felt.

'Are you coming Pips?' I asked. Pippa's growl changed to a whine and she retreated a few steps.

'You're a silly girl,' I said, continuing upwards.

The stairs were constructed against an end wall of the cottage and so, as I reached the landing, I turned into the corridor which ran down the centre of the house, passing the bedrooms on either side and on to the large bathroom at the other end of the house, which had probably been a fourth bedroom before being converted. As I turned I froze and stared unbelievingly down the corridor. Emerging backwards from the open door of the bathroom was a broad male back. He was bent over and pulling something along with him. As he came fully out into the corridor I could see he was holding an unconscious, naked Helen under the armpits and dragging her with him.

'What the hell are you doing,' I shouted angrily, managing to find my voice and taking a few steps towards him. 'Let go of her. Get out of my house.'

Helen's upper body was dropped unceremoniously onto the floor and a swarthy, black bearded face turned unhurriedly towards me. I was stopped in my tracks. I had never seen pure evil in a face before and sincerely hope I never will again, but I knew instantly that the face I was looking into was an open window to a malign, twisted soul. He rose to his full height, which must have been well over six feet and started walking towards me, bending his head to avoid the ceiling beams. He moved silently, with a liquid, almost feline grace which belied his huge frame. I backed away, looking desperately around for some weapon, because his intentions were plain and I knew I could not possibly take him on without one. There was nothing. I retreated until my heels struck the wall at the top of the landing. I thought of escape, but how could I leave Helen to the mercy of this monster. Pippa was now barking frantically at the bottom of the stairs.

I managed to find my voice. 'Get out of my house; now.'

He spoke not a word but smiled, displaying crooked, yellow teeth behind colourless lips. He was right in front of me now. I could almost taste his revolting odour; a smell of wet earth and rotting vegetation. He raised an enormous fist. I'm ashamed to say I didn't care about Helen anymore; I just wanted to run, but was transfixed with fear, unable to move a single muscle. As he brought his fist in a downward arc towards my face I involuntarily jerked my head backwards, shutting my eyes. The back of my head hit the wall, which inexplicably seemed to give way and I felt my body falling backwards and then rebounding forwards.

I had not felt the expected crushing impact from the vicious blow aimed at my face. I opened my eyes to see Pippa, lying on the rug in front of the stove and staring curiously up at me. I was still sitting in my rocking chair, my clean T-shirt soaked with sweat. I took in a great gulp of air and let it out with a long sigh. Gingerly feeling with one hand a small lump rising on the back of my head, where it had obviously hit the back of the rocking chair, I shakily reached with the other for the glass of whisky and threw the remaining spirit down my throat. The single malt burned a fortifying path all the way to my stomach.

'That was one hell of a bad dream Pips,' I said shakily.

Getting unsteadily to my feet I looked around at the clock on the wall behind me; it was nine forty five.

'Why didn't you wake me up, you useless hound?' I said rather unfairly. 'I've been asleep for nearly an hour. Goodness knows what Helen has been doing all this time.'

I walked to the bottom of the stairs. 'Are you OK up there Helen? I called out.

Receiving no reply I climbed the stairs, not without some trepidation and looked down the corridor. The bathroom door at the far end was closed. I walked to the door and knocked.

'Are you all right in there Helen? Do you need anything?' Silence. 'Helen, are you decent? I'm going to come in.' Still no reply.

I tried the door and it wasn't locked, so I opened it slowly. The light was still switched on. I peered around the door towards the bath. The room was unoccupied. She's done a runner, I thought. Why would she do that? I noticed the towels which had been left out for her were crumpled. I felt them and they were damp. What the hell is going on here, I thought. Going back downstairs I went to the back door and looked out to where I had parked her bicycle against the wall. It was gone.

'Helen,' I called. There was no sound except the breeze sighing through the nearby pines and the distant rumble of surf from beyond the dunes. I stepped back inside, closing the door behind me. Pippa had followed me into the kitchen and was sitting, studying me with her head to one side.

'Well this is a rum do old girl. Did you see her leave?' I didn't expect any sensible answer, so I wasn't disappointed when I didn't receive one.

I began to wonder. It appeared I had fallen asleep and dreamt about some monster dragging Helen from the bathroom and attacking me. But what if I had dreamt it all, right from the start? What if I had arrived home from my run, taken a shower, then fallen asleep in the chair and the rest was just one long traumatic nightmare? I had read reports about people thinking they had woken from a dream, but actually they were still dreaming and had subsequently woken again.

I had a thought. I ran upstairs to my bedroom and lifted the lid from the laundry basket. Reaching down I pulled out the T-shirt and leggings I had worn for my run. They were still wet. I put them to my lips and I could taste the salt water. I had for certain been in the sea in those clothes. I went back downstairs and sat by the stove thinking. What more could I do? No obvious answer came to mind.

'Well Pips, I think it's time for bed,' I said after half an hour of fruitless reflection on the evenings adventures, real or imagined.

Pippa followed me upstairs and jumped into her basket by the foot of my bed. I took the shower which I had been promising myself, climbed into bed and turned off the light. I was exhausted and, despite the many thoughts still swirling around in my brain, I think I must have dropped off to sleep almost instantly.

At first I wasn't sure what had awakened me. I looked, bleary eyed, at the luminous dial of my wrist watch on the bedside cabinet; two a.m. It was then I heard Pippa whining softly. I sat up and switched on the bedside light. She was standing with

21

her nose against the bottom of the bedroom door which I had closed before going bed.

'What's up Pippa? You surely don't need to go out again at this hour?' She turned to look at me and then commenced scratching at the bottom of the door. 'Hey, hang on. I've only just varnished that door. Hell's bells Pips, you're a nuisance,' I said, getting up and going over to open the door.

As soon as the door was open Pippa shot across the corridor into the second bedroom, which I had been using as a study. My bedroom overlooks the front of the house and the second bedroom the back garden. Moonlight was streaming in through the uncurtained window. Pippa jumped up, putting her front paws on the window sill.

'And I've only just painted . . . .' I stopped in mid sentence, for Pippa was baring her teeth and starting to growl ferociously; she hardly ever growled and now she had done it twice within a few hours. As I walked slowly over to the window an inexplicable feeling of dread came over me. I had no idea what I would see out of that window, but I somehow knew I would not like it. I was also convinced that it had to be connected with the previous evening's events.

I looked out. Most of the garden, except that portion shaded by the pines, was eerily awash with pale moonlight. I immediately saw what Pippa was growling at. In the centre of the garden, where my recently planted rose bed ought to have been was a large rectangular hole. Standing in the hole, shovelling out soil to one side was a figure I remembered only too well; a very large man with a black beard. To the other side of the hole lay something which appeared to be wrapped in a white sheet. It was long and slim; to my mind it could only be one thing.

Was this another nightmare? I pinched the inside of my arm hard; it hurt. This was no bad dream, unless I could feel pain in a dream. Suddenly, as if he sensed someone was watching him he stopped digging and looked up. We stared at each other for a few seconds. He then he put down his spade by the side of the grave he was digging (for I was convinced that's what it was) and unhurriedly began to climb out.

I ran out of the bedroom and down the stairs, closely followed by Pippa. I had to get a weapon. I ran to the wood burner and picked up the poker from its stand. As I ran into the kitchen towards the back door I was sure I saw a shadow move across the kitchen window. I reached the back door and then my courage deserted me. I stood irresolute, looking at the door. As I did so the handle began slowly to depress. Had I locked the door? I couldn't remember. The handle reached the bottom of its travel. I imagined pressure being applied to the outside of the door to open it, but it didn't move. Suddenly the handle was being shaken up and down, rapidly and violently. At the same time Pippa let out a primordial howl and cowered back against the wall. My hand was gripping the poker so tightly it hurt. Then, after a few seconds, the movements stopped; the handle resumed its normal horizontal position and there was silence.

I stood there, my heart beating so rapidly and heavily I thought it would burst from my chest. The windows; he would try the windows next. I ran around the ground floor, making sure all the windows were secure. At every one I expected to see him climbing in, or a swarthy black bearded face staring in at me, but I saw nothing. Pippa was following closely at my heels; so close I was almost falling over her every time I turned around. I checked the front door and then ran upstairs to secure all the windows there. I left the one overlooking the back garden until last; I didn't want to confront that scene again. Finally I took a deep, ragged breath, walked over to the window and looked out. He was there, but now he was beside the hole, filling it in with the same earth which he had recently taken from it. Of the presumed body wrapped in white there was nothing to be seen. He immediately seemed to know I was there and looked up at the window. I fought an almost irresistible urge to step back into the shadows.

Planting the blade of his spade into the ground and leaning casually upon it, he raised his free arm, favoured me with a ghastly smile and made a beckoning motion. He was asking, no challenging me to go down there. The sheer confidence and brazenness of that casual, mocking gesture so angered me it served to restore my failed courage. I walked resolutely down the stairs and through the hallway to the front door. I did not want to go directly into the rear garden; he could be waiting for me outside the back door. Tightening my grip upon the poker I unlocked the door with my other hand and, raising my weapon, swiftly pulled it open. My eyes were not adjusted to the darkness and I could see very little of the front garden, which lay mostly in the moon shadow cast by the house, but I did not see or hear anything to alarm me.

I had expected Pippa to run past me but she didn't. 'Come on Pips,' I said, stepping out into the garden and beckoning her to follow. She backed up a few paces then, whining pitifully, lay down with her nose between her front paws. 'Well thanks Pippa,' I said. 'You're a lot of help. If I get through this alive I'm going to trade you in for a Rottweiler.'

I walked softly to the gable end of the house and peered around the corner. Seeing nothing, I cautiously crept along the wall to the far corner, took a deep breath and, raising the poker above my head, stepped out into the moonlight. The rear garden lay open before me in the pale lunar light. It was devoid of any presence that I could see, human or otherwise. Trying to look in all directions at the same time I walked towards the rose bed. I'm not sure what I expected to see but, with a mixture of relief and incredulity, all I saw were rose bushes. There they lay before me, moving fitfully in the faint breeze and completely undisturbed by any of the digging out and replacing of earth I had recently observed.

As I stood by the roses I sensed rather than heard a slight movement behind me. I whirled around, at the same time raising my weapon, only to see a rather shamefaced Pippa halted in her tracks before me.

'You're a little late,' I said, sarcastically. 'I could have had my skull smashed in by now.'

Ignoring my rebuke she trotted quietly past onto the rose bed and began to scratch at the damp earth with one paw, looking back at me every few seconds. I watched her thoughtfully. She was not digging as such; she was trying to tell me something.

'Come on Pips,' I said eventually, 'we're going to bed. I'm not going to start digging up my new rose bushes on the strength of a nightmare or hallucination and certainly not in the middle of the night.

I turned and walked back to the cottage and Pippa, after a few seconds, followed me reluctantly. I locked the front door and we went back to bed, but not without a last look out of the study window at the back garden. There it lay, still and serene in the moonlight, as if nothing untoward had happened. Unsurprisingly I lay awake for hours, tossing and turning, before eventually falling into a fitful sleep as the early morning light began to filter through the curtains.

The following day, the fifth of September, was a Friday and I was awakened at 9.30 a.m. by the land line ringing. I picked up the handset by my bed. It was a conference call I had arranged the previous day. I had to bluff my way through the call with three other people, having made no preparations whatsoever. I was relieved to put the phone down at the end of the call.

'This won't do Pips,' I said, getting out of bed. 'I have a living to make.'

After a quick shower the next ten hours were devoted to work and I tried to thrust the previous day's events to the back of my mind. Finally I turned off the Apple-Mac and flexed my aching shoulders. Poor Pippa had only been let out in the back garden all day and every time I looked through the window she was hanging around the roses, looking disconsolate and occasionally scratching at the soil. I made her tea, half of which she ate, unenthusiastically.

'Come on Pips,' I said, 'let's go down to the pub. If you aren't hungry I certainly am and I can't be bothered to cook anything this evening.'

We walked the half mile down to the Black Swan in the village, which was dog friendly, as are many pubs in Northumberland. Having eaten very little over the past twenty four hours I wolfed down the "catch of the day" enthusiastically, washing it down with a pint of locally brewed ale. As I sat back in my chair, replete, I saw Jack Porteous walk in and up to the bar. I had got to know Jack quite well over the past few months. He was chair of the Local History Society and a font of interesting knowledge about the village and its environs.

'Hello Jack,' I called, walking over. 'Let me buy you one.' After getting in two pints we both sat down on bar stools. 'There's

26

something I wanted to ask you,' I said after we had exchanged pleasantries and taken a few sips of the excellent brew.

He smiled. 'I knew there had to be a catch.'

'I just wondered if you might know anything about the history of my cottage.'

'Well, I believe it's over two hundred years old and was originally two fishermen's cottages which were knocked into one. I'm not sure how long ago; certainly before my time.'

'What about the people who lived there. I understand it was rented out for a number of years before I bought it.'

'Yes that's right. No one seemed to stay very long; probably because the owner never looked after the place properly. A chap called McInnes owned it I seem to remember. He wasn't a local and we only saw him here occasionally, when there was some problem or other to sort out.'

'No, I never met him myself; the purchase was completed entirely through the estate agents and our solicitors.'

'I think McInnes was a distant relative of the previous owner who died there. We didn't see much of him either; bit of a recluse. Weddle was his name; big surly bugger. Village gossip was that he died intestate and McInnes was tracked down by one of those companies who do that sort of thing for a percentage of the inheritance.'

My interest had been aroused by Jack's description of Weddle. 'Well you certainly are a mine of information Jack. How long had this Weddle chap lived there?'

'Oh a long time; he'd been there for years before I came to the village and that was in — let me see, sixty seven I think; summer of love and all that. He died about twenty years later. It was

27

weeks before they found his body. It wasn't like this village not to keep an eye on its old folks, but he didn't encourage visitors. As I said, he wasn't the friendly, outgoing type. Why are you asking?'

I hesitated. I was reluctant to say anything about my experiences of the day before. I had already discovered that everyone soon knows everyone else's business in a small village and I didn't want to set that particular hare running.

'I thought I might put together a history of the place to show friends when they visit; see how far I could go back. I'm quite interested in genealogy. It must run in the family; I have a family tree which my mother put together going back to the early eighteenth century.'

'Well, as you know that's an interest of mine too. I'll have a dig around for you if you like; at least to get you started.'

'That's very good of you Jack,' I replied. 'I'll even stand you another pint.'

The next few days at the cottage were uneventful, except that Pippa was still not eating too well and forever hanging around the rose bed looking miserable. I was thinking of taking her to the vets for a check up but on the other hand she was her usual self on our daily evening runs. I was very busy with a new website contract and tried to keep the events of the previous week out of my head. On Wednesday we walked down to the Black Swan again to find Jack there, propping up the bar. He called me over.

'Hey Duncan, I've got something for you about your cottage and Isaac Weddle.'

'He was called Isaac then was he. That's a good Old Testament name.'

'Well he certainly wasn't God fearing. He was an even nastier piece of work in his youth than I recall him being in his old age.'

'Why; whatever did he get up to?'

'Well he was just disagreeable when I knew him, but it seems he was always in trouble with the police when he was younger. Fighting, poaching, robbery; you name it. He lived with his mother until she died in nineteen thirty five and then he lived on his own in the cottage until he died there himself in ninety six. He was ninety four years old then. They say the good die young, so the bad probably outlive us all. I downloaded a few postings from digitised newspaper archives about him; one of them from forty five has a photograph.'

He handed over some print-outs of newspaper reports and got a couple of pints in for us whilst I perused them. The first referred to poaching in nineteen nineteen when he was just seventeen years old; the second to inflicting grievous bodily harm in a fight in Alnwick in nineteen twenty five. Then he was caught burgling a house in Longhoughton in thirty three and there were a couple of others about involvement with the black market during the Second World War. Finally I looked at the one from nineteen forty five. I did not even start to read what he had been up to because this was the report with the photograph. A swarthy, bearded face stared out of the page at me in black and white. Even though the resolution was poor and he looked older than the man I had seen at the cottage, there could be no mistake. A cold shiver ran down my spine.

'Are you all right Duncan? You look as if someone just walked over your grave.'

I tried to pull myself together. 'Could we go over there in the corner and sit down?' I asked quietly. 'I want to tell you something and I'd rather not be overheard.'

'Very mysterious,' said Jack, grinning hugely and following me to the table I had indicated.

We sat down with our pints and I took a deep breath. 'Look Jack, I need you to promise you will keep what I tell you to yourself. I don't want half the village to think I'm a gullible idiot.

'By which you mean the half which doesn't already think so because of that run down heap of a cottage you bought.'

'I'm serious Jack.'

'Fair enough,' said Jack soberly, seeing how serious I was. 'I won't breathe a word.'

I took a deep breath. 'This guy Isaac Weddle; I've seen him very recently.'

'You mean you found his photo on the internet or somewhere? Have you been doing some research of your own?'

'No. I mean I've actually seen him; at the cottage.'

To his credit Jack kept a straight face. 'Are you telling me you've seen his ghost?'

'I suppose I am. Look, I'll tell you the whole story right from the beginning.'

And so I did; from seeing Helen in the sea through to Pippa's continuing odd behaviour over the past few days. When I had finished Jack sat back in his chair and gave a low whistle.

'Well that's quite a tale. You must have been pretty shaken up.'

'I still am, to be honest. I'm finding it difficult to concentrate on work and I'm not sleeping too well. I keep getting flashbacks. I need to draw a line under this somehow.'

'But you haven't seen either of them again since last Friday?'

'No, thank God.'

Jack pursed his lips thoughtfully. 'I'm not one to dismiss the supernatural out of hand, as many would, although I've never experienced anything myself. Do you believe you could have been seeing some kind of re-enactment?'

'Well, I've been trying to convince myself it was all a nightmare or hallucination, but seeing that photograph has really shaken me up again. Perhaps I did see some kind of echo from the past; some memory still present in the house. If Isaac Weddle's spirit is still around in that house it's a pretty malevolent one.'

'As he was in life,' agreed Jack. 'So what we are thinking is that you could have seen an echo of an actual event; a murder in fact.'

'That seems to be the only logical explanation of what I saw. If any of this can be described as logical that is.'

'So, following that through to its logical conclusion, there may be a body under your rose bed.'

'I'll need a little more convincing before I start digging up all the roses I only planted last spring.'

'If, for the sake of argument, the body of this Helen is still buried in your garden, then obviously Weddle was never caught and convicted. I didn't find any reference to him being suspected of murder when I was researching him. He was a low life, but there was nothing on that scale.'

'So, it would never have been reported as a murder,' I said. 'It would have been a missing person enquiry.'

'That will make it harder to find. Thousands of people go missing every year. A lot of them aren't reported at all; certainly not in the national press. We'll need to narrow the time frame down if we're to stand a chance.'

'He looked older in his picture in the newspaper than my image of him. Perhaps around ten years older.'

'The newspaper report was nineteen forty five,' said Jack thoughtfully. 'Unless his mother was in on it, which seems unlikely, the murder must have taken place after she died in nineteen thirty five. That would narrow it down considerably. We should do a search for missing persons, fairly locally at first, from thirty five onwards.'

'I'm really pulled out with a big contract for a new web-site, which I must finish this week. I won't be able to do anything before the weekend.'

'That's OK. As you know I'm retired now. I know all the local sources to look at and you've got me quite intrigued. I'll make a start tomorrow.'

'That's great Jack; thanks.'

'No problem. Your round I think.'

I had just switched off the Apple-Mac on Friday evening and Pippa was looking expectantly at me, anticipating our usual run, when my recently installed front door bell rang. I opened the door and it was Jack. I could tell immediately from the look on his face that he had found something. I invited him in and we went through to the lounge.

'Shall I put the kettle on?'

'I think you'll need more than tea or coffee when I show you what I found this afternoon,' replied Jack excitedly.

'OK. It's a bit early for me but I'll get the single malt out.'

Whilst I did this Jack took some papers from the briefcase he had brought with him and spread them out on the dining table. I brought over two glasses and, handing him one, reached out towards the papers.

'Hang on Duncan. Let me show you chronologically.'

I smiled. I didn't want to spoil his narrative. 'OK, what have you come up with?'

'The first couple of days were quite unproductive. I tried the internet first of course but drew a blank. Many local newspaper archives have still not been digitised; they may never be. So I've been going round looking at the physical archives, which are mostly on microfiche. You can't search by name or subject; you just have to wade through them all.'

'Oh Jack I'm sorry,' I interrupted. 'I didn't want you to go to all that trouble.'

'Don't worry about that Duncan; I think it was worth it. This afternoon I was looking through the Berwick Chronicle archives for nineteen thirty seven. I got to the tenth of September.' He paused for effect and, with a flourish, pulled out a sheet of paper from those on the table. 'Take a look at that.'

It was a photocopy of a report from the newspaper Jack had referred to. The headline read, "Young Eyemouth Woman Missing on Cycling Holiday." I looked at Jack. There was a gleam of excitement in his eyes.

'Go on; read it,' he urged, impatiently.

I looked at the report again and read the following:

"A young lady from Eyemouth was reported missing two days ago by her father Mr Stewart Aitchison, a prominent local solicitor and town councillor. Mr Aitchison told the police that his unmarried daughter Helen —"

I stopped reading and looked up at Jack, who nodded his head vigorously.

" — aged twenty five, who works for her father in his Eyemouth office, left home on Saturday the fourth of September for a cycling holiday in the Scottish Borders. Her declared intention was to cycle to and stay in a hotel in Melrose and use the same as a base to explore the towns and ancient abbeys in that beautiful region. Her original plan had been to travel with a young lady friend who unfortunately was incapacitated by a sprained ankle the week prior to their intended departure date. Mr Aitchison stated he had tried to dissuade his daughter from travelling without a companion, but that she was a strong-willed young woman and had insisted upon going alone. She had been booked into the Bridge Hotel in Coldstream for her first night and then the Queen Mary Hotel in Melrose for the following six days. Miss Aitchison had promised to communicate regularly with her father by telephone but when she had not done so by the evening of the seventh Mr Aitchison rang the Queen Mary Hotel and was told that his daughter had not arrived. He then rang the Bridge Hotel and was told she had also failed to arrive there on the fourth. Mr Aitchison then reported her disappearance to the local police. A search was instigated along her likely route between Eyemouth and Coldstream and officers at all police stations between Eyemouth and Melrose were asked to keep a lookout for her. At the time of going to press we must report that the police have not been able to find any trace of Miss Aitchison, nor have there been any

34

reported sightings by the local populace. Mr Aitchison is a widower and has two other children; a son Michael and a daughter Susan. The family are very naturally distraught. Miss Aitchison is five feet six inches tall and of slim build with blue eyes and medium length fair, wavy hair. She was riding a black BSA Sports Tourist ladies bicycle. If any reader of this report sees or has seen anyone answering to this description they are asked to report their sighting to their local police station immediately."

I looked up. 'Good Lord Jack; that has to be my Helen. The description is spot on. And the name; it can't be coincidence. But we must be thirty miles away from the nearest point on her route.'

'Who's to say she took that route Duncan. Her father said she was headstrong. Perhaps she just changed her mind about where she wanted to go. Or Weddle may have abducted her along the way and brought her back here.'

'If he could drive and had a vehicle.' I was thinking hard. 'If what I saw was a re-enactment as we discussed, then perhaps she did change her mind and come this way and maybe she went for a swim, but it was Weddle who pulled her out, not me.'

That could be why there were no sightings of her,' mused Jack. 'They were all looking in the wrong place. And did you notice the date; the fourth of September. That's the very same date on which you had your encounters last week.'

'But my Helen was real Jack. She was flesh and blood just like you and me. I pulled her from the sea remember. And then there was her bicycle.'

'What about it', asked Jack, looking puzzled?

35

'It was almost dark but I'm sure it wasn't an old fashioned one; it was quite light and modern looking. Oh my God Jack.'

'What now?'

I've just remembered something. Why have I only just thought of this?' I started to repeatedly bang the palm of my hand against my forehead.

'Steady on Duncan, you'll do yourself an injury. What had you forgotten?'

'When I first arrived here there was a lot of rubbish around the garden and in the stone outhouse down near the pine trees. I had to hire two large skips to get rid of it all. It was there at the back of the outhouse under a load of other junk.'

'What was?'

'An old bicycle; a ladies bicycle.'

Jack looked dubious. 'Are you saying Helen Aitchison's bicycle was still there after eighty years?'

'Most of the stuff looked like it could have been that old and the cycle was right at the back.'

Jack gave a low whistle and then took out a further sheet of paper. 'There's another report here from the fifteenth of September; three days later. Her father is offering one thousand pounds reward for information leading to the finding of his daughter. That's equivalent to around eighteen thousand today. You don't have to read it all. This is what I wanted to show you.'

He gave me another photocopy. Incorporated into the article this time was a photograph of Helen Aitchison. It was unmistakeably the same Helen I remembered rescuing from the sea just a week ago. Whether the memory was of an actual

36

event or just a false memory in some way inserted into my brain I could no longer be sure, but it certainly still felt very real.

Jack must have seen the recognition in my expression. 'That clinches it then,' he said quietly. 'We have to dig up your rose bed.'

'We could just tell the police,' I said lamely.

'Is that what you want to do? I thought you didn't want anyone to know about this and anyway we could still be wrong. We will both look like the gullible idiots you described if a hoard of plods come along and dig up your garden, based on our story about an eighty year old possible murder victim and find nothing. We won't be able to keep it quiet from the village then.'

'I suppose you're right. Wait a minute; was she definitely never found then?'

'Well I can't be absolutely sure. I looked through the following two months issues of the newspaper. There were a couple more reports in the weeks following her disappearance, but she still hadn't been found. The only way to know for sure would be to trace her family's descendants and ask them or, as you say, take it to the police. I think the quickest and easiest way to resolve this though would be to dig up that rose bed. If we don't find anything there then we can just forget the whole thing. Put it down to you having too much curry for dinner or whatever and no one need know what prize idiots we've both been.'

I smiled. 'I think I'm the only candidate for village idiot. All you've done is a lot of research based on my wild ramblings.'

'What does that make me then, if not another idiot?'

'Well,' I said glancing outside at the lengthening shadows, 'I'm certainly not going to start digging up the garden now. It isn't a job I fancy completing by torchlight and Pippa has been waiting patiently for her run. I think it will just be a short one this evening Pips.'

Pippa pricked up her ears and put her head to one side at the sound of the word "run".

'You're quite right. I'll be here by ten in the morning if that's OK with you, said Jack. I'd like to see this through.'

'Ten it is then,' I replied, and by twelve we should have the answer.

We finished our whisky and I showed Jack out, then Pippa and I went for our run. We only did about three miles because sunset was fast approaching. As we neared the cottage on our return leg Pippa gave a small yelp and ran on ahead. That's a good sign, I thought. She's ready for some supper. I slowed down to a walk upon reaching the cottage. As I turned in at the back gate I looked around for her and then stopped in my tracks, frozen to the spot. Pippa was sitting calmly in the middle of the rose bed. Beside her and with her hand on Pippa's head was Helen.

Although it was by now almost dark I could see both Helen and Pippa quite clearly in a pale ethereal glow which surrounded them. Helen was dressed just as I had last seen her in khaki shirt and shorts. I couldn't a move muscle; I tried to speak but words would not come. I didn't feel afraid of Helen; I was just unable to function on any level. After a few seconds she smiled at me and lifted her hand from Pippa's head. Immediately the dog stood up and came trotting over to me, quite unconcerned. As she reached me I was suddenly able to move again and, looking down into her large brown eyes, took her head in my hands.

'Good girl Pippa', was all I managed to say.

As I looked up again towards Helen she appeared smaller, until I realised she was slowly sinking into the roses; into the roses and into the earth beneath. She's trying to tell me, I thought. She doesn't realise I already know she's there, where that bastard put her. I'm going to find you Helen, I promised silently. I'm going to take you home.

Jack arrived promptly at ten the following morning. He had brought his own spade. I retrieved another from the outhouse and we began by carefully digging up the roses and placing them to one side. We were able to put a few of them into some old containers I had found. I shut Pippa in the cottage, much to her disgust and we then set about digging in earnest. The soil was light and sandy, so it was relatively easy going. The rose bed was about four by three metres in size and I wasn't sure of the precise spot to dig, although I thought it was at the end furthest from the cottage. We therefore made the hole as large as we felt able to manage; probably about two metres square. After almost two hours we had dug down about a metre over the whole area. We were piling the earth off to the end of the rose bed furthest from the cottage in case we had to enlarge the hole in the direction of the cottage.

Jack paused, leaning upon his spade. 'I'm getting a little old for this kind of work,' he said, breathing heavily and wiping his brow with a large handkerchief. 'He certainly made a damn good job of it. No shallow grave for this guy.'

'I don't think you should speak like that Jack,' I said, rather annoyed at his levity. 'We think there may be a human being down here; a young woman who had her life stolen away. We should show some respect for her.'

'You're quite right Duncan. I'm sorry. I suppose I don't feel as connected to her as you do. You've actually seen her.'

The apparition from the previous night suddenly came back to me. My body gave an involuntary shudder. 'You take a break if you like,' I said, 'and I'll carry on. We must be getting close now, if there is anything here.'

'OK, just five minutes to get my breath back.'

I started work again at the far end of the hole. After a couple of minutes I was just about to dig my spade in once more when I thought I saw something. I put down the spade and knelt on one knee. Reaching down I took hold of a fragment of cloth which looked like it had once been white. I pulled and it came out of the earth with a slight tearing sound. The dry soil had preserved it to some extent, but it was perished none the less. I looked up at Jack. He was staring back at me intently.

'We may be there,' I said quietly. 'I don't think we should use the spades anymore.'

I went to the outhouse and brought back a couple of trowels. We began to remove the earth carefully. Minute by minute more cloth was revealed. Then, as Jack dug in his trowel once more there was a barely audible click. We looked up at each other.

'It could be just a rock,' he said quietly.

'We haven't come across any so far,' I replied.

Bending down I began to scrape the soil away with my fingers from where Jack's trowel had bitten into the earth. Almost immediately I felt something hard and uneven. I continued to brush the soil gently to one side. Gradually a skeletal human hand was revealed.

40

'Jesus!' breathed Jack. 'I don't think, deep down, I really believed it until now.'

We worked on a little longer until an arm began to appear, covered here and there with the remains of the sheet I had seen the body wrapped in on that never to be forgotten night only just over a week ago.

I straightened my aching back. 'Jack, I don't think we should do any more. We need to call the police and let the experts handle it from now on.'

'I must admit I've rather lost my appetite for the task over the last ten minutes,' he replied.

We both got up and climbed out of the hole.

'I know it's only her arm,' I said, 'but I feel I ought to cover it up.'

I brought a clean hand towel from the cottage and placed it over the exposed arm. We then went inside and I picked up the telephone.

'What are you going to tell them Duncan?' asked Jack.

'I hadn't given any thought to that,' I confessed. 'I suppose I'll have to tell them the truth. What other reason could we have for knowing where to find a body in my back garden?'

'None, unless we put it there ourselves. They won't believe us you know.'

'Are you saying there's an alternative?'

'No, of course not. You have to tell the police. Just be prepared. We could be in for a very awkward few hours.'

Jack was wrong. We were actually in for a very awkward few days. A local constable came first, to be followed, as soon as he had established it wasn't a hoax or a dead animal, by a whole forensics team. As they were putting their white tent up and starting to do their work we were questioned, firstly in the cottage by a detective sergeant. As Jack had predicted he didn't believe us, or me to be more precise, even after Jack had shown him all the evidence he had gathered. We were asked to "accompany him to the station". Pippa was dropped off at Jack's house for his wife to look after and we were driven to the police station in Berwick. There we told it all again; but separately this time and, in my case, to a detective inspector and it was all recorded.

'Is that really the best you can come up with?' the DI asked me eventually.

I almost lost my temper. 'Look, you can check out what we have told you. The pathologist will tell you she has been down there for many years and you should be able to extract DNA from her body and match it to one of her direct descendants to prove who she is.'

'So now you're also a forensics expert are you?' he said sarcastically.

'Was that a rhetorical question?' I replied.

He scowled. 'I think you've been watching too many crime scene investigations on the television. What if I was to tell you that you're friend Jack has now changed his tune? Why don't you wise up too and tell us the truth instead of some cock and bull bloody ghost story.'

'Jack isn't telling you any other story because there isn't any other story,' I said, calling his bluff. I was beginning to seriously dislike this man.

Finally the interview was terminated and he left. I checked my watch; I had been there for six hours. He came back a few minutes later.

'I'm releasing you on police bail,' he said, 'but I have a warrant to search your house, so we are going to accompany you there, right now.'

'What about Jack?' I asked.

'That's no concern of yours.'

The forensics team were just removing the body when we got back to the cottage. Three officers searched my house from top to bottom whilst the DI sat with me to make sure I wasn't destroying any evidence. I don't know what they hoped to find but of course they didn't find anything. Eventually they left and I could begin to put the place back together again. As soon as they had gone I phoned Jack's house, discovering he had been bailed an hour earlier than me. The condition of our bail was that we must report to the police station every day. I walked over to Jack's house, collected Pippa and we went for a long run to relieve my frustrations and indignation.

Of course the pathologist's report did confirm that the body in my garden had been there for many years and, after a few days, Jack and I were no longer under suspicion. About two weeks later a different, more amenable, Detective Inspector named Anderson came to see me. He told me they had in fact established, beyond reasonable doubt, that the body from my garden was indeed that of Helen Aitchison. Her extracted DNA had been matched to the grandson of her brother Michael.

'I'm very sorry we put you through the mill,' he said, after telling me all this, 'but you must admit your story was . . . .' he hesitated, 'well, to say the least, very unusual.'

'I understand you had to do your job, though it was a very unpleasant experience.'

'Mister Bryant,' he said, 'I don't quite know how to tell you this, but because of the Helen Aitchison case we have been looking into this guy Weddle. He was a thoroughly bad lot you know.'

'Yes, so I gathered from the newspaper reports which Jack tracked down.'

'The thing is,' said Anderson, 'we have been going back through the archives, looking for other missing persons from Northumberland and the Scottish Borders who were never traced. In particular, women from the period after Weddle's mother died in thirty five. So far we have found five up to nineteen sixty.'

'Are you saying you think he may have murdered other women?'

'It's possible. And he lived in this cottage all his life.'

Suddenly I understood what he was driving at. 'You mean there may be others; other bodies buried in my garden?'

'We can't rule out the possibility. Any decision will be above my pay grade, but we may have to take a further look at your garden. If you were planning any expensive planting schemes or patios I suggest you postpone them for a while.

It was about three weeks later, just before noon, when Pippa raised her head and gave her "visitors coming" bark. I was not displeased. I had been working since eight and was ready for a break. Seconds later the front doorbell rang and I ran downstairs from my study to see who was calling, closely

44

followed by Pippa. I opened the door and then took a step back, speechless.

'Hello Mister Bryant,' said the young woman at the door.

I managed to open and close my mouth but no words came out.

'I'm sorry to disturb you,' she continued, seemingly unperturbed by my silence, 'but when they told me it was you I had to come back to apologise for my behaviour. My name is Fiona, Fiona Stewart.'

'I — I don't; I mean . . . .' my voice tailed off.

She realised something was seriously amiss then and looked more closely at me out of stunning violet blue eyes.

'Are you unwell Mister Bryant?'

I managed to string together a few words. 'No. No, I'm OK. What can I do for you Miss . . . . ?'

'Stewart. I came to thank you,' she said and smiled.

She looked to be in her mid twenties and had a lilting Scottish Borders accent. Her smile transformed an already pretty face into a quite beautiful one. A face I remembered well. Pippa trotted past me and sat down in front of her.

'Hello Pippa. You are just as cute as I remember,' said Fiona, reaching out a hand, which Pippa promptly nuzzled her nose into.

I suddenly began to feel a little unsteady on my feet.

'You're not Helen,' I heard myself saying, but with the odd feeling the words had been spoken by someone else.

'No, not Helen. Fiona. I'm sorry about that. I still don't properly understand it myself Are you sure you're all right Mister Bryant?'

'Look, I'm sorry but I'm feeling a little faint. I think I need to sit down for a few minutes. Won't you come in?'

I turned and walked unsteadily down the hall into the lounge, with Pippa and Fiona following.

'Sit down Mister Bryant and I'll get you a glass of water. That's the kitchen over there, isn't it?'

I nodded and eased myself into the rocking chair by the wood-burner. Fiona came back after a minute or so with a pint glass half full of water.

'I'm sorry it's rather large. It was the only glass I could find,' she said, handing it to me.

'Thank you.' I took a sip and placed the glass on the side table by my chair. 'I'm forgetting my manners Miss Stewart,' I said, reviving a little and pointing to the chair on the other side of the wood burner. 'Please, won't you sit down?

She seated herself delicately on the edge of the proffered chair. Pippa sidled over and lay down across her feet.

'I'm sorry about Pippa, she's incorrigible. Just push her away.'

'Oh that's OK; she's lovely,' said Fiona, smiling and stroking Pippa's head. 'As I said, I came to thank you. I thought one of us ought to. When the police told us where Helen had been found I knew it must be you and it all came back to me.

'Us?'

'Oh I'm so sorry. I'm not explaining myself very well. Helen Aitchison was my great aunt. The police released her b . . . , that is to say they allowed us to bring her home last week. I've come here straight from her funeral this morning. I'm the great grand-daughter of her sister Susan. I wanted to thank you for finding her and sending her home to us. And I wanted to apologise for running away that night. I would have come sooner but I was too frightened; frightened of this house and — and what I saw here. But it feels very different now; I don't feel threatened anymore.'

'You gave me quite a shock at the door. I thought — well I thought for a moment you were Helen.'

'Oh I see; yes of course. My grandmother tells me there is a family resemblance. You must have seen her picture in the newspapers then. It was rather grainy; I'm afraid we don't have a decent photograph of her as an adult. I'm so sorry I gave you such a shock.'

'Believe me Miss Stewart, it's much more than a family resemblance.'

'Oh please won't you call me Fiona? But how could you know that?'

I considered for a moment. 'It's a rather long story Fiona and I'm not sure you will believe any of it, but I promise you it's all true none the less. And won't *you* please call me Duncan?'

'You're intriguing me Duncan and I enjoy long stories; I read Gone with the Wind last month.'

I had to laugh. 'Well it isn't quite as long as that. How much time do you have today?'

'I took the day off work for the funeral, so I'm in no great hurry.'

'Well, it's coming up to lunch time. Would you care to join me for some lunch at the Black Swan? It's only just down the road in the village and I'll tell you the whole story.'

She hesitated slightly and for some reason my heart seemed to give a little lurch in the direction of my throat. Then she gave me the benefit of that radiant smile again.

'Could Pippa come too?'

Pippa raised her head at the sound of her name, her brown eyes looking up into the violet blue ones of her new friend. 'I don't think we could keep her away,' I replied.

And so the story of how Helen Aitcheson's spirit came to me for help and how Jack and I became the means by which she was able to return to her family was told once again over a lingering lunch. Fiona was astounded and she cried a little, but she believed every word.

'I saw him too,' she said at last. 'That's why I ran away.'

'You saw Isaac Weddle?'

'I didn't know it was him then, of course, but from the photograph the police showed to us and now your description, it must have been. I felt frightened as soon as I saw your house that evening. I would have left, but you had been so kind and anyway I couldn't even remember my name. I couldn't, that is, until I came inside and then the name "Helen" just popped into my head. I thought it must be my name I had remembered.'

'When did you see him?'

Fiona looked down at the table and her lips began to tremble.

'Please don't tell me if it upsets you.'

'No. No I must,' she said quickly. 'It all fits together now, you see; fits in with what you've been telling me. It was in the bathroom. I had finished my bath, stepped out and was drying myself. I was standing facing the wall mirror and had just finished drying my hair. As I pulled the towel away I looked up and saw him in the mirror. He was standing right behind me. I wanted to scream but I couldn't make a sound.'

She started to tremble. 'Fiona, it's OK,' I said, putting my hand over hers. 'You don't have to go on.'

She smiled, though her eyes were bright with tears. 'I want to. I need to. I couldn't tell anyone else; they would have thought I was a hysterical female. But you understand. You've seen him too.'

'Yes,' I said quietly, 'I've seen him too.' I continued to hold my hand over hers and she seemed to find it reassuring, for she didn't try to pull away.

She took a deep breath. 'He was smiling. He had bad teeth. I don't know how I did it but I turned around and he wasn't there anymore. I was shaking all over. I managed to put on my clothes, grab my haversack, run out of the bathroom and down the stairs. You were asleep by the fire. Pippa looked up but she didn't bark. I know I should have woken you but I was terrified. I just ran through the kitchen and out of the back door, grabbed my bicycle and rode away. I rode for ages and as I did so I slowly remembered who I was. Eventually I got back to Seahouses to the hotel where I was staying. I had left my purse there as you thought. I tried to come back the next day but I couldn't face it. I was scared but ashamed too. Ashamed of running away when you had saved my life and been so kind to me. I'm so sorry.'

'You've no need to apologise. I know how terrifying he was.'

I reluctantly removed my hand from hers and we sat quietly for a while. It was an easy silence between us; as with old friends, where silence isn't an embarrassment.

'I think your presence may have triggered it all,' I said at last. 'Awakened a memory in the fabric of the cottage; one which had been lying dormant all those years. Perhaps it was the coincidence of you being a descendant of Helen and coming to the cottage on the exact same date that she disappeared all those years ago.'

'I didn't feel threatened by the cottage today. I thought I would be frightened again, but I wasn't.'

'I think he's gone now. They both have.'

We then told each other the stories of our lives (it seemed somehow natural and inevitable that we should do so) and I discovered to my amazement that Fiona was not, as she rather quaintly put it, "walking out with anyone".

After lunch we strolled back to the cottage, detouring along the beach in laughing response to Pippa's insistence. We continued to talk back in the cottage; about exactly what I can't recall, but we conversed as if we had known each other for years. In the middle of the afternoon I received a phone call from Detective Inspector Anderson. He asked me if a Miss Stewart had called to see me. I acknowledged that she had.

'I hope you don't mind. I'm sure you've been trying to forget about it all.'

'That's quite all right Detective Inspector, I didn't mind at all,' I replied, grinning at Fiona.

'Anyway, the other thing I wanted to tell you is that my superiors have decided we won't be digging up any more of your garden. After looking further into the history of Weddle we found that he was mostly in Glasgow during the war, dealing in the black market there; got arrested a couple of times. Then in the fifties and sixties he was working on the trawlers out of Seahouses, so again would not have been home much. In these times of budget cuts we have to be very careful about committing funds and the powers that be didn't feel there was any evidence of his involvement in other missing person cases, so no justification to come ruining your garden.'

'Well thank you for letting me know Detective Inspector; that's quite a relief.'

'Just one other thing. If you were to have any further, shall we call them insights, we would appreciate you letting us know. I promise we will investigate them thoroughly. You were certainly spot-on about poor Helen Aitchison.'

'I promise I will, but I sincerely hope I don't. Good afternoon Detective Inspector.'

Fiona and I sat either side of the wood-burner and talked on and laughed a lot. Much later, as the shadow cast by the cottage lengthened towards the protective pines shielding my garden, I walked her to where her Mini was parked just off the road, on the track leading to my cottage in the dunes.

'I'm glad you came today,' I said, opening the car door for her and wondering how I could prolong these final moments.

She stepped inside the opened door, leaning her forearms along the top. 'Would you like me to come again?' she asked, looking up at me and smiling uncertainly.

I knew I had to seize the moment or I would always regret it. Reaching forward I tentatively pushed a stray lock of fair hair away from her eyes and then, emboldened, gently ran my fingers through her hair. Reaching up she put her arms around my neck and drew me towards her. She closed her eyes and we kissed; lingeringly. Her fragrance was intoxicating. Eventually; reluctantly; we drew apart.

'Is that a yes then?' she asked breathlessly, giving me the benefit again of that stunning smile.

Later, Pippa and I went for our evening run. It was effortless. I felt as though I was running on air; that I could have run all night. When we got back to the cottage I gave Pippa her supper and went up for a shower. I turned up the temperature and luxuriated in the feel of hot water coursing over my body. Steam filled the bathroom as I stepped out of the shower and started to towel myself down. I was facing the mirror on the opposite wall, the one in which Fiona had seen Isaac Weddle. It was misted over with condensation. I wasn't really looking at the mirror, but absently noticed a clear spot had appeared. My eye was drawn to it and, as I watched, the spot slowly became a horizontal line. The mirror had my full attention now. I began to feel distinctly uneasy and stopped towelling. I started to shiver uncontrollably and could feel the hairs rising all over my body as a vertical line was drawn below the horizontal one, forming a capital T on the misted mirror. Letters of clear reflective glass were now slowly appearing on the otherwise opaque surface. I must have been holding my breath because I began to feel dizzy. Finally the writing stopped; the message was complete. I drew moist air hungrily into my lungs and then released it in a long sigh. I closed my eyes for a few seconds and when I opened them again the letters were still there. I smiled. They spelt out only two words. "Thank you"

The Rescue

The temperature is in the mid eighties in "old money", but the heat of the mid morning sun is being disguised by a strong sea breeze blowing onto the beach. Yvonne is off souvenir and present hunting in the local gift shops (an occupation which she enjoys infinitely more than I) using up spare Euros, as our two week holiday draws to a close. I am enjoying our penultimate morning chilling out on the beach in front of the hotel, which has been a good choice, aided by internet reviews, which are not always reliable. It is very close to the beach, its location marred only slightly by the busy road one has to negotiate to get there. However, suite, food and service have all been excellent and we have had no complaints.

We had decided upon a French Atlantic resort as an alternative to the more stifling heat of the Riviera, but it is still very hot and I am relaxing on my beach towel under the protection of a large hired parasol. The familiar sounds of a summer beach are filtering into my drowsy brain and I am trying to avoid thinking of the backlog waiting for me at work next week.

I'm not sure what makes me open my eyes and look down the beach at that precise moment; perhaps it is the loud screams and laughter of two young girls playing on a small stone jetty which juts out about a hundred metres into the sea and used by pleasure craft to embark holidaymakers for trips down the coast. I judge them to be about nine or ten years old, very similar looking with tanned skin, unusually dark hair for their age and identical costumes; probably twins I muse. I am thinking that if Yvonne were here she would be watching them intently, wondering how well they could swim and why their mother was not in close proximity; after all the tide is coming in and the surf is quite high.

I start to look around for the mother, the only obvious candidate being a dark haired slim woman in a black bikini, lying on her stomach between myself and the jetty and apparently asleep. As I am wondering if she *is* the girl's mother some loud shouts and screams bring my attention back to the shore. What I see is an unusually large wave rolling in towards the beach. People in the shallows who have seen it are shouting warnings to those further out, some of whom have started to swim back to the shore. I look again towards the two youngsters on the jetty and I see they are completely oblivious to the danger they are in, preoccupied as they are by a crab, or something else they have discovered out there.

I get up and start to run towards the jetty, passing the dark haired woman on the way but judging there isn't enough time to stop and ask if she is the mother. The girls are about two thirds way out along the jetty and I am certain the wave will break over it, washing them into the sea.

"Girls, Girls," I shout, when about 50 metres from the landward end of the jetty, "run; big wave coming".

It occurs to me as I say this that I don't even know if they speak English, but they have obviously heard because they look up towards me. The wave has almost reached the end of the jetty by now and is starting to break, looking much bigger as it nears the shore.

"Look behind you," I yell, "run here, quickly".

They look around as I say this, scream and begin to run towards me. I have reached the jetty and begin running along it towards the girls. The wave has now broken over the seaward end and is rolling along it, covering it to at least a metre deep. I realise there is no chance they will make it to safety and keep running towards them.

The wave envelopes the girls in a foaming maelstrom, their screams immediately cut off as they disappear from view. I continue to run down the jetty and as the breakers reach me I jump to the side away from the stonework into the sea. I suppose I could have stopped as the girls were washed away and tried to make it back to the shore; I'm not even that good a swimmer. I certainly had no thought of bravery; I wasn't really thinking at all.

As I go under I remember that the beach is quite steeply shelving and I am probably in at least two metres of water. I try to swim to the surface but am being rolled around and am not even sure which way is up. I feel the undertow dragging at me and it is more by good fortune than any aquatic skills on my part that my head suddenly breaks the surface and I can take a gulp of air and a quick look around. Almost immediately I see a dark head and flailing arms about ten metres further out than I and begin to swim towards it. I can see no trace of the second youngster.

The girl obviously cannot swim very well, if at all and it suddenly occurs to me that I have only the most rudimentary notion of how to rescue someone in such a situation. She goes under a couple of times before I can reach her but somehow manages to surface again each time. Some old wives tale flashes through my brain that if she goes down a third time she won't come up again. I finally reach her and manage to grab an arm. As soon as I do so she squirms around and throws her other arm around my neck and we both go under. My scant knowledge tells me I should be trying to get her onto her back, but as I try to do so I lose my grip on her arm and that one also goes around my neck.

As I try to kick back to the surface I begin to fear for us both; I realise I'm not up to this. Her grip is vice-like and I'm beginning to panic myself.

"Let go of my neck and I can help you," I yell. It suddenly occurs to me as strange that I can be shouting but not swallowing any sea water.

"I'm not letting go until you stop thrashing around," she replies.

This is getting really weird, I think. Is this what drowning is like? Can I be imagining having a conversation underwater? I remember reading somewhere that drowning can be quite pleasant if you just give in to it, though I'm not sure how anyone could have shared this reassuring information from beyond the grave. I wasn't expecting to die today, I think. Oh, what the hell, just stop fighting it and succumb to the inevitable.

"That's better Tony; now just take some deep breaths and relax for a few minutes and you'll be fine. You had me worried for a while there."

It occurs to me this isn't a young girl's voice I am hearing. It must be an angel, I reason, but one who's voice sounds remarkably like Yvonne's.

"Are you OK now?" asks the angel who sounds like Yvonne.

I realise my eyes are closed and, in an effort to overcome my confusion, I decide to open them. What is there to lose after all? And there is the angel, lying in all her naked glory beside me on our hotel bed with her arms around my neck and a concerned expression on her lovely face; and it is perspiration I am drenched in rather than sea water.

And that was how I woke up to the last full day of our holiday.

"Bad dream?" enquired Yvonne.

I pushed the palms of my hands against my temples and tried to regain some sense of equilibrium. "Nightmare more like; I really thought I was drowning."

"I'd just taken a shower and heard you shouting and thrashing around," said Yvonne. "You were yelling at someone to run. I came back in, managed to avoid your flailing arms, grabbed you around the neck and held on until you calmed down." She smiled. "You could have had my eye out."

I related to her the events from my nightmare. "It was so real Yvonne. I've never had an experience like that before."

"Perhaps it was the lobster yesterday evening," she grinned, "or your exertions afterwards."

"Your arms certainly felt like a lobsters claws," I replied, "they were vice-like. You should enter the next arm wrestling competition at the Fleece when we get home. I'd have a fiver each way on you".

"Well I can tell you're now fully recovered since you're insulting me. I suggest you take a shower yourself, you certainly need one."

"And then what my dear?" I asked, raising my eyebrows enquiringly and putting on my best silent movie villain leer.

"And then I'm going shopping," she said, squirming out of my attempted embrace, "someone has to buy all the presents for Mums, Dads, nieces and nephews; you certainly won't".

"I'm sure you'll do better on your own, your taste for souvenir tat is infinitely more refined than mine."

"There you go again, more insults. I'm going to buy a new dress now to pay you back for that. Why don't you relax on the beach for a couple of hours and then we can drive up into the hills one last time, where it's a little cooler. We can have a quiet stroll in the afternoon then go for dinner to that little restaurant we found by the river."

"Sounds great," I enthused, "you can wear your new dress. Make it a sexy short one and drive all the local farmers to distraction".

"And you can practice your conversational French with that nubile waitress you fancied."

"I was just being pleasant," I protested. "It's a thankless job waiting on tables. I'll bet she gets paid a pittance."

"I'm sure she makes up for it in tips; with such a lovely pout and legs as long as hers."

"It takes one to know one," I replied generously.

This banter proceeded a pace until sometime later we left the hotel and set off in different directions; Yvonne towards the shops along the seafront and myself across the road towards the beach.

I had started to descend the dozen or more steps to the beach when it suddenly occurred to me that Yvonne & I were repeating the events from my nightmare of a couple of hours ago. I stopped on the steps feeling vaguely uneasy and considered returning to the hotel; after all I could relax just as easily by the pool. After a few seconds hesitation I told myself I would be stupid to give in to such superstitious nonsense and carried on down to the beach.

Upon reaching the beach I trudged across the already baking sand towards the sea, noting that, yes, the breeze was strong and the tide appeared to be coming in. I ignored the lines of parasols, thinking this at least would break the spell, sat down in full sunlight and started to apply liberal amounts of sunscreen. As I was doing so, from behind me, the sound of young girls voices raised in exited chatter reached my ears. The chatter grew louder, mingled with the deeper tones of a woman's voice. My previously vague sense of unease increased a few notches on my mental dial and as the group passed me heading towards the sea it was transformed into a feeling of dread. These were the people from my nightmare, in every detail.

I watched in horrified fascination as the black bikini clad woman spread out her beach towel and lay down on her stomach. One of the girls spoke to her and she replied briefly. I could not catch most of what was said but heard the words Mum and castle from the girls, who promptly started down towards the sea, armed with buckets and spades.

I watched the girls intently as they played close to the shallows, running down frequently to fill their buckets with water to moisten sand for the rival castles they were building. It all seemed perfectly harmless and innocuous until they appeared to grow bored and, after a brief conversation, got up, walked down towards the sea and began to paddle in the shallows. The stone jetty was only about twenty metres away from them. It now seemed inevitable in my mind that their next move would be towards it, whilst their mother lay oblivious, soaking up the sun.

I could stand it no longer; my nerves were jangling. I got up and approached the woman.

"Excuse me," I said. Then, upon receiving no response, "excuse me madam," a little louder.

She raised her head, arching her back and supporting her body on her elbows. She was wearing sunglasses which she now pulled down slightly so that she could look at me over the top of them. She was slim and attractive, but in a hard kind of way and there was a distinct lack of friendliness in her dark eyes.

"Yes?"

"I'm sorry to bother you, but the two girls down by the sea; they're your daughters I think."

She looked briefly towards the girls. "Why do you think that?"

"Well, I saw you all come down onto the beach together and they called you Mum before they went off to play."

"You've been watching my children?"

This conversation is not developing well, I thought. In fact it has the potential to get me into an awkward situation. Ignoring her question (or accusation) I tried to regain the moral high ground.

"It's only that I couldn't help noticing the surf is running rather high and the beach shelves quite steeply and . . . . well it could be dangerous for them to play in the shallows."

"What the hell has it got to do with you?" she said, raising her voice. "Are you saying I'm not looking after my children?"

"Well, no, of course not. It's just that the jetty runs out a long way and the tide is coming in and . . ."

"They're nowhere near the bloody jetty."

I hadn't the nerve to tell her I had dreamt her girls and I had been washed off the jetty to our deaths by a freak wave; she obviously already thought I was either an idiot or a pervert, or possibly both.

"No, not at the moment, but if they were to . . ."

"Piss off."

As I was considering my response to this request a voice behind me said, *"Est ce homme déranger vous madame?"*

"What?" She said, looking over my shoulder. I turned around to see a bronzed Adonis standing behind me. Just the type who would love to kick sand in my face, I thought ludicrously.

"He wants to know if I'm disturbing you", I translated helpfully.

"Yes, he bloody well is", she said, looking at her perceived rescuer; then added "oui" as an afterthought.

"OK, forget it," I said, turning away, "I'm sorry to have bothered you".

I walked quickly back to my spot on the sand, feeling their combined glares boring into my back and lay down. I was determined not to look in the direction of the woman or her girls again. If that was her attitude let her kids drown I thought,

61

somewhat unreasonably, since it was not the girls fault they had a foul mouthed bitch for a mother. I closed my eyes and tried to think about Yvonne in her new dress and enjoying the last full day of our holiday. I think five or ten minutes must have passed before I began to calm down a little.

"Thank as f - - - ing lot."

I opened my eyes and there, standing above me, with her disgruntled looking twins behind her, was the foul mouthed bitch herself.

"You've completely ruined my f - - - ing morning; I just can't relax here now," she declared loudly. "Come on Candice, Nadine, we're going to the pool."

If I felt any relief at this development it was overwhelmed by my embarrassment at this woman berating me in public. I was just grateful to be seeing the back of her.

"Moron." She spat out this final invective over her shoulder as she departed up the beach, followed by her miserable looking girls. If they didn't want to go to the pool they certainly knew better than to complain to their mother, I thought.

I watched them for a few seconds then, sighing with relief, turned back to lie down again. Soon after I had done so I heard shouts and screams coming from down the beach. Looking in that direction I saw with incredulity the large wave of my nightmare rolling towards the shoreline. I watched, transfixed with shocked amazement, as people swam back towards the beach and others ran out of the shallows. The wave broke along the shelving beach and over the end of the deserted jetty, rolling right along it to the shoreward end. The wave had seemingly rolled fairly harmlessly past people swimming further out but had broken over numerous adults and children bathing in the shallows who had not made it to shore in time.

I was about to run down to the sea to lend a hand but glanced first over my shoulder to see if my antagonist had noticed the commotion. She had stopped half way up the beach and was deep in a gesticulating conversation with another woman, presumably a friend she had met and was obviously oblivious to the tumult caused by the freak wave. I was pretty sure I knew what she was telling her friend. In fact she was so immersed in her conversation that she had not noticed the twins had carried on walking up the beach, deeply engaged in some childish discussion as usual.

My earlier feeling of unease returned as I watched the girls nearing the steps leading off the beach. I got up and began to walk quickly after them, passing the mother who, still in animated conversation with her friend, didn't even notice me. My walk turned into a run as I saw with horror an articulated lorry turning onto the seafront road. I was fighting to overcome the anticipation and dread of impending disaster which had gripped me, tightening a steel band around my chest and making my legs feel as heavy as lead as I drove them over the sand. I felt as though I was running in slow motion as in, yes, a nightmare, but one from which, on this occasion, I would not wake.

The twins had now reached the top of the steps and the lorry was approaching along the seafront. I tried to call out to them but was able only to make a croaking sound; my bursting lungs would not permit any warning shout to escape. Still engrossed with each other they stepped off the pavement between two parked cars. I took the steps three at a time but, even before I heard the screech of brakes and their screams of terror, I knew I was too late.

Homecoming

A familiar sound distracted me from the accounts I was trying to bring up to date, causing me to lose my place in the in the column of figures I was attempting to add up in my head. Maths has never been my strong suit but I always scorn the calculator lying in my desk drawer, or the spreadsheet on my laptop, for as long as possible in the expectation, or hope rather, that mental exercise will help to keep the neurons communicating with each other in my ageing brain. I started again at the top of the column until the sound came once more, floating in through the open window and destroying my concentration as effectively as if someone had been shouting random numbers into my ear.

With a sigh I gave in to the inevitable, rose from my desk and walked over to the window. As I looked out across the fields my thoughts began to drift. I tried to resist, but the familiar sound had inexorably drawn my mind back to a day, over forty years ago now, on a very similar sunny morning in May nineteen seventy four, when that same sound, very much louder, had startled me out of a darker reverie.

~~~~~~~~~~~~~~~~~~

As I stood by the rail, gazing across at the sheer sides of Hanjague rising up out of an incredibly clear, cerulean sea, I again wondered why I was there. Why was I going back? Ostensibly because my old school friend Tom Pender had invited me to stay with him and his wife Karen up on their farm near Old Town. I hadn't seen Tom in eight years, although we had kept in touch intermittently and I didn't know Karen at all - she was from Dorset and had met Tom at university. When I say intermittently, this was largely down to Tom's persistence in keeping in touch with me. Tom and I had been best pals at school, but I had been trying for eight years to forget the past. Tom's phone calls and letters describing island life would not allow me to, as I saw it, move on, but I had not the heart to cut him out of my life. Something inside my innermost self would not permit me to break that final thread binding me to the islands. And now he had asked me, or rather I should say begged me, to go and stay with them for a week. Why had I agreed? Some personal demon which demanded I must go on punishing myself? Or was it the underlying trace of anxiety, or even desperation, which I had sensed in his voice?

As I continued to stand, pondering the perceived lack of resolution which had brought me back here, other passengers began to emerge from the saloons and crowd along the rail, looking out at the Eastern Isles. Some were looking rather "green around the gills" from the thirty five mile crossing. Others, such as myself who were good sailors, were bright eyed and smiling with anticipation of our imminent arrival, marvelling at the improvement in the weather from the low, grey cloud we had left behind us in Penzance. I knew this transformation to be quite common, but my overarching emotion was still a sense of trepidation; a feeling that nothing good would come from this return to the home of my youth.

The tide was high, allowing us to take the shorter route over Crow Bar rather than the longer circuit around Peninnis Head and on through St. Mary's Sound. As we entered St. Mary's Pool, the inter-island pleasure launches scurrying out of our way, I scanned the Old Quay looking for Tom. I knew he would not be on the New Quay amongst the beeping fork-lift trucks and tanned, leather faced islanders waiting to unload the containers filled with essential supplies and passenger's luggage. He was even less likely to be amongst the sad faced crowds queuing behind the barriers, waiting to embark at the end of their holiday. I soon spotted him, or rather his unmistakeable shock of curly sun-bleached fair hair, standing at the end of the quay with a slim, attractive woman on his arm, who I immediately recognised, from photos sent to me, as Karen. I managed to conjure a cheery wave and they saw me and waved back. As the fenders bumped against the quay I picked up my only luggage, a large, heavy rucksack and made my way in the crush over to the starboard side to disembark.

Tom and Karen met me half way along the New Quay. I tried to shake hands with Tom but he ignored my outstretched hand and went for the bear hug instead, crushing almost all the breath out of my lungs.

'Steady on Tom, I don't work the land like you,' I protested, grimacing in pain. 'You could do me a permanent injury.'

'It's good to see you again Peter,' he said, standing back grinning. 'It's been far too long. This is my wife Karen.'

'You're photos don't do you justice,' I complimented her gallantly and truthfully, as I took in her wide set, sparkling blue eyes and long, blond hair, set off by a healthy island tan. I reached out my hand, which this time was taken by Karen as she also stretched up and brushed my cheek with her lips.

'It's lovely to meet you at long last Peter. Tom is forever regaling me with stories of all the adventures you both had as youngsters. If only half of them are true you are both lucky to be alive.'

'I suspect all of them are true. Our mothers would never have let us out of the house if they had realised what we got up to.'

'Do you have any more luggage,' asked Tom?

'No. All my worldly goods are in this rucksack.'

'It looks like it too. We parked the car up at Porthcressa; you can't get near the quay when the boat is in. Do you think you can make it so far with that pack?'

'I've been doing circuit training for a month for just such an eventuality.'

We walked back up the New Quay with Karen taking my arm as if she had known me for years and Tom pointing out the few changes which had taken place since I had left for university eight years previously. These consisted mainly of a new Arun Class lifeboat moored in The Pool and a new restaurant by the quay.

'Are your Mum and Dad still well,' enquired Tom?'

'Yes, they're both fine. Dad opted for voluntary redundancy from the bank last year when they closed his branch in Truro. They downsized and used the cash to fund Dad's early retirement. Mum still works part time for a local insurance broker and Dad spends a large part of his time valiantly trying to reduce his golf handicap.'

'Why did they go back to the mainland,' asked Karen? I can't imagine anyone wanting to leave here.'

'Not many can, but I don't think they ever really integrated into island life; they were both confirmed urbanites. Dad was given the a chance of a transfer to the local branch here just as I was coming up to secondary school age and I think they considered all this fresh, clean air would be good for me. It certainly worked. I was a little sickly as a youngster, but when I had been here a couple of years Tom and I could run the whole ten miles around St. Mary's coastline without a break.'

'And we did many times when we were in training for the gigs,' added Tom.

'But when I passed my A levels and decided to remain on the mainland and go on to university Dad took the first opportunity of a transfer back to the mainland, which happened to be Truro.'

We reached the car, a battered Citroen 2CV and Tom heaved my rucksack onto the back seat.

'You sit up front with Tom,' said Karen. 'I'm quite happy in the back.'

I was just about to climb into the front passenger seat when a booming voice assailed my ears. I couldn't fail to recognise that voice, even though I had not heard it for over ten years, since I left the islands to go to sixth-form College on the mainland. I groaned inwardly. Here was one of the two people I had hoped to avoid meeting for a whole week and I had been on the island for less than half an hour.

'Look what the f-----g tides thrown up; Professor f-----g Marshall. I didn't think you'd have the guts to turn up here again.'

As I opened my mouth to make a suitable rejoinder I looked past him and my heart sank in dismay. There, just rounding the corner from Silver Street and loaded down with two large shopping bags, was the other person I had desperately hoped to avoid. She was obviously shocked to see me and froze in mid stride, putting down the two bags. At a glance I saw her long, luxuriant auburn hair, now unkempt and swept severely back from her once strikingly attractive face, which today looked thin, pale and drawn. The flesh around her luminous hazel eyes seemed puffy as if she had been crying and I saw a bruise on her left cheekbone. She was only twenty nine but looked ten years older. It took only a second to take all this in. I was so shocked by her appearance that I was momentarily rendered speechless.

Connor Hicks followed my gaze and turned around to look at his wife. 'Get them f-----g bags in the car Merry,' he said, surprisingly softly. I hated that abbreviation of what I had always thought to be one of the most beautiful of Cornish girl's names.

Hicks then turned back to face me. 'Well Marshall, what the f--k *are* you doing here?'

I found my voice and could not keep the anger and sarcasm out of it. 'Hello Hicks. I'm glad to find the years have mellowed you. You're not half as unpleasant as you used to be.'

The colour rose in Hicks' face and he took a couple of menacing steps towards me. Suddenly Tom stepped between us. He had come up quietly behind me as Hicks and I were having our exchange of words.

'Peter is here as my guest Connor, so just back off.'

Hicks hesitated. He was a big man but a developing beer belly overhung the belt of his faded blue jeans; he didn't look in the best of shape to me. Tom was just as big and clearly very fit. Hicks, a typical bully, was trying to think of a way out without losing face when Meraud's quiet voice sounded over his shoulder.

'Please Connor, let's just get home.'

Finding a convenient outlet for his frustrated aggression, Hicks rounded on her. This time his voice was loud and harsh. 'I told you once to get in the bloody car. If I have to tell you again you're in deep shit.'

'Sorry Connor.' I could see Meraud's lips trembling as she meekly lifted the heavy bags and walked towards a large, dusty four-by-four. An astounding tsunami of affection for her flooded over me and I felt an almost irresistible urge to follow her. I dread to think what would have ensued had I done so, but as I started to move she glanced over her shoulder and our eyes met. I think she sensed what I was about to do and gave a quick shake of her head.

Hicks turned back to face Tom again, who was still standing between us, as I also turned to look him in the eye. I could tell he had followed my gaze and seen the silent exchange between Meraud and myself. His face was like thunder.

'Merry told me all about that bastard,' he shouted, pointing over Tom's shoulder towards me. 'You'd better keep him out of my way while he's here and especially keep him away from my wife. If you don't he's dead meat.'

With that he turned on his heel and followed Meraud to the Isuzu. She was heaving the bags onto the back seat as he got in and before she closed the passenger door I heard him say, 'just wait 'till I f-----g get you home.'

I started to move towards their car, but Tom had also heard and held my arm in an iron grip. 'Leave it Peter. You'll only make it worse for Meraud. Let's talk about this later.'

As the Isuzu pulled away I angrily shook my arm free. 'That guys a bloody animal; he always was. How the hell could Meraud ever have married him?'

'I don't know,' replied Tom. 'Do you?'

The journey to Tom and Karen's farmhouse a little way past Old Town was only a short one; there were no long drives on St. Mary's, unless you kept driving round in circles that is. But I was glad it wasn't any longer because it passed in an awkward silence. Karen had squeezed my shoulder silently in sympathy as I got into the car but none of us spoke a word until we arrived. Tom's question before we set off had struck home and shut me up as effectively as a heavy blow to the solar plexus. It was a fair question, but I wasn't sure I wanted to share the answer with anyone.

We all made small talk as Tom and Karen gave me a short reacquainting tour of the house, which had changed very little since the last time I had visited when Tom's parents lived there - they now lived in a comfortable cottage, converted from an old barn, about two hundred yards away. I was then shown up to my room, which benefited from a gorgeous view out towards Porth Hellick.

'We'll have a spot of lunch and then I'll show you around the farm if you like,' said Tom.

'If you need a hand with anything I'm quite happy to muck in.'

'You may regret saying that.'

Tom took me at my word, but I was grateful for the hard graft and tried to put to the back of my mind for a while the altercation with Hicks at Porthcressa. I tried, but Meraud's thin, haggard face kept returning to me. I resolved that I would confess all to Tom and Karen. Tom had diplomatically avoided any mention of Meraud in his letters and our phone conversations over the years, but he must have known what was going on; St. Mary's is a small island and everyone knows everyone else's business. If only I had asked about her I'm sure he would have told me. But what could I have done. I had burnt my boats long before.

Tom and I returned to the house around six o'clock. 'Dinner at seven OK with you Peter,' asked Karen?

I managed a smile. 'That will be great. I've really worked up an appetite. I'll go have a shower and change.'

After a hot shower, which refreshed my body but did nothing to improve my state of mind, I stood with a towel around my waist looking out of the window towards Porth Hellick, where the strange rock formation known as the Loaded Camel stood reflecting the early evening sunshine. I recalled the many times Meraud and I had sat on the rocky shore below that weathered granite edifice, delighting in each other's company and planning our next few hours, weeks and years together. But it had all come to nothing, because of a tragedy and my own weakness and stupidity.

~~~~~~~~~~~~~~~~

We were in our first few weeks at Exeter University. Meraud and I were in separate halls of residence and one of the guys I had quickly become friendly with mentioned an upcoming party at the Student's Union. Well, true to form, Meraud and I had been too engrossed with settling in and with each other to think about partying. That isn't most people's impression of typical first year students, but we were like a little old couple; very boring. Meraud wasn't that keen to go, but I persuaded her. I remember telling her jokingly that we should get out more. I wish to God I hadn't.

I walked over with Sam, my new friend, and we arrived about nine as Meraud and I had arranged. I was quite surprised to find she wasn't already there. Meraud never kept me waiting; I was usually the unpunctual one. I had a couple of pints of cider whilst waiting for her and Sam introduced me to two girls he knew. They were both very attractive and I was certainly flattered by the attention one of them, introduced to me as Amy, was lavishing upon me. It was nineteen sixty six and the so called sexual revolution was well under way; not that I knew much about it, but Amy certainly appeared to by the way she was flirting outrageously with me. That may sound like I'm trying to blame Amy for what happened that night, but the truth is I was an only too willing participant.

I was surprised and rather annoyed when it got to nine thirty and there was still no sign of Meraud. I began to think she had just changed her mind about coming and assumed I would go back and find her. By ten o'clock and after a couple more ciders I didn't much care whether she came or not. The party was getting loud and the music louder. Sam and the other girl had wandered off somewhere and I was very much enjoying Amy's attentions and responding to them. She then produced some red pills and, saying they would help us to have a great time, popped one into her mouth. If she was taking one, I reasoned, what harm could it do? To this day I'm not sure what it was; LSD perhaps. It quickly had an effect though and I began to feel very happy and optimistic, euphoric even. The colours of our surroundings became more vibrant and I felt almost superhuman; capable of any task I might choose to apply my mind or body to.

Amy pulled me onto the dance floor and we started to move to the driving rhythm of the band. We danced ever closer and Amy, putting her arms onto my shoulders, began to move her body against mine. It wasn't too long before we were kissing passionately as we danced and I was getting very aroused. I didn't give Meraud a second thought. After a little while Amy suddenly pulled back from me for a second and we stared hungrily into each other's eyes.

'What's the matter,' I asked? Her face was flushed and her pupils dilated.

She grabbed my wrist. 'Come on,' she said and started to pull me off the dance floor and towards some stairs.

'Where are we going,' I Mumbled?

She stopped and put her mouth to my ear. 'Somewhere I can have you all to myself.'

She ran up the stairs still holding my wrist and dragging me stumbling after her. We ran down a corridor and round a corner, finally coming to an emergency exit. Amy pushed down the bar and pulled me through the door, closing it behind us. We emerged onto the platform of a fire escape at the back of the building. I really only had eyes for Amy at that point, but I think we were surrounded by blank walls, lit by a weak light above the door and with only a narrow alleyway at the bottom of the fire escape, which presumably led to the front of the building.

'Private now,' laughed Amy, pulling me towards her once more. I didn't really care where we were, so long as her hands were in my hair and her lips on mine. Amy's back was against the platform railing as we began to explore each other's bodies more intimately. Her hand was fumbling with the unusual buckle of my trouser belt; my right hand cupped her firm left breast as I bent to kiss her perfumed neck. Suddenly I heard a small metallic sound and felt Amy's body stiffen slightly.

'You'll have to find somewhere else,' she said. 'This spot's taken.'

At her words I lifted my head and looked back over my shoulder towards the emergency exit. Despite my heightened sense of colour, Meraud's face in the doorway still looked ashen. She didn't say a word; just turned abruptly and stepped back inside, closing the door quietly behind her.

'Come here,' Amy breathed, huskily; grabbing the back of my neck she pulled my head back around to her lips, as her other hand finally solved the puzzled of my belt buckle.

Of course I should have gone after Meraud, but to my eternal shame I didn't. The undeniable truth is at that precise moment, in my drink and drug fuelled exhilaration, I could only think of Amy and her warm, shapely body pressing greedily against my own.

The following morning I eventually managed to open my eyelids, which I was convinced had been glued together, to find myself on an air bed on the floor of a small sitting room with a blanket draped over me. My mouth and tongue were made of sandpaper and someone with a pneumatic drill was trying to make a hole in my skull from the inside. I lay there for a while, trying not to move my head and wondering where I was and how I got there. I had never felt so ill in my whole life, but when my memory of the previous night began to return I felt even worse.

Eventually the door opened and Sam came in. He walked over to the window and opened the curtains. I groaned.

'How are you feeling Casanova? That was quite a night you had.'

I groaned again, but inwardly this time. 'Where am I?'

'My room of course. I'm sorry I couldn't manage to drag you up another flight to yours. I was feeling pretty rough myself.'

'I have to . . . . 'I tried to get to my feet. The room swam around me as the little man in my head intensified his drilling and I fell back again.

'Stay where you are. I'll make some black coffee.'

Sam returned a few minutes later with a large steaming mug of very strong, very black coffee and made me drink all of it.

'Amy is quite a girl isn't she? She really took a shine to you. Even after you were almost too far gone to stand up it didn't seem to put her off. She told me to give you the address of her digs this morning, when you were lucid again.'

'Sam, I already have a girlfriend. You've met Meraud.'

'Well you certainly weren't acting like it last night.'

'I was annoyed with her; that she hadn't turned up. And then Amy . . . .' I put my head in my hands. 'What have I done? Meraud will never forgive me.'

'Well, what she doesn't know won't hurt her. I won't say anything. Providing you attend a few lectures for me and I can borrow your notes afterwards. Only joking,' he added with a smile.

'But Sam, she was there. Meraud was there. She saw Amy and I making out on the fire escape. How the hell did she know we were up there? Did you tell her,' I asked, accusingly?

'Why the hell would I do that,' said Sam, colouring up? 'I never saw Meraud there last night and I didn't even know where you and Amy had gone.'

'I'm sorry Sam; I know you wouldn't. I'm not thinking straight. Someone did though. It must have been someone who knew me; knew both of us. Why would anyone do that?'

'Jealousy maybe. Amy's a stunner. Lots of the blokes fancy her something rotten. Can't think what she sees in *you*,' he added with a grin.

'Well the important thing now is I have to find Meraud quickly and apologise. Somehow I have to make it up to her, although God knows how.'

I managed to get to my feet successfully this time, put on my shoes and weave my way to the door; I was still fully clothed. Thanks for getting me back here last night Sam. I owe you one.'

'Don't you want Amy's address then?' I heard him call, as I closed the door behind me.

I made my way apprehensively to Meraud's Halls of Residence and to the room she shared. After taking a few deep breathes I knocked on the door and her room-mate Beth answered. I wondered if Meraud had told her anything, but she greeted me quite pleasantly.

'Hi Peter. You look rather worse for wear.'

'Thanks Beth. Is Meraud in?'

Beth looked surprised. 'I thought you knew Peter.'

'Knew what?'

'She heard yesterday evening. Her father has had a heart attack. Her mother got in touch with the University and one of the staff came to tell her just as she was about to go out to meet you. She said she was going to try to get in touch with her mother and then go to find you. She was very upset when she got back. I asked if she had found you and she said yes. She was crying. I think her father must be in a pretty bad way.'

My blood ran cold. 'Where is she now Beth?'

Beth looked puzzled. 'Didn't she tell you? She's on her way home. She managed to get on today's flight from Exeter Airport.'

'I must get down there,' I said, turning away.

'You're too late Peter,' she called after me. 'It left two hours ago.'

She must be home by now I thought and went to find the nearest payphone. There was no reply when I rang. They are probably at St. Mary's Hospital, I thought. I waited for another hour before ringing again. This time Meraud's mother answered.

'Hello Aunt Emily,' I said, when she answered. Meraud's surname was Tregarthen, but years ago we had got into the habit of calling each other's parents Aunt and Uncle, although there was no family connection. 'It's Peter. How is Uncle Martin?'

There was silence for a few seconds. 'Aunt Emily?'

I thought I heard a sob. 'He's gone Peter.'

'Gone?' I said stupidly, thinking perhaps he had been transferred by air ambulance to the mainland.

'He had a second massive heart attack this morning. The doctors did their best but they couldn't save him.' There was a pause and another sob. 'Poor Meraud; she was too late.'

My mind was in turmoil. 'Aunt Emily, I'm so, so sorry.'

'Thank you Peter,' she said, her voice breaking. 'You'll want to speak to Meraud. I'll go and get her.'

I heard the sound of the receiver being put down before I could say anything more. She was gone for what seemed an age and I had to put more coins into the box. Finally she came back on the line.

'She won't speak to you Peter.' I could discern the puzzlement in her voice. 'She's very upset, as you can imagine. Perhaps you would try again tomorrow.'

'Yes of course. I'll try again tomorrow. Aunt Emily I . . . .' I heard the sound of the line being disconnected at the other end and stood for a long time, the receiver in my hand, before wandering out into the autumn sunshine, which did nothing to lighten my feeling of utter desolation.

I tried to speak to Meraud several times over the next couple of days. The first time she answered the phone herself, but disconnected as soon as she heard my voice. The next few times her mother answered, but each time she told me Meraud would not come to the phone. On the fifth call I established from Mrs Tregarthen that the funeral would be in a further five days time. The next time I called and asked for Meraud Mrs Tregarthen did not say she would go and find her.

'Peter, what has happened between you and Meraud? She asked me to tell you not to phone again and that she doesn't want you to come to the funeral. This is breaking my heart Peter. First James' death and now this rift between the two of you. I've asked Meraud but she won't tell me anything.'

'I'm sorry Aunt Emily, it's entirely my fault.'

'But what has happened Peter? How have you managed to upset Meraud so much that she won't even speak to you?'

I hesitated. I didn't have the courage to tell her what had happened. 'I'm sorry. I've done a very stupid thing and let Meraud down badly at the worst possible time. Please tell her I love her but that I won't phone again if she doesn't want me to.'

I put down the receiver quickly, before she could say anything else and held my head in my hands, tears pricking my eyes.

~~~~~~~~~~~~~~~

A knock on the bedroom door startled me, dragging me back to the surface of the deep pool of despondency in which my thoughts had been drowning.

'Dinner in ten minutes Peter if that's OK with you?'

I took a deep breath and then exhaled.

'Peter?'

'Yes that's fine Tom. I'll be right down.'

I glanced at my watch on the dressing table. I must have been stood looking out of the window for a good half hour, lost in my dark memories.

That evening Karen produced a fabulous three course meal, but I couldn't really do it justice. We all sat back after the dessert, finishing off the bottle of Pino Noir I had brought over with me. Both of them had studiously avoided the subject which I'm sure was on their minds as well as mine. I drained my glass and very deliberately placed it back onto the table, before looking across at Tom.

'I want to tell you both what happened between us; between Meraud and I. I've never told this to anyone before. I don't come out of it smelling of roses.'

Tom glanced over towards Karen. 'Only if you're sure you want to Peter.'

'I'm sure. I had no idea until this morning, but the obvious nightmare Meraud finds herself in today with Connor Hicks is down to me and I somehow have to find a way to help her out of it.'

'You and Meraud were always inseparable,' said Tom. 'You were an item right from your early teens. None of us ever doubted that you'd always be together. You took the same A Levels, went off to read those subjects at the same university and then . . . .' he gave an eloquent shrug, which expressed his puzzlement better than any words.

I smiled despite my sombre thoughts. 'English Language and Literature and History of Art; my Dad wasn't too pleased. He wanted me to read "something useful" and become a banker like him, or an accountant, but the subjects that enthused Meraud also captivated me.'

And so, omitting the more salacious details, I told them the substance of what had taken place that night eight years ago and its aftermath, which I had been reliving in my bedroom just a couple of hours earlier.

'So I didn't go to the funeral,' I concluded, and Meraud and I haven't spoken to each other for eight years.'

I looked over towards Karen. 'So you see I'm not the nice guy Tom may have made me out to be.'

'Peter, you made one alcohol and drug fuelled mistake,' said Karen, 'and it just happened to coincide with a horrible event in Meraud's life. If her Dad hadn't had his heart attack that day she would have met you at the party as arranged and all you have told us about would never have happened.'

'It's kind of you to say that Karen, but I could have done more. I should have come back to St Mary's and tried to explain to Meraud and begged her to forgive me. Instead I just gave up on her. I tried to forget about the only girl I've ever loved and get on with my life without her. Now here I am, still single after two short, unsatisfactory relationships in eight years, to find Meraud in an obviously abusive marriage.'

'Meraud never went back to Exeter did she,' said Tom? I was at uni' in Bristol, so I didn't find out that you and her had broken up until a few months later. The first time I heard about it was when someone told me Meraud had got engaged to Connor Hicks. I couldn't believe it.'

'I remember you managed to get hold of me on the phone and asked me what was going on. I couldn't believe it either.'

'And you wouldn't tell me why you and Meraud had broken up. I had heard about her father of course, but that left me even more puzzled. I remember thinking a tragedy like that should have brought you both closer together.'

'Well now you know the whole sorry story. When you told me about Meraud getting engaged it should have rung alarm bells. I should have gone to find her and somehow make her see sense. Conner Hicks was always a bad lot at school and leopards like him never change their spots.'

'He always hated you as well, for some reason,' added Tom. Perhaps that's why he set his sights on Meraud as soon as he found out you were out of the way and he knew she wasn't going back to university. And most of Meraud's friends had gone to uni' as well; there was no one to warn her about him.'

'She knew all about him just as we did Tom. That's what I can't understand.'

'I think I may know, said Karen quietly.'

We both looked at her, amazed.

'Think about it. Her Dad had died. Meraud and her mother were left with a flower farm to run all on their own. Surely that's why she couldn't go back to university. And you told me Tom that Connor Hicks father had a flower farm over near Telegraph, before it went bust.'

'Hardly something to make Meraud want to marry him I would have thought,' said Tom. She could just have taken him or someone else on as a farm hand if she needed help.'

'Perhaps she couldn't afford to. You told me flower farming was doing badly in the sixties with all the imports into the UK from the continent. You said there was a lot of rationalisation going on; that only the most efficient survived.'

'It still doesn't seem a good enough reason for her to marry him. Was it because of Meraud that you asked me to come over Tom? I felt there was something you weren't telling me.'

'Well, I've been asking you for years if you recall, but seeing Meraud in Hugh Town a few weeks ago really shocked me; she's wasting away. I couldn't get more than a few words out of her. She seemed afraid of her own shadow.'

'I'm sure he's beating her too Tom. She seems terrified of him and you must have noticed the bruise on her face today. Have you seen Aunt Emily recently?'

'She usually comes to the WI,' said Karen. 'She's always very quiet.'

'I haven't seen her in town for months,' added Tom.

We talked around the subject for another hour or so without coming up with any ideas how we could help Meraud.

'I must try to talk to her on her own,' I said at last; 'find out what's really going on up there on that farm.'

'That may be very difficult,' said Tom. 'We rarely see her about without Connor.'

As it transpired it proved to be easier than Tom thought, but the fall-out was as terrible as it was unpredictable.

The following morning at breakfast, Karen excitedly announced that the next Women's Institute meeting was on Monday evening; the next day in fact. 'I'm sorry I should have remembered last night but I missed the last meeting and had to check my diary this morning for the date. Mrs Tregarthen will probably be there,' she added.

'That's a bit of good luck,' I agreed. 'It could be helpful for us if you could manage to speak with her in private.'

'I could find out if she knows you're here and ask her about Meraud. Perhaps I could give her a message from you.'

And so it was decided that Karen would try to pass on a message verbally to Meraud via her mother, if she was at the WI meeting. She would tell Emily that I was on the island and that I had to speak to Meraud urgently. How we could arrange this was more problematic. It would largely be up to Meraud how she could manage it, since that would depend upon her circumstances; I could meet her anywhere, anytime. This was also assuming, of course, that she would agree to see me, which was by no means certain. Possibly a telephone conversation might be all we could manage.

'Conner goes drinking with his pals in The Mermaid most nights,' said Tom. 'There has to be an opportunity while he is out.'

'It was a pleasant spring day and in the afternoon, after Tom had organised the rest of the day's work on the farm, he awarded himself a few hours off and we all went for a stroll around the northern section of the coastal path, stopping for a picnic on the white sands of Bar Point beach on the northernmost tip of the island. Tom and Karen did their utmost to divert me with a constant flow of island news and gossip and I did my best to put my concerns about Meraud to the back of my mind, but it wasn't easy. The next day was even worse. I helped Tom around the farm but my heart wasn't in it. I was on tenterhooks all day, wondering if Emily would be at the WI meeting that evening and, if so, would Karen manage to have a private word with her.

Karen left for the WI meeting at six o'clock. Tom and I watched TV, played some backgammon and drank too much single malt as the evening dragged on. We heard Karen's car at nine thirty and both rushed to the front door. As it transpired we need not have worried about Karen managing a private word with Emily who had arrived, as Karen explained, and made a beeline for her, pressing a note into her hand whilst greeting her in a normal fashion. She had asked Karen in a low whisper to pass the note to me.

We went into the dining room and sat down around the table. There was no envelope. I opened the note which was folded four times into a small square. It read:

Peter. I must speak with you urgently. Please can you go to Watermill for eight tomorrow evening and I will meet you where we used to picnic. Connor goes out drinking at The Mermaid most evenings until late but if he doesn't I'm sorry I won't be able to come. Meraud.

I wordlessly passed the note over for Tom and Karen to read.

'She's deliberately picked one of the quietist places on the island,' mused Tom. 'There's very little chance that anyone else will be down there at that time.'

I remembered Watermill Cove very well. It was a small sandy inlet on the north east coast of the island. It had been a special place for Meraud and I. Somewhere we knew we were unlikely to be disturbed. I had often recalled over the years the many summer evenings we had spent in that sheltered, secluded cove; gentle waves caressing the white sand as we lay in each other's arms. Sometimes we made love; hesitantly; breathlessly. Sometimes we talked unceasingly for hours, always seeming to find something more to say to each other. At other times we didn't talk at all, comfortable in the tenderness and warmth of a shared stillness.

'Peter?'

I dragged my mind back to the present. 'I was worried she wouldn't agree to even speak to me, but here she is asking me to meet her. I still have no idea what I can say to her; how I can help her.'

'In the end Peter, Meraud must help herself,' said Karen, 'but if she knows we are all here for her it might give her the courage to do that.'

I didn't sleep a great deal that night, the thoughts going round my head again and again as in a whirlpool, but getting nowhere;

coming to no conclusions. The next day seemed interminable. I couldn't raise any enthusiasm to help Tom on the farm and spent most of the day moping around the farmhouse and outbuildings, getting in Karen's way. The northerly breeze, which is the most reliable direction for fine weather in the islands, had veered around to the east; the "dark easterlies" as the locals called them. Wind from this direction always saw a build up in cloud cover which invariably ended in rain. By seven in the evening when I set off for Watermill the cloud cover was almost total.

It was only around two miles walk to the cove, but I wanted to be there in good time. I used a quiet inland route along the nature trail to Holy Vale and then past Maypole before entering Watermill Lane. The lane followed a narrow, densely wooded valley towards the sea. The metalled surface soon gave out and the lane became more rutted as it descended steeply, before eventually becoming no more than a rough track as it neared the sandy cove. A small stream issued from the valley, disappearing as it soaked into the soft shell sand.

On a sunny day Watermill was idyllic, with Yellow Horned Poppy, Common Mallow and Hottentot Fig growing in profusion around the margins of the small inlet. But in the evenings a low westering sun could not penetrate the inner reaches of the cove, where dense trees overhung the beach. On this particular evening of low cloud the place was not as I remembered it, feeling dark and claustrophobic. I glanced at my wristwatch; it was seven forty five. I chose not to venture out into the open towards the sea, but sat down at the top of the beach, where gnarled tree roots projected from a sandy bank, eroded away by wind, sea and rain.

The seconds passed slowly and the minutes were interminable. Eventually I thought I heard the sound of disturbed pebbles coming from the lane. A few seconds more and I was sure. I stood up, my eyes struggling to penetrate the gloom where the lane ended and the beach began.

A figure hesitantly emerged, peering around.

'Meraud,' I called softly, 'over here.'

Startled, her head jerked around in my direction. She looked as nervous and jumpy as a sparrow and I half expected her to turn and run away back up the lane, but she didn't. Instead she turned and walked slowly over to where I was standing. I didn't know how to greet her; whether to shake her hand or try to kiss her cheek, running the risk of a rebuff. In the end I did neither.

'Hello Meraud. It's good to see you.'

'Hello Peter.'

There was an awkward silence. I remembered a time when silences between us had never been awkward. I broke it.

'I'm glad you wanted to meet. I needed to speak with you too.'

'I'm taking a big risk coming here Peter, but Conner's gone down to the pub as usual and I had to warn you. I don't know how long you're planning to stay over here, but you need to be very careful and keep out of his way.'

She looked so frightened and vulnerable. Another wave of affection for her swept over me and I had an overwhelming desire to take her into my arms, which I made a superhuman effort to resist. Instead I reached up and touched the bruise on her cheekbone with my fingertips.

She turned her head away. 'Please don't Peter.'

'Did Conner do that to you?'

'He forgot himself that time. He usually hits me where it doesn't show.'

My legs buckled of their own volition and I sank to the sand with my head in my hands.

'Meraud I'm so, so sorry.'

She hesitated for moment and then sat down beside me.

'You didn't force me to marry Conner. He hates you Peter. Please tell me you'll stay away from him.

'There's nothing new there Meraud, he's always hated me. I never knew why, perhaps it's just because I was an incomer and my Dad was the bank manager. If it hadn't been for Tom he'd have made my life a misery.'

'He hates you more because of what happened between us, or at least he pretends to.'

'You told him?' I was shocked.

'Yes I told him. I'm sorry Peter, I didn't intend to, but after Dad died Conner was really kind to me and Mum. He helped us out on the farm and wouldn't accept any payment. He was a different person to the boy I had known at school. I thought he had matured. Then one day he asked why I wasn't going back to uni. I said I couldn't because of the farm. Then he asked about you and I just poured it all out; I couldn't help myself. I hadn't even told Mum what happened – I still haven't - but I just needed someone to confide in; a shoulder to cry on I suppose and he was there for me. Your Mum and Dad had moved back to the mainland so I didn't expect to ever see you again. He got really mad with you when I told him; said he would beat the shit out of you for doing that to me if you ever came back. I didn't really think he meant it, but at the time I didn't much care whether he did or not.

'I'm not scared of Connor Hicks Meraud.'

'Then you ought to be, especially when he's with his mates. You saw how he behaved the other day at Porthcressa. He'd have gone for you then if it hadn't been for Tom. Please Peter; promise me you'll keep out of his way while you're here.'

'So dare I hope you now care a little bit whether he beats the shit out of me or not?'

She gave me a small smile. 'I suppose time lends some perspective. I can see now that what you did would not have happened had I met you at the time I was supposed to. But you still didn't have to go off with that girl. I can forgive you but I can't ever forget what happened that night.'

'I am truly sorry Meraud. I could try to give you excuses for what I did, but that's all they would be, excuses. There hasn't been a day in the last eight years when I haven't thought about you and been ashamed of how I behaved that night.'

She turned and looked into my eyes, as if she expected to find the truth or otherwise of my words somewhere deep within them. She must have found the truth.

'I believe you Peter, but we have to leave it there and get on with our separate lives. What's done is done; there is no possible future for us.'

'But Meraud it's you I'm fearful for now; Tom and Karen also. How did you ever come to marry Conner Hicks?'

'As I told you, he was kind to me; kind and gentle even. I thought he had changed from the bully we both knew at school. He asked me out and I couldn't think of a good reason to say no. He began to help more and more around the farm and I insisted on paying him. Mum said she liked him too, once she realised it was over between you and I. We became a couple and he gave up his other job down at the harbour to work full time on the farm. He was becoming indispensable. He was hardly drinking at all back then, just a pint or two when we went out in the evenings. Then, about a year after Dad died, he proposed. I didn't love him, but I had come to like him a lot, so I said yes.'

'And when did he start hitting you?'

She looked down, twisting a handkerchief in her hands. 'He began to change soon after we were married. I suppose it was only the farm he was after all along. Mum had made it over to me after Dad died and he knew that. He didn't start hitting me straight away; it was only verbal abuse for the first year or so.'

I was incredulous. 'You mean he's been beating you for five or six years?'

She looked up again and I saw pain and shame in her eyes, as well as tears. 'Not all the time,' she said defensively. 'It's usually only when he's been drinking. Mostly he just shouts a lot.'

I put my hand over hers on the sand and she didn't try to pull her own away. 'You have to get away from him Meraud. You can't go on like this.'

'What can I do?' He would never leave the farm and half of it would be his if I divorced him. And then there's Mum. We don't have anywhere else to go.' She was sobbing openly now. 'It isn't so bad. If I don't annoy him he can be OK for days.'

'Meraud, look at me.' I turned her face towards me with my other hand. She didn't try to resist. Her cheeks were streaked with tears and I desperately wanted to kiss them away. 'You could both come and live with me in Exmouth. I only have a teacher's salary but I'm head of the English Department now. We could manage until you got a divorce.'

'The farm would have to be sold Peter. I don't have the money to buy Connor out. That land has been in our family for over two hundred years. It would kill my mother if it were sold. It's no good; nothing can be done. I've made my bed and I must lie in it.'

As if on an impulse she couldn't resist, Meraud suddenly reached up and tenderly brushed my cheek with her fingertips. A shiver ran through my whole body and my self control evaporated in a second. I tried to pull her towards me but she broke away and quickly rose to her feet. She stood there for a few seconds looking down at me as her tears continued to fall.

'I'm sorry Peter; it's too late for us. There's nothing you can do. Mum and I will get through this somehow.'

With that she turned and ran towards Watermill Lane without looking back.

As she reached the path I found my voice. 'I'll think of something Meraud,' I shouted after her. 'There has to be a way.'

The evening of the following day found me sitting, staring disconsolately down at a bare table in the interview room of the small island police station, which adjoined the constable's house. I looked up as two men came in. The first introduced himself as Detective Inspector Marsden and his colleague as Detective Constable Barclay. They sat down on the other side of the table, each placing a buff folder down upon it. Barclay then proceeded to go through the routine of switching on the recording machine and mentioning their names again and mine along with the time, "for the benefit of the tape".

'So Peter,' commenced the senior man, opening his folder and taking out a few sheets of paper on which I recognised my own handwriting and holding them up for me to see, 'please would you confirm that this is the statement you wrote out and signed earlier today and gave to Constable Davidson.'

'Yes it is.'

'I've read this statement,' continued Marsden, 'and I've also read the statements of Arthur Hopkins and Robert Banfield and interviewed them both. Their statements and yours agree in one respect, that you were all at Peninnis Head with Connor Hicks at around seven thirty this morning.'

I looked up, puzzled.

'Apart from that there are very few factual points on which they agree.'

'I don't understand.'

'It's quite simple Peter. Mr Hopkins and Mr Banfield both give a completely different account of what took place out there than the one you describe in your statement here.'

I opened my mouth to speak again but he held his hand up to silence me.

'D C Barclay and I have had a long day Peter. We had to drive all the way down to St. Just to charter a special flight over here this morning. We've visited the scene, read all the statements and interviewed Mr Hopkins, Mr Banfield and others. It's now eight in the evening and we haven't eaten since breakfast. Why don't you just tell us what really happened out at Peninnis Head early this morning and then we can wrap this up and all get something to eat?'

For a few seconds I couldn't find any words. I couldn't believe what I was hearing.

'This is lunacy. My statement tells you what happened. I'm not going to change it. Why would I?'

'OK Peter,' said Marsden with a sigh, 'so you want to do this the hard way. Tell us then what you say happened out there.'

'I already have done. It's all in my statement.'

'Tell us again.' This was Barclay, speaking for the first time.

I took a deep breath, feeling suddenly scared. I felt my right leg beginning to shake under the table and tried to still it with my hand.

'OK. I woke up early and couldn't get back to sleep. The weather had cleared so I decided to go for a walk.'

96

'What time was that,' asked Barclay?

'About six forty five, I suppose, by the time I set off.'

'Did anyone see you leave the farm?'

'No, I don't think so.'

'All right, carry on.'

'I walked down to Old Town, past the church and out onto Peninnis. I took the lower path along the shore and then up past Pulpit Rock. I followed the path as it reached the head and began to turn west. It was then I heard a sound and looked back to see a man about fifty yards behind me.'

'Did you recognise him?' It was Marsden this time.

'No, I didn't know him. I just assumed it was someone else out for an early morning stroll and walked on. Then, just as I came around a large granite outcrop, I saw Connor Hicks walking towards me with another man I didn't recognise. I looked back. The chap behind me was now only about thirty yards away and had stopped when I did. I noticed he was smiling. I turned back towards Hicks and the other guy and they were still coming towards me; then they stopped.'

'What happened then,' asked Marsden?

'Hicks said "I told you to stay out of my way and now you're going to f-----g wish you had"'.

'Are you sure he spoke to you first and said exactly those words?'

'Yes, of course.'

'OK, carry on.'

'Naturally I was scared; there were three of them. I was blocked on one side by the granite outcrop. My only route away from them was down the steep slope towards the outer head.'

'When did you last see Mrs Hicks?'

Marsden's sudden question startled me. I hadn't mentioned Meraud in my statement. I had wanted to keep her out of it, but I guessed from what he had said earlier that he had almost certainly already spoken to her. There didn't seem any point in concealing our meeting at this juncture. I told him about receiving Meraud's note and meeting her at Watermill the previous evening.

'Why did she want to meet you?'

'She warned me to keep out of her husband's way and I had every intention of doing that.'

'Was that the last time you saw her?' It was Barclay again this time.

'Yes, I told you.'

Marsden and Barclay exchanged glances 'You didn't see her again this morning then by any chance,' asked Marsden? You didn't go to their house?'

'No, of course not. Why would I go to the house of someone I was trying to avoid?'

'You were only trying to avoid Connor Hicks. Perhaps you wanted to see his wife again. Perhaps you couldn't stay away.'

'I told you, I didn't go there this morning,' I said, raising my voice. I was getting rattled.

'OK calm down. Carry on with your story.'

'It isn't a story; it's the truth. Anyway, you said you had been down to the Outer Head, so you know it's just a massive jumble of huge granite outcrops and boulders which look like they've been thrown together by some enormous giant. As I ran down the hill towards the head I glanced over my shoulder and the three of them were following. It occurred to me then that I was running into a dead-end. There was no way out from there except back the way I had come; unless I jumped seventy or eighty feet into the sea that is. Even apart from the height, there is no safe place to jump in down there. It would be suicidal.'

'So why did you carry on,' asked Barclay.

'I was scared. I was sure they were going to beat me up, or worse.'

'But you did find a way out.' Marsden again. Their constant interruptions and changing of questioner was beginning to confuse me, which was probably their intention.

'Yes. I suddenly remembered a deep indentation into the outer head. A channel where the waves rush in about seventy feet below. They disappear under a sheer wall of rock and are forced out under pressure at a blow hole on the other side. The sea was quite rough this morning after last night's wind and rain and I could see where the spray was coming up out of the blow hole. The channel is about twelve feet across at its narrowest point. On the other side is a jumble of enormous boulders on a part of the head which is almost impossible to

99

reach without climbing equipment. The only other way is by jumping over the channel.'

'You remembered all that about the place, Barclay interrupted yet again? 'We understand you haven't been back here for at least eight years.'

'My friend Tom and I used to play down at Peninnis when we were children. We used to do that jump regularly as young teenagers. We were idiots. Our parents would have had heart failure had they known what we got up to out there. Twelve feet doesn't sound much but the landing is onto a huge convex boulder. If you were to land short the incline would be too great to find any grip. You would almost certainly slip back over the edge and into the sea below. It was easier to get off because you can jump down from a higher point back onto the main head. But I also remembered Tom and I had found another way off. It's a crawl of around thirty yards between the boulders and is very tight in places. You could almost call it a cave and you have to be pretty slim to get through. It comes out on the other side of the head. Not many people know about it, not even islanders who have lived here all their lives. I thought if I could still get through it, assuming I didn't kill myself jumping over the channel, I would be out of sight and probably able to get away.'

'So you're trying to tell us you were prepared to make that jump again Peter, even though you knew how dangerous it was,' asked Marsden?

'I didn't feel I had a choice.'

'Where was Mr Hicks by this time?'

'He was following me of course; they all were, but I had gained a little on them. I reached the channel about fifty yards ahead as they scrambled after me down the slope. I looked over the edge and across. It looked wider than I remembered it. I turned and looked back. They were now only forty yards or so behind me. Hicks stopped and grinned.'

'You're a dead man Marshall,' he shouted and then came on.

'Are you sure he said that?' Barclay again now.

'Yes, I'm sure.'

'Word for word?'

'Yes, word for bloody word.'

'OK Peter, just calm down,' said Marsden. 'What happened next?'

'You know what happened next; it's all in my statement your holding in your hand.'

'Yes, but we want to hear it again. Please carry on.'

I knew they were trying to catch me out. Trying to trap me into some inconsistency between what I was telling them now and my original statement. I took a deep breath, gathered my thoughts and recommenced my account.

'My fear of Hicks and his pals was greater than my fear of the jump. I took about ten steps back then ran at the channel and jumped. I landed further down the boulder than I had expected. The slope was very steep there. My feet and hands were scrabbling for grip but not finding any. I was slipping backwards. I looked up in desperation and saw a narrow crack in the granite. I reached up with my right hand and just managed to get my fingers into the crack. I hauled myself up a little until I could get both hands in there. Once I had managed that I was able to pull myself up until my toes found some grip and I could climb up onto the top of the boulder. My heart was beating so hard and fast I thought it was going to burst out of my chest. I turned around and looked back across the channel. The three of them were now all standing on the other side, smirking.'

"Nowhere to go now Marshall; you're f----d," shouted Hicks.

I hesitated in my story and looked over at Marsden. 'I didn't include the next part in my statement because I didn't want to involve Mrs Hicks, but Hick's told me how he came to be there on Peninnis that morning.'

'Go on,' said Marsden.

'I looked back and shouted "What's your problem Hicks?" "You must think I'm stupid Marshall?" he called back. Then he told me he knew Meraud - his bitch of a wife he called her - that she and I would try to meet up, so he had made it easy for us by going down to the Mermaid as usual the previous evening. Then one of his mates had kept watch and followed Meraud down to Watermill Cove. "You and her were so f-----g pleased to see each other you never realised somebody was watching you," he said. Then he told me they were up early in the morning keeping an eye on Tom's farm and that it was his lucky day. "Because you walked straight into our loving bloody arms," he said. As soon as I had set out onto Peninnis they knew they had me. Two of them had gone along the shorter top path to get in front of me and cut me off. "We couldn't have caught up with you in a better place," he said laughing.'

I looked across at Marsden, expecting him to ask me some question or other, but he indicated with a gesture of his hand that I was to carry on. I think they were as absorbed in listening to my account by now as I was in retelling it.

'He turned to his two mates. "OK, go and get him," he said. They looked at each other and then back at Hicks. "You must be bloody joking Conner," one of them said. "I'm not jumping over that. He then said something to the effect that they hadn't signed up for this; that Hicks had said they were just going to rough me up to teach me a lesson. Then he said "If you want him so bad you should have the guts to go get him yourself." Hicks looked furious at this. I could see the colour rising up his neck and into his face. He took a few steps back saying, "Do I have to do every f-----g thing myself?"

It suddenly dawned on me that he might actually jump. He must be absolutely crazy I thought to myself, or drugged up on something. I wouldn't do that jump unless I absolutely had to. And now I've done it I will never do it again. I'd sooner have taken my chances with the three of them where they had stopped me. "Don't be stupid Hicks," I shouted. "There's no need for this. I won't be seeing Meraud again." Perhaps stupid wasn't the best choice of word to use. "Too bloody right you won't," he shouted, taking another couple of steps back. Then he turned, ran forward and launched himself across.'

I paused as I relived the moment in my mind's eye as Hicks came hurtling across towards me. 'Please can I skip the rest of it,' I pleaded, looking across to Marsden. 'It's just like it was happening all over again.'

'We need you to finish your story Peter. Carry on please.'

'It really rankled with me that he was still calling this "my story", but I kept my anger under control.

'He was well muscled but quite a bit heavier than me and overweight. Even so, he landed only slightly lower than where I had. He was also taller than me and his feet were hanging in the air because of the convex shape of the boulder; his finger nails breaking as he scrabbled for a hand hold. He looked up and I saw fear and panic dawning in his eyes. "For Christ's sake help me Marshall," he shouted. I have to admit I hesitated for a second or two. Even if I could reach down and grab his hand there was nothing I could hold onto to prevent him pulling me over with him. Then I remembered the crack in the boulder. If I could get one hand in there I might be able to reach him with my other and perhaps have enough purchase and strength to haul him up until he could reach the crack himself.

I began to climb down again. I saw the crack and jammed my left hand into it. I intended to reach down towards him with my right hand, but the effort of getting my left into the crack caused my legs to swing down towards him. He was still just about hanging on. If he had kept still I think I could have reached down and grabbed him with my right hand, but as my right leg swung across he let go with his left hand and made a grab sideways and upwards for it. That was his undoing. As soon as he let go his other hand couldn't hold him. He made a despairing grab for my leg but missed. I looked into his eyes as his right hand lost its grip and he slid down over the curve of the boulder. There was a hopelessness in them that was harder to look at than the fear. Then suddenly he was gone. The strange thing is he didn't make a sound. He just wasn't there anymore.'

I paused, putting my head into my hands as I recalled that terrible moment.

'Then what happened,' asked Barclay after a few seconds?

'I looked across the channel at the other two. They were still standing there, frozen to the spot. You can imagine the horror on their faces. I shouted for them to run back into Hugh Town to raise the alarm and get the lifeboat launched. They pulled themselves together, turned and ran off.

After my heart rate had slowed a little I scrambled back to the top of the boulder and went to look for our secret way off the outer head. I found it after a few minutes and tried to get through but there was no way. I'm still fairy fit but I've filled out since I was fourteen. I had to back out before I became firmly stuck in there. I returned to wait for help. I suppose I could have tried the easier jump back, but I was too shaken up. I heard the alarm siren for the lifeboat after about fifteen minutes and saw the maroons going up, so I knew it was on its way. It took about another thirty minutes to get there, which isn't bad considering it had to sail all around the Garrison. The island constable had already arrived by then with a few other people. He asked me if I was injured. I said no, but that I couldn't get back over. He told me to stay where I was; that more help was on its way.

The lifeboat obviously couldn't get into the channel, so had to stand off and search for Hicks around the outer head. Eventually an air-sea rescue helicopter arrived and took me off. After making sure I was uninjured they helped the lifeboat search for a while before they began to run low on fuel and dropped me off up at the airport while they refuelled. Then I understand they went back to search some more. The constable was at the airport. He brought me back here and asked me to write out my account of what had happened. I've been here since then; not allowed to see anyone until you had interviewed me. The constable told me a couple of hours ago that the search had been called off. That's all I can tell you and it's the truth.'

'So,' said Marsden, 'you now admit you met Meraud Hicks yesterday evening down at Watermill?'

'I didn't *admit* it, I told you.'

'Only when you figured we already knew. You didn't mention it in your original statement.'

I was getting angry again but tried to control myself. 'I didn't think it was relevant and I didn't want to drag Mrs Hicks into it.'

Its Mrs Hicks now is it? Our witness tells us it certainly wasn't Mrs Hicks when you met up with her yesterday evening.'

I didn't reply.

'Look Peter, we've all had a long day. Why don't you just tell us how you killed Connor Hicks and we can all get something to eat and a good night's sleep?'

I was aghast. I had clearly understood that they didn't believe my account of what had happened, but I wasn't expecting this.

'This is ridiculous. Why would you think I killed Conner Hicks?

'Marsden smiled crookedly. 'You mean apart from the two witness statements I have in this folder telling us you pushed him off that cliff to his death. Perhaps it was because you wanted your ex-girlfriend back, not to mention her farm and her husband was in your way.'

I was getting very worried now. The only witnesses to what had happened were Hicks' accomplices, presumably this Hopkins and Banfield. They had obviously invented a story between themselves to put the blame for his death onto me.

'Hopkins and Banfield are not telling the truth. They had ample time to concoct a story between them before they made their statements.'

'Do you deny you shouted after her as she left Watermill that you would think of a way to get rid of her husband?'

'That's absolute rubbish. I never said that. You can ask her yourself.'

'Unfortunately we can't.'

A sudden panic gripped me. I felt as though a steel band was being drawn tight around my chest.

'Oh my God; what has he done to her?'

Marsden looked at me quizzically. 'What has *he* done to her? I assume you're alluding to Connor Kicks?'

'For Christ's sake, just tell me what's happened to Meraud.'

'This evening she's lying in St. Mary's hospital in a coma, with a fractured skull and suspected bleeding on the brain.'

I closed my eyes, slumped forward and started to bang my head on the table.

Barclay must have jumped up and run around the table because the next thing I knew he had grabbed me by the shoulders and pulled me upright. I opened my eyes and looked across at Marsden. He remained sitting there, impassive.

'Why did you visit Meraud Hicks this morning Peter?'

I stared at him incredulously. 'You must be out of your mind.'

Marsden stood up, said that he was terminating the interview and turned off the recording machine. 'We'll leave it there for today. You'll be held in a cell overnight Mr. Marshall; the only cell actually. We'll resume tomorrow when you may wish to reconsider you're earlier decision not to have your solicitor present. If you don't have a solicitor one can be provided for you.'

He got up and they both walked towards the door.

'Please, I must see Meraud.'

Marsden turned. 'Now *you* must be out of your mind.'

As they closed the door a horrific thought leaped into my brain. 'Aunt Emily; is she OK?'

They didn't reply. The door closed and I was left alone. Soon afterwards Barclay returned with the island constable and escorted me the few yards to the station's only cell. Half an hour later the constable returned with some supper for me. I asked him about Aunt Emily.

'She's at the hospital with her daughter.' He obviously hadn't been told to keep me in the dark.

At least it was a great relief to know that Emily was OK. I spent the night on the hard bunk; tossing and turning, unable to sleep; thinking of Meraud and blaming myself for everything that had happened. If I hadn't returned to the island then Meraud would not now be lying in a coma. I desperately needed to be with her but I couldn't.

Eventually morning arrived. The constable, whose name I had established was Frank, brought breakfast in to me and asked if I wanted a solicitor present at my next interview with Marsden and Barclay. Perhaps foolishly I said no. The hours dragged on into the afternoon with no sign of the detectives. Frank told me they were out interviewing Mrs Tregarthen and others. I asked him about Meraud but he didn't really have any new information. He said as far as he knew there was no change in her condition.

Finally, in late afternoon, the cell door opened and Marsden, who to my surprise was on his own, walked in. Equally surprisingly he came over and sat down across from me on the other bunk in the cell, leaving the door open.

'You're a lucky man Mr. Marshall,' was the first thing he said.

'I don't feel very lucky at the moment.'

'Two holidaymakers - birdwatchers in actual fact - were out early yesterday morning on Peninnis, he continued. 'They were up at the old lighthouse and they both had binoculars.'

My heart leaped and I held my breath; daring to hope.

'They didn't come forward as witnesses yesterday; not wanting to get involved, so they said. But they heard this morning on the island grapevine that you had been arrested. They came into the station and told the constable they had watched the whole incident through their binoculars. D C Barclay and I interviewed them separately and took their statements late this morning. The two statements agreed with each other and backed up your version of events. We then went out to the lighthouse and checked the line of sight down to the outer head and the channel. We were able to confirm it would have been possible to see the whole incident from their viewpoint.'

'Thank God,' I breathed.

'But,' continued Marsden, 'we still had the statements of Hopkins and Banfield. So we brought them in and interviewed them again, separately of course and under caution. Banfield soon broke down when he found out we had other witnesses. He claimed it was all Hopkins idea of course. His new statement agrees in the essential details with yours and the two birdwatchers. Hopkins is sticking to his version of events at the moment, but we're satisfied you were telling us the truth. Both Hopkins and Banfield will be charged with attempting to pervert the course of justice; a very serious offence.

He stood up. 'So you're free to go and I'm sorry we had to put you through all of this.'

'You had your job to do,' I conceded, more graciously than I felt.

'Your friends Tom and Karen Pender are waiting for you in the front office. They've been asking about you since early yesterday, so we phoned them as soon as we knew we were releasing you.'

'Thanks,' I said. What about Meraud?'

'There was no change a couple of hours ago when Barclay last checked. Oh and by the way, we finally managed to interview her mother, Mrs Tregarthen, this morning; she was too upset yesterday. She confirmed it was Hicks who attacked his wife. Mrs Tregarthen was woken around five a.m. this morning by screams and shouting. She got up and rushed to her daughter's bedroom to find her unconscious on the floor. The French windows were open and she saw Hicks walking away across the garden. According to Banfield the three of them had been up all night drinking and snorting cocaine before Hicks told them to keep an eye on Tom Pender's farm while he went to, quote, sort his wife out.'

I met up with Tom and Karen who were greatly relieved to see me. They wanted chapter and verse about all that had been happening, but I said all that could wait and I must go to see Meraud. It took us just a few minutes to drive up to the island hospital, which was down a lane off the road to Old Town. At first they wouldn't let us in to see Meraud, but a nurse took a message up to Emily who was with her. Soon afterwards the nurse came down and said one of us could go up to see her. Tom told me to go.

When I entered the room Emily was sitting by the bed holding her daughter's hand. Meraud's eyes were closed and her head covered by some kind of surgical bonnet. She had two black eyes and the rest of her face was bruised and swollen.

'Aunt Emily,' I whispered from the door.

Emily turned. Her face was red and blotchy; her eyes swollen from crying. 'Oh Peter, look what that horrible man has done to my beautiful girl.'

I walked over and knelt by her chair. I put my arm around her shoulders and kissed the top of her head. 'He won't hurt her ever again Emily.'

She put an arm around my waist whilst still holding onto Meraud's hand and we stayed like that for a while; just holding each other.

'How is she,' I asked at last? 'What does the doctor say?'

I think she has had an x-ray Peter. She has a fractured skull. The doctor has told me a lot of detail but I just couldn't take it all in. I'm Sorry.'

'Don't worry about it; I'll ask him.'

'She was unconscious when I found her Peter. She was lying on her side and I could see she was breathing, so I didn't try to move her. I telephoned for the ambulance and they arrived within a few minutes and brought us both down here. I've been here all the time since then. They offered me a bed last night but I couldn't leave my poor darling.'

'I'm here now Aunt Emily. Why don't you go and have a rest and I'll stay with Meraud for a while.'

'Oh I don't know Peter. I don't want to leave her. I want to be here when she wakes up.'

At that moment a nurse put her head around the door. 'I couldn't help overhearing Mrs Tregarthen. I think your nephew is right. Why don't you come with me to the day room and I'll make you a hot drink. Then you can come back if you wish or have a lie down and rest. We don't want you to end up as our patient as well as your daughter.'

'All right nurse; if you say so. You won't leave her will you Peter?'

'No of course not Aunt.' I flashed a grateful smile at the nurse as she led Emily from the room. 'Please could someone tell Mr and Mrs Pender that I'll be staying for a while and they needn't wait for me? They're down in reception.'

I sat down in the chair vacated by Emily and took Meraud's hand in both of mine. It felt too cold, but her eyes were closed and her breathing appeared regular. A host of contradictory thoughts were swirling around in my head, the primary one still being that if I hadn't come back then all this would not have happened.

I'm not sure how long I had been sitting there when a doctor came in and introduced himself as Dr. Knowles and I gave him my name, without telling him that I wasn't actually related to Meraud. I thought he might throw me out if I did.

'Your Aunt has been persuaded to lie down and is now sleeping Mr. Marshall. She has been sitting with her daughter for over twenty four hours.'

'Please could you tell me how Meraud is doing? I think Aunt Emily was too upset to take it all in.'

'Yes, of course. Mrs Hicks has been in a coma since she was brought in yesterday morning. She has severe trauma, mostly around the head, including a compound fracture of the skull, which means that the skin was broken and the skull visible. She also has a couple of fractured ribs and bruising on her face and both arms. We x-rayed her yesterday and found that the fracture is clean and not depressed; that is it isn't indenting into the brain cavity and cutting into her brain. However, we are still

113

concerned about possible bleeding on her brain and are treating the swelling and monitoring for any increase, which may be an indication of that. If we detect any additional swelling she will have to be flown over to the mainland for a CT scan and probably an operation to relieve pressure on her brain.'

'How long will she be in a coma?'

'Mr. Marshall, I haven't told your Aunt any of this but I will be honest with you. When someone is in a coma, they are deeply unconscious and cannot be woken up. They do not speak or respond to voices, or even pain. Mrs Hicks is breathing without assistance, which is a promising sign. Most people come out of a coma after two to four weeks, but I must warn you that a few people remain unresponsive, or have limited consciousness, for many years. When someone comes out of a coma, it is usually gradual, with small improvements over time. Unfortunately, some people who go into a coma may never regain consciousness. However, there is nothing to indicate that will be the case with Mrs Hicks. Unless complications develop she may well make a full recovery, although brain damage is always a possibility.'

I sat by Meraud's bed for three more days, alternating with Emily. I talked to her a lot, thinking she somehow might be able to hear me. Sometimes I thought I detected small movements in her fingers, but she showed no sign of waking up. Finally the day arrived when I was booked to return to the mainland. I was due back at school the following day.

'Peter you have to go,' said Karen. 'We don't know how long Meraud will remain like this. You can't give up your job. Tom

114

and I will visit Meraud regularly and keep you up to date; and we'll give Emily all the help she needs with the farm.'

'You can't do that forever. You have your own place to run.'

'It won't be forever Peter,' said Tom. 'You'll see.'

And so very reluctantly the following day I joined those sad faced crowds on the New Quay, waiting behind the barriers to embark at the end of their holidays. But I had much more reason for sadness than merely the end of a holiday. I had promised Emily I would fly back as soon as Meraud regained consciousness, but couldn't help wondering to myself if she would ever do so. This tragedy had been entirely my fault. Meraud had been in an abusive marriage, but if I had stayed out of it surely she would have extricated herself somehow, perhaps with the help of Tom and Karen, or others.

It was low tide this time as the passenger ferry left the harbour and so she sailed the long way around The Garrison and through St Mary's Sound. I looked over towards Peninnis Head in the distance as we sailed past. I could not distinguish that vicious, turbulent channel, where Hicks had fallen to his death from the jumble of huge boulders which made up the outer head. His body had not been recovered and I suspected it never would be; probably smashed to pieces on those cruel rocks where many ships had foundered over the centuries. I remained standing by the rail until the Eastern isles disappeared into the haze of another perfect May morning and wondered if I would ever again see Meraud's hazel eyes look into mine with the rekindled love I thought I had seen in that brief moment on the beach at Watermill.

~~~~~~~~~~~~~~~~

The house is what is known in these parts as "upside-down". That is to say the bedrooms are on the ground floor and the living rooms upstairs, affording magnificent views to the north-west across Halangy Down to the headland and the sea beyond. Normally I would celebrate this arrangement sitting nursing a glass of single malt in the evening and watching the sun set over Samson and the Western Isles. It could, however, be very distracting when one is trying to work and today was a case in point.

As I continued to look out, my thoughts still lost in the events of forty-odd years ago, a well-known white shape began to emerge from behind the headland and the Scillonian's siren sounded for a third time, cautioning any small boats in the harbour to make way. The touch of a hand on what passes these days for my waist startled me out of my trance.

'Sorry, did I make you jump?'

'I was miles away. I didn't hear you come in.'

She moved closer, laying her head against my shoulder. 'Penny for them?'

I turned and kissed the top of her head. 'I was just wondering if our new polytunnels are on the Silly Onion.'

She smiled. 'I haven't heard you call her that since we were teenagers, watching her predecessor come around Peninnis.'

Perhaps she felt me stiffen, or sensed disquiet in my silence.

'You weren't thinking about polytunnels at all, were you?'

'Sometimes a sight or sound brings it all flooding back. It doesn't take much; seeing the lifeboat turning out or the face of

116

an old school friend; or a familiar sound like the siren of the Scillonian. I don't see him as often now as I used to. For the first few years I couldn't get through a night's sleep without reaching down for him and seeing the look on his face as he disappeared over the edge. No one deserves to die like that.'

'I don't think he would have given you a second thought if it had been you going over the edge, as I'm sure he planned.'

'There are still folks alive on these islands who think I got away with murder.'

'I very much doubt that, but if there are they are called Hicks and no one pays any attention to them. I am going to get angry with you in a minute. There will always be a few idiots who prefer a good conspiracy theory to the facts. Come on Peter, turn off that laptop. I've set lunch out in the garden. I thought it was warm enough today.'

I followed her through the house and onto the front lawn where Tom and Louise were already well into the carrot cake.

'Sorry Grandma; Grandpa,' said Tom, 'we were hungry; we couldn't wait for you.'

'I'm glad you left us a few sandwiches at least,' laughed his Grandmother. I'll be glad when half term is over. You two are eating us out of house and home.'

'What time are Mummy and Daddy coming for us today,' asked Louise?

'It will be quite late today darling. Your Daddy is sorting bulbs for replanting and Mummy will be helping him after she's finished with the changeover in the holiday cottage. But it's

Friday, so we'll take you down to watch the gig racing after tea if you like.'

'Yippee,' shouted young Tom. 'Will Uncle Tom be rowing?'

'No darling. Don't you remember he had to give up this year because of his bad back?'

'Grandma,' Mumbled Louise through a mouthful of carrot cake.

'Yes sweetheart,' she said, choosing not to scold her for speaking with her mouth full.

'I wish Great Grandma still lived in the cottage.'

My wife didn't reply. She looked across at me and I saw the glisten in her eyes as the tears began to form.

Reaching over, I squeezed Meraud's hand under the table. 'So do we Louise,' I said. 'So do we.'

A Child's Story

I was kneeling, watching my Dad through the spindles, from the landing at the top of the stairs. He was wearing his big heavy coat, the one I could hardly carry. He was staring into the hall mirror. He was just standing there, with both his hands on the telephone table, staring. What was he looking at, I thought? He could only see himself in the mirror.

I jumped up. 'Dad,' I said, 'you're not going out again are you?' He turned around slowly and looked up at me. 'Where are you going; can I come too?' I asked. 'Please don't leave me again; I hate it here on my own.'

Dad stood for what seemed like ages, although it probably wasn't more than a few seconds, with his head a little on one side, as if he hadn't heard me clearly. I held my breath. Then he shook his head slowly. 'No.' He almost whispered the word. 'No,' he said again; then he just turned around and began to put on his gloves.

'Please Dad,' I begged, 'don't leave me here by myself. I hate this house since Mum left. It scares me; it's so big and quiet. Grandma used to come and stay with me. Why doesn't Grandma come anymore? Please take me with you.' I started to cry. I didn't want to because I'm too old now to cry, but I couldn't help it.

But Dad just ignored me. He slowly put on his hat and walked towards the front door. 'No,' he said, 'it isn't possible.' He pulled the collar of his heavy coat up high against the cold, then the big front door opened and closed quietly behind him; he was gone.

I was on my own again, in that big silent house; the house where I could still smell Mum's perfume in her wardrobe. The house where I could still find some of her things; small things, like a handkerchief, at the back of a drawer, or some lipstick. But it was getting harder to find her things now, because when Dad found them he always threw them away. He never did this at once; sometimes he held them in his hands for ages, just looking at them and sometimes he kept them by his bed for days, but he always threw them away in the end. It was also getting harder now to smell Mum's perfume. I knew that soon the scent wouldn't be there at all and I wouldn't be able to find any more of her things either; then she would really be gone forever.

No, I wouldn't be left here on my own; not this time. I would follow Dad and see where he was going. I wouldn't catch him up, because he might bring me back here; just follow him.

The front door wasn't a problem; Dad hadn't even locked it. I stepped out into the front garden and ran down the path. It was very cold, but I didn't mind the cold. I could hear the traffic on the main road in the distance. It was very windy and the dry, dead leaves were swirling all around me. I stopped at the garden gate and looked left and right. There was Dad, walking quickly towards the park. I would have to run very fast to catch up with him, but I could run very fast.

As I ran, I thought about the night that Mum had left. I often thought about that horrible night. The more I thought about it though, the less I understood what had happened. I tried asking Dad, but he never wanted to talk about it. At first he said I would have to be patient and Mum would come back soon, but eventually he started to get annoyed whenever I asked when Mum was coming home. He didn't shout at me, but just said Mum wasn't coming back and he didn't want to talk about it anymore. Then he wouldn't speak for hours, so I stopped asking.

It had been my birthday only a few days before the night when everything changed. I was eight years old. All my best friends came to my party. I even invited some girls, but only because Grandma' made me. Even at my party I could see that Mum and Dad were unhappy. They tried to hide it, but I could tell; so could Grandma'. I caught her crying in the kitchen. She said it was the onions, but it wasn't. We didn't have onions at my party; I hate them.

I had been thinking so much about my birthday party and Mum I almost missed Dad turning into the park. I realised I was catching up with him and he might see me, so I slowed down. Good, he hadn't seen me. I would just follow him quietly. I can be very quiet when I want to. Dad was now walking slowly along a winding path between tall bushes. Although it was November the bushes still had their leaves on, (I think they call them evergreen). It was very dark and I was beginning to get a little scared, but now I had started I was determined to find out where Dad was going. As I walked along behind him I started to think again about the night Mum left. Although I didn't really want to think about it, at least it stopped me thinking of big dark bushes and who, or what, might be hiding behind them.

A few days after my party, I was in bed, but not asleep. I heard Mum and Dad talking very loudly, so I crept onto the landing and listened. I couldn't really hear what they were saying because the lounge door was closed, but I heard Uncle Mike's name more than once. He wasn't really my uncle, but Mum and Dad said they had known him since long before I was born; since sometime they called Uni. So I called him Uncle Mike. He didn't live in our town and I think his work took him a long way away quite often, but when he was able to he always came to see us. I liked him because he always brought me a present and because he made me laugh a lot. He made Mum laugh a lot too.

That night he came again. As I was listening on the landing I heard a car pull up outside the house and beep its horn. I ran into Mum and Dad's bedroom at the front of the house, to see who it was. I was very surprised to see it was Uncle Mike's car, because Mum and Dad always knew when he was coming and told me and he never came so late at night. It was also very strange that Uncle Mike was not getting out of his car; he was just sitting in it. He kept looking up towards the house every few seconds and then he beeped his horn again.

I heard a noise somewhere behind me and I was not in Mum and Dad's bedroom anymore but suddenly back in that cold, windy, dark park again. I also realised that Dad was now sitting on a park bench. He was all hunched up on the bench which was beneath a lamp post. It was a good thing I had heard the noise or I would have walked right up to him. I stepped behind a bush so he wouldn't see me if he looked up. He was just sat there staring at the path in front of him. I heard the rustling noise again, louder than before. I was getting really scared now and crept a little closer to Dad.

Just as I was thinking I should go up to Dad and ask him to take me home, he suddenly turned around and looked straight towards me. I thought he had seen me at first, even though I was still behind the bush. But he hadn't seen me; it was two men he had heard, coming through the bushes. They looked very big and the track suits they both wore had hoods covering their heads, so their faces were in shadow. They didn't see me either, but they had seen Dad. They walked straight up to him. They stood very close and one man bent over him. Dad didn't try to get up. I heard them talking to him, but he didn't say anything. I was very scared, but Dad didn't seem frightened at all. Then I saw that one man was holding something in his hand which glinted silver in the light from the lamp overhead. Slowly

Dad reached inside his coat, took something from his inside pocket and gave it to the man bending over him. The other man laughed and said something, pointing towards Dad's arm. Dad slowly took off his watch, which I remembered was a very nice gold one. Both men then ran off towards the footbridge over the river. They were laughing and shouting as they ran. I heard what they said this time; it wasn't nice. Dad didn't move for a few minutes, then got up and began to walk slowly in the direction in which the men had run.

I remembered that Mum had run too, the night Uncle Mike came to our house for the very last time. Crouched by the bedroom window, I heard the front door open and saw Mum running down the garden path. She was pulling the suitcase she used when we went on holiday; the one with little wheels at two corners, so you didn't have to carry it. I could see and hear everything very clearly. Uncle Mike quickly got out of his car and opened the boot. He kept looking towards the house. He put Mum's suitcase into the boot. It was then that I shouted to Mum through the half open window. She was just getting into the car. She quickly turned and looked up at the bedroom window. She called my name and her hand went up to her mouth. She took a step back towards the house, but Uncle Mike had run around to the passenger side. He said 'for God's sake Jill, get into the car.' Then he grabbed her shoulders and pushed her down towards the car door. Mum did get in, but she was still looking up at me, her hand covering her mouth. Uncle Mike slammed shut the car door, ran around to the driver's side and jumped in. I heard the click of the car doors being locked from the inside, just before the engine started. The car jerked and the engine stopped again, just like our car does with Mum sometimes, when she's in a hurry. Uncle Mike started the engine again and the tyres squealed as the car set off down the road. I watched as the lights grew smaller and then suddenly brighter again as Uncle Mike slowed down at the junction and turned left into the main road. Then they were gone. Everything was quiet again, outside and inside. I have not heard anyone laugh inside our house since that night when Uncle Mike drove away with my Mum.

It was also quiet again in the park as I crept from behind my bush and followed Dad down towards the bridge. He was walking slowly now, head down with his collar still turned up against the cold. I wasn't scared any more. I wanted to catch up with him and hold onto his hand again, as I used to do when I was little and we walked through the park; in the summertime, when it was warm, with Mum holding my other hand. They would laugh with me as they lifted me up and swung my feet off the ground. But I wasn't going to cry again; I was eight and a half years old and I wasn't going to cry.

The medicine cabinet was high up on the wall in the bathroom; higher than I could reach and it was always kept locked. Mum and Dad had told me the things in the medicine cabinet were dangerous and I must never go in there. After Mum had been gone for a long time and I hardly ever found her things around the house any more, I had an idea. I watched Dad and saw where he kept the key to the medicine cabinet. One evening, later that week, Dad was in his study and he thought I was asleep. I got the key and a chair from Dad's bedroom and very quietly took them into the bathroom. I stood on the chair and unlocked the medicine cabinet. There were quite a few little boxes, tubes and bottles in there. I opened some of the tubes and bottles and most of them didn't smell very nice, so I opened the boxes instead. Most of the boxes and some of the bottles had pills inside them, which didn't smell of anything in particular. I knew the pills must be dangerous, even though they didn't smell horrid, but I had a plan. If I took a lot of the pills I would get really ill and if I did then Mum would have to come home again to look after me. I was sure that when Mum came home to make me better and talked to Dad again, she would realise how much she missed him. She would come home for good and they would be happy again and laugh a lot, like they used to do when I was little; everything would be back as it had been. So I took some of the boxes back to my bedroom with a big glass full of water. It took quite a long time to swallow all of the pills; some of them were very big. Before I had swallowed them all I began to feel very sleepy.

Dad was now standing in the middle of the footbridge over the river. He was leaning on the hand-rail and looking into the water. The river was always deep around the bridge, even in summer, but the water didn't move very fast because of something Dad called the weir, which was a little further down. Dad stood looking into the water for ages; I wondered if he was thinking about Mum. Then, slowly, he stood up straight and began to climb over the hand-rail. His big coat got caught on one of the iron scrolls under the rail and he had to reach down to free it. He didn't seem to be in any hurry, but I knew he wouldn't stop now. Soon he was standing with his heels on a narrow ledge on the outside of the bridge. His arms were stretched backwards with his hands holding onto the rail behind him, so that he was leaning outwards and downwards. He was looking towards me now and I knew he could see me at last, but I was too frightened to shout; frightened that he might not let go.

When Dad jumped from the bridge his hat flew off and he looked much bigger as the air got inside his great heavy coat. He splashed into the black, cold water and came under very quickly. He was still looking at me, but now he was smiling. As he sank slowly and quietly down into the deepest part of the river he held his arms out towards me. I saw his mouth open and I heard him calling my name. When he reached me I held onto him very tightly. I realised at last that Mum would never come back again; to that house without laughter that was no longer a home. But now I had my Dad back, and I wasn't going to lose him again, ever.

Remote Control

She picks up the telephone handset but doesn't speak.

'Edith, are you there?'

'Oh John, I'm so sorry.'

'Sorry, whatever for love? What's the matter?'

'I've messed up the TV again John; I can't get a picture. Every time you tell me how to do it I think I've understood and then next day I've forgotten again. I wish you were here.' She starts to cry.

'Don't cry love. I wish I were there to, but you know I can't be. We'll soon sort it out. Is the screen completely blank?'

'There's a message; it says "No Signal"'.

'Oh that's easily fixed. You must have changed the source.'

'The what?'

'The source; the place where the TV is trying to find the signal.'

'How did I do that?'

'I don't know dear. Did you sit on the remote control again?'

'I don't think so. It usually takes me half an hour to find it in the first place. It always seems to wriggle its way down the sides of the cushions on the settee, or hide amongst the magazines, or the dog sits on it. Why can't they make TVs anymore that you can just go over and switch them on, with buttons and knobs to change the channels and turn the sound up and down?'

'Come on now Edith, there haven't been TVs like that since we were both little children.'

'I know, I know, but I just get so frustrated with the darn thing.'

'Why don't you just leave the remote next to the TV, then you'll know where it is?'

'Oh, please don't get annoyed with me John; I never intentionally lose it you know. I just put things down and then can't remember where I've put them.'

'I'm not getting annoyed love, I'm just trying to help.'

'And then there are all the other ones.'

'The other what dear?'

'Remotes of course; I can never remember which one does what.'

'Well I've told you, you only need one for the TV.'

'So why do I have all the others; there are five of them here?'

'Well, one is for the TV, as I've said. Another is for the machine on which you can play DVDs and CDs. You can also record programs on there as well but you don't really need to anymore because the set-top-box has a hard drive that you can record onto and then . . . .'

'A hard what?'

'A hard drive dear.'

'I love it when you talk dirty John.'

'Now behave yourself Edith, I'm trying to explain to you what the remotes do.'

'I'm sorry John; carry on.'

'As I was saying, there is one for the DVD machine and then there is the one which says "Sky" on it which runs from the satellite dish, but you don't need to use that unless the cable service fails.'

'Then why have we got it?'

'Well it was there when we bought the house. We don't subscribe so it doesn't cost us anything. There was no point taking the dish down and throwing away the Sky set-top box if we could use it as a back-up, if needed.'

'What about the little blue and silver one?'

'Ah yes, that's for the amplifier.'

'Why do I need an amplifier? I can still hear perfectly well.'

'I know you can love, but if you want to listen to music or a DVD in stereo you need to use the amplifier to direct the sound through the speakers. You will have to change the source on the amplifier though if you decide to listen to a vinyl record from the turntable.'

'There's that source thing again.'

'Yes but this is a different source, one which tells the amplifier where the sound is coming from.'

'Oh dear, I'll never get the hang of all this. And there's another; an all black one.'

'I think you mean the one which came with the TV and works from the old aerial in the loft.'

'Why do I need that one then?'

'Well you don't really, not since we got the cable service installed when we moved in.'

'So why did we need a cable when we had the satellite thingy and the old aerial in the loft?'

'Well, we got a lot of sport from the cable supplier and we didn't have to pay any extra for it.'

'You mean you didn't have to pay any extra; I'm not interested in sport.'

'What about tennis; you like tennis?'

'Well, apart from tennis. And snooker of course, I like snooker.'

'I think you just like to look at the players bottoms when they bend over the table.'

'Now who's being rude? Anyway, there are only a few minutes to go before Coronation Street comes on and we still haven't got the darn TV working.'

'I'm sorry love; do you have the BT remote there now?'

'Yes, I found it in the bathroom.'

'Why was it in . . . .? OK, never mind, you have it. Can you see the button in the top right hand corner? It's got "AV" on it.

'What does that mean?'

'I have no idea, but it doesn't matter. Just press it and a list will come up on the screen.'

'It doesn't have a screen.'

'What doesn't?'

'The BT remote.'

'I mean on the TV screen Edith.'

'Well why didn't you say so? Was that a tut? Are you tutting at me?'

He sighs. 'I wasn't tutting dear. It must be interference on the line; a bad connection.'

'I'm sure I heard you tut.'

'Never mind that now Edith; have you pressed the button?'

'Which button was that then?' Silence. 'John, are you still there?'

He sighs. 'Yes, I'm still here love.'

'That was definitely a sigh.'

Edith, please would you press the AV button on the BT remote in your hand and a list will come up on the TV screen.'

'I'm sorry John; I'm doing my best, really I am. It's all just so confusing. There, I've done it and I can see the list.'

'That's great Edith. Now keep pressing the AV button until HDMI1 is highlighted on the list and then select.'

'Select what?'

I'm sorry, I meant press the "Select" button in the middle of the remote.'

'I can't see any "Select" button.'

A pause. 'I'm sorry Edith. I forgot it says "OK" on that remote, not "Select".'

'There, you see, even you get confused. Oh drat, the list has disappeared now. It just says "No Signal" again.'

'The list goes off after a few seconds if you don't do anything. Just keep pressing the AV button until HDMI1 is highlighted on the list and then press the OK button.'

Seconds pass, then . . . . 'I've done it. I have a picture. Now I just need to find the right channel.'

'I think you can manage that on your own. I'll leave you to your Coronation Street.'

She puts down the BT remote on the coffee table. 'John?'

'Yes love?'

'Thank you. I would never have been able to do that by myself.'

'Write it all down now, whilst you remember it.'

'But Coronation Street is on in two minutes.'

'Of course; I'm sorry; you must get your priorities right.'

'You're being sarcastic now, but I don't mind. I know you never did like Coronation Street.'

'I'll let you get on with it then. You know where I am if you need me.'

'John?'

'Yes love?'

'Why did you have to go? You know I always wanted to go first.'

'We can't always have what we want love and I'm here anytime you need me.'

'It isn't the same as you being here, with me; just the two of us.'

'I know, I know.'

'And why the phone?'

'Well, it seemed like the best place. You just have to pick up the handset and here I am. You don't even have to press any buttons.'

She laughs. 'I never was any good with the TV and all these dratted remote controls.'

'I was never any good with the washing machine and the dishwasher. If you had gone first I'm sure you would have helped me out with those.'

'But I didn't.' She sniffs.

'No; no you didn't. I'd better go now. Find your channel and watch Coronation Street.'

'I love you John.'

'I love you too Edith. Goodnight.'

'Goodnight love.'

The connection goes dead. Edith absently puts the telephone handset down beside her on the settee and it slips between the cushions. She picks up the Sky remote control and presses 3. Nothing happens. She sits back on the settee and closes her eyes. Two large tears emerge from under her eyelids and roll down her cheeks. She is lost in her memories. Eventually she opens her eyes again and realises she has the wrong remote in her hand. Picking up the BT one she presses 3 and the programme on the TV changes. A familiar theme tune fills the room. Coronation Street has just finished.

My Exciting Adventure

I am four seasons old and my name is Ruby. I am a girl. My humans, Tony and Sue, sometimes tell others they meet that I am called Labradoodle, but I think Ruby is a nicer name and they always call me that when we are on our own. I am quite proud of my curly black coat (although I don't much like having it brushed) and long legs that mean I can run very fast.

I have lived with Tony and Sue almost all my life. I don't know anything about my father and I only have dim memories of my mother; her soft, warm body and the lovely milk she shared between me and my little brothers and sisters. Tony and Sue are very kind to me though and I am really happy with them.

We live near to the sea in a place which Tony & Sue call Northumberland and when we go there I love to run into the water to cool off after bringing back the ball which Tony keeps throwing away. I don't know why he does this but he seems to enjoy it and I don't mind bringing it back so that he can throw it again. I don't much like swimming though, but if Tony throws the ball into the sea I grit my teeth and bring it back because otherwise he would lose it. I usually get my own back by shaking all the seawater out of my coat next to him which makes him shout and Sue scream if she is with us. He usually doesn't do it again after that.

I love to chase around with other folk like me that we meet when we are out but they are sometimes quite grumpy and some are really unfriendly for some reason. I find it difficult to tell who are going to be the unfriendly ones but Tony and Sue, especially Sue, seem to know and usually blow their whistle to let me know before I get into trouble and I run back to them as fast as my legs can carry me, which is pretty fast..

There are also a lot of different folk which Tony calls sheep which seem to live all over Northumberland. None of them seem to have any real home and live out in the fields, which must be really miserable when it's cold or rainy. They seem like they could be fun to run around with but Tony has taught me that they don't like to be chased and get upset if they are, so now I ignore them, even though they are always staring at me as we go past.

One day Tony and Sue started to put a lot of their stuff (humans do seem to have an awful lot of stuff) into the big shiny machine they use to take us to places too far away to walk. I don't know how it works but it certainly goes a lot faster than I can run and it's great fun to put my head out of the window and take in all the different smells as we go along. Tony and Sue call this machine Rover and it's always exciting to go in and the trip usually ends in a long run somewhere which I have never been to before. Knowing this I never have any hesitation in jumping into the back of Rover.

This time we went a really long way into some big hills which had lots of sheep on them. It was so far that I eventually went to sleep and only woke up when Rover stopped going smoothly along and began to bounce up and down. When I looked out of the window we had turned off the usual flat road onto a bumpy narrow one made of loose stones and were heading towards a long white house at the bottom of a steep hill.

Hi Mum. Just to let you know, we are going to spend a long weekend with Mark and Sam up in the Cheviots. Tony may help with the lambing if needed and Sam and I hope to have a good natter, if she has any spare time, which she rarely does. Ruby will like the change of scenery too. I will e-mail again when we get home next Tuesday. xxx Sue.

As we got near to the house two humans came out and waved to us and Tony and Sue waved back. They got out of the car and there was a lot of talking and kissing. They had forgotten about me so I let them know I was there.

"Oh, sorry Ruby", said Sue and came to let me out. "This is Mark & Sam", she said to me, pointing. I ran over and made a fuss of them and they laughed and rubbed behind my ears, which I like. They seemed OK.

We went inside the house, which was not like our home at all. The walls were very thick and Tony, who is taller than most humans, had to bend down a little to go through the doors. We went into the place they called the kitchen where there was a big fireplace with a roaring fire, because it was quite cold outside. Near to the fire was a small human who was holding a little lamb; I think that's what they call a baby sheep.

"Hi Fiona", said Sue, "what are you up to?"

"I'm looking after Charlie", replied Fiona, "he hasn't got a mother".

"His mother rejected him", said Mark, "so we are bottle feeding him".

I went over to investigate and had a sniff at Charlie; he didn't seem to mind and licked my nose. Fiona giggled at this.

"Will Ruby be OK with him?" asked Mark.

Tony smiled. "He'll be safe enough with Ruby; she doesn't bother sheep."

Later on that day, after Tony, Sue and I had had a good walk around the farm, it had gone dark and the grown up humans were all in the lounge sitting around the wood burning stove and talking a lot, like humans do. Fiona had gone to bed and I had been dozing in front of the fire in the kitchen. I woke up and didn't see Charlie anywhere. After a sniff around I still couldn't find him but could smell his scent on a little door cut into the back door of the house. I thought I should go and find him if he had gone outside, but I was too big to get through the little door, so I went into the lounge and asked to go out.

"You don't really want to go out again do you Ruby, we've been out all afternoon", said Tony. "Oh, all right then". He gave in after I persisted and came to let me out of the front door. He opened the door and I ran outside.

"She'll be OK", said Tony to the others. "She'll be barking to come back inside in a few minutes."

After Tony had shut the front door I ran around to the back of the house, picked up Charlie's scent and began to follow it. The trail led towards a big building inside which, earlier in the day, Mark had shown us were other sheep and young lambs. Perhaps Charlie was trying to find his mother, I thought. Just then I heard a small scream and then another one. I ran towards the screams and as I came around the corner of the barn I saw Charlie and an animal a little smaller than me with a red coat. It had got Charlie by the neck in its mouth and was dragging him away from the farm towards the gate leading into the fields.

I growled and ran towards the red animal. It dropped Charlie and snarled at me. I didn't like the look of it but that didn't stop me. I ran straight at it and jumped right in. It didn't smell very

138

nice; in fact it stank. We were both trying to bite each other but I managed to get my teeth into its throat first and I shook it as hard as I could. After a little while it stopped struggling and I knew it must be dead. I had never killed anything before and I wasn't sure if I would get into trouble; but it would have killed poor Charlie so I didn't think I had done anything wrong.

I looked around for Charlie. He was lying whimpering on the ground nearby and there was blood all around his throat. I picked him up as gently as I could by the scruff of his neck and carried him back to the front door of the house. Still holding Charlie I scratched on the door but no one heard me, so I put Charlie down and barked. Tony then came and opened the door.

"What have you been up to then Ruby?" he said as he opened the door. He then saw Charlie and stood very still in the doorway. "Oh shit" he said.

"What's the matter Tony", I heard Sue say.

"It's Ruby", said Tony, "I think she's attacked Charlie".

"Oh no, she can't have", shouted Sue as she ran to the door, followed by Mark and Sam.

I tried to tell them that I hadn't attacked him; that the red coated, smelly animal did it, but they weren't listening. Mark picked up Charlie and carried him inside and I followed. He examined Charlie and found where he had been bitten.

"I think he may be OK", he said. "I should be able to stem the flow of blood and I have some antibiotics which the vet left with us. I'll start him on them to stop any infection. The vet is due to call again tomorrow, so he can have a look at him." He then looked at me.

"Tony, I can see blood all around your dog's muzzle", he said. I noticed he wasn't calling me Ruby anymore. Tony examined around my mouth.

"I'm so sorry Mark. She's never done anything like this before."

"There's always a first time", said Mark.

"Oh Ruby, how could you", sobbed Sue.

I tried to tell them I had actually saved Charlie from the nasty red animal but I just couldn't make them understand.

"Come on Ruby", said Mark, dragging me protesting into the Kitchen, "I'll clean you up and then you'll have to sleep in the utility room tonight, where you can't get at Charlie again".

"How could Charlie have got out", I heard Sue say from the other room.

"I think he must have got out through the cat-flap", said Sam. "He's done it before. I always put him in a small pen at night when we are not there to watch him, but unfortunately I forgot tonight."

"I don't understand", said Sue. "Ruby didn't try to harm Charlie him when they were both in the kitchen on their own and she must have brought him back to the front door. I'm sure she didn't mean to hurt him."

"Well she made a pretty good job of it", grumbled Mark. "There are deep bite marks in his neck, but fortunately they seem to have missed the main artery. Anyway, I'll have to get back now and help Tom with the lambing".

I didn't hear anything else because Tony took me with my bed to what he called the utility room.

"You've been a very bad girl", he said "and you will have to stay here until the morning. We may even have to go home tomorrow after this".

He then shut the door and left me in the dark. I considered barking to be let out but thought better of it and settled down to spend a cold miserable night in the darkness. I didn't even get any supper.

Oh Mum, an awful thing has happened. Ruby has bitten a little lamb which Mark & Sam were bottle feeding. We are all very upset; it's so unlike Ruby. We can't believe she has done it after all the training we have given her. We may have to come home early now. Mark thinks the lamb will be OK though. xxx Sue.

Next morning Tony opened the door and put a lead around my neck.

"I'll take you out now Ruby", he said, "but I'll have to keep you on your lead from now on".

As we went through the kitchen Mark came in at the back door looking exhausted.

"My goodness, have you been up all night?" asked Tony.

"Yes and I'm completely shattered, but we've delivered another twelve lambs", replied Mark. "Tony, could you come over to the barn with me, I want to show you something."

"Oh no", cried Sue, who was in the kitchen helping Sam to make breakfast for the family, "don't tell me Ruby did some more damage last night".

"Bring Ruby with you", said Mark, looking serious "and don't bother with her lead".

Tony and Sue looked very puzzled, but Tony took off my lead and we all trooped out of the kitchen door and towards the barn. We walked around the corner of the barn where I had been the night before and towards the gate into the nearest field where I had fought with the red animal. As we neared the gate I saw the animal still lying there.

"Do you see that?" asked Mark.

"My God, it's a dead fox", exclaimed Tony.

So that's what they call it, I thought to myself. I'll remember in future, but I hope I never meet another one.

"Do you see, it's been bitten in the throat", said Mark, lifting up the animal's head. "That's what killed it; but if you look closely you'll see it also has blood around its mouth."

"Oh Mark", said Sue, "do you think it may have been this fox which attacked Charlie?"

"And Ruby killed it?" added Tony.

"I think that's the only explanation", said Mark. "Both our dogs were locked up in their kennels at dusk yesterday, so it couldn't have been either of them."

"Oh Ruby", sobbed Sue, falling to her knees and flinging her arms around my neck, "we're so sorry; you saved Charlie's life and we didn't understand. You're a hero".

We'll yes, I suppose I am, I thought to myself. It's a pity you didn't realise that last night though and then I wouldn't have had to spend all night in that cold, dark humility room; or whatever it is you call it.

> *Hi Mum. Thank goodness everything is all right with Ruby. Mark found a dead fox that must have attacked Charlie the lamb when it got out of the house last night. It could only have been Ruby who killed it and brought Charlie back to the house. Everyone is making a great fuss of her and she is lapping it up. See you next week. xxx Sue.*

After I was cleared of biting Charlie our visit to Mark and Sam's farm went swimmingly. I had some long walks in the hills with Tony (without my lead) and had some meals that were big enough for two of me, but I managed to eat them all up.

"We'll have to give you plenty of long runs on Cheswick beach when we get home", said Tony, "you'll be getting fat the way you're eating here".

What a cheek, I thought; I'm only eating what you give me, although I'm not complaining.

I was also getting on very well with Charlie, who everyone, particularly Fiona, was making a great fuss of. The vet had called later that same morning, approved the antibiotics which Mark had started Charlie on and pronounced that he should make a full recovery in a week or so. Although Charlie did not seem inclined to go exploring outside anymore, I still kept a close eye on him and in the evening slept next to his pen to keep him company.

"Ruby seems to have taken Charlie under her wing", said Sue on our last evening. "It's a pity we have to leave tomorrow. I think she will be quite distraught."

"So will Fiona", mused Mark, "when Charlie is old enough to go into the fields".

"And then in a few months . . .", said Sue, her voice trailing off.

"That's the nature of sheep farming", said Mark, "and Fiona will have to come to terms with it. She's never been so attached to a lamb before though; it's going to be difficult for her to let go".

"Oh, it's such a shame", said Sue, tears coming into her eyes, "could you not make an exception with Charlie".

"Sorry", said Mark, "all the animals and humans have to earn their keep on this farm, one way or the other. We can't afford any passengers".

Later that day we all got into Rover and set off for home. I said goodbye to Charlie before we left, but he looked very sad and bleated pitifully as we all left Mark and Sam's cosy kitchen for the last time.

After we got home I couldn't get Charlie out of my head. Every time I saw other sheep in the fields I wondered how he was getting on; if he now had to live in the cold and sometimes rainy fields like them and how little Fiona must have cried when her Dad took him away.

One evening, when Tony and I were out for a walk and after we had been home for quite a while, I saw a farmer near to our house rounding up a lot of sheep with other folk like me who worked for him. I said hello to them but they were far too busy to answer me. They were driving the sheep into a machine something like Rover, but much bigger. It had a lot of small openings in the sides which the sheep were trying to look out through. When all the sheep were inside they closed the big doors at the back and the machine drove away. I wonder where they are going, I thought to myself.

"Charlie wasn't there Ruby", said Tony, as he saw I was taking a great interest.

I know that, I thought to myself. I'm not stupid. Still I would like to see Charlie again; he was such a friendly little chap. I don't suppose I ever will though.

The next day was one of the ones where Tony didn't have to go to what he called work. After I had been for my usual morning run on the beach and brought Tony's ball back so many times I lost count, we got back home and I could sense immediately that something was different. Sue seemed on edge and kept looking out of the front window.

"They won't be here for an hour or so", said Tony, "so you might as well relax".

Oh good, I thought, they must be expecting visitors. I always get made a fuss of when visitors come.

Eventually I heard a sound coming down our lane and so I went to the front window to see what it was. Tony and Sue heard it too and ran to the front door. A big machine, something like Rover but a bit bigger turned into our garden and stopped outside the house. The front of the machine was like Rover but the back was all closed in with no way to see in or out.

The doors opened and to my surprise Mark, Sam and Fiona got out. There was a lot of hugging and kissing as grown up humans do and Fiona came over, put her arms around my neck and kissed me. I didn't really mind; she's a nice kid.

"Well", said Sue, "come on Mark, we can't wait any longer can we Tony?"

"Well you certainly can't", replied Tony. "You've been on tenterhooks for hours."

Mark smiled, walked around to the back of the machine and opened a big door.

"We're here", he said," come and see your old friends".

And would you believe it, out popped Charlie. He was much bigger but I recognised him and his scent straight away. I said hello and Charlie ran straight over to me and I let him lick my nose. After all, having just been kissed by Fiona, how could I refuse, although it was a little beneath my dignity to be licked by a lamb; or full grown sheep now, I thought to myself.

Hi Mum. Charlie has arrived! He and Ruby have renewed their friendship and they are now both in the paddock. Ruby is watching over him like an older sister and Charlie is munching away happily. I'm sure he will do a great job keeping the grass beautifully cropped and save Tony a big chore. I think he will be very happy with us and it is a win, win for everyone. We have paid Mark the going rate, Fiona is deliriously happy that Charlie is not going you know where, Ruby has a pal and Tony doesn't have to cut the grass anymore. See you next weekend. xxx. Sue.

146

And that's nearly the end of my story. Charlie the sheep came to live with us and he says he is very happy here, particularly since he has a little shed to live in out of the cold when he is not eating grass, which he does quite a lot of. He doesn't seem to miss his sheep friends; in fact he told me that all the boys went off somewhere in a big machine (it sounded just like the one I saw) the day before Mark and Sam brought him here. I wonder sometimes where they all go to.

Charlie and I see each other every day and we have lots fun together, although Tony won't let him come with us on our walks. I let him chase me around the paddock but, remembering what Tony taught me, I never chase him. Sue and Tony introduce him to all our visitors and she tells everyone who will listen about my exiting adventure and that Charlie and I get on like a house on fire; whatever that means.

The End.

Acknowledgements:

1) As you have probably guessed, I don't really speak English, although I understand a lot of it quite well. So I must thank Tony for translating my story into English from the original dogeral (not to be confused with doggerel, which Tony says is something quite different).

2) I also must thank Sue for allowing me to include her e-mails to her Mum, which gives you an idea what the humans were thinking during my adventure.

A Helping Hand

A slightly built figure stood in dappled sunlight, in the farthest corner of a country churchyard in North Yorkshire. Closer approach by an observer would have revealed a man in his late thirties, dressed in a dark suit, white shirt and navy blue tie, bending over the headstone of a small grave. The grave in question lay at the extremity of shadow cast by an ancient oak and the shifting contrast of sunlight and shade was making the inscription on the smooth, white marble somewhat difficult to read.

Gary Bradshaw produced a small notebook and slim, gold ballpoint pen from the inside pocket of his expensive, made-to-measure suit and cast a quick glance around his immediate environs. He then sat back on his haunches by the grave and, balancing the notebook on his right thigh, began to slowly copy the inscription from the headstone. It read, "In loving memory of Christopher Bateman, Son of Thomas and Mary Bateman. Born 5th August 1929. Departed this life 23rd April 1937, aged 7 years. Forever in our Hearts", and below "Suffer the little children to come unto me and forbid them not, for of such is the kingdom of God. Mark 10:14".

It had taken Gary most of the day to find the grave he sought. This was the fifth churchyard he had visited. He had dressed for the day in his most sober suit which, considering the places he was searching, he judged would serve to draw as little attention to himself as possible. Even so, he chose not to stay in any churchyard longer than twenty minutes. Given the short periods of time he had allowed himself it was not easy to find the resting place of a young male under 10 years old. However, this one appeared to match his criteria perfectly. The grave was uncared for; obviously forgotten. The parents were perhaps deceased, or had moved away from the area. Or, Gary reflected cynically, perhaps "forever" did not last as long in Yorkshire as in London. He permitted himself a satisfied smile as he rose, somewhat stiffly, to his feet and appreciatively patted the smooth marble.

'Well, Chris' old son,' he said, under his breath, 'you would have been 38 years old now, if He hadn't suffered you to go to Him; just about my age in fact. Still, you may get a second chance to make a name for yourself. All you have to do is to leave Him and follow me .'

He turned and sauntered towards the distant lych gates, shimmering in the heat haze. As he did so the warm breeze increased, ruffling his dark hair. It felt almost as though soft hands were catching at his own, as the light wind played between his fingers. The feeling was not unpleasant and, as he walked, he removed his jacket, folding it carefully over his left arm to take advantage of the breeze and make himself more comfortable in the heat of the July sun.

It certainly was a lovely Yorkshire day in this "summer of love", Gary reflected. It would be even hotter where he was going; for months on end, not just the typically English few sunny days followed by a thunderstorm. Spain was the place he had in mind. A few of his acquaintances, tax exiles you might say, were already over there, enjoying their ill-gotten gains on the Costas. However, first he had to organise his new identity. The police had come uncomfortably close on a couple of occasions recently. He needed to seek new horizons and quickly.

A passport in the name of Christopher Bateman would not be a problem. Gary had all the necessary know-how and contacts to obtain a new identity for himself in true, "Day of the Jackal" fashion, though that novel was, at the time of which we speak, merely an idea sketched out in an up and coming authors notebook.

Gary's substantial fortune, liberated from numerous gullible old ladies, was already secreted away overseas, in various numbered bank accounts. There had also been gullible old men, but the ladies fell more easily for his dark, good looking, clean cut charms. Rich old dears who could not resist a sound investment opportunity, particularly when proffered by such a beautifully mannered, well spoken, handsome young man; so obviously of good family and representing such respected institutions.

Still, Gary smiled to himself as he walked along the tree lined lane leading from the small Norman church, all good things must come to an end; to be followed by bigger, better good things. A new name, warmer climes and even richer old ladies. He had already been working hard on his Spanish; Gary was nothing if not thorough.

These pleasant thoughts were occupying Gary's mind as he reached his MGB GT, parked unobtrusively a quarter of a mile from the church. He reached over, carefully placing his jacket on the passenger seat, before swinging himself, with practised ease, into the low sports car. As he did so the freshening breeze seemed to tug at the open driver's door, pulling it from his fingers before he could close it. Immediately afterwards his jacket, seeming almost to take on a life of its own, slid from the passenger seat.

'That bloody wind must be getting stronger,' he muttered petulantly, as he closed the door with an extra hard pull and, picking up his jacket, laid it carefully on the folded down rear seat. 'Probably the thunderstorm, arriving earlier than forecast.'

As rural Yorkshire was left behind and large raindrops began to spatter on the windscreen, Gary reflected upon a day's work well done. As he headed south into the storm coming north, the miles slipping by under the MGB's wire wheels, he began to think about the original owner of his, soon to be, new identity. Seven years old. Poor little mite couldn't have had much of a life, he thought, especially stuck out there in the middle of nowhere. Never got to see the bright lights; have some fun; discover the opposite sex.

'You stick with me old son,' he said aloud. 'I'll show you bright lights; and the rest.'

I should have had a son, he thought. It wasn't too late by any means. There would be many good looking Spanish girls who would appreciate the lifestyle he could offer them. As his son grew up he would show him all the "tricks of the trade". He would be a "chip off the old block".

Over the next few weeks Gary maintained a low profile, in an anonymous furnished flat he had rented rather than return to his usual address. The flat was utilitarian in the extreme, with decoration in neutral colours, functional furniture and somewhat less than functional appliances. Surprisingly though, Gary looked forward to returning to this hideaway, after the finalisation of his plans necessitated a personal visit to one or other of his acquaintances. He found something indefinably welcoming and comfortable in its bland interior; an easy feeling, almost as though he was sharing the place with a good friend who had just stepped out for a moment.

Gary also found that his contented, tranquil frame of mind was making him rather untidy; leaving various possessions scattered around the flat: on the bed; on the floor; in the bath. Although he was generally a fastidiously tidy person and in fact could not remember when and why he had left his personal items in sometimes rather odd places, this new trait in behaviour and apparent forgetfulness did not concern him unduly. He attributed it to a relaxing withdrawal from his normally stressful way of life.

In this easy atmosphere he had begun to identify with Christopher; almost to believe he really was giving the boy a second chance of life. As he finalised his plans and waited for his new passport, Gary began to talk to Christopher; seeking his approval on the minutiae of his plans; giving him progress updates each time he returned to the flat. Finally the day arrived when his arrangements were almost complete.

'There's one last thing I must do son' he said, speaking aloud, as was now his habit. 'I still have some funds in William and Glyn's in Hampstead, which I need to withdraw for petty cash. I'll go over there tomorrow morning and organise that, then get straight down to Portsmouth for the ferry. Yes, of course you're coming; I wouldn't leave you behind now, would I?'

The following morning found Gary standing across the street from the Hampstead branch of William and Glyn's bank. The sun was shining again, giving the promise of yet another hot summer's day. Life was good, he thought and could only get better. As he waited to cross the street, he suddenly felt a small, warm hand slip into his own. It was unmistakably another hand which now clung to his; small and soft; a child's hand. Garry smiled and looked down, but could see nothing, except his own left arm being pulled forward away from his body with increasing urgency. For some inexplicable reason it did not occur to Gary that this was strange, or even unusual. Instead, in answer to the insistent tugging, he took two steps forward.

The Routemaster was travelling at only 25 miles an hour when it hit Gary, or so the driver subsequently maintained. In any event, Gary never saw what hit him. Still looking down to his left, he was killed almost instantly as the vehicle struck him full on. His head smashed against the engine housing, before the bus continued on over his body, inflicting further terrible injuries. The screech of brakes; passers-by shouting, screaming and running to the scene; ashen faced driver leaping from his cab. Gary neither saw nor heard any of these things; he was already on his way to a hotter place.

Thirty five years have passed since Gary Bradshaw's sudden, gruesome death on that hot August day in 1967. Two recently retired policemen are sitting outside a Kent hostelry on another hot summer's day, enjoying the "real ale", a speciality of that county and reminiscing about their significant past contributions to the maintenance of law and order. Eventually the conversation turns to unusual cases in which they have been involved in years past. After a number of these have been dredged from the memory banks and related, ex Detective Chief Inspector Sam Tudor of the Met' falls silent, staring into his pint with some show of introspection.

'What's up Sam?,' asked his companion, ex Detective Superintendent Mark Rawlinson, (both men had risen to dizzy heights in the force). 'Penny for them.'

'I was just thinking about a very odd case I was involved in, back in '67,' said Sam, 'when I was a young constable on the beat, working in Hampstead. It was a road accident; youngish bloke was knocked down by a bus; killed instantly .'

'Nasty,' says Mark. 'Doesn't happen that often thank God, but what was odd about it?'

'Well, it wasn't so much the accident itself but the aftermath, so to speak. We got there pretty quickly because it was in the centre of town. There was this old lady who had been standing right behind the bloke when he just stepped out in front of the bus. When we arrived the old dear was hysterical.'

'That's understandable, given what she'd just witnessed.'

'Well yes, but it wasn't just that. She had everyone in the street looking under the bus and under parked cars nearby. She said the guy who was knocked down had a child with him, a blond boy about six or seven years old. She swore she saw them both distinctly as they walked out into the road, right in front of the bus. The boy was holding this chaps hand; pulling at it, she said. She reckoned if the guy hadn't been taking so much notice of the child he would never have stepped off the kerb without looking, as he did. Well, I and the other constable looked all around too of course, but there was no child to be found and no one except the old lady had seen one.

'Traumatic events can make people think they have seen things they haven't' mused Mark. 'You only have to remember how many conflicting versions of the same incident different eye witnesses can give.'

'Yes, that's very true. Anyway, this old dear was the only one who actually saw the guy walk into the road. It was fortunate for the bus driver she did too, even though we had to take her account with a pinch of salt, in view of the child business. She was still insisting a kid had also been knocked down when the paramedics sedated her and carted her off to the hospital.'

'Mmmm; but apart from the old girl, not that unusual,' said Mark, taking another long pull on his pint.

'Ah, but the really weird things came later. When we looked in the deceased's pockets he wasn't short of identification, including a passport in the name of Christopher Bateman for himself and his son, also called Christopher, together with two ferry tickets; Portsmouth to Santander, for the following day. The son was shown as being seven years old, just about the age the old lady had described.

'So, he did have a son. I assume you found him eventually?'

'Well, sort of. When we traced the name back through the passport application we found that Christopher Bateman had been dead for thirty one years'

'Excuse me?'

'Christopher Bateman died in 1937, in Yorkshire'

'Ah,' said Mark, suddenly seeing the light, (one doesn't rise to chief superintendent in the Met. without being pretty sharp), 'I don't imagine you mean a ghost was run over, so this poor sod must have stolen the identity of the child who died. It was pretty easy to do in those days. In fact it's even easier now come to think of it, but not as easy to obtain a passport like that. So, who was the guy really? Sounds like he may have had something to hide; probably had a police record.'

'We never found out,' said Sam quietly. 'His face was so smashed up there was no chance of identification that way. We had no record of his fingerprints on file and of course there was no DNA testing in those days. Even if there had been, I doubt we would have found him on the database. I think he must have been very adept at covering his tracks. If he was a bad 'un he certainly had never been caught. That wasn't quite the end of it though. We looked into the dead child's family details, thinking they might lead us to our man's identity. We thought he might be a relative, or family friend. It was a long shot and, not surprisingly, it drew a blank. We did discover one interesting thing though — about the child's death.'

'And what was that then?'

'He died in an accident; run over by a bus.'

'You're kidding me.'

'No; in Pickering; spring of 1937. We made further investigations then of course. Christopher Bateman was an only child. The parents were devastated, naturally; particularly since the mother couldn't have another child because of complications during Christopher's birth. The father was a doctor. He blamed the mother for not keeping a proper eye on the boy when they were out shopping. Husband and wife separated soon after the boy's funeral. The father went off to work as a doctor for the Missionary Society in China. He died in a Japanese internment camp, late in the war. The mother hung herself in 1945, when she heard the news.'

'Bloody Hell !'

Both men remained silent for long minutes, in sober reflection. Two dogs started a fight in the pub car park and the sound of their barks and squeals of pain mingled with sudden inebriated laughter from an adjacent table. These disturbances did not register at all with the two friends.

'It was a hell of a coincidence wasn't it?' said Sam, eventually. 'Or perhaps the old lady had it right all the time.'

Mark looked up from contemplating the large wasp hovering persistently around the rim of his pint glass.

'There are more things in heaven and earth, Horatio, than were dreamt of in your philosophy,' he misquoted gravely.

Sam sighed. 'I've told you before not to call me Horatio.'

Both men smiled, before taking another long draft of the amber liquid.

'Your round I think,' they said, in unison.

Not Cricket!

It was a late afternoon in early July in the village of Crompton Bassett. We were in the middle of one of those long hot summers we enjoy only every seven years or so in this country. The familiar and reassuringly English sound of willow on leather, punctuated by the occasional "howzat", drifted across to me as I relaxed in my deckchair after a hard bowling stint, which had rewarded me with my best figures of the season; five wickets for the cost of only twenty nine runs. Long Stretton had been bowled out for only one hundred and forty six and we were well on our way to victory, needing only a further twenty three runs with six wickets still in hand. As I contentedly, and I confess a little drowsily, watched the match from under the brim of my cricket hat, I was confident that my limited batting skills, due in as I was at number ten, were very unlikely to be needed for this game.

Tom Patch, our next door neighbour, had just hit a fluid cover drive which would probably not quite reach the boundary before being intercepted by a still enthusiastic Stretton fielder. Tom turned and was halfway down the wicket on his second run when he seemed to stumble over some unseen obstacle. Off balance, he staggered on for a few paces before falling full length, face downwards. He lay perfectly still, making no attempt to regain the safety of his batting crease. The fielder retrieved the ball just inside the boundary and threw back to the wicket keeper who automatically took off the stumps, but without making any claim for the wicket. The nearby fielders and Simon Armitage, our other batsman, were already running towards Tom. I stood up and watched anxiously as Simon turned Tom onto his side.

'Hey Peter, get over here quick', shouted Simon, after a few seconds. But Peter Simmons, one of our local GPs and another team member, was already halfway across the pitch, running full pelt. He reached the group around Tom and as I also ran towards them I could see that he had turned Tom onto his back and started to administer CPR. Peter looked up, saw me, and shouted for me go back and bring the portable defibrillator, one of which we were fortunate enough to have at the clubhouse. I turned around to run back but Brian Bannister, our team captain, was already on his way with it.

Peter looked up again. 'Someone call for an ambulance quick', he shouted towards the pavilion, before grabbing the defibrillator from Brian and starting work.

It was a full half hour before the ambulance arrived, but long before then it was all over. After fifteen minutes Peter told us that Tom had gone. 'I'm sorry guys, there's nothing more I can do', he said. 'It must have been a really massive heart attack. He never showed any life-signs after I reached him.'

We carried poor Tom back to the pavilion and laid him on one of the long benches by the wall. We were all in shock. All the women and many of the men were in tears. The ambulance finally arrived and the paramedics confirmed that there were no life-signs. They took Tom away in the ambulance. Peter went with them.

All of us left in the pavilion just stood around, too stunned to speak. After a few minutes Brian and the opposing captain – I think his name was Stuart – who had been quietly talking, stood up and Brian knocked on a table a few times to gain everyone's attention. The gist of what he said was what a terrible shock this was to everyone and what a fine friend and team mate Tom had been to us all. He was unmarried and Brian was unaware who his nearest relative was. Did anyone here know? No one did. Then no doubt the hospital would set in motion the task of finding and notifying them. He ended by saying that obviously the game was abandoned but, since the post match tea was already prepared, we should all sit down and do it as much justice as we could manage. He was sure Tom would have wanted us to do this. Needless to say, this proposal was greeted without much enthusiasm, but never-the-less we all sat down and went through the motions.

Later, Fiona my wife and I were walking around the cricket pitch back to our house - our back garden abutted the pitch and, as I said, Tom's house was next door to ours. 'Paul', she said suddenly 'I've been thinking how little we actually know about Tom.'

'He was a rather private person', I agreed, 'but always very friendly and neighbourly. I don't recall seeing many people visiting him though, in the six years we've lived here.'

'Martha told me as we were clearing up that he actually owns the cricket ground.' I must have looked astonished because she added. 'It's true apparently. Jean agreed with her and they've both been members for millennia.'

'Well, he's on the club committee of course. Was I should say; I just can't get my head around thinking of him in the past tense yet. But no one has ever mentioned at the meetings whilst I've been there that he owned the ground and I've been on the committee myself for three years now.'

'Perhaps there was just no reason for it to come up. Apparently his father owned a lot of land, including the cricket field. He sold most of it off for development in the eighties but not the cricket field because Tom was already a keen young player back then. The new primary school was built on one side of the ground and new houses around most of the rest of the perimeter, one of which is ours of course. He bought the one next door to us for Tom as soon as it was built, when he was in his late teens and he has lived there on his own ever since.'

We reached our back garden gate which, like Tom's, gave us direct access to the cricket field and I held it open for Fiona. 'Well, it's been a tragic day and if what you say is correct it could spell the end for the club. The cricket field isn't in the green belt and whoever owns it could make a fortune selling it to a developer, assuming they can get planning permission.'

'Oh, I think the club will be fine. Jean said that Tom had promised to bequeath the land to the club.'

'Well I hope Jean is right,' I said, as we walked up the garden to the house, 'or we could have a new housing estate to look at instead of a lovely cricket ground.'

We had another home game the following Saturday against Charington. Everyone was still very subdued after attending Henry's funeral the previous day and we didn't play well. The opposition posted one hundred and ninety six for five in their forty overs and we never looked like getting anywhere near that total. My seven overs had cost us fifty two runs for only one wicket and I was pretty unhappy about it. Consequently, when I went in after the fall of our eighth wicket for only one hundred and twenty six, I was determined just to have a slog.

I got outside the line with the first delivery attempting an off drive. The ball clipped the top of my back pad and there was an appeal for leg before, but fortunately the umpire judged the ball to be missing off stump, or too high. Undeterred, I went for a pull shot with the next delivery, which was pitched a little short. This time I connected well and the ball sailed, rather higher than I had intended, in the direction of our garden. As I set off to run there came a shout of "catch it", which I couldn't understand because I was sure there hadn't been any fielder down there. Upon reaching the bowling crease I looked over and saw the ball bounce across the boundary and come to rest against Tom's garden gate with a fielder in fruitless pursuit.

As I turned to walk back to the batting crease the bowler said, 'sorry skip, I thought we had someone down there'.

'Well if you'd asked me to I would have put someone there,' their skip replied, rather testily.

This exchange rather cheered me up and had the opposite effect upon the bowler who sent down a bouncer next ball. Now, full of confidence, I went to hook. The ball caught the top edge of my bat, sailed high into the air and dropped steeply into the waiting gloves of their wicket keeper. Deflated and miserable I trudged back to the pavilion.

Our final pairing put on another eleven runs for the last wicket before we were all out for one hundred and forty one. We had lost by fifty five runs. It was a dispirited bunch of players and spectators who made their way homeward after the match.

Early the next week Brian Bannister, who was also the club president, called a special evening committee meeting. Most people had already arrived and were sat around the table looking pretty glum when I walked in.

'We are just waiting for Peter now,' said Brian, 'but he has a surgery of course, so he may be a little late.' As he said this the door opened and Peter Simmons entered.

'Ah good,' said Brian. 'Thanks for rushing over Peter. We can start now. As all of you know, our poor friend and fellow member Tom Patch owns, that is to say owned, the land on which our cricket ground stands.' A few heads around the table nodded. 'Many years ago Tom very generously promised to bequeath the land to the club in his will. He had never married and at forty seven appeared to be a confirmed bachelor. He was also an only child and had no close relatives as far as we know, his parents both being deceased, so no one would be losing out by his willing the land to the club.'

Here Brian took a deep breath. 'Tom's solicitor is Nigel Swallow, who I know very well. A few days ago, since I had not heard anything from Nigel about Tom's Will, I spoke to him and said I had been expecting him to contact me   because of Tom's expressed intent to bequeath the cricket ground to the club. Nigel then told me that Tom had not made a Will; he had in fact died intestate.'

No one spoke for quite a while after that revelation. 'I suppose he thought there was no hurry,' I said eventually. 'After all he was still a relatively young man.'

'As you say Paul, he was in the prime of life; apparently fit and healthy,' agreed Peter. 'But unknown to him and everyone else he had an unsuspected genetic heart defect which resulted in a sudden cardiac arrest which I couldn't reverse, even with our defibrillator.'

'So what happens now?' Martha Bell asked.

'Nigel told me they had engaged a specialist company to carry out searches, looking for any living relative,' said Brian. 'And they have found one; a third cousin.'

'I never could quite get my head around what a second cousin is,' I said, 'never mind a third.'

'It means a child of Tom's parent's second cousin,' said Martha helpfully.

We were all probably still looking confused, so she added. 'In other words Tom's great grandfather must have had a brother or sister and their great grandchild will be Tom's third cousin.'

'Well, as I said, according to Nigel they have found one,' continued Brian. 'It's a man and he lives in Richmond. He was contacted last week. Apparently he had outstanding business commitments which he had to fulfil first, but he is flying over here tomorrow.'

'Why fly from Richmond?' Simon asked. 'Does he have his own helicopter?'

'Sorry, I should have said, that's Richmond in Virginia.'

'Well, well', said Peter, 'I don't suppose he will know too much about cricket then.'

'I assume he will be seeing Tom's solicitor soon after he arrives', continued Brian. 'I have asked Nigel to mention to him about Tom's promise to bequeath the cricket ground to the club, but quite honestly I don't hold out much hope for that promise being honoured. I suspect the temptation to cash in on the land will be too great for him to pass up.'

'Unless he's a philanthropic millionaire American who loves cricket', ventured Jim Lowe, another Committee member.

'I don't think we should be too optimistic in that regard,' muttered Brian bleakly.

Soon after this the meeting broke up, with Brian promising to keep us all informed of any developments he managed to glean from Nigel Swallow. 'Of course he shouldn't really tell me anything', he said, 'client confidentiality and all that, but we have been friends since our school days and I don't think he will hold out on me.'

I brought Fiona up to speed as soon as I got home, after resisting the temptation to join some of the guys drowning their sorrows in the Crown and Thistle. We were both feeling pretty glum about it all and proceeded to finish off half a bottle of gin.

'I wonder where this American will stay', mused Fiona later, in bed. 'Perhaps he will stay at Tom's house, since presumably he now owns it.'

This turned out to be prescient of Fiona because, sure enough, when we both got home from work the following day there was a Ford Focus on Tom's driveway, bearing a hire company's logo and we could see someone moving around in the kitchen.

'We should go over there and check if everything is OK and introduce ourselves', declared Fiona. 'After all it might be a burglar for all we know.'

'Well, I certainly don't want to introduce myself to a burglar.'

'Don't be such a wimp Paul. I'm sure you could see off a burglar if push came to shove.'

Not liking to be called a wimp, which I think is only one step removed from an outright coward, I agreed we should go round and introduce ourselves to the American, or burglar.

Following my ring on the bell, Tom's door was opened by a tall man - at least six feet two - who looked to be in his early forties. He was quite heavily built, but it appeared to be all muscle. He sported a full head of wavy, sandy hair, which he wore quite long, strong jaw, blue eyes and a fair, healthy looking complexion. I supposed he could be considered quite handsome, if one liked that sort of thing.

'Hi, can I help you folks?'

'We live next door, said Fiona, before I could open my mouth. 'We saw the lights on and assumed you were a relative of poor Tom, so we came to introduce ourselves and offer our condolences. Also if we can be any help to you, please don't hesitate to ask. I'm Fiona and this is my husband Paul.

'Well that's real kind of you Fiona,' he said, smiling broadly and extending a large hand, 'and Paul,' he added, somewhat as an afterthought. 'I'm Henry Patch; very pleased to meet you both. Won't you step inside?'

'Oh we don't want to intrude,' I interjected, as I saw Fiona taking a step towards the door. You must be tired after your long flight.'

'How do you know I've had a long flight?'

'Well, you're obviously American and you've only recently arrived,' I said, thinking quickly. 'I just assumed you must have flown over today.'

'Well that's very perceptive of you Paul and you're quite right in your assumption. My flight from Richmond International landed at Heathrow around noon. It's taken me four hours to drive out here, half of which was just getting out of London in your terrible traffic. I collected the keys from Cousin Tom's solicitor and here I am.'

'Haven't you eaten at all?' asked Fiona brightly. 'Why don't you come over and have dinner with us?' I turned towards her. She was gazing up at Henry Patch with those large, luminous eyes of hers. Oh my God, I thought, she's smitten.

'Well, again that's real kind of you Fiona, but I don't want to intrude. I was just going to finish unpacking and then see if I could get a meal at one of your English pubs. I think I noticed one just down the road.'

'Oh you don't want to do that. The Crown and Thistle is just a locals drinking den. The food isn't very good. I have a lamb casserole in the oven and there's more than enough for three. Do come. It will be no trouble at all.'

'Well . . . .,' he hesitated, looking at me. I almost felt Fiona's metaphorical kick on my shins.

'As Fiona says, it's no trouble and we'd love to have you.'

'Well this sure is real English hospitality. When would you like me to come over? I just need a little more time to unpack and freshen up.'

'Oh, shall we say about seven? That gives you an hour or so,' replied my darling wife.

'Why on earth did you invite him over for dinner?' I asked, after we got back inside our house. 'We've only just met him. He may be a psychopath for all we know.'

'Don't be silly Paul. He looked rather nice.'

'You quite fancy him don't you?'

'Well he is rather dishy, but that isn't the reason I invited him. Don't you want to know what his intentions are regarding the club? We'll have the perfect opportunity to find out, particularly after we've plied him with a few drinks.'

Well, ply him we did, during and after doing justice to Fiona's marvellous lamb casserole, of which there wasn't enough for my usual second helping. However, for desert Fiona produced her home cooked gooseberry pie, which I had been looking forward to demolishing over the next few days. We had repaired to the lounge and were sitting comfortably replete when Fiona broached the subject.

'Did you know Tom well?' she began.

Fiona gradually and expertly ascertained from Henry Patch that he had never heard of Tom Patch prior to receiving a phone call from the agent engaged by Nigel Swallow, telling him that he might be in line for an inheritance from a long lost cousin. He told us his great grandfather had emigrated from England as a young boy in the early twentieth century and married a girl from Norfolk in Virginia. Very little information about the

English side of the family had been passed down the generations and no one had been sufficiently interested enough to look into it.

'I own a large automobile dealership with branches all through Virginia and into North Carolina,' he said modestly, 'and it keeps me very busy. I thought it was probably some kinda' scam and so I passed the guy over to my attorney to deal with. I thought no more about it until a week or so later when Phil - he's my attorney - rang back to say the guy was kosher and I really had inherited a piece of real-estate over in England. I had been promising myself a vacation and so I decided to fly out here as soon as I had finalised a coupla' deals and take a look at what I got. I need to sign a few papers with Tom's attorney over here; solicitor I'm told you call 'em. I could have gotten all the papers sent over to the States but I hadn't been to England since my honeymoon eighteen years ago and never to this part of the country. So I thought what the hell, go over and have a look-see. It's really pretty cute, what little I've seen of these parts so far. The last time I was here we mostly stayed in London, with just a few days in York.'

'So was your wife unable to come with you this time?' asked Fiona.

'Oh, Helen and I were divorced twelve years ago,' he said, waving an arm dismissively. 'She took me for half a million. I won't make that mistake again.'

'Did you know that you now own our village cricket ground?' I asked, becoming irritated with the casual references to his wealth and thinking we might as well get to the point.

'Cricket. That's kinda' like baseball isn't it.'

'In so far as you hit a ball with a bat, I suppose yes. But that's where the similarities end.'

'So they play this game of cricket on the piece of land I own?'

'Yes, it's at the bottom of our gardens.'

'Well I'll be dammed.'

'We don't wish to pry of course, but naturally we can't help wondering what you are planning to do with it,' said Fiona innocently.

'Oh I'll leave all that to Phil my attorney. He'll make sure I get the best price for the land and the house. He tells me the land could be worth quite a tidy sum to a developer. He says the house and land together should bring in over a million. Pounds that is, not dollars,' he added with a grin.

A feeling of despondency washed over me. Here were our worst fears being realised.

'Tom Patch was a keen cricketer,' I said. He had promised to leave the cricket ground to the club, but he died suddenly before he had made a Will.'

Henry Patch looked at me narrowly. 'Well that's bad luck for the club. I guess they'll have to buy it from me now.'

I was considering my reply to this bald statement when Fiona interjected. 'There isn't any possibility of that. The club doesn't have that kind of money.'

'Well that's tough. I suppose they'll have to move. Buy some cheaper land somewhere. Well I got to go. I'm feeling the jet-lag kicking in. It's been real kind of you folks to invite me over for dinner. After my last visit I thought all the English were surly, self serving, supercilious bastards - pardon me Fiona - but you guys have changed my opinion somewhat.'

'Well if you stayed in London I can see where you might have formed that opinion,' I replied. 'On the other hand a lot of uneducated English people think most Americans are gun-toting, obese, white supremacists. And there lies the danger of stereotyping.

Henry laughed uncertainly, not sure if he should be personally insulted. 'Well I suppose I asked for that,' he said eventually. 'Anyway, I'll be here for a week or so. I'd like to return your hospitality and take you both out for a meal.'

'If I did quite fancy him I don't anymore,' said Fiona, when Henry Patch had taken his leave.

I smiled sourly. 'I felt like punching the guy in the face. The club has had it. We only have a couple of thousand pounds in the bank. How could we buy any other land, even if we could find someone willing to sell to us? And even if we somehow found some land and raised the funds it would take a couple of years at least and a lot more money to develop a good enough playing surface from a meadow.'

We sat around for a while getting more inebriated and trying to decide if we knew any Americans we actually liked. We drew a blank; not that we knew many. At around ten o'clock we decided upon an early night and both fell almost immediately into an alcohol induced deep sleep.

I was woken by Fiona's hand shaking my shoulder insistently.

171

'Wake up Paul. Oh do please wake up.'

'Whassamatter?'

'Come over here to the window.'

I glanced at the luminous dial of the bedside clock. 'It's three a.m. Fiona.'

'Just come over here. You must see this.'

Still grumbling I did as I was told. Our bedroom is on the corner of the house and has two windows, one looking over the rear garden and the other towards next door which is about twenty metres away. Fiona was peering between the curtains of the window looking towards Tom's house. As I arrived she threw open the curtains. I blinked a few times at the sudden influx of light into our bedroom.

'All the lights are on,' she observed, unnecessarily. 'It looks like he must have every light in the house burning.'

'Well certainly all the ones on this side of the house. What the hell is he up to at three a.m.?'

'Come over here now,' my wife whispered, padding over to the other window. I followed obediently.

She parted the curtains to this window only slightly and pointed diagonally across our garden towards that of next door. 'Do you see him?'

The light from Tom's house was flooding down the garden, illuminating shrubs and trees and forming long shadows behind them which seemed to reach out menacingly towards the figure of Henry Patch, who was sitting hunched on a garden bench

172

and looking up towards the house. It looked like he was wearing only pyjamas.

'You should go and check if he's OK.'

'Fiona, it's the middle of the night. Perhaps all Americans sit in their gardens in their night clothes at three a.m. in the morning, weather permitting. Maybe it's demanded by the Constitution that they sit and look towards The White House whilst singing The Star Spangled Banner.'

'Very amusing Paul. There must be something wrong. Please go and see if he's all right.'

'Perhaps my gooseberry pie which he ate half of reacted badly with the lamb casserole and he just needed some fresh air. And he had to switch all the lights on so he could see where he was going.' I added, mentally congratulated myself on this quite logical hypothesis.

Fiona didn't appear to follow my line of reasoning. 'Well if you won't go then I must,' she said, walking over to the bedroom door and reaching for her dressing gown.

'Ok, OK, I'll go,' I sighed, knowing she meant it.

I put on a long raincoat over my pyjamas and made my way around to the front of Tom's house. As I walked up the side of the house I looked up and saw Fiona watching me. I waved and she waved back then moved away from the window. I guessed she was going to the other window to get a ringside view of whatever transpired. I came around the corner of the house and began to walk down the garden path towards Henry Patch. My extraordinarily elongated shadow cast by the houselights mingled with those of the shrubs and trees as I advanced towards him. I now saw that he was sat bolt upright, looking straight at me. His body seemed rigid. Somehow I was sure he was unable to move. I stopped before I got too close.

'Are you OK Henry?'

My voice seemed to jerk him out of his trance. His right hand flew behind his back and then emerged holding . . . . nothing. I was immediately convinced he had been automatically reaching for a firearm which, fortunately for me, wasn't there. I then realised he could only see a silhouette of me because of the house lights.

'It's Paul from next door Henry. I was just wondering if you had a problem.'

His posture noticeably relaxed. 'Jeez Paul, you really scared the hell outa' me.'

'I'm really sorry about that,' I said, moving closer. 'Fiona saw all the lights on and you sitting out here. We thought you might be unwell . . . . or something.' My voice tailed off.

I saw him take a deep breath and then force a smile. 'Well, again that's very neighbourly of you to be concerned; especially at this time of night. You would take your life in your hands walking onto someone's property in Virginia in the middle of the night.'

'I can well believe it,' I replied, sensing an admonishment in his words.

'I couldn't sleep,' he added. 'Just getting a breath of fresh air. I think it's the jet-lag.'

'Well I'll get back then and reassure Fiona that you're OK.'

'She's a real fine woman your Fiona. Tell her thanks again.'

'I will.' I began to walk back up the garden.

Henry followed me up to the house. A little too closely for comfort I thought; invading my personal space. As we reached the house his right hand shot out and grabbed my left arm very tightly. It almost seemed to be an involuntary movement. I looked down at his hand on my arm. He appeared to only then realise what he had done and, with an apparently conscious effort, loosened his grip but still held my arm.

'I was wondering about . . . .,' he began, then hesitated and started again. 'I was wondering if you'd like to come in for a nightcap. I found an almost full bottle of single malt in a cupboard.'

'It's a little late for me to be drinking whisky. I have to go to work in four hours; but thanks anyway.'

His hand still held my arm. 'I'd really appreciate your company Paul; just a quick one.'

I wasn't sure he was going to let go of my arm, even if I said no again.

'All right, just the one. Then I'll have to get some sleep.'

The French doors had been left open and he stood aside to let me in first. The smell of Tom's pipe was still easily discernible, as if he had just stepped out of the room.

Henry followed me in and walked over to the drinks cabinet, his eyes darting all over the room as if he had never seen it before. On the drop down door of the cabinet stood an opened bottle of Scotch. He poured a couple of stiff ones and handed one to me. 'Take a seat Paul.'

We both settled into Tom's comfortable armchairs facing each other.

'About this cricket Paul. Do you play?'

'Yes, I'm a member of the club. So is Fiona; non-playing that is.'

'How's the game played then? You say it's nothing like baseball.'

I did my best to give him a general rundown of the game without going into too much detail. He seemed genuinely interested, which surprised me and asked quite a few questions.

'Look, we have nets tomorrow evening. Why don't you come along and have a look see, if you don't have any prior engagement that is. You could even hit a few balls if you would like to.'

'Nets?'

'I mean practice. We call it nets.'

'Well that's uncommonly decent of you Paul. I'd like that.'

'I'll call for you at six o'clock then. We can get onto the cricket ground from our back gardens. Now I really must go,' I said, draining my glass and standing up.'

He stood up as well and seemed on the verge of trying to persuade me to stay longer but held himself back. He followed me over to the French windows and as I walked out onto the patio he turned quickly and looked back into the room. I bid him goodnight, but he didn't seem to hear me.

Fiona was sitting up in bed when I returned and wanted to know chapter and verse about what had transpired. I related it all to her as succinctly as I could and then told her I just had to get some sleep.

'He seemed really on edge about something', I said as I lay my head on the pillow.

As I was drifting off to sleep I felt Fiona get out of bed. 'All the lights are still on,' she said.

The next day at the appointed time Henry was waiting for me at the bottom of his garden. I thought he looked rather haggard but greeted me cheerfully enough. He asked a few more questions about cricket as we walked over to the club house. His interest from the previous night appeared not to have abated. Some junior members were practicing in the nets and we watched them for a few minutes until they gave way to the seniors. I introduced him to Brian Bannister and a few others by his first name only, as a visiting American friend interested in cricket. I thought if I told them who he really was some of them might start badgering him about the club's future and that might be counter-productive. Officially only Committee members knew of the situation, but the Committee leaked like a sieve. In any case, after our conversation the previous evening, I didn't hold out any hope of him changing his mind and any ensuing argument would just sour the atmosphere.

We practiced for half an hour or so, taking it in turns to bat and bowl whilst Henry watched. Brian then asked him if he would like to try his hand and he agreed enthusiastically.

'Would you like to bat or bowl?' asked Brian.

'Oh batting seems easier.'

Brian smiled knowingly. 'You'll need to get padded up then; Health and Safety you know.'

I helped Henry on with his pads and he went down and took position in front of the wicket grinning hugely. His earlier haggard look had disappeared completely. I took a ball and started my run up. Henry raised his bat and held it like a baseball bat.

I stopped. 'You'd better to take guard like you saw the others doing,' I called.

'I'm fine Paul. I feel more comfortable like this.'

Suit yourself I thought. I continued my run up and sent down quite a friendly long hop. Henry brought his bat around from a great height and hit the ball cleanly high out over my head towards the far side of the pitch. I heard quite a few barely suppressed chuckles from my team mates. I wasn't best pleased and vowed to give him a less friendly one next time. The next bowler sent down a better ball which Henry dispatched with a little more difficulty into the on-side netting. The third ball he received suffered a similar fate. Henry was enjoying himself enormously. The fourth was a little wide but he reached it and thumped it into the off-side netting. And then it was my turn again.

'Try him with a yorker Paul,' Brian whispered. 'He won't be able to handle it holding the bat high like that.'

I duly ran up and, though I say so myself, sent down a perfect yorker which pitched just by his feet and took out his middle stump. Henry got nowhere near it.

'Hey Paul, is that allowed?' he called.

'That's why you need to take guard properly,' called back Brian.

Henry took a few balls using a more orthodox guard and middled most of them. He then tried his hand at bowling with a lesser degree of success.

Whilst all this was going on Brian drew me to one side. 'That's him isn't it, Tom's long lost cousin?'

'Yes,' I admitted, 'but there's no hope of him honouring Tom's wishes'. I recounted briefly the events of the previous evening, omitting our dead of night encounter.

Brian looked thoughtful and buttonholed Henry at the end of the session. 'You're definitely a batsman rather than a bowler Henry, but you have good hand eye coordination. A couple more practice sessions and you could be pushing for a place in the team. How long are you over here for?'

'Well thank you kindly,' grinned Henry. 'I've had a great time. I used to play minor league baseball when I was younger but I haven't held a bat for a few years now. I'm only here for a few more days or I might have tried to make the team.'

'Well you're welcome here anytime,' said Brian. 'We are playing away at Escombe Magna on Saturday. If you are interested and still around, why don't you come along with Paul and watch the match.'

'Well that's mighty kind of you Brian. I don't fly out until Monday, so I may just do that.'

Henry had a thoughtful look on his face as we walked back in the lengthening shadows of an English summer's evening. 'A nice bunch of guys you have there,' he said eventually. 'You didn't tell them who I was?'

'No I didn't.'

He said nothing further until we reached our garden gate. I'd sure like to come along on Saturday, if that's OK with you?'

'No problem. I'll be leaving about ten thirty. I'm taking a couple more of the team in my car but there's room for one more. I'll see you then if not before.'

He didn't make any move towards his own gate and I wondered if he was hoping for an invite up to the house, but I didn't oblige.

'Goodnight Henry.' I opened my gate and entered the garden.

'Goodnight Paul.'

I walked up to the house and glanced back as I opened the back door. He was still standing there in the gathering dusk, looking up at Tom's house.

I put my gear down in the utility room and walked through into the lounge. Fiona was reclining on the settee in her silk nightgown, the one which clung seductively to her slender body, displaying and enhancing every curve. She was cradling a drink in one hand and leafing through a magazine with the other.

'Did he go with you?' she asked, looking up.

'Yes, and he had a bat and a bowl.'

'How did he do?'

'Too bloody well; the guys a natural batsman. Twice as good as me.'

'He can't be that good then, if he's only twice as good as you.'

'I'd resent that if it wasn't true and you didn't look so sexy. Where have you hidden the gin?'

'Go take a shower and I'll bring a glass up for you. Then you can show me something you're really good at.'

I didn't need telling twice. I was reasonably sure she wasn't referring to my bowling.

Two days later Saturday morning duly dawned. On Thursday and Friday Henry had kept the house lights on again all night but we hadn't seen him at all and certainly not in the garden in the small hours. At ten fifteen a knock came to the front door. I was finishing packing my gear upstairs and Fiona answered. I heard her saying hello to Henry. When I came down they were both in the kitchen.

'Are you still OK with me coming along Paul?' asked Henry.

'Certainly; I'm almost ready.'

'I've been kinda' busy the last couple of days but I would like to take you both out for a meal on Sunday if you're free. I'll be flying back home to the States on Monday afternoon.'

We agreed to go out with him on Sunday evening. We had earlier decided to go if he asked us. It would have been impolite not to, although neither of us was particularly keen on the prospect.

I picked up Simon and Jim and drove the twelve miles to Escombe Magna. It was a bright morning with the promise of another fine sunny day and I was looking forward to hopefully banishing the memory of the previous Saturday's defeat, although the perilous future of the club was always in the back of my mind. We arrived at the ground which was in a beautiful setting just outside the village and close to the river. When it was time to toss up we were still missing two players, Colin Peters, our wicket keeper and Matt Taylor. That meant we only had ten men including Gary Bunn our reserve. Brian was anxiously checking his watch when his mobile phone rang. He walked off a little distance to answer it.

When he came back he was wearing a deep frown. 'That was Matt. He and Colin have had an accident. They were trying to avoid a deer which jumped over a fence and out into the road right in front of them. They swerved and ran into a ditch. The car will have to be recovered. They don't have any broken bones but are being taken to hospital to be checked over. There's no chance that they can play today.'

'Who can we phone to come over?' I asked.

'We were always going to be struggling this week. We have three people on holiday. I could see if one of the juniors is available I suppose.'

'Are you ready to toss up Brian?' This from the opposing captain who had strolled over.

'Yes of course Steven,' said Brian, 'but we have a problem'.

Brian explained the situation and said he would try to contact one of our juniors who might be able to play. 'We will have to start with ten men.'

'I'd sure like to play,' said a voice with a distinctive southern American drawl.

'I'm afraid that isn't allowed Henry,' said Brian. You need to be registered with the league to play in matches. Brian turned to Steven. 'Henry is a friend of Paul's. He's over here on holiday for a few days. He just came along to see how the game is played.'

'Well,' said Steven, smiling at Henry, 'I won't say anything to the league if you would like to play Henry. Just use the name of one of your missing players.'

'Well that's really good of you Steven but he doesn't have any cricket boots or whites.'

Steven eyed up Henry. 'We have some spare kit in the clubhouse. What's your shoe size Henry?'

'It's eleven in US size. I don't know if that's any different in the UK.'

'I think it's about ten in UK size. We should be able to sort you out, if that's all right with you Brian.'

'If you're sure you don't mind.'

'No problem. Shall we toss up?'

Steven won the toss and elected to bat. 'I'll get our openers to pad up. Come along with me Henry and we'll get you kitted out.'

That was very obliging of him', I said to Brian, as Steven strolled off with Henry.

'Do you think so? Maybe he just sees a better chance of winning if we play someone who has never played cricket before.'

'That's a little cynical,' I replied, smiling. 'He may get a surprise though.'

Henry came back after a few minutes looking quite the part. 'Can I have my catching glove Brian?'

'I'm afraid only the wicket keeper gets gloves in cricket Henry. Oh damn, I forgot we haven't got a wicket keeper; any volunteers?'

'I'll wicket keep if I get to wear some gloves,' piped up Henry.

'It's a specialist job Henry. You had better stay in the outfield until you get the hang of what's going on.'

'Paul explained the game to me and I've played quite a bit of baseball. I'm sure I could wicket keep.'

Brian looked dubious.

Why not try Henry for a few overs?' said Simon. 'We could always change if it isn't working out and I don't think anyone else fancies the job.'

'Why not give him a go,' I added, smiling. 'What could possibly go wrong?'

'Quite a bit; we could lose a lot of runs before we find out it isn't working.' Brian considered for a few seconds. 'All right Henry, we'll try you out for a few overs, but if I decide to change I don't want any arguments. You'll need pads as well as gloves.'

'You're the boss Brian.'

I was bowling the first over. Henry had taken up position, standing back to my medium-fast bowling. His expression was that of a cat who had just unexpectedly found a rather large saucer of milk. Brian put in a couple of slips to start with.

My first delivery was a loosener, pitching a little short of a length. Their opening batsman executed a cover drive which he did not quite time. The ball got past our cover point but Gary was able to recover and chase it down half way to the boundary. The batsmen took two runs. My second ball pitched on a good length and, moving away off the seam, beat the outside of the bat. Henry moved lithely to his right and took the ball easily. Brian and a couple of the guys shouted well done. My third was right on middle stump and again on a length. The batsman played a defensive shot on his back foot and the ball trickled back down the wicket to me. Annoyingly, with my fourth delivery I strayed towards leg stump. The batsman, looking to deflect the ball down towards long leg, caught it much too fine. Henry had taken a couple of steps to his left as he saw where the ball was going to pitch and now, moving with superb agility for a big man, he dived to his left and took a magnificent one-handed catch. Landing, he executed a couple of victory rolls then stood up holding the ball aloft. "Howzat" came the cry from everyone except Henry. The umpire raised his finger and we had our first wicket. Ecstatically, we all ran over to Henry to congratulate him.

'Sorry Paul,' said Henry after the hubbub had died down.

'Whatever for? That was a brilliant catch.'

'I forgot to say howzat.'

After our initial success we struggled a little for the next wicket. Henry however was taking cleanly everything which came in his direction. Simon took the next wicket after the opposition had reached thirty seven runs when his out-swinging delivery was edged to slip, which fortunately Brian had kept in place. Soon after that two more wickets fell in quick succession; a leg before wicket, then a caught and bowled by me. Their middle order then staged something of a recovery until their fifth wicket fell to a run-out. They foolishly went for a third run after a pull shot had just failed to reach the boundary. Jim had chased it down and threw back accurately to Henry who caught the ball and took off the stumps in one fluid movement. Their score was now only ninety four for five wickets. Henry must have taken in everything I told him about the game and then some, I thought to myself; he's a natural.

The remaining wickets fell at fairly regular intervals. I got the next, taking out the batsman's off stump, then Simon also got another with a leg-before. Brian then put himself on with his leg breaks and took two wickets; one a fine edge to Henry, who was now standing up to Brian and the other when the batsman foolishly tried to hit against the spin and Peter took a good diving catch at midwicket. I then managed to get the final wicket with a well pitched up ball, taking out the middle stump when the score was on one hundred and forty two.

We then all took refreshments in the pavilion and I noticed Steven Lindsey, the opposing captain, was looking rather sourly at Henry.

When our innings started Brian and his opening partner Frank Murphy put on thirty six for the first wicket before Frank fell to a leg before decision which I thought was very harsh. I was watching from pretty well behind the bowlers arm and I didn't think the ball had pitched in line with the stumps. After that the wickets began to fall with worrying regularity. Brian was still there on forty eight when our fourth wicket fell with the score on only eighty one. Brian got his fifty in the next over but fell soon afterwards for fifty nine. We were now five wickets down for only ninety seven runs, hardly better than Escombe's performance.

The sixth wicket partnership of Jim Booth and Simon Armitage put on another eighteen before Simon mistimed an on drive, getting a leading edge which gave an easy catch to the bowler. One hundred and fifteen for six; still twenty seven runs behind with only four wickets to spare. And one of those wickets was Henry's, who had never played in a cricket match before. I didn't think hitting a few friendly balls in the nets would be enough to prepare him for a real match if he had to bat.

I started to pad up and as I did so the dreaded cry of "howzat" went up. I looked up to see the umpire's finger raised. Chris

Patterson had fallen first ball. As Jim Lowe walked to the middle, passing Chris trudging back to the pavilion, he gave him a commiserating pat on the back, which I don't think Chris appreciated too much.

All our players were watching intently now as the two Jim's endured a torrid four overs. Escombe put their two opening fast bowlers back on and threw everything at us, bringing in the field and looking for the kill. But they survived and gradually began to eke out the runs needed once Escombe's two best bowlers had reached their maximum allowed overs and had to be taken off. I was beginning to think that I wouldn't be needed after all as our total reached one hundred and thirty two. Only eleven more runs needed to win with three wickets still in hand. And then disaster. Jim Lowe got an inside edge onto his stumps and was out for seven.

As I walked nervously out to the wicket with cries of "good luck Paul" ringing in my ears I consoled myself with the thought that Jim Booth was still there on twenty five and looking solid. I just needed to survive the last two balls of the over and then Jim would be on strike. I was hoping he would be able to get the eleven runs needed before I had to face another ball.

One of the Escombe players I knew called out as I reached the crease. 'Have you come to show us how to bat Paul?'

'Piss off Stewart.'

'Such repartee Paul; you ought to be a stand up comic. I'll buy you a pint if you score a run.'

'I'll buy you two if I don't.'

They had an off spinner on and I had seen that the wicket was taking spin. I looked around after reaching the crease, ostensibly to note the field placings but really to delay as long as possible the moment when I would have to face that first ball. I saw that they had brought in a fielder to short leg to take a bat and pad or a ball which they hoped I might edge round the corner with the spin.

I took guard on middle stump and waited nervously for the first ball. I was resolved to just defend and get Jim on strike, but the first ball was delivered wide of my off stump and short of a length and I instinctively just threw my bat it. I had allowed for the spin but the ball went straight on and I didn't get within six inches of it. Their wicket keeper took the ball cleanly, swept off the bails and shouted for a stumping. Horrified I looked around and saw that the toe of my raised back foot was just inside the batting crease. But had it been when he took the bails off? I looked around to the square leg umpire who, to my enormous relief, was shaking his head. Not out.

Jim walked down the pitch towards me and I met him in the middle. 'Take it easy Paul,' he said quietly. 'Just play a calm defensive shot and you'll be fine. I'm sure I can get the runs we need in the next over.'

'Sorry Jim,' I muttered abjectly. 'Rush of blood.'

The next delivery pitched on a length and spun. Again I got nowhere near it but the bounce was high and it clipped my thigh before eluding their wicket keeper and running down towards deep fine leg where there was no fielder. I turned and saw short leg giving chase.

'Yes,' called Jim and I ran hard.

'Go for two,' he shouted as he passed me.

I turned at the bowlers end and started back as the fielder reached the ball. Jim had a head start on me and was already half way back down the wicket. The fielder picked up the ball, turned and threw in one movement, but I got home safely with half a second to spare. The umpire signalled two leg byes. I breathed a sigh of relief. Nine to win and now it was up to Jim.

Their skipper put the field back for Jim, trying to cut off any boundary. They had a pretty ordinary medium paced bowler on and Jim connected cleanly with a cover drive on the first ball of the over. We ran an easy two and could possibly have managed a third but Jim held his hand up and shouted no after the second run. He wanted to stay on strike and I couldn't blame him. Only seven needed to win now and Jim still had five balls of the over left to do it before I would have to face another ball.

I hadn't rated their bowler, but with his next delivery he sneakily put in a well disguised slower ball which Jim didn't pick. Consequently he was early on his shot and skyed the ball towards the mid-on fielder who was positioned well back towards the boundary. Hearing Jim calling for the run I set off. As I reached the batting crease and turned for a possible second run I saw the fielder diving forward to take the catch. We were now nine wickets down, still needing seven runs to win and only myself and Henry left to make them.

Henry jauntily arrived at the wicket and was grinning happily as we met in the middle. 'This is great Paul. I didn't think I would get a chance to bat.'

'You probably won't. I crossed with Colin when he holed out so I'm on strike. The way I'm batting I'll be out before you have to face a ball.'

'Think positive Paul. Just seven more needed and Brian says we have plenty of overs left.'

'I don't think the overs left will be relevant.'

I turned, walked back to the crease and took guard. My heart was pounding and my knees trembling. And I do this for pleasure I thought ruefully as the bowler started his run up. The delivery was a little wide of my off stump and, attempting a square cut, I caught a thick top edge. Turning I saw the ball sailing over gully and started to run as the fielder gave chase. As I reached the bowling crease, turned and started down the wicket for a second run, I saw that a fielder, running round from deep point, had just gathered the ball and was turning to throw.

'Run Henry,' I shouted, but he was still in the batting crease and had his hand up.

'Get back Paul,' he called.

Shit! I was half way down the wicket. The fielder had seen this and was about to change his throw to the bowlers end. Henry obviously wasn't going to move and there was no point in both of us ignominiously ending up at the same end. I skidded to a halt and started to run back to the bowling crease. The fielder threw the ball and I knew I wasn't going to make it. The ball was in the air, the bowler was waiting to take off the stumps and I was still yards out of the crease. The throw saved me. It was wide of the bowler who had to dive to his left to take it. He held onto the ball, hit the ground and threw at the wicket as I dived for the crease. The tip of my bat crossed the crease as the ball just missed the stumps and hit me on the shoulder. I was fuming. Getting up and dusting myself down I was about to march down the pitch and remonstrate with Henry.

'Sorry Paul. I didn't think we could get that second run.'

I bit back what I was itching to say to him. There was nothing to be gained from having an argument at this juncture. We conferred in the middle.

'OK Henry; we got away with it. You have three balls left to face. He'll probably try to pitch it well up to prevent you getting a good strike on the ball. As you said we have a few overs left so there's no hurry. Just try to keep your wicket intact until I can get back on strike.'

Henry looked at me quizzically. I knew what he was thinking. Getting me back on strike was probably the fastest way to lose the game.

'Don't worry about me Paul. I know what to do.'

He marched back to the batting crease and took guard in the conventional manner. As the bowler commenced his run up I moved forward as far as I could whilst still keeping the tip of my bat in the crease. I was determined to take a run if even the smallest opportunity presented itself.

The bowler completed his run up and delivered the ball. As he did so Henry raised his bat high and took two steps down the wicket. If he missed the ball now he would be stumped and the game would be over. Henry brought his bat down and round in a powerful arc. By moving down the wicket he was able to take the ball on the full and he connected perfectly. The ball sailed high over mid-on position towards the boundary. I knew there was a fielder out there and as I started to run I looked anxiously over my shoulder. The fielder was standing just inside the boundary. Henry had hit the ball very high; too high. The fielder had picked up the flight and the ball was heading straight for him; he would not have to move an inch. Groaning internally I turned and started on the second run. The ball was descending from an enormous height. The fielder leaped upwards and backwards and took a magnificent one handed catch at the extremity of his reach. Off balance as he landed, he fell backwards, hitting the ground hard but retaining his grip on the ball. It was all over; we had lost. He held the ball up in triumph as he lay there. In triumph that is until he saw where he was. He had not realised how close to the boundary he had been standing and had fallen back over the boundary line and out of the field of play. His elation turned to despair. The umpire signalled a six. We had won.

Cheering broke out from our team and, forgetting my frustration with Henry, I hugged him as we met in the middle of the wicket.

'But he held the catch,' Henry uttered, confused.

I explained to him and his puzzled expression turned into his habitual cheery grin. As we walked off the pitch we were met half way by the rest of the team. Henry was mobbed and he lapped it up. I got a few slaps on the back but Henry was the hero and I have to admit he thoroughly deserved it. There was no way I could have connected with the power and precision he had displayed.

Later, in the pavilion, as we all enjoyed a beer, Steven Lindsey strolled over.

'Well played guys,' he said, 'it was a good game.' He was trying to smile but it did not reach his eyes. He turned to Brian. 'I thought you said Henry had never played before.'

'Well I didn't say that,' replied Brian, 'but he only had a couple of hours with us in the nets last week. If you're unhappy Steven you can still report us for fielding an unregistered player.'

'Oh no, I gave you my word and I'll stick by it. I'll bet you wish Henry could play for you every week though. Well done Henry,' he said, giving him a pat on the shoulder, before turning and walking over to the bar.

'He's sure sore,' said Henry, 'though he's trying to hide it.'

'He'll get over it,' replied Brian. 'My round I think.'

The following evening Henry treated Fiona and I to the dinner he had promised us at the Three Fishes down by the river. It was several cuts above the Crown and Thistle in the village. We had a very pleasant meal and the Chablis flowed freely. Fiona was on her usual good form and I saw that Henry barely took his eyes off her all evening. I was very glad he was flying back to the States the next day. After the meal we moved to the lounge bar for coffee.

Although we had maintained a friendly and cordial atmosphere with Henry throughout the evening - and in truth he wasn't such an ignorant Yank as I had at first thought - the fate of the cricket club was hanging over Fiona and I like a dark cloud. We had agreed beforehand that we would not let the evening end without making a last ditch attempt to persuade Henry to allow the club to continue playing on the cricket ground, at least until we could somehow raise enough funds to find an alternative location.

'I've had a real fine time over here,' said Henry, putting down his coffee cup with some deliberation. 'It's been an education. I'd like to thank you both for your hospitality; you and all the other guys in the cricket team.'

This was the moment I knew we had to raise the subject of the cricket ground. 'We're glad you've enjoyed your stay,' I said. 'I don't suppose we'll be seeing you again'

'Well, as a matter of fact I hope you will. I wanted you two to be the first to know. I've decided to sign over the cricket ground to the club, as a gift.'

We both stared at him open mouthed and speechless. 'Well that's tremendous and really unexpected news Henry,' Fiona said eventually, 'but are you sure. You'll be losing a lot of money.'

'Oh I don't need the dough and in any case I spoke to Mister Swallow last week and he told me I'd make close on half a million dollars for the house alone.

'That sounds about right,' I said, 'particularly if it looks out onto a cricket field rather than more houses.'

'I only have one condition.'

I glanced at Fiona nervously. I had a sudden nightmare vision of him asking her to be his personal assistant and her accepting and flying back to the States with him.

'Don't worry guys,' Henry laughed, 'my only condition is that I be allowed to play for the team whenever I come over here.'

I smiled in relief. 'I don't think that will be a problem. Brian will welcome you into the squad with open arms. He'll probably register you with the league as soon as he hears. I don't suppose any of the other teams will fall for the visiting Yank hustle again, not once they all hear about our epic victory against Escombe.'

Brian was ecstatic when I phoned him late that evening. 'That's incredibly generous of him. How many times does he plan to come over?'

'He thinks he can spare a couple of weeks a year. He says he'll make sure they are during the cricket season.'

'I don't think anyone will mind dropping out of the team for a game to accommodate the man who saved the club.'

Much later that night, around two in the morning, I was lying, still wide awake, beside Fiona. We had enjoyed a most pleasurable but exhausting couple of hours after getting home, but the amazing events of the last two days were still whirling around my brain and sleep would not come. I got out of bed, intending to bring a glass of water from the bathroom. As I walked towards the en-suite something drew me to the window overlooking Tom's garden. I gently drew aside the curtain and looked down. There was Henry standing on the patio, looking towards the cricket ground. I saw the glint of a glass in the moonlight as he raised it to his lips. Probably finishing off Tom's single malt I thought. There was an air of contentment about the way he stood there imbibing the sights and sounds of a soft English summer night, as well as the scotch. For the first night since he had arrived the house behind him appeared to be in total darkness; I could not see a single light burning.

And so the cricket ground at Crompton Bassett was saved. Early Monday morning found us both standing, dressed for work, on Tom Patch's drive as Henry loaded his two cases into the hired Ford Focus and turned to us.

'Well goodbye for now folks. It's been a real pleasure meeting you both and all the guys at the cricket club. I surely can't wait until my next visit.'

Henry shook my hand and bent to kiss Fiona's proffered cheek. He then got into the car, started the engine and lowered the driver's window.

'Thanks for everything Henry,' I said. For saving the cricket club and also for the most exiting victory we've had in a long time. I'm sure if Tom is watching he'll be very happy right now.'

'I know he is Paul. Tom's a great guy and he sure knows a thing or two about cricket, but I wouldn't want to run into him every day.'

Henry found first gear with a crunch that made us both wince. 'I'll never get used to this stick-shift,' he grinned and in a spray of gravel was off down the drive.

I glanced across at Tom's house standing solid and unremarkable in the warm morning sunshine and wondered about the extraordinary events of the past two weeks. Putting my arm around Fiona's waist I drew her gently to my side until I could feel the reassuring warmth of her body next to mine through her thin summer dress.

Henry gave us a cheery wave as he turned right into the avenue and was gone.

Fiona turned and looked up at me, her normally smooth, untroubled brow wearing a puzzled frown. 'Whatever do you suppose he meant about poor Tom?'

I tenderly kissed her moist upturned lips 'I have absolutely no idea.'

The Old News Seller

It had been a typically rough Monday at the office for Jon Meade and he was making his weary way along the busy city street towards the station to catch his commuter train home. It was late autumn; the shortening days light almost spent and a strong, cold, northerly breeze was swirling fallen leaves and litter around his feet. His brain was still in work mode, reviewing the last deal he had made that day and thinking he should have held out for the extra five percent he now knew he could have achieved. Certainly he was not paying very much attention to his immediate surroundings, having walked this route twice a day every week-day for the past five years or so.

'Evening paper sir?'

Meade glanced to his right, to where a narrow alleyway opened off the main thoroughfare; an alleyway which he did not recall having ever noticed before. Initially, seeing nothing, he thought he must have imagined the wheezy cry until . . . .

'Last one sir.'

He peered into the gloom and there, standing just inside the alleyway, was the indistinct and diminutive figure of an old man. He was dressed, as far as Meade could make out, rather shabbily in a dark overcoat and crumpled trousers. His pale hands held the sides of a tray, the weight of which was ameliorated by a cord fastened around his neck. This tray appeared to contain, as he had implied, a single newspaper.

'I've never seen you here before,' Meade said, feeling almost sorry for the old man, standing there in the cold, trying to sell his last newspaper so that he could go home; if he had a home to go to.

'I'm always here sir; not everyone sees me.'

'I'm not surprised,' Meade replied shortly, 'you should stand in a more prominent position. How much is it?'

'Just one pound sir.'

Meade groped in his jacket pocket, located a pound and proffered it. The ice cold of the old man's wrinkled hands shocked like an electric current as he took the coin and Meade involuntarily jerked his own hand away. The news-seller seemed not to notice and, carefully folding the newspaper, he handed it over. As he did so his face was illuminated by a car turning right from a side street opposite and the two men's eyes met briefly. There was intensity and intelligence in those grey eyes which belied the man's dilapidated appearance and Meade was momentarily taken aback by his piercing gaze.

'Have a pleasant evening sir and be careful how you go.' The old man smiled, showing surprisingly white and even teeth. The car completed its turn and he was submerged again in the evening gloom.

'Thank you,' Meade muttered, unaccountably relieved that the returning twilight had enabled him to break eye contact, 'and the same to you.'

Meade turned and hurried on towards the station, slipping the newspaper into the side pocket of his briefcase. For some reason he felt vaguely uneasy as he remembered the intensity in the old man's eyes, as if he were looking hard for some kind of reciprocal recognition. Recognition of what? Meade gave a mental shrug and tried to dismiss these unproductive thoughts from his head as he entered the station, crossed over the footbridge and joined the other homeward-bound commuters on the opposite platform.

His train duly arrived and he was fortunate to grab an empty seat, beating a heavily pregnant woman to it by a short head (or stomach in her case, he thought). Meade gazed resolutely out of the carriage window as he felt her indignant eyes boring into his skull.

'Would you like this seat,' a nearby male voice asked, from behind Meade's head. 'I'm not going much further.'

Meade heard the woman thank the stranger and sit down. The age of chivalry is long dead, he told himself. If you merely open a door for a woman these days they glare at you as if you were making a pass at them. If they espouse feminism and want equality in everything they have to live by the consequences. Justifying his behaviour with this misogynistic thought he took out his newspaper and read the front page headline.

'Death on the Rails.' It announced dramatically. The article went on to say that one of this morning's northbound commuter trains into the city had been halted for three hours after a man's body had been discovered by the line. The unfortunate man had apparently been hit by a train and was pronounced dead at the scene. A police investigation was ongoing. The man's name was being withheld until next-of-kin had been notified.

My train must have got through just before that all happened, thought Meade. He considered how fortunate he had been. A three hour delay would have prevented him doing hundreds of thousands of pounds in transactions and potentially losing a great deal in bonuses. As he was congratulating himself on his good fortune he remembered he had not had time to minute the details of a client meeting held earlier in the afternoon. He therefore slipped the newspaper back into his briefcase, took out his laptop and started work. He had just completed his notes as the train pulled into his station.

Meade's home was a large, attractive, three storey Georgian town house. It was central in a crescent of identical properties overlooking, to the front, communal gardens which could be accessed by residents via a gate in the six foot high ornamental railings, kept locked to keep out the general public. The crescent was conveniently situated within walking distance of the station, in the small commuter town in which Meade and his wife Claudia resided. Meade and Claudia had bought the house five years ago when he was head-hunted to his current position.

I'm home, Meade intoned as he entered the large high ceilinged hallway. Claudia duly emerged from one of the rooms leading off the hallway. She was wearing riding jodhpurs, with her long, strawberry blond hair, recently released from a riding helmet, cascading luxuriantly over her shoulders.

'Hello darling,' she purred, flinging her arms around his neck and giving him the benefit of a lingering kiss full on the mouth, 'I hope you haven't had too horrid a day.'

His olfactory receptors were assailed by a heady mixture of thoroughbred horse and expensive perfume.

'I think dinner is almost ready,' she added, 'I'll go check with Mary.'

'Have you been riding today?' he asked, reluctantly allowing Claudia to disengage herself from their embrace. 'It's been rather cold.'

'Only inside the equestrian centre,' she flung over her shoulder as she made her way down the hall towards the back of the house.

Meade admiringly watched her tall, lithe figure undulating towards the kitchen in her skin-tight jodhpurs.

Their marriage had been one of convenience. Claudia came from a minor aristocratic family, latterly fallen on harder times than they had experienced in the last three hundred years or so. She needed someone able to resurrect the lifestyle to which she had formerly been accustomed as a child and to support her twin expensive passions of riding and sailing. Meade was a *nouveau riche* 'something in the city' in need of a trophy wife to parade around his colleagues and to ease his way up the greasy pole and into the social circle to which he aspired. That said, they had been and still were, young, handsome and lustfully attracted to each other, a fact which their mutually mercenary marital objectives did nothing to detract from.

After dinner a few friends had been invited around for drinks and the wine and spirits flowed freely, though not freely enough to inhibit the athletic sex which Jon and Claudia afterwards engaged in until the small hours.

The following morning Meade, somewhat worse for wear, just managed to catch the 7.50 a.m. train into the city and, Lord be praised, find a seat. He made a mental note to buy a first class season ticket next time around, with a reserved seat. After all, I can afford it so why the hell not, he thought. After about half an hour the train decelerated, eventually coming to a complete stop. Groans and mutterings ensued from Meade's fellow commuters. A further ten minutes later an announcement came over the loudspeakers.

'We regret to inform passengers that there has been an incident on the line and this train will be delayed. We will make a further announcement when more information becomes available.'

The mutterings became louder. Mobiles, laptops and tablets were produced and many excuses began to be made for late arrivals at work and missed appointments. Meade did likewise.

A full half hour went by with no further developments and then the loudspeaker came to life again. 'Further to our previous announcement, we regret to inform passengers that the police have temporarily closed the line following a serious incident and this train will be delayed for at least a further two hours. We apologise to passengers but the delay is beyond our control.'

As the announcement ended an unfortunate ticket collector appeared and was assailed from all sides with questions, abuse and threats of litigation against the train operator. To his credit he remained calm and polite throughout all this, whilst continuing to check tickets. As he made his way down the carriage Meade heard him tell a nearby passenger that he understood a man's body had been found beside the tracks, causing the police to close the line. As Meade's ticket was checked he remarked conversationally that it was an unfortunate coincidence to have two such incidents on the same line on consecutive days.

'Which two days would that be then sir?' replied the ticket collector.

'Why today and yesterday of course,' said Meade.

'You must be mistaken sir; there was no incident on this line yesterday.'

Before Meade could argue the matter he had moved on down the carriage.

I'm sure it was this line, thought Meade and then, remembering he had not had any opportunity to read the rest of his newspaper the previous evening and it was still in his briefcase, he reached down, took it out and read the article again. It undoubtedly refers to this line, he thought. The man is an idiot; he doesn't know what day it is. As he was glancing over the rest of the front page the date caught his eye. Puzzled, he checked the date on his Breitling Navitimer and then looked back to the newspaper. There could be no mistake; the newspaper showed the current days date.

Meade was shaken. He glanced at the man sitting next to him engrossed in a novel, half intending to verify the date with him, but hesitated. It's just too absurd, he thought. I don't want to make a fool of myself. He leafed through the rest of the newspaper; today's date was on all the pages. He looked at the sports pages. There was a report on Monday evening's premier league match. The report was accurate; he had watched the highlights on this morning's breakfast news. A thought suddenly came into his head. He turned to the business pages and, looking at the day's early news, the thought began to crystallise into a scheme. What would be the harm in making a few small changes to his portfolio of shares to see what would happen? He took out his laptop and dashed off an e-mail to his broker with a number of selling and buying instructions.

Eventually, four hours later, Meade arrived at his office and spent the rest of the day playing catch up. Just after 6.00 p.m., exhausted, he finally felt able to turn off his screen and leave. Just as he was about to do so he remembered the e-mail to his broker and checked the closing share prices. To his delight he estimated he had made around five thousand pounds on the day. He smiled to himself. Not bad for a three minute e-mail.

He had no idea how this time-shift, or whatever it could be called, had occurred, but he was a pragmatic individual and wasn't inclined to think too deeply about it. In true entrepreneurial fashion, he told himself, he had taken full advantage of his good fortune and that was the end of it. But was it? He couldn't help thinking that he should have made more of his opportunity. After all, five thousand pounds was neither here nor there, he could make that most days in bonuses.

As he left the office he was beginning to think he had missed a great opportunity. Consequently, as he passed the gloomy alleyway in which he had encountered the old news-seller the previous evening he peered down it carefully. It was quite dark by this time and, seeing nothing, he took a couple of steps into the shadows. As soon as he moved into the alleyway the busy street sounds suddenly diminished, becoming somehow muffled, as if he had just put on a pair of ear defenders. The dirty brick walls close on either hand, what he could see of them, also looked odd; seemingly shimmering, as in a heat haze. He had the disconcerting impression that if he reached out to touch them they would be pliable; that his hand might even go straight through them.

'Looking for me sir?' The question, perfectly clear to his ears, came from a wheezing voice close behind him.

Meade's heart seemed to jump right up into his throat and he spun around to see a diminutive silhouette standing in the entrance to the alleyway, backlit by the shop window displays across the street.

'You gave me quite a start,' said Meade shakily, recognising the news-seller. 'I was looking for you just now. I don't know how I missed you.'

'It's easy to miss me when you're looking too hard.'

'I've no idea what you're talking about,' replied Meade testily; annoyed that the old man had given him quite a fright. 'Look, do you have a newspaper to sell or don't you?'

'You're lucky again sir; this is my last one.'

Meade took out a pound. Finding himself disinclined to touch those icy fingers again, he dropped it onto the fellow's tray.

The newspaper was folded as before and placed into his hand. Meade felt a visceral urge to exit that gloomy alleyway a quickly as possible. Stepping tentatively around the small dark figure he regained the normal sights and sounds of the busy high street, opening the newspaper as he did so. By the light issuing from the nearest shop window he looked keenly at the date on the front page; it was tomorrows.

'Look here,' he said, turning quickly around, 'are you aware that . . . .'

The old man was nowhere to be seen. Meade looked up and down the crowded street, then into the alleyway. He found himself reluctant to step again into the darkness before him. The people passing in both directions seemed oblivious to anything unusual having happened; they were just going about their normal business.

Meade took some deep breaths, making a conscious effort to regain his equilibrium; then, shrugging his shoulders, resumed his walk to the station, tucking the newspaper into his briefcase as he did so. He resisted the temptation to read the newspaper on the train, not wanting any of his fellow passengers to notice its unique qualities.

Dinner was almost ready when he arrived home. Claudia is high maintenance he thought, but she certainly knows how to organise a household. He deposited his briefcase in his study, changed quickly and went down to dinner.

After dinner, as they finished off a bottle of Sedlescombe 2012 Regent-Rondo, Meade told Claudia he had a little work to finish. He placed his napkin on the table, meaning to rise and retire to his study. Stepping nimbly around the table she leant over him, giving his eyes the benefit of her ample cleavage and his mouth a lingering kiss.

'Don't be too long darling,' she murmured. 'We have the evening all to ourselves. It would be a pity to waste it on silly work.' As her right hand teased the short hairs on the back of his neck, the fingertips of her left traced an intricate pattern on his chest though the thin material of his casual shirt.

'You're insatiable,' he grinned, grabbing her left wrist as her fingers wandered lower.

'How do you know?' she whispered into his ear, 'you haven't really tested me yet.'

'That sounds like a challenge', he replied, attempting without success to keep the hoarse tremor out of his voice.

Claudia did not reply directly, merely arching her delicately plucked eyebrows questioningly.

'I must do this darling; it won't take long'.

He reluctantly extricated himself and, gaining the sanctuary of his study, took the evening newspaper from his briefcase. Ignoring the front page headlines about the dawn arrest of two suspected Islamic terrorists he quickly turned to the business pages. His attention was immediately drawn to a headline 'Substantial new gold deposits discovered in Peru'. The article went on to report that the New England Mining Corporation had discovered large, previously unsuspected gold reserves in the Cajamarca region of northern Peru.

That's the one, though Meade, smiling to himself. He consulted the contacts list in his android and then pressed the short dial icon for his broker's home number.

'Evening Charles,' he said, responding to the curt hello at the other end of the line. 'Sorry to ring you at home; I hope I'm not interrupting anything.'

'Oh hi Jon,' replied Charles Reardon, recognising Meade's voice. 'No problem. Are you and the delectable Claudia inviting us to another dinner party; I think it's your turn.'

'Soon Charles, soon. I'm afraid this is business though. I need you to do something for me immediately the markets open in the morning. I thought I would ring you now so you could make it your first task tomorrow. I know how busy you get as soon as you walk in.'

'Well it must be important for you to call me at home; go ahead.'

'I want you to dispose of all my worst performing shares, up to a value of around half a million pounds sterling and put it all into New England Mining Corporation stock.'

There was silence on the other end of the line; Meade waited it out.

'What have you heard Jon?'

'Nothing Charles, it's just a hunch.'

'A hunch my arse; you know something. NEM Corp is mainly gold mining is it not?'

'I believe so,' said Meade coolly.

'You believe so.' Reardon chuckled. 'You're a sly old fox Jon; you definitely know something.'

'How could I? You know I don't have anything to do with mining, let alone gold mining. As I said, it's just a hunch, otherwise it would be insider dealing and I would have to be pretty stupid to risk that.'

'OK, have it your own way. I'll do as you ask first thing tomorrow. I hope you know what you're doing.'

'Thanks Charles. I'll check with Claudia about the dinner party; you know she organises our entire social calendar.'

Meade rang off and sank back for a moment into his burgundy leather swivel chair, a little doubt creeping into his mind. I hope this isn't a big mistake, he pondered. If this goes pear shaped I'll find that little fart and wring his neck for him. Oh what the hell; live for the day. With that thought in mind he turned off the desk lamp and went in search of Claudia.

About 11.00 a.m. the following morning the news Meade had been eagerly anticipating came through on his screen from Reuters. He uttered a sigh of relief and then gave full attention again to the job he was being paid for. If this carries on, he thought, I'll be able to retire before I'm thirty five.

Charles Reardon rang just before Meade left the office. 'At today's close you've made nearly two hundred and fifty thousand on top of your half a million you canny bastard,' he said as soon as Meade accepted the call.

'Yes, so I see,' replied Charles. 'It was a good hunch.'

'You're still sticking to that line then are you.'

'There is no other line.'

'OK, have it your way. Do you want to hang on to the shares?'

'Yes, for the moment. Sorry, I've got to rush now. I'll speak to you again soon.'

Meade rang off and left the office. As he made his way along the high street he slowed down as he neared the place at which he had previously encountered the old news-seller, but could not see him. He turned and retraced his steps, having passed the alleyway without noticing it. Another five minutes later he had still not found the news-seller; he couldn't even find the alleyway. This is ridiculous, he thought to himself. Why can't I find the damned place? He glanced at his watch and, frustrated, realised he could delay no longer if he was to catch his train.

An hour or so later Meade shut his front door behind him and started to take off his overcoat.

'Hi darling, I'm back.'

As he moved to hang up his coat something on the hall table caught his eye. There, neatly folded, lay an evening newspaper.

'Hello darling,' said Claudia, emerging from the rear of the house. I'm afraid dinner will be a little late this evening. I had to give Mary the afternoon off because her father is . . .'

'Where did that newspaper come from?' asked Meade, rather rudely interrupting his wife.

'What? Oh that. It was delivered.'

'Delivered?'

'Yes, about half an hour ago. There was a knock on the door. I checked the CCTV and there was this little old man standing there. He looked rather disreputable, so I asked . . . .'

'What did he look like?' asked Meade, interrupting again.

'Well if you would give me half a chance I would tell you.'

'OK, OK, I'm sorry. Go on.'

'As I was saying, he looked rather disreputable. He had on a dark overcoat and there was some tray thing hung around his neck. I couldn't really see his features very well. Anyway, I asked him what he wanted over the intercom. He said he was delivering the newspaper you had ordered. It all seemed a bit odd to me. I asked him why he didn't just put it through the letterbox and he said he wanted paying. I still didn't much like the look of him and I wasn't going to open the door, being on my own in the house.'

'So what happened?'

'I told him to either put it through the letter box or take it away, but that I wasn't opening the door. Then he said 'Tell Jon I'll catch him later' and pushed it through.

'He said what?'

'Tell Jon I'll . . . .'

'How the hell did he know my name?'

'How should I bloody know? I've never seen him before in my entire life and I would appreciate it if you would let me finish a sentence occasionally.'

Meade took a deep breath. 'I'm sorry darling, it's just that . . . . Oh it doesn't matter, it's only a newspaper.'

'So who is he?'

'It sounds like the same chap I bought a newspaper from a couple of times this week; but that was in the city. I've no idea how he could know my name or where I lived.

'That's a bit scary Jon.'

'Oh I think he's harmless enough,' said Meade, totally without conviction. 'I'll get changed whilst you finish dinner. What are we having?'

'I'll let you know when I do.' She turned and headed back towards the kitchen.

Meade groaned inwardly. Claudia was a peerless organiser, but her talents did not extend to the culinary arts. He picked up the newspaper and looked at the date. It was tomorrows of course; why wouldn't it be? He took it into his study and sat down. The front page headline caught his attention immediately. The portrait of an attractive young woman looked out at him from beneath the headline *"Kenton Woman Battered to Death"*. My God that's here, he thought. He skim read the article. A twenty three year old woman named Karen Lewis had been found with severe head and other injuries in Ashton Terrace just after 10.00 p.m. the previous evening, after police and ambulance services responded to a 999 call. The woman had been rushed to hospital but was pronounced dead on arrival. The article went on to report that the assailant had not yet been apprehended but that the police had a good description and were hopeful of making an early arrest. There were details about the young woman. She was a post graduate student studying for a master's degree in economics. There was no obvious motive for the attack. Her fiancé and family were distraught etc. etc.

Meade turned to the business pages but could not take in any detail. He put down the newspaper and sat quietly behind his desk, deep in thought. He was troubled. He had in his hands the knowledge which could save a young woman's life. If he phoned the police, what would he say? If he merely told them he suspected this woman might be murdered tonight they would want to know why he thought that. He obviously could not tell

213

them the truth. Even if he was believed he did not want anyone to find out about the newspapers; he wanted to keep that little secret all to himself. In any case, if his recent share dealings came to light he could be in deep trouble. If he didn't give them any background and, thinking he was some crank they did nothing, then when the woman was killed, he would be the chief suspect. He could make the call anonymously but he was sure they would be able to trace it back to him. After a few irresolute and agitated minutes he rose and went upstairs to change for dinner.

'You're not very good company this evening,' said Claudia some time later, as she washed her boeuf bourguignon ready meal for one down with her third glass of Château Simard 1996 St-Emilion.

'I'm sorry,' said Meade, distastefully pushing away the remains of his sweet and sour chicken and egg fried rice, 'I've had a lot on my mind.'

'It isn't that thing with the newspaper bothering you, is it?'

Meade forced a smile. 'Oh that's nothing. I'm sure there must be a logical explanation. Look, I have some good news. I had a tip off and made quite a killing on the stock market today.'

'Oh do tell,' said Claudia, suddenly animated. 'How much did you make?'

Meade paused for effect. 'Around a quarter of a million,' he said carelessly.

Claudia gasped. 'You're joking.'

'I never joke about money.'

'Oh my clever, clever darling, you're in for a very special treat tonight.'

'Even better than last night,' he grinned. 'I'm not sure I have the stamina.'

'Oh, that was just the overture.' She came around the table and eased herself into his lap, running her fingers through his hair as she did so.

'Jon, do you remember that Jeanneau Sun Fast 3600 we were talking about.'

'You were talking about,' he corrected. 'How could I, you even talk about it in your sleep?'

'I'm sure I don't. Anyway, we could afford it now. It's only about a hundred and seventy five thousand. If we ordered it before Christmas they could deliver by April, just in time for next seasons sailing. I would be *very* grateful.'

'*Only* one hundred and seventy five thousand?'

'Including VAT.'

'Oh, that's OK then. What about that Porsche 911 cabriolet I've been looking at.'

'Oh, we can afford your silly old Porsche as well.'

'What's this *we* business? I made the quarter of a million.'

'But what's yours is mine,' she breathed, 'and what's mine is *definitely* yours,' she added, smiling with feigned innocence and fluttering her eyelashes. 'Look, Mary can clear all this up in the morning. Let's go and watch something sexy on the home cinema to really get us into the mood.'

An hour later, despite being half way through a particularly erotic drama and with Claudia draped seductively all over him, Meade was still not in the mood. He could not get out of his head the image of Karen Lewis staring accusingly at him from the newspaper. To his agitated mind she seemed to be saying 'you selfish pig; you could have saved my life.'

He glanced at his watch; it was nine fifteen.

'Look Claudia, I'm sorry but I just can't concentrate. I'm going to go out for a run to get all this work stuff out of my head. I won't be long.'

'A run; at this time?' Claudia was astounded.

'Yes, I know it's probably stupid, but I can't give you the attention you deserve whilst all these figures are running around inside my head. I'll only be half an hour or so and then I'll make it up to you.'

'You'd better.' She looked genuinely upset and aggrieved, which was understandable he supposed, since the deployment of her considerable charms over the past hour had been ineffectual.

Meade descended to the basement, which incorporated a sizeable gym and wet room. He changed into running shoes and a dark grey jogging suit, but did not immediately leave. Sitting on a bench, irresolute, his mind was in turmoil. He had made a lot of money that day which he did not deserve and in a way he did not comprehend. How could he just let this young woman die when he was probably the only person on earth who could save her? He did not doubt for a second that this terrible event was going to take place in - he looked again at his watch - half an hour. That the newspaper was genuinely tomorrow's, just as the previous two editions sold to him had been for the following days, he had no doubt

Meade was a man whose conscience rarely bothered him, but he knew if he did nothing now, when he could possibly save an innocent woman's life, it would haunt him for the rest of his. He knew Ashton Terrace; it was on one of his jogging routes. It was a street made up of large Victorian houses, most of which had been converted into flats. The houses were generally of three storeys; four if you included the basements, which most of them had. It was around one mile away; he could make it in time. He made up his mind, stepped outside via the basement door and began to jog at a steady pace. After about five minutes it occurred to him that perhaps he should have taken some kind of weapon. If he encountered a potential murderer he might need something. He glanced at his watch again, it was 9.42 p.m. Damn; it was too late to turn back now. He ran on, cursing his lack of forethought.

He arrived at Ashton Terrace at nine forty eight. Since he had no idea from which direction Karen Lewis or the assailant would approach he took up position about half way along the street, which was no more than two hundred metres long. He looked around for anything he could use as a weapon to defend himself, but could see nothing. The minutes dragged by. The street was quiet; not a single person to be seen. Most of the buildings had lights at many of the windows, an indication that they were indeed flats and music or voices faintly reached his ears from some of the nearer ones. He looked yet again at the illuminated dial of his Breitling; 9.57 p.m. He fervently wished that nothing would happen and he could make his way home.

It was a faint but regular clicking sound which first reached Meade's ears; a woman's high heels. Seconds later a slim figure turned the corner into the street from the southern end, walking towards him, but on the other side of the street. Meade looked quickly around in all directions. He could see no one else, but there might be someone hiding in the shadows. On the steps leading down to one of the basement flats, or in the mostly unlit areas fronting them would be an obvious place. It then occurred to him that if he waited until the assailant appeared he would, of necessity, be obliged to confront him and would quite possibly be too late if the man reached the woman first. Prevention would be much better. If the attacker saw that he did not have a clear field he would probably abandon the attempt. Meade's brain processed these thoughts in less than a second and he started to cross the street towards the young woman, who was now less than thirty metres away.

As Meade approached he saw her stride shorten and she looked quickly over her shoulder. Then, seeming to gather herself, she started forward again at a quicker pace, but halted completely as Meade came within a couple of metres of her.

'Excuse me,' said Meade, 'are you Karen Lewis?'

'Who are you? I don't think I know you.'

Meade glanced around to make sure no attacker was approaching from behind him. Karen obviously misinterpreted the reason for his action and took an involuntary step backwards.

'You don't know me but I need to talk to you. Your life is in danger.'

'Please leave me alone.' The pitch of Karen's voice rose and she retreated further.

'No; listen. I'm here to help you,' said Meade, taking a step forward.

'Get away from me.'

'Look, I believe someone is going to attack you, in this street, at any moment.

'Oh my God, please don't hurt me?'

'I'm not going to hurt you; I'm trying to help you, said Meade, becoming exasperated.

Meade reached out towards her and took another step forward. 'Listen to me. If I stay with you I can protect you; he may not even try it.'

'You; stay with me. Do you think I'm insane? Don't come any nearer or I'll scream.'

As Karen said this she took another step backwards, but the heel of her shoe encountered nothing but thin air. As she overbalanced and started to fall backwards she tried to grab onto the railings past which she was falling, at the same time letting out a terrified scream. Meade lunged forward, making a despairing but unsuccessful attempt to catch hold of her arm. Karen fell backwards down the steps leading to a basement flat. There was a sickening crunch as her head hit about six steps down and she tumbled head over heels down the rest of the steps to the area in front of the flat, where her body lay, twisted and unmoving.

Meade was in shock. For a couple of seconds he stood immobile at the top of the steps; unbelieving; unable to react. Then an outside light was switched on below and the door to the basement flat opened. The area, the steps and Meade were flooded with a harsh unforgiving light. A large male figure appeared, silhouetted in the doorway.

'What the bloody hell is going on?'

He then saw the body lying broken beside his front door and looked up.

His eyes met Meade's and held them. He started to move towards the steps.

'You f-----g bastard.'

The expletive galvanised Meade's body into action, but arguably not his brain. He turned and ran. As he ran faces began to appear at nearby windows. The large man reached the top of the steps leading from his flat, but there he hesitated. Meade was young and fit and was already thirty metres down the street. Realising he would not catch Meade he turned back to render what assistance he could to the woman he would soon discover was his near neighbour, Karen Lewis.

Meade reached the end of the street and turned left. He was trying to rationalise why he had run. He should have stayed to explain what had happened; tried to help Karen. But he had panicked and now it was too late to go back. And of course he knew anyway that Karen was dead; he had already read about it in the newspaper. What an idiot he had been. He should have stayed out of it and then none of this would have happened. Would Karen still be alive, or had there really been someone else lying in wait for her? If so, that person must have had a motive. Perhaps he was the one the police would apprehend.

His brain was now functioning again. He was heading towards the river. He remembered there was an old narrow wynd a few hundred yards down this road which would allow him to quickly double back to a quiet park, the other side of which was his own house. If he could get home without being seen he would be OK. He had never touched the woman, so there could be no DNA evidence linking him to her. How good a look had the man got of him? He remembered the newspaper article 'the police had a good description and were hopeful of making an early arrest'. He would have to ask Claudia to say he had been with her all night. She would back him up; he was her meal ticket after all. With these thoughts running through his head he almost missed the entrance to the wynd.

He skidded to a halt and then ran into the narrow opening between two high garden walls. He felt safer now. He didn't think anyone had seen him enter. As he ran further down, the light from the street behind him grew dimmer and he had to slow down or run the risk of tripping up on a loose cobble or running into some waste bin or other street furniture.

Suddenly. 'Hello Jon.' A voice he instantly recognised croaked from the darkness.

Meade halted, dumbstruck.

'I see you've made Friday's front page Jon,' the old news-seller's voice continued evenly. 'Would you like to read all about it?'

A pale yellow light appeared from somewhere, illuminating the old man's face and the newspaper he was holding. Meade could not determine from where the light was issuing, but he could just distinguish a face staring out from the front page of the newspaper. His face.

'Who the hell are you?' Meade managed to ask breathlessly, his voice breaking with emotion mid-sentence.

'You could say I was a traveller Jon . . . . and an observer.'

'An observer? An observer of what.'

'Why homo sapiens of course, or the human race as you prefer to call yourselves.'

'Homo bloody sapiens. You're insane you little f--k. This is all your doing. You set me up for all this shit.'

The old man smiled, showing his even white teeth.

'On the contrary Jon, I think you must agree it was entirely your own actions which have brought about your current predicament.'

Meade became aware that the news-sellers voice had changed. It now sounded younger and cultured, with a strange accent he just could not place. He was suddenly filled with an all consuming rage and an uncontrollable desire to exact revenge upon this man. He raised his fist and took a step towards his nemesis. As he did so it felt as though a giant fist had enveloped his own, immobilising not only his arm but his whole body. As he stood, unable to move a muscle, the man's figure, now larger and much younger looking started to shimmer and become indistinct.

'I'm sorry I shan't be able to appear for the defence Jon and I'm afraid you won't be able to find any of those newspapers you bought from me. Oh and of course there won't be any image of me on your CCTV.'

Meade made a supreme physical effort to release himself from the unseen constraints binding him, but to no avail.

'Thank you Jon, my visit has been extremely enlightening. I'm sure my report will be well received.'

The man's body was becoming translucent, appearing to separate into individual molecules, each one glowing eerily in the darkness before winking out. As it did so Meade caught the briefest glimpse of someone or something else within.

'I think you'd better run now Jon,' was the last thing he heard before the last glowing points of light disappeared.

Meade found himself once more alone in the darkness and heard the distant but clear sound of approaching sirens. Suddenly he realised he could move again. He ran.

Jon Meade sat working at his desk in the same, now rather worse for wear, burgundy leather swivel chair and in a rather more modest house than the one he had occupied thirty years previously. He heard the front door bell ring and looked up, listening. There was the sound of the front door opening and then Claudia's voice in conversation with a deeper male one. He could not distinguish any words and after a minute or so there was silence again. Meade then heard the sound of approaching footsteps, the study door opened and Claudia entered. The years had been kind to her. The strawberry blond hair was cut shorter but there was only a hint of grey at the temples, which she scorned to disguise. Her figure had retained its youthful slenderness and she still moved with a lithe grace which belied her fifty seven years.

Meade looked up smiling. 'Do we have a visitor?'

'Yes, it's a man. European I think, although I can't quite place his accent. He apologises for calling without any appointment but says he's from head office.'

'Geneva? What's his name?

'It sounded like Newseller; odd name. What should I tell him; I know you wanted to finish that report this afternoon.'

'Oh that's OK; I'd better see him; although I don't recall anyone at head office by that name.'

'I'll show him in then.'

Claudia returned a few seconds later, followed by a visitor Meade did not recognise. He was tall, slim and fair haired, with an unusually pale, smooth completion. If Meade had been asked to guess his age he would have struggled.

'Mister Newseller, this is my husband Jon,' said Claudia.

The visitor held out his hand and smiled, showing white, even teeth. 'Yes, we have met before. Hello once again Jon.'

Meade took the stranger's hand. His handshake was firm but the hand surprisingly cold, despite the warm, sunny July day outside.

'I'm sorry but you have me at a disadvantage, Mister . . . . Newseller? I I'm afraid I don't recall us having met before.'

'Well I suppose that is hardly surprising, it was thirty years ago and I recollect you were in rather a hurry at the time.'

Meade felt a cold shiver run down his spine and he glanced quickly at Claudia who was hovering, looking uncertain and puzzled.

'You're not from head office in Geneva are you Mister Newseller.'

'Well no, not from that head office. I apologise for the subterfuge but you may have tried to make it more difficult for me to see you had I introduced myself properly; although the name I have chosen to use should have given you a clue.'

'Is everything alright Jon?' asked Claudia tremulously.

Meade glanced at her again. 'Yes, it's OK darling. There's no need for you to stay.'

'Oh I think it would be useful for Claudia to stay. I believe she will find what I have to tell you of interest.'

'What do you want with us? Haven't you done enough damage?'

'On the contrary, from what I have observed the outcomes have been entirely satisfactory.'

224

'Jon, please tell me who this is,' said Claudia, coming around the desk and placing a protective hand on Meade's shoulder.'

'Satisfactory,' said Meade incredulously. 'An innocent young woman died and I almost ended up in prison for murdering her.'

He felt Claudia's fingers digging into his shoulder and put his hand over hers.

'Unfortunately I could not have prevented Karen Lewis's death Jon. There are some things which cannot be changed. But your life was saved and that of another.

'My life saved!' said Jon incredulously. 'I would have gone to prison but for Claudia giving me an alibi. She believed everything I told her about what happened that night, even though I could hardly believe it myself.'

'But you did not go to prison. That was not just because of Claudia. You found your CCTV camera showed nothing when you checked it after you arrived home. It was not only my image which was erased but also the image of you leaving your basement at 9.35 p.m. that evening. Did you never wonder why there was also no image of you on the six CCTV cameras on the route you took that night?'

'That was you?' breathed Meade.

'There was nothing else to link you to the scene but the description of the one eye witness. So, not only did you not go to prison, you were also able to successfully sue a number of newspapers for the character assassinations they printed about you after you had been arrested.'

'I gave all that money to charity,' asserted Meade.

'You did indeed. You also gave to charity the quarter of a million you made on the NEM Corporation shares. You then gave up your lucrative job in the city to work for a charity yourself at half the salary. A charity you have continued to work for with great distinction for the last thirty years.'

'Humanity Against Religious Extremism,' confirmed Meade.

'Yes, you certainly got that up and running,' said the visitor, smiling at his own witticism. 'And Claudia; you gave up riding horses for saving them. How many do you have at the sanctuary currently?'

'Almost one hundred,' replied Claudia automatically, then: 'How on earth do you know about this?' Despite her incredulity Meade could feel the grip of her fingers on his shoulder relaxing a little.

'I know that time was traumatic for you both,' said the visitor, ignoring Claudia's question, 'but if I had not intervened when I did Jon would have continued on his trajectory to disaster and been ruined in the banking crisis and stock market collapse a few months later. I will not go into detail about the subsequent years, but you two would certainly not have been together today and still obviously very much attached to each other.'

'The experience I endured would have changed anyone's perspective on life. But you said someone else was saved?' said Meade, after a few seconds silence.

'Yes I did; the young man whom Karen had broken off her engagement to a few days previously. He was waiting for her nearby, as you suspected. If you had not intervened he would have approached and tried to persuade her to change her mind. Karen would have refused and he would have become agitated. The altercation would have ended as it did for you, with the

226

difference being that no one would have believed it was an accident and he would have been incarcerated for a very long time. As it was, he watched your encounter, then slipped away unnoticed. The police were so convinced by the eye witness's description of you they dismissed him from their enquiries after perfunctory questioning. He lied about being there of course and again, thanks to my efforts, there was no CCTV evidence to contradict that. He was consumed with guilt however and I suspect he would have come forward to aid your defence had the case gone to court, but you were both spared that. He too has become a better human being over the intervening years, but there is no necessity to go into details about that.'

No one spoke for a while. 'Why has it taken thirty years for you to come here and tell us all this?' asked Meade eventually.

'You're measurement of time has no relevance to me, but this is the first opportunity I have had to return   and I am pleased to find the results of my actions have been satisfactory. I could not have planned the eventual outcomes; all I could do was stop you in your tracks, set you on a new course and the rest is the future, as we say. Your story has been one of my greatest successes.'

'Are you saying you do this all the time?' asked Claudia incredulously.

'I do not make a habit of,' said the visitor soberly, 'my role is mainly to observe, but in your case the range of potential improved outcomes justified an intervention.'

'You're telling us we are not in charge of our own destinies.'

'On the contrary Claudia, once I had applied a small course correction you were both *entirely* the agents of your own successes or failures.' He smiled. 'Jon really was a rather unpleasant individual when I intervened; it would not have taken you very much longer to discover that.

'Surely it isn't possible to go back in time and change historical events.'

'One human being's future is another's history. Any of you can change the future for the better; it's just you mostly choose not to do so. Well, I must leave you now. I shall depart more conventionally than the last time we met Jon.'

'Who are you and where do you come from?' said Meade, finally finding his voice again.

'You asked me that once before,' replied the visitor, as he walked to the door of the study. 'I regret you're still not ready for that revelation. Goodbye to you both; we shall not meet again.' With those words he closed the door gently but firmly behind him.

~~~~~~~~~~~~~~~~~

In Einstein's equation, time is a river. It speeds up, meanders, and slows down. The new wrinkle is that it can have whirlpools and fork into two rivers. So, if the river of time can be bent into a pretzel, create whirlpools and fork into two rivers, then time travel cannot be ruled out.

Michio Kaku (1947 -)

The Coastal Retreat

The painting was large. Very large, thought Adam, as he sat on a comfortably upholstered leather bench facing it and surreptitiously eating his chicken and bacon sandwich. He did so in defiance of gallery regulations which prohibited the eating of food on the premises. It was raining outside and he had to eat his lunch somewhere, he reasoned. The painting must have been around three metres wide by two high, he thought to himself and took up most of the end wall of the long gallery in which it hung. Unusually for its large dimensions it was a relatively modern work; around the turn of the nineteenth to twentieth century's according to the information plaque on the wall to the left of the painting. He didn't recognise the artist's name, but the plaque informed Adam that he was one of the "Devon School" of painters who followed closely upon the heels of the Pre-Raphaelite Brotherhood of the mid to late nineteenth century, employing their vibrant use of primary colours but painting rural and coastal West Country scenes, mostly in Devon.

The subject matter of the painting was pastoral, as one might expect. It showed the seaward extremity of a verdant valley, running down to an idyllic cove sheltering a white, shell-sand beach. Two children were playing on the beach; probably girls, but they were too distant for Adam to be totally sure. To the left of the dusty, rutted lane leading to the beach stood a thatched cottage, elevated and set some way back from the lane. Between the lane and the cottage was a large garden containing a profusion of herbaceous flowers and shrubs on either side of the path leading to the cottage door. A small stream ran by the side of the lane furthest from the cottage, issuing onto the beach and meandering across the sand. A sunny, sloping field lay over a hedgerow on the other side of

229

the lane, within which a group of workers were engaged in haymaking in a traditional, non-mechanised manner.

Rather "chocolate box" thought Adam, but certainly very well executed and pleasing to the eye. One could almost lose oneself in the sheer enormity of the scene. Hearing footsteps, he glanced over his shoulder and saw a gallery attendant walking in his direction. He hurriedly stuffed his half eaten sandwich into the inside pocket of his raincoat and innocently returned his gaze to the painting.

'Do you like it?' The female voice came from behind his other shoulder.

Turning around he saw a young woman who appeared to be in her mid twenties; around his own age. She was slim, of medium height and dressed rather shabbily in a light-brown raincoat. This was unbuttoned displaying a blue and white check shirt and blue denim jeans beneath. On her feet were well worn white trainers which, thought Adam, explained why he had not heard her approach. The hood of her raincoat was thrown back revealing dark, almost black hair, pulled back rather severely into a pony tail. However, this had the advantage of fully revealing attractive features with high cheekbones, full lips and, not least, large expressive almond eyes with long dark lashes, which were currently not looking at Adam but at the painting. He wasn't entirely sure he had heard her correctly and that she had been addressing him. She almost immediately dispelled these doubts.

'I meant the painting rather than your sandwich,' she said, giving him the benefit of a mischievous smile. 'They must have recently brought it out of storage. It wasn't on display when I was here last.'

Adam felt his pulse rate increasing. He was naturally shy and was not accustomed to attractive women addressing him out of the blue. He opened his mouth but his vocal cords seemed to be momentarily paralysed. Her smile became quizzical and her eyebrows rose questioningly.

He became aware that he was blushing and finally managed to say, 'do you come here often then?' Even as he spoke the words he was inwardly cringing at the banality of the question.

Her smile became a grin as she answered. 'Oh yes, all the time; it's warm in here and there isn't an entry charge.'

This answer made Adam wonder if she might be homeless, but he couldn't ask that outright. Her clothes had seen better days but they were clean and her complexion, devoid of any make-up, looked healthy and vital.

She seemed to read his mind. 'I have a flat just out of town, or what passes for one, but I can't afford to use the heating on my benefit payments.'

She held out her hand. 'I'm Emily.'

He took the proffered hand, which was slender, but the grip firm and assured.

'Adam; pleased to meet you. I was just thinking it's a beautiful painting, but a rather idealised scene. I'm sure rural life at the turn of the nineteenth century wasn't too great for most people.'

'Rather Helen Allingham you mean?' replied Emily. Then, seeing Adam's blank expression, she explained. 'She was a watercolour artist who was painting similar scenes around that time. She was criticised for being overly sentimental in her representation of rural life and picturesque farmhouses and cottages. On the other hand her paintings left us with an important historical record of many period dwellings which were often demolished soon after she painted them.'

Adam was impressed. 'You're very knowledgeable. Is she one of your favourite artists?'

'Not particularly, but I took a degree in Art History, for what good it's done me. Sebastian Menhenick, who painted this, was an interesting character too. Did you know he was a Druid?'

'I'm afraid I had never heard of him until today,' confessed Adam. 'His name is quite a mouthful.'

'The surname is Celtic Cornish. He isn't particularly well known and he wasn't very prolific. I think this may be the only one of his paintings on public display. The others, which are all just as large, are in private collections.'

'You certainly need a lot of wall to hang one. Aren't Druids the folks who turn up at Stonehenge every summer and winter solstice?'

'Yes,' replied Emily, 'but there's a lot more to them than that. Druidry is a spiritual path; a religion to some, a way of life to others. All Druids sense nature as divine or sacred. Every part of nature is treasured as part of the great web of life, with no one creature or aspect of it having supremacy over any other.'

'Wow, you seem to know a lot about them,' said Adam, impressed yet again by this young woman. 'Are you a Druid yourself?'

Emily laughed. 'Well, certainly not a practicing one, but I must say I'm sympathetic with their beliefs. I only know so much about them because I chose to do a dissertation on the Devon School of painters at Uni. and Menhenick was a leading light. Druids also believe that the world we see is not the only one that exists. A cornerstone of Druid belief is in the existence of the Otherworld; a realm or realms which exist beyond the reach of the physical senses, but which are nevertheless real. This Otherworld is seen as the place we travel to when we die. But we can also visit it during our lifetime in dreams, in meditation, or under hypnosis. Celtic mythology, which inspires so much of Druidism, is full of descriptions of this Otherworld. Sorry, I'm boring you.' Emily had seen Adam glancing at his watch.

'No. No not at all. It's just that I'm on my lunch break, but I still have forty minutes left. Look, would you like a coffee, or tea. We could go to the café here. It isn't expensive,' he added. He couldn't believe he had just said that. He was usually quite shy and they had only met a few minutes ago.

Emily looked embarrassed. 'I'm sorry but I only have enough money left for my bus fare home.'

'Oh that's alright; I can stand you a coffee. It's only a couple of pounds and you can continue my education there.'

Emily hesitated, but only for a second. 'OK,' she said, 'a coffee would be lovely.'

Inside the gallery café Adam brought over two filter coffees and sat down opposite Emily at the table she had chosen. It looked out over a rainy square, where people were hurrying to escape the continuing downpour.

'You work in the city then?' she asked.

'Yes, just around the corner in fact; in the call centre of an insurance company. You're not working at the moment then?'

'I was made redundant from the bank three months ago. Lots of the high street branches are being closed. Everyone is banking on line now, or so they tell us, but people don't really have a choice if they close all the branches. I haven't been able to find anything else yet, although I must have sent my CV out a hundred times. Anything will do, just to get off benefits, such as they are. I should have got out of the bank sooner. I could see which way the wind was blowing; we all could. Do they have any posts vacant where you work?'

Adam gave a short, rueful laugh. 'You can have mine,' he said. 'You're welcome to it.'

'It can't be that bad. At least it must be better than food banks and wearing your overcoat at home because you can't afford to turn on the gas fire.'

'I'm sorry,' said Adam, 'of course it's better than that, but it's still pretty bad. It's depressing how many people feel they can be obnoxious with someone when they aren't face to face and will probably never speak to them again'.

'But are there any vacancies?' insisted Emily. 'I really, really do need a job.'

'Well, there is a high staff turnover because not many people can stick it out for too long. I'll ask if you really want me to.'

'Oh please, would you?' she exclaimed, clasping her hands together as if in prayer. 'That's really good of you.'

'No problem,' said Adam, thinking to himself that this might at least be another opportunity to meet this vivacious girl again. 'Could you be here tomorrow after I start my lunch break; say one fifteen?'

'Well I do have a session with my personal trainer at eleven-thirty and my investment broker at two, but I think I could just about squeeze you in,' said Emily seriously.

For a split second Adam was confused before the joke sank in, then he grinned hugely. 'You had me going for a second there.'

This girl was something else. How could she possibly be out of work?

The two drank their coffee, chatting easily about their favourite bands and a little of their own lives to date. It transpired that they had both been at Durham University, but two years apart, Emily being two years younger at twenty three, but had obviously never met. Adam managed to refrain from saying what a small world it was; one banal cliché was enough for one day. Their difficulties in finding any employment in their study fields, post the financial meltdown, had also been very similar, both eventually taking the only jobs they could find at the time. Adam had moved on a couple of times but Emily had stayed at the bank until losing her job.

Adam looked again at his watch. 'I'm sorry but I have to get back. They're very strict on timekeeping amongst other things. If you amass three demerit points it's a disciplinary meeting and a written warning.'

'Sounds like a lot of fun,' said Emily. 'May I walk round with you, to see where it is?'

'Of course, but aren't you in a rush to see your architect?' Adam regretted this as soon as he had uttered the words. Telling a joke against oneself was OK but she might not think it so funny coming from him.

'Touché,' smiled Emily, not seeming to mind at all. 'I asked for that one.'

They both put on their coats and wandered out into the rain, which thankfully had eased off considerably. Adam had his hands in his raincoat pockets and as they walked along conversing easily, just like old friends, Emily slipped her arm into his, as if it were the most natural thing in the world for her to do. Adam liked that; it felt very good.

'Could your parents not help you out a little until your find another job?' asked Adam. He immediately regretted the question as Emily remained silent. 'I'm sorry; I shouldn't have asked such a personal question. It's none of my business.'

'That's OK,' replied Emily after a moment, 'I don't mind. My father had a very stressful job in sales and marketing. He was a heavy smoker; a thirty a day man. We had a small cottage in the Dordogne where we used to go every summer. It was idyllic. Mum and I would stay for the whole of the school holidays but if Dad made it over for a week we were lucky. One day we were waiting at the airport in Limoges for him and he didn't get off the flight. Mum was really pissed off and tried to get hold of him on his mobile but it went straight to voicemail. She then rang his secretary who said as far as she knew he was on his way to us, but she would make enquiries. As soon as Mum ended the call her phone rang and it was the hospital. Dad had had a massive heart attack on his way to the airport. He was rushed to hospital but pronounced dead on arrival. I was sixteen at the time. Dad was only forty eight.'

'Emily, I'm so sorry,' said Adam, regretting even more that he had asked the question. 'I can't imagine how awful that must have been for you both.'

'Well, Mum seemed to get over it pretty quickly. Dad was very well insured, so financially we were OK. There was a French guy my parents were friendly with, although I never liked him. He had a company running excursions on the Dordogne River. Next summer Mum got very friendly with him. After that she began to go over there three or four times a year, leaving me to fend for myself. In the summer when I was eighteen, just before I went up to Durham, the bastard made a pass at me. Of course Mum wouldn't believe me when I told her; said I was making it up because I didn't like him. Soon after I started Uni she told me she was selling up and moving over there to marry him. I wouldn't go to the wedding and I haven't been over there again since. I've hardly spoken to my mother since then either.'

Adam couldn't think of anything to say after this revelation, but before any awkward silence could develop they arrived at the late Victorian edifice which housed the insurance company's divisional operations.

'Well, this is it.'

'It's very grand,' said Emily, looking up. 'I'm sorry to lay all my family woes on you Adam, just when we were having such a good time.'

'It was my fault. I shouldn't have asked such a personal question. I'm sorry Emily, but I'll have to rush. Are we still OK for one fifteen tomorrow?'

'Of Course; I'll see you where we first met, by The Coastal Retreat. I have a feeling it's a lucky painting.'

'You may not think it's so lucky if you actually manage to get a job at Scrooge and Marley's,' he smiled, trying to lighten the mood again. He suddenly realised that, until a couple of minutes ago, he had been smiling so much his face had begun to ache.

'Don't put more than one lump of coal on the fire,' she retorted, 'or you'll be out on your ear and Tiny Tim won't get any supper.' With that she disengaged her arm and gave him a dazzling smile, before turning and walking off into the drizzle, back the way they had come.

Adam stood watching her for a while before looking again at his watch. 'Oh bugger,' he muttered and ran up the steps and into the building, taking them three at a time.

He had great difficulty concentrating that afternoon and was more relieved than usual when his shift ended at six o'clock. As soon as he had signed out he ran up two flights to the Human Resources department only to find the door locked; they had all gone home. Typical, he thought, just bloody typical. I'll have to get in early in the morning and try to find someone to ask about vacancies before I start my shift. With that he left and caught the metro to the one bedroom flat he rented in the suburbs. The flat was a trade off. It cost him a fortune to commute into the city, but it would have cost him even more to rent close to the centre.

Of course he had no chance of ever saving enough to buy a place of his own. He was from working class Durham mining stock. His father had lost his job when the mines closed in the eighties and had then drifted from one low paid labouring job to another until emphysema had caught up with him in his early sixties. His mother had been diagnosed with breast cancer a year later and had only out-lived her husband by two years. She had died just after Adam started Uni. He didn't care to think about how much student loan he owed. At least there isn't much prospect of ever having to pay it back he thought ruefully; not the way my career has been progressing so far.

Then he thought of Emily and his mood lightened. The mental snapshot of her attractive, intelligent face looking up at him in the rain before she turned and walked away was etched into his memory. They had both endured a tough few years, but perhaps this could be a turning point for them. He would get a better paid job with some prospects. He had been drifting disconsolately these past two years. He felt good about Emily.

He knew there had been a connection between them and was convinced she had felt it too.

He threw a ready meal into the microwave and turned up the thermostat on the central heating. At least he could afford his heating bills; just. A mental picture of Emily sitting in a thick coat in her cold flat filled him with a determination to help her. Together they could turn things around. They were both young and university educated with first class honours degrees, even if they were in the humanities, which didn't seem to count for much with employers.

The next morning Adam took an earlier tram into the city, arriving at work half an hour before he was due to start his shift. He ran up the stairs past his floor to Human Resources. He had a personal keep fit policy of never using a lift when stairs were available. Fortunately a few staff were already in the department, but the young woman on reception whom he asked about vacancies in Claims Processing looked at him rather oddly and asked him to wait whilst she brought over her manager.

Adam didn't see why it was necessary for a manger to attend to him but waited patiently until a rather severe looking middle aged woman returned with the receptionist.

'Are you asking about a vacancy for yourself?' the woman asked, without preamble.

'No, I work in there. I was asking for a friend,' Adam replied.

'Then you obviously have not yet been to your desk,' she continued.

'I'm not due to start my shift until nine,' said Adam, somewhat indignantly, thinking the woman was accusing him of being late.

'I'm well aware of that. There are no vacancies in your department. I suggest you go down to your office and all will be made clear to you.'

'Made clear?'

'Yes. I'm sorry but I cannot discuss the matter further with you. You need to speak to your manager.' With that she turned and strode away.

Adam glanced at the receptionist who was studiously avoiding eye contact, then turned and walked down to his department and to his desk. On his and all the other desks were white A4 envelopes. He tore open the one with his name on it and read the enclosed letter with increasing incredulity. As he finished reading he heard footsteps behind him and turned to see Robert Clayton the department manager approaching.

'Why are you in here so early Cross? You're shift isn't due to start for another twenty minutes,' said Clayton.

'It isn't going to start at all is it?' Adam countered.

'Well yes; quite. There will be a meeting at nine when everyone has arrived. I'll answer any questions then, but suffice it to say the company's Claims Processing operation has been outsourced with immediate effect, so you will all be asked to gather up any personal belongings in boxes which will be provided and you will be escorted from the premises by Security.'

'I take it you won't be escorted from the premises?' said Adam bitterly.

'Not that it's any of your business, but I'm being transferred to central office. I'll have to uproot my family and take a pay cut,' replied Clayton, turning on his heel and walking back towards his office, beside which, Adam now noticed, were standing two security staff.

'Well, tough on you,' Adam called after him.

The meeting was duly held just after nine o'clock when all twenty four of the call centre staff had arrived for work. This included two supervisors who were also being made redundant. Clayton was the only one who wasn't losing his job. It transpired that the decision to outsource Claims Processing had been taken by the Board six months previously and had been in planning since then. All the new staff in the Indian company taking over had been trained up over that period. All the telephone lines had been transferred overnight and the new staff were already taking calls from nine a.m. GMT. It was a "fait accompli", but that didn't stop the atmosphere becoming somewhat ugly and two more security staff arrived.

'I didn't know we had so many security staff,' said Adam, to a colleague; now ex-colleague.

'I'm sure we don't normally,' came the reply. 'The bastards certainly kept this very quiet.'

Adam didn't reply. Looking at it objectively he could understand why the company had kept it all under wraps. Disgruntled staff on the telephones to customers and using the computer systems would have been too risky to allow. That didn't make it any more palatable though.

For himself, Adam wasn't too bothered. He had been thinking of looking for something better for some time and this just gave him the push he needed; that, together with meeting Emily the previous day.

He didn't have any personal possessions in the office and so didn't need one of the ubiquitous cardboard boxes. Some of the women staff were quietly sobbing as they were all escorted from the building.

Well, I now have over three hours before I'm due to meet Emily, Adam thought to himself. There isn't really time to go back to the flat and return, apart from the expense. At least it isn't raining. So he wandered around the city for three hours, looking in the department stores, visiting a museum and managing to spend an hour over a cup of coffee whilst reading the previous evening's local paper and looking through the situations vacant pages.

With a high degree of pleasurable anticipation he entered the art gallery just after one o'clock and made his way to the long gallery. He couldn't see any sign of Emily, but it wasn't quite quarter past the hour so he wasn't unduly concerned. He wandered down the gallery, not really looking at any paintings but glancing over his shoulder every few seconds to see if Emily had arrived. Eventually he reached the far end of the long gallery and sat down on the leather bench facing Menhenick's painting. It was now twenty minutes past one and he began to worry a little. At one thirty he was very worried. Had she stood him up or had something delayed her.

For the first time that day he actually looked up at the painting. It represented a lost way of life, he thought to himself; or a way of life that had probably never existed in reality. It had that otherworldliness about it of the kind Emily had spoken of, which presumably the painter Menhenick believed in. He looked more closely. There was something about the painting which wasn't quite right, but he couldn't put his finger on it. He looked at the men and women haymaking in the field and then down to the two girls playing on the beach. Were the girls moving? No of course not. How could they be? His eyes must be playing tricks on him. He turned around as he felt a slight draft, as if someone had just opened a door. Was it Emily? But he was the only one in the long gallery and the draught wasn't coming from that direction; he could now feel it quite distinctly on the nape of his neck. He turned back and looked again at the painting and then he spotted the difference at last. A woman was standing by the now open cottage door and her hand was raised. She was waving. Her hand actually appeared to be moving. Adam closed his eyes, rubbed the lids with his thumb and forefinger and then looked up again. The draught had now become a breeze and it seemed, incredibly, to be blowing out from the painting. The woman was still waving. He couldn't be sure at that distance, but she appeared to be really just a girl of about his own age with dark, almost black hair and wearing something blue. She looked familiar.

Adam's heart rate was increasing exponentially and he was beginning to feel light headed. He told himself not to be stupid and to calm down. He *had* to be hallucinating. The events of the morning must have taken more of a toll on his nerves than he had realised. But he needed to take a closer look at that girl. He stood and walked slowly forwards. As he neared the painting it filled the whole of his peripheral vision. Was that really the sea he could smell and seabirds he could hear? Impossible! The floor of the gallery was no longer smooth. He looked down and saw a rough, pebble strewn road beneath his feet. Adam was sure he had heard his own name being called out, but it felt more like an electrical pulse passing across his brain than any actual sound. Then, looking up, he saw the girl running towards him through the cottage garden towards the gate. She was still waving and calling his name. Her dark hair, now loose, was wind-blown and tumbling around her shoulders. As she came closer he saw almond eyes wide and sparkling in the sunlight.

~~~~~~~~

The little girl stood holding her mother's hand and looking up at the very large painting which took up most of the end wall of the long gallery in which it hung.

'That's Devon Charlotte,' said her mother. 'We're going there next summer for our holidays.'

'I know that Mummy. You told me last time we were here.'

Denise smiled to herself. Charlotte was only just four years old and already her memory was getting better than her mother's.

'There's something wrong with the picture,' Charlotte added.

'Wrong darling; what do you mean by wrong?'

'It's different.'

'Paintings don't change dear. A very clever man painted that over a hundred years ago; long before grandma was born and it hasn't changed since then.

'But it has changed Mummy,' said Charlotte, petulantly stamping her right foot.

Denise was beginning to get a little exasperated with her daughter, but she didn't want her to make a scene inside the gallery, especially with the attendant standing only a few yards away. She decided to humour the little girl.

'Well I'm sure you must be right darling, if you say so. How has it changed?'

'It's the cottage Mummy. It looked sad and empty the last time we came, but now smoke is coming from the chimney. Someone must be living there now.'

'Well that's nice dear. It's a lovely cottage. I'm sure they will be very happy there.' She looked quickly at her watch. 'Come along darling, we have to pick up Sam from school in half an hour and then we're all going to grandma's house for tea.'

Charlotte appeared satisfied with her mother's capitulation and walked hand in hand with her back down the gallery towards the entrance.

Stanley, the attendant, watched them go, then strolled slowly over to the painting and began to study it minutely. He was the longest serving member of staff, having worked at the gallery for over twenty years. He had helped hang the painting a few weeks previously when it had been taken out of storage to be included in the gallery's Devon School exhibition. That had been quite a job. It had taken six staff to do it. Stanley could now see that there was indeed a wisp of smoke curling up from the cottage chimney. My, that little girl must have good eyesight, he thought to himself and a very retentive memory. He couldn't recall having seen any smoke when they had hung the painting, but it was very large and contained a lot of detail. He couldn't be absolutely sure.

His gaze then shifted to the two girls playing on the beach and recalled when the work had last been on public display over fifteen years previously. He remembered that time particularly well because two twin sisters had run away from a local children's home. They were thirteen years old. Exhaustive searches had been carried out for them all over the city. A member of the public had even reported having seen them in the gallery and the police had arrived. They had asked a lot of questions and combed the whole building but found nothing. The searches went on for about two weeks before the police decided the twins must have somehow left or been taken out of the city and the investigation was gradually wound down. As far as Stanley knew the girls had never been traced.

At the time, no one could understand why the twins had run away. They had been at the children's home for a number of months because the authorities did not want to split them up and it had been proving difficult to find a foster home to take both of them. However, Stanley recalled that a few months ago there had been headlines in the local and national press about the arrest of an ex warden of that very same children's home. He had retired ten years previously, but was now accused of historical sexual abuse against children within his care at the home. According to the report Stanley had read, the abuse had allegedly taken place over a period of almost thirty years.

Stanley pursed his lips and thoughtfully scratched the back of his head. Had those two young girls always been there on the beach? He couldn't be sure; just as he couldn't be sure that smoke hadn't always issued from the cottage chimney. And what had happened to the young woman and then the young man he had seen entering the long gallery only the day before? When he had followed a little later there had been no sign of them. How could they have got past him? An absurd thought began to form in his mind. He turned his attention again to the cottage and peered intently at the windows, trying to see if anything was visible inside, but to no avail.

A faint breeze ruffled Stanley's thinning hair and he imagined he heard the distant sound of children's laughter. He took a couple of involuntary steps backwards and looked down the long gallery. No one had entered; he was alone. His gaze fell once more upon Menhenick's painting. He wondered if a young couple now lived in that cottage by the sea and if they were happy there? Even whilst his brain was forming these questions he realised that deep, deep down in his inner, spiritual consciousness he already knew the answers.

The Missed Train

It was a cold, wet Wednesday evening in late October, as I made my hurried but unavoidably erratic progress down Euston Road towards the station, weaving in and out of a solid phalanx of humanity moving in the opposite direction. I did not need to hear the raucous chanting to know this was, unfortunately for me, a match night; City were in town.

Passing a news stand I judged I had just enough time to grab an evening paper to read on the train, thereby avoiding queuing at one of the Euston kiosks. I had just handed over the correct change and was about to resume my personal battle with the City fans when:

'Hello Martin.' The female voice sounded somehow familiar. As I turned I was dreading the consequences of, firstly meeting an acquaintance when I was in a tearing hurry and secondly not being able to remember her name, which was invariably very embarrassing. I needn't have worried, at least not on the second count. As I looked down into those wide, expressive green eyes beneath the long, somewhat out of control red hair, I recalled how she had always reminded me of a Pre-Raphaelites' muse.

Bethany Zanolini gave me that slightly crooked, sardonic smile I remembered so well.

'Cat got your tongue Martin? It's not like you to be lost for words. 'She reached up and gently pushed my chin upwards with two fingers. I realised then how silly I must have looked, standing there with my mouth open in surprise.

I managed to swallow the lump that had somehow developed in my throat.' Hello Beth,' I eventually said, in a voice meant to sound surprised, though matter of fact, but which came out rather too huskily. 'What are you doing here?'

'I live here, don't you remember.'

'That was a long time ago,' I managed to reply, striving to regain my equilibrium.

'Almost eight years. I don't think I shall be leaving anytime soon; the big city has taken hold of me now.'

'You don't look a day older,' I said and meant it.

'You always did know how to make a girl feel good about herself,' she laughed; that deep infectious, girlish giggle I remembered so well.

'How about you?'

'What? Oh, I'm just in town on business. I live in Shrewsbury now. I managed to buy into a partnership up there.'

'Impressive. When did you move up to the frozen north then?'

I hesitated. 'Well, as a matter of fact pretty soon after . . . . that's to say . . . . '

'Soon after you dumped me?' she asked, raising her eyebrows questioningly.

I felt my neck and face reddening. 'I'm sorry Beth, I was . . . . I mean, I just wasn't ready to commit back then.'

'It's OK Martin, no hard feelings; water under the bridge and all that.'

'Fact is I'm rushing to catch the last train that will give me a connection. I have to change at Birmingham. '

'Perhaps you won't make it now.' She gave me the benefit of that familiar mischievous smile again. 'Maybe you'll have to stay in town.'

I glanced at my watch. If I ran I might still just make it. Damn Peterson for going on ad nauseam about a minor takeover, all the relevant details of which had been ironed out weeks ago. The man suffered from verbal diarrhoea. Still, if he hadn't I wouldn't be here now, with Beth.

'Do you remember Antonio's?' she said, breaking into my thoughts. 'We used to have drinks there before going to the cinema, or to a show. There always used to be a nice crowd in there.'

Antonio's was the place where we had first met nine years ago. Of course I remembered and Beth knew that I remembered.

'I must go Beth,' I said, desperately trying to break eye contact but unable to drag my gaze away. 'I have a meeting first thing in the morning.'

'The Euston Court is just around the corner. Why don't you take a room for the night and catch an early train in the morning. You look done in; all this rushing around isn't good for a thirty something. Can't you postpone your meeting?'

'Well . . . .' I hesitated. I had probably missed my train now anyway and I didn't really have a meeting in the morning.

'We can go to Antonio's and you can tell me what you've been doing with yourself for eight years. There may still be people there we know. It would be fun; just like old times.'

'You haven't been there since we . . . . since I . . . . ?'

'No, I didn't want to go back; it wouldn't have been the same.'

I suddenly felt desperately ashamed of myself. What a self-centred, unfeeling idiot I had been back then. I gave in. I knew I had wanted to all the time.

'OK,' I said, 'why not. Do you want to come round with me whilst I book a room?'

'Oh, I need to change out of these horrible work clothes,' she said, looking down at her crumpled, rain drenched coat and grimacing. 'I'll get changed, put on a new face and meet you in Antonio's at nine.'

Suddenly she took both my hands in hers, stood on tiptoe and kissed me lightly on the lips. I could smell the same perfume she had always worn and the freshness of her hair as it brushed my cheek. It felt for a long moment that we had never been apart. I was drowning in the depths of those cool green eyes; finding it difficult to breath.

'Your hands are ice cold,' I spluttered, trying to cover my confused thoughts.

'Forgot to put on my gloves,' she smiled. 'Always did have poor circulation. I'll see you at nine then.' She turned and walked quickly away into the rain.

I stood there watching her glide effortlessly through the crowd, which I had had so much difficulty penetrating, until she disappeared around a corner. My heart was beating very hard and very fast; I hoped my rib cage was strong enough to contain it. Eventually I turned, crossed the road and made my way to the Euston Court Hotel.

As I took the lift up to my room I tried to tell myself I shouldn't be letting this happen. What's over is over Martin; one should never try to go back. On the other hand, what was the harm in a pleasant evening over few drinks with an old friend? But I wasn't even fooling *myself*. I knew, having touched those lips again and looked into those eyes, that an evening would not be enough.

This is ridiculous I thought, as I threw my briefcase and laptop onto the bed, I don't even have a toothbrush. Well, I suppose that's soon rectified. I obtained a toothbrush from the small shop in the hotel foyer - they must be used to people making unplanned stays - took a shower and dressed again. My watch told me it was just 8.30 p.m.. Should I phone home and say I had missed the train and had to stay in town? I stared at the short dial screen on my mobile. Helen's smiling face stared back at me, somehow accusingly. I knew I hadn't the nerve to ring; she always knew when I was hiding something; not telling the whole story. I could text. No, that was no good; she hated me texting when I could have phoned. She would expect me to be well on my way home by now. I managed to persuade myself that Helen would be getting the twins to bed and wouldn't want to be disturbed by the telephone. I would ring later when I knew they would be settled.

I took a cab to the end of Piccadilly and walked the last few hundred metres to Antonio's. Except it wasn't Antonio's, it was a fast food restaurant. Could I have misremembered where it was? I didn't think so. I was a little late but there was no sign of Beth. I walked in and up to the counter.

'Yes sir, what can I get for you?' an over-weight, over-cheerful young man asked, tucking a stray lock of greasy hair back under his logo emblazoned baseball cap.

'I'm sorry, I don't want to eat. Could you tell me how long this restaurant has been here; I was looking for a place called Antonio's.

'I've only worked here for two years' he said. I gave up on that line of questioning.

'I was supposed to meet someone here. You haven't seen a woman come into here in the last half hour; slim, attractive, about thirty but looks a lot younger, red hair, green eyes, fair complexion, around five feet six?

'I haven't seen anyone like that.'

'Are you sure?'

He grinned.' I think I would have remembered if that description is anything like accurate. Look, I'm sorry mate but there are customers waiting behind you. Do you want to order anything?'

'No. No its OK, I'll wait outside.'

I went back outside and felt for my mobile, meaning to search for Antonio's but realised, to my annoyance, that in my hurry I had left it in the hotel room. I waited in the rain for half an hour. I knew then she wasn't coming. Perhaps we had got our wires crossed and she had meant somewhere completely different. Perhaps Antonio's had moved and she had forgotten I wouldn't have known that. Why didn't I ask for her mobile number when I had the chance? Eventually I hailed a cab and returned miserably back to the hotel. I could have been nearly home by now, I thought ruefully. Never try to go back.

As soon as I reached my room I saw my mobile on the bed. There were eight missed calls from home spanning the last hour. Oh shit, I'm in trouble about something, I thought; better ring now.

Helen answered on the first ring; she must have had the phone in her hand. Her voice sounded almost hysterical.

'Martin, is that you. Are you all right?'

'Of course I'm alright; why wouldn't I be? Look I'm sorry I didn't phone earlier, the meeting went on very late and — '

'You didn't catch the train?'

'No. I missed it. I'm in a hotel. I popped out to get a bite to eat and forgot to take my phone.'

'Oh, thank God.'

'What do you mean? What's the matter?'

'The train you were supposed to be on; there's been a very bad accident, just short of Birmingham; people have died.'

For the second time that evening I found it difficult to articulate my thoughts.

'Martin, are you still there?'

'Yes, I'm still here,' I managed to say.

'You're sure you're all right?'

'Yes, I'm fine; just shocked. Are the twins OK?'

'Yes, I put them to bed before I heard it on the TV. It's all over the news channel right now.'

'I'm sorry I didn't ring earlier, you must have been very worried.'

'Very worried!' she repeated, her voice breaking.' Can you imagine what it was like hearing your phone repeatedly ringing out then going to voice-mail? I was thinking about the disasters we've seen on the news, where people's mobiles just go on ringing whilst their owners are lying dead in the wreckage.'

'I'm really, really sorry, but I am OK. I'll be back in the morning.'

'You'll have to come home by another route. That line will be closed for days.'

'I love you.'

She hung up without replying, which rather annoyed me. OK, I should have rung, but at least I was alive.

I switched on the BBC news channel and it was all there; the crumpled, overturned carriages harshly lit by arc lights, with the rescue services crawling all over them in the pouring rain. Eventually a reporter at the scene gave the up to date picture. The express from London had somehow derailed on a bend about fifteen miles short of Birmingham and collided head-on with a local train heading south. It was thought the express would have been travelling at over ninety miles per hour. More than one hundred dead and injured had already been taken to local hospitals but many more were still trapped in the wreckage. The rescue services had not yet released any details of casualties but it was believed, said the reporter, over forty had died, most of them in the first two carriages of the express. Thankfully the local train had been almost empty.

I opened my wallet and looked at my reservation; I would have been travelling in the second carriage. I switched off the TV and began to unbutton my shirt but my hands were shaking. I gave up, turned off all the lights except the one by the bedside table and lay down on the bed in the semi darkness, trying to compose myself.

There was only one thought on my mind. I needed to find Beth and thank her. She couldn't have known of course, but if it hadn't been for her I would probably now be lying dead or badly injured in that train wreck.

After half an hour I was feeling calmer. I got up, opened my laptop on the small dressing table and clicked onto the internet. I thought Beth might have a Facebook page or be on a professional network that would enable me to track her down. I had almost got back in touch with her often in the weeks following my move up to Shrewsbury, after my successful job interview in Birmingham; the interview I had not told her about.

Beth and I had been together for almost a year. She was beautiful, vivacious, funny, adorable — I always felt exceptionally proud and pleased with myself whenever we walked into a room and all male eyes would suddenly turn towards her. I had known soon after we met that I was in love with her and her with me. I knew she wanted to move in with me (permanently that is, not just for a few nights each week) although she never asked outright; but I enjoyed having my own space. Then she asked me if I'd like to meet her parents, Lorenzo and Margaret; her father, she told me, was Italian and her mother English. She was naive and old fashioned in many ways; that was part of her charm; one of the ways in which she was different from other girls I had dated. However, I was only twenty five and, yes, conceit was not one of my most endearing traits. I somehow convinced myself that I didn't want a long term relationship; that I had plenty of time left to "play the field". So, when I was head hunted, I allowed myself to be persuaded that a move away to pastures new was the best thing for both of us; well, for me anyway.

The evening I told Beth that I was ending our relationship was not good. There were a lot of tears, but somehow I stood firm. I heard myself uttering the usual hackneyed platitudes, whilst at the same time feeling thoroughly ashamed of myself.

After only a week I knew I had made a big mistake. I had been sorely tempted to contact Beth after I had moved, but my pride and conceit wouldn't let me. I don't think I could have held out very much longer though; I was lonely and missing her so much. It was then that I met Helen, the senior partner's daughter and only child and we hit it off straight away. Helen was and is a lovely person, but my feelings for her did not have the same intensity as those for Beth; the ache wasn't there when we were apart. None the less we were good together and, to my shame, my mercenary instincts came to the fore. She was who she was and I knew she loved me.

We've been married for six years now and her father's wedding present was the partnership I told Beth I had bought. In reality I could not have afforded to do that for years. Three years ago Helen gave birth to beautiful twin girls. We are very happy and I have grown to love Helen in a different way to my love for Beth. Until I saw Beth again this evening I had forgotten how different.

I keyed Beth's name into Google, not really expecting to find anything; Bethany Zanolini was not exactly a common name. However, almost immediately a recent Evening Standard headline caught my eye.' **"Hit and run victim still in coma"** and, in the text below, the name Zanolini. With some trepidation I clicked onto the article. It couldn't be anything to do with Beth; either that or she was just mentioned as a witness, or someone who had given first aid; she was a nurse after all.

As I read the article I began to feel dizzy, the screen blurring before my eyes. I had heard the phrase "my blood ran cold" but now I knew what it felt like; this could not be true.

"Bethany Zanolini, the thirty year old woman who suffered severe head injuries in a hit and run incident in Fulham on Tuesday evening last week is still in a coma at St Stephen's hospital, where she was taken after the incident."

The article went on to say that the vehicle involved had not yet been found or the driver identified and there was a photograph; it was Beth. But how could it be; I had been talking to her less than four hours ago. The article was dated the previous Friday.

I slowly leaned back in the chair and tried to take some deep breaths. Eventually my heart rate began to reduce to something approaching normal. I thought about how she had glided through those crowds so easily, when I could hardly make any headway at all. No, it isn't possible. I had spoken to her; she had kissed my lips; she was real. There had to be a logical explanation for the last four hours. Perhaps I had missed the train, lain down on my hotel bed and was dreaming all of this. However, dream or reality, one thing was certain.

'You probably saved my life Beth,' I murmured quietly to myself. 'I owe you one.'

'Can I take it now?' a familiar voice whispered from the shadows behind me.

A tingle ran down my spine and the hairs on my arms and the back of my neck began to rise. I wasn't sure if, physically, I would be able to turn around. I could smell that perfume again; the air conditioning wafting it gently across my face. I slowly looked up and saw her face indistinctly in the dressing table mirror. I closed my eyes, slowly got to my feet and turned around. I tried to tell myself that it was my imagination; that she would not be there when I looked again, but I knew I wanted her to be.

It felt like an age before I had the courage to open my eyes. As I did so she moved out of the shadows towards me. She was wearing a short green evening dress, matching her eyes and perfectly complementing her hair, now cascading over her bare shoulders. The emotion I felt as our eyes met was the most overwhelming love I had ever felt for anyone in my entire life. This had to be real; this was no hallucination.

'Beth, I don't understand; is it really you?'

She moved forward and gently put her fingers to my lips. I felt her warm body pressing against mine. Her perfume was intoxicating.

'Just kiss me.'

We embraced. That kiss seemed to last a lifetime and I hoped it would never end. Finally it was Beth who stepped away and held me at arm's length. Her face was flushed; her lips wet; her eyes bottomless green pools.

'I can't stay,' she murmured. 'I just had to see you again, one last time.'

'How can you even be here?'

She smiled; not the sardonic amused smile I had seen earlier that evening, but one which somehow managed to be sorrowful and resigned at the same time. It was with a desperate feeling of hopelessness that I somehow knew it would be the last time I would see that smile.

'Sometimes it's allowed,' she said quietly 'in very special circumstances.'

'You just saved my life Beth,' I said, my voice breaking. 'You tried to save it eight years ago, but I wouldn't let you. You can't go now; please stay with me.'

'I'm sorry, I have to go.'

Tears filled my eyes. 'What can I do? I must be able to do something to help you.'

'Just make Helen happy,' she murmured 'and be a good father. That's the best you can do.'

She turned, walked to the door and hesitated there. I could see her bare shoulders shaking; then she opened the door and stepped outside without looking back. The last thing I saw was a glimpse of green dress as the door closed gently behind her.

Somehow I managed to stumble over to the door, wrench it open and step outside.

'Bethany.' The sound of her name came from somewhere deep down in my soul and reverberated along the endless hotel corridor. There was no one there.

I arrived at the hospital about half an hour before midnight. I told the receptionist I was Beth's cousin and that I had just arrived back in the country that evening. I knew they would not let me see her if I said I was just a friend and I desperately needed to be with her; to hold her hand. If I could do that an explanation for the last few hours might somehow be revealed. The receptionist asked me to wait and after a few minutes a senior nurse approached me.

'Mr Gibson?' she enquired.

'Yes, I'm Martin Gibson' I replied.

She introduced herself as Nurse Marjorie Patterson and, at her request, I followed her to a small, sparsely furnished room off a nearby corridor. She closed the door, invited me to sit down and took the chair opposite.

'I'm sorry Mr Gibson; I have to give you some bad news. The trauma to Miss Zanolini's head was very severe. We operated to relieve the pressure on her brain but she slipped into a coma.

I'm afraid there was nothing further we could do for her. She passed away earlier this evening.'

I sat silent; unmoving; the walls of the small room seemed to darken and lean in towards us.

'Did she . . . . was she able to say anything before . . . I mean . . . .'

Marjory Patterson reached over and put her hand on mine. 'Bethany never regained consciousness Mr Gibson. I'm very sorry for your loss.'

I took a deep shuddering breath. 'What time did she die?,' I managed to ask.

'Less than an hour ago. I'm afraid you were just too late.'

'I wasn't too late.'

'I'm sorry, I don't understand.'

'I don't think I could explain. Would it be possible to see her.'

'Her parents are still with her. Would you like me to ask them if you could go up.'

'No,' I said quickly 'I don't want to disturb them. Please could I just sit here for a few minutes?'

'Of course. Just ask for me at reception when you're ready. Nurse Patterson,' she reminded me.

She left, closing the door behind her. I sat, holding my head in my hands. Beth had died less than an hour ago, but around that time we were both in my hotel room; I was holding her in my arms. It could not be possible, but by some miracle Beth had saved my life that evening, just as she was losing the battle for her own.

I couldn't stay in that room; the nurse might come back; might even bring with her Lorenzo and Margaret Zanolini. How could I explain who I was; why I was here pretending to be their nephew? After a few minutes I rose and left that small impersonal room.

Avoiding the receptionist's enquiring gaze I walked quickly out through the main doors and into the neon night. A church clock somewhere near was striking the hour; it was midnight. I gazed down at the empty cigarette packets and sandwich wrappers swirling around my ankles, dislodged from the overflowing waste bins by a cold easterly wind from the distant English Channel. Ignoring the tears coursing down my cheeks, I turned up the collar of my overcoat and walked back to the hotel in the rain.

Fever

'I can't raise Tauranga', he said, walking into the bedroom and closing the door gently behind him.

She was lying on her back on the disordered bed with her eyes closed. Her face bore a sheen of perspiration and a nightgown clung damply to her emaciated body. She slowly turned her head towards him, opening her eyes as if with a great effort.

'I'm so cold Jack; so cold.'

He stepped quickly over to the bed and began to pull the discarded duvet across her.

'No, not that,' she said. 'I just want you to hold me Jack. Please; just hold me very tightly.'

He lay down beside her on the bed, slipping one arm beneath her head and drawing her close to him. She turned her body towards him with a whimper of pain and then, sighing, laid her head upon his chest. He could feel the fever in her body through his clothing. He put his hand upon her brow, stroking back the fair matted hair from her sunken blue eyes. Her temperature must be over a hundred and four he thought.

They lay there for a while; he staring out of the window at the November spring sunshine; she, eyes closed again, breathing shallowly and unevenly against his chest.

'Claire', he said quietly, after some time had passed.

'Tauranga', she said, without opening her eyes.

'Yes, Tauranga. I can't reach them on the radio. They aren't responding to my call sign.'

263

She didn't reply.

'I'll try them again later', he continued, 'but I think they've had it. There were just two of them yesterday when we spoke.'

'Are we the only ones left now?' she asked.

'There may still be some pockets of people who don't have a radio; it's very old tech now after all. The internet and mobile phone networks have been down for some months and the land lines died in October. I'm so sorry Claire. I thought we might be safe out here at the cabin. I thought it might pass us by.'

'It isn't your fault Jack', she said, opening her eyes and looking up into his. 'It was only ever a foolish hope, but we had to try something.'

He bent his head down to kiss her brow.

'No Jack', she said weakly, trying to pull away, 'the virus; you'll catch it.'

He kissed her anyway, the heat from her forehead seeming almost to burn his lips.

'If I don't catch it today I'll catch it tomorrow. What does it matter?'

'You mustn't talk like that Jack. You should get away from here; Whangerei perhaps. It may not reach there.'

'You could never stand the journey. Even if we had enough fuel, which we probably haven't.'

She let her head fall back upon his chest. 'I'm talking about you my love, not me. I'm dying Jack. We both know that. When I'm gone you should try for Whangerei.'

A spasm of coughing overtook her which lasted for some minutes. He held her close until it passed. Noticing red flecks upon her dry, cracked lips, he dabbed them away with his handkerchief. She didn't seem to notice.

'Would you like some water?' She murmured something unintelligible, which he interpreted as yes. He reached over for the glass of water by the bedside, raised her head a little and held the glass against her lips. She managed to swallow a little, with difficulty.

'Don't try to talk so much. You always were an incorrigible chatterbox.' Her mouth formed into a thin smile. 'The fever will pass and then you could be immune to the virus.'

She said nothing. She didn't have to. Jack was a medical doctor and knew he was talking nonsense. If this one doesn't kill us he thought, the next one will, or the one after that. Wave after wave of pandemics had swept around the world over the past seventy or so years. It had started with HIV in the nineteen eighties. We thought we had beaten that. Then came Ebola, Zika, Hendra, Coronaviruses, Tularaemia, Marburg Virus, Nipah Virus, Bolivian Hemorrhagic Fever, Super Malaria and various Avian and Swine influenza viruses crossing the human-animal interface; the list went on. Each time vaccines were manufactured the virus would mutate, or another would emerge, more virulent than the last. Then there were the antibiotic resistant microbes; so called Superbugs. Many microorganisms such as Tuberculosis and Staphylococcus Aureus developed resistance to antibiotics. These pathogens led to the re-emergence of diseases that were thought to be under control, such as multidrug-resistant Tuberculosis and Severe Acute Respiratory Syndrome.

In the beginning each new outbreak killed only hundreds of thousands, then millions. As the pharmaceutical giants became overwhelmed with demand it became impossible to produce vaccines quickly enough and hundreds of millions died. Finally, as humanity's capability to fight back was undermined and eventually destroyed by the decimation of its population - in particular scientists and doctors, the only people who could have saved it – a billion could die in each pandemic.

At first, New Zealand in its relative isolation had escaped the worst, but with an economy dependent upon imports it was only a matter of time before its own people began to die. And then of course there were the thousands of people of other nationalities, who saw in New Zealand a last refuge and arrived by the boatload. He remembered the gradual breakdown of law and order; the emergence of what could only be termed local warlords. The veneer of civilisation had certainly been wafer thin.

A shudder ran through Claire's body and Jack stirred from his dark reverie. 'Would you like some more water?' he asked.

'Hold me closer Jack. I'm falling and I can't stop myself.'

'I have you sweetheart. You're safe now. I won't let you fall any further.'

After a few minutes she quietened and looked up again. 'It's getting very dark in here and I'm so cold.'

'Let me pull the duvet over us. You'll be warmer then.'

'Jack, is it sunny outside; sunny and warm?'

He looked at the brilliant morning light streaming in through the bedroom window. 'Yes sweetheart, it's a lovely day.'

'Please take me outside. I want to see the grass and trees and the flowers by the lake. I'm sure I'll be warmer outside.'

She weighed no more than a small child and he picked her up easily and carried her out into the sunshine on the porch. He sat down on the bench hammock and, pulling a rug over them both, began to swing gently to and fro, cradling Claire in his arms.

'That feels good,' she murmured. 'The sun is warm and I'm not falling anymore. I could stay here with you all day.'

'Then we shall.' He smiled. 'There is nowhere else I'd rather be.'

She started coughing again and he held his handkerchief to her mouth so that the red flecks would not stain her white nightgown.

'How did all this happen Jack? Where did we go wrong?'

'We were laying waste to the earth,' he said. 'Perhaps it fought back in the only way it knew how. In a hundred thousand years homo sapiens' will be just another extinct species and the earth will have recovered, ready for some other life-form to evolve and take our place. Perhaps they will make a better job of it than we did. He laughed quietly. 'Homo sapiens; wise person. That's turned out to be a really poor joke.'

Claire did not reply and so he continued to swing back and forth as the sun rose higher in its cathedral of sky. He remembered how they used to sit here on endless summer evenings, sipping beer or wine after dinner. Sometimes happily with friends or family, but best of all when they were alone; just the two of them.

Jack's thoughts began to wander and he rather lost track of time. Eventually, rousing himself from his daydream, he became conscious of how still and quiet she had become and with a smile looked down upon her once lovely face. Claire's unblinking blue eyes were gazing sightlessly up towards the nearby trees whose leaves moved almost imperceptibly in the gentle breeze drifting up from the lake. He gently placed his middle and index fingers onto her neck above the carotid artery, feeling for the pulse he knew he would not find. After a few seconds he used those same fingers to tenderly close both her eyes, then he lovingly kissed her pale lips. As hot, salt tears rolled down his cheeks, he began to swing again. Back and forth; back and forth. Summer is almost here, he thought and there is nowhere else I'd rather be.

Michael

She hesitated; irresolute. The wide avenue stretched away from her for around three quarters of a mile to the junction with Station Road. A right turn there and a further two thirds of a mile would bring her to the station. But she was running late and her train was due in twenty minutes. If she missed it she would have to wait a further forty minutes for the next one. And there on her right, seductively, lay a path. A path she knew traversed the edge of The Common, cutting across the corner of the two thoroughfares. If she crossed The Common she might just be in time to catch her train. But it was six-thirty on a cold, windy March evening and it was getting dark.

She made a decision. The click of her heels on the pavement turned to the crunch of gravel on the path as she set off into the trees which screened The Common, protecting it from the noise and traffic pollution of the two highways. As she walked deeper into The Common the trees began to thin out, being replaced by gorse, rhododendron and other wild shrubs.

 The traffic noise was gradually fading. As she strode on she could still see the reassuring glow of street lights in the distance between the trees, but they were getting further away all the time. It was now almost dark but a full moon suddenly came out from behind a ragged bank of cloud, helping her to follow the path which had been growing fainter.

She quickened her pace. Another five minutes and she would be past the furthest point away from the two highways and start to approach Station Road. She glanced at the luminous dial of her watch; she might just make it. And then she heard the sound. Was it the snapping of a dry twig? She stopped and listened intently. She wasn't sure which direction the sound had come from; probably just an animal. She must hurry. She started to jog. She considered taking off her shoes but the gravel underfoot was too rough. Then the sound came again; unmistakeable. She had not seen another living soul since she had set off across The Common. Running on she could just discern the lights of Station Road ahead of her.

Then she saw him; keeping pace with her about thirty yards to her right. He was tall, wearing a long dark coat. A low animal-like whimper escaped her lips and she tried to run faster, but it impossible in heels and a skirt. She could tell he was getting closer; his course intercepting hers. Her breath was now coming in short shallow gasps and there was a pain in her side. Suddenly he increased his pace and cut across the gap between them. She screamed as he made a grab for her shoulder bag and caught it. She held on and was swung bodily around. The moonlight showed her the pale gleam of a knife in his other hand. She screamed again.

~~~~~~~~~~~~~~~~

He was a large man and it was a small, windowless room. A grimy mattress took up much of the floor space. He sat cross-legged on a corner of it, wearing a dirty, long, black trench-coat. Various items of clothing and detritus lay around the room. The only light was provided by a candle balanced on a small crate by the mattress.

He cleaned a spoon by licking it before placing a measure of black tar heroin into it, then used a syringe to suck up a small amount of water and squirted this into the spoon. He then heated the bottom of the spoon with his lighter to make the heroin dissolve better, stirring gently with the plunger he had taken from the syringe. After cleaning the plunger he replaced it in the syringe, then dropped a very small ball of rolled up cotton into the heroin solution and watched it puff up. Pushing the tip of the syringe into the centre of the cotton ball he pulled back the plunger until all the heroin solution was sucked in.

Cleaning an area on the bend of his arm as best he could, he then placed the needle of the syringe almost flat on the skin and inserted it, in a well practiced manner, down into the length of the vein. He pulled the plunger slowly back a tiny bit to ensure blood came in. This told him the needle was in the vein. Satisfied, he then injected the heroin. Almost immediately he felt a pleasurable sensation, the heroin "rush". This was accompanied by a warm flushing of his skin, a dry mouth, and a heavy feeling in his arms and legs. He began to feel drowsy. His heart function and breathing were slowing.

As his drowsiness increased he reached over and picked up a credit and a debit card from the crate. He cursed softly to himself. If the stupid bitch hadn't screamed so much he would have got her pin numbers out of her as well. Then he would have had a lot more than just the cash from her purse. Instead he had been forced to shut her up. It was her fault. Why couldn't she just have kept quiet and given him what he wanted; what he needed. Instead he had just enough cash to buy a couple of shots. He threw the cards away disgustedly into the far corner of the room. Lying back on the mattress he drifted into a deep sleep, his breathing and heart rate slowing further.

~~~~~~~~~~~~~~~~~

I left work late yet again. As I walked down Studley Avenue leading to Station Road I glanced at my watch. It was six-forty. I had no chance of catching the six-fifty train and the next one wasn't due until seven-thirty; I had plenty of time. As I passed the path leading onto The Common I saw the "Path Closed. Police Incident." sign. It was a cold, cloudy evening and already almost dark. I could see nothing as I peered down the path, but could imagine only too easily the yellow "Crime Scene" tape and the white tent surrounding the . . . . I felt a cold shiver running down my spine. Someone walking over your grave my mother would say. I hurried on.

The click of my heels sounded loud and hollow on the pavement. There was hardly anyone else walking along the avenue and they were all on the other side. I glanced frequently and nervously into the trees lining the edge of The Common, but saw nothing untoward. I considered crossing over to the other side of the road but told myself not to be stupid; The Common was probably saturated with patrolling police officers.

After fifteen minutes I had reached the junction with Station Road and turned right. Another ten minutes saw me approaching the bright lights of the station. The trees and shrubs on the edge of The Common pressed closely up to the road here, the shrubs encroaching onto the pavement in places and the trees overhanging, but there were more people about now and I was less anxious.

I decided to cross the road where there was a pedestrian crossing. As I reached it I saw a shabby old man shuffling across towards me. He was completely ignoring or oblivious to the oncoming traffic and horns were sounding impatiently. I waited by the roadside for a gap in the traffic to materialise. Somehow he managed to reach my side of the road unscathed. Approaching me he muttered something about his bus fare home. Obviously he wanted money.

I could smell the alcohol on his breath from two metres away. He was blocking my way to the pedestrian crossing and I decided to give him a two pound coin to get rid of him. There were other pedestrians about now, so I wasn't nervous about being mugged; I didn't think he would have the strength anyway. As I reached into my shoulder-bag and found my purse I glanced up and saw that he had raised his head and appeared to be staring straight through me with an expression I can only describe as a combination of shock and disbelief across his dirty features. I quickly swung around to see what he was looking at. The street lights penetrated only feebly into the thick shrubbery by the roadside and the trees beyond. But was there something there; something pale amongst the shadows; something pale which moved?

I heard a strangled cry and turned back to find the old man running, or attempting to, back across the road. Horns sounded again, brakes squealed, but he miraculously managed to reach the other side in one piece and limped off away from the station. I looked around again but the pallid, human-like form I thought I had seen was gone. Had he seen it also? He must have. I hurriedly but safely crossed the road, breathing a sigh of relief to be on the far side, away from The Common. Glancing at my watch I saw I still had another twenty minutes before my train was due; perhaps just enough time to grab a coffee in the café outside the station.

As I neared the entrance a man approached from the opposite direction with a large German Shepherd. I love all dogs; my partner Ian and I have a Golden Retriever we call Sherlock. He would be waiting for me now I thought; sat in his favourite armchair in the bay window, listening for the sound of my footsteps coming down the road. I know all dog owners will say this about their own dogs but Sherlock is a very clever dog. I am sure, had he been able to write, he would have penned a monograph, in the style of his famous namesake, on the audio characteristics of the hundred most common types of footstep. I could not resist reaching out my hand towards the German Shepherd as it passed, but he bared his teeth and snarled at me. I withdrew my hand quickly as the owner muttered a curse and pulled roughly on the dogs lead. I was having an eventful evening.

Upon entering the café I saw it was rather crowded. A waitress was serving a table by the window and looking past her I saw a single unoccupied table for two at the far end. I made my way to it and sat down with relief to regain my breath and composure in the warm convivial atmosphere. An older couple, probably in their sixties, were sitting at the next table. The local evening paper lay between them unopened, its front page bearing the stark headline *"MURDER ON THE COMMON"*. I could not avoid overhearing their conversation.

'But why was she out there anyway?' the man said. 'At night and in the dark.'

'We don't know it was in the dark,' answered the woman. 'The police haven't said so.'

'It must have been last night because that dog walker didn't find the body until this morning.'

'Poor lass,' continued the woman. 'The paper says she was only in her twenties. Such a waste of a young life.'

'They haven't identified her yet. Or if they have they're not saying.'

The conversation moved on to the recent rail fare increases and whether it would be cheaper to come into town by car in future. I looked across and tried unsuccessfully to catch the eye of the waitress. If I didn't get served soon I would have to forget my coffee.

A young couple came in holding hands. They looked around for a table and started to make their way across the café towards where I was sitting. They determinedly held onto each other as they manoeuvred between the crowded tables; so sweet. I couldn't see another table free. They probably thought I had finished since I had nothing in front of me. I was hogging a table for two and was running out of time anyway. I got up and stood aside as they passed me and sat down, smiling and chatting. They were so lost in each other I don't think they even noticed me.

Buttoning up my duffle coat again I exited into the cold, turning left to walk the few yards to the station entrance. A woman was passing, holding a pretty little girl by the hand; probably about four years old. I smiled at the girl as they passed but she shrank into her mother's side, grabbing at her coat with her other hand.

'Mummy, I don't like that lady,' I heard her say. I was quite hurt by that because I like children almost as much as I like dogs. I turned around, looking at their retreating backs.

'Which lady was that darling,' I heard the mother say, but any further conversation was lost in the traffic noise.

I turned into the station entrance, beginning to feel a little upset and unloved; first the dog and then the child. I dug around in my shoulder-bag, eventually finding my season ticket and made my way onto the platform just as my train was pulling in.

The evening rush hour was now abating and the train was not too crowded. I managed to find a window seat and sat down for the thirty-five minute commute home. The train moved off smoothly and, settling down comfortably into my seat, I watched as the backs of tenements and factories gradually gave way to suburban houses and then to open fields, just discernible in the gloom. The heat of the carriage and soporific train sounds were starting to make me feel drowsy after my long working day.

'Excuse me. Is this seat free?'

I saw the indistinct, pale reflection of a man in the window and, dragging my gaze away from the twilit fields drifting past, looked around and up. A tall and quite good looking man with a kindly face and laughter lines radiating from the corners of his eyes stood above me in the aisle. It was difficult to be certain of his age. He had a smooth, fair complexion, without any blemishes, but with something of an aura of age about him. A friendliness and warmth seemed to emanate from him. Funnily enough though, the thing which struck me as most peculiar in his appearance was his dress. He was wearing a lightweight, linen suit, more appropriate to a warm, sunny summer's day than a cold March evening. It was almost white in colour, reminding me of the journalist who had become an independent Member of Parliament a few years previously; Martin something-or-other. He always wore white suits, as an outward sign of his incorruptibility I suppose.

Despite the man's pleasant appearance I was displeased at being disturbed from the first quiet moments I had enjoyed all day and found myself tempted to say there were a number of other seats free, any of which he could choose. Instead, good manners prevailed, although I confess a trace of grumpiness may have been evident in my response.

'Yes, it is.'

'May I sit?'

'If you wish.'

He eased himself into the adjacent seat. 'Thank you.'

I turned my face back to the window and closed my eyes, hoping he would take the hint and not disturb me for the remainder of my journey.

'I've been looking for you Sophie.'

He had my attention again. 'Looking for me?' I was nonplussed. 'I'm sorry, do we know each other?'

'Not yet,' he replied, smiling pleasantly. My name is Michael. I've come to take you home.'

I was taken aback by this totally unexpected and ridiculous remark and not a little concerned, despite his friendly smile and demeanour.

'How do you know my name? I don't think we've met before and I don't need anyone to take me home thank you. Now if you will excuse me.' I reached for my bag, preparing to move to another seat.

'I am sorry if I have upset you Sophie, but if you are intending to move I need to ask you a question first,' he said, still smiling.

For some inexplicable reason I felt unable to rise, despite the fact he was making no physical effort to restrain me. As I sat, irresolute, he reached into his jacket pocket and took out what appeared at first glance to be a small, black picture frame. I say a picture frame because I could initially see through it. However, a kind of mist immediately began to cloud the interior of the frame and within a few seconds this had coalesced into the features of a young man. I sat, transfixed and amazed by this image, which appeared to be of a man in his twenties but with a thin, haggard face, which made it difficult to be sure.

'How did you do that?'

He ignored my question. 'Do you recognise this man Sophie?'

'No, I've never seen him before.'

'Please, look closely. Take your time.'

Despite my growing apprehension I did as he asked and looked more carefully. There did seem to be something familiar about those gaunt features; the hollow cheeks; the eyes which seemed to recede into his skull.

A though occurred to me. 'Are you a policeman?'

'You could say that,' he replied quietly. 'I find people who are lost; people who need to find their way home.'

'Is *this* man lost? Does *he* need to find his way home?'

'He is lost, but he is lost down a path of his own choosing.'

A sudden realisation hit me like a physical blow and I shrank back into my seat. 'He's the man on The Common. The man who killed . . . .' I couldn't say it.

'You recognise him now.' It was a statement, rather than a question.

In my mind's eye I saw the cold gleam of a blade in the moonlight; the hollow staring eyes. I heard the muttered curses. I felt the . . . . A wave of nausea swept over me. Michael reached out and touched my arm. I looked around into his blue eyes. Eyes full of sadness and compassion.

'Have they . . . . have they caught him yet?'

'Early tomorrow morning,' he said quietly in a monotone, as if reading from a prepared text, 'on the other side of the city, two workmen will be checking out an old warehouse they are preparing to demolish, to make sure there is no one inside. They will find his body in a small office in the warehouse. The police will be called and will find debit and credit cards in a corner of that office which, together with subsequent DNA evidence, will identify him as the murderer. The post-mortem will reveal he died from a heroin overdose.'

I began to cry. 'How can you know all this?'

'I think you have already worked out the answer to that question Sophie.'

'I want to go home,' I sobbed, the tears running down my cheeks. 'I want to go to Ian and Sherlock.'

He looked sadly into my eyes, obviously distressed himself. 'I'm sorry Sophie. You can't go on like this you know. You have to let go. Some people can see you; you frighten them.'

I sat for a moment looking up into those blue eyes, searching in them for a way out, but I knew he was right.

'Are you ready to go now? Are you able to stand?'

I nodded, shakily. 'I think so.'

We both stood and he offered his hand. I took it and he led me down the centre isle of the carriage. I glanced backwards. The interior of the carriage and its occupants seemed to be dissolving and receding at the same time; the passengers taking no notice of us. I turned around again and saw a soft, white light coming from the end of the carriage we were walking towards. Now it was surrounding us, appearing to come from everywhere and nowhere. Michael's suit no longer seemed incongruous; it was perfect.

I looked at Michael. 'Will you be coming for him too?'

He looked down at me and his face for the first time was sombre and troubled.

'No. Someone else will be coming for him.'

We walked on together; further into the light. We were now in a warm summer flower meadow, ablaze with colour. I was intoxicated by the sweet perfume. The soft white light pervaded all.

'Where are going Michael?'

He looked down at me and the smile had returned to his handsome features.

'We are approaching Haddersley.'

'Haddersley?' That name seemed somehow familiar.

'This service will terminate at Haddersley.'

'Haddersley. Michael, that's my station. I must get off.'

My brain jerked back into the moment and I looked wildly around. I was still sitting in my seat in the carriage. A few people close by were getting up, reaching for bags and looking at me curiously. My heart was pounding and I could feel a rivulet of perspiration running down my spine.

'Are you all right love?'

A kindly looking middle aged lady was looking down at me with a concerned expression on her face.

I tried to smile, but it probably came out as a grimace. 'Yes, I think so. I mean yes, of course. I must have fallen asleep; must get off.' I rose unsteadily to my feet continuing to look up and down the carriage.

'Are you looking for your friend?'

'My friend?'

'Michael,' she said. 'You were calling for him, just now.'

'Have you seen him?' I almost shouted, staring at her wild eyed. She must have thought I was a mad woman.

'No dear. You've been sitting there on your own since you got on the train. I thought you were asleep.'

I was beginning to calm down. 'Of course I was. I just had a very vivid dream, that's all. Overwork and a rushed lunch probably. I'm sorry if I worried you.'

'That's all right love,' she said turning away. 'You take care of yourself now.'

The train slowed to a halt. I picked up my shoulder bag and walked, a little unsteadily, down the carriage and stepped off onto the platform. I crossed over the bridge to the village side of the tracks and out of the station entrance. As I did so a golden whirlwind, trailing a lead, launched himself at me, almost knocking me over.

'Sherlock! Where on earth did you come from and where's Ian?'

'I'm sorry Sophie,' panted Ian, rushing up. 'He saw you before I did and I wasn't holding the lead firmly enough.'

I laughed and it felt so good. 'What are you doing here?'

'Well, when you rang from work to say you probably wouldn't make the six-fifty, I started to prepare dinner. But when you hadn't arrived by seven-thirty Sherlock started to get really worried, so I put the dinner on hold and decided to walk down and meet you off the train.'

I managed to disengage myself from Sherlock and stood up. Flinging both arms around Ian's neck I gave him a very long, very passionate kiss.

'I love *you*; and you too Sherlock,' as he tried to insert himself between us.

'Well, I'll have to meet you at the station more often,' grinned Ian, breathlessly.

After dinner I told Ian all about the events of the evening, from leaving the office to being assaulted by Sherlock, including my dream, or hallucination, on the train.

'You've been working too hard Sophie. Having to walk past The Common, then hearing the old couple in the café talking about the murder; it just all got inside your head and came out in a bad dream when you fell asleep on the train.

I supposed Ian must have been right, so I tried to put it all out of my mind. We had a late dinner and then settled down to watch a DVD. Afterwards, as we were about to go up to bed, Ian suggested we put on the local news to see if there was anything more about the murder. I wasn't overjoyed, thinking this might spoil a pleasant evening, but agreed.

It was the first item on the bulletin. The newsreader said:

"The young woman, whose body was found on The Common at Leombridge early this morning, has been named this evening by the police as Sophie Williamson, (a photograph of a young woman appeared on screen) a twenty eight year old married mother of two young daughters aged two and four. Her family have been informed and have asked the press to respect their privacy at this very difficult time. The police say that Mrs Williamson had been stabbed seven times in the neck and chest in a frenzied attack and would have died very quickly from her wounds. The police are appealing -"

'Please turn it off Ian, it's horrible.' He quickly did so.

'That's weird Sophie; the poor woman having your first name. She even looked rather like you. She could have been your older sister.'

I started to cry; I couldn't hold it in. The news bulletin had brought back my dream as vividly as I had experienced it for the first time on the train. I had even seen the knife in the moonlight and felt it slice into my body. I began to shudder uncontrollably. Ian put his arms around me and I laid my head

283

against his chest. I was now sobbing hysterically. Sherlock jumped up whining and put his head into my lap.

'I'm sorry Sophie. I shouldn't have put it on. I'm an idiot.'

Eventually I began to regain my composure. 'You couldn't have known there would be so many similarities to my dream. How could I have seen all that?'

'Are you sure you didn't hear something on the radio during the afternoon, or one of your colleagues talking about it at work?'

'I'm sure I didn't hear anything earlier today and anyway the newsreader said she had only been named by the police this evening. Also the old couple in the café said she hadn't been identified, so there can't have been any details in the evening paper.'

'Let's go to bed darling. Try to put it out of your mind and get some sleep.'

Easier said than done; I spent a restless night tossing and turning and looking at the luminous dial of the bedside clock every half an hour. I think I must have fallen into a fitful sleep around four a.m. because Ian woke me with a cup of tea at seven.

'Why don't you call in sick?' he said, as we drank our tea. 'You don't look well at all. I'll ring the office for you if you like.'

'Thanks but I'll be OK. I have to be at an important planning meeting today.'

'Well, if you're sure.'

I smiled. 'I wish I could work from home like you. I'll bet you and Sherlock have a great time.'

'Of course we do. When we aren't watching daytime TV we're in the park socialising with all the neighbourhood dogs and housewives.'

'You'd better not be socialising too much with those housewives. Some of the ones I know would eat you alive.'

He grinned. 'Thanks for the warning.'

I spent another hectic day in meetings at the office and in visiting two important clients before getting away early enough to catch the six-fifty train. The British climate had worked another of its minor miracles overnight and it had been a lovely, warm spring day. The evening sun was now setting gently over the retail park, bathing the trees on the edge of The Common in a golden glow and making them seem remarkably unthreatening. Another week and we would be in British Summertime and I would be arriving home in daylight, always a cheerful thought. I saw the police sign was still up by the path leading onto The Common, but this time I had crossed over Studley Avenue and I stayed on that side all the way to the junction, crossing over Station Road there so that I was again well away from the edge of The Common.

Arriving at the station I couldn't avoid passing the news-stand. I tried not to look but some irresistible urge drew my eyes to the front-page headline in the local evening paper. *"MURDER ON THE COMMON: KILLER IDENTIFIED?"* I couldn't help myself. I paid for a copy and put it into my shoulder bag without reading any further and made my way onto the platform.

The train arrived on time for once and I boarded the second carriage as usual. It was warm on board and I took off my jacket before walking down the aisle looking for a seat. This earlier train was more crowded than the seven-thirty had been the previous evening but I saw two adjacent seats still unoccupied. They looked to be the same seats, or very close to the same, that I and Michael . . . . I hesitated, berating myself angrily. Telling myself not to be ridiculous, I moved to sit down and then faltered in my resolve. I suddenly felt an aversion to sitting in either of those seats. More than that; it was almost as if some unseen physical force was preventing me. I could feel my heart rate starting to increase and goose bumps rising on my bare arms. Seeing an aisle seat unoccupied three rows back I quickly moved on and sat down. I watched other passengers walking down the aisle and also hesitating by the empty seats, but none of them sat down. They all moved on, their faces wearing a puzzled frown.

The train moved off. Whilst keeping half an eye on the unoccupied seats I took the evening paper from my bag and started to read the headline story.

"At a press conference early this afternoon Leombridge Police announced that a man's body had been found by workmen at a disused warehouse on the northern edge of the city. Items found with the body have linked the deceased to the murder of young married mother Sophie Williamson, whose body was discovered on The Common early yesterday morning. The police say that DNA tests will be carried out to ascertain if blood found on the deceased man's clothing is that of the murdered woman."

I stopped reading and pressed the paper down onto my knees to stop my hands trembling. Again this was happening just as

Michael had . . . . pull yourself together, the logical side of my brain tried to tell me. There had been no Michael. He had just been a character in a dream you had on the train; but a dream which had predicted not only details about the murdered woman but also the finding of the murderer. Despite trying to resist it a deep conviction was forming in my mind that later news stories would confirm the man had died from a heroin overdose and that DNA evidence would prove he was the murderer. As my common sense was being tested by this growing certainty, something beside the unoccupied seats caught my eye.

There appeared to be some disturbance in the air; a sort of shimmering, like heated air rising from a road surface on a hot summer's day. I stared intently. Was there the faintest hint of a presence within the disturbed air; a kind of moving silvery light? I closed my eyes for a few seconds. When I opened them again the apparition, if I can call it that, had moved further away from me down the carriage, but I could still see it. Apparently no one else could. The other passengers seemed oblivious, continuing to read their newspapers, books, or tablets or work on their laptops. I thought I could now distinguish two separate silvery elements flickering within the shimmering air. The automatic door at the end of the carriage suddenly opened and my heart missed a couple of beats; something had triggered its sensors. A few people now looked up but apparently still didn't see anything untoward, presumably assuming some malfunction. Why just me? The apparition moved through the open doorway. The door closed again and I saw nothing more. My hands were now shaking again. Realising I had been holding my breath I tried to start breathing normally again.

The train began to slow for a station. Gathering all my courage I rose and walked up three rows to the unoccupied seats. I didn't sense anything abnormal there anymore. I took a deep breath and sat down by the window. Nothing happened. I was sitting in an ordinary, slightly grubby, commuter train seat. A few people got off the train and after a minute or so it began to move off again. I watched the end of the platform slip away backwards to be replaced by suburban gardens as I began to regain my composure.

'Excuse me. Is this seat free?'

I looked around and up. This could not be. I saw again the kindly face with the laughter lines radiating from the corners of his eyes. And he was wearing that same . . . . I froze. I couldn't move or speak.

'Miss?'

I made an enormous effort. 'Excuse me?'

'The seat,' he said, pointing. 'I was asking if it was free.'

'Yes. Yes it's free.'

'May I sit?'

'Of course.'

He eased himself into the adjacent seat.

'Thank you,' he said, glancing over towards me again, 'Sophie'.

'What did you say?'

'I'm sorry, that was over familiar of me. I do hope I haven't offended you.'

'How do you know my name?' I managed to ask. I could hear the hysteria rising in my voice.

'You're still wearing your name badge; from work I presume.'

'Oh yes, of course,' I just managed to say, glancing down briefly at the company identity badge I had forgotten to remove. I still couldn't drag my eyes away from his face. I was obviously making him feel uncomfortable.

'Was there something else bothering you?'

I had to ask; I couldn't help myself, though the thought of the answer I was expecting terrified me. Taking a deep shuddering breath I asked the question.

'I was wondering if we had met before. Is your name by any chance M-'

'Martin Bell? No it isn't. He smiled, the laughter lines deepening at the corners of his eyes. I'm often asked that. People tell me there is a physical resemblance, but quite honestly I think it's just the suit.'

'The suit,' I repeated.

'Yes. Martin Bell always wore a similar coloured suit; still does I believe. My name is Frances; Frances Enderby. Pleased to meet you.' He held out his hand.

A Final Word

I have been unable to find any logical explanation for what happened to me over those two days five years ago and I have not had any similar experiences since, thank God. I have never told this story to anyone before now, except to Ian of course.

At the time I was only recently qualified and employed by a firm of architects in Leombridge. I was working really hard to progress within the company; trying to make a name for myself. Working too hard is Ian's only unconvincing explanation for the events I have related to you.

Ian and I married four years ago and now have two beautiful daughters, Clara and Rachael. I think my two periods of maternity leave were rather frowned upon by my employers but nothing was said of course. However, I gained the distinct impression that I would not progress within the firm.

Ian has now had two novels published which have been quite successful and so we decided it wouldn't be too much of a financial risk for me to set up on my own. This will enable us both to work from home and have a better family life with the girls. I even suggested to Ian that he might include my story, unattributed of course, in his next book, but he thought his readers would find it too implausible.

I am now working my final month before becoming self-employed and from the beginning of April will be very pleased not to have to walk by The Common any more. I certainly would never venture onto it, especially on dark winter evenings. Even more especially since, whilst writing this narrative, I have realised I am now the same age as poor Sophie Williamson when she was murdered and my daughters are presently aged two and four, as were hers.

I read somewhere recently that, in the Judaic tradition, there are named seven archangels who stand in the presence of God. However, only one of these is mentioned in The Bible. His name is Michael. Just a coincidence I'm sure.

Printed in Poland
by Amazon Fulfillment
Poland Sp. z o.o., Wrocław